CRUISING ASSOCIATION HANDBOOK

SEVENTH EDITION (REVISED)

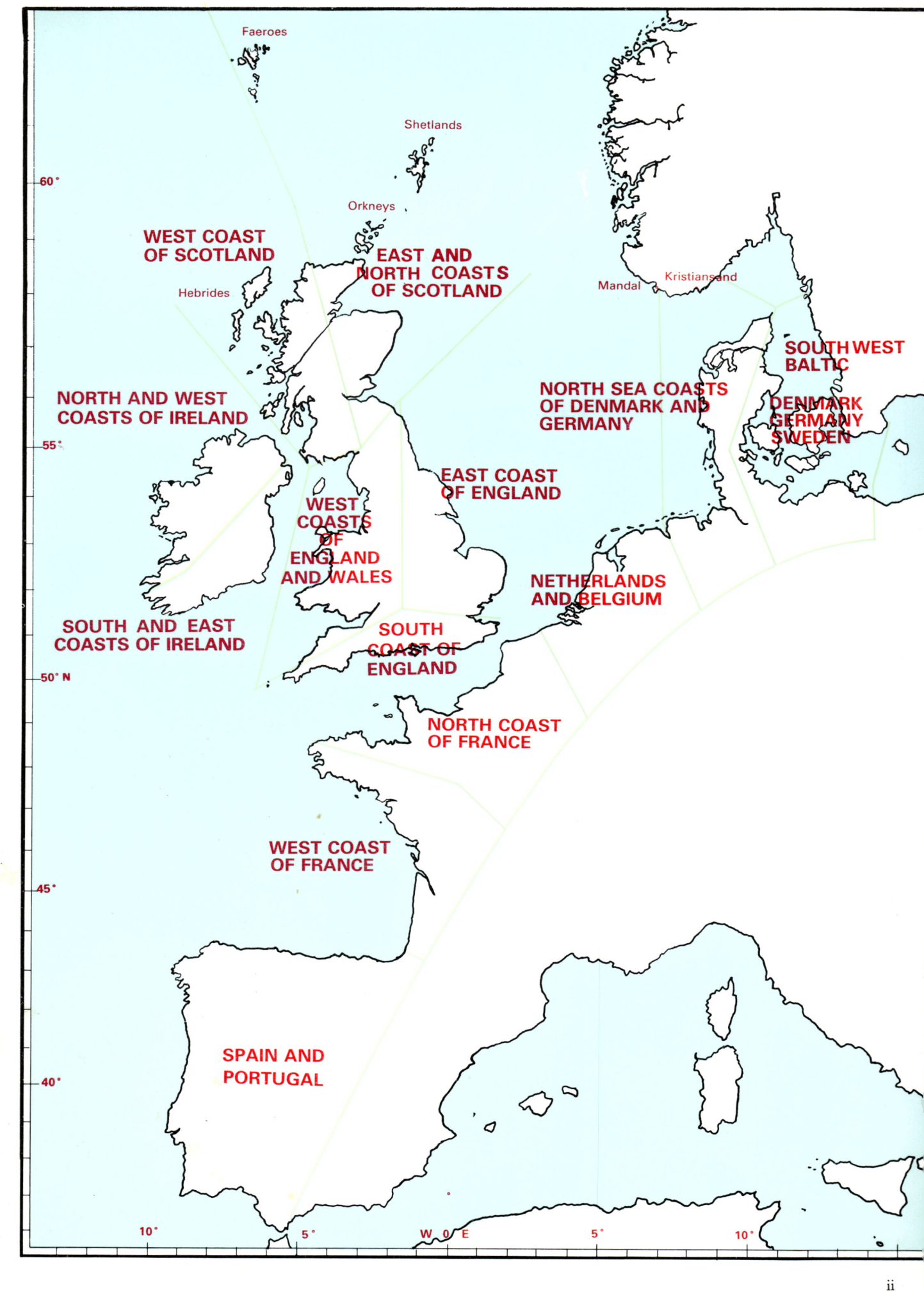

CRUISING ASSOCIATION HANDBOOK
(7th Edition Revised)

 *Published by the Cruising Association*

Published by The Cruising Association
Ivory House, St Katharine Dock, London E1 9AT

Plans produced by Imray, Laurie, Norie & Wilson
Wych House, St Ives, Huntingdon,
Cambridgeshire, PE17 4BT

Typesetting and camera-ready artwork produced by Raven Marketing Group, Cromwell Court, New Road, St. Ives, Cambs. PE17 4BG

Reprographics by Morgan's Photo-Repro, St Ives, Cambs.

Printed in Great Britain by Tabro Litho Ltd, Ramsey, Cambs.

ISBN 0 9503742 6 1   7th Edition (Revised) 1992

DISCLAIMER

Whilst all reasonable care has been taken in the preparation of the contents of this book, the reader/user is responsible for the safe navigation of his/her own vessel. Every effort is made to ensure that the information and plans contained in this book are up to date and accurate, but the Cruising Association, the editor and other members responsible for this compilation accept no responsibility for the result of any errors or omissions and responsibility is expressly disclaimed for any injury, loss or damage howsoever caused or contributed to by negligence upon such information.

THIS HANDBOOK SHOULD ONLY BE USED IN CONJUNCTION WITH THE PROPER UP TO DATE (OR UPDATED) CHARTS (OF THE APPROPRIATE SCALE) AND NOTICES TO MARINERS

COPYRIGHT

All rights reserved. No part of this publication may be reproduced, stored in a retrieval system or transmitted in any form or by any means electronic, mechanical, photocopying, recording or otherwise without the prior permission of the publishers.

ACKNOWLEDGEMENTS

The Cruising Association is most grateful for permission to reproduce information from various official sources and charts and acknowledges the following hydrographic authorities from whose charts our plans have been based:

British Admiralty Charts and Tide Tables (Crown Copyright) with the permission of the Controller of Her Majesty's Stationery Office.

Deutsches Hydrographisches Institut, Hamburg

Service Hydrographique et Oceangraphique de la Marine, France

Boligminsteriet Kort-og Matrikelstyrelsen Søkortafdelingen, Denmark

In addition although not directly used we would like to acknowledge the help various contributors will have had from perusal of charts prepared by:

Instituto Hidrographico de la Marina, Spain

Ministerio da Defesa Nacional Marinha Instituto Hidrografico, Rua das Trinas, 49 1296 Lisbon Codex Tel 601191/6: 65990 Hidrog P – Telefax: 660515, Portugal

The National Swedish Administration of Shipping and Navigation Hydrographic Department, Sweden

The Hydrographic Department of Norway

The above sources do not assume responsibility for information published from their charts

In all the above cases we have advised our readers on the use of both British Admiralty charts and those from the particular country concerned.

Contents

	Page
SOUTH COAST OF ENGLAND	1
EAST COAST OF ENGLAND	69
EAST & NORTH COAST OF SCOTLAND ORKNEY, SHETLANDS & FAEROES	117
WEST COAST OF SCOTLAND	143
WEST COAST OF ENGLAND & WALES	165
IRELAND, SOUTH WEST, SOUTH & EAST COASTS, NORTH & WEST COASTS	201
SOUTH WEST BALTIC, DENMARK & GERMANY	243
NORTH SEA, COASTS OF DENMARK & GERMANY	263
NETHERLANDS & BELGIUM	273
NORTH COAST OF FRANCE & CHANNEL ISLANDS	299
WEST COAST OF FRANCE	351
SPAIN & PORTUGAL	381
INDEX	406

FOREWORD

BY THE PRESIDENT OF THE CRUISING ASSOCIATION

It is my privilege to introduce the 7th edition (Revised) of the Cruising Association Handbook; each edition has been an improvement on its predecessor in both content and presentation, but in this there is a great step forward. The A4 format gives a far more efficient use of space enabling more information to be contained in fewer pages, and a layout in which most of the harbour plans are incorporated within or adjacent to the relevant text.

Many ports on Spain and Portugal formerly covered by brief notes now have full sailing directions and harbour plans whilst for the first time the Faeroe islands have been included with five ports. Harbour plans now appear in four colours making for greater clarity. Its comprehensive nature makes it a valuable aid to navigation over the whole coastline of N W Europe; a yacht on passage will have detailed plans and information on ports of call contained in one book.

All this has been achieved through the enormous fund of information available from the Association's Hon Local Representatives, and members during the course of their cruising. Our thanks are due to all those who have given information, however small, to fit in the jigsaw. This is collated by Hon Regional editors working as a team under the Hon Editor, Tony Brett-Jones and the Handbook Committee responsible for the production ably chaired by Bill Clark-Lewis and then John Morl. Cruising sailors generally owe a great debt of gratitude to all these people who have voluntarily contributed so much of their time and experience; the contribution made by so many volunteers makes this book of inestimable value, and the cover price in no way reflects its true worth to all who cruise in small ships.

R M BROWNE

THE CRUISING ASSOCIATION

The Cruising Association was founded in 1908 'to encourage cruising in yachts and boats and to protect the interests of yachtsmen'. It had some 5,300 members in 1992, the majority resident in the British Isles but several hundred living in Europe and other parts of the world. Its meeting rooms, chart room, offices and reference library are at Ivory House, St Katharine Dock, London E1 9AT, tel 071 481 0881.

The Library contains some 8,500 books, and may well be the most important collection on sailing and allied subjects in private hands on the eastern side of the Atlantic. There is a large collection of charts and Sailing Directions for cruise planning purposes, and files of information are kept on cruising areas all over the world, in which news from members and other sources are collated.

Publications The most well-known is, of course, this *Handbook*, as it is sold to the public as well as members. Members are entitled to buy copies at a substantially reduced price. The *Handbook* is updated by annual lists of Corrections, available from the Association's headquarters to callers or by post. As noted elsewhere, the *Handbook* should never be used without all current Corrections. Shorter Guides to special areas are also published: in print in 1992 were *Notes on French Inland Waterways* and *Visiting Yachtsman's Guide to the London River;* also in collaboration with the RYA *Planning a Foreign Cruise C1/91 (USSR to Portugal)* and *Planning a Foreign Cruise C2/92 (The Mediterranean)*. Turning to publications available to members only, *Cruising* the quarterly Journal of the Cruising Association contains news, logs and articles. *Harbour, Anchorage and Navigation Notes* are also quarterly, circulating the most recent news from members and other sources on ports, harbours and other navigational matters. The *Year Book* is published annually, and contains lists of members and boats, Honorary Local Representatives, Association Boatmen and much other useful information.

Honorary Local Representatives are yachtsmen, usually members, whose detailed knowledge of the ports they cover is available to other members in the form of advice or assistance.

Association Boatmen are professionals, often organisations rather than individuals, who are recommended as giving reliable and good service at a particular port. They can often arrange moorings, look after boats that are left in their care, and of course provide normal repair and maintenance facilities. The services which they can offer are detailed in the *Year Book*.

Crewing Service To assist the owners and crews to get in touch with each other, the Association provides a service circulating the names and addresses of owners seeking crew and vice versa. This is open to non-members on payment of a fee.

Enquiries on cruising matters The C.A. is associated with numerous cruising clubs in Britain and elsewhere. Full details are to be found in the *Year Book*. It thus has access to an unrivalled body of cruising knowledge, available to members through the secretariat.

Educational and social events The Association organises a full programme of lectures, training and purely social events during the winter both in London and in area sections throughout the country. Also numerous meets where members gather together in ports in Britain and overseas are held during the sailing season.

Challenge Cups Several Challenge Cups are awarded every year, mainly for logs of cruises in various categories, but also for outstanding cruises or acts of seamanship. Enquiries about membership should be addressed to the General Secretary, Cruising Association, Ivory House, St Katharine Dock, London E1 9AT – 071 481 0881.

ACKNOWLEDGEMENTS

As Hon Editor for the 7th edition (revised) of the CA Handbook which contains so many new features my thanks are due to the team of regional editors for the many drafts they produced and the help and co-operation they gave each other and me working as a team to produce this edition. I gladly acknowledge this by setting out the names and the regions covered:

Bob Parker	South coast England
	North coast France
Don Willis	East coast England
John Morl	
Paul Gore	East & North coasts Scotland Orkneys & Shetlands
David Williamson	West coast Scotland
Arthur Orr	Ireland
Tony Brett-Jones	
Donald & Barbara Woods	Denmark & Skaggerak
Kevin Seymour	
Bill Clark-Lewis	Germany
Kevin Seymour	
Bill Clark-Lewis	Netherlands & Belgium
Stuart Bradley	
Peter Doyle	West Coast France
Margaret Elliott	
Margaret Elliott	North & West Coast Spain & Portugal
Vernon Marchant	French Inland Waterways
Tony Brett-Jones	West Coast England & Wales, Faeroes

In addition I am indebted to Peter Ambrose for his administrative work, Willie Wilson of Imray Laurie Norie & Wilson who prepared the plans, for his advice on layout and production which were invaluable and Brian Smith of Cromwell Graphics who helped us iron out the problems transposing the text from personal word processors to typesetting.

There are many more such as our Honorary Local Representatives (HLRs) around the coast, many Harbourmasters, as well as our own members, without whom the detail in this book tailored to suit the person cruising, would not be possible.

Honorary Editor TONY BRETT-JONES CBE

EXPLANATORY NOTES

Cut off Date – 29 August 1991

Layout of Handbook: The sailing directions in this Handbook are laid out on standard principles although these may be varied where necessary to bring clarity to the user.

Ports in Great Britain are presented starting from the Isles of Scilly in an anti clockwise direction. The coastline is divided into sections as listed below with a graphical index in front of each. Ireland is treated similarly starting from Valentia. The continental coast is arranged working from North to South starting from the South West Baltic down to Gibraltar.

Passage Notes are given at intervals throughout the text.

Although consistency has been striven for throughout the various regions this has not always been adopted as what is essential in one area becomes unneccessary in another. Limits on space dictate the optimum approach.

Graphical indices appear in front of the following sections:-
- South coast England
- East coast England
- East & North coasts Scotland including Orkneys, Shetland, & Faeroes
- West coast Scotland
- West coast England and Wales
- South West, South, and East coasts of Ireland
- North and West coasts of Ireland
- South West Baltic, Denmark & Germany
- North Sea coasts of Denmark, Germany, Holland and Belgium
- North coast of France including the Channel Islands
- West coast of France
- North and North West coast Spain, Portugal and South West Spain

Times given as Dover ±xh are in relation to HW at Dover (see also below). Otherwise they are given in relation to local High Water or in a few cases in local kept time.

All courses and bearings are given TRUE unless specifically stated otherwise and bearings of lights and transits etc are given from seaward.

The plans are in colour but we are specifically not allowed to mimic those used on British Admiralty charts. Deep water is white, water below the 2m line is normally coloured blue but in a few areas in France and Spain where it is not possible to include a 2m contour line the blue will be inside the 5m contour. Drying areas are yellow and land green. Lights and marinas etc are magenta.

Dredged depths are followed by m as 3.5m indicating 'Dredged to 3.5m'

The cable (ca) one tenth of a nautical mile is used extensively in the text in preference to giving distances in metres as it can be easily measured from the latitude scale on each plan. If it is required to convert metres to cables the conversion is one cable to 185.2 metres. A short conversion table is set out below:-

m	ca
10	0.05
20	0.10
30	0.16
40	0.22
50	0.27
100	0.54
200	1.08
500	2.70

As is customary winds are given in respect of the compass point from which they originate. But winds blowing on to a shore are described as onshore winds whilst those blowing from off the land are described as offshore.

In the case of tidal streams they are always described in the direction towards which they are flowing, eg a south going stream.

Corrections: Corrections are issued annually and users must ensure that they use the Handbook in conjunction with the up to date Corrections. These will probably be issued in cumulative form and available from the Cruising Association for a small charge.

Other Navigational Information: Users should not rely on the Handbook only. It is essential to carry up to date Admiralty or foreign charts. It is recommended also that Admiralty Pilots, Lists of lights, Tide Tables and Notices to Mariners are also carried.

Those cruising to the smaller harbours and anchorages or wishing to cruise any area extensively are advised to carry the local pilot or guide to the area. Recommendations of suitable publications are made in various parts of the text.

Notes on Tidal Data: Chart Datum (CD) is the level from which the depth of water or drying height is measured and is approximately the same as Lowest Astronomical Tide (LAT). All BA metric charts refer to this datum. Mean High Water Springs (MHWS) is in effect the average height of spring tides throughout the year. Mean High Water Neaps (MHWN), Mean Low Water Neaps (MLWN) and Mean Low Water Springs (MLWS) represent similar averages. Mean Tide Level (MTL) is the average of these four levels and this enables one to calculate the range of tide (the height between sucessive high and low waters) knowing only the rise of high water (the height to which High Water will rise above chart datum on any particular day). Twice the difference between the Rise and MTL gives the range thus enabling one to calculate the minimum depth of water on that tide.

ILLUSTRATION of USE of MTL to CALCULATE RANGE and LW from KNOWN HW (5.0m)

Handbook Info	Rise m	Tide Table Calculation
MHWS	5.5	
		5.0m
MWHN	4.4	
MTL	3.2	Range 2(5.0-3.2)=3.6m
MLWN	2.2	
		∴ LW 1.4m
MLWS	0.8	
Chart Datum	0.0	

VARIATION IN PREDICTED HEIGHTS OF TIDES
The use of Mean Tide level to calculate the range for the tide is only approximate as the rise of tide before HW may often be slightly different from the fall after it to the next LW.

There are many meteorological effects on tides where the conditions will cause differences from the levels assumed in the tidal prediction. The main effects are briefly summarised:-

Barometric pressure:- a difference of 34 millibars from the average (1013 mbs) will cause a lowering of the predicted tide of .3m with high pressure and a similar rise with low pressure.

Wind:- A strong wind blowing for some time in the general direction of the coastline will cause a higher than predicted tide and the reverse with a wind off the shore. The effects will vary widely in different areas.

Seiches:- Sudden changes in weather such as the passage of an intense local depression or line squall may set up a wave (trough) known as a seiche having a period from a few minutes to an hour or so. The effect can be up to 1 metre in extreme cases. Some harbours are more prone to the effect, Fishguard and Wick being examples.

Storm Surges:- Occur particularly in the North Sea where a constant gale force wind blowing from a Northerly quarter will cause a positive surge resulting in a rise above predicted levels of up to 2.5m in extreme cases. Negative surges also occur in the Southern North Sea up to 2m below predicted levels. About 15 surges per year more than 0.6m may occur although the extreme cases are very rare.

For all these reasons therefore it is prudent to allow a considerable margin when calculating depths of water for anchoring or passages in shallow water.

Use of HW Dover: The time of High Water at ports is related to HW at Dover. The direction of tidal streams is dealt with similarly. The provision of this information has been found useful over many years as the times of Dover tides are so readily available. But it must be emphasised that the differences are approximations only intended primarily for cruise planning or as a last resort when other more accurate information is unavailable. Much greater accuracy will be obtained by using Amiralty Tide Tables or applying the appropriate differences to a standard Port.

The differences on Dover are the mean of extremes and in some areas (Cornwall and parts of West Scotland being two examples) the variation between the constant at spring and neap tides can be nearly two hours. It is therefore possible that the actual time of local HW on a particular day can vary by nearly an hour from the figures given in the Handbook. Nevertheless it is still felt that the figures are useful as a general guide when planning, deciding on alternatives or as a fall back in the last resort.

Yachtsmen using the Admiralty Tide Tables will be aware that when a secondary port in say zone time −1 hour (−0100) is related to a Standard Port on GMT eg St Malo/St Helier or Corcubión/Lisboa, that the correction to be applied using these tables includes the allowance for the difference in zone time.

In the Handbook however where a time difference between local HW and HW Dover is given this should be applied by a simple addition or subtraction to the time of HW Dover on the day required. If the Dover tables give the time in GMT then the resulting answer for HW at the local port will be in GMT. If it is then required to express the answer in Zone Time or local Kept Time such as French or Spanish Summer Time then a further correction must be made.

In most of the Solent where there is a lengthy stand at HW, or double HW, it is necessary to refer to Low Water. Thus LW: Dover +5h means local LW occurs 5 hours after HW Dover.

The figures given for the heights of tides at MHWS etc are self explanatory. All figures are in metres although the reminder of this is only given in each case for MHWS. It should be noted that certain tides included are based on local observation or interpolation. It was thought in these few cases an educated estimate was better than no information at all.

The mean spring range at Dover is 5.9 metres and the mean neap range 3.3 metres. The height of tide predicted as MHWS will therefore be attained on a day when the Dover range is 5.9m and this will apply (one day) anywhere in Europe. Where tides occur substantially outside the mean levels eg equinoctial tides, then tidal streams will also vary from those shewn. Thus if the text says 'Streams attain 4kn at springs' these may in fact be say 5kn where the tidal range for Dover is say 6.9m instead of 5.9m

Depths: All depths given in the Handbook, except where otherwise stated, refer to the depth at chart datum. Thus if advice is given to anchor in 3-4m and the height of tide (vertical distance at any one moment between sea level and chart datum) is 2m then the boat will be anchoring in 5 to 6m. This applies to all depths given in channels and over bars, to soundings and to all depths mentioned except where specifically referred to other heights.

Calculation of Height of Tide: For many purposes the Rule of Twelve gives sufficient accuracy although care must be taken in certain instances. This states:-
HW or LW 1 hour Rise or fall 1/12 of its range
HW or LW 2nd or 5th hour Rise or fall 2/12
HW or LW 3rd & 4th hours Rise or fall 3/12
Thus HW −4 hours the tide will be 9/12 ¾ of the range below HW level; 2 hours later it will be 3/12 ¼ of the range below HW level for that day.

In most ports the error involved in using this rule is unlikely to exceed 5-10% of the range, and weather and other factors may mean that the predictions are less accurate than this in any case. However the rule must not be used in ports with freak tides such as those in the Solent with double high waters or the Seine estuary which has a prolonged high water stand. For these, local advice must be taken or tide tables with tidal curves used which enable these tides, and indeed all tides, to be calculated with accuracy.

French Traffic Signals
Pending the introduction of the International Code of Signals, the existing French Full and Simplified Codes may be seen for many years, ie:

Full	Simplified	Meaning
3 cones pt down (vert) or 3 Glts (vert)	---	Port open Entry or Departure Permitted
3 Balls (vert) or 3R lts (vert)	---	No entry: Emergency
Ball/cone(pt up)/ Ball (vert) or RWR lts (vert)	R Flag or R lt	No entry: (normal)
2 cones pt to pt/ ball (vert) or GWR lts (vert)	R over G flags or R over G lt	No entry or Departure
2 cones pt to pt/ cone pt down (vert) or GWG lts (vert)	G flag or G lt	No Departure

Entry can therefore be made when the 'No Departure' signal is displayed and vice versa or when there is no signal or when the International Signal 3 G lts (vert) is displayed meaning 'Proceed'.

These signals may be supplemented for special needs eg ferry or tanker traffic at Calais. In such cases details will be found in the port entry.

Abbreviations: The standard Admiralty abbreviations to be found in BA Chart 5011 are used where relevant. A limited number of additional abbreviations are used for economy in the text and clarity on the plans. Below is a summary of those used together with the commoner ones found in BA 5011.

Tides:
HW	High Water
LW	Low Water
MHWS	Mean High Water Springs
MHWN	Mean High Water Neaps
MTL	Mean Tide Level
MLWN	Mean Low Water Neaps
MLWS	Mean Low Water Springs
HWD	High Water Dover
LAT	Lowest Astronomical Tide
Kn	Knot(s)
DS	Direction of Stream

Direction:
N	North/Northerly/Northernmost
E	East etc
S	South etc
W	West etc

Lights:
As set out in BA Chart 5011 (metric) thus:
F	Fixed
Oc	Occulting
Oc(2)	Group Occulting
Iso	Isophase
Fl	Flashing
LFl	Long Flashing
Fl(3)	Group Flashing
Q	Continuous Quick Flashing
VQ	Continuous Very Quick Flashing
Alt	Alternating
s	second(s)
Vert	Vertical

Colours:
W	White
R	Red
G	Green
Y	Yellow
Bu	Blue
Vi	Violet

Miscellaneous:
Approx	Approximately
ATT	Admiralty Tide Tables
BA	British Admiralty
bn	beacon
br	bridge
ca	cable
card	cardinal
CD	Chart Datum
cg	coast guard station
con	conical
ch	church
conspic	conspicuous
EC	Early closing
F5	Beaufort wind scale Force 5
HM	Harbourmaster
h	hour
hbr	harbour
ht	height
I	Island (plan)
Is	Island (text)
Kn	Knot(s)
L	Loch or Lough (plan)
LB	Lifeboat station (plan)
ldg	leading
Lt(s)	Light(s)
M	Miles (nautical)
m	metre(s)
mte	monte (Spanish only)
PH	Public House
PO	Post Office
pt, pte	point
pta	punta (Spanish only)
rk	rock
Ro Bn	Radio Beacon
rly	railway
SC	Sailing Club
sph	spherical
stb	starboard
tel	telephone
tfc	traffic
tr	tower
TSS	Traffic Separation Scheme
VHF	VHF channel
Wks	Wrecks
YC	Yacht Club

Sun, Mon, Tue, Wed, Thur, Fri, Sat: Days of week
Jan, Feb, Mar, Apr, May, Jun, Jul, Aug, Sep, Oct, Nov, Dec: Months

Charts:
BA	British Admiralty
B	Belgian
D	Danish
F	French
G	German
N	Netherlands
NS	Norwegian (Norske Sjorart)
S	Spanish
P	Portugese

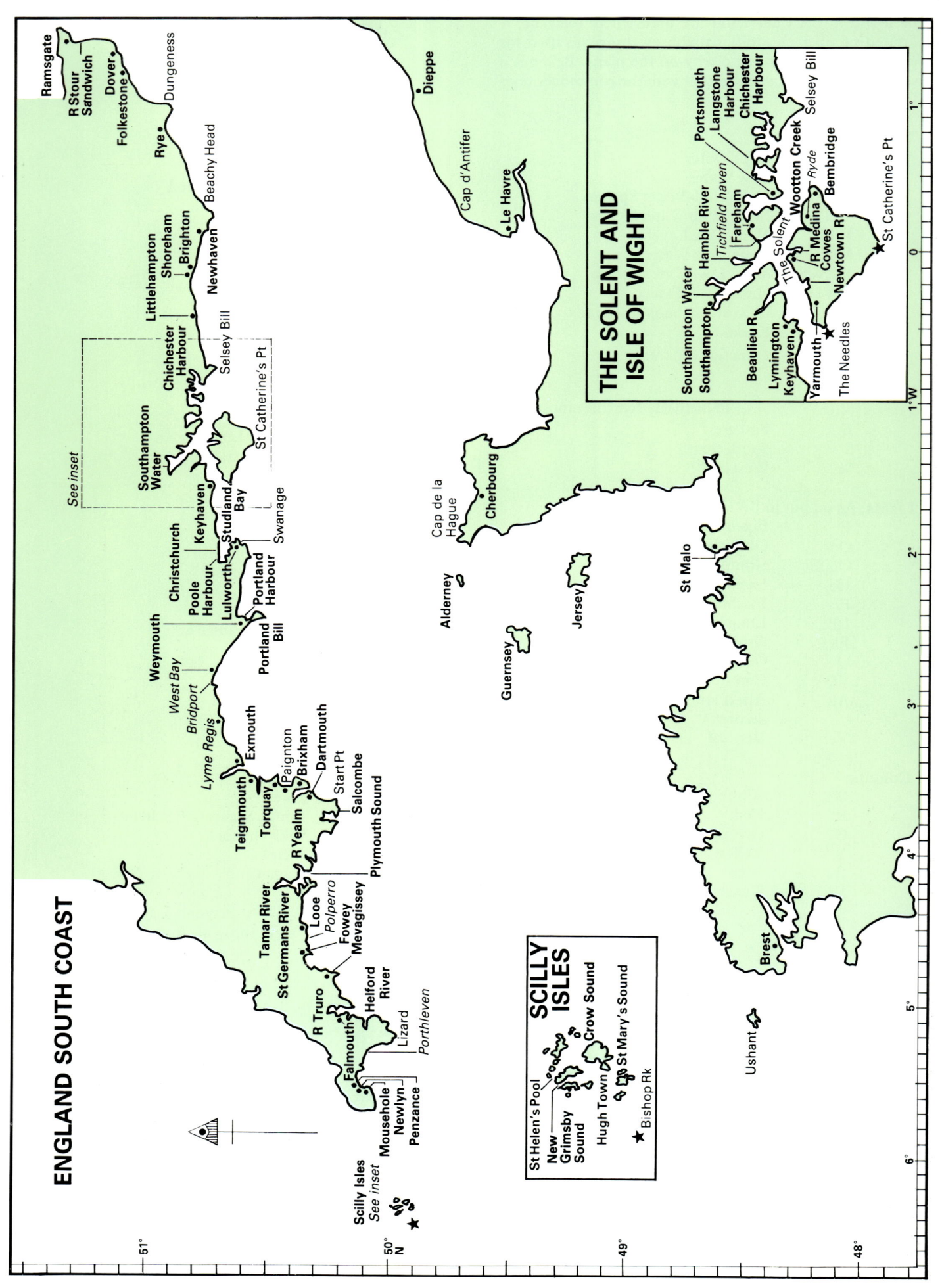

1 *ENGLAND, SOUTH COAST*

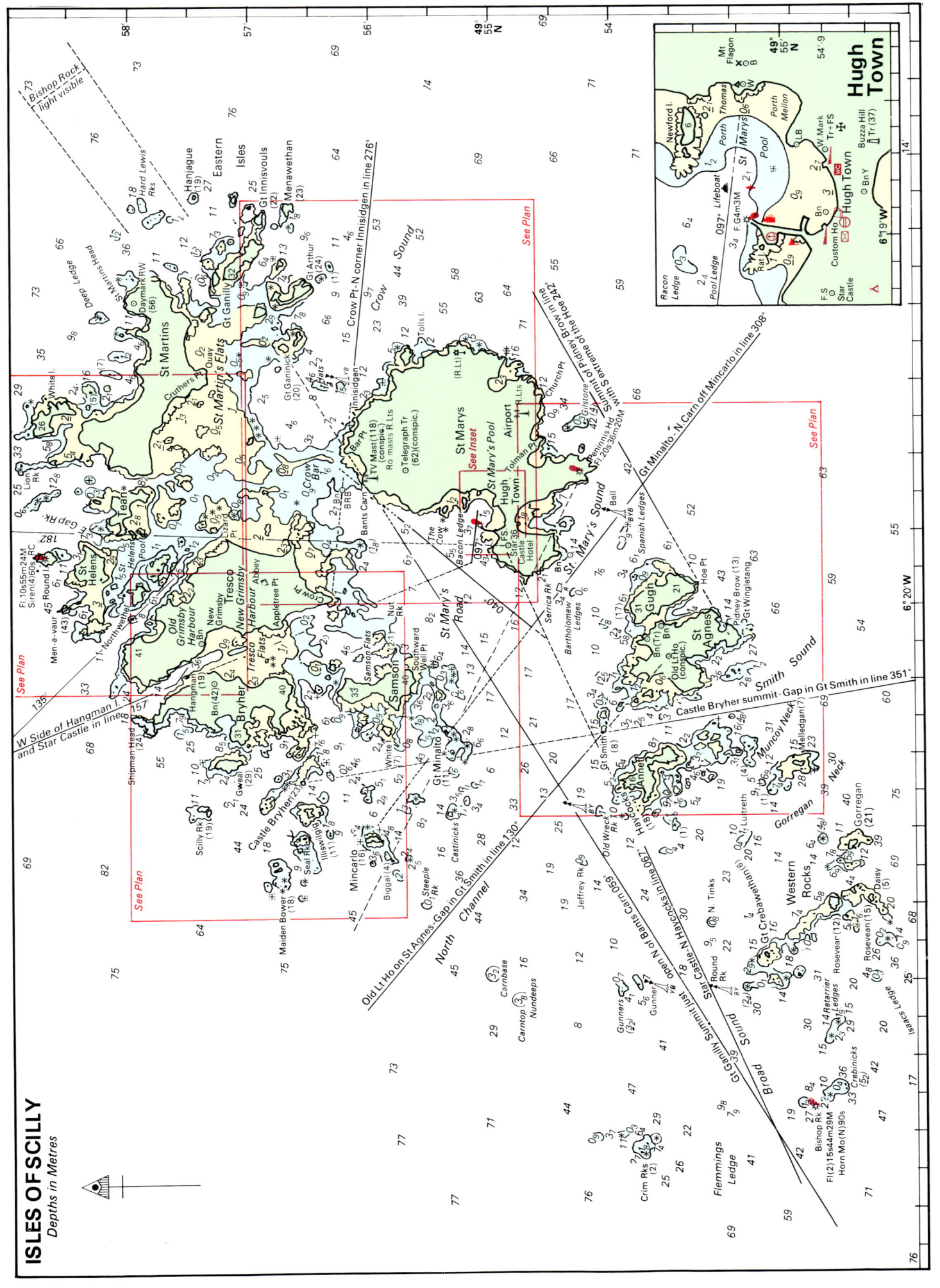

ENGLAND, SOUTH COAST

SCILLY ISLES TO RAMSGATE

PASSAGE NOTES: SCILLY ISLES TO PENZANCE
Charts BA 2565; 1148 and 777

Passage Lights

Bishop Rock	Fl(2) 15s 24M, horn 90s
Round Is	Fl 10s 24M (021°-288°), horn(4) 60s
Penninis Head	Fl 20s 20M (231°-117°)
Seven Stones	Fl(3) 30s 25M, horn(3) 60s.
Wolf Rk	Fl 15s 23M, horn 30s
Tater-Du	Fl(3) 15s 23M, horn (2) 30s; and FR 13M (241°-074°) (over Runnelstore)

Streams related to Dover
Scilly Is to Land's End: +1h NW; +3h N; +5h NE; −4h SSE; −1h SSW.
Runnelstone −6h to −3h E; −3H to +6h NW.
Land's End HWD N; −5h S.
When going E from the Scillies to Penzance make for the Wolf Rk lt ho; deep water up to ½M off on all sides. Then pass well S of the Runnelstone lt buoy, S card Q(6)+Fl 15s, liable to drift, and follow the coast at least 1M offshore.

ISLES OF SCILLY   Charts BA 34 or 883
HW St Mary's: Dover +6h
MHWS 5.7m   MHWN 4.4   MTL 3.1   MLWN 2.0   MLWS 0.7
The tidal streams are rotary clockwise ¾ to 1½kn but more at various points. Off St Martin's Hd there is a tide rip to S and SE for 3M.
DS: Off Gilstone: Dover +2¼h NE 1.8kn; −4¼h SW 2.5kn.
St Mary's Road: Dover +1¾h E; −5¾h W (varies between SW and NW) both about 1kn.
St Mary's Sound: Dover +2¾h SE; −4h NW, both 2kn.
Crow Sound: weak and irregular except from Dover −1¾h to +5¼h when it runs SE at first, changing through E to N; max 1.4kn at 2¾h NE.
New Grimsby Hbr: Dover −4h N; +4h S both 1kn. Off the entrance: +1¼h E; −5¼h W, both 2½kn.
N of Round Is, streams are up to 4kn ½M off.

Approaches Principal landmarks are:
Round Is lt ho (W circular 55m);
St Martin's Is daymark (R & W horizontal bands 56m);
St Mary's Is - TV mast 118m, radio masts and telegraph tr 62m, and Penninis Head lt ho (W circular iron 36m);
St Agnes Is disused lt ho (W stone 23m); and Bishop Rk lt ho (grey circular 44m).
From E, St Martin's daymark comes up first; from S, St Mary's TV mast. There is an aero radio bn on St Mary's, 49°54'.8N, 6°17'.4W, 321 khz continuous, call sign STM (NON 2A), range 15M.
Main Approaches are:
(1) From NNW: (a) to New Grimsby Hbr, between Bryher and Tresco. Beware cross stream in approach. Round Is lt is 1½M to port (Ro Bn), otherwise unlit. (b) to Old Grimsby Hbr on NE side of Tresco. Strong cross stream in approach, unbuoyed and unlit. From N of Tresco steer 135° for mid-pt between Northwethel and Merchants Pt.
(2) From N: E of Round Is to St Helen's Pool and Old Grimsby. Bar 0.3m; unlit.
(3) From E: Crow Sound. Crow Bar 0.9m; buoyed, unlit. Steer for TV mast and round NE of St Mary's Is 4 ca off.
(4) From SE: St Mary's Sound. Easiest; buoyed, unlit.
(5) From S: Smith's Sound W of St Agnes. Unbuoyed rks either side. Ldg marks require good visibility. Not recommended; use St Mary's Sound.
(6) From SW: Broad Sound 4 ca N of Bishop Rk, 059°. Buoyed, unlit.
(7) From W: North Channel. Old lt ho on St Agnes in line with with gap in Gt Smith 130°. Cross tide, outlying rks, unbuoyed.

Entrance (1) New Grimsby. Keep the W side of Hangman Is (conspic pinnacle 19m) in line with Star Castle on St Mary's 157°.
(2) St Helen's and Old Grimsby. Leave Round Is 1¼ca to W and keep Star Castle in line with E Gap Rk (2m) 182° until past E extreme of St Helen's Is whence steer 201° between E and W Gap Rks over 0.3m bar into St Helen's Pool.
(3) Crow Sound. (N.B. Only 0.9m on Crow Bar.) Leave Hats S card buoy close to stbd and clear Bar Pt by 1½ca; pass 50m either side of Crow bn (2 balls vert). Follow island round to pass between Bacon and Cow ledges (latter dries 0.6m) by keeping B vert strip on white shelter on promenade in line with Buzza Tr on skyline 151°.
(4) St Mary's Sound. Round S of St Mary's keeping ½M off Tolman Pt to clear Gilstone; close round Penninis Head leaving Spanish Ledge (E card) and Bartholomew Ledge R can buoys to port with N Carn of Mincarlo in line with W extreme of Gt Minalto 308° until NW corner of St Mary's is in line with St Martin's daymark; follow this line (040°) and enter St Mary's Pool with W arrow mark on E side of hbr in line with large B cross on hill top.
(5) Smith's Sound. (Not recommended). Castle Bryher (islet to W of Bryher) in line with gap between the summits of Gt Smith 351°. 5M minimum visibility needed. Passing Menpigrim and Buccabu pay off ½ca to E. Regain line to leave Gt Smith ½ca to stb.
(6) Broad Sound. Enter 4ca N of Bishop Rk lt ho and S of Flemings Ledge. Ldg line Gt Gannilly summit (8½M off) just open N of Bants Carn 059°.
(7) North Channel. Keep on approach ldg line (see above) until on ldg line for Broad Sound.

Interior Channels (1) St Mary's to New Grimsby. Leave 2h after LW for 1.3m draught and at half flood for 1.8m. Leave Nut Rk to port and Hulman Bn 50m to stb until Merrick Is is in line with right hand edge of Hangman Is. On this transit keep Little Rag Ledge Bn to port, Chink Rks to stb, Gt Crabs Ledge to port, Plump Rks to stb, Merrick Is to port and Plumb Is to stb, direction generally 340° but varies.
(2) To Old Grimsby: at half tide keep Crow Bn in line with middle TV tr to Lizard Pt whence steer for middle of gap between Tresco and Northwethel.
(3) To St Helen's Pool: at half tide from Hats anchorage, N of St Mary's, steer on the centre islet of Men-a-vaur in line with the landing cairn on SW corner of St Helen's, 322°. As the anchorage nears the islet will be obscured by the cairn.

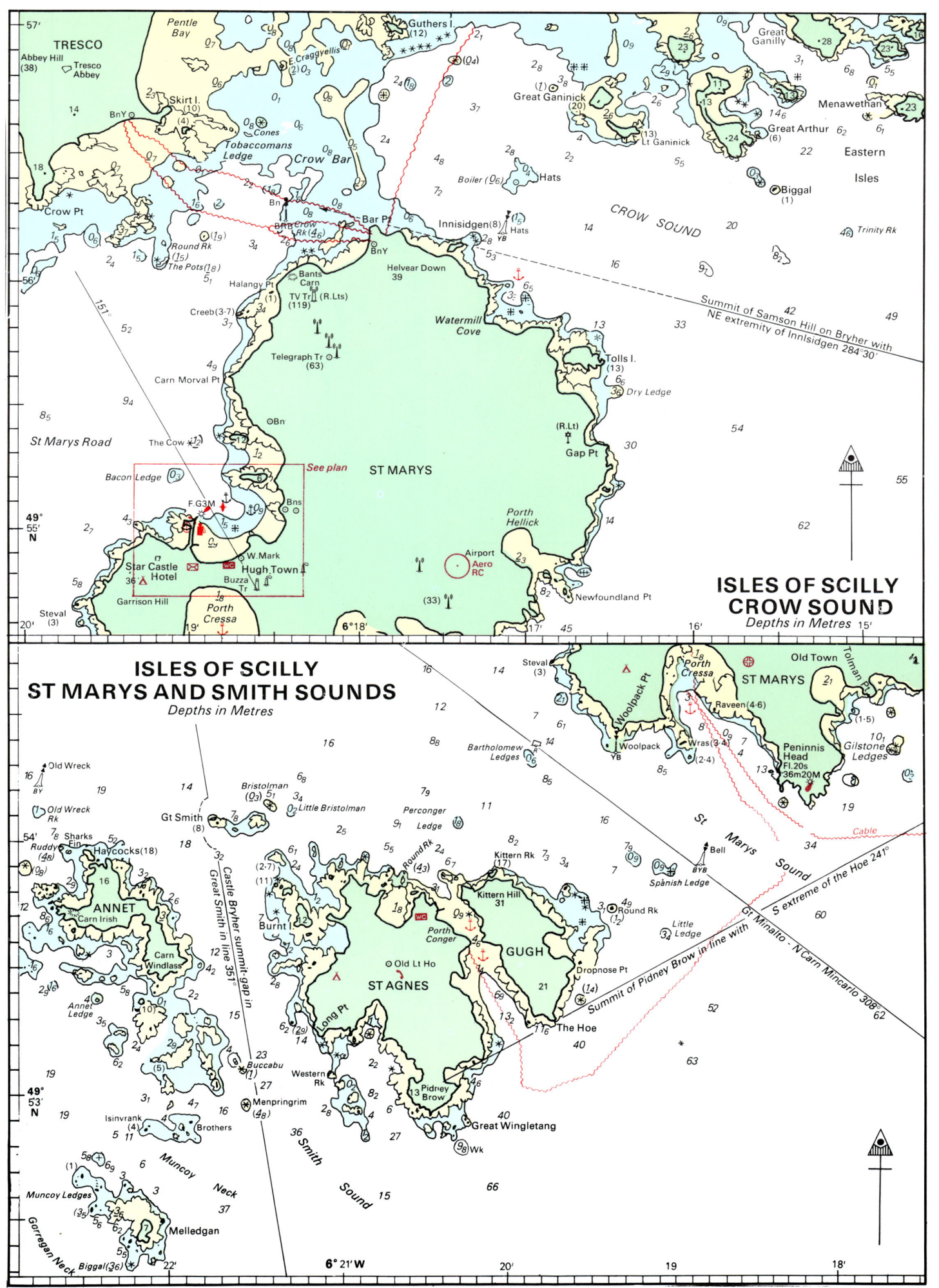

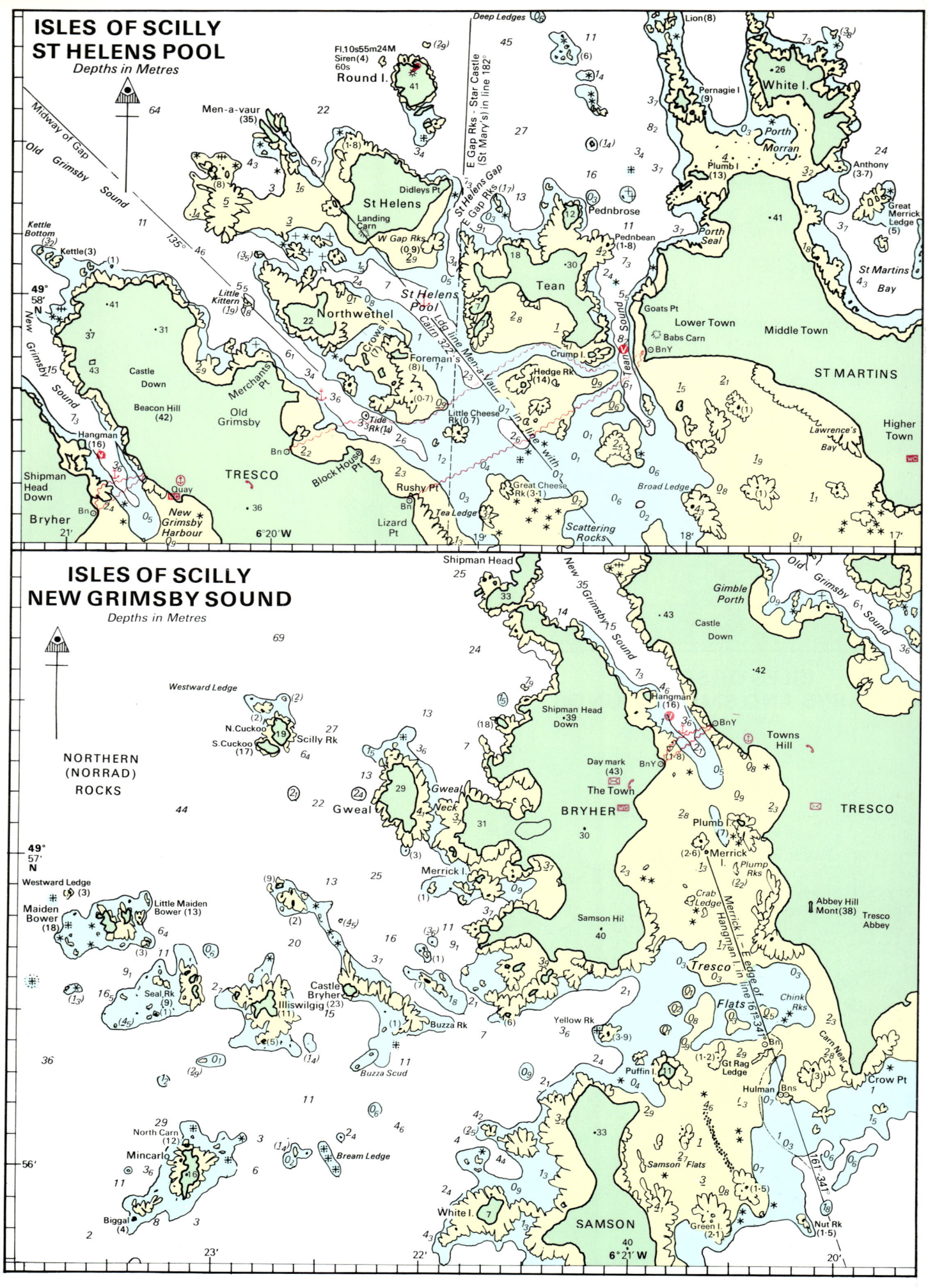

Anchorage. Yachts may lie alongside St Mary's Quay. None of the following anchorages offer all round shelter: it is important to consider wind direction, probable wind shift and direction of swell.

(1) St Mary's, Hugh Town. NE of line between pier and lifeboat station. Uncomfortable in winds SW to N. Clear Customs here. Busy in season; charges.
(2) St Mary's, Porth Cressa. Untenable in strong winds from SE to W, sheltered from W through N to E, but swell possible from W or ESE. Beware submarine cable, although it has concrete protection.
(3) St Mary's, Watermill Cove. Sheltered from S through W to NW.
(4) New Grimsby Hbr. Best and most sheltered anchorage. Sheltered SSW through W to NW and from NNE through E to SSE. Submarine cables. Visitors mooring buoys (charged) are encroaching on the anchorage.
(5) Old Grimsby. Sheltered from SSW to W. Subject to swell, even from W. Strong spring tidal streams.
(6) St Helen's Pool. Anchor astride line joining centre of Men-a-vaur to landing cairn on SW tip of St Helen's Is. Can be lonely but comparatively sheltered; some scend at HW.
(7) St Agnes/Gugh. These two islands are connected by a bar drying 4.6m, providing anchorages to the S in the Cove for winds from WSW through N to NNE, and to the N in Porth Conger for winds from E by S to W. Bar covers at HW springs when anchorages may be uncomfortable for HW±1½h.
(8) Visitors' buoys in Tean Sound, W of St Martins.

Supplies Fuel and water on quay at Hugh Town; water also on quays at Bryher and Tresco. Shops at Hugh Town and stores at St Agnes, Bryher and Tresco. Pubs or hotels at Hugh Town, Tresco, Bryher, St Martin's and St Agnes.
Tel & VHF HM (0720) 22768/ch 16 and 14 in working hours.
Customs (0720) 22571. Coastguard 22651/ ch 16, 67 (bad weather).

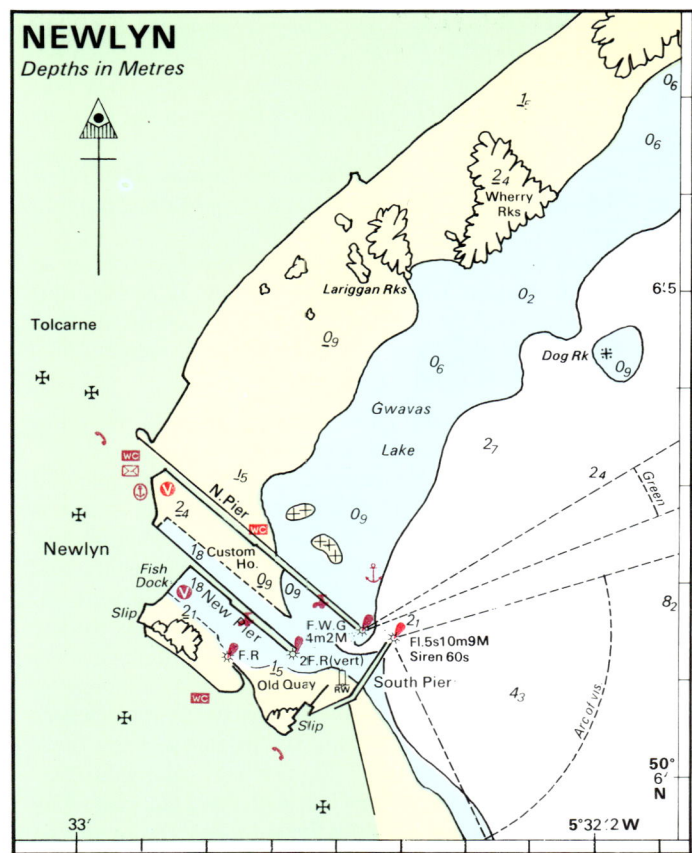

NEWLYN Chart BA 2345
HW: Dover +6h
MHWS 5.6m MHWN 4.4 MTL 3.2 MLWN 2.0 MLWS 0.8
From last quarter flood to first quarter ebb the tide flows NE in the N part of Mount's Bay.
For those coming from the Bristol Channel going S this is a useful port of refuge in the event of a bad weather forecast, affording protection in gales from S through W to NE.
Approach From Penzance leave Gear Rk to stb and steer for pierheads. From S, leave St Clement's Is ½M to port, steer N with Low Lee E card buoy, Q(3) 10s, to port until lt ho on S arm of hbr bears 305°, which course clears Carn Base Rks. By night, keep in W sector of Penzance lt ho (Iso WR 2s W 268°-345°) until Newlyn lt (Fl 5s) bears 305°.
Entrance Beware of emerging fishing boats. Turn to stb, leaving to port RW spar buoy at end of slipway.
Berthing 1. Anchor outside in Gwavas Lake, N of end of North Pier; good holding and sheltered in W winds.
2. Berth along W side of Central Pier in 2m rather than alongside Northern Pier which is for fishing boats which may leave at a very early hour. Crowded in summer.
Supplies Fuel from tanker; water on quays. Shops. EC Wed.
Tel/VHF HM: (0736) 62523/ch 16, 12 Mon-Sat.

MOUSEHOLE Chart BA 2345
HW: Dover +5¾h
MHWS 5.5m MHWN 4.6
A small pier drying hbr S of Newlyn, 4m springs, 2.6m neaps, sand and rk. Entrance closed in S gales. Good anchorage S of entrance. Water, shops.

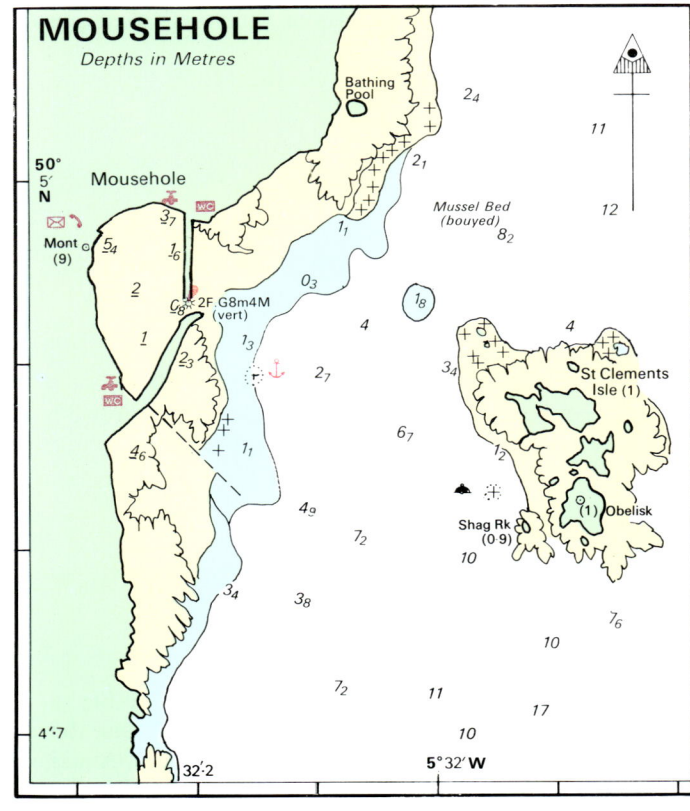

ENGLAND, SOUTH COAST 6

PENZANCE
Chart BA 2345

HW: Dover +6h
MHWS 5.6m MHWN 4.4 MTL 3.2 MLWN 2.0 MLWS 0.8
Tide flows NE in N part of Mount's Bay from last quarter flood to first quarter ebb.

There is a wet dock with sheltered berths open HW−2 to HW+1 (yachts welcome), an outer drying hbr and outside anchorage.

Approach From the E leave Mountamopus S card buoy to stb. From W clear Low Lee E card buoy, Q(3) 10s, and Carn Base Rks off Penlee Pt, the Gear Rk (bn) and the Battery Rks to SW of S Pier. At night keep in W sector (268°-345°) of lt Fl WR 5s on S pier head.

Signals 2 R lts (vert): gates open. R over G lts: gates closed. Signal mast on N side of dock entrance.

Entrance Keep clear of Cressar Rks to N of approach and be prepared to stand off if ship arrival or departure is imminent. When waiting for dock opening either anchor (in fair weather) E of end of Albert Pier, or wait in tidal hbr, or alongside lt ho pier if not required by Scilly steamship. In bad weather and at weekends the ship may use the Albert Pier, but her normal berth is alongside the Lt Ho Pier and she occupies this only from 1900 to 0930 and on Sats in summer from 1230-1400. The berth is therefore usually available while awaiting the opening of the dock gates between 1000 and 1830. There is 1.8m alongside between the lt ho and the ladder halfway along the pier. The S wall is swept by seas in S and SE gales and it may not be possible to open the dock gates in winds of storm force from those directions. Otherwise they open from HW−2h to HW+1h.

Berthing (1) Anchor in fair weather, with winds SW-W-N, 2ca or more off the Lt Ho Pier, clear of fairway but not E of lt ho because of swell.
(2) Drying moorings may be available in tidal hbr.
(3) Visitors' alongside berths in wet dock.

Supplies Diesel from hbr staff day or night when dock gates are open. Water on quay. Chandlery and 10-ton crane. All facilities. Rly, buses to Land's End, St Ives. Steamer and helicopter to Isles of Scilly. EC Wed (suspended in summer).

Tel/VHF HM: (0736) 66113/ch 16, 12, 9. (Penzance Hbr)

Customs as Plymouth.

PASSAGE NOTES: PENZANCE TO FALMOUTH
Chart BA 777

Passage Lights
Lizard   Fl 3s 29M Siren 60s
St Anthony Hd   Oc WR 15s 22/20M horn 30s
                (R over Manacles)

Streams related to Dover
Mount's Bay (middle): rotary clockwise. −6h E; +½h W (weak).
Lizard: −3½h W; +2h E.
Lizard to Falmouth −3h SW; +3h to −4h NE.
Bound to Falmouth from Mount's Bay it is desirable to reach the Lizard at the turn of the tide to the E because the ebb stream out of Falmouth makes progress slow. Avoid the Boa, an 11m shoal 3¼M W of the Lizard Lt Ho, in

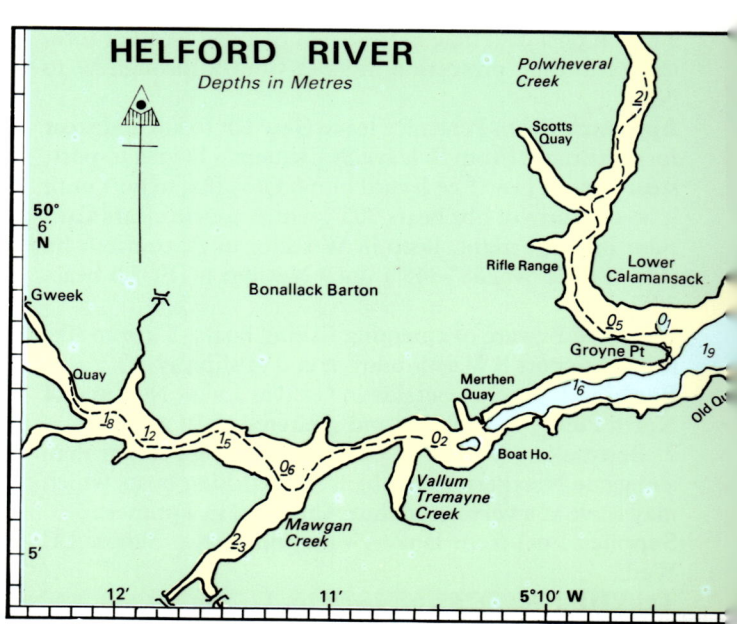

7 ENGLAND, SOUTH COAST

strong SW winds because of breaking seas. Off the Lizard dangers extend ½M to seaward, and a race extends to the S and SE for 3M. The violence of the seas varies with the tide and wind, but it is particularly bad in strong westerlies against an ebb tide. In bad weather keep at least 3 to 4M offshore. Otherwise, to clear Lizard dangers keep Godolphin Hill open of Rill Hd, 337°, until Lowland Pt opens E of Black Hd, 036°.

Black Hd should be cleared by ½M and the Manacles E card buoy, Q(3) 10s, given a wide berth to seaward. In E winds a confused sea builds up between Black Hd and the Manacles; with the flood tide a race may develop, dangerous at springs. In such conditions if heading for Falmouth it is best to make for the Y lt buoy, Fl Y 10s, at 50°00'N, 4°59'W and not steer for Falmouth until due S of St Anthony Lt. From the Manacles to Helford R and Falmouth the passage is straightforward, but there are unlit buoys off Porthallow.

Anchorages St Michael's Mount Good anchorage in offshore wind 1-1½ca W of W arm of hbr (or, with permission, dry out inside W arm). Avoid Outer Penzeath Rk ½M to W.
Loe Pool Good anchorage ¾M SSW of Pool. There is no navigable water between the sea and the Pool.
Mullion Good anchorage in E wind N of the island.
Housel Bay between Lizard Pt and Bass Pt, 6ca ENE. Large hotel conspic at head. Two RW striped bns on Bass Pt bear 292°
Parn Voose Balk Bn RW mast, W diamond top, at head of cove in line with a W patch 4½ca SSE bears 325°. This transit's intersection with 292° transit of Bass Pt bns marks Vrogue Rk.
Cadgwith Cove SW of lifeboat station at Kilcobben Cove. (N.B. It is imperative to get out to sea from the above three anchorages if onshore wind is expected.)
Porthoustock Cove midway between Manacle Pt and Pencra Hd, ½M N with conspic RW radar tr. Beware rks awash on N side of entrance for 1ca offshore.

PORTHLEVEN Chart BA 2345
HW: Dover +6h
MHWS 5.5m   MHWN 4.3   MTL 3.1   MLWN 2.0   MLWS 0.8
A drying hbr 8M NW of Lizard. Entrance closed in bad weather. Used mainly by small fishing boats but room for a few yachts. 3.6m on sill at springs, 2.7m at neaps. Visitor's berth is along E quay immediately to stb. Water, shops, boat and engine repairs.

HELFORD RIVER Chart BA 147
HW: Dover −6¼h
MHWS 5.3m   MHWN 4.2   MTL 3.0   MLWN 1.9   MLWS 0.6
A sheltered river with several creeks, navigable to Gweek, 4½M within entrance.
Approach from NE: to clear the Gedges keep Pennance Pt well open of Rosemullion Head until Bosahan Pt on S side of the entrance is well open of Mawnan Shear on N side. From S, bring N extremity of the pt ¼M NNW of Helford Pt just open of Bosahan Pt, 270°.
Entrance is between Rosemullion Hd in N and Nare Pt in S. G con buoy Fl G 5s (seasonal) lies about 1ca SE of the Gedges (August Rk). Give Nare Pt a wide berth at all states of the tide. Keep Helford Pt open of Bosahan Pt to clear a reef off the E end of the latter. To port a N card buoy marks the Voose, a drying ledge 1M WNW of Dennis Hd. NW of the Bosahan Narrows a G con buoy is moored on the edge of the N bank; it is difficult to see among moored craft.
Gillan Creek is entered S of Dennis Hd. Enter to N of E card buoy, midway between the buoy and Dennis Hd. The buoy marks a rk (dries 1m) almost in the centre of the entrance. The passage S of the buoy is not recommended without local knowledge, due to offlying rks.
Berthing Oyster beds lie in river and creeks.
Anchoring (1) Off Durgan or Grebe Rks, 2½-3½m, disturbed in S to E winds;
(2) Off Helford, 5½-11m, among or at W end of moorings; strong tide. Edge of mud across Penarvon Cove is steep-to.
(3) Near entrance to Navas Creek along the N shore out of the tide, 1¾m or more. Uncomfortable if far out in the stream in fresh E or W winds.
(4) Quiet anchorage inside Navas Creek, among moorings, in 'Abraham's Bosom' pool, 2m. N.B. 0.9m bar at entrance. Land at Oyster Fisheries Quay.
(5) Gillan Creek. Pool with 1½-2m inside the entrance but no shelter in E winds unless on the mud 1M up the creek. There is 1½-3m either side of and just beyond the mid-channel rk, shoaling rapidly to under 1m.

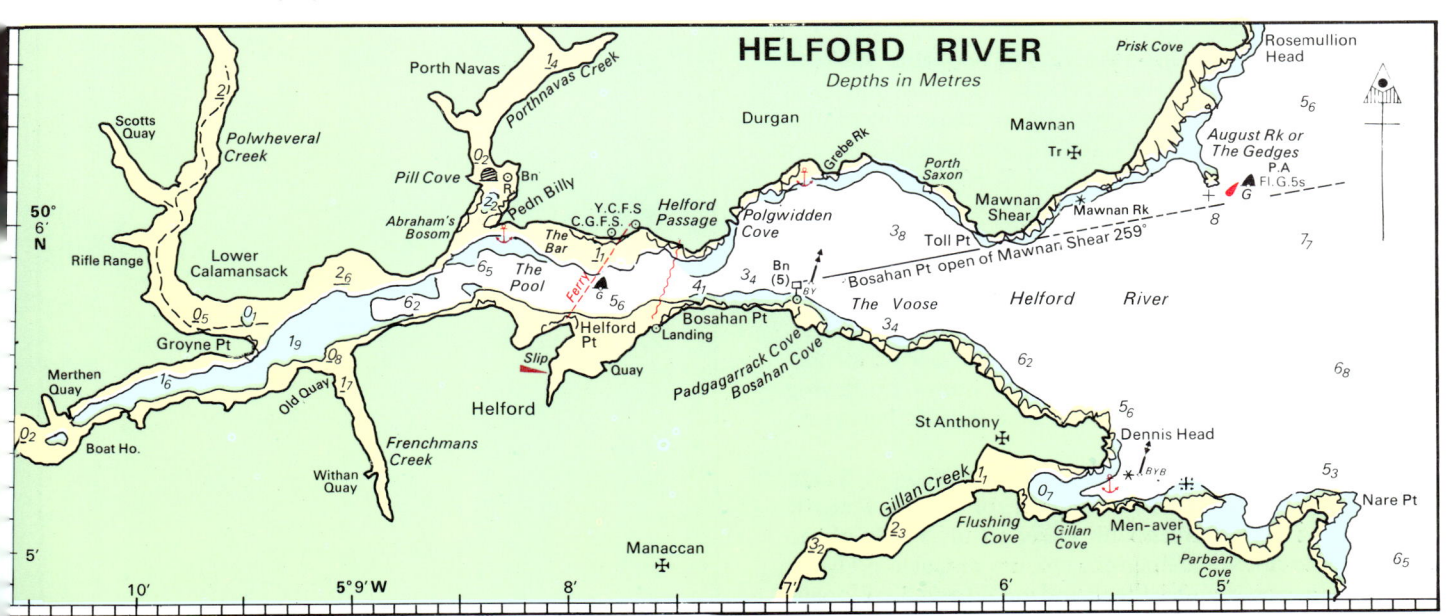

Moorings Visitors' moorings (those with green pick-up buoys) off Helford. Consult Sailaway, St Anthony, for Gillan Creek.

The river may be explored at HW to Gweek, Mawgan and Polwhetheral.

Supplies Fuel (not in bulk) and water at St Anthony (Sailaway), Gillan Creek and at Porth Navas YC. Water at Durgan and Helford River SC. Stores at Helford. Landing at pontoon on Helford Pt (charge) or at SC.

Tel/VHF: Moorings (0326) 280422/ch 37.

FALMOUTH & TRURO RIVERS Charts BA 32
HW: Dover −6h. DS: Dover −3h SW; +3h NE.
Falmouth:
MHWS 5.3m MHWN 4.2 MTL 3.0 MLWN 1.9 MLWS 0.6
Truro:
MHWS 5.3m MHWN 4.2 (dries)

The Fal estuary provides excellent shelter and anchorages, with several drying creeks and navigation at HW via Truro River to Truro.

Approach From E, St Anthony Lt is not visible until it bears NW. From SW, coast between Pennance and Pendennis Pts has drying rks up to 1ca from shore.

Entrance is divided into two channels by Black Rk conspic B bn and E card buoy Q(3) 10s. When this rk is covered there is 2.7m over the banks inside the river as far as Trelissick.

Inner Hbr, Falmouth & Penryn River When the N arm Q lt comes on with the R Fl lt on the E breakwater, 293°, the fairway to Falmouth is open. However, except when approaching directly from the E, these lts may be obscured by a strong W lt illuminating the jetty. Governor buoy, unlit, can be avoided when approaching from SE by keeping lts on E and N arms of the quays open either way. The river continues 1M to W above Falmouth to Penryn but there are oyster beds on the mudflats on both sides of the channel. Above the wharf at Boyer's Cellars the river dries. At Penryn, Town Quay has 4.3 to 3.0m at HW.

Berthing Anchor off Custom House Quay, close NE of Visitors' Yacht Haven (buoy anchor and keep clear of approach to docks).

Moorings: 1. There are two trots of bookable Harbour Authority moorings for visitors between Greenbank Quay and Prince of Wales Pier; green buoys marked K1 to K7 and T1 to T5. In season T1 and T2 may be replaced by a pontoon.

(2) RCYC have some buoys marked for visitors and others may be had from local yards.

(3) Marinas at Falmouth: Visitors' Yacht Haven, North Quay (Apr-Oct): 40 yachts alongside, 1.8m; best for shopping, water and short stays. Yacht Marina, North Parade, ½M above Greenbank Quay: 30 pontoon berths for visitors; dredged access channel 2m, lt buoys Q; drying pipeline across middle of basin - take outside berth and enquire.

Landing places at Custom House Quay or Visitors' Yacht Haven, Fish Strand Quay, Prince of Wales Pier, R Cornwall YC and Greenbank Quay all on S side of the channel (do not leave dinghies moored at Custom House Quay or Prince of Wales Pier); and at Old and New Quays at Flushing on the N side. Hard at Flushing Quay and several good ones both sides of hbr.

St Mawes Creek From Castle G con buoy, leave St Mawes S card buoy (Lugo Rk) well to port. At half tide there is not less than 1.8m between the buoy and the Pt. There is about 1.2m up to Porthcuel but channel is tortuous, unmarked and with many moorings.

Berthing Anchor off two beaches beyond the pier, 2m or more. In SW wind there is good shelter round Amsterdam Pt clear of moorings, dries. Avoid Black Rk close inshore abreast N end of wood on E side. St Mawes SC has moorings. Landing on slipway at SC at Polvarth except LWS.

St Just Creek Good anchorage in 3m inside Messack Pt under N shore.

Mylor Creek Navigable to Mylor Br by dinghy. Mylor Yacht Hbr has 12 moorings and 4 pontoon berths for visitors.

Restronguet Creek Anchor off entrance, no room inside. Landing at Ferry Ho or Pandora Inn pontoon. Deveron (1½M) may be reached by dinghy on the tide.

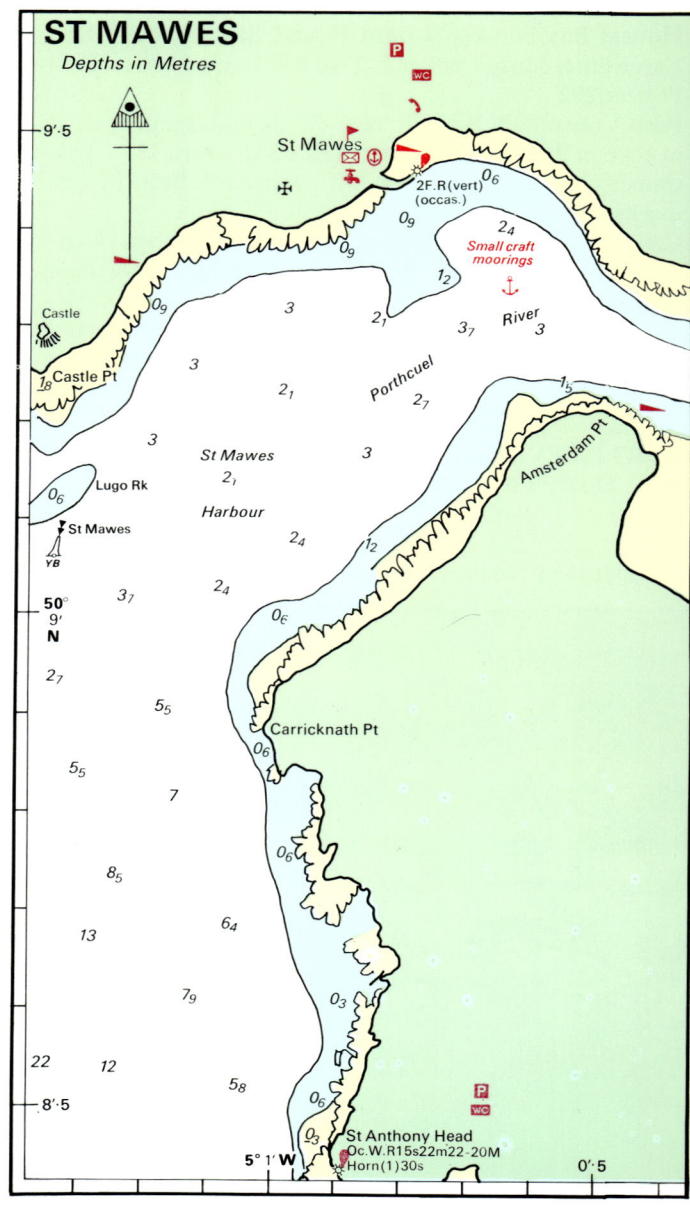

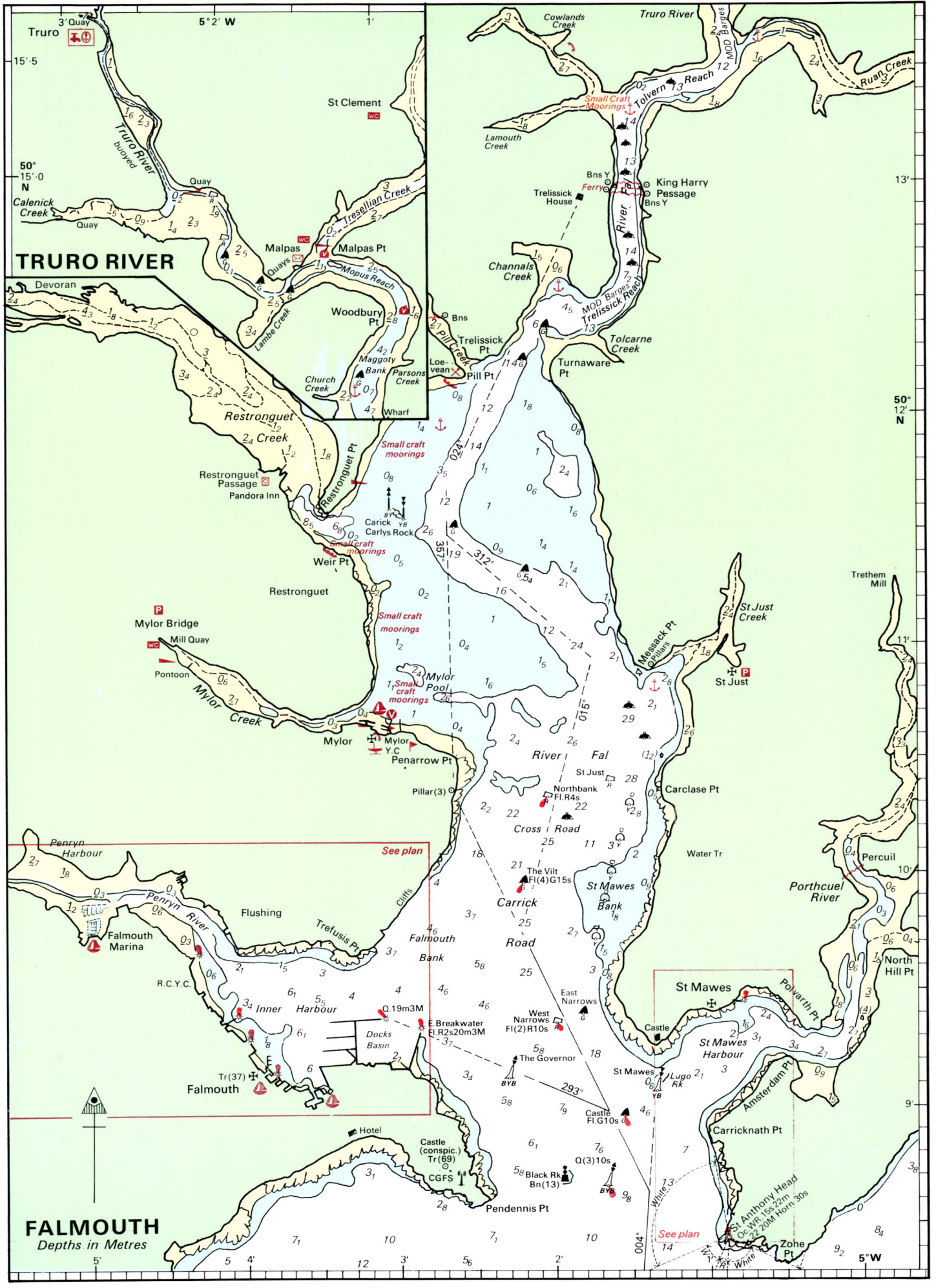

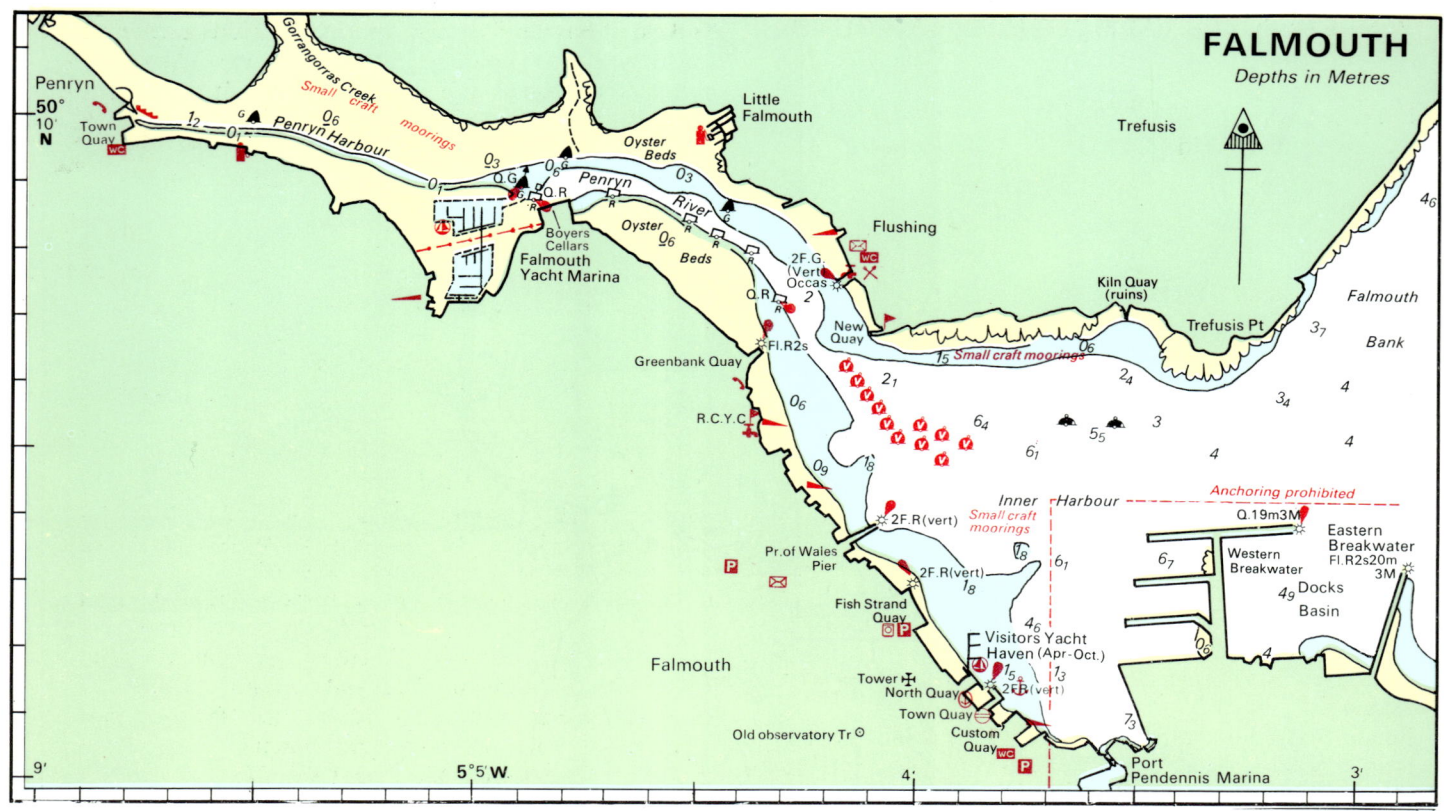

Truro River There is plenty of water up to Malpas except at Maggoty Bank (G con buoy). Concrete mooring clumps, drying, are reported near the W bank 3ca S and ½ca N of the ferry at King Harry Passage. They are marked by a W post. Malpas is the limit of LW navigation. With a draught of less than 1.5m, Truro can be reached on the tide following the buoyed channel.

Berthing Anchor (1) Off Loe beach. Good, clean, quiet anchorage in 2m inshore off Loe Vean. Summer moorings are laid all the way between Restronguet and Loe Beach: anchor outside these. Riding lts advisable.

(2) Channels Creek.

(3). Above King Harry Ferry off the entrance to Cowlands Creek on the N side.

(4) Off the mouth of the River Fal (Ruan Creek) where it joins River Truro near Tregothnan. Beware of drying concrete blocks close inshore off ruined cottage on N side of entrance to Ruan Creek

(5) On Maggoty Bank according to tide.

Moorings off thatched restaurant at Tolverne, opposite entrance to Cowlands Creek; 4 Carrick visitors' buoys off Malpas Pt; and at Malpas Marine. Mooring alongside quay at Truro possible; dries, soft mud.

Supplies Fuel and water at Falmouth Yacht Haven and Yacht Marina, Falmouth Boat Const Co, Mylor Yacht Hbr. Water at RCYC, St Mawes (tap opposite hbr steps), Porthcuel, Truro and Malpas Marine (also engineer). When Falmouh is crowded in the season it is pleasanter to go to Truro at HW for water and supermarket.

Telephone/VHF Falmouth Hbr Office (0326) 312285, 314379/ ch 16, 12.

HM Launch: ch 16, 12. Falmouth Visitors Yacht Haven and deep water moorings as for Hbr Office.

Falmouth Yacht Marina: 316620/ ch 80, 37.

Falmouth Boat Const Co: 74309.

RCYC: 311105/ ch 37 (for boatman).

St Mawes SC: 270686 or 270808 for moorings.

Mylor Yacht Hbr: 72121/ ch 37.

Truro hbr office (0872) 72130, 224231/ch 12 ('Carrick').

Fal River patrol ch 16, 12 ('Carrick 3').

Penryn HM (0326) 73352.

Malpas Marine (0872) 71260.

Customs as Plymouth.

PASSAGE NOTES: FALMOUTH TO PLYMOUTH
Chart BA 1267

Passage Lights
St Anthony's Hd	Oc WR 15s 22/20M horn 30s (R over Manacles)
Eddystone	Fl(2) 10s+F R 24/13M horn (3) 60s

Streams related to Dover.
Rectilinear in W, rotary clockwise in E.
5M E of St Anthony's Hd: Dover +3h NE; −3½h SW.
Plymouth: +4h E; −2h W.

Leaving Falmouth bound E, keep at least 1M offshore to clear the Bizzies, a shoal patch off Greeb Pt, and the Whelps off Nare Hd. In bad weather keep at least 2M off Dodman Pt (conspic stone cross) because of overfalls. If going inshore to Fowey, give a wide berth to Gwineas and Yaw Rks (E card Q(3) 10s) ¾M S of Chapel Pt, and Cannis Rk (S card Q(6)+L Fl 15s) 4ca SE of Gribbin Hd. E-bound from Fowey keep well clear of Udder Rk (S card) 3M to E, and Ranneys Rks off Looe Is. Rame Hd appears conical and has a small chapel on its summit. No offlying dangers.

Bound up-Channel offshore give a wide berth to Eddystone Lt Ho, especially in bad weather; also avoid Hand Deeps, 3¾M to NW (in F R sector), dangerous overfalls.

With light winds along the shore it is often possible to carry a breeze close inshore by the Dodman and Fowey, while a direct course to Plymouth might end in being becalmed.

Bound from Fowey or Plymouth to Falmouth, there is a considerable set into the bight E of Falmouth. Remember St Anthony Lt first appears when bearing NW.

Anchorages Gorran Haven, 1M WSW of Gwineas Rk. Good anchorage in W winds in 6m. **Portmellon,** a small sandy cove in SW corner of Mevagissey Bay. Good anchorage in W winds, 5m.

St Austell Bay: in S corner, 5m. In SW winds anchor off Ropehaven, good holding. **Polkerris,** 1½M N of Gribbin Hd: good anchorage in E winds, 5m. (Hbr dries.)

Whitesand Bay: offers a long stretch of clear coast with shelving shore in which to close the land in poor visibility. Good anchorage in calm weather and offshore winds.

MEVAGISSEY
Chart BA 147

HW: Dover −5¾h. DS: Dover +3h NE; −3h SW.
MHWS 5.4m MHWN 4.3 MTL 3.1 MLWN 2.0 MLWS 0.7

Mevagissey is a fishing harbour which can accept only a few visiting yachts. It provides good shelter except in strong E winds.

Entrance Beware of Black Rk (dries 0.3m) to N of entrance 20m wide and 2.1m depth.

Outer Hbr has 2m alongside S pier with drying rks along S and N sides. Inner Hbr dries and is reserved for fishing boats except when taking on fuel or water.

Berthing Moor alongside S Pier, clear of steps, and report to HM (or car park attendant in hut at root of quay). Do not pick up a vacant buoy. There is a good anchorage in ofshore winds off Porthmellon ½M S of hbr.

Supplies Fuel and water at W side of Inner Hbr. Boatyard and slip. EC Thur (suspended in summer).

Tel: (0726) 843305/842496. Night 843332.

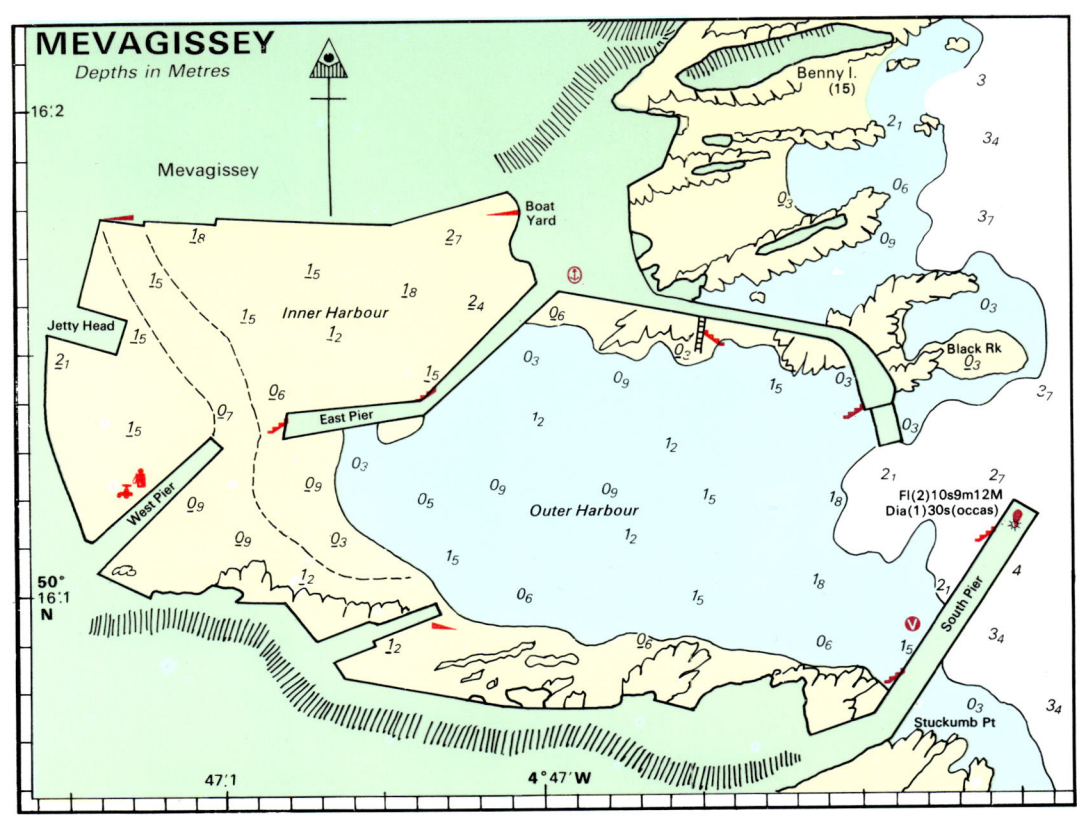

ENGLAND, SOUTH COAST 12

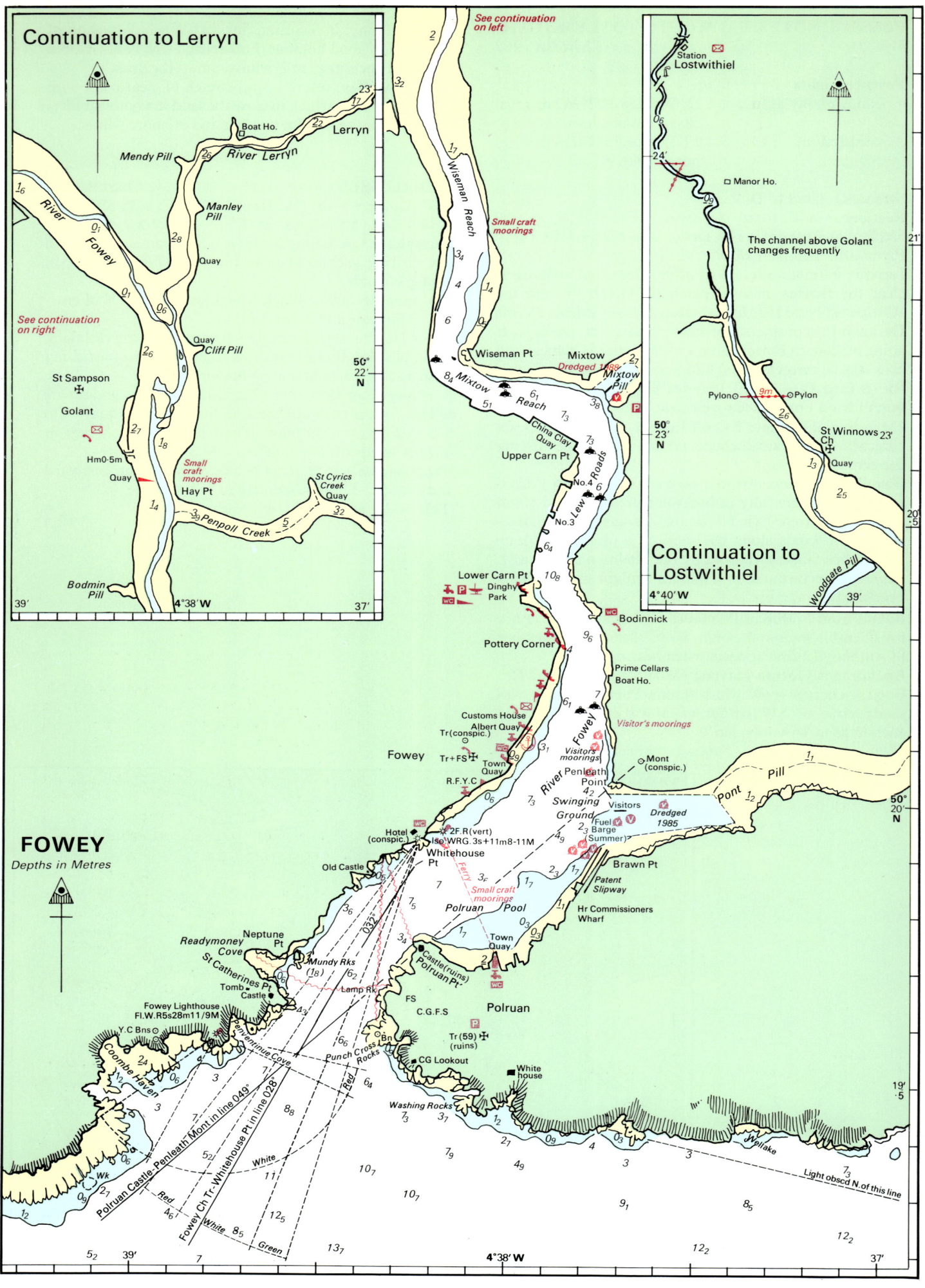

FOWEY
Chart BA 31

HW: Dover −5¾h . DS: Dover +4h E; −2h W.
MHWS 5.4m MHWN 4.3 MTL 3.1 MLWN 2.0 MLWS 0.6

Fowey has many sheltered moorings for yachts but is also a commercial port used by large ships for the export of china clay.

Approach From E keep RHWS tr on Gribbin Hd bearing more than 273° to clear the Udder Rk 3M E of Fowey (S card bell buoy). To pass between the Udder and the mainland keep Looe Is shut in by Nealand Pt. From SW to clear the Cannis Rk, ¼M SE from Gribbin Hd, keep Dodman Pt open to seaward of Gwineas until Tr of Fowey Parish ch is open of St Catherine Pt. To pass between Cannis and the mainland (1.2m) keep the old castle on Polruan Pt in line with conspic memorial on Penleath Pt (048°).
At night keep a mile offshore and alter course N when in G sector of Whitehouse Pt lt (Iso WRG 3s) and bring lt ahead steering 025°. From SW bring the lt bearing 025° and keep in W sector.

Entrance Fowey ch tr in line with Whitehouse Pt, 028°, leads in mid-channel. To clear Lamp Rk on E side, keep the houses in Bodinnick shut in by Fowey Town Quay. To clear Mundy Rk on W side, keep the FS at the YC open of the end of Whitehouse Pt breakwater.

The River is often crowded with shipping and it is inadvisable to attempt to reach Wiseman's Pt without reliable power. The upper reaches can be explored by dinghy to Lostwithiel and Lerryn. Do not pass E of the ships laid up on E side of fairway between Penleath Pt and Bodinnick as they may be connected to the shore by breast lines. Overhead cable (9m) crosses river ½M S of Lostwithiel.

Berthing Anchoring in Wiseman's Reach is now allowed only with permission of HM. Anchoring off Polruan, clear of the swinging area, is also subject to permission, normally given only when pontoons are full. Give 90m berth to large can mooring buoy, used for swinging, off Pont Pill. Avoid anchoring between Penleath Pt and Wiseman's Pt as large ships are swung in channel. There are no floating anchorages in upper reaches.

Moorings Pontoon at Albert Quay is short-stay and for water only. There are 19 W or Y visitors' buoys, marked 'FHC Visitors', and a 90ft pontoon just N of Penleath Pt; pontoon and buoys are uncomfortable in S winds above F4 (and removed in winter.) There is more shelter in Pont Pill on five trots of fore and aft moorings (each taking two boats) and another pontoon. There is a third pontoon, with the SW end reserved for visitors, further upriver at Mixtow Pill (dredged), but the surrounding landing places are private except for the head of the Pill, accessible at HW. Otherwise land on slip by hotel opposite Bodinnick.

Supplies Fuel on Polruan Quay; Water on Albert and Polruan Quays. All stores, EC Wed.

Tel/VHF HM (0726) 832471/2; ch 16,12,11. Hbr Patrol Boat (Apr–Sept) ch 12. Water taxi ch 16, 6. Customs as Plymouth.
Fuel Barge 'Fowey Refueller' (0836) 519341/ch 16.

LOOE
Chart BA 147

HW: Dover −5¾h.
MHWS 5.4m MHWN 4.2 MTL 3.0 MLWN 2.0 MLWS 0.6

A drying hbr with 3-4m alongside E quay at HW and 1.2-3m along W one.

Approach From W, to clear the Rennies keep the mainland showing above the top of Looe Is; overfalls S of the Is on the ebb. Steer in when E Looe Ch is well open of W point of the entrance. At night, coming from W keep in W sector of pier-head lt Oc WR which opens at 313°. If beat-

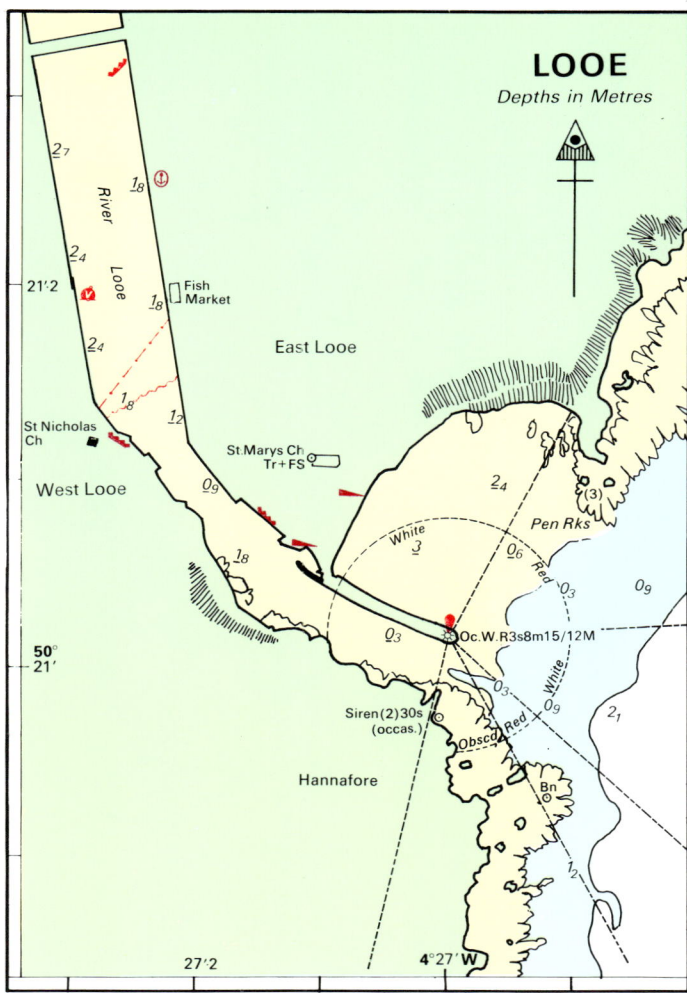

ing in from E, remember that rks run out 1½ ca from the shore NE of the entrance. Passage between the Is and the mainland should not be attempted except at HW with local knowledge. Dangerous half-tide rk (Dunker) ½ ca off NW corner of Is.

Signals R flag at root of jetty when conditions outside hbr are unsuitable for small craft.

Entrance Stream runs at 3kn through the narrows on both flood and ebb. On the flood there is an out-going eddy on both sides of the river from the inner end of the narrows to beyond the visitors' berth on the W side of the hbr, causing problems coming alongside. A bank runs down the centre of hbr from the br to opposite St Nicholas Ch giving ½m less water.

Berthing Anchorage outside. Sheltered in W winds, open to SE and E, and S by W. Bring pier-head on with St Nicholas Ch, W Looe, and anchor in 3m, sand and mud, abreast the W marks on the rk at W entrance of the hbr. Inside mooring: hbr is crowded when fishermen are in and yachts are not allowed to lie alongside fishing boats. Visitors' berth is immediately up-river of the third set of steps on the W side of the hbr by a fishermen's shelter.

Supplies Water on quays; fuel in cans at E Looe. Shops EC Thur.

Tel: HM (05036) 2839 or night 2647.

POLPERRO
Chart BA 148

HW: Dover −5½h.
MHWS 5.4m MHWN 4.3 MLWN 2.0 MLWS 0.6

A small drying hbr with room for only a few visiting yachts and a fair weather anchorage outside the pier. Entrance closed in bad weather. Fuel, water, shops.

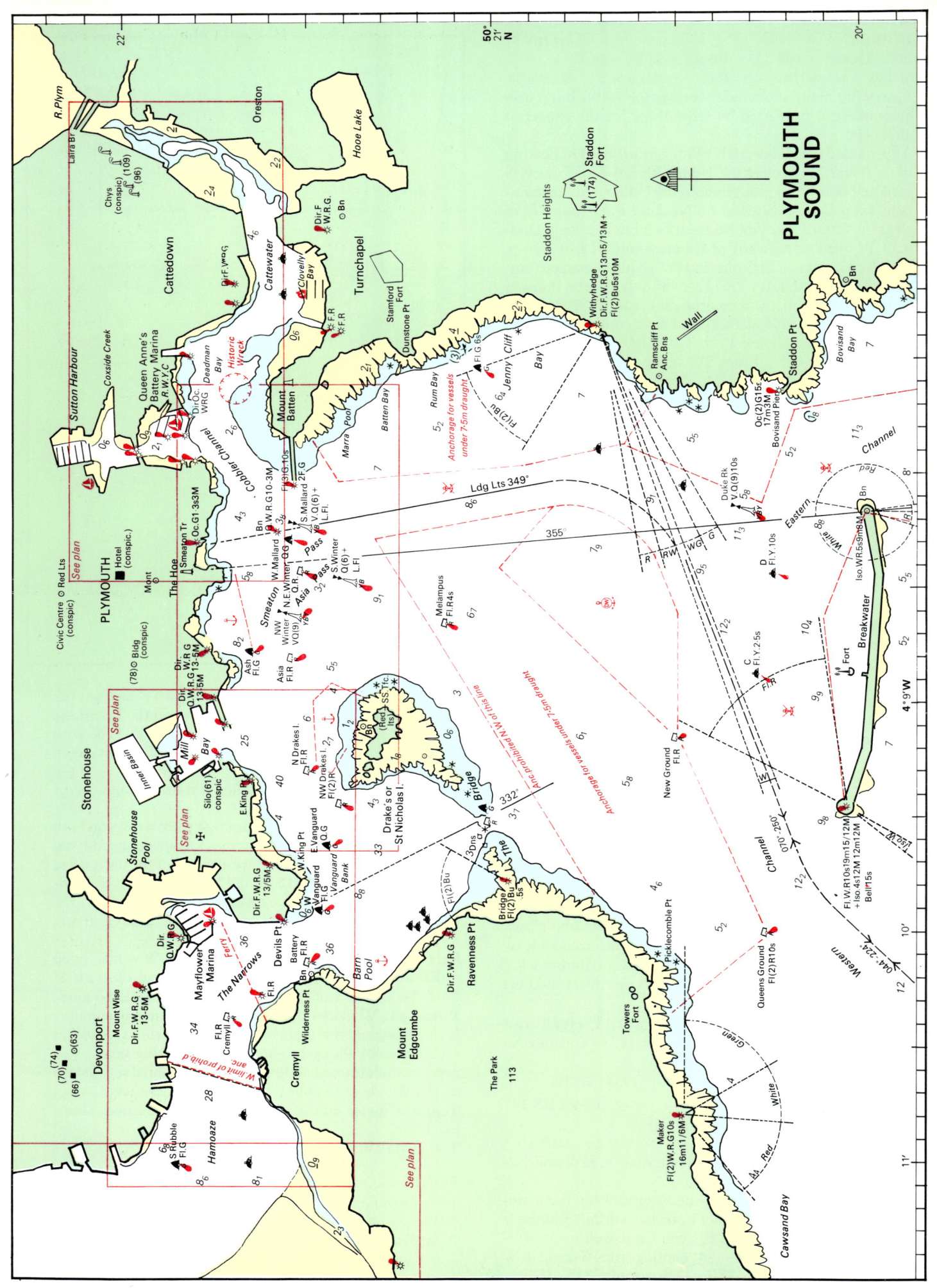

PLYMOUTH

Charts BA 30, 1901, 1967; 1902 Hamoaze; 871 Tamar. HW: Dover −5½h. DS: Dover +4h E; −2h W.
MHWS 5.5m MHWN 4.4 MTL 3.2 MLWN 2.2 MLWS 0.8
At Cotehele Quay HW is up to 20min after HW Devonport; LW is LW Devonport +¾h.

Plymouth is a Naval Dockyard Port, under a QHM, with considerable commercial traffic as well as extensive yachting facilities. The hbr is protected by a breakwater with E and W entrances.

In E entrance streams are rotary clockwise, Dover +5h N; −3½h S.

In W entrance, streams are rectilinear, Dover +2¼h NE; −4½h SW.

Internally the streams run strongly NNW and SSE across The Bridge. In Asia Pass the flood (1kn springs) sets towards the shoal running NE from Drake's Is; the ebb sets towards Winter Shoal. S of Vanguard Bank the flood (2kn) sets towards Barn Pool, the ebb SE towards The Bridge. In The Narrows at the S end the flood (2¾kn) sets NE out of Barn Pool and the ebb towards Vanguard Bank. At the N end the flood sets towards Mount Wise and the ebb towards Devil's Pt. In Hamoaze S of Rubble Bank the ebb starts Dover-6h and sets towards Millbrook Lake; flood starts Dover +½h.

Approach From E, round the Mewstone and steer 292° with Stock Pt on with N side of the Mewstone astern and follow directions for E or W entrance. From W, in bad weather or with wind against tide, give Rame Head at least ½M clearance and steer to leave breakwater lt ho (Fl WR 10s & Iso 4s) well clear to stbd.

Entrance In strong S winds the sea breaks heavily on Knap and Panther shoals, to SSW of breakwater lt ho, and on the ebb in the E entrance, which also has a dangerous sea in strong W winds. For the E entrance bring the lt bn, Iso W R 5s, on E arm of breakwater in line with Smeaton's Tr (RW bands) on the Hoe, 355° (at night keep in W sector of breakwater lt). Give breakwater end 1ca clearance, thence proceed on one of the internal routes below.

For W entrance, leave the breakwater lt ho well clear to stb.

Signals Signals to control the movement of ships longer than 20m in the main channels may be displayed at a mast on Drake's Is or at FS at Devonport N Dockyard:

3 R Fl Emergency.	All unauthorised movements stopped.
1 R Oc over 2 G Oc	Outgoing tfc only may proceed on recommended track.
2 G Oc over 1 R Oc	Incoming tfc only may proceed on recommended track.
2 G Oc over 1 W Oc	Give wide berth to HM vessels on recommended track.

Craft under 20m may proceed in the contrary direction so long as they do not impede the main channels.

North of the Breakwater, craft longer than 45m have right of way over smaller craft whether under power or sail.

The main channels have W bns 9m high with △ Or/W day marks, mostly lit: W on course; Alt WR or WG slightly off channel; FR or FG further off channel.

Lt Q Y is displayed at all major dir lts when main power supplies are interrupted.

The Sound. Anchorages Yachts can approach to 1½ca of the shore, apart from the area of the Bridge, SW of Drake's Is.

(1) Cawsand Bay, W of breakwater, except in E and SE winds. Anchor close inshore on S side of bay.

(2) Jenny Cliff Bay, E side of The Sound. Sheltered from NE through E to SE.

To Cattewater, Sutton Hbr and Cobbler Channel Pass ½ca W of Mount Batten breakwater Fl(3)G 10s 4M to Fisher's Nose Fl(3) R 10s W of entrance to Sutton Hbr. At night pick up dir lt off Queen Anne's Battery Oc WRG 7.5s, 050°. For Sutton Hbr Marina steer N, when abreast of Fisher' Nose, for entrance between pier-heads Fl R and Fl G 3s, with Queen Anne's Battery Marina to stb, marked by four pairs of 2FG(vert) lts on breakwater and pontoon heads. For Cattewater continue to steer 050° on dir lt on Queen Anne's Marina breakwater, then Cattedown ldg bns 102° followed by Turnchapel ldg bns 129°, depth 4.9m. Laira Br, at the N end of Cattewater, has clearance of 4.9m in the centre.

Berthing Anchoring in Cattewater is difficult: space may be found in Clovelly Bay. There are Cattewater Hbr Commissioners visitors' buoys S of Sutton Hbr entrance and four belonging to RWYC (Or with W tops) S of QAB breakwater; moorings may also be available from Turnchapel yacht yards. Two marinas at Sutton: Sutton Hbr Marina in N (boats up to 45ft) and Queen Anne's Battery Marina (60 visitors' berths, up to 100ft).

To Millbay Docks From Melampus R can buoy either steer NNW over Asia Knoll shoal, 5.5m, or follow Asia Pass round Asia buoy (Fl(2) R 5s). By night approach from The Sound with Millbay dir lt (Dir Q WRG) bearing 326°, within W sector to Asia lt buoy and NW Winter (W card VQ(9) 10s) and thence to entrance between pier-heads (QR and QG).

Berthing Anchor off W Hoe, 3½-7½m, in all but S winds, very uncomfortable in SE wind. Bottom foul, buoy anchor. Steamer wash day and night.

Hamoaze and Mayflower Marina From Melampus R can buoy make for Asia Pass buoys and follow buoyed chan round to the Narrows where Mayflower Marina is to stb. By night follow dir lts (all F) from Asia Pass: Western King 270°, Raveness 225°, Mount Wise 343°.

Another route by day is via The Bridge to SW of Drake's Is. It is unlit, lies between E and W Bridge buoys and has only 2.1m. There are obstructions on the bottom close to the chan either side of the buoys and in bad weather the sea breaks heavily in the approach. Across The Bridge the streams run strongly NNW and SSE. Ldg line is Devil's Pt Bn (W post) on with large house with three chimneys 332°, keeping in centre of channel between the Bridge buoys.

Berthing Anchor (1) in NW corner of Barn Pool at W end of Drake Channel; bottom very steep-to; good shelter from W winds.

(2) N of Drake's Is to E of private pier – buoy anchor.

(3) Millbrook Lake, 3ca W of Mashford's Yard at Cremyl. Moorings available in Stonehouse Pool from yard adjoining Admiral's Hard; and at Ballast Pound Yacht Harbour off Torpoint, 2ca S of chain ferry. This yacht hbr has also drying quayside berths accessible HW±2h. Mayflower Marina at Ocean Quay has berths for craft up to 19.8m long, 3m draft.

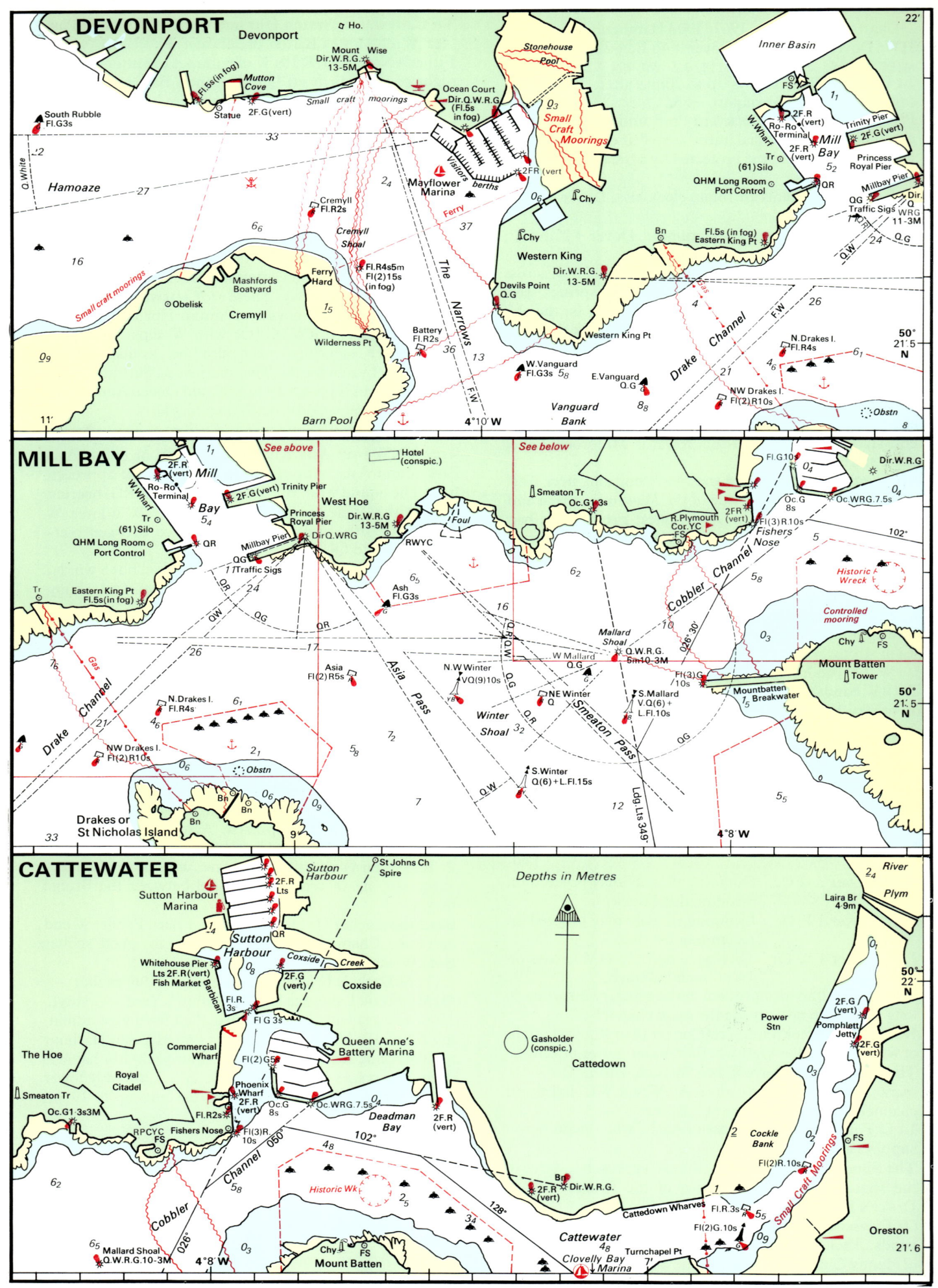

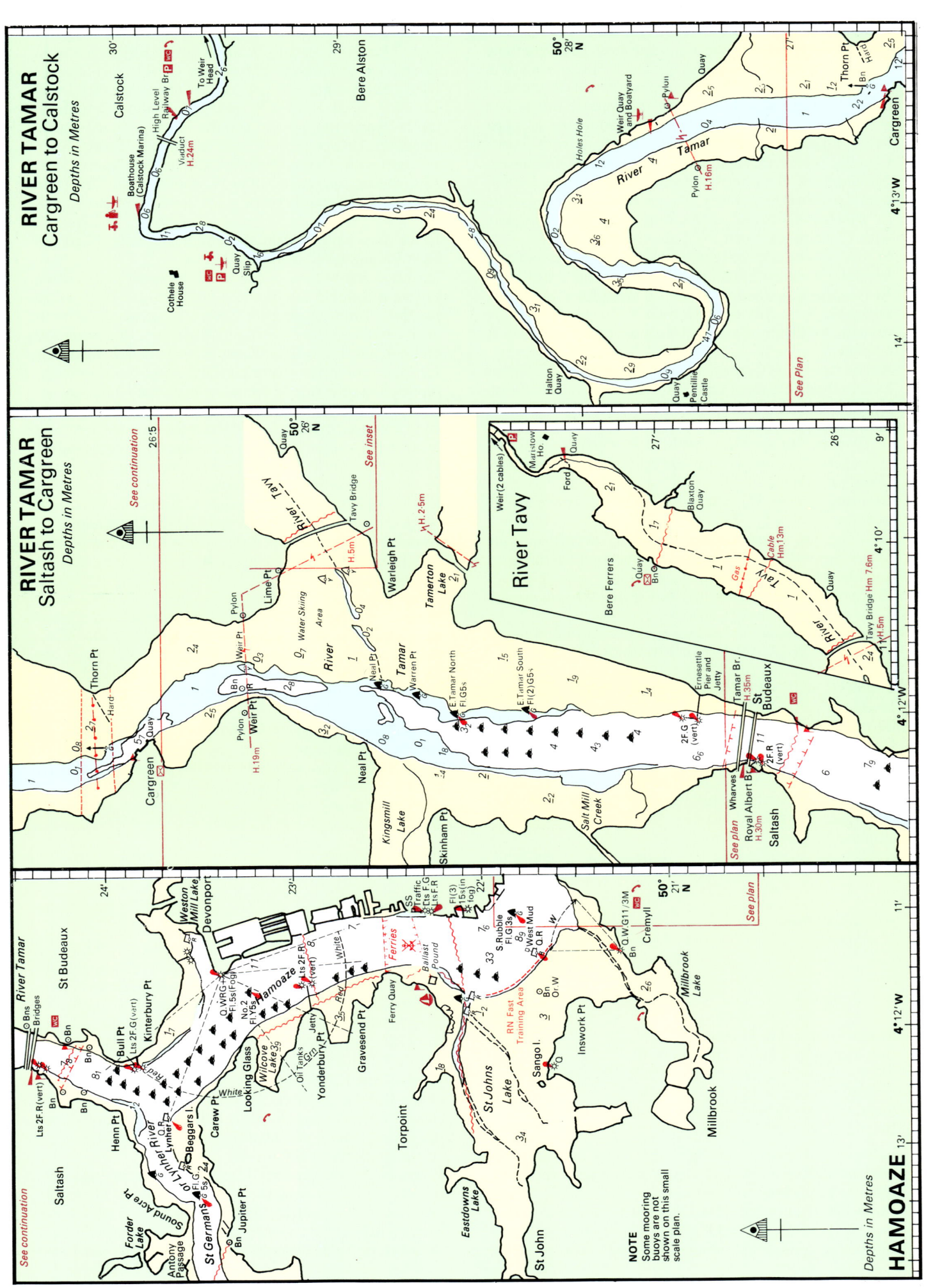

The Tamar and its Tributaries The Tamar has lt bns as far as Warren Pt 50°25′N. Above Skinham Pt LW depths are generally less than 2m but some stretches have more (see notes below on mooring). Calstock can be reached at HW and craft with 1.5m draft can reach ¼M off the head of navigation at Weir Hd at HWS. Navigation in this area at LW (even LWN) is not recommended owing to debris (water-logged tree trunks) and the unreliability of charts. Channel winds through mud-banks and is unmarked. Although the chain ferry between Torpoint and Devonport is required to give way, yachts should avoid impeding its passage. Overhead cables cross 4ca below Cargreen with 19m clearance and 1¼M above Cargreen, 16m.

St John's Lake dries but a narrow channel, buoys and bns, has 0.4 to 1.8m to Trevol Pt, jetty with 1.9m at head.

St German's or Lynher River is buoyed for 2¼M and is navigable by yachts to St German's Quay and with 2m draught to Tideford at MHWS; also to Notter Br on R Lynher.

Anchorages in St German's River: Off Anthony Village or Dandy Hole off S tip of Erth Hill, 3m, sheltered, but landing difficult at LW. Keep clear of bend at W end of reach, used by salmon fishermen with nets.

R Tavy has an overhead cable at its entrance with 5m clearance. Craft with 1.5m draught can reach the falls (2½M) at MHWS.

Berthing Anchor: (1) Saltash Bay on W side above the brs in 3½m.
(2) Cargreen. Good holding in 3-3½m except opposite quays. Several deep-water holes may be found in this area, good holding but stream strong.
(3) Cotehele: ¾M above quay but spring streams strong, as at (4) in pools above Calstock.

Supplies Alongside fuel and water at the marinas; water at St Germans SC. All facilities in Plymouth; PO and shop at Cargreen.

Tel/VHF (all 0752). QHM, Longroom 663225/ ch 16, 14, 12, 8. Cattewater Hbr Commissioners 665934/ ch 16, 12 (Mon-Fri). Sutton Hbr Marina 664186/ ch 16, 80, 37. Queen Anne Battery Marina 671142/ ch 80,37. Millbay Marina Village 266785/ch 80,37. Mayflower Marina 556633/ ch 80,37. Ballast Pound Yacht Hbr 813658. Clovelly Bay Co 404231/ch 80. RWYC 660077; R Plymouth Corinthian YC 664327. Customs (0752) 220661.

PASSAGE NOTES: PLYMOUTH TO TORBAY
Charts BA 1613

Passage Lights
Start Pt   Fl(3) 10s 25M+
             FR (over Skerries) 12M,
             horn 60s
Berry Hd   Fl(2) 15s 18M, vis 100°-023°

Streams related to Dover.
Bolt Tail to Bolt Hd: +5h E; −2h W.
3M S of Start Pt: +5h ENE; −1¼h WSW 2kn.
Start Pt inshore: +4½h E; −1¾h W 4kn.
Start Bay: +4¼h NE; −1¼h SW.
Berry Hd: +5¾h N; −1h S.

Between Plymouth and Bolt Tail keep at least ½M offshore in fine weather to clear rocky ledges. In strong onshore winds keep well out to sea.

From Bolt Tail to Bolt Head there are cliffs up to 120m; conspic radio masts 1¼M E of Bolt Tail. Heavy swell possible, keep at least ½M offshore.

In strong winds the race off Start Pt may be severe for 1M or more SE, and up to 2M with strong SW wind against tide. There is a set into West Bay especially in S winds. Bound for Dartmouth either pass outside the Skerries (Berry Hd bearing 021° between Scabbacombe Hd (Downend Pt), 50°21′N, 3°31′W and E Blackstone Rk to the S, clears Skerries to SE) or take the inner passage, usually smoother, between Start Pt and Skerries, ¾M wide. Keep at least 4ca off lt ho until it bears 320°, at least 2ca S of Start Rks, thence pass close to the Pt. Southernmost white ho (conspic) at Beesands bearing 320° leads through.

In fog do not try to make the land between Bolt Tail and Start Pt: aim for Start Bay or Torbay.

Start Bay may be entered in a calm with no swell if position known within 2M (check with Start Point and Berry Head Ro Bns). From SE aim for Torcross, sounding continuously, 40+m depth up to 5ca off Skerries, 2-3m on its SW end, 5m in the middle and over 4½m on its NE end. Start Pt fog signal often inaudible here and Decca bearings reported as difficult. When soundings reach 14m you are over the bank: steer WNW and anchor in 8-9m. Sand, good holding, little traffic and sheltered between SSW and N. If shallow soundings not met when expected, stand off to E and wait for it to clear, N of shipping lane. With any swell keep away from the Skerries.

E-bound from Dartmouth keep ¾M offshore to clear E Blackstone and Nimble Rk and keep 1M offshore of Hope's Nose to clear Ore Stone. Coast is then free of dangers to Exmouth apart from Dawlish Rk, 3.5m, ½M off the town.

Anchorages:

R Erme. Keep close to port on entry to avoid reef off Fernycombe Pt on stb. Anchor off cove W of pine-clad hill.

Burgh Is. Pool N of Murrays Rk (R bn, cross top) 2m, sand. Exposed at HW, otherwise protected from E to N. Keep well to E in approach as there is an underwater rk E of Murrays.

Hope Cove. Anchor in offshore winds only. Poor holding. Beware rk drying 2.7m ½ca offshore.

Start Bay in offshore winds off **Hall Sands** or **Torcross** close inshore. Run for Dartmouth if wind backs S.

Torbay, Elberry Cove in SW corner of bay in 5m, 3ca offshore.

RIVER YEALM
Chart BA 30

HW: Dover −5½h.
MHWS 5.4m MHWN 4.3 MTL 3.1 MLWN 2.1 MLWS 0.7

In the river the flood starts at Dover +1h (1½kn) and the ebb at −5½h (2kn but 4kn off Warren Pt in freshets).

Approach To clear outlying rks on E and W of approach, keep Cawsand open of the Mewstone 298° until, coming from W, Wembury Ch (St Werburgh's on BA charts) bears 030° which clears Slimers Rks on W of approach; or, coming from E, Wembury Ch bearing 006° clears Ebb Rks on the E of the approach. Misery Pt well open of Season Pt clears Church Ledge. Stand in between these limits until the outer marks are identified. Entry should not be attmpted in strong SW winds.

Entrance A sand bar runs S from Season Pt leaving a narrow channel close along the S shore. The outer ldg marks (BW bns, △ topmarks) lead over the S end of the bar where it dries 0.5m and lead 089° into Cellar Bay. To clear Mouthstone Ledge do not stray S of the line until past

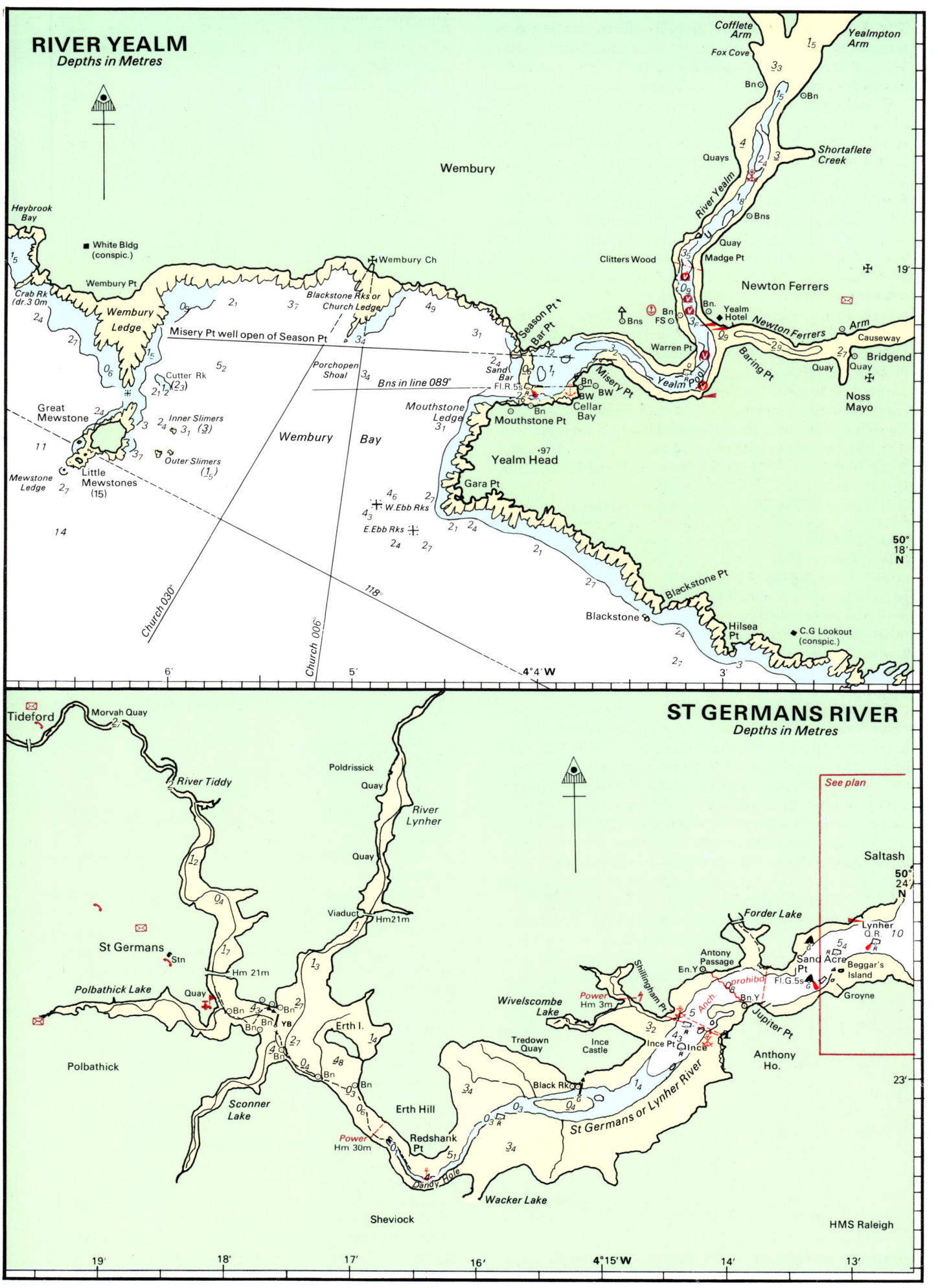

Mouthstone Pt. After this the best water is midway between the line and the rks on the S shore leaving the Bar buoy, R can Fl R 5s (Good Fri-Oct 31) to port. There is a gap of 40m between the buoy and the S shore with a least depth of 1.5m. After the buoy there is a G △ bn on W backboard on S shore. When abeam, steer NE for the single RW bn opposite Misery Pt. Thence keep mid-channel leaving to port R can buoy marking drying spit SE of Warren Pt.

Berthing Anchor in fine weather in Cellar Bay (open from W to NW). The river is crowded with moorings but mooring to two anchors may be possible in the Pool; boats which can dry out may be able to anchor in the entrance to Newton Arm or off Noss Creek. For visitors there is a mooring for craft up to 75ft off Misery Pt; further in are two moorings, each taking three craft or 25 tons; a line of pontoons in the Pool with some 25 berths; two small moorings for craft under 26ft off the old lifeboat ho; and a trot of fore and aft moorings (yachts may moor up to five abreast) on W side N of Yealm Hotel. Residents' moorings may have a label showing if they are vacant.

Supplies Water at slip near Yealm Hotel; no fuel. Newton – PO/Store, grocer, butcher, chemist, bank (Tues and Thur 10-2), pub, YC; Noss PO/Store, 2 pubs. EC Thur. Bus to Plymouth.

Tel HM: (0752) 872533; Customs as Plymouth.

SALCOMBE   Chart BA 28
HW: Dover −5½h
MHWS 5.3m   MHWN 4.1   MTL 3.0   MLWN 2.1   MLWS 0.7
In the Range the stream is inward from HW Dover +2h to +4h and outward from −2½h to −1½h. Max 1½kn. At other times the stream is mainly easterly or westerly following the main channel flow. Inside the stream can reach 3kn below the ferry landing.

Approach From W give the Mewstone and Cadmus Rk clearances of 2ca and 1ca respectively. Starhole Bay provides temporary anchorage in W winds to wait for a suitable time to cross the bar. From E give Prawle Pt clearance of 2ca and steer 298° for the pinewood S of Bar Lodge, a tall narrow building with a red roof. (Note also ldg line on plan for clearing Rickham Rk, 2.7m). From 2ca off Mewstone steer N for about 4ca to a position about 1ca off the Eelstones and follow entry directions.

N.B. Decca reported as not accurate in The Range.

Entrance At the N end of the gradually shoaling Range is The Bar (1.5m), extending SW from Limebury Pt. It is dangerous in onshore winds between E and S, particularly on the ebb. With a swell, crossing should not be attempted until there is a considerable rise in tide. The deepest water is ¾ca W of the ldg line, Poundstone Bn (RW with R can top) in line with Sandhill Pt Bn (RWHS, diamond top) to W of red-roofed house, 000°. Leave Bass Rks to port, Wolf Rk G con buoy to stb, Blackstone GW bn to stb, RW Poundstone Bn to port and round up 043° with Ox Pt lts in line.

By night, By night enter in W sector (358°-003°) of Sandhill Pt dir lt, Fl WRG 2s. Blackstone Rk sectored lt Q WR shows R until the Wolf Rk is cleared, then bring Ox ldg lts front Q (may be obscured by anchored vessels), rear Q, in line 042°.

The River is marked by bns to Kingsbridge where Squares Quay dries 3.4m and has 1.3m HWS and 0.2 HWN.

Berthing Anchorages (1) Off Marine Hotel on E side of estuary. Uncomfortable in swell and poor holding.

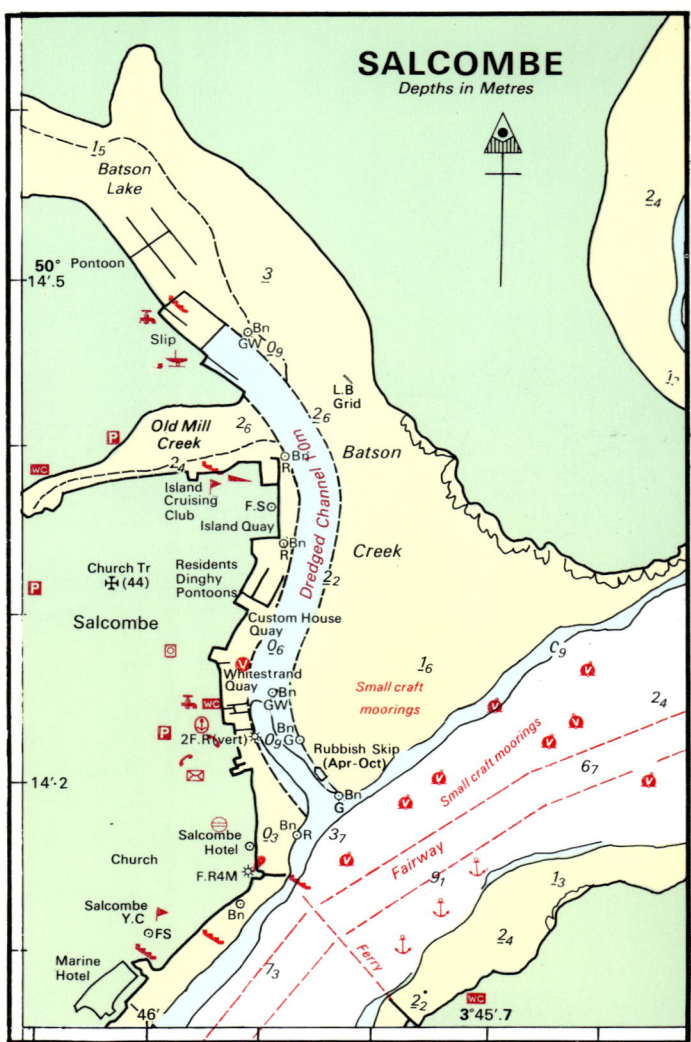

(2) In settled weather, in deep water to E of fairway off the town.
(3) In settled weather with modest draught, off Sunny Cove on the E side.
(4) Off Halwell Pt.
(5) W of Salstone Bn.
(6) Frogmore Lake: Narrow pool (2m) just before bay on S side.
(7) For Kingsbridge by dinghy, anchor off junction to Balcombe Lake.

Moorings: Visitors' pontoon at Whitestrand allows short stay (2h) for shopping; no double banking.
Visitors' moorings mostly Y and marked 'V', off the town, N of the fairway, and off entrance to South-pool Creek. With strong winds from SE to W, it is well worth going into The Bag where there is complete shelter.
Alongside: visitors' pontoon on W side of Bag, not connected to shore.
Drying berths at Kingsbridge alongside car park on W bank or pontoon on E. Check availability with River Officers. Navigable HW±2½h.

Facilities Landing at Ferry Pier (dinghies cannot be left), at Whitestrand pontoon and at Creek Boat Park Slip (tidal). Boatyards at Salcombe and Lyncombe. Fuel and water at barge on Middle Ground (only 3 days/week in winter). Water also from Whitestrand pontoon or from water boat (fly bucket from halyard). Refuse barge off Whitestrand (Apr-Oct).

Tel/VHF HM: (054884) 3791/ ch 14; Hbr Water Taxi ch 14; Island Cruising Club 3481/ ch 37; Salcombe YC 2593. Customs as Plymouth.

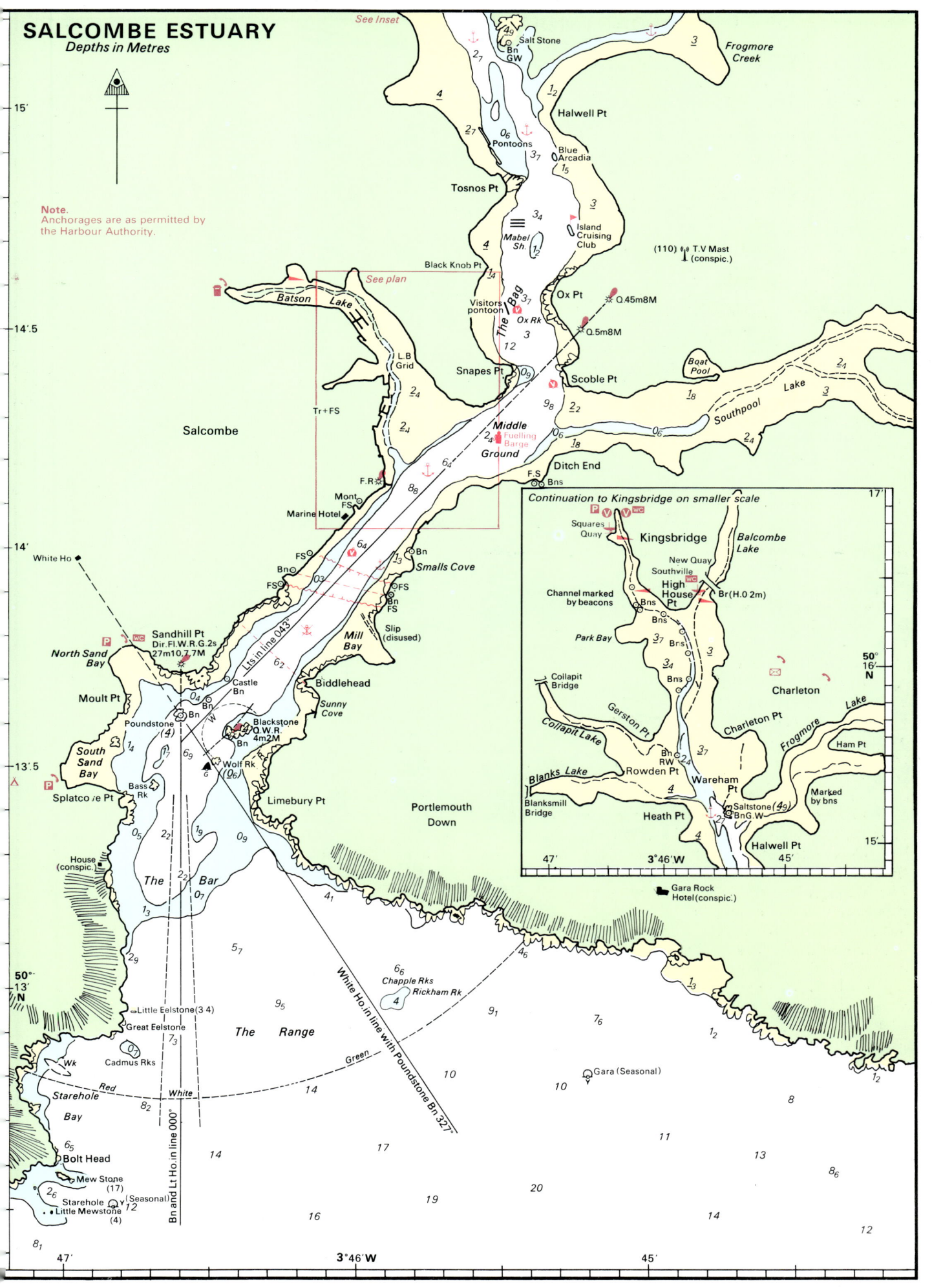

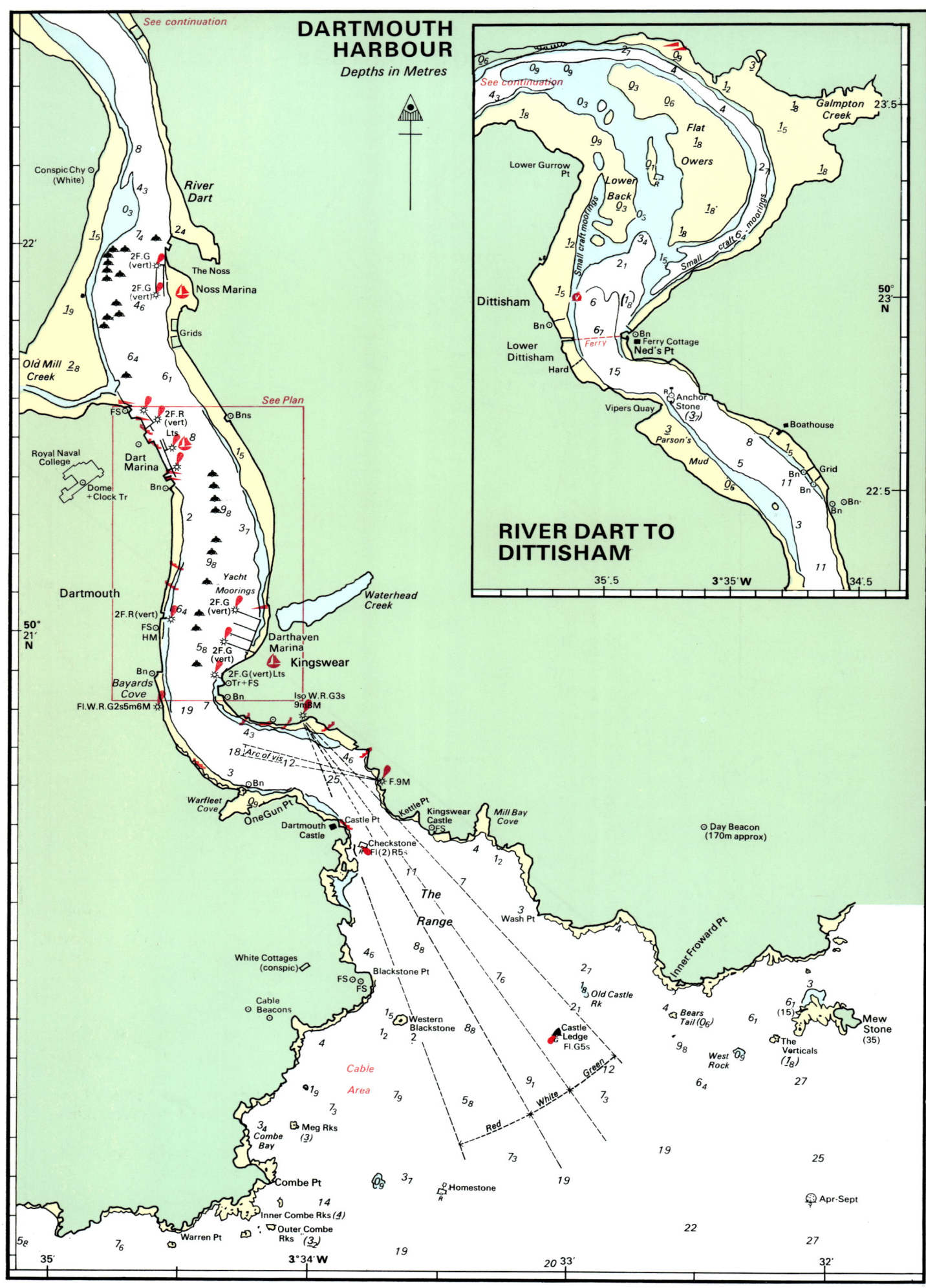

DARTMOUTH

Chart BA 2253

HW Dartmouth and Dittisham: Dover −5¼h; Totnes −5h. DS outside: Dover −1h SW; +5¾h NE; both 1½kn max. Flood into hbr starts Dover +1h.

MHWS 4.8m MHWN 3.6 MTL 2.7 MLWN 1.8 MLWS 0.4

Approach SW set may be experienced on the flood and NE on the ebb, except near the ends of both. To the E above Froward Pt there is a truncated stone pyramid bn 24m (177m above HW).
From E, give Mewstone Rk (38m) a clear berth to stb (crab pots) and then keep E Blackstone well open of it to clear rocky ledge extending 3ca WSW. After this distance make for Castle Ledge G con buoy (Fl G 5s). From W, keep outside the Homestone buoy (R can) and keep E of W Blackstone Rk (2.4m). Keep away from Combe Pt at all times. From S, Skerries bell buoy, 3½M from the entrance, is a good guide.
At night, from E keep lts of Berry Hd and Start Pt both just visible until Castle Ledge buoy, G con (Fl G 5s), is visible. Steer for this until in W sector of Kingswear (see below). From W, keep both Berry Hd and Start Pt lights visible until in Kingswear W sector.

Entrance is easy under power but squalls off the high land either side of the entrance may make sailing difficult, particularly with winds from SW through W to NW. Checkstone buoy is just E of a rocky ledge and must be left well to port. At springs localised streams up to 3kn may be experienced off Battery and Castle Pts with associated heavy swell in the entrance. The swell and fast tides disappear inside the estuary.
At night keep in W sector of Kingswear lt (Iso WRG 3s 9m 8M; W 325°-331°) until within W sector of Bayards Cove lt, Fl WRG 2s, W 289°-297°. (There is a FW lt NNW of Kettle Pt for vessels leaving; it is useful to keep it astern on this leg). Keep in the W Bayards Cove sector until the G lts on Kingswear pontoon are well open, when course should be altered to pass through the fairway to the anchorage E of the main hbr buoys.

The River Dart is navigable to Dittisham at any state of the tide and to Totnes after half-flood. It is controlled all the way by the Hbr Authority; dues are levied on all vessels. The S-most ferry has right of way and the cable ferry should be given a clear berth as under strong wind or tide the cables can be very close to the surface. Between Noss Pt and the Anchor Stone the channel hugs the E bank. Dittisham Lake, ½M wide, has two navigable channels separated by Flat Owers (dries 2m). Large vessels use the W channel. Above this the channel is winding, marked to Totnes by buoys and bns. Keep High Gurrow and Blackness Pts close to port, Pighole and Mill Pts close to stb; alter course to port to cross the river, pass close N of White Rock and make for buoys off Langham Wood Pt, leaving latter close to port. Then follow the buoys, keeping to outside of bends. At springs the river dries for 2M below Totnes but yachts of 1m draught can proceed there 1½h after LW.

Berthing During working hours the River Officers (VHF 11, 'Dartnav') are on duty near the Town Jetty and up-river at Dittisham. Dinghies may be left at pontoons adjacent to Dartmouth YC and at new pontoons N of Lee Court Flats.
(1) Anchor E of the town and of the ships' buoys in 4½m. Good holding but beware the chains of large moorings.
(2) Visitors' buoys and pontoons between buoys: enquire of River Officers.

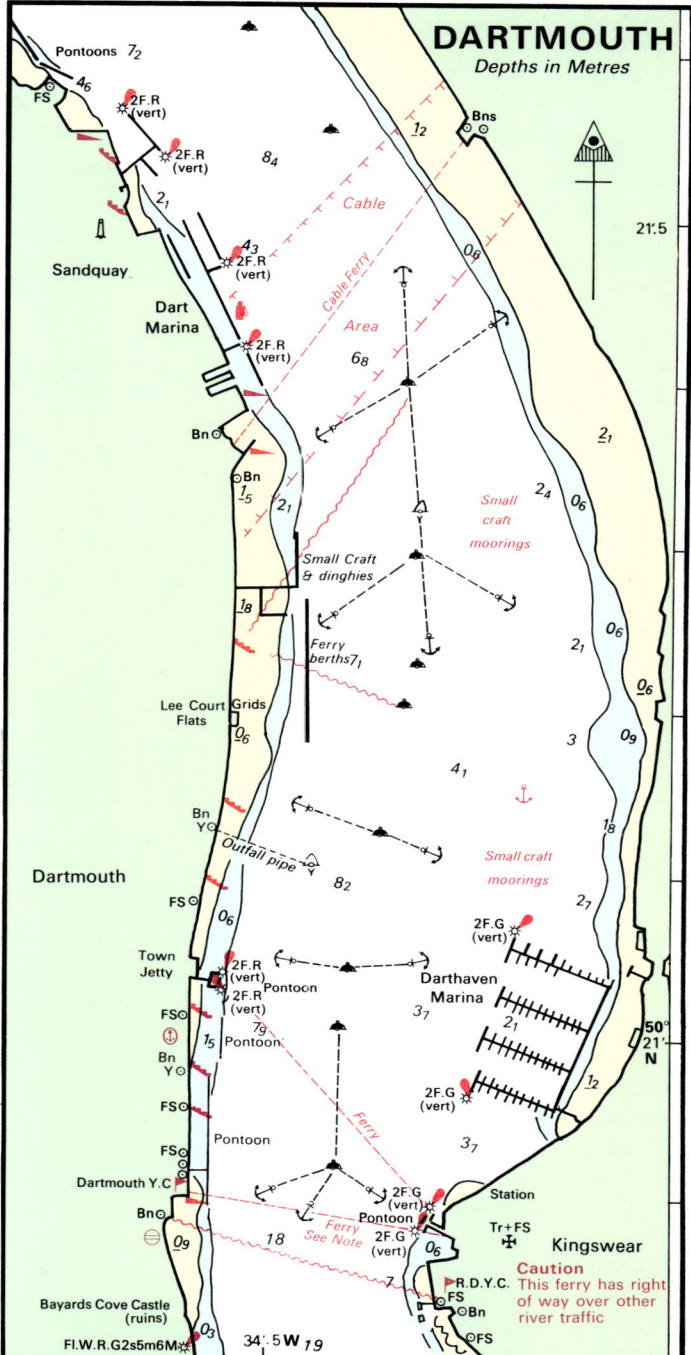

(3) Visitors' pontoons adjacent to Dartmouth YC (max 30ft) W bank; Yachts may use S end of inshore side of Town Jetty for 1h free; also for craft under 26 ft at pontoons on W bank N of Court Flats.
(4) Darthaven Marina pontoons (E side).
(5) Dart Marina pontoons (W side, just above cable ferry).
(6) Fore and aft moorings sometimes available at R Dart YC on E bank.
(7) Anchor on W side of river below Anchor Stone (R can) off Parson's Mud clear of moorings and out of main channel.
(8) Visitors' moorings off Dittisham, clearly marked with holding capacity which must be observed.

ENGLAND, SOUTH COAST 24

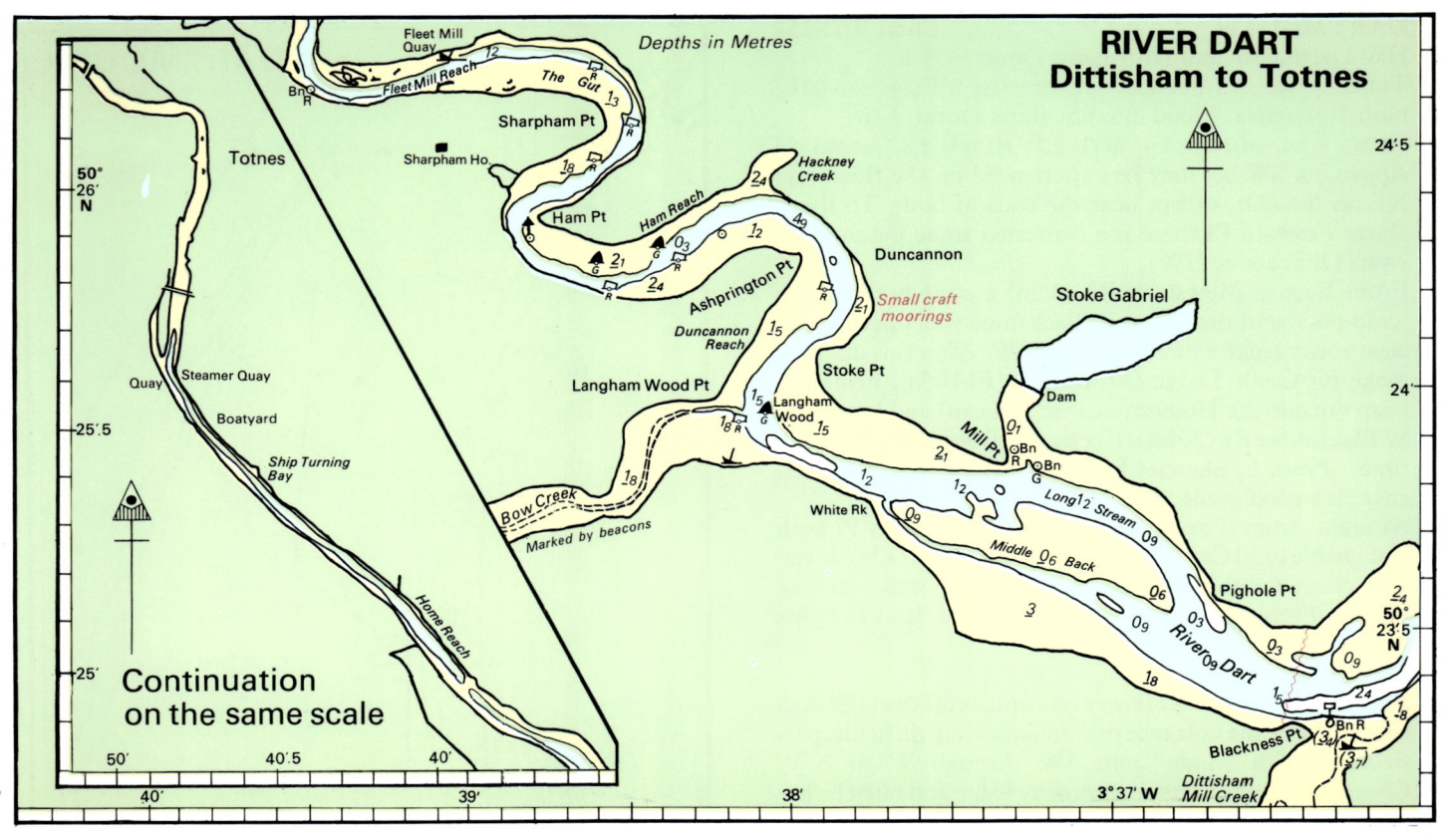

(9) Above Dittisham consult River Officer, waiting for him at Visitors' moorings if necessary. Keep well clear of fairway which is used by large timber vessels up to Totnes.
(10) Totnes: Mill Tail Quay (dries soft mud) by pub on W bank. (Steamer Quay on E bank is for passenger vessels.) There are NO visitors' facilities at Noss Marina.

Supplies Diesel and water at Dart Marina and fuel barge; petrol from garage near small craft pontoon. Water at North Embankment (by WCs) and South Embankment, Dittisham, Galmpton. Water and stores at Dittisham, Galmpton and Totnes.

Tel/VHF HM (0803) 832337/ ch 16, 11; Dartmouth YC (0803) 832305; Coastguard (08045) 882704/ ch 16, 67; R Dart YC (080428) 272; Dart Marina (08043) 3351/ ch 80/ 37; Darthaven Marina (080425) 545/ ch 80/37; Yacht Taxi 833727/ch 16, 6, 8, 73. Customs as Plymouth.

BRIXHAM Chart BA 26
HW: Dover −5h. DS: Dover −1h SW; +5h NE.
MHWS 4.8m MHWN 3.6 MTL 2.7 MLWN 1.9 MLWS 0.6
Brixham is a busy fishing port with limited accommodation for yachts. In N-NE winds there is considerable scend in outer hbr and Torquay is preferable.

Approach Steer for RW Fairway buoy, Q bell, bearing 308°, 1.2ca, from Victoria Breakwater lt ho. From N clear rks off Hope's Nose by keeping W edge of Cod Rk, off Berry Hd, bearing more than 195° and open E of Berry Hd. From S, clear dangers S of Berry Hd by keeping Hope's Nose open E of Berry Hd, 359°. From Berry Hd (25m depth close inshore) steer 284° for Fairway Buoy.

Signals 3 R balls or lts at the inner hbr entrance indicate hbr is closed.

Entrance Craft must round the Fairway Buoy to seaward and head for appropriate fairway. For the Town Dock area of the Marina, use the Lifeboat Fairway. The main fairway is marked by two pairs of lateral lt buoys; watch illuminated sign at entrance of MFV Basin for warning of emerging craft. Give way to craft manoeuvring off fuel berth at MFV basin and to LB when leaving hbr giving emergency signals.

Berthing Marina in SE corner of hbr. In summer a pontoon is moored off Brixham YC, subject to MFV wash. There is no room to anchor in the hbr and holding in Fishcombe Cove is very poor.

Leaving the Marina, give way to MFVs leaving the MFV Basin or manoeuvring off fuel berth, and to craft entering hbr from seaward.

Supplies Diesel at Oil Jetty; water at end of pier, Breakwater Hard, New Pier and Oil Jetty. All facilities. EC Wed.

Tel/VHF HM (08045) 3321/ ch 16, 14.('Brixham Port'); YC 3332; Marina (0803) 882711 ch 80/37; Customs as Plymouth.

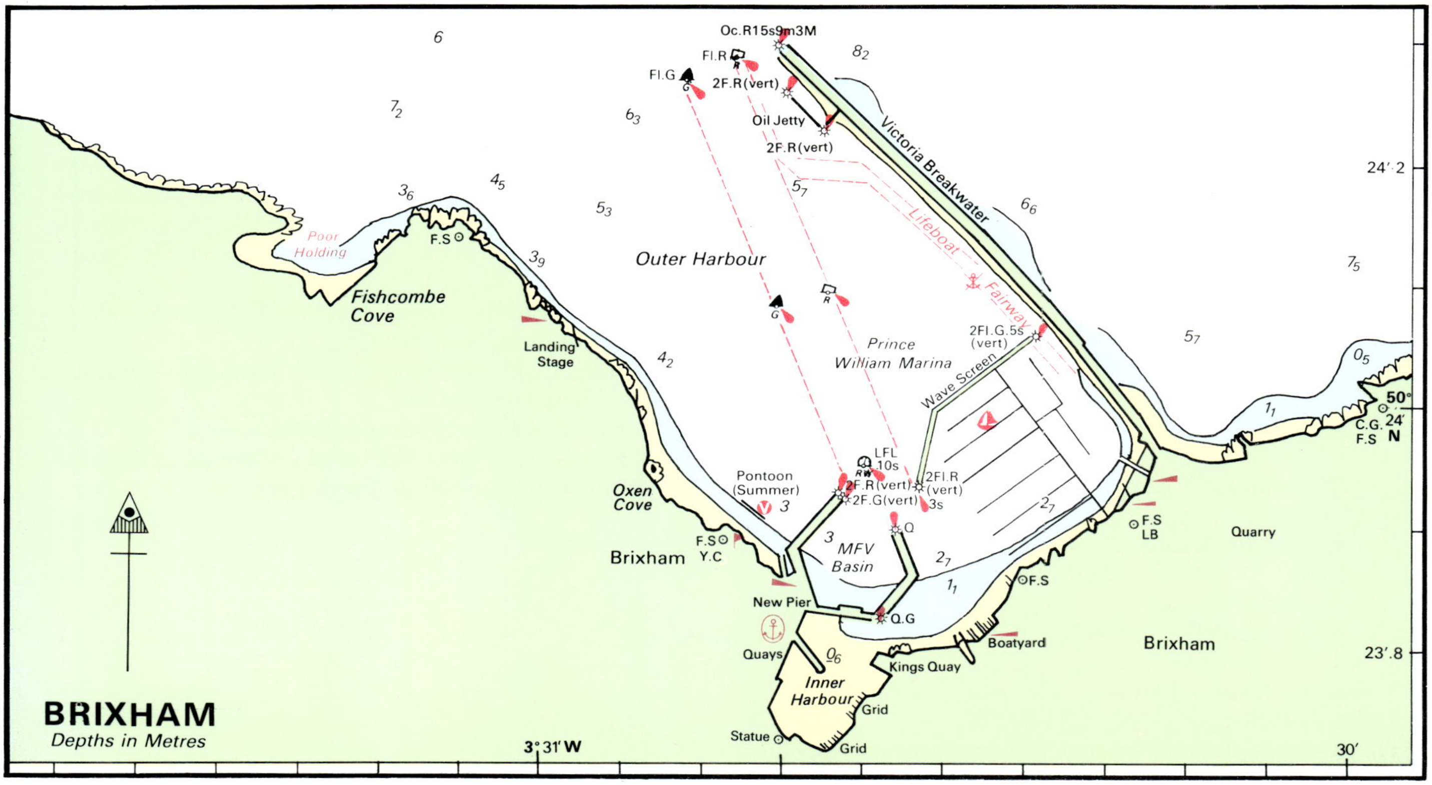

PAIGNTON
Chart BA 26

Tidal data as for Torquay. A small drying hbr with very limited accommodation for yachts, either on a vacant mooring or alongside quay. Water, fuel at garage, shops.

TORQUAY
Chart BA 26

HW: Dover −5h. DS: Dover −1h W; +5h E.

MHWS 4.9m   MHWN 3.7   MTL 2.8   MLWN 2.0   MLWS 0.7

A sheltered hbr with marina, commercial traffic and passenger launches. Busy in summer.

Approach From E a ch tr and a spire stand out on the skyline above Babbacombe. There is a safe passage between the Orestone and the Flat Rk off Hope's Nose. It is not safe for strangers to pass inside the Thatcher even at HW. The Orestone with its own length open of the Thatcher will clear all shoals along the N shore of Torbay.

Signals 3R balls or lts vert: hbr closed, or incoming traffic must wait until entrance is clear.

Entrance faces W. G con buoy QG is moored (Apr-Sept) off W end of Haldon Pier. Much traffic in summer: keep well to stb in entrance.

Berthing 500 berth marina occupies W half of outer hbr with some 50 berths for visitors (signposted). Harbour Authority moorings sometimes also available. Haldon Pier is used by large commercial vessels. Inner hbr dries and is for small local craft. Good anchorage outside the hbr: keep clear of buoyed fairway. Landing inside Haldon and Princess Piers.

Supplies Fuel at South Pier; water too, and at Haldon Pier and marina. Small to medium craft may dry against wall in inner hbr. All facilities. EC Wed and Sat.

Tel/VHF HM (0803) 292429/ ch 16, 14; Marina 214624/ ch 80/37; R Torbay YC 292006; Customs as Plymouth.

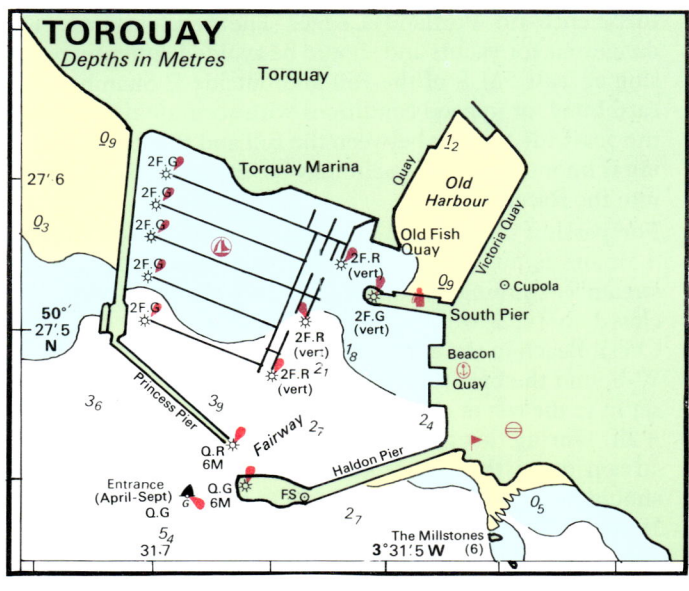

ENGLAND, SOUTH COAST

PASSAGE NOTES: LYME BAY (TORBAY TO WEYMOUTH). Chart BA 3315.

Caution In Lyme Bay if S-SW gales blow up there is no refuge in onshore winds.

Passage Lights

Portland Bill	Fl(4) 20s 29M + FR (over Shambles) 13M, dia 30s (From 221° to 244°, changes 1 Fl to 4 Fl then 4 Fl to 117°, changing from 4 Fl to 1 Fl by 141°.)
W Shambles W card buoy	Q(9) 15s Bell.
E Shambles E card buoy	Q(3) 10s, horn(2) 30s, bell
Portland Hbr East Ship Channel	Fl 10s 20M horn 10s.

Streams related to Dover.

Inshore off Bridport: +6h E; HWD W.
On W-going stream Portland Bill produces an eddy in West Bay with a N set felt up to 10M off the Bill and a S set felt as far as 6M S of the Bill.

Portland Bill Streams:

(Caveat: Yachtsmen approaching Portland Bill from E may be using BA Charts with streams related to HW Portsmouth or Dover; but for the Bill they are shown on charts 2615 and 3315 related to HW Plymouth. Those below are related to Dover.)

W of the Bill:	from +2h to −¾h (about 9½h) S, 3kn.
	from −¼h to +2h N, 1.1kn.
Off the Bill:	from +5h E to SE (max 6kn at −5h)
	from −1h SW to W (max 7+kn at +1h)
E of the Bill:	from −5¼h to +5h (about 10¼h) S, 4.5kn
	from +5h to −5¼h N, 1.8kn.

From Exmouth to Portland Bill there are two conspic features: Beer Hd 130m, the W-most chalk cliff on S coast; and 3M before Bridport is Golden Cap 186m.

Portland Bill

The strong S streams either side of the Bill, running for 9 or 10h, meet the main Channel streams causing violent turbulence on Portland Ledge. The resultant race is dangerous for yachts and should be avoided either by passing at least 5M S of the Bill and outside E Shambles E card buoy; or in good conditions with accurate timing, by the 5ca-wide passage between the Bill and the Race. Timing is important or the yacht may be set out of the channel into the Race.

For passing inshore the best time E-bound is at Dover +5h and is possible to −5h. Between these times the S stream is running out of W Bay and the land must be closed to 1-2ca well N of Is of Portland: keep close to Chesil Beach in the approach and round the Bill at 1-2ca. W-bound the best time is Dover −1h (earlier risks being set in to the last of the E-going Race) and is possible until +2h. During this period the yacht will have a strong fair stream down the E side of the peninsula and the land should be kept within 1-2ca down to the pitch of the Bill. If the tide has turned to the W when the pitch is reached, steer NW into West Bay to avoid being set into the Race.

Caution (1) In winds of F 6+, and in weaker E winds, the inshore passage ceases to be relatively smooth.
(2) Lobster pots and their buoys are a hazard in the passage and along the E coast.

The Shambles The passage between the Race and the Shambles needs extreme care. Strong tidal streams may cause heavy seas; allow for strong set into the race or onto the Shambles. Ldg marks are Portland Hbr 'A' pierhead lt in line with Grove Pt 358°, leading 3ca W of The Shambles.

Anchorages Babbacombe (close N of Long Quarry Pt) in offshore winds off local moorings.
Exmouth, outside anchorage near Fairway buoy if waiting for the tide in fair weather
Littleham Cove just N of Straight Pt.
Beer Roads, E of Beer Hd: good anchorage in offshore winds through W to SW in Bay of Beer.

27 ENGLAND, SOUTH COAST

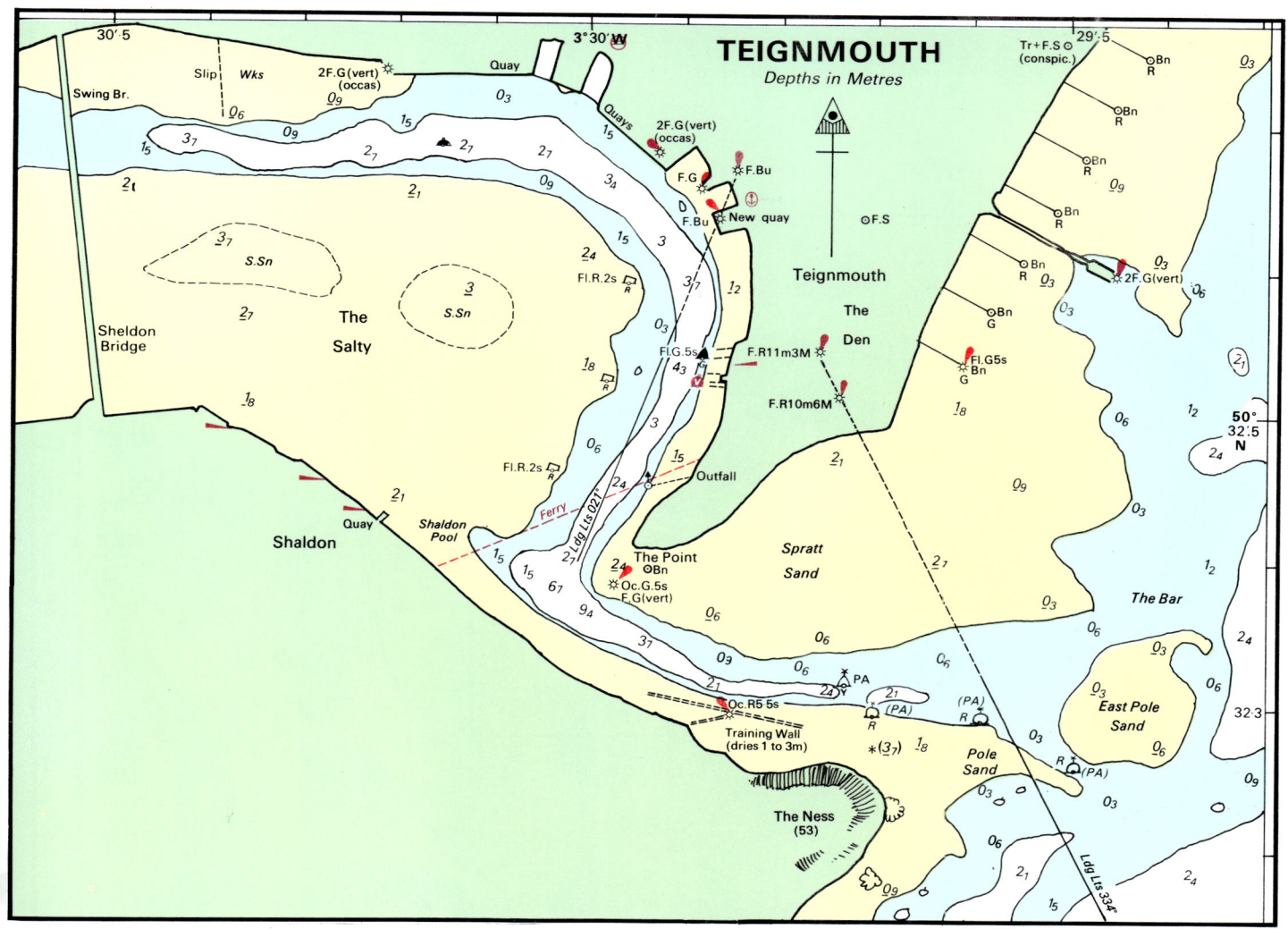

TEIGNMOUTH
Chart BA 26

HW: Dover −5h. DS: Dover −½h W; +5¼h E.
MHWS 4.8m MHWN 3.6 MTL 2.7 MLWN 1.9 MLWS 0.6

A commercial port with limited accommodation for yachts. Entrance difficult and not accessible in strong onshore winds from NE to S.

Approach R Teign is N of the Ness, a red sandstone headland with pines at summit.

Entrance A sand bar, extending from the Ness to Teignmouth Pier, is constantly changing. Tides scour channels which are marked by buoys for the use of pilots; they are frequently moved as the channel changes and must be used with caution. The bar is dangerous in onshore winds and with a swell. Without local guidance, approach should be with offshore winds and at the last quarter of the flood. Approach is best from S with foot of pier bearing about 355°. Sound to skirt N edge of Pole Sand noting, but not depending on, pilots' buoys (do not confuse with fishing buoys) to bring W bn tr on training wall between two vert W strips on grey wall on shore; steer on that line until 50m from bn, then keep in middle of channel Past Ferry Pt and steer 021° for New Quay leaving R can buoys well to port. Beware of set along the Shaldon shore and unmarked shoals above the quay on stb side. Stream off the Pt runs at 4kn and is strong throughout the hbr especially for last half of the ebb.

Inadvisable to attempt entrance at night or to leave when ebb is running strongly.

Berthing In settled weather anchor outside 2ca E of end of pier, 2m. Fore and aft mooring for visitors 1ca N of The Point. Quiet anchorage above the bridge, clearance 4m. Drawbridge section has 2m depth at MHWS.

Supplies Water at quays. Fuel by tanker. Scrubbing hard on S side of New Quay. Shops: EC Thur.

Tel/VHF HM (06267) 2311/ ch 16, 12 (office hours).

ENGLAND, SOUTH COAST 28

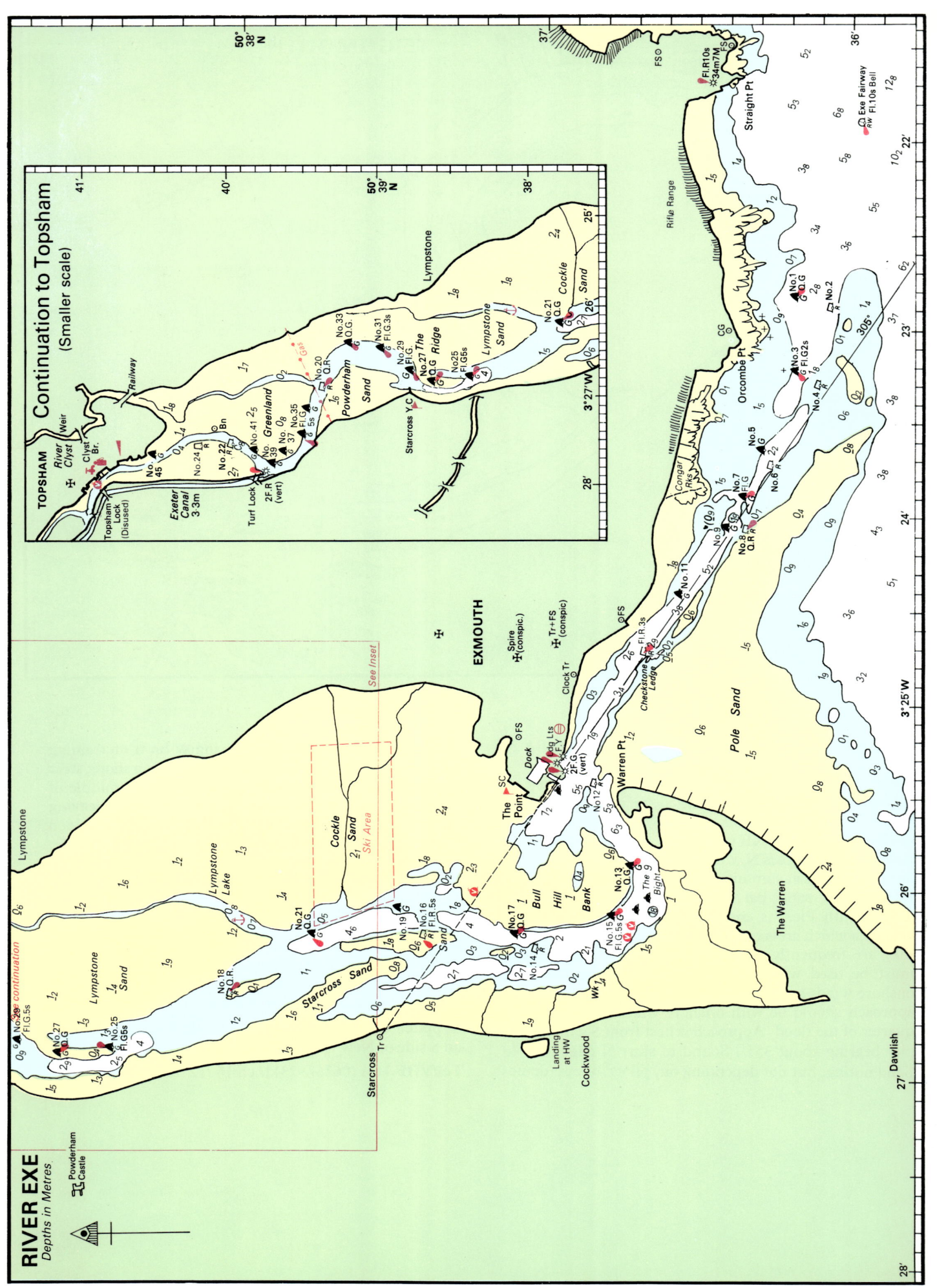

RIVER EXE
Chart BA 2290

HW: Dover −5h. DS: Dover +4¾h E; HWD W.
MHWS 4.6m MHWN 3.4 MTL 2.5 MLWN 1.7 MLWS 0.5

A pleasant estuary with many moorings (few for visitors) but still places to anchor. Exmouth Dock now closed to commercial traffic. Aproach dangerous in strong onshore winds.

Approach From SW steer for Straight Pt, a low promontory backed by red cliffs, until Exmouth ch bears 320°, then make for Exe Fairway buoy, sph RWVS Fl 10s, ¾M S of highest part of cliff. From E, Mamhead Tr, 218m, 3M inland, in line with Langstone Pt, 269°, will clear Pole Sand and ledges S of Orcombe Pt. Beware firing range off Straight Pt: R flag and RM launch (VHF 16) when firing.

Entrance A long shifting shallow bar (1.5m) with rks on NE and Pole Sand on SW extends SE as far as Orcombe Pt. Entrance should not be attempted in strong onshore winds. Otherwise best at half flood. When past Orcombe Pt bring conspic R tr on foreshore at Starcross on with end of pier at NW end of Exmouth Esplanade, 305°, leading between Conger Rks and Pole Sand. Keep close to stb buoys from No 5 to No 11 as Pole Sand encroaches into the channel. After No 11 buoy the ebb runs strongly and if then entering, keep to stb of channel until halfway between No 10 and the shore; thence, to avoid shoal patch off Clock Tr, steer to a pt just W of Dock pier-head, then turn up into the Bight.

Entrance at night is dangerous, but Straight Pt lt ho (Fl R 10s 246°-071°) enables course to be set for Fairway Buoy (Fl 10s). Leave No 1, (QG), and No 7 (Fl G 5s) G con buoys to stb and No 8 R can buoy, Q R, to port. Then pick up FY ldg lts 305°.

River Exe Proceeding up-river follow the curves of the centre of the channel rather than straight lines between the buoys. Bull Hd obtrudes between 13 and 15 buoys. The channel is buoyed to Topsham. Turf lock gives access to a canal leading to Exeter, used by commercial craft. Daily convoy to Exeter (max headroom 11m under M5), lock opening HW Exmouth -1h.

Berthing Anchor (1) In the Bight, 3-5½m, sand.
(2) Off Starcross S of pier, but many moorings.
(3) In Lympstone Lake.
(4) Off Turf lock, clear of fairway and entrance (strong ebb).

There are visitors' buoys opposite No 15 buoy and one to E of line between Nos 17 and 19 buoys. (Ferry service from yachts in river to the Dock.) Alongside mooring in Exmouth Dock (dries, soft mud; moor in entrance for HM to open br) and in canal via Turf Lock (opens HW Exmouth-1h, weekly charges reasonable). Limited buoys and pontoon berths for visitors (shallow at springs, sand/mud) at Topsham (Trout's boatyard). Land at Dock entrance, Starcross or on the beach S or N of hbr entrance. It is dangerous to anchor off the Point especially with spring tides or SE wind against tide as streams may reach 5kn.

Supplies Water from Dock and Topsham. Shops at Exmouth (EC Wed) and Topsham.

Tel/VHF HM River & Canal (0392) 74306/ch 12 ('Port of Exeter'). Dock (0395) 272009; Trout's Boatyard Topsham (0392) 873044; Ferry service from river to Dock: ch 37 ('Conveyance'). Customs as Plymouth.

LYME REGIS
Chart BA 3315

HW: Dover −4¾h
MHWS 4.3m MHWN 3.1 MTL 2.4 MLWN 1.7 MLWS 0.6

A drying hbr with very limited alongside accommodation for 12 visitors. Enter HW ±2½h. Outside anchorage and red visitors' buoys, bad in heavy weather from S to E. Fuel, water, shops.

WEST BAY (BRIDPORT)
Chart BA 3315

HW: Dover −5h
MHWS 4.1m MHWN 3.0 MTL 2.3 MLWN 1.6 MLWS 0.6

A small artificial hbr, mainly drying, with some commercial traffic. Enter HW±2h. Inside berthing difficult; outside anchorage abreast the piers. Supplies limited.

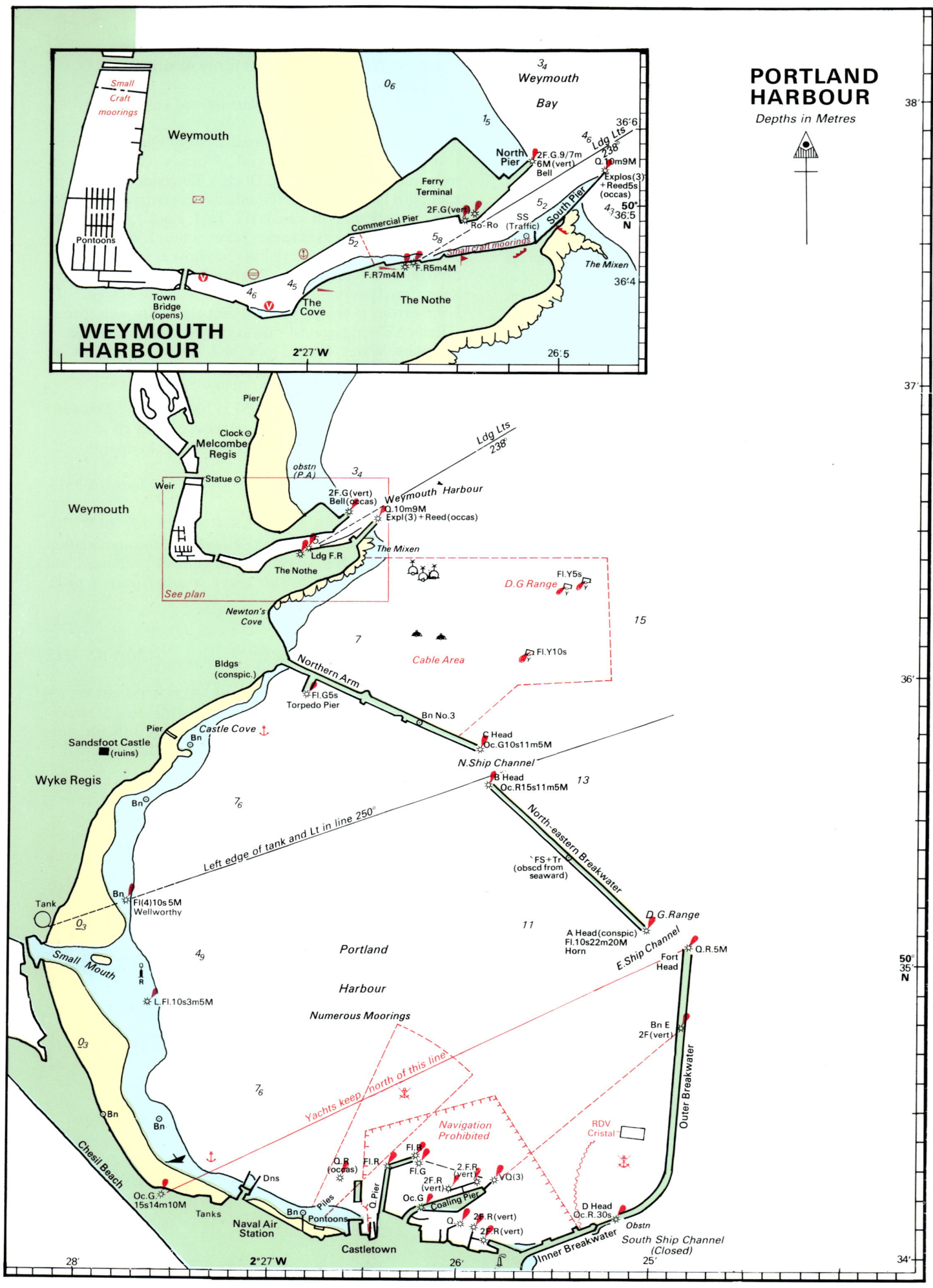

PORTLAND HARBOUR Chart BA 2268, 2255
HW: Dover −4½h

MHWS 2.1m MHWN 1.4 MTL 1.1 MLWN 0.7 MLWS 0.2

Streams are imperceptible in the hbr but run up to 1kn in the entrances, with eddies.

Portland is a naval base under the direction of QHM. Navigation and anchoring are prohibited in some parts.

Approach From the W the main hazard is Portland Race; from S the Shambles and from E, Lulworth gunnery ranges. Study Passage Notes. The hbr is at N end of the wedge-profiled Portland peninsula.

Signals Due to frequent movements of naval vessels, craft are asked, when 3M from pierhead A, to report to QHM on VHF 13.

Entrance Keep clear of craft over 20m long. The South Ship Channel is closed. Enter via North Ship Channel, white tank in transit with Wellworthy Bn (Fl(4) 10s), 250°. Leave via East Ship Channel.

Berthing Yachts should keep N of line Fort Head-Chesil Beach. Anchor (1) Off Castle Cove in NW corner of hbr, outside moorings (beware reef running 1ca ENE from foot of Sandsfoot Castle to bn). Uncomfortable in S winds. (2) Off Castletown or W of the hard ½M W of Castletown. Exposed in westerlies. Note prohibited area on plan. Permission to enter from QHM on VHF 13.

Supplies Fuel from garages. Water from SC dinghy park. Shops. EC Wed.

Tel/VHF QHM (0305) 820311, ext 2104/ ch 13, 14. Customs 774747.

WEYMOUTH Chart BA 2172
HW: Dover −4¾h. DS: Dover +5¾h E; HWD W. Tides 4h flood, 4h ebb, 4h slack.

MHWS 2.1m MHWN 1.4 MTL 1.1 MLWN 0.7 MLWS 0.2

Owing to an eddy, stream in Weymouth Roads is W-going (not more than ½kn) at all times except Dover −5¼h to −3¼h.

Weymouth is a commercial port with a cross-channel ferry terminal and accommodation for yachts.

Approach See Passage Notes re Portland Race and Lulworth Gunnery Ranges.

Signals are shown (vert) from a mast on S pier:

3 R Fl lts — Port closed; emergency.
2R over G lts: Entry and departure forbidden.
3R lts: Vessel leaving, keep fairway clear.
3G lts: Vessel arriving; **do not attempt to leave hbr.**
GWG lts: Vessels may proceed only when instructed.

Storm and International Code Signals are displayed from FS on N pier.

Entrance Keep to N of transit through the ends of hbr piers and steer in as soon as entrance is wide open. Two R diamonds (R lts at night) on S side of hbr in line 238° lead between the piers. Hydrofoils operate from ferry terminal Mar-Oct.

Berthing Instructions may be given from office on N pier, by VHF (16, 12) or by Piermaster in Cove area; (otherwise berth as convenient above LBS until instructed by staff). Anchoring in the hbr is forbidden; there are 185 berths for visitors, mainly in the Cove area and on the town side of the hbr at berths 4-8. Swell runs up the hbr with winds from E-NE. There are pontoon berths for local yachts above the br: 2h notice is needed for opening; R and G traffic lts. In fine weather there is a good anchorage outside the hbr 3 or 4ca N of S pier-head, 2½-3½m.

Supplies Water at pierhead and at fuel pt at No 5 berth. All facilities; EC Wed.

Tel/VHF Piermaster (0305) 760276;HM 760620/ ch 16, 12 (working day or when vessels expected). Customs 774747.

PASSAGE NOTES: WEYMOUTH TO POOLE
Chart BA 2615

Hazards are Lulworth Gunnery Ranges and St Alban's Race.

Passage lt is Anvil Pt Fl 10s 24M.

Streams related to Dover

Lulworth to St Alban's Hd close inshore: +5h E; −2h W
W side of St Alban's Hd: SE almost continuously.
3½M S of St Alban's Hd: +5¾h E; −¼h W; 4-5kn.
Durlston Hd: +5½h NE; −½h SW; 3kn.
Peveril buoy: +5h NNE (1½kn); −2¼h SSW (3kn).
Old Harry: +5h E; −1¼h W.

When coming from S or W of Portland Race study Passage Notes for Lyme Bay.

Inshore E of Weymouth there is an obstruction, least depth 4m, 3ca SE of Redcliffe Pt, and rks running out 3ca from Ringstead Pt. There are no dangers outside 2ca as far as Lulworth Cove. E of that avoid Kimmeridge Ledge extending seaward more than ½M.

Lulworth Gunnery Range for tank firing extends from St Albans Hd to a pt 5M S of Lulworth Cove. In addition there is a naval gunnery range, firing from 2°17′.5 W (approx) at targets marked by three DZ lt buoys (Fl Y, from W to E, 2s, 5s, 10s) 2½M S to SW of St Alban's Hd.

When the Army ranges are in use, code flag U and a R flag with R Fl lts are displayed from FS on Bindon Hill and St Alban's Hd; range safety boats are stationed at the edges of the danger area. Army firing is mainly in the daytime, Mon-Fri, but sometimes there is night firing mainly Tue and Thur. There is also firing on six weekends a year. There are several no-firing periods, usually including the whole of August. Firing times are broadcast with shipping information by Radio Solent at about 0745 on weekdays and by Portland Naval Base on VHF 13, 14 at 0945 and 1645 daily.

In theory yachts may pass through the firing area; some do. The Range Officer is responsible for ceasing fire, but as this disrupts the firing schedule, yachtsmen may find themselves under very considerable verbal pressure from the range launches to pass clear of the area on the recommended tracks: from Weymouth Pierhead 121° to a turning pt at 50°30′N, 2°09′W, thence 062° to clear Anvil Pt, a course which clears St Alban's Race.

Naval firing is less regular. There are no visual signals ashore but warships patrol S of Lulworth Banks and fly R flags during firing.

When any firing is in progress listen on VHF 8.

St Alban's Hd is easily identified with chapel and CG hut on top. Off the Hd the dangerous race varies in position and severity. It extends 3M seaward, less in S winds. Overfalls extend 2½M further SW on the ebb than on the flood and are much more dangerous. Either avoid the race by giving the Head a berth of 3½M or in good weather and offshore winds use the ½M-wide passage between the Hd and the race; the latter has an early fair eddy but there is an almost continuous eddy down the W side of the Hd.

There is deep water to close inshore between the Hd and Anvil Pt (W lt ho). From Anvil Pt to Peveril Pt rough water is frequent. Durlston Hd has a castellated building on top; Peveril Pt (CG and FS) has a rocky ledge running ¼M to seaward with R can buoy at end. Stream sets towards the ledge. In bad weather a dangerous race runs seaward of the buoy especially to SE with W-going stream. Between Swanage and Poole lobster-pot buoys are frequent.

There are VHF Ro Bns (ch 88) at Anvil Pt and (AL) High Down (HD) 50°39′.70N 1°34′.60W on Isle of Wight, working in conjunction (N.B. They give position lines in true, not magnetic, bearings).

Anchorages Worbarrow Bay. 1M E of Lulworth Cove, sheltered from WNW-ESE. Anchor in E half of the bay to avoid pipe-line running SSE from Arish Mell Gap: inshore end marked by BY bn, can top. This is in the Gunnery Range area and mooring is forbidden when firing is in progress.

Chapman's Pool W of St Alban's Hd. 1.6m in centre of Pool; depths inshore unreliable due to cliff falls. Open from S to SW and swell from SE. If becalmed, W of Kimmeridge Ledge, clear of rocky bottom, may be preferable. See also separate entries for Lulworth, Swanage and Studland.

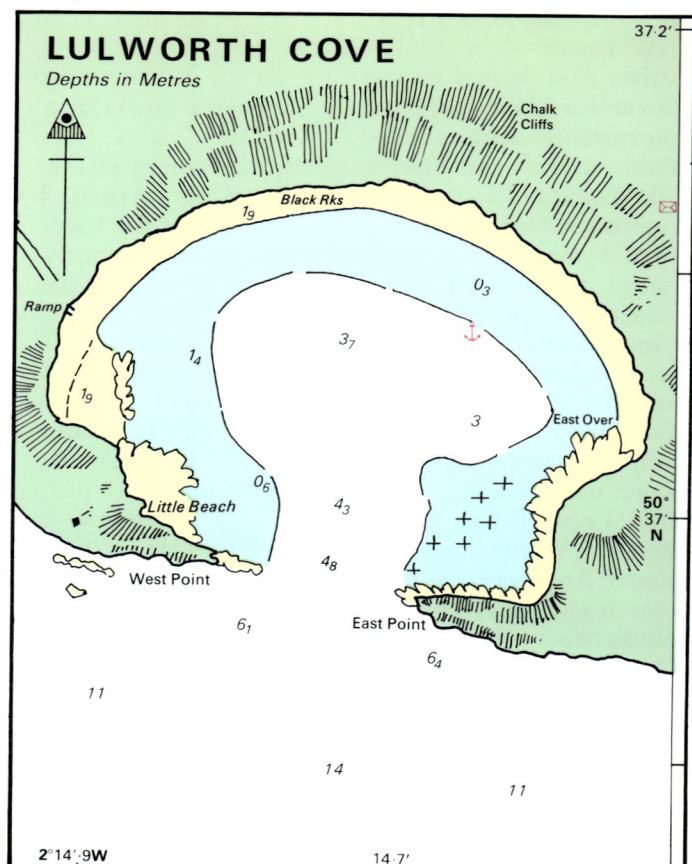

LULWORTH COVE   Chart BA 2172

HW: Dover −4¾h. DS: Dover +5¾h E; HWD W.
MHWS 2.3m   MHWN 1.5   MTL 1.2   MLWN 0.9   MLWS 0.3
A circular basin with a narrow entrance. In S winds a heavy swell rolls in, dangerous with strong winds. Otherwise a yacht with good ground tackle may ride out bad W weather safely but uncomfortably.

Approach From W keep ½M offshore to clear Ringstead Ledge. Lulworth lies 3M E of White Nose where the cliffs change from clay to chalk. Near the hbr the shore is steep-to. From E, Arish Mell Gap open of Worbarrow Hd clears Kimmeridge Ledges.

Entrance Channel is 80m wide with 4.8m depth. The wind may be fluky or squally in the entrance. Rocky ledges extend into the hbr NNW and ENE from each side of the entrance. The W ledge obtrudes more into the entrance and a yacht should therefore keep 1/3rd of the way over from the E cliff and head for the junction of green and white cliffs on N side of hbr. Do not deviate to port or stb until fully halfway across the cove.

Anchorage in NE corner of cove in 3m, good holding. Avoid obstructing the fairway to NW corner of the bay, used by tourist boats to land passengers. Mooring buoy in NE part is for MOD vessels. If there is any suggestion of the wind going into S, get out.

Supplies Garage, hotel, stores, PO. Water at car park.

SWANAGE   Chart BA 2172

Double HW: springs Dover −2¼h and +¾h; neaps −5h and +1½h. DS: Dover +5h E −1h W.
MHWS 2.0 & 1.5m   MHWN 1.4 & 1.6   MTL 1.5   MLWN 1.1   MLWS 0.3

Approach From W give Peveril Ledge buoy a good berth as tide sets across the ledge. There can be a sharp race off the pt extending beyond the buoy.

Anchorage There is good shelter from W winds. Anchor 1ca WNW of head of pier, good holding but foul in places. Land on beach.

Supplies Water at pier. Shops, EC Thur.

STUDLAND BAY   Chart BA 2172

Tidal data as Swanage. A good anchorage, sheltered from S through W to WNW. Good holding except on visible weed patches. Anchor about 2ca off the beach, 2½m abreast the Yards, three prominent projections in the cliff. Riding lts desirable but many yachts do not hoist them - care needed if entering at night.

Supplies Shops up steep hill. Pub nearer at hand.

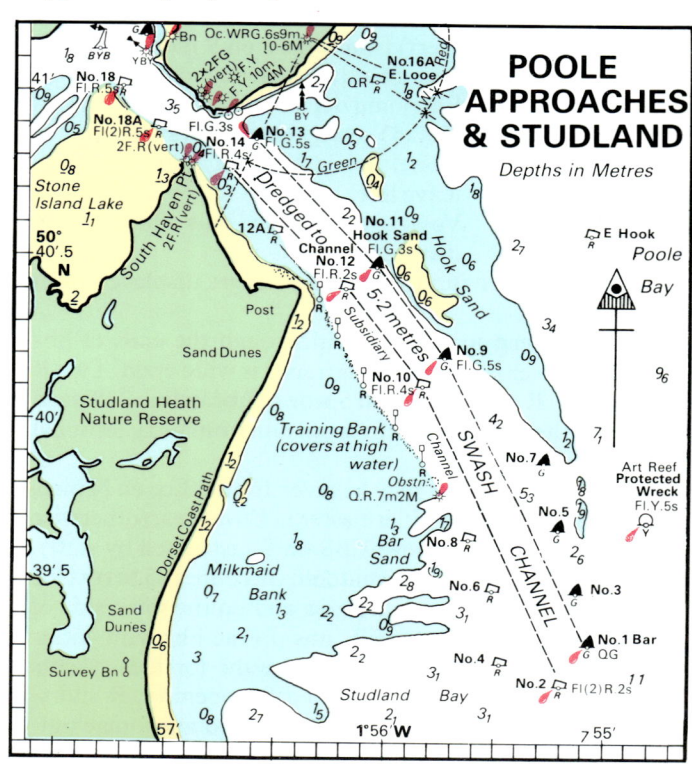

33 ENGLAND, SOUTH COAST

POOLE HARBOUR   Chart BA 2611

An extensive natural hbr with quays at the town, many channels and islands, several marinas and anchorages. There is considerable commercial traffic, including that from the oil-field base at Furzey Is.

Low Water (Town Quay) is HW Dover +5¾h.

HW Springs (when LW is between 2.30 and 8.30, a.m. or p.m.) is about 5h after LW; a second, lesser, HW is 4h after that, 3h before next LW.

HW Neaps (LW between 8.30 and 2.30, a.m. or p.m.) is just over 3h before the next LW. There may also be a first, lesser, HW at neaps or there may be a rise, a stand for 2h and then another rise to main HW. Range only 0.5m.

HW related to Town Quay is: Entrance −½h; Russel Quay +¾h, Wareham Quay +1¼h.

Variations in tide levels above CD in different parts of the area are small and levels can be taken as:

MHWS 2.0m MHWN 1.6 MTL 1.2 MLWN 1.1 MLWS 0.3 but Wareham

MHWS 2.2m MHWN 1.7 MTL 1.4 MLWN 1.1 MLWS 0.7

These heights are subject to a variation of ±0.3m according to barometric pressure and wind direction.

Streams in entrance are ingoing: Dover −6h 3kn; outgoing −1¼h, 4¾kn. Outgoing stream is weak for first 3h.

Approach From W keep Anvil Pt lt ho open until you pick up the Poole lts which must not be closed in. Avoid Handfast Pt tide-rip on the ebb or in a breeze. From E, keep Swanage open of Ballard Pt to clear shoal patches 2.4m and Hook Sands. There is a RDF bn at Haven Hotel, 50°40′.95N, 1°56′.73W. 303.4khz, 'PO', 10M.

Bar MHWS 5.5 MHWN 5.2 MLWS 3.7m.

Strong winds between S and E cause a heavy sea.

Entrance From Fairway lt buoy RWVS, Fl 10s, bell, 6½ca NE of Handfast Pt, steer for buoyed and lighted Swash Channel, 1ca wide. After No 8 port buoy the W side of the channel has a training bank which covers at half tide. There is a lt, QR 7m 2M at the seaward end beyond which it is marked by bns, R can tops.

There is a subsidiary channel (3m) for small craft entering and leaving the hbr via the Swash Channel. This is to the W of the dredged channel, between the R can buoys to stb and the R bns to port, from No 2 buoy to No 12A, leaving latter to port.

East Looe Channel is another subsidiary entrance for small craft from E; 1.5m, parallel to the shore close to S side of Sandbanks. Approach in W sector (294°-304°) of East Looe Lt Oc WRG 6s. Do not attempt in swell or onshore winds.

It is inadvisable to enter the Swash Channel, from E, N of No 1 G con Bar buoy except in good weather at HW and then not N of No 5 buoy. The S part of Hook Sand has only 1.2m and N of No 9 it dries.

Sandbanks chain ferry runs between S Haven Pt and Sandbanks. It must be given a clear berth as the chains are near the surface at each end of the ferry.

Interior Channels It is advisable to keep to the marked channels: outside them the water is generally shallow.

South Deep Channel is to port after No 18 buoy, Fl R 5s, and leads to the network of channels S of Brownsea Is and the oil base on Furzey Is, to which pt there are lt bns (mainly stb).

Anchoring Avoid oyster beds, marked by YW buoys and stakes from Stone Is to Cleavel Pt. Otherwise anchor: (1) In Brownsea Road close into houses on Brownsea, 0.6m to 2m, strong stream. Beware cables between North Haven and Brownsea.

(2) In South Deep off Goathorn Pt or above Furzey Is; keep out of fairway – tripper boats.

(3) For shallow bilge-keel craft, Blood Alley Lake, 0.3m, mud.

Middle Ship, Small Craft, Northern and Little Channels The main channel bears NNE round N Haven W card lt bn, Q(9) 15s, after which the array of buoys, bns and moored yachts may appear confusing. At No 20 Middle Ground S card buoy, Q(6)+LFl 15s, the Northern Channel (marked as Main Channel on some charts) is to stb, NE, and Middle Ship Channel (used by large vessels) to port, due N. Both are buoyed and lit and bear round to W to Poole, joining again at No 51 (Diver) W card bn, Q(9) 15s.

Small craft are advised to take the Northern, rather than Middle Ship, Channel; but if following the latter there is on SW side, from No 46R can buoy, a Small Craft Channel marked on its S side by R stakes with R can tops. It is 30m wide, for craft with up to 1.5m draught, and goes as far as No 54 R can buoy just after the junction with Northern Channel (which passes the Salterns Marina). Entrance to Poole Quays is via Little Channel after No 55 (Stakes) S card buoy, Q(6)+LFl 15s.

Poole Br opens about every 2h, 0930 to 2330. Signal to open 3 long blasts. Traffic lts. Only 2m clearance closed.

Berthing Anchoring is forbidden in Middle Ship, Northern and Little Channels. Moorings are sometimes available from yards.

Alongside berths: (1) Town Quay. Can be crowded and difficult to clear on ebb with several craft outside; very uncomfortable with strong winds from S to E.

(2) Salterns Marina off Northern Channel.

(3) Above the br: Quay West Marina and Cobb's Quay Marina.

Wych Channel 5ca NNW of No 20 buoy a BYB E card bn marks the N edge of the entrance to Wych Channel, rounding Brownsea Is to N, marked with stakes. There are two shallow (1m) short-cuts across the mud linking Wych to the main channel: Ball's Lake, near the NE tip of Arne peninsula, and Wills Cut from NW corner of Brownsea Is. Each is marked by stakes.

Berthing Anchor: (1) Clear of moorings (e.g.to NW of Brownsea Is) clear of oyster beds or off Pottery Pier.

(2) Shipstal Pt 1m.

Wareham Channel is the continuation of the main channel after the entrance to Poole Quay and leads to the entrance to R Frome and thence to Wareham. It is buoyed and staked and is lit at the main turning pts as far as No 84 buoy, SW of Boundary Stone, after which it dries; it is navigable at HW to Wareham for craft up to 1.5m draught.

Berthing Anchor off Russel Quay or elsewhere according to draught and oyster beds S of Hamworthy Pt.

Alongside Berths: (1) Ridge Wharf in R Frome.

(2) Redcliff YC.

(3) Wareham Town Quay is not recommended except for very short stay as tourist launches are liable to berth alongside.

Supplies Fuel at Cobb's and Salterns Marinas, Ridge Wharf, fuel barge (near junction of Middle Ship and Wych channels), and most yards. Water at marinas and Town Quay. Shops at Poole (EC Wed) and Wareham.

Tel/VHF (all 0202 unless shown differently) HM 685261/ ch 16, 14 (Mon-Fri); Cobb's Quay 674299/ ch 80,37 ('CQ Base'); Quay West Marina 675071; Salterns Marina 707321/ ch 80,37 ('Gulliver Base'); Ridge Wharf (09295) 2650; and for moorings: Sandbanks Yacht Co 707500; Harvey & Sons 666226; Dorset Yacht Co (Hamworthy) 674531; Customs as Southampton.

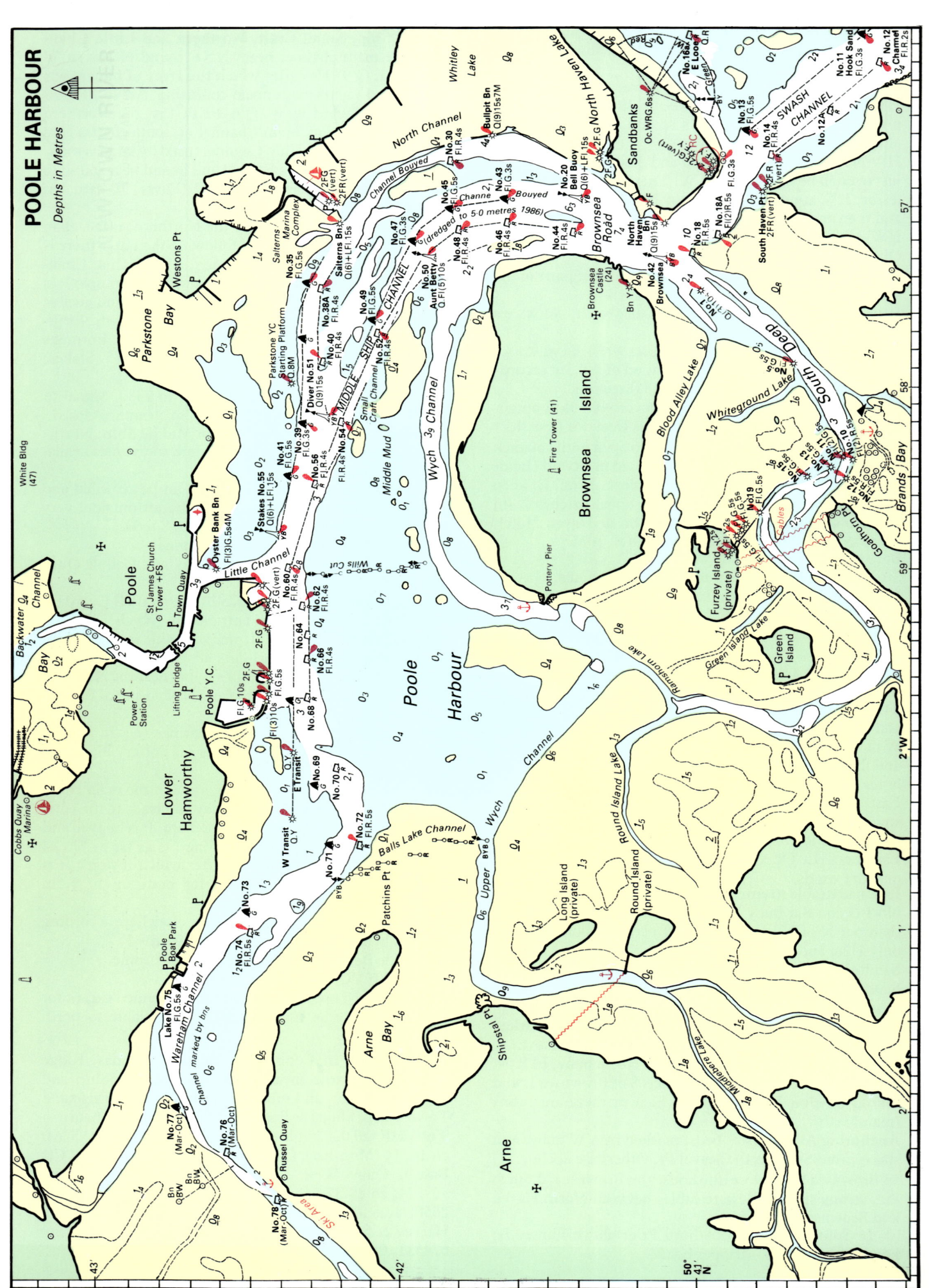

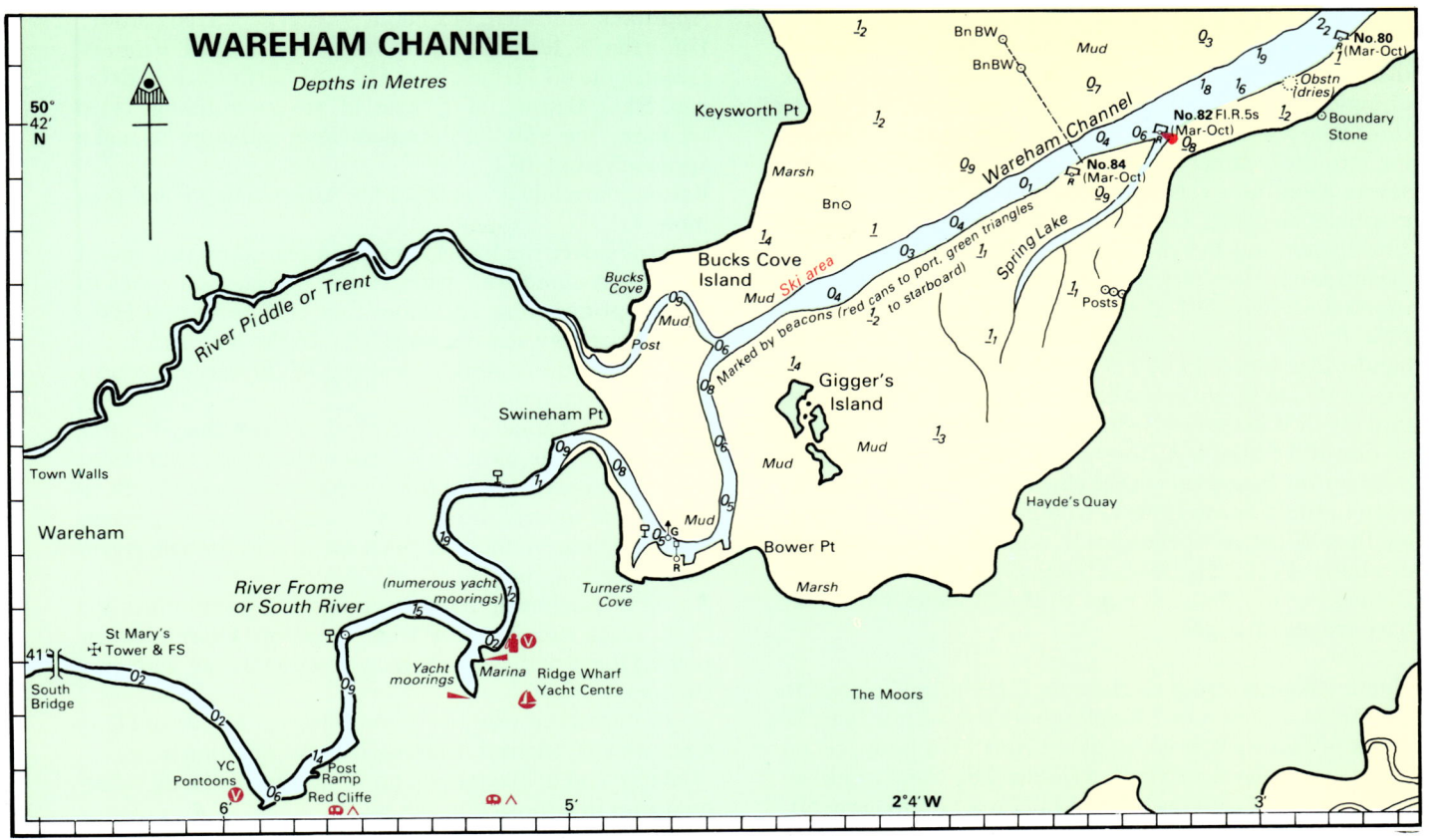

PASSAGE NOTES: POOLE TO CHICHESTER
                                    Chart BA 2450
The main hazards are Christchurch Ledge and the Shingles Bank on NW side of the Needles Channel.

Passage lts
Anvil Pt	Fl 10s 24M;
The Needles	Oc(2) WRG 20s 17/14M, Horn(2) 30s, R sector over Shingles and to SE;
St Catherine's Pt	Fl 5s 30M+F R 17M to NW;
Nab Tr	Fl(2) 10s 19M, Horn(2) 30s

Tides From Christchurch to Southampton there is a stand around the time of HW Portsmouth during which some places have a small fall followed by a second HW; others have a second HW only at springs. In places the time of HW in relation to HW Dover varies so much between springs and neaps that it is better to relate tides to the time of LW, which is fairly constant in relation to HW Dover. Where this is the case the tidal data will be prefaced accordingly. Thus for example **Low Water** Lymington is 5¼h after HW Dover.

Streams related to Dover:
Poole Bay, offshore: +5½h NE; −½h SW;
inshore +5h E; −1¼h W; 1kn.
Needles entrance: +5½h E; −½h W.
North Channel to Hurst approx: +5h E; −1h W.
Ryde Pier, N of: +4¼h E; −1½h W.
S of IOW: +5½h ENE; −¾h WSW; 5kn between
St Catherine's Pt and Dunnose.
Nab Tr: HWD W; +1h SW; +6¼h E; −4h ENE;
−2¾h NE; −½h N

The E stream sets towards Christchurch ledge and across the Shingles. The W stream sets well S of Durlston Hd and Anvil Pt. Streams are weak inside the line Handfast Pt to Hengistbury Hd and in Christchurch Bay but are strong across Christchurch Ledge and the Shingles. Between Poole and Wight the flood sets strongly into Poole Bay. The area Anvil Pt to the Needles is covered by the pair of VHF Ro Bns (VHF 88) at Anvil Pt and High Down (N.B. they give true, not magnetic, bearings).

Hengistbury Hd is prominent with dark red cliffs, 18m high and a look-out, conspic, with FS 4½ca to W.

There are overfalls on Christchurch Ledge on the ebb. Christchurch Priory open SW of the look-out on Warren Hill (W side of Hengistbury Hd), 333° leads SW of it. If crossing the Ledge in fair weather aim for a point about 1½M SE of Hengistbury Hd. Close inshore there are rks, awash at LW, ½ca off the hd of the groyne. In fog the position of Needles Lt can often be guaged from the fact that fog lies lightly to W of the entrance, but hangs in a dark and heavy patch on the cliff over looking the lt.

Entrance to the Solent is via the Needles Channel or the North Channel.

Needles Channel With wind against the ebb, the entrance is uncomfortable, at times dangerous, and N Channel is then to be preferred. Remember the tide sets across the Shingles on both the ebb and flood: this calls for extreme care when SW-bound with the ebb. The Bank is encroaching into the channel and parts dry as much as 1.5m; after severe gales there can be deposits above HW level which gradually disperse. The ldg line (042°) of Hurst High and Low lts now touches the edge of the bank where there is a drying patch 3½ca NE of SW Shingles buoy; to NE it passes on the wrong (W) side of Shingles Elbow R Can buoy, Fl(2) R 5s. Entrance is made between SW Shingles port-hand pillar buoy, Fl R 2.5s, and Bridge W card buoy, VQ(9) 10s, in W sectors of Hurst ldg lts, Iso 4s and 6s, and initially in W sector of Needles lt but entering its R sector on line of the buoys. As soon as the two buoys are cleared, steer for the Island side of the channel with Hurst High Lt open to the E of the Low lt. At night this brings you into another W sector of Needles lt, leading onto Warden G can buoy. Fl G 2.5s, clear of dangers off the Island shore. Remember too that the edge of the Shingles bank may have moved after gales.

North Channel From Christchurch Ledge make good to NE (flood setting onto Shingles to stb) in the northern W sector of Hurst High lt (Iso 6s) to North Hd buoy, G con Fl(3)G 10s, then steer SE with Golden Hill Fort (white) on with Bramble Chine, parallel with Hurst Spit to leave NE Shingles E card buoy, Q(3) 10s to stb. Streams run strongly in the channel, mainly in its direction.
Caution: A spit, the Trap, runs S from Hurst Pt with 0.3m at its inshore end - the tide sets onto it. There is generally turbulence or overfalls in Hurst narrows.
Solent hazards are the mud flats off the Hampshire coast, Bramble Bank (dries 1.3m) in the entrance to Southampton Water, and the submerged obstructions inshore of Horse Sand and No Man's Land Forts.

South of Isle of Wight At night rounding St Catherine's Pt from NW keep in Needles W sector until St Catherine's lt bears 064° and keep S of latter's FR sector. To clear the worst of the race (bad in strong wind against tide conditions, severe to SE of the Pt with W gales) keep 2M offshore.

Anchorages are to be found in suitable conditions off the coast in Poole and Christchurch Bays and in the Solent, especially **Hurst**: close inside the Pt off the lt ho, stream generally W-going, wash from tide-cheating fishing boats; **Alum Bay** (mind drying rks 1 and 2ca W of coloured cliffs) and **Totland Bay**; W of entrance to **Yarmouth Hbr,** strong stream on ebb, mind Black Rk (dries 0.4m) 3½ca WNW of entrance; **Osborne Bay**; and N of **St Helen's Fort**.

CHRISTCHURCH   Chart BA 2172, 2219
DS: Dover +5h E; −1¼h W
Low Water: Dover +5h. At springs there is 5h rise, 3½h stand, 4h ebb. At neaps there is 5½h flood, 2¾h stand and 4¼h ebb. The ebb in the entrance is fierce after the second HW. In the hbr, tide height can be critical - see Poole tidal curves in ATT.
MHWS 1.8 & 1.5m   MHWN 1.4   MTL 1.0   MLWN 0.6
MLWS 0.4
Entry safe for draughts up to 1.2m (1.5m at springs) except in fresh winds between S and E.

Approach Entrance lies about ¾M NE of Hengistbury Hd. From E, leave the Solent via North Channel. From W give groyne off Hengistbury Hd ¾M berth to clear Beerpan Rks. Beware of groyne of stones running 1½ca offshore, 3ca SSW of entrance. Keep offshore to make approach from SE.
Bar has normally 0.3 to 0.6m but varies in depth and position.
Entrance over the bar is marked in season by two lateral buoys and about four pairs of sph buoys. Best times to enter: springs from 2h before first HW to second HW; neaps at or between the two HWs. In the Run and in the hbr, ebb continues until 1½h after LW. Beware fishermen shooting nets in the run.
Inside, the channel is well buoyed to Grimsbury Pt after which moorings indicate it. After Mudeford Quay bear sharply to port and give first G sph buoy a wide berth to stb. Leave moored boats to stb until the pontoon jetty, after which leave them to port. Depths in the two rivers vary from 0.6m to 1.3m.
Berthing Anchoring room is limited but possibilities are (1) In reach running SSW from Mudeford Quay between Black House and pontoon jetty; restrict swing with two anchors.
(2) In unmarked channel (0.9m) close to N side of Hengistbury Hd, entered from reach above pontoon jetty.
(3) At SE end of Steep Bank on W side immediately below moorings in approach to rivers.
(4) In Clay Pool at junction of the rivers.
Moorings: enquire at Christchurch SC, G Elkins or Christchurch Marine.
Supplies Fuel at Christchurch Marine; water from Mudeford beach or Christchurch SC. Limited supplies from Mudeford beach cafe. Shops at Mudeford village and Christchurch.
Tel Christchurch SC (0202) 483150; Christchurch Marine 483250; Customs as Southampton.

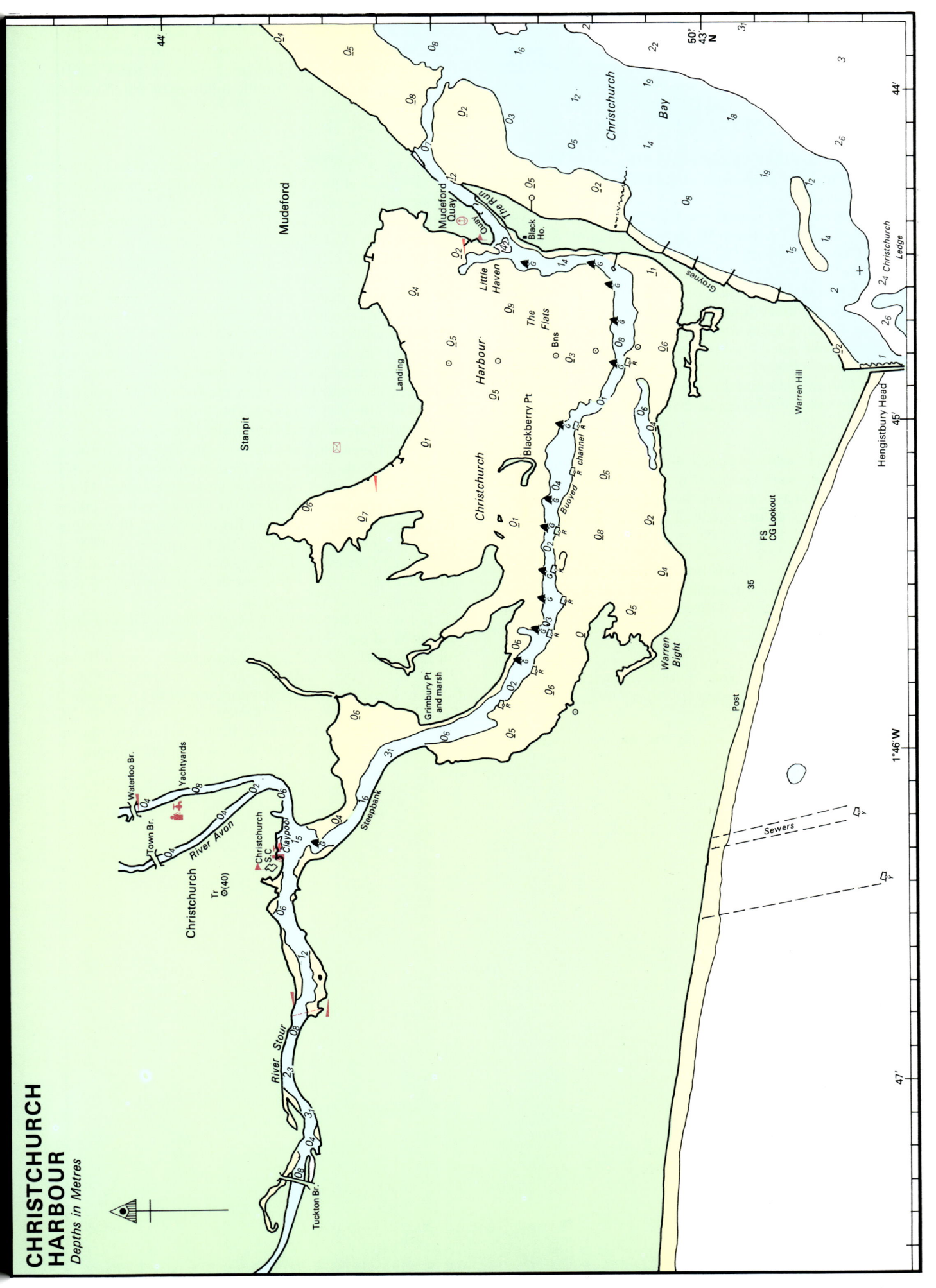

KEYHAVEN
Chart BA 2021

At Hurst Pt: **Low Water:** Dover +5¼h. Springs: rise for 6½h to 1st HW, fall for 1h, stand and small rise to 2nd HW for 1½h, fall for 3½h. Neaps: Rise for 7½h, followed by fall, with no stand or 2nd HW.

MHWS 2.7 & 2.5m MHWN 2.3 MTL 1.8 MLWN 1.3
MLWS 0.5

DS (Hurst Narrows): Dover +5¾h NE; −¾h SW; 4kn. A small attractive creek with limited room near the castle for anchoring.

Approach From E, keep Hurst Low lt open twice its own width S of High Lt. From W, give the Trap off S side of Hurst Castle a berth of 1½ca.

Entrance The bar changes. Do not attempt entrance in strong E winds. The leading line, marked by two small Y St Andrew's crosses (inconspic) which are moved from time to time, is generally about 285°. The entrance is marked by two small buoys, G and R. Inside, the channel is marked by a few stb buoys, one port buoy off the entrance to Mount Lake and the line of private moorings. Pass round the bows of all moored craft as the areas astern are shallow

Berthing The river is congested with private moorings but space to anchor may be found in the bay just inside the entrance. The heavy mooring there is used by the tender for maintenance at the castle. Land on the spit or at Keyhaven hard.

Supplies Fuel at W Solent Boat Builders in emergency only; otherwise by can from Milford. Water at Keyhaven YC and at River Warden's Office. Inn at Keyhaven; shops at Milford. EC Wed.

Tel Hbr Authority: New Forest District Council, (042128) 3121. River Warden (0590) 645695; Keyhaven YC: (0590) 642165.

YARMOUTH IoW
Chart BA 2021, 2040

Low Water: Dover +5h. Springs: rise for 6¾h to 1st HW, fall for 1¼h, stand and small rise to 2nd HW for 1h, fall for 3½h. Neaps: Rise for 8h, followed by fall. No stand or 2nd HW.

MHWS 3.1 & 2.8m MHWN 2.5 MTL 2.0 MLWN 1.4
MLWS 0.6

DS: Dover +5¼h NE; −¾h SW. Stream runs hard across the outer half of pier but weaker near the entrance where hbr stream takes over.

Approach From W keep 2ca offshore until abreast the breakwater to clear Black Rock and then aim for the pier, about a third of its length from the head, until ldg marks in line. From E beware anglers' lines in rounding pier.

Entrance Illuminated notice 'Harbour Full' or R flag by day at end of ferry jetty: no spare berths, anchor outside. It is inadvisable to enter under sail because of ferry movements and, in season, congestion. Ldg lts F G front and rear, BW diamonds on grey posts, 188°. There are 2FR(vert) each side of the ferry ramp and Fl G 5s on dolphin at W side of entrance. At the dolphin beware of traffic emerging on stb hand from outer line of piles.

Berthing Moor as directed by Berthing Master or between piles or alongside Town Quay (uncomfortable with N-NE wind). Berthing on S quay only with permission. Moorings sometimes available from the two yards for a longer stay. Br opens about every two hrs in summer; by arrangement in winter. River navigable by dinghy at HW to Freshwater Causeway. 12 Visitors' moorings are available (Apr-Oct only) NW of hbr entrance, following 4m contour except two at W end in 2m.

Anchor outside according to height of tide, clear of entrance to W of pier. Sand, shingle.

Supplies Fuel and water at S Quay, water also at Town Quay. Shops (EC Wed), also at Freshwater (EC Thur). Buses to Freshwater and Newport. Ferry to Lymington.

Tel/VHF (0983) Berthing Masters 760300; R Solent YC 760256; Harold Hayles Boatyard 760373; Buzzard Marine 760520; Water Taxi ch 10; Customs as Southampton.

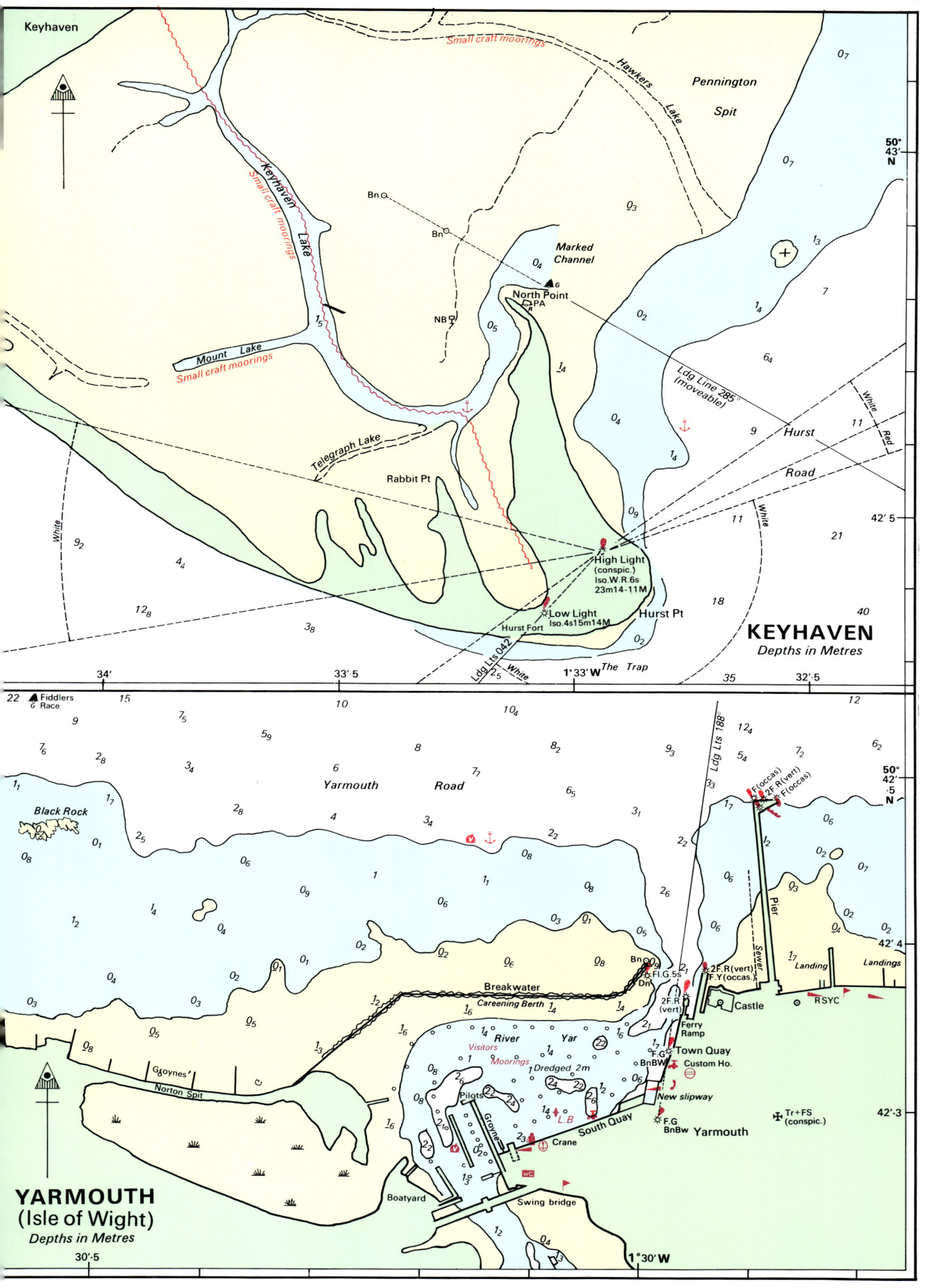

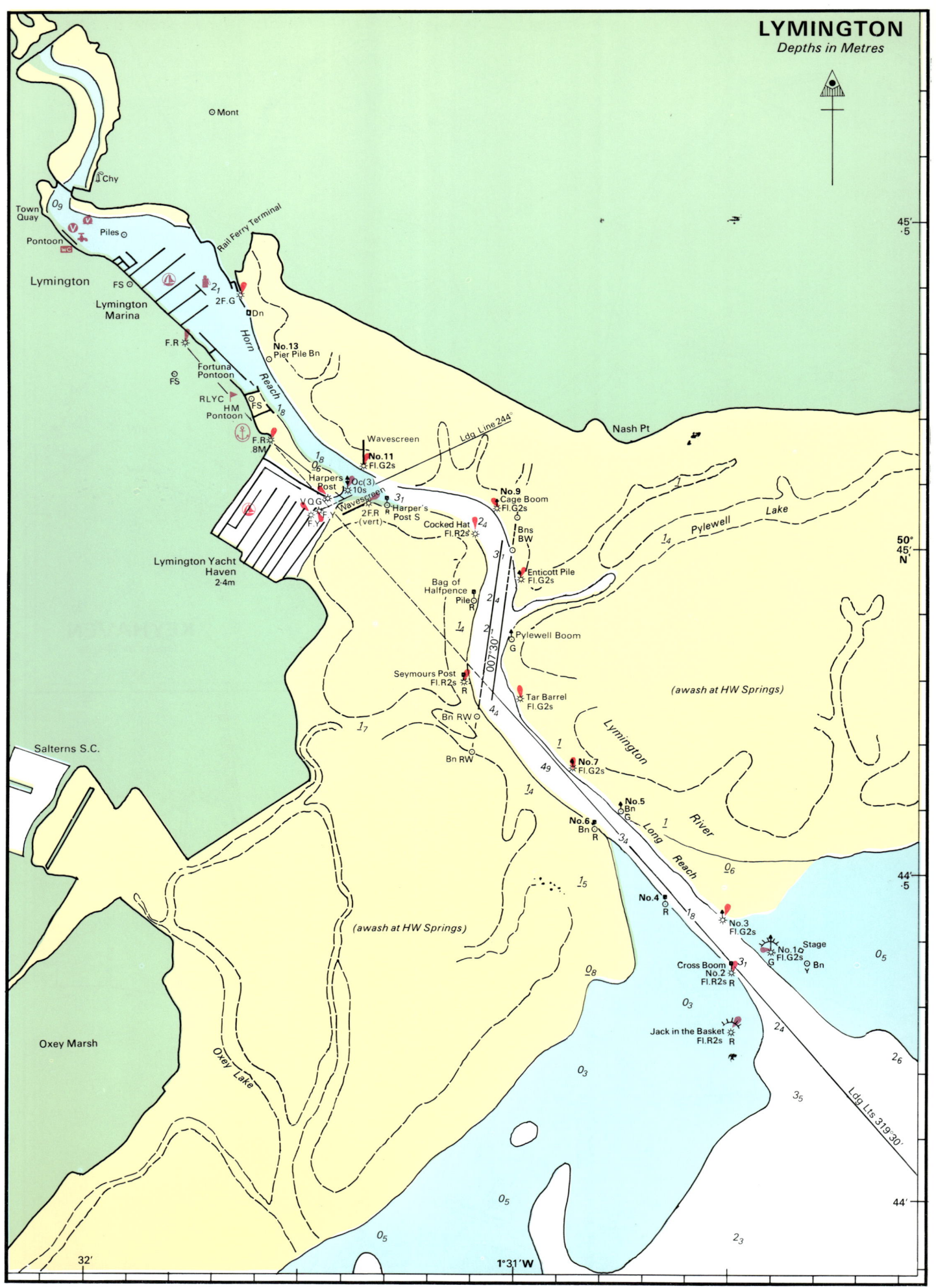

LYMINGTON
Chart BA 2021

Low Water: Dover +5¼h. Springs: rise for 6¾h to 1st HW, fall for 1¼h, stand and small rise to 2nd HW for 1h, fall for 3½h. Neaps: Rise for 8h, followed by fall. No stand or 2nd HW. DS: Dover +5¼h NE, −¾h SW.

MHWS 3.0 & 2.9m MHWN 2.6 MTL 1.8 MLWN 1.3 MLWS 0.5

Approach Keep Hurst Low Lt fully twice its own width open S of the High Lt to clear the mud banks either side of the entrance; at night do not go N of W sector of Hurst High Lt until on line of F R ldg lts, 319°. The RLYC starting platform on E corner of entrance is conspic landmark.

Entrance All craft must give way to Sealink ferries which take up much of the channel. They may pass abreast between Cocked Hat pile and Seymours Post (the sector on ldg line 008°). Keep well to stb but remember that in passing they lower the water level and the mud flats are steep-to. The channel is marked by lt bns as far as ferry terminal opposite Lymington Marina. The bns are on the edge of the drying mud flats; follow the natural curves of the river rather than going in a straight line from bn to bn. This is important between bns no 9 and 11, and between latter and edge of ferry terminal. The final stretch to Town Quay is not lit but is navigable at night with care by following lines of moored boats. Entrance to Lymington Yacht Haven is marked by Harper's Post E card Bn, Q(3) 10s and 2F G(vert) on S end of breakwater. Leave both to stb on ldg lts F Y 244°.

Berthing Anchoring in hbr is prohibited. Visitors' berths at Lymington Yacht Haven, Lymington Marina and at Town Quay (pontoons alongside and fore and aft buoys).

Supplies Fuel and water at marinas, water at Town Quay; all facilities. EC Wed.

Tel/VHF (0590) HM 672014; R Lymington YC 672677; Lymington Yacht Haven 677071/ ch 80,37; Lymington Marina 673312-6/ ch 80,37; Customs as Southampton.

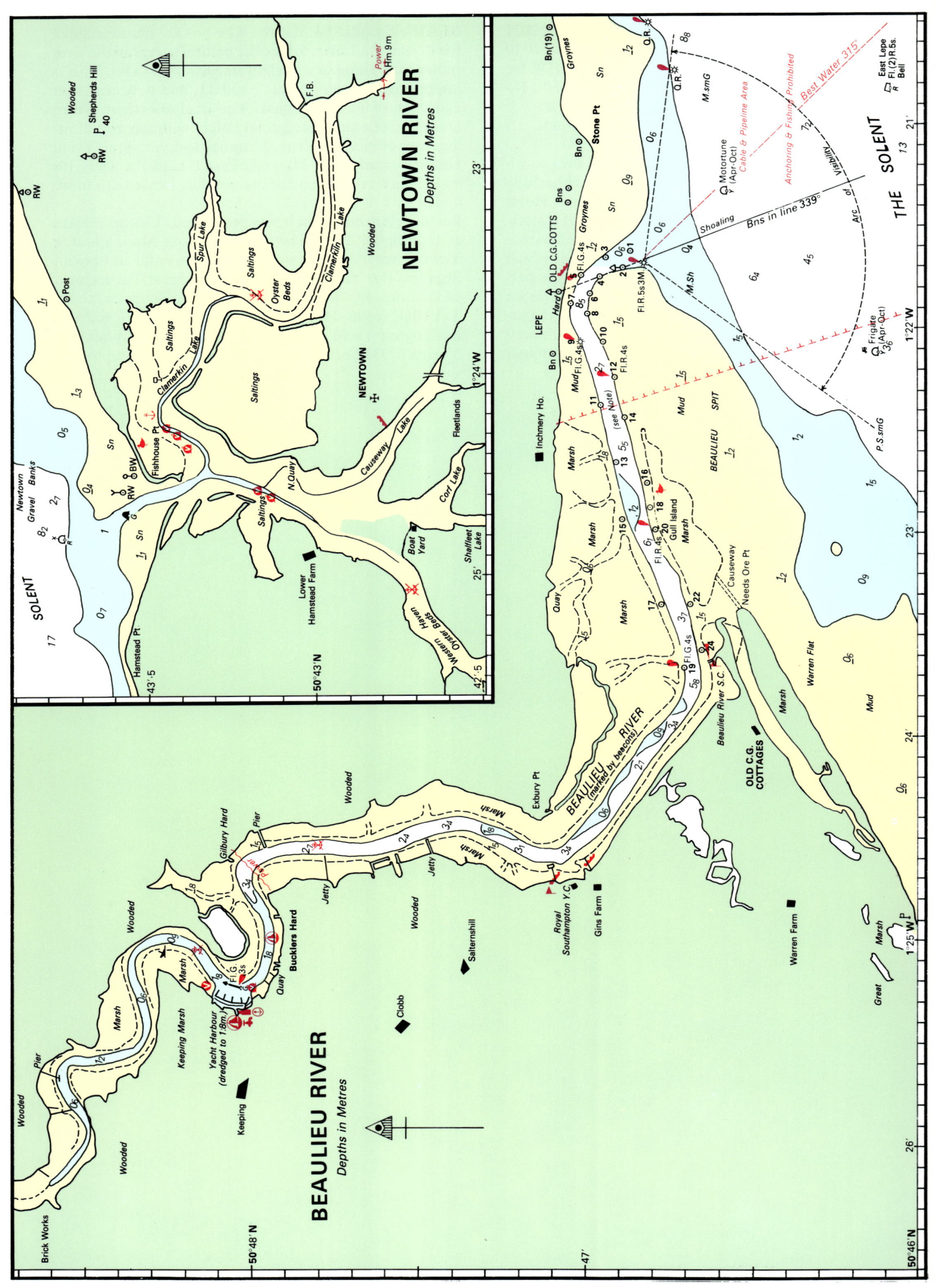

NEWTOWN RIVER IoW Chart BA 2022
Low Water: Dover +5¼h. Rise for 6¾h (springs), 7¼h (neaps).
DS: Dover +5h E; −¾h W.
MHWS (Solent Banks) 3.4m MHWN 2.8 MTL 2.1 MLWN 1.5 MLWS 0.5

An unspoilt sheltered natural hbr owned by the National Trust.

Approach The entrance lies ¾M E of Hamstead Ledge G con buoy Fl(2) G 5s. From E, Yarmouth Pierhead open of Hamstead Pt skirts the edge of Newtown Gravel Banks (3½m).

Entrance Ldg bns (130°): front RW, Y top, rear BW disc top, off Fishhouse Pt lead over the bar (1.5m) with a very small R sph buoy to port in approach and similar G sph to stb opposite first bn. Thereafter channels are marked by R and G stakes with can or pointed topmarks. Beware of overhead power lines near the head of Clamerkin Lake, clearance 12m.

Berthing There are R or W numbered visitors' buoys to port in Clamerkin Lake or ahead in main channel. Anchorage in Clamerkin Lake as far as the two 'Anchorage Prohibited' notice boards (oyster beds) or in main channel to abreast of Lower Hamstead Landing. Landing on Fishhouse Pt is prohibited from Apr - Jun (nature reserve). Land at Shalfleet Quay, Newtown (both dry) or Lower Hamstead on W side of entrance.

Supplies Porchfield or Shalfleet; bus to Yarmouth or Newport. Water at Newtown and Shalfleet Quays and Lower Hamstead. Small yard at Shalfleet Quay.

Tel: Berthing Master Calbourne 424.

BEAULIEU RIVER Chart BA 2021
Low Water: Dover +5¼h rise for 7h (springs), 7½h (neaps). DS: Dover −1h W; +5h E.
MHWS 3.4m MHWN 2.7 MTL 2.0 MLWN 1.5 MLWS 0.5

Approach Give the shore a berth of 3ca S off Stansore, Stone and Needs Oar Pts. Near E Lepe buoy, terraced cottages will be seen to N and white boathouse on shore below. The boathouse on with the W-most cottage leads towards the entrance.

Entrance Ldg marks (339°), both fluorescent Or triangles over rectangles: rear in trees 1ca west of cottages; front in water 3ca from shore mark. Best depth on bar is to E of ldg line with dolphin bearing 315°. Close to stb in summer is a sph racing buoy and to port, ¾ca S of front bn, is a dolphin Fl R 5s at end of Beaulieu spit. Channel is well marked, initially by bns with R and G reflectors, of which three stb and two port are lit; after the bns there are perches. Least depth 1.5m to Buckler's Hard.

Berthing Anchor in first reach up to Needs Oar Pt clear of fairway; strong stream. Anchoring prohibited within 1M either side of Buckler's Hard. Marina (2m) and pile moorings at Buckler's Hard. Report to HM within 24h of arrival.

Supplies Water and fuel, hotel, shop and Maritime Museum at Buckler's Hard. Shops at Beaulieu, 2M by footpath.

Tel HM & Yacht Hbr (0590) 616200 or 616234.

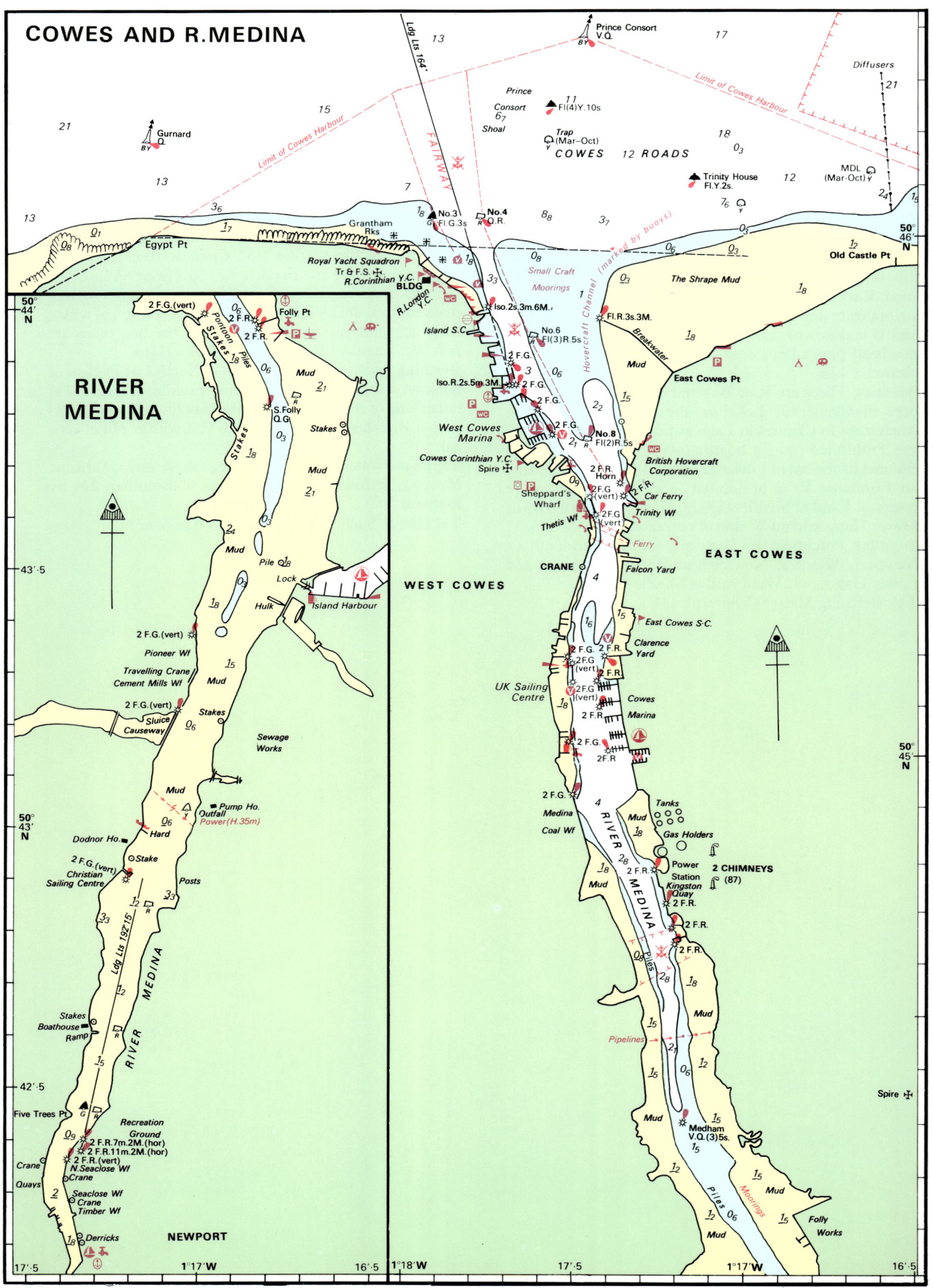

COWES & RIVER MEDINA IoW Chart BA 2793

HW: Dover +½h. DS:Dover +4½h E; −1¼h W. In R Medina, flood Dover +5¾h, ebb +½h.

Cowes:
MHWS 4.2m MHWN 3.5 MTL 2.5 MLWN 1.7 MLWS 0.6

Newport:
MHWS 4.1m MHWN 3.4

A busy port and yachting centre with ferries and hydrofoil to Southampton. Accessible at all states of tide and with good all-round shelter in upper reaches.

Approach E side of entrance is occupied by Shrape Mud, covered at half-flood, leaving only a comparatively narrow channel along W Cowes shore. From E, keep 2ca off Old Castle Pt.

Entrance Channel is buoyed and between May 1st and September 15th entry must be made between the first G (No 3, Fl G 3s) and R (No 4, QR) buoys. Ldg line 164°: front Iso W 2s, rear Iso R 2s. Depth 2½m. When W lt is abeam, more useful to steer on the S set of 2F R (vert) lts on Trinity House Wharf. Beware of the 'Floating Bridge' (chain ferry) just S of this. Below the ferry the ebb runs hardest on E side, but above it, hardest on the W side.

Cowes Berthing Anchoring prohibited. Visitors' moorings on large buoys on stb side soon after entry (much wash); at marked piles just S of West Cowes Marina or both sides ¼M S of Floating Br; also on pontoon off Shepards Wharf on W side N of floating br (shore access). Marinas on stb, West Cowes Marina, and port, Cowes Marina.

Supplies Fuel and water at West Cowes Marina and fuel jetty; water also at Town Quay and Cowes Marina. All facilities in Cowes. EC Wed.

River Medina Above Cowes there are open rural surroundings to Newport. River is navigable for boats up to 1.5m draught to Folly Inn and boats can reach Newport at about HW Portsmouth ±2h with 2.1m draught at Springs and 1.1m at Neaps; data for times of HW at Newport are lacking. Channel is buoyed but not lit above Folly Inn. ½M above the inn is Island Yacht Hbr entrance lock. Ldg line to Newport 192°, both marks W diamonds, F R.

Berthing Piles with pontoons between marked for visitors opposite Folly Inn; pontoons at Island Yacht Hbr; lock open HW ±3h, 1.8m draught. At Newport twin-keeled boats tie to a pontoon, fin keels to the quay. Bottom soft mud. Showers and toilets for yachtsmen on quay

Supplies Fuel and water at Island Yacht Hbr; water at Newport Town Quay. Shops in Newport, EC Thur.

Tel/VHF: (0983) HM: 293952/ ch 16,69; Chain Ferry ch 69; West Cowes Marina 294861/ ch 80,37; Cowes Marina 293983; HM Newport (includes Folly Pt moorings) 525994/ ch 16, 6 (office hours); Island Hbr 526733/ch 80,37; Customs as Southampton.

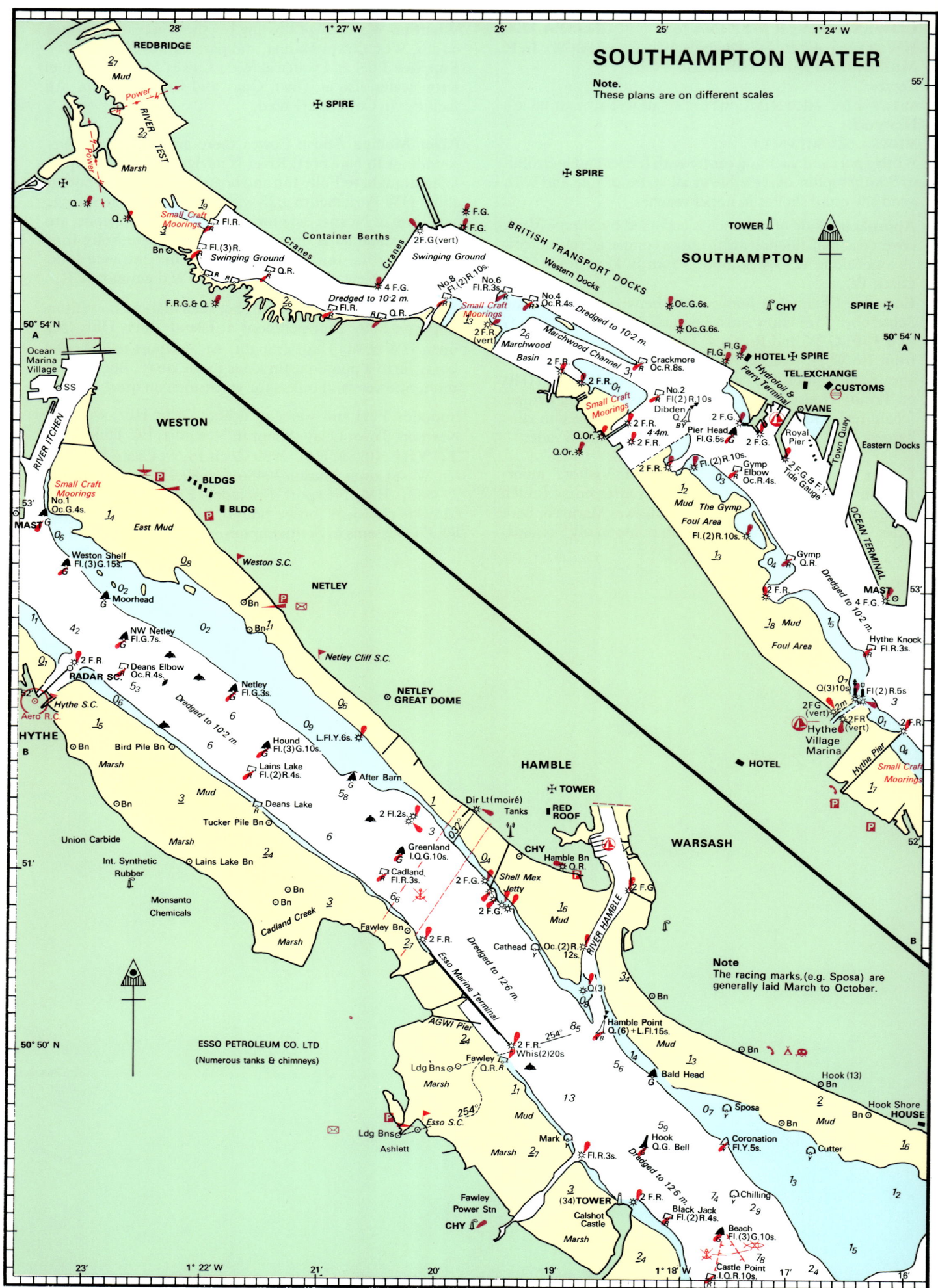

SOUTHAMPTON WATER Chart BA 1905, 2041

HW Calshot: Dover +½h; Southampton: +0h. DS: Calshot: Dover HW to +5h mainly SW, +5¼h to −1h mainly NE. At Southampton: Dover +6¼h flood, HWD ebb. The tide flows for 1½ to 2h, slack 1 to 1½h, flows 3½h to 1st HW, ebbs 1h, flows 1¼h to 2nd HW, ebbs 3¼h to LW.

At Southampton
MHWS 4.5m MHWN 3.7 MTL 2.6 MLWN 1.8 MLWS 0.5

A very busy commercial hbr and oil terminal with good facilities for yachts.

Approach When vessels over 100m are in the Western Approach Channel (including the Thorn Channel and Calshot Reach), craft under 20m are not allowed in the main channel off Calshot, i.e. N of the line Bourne Gap buoy to N Thorn buoy and S of the line Calshot Pt buoy to Reach buoy. As Calshot side is steep-to, it is better to keep outside the main channel to E. E-bound outgoing ships fly code flag E over Answering pendant, W-bound Answering pendant over flag W. Listen on VHF 12 to Port Radio. Coming from Cowes beware Bramble Bank, dries 1.3m, and keep well to W near W Bramble W card buoy, VQ(9) 10s and Thorn Knoll G con buoy, Fl G 5s. From E take North Channel, buoyed and lit, entered from E Bramble E card buoy VQ(3) 5s.

Southampton Channel is clearly marked. For Ocean Village and R Itchin, leave it after Weston Shelf G con buoy, FlG(3) 15s and pass one G con buoy, Oc G 4s, four lt stb bns and a jetty (2x2F G(vert)). Ocean Village Marina is to port before br.

Berthing Anchorage: (1) Ashlett Creek (just SE of Fawley oil wharf), below the notice board. The creek itself dries and is full of private moorings. Land at Public Quay near HW or at LW hard, 0.3m. All stores, EC Wed.
(2) Netley, outside moorings in 2m.
(3) Hythe Pier, N of pierhead, 2m, clear of ferry. (These three anchorages are exposed to wash from commercial traffic).
(4) Marchwood near former power intake at top of permanently navigable water; local YC. Or clear of moorings in former power stn basin.
(5) Calshot Castle inshore near Activities Centre. Shallow.
Marinas: (1) Town Quay Marina.
(2) Ocean Village in R Itchin, W side below Woolston Br, traffic lights on stb side of entrance. Bus to town centre.
(3) Shamrock Quay above the br (24.4m clearance) to port; stream strong on outer pontoons. All boatyard services.
(4) Berths for shallow draught boats, and those capable of taking the ground, at Kemp's Shipyard above Shamrock Quay to stb.
(5) Hythe Marina (entrance locks) has very limited accommodation for visitors. Channel dredged 2m; waiting pontoon.
Supplies Fuel and water at Kemp's Shipyard, Hythe Marina and Itchen Marine at America wharf. Water also at Ocean Village and Shamrock Quay. Shops in town centre and new complex at Ocean Village.
Tel/VHF (0703). HM 330022/ch 16, 12; Hythe Marina 849263/ch 80,37; Ocean Village Marina 229385/ ch 80,37; Shamrock Quay 229461/ ch 80,37; Kemps Quay 632323; R Southampton YC 223352; Customs 827350.

See page 51 for Hamble

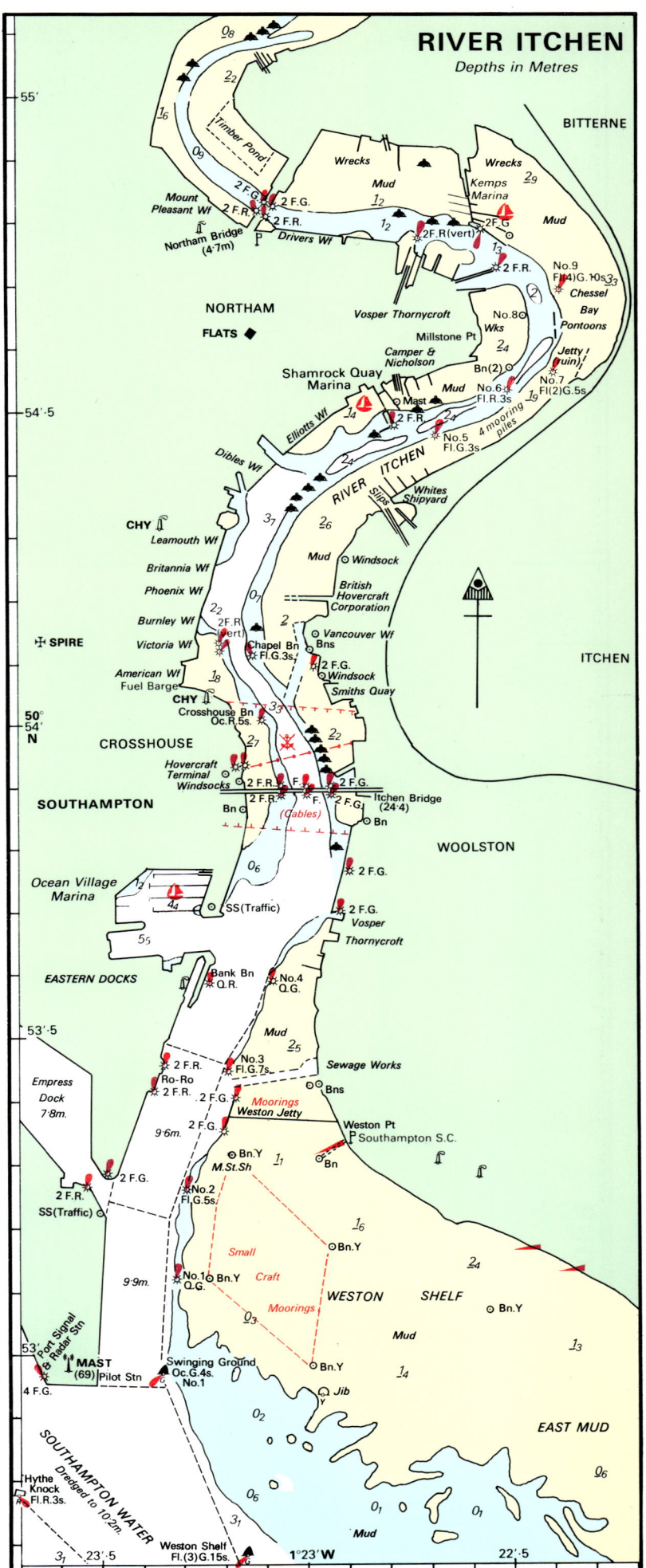

ENGLAND, SOUTH COAST 48

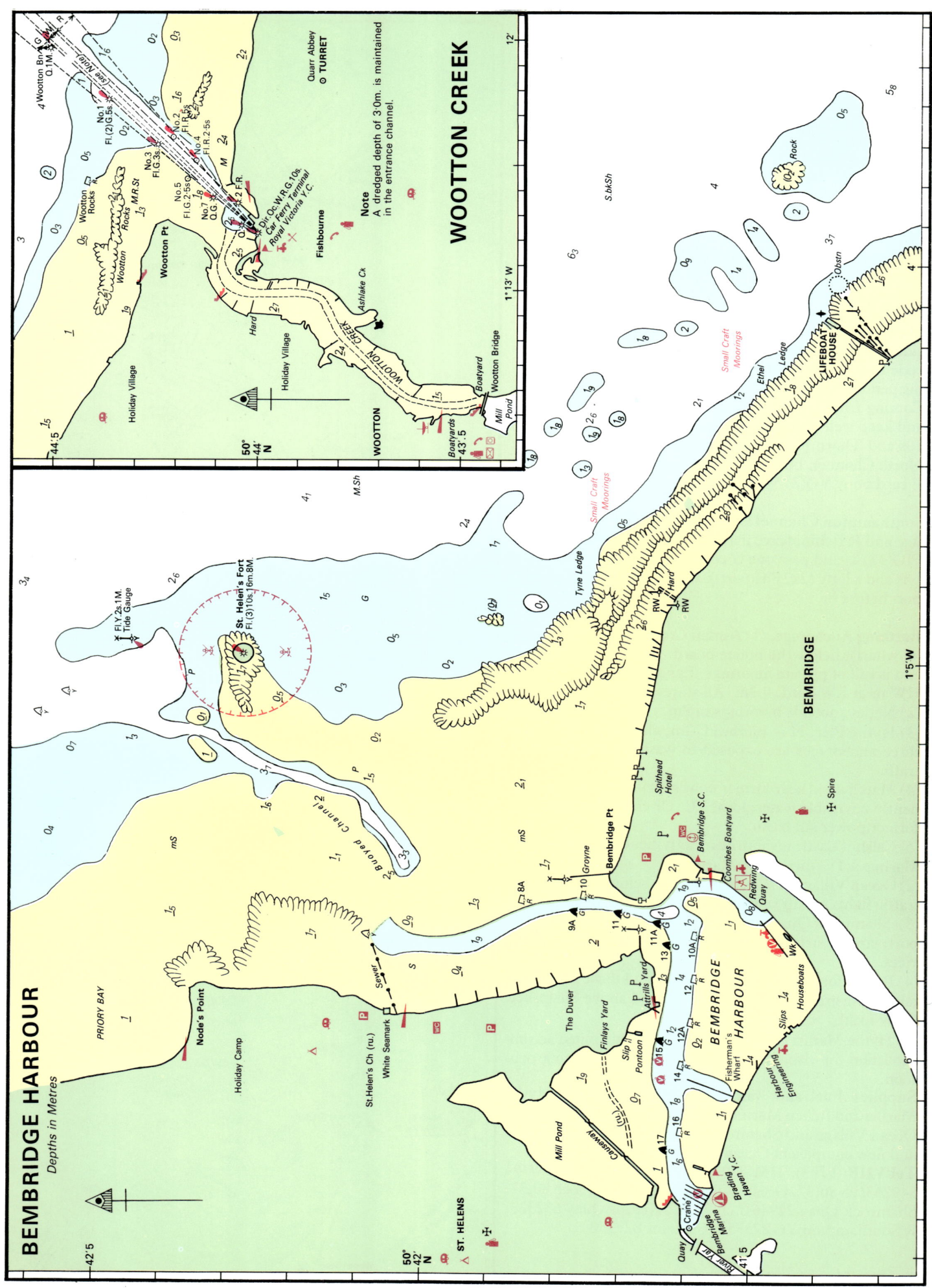

Hamble & Titchfield Haven – see next page

WOOTTON, IoW   Chart BA 2022
HW: Dover +¼h. DS: Dover +4¼h E; −1¾h W.
MHWS 4.5m   MHWN 3.7   MTL 2.6   MLWN 1.8   MLWS 0.7
A winding creek with many moorings and a car-ferry terminal at entrance.

Approach From W keep N of the line Old Castle Pt to the second pile from seaward to clear Wootton Rks. From E keep at least 4ca offshore. When Wootton Rks are covered there is 0.9m on the mud flats.

Entrance Channel, dredged 3m, is marked on stb by N card bn, four stb and two port lt piles. Do not attempt when a ferry is entering or leaving, generally around the hour and half hour. A dir lt, Oc WRG 10s, is at the ferry terminal. If going further up the creek, turn to stb after the fourth stb pile (No 7, QG), and follow line of moorings. Wootton Br (impassable) is accessible for shallow draft boats but channel is not marked and landing is only possible at HW±2h

Berthing Some visitors' berths alongside pontoons (1.3m) at Fishbourne Quay opposite ferry terminal. Dredged approach for 2m draught HW±4h. RVYC visitors' moorings: four piles and four large buoys; moor fore and aft; dry at springs. Anchoring forbidden in the fairway. Or anchor offshore 3ca N of Wootton Pt, 2.1m.

Supplies Water at RVYC; inn/restaurant; papers at ferry terminal; small store at Fishbourne; PO and shops at Wootton Br. EC Wed.

Tel Fishbourne Quay (0983) 883132; RVYC 882308.

RYDE HARBOUR   Chart BA 394
A new small craft drying hbr (sand/mud) E of Ryde Pier and Pavilion (conspic). Pontoon berths and quay for fin keels. Max draught 2 m, no multihulls. Accessible HW-2½h to +2h by buoyed and lighted approach across Ryde Sands, 197°. Tel: HM (0983) 613879).

BEMBRIDGE IoW   Chart BA 2022
HW: Dover +¼h. DS: Weak and variable except from Dover +3¼h S for 1h, 1-1½kn.
MHWS 3.1m   MHWN 2.3   MTL 1.3   MLWN 0.4   MLWS 0.0
A natural hbr much of it drying, (0.3m) in entrance.

Approach Aim for N side of St Helen's Fort, Fl(3) 10s, making sure the tide has risen enough to clear the gravel banks that surround it. Do not approach within ½ca of the fort on seaward side.

Entrance The channel starts at the tide gauge, Fl Y 2s 1M, 2 ca N of the fort and is buoyed but unlit. With spring or medium tide vessels with up to 1.8m draught can enter from HW-3 to +2h, but with tides under 4m, depth between buoys nos 6 and 8 may not exceed 1.5m. There is a minimum depth of 1m between no 10 buoy and the marina; otherwise the channel dries every tide with the least depth between buoys 6 and 8, which is the depth shown on the tide guage at the entrance. Max flow across the entrance is 1½kn.

Berthing can be difficult. Anchoring is forbidden except for boats that can dry out, anchored fore and aft, in sandy bay on E side by Bembridge SC. Pontoon berths at marina. Buoys are private.

Supplies Fuel at yard, water at marina and quay. Shops up the hill in Bembridge or at St Helens. EC Thur.

Tel/VHF Bembridge Marina (0983) 874436/ ch 80, 37.

HAMBLE
Chart BA 2022

DS off Hillhead: Dover +2½h E, −2h W. NW side of Bramble Bank: +4½h NE, −¾h SW.

Although the Hamble is congested with moorings and marinas, there is provision for visitors. Traffic at weekends is heavy, engines should be used, and wash can be uncomfortable at moorings.

Approach Steer for Hamble Pt buoy, S card Q(6) + L Fl 15s and leave it 30m to port. Follow ldg line 346°, front Oc(2)R 12s, rear Q R, to ldg line 026°, front Q G, rear Iso G 6s, past Warsash jetty, 2F G (vert). Above this some piles are lit, all have R or G reflectors. Do not cut corners, which are shallow, particularly on E side opposite Mercury Y Hbr and on W side approaching Swanwick.

Bridges at Bursledon have 4.0m headroom.

Berthing Anchoring forbidden above bns 9 and 10. Hbr Board pile moorings for visitors to port opposite Warsash (piles B1-4) and to stb opposite Port Hamble (piles 9-16). Marina berths at Hamble Pt, Port Hamble, Mercury Y Hbr, Universal Marine at Sarisbury Green, and Swanwick Marina. Moorings sometimes available from RAF YC. Landing on public hards at Warsash, Hamble, Swanwick Shore; at HM's jetty; and Jolly Sailor Inn at Bursledon.

Supplies Fuel and water at Warsash and marinas (save Universal). Provisions and chandlery at Warsash, Hamble and Swanwick. EC Wed.

Tel/VHF Warsash HM: (04895) 76387/ ch 68; Hamble Pt Marina (0703) 452464/ ch 80,37; Port Hamble Y Hbr (0703) 452741/ ch 80,37; Mercury Y Hbr (0703) 452741; Universal Marine (04895) 74272; Swanwick Marina Moody's (0489) 885000/ ch 80,37; RAF YC (0703) 452208; R Southern YC (0703) 453271. Customs as Southampton.

TITCHFIELD HAVEN (Or Hillhead Haven)
Chart BA 2022

A small drying creek, base of Hillhead SC. 1.8m draft at HW but dries to ¼M offshore.

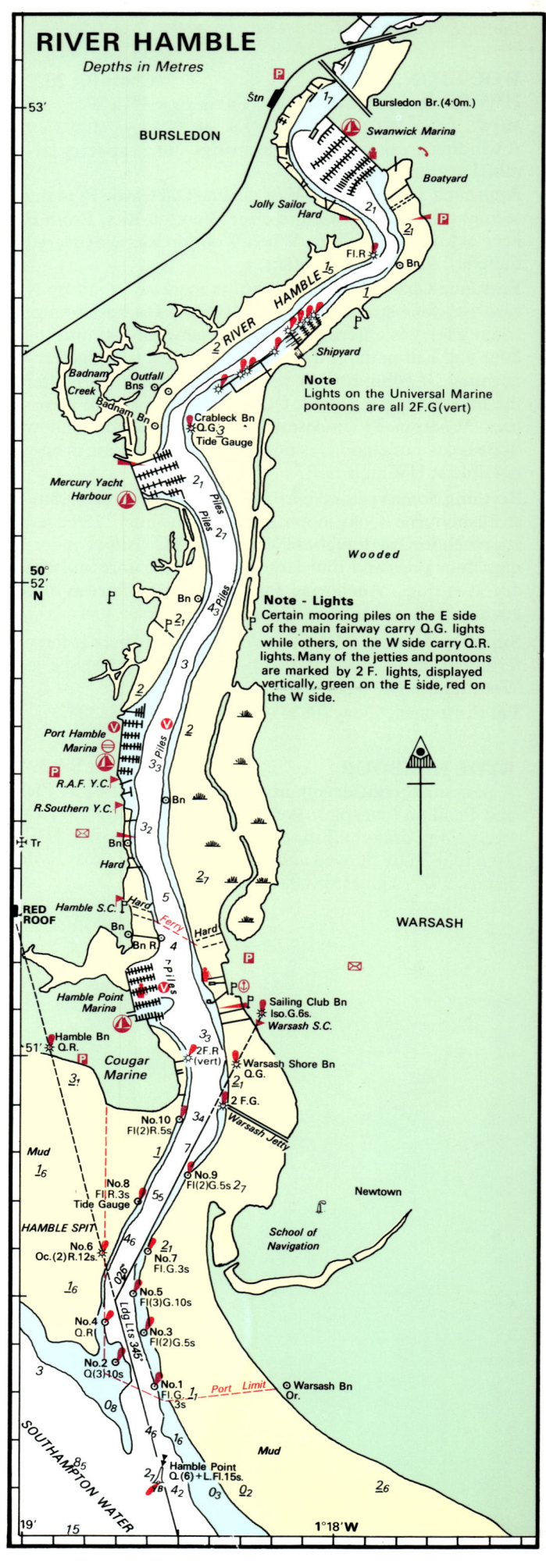

51 *ENGLAND, SOUTH COAST*

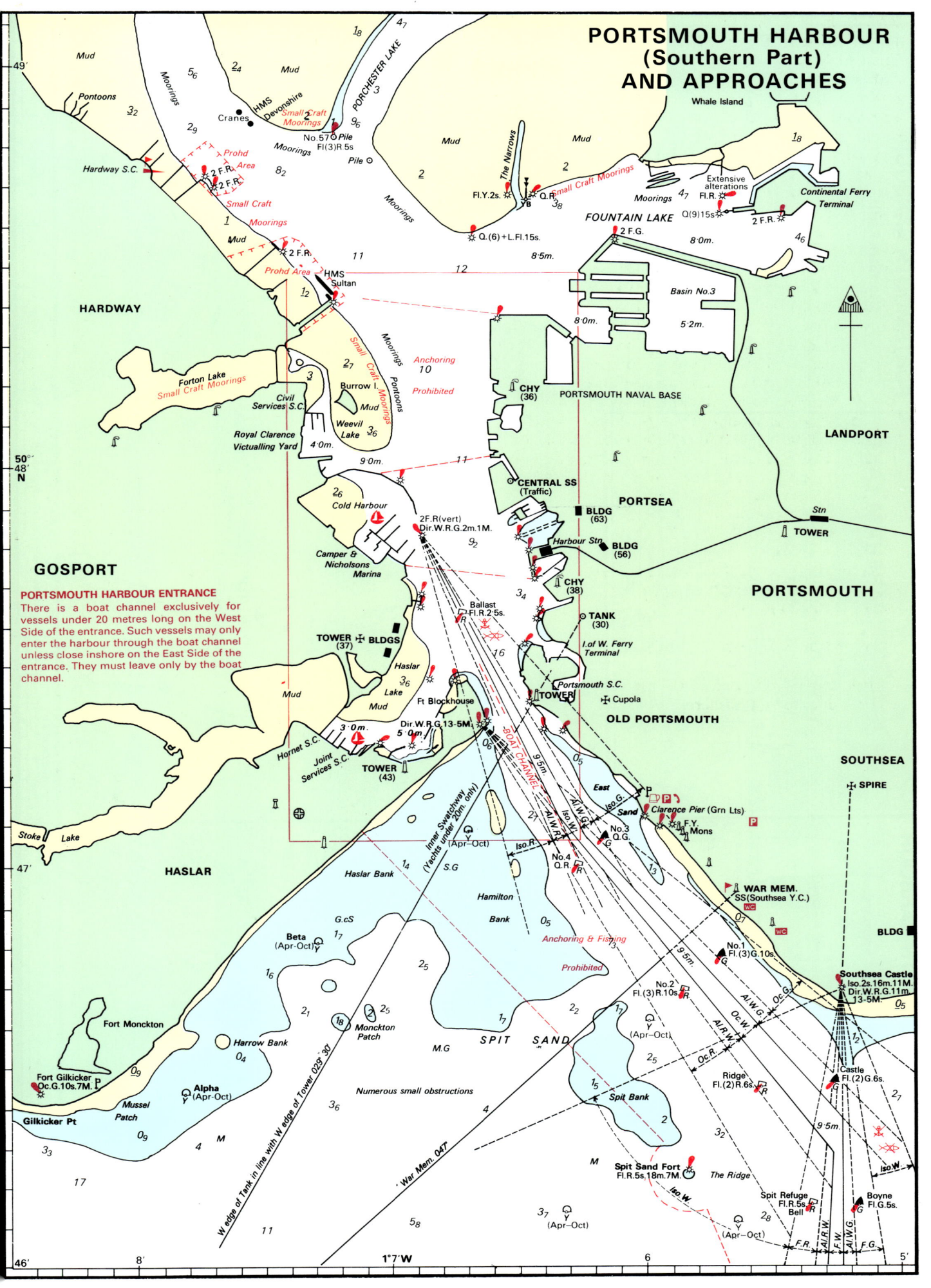

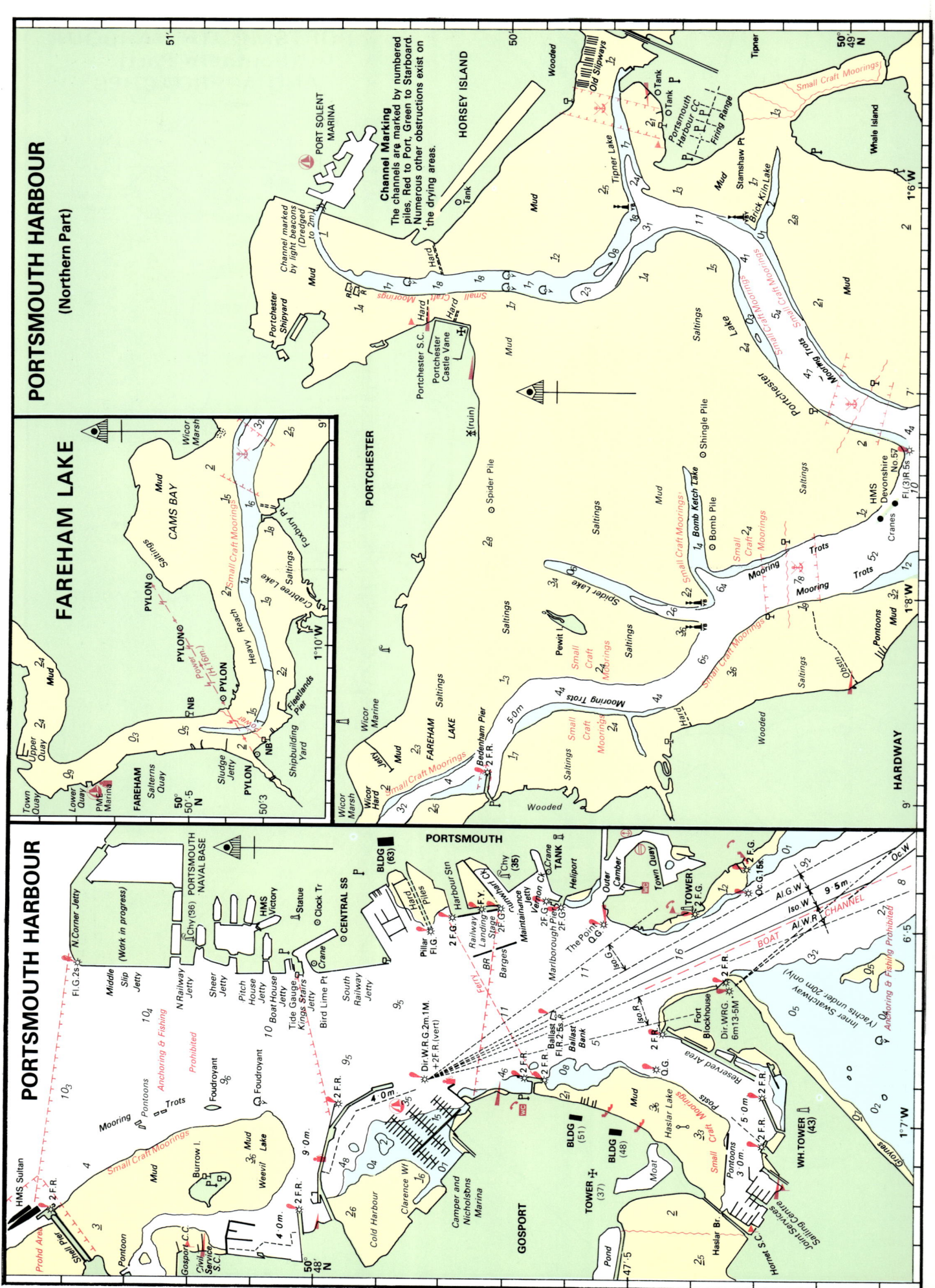

PORTSMOUTH Charts BA 2631, 2628, 2629
HW: Dover +¼h. DS Dover +3h E; −2h W.
MHWS 4.7m MHWN 3.8 MTL 2.7 MLWN 1.8 MLWS 0.6
A busy naval and commercial port with ferry terminal and marinas, under control of QHM. The town has much to offer in maritime history.
Approach From Langstone and Chichester Hbrs there is an inshore passage (1.2m) through the submerged barrier N of Horse Sand fort. Pass close N of dolphin, QR, marking the gap about 1M NNE of fort. Otherwise pass S of fort for the main channel, St Jude's Ch on with Southsea Castle 003°; by night in FW sector of the castle dir lt. From W either 1. Steer for Horse Sand Fort and take the main channel or 2. Take the Swashway over Spit Bank (1.8m), with War Memorial bearing 048°, unlit, or 3. Inner Swashway, forbidden to craft over 20m long, keeping W edge of tank (conspic) in dockyard on with W edge of round tr 029°, 0.5m, passing very close to N tip of drying shoal 1¾ca S of Fort Blockhouse; unlit.
Signals which may be displayed at Gilkicker, Blockhouse and Central Signal Stations, and which do not affect craft in Small Boat Channel, are as follows. Instructions from QHM will be on VHF 11 or 13.

	Signal	Meaning
day	R flag W diag	Large vessel underway; other vessels may be ordered to wait.
night	R/G/G lts	
day	R flag W diag/ B ball	Large vessel leaving. Vessels may leave; those entering will be kept clear
night	W/G lts	
day	B ball/R flag W diag	Large vessel entering. Vessels may enter; those leaving will be kept clear.
night	G/W lts	
day	Int Code pennant over pennant ZERO	Flown on warship under way: 'Keep clear of me.' Instructions from QHM
day	Int Code pennant over pennant NINE	Warship underway. Instructions from QHM
night	3 G lts vert.	
day	Flag E	Submarine entering or leaving Haslar Creek. Instructions will be issued by QHM but all craft under 20m must keep clear. (The amber lt at Blockhouse pierhead will FLASH when subs are actually underway.)
night	R lt	
	Amber lt	
day	Int Code pennant over Flag A	Flown by ship or boat. Have divers down.
night	2 R lts hor.	

Entrance Vessels under 20m in length must enter either by Small Boat Channel or very close along stb shore. The Small Boat Channel runs from No 4 Bar buoy Q R close along Fort Blockhouse wall, leaving two unlit R stick bns, BC2 and BC4, close to port and extends 50m from shore. It may be entered or left only at N or S ends or from W. Vessels entering by this channel must pass W of Ballast R can buoy Fl R 2.5s. When leaving, all vessels under 20m must use this channel. Yachts with engines must use them from No 4 buoy in S to Ballast buoy in N. Vessels without engines must conform to these regulations, if necessary waiting until they can do so or by arranging a tow. By night the Oc R sector of Fort Blockhouse lt and the Iso R sector of the lt on dolphin off Gosport Marina show over Small Boat Channel.

Hbr is difficult to enter on the ebb which runs strongest (5+kn) in third and fourth hours. Flood runs strongest in last two hours (3¼kn) but an eddy runs along E side of hbr during part of the flood. There is slack in entrance for ¾h during second and third hours of the flood.
Portchester Lake has 4.3m at its lower end and 1.8m near Portchester. There is a rifle range at Tipnor abreast piles 89-92. If R flags are flying, you may still pass but do so quickly. Channel is marked by R and G posts, nine lighted. The channel to Port Solent (dredged 2m, lt piles) starts just E of Portchester Castle.
Fareham Lake is marked by R and G poles, the stb ones have reflectors. There is a least depth of 4.5m to Bedenham Pier but it dries out ½M below Fareham town.
Berthing Anchor near Portchester Castle, 1.8m, hard for landing; or ¾M below Fareham, 1.5m. Riding lt necessary. Visitors' moorings at Hardway SC above Gosport. Alongside berths at Camper & Nicholson's Marina, Gosport (crowded in summer) and Port Solent Marina (lock, 24h service) ½M NE of Portchester Castle. Buoys at Wicormarine, Fareham; and drying pontoons at Fareham Y Hbr. The Camber is a busy commercial basin where only temporary berthing by yachts is a practical proposition.
Supplies Fuel and water at C & N Marina, Port Solent, Hardway Marine, Wicormarine, Portsmouth Marine Engineering. EC Fareham Wed; variable in Portsmouth and Gosport.
Tel/VHF QHM (0705) 822351 Ext 22008/ ch 11, or 13 if so instructed; ; C & N Marina 528411/ ch 80,37 ('Camperbase'); Port Solent 210765/ch 80,37; Hardway Marine 580420; Wicormarine (0329) 237112/ ch 80,37; Fareham Yacht Hbr (0329) 232854/ch 80,37; Customs as Southampton.

LANGSTONE HARBOUR Chart BA 3418
HW: Dover +½h. DS on Winner: rotary anti-clockwise, Dover −2½h N; +2½h S, less than 1kn, but 2.4kn +3½h to +5h. In entrance stream is strongest for fourth and fifth hours of the flood (3.4kn) and second and third of the ebb (3.1kn).
MHWS 4.8m MHWN 3.9 MTL 2.8 MLWN 1.8 MLWS 0.6
A natural hbr with narrow channels lacking anchorages convenient to shore. Has a large water-skiing area.
Approach From Portsmouth there is a gap in the obstruction between the shore and Horse Sand Fort - See Portsmouth Approach. Otherwise from W pass S of Horse Sand Fort and keep No Man's Land Fort open to S of the latter until entrance is open. From Chichester, steer S for 4ca past Bar Bn and then steer for Winner S card buoy, unlit. With a heavy sea or strong S wind the shallows can be dangerous for 1½M offshore.
Entrance is bounded on either side by gravel banks, steep to on E side of fairway. These may move in gales and their height varies. The connecting bar has a least depth of 2m and is dangerous in onshore winds especially near LW on the ebb. Bring Fairway Buoy, RW sph, Fl 10s, on with centre of hbr entrance, 354°. Alternatively, concrete dolphin off Eastney Pt, QR, in line with outfall jetty to N, 2F R(vert), 344° has 1.7m on the bar. Inside, Langstone channel is buoyed, lit and dredged 1.8m at its N end and leads to Havant Quay used mainly by gravel dredgers. The drying channel leading to Chichester Hbr round the N of Hayling Is has 3.7m at MHWS with a br clearance of 1.7m.
Channel through Lock and Eastney Lakes to Langstone Marina has bns and is dredged 1.5m.

ENGLAND, SOUTH COAST

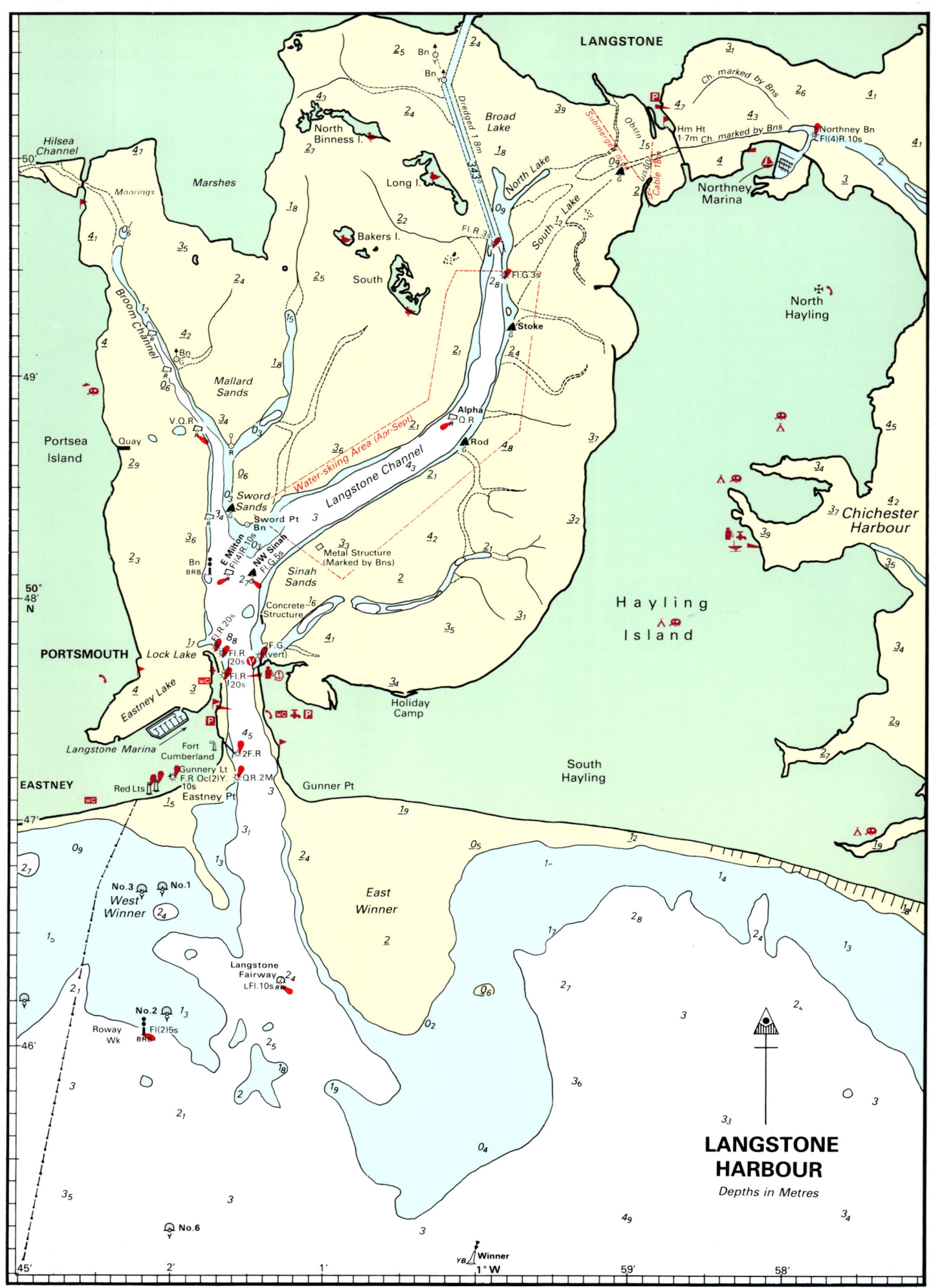

LANGSTONE HARBOUR
Depths in Metres

55 ENGLAND, SOUTH COAST

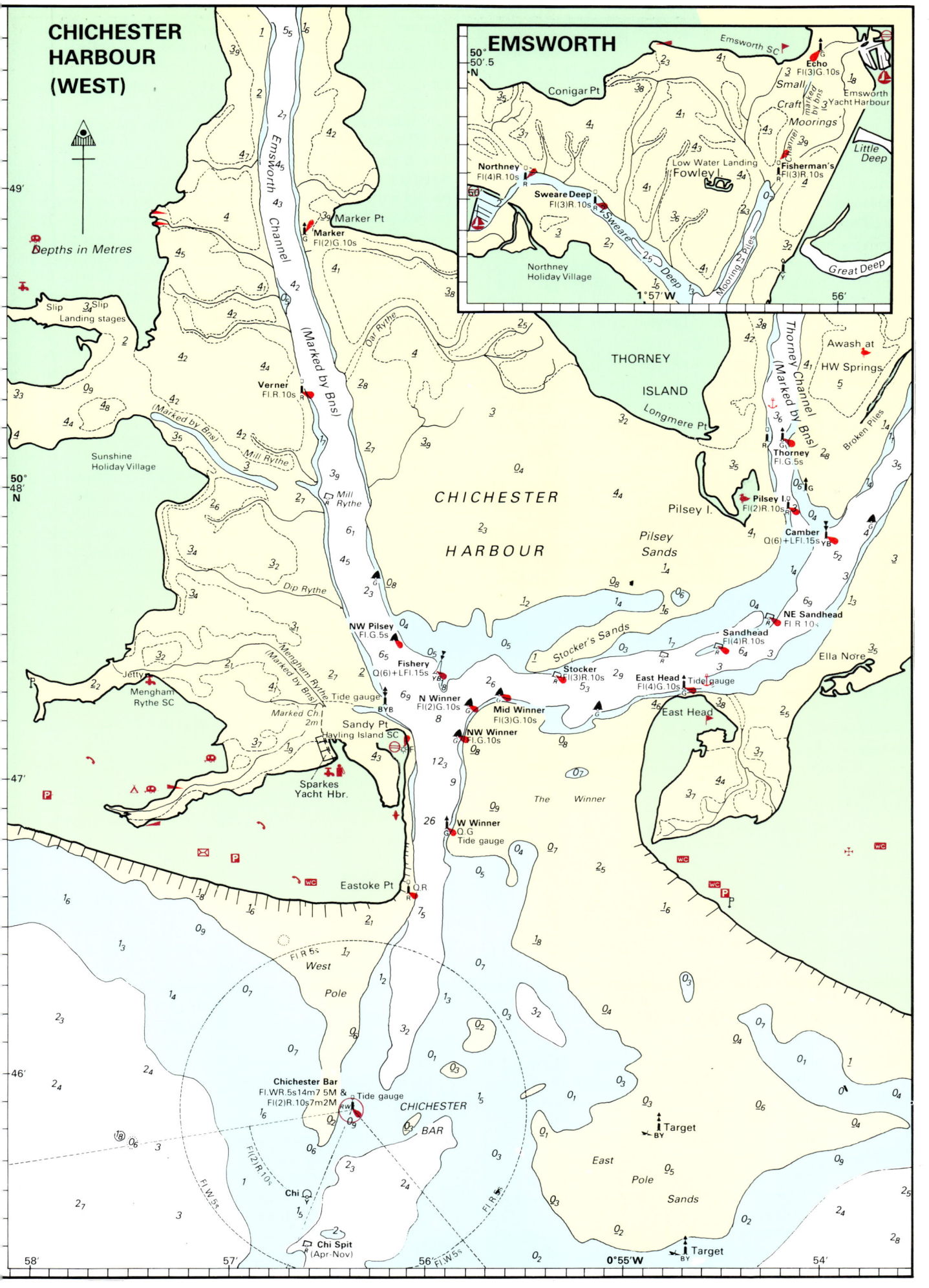

Langstone Harbour continued

Berthing All visiting vessels must report to Hbr Office. Six visitors' buoys to stb off Ferry Boat Inn for craft up to 30ft – no doubling up; not for use in SE gales. (Advisable to make advance arrangements with HM, especially if staying overnight.) Anchor (with HM's approval) in upper reaches of Broom and Langstone Channels, but both are in use by gravel dredgers day and night; the latter channel is a water-skiing area and mooring may be uncomfortable.

Pontoon berths at Langstone Marina. Access HW±3h; waiting pontoons.

Supplies Fuel and water at Marina and HM's office. Diesel on ferry pontoon (do not berth on shore side of latter); petrol on wall (tidal). Provisions in West Town, Hayling Island (1½M).

Tel/VHF HM (0705) 463419/ ch 16, 12. Langstone Marina 822719.

CHICHESTER HARBOUR   Chart BA 3418

HW (entrance) Dover +½h. DS (off bar): Dover +3½h SE; −1¼h NW. In entrance flood reaches 2.8kn, ebb 6.4kn

MHWS 4.9m MHWN 4.0 MTL 2.8 MLWN 1.8 MLWS 0.7

A major yachting centre in largely unspoilt natural hbr with marinas, moorings and anchorages near pleasant villages. Virtually no commercial traffic except fishing boats. Bar restricts entry and exit and is dangerous in strong onshore wind against an ebb tide. In quiet weather access is straightforward with care.

Approach From E keep 1½M offshore (in poor visibility the 5m line); from S keep Nab Tr bearing 186°; from W stay on 5m line or with old target (S card) in line with Cakeham Tr, 064°. From all three directions get Eastoke Bn, Q R, open to E of the Bar Bn Fl WR 5s; at night get in W sector (322°-080°) of Bar Bn; but keep to E of SW part of sector covered by lt Fl(2)R 10s.

Entrance The bar is dredged to 1.5m below datum giving a depth of 2m at MLWS, but after severe gales the bottom may vary by ±0.75m. There is a drying patch 2ca SW of Bar Bn on which onshore swell can break dangerously. Aim to cross at slack water or between HW -3h to HW +1h. On the ebb the stream sets to SW onto West Pole Sands. Leave Bar Bn ¼ca to port (its tidal gauge reads depth above datum, NOT depth on the bar) and steer to pass between Eastoke Q R and West Winner Q G bns. Follow the W shore until abreast of Hayling Is SC (all-round W lt) where channel divides at Fishery S card buoy Q(6)+LFl 15s.

Itchenor Channel goes to stb with three G con buoys (Fl, Fl(2) and Fl(3) all 10s) in an arc marking NW edge of the Winner. Channel to Emsworth and Northney Marina continues to N, buoyed and lit.

Bar Bn has a Ro Bn, sign CH freq 303.4kHz, 10M but frequently only 2M, sequence 1,4. The transmission sequence is CH CH CH CH, 4s dash, 1 - 8 dashes (wind direction), 4s dash, 0 - 8 dots (wind force), 12s dash, CH CH, 5s silence. Wind information is clockwise one dash for NE, eight dashes for N. Wind force Beaufort Scale averaged over three minutes, the number of dots being the lower limit of the force number. No dots means calm. This bn can be unreliable.

Within the hbr anchored yachts must hoist a B ball, and an anchor lt at night, and must not be left unattended for more than four hours.

Emsworth Channel is free of moorings between the entrance to Mill Rythe and the junction with Sweare Deep. It is marked by half-tide perches and three lt bns (two port, one stb). Sweare Deep is also lit (Fl(3)R and Fl(4)R both 10s) as far as the entrance to Northney Marina (but near LW follow the moorings to stb rather than going straight from one bn to the other). Although there is a lt bn, Fl(3)G 10s, at the head of the Emsworth branch, the stretch between it and Fisherman's Bn (Fl(3)R 10s) to the S is so congested with moorings that night passage for a stranger is not recommended, nor is Emsworth Yacht Hbr easily accessible in the dark. It would be better at night to tie alongside one of the boats on the piles to port. Landing is possible at Sparkes Boatyard (approach dredged 2m) or at HW at Mengham Rythe SC and at the head of Mill Rythe; each is navigable at MHWS for draughts up to 1.5m. Landing at Emsworth for any time presents problems as the muddy hard dries out for almost ½M. For passage through Sweare Deep to Langstone Hbr see entry for that Hbr.

Berthing Anchor out of the fairway to N of Hayling Is SC moorings (use tripping line). Visitors' buoys available from the club.

Berths at Sparkes Yacht Hbr, near Sandy Pt (pontoon and buoy); Northney Marina (pontoons, 1.8m draught, sill dries at datum); Emsworth Yacht Hbr (pontoons, sill dries 2.4m); southern 5 pile berths in Emsworth Channel (above Sweare Deep junction), max of two abreast (Hbr Conservancy). Half-tide buoys and pontoons also at Hayling Yacht Co at head of Mill Rythe.

Chichester Channel is buoyed and lit as far as entrance to Chichester Yacht Basin. Land at East Head, Itchenor Hard, Bosham side of Itchenor ferry (dries out for 2ca) and Dell Quay. At entrance to Bosham Channel leave Fairway G co buoy, Fl(3)G 10s, (not readily distinguishable against background of moorings) to stb for fairway through the trots.

Berthing Anchor N and NE of East Head (uncomfortable with winds from NW to NE; swimming dangerous) or W of the Fairway buoy on S side of channel. Anchoring is forbidden in Itchenor Reach. Six Conservancy visitors' buoys off Itchenor take up to six vessels each (depending on size); visitors' pontoon (Apr-Sep) on S side above Itchenor SC. Marina Berths at Birdham Pool (1.6m draught, lock HW±3h) and Chichester Yacht Basin (lock HW±4h).

Thorney Channel Entrance has two pairs of ruined groynes down to LW mark at each side of entrance: first pair NE from tip of Pilsey Is, (port side of gap has bn, Fl(2)R 10s); second runs E from S tip of Thorney, stb bn Fl G 5s. Rest of channel is marked by perches, some well above LW mark. Pilsey Is is a nature reserve and access above HW mark is not allowed. Thorney Is is MOD controlled but the public are allowed to use the foreshore path all round the Is. Land at stage by the ch.

Berthing Anchor off Pilsey in the stretch between the two pairs of ruined groynes. Shore is steep-to and current strong. Sheltered from strong NW winds when East Head is untenable. Anchoring also possible further up the channel clear of moorings.

Visitors' buoy available from SC near church.

Drying berths (jetty and buoy) at Thornham Marina (about HW±1h) at head of channel.

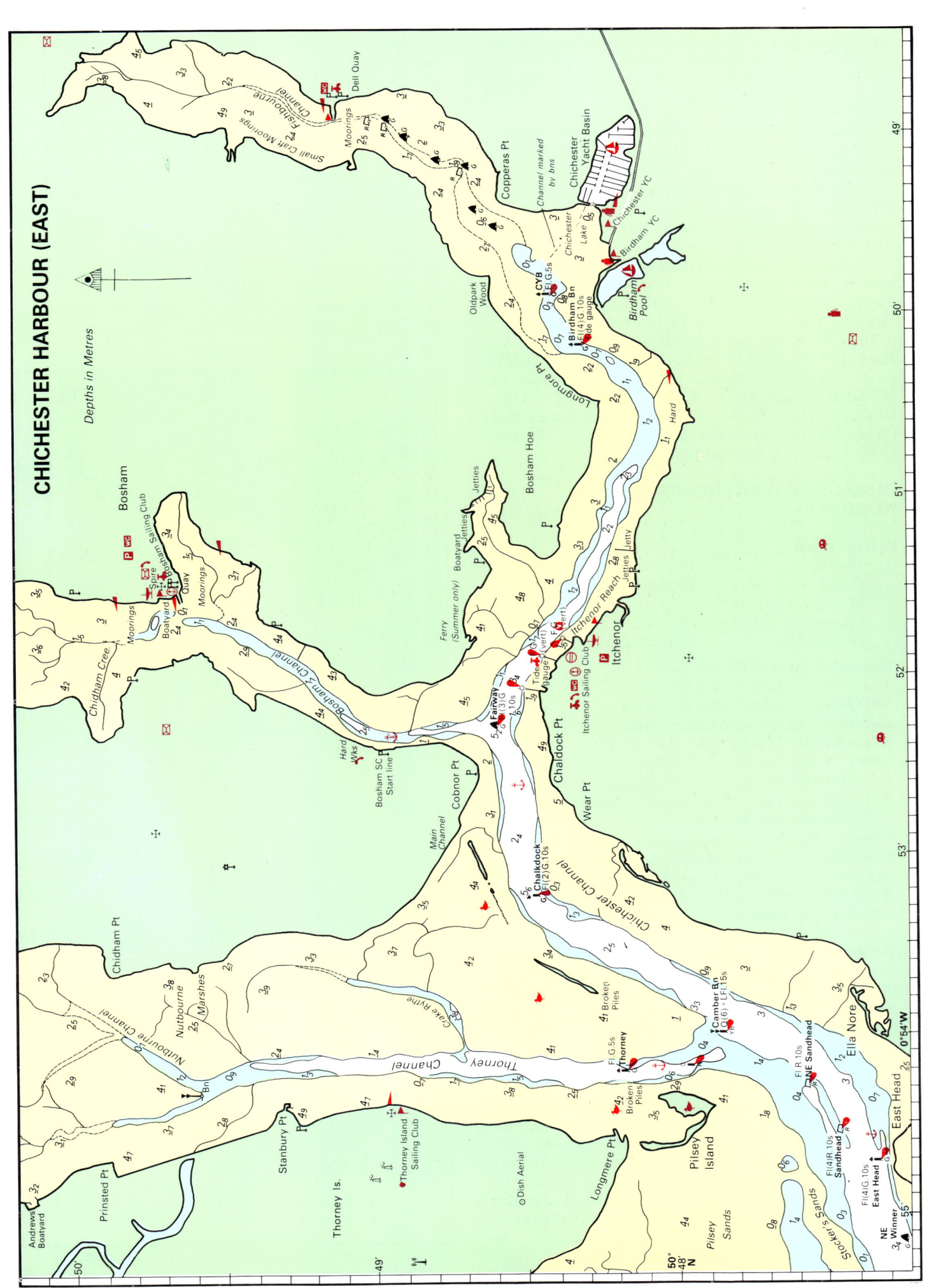

Bosham Channel is unlit; depth 4m until near the quay when it falls to 1m. There are no visitors' buoys (all moorings are private) but it is possible to dry out alongside the quay - charges. Alternatively Bosham, an attractive village, can be reached by dinghy with the tide or, in the season, by the ferry from Itchenor.

Supplies Fuel and water at Sparkes Yacht Hbr, Hayling Yacht Co, Northney Marina, Emsworth Yacht Hbr, Birdham Pool (at HW to stb outside lock, diesel only), Chichester Y Basin (lock dues) and water at pontoon off HM office (Itchenor) and Bosham Quay. Provisions at Emsworth, Mengham, Chichester Yacht Basin, Birdham and Bosham (EC Wed). None at Itchenor. Chichester (EC Thur) best reached by train from Emsworth or bus from Bosham, Birdham or Itchenor cross-roads.

Tel/VHF HM (0243) 512301 / ch 14 ('Chichester'); Patrol Launch (when manned) ch 16,14 ('Aella'); Coastguard (0705) 552100; Sparkes Y Hbr (0705) 463572/ ch 80,37; Hayling Y Co (07016) 3592; Northney Marina (0705) 466321/ch 80,37; Hayling I SC (0705) 463768/ ch 37('Sandy'); Emsworth Y Hbr (0243) 375211/ch 80,37;Thornham Marina (0243) 375335; Birdham Pool (0243) 512310; Chichester Y Basin (0243) 512731/ch 80,37; Customs as Southampton.

PASSAGE NOTES: CHICHESTER TO NEWHAVEN   Charts BA 1652, 2045

Passage lights
```
    Nab Tr              Fl(2) 10s 19M Horn(2) 30s
    Owers               Fl(3) 20s 22M Horn(3) 60s
    W entrance to Looe
    Channel, Boulder buoy, Fl G 2.5s
    Beachey Hd          Fl(2) 20s 25M Horn(1) 30s
```

Streams Related to Dover.
The Looe: +4¾h E; −1¼h W; 2½kn.
S of Owers: +5¾h E; −¾h W; 2¾kn.
E-going stream sets onto Outer Owers.
Selsey Bill: HW Dover +¼h.

| MHWS | 5.3m | MHWN | 4.4 | MLWN | 1.8 | MLWS | 0.6 |

Leaving Chichester bound E, keep clear of wreck 2¾M SE of Chichester Bar bn, marked by S card bn Q(6)+LFl 15s and W card bn Q(9) 15s.

There are three ways of passing Selsey Bill: at night or in poor visibility, outside S of the Owers Lt Ho buoy; by day and in good visibility, through the Looe, passing 1½M S of the Bill; or by day around HW in good visibility with light or offshore winds, close inshore.

E-bound through the Looe, steer about 097° between the two entrance lt buoys, R can and G con Fl G 2.5s; when the Mixon bn, 9m with square cage, bears N 2ca, alter course to 077° to clear East Borough Hd (due to be marked by E Card buoy Q(3) 10s).

The inshore route should be made within 2½h either side of HW. From E approach LB ho, ½M NE of the Bill, on a bearing of not less than 280° and follow round the line of the Bill, keeping about 40m off the ends of the groynes until windmill (conspic 1M NW of Bill) is abeam; then head out for Nab Tr 238°. Shallowest water will be between the end of the High Street and CG tr. When ¾M clear of the shore, course may be set for Chichester Bar Bn, leaving the old target (S card) on Pole Sand close to stb. This route is said to have many fishing buoys.

For the inshore passage from W, head for the windmill with Nab astern and follow the line of beaconed groynes. The direction of the stream changes considerably earlier than in the Looe; on the early spring ebb there may be a current of 6-7kn just to the E and round the Bill. If going E, the effect may be reduced by a wider sweep offshore. Pagham 'Harbour' is only a basin of mudflats. Access is difficult and as it is a nature reserve, landing and anchoring are forbidden.

Between Selsey Bill and Beachey Hd the effect of a foul tide may be escaped by keeping close inshore, where the tide may turn 1½-2h before the main offshore stream. But be careful between Angmering and Shoreham where shallows extend a considerable way offshore.

Anchorages In W and N weather, in **The Run** N and S of Selsey LB ho, clear of moorings (2m).

In offshore winds, on NE side of **Bognor Rks,** between them and the shore. SE winds bring in a heavy sea.

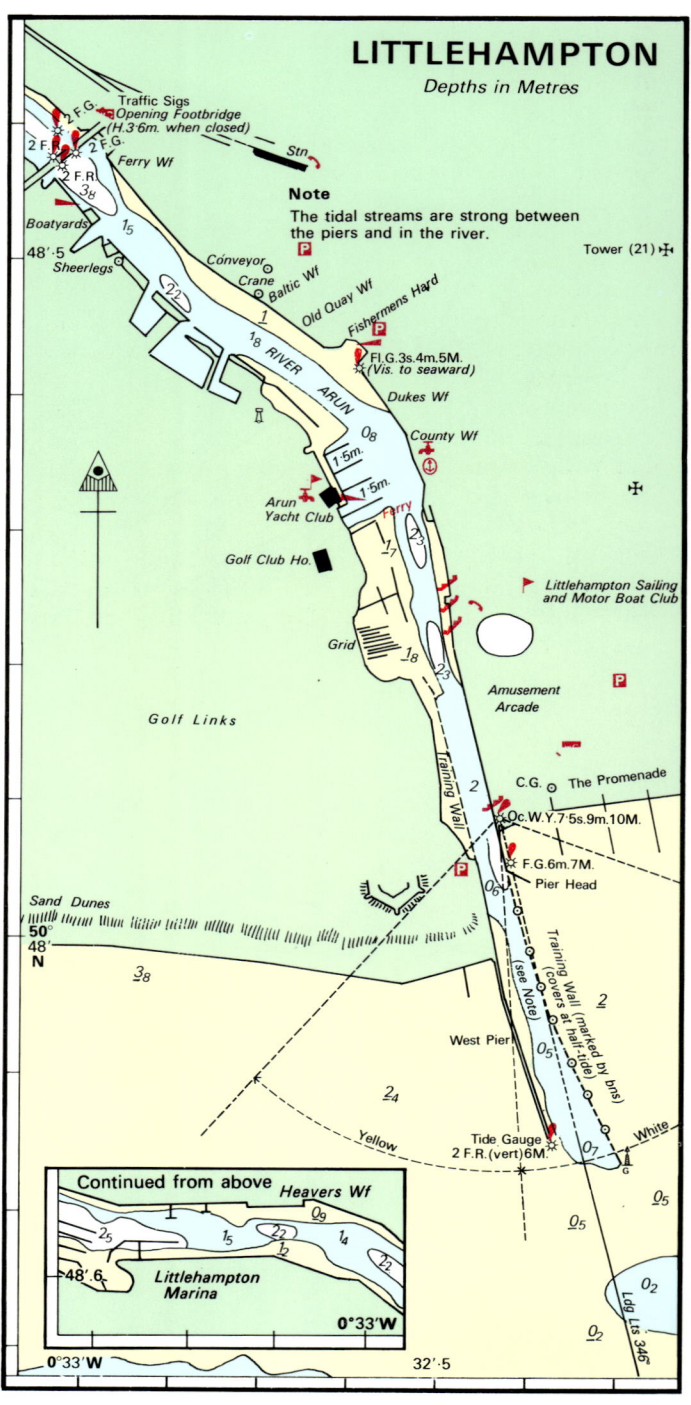

59 ENGLAND, SOUTH COAST

LITTLEHAMPTON Chart BA 1991

HW: Dover +¼h. DS: Dover -1h W; +4½h E.

MHWS 5.7m MHWN 4.6 MTL 3.1 MLWN 1.7 MLWS 0.5

This commercial port is the estuary of R Arun; navigation is limited by a br ¾M from the entrance. The bar dries 0.1m.

Approach Leaving Looe Channel at E Borough Hd buoy make good 040° to Winter Knoll S card buoy, Q(6) + LFl 15s, 2¾M SSW of entrance. From E aim for the Y sewer buoy, Fl Y 5s, 2¼M SSE of entrance. Pilot boat with lts or flag signifies commercial vessel is about to enter or leave and all small craft must keep clear of the narrows. Do not attempt entrance in strong onshore winds.

Entrance Lies between a pier on W side, 2F R(vert), and shorter pier and training wall extension on E side. The extension, which covers at half tide, is marked by seven perches and at its end is a bn with diamond topmark. Keep on ldg bns on E pier, 346°: front iron column, F G; rear 9m W concrete tr Oc WY 7.5s (Y sector covers approach over W pier, W sector covers the entrance). Stream is slacker on W side of hbr on the flood; it rushes round the pierhead from E and causes an eddy. After HW-2h keep to E centre of fairway in the entrance to allow for W-going set; ebb can reach 5kn. There are shoals within 25m of W pier and alongside the training wall. Continue in centre of channel to Fisherman's Quay, F W lt.

The swing foot br has 3.6m closed; requests for opening must be made before 1630 the preceding day (not Suns or Bank Holidays). 4ca upstream is a fixed br, clearance also 3.6m. There is a marina to port above the foot br. River is navigable to Arundel for 1.2m draught and dinghies can get to Amberley.

Berthing Report to HM on County Wharf where there are two alongside berths. Hillyards and Arun Yacht Club Ltd have berths on port side below foot br.

Supplies Fuel at Marina above br; water near HM's office. EC Wed.

Tel/VHF HM (0903) 721215/6; Hillyards (09064) 3327; Arun Yacht Club (0903) 716016; Littlehampton Marina (0903) 713553/ ch 80,37; CG (0705) 552100; Customs as Southampton.

SHOREHAM Chart BA 2044

HW: Dover +¼h. DS: Dover −1¾h W; +5½h E.

MHWS 6.2m   MHWN 5.0   MTL 3.4   MLWN 1.9   MLWS 0.7

Comprises the estuary of River Adur (dries) and a non-tidal basin, approached through locks, with commercial wharves and a marina.

Approach Lt ho is Fl 10s, 15M. Avoid from W, Church Rks, 0.9m, over ¼M offshore and 1½M W of entrance; from E, Jenny Ground 1½m, 3ca offshore and 1¾M E of entrance, and unlit S card sewer buoy 3ca ESE of entrance. Shallows in approach can be very rough in strong onshore winds particularly on the ebb, when Newhaven is a better refuge.

Signals Tidal: Front ldg lt on Middle Pier also indicates tide level: R not more than 2m above CD, G 2-3m, W more than 3m above CD. In good conditions anchoring is possible while awaiting entry 1 to 1½M from lt ho, bearing 360° in 7m.

Entry: International Port Traffic Signals from Middle Pier, roof of LB ho and at locks.

Entrance Keep front ldg lt on Middle Pier watch house (F W, R or G depending on depth, with Horn 20s) in line with lt ho Fl 10s, 355°. Keep to middle and avoid eddies along the piers. Turn to port for Adur; beware groyne extending N from W pier, awash at half-tide, marked with port perches. Tide sets against E end of Kingston Wharf. Turn to stb for locks.

Berthing Drying moorings are sometimes available in the Adur (W arm) from Surry Boat Yard. Otherwise anchoring in this branch is not advised except in emergency. Entry to the E basin is through the locks: yachts sometimes by the smaller, northern, Prince George lock (consult, lock office). Locking inwards weekdays is approx: HW -3¼h, -1¼h, +1h and +3¼h; but Sats, Suns and Bank Holidays, Apr-Oct incl, HW -3¼h, -2h, -½h, +½h, +1¾h and +3¼h. Enquire for outward times. Visitors' moorings rarely available except by prior arrangement from Lady Bee Marina (to port after entry) or from CA Boatman. While awaiting lock opening, anchor S of slipway on Mackley's Wharf just N of 1.5m channel.

Supplies Fuel and water at Lady Bee. EC Wed.

Tel/VHF HM: (0273) 592366; Control Station ch 14 ('Shoreham Hbr Radio'); CA Boatman 592456; Lady Bee Marina: 593801/ ch 80,37; Surry Boat Yard: 461491; Customs as Southampton.

BRIGHTON Chart BA 1991

HW: Dover-¼h. DS: -1½h W; +4½h E. Streams weak.

MHWS 6.5m   MHWN 5.1   MTL 3.5   MLWN 1.9   MLWS 0.6

A man-made marina with 1800 berths in tidal hbr; and inner hbr through lock with yard and domestic moorings. Entry not advised in SE gales.

Approach No outlying dangers. Landmarks are Roedean School on cliffs to E and tall hospital block with W vert stripe to W. Entrance lt ho is Fl(4)RW 20s,(R over rks to E of entrance). RoBn ('BM', 303.4khz, 5-8M).

Entrance Avoid shoal obstruction adjacent S and N of E breakwater hd. Channel turns to E, marked by lt buoys port and stb. Entrance to inner hbr marked by 2R(vert) port and 2G(vert) stb lts.

Berthing Visitors' reception pontoon is immediately inside hbr.

Supplies Fuel, water, provisions, laundromat and scrubbing grid.

Tel/VHF HM: (0273) 693636/ ch 80,37,11,68 ('Brighton Control'); Customs as Southampton.

NEWHAVEN Chart BA 2154

HW: Dover. DS −5½h E; −¼h W.

MHWS 6.6m   MHWN 5.2   MTL 3.6   MLWN 1.9   MLWS 0.5

The estuary of R Ouse. A busy commercial and ferry port with a marina. It is accessible with care in all weathers.

Approach The hbr lies immediately E of the line of cliffs running from Brighton to Newhaven. To its E the coastline is low. From W at night the lights of Seaford make a good mark to steer on. From E in heavy weather keep breakwater lt ho (Oc(2) 10s Dia 30s) to stb until E pier lts are open to clear shallows E of entrance.

(continued on page 63)

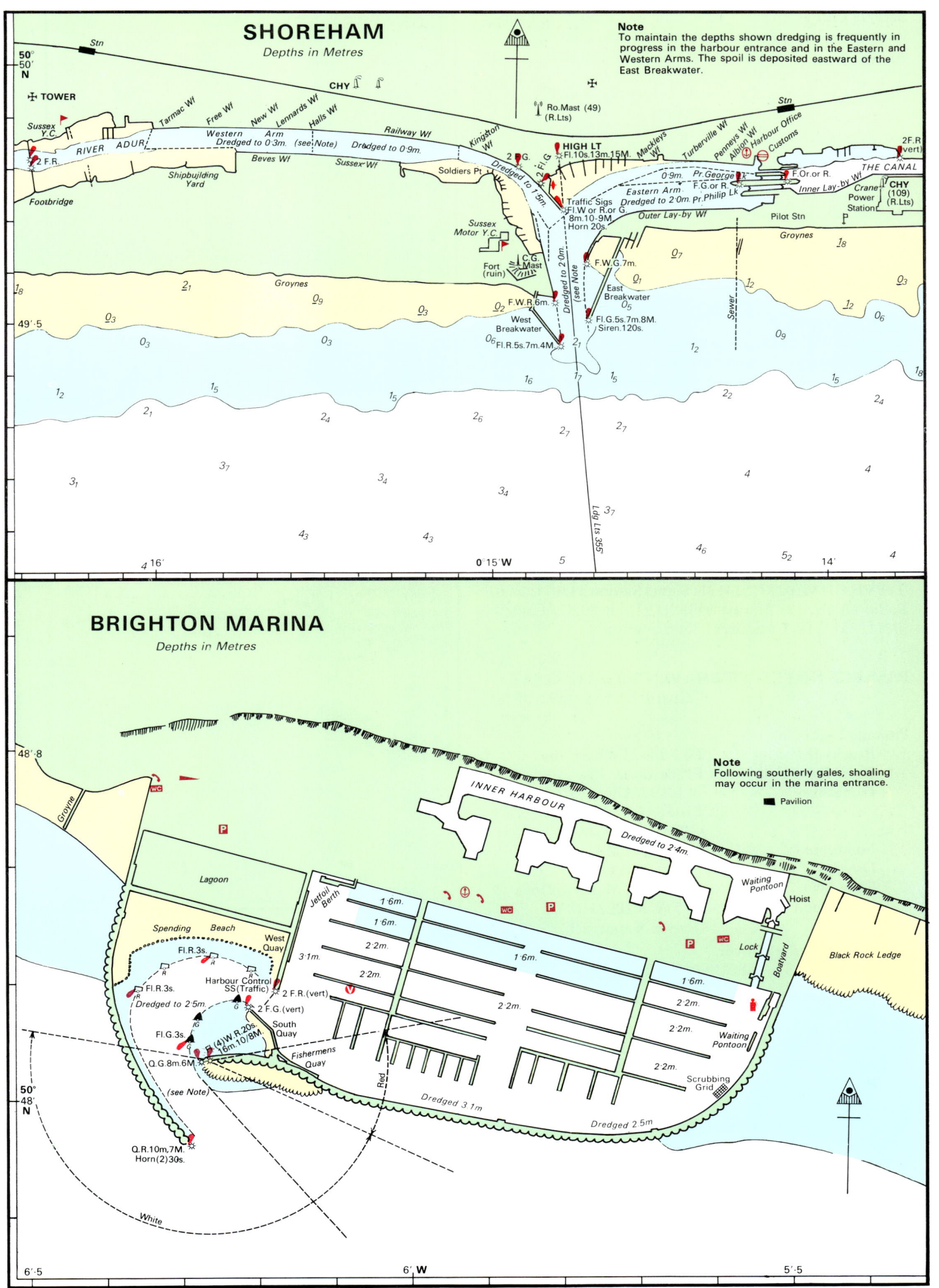

Signals Entry signals on mast at base of lt ho do not conform to the International System but are as follows:

By day: signals use a R △ pt down and R ball(s).
R △/R ball: entry only. R ball/R △: departure only.
R ball alone: entry and departure permitted for small vessels.
R ball/R △/R ball: entry and departure prohibited.

By night: G and/or R lts.
G: entry only.   R: departure only.
G/R: entry and departure permitted.
R/G/R: entry and departure prohibited.

Swing br: Fl G: br opening or closing. F R: pass N to S. F G: pass S to N.

Entrance Within the breakwater keep the W side of the hbr open to clear the mud on W side between it and the W pier. Beware hawsers across river from ships warping off quay or from dredger (latter displays international signals). Inside, Newhaven Marina is to port. Swing br opens on demand through Port Radio. Above the br to port is Cantell's Yard. At HW river is navigable to Lewes, 3m headroom.

Berthing at (1) Newhaven Marina: tie to visitors' pontoon, accessible for 1½m HW±2½h. (2) Cantell's: drying pontoons, accessible HW±2½h.

Supplies Fuel and water at Marina, water at Cantell's. Shops. EC Wed

Tel/VHF HM (0273) 514131; Signal Station 513071; Port Radio ch 16, 12; Marina 513881/2/3, ch 80,37; Cantell (07912) 514118; Customs as Southampton.

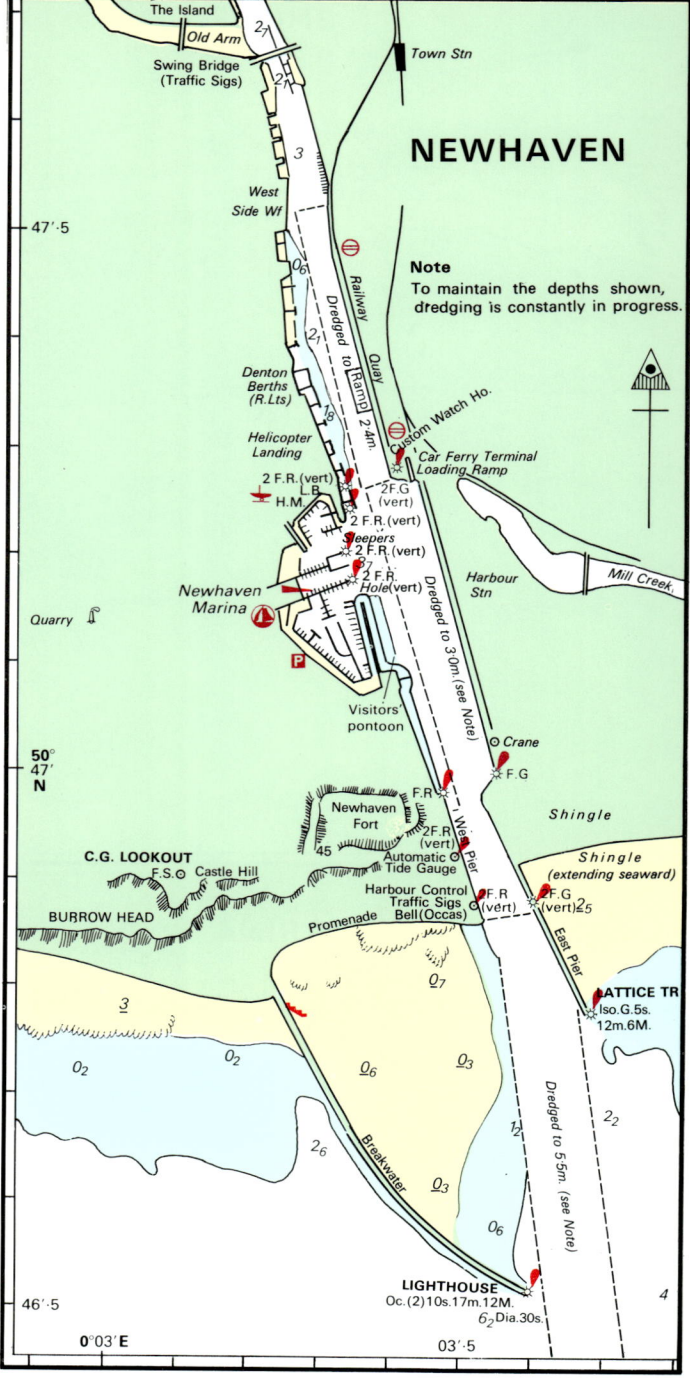

PASSAGE NOTES: NEWHAVEN TO RAMSGATE
Charts BA 536, 1892, 1828

Passage Lights

Beachy Hd	Fl(2)20s 25M horn 30s
Royal Sovereign	Fl 20s, dia(2) 30s
Dungeness	Fl 10s 27M horn (3) 60s and FRG (R 057°–073°;196°–216° G 073°–078°) 11M
Folkestone	Fl(2) 10s 22M Dia(4) 60s
Dover	Fl 7.5s 20M Dia 10s
S Goodwin Lt F	Fl(2) 30s 25M, horn(2) 60s
N Foreland	Fl(5) WR 20s 21/18M. (R over N approach)

Streams Related to Dover.
Beachy Hd (2M S) +¼h W; −5¼h E.
Dungeness (2M SE) +4½h SW; −2h NE.
S Goodwin LV +4h SW; −2h NE.
Gull Stream +4½h SSW; −1½h NNE.
N Foreland (3M SE) +4¾h SSW; −1¼h NE.
Inshore: S Foreland to Deal +4¼h S; −1¾h N. Ramsgate to N Foreland +4¼h S; −1¾h N.
Streams run at 2½kn off Beachy Hd, Royal Sovereign and Dungeness but at only 1½kn between the latter. Passing Dungeness at the beginning of the W stream, one has only 2h of fair tide. It is better to pass with the last of a fair stream, fight the weak foul stream between Rye and Hastings and take the next fair stream off Eastbourne. If faced with foul tide when W-bound at Beachey Head consider anchoring off Eastbourne and wait for next tide. E-bound with adequate speed a fair tide can be carried for 10h to N Foreland.

Anchorages Seaford Road ¼M offshore abreast the ch. Sheltered from ESE to NNW, little stream, good holding.
Eastbourne E of pier; sheltered from W by N to NE.
Rye In N winds, anchor 1M–1¼M (according to draught) NNE of Rye Fairway buoy, Q.
Dungeness W Road In NE winds anchor 1M inside the Ness out of stream, but uncomfortable scend from E winds.
E Road Good anchorage NE off the Ness in 5–6m with water tr (conspic) bearing 029° and Dungeness new lt ho 197°. Sheltered with wind round to SWxS.
Small Downs 1M N of Deal Pier off Sandown Castle, less than ½M offshore. Sheltered from SSW through W to N. Good holding, some stream.
Anchoring in Pegwell Bay is not recommended as the fetch from W is too great when flats are covered.

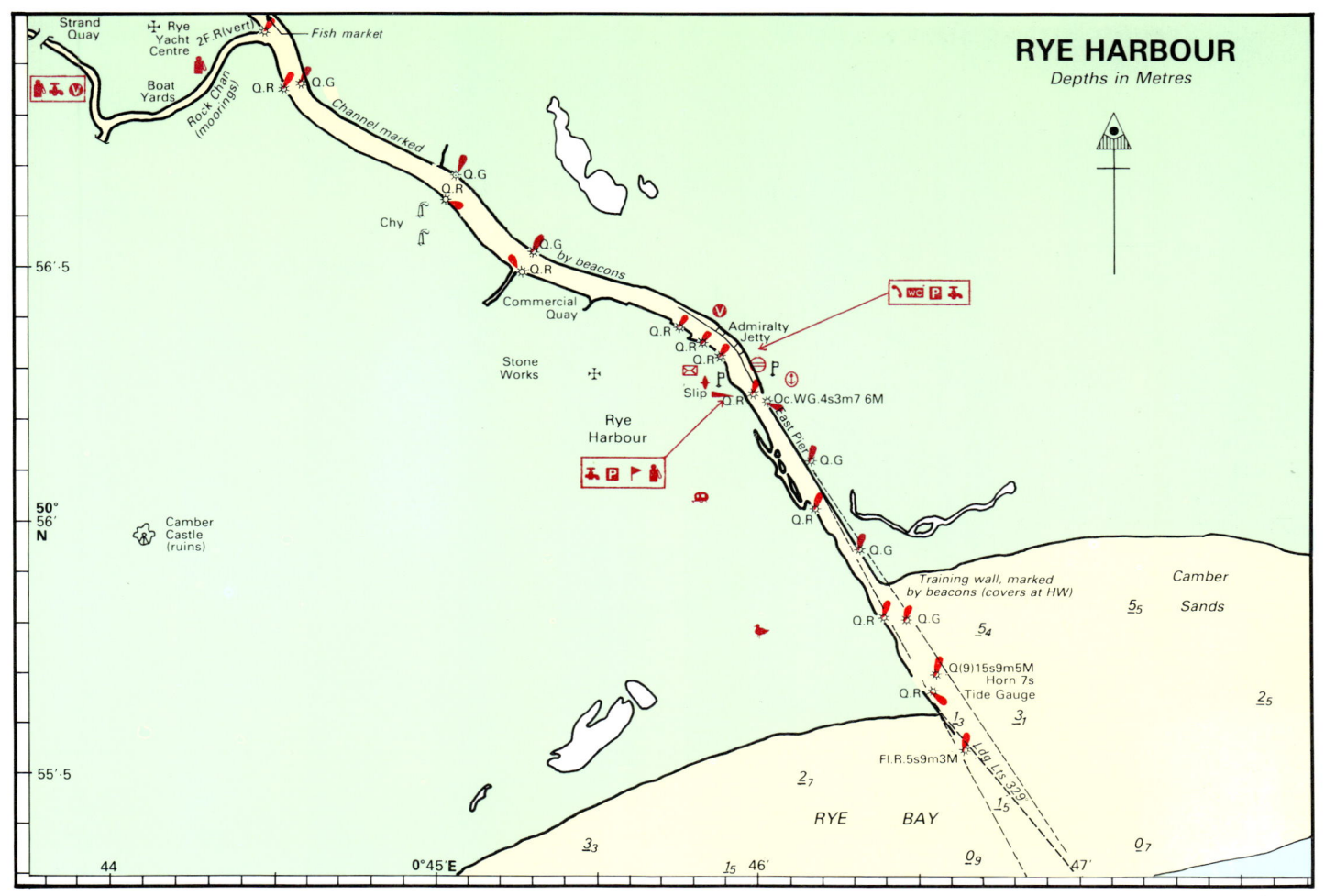

RYE
Chart BA 1991

HW: Dover. DS: −4h E; +3h W
In approach:
MHWS 7.7m MHWN 6.0 MTL 4.1 MLWN 2.2 MLWS 0.9
Hbr: MHWS 5.3m MHWN 3.6

Flood does not enter hbr until LW+2½h and then sets rapidly reaching 3-4kn. At springs HW-1h it flows over E and W piers, when stream slackens in fairway. This is best time to enter.

Estuary of the R Rother is navigable to Rye at HW but the whole river dries well before LW. It should not be entered in onshore winds over force 5.

Approach From W follow Fairlight cliffs (CG and conspic square ch tr on skyline). Entrance is 4M to E. From E follow coast from Dungeness about 1M offshore until W groyne and tripod bn are visible and make for Fairway buoy, spher RW Fl 10s, 1.8M from entrance. It is prudent to enter from the buoy as there may be nets on either side of the fairway. Approach dries ½M offshore, shoaling gradually to the entrance. Depth 4.8m springs, 3.6m neaps.

Signals at HM office. Tide: (night only) F G 2-3m on bar; F purple over 3m.

Traffic: by day or night, Q Y: ship moving in or out. By day one B ball: large vessel inbound; 2B balls (hor): outbound; 3B balls in △: vessels in- and out- bound. Listen on VHF 14.

Entrance From Rye RW Fairway safewater buoy, Fl 10s, by day make good 329°. By night steer 330° on E pierhead lt, Q(9) 15s 5M horn 7s. Bns on W retaining wall, which covers near HW. Outer E pier is a training wall which covers at springs when last hour of flood and first ebb set diagonally over it. Shingle piles up on W side of entrance. There is 4.5m (MHWS) in mid stream (up to 0.6m less with strong E winds) to Rye Hbr village, 1M up, in W sector of ldg lt OC WG 4s.

Three QR port and three QG stb lts mark channel to Rye Hbr village and 3 QR mark limit of private moorings on W bank off the village. Between these and the bend into unlighted Rock Channel there are three stb FlG and two port FlR. 2 FR(vert) on N side of entry to channel are boatyard lts and may be unreliable. Take a wide sweep into Rock channel which is narrow but marked by buoys at entrance and thereafter by bns.

Berthing All berths dry. Report to HM office opposite Rye Hbr village. A few berths are available at seaward end of catwalk near the office. Otherwise proceed to Strand Quay at Rye (soft mud) which is better for deep-keeled yachts. Fish Market staging at Rye is for fishing boats only.

Supplies Fuel, water, shops and yards at Rye. Water, store, inn and PO at Rye Hbr village.

Tel/VHF HM (0797)/ 225225ch 16, 14; Customs as Dover.

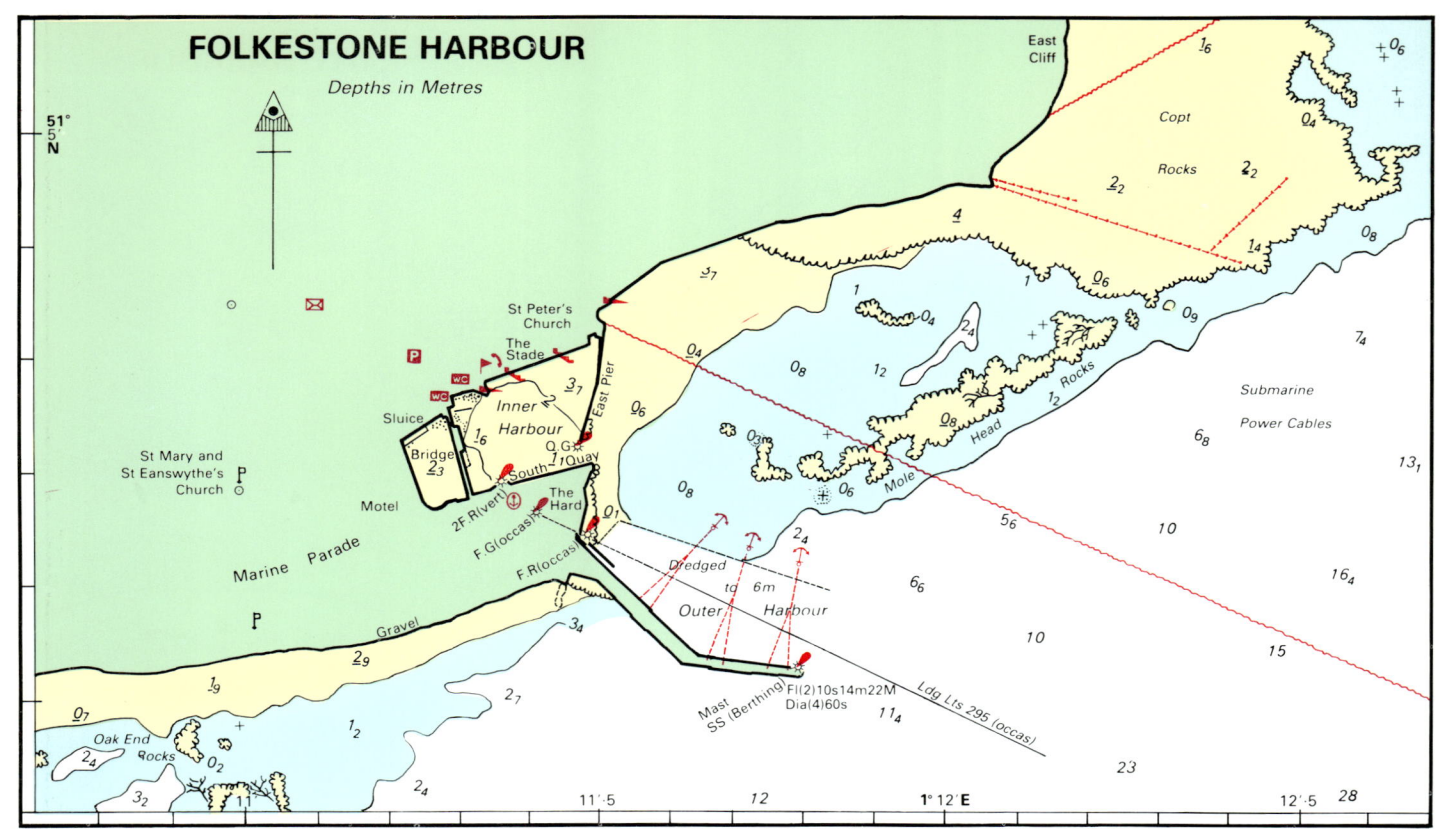

FOLKESTONE
Chart BA 1991

HW: Dover −¼h. DS: Dover −2h E; +5h W.

MHWS 7.1m MHWN 5.7 MTL 3.9 MLWN 2.0 MLWS 0.7

A busy ferry terminal with very restricted accommodation for yachts which can take the ground. Inner hbr entrance dries. Not a good refuge in bad weather.

Approach There are rks to W of breakwater and to E of entrance. Do not enter if B flag is flying at pierhead (ship entering or leaving).

Berthing Anchor (not in E winds) outside Inner Hbr to E of pier. Otherwise drying buoys available from HM or YC.

Supplies Fuel, water, shops. EC Wed.

Tel/VHF HM (0303) 54947/ ch 16, 22; Folkestone Yacht & Motorboat Club 51574. Customs as Dover.

DOVER
Chart BA 1698, 1892

DS: −2h E; +5h W

MHWS 6.7m MHWN 5.3 MTL 3.7 MLWN 2.0 MLWS 0.8

A very busy ferry, hovercraft and jet-foil terminal, but with accommodation for yachts.

Approach From E observe Separation Zone regulations.

Signals International Traffic Signals (no exemptions) are displayed day and night on the port side of the Western entrance and the starboard side of the Eastern entrance (and also at the entrance to Wellington Dock).

Entrance Permission to enter, or leave, must be obtained from Port Control on VHF 74; if 74 not fitted, call on 16 and ask for transfer to 12. With Aldis, SV to enter, SW to leave. Q lamp from Control tr means 'Keep clear of entrance you are approaching'. Permission given, listen on VHF 74 until berthed.

Stream sets from N to S across the E entrance except from HW −2h to +3h. In strong winds the heaviest sea is from HW to +4h when entry should be avoided. W gales cause a race off the S breakwater. In onshore winds there is a confused sea off the W entrance. Keep up-tide until entry permitted. Enter under power at all times and do not try to pass between the Southern Breakwater and the wreck buoy inside the Western Entrance.

Berthing Free anchorage in the corner on N side of Prince of Wales Pier, 3½-7½m, inshore of Y buoys. Exposed from NE through S to SW; in gales a heavy sea builds up and yachts should not be left unattended; landing on POW pier not allowed. Camber Docks are for commercial use. Some visitors' W buoys in outer hbr but visiting yachts are generally berthed in Wellington Dock. Permission to enter Wellington Dock must be obtained from Port Control on VHF 74 (or 12) or from Hbr Patrol Launch. Yachts must wait in the yacht anchorage area until told (VHF 74 or by launch) to go to pontoon on Crosswall Quay at entrance to Granville Dock, where berthing instructions will be given. Gates open HW -1½h to +1h. Small Fl Y lt shows 5min before br opens.

Supplies Fuel, water, showers and toilets in Wellington Dock. All facilities. EC Wed.

Tel/VHF HM (0304) 240400; Wellington Dockmaster 206560; Port Control ch 16, 74, 12; R Cinque Ports YC 206262; Dover Coastguard (for Channel Navigation Information) ch 80, 76 or 16: information broadcasts H+10, H+40 on VHF 11; Customs 202441.

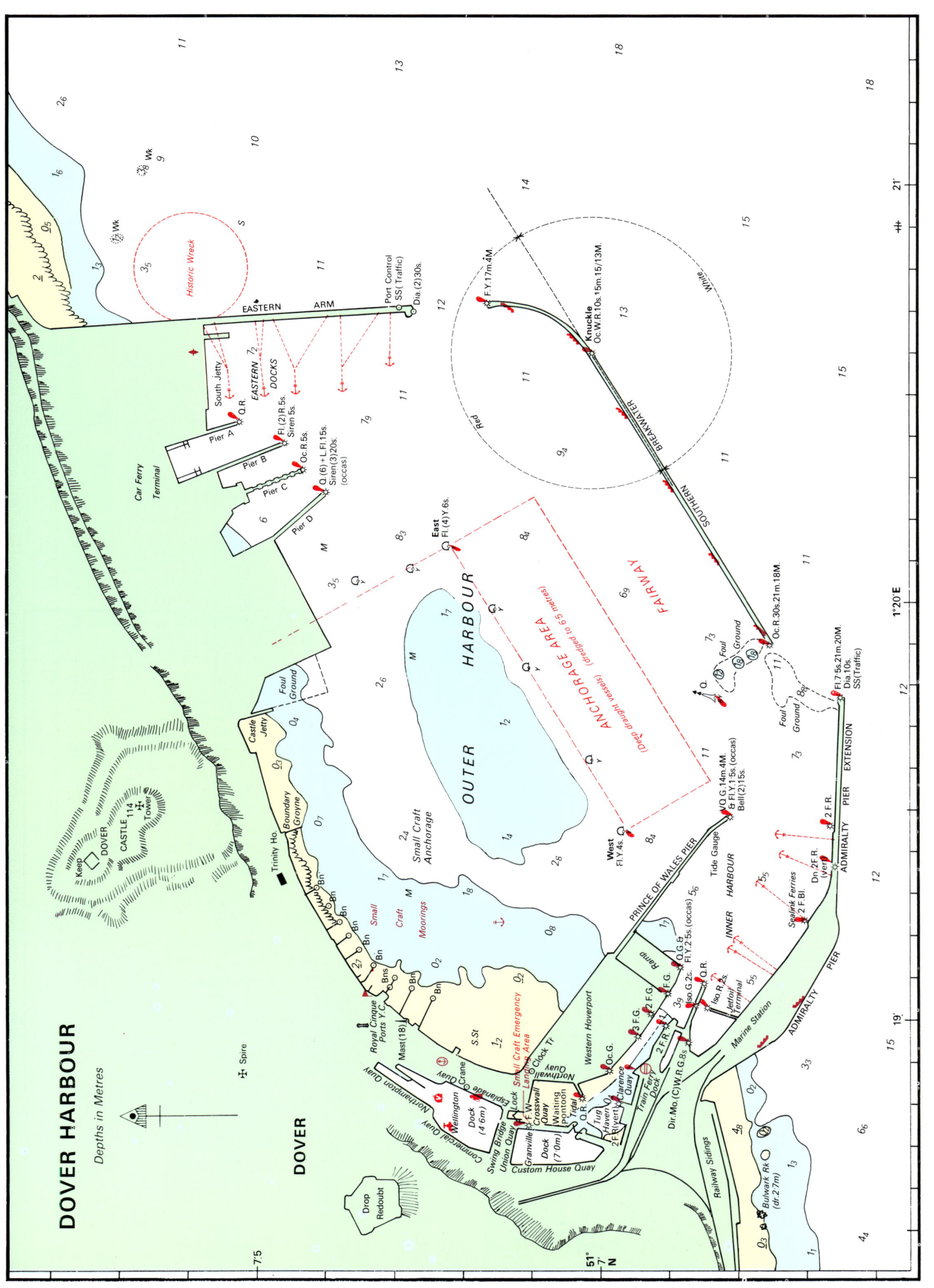

STOUR & SANDWICH Chart BA 1827, 1828
HW: Dover +2¼h. DS (offing): Dover −h NE; +4h SW
Flood in entrance probably starts about Dover −4¾h; ebb +2h
Sandwich: ebb runs for 9h, flood for 3h
Richborough:
MHWS 3.3m   MHWN 2.7   MLWN 0.3   MLWS 01
Estuary of R Stour. Entrance dries but 3-4m at HW.
Approach at HW±2h. Make for safewater pillar lt buoy, Fl 10s,'SFB', about 3M SW of Ramsgate Outer Hbr and then follow line of G con buoys to Sandwich Approach Tr Fl R 10s 3m 4M.
Entrance Channel is buoyed to tripod at entrance to R Stour after which posts mark channel to Sandwich. 3m at

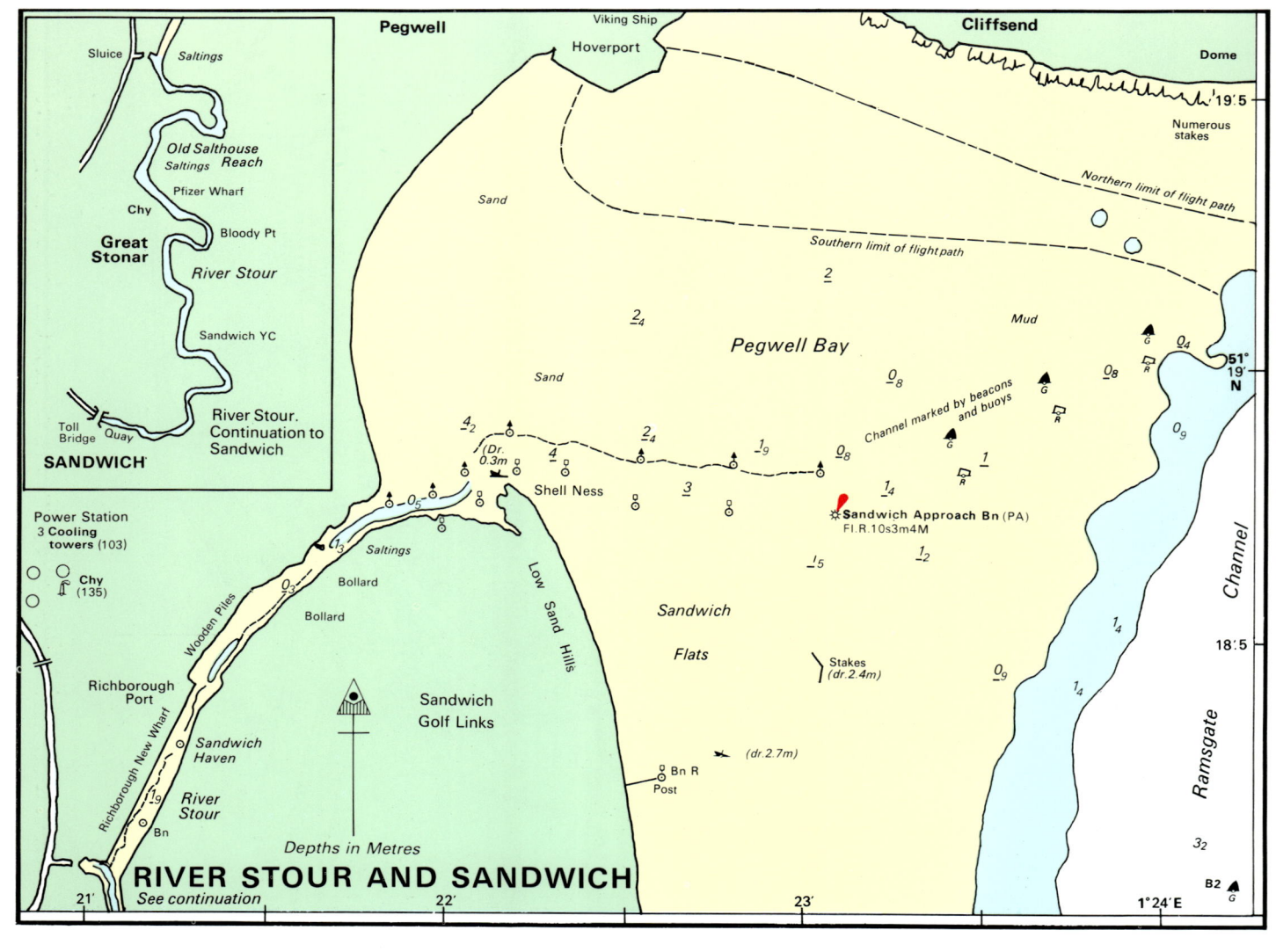

springs, 1.9 at neaps; keep to middle channel. Br at Sandwich opens after which river is navigable for some 12M with 1.2m draught and 3.5m headroom.

Berthing Richborough Quay is used by small tankers and is private. Drying berths at Sandwich SC and Sandwich Marine (HW±1½h) or berth at Town Quay. Bottom is shallow layer of mud on chalk.

Supplies Water at Marina or Quay. Shops.

Tel Sandwich Marina (0304) 613335 & 613783.

RAMSGATE   Chart BA 1827, 1828

HW: Dover +¼h. DS (inshore); Dover -1h N; +5h S.2M SW of Gull buoy: -1h NxE; +5h SSE.

MHWS 4.9m MHWN 3.8 MTL 2.6 MLWN 1.2 MLWS 0.4

Ramsgate Hbr consists of the Royal Hbr, with an Inner Hbr Marina, to N and a RoRo hbr to S. All share the same approach channel.

Approach Yachts must report to Ramsgate Port Control on VHF 14 before entering main channel and remain listening. From S, approach by the Ramsgate Channel, leaving G con buoys fairly close to stb, or by the Gull Stream and the main approach channel.

Signals International Port Traffic signals on W pier control movement in and out of Royal Hbr.

Entrance There is a dredged approach channel from E Brake E card buoy Q(3) 10s, at 51°19'.27N, 1°29'.06E, westward for 1.15M, with 3 port and 3 stb lt buoys before entrance between N and S breakwaters. It may be entered from N at the Dike S card buoy Q(6)+LFl 15s; or at ½M off the breakwaters from S. At night steer 270° on dir lt Oc WRG 10s.

After clearing the breakwaters steer to stb, giving a clear berth to 'Harbour' G con buoy, Fl G, for the Royal Hbr whose entrance is 3m or less, variable. Keep clear of ferries especially in the turning area between breakwater entrance and the ferry terminal. Yachts should pass quickly through the area between the outer breakwaters and Royal Hbr; do not stop to raise or lower sails.

Berthing With winds from WNW to NNE small craft can anchor near hbr entrance S of breakwater and entrance channel, 2½-3½m. There are berths for shelter or short stay in the outer Royal Hbr (where yachts may not be left unattended) or visitors may enter the yacht hbr, through the lock (at least HW −2h to +1h).

Supplies Fuel, water, boatyard, shops. EC Thur.

Tel/VHF HM (0843) 592277; Port Radio ch 16, 14; Customs Freephone or (0304) 202441.

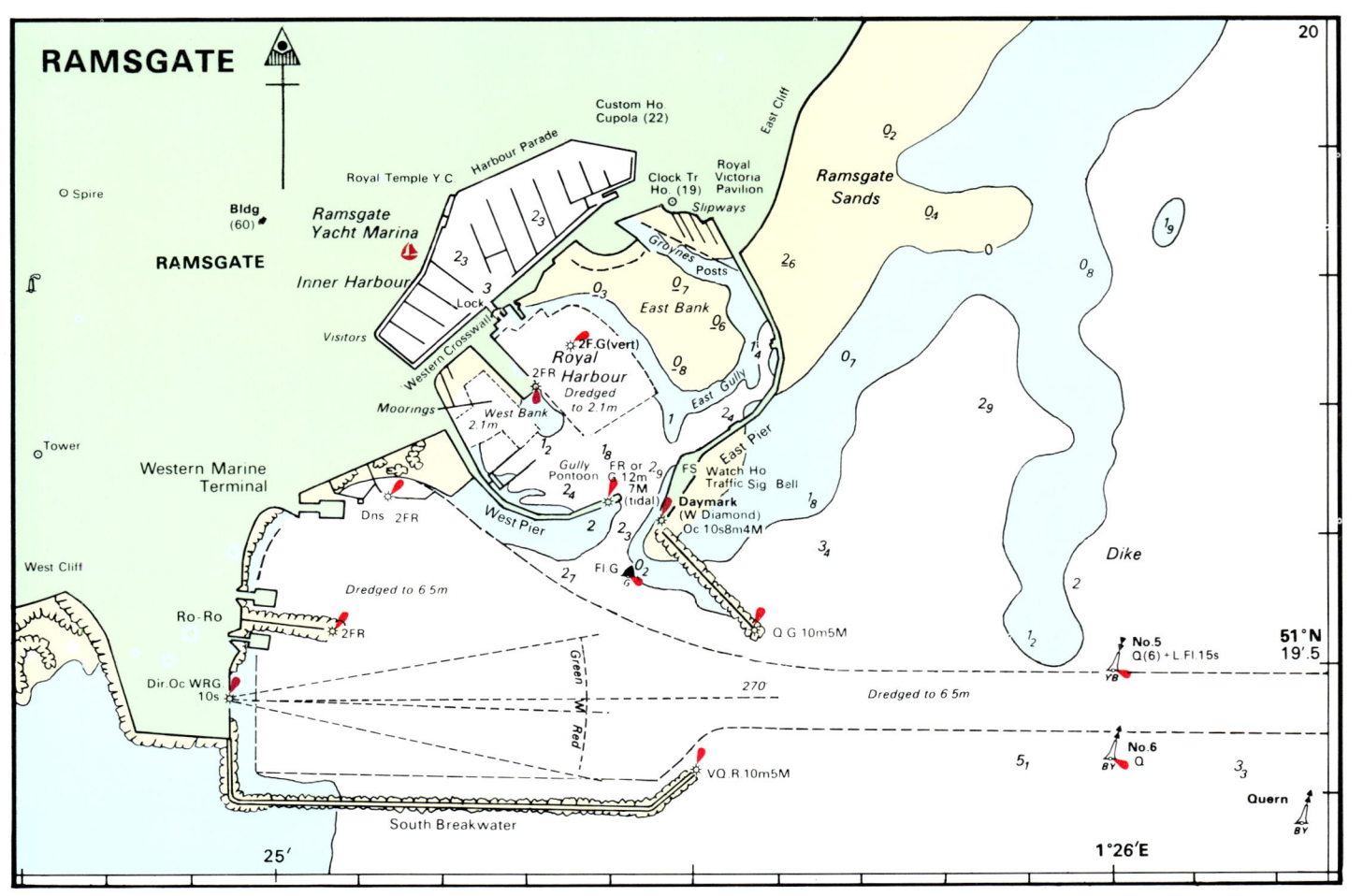

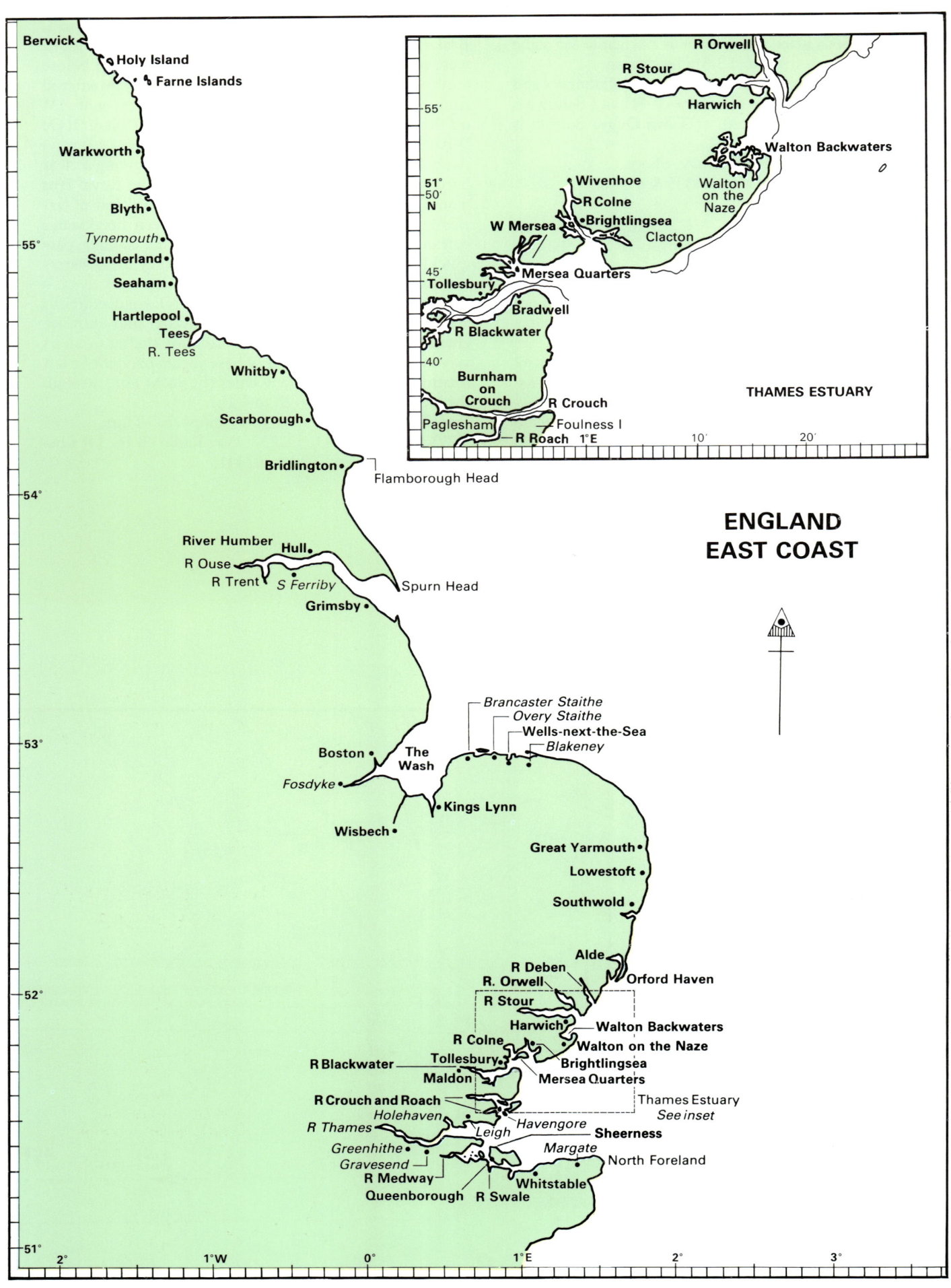

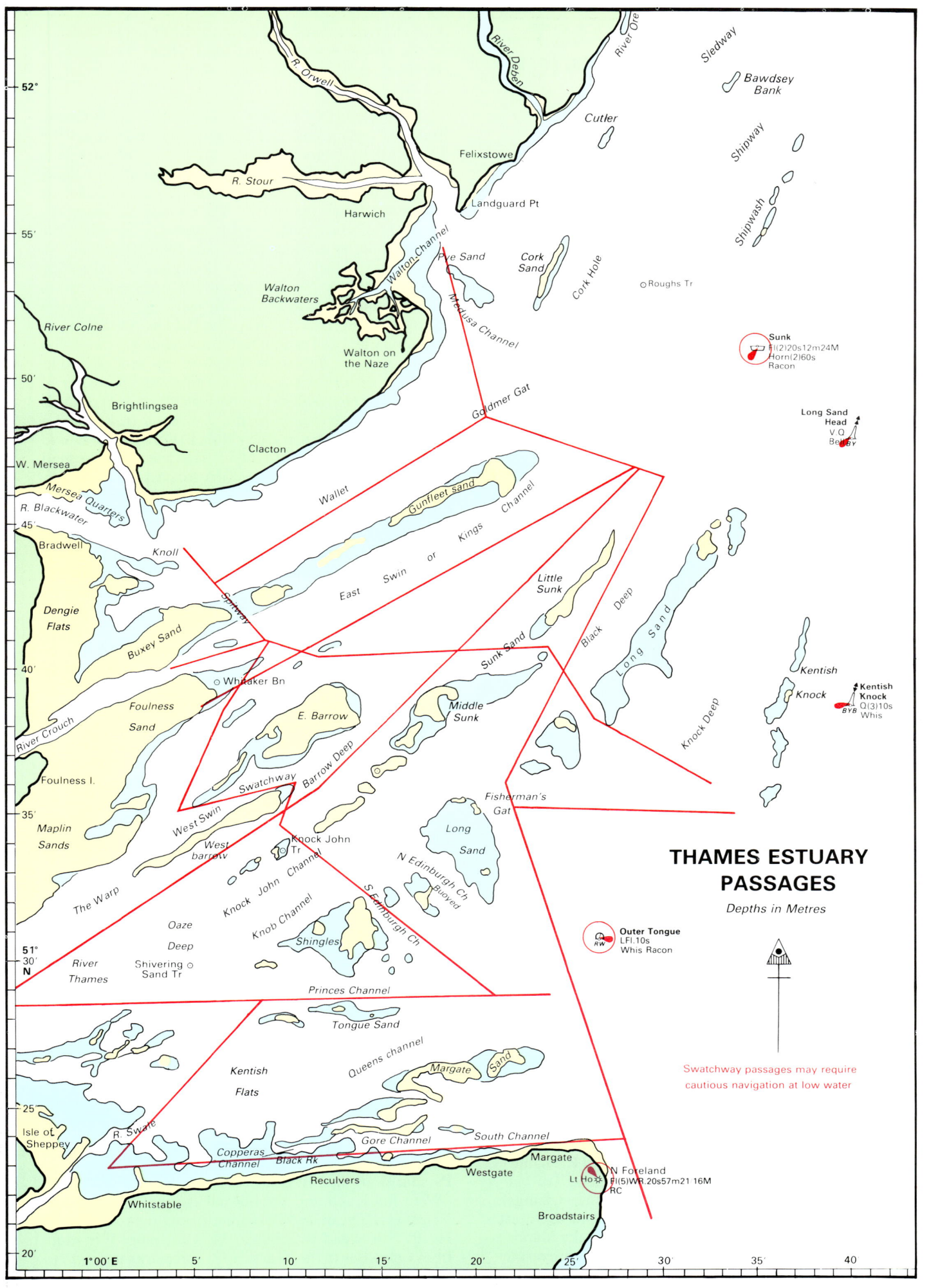

ENGLAND EAST COAST – N FORELAND to BERWICK

PASSAGE NOTES: NORTH FORELAND TO HARWICH   Charts BA 1183, 1607, 1975, 2052
In the Thames Estuary sandbanks are extensive and change frequently and it is essential to carry up to date and fully corrected charts. The N Kent coast has chalk cliffs as far as Westgate and is backed by hills; there are low cliffs at Warden Pt on the Is of Sheppey. From the Is of Grain to Clacton the shore is low. From Clacton to the Naze and at Bawdsey, to the N of Harwich, there are low sandstone cliffs. Conspic objects are N Foreland Lt Ho, Reculvers twin trs, the power stn chimney at the mouth of the R Medway, two lattice masts on Foulness Is, the nuclear power stn at Bradwell, the Naze Tr and Felixstowe container port at the entrance to Harwich Hr. The estuary is notorious for the short steep seas raised in wind over tide conditions, particularly bad in NE winds in the Mid Barrow region and off Clacton. Tides run up to 3kn at springs, mainly in the direction of the channels; those in the S are rotary.

Tides DS: All related to Dover.
(1) The interaction of the Estuary and Downs tides off N Foreland is summarised as follows:
  (a) −1¼h to +¾h N and W from the Downs to the Estuary.
  (b) +¾h to +4¾h Downs tide runs N, Estuary tide runs E.
  (c) +4¾h to −4¾h E and S from the Estuary to the Downs.
  (d) −4¾h to −1¼h Estuary tide runs W, Downs tide runs S.
(2) At intermediary points:
  (a) −4¾h W, +2h E, in The Princes Channel.
  (b) −5h W, +1½h E, at Tongue Sand Tr.
  (c) −4½h W, +1¾h E, at Great Nore.
  (d) −5h SW, +1¼h NE, at Barrow No 8 buoy.
  (e) −5½h SW, +¾h NE, at Barrow Deep.
  (f) −5h WSW, +1¼h ENE, at Whitaker buoy.
  (g) −4h W, +1½h E, at Columbine buoy.
(3) At N extremity of the Estuary:
  (a) −5¾h SW, +½h NE, at Sunk LV.
  (b) −5½h SW, −5h WSW, +¾h NE, +1¼h ENE at the Naze and the N end of the Wallet.

The passage notes are arranged as follows:
(1) Inwards and cross Estuary from the S.
(2) Inwards from the N.
When traversing the Swatchways across the tide, a careful check must be maintained on soundings. For efficient passage making in the Thames Estuary tides must be used to their best advantage. Coming from the S this necessitates stemming an adverse tide in the Downs to make the first of the flood at N Foreland.

(1) N Foreland to the Swale, R Medway and R Thames
(a) Through the Horse and Gore channels, S of Margate Sands to the Spile in Four Fathoms Channel. This passage is sparsely buoyed and lit and there are unmarked shallows and drying patches from the Margate Hook Spit to the Spile. In onshore winds there are no secure anchorages other than the E Swale and R Medway.

(b) E of Margate Sand and through the Princes Channel the passage is well buoyed and lit; there is considerable commercial traffic. For tidal stream see above.

(2) N Foreland to R Crouch, R Blackwater and R Colne
From N Foreland pass E of Margate Sand and through the S Edinburgh Channel, marked only at the NW end by the N Shingles buoy Fl R 2.5s, cross the Knob and Black Deep Channels where extreme caution is necessary as tides run athwart the course. The swatchway across the Knock John Channel may be followed after rounding the Tizard Bank by keeping the Knock John R can buoy in transit with Knock John No 1 G con astern and sailing from the Barrow No 9. Toward LW it is necessary to watch soundings as there may be less than 1m at lowest springs. In the Barrow Deep the Barrow Swatchway is now unmarked and cannot be recommended to those who are not familiar with these waters except in ideal conditions and with constant reference to depth. It is safer to pass Barrow No 7 and circumnavigate the N part of the E Barrow Sand. If sailing to the R Crouch make good a course between Barrow Deep No 5 Fl G 10s to the E, and S Whitaker Fl(2) G 10s to the W. This leads over the sand with sufficient depth except possibly for deeper draught vessels at LW. To lay a course for the R Blackwater or R Colne, after rounding the E Barrow sand, head for the N Middle, N Card buoy, leaving it to the S and pass close to the Whitaker E Card buoy making straight for the Swin Spitway safewater buoy and on to the Wallet Spitway. Buoyed channels lead directly to the two rivers.

(3) N Foreland to Harwich
The direct route leads E of Margate Sands and 2M E of the Tongue Sand Tr via Fisherman's Gat and entering Black Deep. This passage is without buoyage and if in any doubt of one's position it may be prudent to take the longer route through the N Edinburgh channel keeping well out of the way of ferries and other traffic. Leave the Black Deep at Sunk Head Tr to pass approx 1M NE of the Wallet No 2 buoy, heading for the Medusa Channel to Harwich. Alternatively enter Barrow Deep as in (2) above following deep water beyond the Gunfleet Spit Buoy Q(6)+L Fl 15s Bell, holding this course until clear of Gunfleet Sand and then take the Medusa N to Harwich approaches.
The offshore route lies either through the Knock Deep or outside of the Kentish Knock to Longsand Head, The Roughs and Cork Sand QR buoy before joining the mandatory Yacht Track S of the commercial dredged channel to Harwich.

(4) Sunk Lt F to Rs Medway and Thames
The main routes are Barrow and Black Deeps or E and W Swins to avoid shipping. Although fewer buoys mark the passages than hitherto, they are well lit.

(5) Sunk to R Crouch
The E Swin leads on to the Whitaker Buoy from which the R Crouch is entered on a heading of approx SW.

(6) Sunk to Rs Colne and Blackwater
Passing W of the NE Gunfleet Buoy into the Wallet sail SW to the Knoll and the buoyed channel to Colne Bar Fl(2) G 5s. The more Nly channel brings the Inner Bench Hd Fl(2)R 5s and R Colne on 342°, the more Wly route from Colne Bar to the Bench Hd G con marks the entry to R Blackwater.

(7) Harwich to the Whitaker Buoy
Yachts entering or leaving Harwich must take the prescribed Yacht Track to avoid all commercial traffic. From the Medusa channel either a route to the NE Gunfleet and E Swin may be taken, or a course may be followed from E of the Stone Banks buoy to give an offing of 1M at the Naze. From the Wallet to the Swin, the Spitway has a least depth of 1.2m and leads on to the Whitaker buoy.

(8) Whitaker Buoy to E Swale
Through E and W Swins to the SW Barrow Buoy, then given sufficient rise of tide, to the Spaniard Buoy E Card Q(3)10s, 2.5M NE of the Columbine Buoy at the entrance to the E Swale. To avoid the Red and Middle Sands, from the SW Barrow buoy lay a course to pass close to the Shivering Sand Tr and the Girdler Bn before making up to the Spaniard.

Passage Lights
N Foreland Lt Ho   Fl(5)WR 20s 57m 21/18M
Sunk Lt F   Fl(2) 20s 12m 24M Horn(2) 60s Racon
Galloper S Card Lt   Q6+LFl 15s whis Racon

MARGATE   Charts BA 1607, 1827
HW: Dover +1h   DS: Dover +2h E, −4½h W
MHWS 4.8m MHWN 3.9 MTL 2.6 MLWN 1.4 MLWS 0.5
Hbr is open to the NW, has 1.2m MHWS and dries 2.7m. Bottom sand and mud. This hbr is not recommended for use without special reason and care must be exercised in avoiding the unmarked ruins of the pier.
Anchorage In ordinary conditions reasonable shelter can be found just W of Margate, or N of Margate Pier.
Supplies All stores. EC Thur.

WHITSTABLE   Chart BA 2571
HW: Dover +1¼h
     DS (Spaniard buoy): Dover −4½h W, −1¾h E
MHWS 5.4m MHWN 4.3 MTL 2.9 MLWN 1.5 MLWS 0.5
Approach There are drying patches at LW in Whitstable Bay. Care should be exercised to avoid oyster beds, marked by flag buoys. To find the best water the approach should be made on a course of 155° from the Columbine Spit G con buoy or 182° from the Whitstable Street N Card VQ buoy, taking care to avoid the Whitstable Street drying spit 3 ca to the W. By night approach in the G sector of the Fl WRG 5s lt at the end of the W pier, until the R ldg lts 122° are in line. The tide runs across the entrance at a maximum speed of 2kn, W on flood and E on ebb. Ebb begins approx 1h before HW.
Entrance The hbr dries to 1.2m at LAT with shingle between the piers and mud inside, best water close alongside the W pier.
Traffic signals from E side of hbr: F R lt by night or B ball by day signifies no entry. Tidal signals on mast on E quay; R flag indicates more than 3m in the hbr.
Berthing Only permitted for a limited length of time for Customs clearance or other essential services. A mooring in the bay may be obtained from the Secretary of Whitstable YC (0227) 272343.
Anchorages Good anchorage in the bay for draught up to 1.5m close by the yacht moorings W of the hbr entrance and clear of fairway: also in Tankerton Bay 1M E of hbr.

RIVER MEDWAY   Charts BA 1834, 1835, 3683
HW: Sheerness: Dover +1½h
    DS (Sheerness narrows): Dover −4½h S, +1¾h N
Sheerness:
MHWS 5.7m MHWN 4.8 MTL 3.1 MLWN 1.5 MLWS 0.6
Upnor: HW Dover +1¾h
MHWS 5.9m MHWN 4.9 MTL 3.2 MLWN 1.4 MLWS 0.5
The Medway is accessible at all times; it is well marked and navigable within limits to Tonbridge.
Approach A traffic warning lt Fl 7s is exhibited from Garrison Pt on the E side of the entrance when tankers of 6,000 dwt and over are moving. A chy 74m conspic on the E end of the Isle of Grain is a good landmark for the entrance.
(1) Ample water outside channel for small craft (but beware wreck WNW of No 7 buoy and tidal set on to vessels in anchorages). Exercise caution at night when wreck lights and lights of anchored shipping can be confused with shore lights.
(2) From Sea Reach through the Nore Swatchway leaving the Nore Swatch R can Fl(4)R 15s to stb, thence join the main channel at No 11 G con buoy Fl G 10s.
(3) From the SE a course may be steered in 2m from the Spile G con Fl G 2.5s in the Four Fathom Channel to join the Medway Channel at No 8 R can buoy Fl R 5s.
(4) An inshore passage (0.6m LAT) may be taken on a rise of tide from the Spile buoy leaving the tripod post E of the Cheyney Rks (drying) to port entering the Medway at the West Cant.
Entrance Stream runs at 3kn. On the ebb considerable advantage may be gained from an inflowing eddy that runs close in by the seaward side of Garrison Pt, or the main strength of stream avoided by keeping to the W. Sheerness is a busy commercial port unsuitable for small craft. There are two small boat basins:
(1) Boat basin to N within the bonded area, and to be avoided;
(2) The S basin; Normally open to small craft and can be used to obtain Customs clearance, but dangerous. The entrance is frequently blocked by the mooring lines of the Ro-Ro ferry and should be checked before attempting entry. Better to clear in at Queenborough.

ENGLAND, East Coast 72

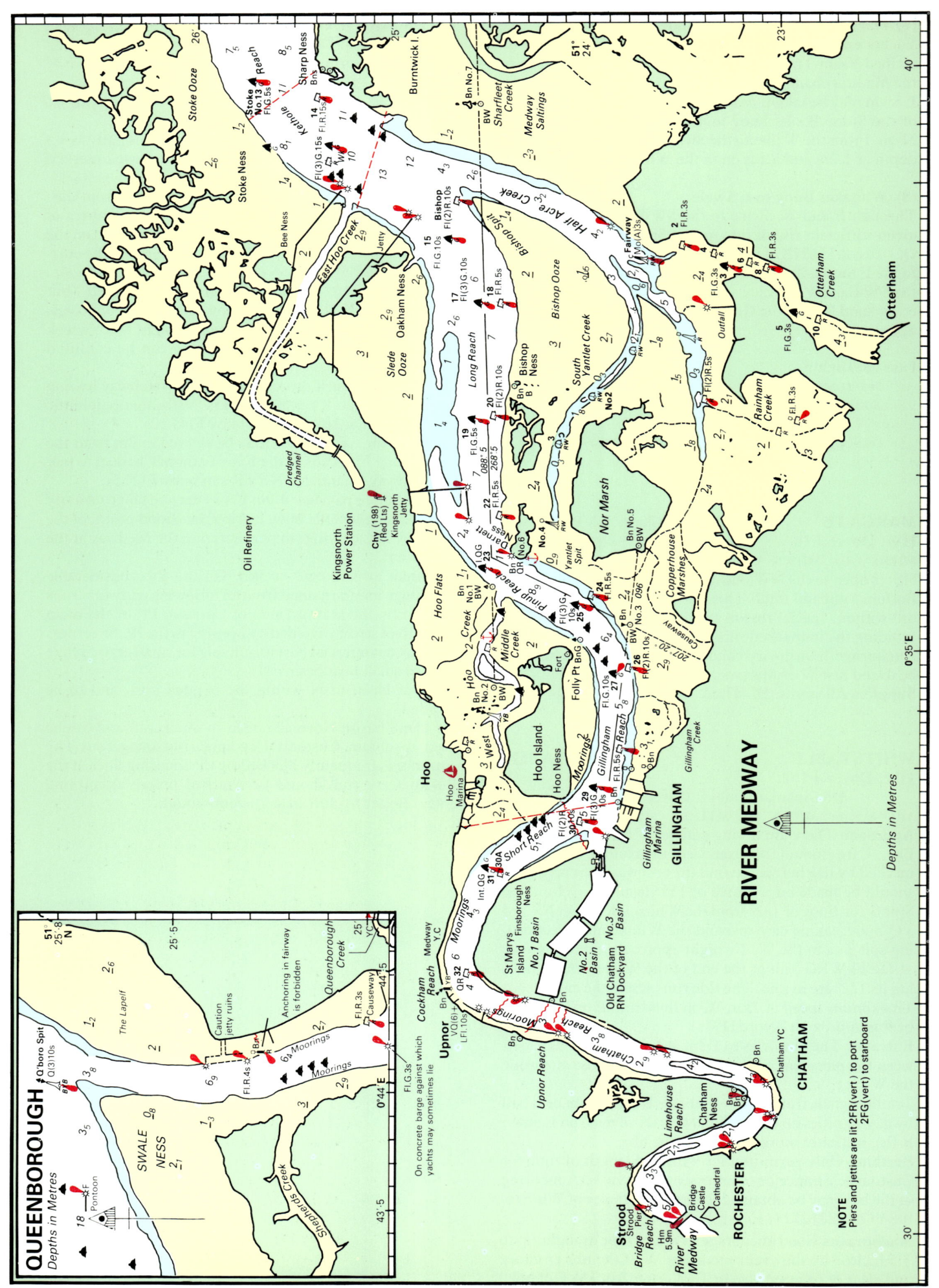

From Garrison Pt to Rochester the channel is well buoyed and lighted. Beware numerous unlit buoys outside channel; 8 ca upriver from Sheerness the entrance to the West Swale is marked by the Queenborough Spit E Card buoy Q(3)10s. A further 1½M on in Saltpan Reach the entrance to Stangate Creek on the S side of the river is marked by the Stangate Spit E Card buoy VQ(3)5s which lies S of the fourth of the mooring buoys off the oil wharves on the Isle of Grain shore (N side of the Reach). These wharves extend from Victoria to Elphinstone Pt. Large tanker movements take place in this area and small craft must keep well clear. The Medway Ports Authority prohibits any unauthorised vessel from coming within 100ft of the jetties or the vessels moored there.

From Kethole Reach inwards the river appears deceptively wide towards HW, but the deep-water channel is only about 2 ca wide, buoyed. Speed limit of 6kn from Gillingham Reach inwards. At the S end of Chatham Reach a sharp lookout should be kept for vessels and their attendant lighters proceeding to and from Rochester. Navigation for vessels with high fixed masts stops at Rochester Bridge, headroom under the middle span 5.96m above MHWS giving 11.36m at MLWS but with depths of less than 1m in places. Passage under Rochester Bridge should not be attempted by vessels of over 0.8m draught at MLWS. Centre arch has least water, is subject to difficult tidal eddies and leads directly onto shoal patch. When depth is critical take Strood arch obliquely, lining up buttress on Strood side with MV Rochester Queen on Rochester bank above bridge; straighten up into channel along outside line of RCC moorings. If heading for MPA visitors' buoy on Strood side, follow same approach, cross river when above these moorings and fall back onto them.

Progress beyond this point to Allington Lock 12M, the end of the tidal part of the river, is inadvisable before half flood. Navigation from Allington Lock is only suitable for motor cruisers. The lock is operated from HW−3h to HW+2h and manned at all times Maidstone (0622) 52864. Maximum draught from Allington Lock to Maidstone is 2m; craft proceeding upriver against the stream should give way to craft going downriver. Headroom under Maidstone Bypass Bridge is 9.45m at MHWS.

Medway Ports Authority maintains a Port Operation Service at Garrison Pt Sheerness (07956) 3025/6 for the purpose of providing radio and radar assistance to all vessels navigating in the River Medway. Medway Radio maintains a constant watch on VHF 16 and 14, the latter being the port operation channel.

Anchorages (1) Stangate Creek (see Entrance) affords a quiet sheltered anchorage clear of traffic, in among the marshes. No facilities. To enter the creek leave the Stangate Spit E Card VQ(3) 5s buoy to stb. At night if the refinery flare is visible keep to mid channel of the Medway until the flare bears 002°. Maintain this back bearing to the entrance and then steer 179° up the creek onto Ldg lights 171°. Anchor well clear of this line and use riding lt: barges use channel day and night. Avoid a G Con buoy on the W mud flats ½M from the entrance and leave R can buoy to port, also the mud flats on the E side for ¾M from the entrance to the first headland, after which the creek is clear of wreckage with good anchorage to either side.

(2) Sharfleet Creek leads out to Stangate on the stb hand ½M from the entrance. Good anchorage on the S side just inside, or on either shore further in, clear of oyster beds. Landing places at public piers: in Limehouse Reach, Ship Pier, and Blue Boar Pier, Bridge Reach, and in Tower Reach, Esplanade Pier. (Note the Esplanade Pier is occupied by the restaurant vessel 'Rochester Queen' and the gate to the Pier is kept locked when the restaurant is closed). Other landing places: Commodore Hard, Gillingham Strand (suitable for launching), Gillingham Pier steps just downstream of the dockyard entrance, Upnor Causeway upstream of the Arethusa shore establishment, Sun Pier, Chatham (dinghy landing only at downstream pontoon), Town Quay steps downstream of Rochester Bridge (suitable for dinghies), Strood esplanade steps upstream from Rochester Bridge, and the Medway Bridge Marina. Medway Ports Authority maintains six visitors' buoy above Rochester Bridge on the Strood side. There is a marina by the motorway bridge on the S side of the river, and another at Hoo providing electricity, showers, boat hoist, scrubbing berth and some provisions. VHF M or tel: (0634) 250311. Access HW ±3h.

General supplies can be obtained from all the above places. Diesel from Gillingham, Medway Bridge, Cuxton, Allington Marina (all HW access only) from pier just upstream of Gillingham Marina (lock opens 0800 - 2100 hrs only) and from pontoon near tug moorings at Chatham. (Water hose here also and Calor gas from nearby shop). Moorings may be available from Yacht Clubs. REYC permits use of vacant moorings free for 24 hours - details on Upnor Jetty just downstream of Upnor Castle.

The wreckage of HMS Bulwark in Kethole Reach is marked by a R can buoy. It may be passed on either hand but vessels should not anchor in the vicinity.

QUEENBOROUGH Chart BA 2572
HW: Dover +1½h   DS: Dover −4h S, +2½h N
MHWS 5.7m MHWN 4.8 MTL 3.1 MLWN 1.5 MLWS 0.6
A convenient and sheltered port easily accessible by day and night.

Approach and entrance From the R Medway leaving Queenborough Spit E Card buoy Q(3) 10s close to stb. Further into the creek two dolphins Fl R 6s and FR marking the ruins of the rly pier must be left to port. The area of the derelict pier is dangerous and stumps are exposed at half-tide. Do not attempt to land at remains of pier with rly footbridge over. A course of 178° from the Queenborough Spit leads up the fairway.

Berthing At two visitors' buoys immediately S of causeway for up to 6 yachts each, or with prior permission the E side of the concrete barge opposite the causeway. The HM Sheerness (0795) 662051 normally patrols at HW on weekends and Bank Holidays. Diesel in creek, chandlery, stores, Rly to London.

E. SWALE AND HARTY FERRY
Charts BA 2571, 2572
HW: Dover +1¼h
MHWS 5.7m MHWN 4.8 MTL 3.1 MLWN 1.5 MLWS 0.6

Approach and entrance To maintain the best depth of water 2m through the entrance, approach from the Columbine G con buoy on 234° to close N of the Pollard Spit R can buoy QR, thence 227° leaving the Sand End G con buoy Fl G 5s wide to stb. Thence 237° towards Faversham Creek N Card buoy which may be lying dried out in the creek entrance, altering course to pass close N of the line moorings.

Berthing A mooring may be obtained from Tideway Services boatman operating from a fishing boat moored at the E end of the moorings. Uncomfortable in strong NE winds.

Anchorages (1) At the W end of and in line with the moorings, clear of the fairway used by barges and fishing boats, in 3m. More comfortable shallow-draught anchorages may be found in South Deep. Inn close by the hard on N side, some food obtainable. Oare and Faversham are accessible from the hard on the S side. Boatyard and Inn at junction of Faversham and Oare Creeks.

(2) In the South Deep between Fowley Is and the S shore in 1m. To approach follow the S bank for approx 1M from Harty Ferry hard leaving a small Is marked by a E Card buoy to stb until the moorings are sighted.

Conyer with all facilities may be reached on the tide; the tortuous channel is well marked with perches, △ tops to stb, round tops to port. Limited space. Conyer Marine if previously contacted will assist vessels on VHF 37.

PASSAGE NOTES: QUEENBOROUGH TO HARTY FERRY THROUGH THE SWALE

Least depth at MLWS 1m. All times relate to Dover.
DS: −4½h to −4h: slack everywhere.
Queenborough: −4h S, +2½h N.
Kingsferry: −4h SE, +3½ NW. (i.e. in from Medway for 7½h, out towards Medway for 4½h).
Fowley Is: −4n to +1½h streams run in at both ends and meet here. From +1½h to +5h the stream is E-going. From +5h to −4½h streams separate here and run out at both ends.
Harty Ferry: +1½h E, −4h W.

Streams are strongest soon after they begin and the greatest rates, about 4kn at sp, occur near Kingsferry. It is easier to carry a fair tide when bound E.

Directions Just beyond Queenborough the channel turns to stb and the deepest water is close to the wharves on the port hand. A G con buoy marks the Horse Shoal (dries). Leave this to stb, passing S of the shoal. Approx 1M further on there is a wreck on the port hand: keep well clear. A further ½M beyond the wreck electric cables run across the river bed marked by beacons on either bank; a drying bank lies in mid-channel hereabouts: avoid by keeping to the stb side. Kingsferry Bridge lies ¾M further on. The br lifts on request, rly traffic permitting. Clearance at MHWS: closed 3.3m; lifted, up to 28.9m. To request opening, if possible telephone bridge keeper in advance Sittingbourne (0795) 73637 giving ETA at bridge. A listening watch is maintained on VHF 10 or a message may be passed through Medway Radio on VHF 14. A flag or round object in the rigging or one long followed by four short blasts indicates that passage is requested. Traffic signals are shown only when br is about to open or about to be closed.

Fl R and Amber	– Bridge about to open
Green	– Bridge open for passage
Fl R	– Bridge closing
No Lights	– Opening not imminent

There is a good hard here and anchorage for a short stay on S shore taking the mud. Beware of sizeable commercial vessels using the fairway on way to and from Ridham and Grovehurst docks, also Milton Creek.

From Kingsferry Bridge to Milton Creek the banks are a fair guide: keep near to the two wharves just before this creek and follow the outside curve of the river. From between the N (G con) and S (R can) ferry buoys steer to pass between the two noticeboards; when exactly between them turn to stb and pass close N of R can buoys 8,6,4,2, laid at ½M intervals. At LW the channel is only a few metres wide here and bounded by large areas of mud which cover at half-tide. Least water (nearly dry at LAT) is near Fowley Is and at Elmey, where the causeway stands ½m above the river bed. A bar exists approx ½ ca beyond No. 2: sound along the edge of the spit off Fowley Is towards a post marking the stb hand entry to Conyer Creek, thence make good 097° until No 1 G con buoy is abeam (this buoy dries and should be given a good offing), thence 123° to Harty Ferry anchorage. Distances: Queenborough to Kingsferry Bridge 2½M; Kingsferry Bridge to Harty Ferry 7M.

GRAVESEND   Chart BA 1186
HW: Dover +1½h.
MHWS 6.5m   MHWN 5.4   MTL 3.5   MLWN 1.6   MLWS 0.5

Approach Care is required when passing through the outer ship moorings as the tide runs very hard.

Berthing In Canal Basin. To enter apply Lock Foreman (0474) 352392, 337488 or 337489 on the port side of the lock.

Entrance is at the E end of the promenade, approach by a narrow gut between drying banks. Sound in carefully as channel is subject to continuous alteration. Vessels drawing over 2m should seek assistance from the YC. The gates are opened from 1h before to HW if HW is between 0700 and 2100; otherwise the Lock Foreman will attend if given 24h notice. The basin is owned by the Council and charges are for 24 hours, 48 hours, 7 days, and longer periods. The moorings within the basin are maintained by Gravesend SC (0474) 533974; visitors may on request be allocated a mid-basin mooring instead of lying against the dock wall. The Club welcomes visitors and may assist, by prior arrangement, with masts (up to 40ft). Small crane. Water, tel at Club. Rly, ferry. EC Wed.

Anchorage Strangers should anchor off the E end of the promenade well clear of all moorings; tripping line essential. Close inshore the stream is weaker, but on springs the shore dries out to the inner line of YC moorings. Two orange YC buoys marked 'GCS 5 tons' may be picked up by visitors waiting to enter the basin. Some traffic and wash will be experienced.

GREENHITHE   Chart BA 2151
HW: Dover +2h
MHWS 6.2m   MHWN 4.9

Sheltered in SE through S to SW winds; most exposed to NW. Anchor off causeway, end marked by a buoy which indicates the drying edge of the mud. Sound carefully, as mud is steep-to in places, and it is advisable to rig tripping line.

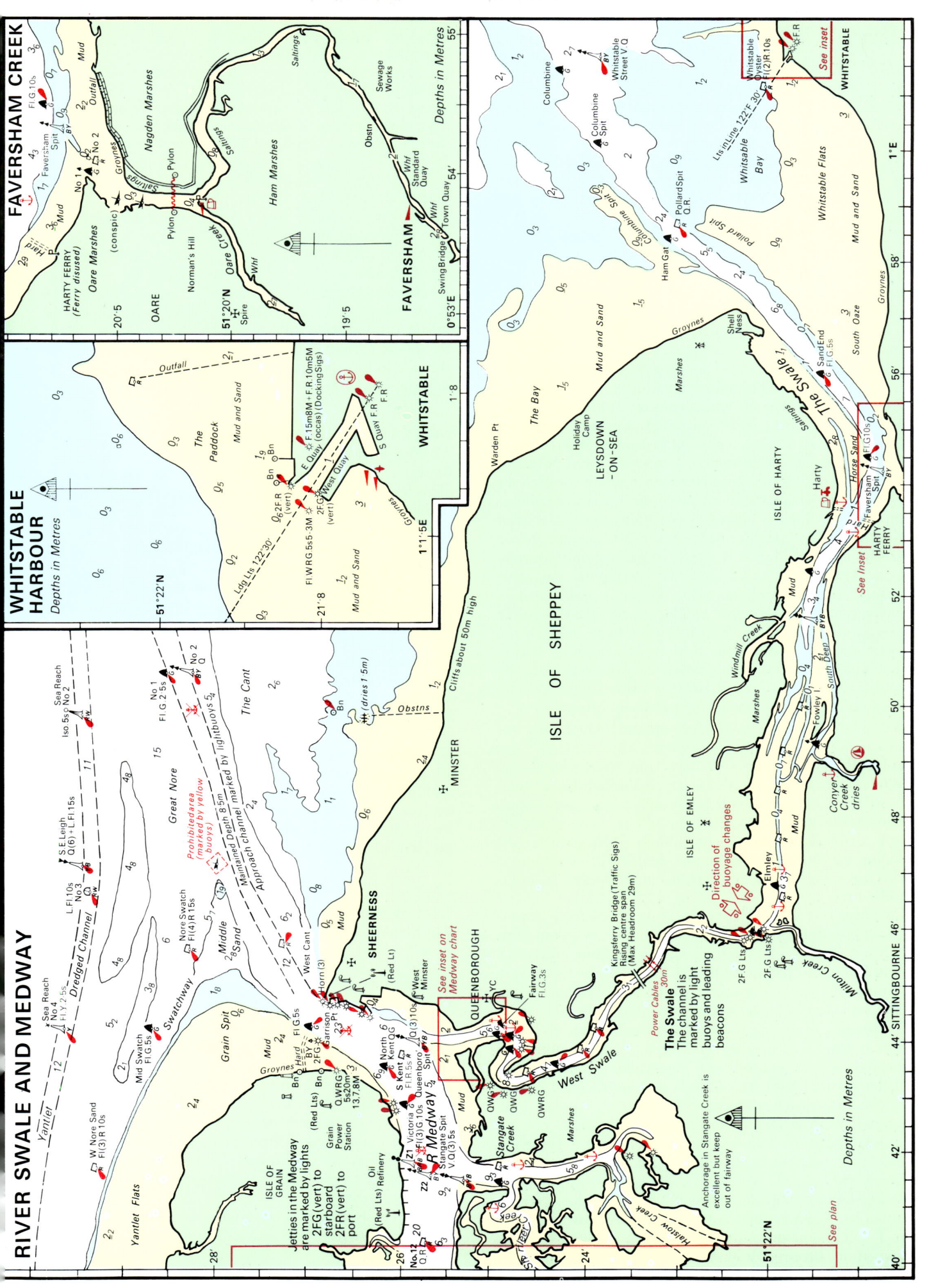

THE LONDON RIVER OR RIVER THAMES
Charts BA 1185, 1186, 2484, 2151, 3337, 3319
See also Cruising Association Visiting Yachtsman's Guide to the London River and PLA Guide to Users of Pleasure Craft on the Thames Tideway. Persons in charge of vessels navigating in any part of the R Thames must comply with rules relating to sound signals.

To make reasonable passage times in the River Thames it is essential to use the tides, running at 3-4kn, to the best advantage, beginning the upriver passage at LW in Sea Reach.

Approach The Sea Reach deep-water channel is marked by safe water and special buoys. It is restricted in width to 150m either side of the buoys and is maintained at a depth only just sufficient for the deepest draught vessels using the port, so their passage must not be impeded in any way. The N and S navigable margins of the Reach are well marked and should be used by all small craft.

Thames Barrier A control zone exists between Margaretness and Blackwall Point for regulating traffic through the Thames Flood Barrier, which consists of nine piers. Passage of all craft strictly controlled. Contact Woolwich Radio on VHF 14 for permission to proceed when passing Margaretness Point inward or Blackwall Point outward. Yachts without VHF should navigate inwards through the northern-most span and outwards through the southern-most span which is open to navigation. Contact Barrier Control (01-855-0315 or 5186) before proceeding. Green arrows are exhibited at the ends of piers open to navigation. The arrows point inwards toward the navigable span(s). Red crosses denote closed span(s). Spans open to navigation in one direction will be closed to navigation in the opposite direction. The tide runs hard through the open spans. No stopping, turning or anchoring within 100m of the Barrier. Permanently closed spans (A to the south, H, J, K, to the north) display an equilateral triangle apex downwards contructed of red discs or lights.

Large notice boards (yellow background, black text) are situated at Erith Rands, False Point, Thamesmead, Cuckolds Point, Brunswick Wharf, and Blackwall Point. When amber flashing lights are exhibited from these boards, a loud-hailer will broadcast instructions which must be obeyed. When red flashing lights are exhibited, stop, since all navigation is prohibited. During surge conditions the Barrier will be closed, advice will be broadcast by Gravesend Radio on VHF 12 and Woolwich Radio VHF 14.

Entrance Bound up-Thames from the R Medway, where Queenborough provides a convenient stopping-over point, a start can be made using the last hour of ebb to clear Garrison Pt and standing well clear of the Grain Spit start the inward passage through the Nore Swatch. A fair tide can then be held with reasonable speed as far as Richmond. Outward bound from Richmond, the best time to leave is as soon as the weir is drawn, sounding to maintain a sufficient depth of water outside the strongest of the stream. A fair tide should be found from London Bridge onwards. With no more than average speed a foul tide will be met long before comfortable shelter can be found outside the Thames, so it is preferable to bring up and await the next favourable tide before reaching Gravesend.

Bridge lights navigable arches of Thames bridges carry 2 amber lts close together. A R triangle point down by day, or 3 R lts point down at night, denote bridge closed to navigation, except at Richmond Weir where 1 R shape or lt is shown when it is closed.

Berthing Not allowed at the privately owned piers and those belonging to the PLA, except for a short period with the express permission of the Piermaster. Gravesend Canal Basin by prior arrangement (0474) 352392. At Grays Thurrock a YC mooring buoy may be obtained by prior arrangement. St Katharine Yacht Haven: entrance through lock on N bank just below Tower Bridge (071 488 2400). All facilities. The HQ of the Cruising Association in Ivory House (071 481 0881) overlooks the basin. New marina at S Dock Rotherhithe. Lock opens HW ±2h indicated by lts (Bu below R) for vessels of 2m draught.

Avoid securing alongside groups of barges on swinging moorings which on the turn of tide may well foul each other, crushing craft lying between them.

Anchorage Greenhithe (see previous entry). Erith on S bank below jetties and Erith YC moorings, below and inside the lighter roads. Margaret Ness to Cross Ness, inside the lighter roads on the S bank. Greenwich, below the pier in line with it and abeam of the Naval College. It is always advisable to buoy the anchor.

NOTES ON THE RIVER THAMES ABOVE HAMMERSMITH

Between Hammersmith and Richmond the tide remains at a low level for several hours, making practically the whole of the flood in the final 2h before HW. The ebb is more or less normal. Floodwater running down the Thames can affect this behaviour considerably and strong winds at sea cause fluctuation in the tides.

Between Richmond and Teddington, for the first 2h after the weir is drawn the tide flows up to Teddington, at other times a very weak tide, if any flows down river. At exceptional springs the tide may flow over Teddington Weir and one can sometimes carry it as far as Kingston or Hampton Court. In winter Richmond Weir is sometimes left drawn and the tide above Richmond behaves in the same manner as that below. When the river is swollen the flow of water under Richmond Bridge can be dangerous.

Shooting bridges The stream swirls round the buttresses of all bridges and to avoid being swept into them, arches should be taken squarely. They should be approached so that the insides of both sides of the arch to be taken can be seen from a distance. Hammersmith is the lowest bridge with a headroom of 3.8m at MHWS.

The lock for the Grand Union Canal, Brentford, is in Syon Reach, and is normally open from HW−2h to HW+3h (Local HW London Bridge +1hr). Brentford Marine is also in Syon Reach.

NOTES ON THE RIVER THAMES ABOVE TEDDINGTON

Above Teddington the river is controlled by the Thames Water Authority (TWA) and all craft must be licensed. There are special rates for power-driven craft visiting the Upper Thames for either 14 days or a calendar month.

The Authority does not register vessels capable of being driven at high speed. All vessels must be navigated with caution and in such a manner as not to endanger lives or cause injury to persons, other vessels, moorings, river banks or property.

Sound signals on power vessels are compulsory. Vessels are required to have port, stb and stern lts visible 2M and masthead lts visible 5M. International rules of the road and sound signals apply.

No waste, litter or sewage may be discharged into the river above Teddington Lock, Kingston Corporation (sewage pumping station near rly bridge), Shiplake Temple, Boveney, Shepperton, Days and Abingdon Locks provide facilities for refuse disposal. TWA inspect and if necessary seal pipes discharging into river.

TWA have regulations regarding fire risk which are available from Head Office, Nugent House, Vastern Road, Reading, R61 8DB (0734) 593333.

The river is dredged so that in summer it can be navigated as follows:

	Draught (m)	Miles from Teddington
Teddington to Staines	2	17
Staines to Windsor	1.7	25
Windsor to Reading	1.4	55
Reading to Oxford	1.2	93½
Oxford to Lechlade	0.9	124½

Key bridge heights are:	(m)
Teddington to Lock Cut	5.8
Desborough Chan	5.2
Windsor	4
Cookham	3.8
Clifton Lock Cut	3.6
Folly (Oxford)	3.1
Osney	2.3

These are heights in dry weather with the water level at datum. In times of winter flow or flood they will be less. Lock-keepers will advise whether the water level is above or below datum.

The best navigational guide to the Upper Thames is that published by the Association of Thames Motor Boat Clubs and the best charts those published by Stanford and Salter. The latter also publish a good guide.

Dredgers: pass on side showing W flag.

Yachts may moor to the towpath for not more than one day. For available moorings consult local boatmen. Near all the larger towns small self-drive motor launches are for hire and their occupants may not have any knowledge of the rules of navigation.

In summer there is no tide above Teddington and the river flow is under 1kn. In winter spring tides may flow as far as Molesey Lock and after rain (usually Nov and Feb) the ebb stream can run up to 12kn exceptionally.

Locks operate till dusk except Molesey and Teddington which are always manned. During winter months locks may be closed for repairs: TWA will advise.

HOLEHAVEN
Charts BA 1186, 1185
HW: Dover +1¾h
MHWS 6.2m MHWN 5.2 MTL 3.3 MLWN 1.4 MLWS 0.5

Approach and entrance Approaching from Sea Reach the entrance to the creek (0.3m at LAT) lies immediately W of the last oil jetty on Canvey Is, the fourth from seaward and well inside the large new jetty running out from Holehaven. ½M inside the Creek a bridge crosses it, connecting this new jetty to the Canvey shore. It has 9m headroom at MHWS and a navigable opening 30m wide.

Berthing S of the pier crowded moorings lie in 2m at LAT, one of these may at times be available with permission from the Piermaster. Care should be taken as considerable tanker movements Holehaven/Shellhaven/Gravesend. VHF 12 Thames Navigational Service.

Supplies Canvey village 1M, shops, PO, bus to Benfleet (3M), rly. EC Benfleet - Wed; Canvey - Thur.
Tel: Outside Lobster Smack Inn close to causeway.

LEIGH
Chart BA 1185
HW: Dover +1½h
MHWS 5.7m MHWN 4.8 MTL 3.1 MLWN 1.4 MLWS 0.5

Approach From Leigh Channel 8 ca WNW of Southend Pier lies the Leigh G con buoy marking the W side of the entrance to the Ray Gut which has 2.4 to 4m. This buoy should be left to port. Silting occurs and the approach should be made with caution.

Entrance After leaving Leigh G main channel buoy close to port a further small can unmarked (known as Sand Edge) should be left to port; then head for moored fishing boats leaving them fine to stb for best water. Offshore from Leigh the sands dry 4m for a distance of 7 ca to the Ray Gut. Drying moorings off Two Tree Island in Hadleigh Ray. (Water and emergency telephone, 2 mile walk to Leigh rly and Town). Benfleet Creek continues westward after ½M marked by numbered port hand marks, to South Benfleet, (Canvey Road Bridge blocks navigation) rly, Benfleet YC, water and Dauntless Boatyard. Ask local advice.

Anchorage in the Ray Gut 2½ to 4m suitable whilst waiting for flood tide for London. Area is patrolled by Southend CBC Launches 'Alec White' and 'Loway' (VHF 12 & 16) and Essex police launch 'Vigilante III' (VHF 12).

Berthing Alongside Bell or Victoria Wharf; both public. Craft must be prepared to take the ground.

Supplies Fresh Water Leigh SC or Essex YC, Tel outside Smack PH, all facilities in the Town, EC Wed.

HAVENGORE CREEK
Chart BA 1185

This HW short-cut runs between the R Thames and the R Crouch and is available for shoal-draught vessels only. Navigate in daylight only, approx 1½h before and up to HW. The route has 2m at MHWS and 0.9m at MHWN. The height of tide may be reduced by up to 1m by S winds or high barometric pressure. A new lifting bridge was completed in November 1988 (see Entrance).

Approach The Maplin Sand is a Min of Defence heavy artillery firing range; at times the passage of all vessels through this area is strictly controlled. For the latest information tel (0702) 292271.

Leaving the Warps 1½ to 1h before HW, to ensure that some rise remains, pass E of the wooden survey platform, which lies ½M W of the E Shoebury G Con buoy and make good a course of 337° leaving the H topmark bns to port. These mark the Broomway, which runs approx at right angles to the course line and lie some 3 ca from Havengore Creek entrance. There are numbered port hand buoys marking the last few cables and a RWS offing buoy maintained by Wakering YC (sometimes off station).

Entrance The entrance may be located by sighting the lifting bridge which crosses the creek. To contact the bridgekeeper tel (0702) 292271 ext. 3406 (on duty for 2hrs either side of HW daylight only). When the sea wall is reached the channel deepens to 0.6 to 0.9m with steep sides. It may be marked by withies. Sounding in between the entrance points, the bottom is mud to the SW side of fairway and sand to the NE. All this part dries 2½ to 3h after HW. Passing through the bridge, take great care if the flood is still making, as the tide does not run true.

Once inside the line of the land the channel gradually deepens. To go to the R Roach and Burnham take the first turning on the stb hand after entering the Haven and continue N till reaching the Roach, then turn E for the Crouch.

To go through the Haven from Burnham, stand up the Roach. Take first creek port hand and then the third on port hand again, the first and second branches leading to Shelford and New England respectively, obstructed by fixed bridges. If the branch to stb is taken, the Roach may be reached once more and Potton is circumnavigated at MHWS. The nearest berth to the Haven where a vessel can lie afloat is just before entering the third turning, where there is 1.2 to 1.5m at MLWS. When the mud on the bank of the channel at this point is covered there is 1m of water at the entrance to the Haven.

Streams at Havengore run strongly; the ebb and flood part and meet about ½M inside. There is more water at the entrance in NW winds, less in SE or SW. At slack neaps the waters sometimes fail to meet.

RIVER CROUCH Chart BA 1975, 3750
HW (Burnham): Dover +1h

MHWS 5.3m   MHWN 4.5   MTL 2.4   MLWN 1.4   MLWS 0.5

Accessible at all times. The coastline is low and there are few distinguishing marks; the spire of Foulness ch may be seen inland in good visibility and there are two conspic lattice trs well to the S at Eastness on Foulness. The tides run hard, up to 3kn on a spring ebb and follow the line of the channel. The river has a least depth of 2m in or close by the channel at the Sunken Buxey. The channel is narrow in places and shoals rapidly at the edges. Vessels drawing up to 2m can reach Battlesbridge, the upper limit of the river at MHWS but the upper reaches are crowded and tortuous making passage difficult.

Approach (1) From the Whitaker E card buoy Q(3) 10s Bell the fully buoyed and lighted channel may be followed as far as No 15 buoy 0°47′.3E. In all 25 buoys now mark the channel. Entering the river between the Outer Crouch G con buoy and the Crouch R can buoy the channel narrows. Sound along the 5m line either side in bad visibility. Fairway is marked by G con buoys QG odd number 1 - 15 and R can buoy No 2 QR.
(2) Across the Swin Spitway. From the Swin Spitway safe water pillar with topmark Iso 10s bell leave the Ridge R can buoy with topmark to port and thence to the Sunken Buxey N card buoy (Q) as in (1) above. Note that (1988) shallow patches are appearing at LW on the direct course Swin Spitway to Ridge buoy. The best water lies to the S. If in doubt steer S from the Swin Spitway for 1M, then 250° to the Ridge.
(3) From the Wallet through the Raysand Channel. This channel dries 1.2m at the S end; seasonal variations in the line of deepest water occur. Passage should be attempted only on a rising tide taking care to avoid being set upon the Knoll and the Bachelors Spit by the flood, sounding across into the Crouch channel use the Buxey bns and the bns marking the old target wrecks on the Dengie Flats to fix position. In summer a Y buoy is often in position at the S end of the channel indicating best water.

Entrance Inside the entrance the river is clear of dangers for approx 2M as far as the mouth of the R Roach. In this area neither bank should be approached too closely. During the summer two Y race buoys laid on the N side indicate the line of safe limit to the N. A further Y race buoy laid off Wallasea Ness on the W side of the Roach entrance marks the NE extremity of Brankfleet Spit which should be left to port when proceeding up the Crouch. After Burnham Essex Marina is situated on the S bank closely followed by Baltic Wharf at which timber ships berth. At the NW end of Cliff reach, Althorne Creek leads to Bridgemarsh Marina. Between Creeksea and Fambridge, Bridgemarsh Is is completely covered at HW making identification of the channel difficult. Keep to the centre of the channel and do not enter bights in the river bank; the line of the S bank indicates the channel. About ½M E of Fambridge on the N bank there is a sunken sea wall deceptive at HW. At Fambridge moorings line both sides of the river; the entrance to Stow Creek lies on the N side of the river leading to W Wick Marina. The best water in the creek is on the E side.

Berthing (1) At Burnham on mooring buoy, by arrangement with one of the yards. Do not leave boat unattended on buoy until permission secured.
(2) At Wallasea Is on application to the Essex Marina. Fuel Barge. Stow Creek on the N bank leads to W Wick Marina, limited accommodation with slipway, water and diesel.
(3) Burnham Yacht Hbr. 550 berths, dredged to 3.5m below chart datum, 24 hr access. Entrance marked by a safe water pillar buoy LFl 10 s and lighted entrance bns to port and stb Fl 10s and is the first entrance through the sea wall approx ½M W of Town Quay on N bank. Metered elec, water on pontoons, diesel. Travel lift to 35 tons. Visitors' berths opposite entrance. HM VHF M or (0621) 782150. Chandlery (0621) 783133. All facilities shops etc close by.
(4) Bridgemarsh Marina in Althorne Creek.

Anchorage Note: Crouch Harbour Authority Bye-laws prohibit any vessel from anchoring in such a manner as to obstruct any fairway. Riding light should be shown.
(1) Burnham, ½M below the town, clear of power cables marked by bns on banks and buoys in midstream.
(2) In any clear berth on the N shore ½M above the town. Do not anchor among moorings as the ground is foul. All facilities, rly, EC Wed.
(3) Cliff Reach. Keep well over to the S bank abeam of the Baltic Wharf to avoid a spit which extends from the N bank a quarter of the way across the river. Anchor in the bay of the S bank beyond the moorings in 5½m if the wind is W and off the red cliff further up river on the N bank in 3½m if the wind is E. Lion Creek has 2.4m in centre MHWN.
(4) N Fambridge. Good anch in 2.5 to 3m clear of moorings or by arrangement with yard, pick up mooring buoy. Avoid telegraph cable from slipway on N bank to steps on S bank. Slipway, floating pontoon, rly. EC Thur.

RIVER ROACH Chart BA 3750
Entrance From seaward do not cut the corner at Nase Pt as the mud is extensive and unmarked. From Burnham do not pass inside Branklet buoy near LW. 1½M beyond the entrance is Horseshoe Corner where the river turns W; on the port hand in this reach is Yokefleet Creek leading to Havengore. 4M further on the river bears away SW and the moorings at Paglesham will be seen. Landing on Foulness is prohibited. Beyond Paglesham the river shoals rapidly.

Anchorages (1) Close under the W Bank under the high sea wall in the bay above Wallasea Ness in W winds and off the quay on the E side ¾M further up in E winds.
(2) Inside the entrance to Yokefleet Creek in 2m.
(3) Off Paglesham clear of the moorings and S of the fairway marked by unlit buoys numbered 1 to 4.

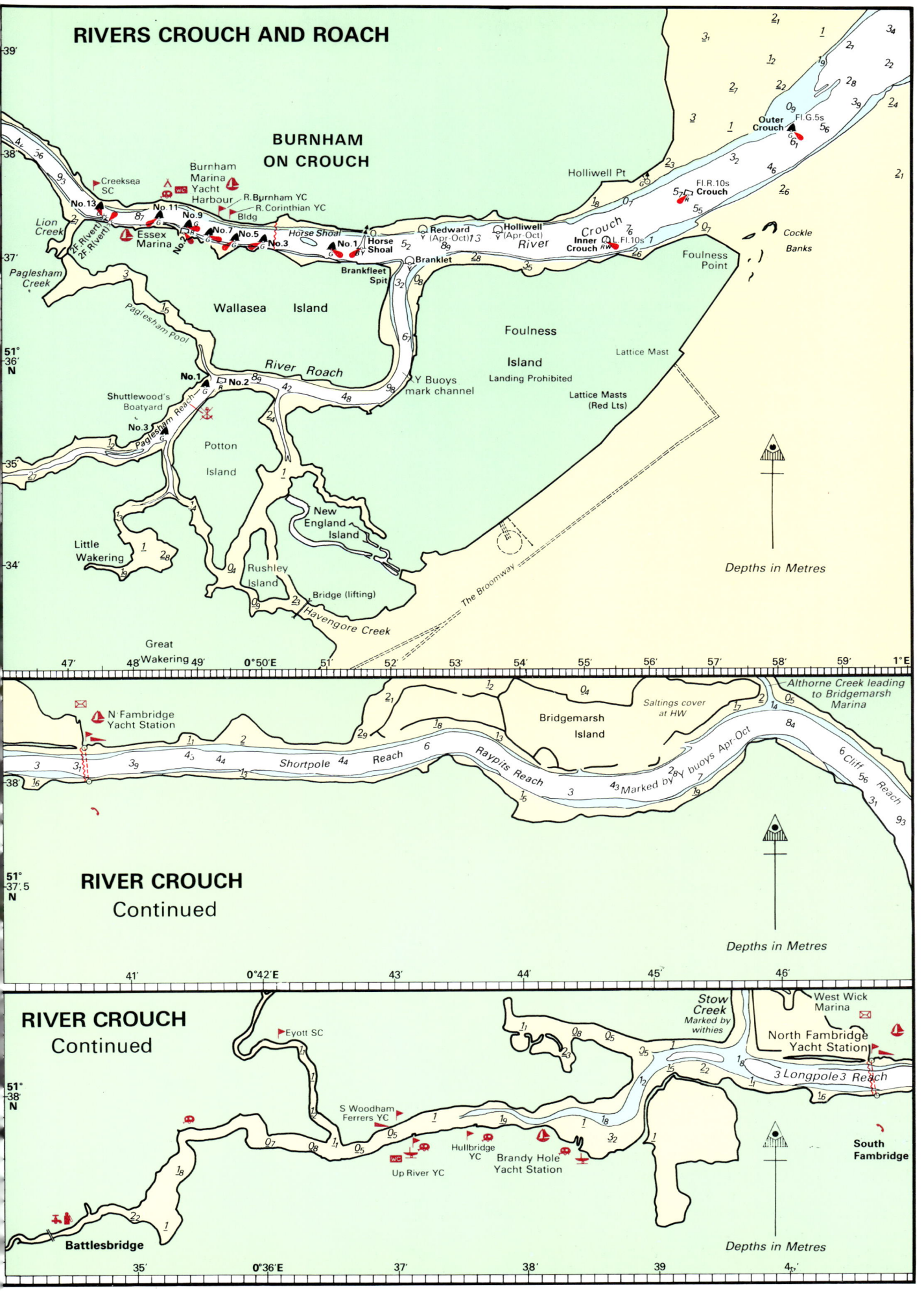

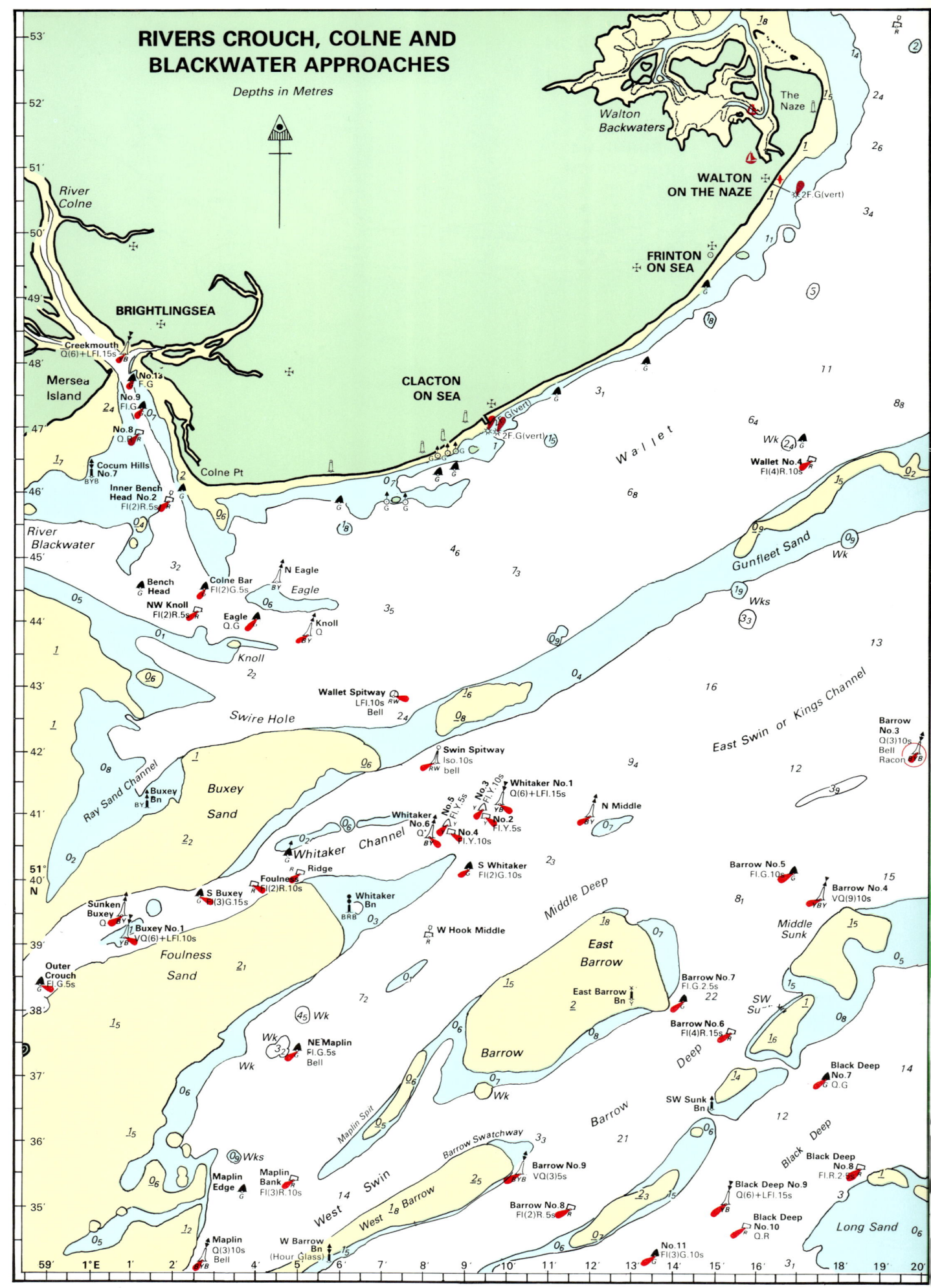

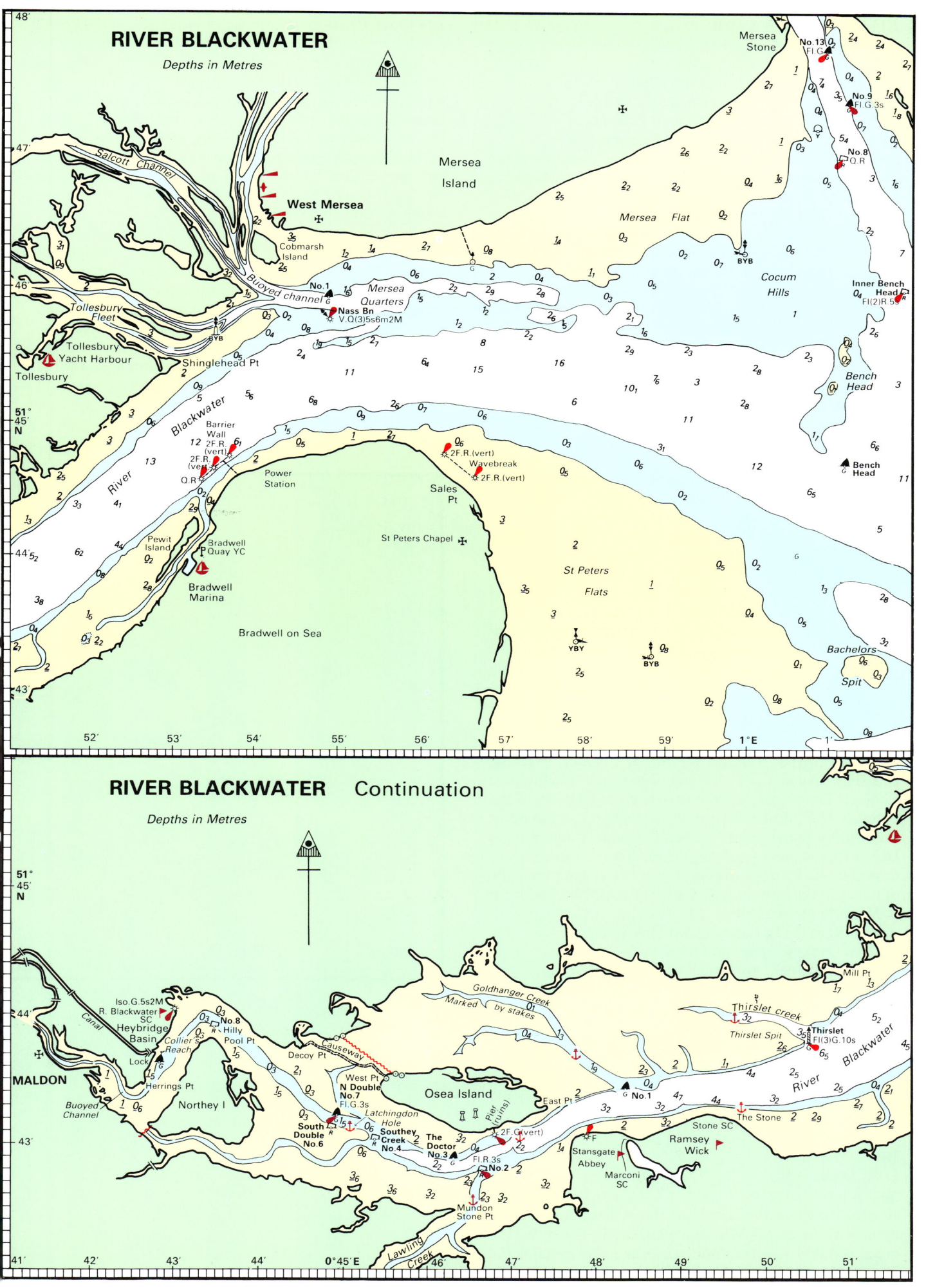

RIVER BLACKWATER Chart BA 3741

HW (Bradwell): Dover +1h: HW (Osea Is): Dover +1¼h
HW (Maldon): Dover +1¼h
DS: Knoll buoy Dover −5h W, +2h E
   Osea Is   Dover −4¾h in, +1½h out
   Maldon   Dover −4¼h in, +1½h out

The river is navigable as far as Maldon on HW.

Approach From the Wallet the approach may be made from the Knoll N Card buoy (Q) or the North Eagle N Card buoy. Both channels are clearly marked with a least depth of 3.8m but the N Eagle is unlit.

Entrance From the Bench Head G con buoy make good a course of 290° keeping the Bench Head and NW Knoll buoys in transit astern. When the Bradwell Power Station barrier wall stands well clear of the land, alter course to make good 270° until the barrier wall is in line, after which the channel runs in a direction of 243° towards Stone Pt, conspic and easily seen, on the S shore with moorings laid off it. Large laid-up vessels are often moored in the deepest water and serve to indicate the channel. With Osea Is ahead, to be passed to the S, stand in towards the Stone shore which is fairly steep-to. A narrow shoal patch 0.4m lies off Osea Pier from 2 ca E of the pier, W to No 3 G con buoy. From midstream off Stansgate Pt a course of 247° made good will clear this shoal. Numerous moorings, owned by the Marconi YC, extend well into the channel off the Pt. The channel is buoyed above Osea Is.

Between the first and second R can buoys above Osea is Latchingdon Hole. After rounding Northey Island turn into Colliers Reach, when Heybridge Basin lock will be seen on the stb side halfway down the reach. The channel dries with hard bottom for ½M below the lock. At night a G lt Iso 5s is shown from the Blackwater SC clubhouse at Heybridge showing the channel from the Doctor buoy.

Berthing (See also entries for Bradwell and Mersea Quarters). Lawling Creek opposite Osea Pier; moorings may be available on application to Dann Webb & Feesey. At Heybridge Basin there is a depth of 4m in the approach channel at MHWS. The lock opens at times varying from HW −1h to HW. Contact Heybridge Lock on VHF M, call sign "Basin Lock". Water near Inner Lock gates. Shops at Heybridge (1½M); vessels up to 3.6m beam can enter at HW. Lock Keeper is not obliged to attend at night: prior notice of arrival then advisable. Canal navigable to Chelmsford for 3.6m beam, 0.6 draught, 2m air draught. Maldon: a drying berth on staging may be obtained at the boatyard. There is 3m at MHWS and 1.5m at MHWN in the channel. EC Wed.

Anchorages (1) In Latchingdon Hole in 2m.
(2) E of Osea pier-head and for ½M downstream
(3) Thirslet Creek, good anchorage in 3.3m or less.
(4) Goldhanger Creek, anchor in 2m. Goldhanger Spit is marked by a G con buoy to be left well to port entering the creek.
(5) Lawling Creek, opposite Osea Pier; good anchorage in 2 to 2½m, within 2 ca of the entrance.
(6) Off the Stone. Clean landing on shingle near PH.

Approach From the E approach from close S of the Power Stn barrier wall, then alter course to leave entrance bn approx 3m to stb. From the W turn onto this line from close to the W end of the barrier wall.

Entrance The narrow entrance channel is marked by a prominent square pile (QR) surmounted by a box. Follow line of withies round leaving them about 3m to stb and leaving R can buoys to port until triangular leading marks on sea wall come into transit. Turn to stb immediately on passing G con buoy and follow line of moorings. Deepest water is on port side of channel.

Berthing Bradwell Marina can accept visitors. VHF M. Entrance channel marked by withies. Regular dredging of marina aims to maintain 1½m at MLWS at all berths, but silting occurs and less depths at some berths from time to time. More water at end of 'A' pontoon. Fuel, water and electricity. Customs clearance. Buoy sometimes available in creek. Do not anchor: bottom foul with mooring chains. Stores, inn, chandlery, club, restaurant and bar at marina, also Bradwell Quay YC nearby, open at weekends, bar and food available.

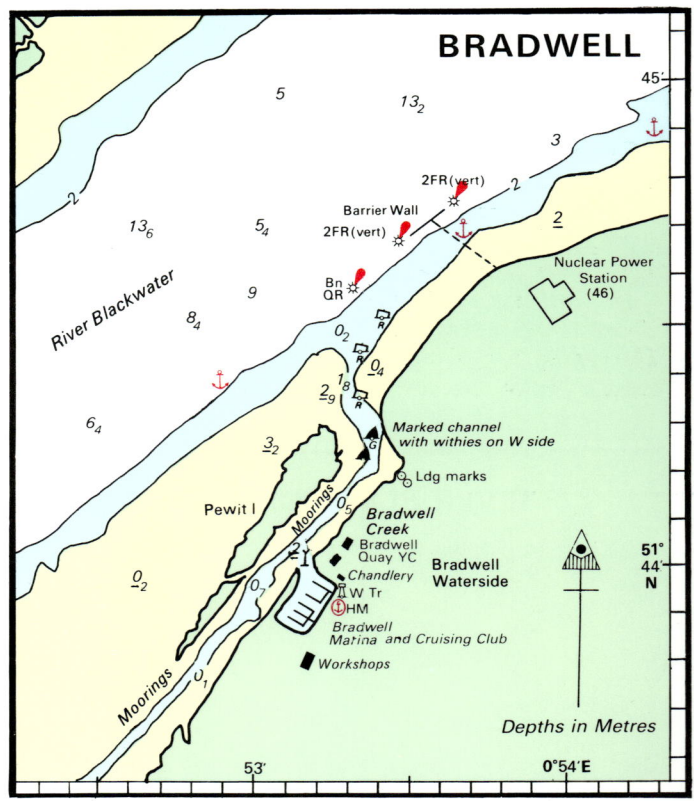

BRADWELL Chart BA 3741

HW: Dover +1h

MHWS 5.3m MHWN 4.2 MTL 2.8 MLWN 1.4 MLWS 0.5

A small inlet on the S side of the R Blackwater, with approx 0.6m at MLWS. Situated inside Pewit Is, the creek is full of small craft moorings and also contains the approach channel to Bradwell Marina.

MERSEA QUARTERS
Chart BA 3741

HW: Dover +1h

MHWS 5.2m MHWN 4.0 MTL 2.8 MLWN 1.4 MLWS 0.5

Mearsea Quarters has 2 to 7m and is reached by a channel separated from the R Blackwater by the Nass Spit marked by an E card bn, without topmark, VQ(3) 5s 2M. The bn has a tidegauge showing ht of water over the sill at Tollesbury Marina. Vessels rounding the Nass at LW should keep well to the E and N of the bn as the spit is extending and dries 1ca W of the bn and only 1.2m will be found close E.

Approach From the NW Knoll buoy it is 288° 4½M to the Nass bn. This is difficult to pick up from a distance and black shed on Packingmarsh Is between Sunken Is and Cobmarsh Is is a useful mark until the bn is sighted. Coming from R Colne, keep the shed well open of the W end of Mersea Is to clear the Cocum Hills shoal.

Entrance Pass 2 ca to the NE of the Nass bn and make good course 285° up buoyed channel. After some 4 ca on this course from the Nass bn the channel divides within Mersea Quarters. By maintaining course and bearing to stb the Mersea Fleet is entered which in turn further divides into three fleets, the two stb ones of which lead to the Mersea inner moorings and hard. By bearing to port in Mersea Quarters and following the port hand buoys on a SW course Tollesbury can be reached.

Berthing (1) **Tollesbury.** Tollesbury Fleet carries about 2m for 2M. There is a horse in midstream within the entrance, marked by R can buoys about 1 ca apart. A G drum marks the E end of Gt Cob Is. To proceed to Tollesbury via the S channel, leave this G buoy to stb and follow channel which is marked by four G con buoys to stb and one R buoy to port marking Shingle Hills. The channel is also marked by withies. There are some deep-water moorings in S Channel near the entrance to Woodrolfe Creek and there is a rough hard where one can land by dinghy. It is advisable to keep as close as practicable to the moorings. The entrance to Woodrolfe Creek is marked by a E card topmark buoy to be left to stb and there is a tide gauge to indicate depth of water on harbour sill. While waiting for the tide it is possible to pick up a boatyard mooring marked WB. The marina is at the head of the ¾M Woodrolfe Creek, reached over a sill which has 1.8m at HW neaps. Inside, the hbr is dredged to about 2.4m below sill level.

(2) **Mersea.** Thorn Fleet, W of Packingmarsh Is which can be identified by its conspic black shed, carries 1.7m. Mersea Fleet, the channel between Cobmarsh Is and Packingmarsh Is and extending N to the Gut, is locally called the Creek and has 1.5m, but 1m on bar abreast shed. Thorn Fleet is the best channel but care should be taken to follow the line of deep keeled moored craft as many moorings on the E and W edges are half drying. No attempt should be made to deviate off a general N/S line past Packingmarch Is. These creeks are too crowded with moorings to anchor, but a vacant buoy can usually be found on enquiry; secure between the mooring posts in the upper part of Thorn Fleet and lower Ray Channel, or ask advice from the WMYC boatman (VHF M call sign "Whysea One" usually cruising in the white club launch during working hrs at weekends). The CA boatman operates on Saturdays and Sundays in a large blue launch. Land at floating jetty opposite the Gut and about 18m N of WMYC or at the hard just below Clarke & Carter's shop. Water, diesel and stores, yacht chandlers and yards, scrubbing posts (apply WMYC) wet dock (enquire at Clarke & Carters) PO, tel. Store at end of jetty and more extensive shopping in Mersea Town, 1M. EC Thur.

Anchorages (1) In the outer Quarters SE of the moorings, 2 to 7m. Uncomfortable in SE winds, buoy the anchor.
(2) Salcot Channel S entrance marked by bns carries 1.8m to Sunken Is.

Strood Channel may be sailed in a dinghy up to the causeway. Anchoring prohibited owing to oyster beds, but some mooring buoys may be found for shallow draught vessels.

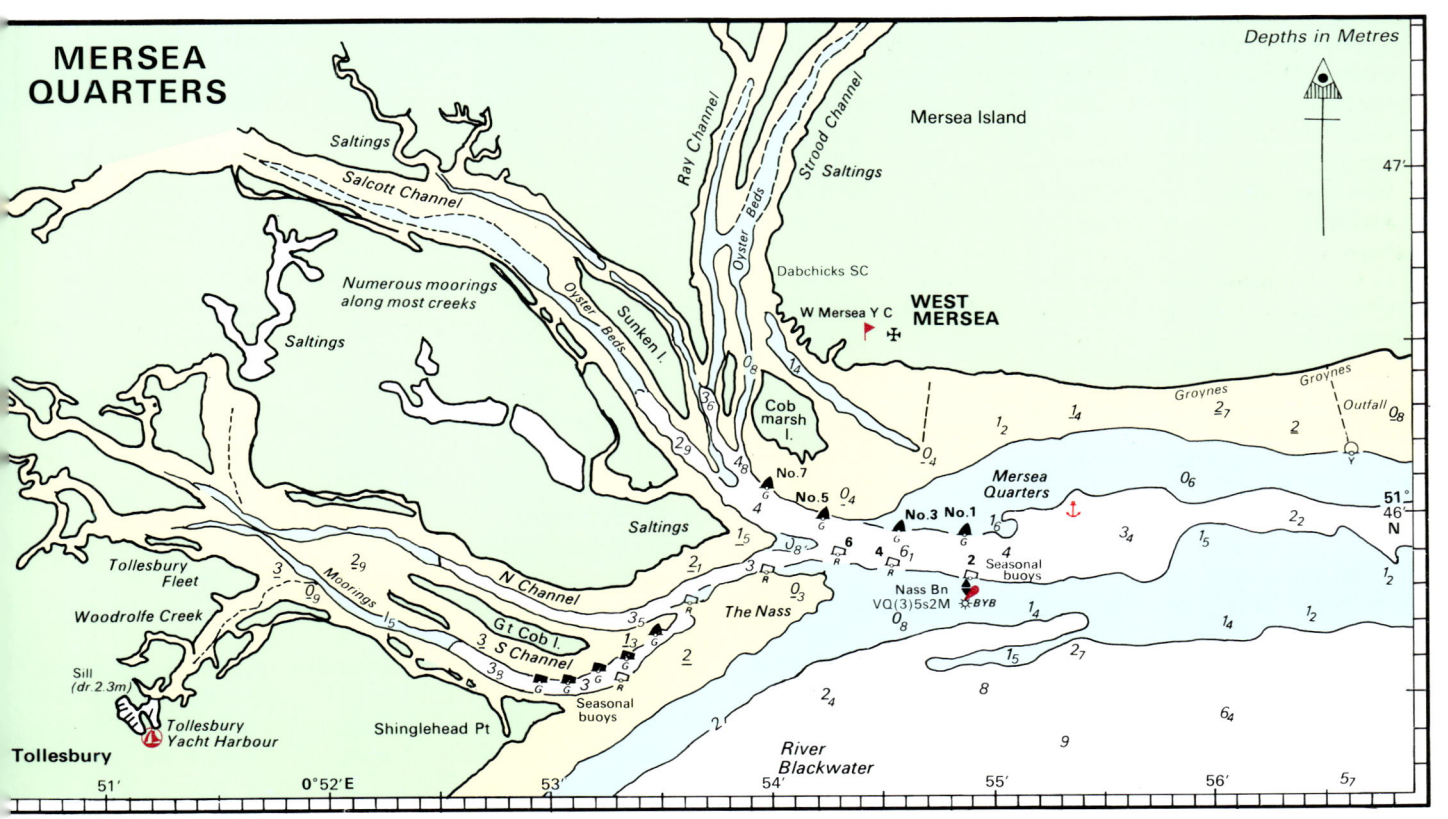

ENGLAND, EAST COAST

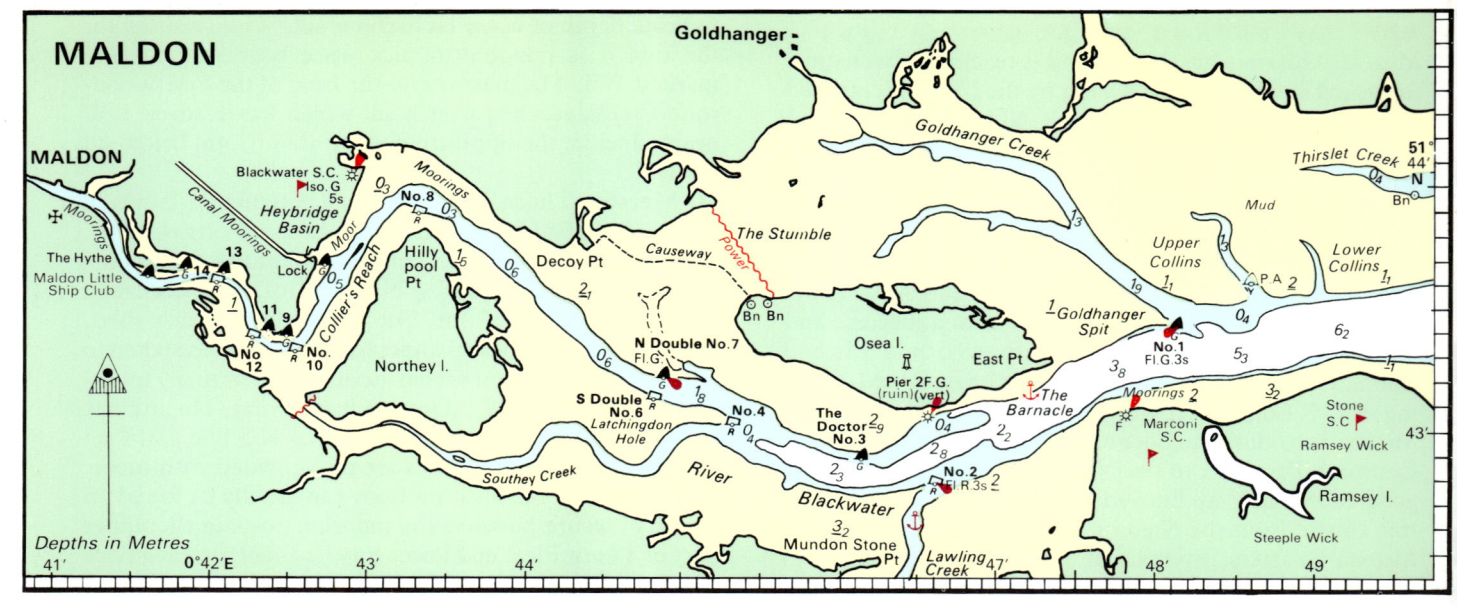

RIVER COLNE   Chart BA 3741
HW Brightlingsea: Dover +¾h
HW Wivenhoe: Dover +1¼h

Approach from Seaward At any state of tide, by day or night. From Knoll buoy Q, 287° to Eagle buoy Q G, thence 302° to Bar buoy Fl(2) G 5s, thence 342° to Inner Bench Head buoy Fl(2) R 5s. At any state of tide, by day. From N Eagle buoy (unlit) 266° to Colne Bar buoy, thence to Inner Bench Head as above.

Given sufficient rise of tide, by day, to allow for drying at LAT, from N Eagle buoy 311° to Inner Bench Head.

N.B. Between Colne Bar buoy and Inner Bench Head buoy the tide sets E or W up to 1½kn on spring ebb and flood tides respectively.

Approach from River Blackwater At any state of tide, from Bench Head buoy (unlit) 024° to Inner Bench Head buoy gives least depth of 2.4m at LAT. Given sufficient rise of tide to clear Cocums at LAT 0.6m, from Nass Beacon 086° to ½M south of E card bn (Molliette) on Mersea Flats, thence 036° to enter channel south of No 8 buoy.

Entrance From Inner Bench Head buoy 336° to No 8 Q R buoy, thence, 351° to close W of No 13 Fl G buoy gives a min of 3m at LAT.

Anchorages In Pyfleet Channel, east of Peewit Island and clear of oyster layings, marked by withies. Anchoring in Brightlingsea Roads, particularly to seaward of R can buoy marking wreck on E Mersea shore, should be avoided if possible, as this area has deep water and is used by commercial vessels which may be up to 100 metres long. The swinging arc of such vessels when anchoring or when swinging at low water, can take up the full width of the roads. If it is necessary to anchor in this area always show a GOOD anchor light.

Landing at Mersea Stone Pt or after half flood at E Mersea hard, and on the beach at Bateman's Tr ½M from Brightlingsea.

Supplies Water at standpipe behind huts at Bateman's TR, all facilities at Brightlingsea.

BRIGHTLINGSEA   Chart BA 3741
HW: Dover +¾h
MLWS 5.0m MHWN 3.8 MTL 2.7 MLWN 1.2 MLWS 0.4

Entrance From No 13 G con buoy (QG) stand out in mid-channel until abeam of Brightlingsea Creek S card buoy Q(6)+ LFl 15s, close with it in 0.6m and proceed on 041° keeping the orange rectangular ldg marks in line. These can be seen under the conspic cupola of the Anchor Hotel. Follow ldg marks as far as R can buoy Fl R 5s then turn to leave fishing vessel moorings and N card Lt Bn BY Q to stb. By night FR ldg lts are shown; two FR(vert) mark the end of Brightlingsea hard on the N side of the channel. Also 2 FR(vert) at either end of Colne YC hammer head jetty and 2 FR (vert) at SW corner of Olivers Wharf close E of Colne YC. Yachtsmen should watch out for commercial vessels manoeuvering in the vicinity of the quay at Olivers Wharf.

Berthing Apply to HM (020 630 2200) for the use of a swinging mooring or the trots or piles. There is little water at the W range of mooring piles at LWS: do not attempt to pass between the W side of the pilings and the shore near LW. There are posts for scrubbing on the N shore. Landing at the hard. Colne YC have a pontoon connected to the shore by catwalk E of the hard; water hose. The club is well equipped and friendly. All facilities close by hard. HM in the Boat Park, Waterside. EC Thur. Alresford and Geeton Creeks dry. Navigable by shallow draught barges at HW. When the E banks up-river are covered there is approx 2m in the channel.

WIVENHOE
HW: Dover +1¼h

Commercial traffic in the river is heavy. There is 4½m in the channel at MHWS, and over 3m at MHWN. Do not anchor in the fairway.

Berthing A berth may be obtained on application to Colne Marine & Yacht Co, (020 622) 2417. Landing at Wivenhoe SC hard, water available. A temporary stop may be made around HW at Rowhedge on W bank 1½m above Wivenhoe for shops, PO, PH and water.

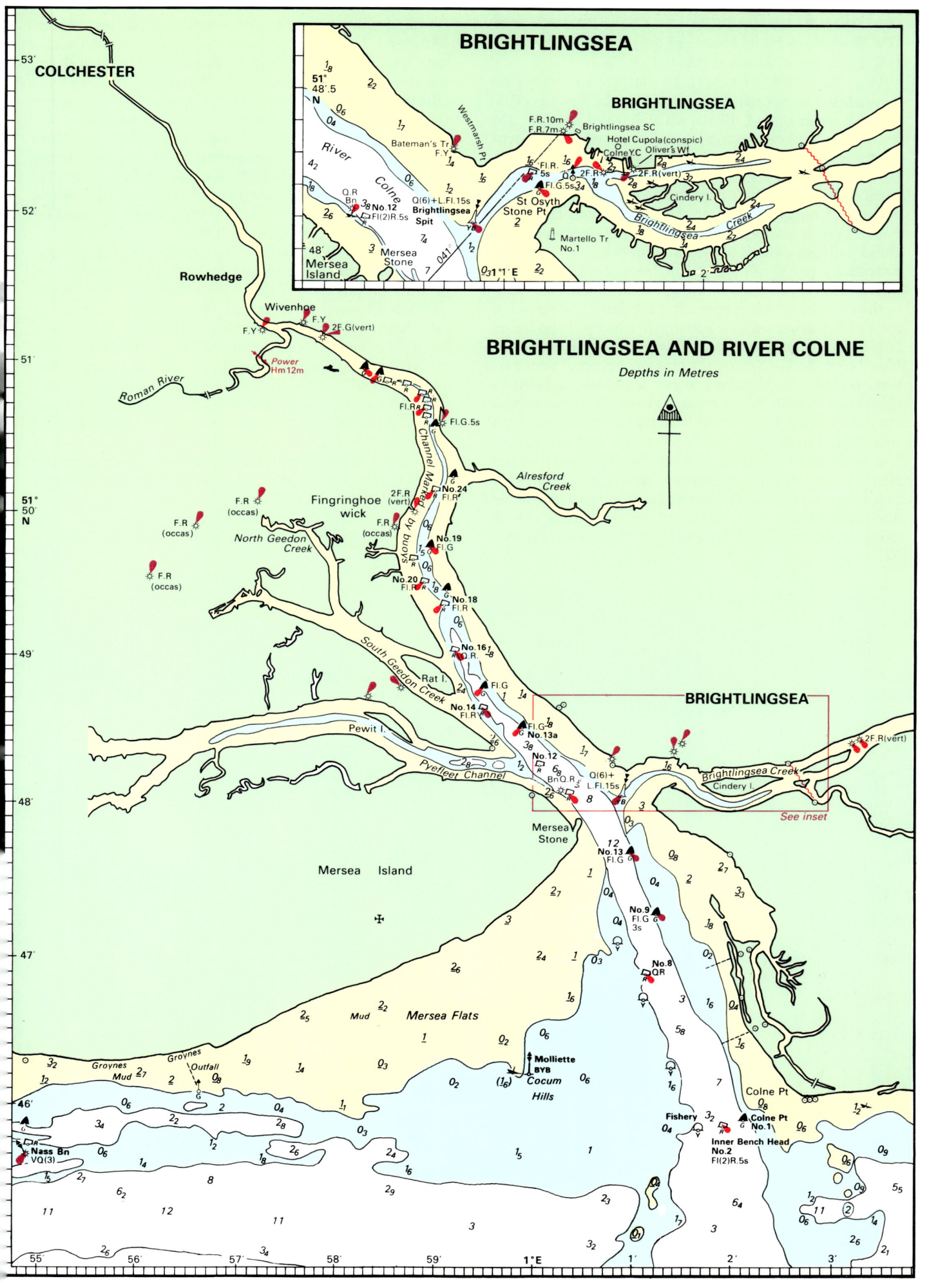

WALTON BACKWATERS   Charts BA 2052, 2695

HW Walton-on-Naze: Dover +¼h.
HW Stone Point: Dover +½h

MHWS 4.2m   MHWN 3.4   MTL 2.3   MLWN 1.1   MLWS 0.4

Approach The approach is marked by the Pye End RW Sph safe water buoy L Fl 10s which lies in 1.2m 335° 2M from Stone Banks R can and topmark buoy when approaching from the S. From the N, 240° 6ca from Landguard N Card buoy (Q) at the entrance to Harwich hbr. The buoy is small and often difficult to pick out. The conspic Naze Tr is situated on the E side of the Naze. From the Stone Banks buoy a course maintained with Harwich ch spire ahead will lead close E of the Pye End buoy.

Entrance 7 ca SW of the Pye End buoy. No 2 R can buoy marks the NE extremity of the Pye Sand and the entrance to the channel which deepens and runs in a SW direction for 1½M, marked on the shelving W side by G con buoys Nos 3 to 7 and on the steep-to seaward side by R can buoys Nos 2 to 8. At No 8 buoy the channel becomes very narrow. Bound into Hamford Water leave Island Point N Card buoy to port. When bound into the Walton Channel keep close to the R can buoys to avoid the spit running out from Island Pt marked by a G con buoy. A R can buoy is laid off Stone Pt. The remainder of the channel to port and stb is marked by withies; the line of moorings indicates the best water. Approx 1.2M past Stone Pt the entrance to the Twizzle running W to stb and Foundry Creek, which dries carries on to the S, leading to the Walton and Frinton YC.

withies; the line of moorings indicates the best water. Approx 1.2M past Stone Point the entrance to the Twizzle running W lies to stb and Foundry Creek, which dries, carries on to the S, leading to the Walton and Frinton YC.

Berthing A mooring buoy may be obtained on application to the CA boatman. At the WFYC quay, which dries out, limited to 2h for visitors. Water hose. There is a basin behind the YC with sluice opening an hour or two before HW by arrangement with Bedwell & Co Frinton (0255) 675873; craft up to 2m draught can lie afloat. In the Twizzle there are piles and a marina (1M from town) operated by Titchmarsh Marina (0255) 672185.

Anchorages Off Stone Pt, leaving a fairway to the W side of the Channel. Care should be exercised if landing on Stone Pt as this is a bird sanctuary. Or anchor elsewhere in Walton Channel or Hamford Water clear of moorings which are laid across the channel and these areas must not be used as an anchorage. Hamford Water uncomfortable in NE winds. There are oyster beds in Kirkby Creek; considerable care must be exercised when selecting an anchorage and guidance be sought from the Notice on the bank and the buoys in the creek marking the limits. Due to movement of ships carrying explosives, Oakley Creek is no longer a recommended anchorage. Landing at the WFYC hard approx HW ±2h, shops ¼M open 7 days a week in season. All facilities.

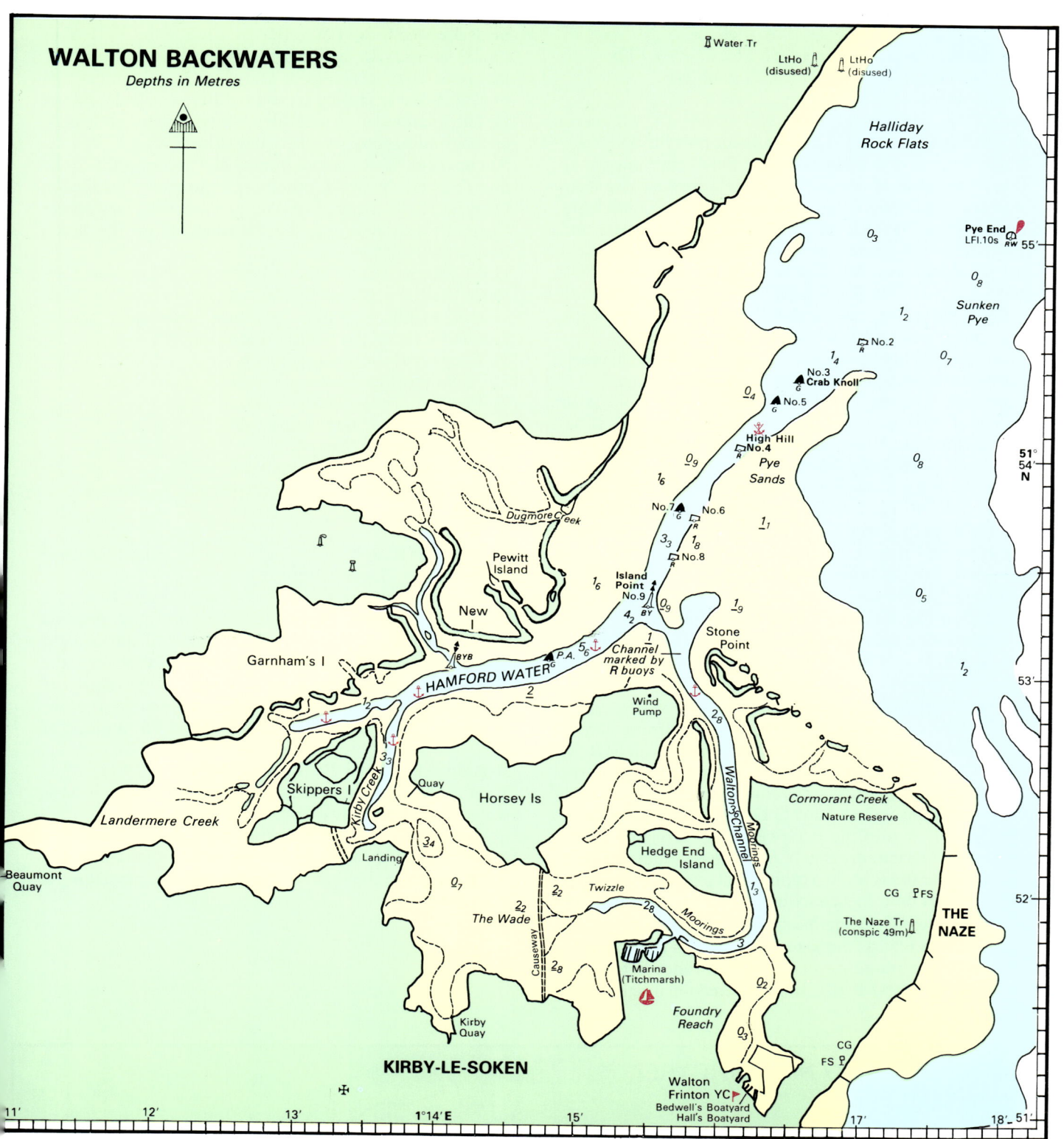

HARWICH   Charts BA 1491, 1593, 2052, 2693

HW: Dover +¾h
DS: Landguard Pt Dover +5½h Flood, −½h Ebb
DS: Dover (Cork buoy) −6h SW, +¼h NE:
(Naze) +6¼h S, −¼h N
MHWS 4.0m   MHWN 3.4   MTL 2.2   MLWN 1.1   MLWS 0.4

Accessible at all times. This is a major port for both ferry traffic and heavy container vessels. Small craft must at all times keep clear of commercial vessels approaching from seaward or manoeuvring within the hbr area. Harwich hbr Patrol vessel "Godwit" VHF 11 will provide advice and assistance when requested in addition to the special yacht patrol which operates May to Sept at weekends 0800-1600. Harwich Hbr Radio VHF 71 is extremely busy with commercial operations and should not be used by pleasure craft but it is advisable to monitor the frequency.

Yachts should not be navigated in the deep water channels and when crossing them, should do so at right angles.

Approach Well marked. From the S by night make good course of 355° from the Medusa G con buoy (Fl G 5s) towards the Inner Ridge buoy (Q R) to avoid the unlit Stone Banks and Outer Ridge buoys.

From the E keep 3ca S of the deep water channel to the Cork buoy QR, leave close stb maintaining a course made good 270° to pass well S of Y lighted deep water channel buoys to the Pitching Ground buoy Fl(4)R 15s and on to pass close S of the Inner Ridge buoy QR.

From the N at or near LW, stand out from shore to pass seaward of the Wadgate Ledge G con buoy Fl(4) G 15s before crossing the deep water channel between The Platters and Rolling Ground buoys and join the yacht track described below.

Entrance From the Inner Ridge buoy the required yacht track leaves all channel marks close to stb turning NW at Landguard N Card, more Nly at Cliff Foot R can Fl R 5s, then NW from N Shelf QR to the Grisle buoy and on to the Guard buoy. From thence the channel must be crossed to the Shotley Spit S Card buoy Q before taking either the N route to follow into the R Orwell or to turn due W for Shotley Pt Marina, or, stay N of the deep water channel, continue into the R Stour keeping well clear of manoeuvring ships and unlit mooring buoys.

Berthing There is a large marina at Shotley Pt. From the Shotley Pt bn take a course towards Ganges buoy Fl G 5s ½M W before rounding up for the entrance between 2 bns, BYB to P and B stb. Inogon directional lights lead directly to the lock, control is by traffic lights. Channel is dredged to 2m LWS. Berths, Clubhouse, VHF M or (0473) 348982. All facilities.

It is possible to lie alongside Harwich Quay 1h either side of HW. Good fendering is essential and vessels should not be left unattended as considerable wash may be experienced from passing vessels. Quay dries LW.

Anchorages Well inshore immediately to seaward of the moorings on the Shelf, otherwise upstream of Parkeston Quay in the R Stour. Landing at Harwich Quay where Custom's clearance may be obtained, or on the beach beside the HTSC.

HM Customs (0255) 502246/598966 or "Freephone Customs Yachts". Special Sound Signals are used by large vessels within the hbr area and yachtsmen should familiarise themselves with these as follows:

1) Four rapid short blasts + one =
   "I am turning short round to S"
2) Four rapid short blasts + two =
   "I am turning short round to P"
3) One prolonged blast =
   "I am leaving berth or mooring"

For other Marinas etc see entries for R Stour and R Orwell.

RIVER STOUR   Chart BA 2693

HW Mistley: Dover +1¼h
MHWS 4.2m   MHWN 3.4   MTL 2.2   MLWN 1.0   MLWS 0.3

Entrance Leaving Parkeston Quay to port proceed upriver in a W direction. The river is broad and straight for a distance of 2.5M until approaching Wrabness; the channel is buoyed and lit as far as Mistley. There is approx 0.6m at Mistley. The R Stour is navigable as far as Manningtree, 5M upriver of Wrabness, for 1.2m draught at HW.

Berthing (1) Shotley Point (0473) 348908 and VHF 37 or 80. Entrance well marked. Call for instructions to lock which is continuously manned. All facilities.
(2) Wrabness. A vacant mooring buoy may be used for a short period but yachts should not be left unattended.

Anchorages In the R Stour clear of the channel, riding lt essential.

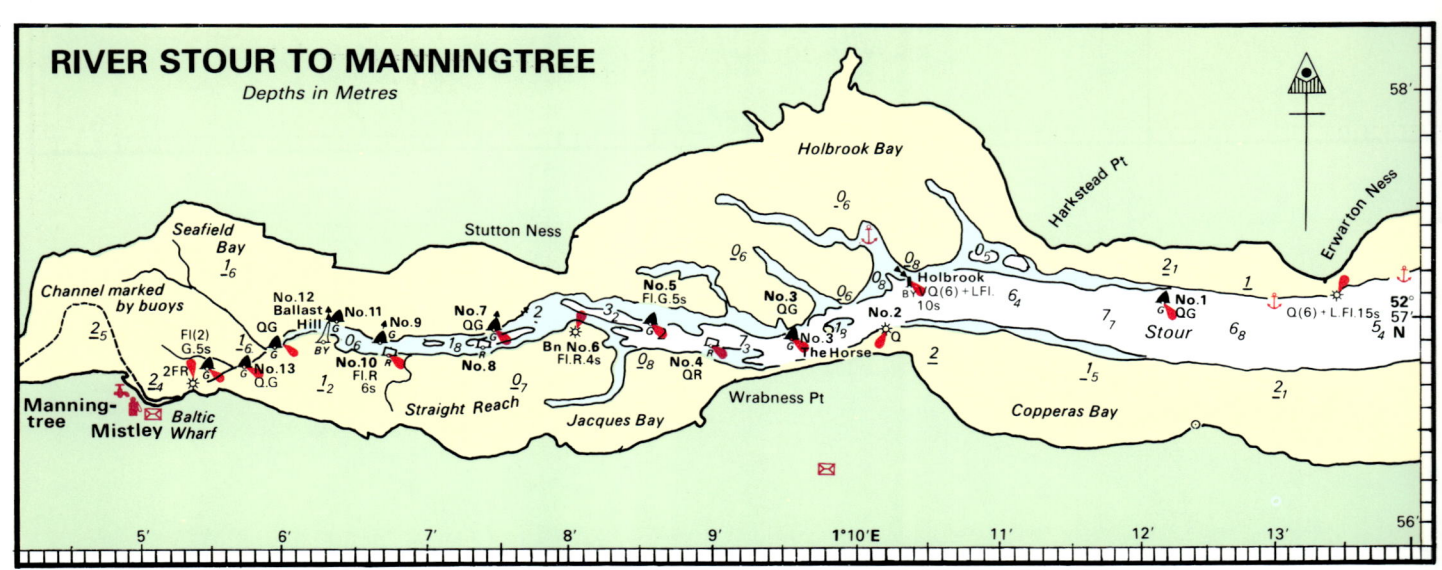

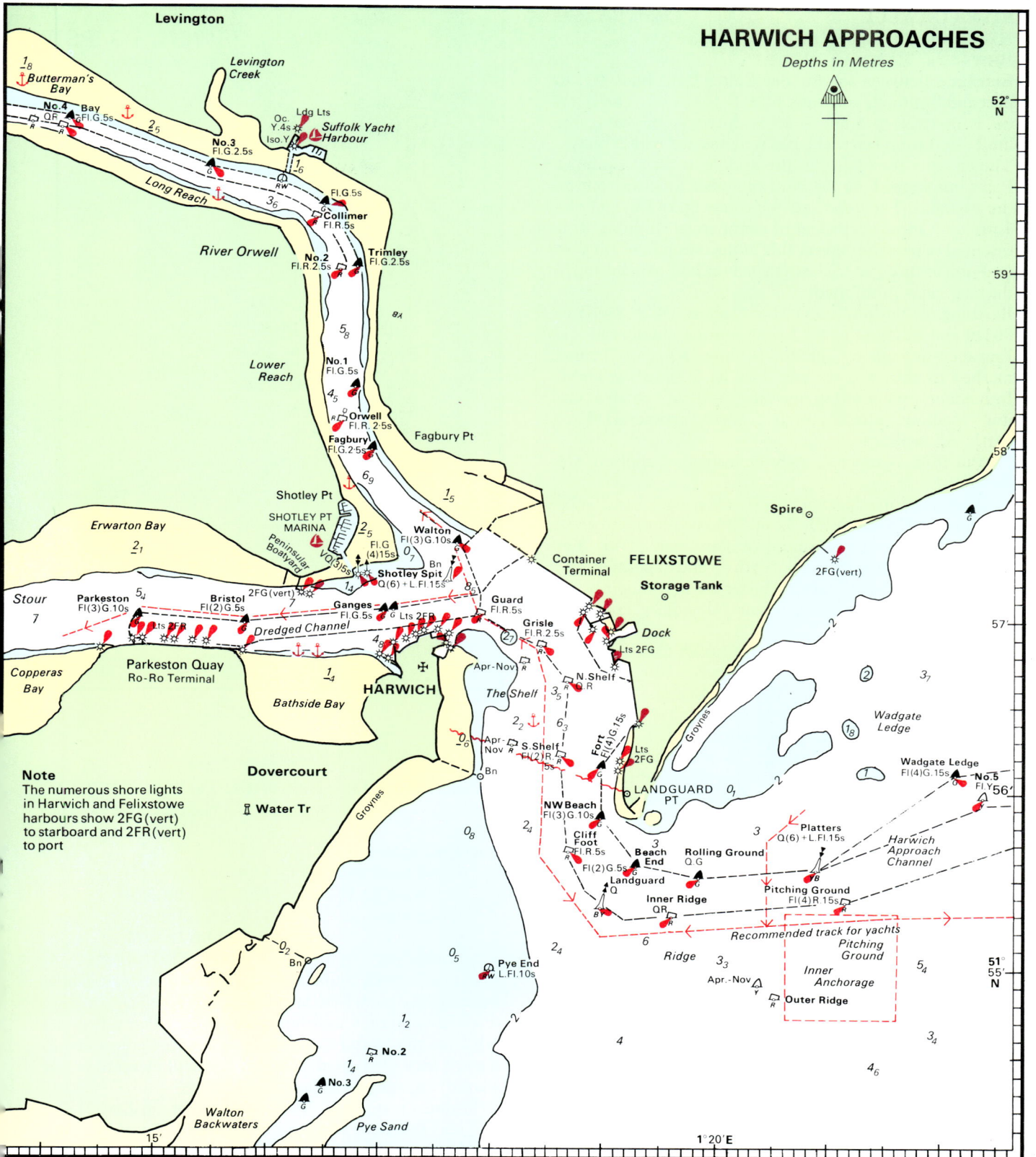

RIVER ORWELL

Charts BA 2693

HW Ipswich: Dover +1h

MHWS 4.2m MHWN 3.4 MTL 2.3

Entrance Between the Shotley Spit S Card buoy (Q) to port and Walton G con buoy Fl(3) G 10s to stb. The channel is dredged to 5.8m as far as Ipswich, the navigable limit 9½M from Harwich. It is well marked with lt buoys. The channel runs fairly in the middle as far as Collimer Point but above here the mud extends a long way out on the stb hand. The flood and ebb run at up to 3kn and pleasure craft must keep clear of commercial shipping. It is essential to pass the correct side of the G con buoy off Potter Point as this spit dries extensively at LW. Anchoring in the channel is prohibited.

Berthing (1) Suffolk Yacht Hbr Nacton (0473) 88465 or 88240 and VHF 37 or 80 during normal daytime hours. Entrance marked by sph RWS buoy, 1.2m in channel marked by port and stb bns. Ldg lts Y shown at night. Immediately on entering hbr turn to stb and berth at visitors' pontoon adjacent to fuel berth, contact HM for berth. All facilities.

(2) Pin Mill. A mooring may be available: apply to CA boatman.

(3) Woolverstone Marina. MDL (Marinas) Ltd (0473) 84206 or 84354 and VHF 37 or 80 have pontoon berths and swinging moorings. Entrance at any state of tide. For visitors' berth call on VHF or berth on end of pontoon and immediately contact Marina Master for berthing instructions. All facilities including repairs, chandlery, crane and laundrette.

(4) Fox's Marina at the W side in Ostrich Creek near No 12 buoy. Enter channel S of No 12 buoy, through dredged channel with approx 2m MLWS. Visitors' berth by arrangement, VHF M Ipswich (0473) 689111. All facilities including repairs, spraying and hoist.

(5) Ipswich New Cut, Debbage Yacht Services, Ipswich (0473) 601169. Enter New Cut on port hand when close to Dock Gates leaving sph R buoy close to port to avoid spit on stb hand. Access from half-tide for 1.2m draught; limited number of pontoon berths but boats dry out in soft mud. All facilities including repairs, 20 ton crane and boat transport.

(6) At the N end of Ipswich Dock, Neptune Marina (0473) 34578/84366 VHF M, has some facilities including lift out cranage and road transportation but no fuel or chandlery. Berths by prior arrangement. Enter through lock as for Wherry Quay.

(7) Oysterworld Centre offers most facilities, except petrol (0473) 230109, VHF M. Visitors' berth by prior arrangement.

(8) Ipswich Dock. Limited berthing available. Enter through lock. Contact Wherry Quay VHF M or (0473) 53999 or Ipswich Port Radio, VHF 14 prior to arrival. Advance notice required for entry into Dock. HM Customs (0473) 52837 or "Freephone Customs Yachts".

Anchorages (1) Above Shotley Point on W side opposite No 1 buoy. Shore is steep-to, beware tel cable. Landing on isolated beaches at HW, good shelter in W winds.

(2) In Long Reach on S side, well clear of main channel, show riding lt.

(3) In Pin Mill bay below moorings, riding lt.

PASSAGE NOTES: HARWICH TO SOUTHWOLD

Charts BA 2693, 1543

Passage Lights

Outer Gabbard Lt F	Fl(4) 20s 12m 24M
Shipwash Lt F	Fl(3) 20s 12m 24M
Orfordness	Fl 5s 28m 30M +
	F GR 14m 15/14M
Southwold	Fl(4) WR 20s 37m 22M

Leaving Harwich round Landguard Point keep close N of the buoyed channel and stand on as far as the Platters buoy to avoid numerous shifting shoals E of the Point. Proceed NE from the Platters leaving the Wadgate Ledge buoy to port. A least offshore distance of ½M will thereafter clear all outlying dangers as far as Orfordness.

Orfordness is steep-to. An eddy runs close inshore N and S. Tides run hard and with wind over tide a steep, confused sea is raised. To avoid the Aldeburgh Ridge 7 ca offshore, stand close inshore or pass outside E of the Aldeburgh Ridge buoy.

DS: Dover −6h SW, +¼h NE

To pass inside Sizewell and Dunwich Banks from the S, make a position with Thorpe water tr in line with a grey churchlike building close N of the conspic tr 263° 2 ca, and with Sizewell Nuclear Power Stn main buildings bearing 330°. Thence make good 348° on Minsmere ex CGS (W cottages on S end of Cliff N of Minsmere Level, 52°15'.1 N, 1°37'.8E). Maintain this course, passing 2 ca inside the shallowest part of bank until Southwold Lt Ho comes in line with Southwold Hbr pierheads: this leads clear inside

Dunwich Bank. The shore is sand and shingle, steeply shelving; from N of Shingle Street no inshore shoals, except for the rocky reef projecting from Thorpeness (many lobster pots), to about ¾M S of Southwold Haven entrance. Inshore hazards are clearly visible.

With winds between SW and NW there is good anchorage in 3½ to 5m, sand, anywhere between Sizewell and Dunwich.

RIVER DEBEN   Chart BA 2693
HW: Dover +¼h   DS (offing): Dover +¼h NE, −6h SW
MHWS 3.7m   MHWN 2.9   MTL 2.0   MLWN 1.0   MLWS 0.5
Bar 0.3 to 1m, varying in depth and position. The banks are liable to shift at any time.
Approach The entrance lies between Felixstowe and Bawdsey Cliff. Prominent shoreline features are two Martello trs (marked T and U on Chart BA 2693) to the W, and a radio tr N of the entrance. The lie of the channel alters frequently; there is a safe water offshore buoy (WE Haven) from which the bar buoy (G con) can usually be seen. The entrance is rough in onshore winds and on the ebb: under these conditions entrance should not be attempted without local knowledge. Except in good conditions strangers are advised to arrange for pilotage or to follow in a local vessel of suitable draught and experience: hail to confirm.
Entrance The channel may change dramatically and up to date information should be obtained but if in settled weather on a rising tide entry is attempted unaided the following points may assist. Beware of strong cross currents in entrance which render course keeping hazardous and follow transits where possible. From the Haven buoy continue to head N until the Bar buoy G con is in line with the White Ho (Golf Club) to S of Martello Tr 'T', before turning in. From here (June 1991) lay a course to pass just S of the Bar buoy heading initially for the White Ho (Golf Club), then just S of large farm blds atop the hill on 276°. Maintain this track until the ldg marks (The Metes) come on line; R rectangular board at rear; forward mark W △ on R. Do not turn immediately on to this ldg line but continue for about 50m until closer to W shore then run up river; passing Martello tr 'U' take mid channel when abreast of Felixstowe Ferry SC avoiding obstructions on W shore close to the slip. The Horse Shoal and the Horse Shoal R can buoy are left to port before following the channel near mid stream as far as Shottisham Reach. Above this point the channel is buoyed or marked by perches △ to stb ▽ to port.

Berthing (1) Ramsholt: a mooring may sometimes be obtained from the Boatman. Woodbridge (0394) 34318
(2) Waldringfield (0473) 36260. Visitors' moorings from Waldringfield Boatyard Ltd. Gas, chandlery, provisions and PO. Petrol 1M.
(3) Woodbridge, Tide Mill Yacht Hbr (0394) 385745, on the port hand just beyond Woodbridge Docks. Dredged entrance channel marked by bns carries 2m at MHWN, 3m at MHWS, with 2m inside. In general, if a yacht has enough water to reach Woodbridge there is enough water to enter the Yacht Hbr. Tide gauge. All facilities, including gas and diesel, craneage up to 12 tons. Rly. EC Wed. Most shops stay open during Summer season.
Anchorages Off the E bank at Felixstowe Ferry above the ferry. Ramsholt, clear of the moorings. Off Waldringfield: provisions.

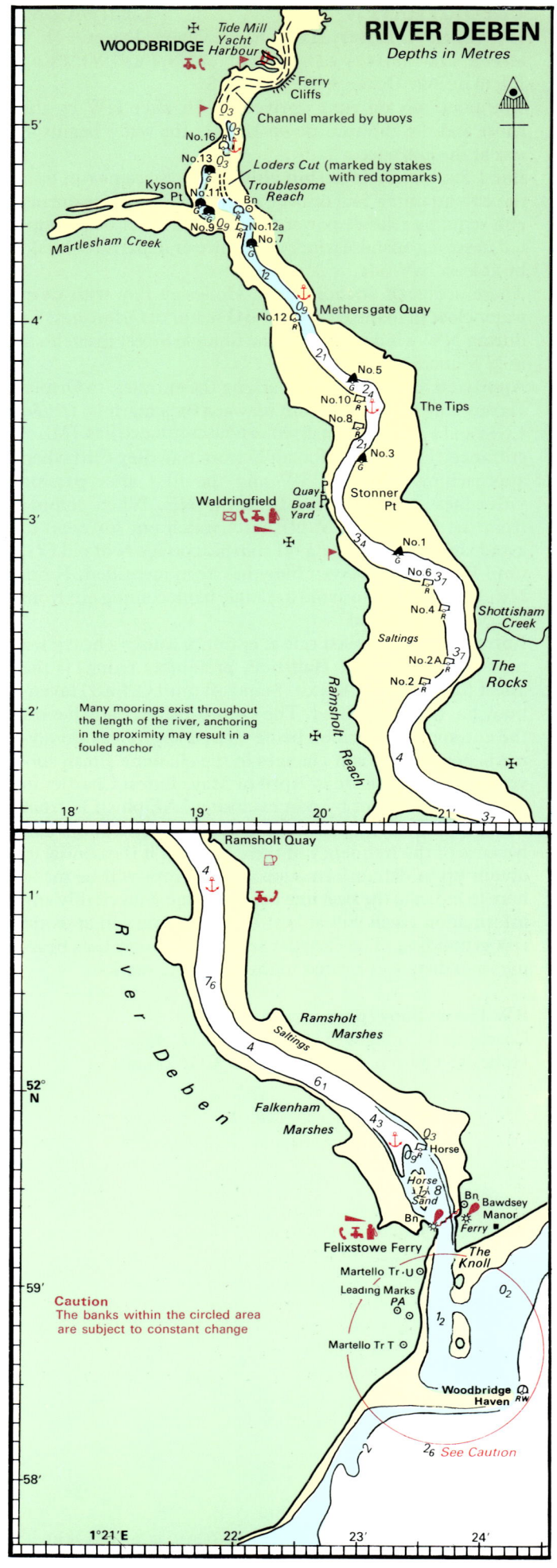

ORFORD HAVEN
Chart BA 2695

HW (Bar): As Dover. HW (Orford Quay): Dover +1h
MHWS 3.2m MHWN 2.6 MTL 1.7 MLWN 0.9 MLWS 0.2
DS in offing: Dover +¼h N, −6h S.

The flood stream runs upriver for 1h after HW by the shore and the ebb runs down 1h after the water begins to rise at the entrance.

Bar 1.2m but liable to shift after a gale. Streams run fast, the ebb attaining 5kn or over at springs. Entrance during ebb requires reliable power, and should never be attempted in strong onshore winds. Entrance or departure should be at least half-tide.

There are good anchorages in Hollesley Bay with deep water close in to the beach in the G sector of Orfordness Lt during NW winds, and S of the Shingle Street martello tr in NW and SW winds.

Approach Shingle Street, marking the entrance to Orford Haven may be located from seaward by a martello tr, old CGS, and a cluster of small white houses situated just 1M S of entrance. The tr is the fourth N from Bawdsey Cliff when approaching from the SW and the first after passing Orfordness when coming from the NE. When coming from the SW keep ½M offshore (watch out for nets) to avoid shingle banks lying off conspic cottage N of old CG, until RW Orford Haven buoy has been identified. From NE, keep ½M off to avoid a shingle bank coming out from the N entrance head.

Entrance Wind against tide at entrance causes a heavy sea near and on the bar. Half-tide, preferably rising, is the safest time for entry or exit. Stand off until Orford Haven buoy has been identified. The Orford Haven buoy lies off the entrance, its position being altered as often as surveying is possible, to suit changes in the channel. Fresh surveys are usually made in April or May. Latest Chartlet in CA Regional File or by post enclosing SAE plus £1 from Aldeburgh YC. The entrance changes most winters and because of the frequency of these changes it is essential to obtain up to date information. No attempt will be made here to indicate the best line because almost inevitably any information given will at best be out of date and at worst risk grounding. The Chartlet referred to above uses bearings and distances related to the following marks:-

RW Haven buoy (posn varies)
Coastguard Cottages (52° 02′.1N 01° 27′.4E)
Hollesley Church Tower (11ca NW CG Cottages)
Bungalow (1ca NE CG Cottages)
Ldg bn (5ca NE CG Cottages, Orange Diamond Topmark)
Prominent grey chimney (1M N of ldg bn)

Once inside the best water is close to the seaward side of the river up to the N of Havergate Is. The channels here may be marked by bns. Water skiing is carried out in Long Reach. The Ore/Alde has 2.7 to 7.6m to Slaughden except in Pigpail Reach and over the horse 4ca S of Aldeburgh Martello tr. When approaching Dove Pt the deeper water is closer to the E bank. Above Slaughden Quay from Cob Is the channel is marked by bns with R cans or G flags (unreliable). Explore only on the flood above half tide.

The W side of Havergate Is has more room for beating up, the E side is straighter.

Anchorages Avoid the mouth where streams run hard.
(1) Approx 1M above N Weir Pt close to the E bank. Streams still run strong and holding unreliable, 4½m.
(2) Just inside Butley River in 2m. Channel narrow; also 1.25m up Butley River to N of Brick Quay on W bank.
(3) In the Gulls, 3½M from entrance on the W side of Havergate Is and E of the entrance to Butley Creek in 7½m.
(4) Just S of Orford, 4½M from entrance in 4½m.
(5) Off Slaughden in Westrow Reach (9M) in 4½m.
(6) For a short time in fine weather between martello tr and YC in 2m.
(7) At Iken Cliff, 1½m in channel at LW. Keep clear of fairway. It is very narrow above the Black Heath Reach. Riding lts advisable.

Care should be taken to avoid anchoring on the starting lines of the AYC at Slaughden and the Orford YC at Orford. The moorings in the Ore and Alde at Orford and Aldeburgh lie athwart the stream, thus to avoid fouling, anchor in the centre of the channel or just below the Aldeburgh YC.

Landing prohibited (1) on Havergate Is, a bird sanctuary; (2) on E side of river from NE corner of Havergate to 1M S of Aldeburgh martello tr, Ministry of Defence.

Landing permitted at Orford and Slaughden quays, most facilities at Aldeburgh. Lay ashore on S side of Slaughden Quay. Waterhose on Quay. Hotels and shops at Aldeburgh and Orford.

Supplies EC Wed.

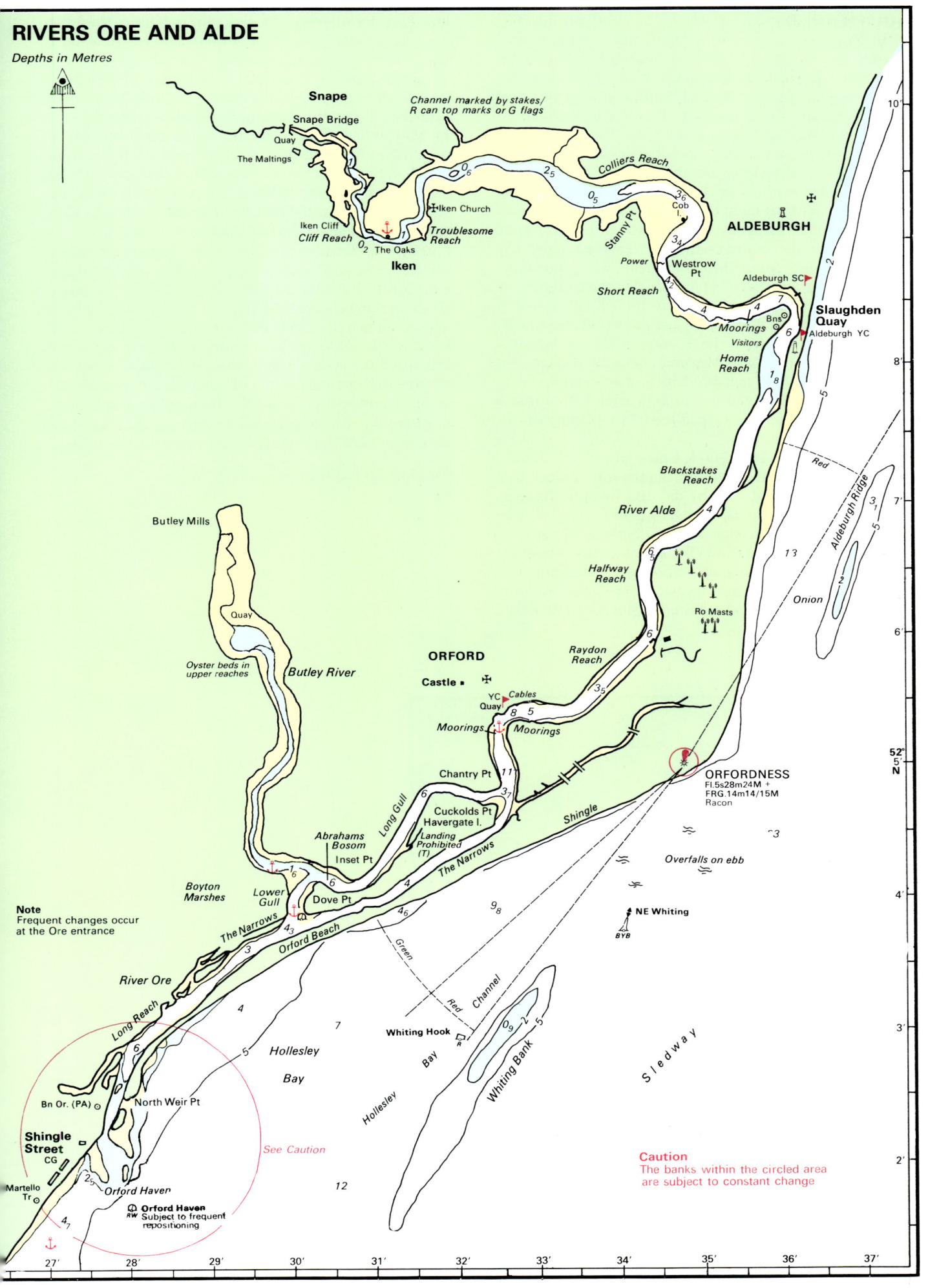

SOUTHWOLD

Chart BA 2695

HW: Dover −1h   DS: Dover +¼h N, −6h S

MHWS 2.5m   MHWN 2.2   MTL 1.5   MLWN 0.9   MLWS 0.4

The hbr is formed by the mouth of the R Blyth which enters the sea approx ¾M S of Southwold, between two piers 137m long and 36m apart. The N Pier foundations are badly eroded and liable to collapse. The banks at the entrance are liable to change with E gales or a period of E winds, and during winter months sand and shingle banks may build up to reduce entry to near HW. Visitors should not attempt entry at night or in poor visibility, or with the wind more than moderate from S through E to N, when the entrance is dangerous on the ebb. It is sheltered in SW to NW winds. Altogether a difficult and potentially dangerous entrance, to be approached with caution.

Approach Arrival should be timed for ½h either side of local HW when the tide is slack and there is the best water. If carrying the ebb from the S, plan to take the new foul flood close inshore off Minsmere ex-CG cottages, or anchor 1-2 ca SE of pier-head in 5 to 6m, sand. Entry should not be attempted before 2-3h after LW. From S and even more from N, keep at least 3 ca offshore for the last mile before entrance.

Entrance Contact HM Mr A Chambers (0502) 724712 VHF 12 for latest information on depths and channel. HM to be appointed. Red flags by day and by night three lts Fl R 1½s indicate entrance dangerous and should only be attempted with local knowledge. Otherwise N pierhead shows Fl G 1½s, S Pierhead QR. It is essential to have the vessel under full command before being committed to entry. The channel is narrow and there is little room to manoeuvre inside; the tide runs up to 3kn at half flood and 5kn after half ebb.

There is a drying sandbank along the outside of the S Pier and a large shoal spreading N and seaward from the N pier. The channel edge with the N shoal can usually be seen from close to. The exact location and direction can change overnight, especially during E winds. Day-to-day information is essential during November to March. During May to September it usually settles down and can be expected to lie somewhere between transits N Pier lt on with Southwold Lt Ho, 015°, and hbr fully open on heading 305°. Least depth at MLWS is then usually about 1m with least water in the last 50-100m to pier-heads. Concrete blocks lie up to 5m out from S pier-head.

Entrance is between the two piers. Unless previously advised otherwise, enter at least 5m clear of S pier-head. Steer for the knuckle at inner root of N pier, pass close to G bns marking concrete blocks sunk off knuckle, and continue close to wall below caravan site. S bank here is shoal. Stand out to mid-river after clearing derelict stage above 4kn speed restriction sign. Follow stb side of river, but keeping well out towards middle until after ferry to Corporation visitors' pontoon outside Harbour Inn, Blackshore.

Berthing On visitors' stage below Harbour Inn, only 1.2m alongside at LWS. Bottom is steeply shelving, hard mud.

Supplies All facilities, repairs. EC Wed.

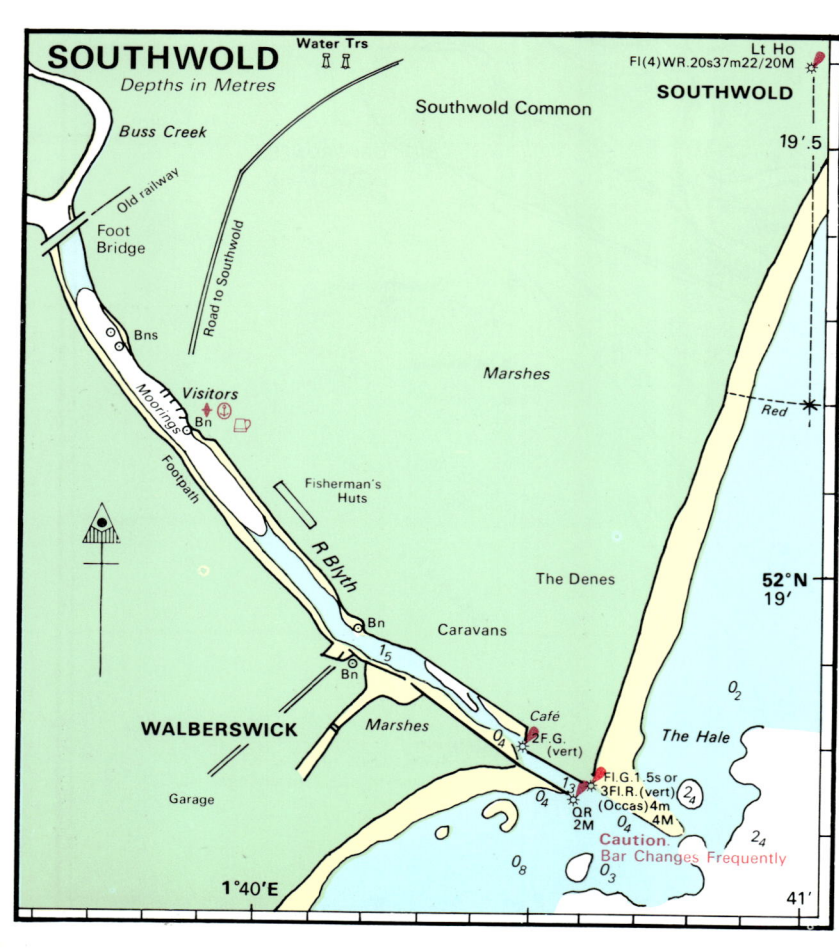

ENGLAND, EAST COAST

PASSAGE NOTES: SOUTHWOLD TO GREAT YARMOUTH
Chart BA 1543

Passage Light
Lowestoft   Fl 15s 37m 28M+FR 30m 18M

From Southwold to Lowestoft there is an inshore passage in 6m approx 1½-2 ca offshore. In poor conditions use the outside route. To keep to the E of Barnard Shoal off Benacre Ness from the S, keep Southwold Lt Ho bearing nothing less than 218° until Kessingland ch bears 297°. This leads ½M clear of the end of the shoal. If Southwold ch is not visible, Covehithe ch bearing 240° leads to the same position, but across the S end of the shoal in less than 5.5m.

From Lowestoft to Great Yarmouth a safe distance of ½M offshore can be maintained.

LOWESTOFT   Charts BA 1543, 1536
HW: Dover −1¾h

DS (S Channel): Dover −6¼h S, +¼h N

MHWS 2.4m   MHWN 2.1   MTL 1.5   MLWN 1.0   MLWS 0.5

Accessible at all times, least depth in entrance 4.3m.

Approach Beware of the shallow patches on the bank E of the N Road. With wind against the tide a nasty sea gets up off Lowestoft Ness opposite the Lt Ho. Approach only from the N via the Hewitt Channel as the Newcome Channel has silted and become unreliable. Vessels should remain inside the buoyed channels as the banks are continually changing and deep water shown on charts outside the channels may have silted.

Entrance With foul wind and ebb tide make the entrance from S pier. Keep N pier just shut in by S pier, enter carrying good way past the S pier-head, and be prepared for eddy. The yacht basin is a cul-de-sac at the SW corner of the hbr. The turreted building on the promenade pier makes a wind eddy and often causes vessels to gybe. Inside the basin there is no room to come about.

A Fl W traffic control lt, which must be obeyed, is shown below the Oc R lt on the S Pier Lt Ho. When this W lt is flashing vessels may leave subject to clearance from hbr control VHF 14 or tel 572286, but none may enter. At all other times vessels may enter but must not leave the hbr. Yachts may pass through the first bridge into the inner hbr when it is opened for commercial traffic. Yachts should not approach the bridge without a G lt on the N wall, neither may they moor in the br channel.

Berthing Yachts should secure to inner S pier pending allocation of a club mooring, but only as a temporary measure, as the bad state of disrepair makes this hazardous. Yachts lie in three tiers on the port side of S basin. Wire hawsers have been run between the three dolphins in centre of basin and S pier, with lines of buoys in between. Secure warps to hawser and appropriate buoy. Lowestoft Cruising Club can offer pontoon berths on the N shore at the W end of the inner hbr. Port VHF 14, 16. Docks Manager (0502) 572286, Customs (NW side of bridge) (0502) 562161, CG (0493) 851338. Weather reports RAF Honington (0359) 6466. There is a dry dock and slipway. Land at steps at town end of basin. The YC has private steps where water may be obtained. All facilities. EC Thur. Lowestoft Hbr bridge opens for yachts giving more than 1h notice by VHF 14 to Lowestoft Hbr Radio or tel (0502) 572286. The bridgemaster may also be contacted in person at the following times:

Mon to Sat	0700	0930	1900	2100
Sun	0700★	0930	1400	1900	2100
Oct to April	0800★			

The rly swing bridge opens on request if clear. Mutford Locks open Wed 1300-1600 on 48h notice and summer Sats 0800-1200. These allow access to Oulton Broads and the southern Norfolk Broads.

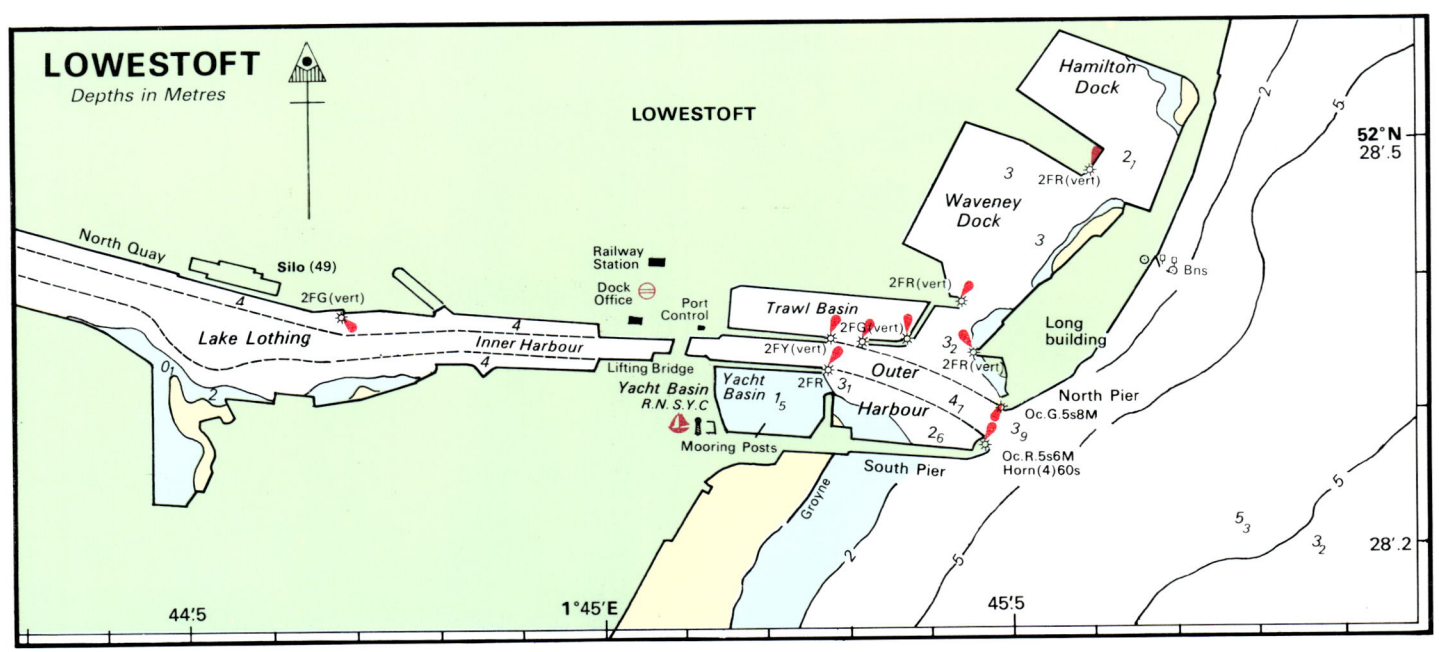

GREAT YARMOUTH

Charts BA 1543, 1536

HW: Dover −2¼h   DS: Dover +6h S, −½h N
MHWS 2.4m   MHWN 2.0   MTL 1.5   MLWN 1.0   MLWS 0.5

This port is the busiest offshore industry support base in the UK. It is essentially a commercial port and no special facilities exist. Published navigational directions must be strictly observed, particularly the one-way traffic system at the hbr entrance. The rectangular building on the E end of the S pier has now been painted white and is illuminated at night. On its roof 3FR vert 2m apart indicate entry prohibited (2B balls vert during daytime). At the root of the S pier is the Port Control Office from which 3 FR vert 2m apart prohibit downstream movement beyond the slipway (3R balls vert in daytime). Also on the S Pier at its E extremity, 2 FR vert 2m apart are in line with 2 FR vert established 25m NW and placed on the top and northern side of the pier. Tidal signals are displayed from S pier head from the white painted building as follows:

Q amber indicates tide flooding between pier heads.
Fl mauve indicates tidal flow in excess of 1kn.
Port Control (0493) 663476, Yarmouth Radio VHF 12 is manned continuously and will advise on tidal and weather conditions.

Radio-equipped yachts should make contact before entering or shifting berth and prior to departure.

Entrance There is 4.3m in the entrance and 4.8m up to the town with up to 1m less during strong SE winds. Small craft can enter at most times, but preferably at slack water; the stream runs up to 4kn or more. It makes up the hbr until 1½h after HW at the pier-head, and out of the hbr until 1½h after LW at the pier-head. Entering with the flood, beware of the eddy which sets across the S pier-head towards the N pier. Entrance should not be attempted in strong SE winds, when a dangerous sea occurs especially on the ebb tide. Passage under sail within the port limits is not normally permitted. Anchoring in the hbr prohibited except in emergency. Vessels are strongly advised to keep an anchor cleared ready to drop especially if navigating up-tide of the bridge.

Berthing If clearing Customs, report to the Waterguard on the Fish wharf. Visitors should not berth on Bunns Quay but on newly repaired wall at N end of Town Quay close to S side of Haven Br. Space may sometimes be found at the S end of the Fish wharf among the local workboats, or on W Quay, but both are subject to heavy wash and risk of damage by manoeuvring ships. Beware of vandalism. There are boatyards and marinas above Haven Bridge. Port dues and Norfolk Broads temporary licences at The Haven Commissioners, 21 South Quay.

Supplies All facilities and stores, EC Thur.

Up-river, Great Yarmouth is the northern gateway to the Norfolk Broads via the R Bure (two fixed bridges, headroom about 2m at HW) and R Yare. (Lifting bridge at E end of Breydon Water). To enter, the lifting Haven Bridge (headroom when closed 4.2m at MLWS, 2.4m at MHWS) must be passed, preferably at slack water. For the S rivers, the new Breydon Lift Bridge must also be passed. This lifts in conjunction with the opening of the Haven Bridge. Yachts are expected to fit in with booked openings for commercial shipping if possible: contact the Bridge Officer (VHF 14 or (0493) 855151 in office hours). Bridge signals control the passage of traffic as follows:

a) Southern side of E Pier: 3 FR vert signal, freedom of passage to Northbound vessels.
b) Northern side of W Pier: 3 FR vert signal, freedom of passage Southbound.

Priority at all times is given to shipping and yachts must keep clear. Keep to marked channel across Breydon Water.

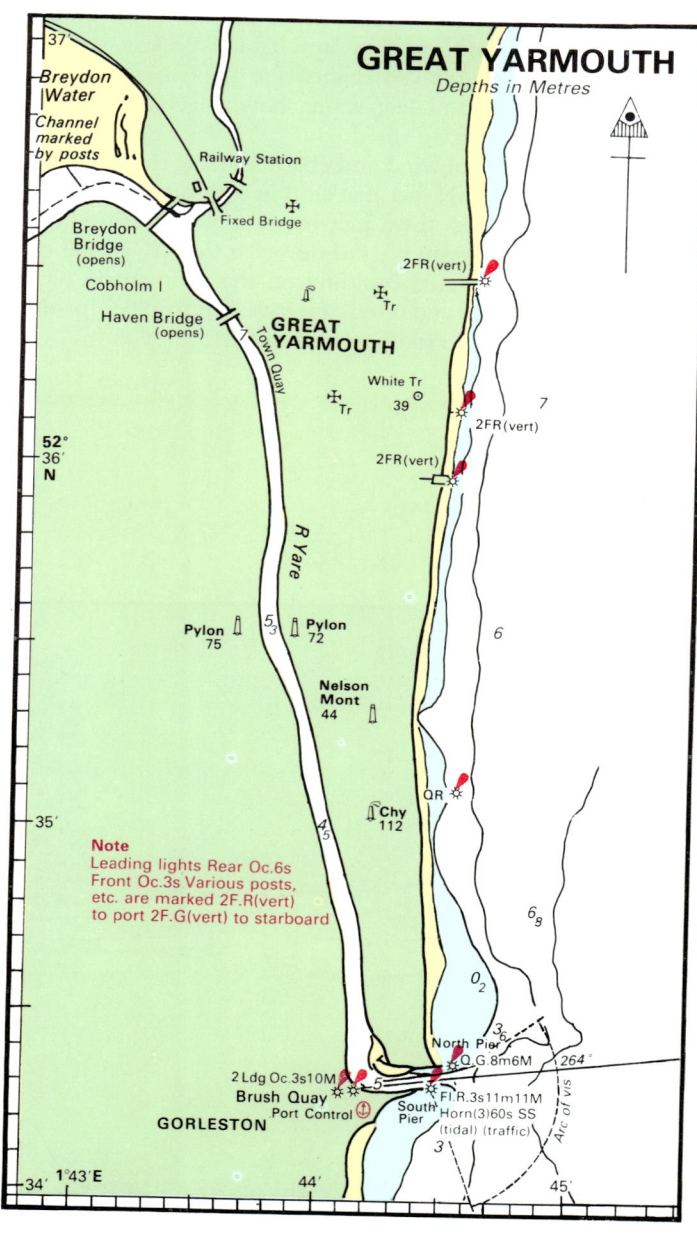

NORFOLK COAST Charts BA 108, 106

Yarmouth Road	DS: Dover +6h S, −¼h N
Cromer	DS: Dover +4½h ESE, −1¼h WNW
Smith's Knoll	DS: Dover −5¾h SE, +½h NW

Inshore, the tidal streams run parallel to the coast and they run true in the channels parallel to the coast. In the outer channels the streams run true when they are strongest, but there is a set across the shoals towards the beginning and end of each stream. The SE stream changes through SW to NW, and the NW stream changes through NE to SE. On this coast generally the NW stream is strongest at LW by the shore, and the SE stream strongest at HW.

Blakeney Overfalls DS: Dover −2h W, +3h E

The inshore Wash streams and the Norfolk coast streams meet and separate near Scolt Head.

W of Scolt Head	DS: Dover −6h E, +¼h W
E of Scolt Head	DS: Dover +4¼h E, −2h W

Caution North Norfolk. Before starting on passage to the N Norfolk coast, consider that no hbr there is accessible during fresh winds appreciably N of E or W and some become dangerous before this. It should also be kept in mind that, hbrs along this coast dry at low water, adding further to problems likely to develop in worsening weather. Under bad conditions the outer entrances are a mass of broken water, and marks and buoys become very difficult to see. Grounding can easily result in the loss of the vessel. Conditions in entrances are rapidly worsened when the ebb begins or if there is any swell running from an onshore blow. Under these conditions entrances may be unsafe even in a light breeze. The most dangerous conditions are when there is a lot of water running out, i.e. at spring and surge tides. The nearest alternative safe hbrs are 50M or more away and call for accurate navigation among the sands to reach them. Passage should not be started, even in fine weather, without preparing for this possibility.

It is difficult to assess conditions in the entrances from outside. Blakeney, Wells and Burnham Overy are all very exposed to onshore winds and conditions deteriorate rapidly. Brancaster is more sheltered and usually has appreciably less sea while its long channel is well sheltered once the entrance is gained. In poor conditions avoid Blakeney and Burnham Overy. The choice is between Wells or Brancaster, or staying outside. Wells is lit far enough in to reach a safe anchorage if the bar can be crossed and its marks are fairly easy to see but the sea builds up in the entrance much more quickly than at Brancaster.

Brancaster's greater shelter is largely offset by the difficulty of identifying the small buoys especially in broken water and entry after dark is not possible. If in doubt it is prudent not to attempt either unless it becomes possible to follow a fishing vessel of similar draught.

In safe conditions, boatmen will pilot vessels in by prior arrangement. Tel description of vessel, or, better, advise CG of intended passage so that pilot can check passage past Cromer for ETA.

BLAKENEY Chart BA 108

HW (bar): Dover −4¾h (town): Dover −4½h
DS: Dover −1h NW and W, +6h E and SE

Bar: MHWS 5.7m   MHWN 4.5

14M W of Cromer, 5M E of Wells. Very exposed to winds from a N direction and conditions in the entrance deteriorate quickly. A poor hbr for cruising yachts: most of it dries and any craft drawing more than 1.5m must expect to take the bottom at LW. Without local knowledge this hbr should be approached only under ideal and settled conditions.

Approach From the E, Salthouse ch is sighted when the shingle bank begins; other conspic marks are Blakeney ch with large and small trs, Langham ch tr, turret and FS above trees on skyline 3¼M inland. A G con buoy lies close to the edge of the sand ½ ca NE of a wk.

From the E the shore may be kept close to until abeam of the CG lookout, with a conspic chimney standing on the neck of Blakeney Pt. The Pt is of grass topped sand dunes and where the sand begins the offing should be increased to 2 ca until the G con buoy is sighted marking a wreck. From the E steer just S of the buoy, from W steer to pass approx ¼M N of it to 100m E of the buoy until on a bearing N of W then enter channel. From the W give the Binks, the low sandy pt with a clump of fir trees ½M E of Wells LB Ho, a berth of 1M and make G con buoy.

Entrance Marked by B cyl buoys numbered 2-10 which are left to stb on entering. Shallow, frequently varies in position and depth. Impassable in fresh onshore winds and in lighter ones during the ebb or if a swell is running. In these conditions stranding will probably lead to the loss of the vessel. Should not be attempted by strangers without a pilot except under ideal conditions in a shallow-draft vessel, within 1h before HW at the entrance, in calm weather with good visibility, and with full understanding of the risk of stranding in an exposed position. If notified in advance Maj Andrew, Chairman Blakeney Boatmen's Association (Cley (0263) 740306) or Mr. Stratton-Long CA Boatman (Cley (0263) 740362) will provide pilotage.

Without up-to-date reliable knowledge of its current position, the stranger's only guide to the entrance is the appearance of the sea. The bottom is steep-to, soundings reducing abruptly from more than 7m to nothing, so that the sounder is of little help. Locally used transits are not easily identified and vary. Beware tidal set across the entrance during the last quarter flood. Within the entrance the channel usually trends first towards the SSE then in a SW direction thence towards the S.

Orange floats laid by fisherman on the W side of the channel should be left close to stb. Shallow flats run off a long way NW and W of Blakeney Spit, which should be left to port. The channel is obstructed by mussel lays standing up to 0.8m above the sand and drying at half-tide. The lays are protected by several Fishing Orders and vessels must be certain of sufficient water to pass over without touching. Soundings and the perch to stb marking the entrance to Simpool are the best guides here. Hammond's wk, 1 ca N of Simpool, is ½ ca up on the sand. Past Simpool the channel curves to the E to pass approx 1 ca S of Blakeney Spit, which continually alters in shape. The channel inside the hbr is marked by bns.

Berthing The CA Boatman may be able to provide a mooring in the Pit, SE of old LB Ho, in 1m, 2M to village. The flats inside the hbr cover approx 1.5m to 1m at neaps. Shallow-draft craft able to sit upright can anchor and dry out, but it is a long way from the village, and muddy. Avoid narrow and crowded gut at quay, land from dinghy at hard near quay or in Morston Creek at HW.

Supplies Water, stores, petrol, diesel, chandlery, gas at Blakeney; launching hard, hotel. Water, stores and pub at Morston.

WELLS-NEXT-THE SEA   BA Chart 108

HW: Dover −5h (at Bar)   DS: Dover +4¼h E, −2h W
MHWS 6.0m   MHWL 5.8   MLWN 2.6   MLWS 0.9

Wells is 5M W of Blakeney and is the only lit hbr in N Norfolk. The hbr dries but the quay is accessible to 3m draft craft at MHWS, 1½m draft at MHWN. As with all hbrs on this coast, it should not be attempted by strangers in bad weather without local assistance, conditions may become treacherous on the ebb especially if winds are from a northerly quarter.

Approach From E, pass Blakeney leaving the Binks, a low sandy point with a clump of fir trees, 1M to port. Maintain soundings to keep clear of shallows extending up to 2M offshore. Locate Wells Fairway RWVS buoy Fl every sec, Radar Reflector.

From W make Bridgirdle R can buoy from whence the Wells Fairway buoy lies approx 166° 4½M and ¾M approx outside the channel entrance to Wells.

From the Fairway buoy, Holkham Obelisk and the ch tr are visible among trees which otherwise obscure the town, approx 3M to SW. The two entrance buoys No 1 stb and No 2 port are in transit when sighted from the Fairway buoy.

Entrance Drying sands shift frequently necessitating changes in the buoyage positions. It is therefore essential to identify and follow the marked channel, local fishing craft or the official pilot being ready to assist at appropriate times. Contact the HM, Capt G Smithers VHF 12 (0328) 710655 callsign "Wells hbr radio" for entry and berthing instructions, as there may be restrictions applied on small craft movements especially at times of spring tides to permit the passage of large commercial vessels. Best time to enter is within 2h of HWS or 1½h of HWN preferably on the flood and only in ideal conditions. The channel which dries for much of its length, is well buoyed as follows:-

stb marks, G con, odd numbers 1 - 13
port marks, R can, even numbers 2 - 16

Stb Buoys 3 & 5 Fl G remainder Fl and all porthand marks Fl R. Since these are presently battery operated, some allowance should be made for possible unlit marks. Closer in, bns replace buoys.

The hbr mouth has a conspic W LB Ho with R roof on its W point and close W of this is the CG lookout with an Or balcony. Extending W is a long line of trees on the sand hills fronted by beach huts. To the E, the fir trees on the Binks lie 1½M E of the LB Ho. Follow the mid channel course until opposite the LB Ho, where R bns to port indicate, the channel's turn from SE to SW. Leave buoys 13 and 15 well to stb, keeping close to R bns head towards G Bn by the W shore. Take a long turn to port to pass between buoys 14 and 17 continuing close to R bns as far as No 16 buoy. The quay now lies directly ahead but note that yachts may lie only in the area between the silo and the angle of the quayside, probably alongside another vessel as directed by the HM.

Berthing If an alongside berth is required contact the HM preferably before entering hbr to be certain that a place exists and note that pleasure craft must not be left unattended at spring tides from HW −1½h until all shipping movements have been completed. Alternatively contact, Osprey Marine Services VHF37(M) who have six only visitors deep water moorings in an area just S of the LB Ho. Ladders may be necessary when alongside. Presence of cats, dogs etc on board must be notified to HM.

Supplies Diesel up to 100 galls on request from bowser, 24 hours notice required for larger amounts. Fresh water on request. Repairs, slip, crane, chandlery.

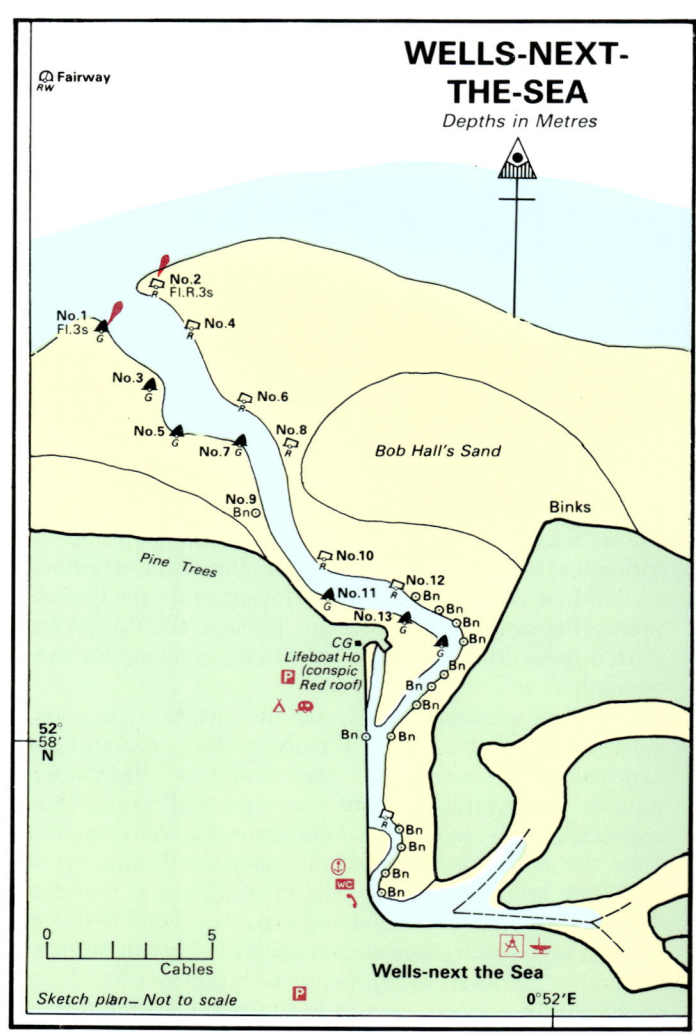

BURNHAM, OVERY STAITHE   Chart BA 108

HW Dover: −4½h   DS: Dover +4½h E −2h W

MHWS 3.7m   MHWN 2.8

A small unlit drying hbr 4½M E of Brancaster, 2½M W of Wells. Not to be attempted without local knowledge except by day and in fine settled weather, in shoal draught craft with the tides making up towards springs.

Approach Conspic marks are Scolt Hd, high sandhills to the W, and Gunn Hill, a high, steep sided, flat topped sandhill close to the E. The highest part of the rising ground inland lies to the W of the hbr. The entrance lies about 255° 2½M from the Wells buoy and 149° 3M from the Bridgirdle buoy. This latter course passes close E of the shallow part of Bridgirdle Shoal and E of the shallow patch extending ¾M offshore N and NW of Gun Hill. The inner part of Bridgirdle Shoal may also be crossed in suitable conditions in about 2m by following the shoreline of Scolt Hd at 4 ca offing and then standing off at ¾M to round the shallows before approaching entrance.

Entrance Banks, channel and buoyage are so variable that no entry directions can safely be recommended. Pilotage and mooring can be arranged by the CA Boatman (0328) 738348.

Berthing Craft to be left unattended or in the care of the boatman should moor as directed off the staithe, accessible to 2m draft at MHWS, 1m MHWN, dries with a hard bottom.

Supplies All facilities.

BRANCASTER STAITHE   Chart BA 108

HW Dover (Bar): −4½h   DS: Dover +1¼h W −6h E

An unlit hbr 10M E of Hunstanton, 12M from Wells. Not to be attempted by strangers except in settled weather, even then preferably with local assistance.

Approach Conspic marks are Scolt Hd, high sandhills, to E; golf clubhouse Lt Fl 5s 8m 3M close to foreshore near entrance. The wk shown on the chart is in three parts, not usually visible at HW; it is marked with a mast and two black balls. The highest part of the rising ground inland lies to the S of the hbr. From seaward make Bridgirdle R can buoy whence the entrance lies about 236° 4½M. In poor visibility, shallowing after passing deeper in Brancaster Road warns that the coast is near. From E, either make Bridgirdle buoy or, in suitable conditions, after passing the entrance to Overy Hbr close the coastline of Scolt Hd Is to 4 ca and follow it at this distance to pass over the inner part of the shoal in about 2m, continuing on this course until the clubhouse bears 187°.

Entrance Banks, channel and buoyage are so variable that no entry directions can be recommended as safe. Pilotage essential. Pilotage and moorings can be arranged by CA Boatman.

Berthing A visitors' mooring may be available: anchored vessels must be prepared to take the ground. Small boatyard, all facilities.

PASSAGE NOTES: CROMER TO RIVER HUMBER

Inshore and along Lincolnshire coast DS: Dover +2h S and SW, −5h NE and N.

Inner Dowsing Lt Ho DS: Dover +3h W turning S, −3h E turning N.

From the Blakeney Overfalls buoy pass between the Docking and Race buoys, leaving the Inner Dowsing Lt Tr approx 1M to port. From a position with the Protector Overfalls buoy 1M to port, the Rosse Spit buoy marking the approach to the R Humber will be sighted. Make for Haile Sand buoy before altering course to westward to enter buoyed channel. Off lying banks whilst not directly dangerous to yachts may present heavily breaking seas in bad weather and should be avoided. Oil and gas installations offshore must be passed at a greater distance than 500m. At night these are lit and a main Lt Fl 15s morse U indicates their position; in fog, horn 30s morse U.

Passage Lights

Newarp Lt F	Fl 10s 11M
Happisburgh	Fl(3) 30s 41m 14M
Dowsing Lt F	Fl(2) 10s 23M
Spurn Lt F	Q(3) 10s 8M

THE WASH   Charts BA 108, 1200

The spring tide range about 7m and neaps 2.7m, so that it is safe to expect to find 2m more than charted at MLWN.

In main channels DS: Dover +1½h in, −4¾h out

Approach From the E: (1) Docking Channel, the ship route and well buoyed, but a long way round.

(2) To the Woolpack R can buoy Fl R 10s, N of the Middle Bank, thence head in a SWly direction towards the Roaring Middle Lt Fl Q Bell. This passage is narrow and seas break on both sides in NE winds.

(3) Through the Bays, between Middle Bank and Sunk Sand. There is approx 5m at LW between the banks but less than 2m in the approach from the E. The channel is not buoyed and is difficult to follow.

(4) Inside the Sunk Sand at MLWS approx 1.5m of water can be found, more than shown on chart. At LW keep 2-3 ca off W sands and follow the coast round Gore Pt. Approx 1M N of Hunstanton there is a mussel bank which runs out from the land and stands out black when uncovered. As Hunstanton is approached keep 2 ca approx from the shore and pass close W of Y can sewer buoy off S beach. From this buoy make good 240° passing close to the Kings Lynn No 3, E card Lt buoy. If bound for Kings Lynn leave buoy to stb and follow channel into Cork Hole. When bound for Boston or Sutton Bridge, leave No 3 buoy to port and proceed by Kings Lynn No 1 N card buoy. From the N, Lynn Well is the best approach.

In general the Wash is not easy once out of the main channels. It is best to wait until half flood before entering any of the rivers, unless a smack is followed. (Boston smacks draw approx 2m).

ENGLAND, EAST COAST

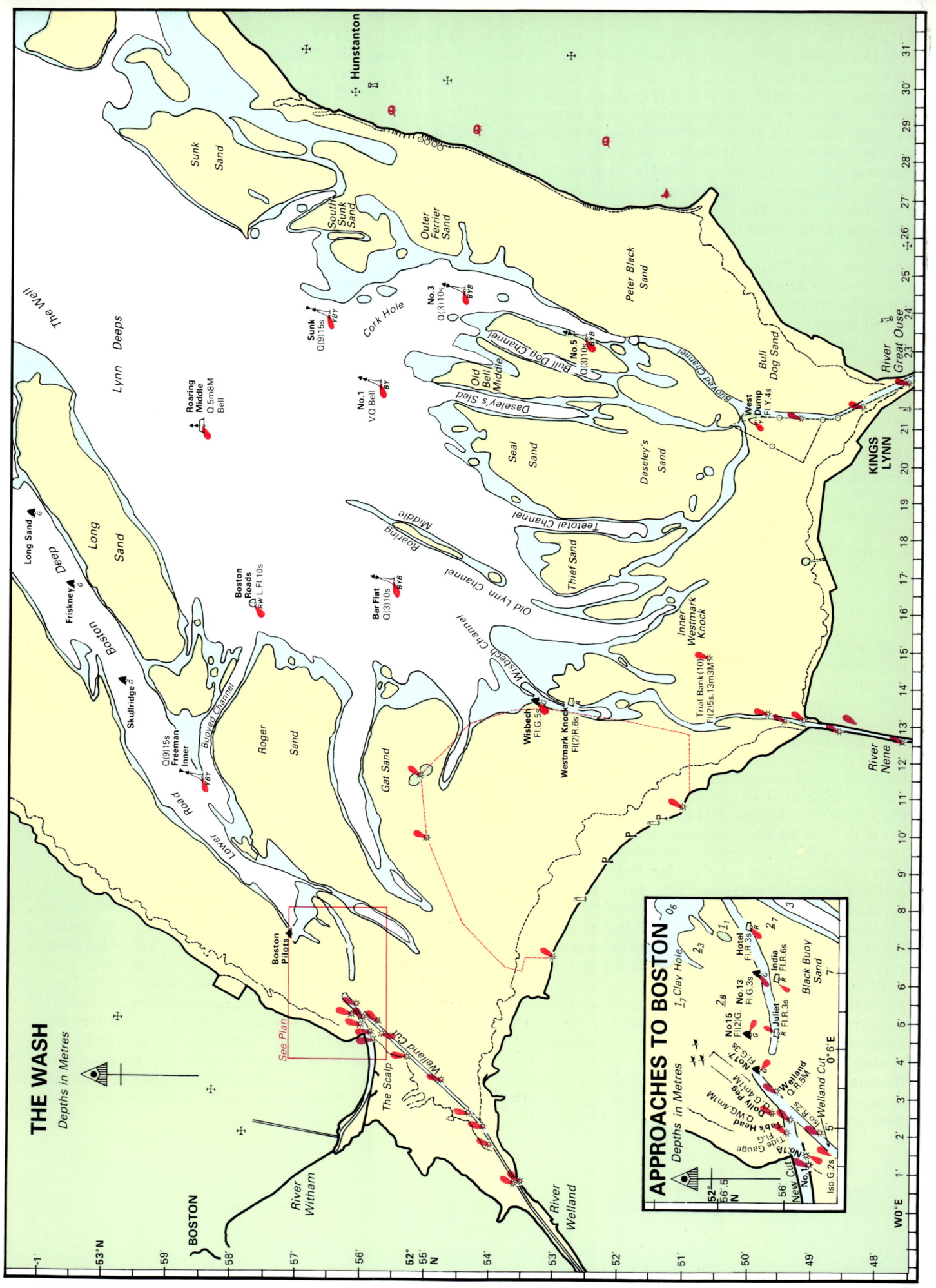

KINGS LYNN

Chart BA 1200

HW: Dover −4¾h

MHWS 6.9m   MHWN 5.1   MTL 3.7   MLWN 1.8   MLWS 1.0

The channel is constantly changing, but it is well buoyed. 1.5m draught vessels can get up about 2h after LW. In Lynn Cut and the river 9-10h ebb and 2-3h flood are usual; ebb in the river may run up to 5 kn. The hbr is open at all times subject to draft. The dock is normally open HW −1½h to HW and this is the best place to stay (accommodation limited, substantial entry charges). Yachts may be left here with the permission of the Dock Master (0553) 691555 or 775041. Anchoring is prohibited below the docks or in the vicinity of the Quays. Drying berths available at S Quay in the centre with the permission of HM (0553) 773411. Do not leave craft unattended. Friar's Wharf - Boat Quay is now closed.

VHF 14,16 normal working hours and in addition HW−4h to HW (Docks HW−2½h to HW+1h).

Between the training walls and the docks the river is spanned by electric cables 47m clearance above MHWS.

Supplies Facilities limited. EC Wed.

FOSDYKE

Entered by the Welland Cut which runs SW from the Boston R at the Cut end. It is marked by lighted bns on top of stone banks on either hand, at approx 64m intervals. Strong spring tides (4kn, less at neaps), navigable from HW −2h to HW +3½h for vessels up to 1.3m draught Substantial commercial traffic now using the river which is therefore unsafe to use as an anchorage overnight. A possibility exists for mooring above the new br by arrangement with the HLR or boatman.

BOSTON

Chart BA 1200

HW:Dover −4¼h

MHWS 6.6m   MHWN 4.8   MTL 3.3   MLWN 1.8   MLWS 0

Approach The Freeman channel is the best approach. Wainfleet Swatchway needs care and should be attempted only in clear weather. Parlour channel is unbuoyed and should not be used without local knowledge.

Entrance The channel leading from High Horn (No 9 G con Fl G 3s) buoy to No 17 G con buoy, Fl G 3s is constantly changing but is well buoyed and lit. The top end is shoaling each year and in places almost dries at LW. Half flood is the best time for entering the Cut.

Anchorage 5ca SW High Horn buoy to await tide. Berthing Not available in Boston Dock except in emergency. Very few moorings available in hbr. Yachts which can lower their masts are advised to do so by the dock then pass into fresh water at the Grand Sluice, first and second levels being approx −2½h and +2½h HW Boston respectively. A berth is usually available at Boston Marina immediately after passing Grand Sluice. Vessels with fixed masts may dry out at pontoon on E bank just above the Swing br or (Rly) normally left open. Further navigation is prevented by 3 fixed brs before the sluice. There is an underwater cable near St. Botolph's Ch. Due to variability of levels in Grand Sluice it is advisable to contact the Sluice Keeper before planning a visit, (0205) 64864 or VHF 74. If in difficulty on arrival secure if possible near HM office at dock entrance and seek advice HM (0205) 62328, VHF 16 (Boston Dock).

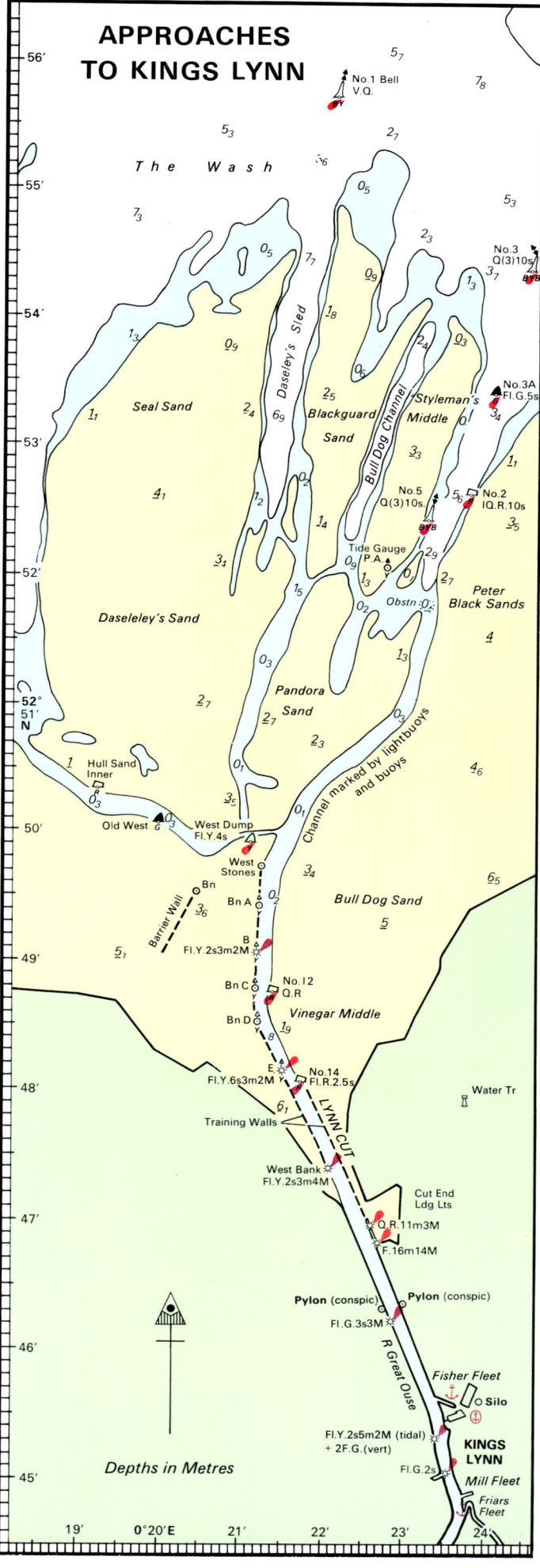

ENGLAND, EAST COAST

WISBECH
Chart BA 1200

HW: Dover −4¾h

MHWS 7.4m MHWN 5.5 MTL 3.5 MLWN 2.2 MLWS 0.6

Vessels of 4.8m draught (at springs) and 3.4m (neaps) can reach Wisbech. The entrance is not easy for a stranger. The Outer Gat tends to extend to the E, the bns and buoys are frequently moved without notice to follow changes in the channel.

Approach The Wisbech channel leaves the Old Lynn channel S of the Bar Flat E Card buoy Q(3) 10s; from there it is 225° 2.6M to Wisbech No 1 G con buoy (Fl G 5s). Thence inwards West Mark Knock R can (Fl (2) R 6s) to port and on stb hand E Card buoy (VQ), 178° leads to Fenland G con buoy(Fl(3) G 10s). Leave this 2-3 ca to stb and the perches after it a good ca to stb since they are well up on the mud.

Entrance The Channel passes between two 19m trs and enters the Wisbech Cut, whence it is 3½M to Sutton Br, 12M to Wisbech. Fl lts R to port, W to stb, are shown from posts along the cut. Spring tides run 4kn in the R; neaps very much less. There is a swing br at Sutton Br, letter 'B' (−...) on horn to open. Radio watch from HW−3h to HW, Sutton Br VHF 16,9,14 or tel Sutton Br 350 364 or 2182/2246 kHz.

Berthing Sutton Br: if intending to use the port, contact HM in advance. Wisbech: moor at quay on port hand opposite the grain elevator and contact HM.

Supplies Facilities limited, fuel from town in cans - gas available.

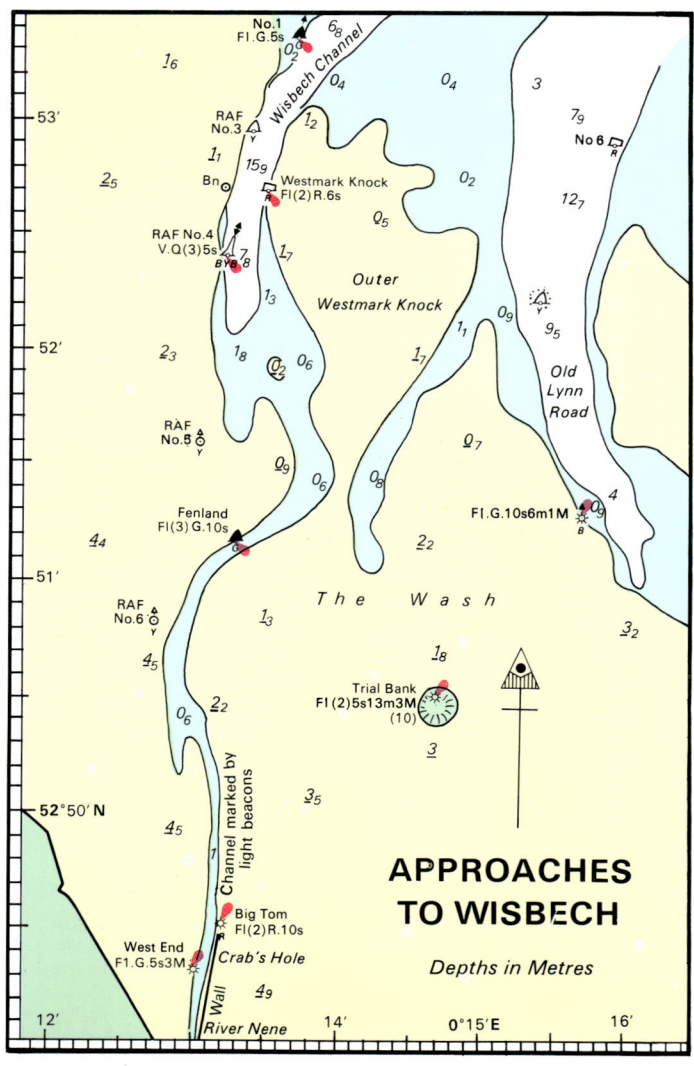

APPROACHES TO WISBECH

Depths in Metres

RIVER HUMBER
Charts BA 107,109,1188,3497

HW (at Grimsby) Dover −5¼h

MHWS 7.0m MHWN 5.5 MTL 4.0 MLWN 2.7 MLWS 1.0

Spring tides run at 4½kn at Immingham, 5kn at Hull. From S after sighting Rosse Spit R can buoy, Fl(2) R 5s, care should be taken if early on the flood to avoid being set into shoal water on the port hand. Keep well to the N and leave No. 2 Haile Sand R can buoy Fl(3) R 10s to port. The Chequer Shoal Lt float VQ (6) +L Fl 10s should then be seen and passed on either side. Entering the fairway of the Humber, pass between the Bull N Card Lt float (VQ Horn(2) and Spurn Pt, keeping fairly close to the latter, taking care W of Immingham to avoid Foulholme Spit and Skitter Sand.

From N, if at first hour of flood abeam of Dimlington high land or Kilnsea trs, steer for the Spurn Lt float. Keeping well outside the Binks, a bank of large boulders and shingle over which a confused and broken sea is raised by wind over tide conditions. Give Outer Binks E card buoy a wide berth to stb. Thence to Grimsby, Immingham and Hull, the river is well lit and buoyed and the channel free from obstructions.

Berthing

(1) **Humber Mouth Yacht Club.** Drying moorings are reached via a channel which runs roughly N-S. The channel is marked by B stb hand barrel buoys (about 14 in number). It is essential to identify them before attempting to reach the moorings. The best approach is on line from the Haile Sand Fort to the Cleethorpe Sewer Outfall. Following this course will result in crossing the line of the marker buoys between Nos. 2 and 3. The anchorage is safe for boats which can take the ground though it is uncomfortable at HW springs when the Haile Sand Bank covers.

(2) **Hull Marina** Accessible to craft of 2m draught 4h either side of HW. Anchor outside if waiting. Outer entrance marked by 3 traffic signal lights (2G over W to enter). Marina is westward (up river). Allow for strong set, 4kn, past outer entrance. Lock operates on request HW ±3h if this is between 0700 and 2200 VHF 37(M) "Hull Marina". Pontoons have electricity and water, fuel barge nearby. Travel hoist (0482) 25048.

From seaward leave Spurn Pt between LW and half flood to carry favourable stream to Hull.

(3) **Grimsby** The entrance is marked by hydraulic tr 94m. Vessels enter hbr by lock on stb side of tr available HW −3½ to +2½h. Yachts wait on left of entrance to disused E lock in the Royal Dock Basin which is partly tidal and recommended for a short stay only. Minimum depth approx 6ft at LW. The basin is uncomfortable in strong E winds.

Contact Grimsby Royal Dock VHF 9, 18 or (0472) 359181 (or 361344 out of office hrs) for permission to enter Royal Dock and proceed via the Union Dock to S arm of the Alexandra Dock under new road br (ht 10ft) to Grimsby Marina (0472) 360404.

Visiting yachts with fixed masts may be directed to alternative berths or accommodated by the Grimsby Cruising Association (0472) 343232. Pontoons have been established in NW corner of the Fish Dock. Entrance is through the lock at HW ±2h at no charge but expensive at other times.

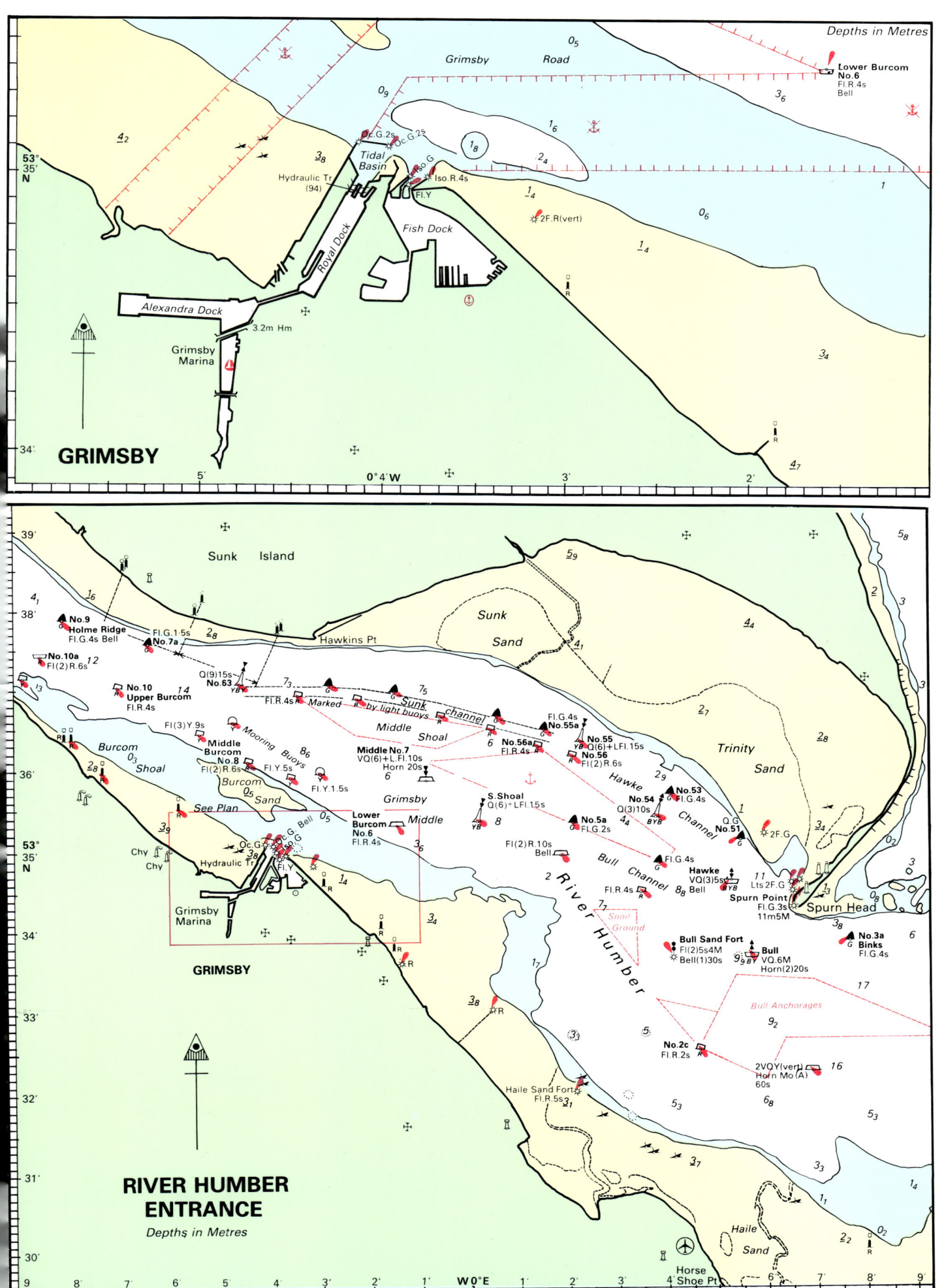

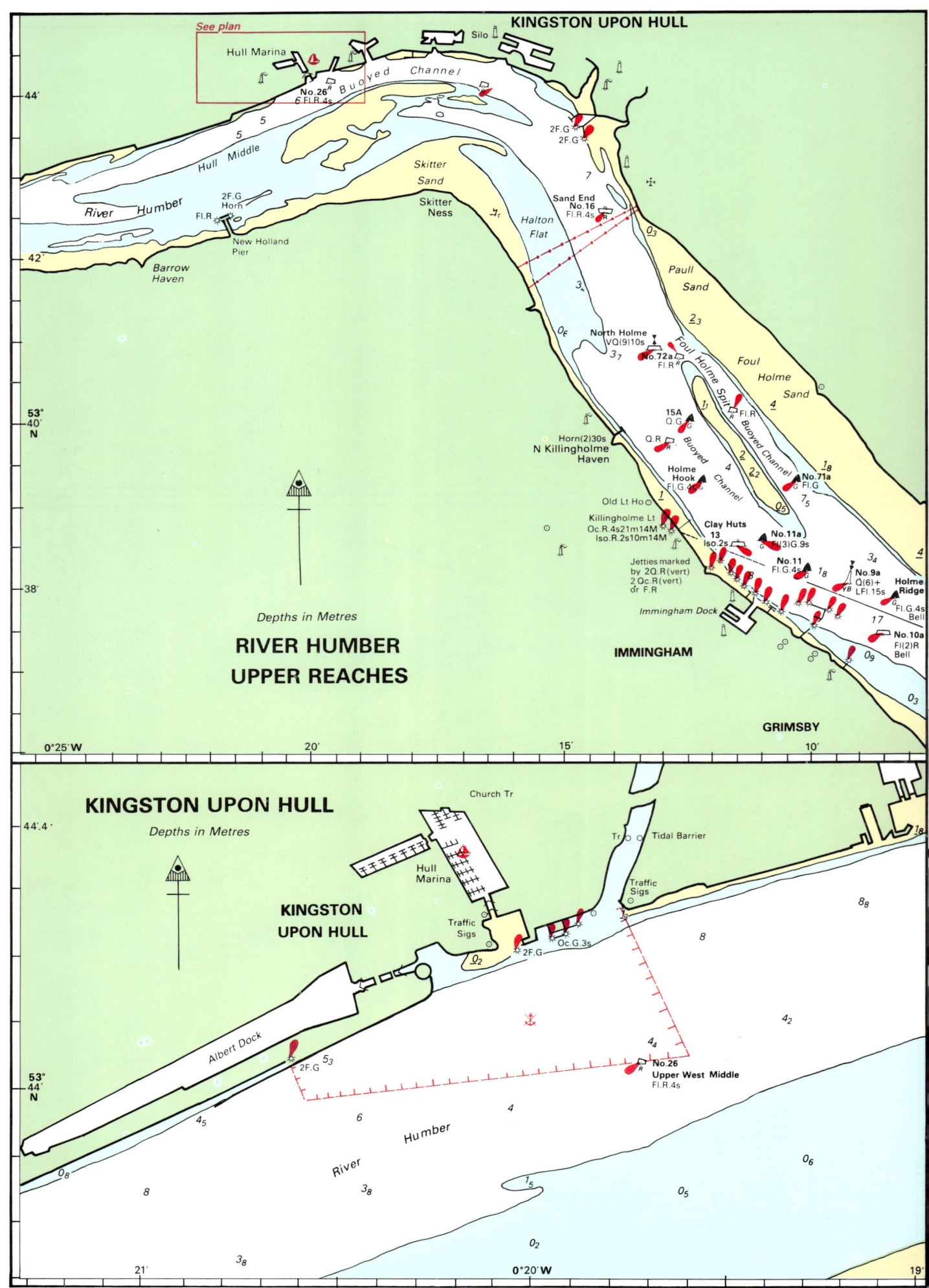

(4) **South Ferriby:** apply to lock keeper for berth or call "S. Ferriby Marina" VHF 37(M) or Barton-on-Humber (0652) 635620. Berthing, shore storage and repairs.
(5) Visitors are welcome at Humber Yawl Club moorings in Brough Haven.
(6) The Humber YC have developed a basin at Winteringham Haven on the S bank. Buoyed entrance, available for 1.5m draught 1½h either side of HW neaps to 2½h either side of MHWS. Beware of submerged saltings downstream of entrance at HW Springs.

Anchorages At the entrance to the river in the N channel a good anchorage situation inside Spurn Pt completely sheltered in N and E winds, uncomfortable in strong NW winds particularly on spring ebb. Bring up in 2 to 3½m opposite the Lt Ho off brickyard chimney, Killingholme, in S or W winds, S off Hawkins Pt sheltered in N winds. Off Cleethorpes about 1M offshore in fine weather: untenable in strong winds.

For the most up to date information on navigation above Hull, contact "Associated British Ports" who have responsibility for Humber estuary ports, as the channel and its buoyage are constantly changing.

The Humber is a busy commercial river and much information regarding shipping movements and regular weather information is given by VTS Humber VHF 12.

RIVER TRENT   Chart BA 109

British Transport Docks Board chart "Barton Haven to Burton Stather" R Trent (tidal) chart, published by the "Trent Boating Association" is now available from T. Pattison Esq., 12 Baker Ave., Arnold, Notts. Nottingham (0602) 262055.

Navigable to Keadby Br. Lock on the W bank below br gives access to canal.

Crane available: with mast unstepped, navigable to Nottingham. Depth at MLWN 1.6m, air draught at MHWS 4.2m.

RIVER OUSE

Goole provides access to the Aire and Calder Canals also a small marina/boatyard about ½M up canal from docks. Best to arrive just before HW. Locks operate working hours but only when the tide serves during weekends.

PASSAGE NOTES: HUMBER TO BERWICK

Principal Passage Lights

Flamborough Hd	Fl(4) 15s 65m 29M
Whitby High Lt	Iso WR 10s 73m 23M
The Heugh (Hartlepool)	Fl(2) 10s 19m 19M
Sunderland (Roker Pier)	Fl 5s 25m 23M
Tynemouth	Fl(3) 10s 26m 26M
Blyth (Coquet)	Fl(3) WR 30s 25m 23/19M
Farne Is (Longstone)	Fl 20s 23m 24M

For most of its length this passage offers no navigational difficulties, with no offshore hazards to affect a yacht. The poor supply of harbours available in strong onshore winds must always be borne in mind. In bad weather no attempt should be made to take the passage inside the Farne Islands where tides are strong and sea conditions can be very difficult. In such circumstances keep at least 1M E of the Longstone Lt Ho.

YORKSHIRE COAST   Charts BA 121, 129, 134
Spurn Pt to Bridlington   DS: Dover +1½h S, −4¾h N
Flamborough Hd   DS: Dover +¼h S, −6h N

Flamborough Hd to Tees, streams are weak. As the streams turn offshore first, 1½h to ½h may be gained by carefully watching the time of change and closing or standing offshore. The ebb sets N and the flood S. In poor visibility sound continuously, as an indraft into all the small bays is likely to set vessels into Bridlington and Filey Bays. Bound N from Spurn, one may coast as far as Flamborough Hd at a safe distance offshore of ½M, and may anchor anywhere between Spurn and Flamborough Hd in offshore winds. With onshore wind do not attempt to anchor except in Bridlington Bay, as a sea is quickly raised.

Anchorages (1) Bridlington Bay. With the wind from NNW to SSW anchor approx ¼M off the pier end, from the NNW round to the NE, bring up under Danes' Dyke or near the S Landing.
(2) Filey Bay. Proceeding round Flamborough Hd keep the lantern of the Lt Ho open above the cliff tops and stand off Filey Brigg by the Filey Brigg E Card buoy. The bottom is clay covered with sand, with foul ground beginning with Scarborough Rk appearing outside Car Naze. Do not remain in the bay with the wind E of NNE. In winds from W of S anchor 4 M S of Filey under Speeton Cliffs. From Filey Brigg Buoy stand 1M offshore to avoid numerous wrks.
(3) Scarborough Bay. Smooth bottom sand over blue clay with good holding ground. Open to winds from NNE to SSE. Anchor with the Castle bearing 332° and Spa Ho from 260° to 290° in 5 to 7m.
(4) Whitby Bay and Sandsend Bay. Leaving Scarborough, proceeding N, anchor in either of these bays. Beware of Up Gang Rks lying ¾M offshore midway between Whitby and Sandsend with 0.5m over them and 11m close by.
(5) Runswick Bay. When entering to anchor, give Kettleness a wide berth.

BRIDLINGTON
Chart BA 1882
HW: Dover +5¾h   DS: Dover +2h SE (in offing)
MHWS 6.1m   MHWN 4.7   MTL 3.6   MLWN 2.3   MLWS 1.1
Bar Sand bar across hbr entrance: approx 0.6m at LAT. Hbr dries.
Approach Approach from S so that hbr entrance is open. N pier head Fl 2s 7m 9M horn 60s. Signal stn 50m approx W from head of S pier shows FR at night or a R flag by day when depth available is 2.7m or above; when there is less water, FG at night but no day signal is shown. A W flag with a central B disc, under a R flag by day indicates entrance is not clear.
Anchorage Anchor in Bridlington Bay approx ½M SE from piers.
Berthing Against quays or on mud; anchor outside and enquire for berth. Fresh water can be obtained from points along S pier on request to the Watchkeeper at the fish quay. Fuel is delivered by a road tanker from a local garage.
The Royal Yorkshire YC is situated at the approach to the S pier.
Supplies EC Thur. All supplies, repairs, crane, shipwright.
Tel: HM (0262) 670148 VHF 16 12 (14 occas).

SCARBOROUGH
Chart BA 1612
HW: Dover +5½h   DS: (in offing) Dover +2h SE
MHWS 5.7m   MHWN 4.6   MTL 3.4   MLWN 2.3   MLWS 0.9
The Old hbr is reserved for the fishing fleet, the E hbr, available from half flood to half ebb, dries out completely at MLWS. No vessel should attempt to enter in onshore gales (NE through E to SSE).
Approach When a B ball is hoisted at the Lt Ho FS or by night Iso 5s is shown, there is more than 3.7m depth available in the Old hbr. The E hbr entrance has a concrete sill liable to silting and carrying approx 1.5m less water over it. R flag indicates entry forbidden.
From the S give the shore a berth of somewhat less than ½M, closing in fine weather to 45m as the pier wall comes abeam. An eddy from the S bay sets round the pier-head and along the outer wall of the hbr from quarter flood to HW. It runs NE at 1½ to 2kn springs, increased by E and SE winds. Make allowance, especially coming from S. Beware isolated rocks drying 0.6m, in an area SSW of E pier-head up to a distance of 23m.
Entrance Small craft run a great risk taking the entrance from the E and NE in bad weather, as the sea breaks for some distance outside piers.
Berthing Yachts take up a quay berth if one is vacant or as directed in E hbr which is entered between E and Vincent Pier (very narrow). Yachts are only allowed in the Old hbr in an emergency: anchor off and go ashore for instructions. A fender plank is necessary when lying alongside: vessels should not be left unattended. The hbr is safe but there is a good deal of swell in strong NE and E winds. There are three visitors' berths at Vincent Pier and Old Pier close to Lt Ho, secure and seek instructions from Lt Ho keeper. Spars available on loan.
Anchorage Anchor 1 to 3 ca from outer pier E of a line Scarborough Castle–Vincent Pier Lt Ho.
Supplies All facilities Water at Lt Ho. EC Weds
Tel: HM (0723) 373530 working hours or 360684 out of hours.
VHF 16,12,14 (call Scarborough Lt Ho).

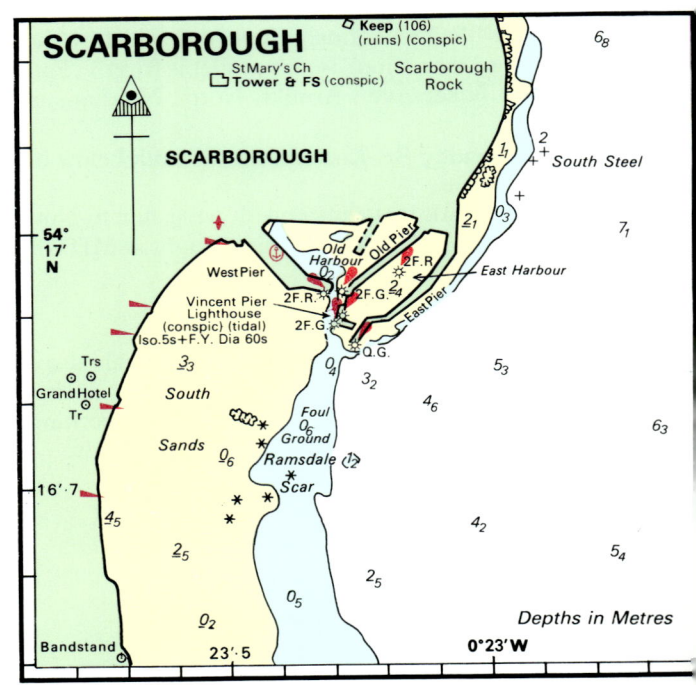

WHITBY   Chart BA 1612

HW: Dover +5¼h

DS: Dover +2h SE, −4h NW (in offing)

MHWS 5.4m   MHWN 4.3   MTL 3.1   MLWN 2.0   MLWS 0.8

Harbour available between HW±3h for craft drawing 2m. When the concrete ledge round the foot of the pier heads is awash, there is 2.4 m on bar, 2m between the pier heads, 1m within the inner pier and 2m at the quay side on W of hbr.

Approach When approaching from SE it is essential to round Whitby Rock buoy, leaving it to port before making up to the hbr. From all other directions the approach is straightforward. At the Whitby Rock Buoy, approx ¾M from the hbr mouth, the tide turns some 2h after HW and LW.

Entrance Unlighted ldg marks are a white △ (lower) and a white circle with B line vert (upper), sited on the E side of the hbr and mark the approach line 169°. Hold this course until 2 similar marks on the E Pier, carrying FY lts, are observed. Leaving these in line over the stern, a course 209° follows the channel maintained at a depth of 1.5m into the hbr.

Whitby Hbr Radio VHF 16 office hours; Swing Br Radio VHF 16, HW±2h normally opens only on the hour and half-hour. Some special openings may be made on Sat and Sun in the summer season at 0900 and 1800 regardless of state of tide. For details contact HM or Whitby YC (0947)603623.

A B ball is shown on W pier Lt Ho or FG by night when vessels over 100 ft are expected and there is not less than 3m over the bar.

Berthing In lower hbr on W side on the quay between br and Marine Hotel, dries, mud. For a short stay, on the fish quay S of HM's office, with fishing boats. Advice from HM. Pass through the br, see above, visitors' berth at marina on stb side with approx 1.5m at N end to 0.7 at S end, less on inshore side of pontoon; also between swing br and N end to the pontoon on the W side, subject to shoaling after heavy spate down R Esk. Or secure to piles on port hand. Beware of stone causeway approx 20m upstream of S end of pontoon extending across R and drying at LW.

Anchorage Outside ¼ to ½M NNW of W pier opposite spa buildings in 5m, sand.

Supplies All facilities EC Wed. HM (0947) 602354.

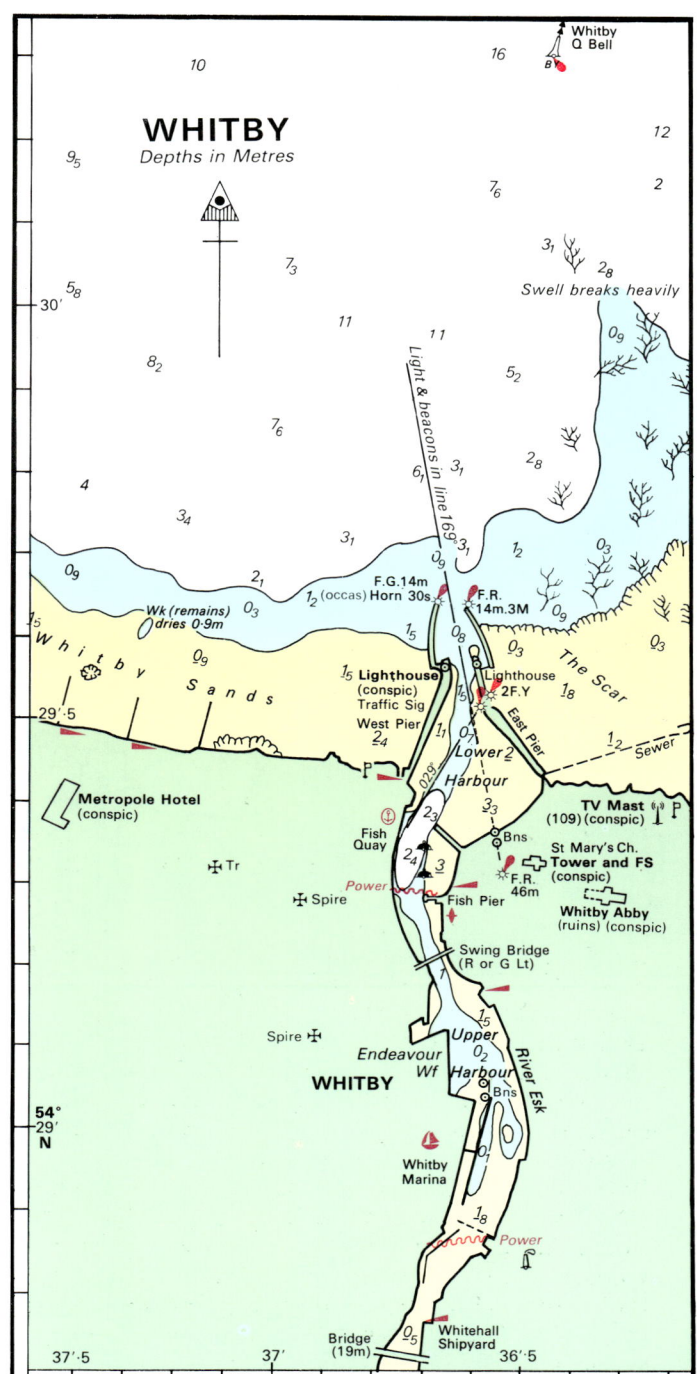

ENGLAND, EAST COAST

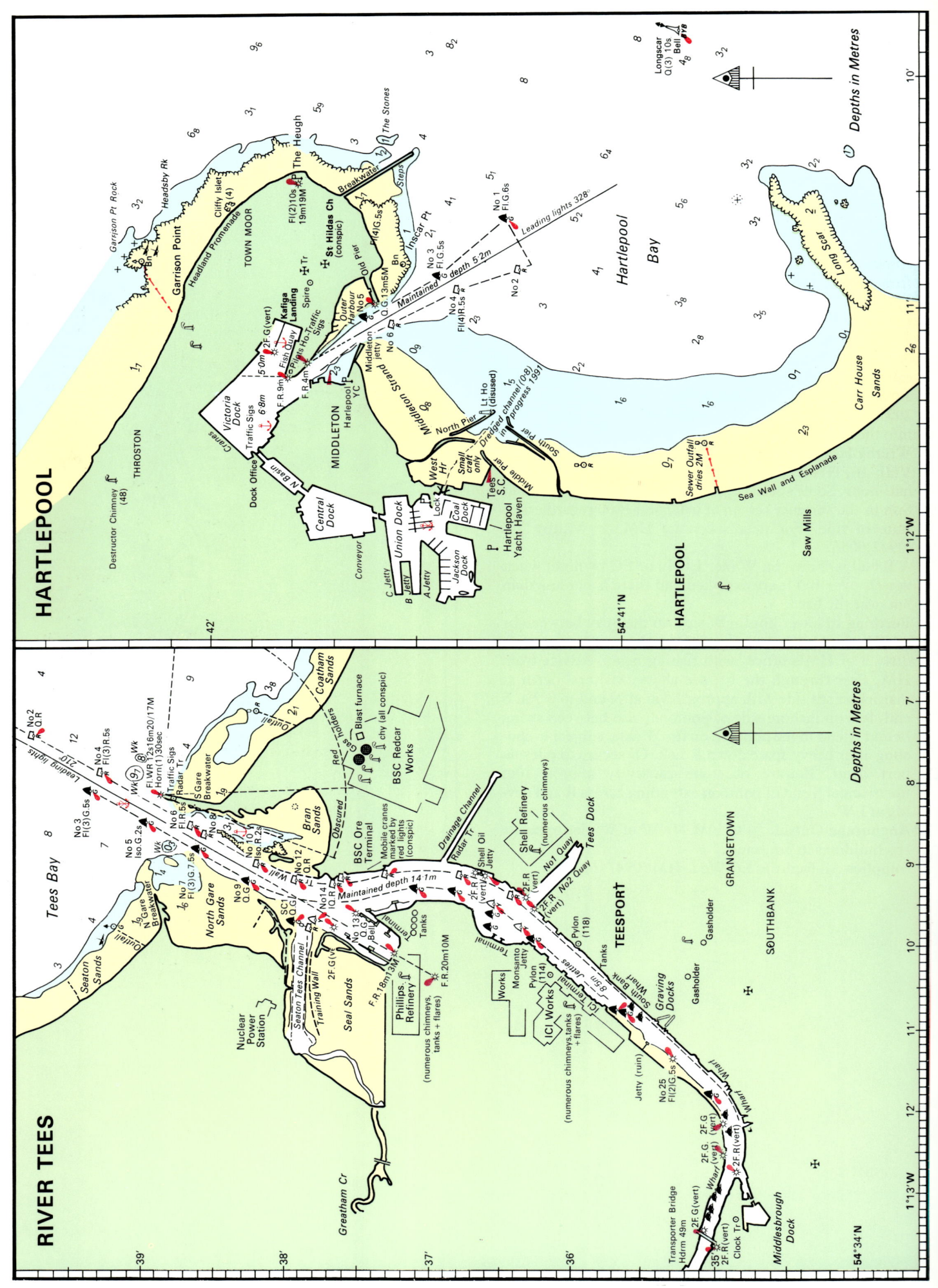

RIVER TEES   Chart BA 2566
HW: Dover +5h (at entrance)
           DS: Dover −4½h NW, +1½h SE (in offing)
MHWS 5.5m   MHWN 4.3   MTL 3.2   MLWN 2.0   MLWS 0.9

Approach In heavy weather, Hartlepool with more sea room is preferable to the Tees. Tees Fairway safe water pillar buoy, Iso 4s Horn, Racon, marks the approach to the main channel dredged to 15.4m, marked by port and stb Lt buoys.

Entrance 210° leads up fairway, to abeam of Seaton channel turning. Channel buoyed and lit to beyond Middlesborough. Advice obtainable from "Tees Hbr Radio" VHF 16, 12, 11, 14, 22.

Berthing Contact or proceed to HM office at Tees Dock 2¾M from entrance for instructions.

Buses to Middlesborough, 2M walk to Seaton Carew; hotel, shops.

Anchorages (1) Paddy's Hole, 202° 6ca from S Gare Breakwater N end, on E side of entrance up to 1.2m draught.

The approach is buoyed: a mooring may be obtained from S Gare Warden.

(2) Near Pilot jetty on either side of piles. Water from Pilot Stn, S Gare Marine Club.

(3) Moorings may be available by arrangement with the Secretary of Castlegate Marine Club.

In emergency contact HM Tees Dock (0642) 452 541

Navigation up River ½M above Middlesborough Dock (closed) is a Transporter br 49m at MHWS. 2M further is Newport br, 36m with a span raised (6.4m closed: 24h notice required to open) closely followed by the A19 road br (18m). 2M beyond this are the Stockton-Victoria br (5.5m) and Rly br (6.3m). Between Stockton and Yarm there is a pipe br and a HT electric cable; lowest has 7m at MHWS.

Proceed up Yarm R at half flood and descend early on the ebb.

Supplies EC Wed.

HARTLEPOOL   Chart BA 2566
HW: Dover +4½h   DS: Dover −4¾h N, +1¼h S
MHWS 5.1m   MHWN 4.0   MTL 2.9   MLWN 1.8   MLWS 0.8

Tidal stream at entrance is rotatary: Dover −1h NW ¼kn; +2h 200° 1kn; +5h SE ¼kn; −4h 010° ¾kn.

Approach Conspic landmarks are St. Hilda's ch 2½ca WSW of Heugh Lt Ho. The Lt Ho lies NE of the hbr entrance.

In heavy weather approach towards the Long Scar E Card buoy (Q3) 10s Bell and give the Heugh a very good clearance to avoid the backwash which upsets the swell for some distance E and S of it. From the S, make for Long Scar buoy to avoid the Long Scar shoal lying 6 ca SW of the buoy.

Entrance The channel is marked to stb by three G con buoys, the outer one Fl G 6s, and to port by three R can buoys. By night ldg lts FR are shown from the E side of the hbr entrance on 329°; by day R fluorescent boards.

Berthing (1) Temporarily in W hbr by arrangement with Dockmaster. Unbuoyed, unlit, dries, suited only to shoal draught boats able to take the ground.

(2) A long pontoon from the middle of the E quay extends NW (and is opposite the Fish Quay) in Victoria Dock. This is known as Kafiga landing, operated jointly by the Hartlepool YC and the local Boatowners Association 2 FG vert on outer end.

(3) At No 5 Graving Dock which is tidal; apply to Hartlepool YC for mooring. Basin sill 0.7m MLWS, berths up to 10m.

(4) At Victoria Dock, moorings available by arrangement with Dockmaster VHF 16, 11, 12 or (0429) 266127. Small craft may be slipped at Hartlepool YC on small promontory at landward end of Middleton jetty to port when entering. Tees SC on S corner of W hbr (available to small craft only).

(5) A large new marina development is in progress (July 1991) with berths for 82 craft initially (ultimately 450) in the Union Dock entered via a channel dredged to 5ft through W Hbr leading to lock in W wall. Approach from No 2 Channel buoy on 279° 4ca to W hbr entrance between outer piers. Channel to lock gates has waiting buoys for craft intending to enter. Lock operates HW -3h to HW +3h between 0800 and 2200 hrs or at other times by prior arrangement. Follow sector light RWG 307° by keeping in W sector. Lock sill is 0.8m below chart datum, marina is to port after locking in area shown as 'Coal Dock' on plan. Fresh water all berths, electricity to 80%. Diesel. Call Yacht Haven VHF 37 and 80. Staff on duty 24hrs for security and assistance. All facilities. Lift to 40 tonnes.

(6) Tees SC is situated just S of lock in W Hbr. Facilities for small craft only. Slip.

Supplies EC Wed. All facilities.

SEAHAM
Chart BA 1627
HW: Dover +4¾h   DS: Dover −5h N, +1h S
MHWS 5.2m   MHWN 4.1   MTL 3.0   MLWN 2.0   MLWS 0.7

Approach Keep ½M offshore until E of hbr entrance. FS at NE corner of S Dock in line with N Lt Ho (W with B bands) leads in clear of E Tangle Rk 1.9m.

Entrance There is 5m in the entrance with a 5m channel dredged to the S Dock and 1m elsewhere in the Outer (tidal) Hbr. The S Dock is manned 2½h before to 1½h after HW. Yachts lie along quay as directed by HM. The hbr is large, well protected, has limited berthing and the entrance is normally easy. Extensive improvements in hand. Water on quay, limited facilities.

In severe NE and E winds the hbr may be closed.

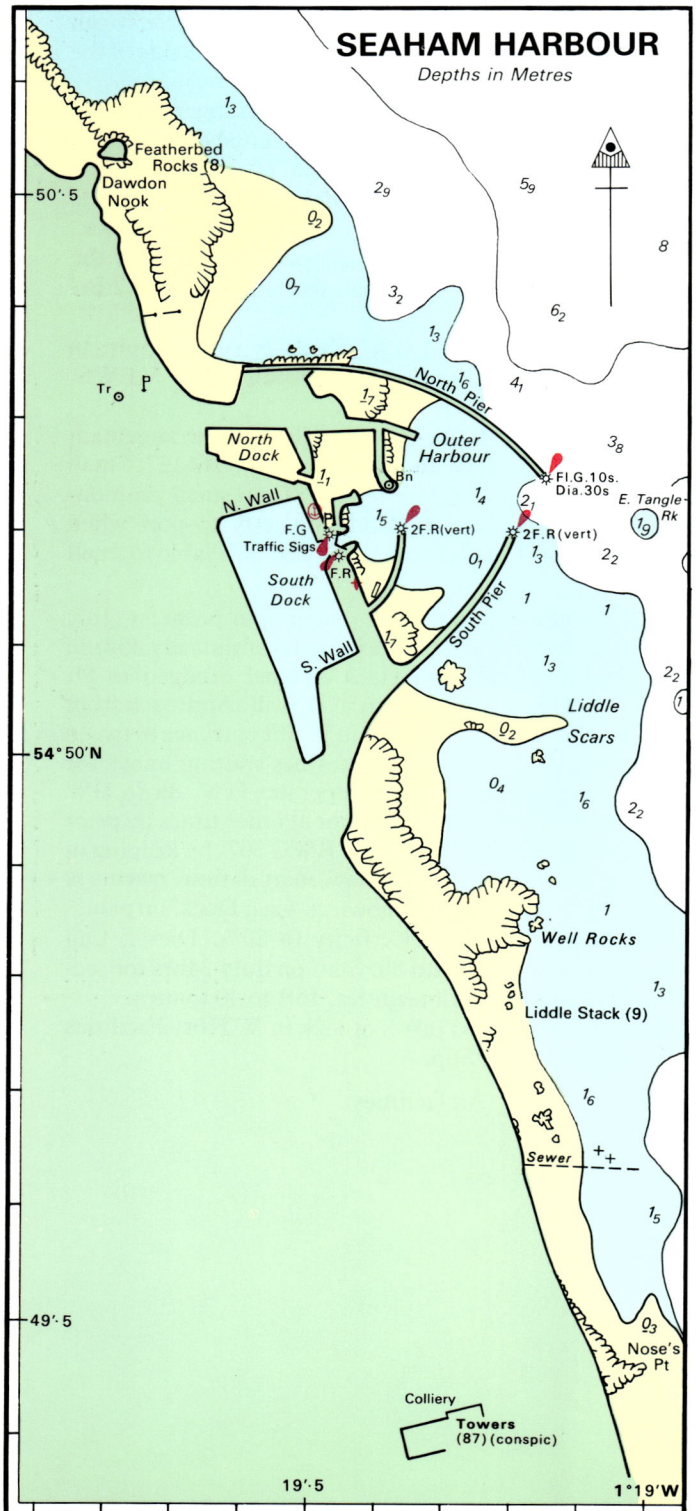

England, East Coast

SUNDERLAND

Chart BA 1627

HW: Dover +4¾h   DS: Dover −5h N; +1h S
MHWS 5.2m MHWN 4.2 MTL 3.0 MLWN 2.0 MLWS 0.8

Approach The entrance to the R Wear is made between two recently constructed, crescent shaped piers, the northern most Roker Pier has Lt Ho conspic at its hd Fl 5s 25m 23M Siren 20s. The new S Pier Fl 10s has a R can buoy Fl R 5s just N of it which must be left to port on entering.

Entrance Enter between Roker Pier and the R can buoy and then on a course between the inner piers, depth 5m. Entry signals: (1) from Pilot Stn on old N pier; 3 FlR (vert) = Danger in hbr – no entry and no departure.
(2) from Pylons at S Docks and No3 gate to control traffic through S Dock entrance. There are no yacht facilities in S Dock and consequently these signals are not generally relevant to small craft.

Berthing On Sunderland YC moorings in N Dock Basin or by permission pick up a mooring N or S side of river beyond dock entrance, or enter N dock VHF 16,14.

Anchorage Clear of fairway inside Roker Pier in 3m.

Supplies All facilities EC Wed.

Tel: HM (0783) 672626

TYNEMOUTH

Charts BA 1934, 152

HW: Dover +4¾h   DS: Dover −5h N; +1h S
MHWS 5.0m MHWN 3.9 MTL 2.9 MLWN 1.8 MLWS 0.7

The channel of the R Tyne from the sea to Jarrow Quay Corner is dredged to 9m.

Approach Bring ldg lts FW in line 258° (Two W trs) to pass between N pier head Fl(3) 10s 26m 26M Lt Ho conspic Horn 10s and S pier head Oc WRG 10s 15m 13-8M Bell 10s.

Entrance Pass between the piers in mid channel. Stream runs hard and raises a steep sea in E winds: keep to N side entering and S side leaving.

Berthing For short stay, alongside fish quay. For a longer stay, 2M upriver in the Albert Edward Dock by permission of HM VHF 16, 11, 12, 14 or 091 257 0407. Since berthing facilities are very limited it is essential to obtain prior permission either from HM or YC secretaries.

Anchorage 200m N of the G con No1 buoy W of the N pier head.

Supplies All facilities EC Wed.

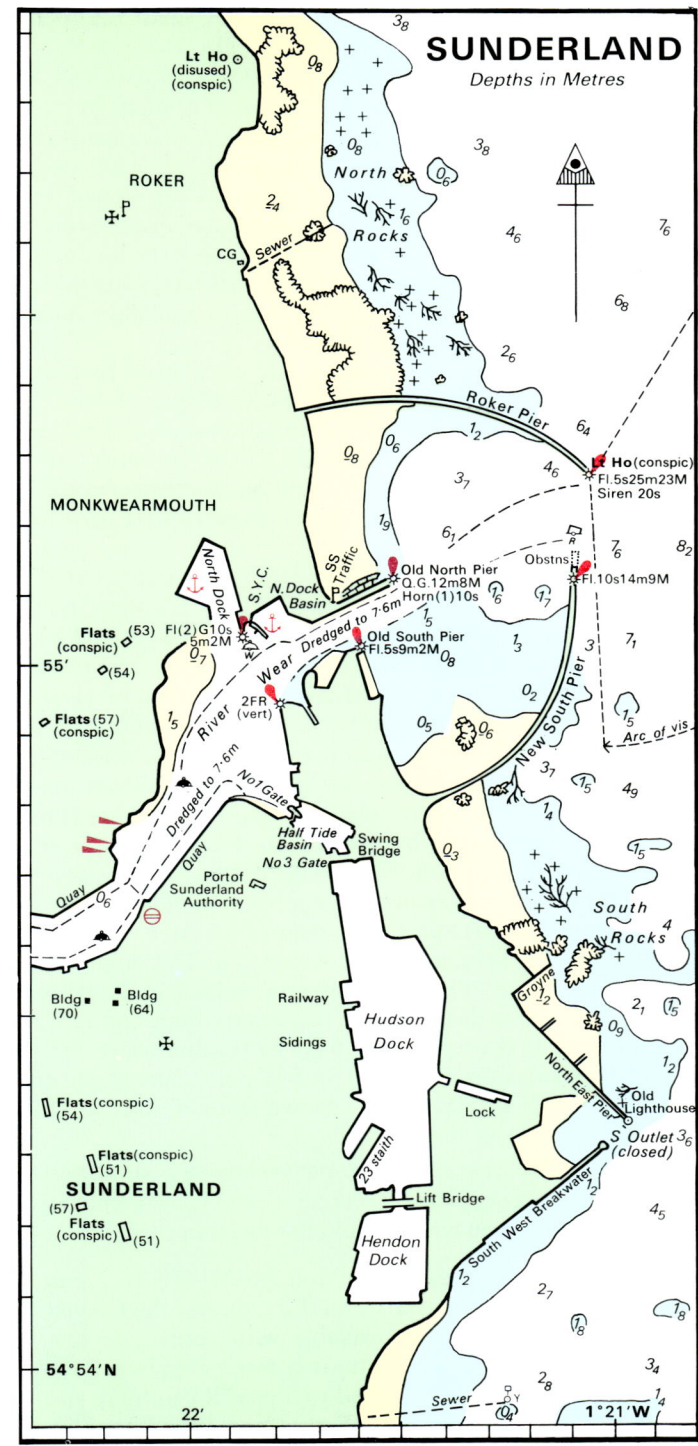

ENGLAND, EAST COAST

BLYTH   Chart BA 1626
HW: Dover +4½h   DS: Dover −5h N
MHWS 5.0m   MHWN 3.9   MTL 2.9   MLWN 1.7   MLWS 0.8

Approach The hbr may easily be located at night by the industrial Lts. The entrance opens to the S with sands to W and rks to E abreast of breakwaters. From S, when past St. Mary's Is bring Lts F Bu in line 324° on lattice trs with Or diamond topmarks 11 and 17m respectively. From N, to clear the Sow and Pigs Rks leave the Sow and Pigs R can buoy to stb and proceed in a S direction towards the fairway G con buoy Fl G 3s, bell from whence steer mid way between the piers on 324°

Entrance Enter between the piers, turn hard to port round the N end of the inner W pier Fl(2)R6s into S Hbr.

Berthing Visiting yachts are usually accommodated by the Royal Northumberland YC in the S Hbr, or berth temporarily and contact HM on inner W pier for instructions. **Tel:** HM (0670) 352678. Blyth Hbr Control VHF 16,12.

WARKWORTH HARBOUR   Chart BA 1627
HW: Dover +4½h (Croquet Rd)   DS: Dover −5h N
MHWS 5.1m   MHWN 4.0   MTL 2.9   MLWN 1.8   MLWS 0.8

Bar 2.2m at MLWS. Rock covered with sand, care must be exercised in conditions of swell. Dangerous breakers may occur when strong wind is between N and E.

Approach From N pass inshore of Pan Bush buoy leaving at least 2ca to port and steer for hbr entrance midway between piers. From S leave Hauxley buoy and Coquet Is to port until NE Coquet buoy has been cleared before turning in towards hbr entrance. Watch out for lobster pots. Passage inshore of Coquet Is is not recommended without local knowledge as buoyage in channel has been removed. In NE winds there are dangerous seas on NE Coquet and Pan Bush shoals. The area between Pan Bush and the hbr entrance is very dangerous in these conditions and entry should not be attempted, Blyth is a better alternative. A Fl R 5s Lt is exhibited from Lt Ho, RW hor stripes at end of S pier. On N pier Fl G 6s is shown from W iron Lt Ho about 6m from seaward end.

Entrance Lies between the two piers 68m apart. Approach with care as S going stream sets across and is dangerous in N to E winds when entry should not be attempted.

Berthing Yachts lie at S Jetty in 0.7m MLWS to 2.1 m MLWN. Further upriver beyond the quays, the Coquet YC may have moorings available with similar depths. Amble Braid Marina 250 berths may be entered by following line of quays, keeping well to S pass R can buoy and turn in S of jetty marked by E card bn. Access 2m 3½h either side of HW Springs and 3h either side of HW neaps. VHF 80, call 'Amble Braid Marina'.

Supplies Local boatyard with 18 ton hoist and slipway. There is a scrubbing grid in the Fish Dock near the RNLI shed. All facilities. Bus to Newcastle and Alnwick.

THE CRUISING ASSOCIATION

Founded 1908 - Membership 5500

Library 8500 volumes - Chart Room 2500 charts

Pilots & Navigational Information

Worldwide Regional Files

250 Hon Local Representatives Worldwide

Quarterly Magazine & Navigation Notes

Bi monthly Bulletins

Crewing Service - Local Area Sections & Meets

The Cruising Association, Ivory House,
St Katharine Dock, London E1 9AT
Tel: 071 481 0881

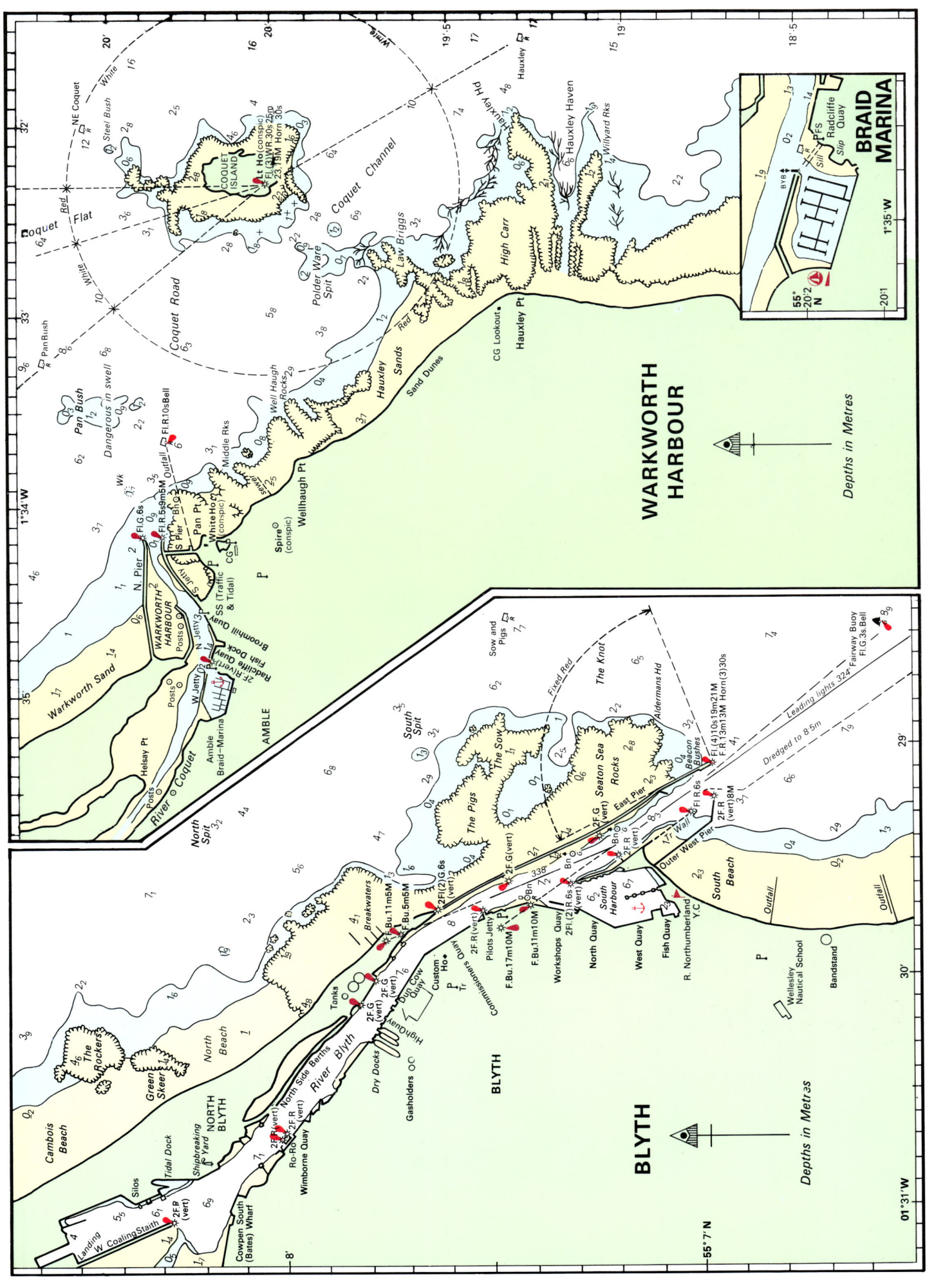

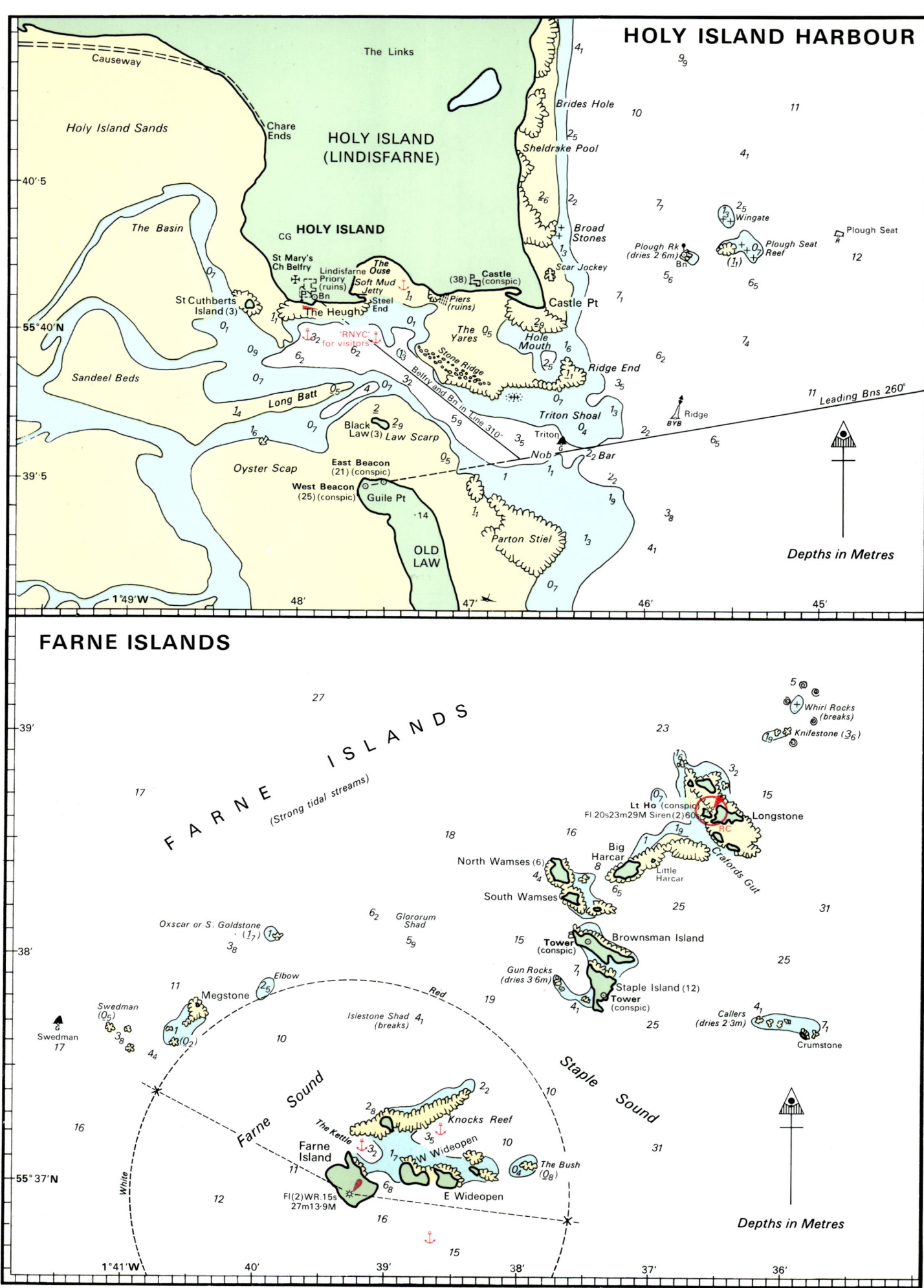

HOLY ISLAND
Chart BA1612
HW: Dover +4h DS: (in offing) HWD SE, +6h NW
(in hbr) −2¾h flood, +3¾h ebb
MHWS 4.8m MHWN 3.7 MTL 2.6 MLWN 1.5 MLWS 0.6
A natural hbr with 3 to 7m inside. Strong streams and eddies.

Approach From S keep Plough Bn on Plough Rk open to E of Emanuel Hd (the most NE point of Holy Is approx 1M N of Castle Pt) until the bns on the Old Law are in transit then steer in on 260°. Least depth on line 1.3m. From N through Goldstone Channel, leave the E card Ridge buoy off Castle Pt well to stb. Strangers should avoid the passage W of Plough Rk. Entry under sail is possible only with a fair stream or leading wind.

Entrance Bring bns in line and steer on 260° leaving the Triton G con buoy to stb until the triangular bn on the Heugh (caution: do not confuse with tall narrow stone War Memorial further W) comes in line with St. Mary's ch belfry 310°, steer on this bearing to anchorage.

The ebb runs at 4kn in the channel, the entrance is long and narrow but is easy in fine weather with the help of ldg marks. The Old Law Bns are conspic stone obelisks: the Heugh is a little cliff with a ch behind it. At LW the Law Bns must not be opened to N until Emmanuel Bn is closed behind Castle Pt. The marks are unlit and it is unwise to enter unless they are discernible.

Anchorages Vessels exceeding 2m draught, bring up off Heugh bn where there are six visitors' moorings marked RNYC. Vessels drawing 2m can lie 1 ca S of Steel End. In W gales boats should lie to 2 anchors due to scend at HW. Small craft able to take the ground are more secure in the Ooze, soft mud, except in S and SE breezes when it should be avoided.

Supplies Water tap in square, stores at P.O.
Tel: HM Holy Is 207 or 217.

BERWICK
Chart BA 1612
HW: Dover +3½h DS: Dover −4¾h N
MHWS 4.7m MHWN 3.8 MTL 2.6 MLWN 1.3 MLWS 0.6
Bar 0.6 to 1.8m. Inside hbr 2.4m

Approach From S, to clear shoals in Berwick Bay keep Megstown and Farm Is lt tr in line astern. 142° from N, stand off from shore ¾M. Approach breakwater had with Lt Ho in line with Town Hall spire 294° or S of this line.

Entrance Enter parallel with breakwater and approx 10m off. Keep steering for bn QG after breakwater turns NNW until Spittal ldg marks (Lt bns B&Y FR with △ topmarks) come in line 207°. Maintain this line until E of 2nd G con buoy QG then steer for NW end of Fish jetty. Do not keep too close to G con buoys which are laid in shoal water outside the channel. From here steer for the end of the pier at Tweed Dock.

Berthing Temporarily at W end of fish jetty: do not leave boats unattended. Otherwise Tweed Dock is normally left open and yachts may enter or leave at most states of the tide except at LW±2h. There is 0.6m in entrance. Berth as indicated by HM VHF 16,12 usually alongside another vessel. Depth approx 1m at MLWS, bottom soft mud.

Supplies All facilities EC Thur.

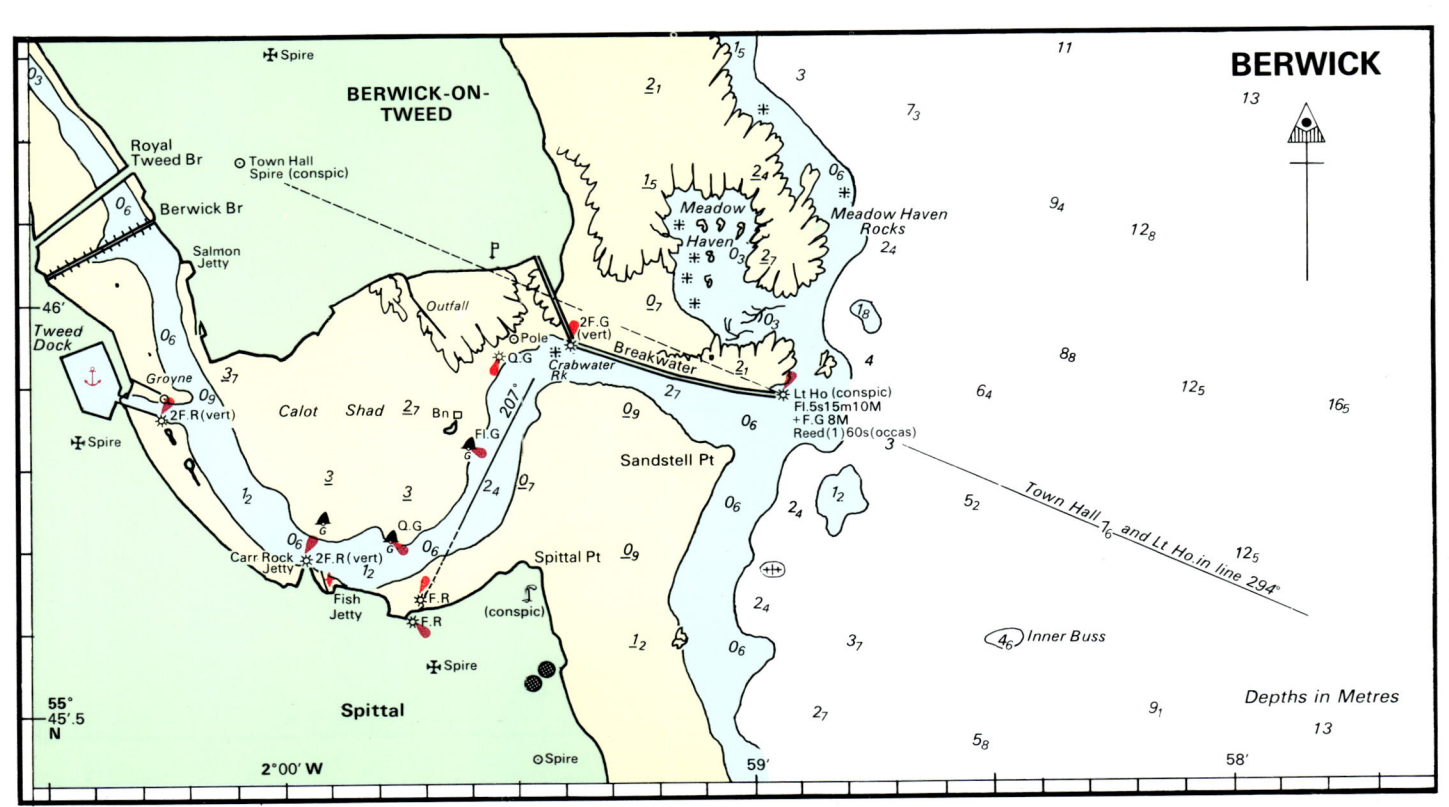

ENGLAND, East Coast

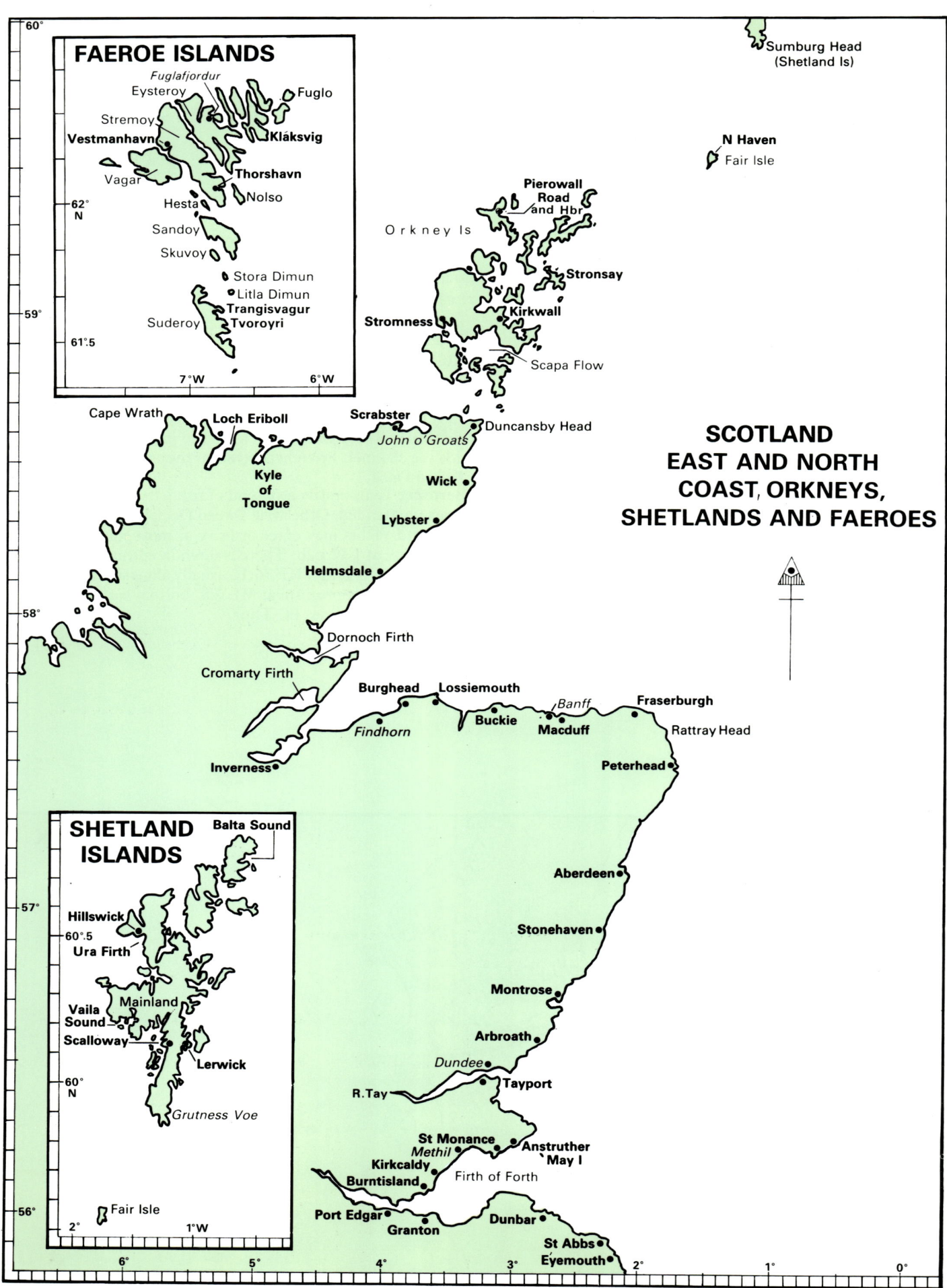

117 *SCOTLAND, EAST COAST*

SCOTLAND

EAST COAST The Border to Duncansby Head

General
For more details refer to:-
Clyde Cruising Club Saiing Directions (CCC SD): N and NE Coasts of Scotland;
Forth Yacht Clubs Association Pilot Handbook: (Berwick to Fraserburgh);
R Northumberland YC Sailing Directions: (Humber to Rattray Head).

A yacht cruising this coast needs to be able to make offshore passages of 100 miles and to keep the sea in adverse conditions. Many of the harbours are unavailable in strong on-shore winds; and a large swell, which may make entrances dangerous, persists for some days after heavy Northerly winds have died down.

It must be remembered that, with the exception of the Forth yachting centres (Granton, Port Edgar), all the harbours on this coast are working harbours, busy with fishing and the oil industry. You are advised to check entry signals for each port: in several cases in this area G means "hbr closed"!

PASSAGE NOTES: BERWICK TO ARBROATH
On a direct passage the crossings of the Forth and Tay estuaries pose no great problems; but bad seas can be experienced off the Forth, particularly in E winds against the tide. The Tay is shoal for several miles out and should be given a wide berth. St Abbs Hd (90m) has appearance of an island from NW and SE.

Passage Lights
St Abbs Head	Fl 10s 68m 29M
Bass Rock	Fl(3) 20s 46m 10M
Isle of May	Fl(2) 15s 73m 22M
Fife Ness	Iso WR 10s 12m 21/20M

CLYDE CRUISING CLUB
1. Clyde Area Sailing Directions
2. Mull of Kintyre to Ardnamurchan Sailing Directions
3. Ardnamurchan to Cape Wrath Sailing Dire tions
4. Outer Hebrides Sailing Directions
5. Shetland Sailing Directions
6. Orkney and North and North East Coasts Sailing Directions
7. Amendments to Sailing directions
8. Sketch Charts

1982 Edition. Covers West Coast of Scotland from the Solway Firth to Cape Wrath and includes the Hebridces.
Set of Chartlets - size 15" x 19"
Fully revised amendments to all seven volumes of the Sailing Directions updated annually and collected in one booklet.

Kate Johnson, Clyde Cruising Club,
c/o RA Clement & Co
29 St Vincent Place, Glasgow G1 2DT
Tel: 041 221 0068
Fax: 041 204 3744

THE CRUISING ASSOCIATION

Founded 1908 - Membership 5500

Library 8500 volumes - Chart Room 2500 charts

Pilots & Navigational Information

Worldwide Regional Files

250 Hon Local Representatives Worldwide

Quarterly Magazine & Navigation Notes

Bi monthly Bulletins

Crewing Service - Local Area Sections & Meets

The Cruising Association, Ivory House,
St Katharine Dock, London E1 9AT
Tel: 071 481 0881

EYEMOUTH
Chart BA 1612

HW: Dover +3½h. DS: Dover +½h SE; −5h NW
MHWS 4.7m MLWS 3.7

A busy fishing hbr, safe in any weather but not to be approached in strong winds from between N and E. Bar varies but normally 1m MLWS.

Signals R flag by day, FR lt by night: hbr closd.
Approach Keep ½M offshore until ldg marks come in line on 174°, Orange poles (FG). E pier-head lit Iso R 2s. Approach after half flood, and if any sea only near HW. (Passage S of Hurkar Rks is unmarked; keep mid-channel, borrowing slightly towards Hurkar)
Entrance 16m wide. Keep to ldg line until hbr is well open, then round E pier fairly close and keep rather to E of centre of channel. Be prepared to stand off for fishing vessels leaving hbr.
Berthing Usually across N end of Middle Quay; 2m, soft mud. Beware strong current from Eye Water after rain.
Facilities Water on quay, stores, repairs. EC Thur.
Tel/HM (08907) 50233, VHF 16, 22.

ST ABBS HARBOUR
Chart BA 160

HW: Dover +3½h DS: HW Dover ESE; −6h WNW.
MHWS 4.7m MLWS 3.7

Small attractive hbr 1M S of St Abbs Head. Inner hbr dries; outer hbr has about 1m LWS. Not to be attempted in strong on-shore wind/seas.

Bar 1m.
Approach From S identify by clifftop village and high SE-facing cliffs whitened by birds; from N round St Abbs Head which is steep-to. Make for Maw Carr, a prominent steep-sided reddish rock (15m) about 120m NNW of entrance. Conspic Y LB ho identifies hbr.
Entrance Bring E edge of NW pier and centre pier in line and steer exactly on this line. Channel through rocks is narrow but all dangers show. Ldg line lit FR.
Berthing As directed; best along S end of NE pier (at Springs diagonally across corner).
Facilities PO, PH.

DUNBAR
Chart BA 734

HW: Dover +3¾h
MHWS 5.2m MHWN 4.2 MTL 3.0 MLWN 2.0 MLWS 0.7

A pleasant resort town with picturesque hbr. 1m MLWS in entrance. Good anchorage outside, sheltered from W through S to E, clean sand, good holding.

Approach On ldg line 198°, white disc over △ on concrete posts on grassy slope E of swimming pool.
Entrance 10m cleft cut through rocks to port, invisible until open.
Berthing In 1.2m alongside as near to Castle as possible, sand. N quay dries, uneven, sand at E end. Uncomfortable surge with on-shore swell. In bad weather HM will open br admitting to Old Hbr, dries out, mud.
Facilities Stores. EC Wed.

PASSAGE NOTE: DUNBAR TO GRANTON
Between Dunbar and Granton there are a number of anchorages and small harbours. Most significant are **North Berwick** and **Fisherrow** – both are restricted and subject to surge. Yachts are not normally allowed into **Leith Docks.** Keep ½M offshore.

GRANTON
Chart BA 735

HW: Dover +3¾h
MHWS 5.6m MHWN 4.3 MTL 3.0 MLWN 2.1 MLWS 0.8

Headquarters of R Forth and Forth Corinthian YC's. Hbr divided by central pier; yachts use E arm. Much of hbr dries.

Entrance 3m. Beware pilot boats.
Signals Tide signals on middle pier. Red flag W cross (FG lt) = No Entry. Yachts drawing less than 3m can ignore these signals with caution.
Berthing Secure temporarily near Pilot Berth on E side of middle pier (piled, awkward) and report to HM.
Facilities All. Buses from gate to Edinburgh and Leith.
Tel/HM 552-3385 VHF 16, 20, 71 ("Forth Navigation Service")

PORT EDGAR
Chart BA 736

HW: Dover +4h.
MHWS 5.6m MHWN 4.5 MTL 3.0 MLWN 2.1 MLWS 0.8

Large efficient yachting centre in old Naval Harbour on S shore immediately above the brs.

Approach Follow the buoyed shipping channel N or S of Inchkeith as convenient and pass through centre of road and rail bridges.
Entrance Pass W of floating breakwater of lorry tyres (lit 4 x QY) leaving W breakwater (Fl R 4s Dir 244°) to stb.
Berthing Visitors' berths on end of pontoons. If over 40 ft apply prior to arrival.
Facilities All, Sailboard and dinghy hire and instruction. Laundry collects/delivers (Tel 331-1893). Shops, etc, in S Queensferry, ½M E.
Tel/HM 331-3330 VHF 80, M. (0900 - 1900)

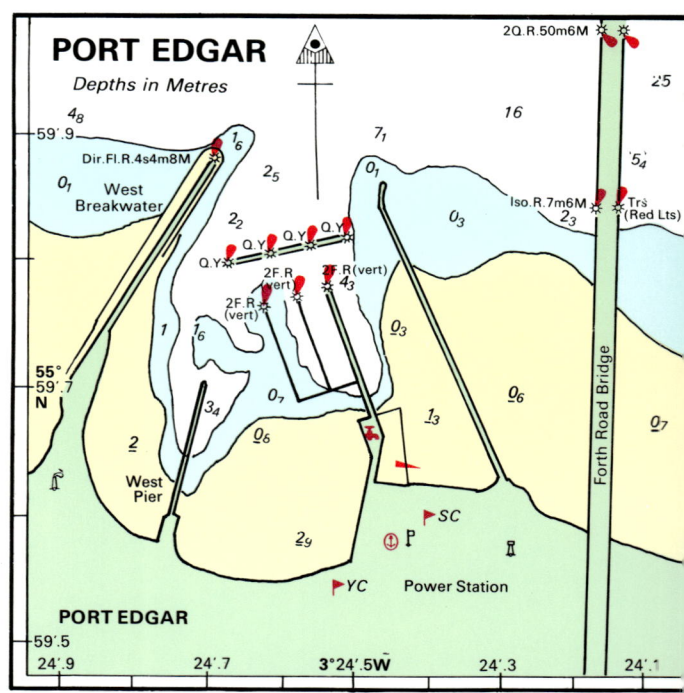

PASSAGE NOTE: N SHORE FIRTH OF FORTH
Of the harbours on the N shore of Forth, **Pittenweem** is a restricted and very busy fishing hbr, yachts unwelcome except week-ends. Most are inaccessible in strong E-SE winds but then **Methil** is available.

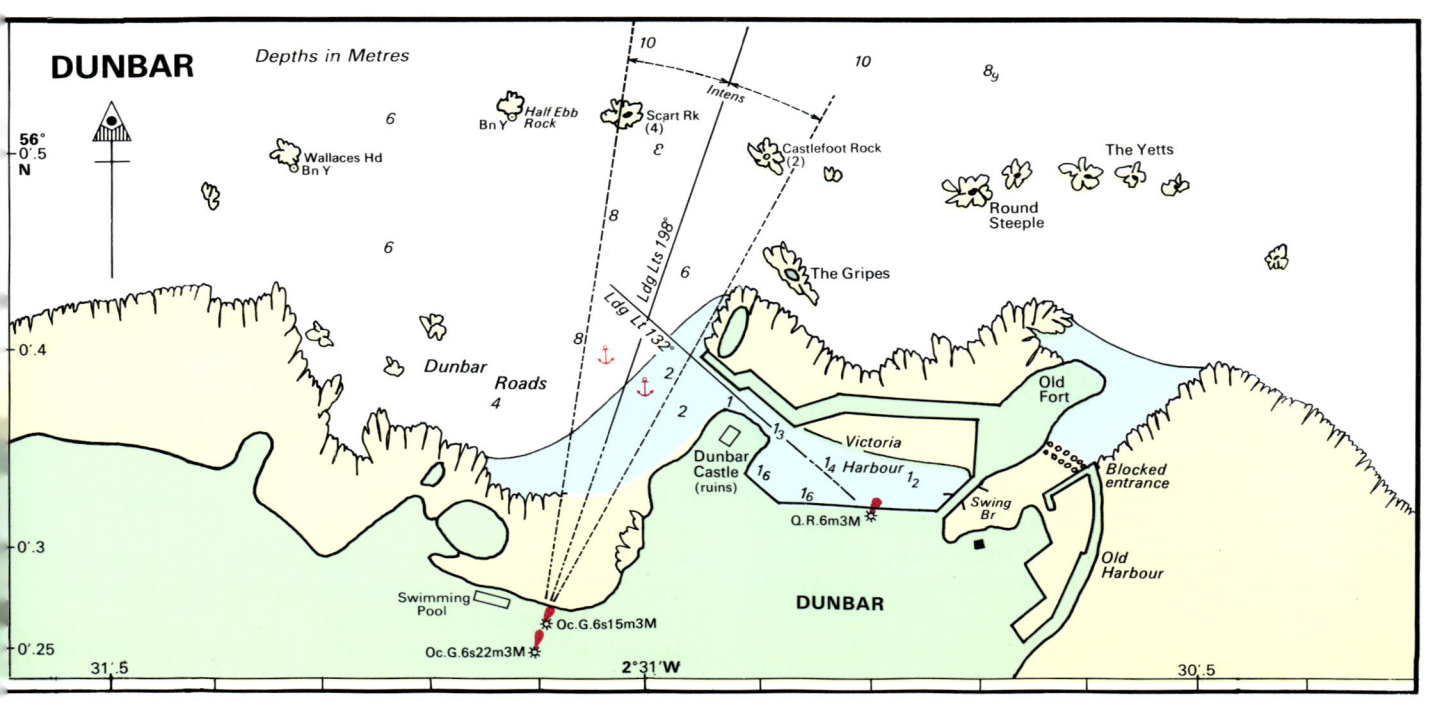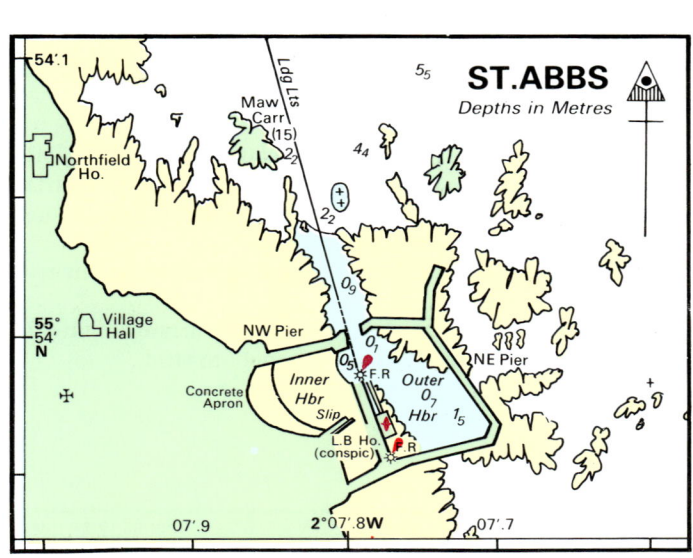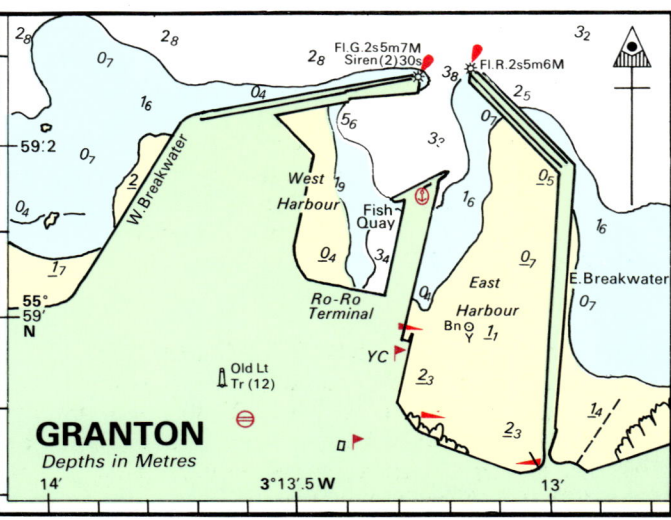

SCOTLAND, EAST COAST

BURNTISLAND
Chart BA 739
HW: Dover +3¾h
MHWS 5.5m MHWN 4.5 MTL 3.0 MLWN 2.1 MLWS 0.8
Commercial hbr with oilrig fabrication yard. Outer tidal harbour and two wet docks. Accessible at all states of tide and in most weather, heavy surge in winds SE to SW.
Berthing Yachts may sometimes use E dock. Outer hbr unsuitable for yachts in strong winds and E dock wide open to W wind. Lock into E dock HW−2h to HW. Short stay only.
Facilities Water, stores, trains to Edinburgh and Dundee.
Tel/VHF 16; 20,71 ("Forth Navigation Service")

KIRKALDY
Chart BA 739
HW: Dover +3¾h
MHWS 5.5m MHWN 4.4 MTL 3.0 MLWN 2.0 MLWS 0.7
A pier hbr facing S. Avoid in strong E winds when seas break a long way out. Busy with small coasters. Contact hbr in advance of entry; Methil Hbr Radio (ch 16; 14) will relay messages.
Entrance Keep close to E pier. W of hbr is shoal.
Berthing Seek berth alongside E pier in 0.5 to 1.5m, or by steps along outer section of S pier. Yachts can sometimes use wet dock (entry HW−2h to HW).
Facilities Water, stores, trains, buses.

METHIL
Chart BA 739
HW: Dover +3½h
MHWS 5.5m MHWN 4.4 MTL 3.0 MLWN 2.0 MLWS 0.7
Situated ½M W of conspic power station and just E of oilrig yard. Once a major coal port, now quiet but industrial and rather dirty; important because it is available in strong E to SE winds. Avoid in SW winds.
Entrance Faces S. Straightforward, given sufficient rise of tide.
Berthing Lock into No 1 or No 2 dock by arrangement. Or by ladders at head of "Long Channel" to stbd.
Tel/VHF 16; 14, ("Methil Hbr").

ST MONANCE
Chart BA 734
HW: Dover +3½h
MHWS 3.5m MHWN 2.5 approx.
Small pleasant fishing hbr, dries completely, sand and mud.
Approach After half tide; avoid in bad weather.
Entrance Between E breakwater (Oc WRG 6s) and pole bn on rocks to W.
Berthing In E hbr on outer pier.
Facilities Water, stores, local buses; boatbuilder, engineer. EC Wed.

ANSTRUTHER
Chart BA 190
HW: Dover +3½h
MHWS 5.5m MHWN 4.4 MTL 3.0 MLWN 2.0 MLWS 0.7
Hbr dries, inner hbr soft mud. Conspic lt tr on W breakwater and moored lt vessel inside.
Approach from S and enter on line of ldg lts, 019°. Avoid in heavy weather from E to S.
Berthing As directed; if possible alongside W pier in inner hbr just above first knuckle.
Facilities All; EC Wed. Admirable Fisheries Museum.

Off-shore Anchorages
Isle of May Shore is bold except NW end, bottom rocky, holding poor.
Shelter from E winds at W Tarbert and Altar Stones; from W winds at E Tarbert. Kirkhaven small boat hbr requires detailed knowledge; enter from South.
Largo Bay On N shore of Firth of Forth. Good anchorage in N and E winds.
St Andrew's Bay (N of Fife Ness) Good in S winds through W to NW. Anchor about ¼M E of St Andrews hbr pier in suitable depth, sand. Rks beyond pier hd marked by bn.

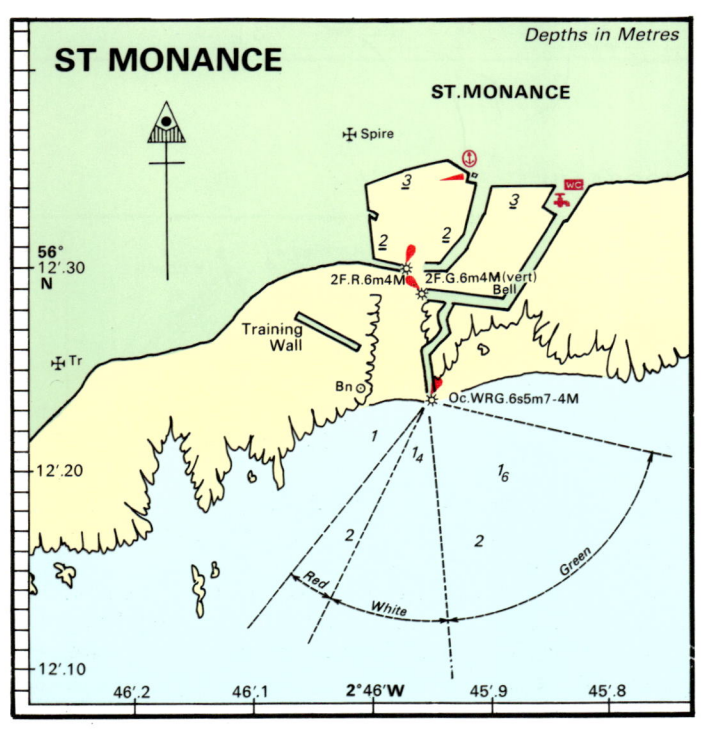

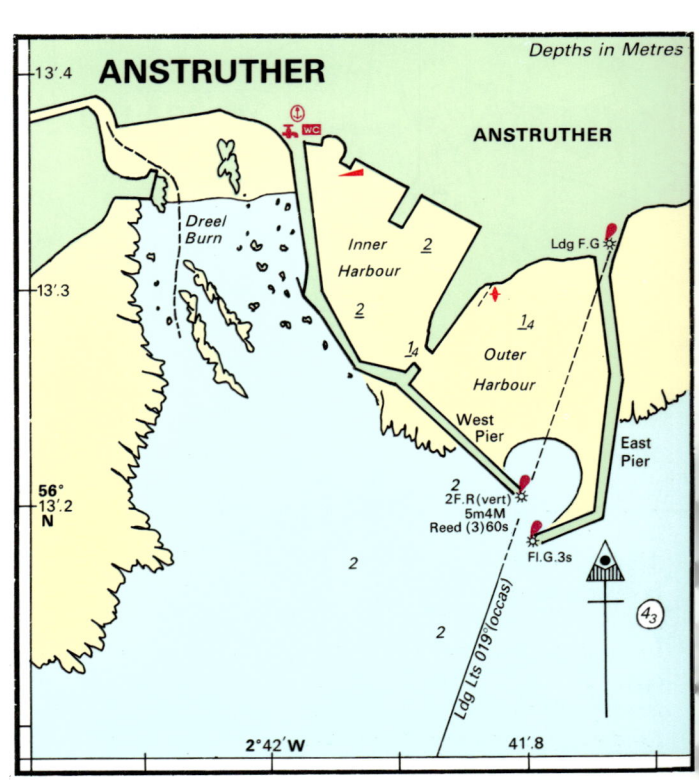

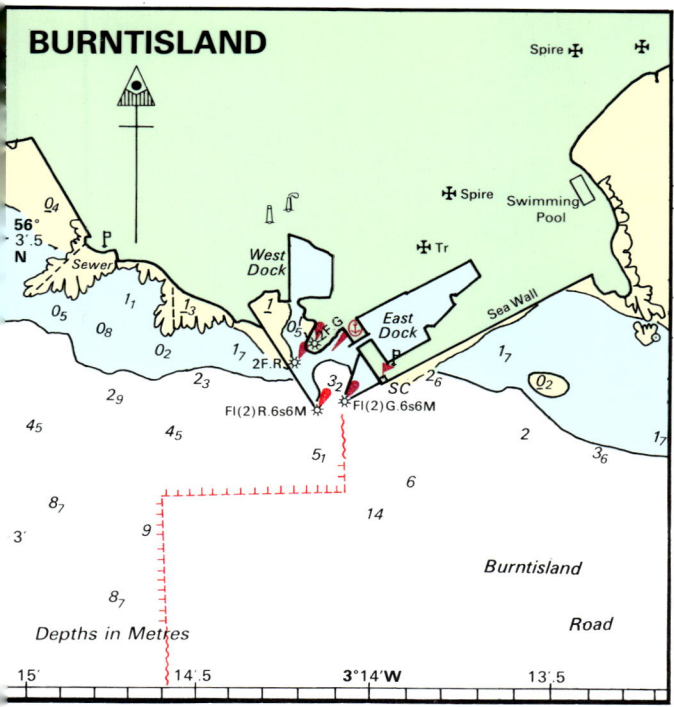

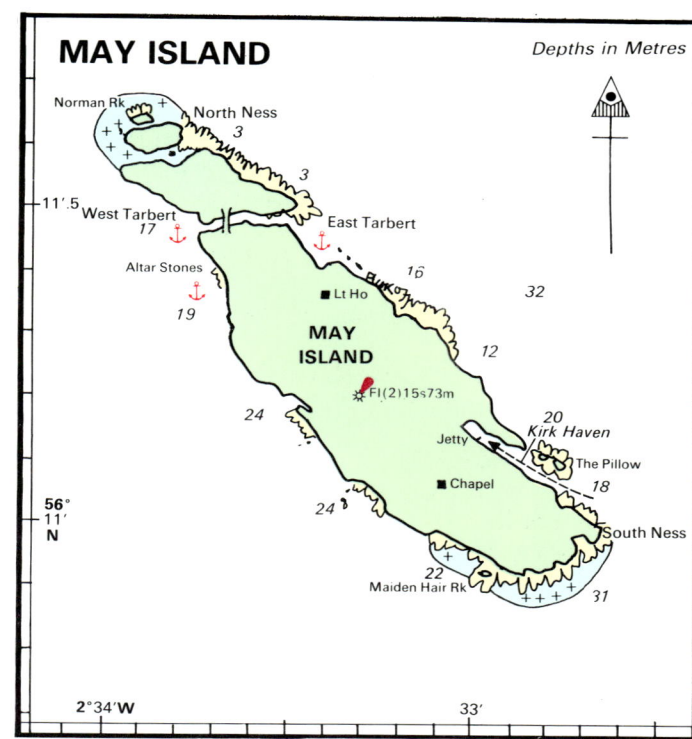

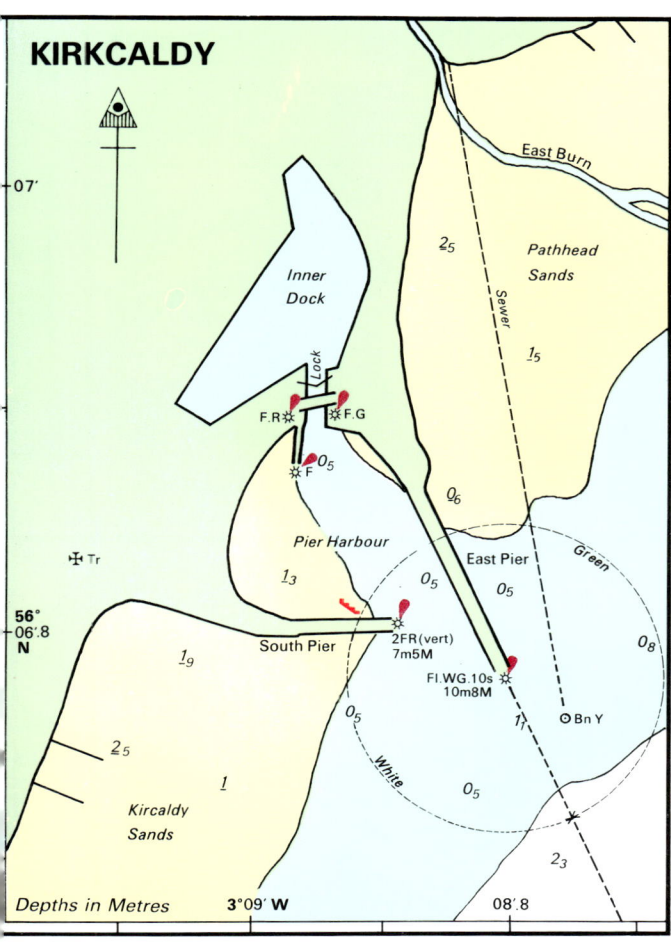

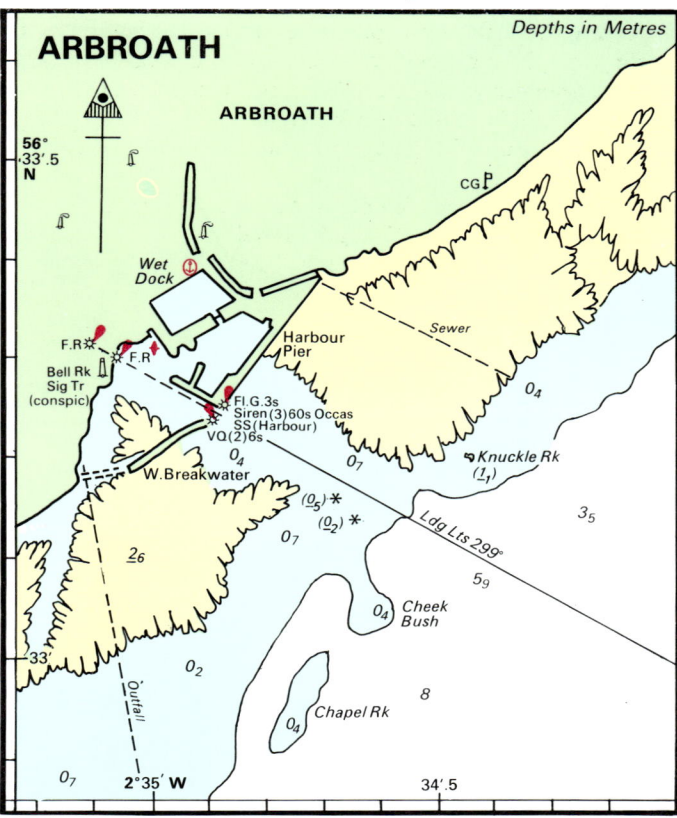

ARBROATH   Chart BA 1438
HW: Dover +3¼h
MHWS 5.0m   MHWN 4.1   MTL 2.9   MLWN 1.8   MLWS 0.7
Fishing hbr. Outer hbr dries; wet dock, sometimes left open (chiefly Fri-Mon). Identified by conspic white swimming pool ½M W of entrance and white signal tower. Useful passage hbr in off-shore weather for boats willing to dry out.

Approach Channel bounded by drying rock ledges for ¼M from a bar (0.5m). Outlying dangers Knuckle Rk (stb) Cheek Bush and Chapel Rk (port).
Entrance Steer with twin towers of church on with gap in piers until white pole ldg marks (FR) located, 299°. Keep strictly to line. Moderate SE swell causes very awkward swell in entrance.
Facilities All. EC Wed.

SCOTLAND, EAST COAST   122

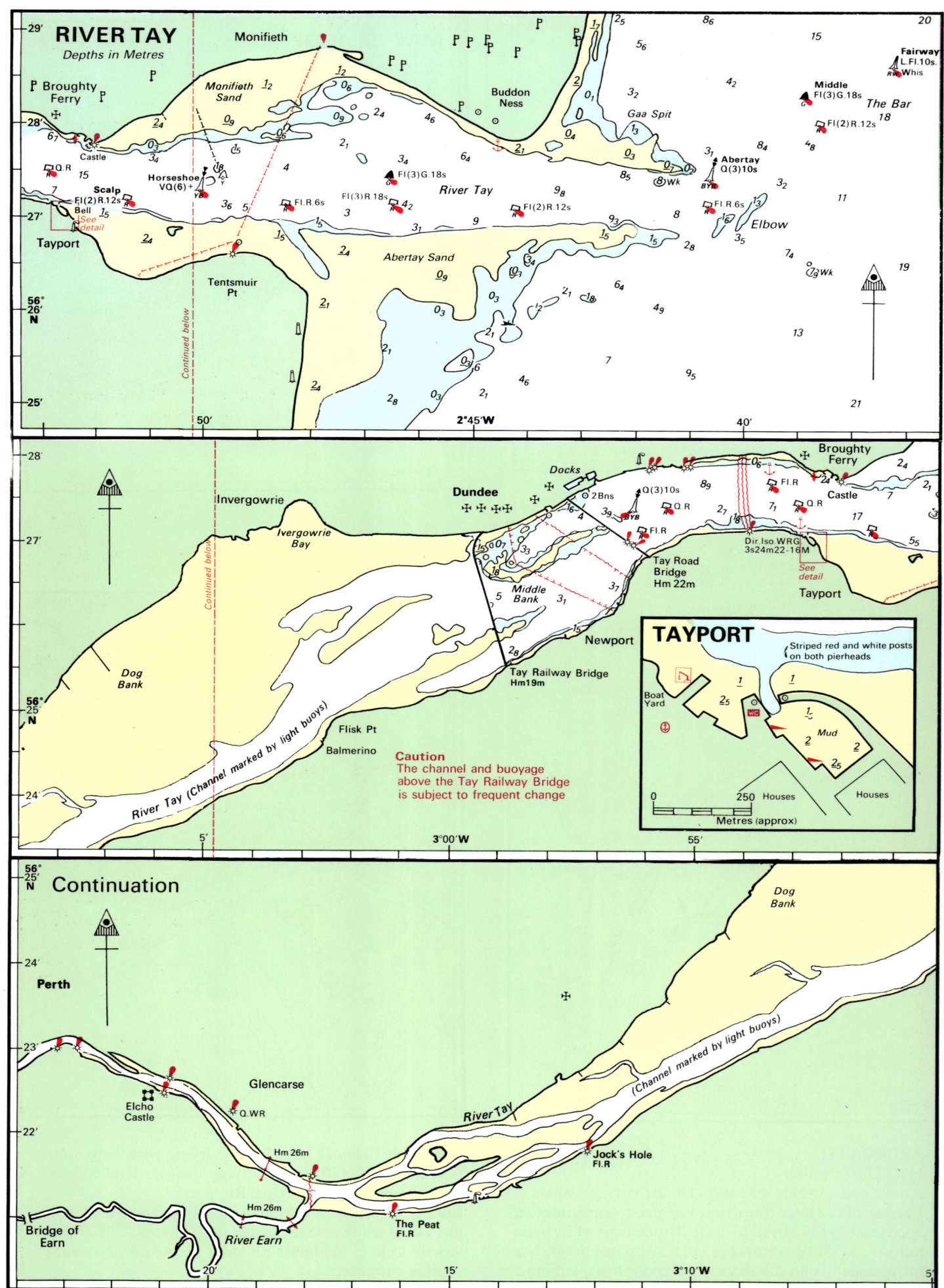

RIVER TAY
Chart BA 1481

HW: Dover +3½h (Bar) +4h (Dundee). DS off bar: Dover −1¼h SW; +4¾h NW

A major river leading to port of Dundee and navigable on tide to the deep-water hbr of Perth. Approaches are shoal a long way off-shore. Once in the river ebb stream is stronger on N shore, flood on S.

Approach With draught of 1.5m enter channel between R and G Middle lt buoys. (With deeper draught or in onshore weather enter from Fairway safe water buoy 4½M ENE of Budden Ness.) From S, after half tide and with smooth water, it is possible to join the channel near Abertay R can buoy (Fl R 6s), keeping the old lt houses on Budden Ness in transit. Do not attempt to cross Abertay sands which extend 5M out from S shore – stakes. On-shore marks can be difficult to identify in poor visibility.

Bar 5.5m between Gaa Spit and Elbow. Dangerous in strong E wind or heavy on-shore swell.

Entrance Channel is buoyed. From Abertay E card lt by (Q3 10s) steer on steep-to shore at Tayport with Dir lt ho (Iso WRG 3s) brg 269°.

Anchorages/Berthing (1) Tayport – see separate entry.
(2) Temporary anchorage on S side just N of Lucky Scalp E of Tayport. On N side close inshore SW of Budden Ness, out of main ebb stream.
(3) Good anchorage clear to W of Tayport entrance, to N of line of high and low lights (low lt disused).
4) In W Ferry Bay 8ca WNW from Broughty Castle by R Tay YC moorings. (Mooring may be available from club; stream runs strongly.) Broughty Hbr dries; available HW ±3h, keep to W wall. Slip, crane.
Both (3) and (4) rather exposed.
(5) Dundee Docks Entrance 4ca E of Road Bridge. Anchorage off not recommended. Yachts can enter wet docks by prior arrangement; commercial port, perfect safety. Lock HW -2h to HW. Strictly no smoking. EC Wed.
(6) Pleasant anchorages above brs off Balmerino and further W. (Local knowledge needed above Jock's Hole.) Dundee Port authority, VHF 16; 12, "Dundee Hbr Radio", covers all shipping movements.

TAYPORT
HW: Dover +4h

Completely sheltered hbr 7M from Abertay R and BYB buoys, offering an excellent passage stop. Mostly dries to very deep soft mud. Upper end of hbr taken up with local boats. No commercial activity, visitors welcome.

Approach Just W of Larrick Bn (conspic pile lt) head for hbr mouth on 180°. Beware strong cross-stream and moorings W of entrance.

Entrance Keep close to E quay wall for best water (3h either side of HW for 1.5m draught).

Berthing On inside of NE wall. Check with HM. Top of hbr dries very early on ebb.

Facilities Pleasant small town; boatyard. Power, water on quay.

Tel/HM (0382) 553534.

PASSAGE NOTES: ARBROATH TO RATTRAY HEAD

Not a stretch of coast to be trifled with in on-shore weather. An offing of ¾ to 1M (but 2M in on-shore weather) is sufficient as far as 57°20′N. S of Cruden Bay a reef, "The Scares", runs 1M to seaward, buoyed Fl R 10s off end. In thick weather the 30m contour gives clearance of all dangers, closing the coast at Buchan Ness just S of Peterhead. Peterhead alone offers safe entry in almost any conditions.

Tide The ebb, NE-ly, starts Dover −6h off Bell Rk and 2½h earlier (Dover+4h) 5M off Rattray Hd. Similarly the flood sets in later the further S. The inshore streams change some 2h earlier.

Rattray Head Seas can be dangerous in heavy weather. Best rounded at slack water, 1M off (this clears inshore dangers and leaves area of steepest seas to seaward). In bad conditions pass five miles off and if necessary more.

Passage Lights and DF Bn.
Scurdie Ness	Fl(3) 20s 38m 23M
Tod Head	Fl(4) 30s 41m 29M
Girdle Ness	Fl(2) 20s 56m 22M
Buchan Ness	Fl 5s 40m 28M
Rattray Hd	Fl(3) 30s 28m 24M
Aero RC Scotstown Hd	3M S of Rattray Hd
	383kHz, SHD, cont, 80M

Off-Shore Anchorage
Lunan Bay offers temporary anchorage in off-shore winds, either close to S shore (no further W than Ethie village) or under Boddin Pt at N end. Subject to swell.

Montrose – see next page

STONEHAVEN
Chart BA 1438

HW: Dover +2¾h

MHWS 4.5m MHWN 3.6 MTL 2.6 MLWN 1.7 MLWS 0.6

A good small fishing hbr 9ca N of Dunottar Castle (ruins). Outer hbr dredged 1.5m along piers but liable to silting; inner dries. Sand and mud.

Inner hbr closed with booms in bad weather.
Avoid in heavy onshore weather. Outer hbr subject to surge with swell offshore.

Approach Steer just S of W, giving good clearance to Downie Point and Bellman Rks. Pierhead lit Dir WGR.

Entry Keep up to stb after passing outer pierhead.

Berthing In offshore weather alongside pier in outer hbr. Otherwise enter inner hbr and dry out against quays as directed.

Facilities Stores, water; fuel ½M. EC Wed.

Tel/HM (0569) 62741.

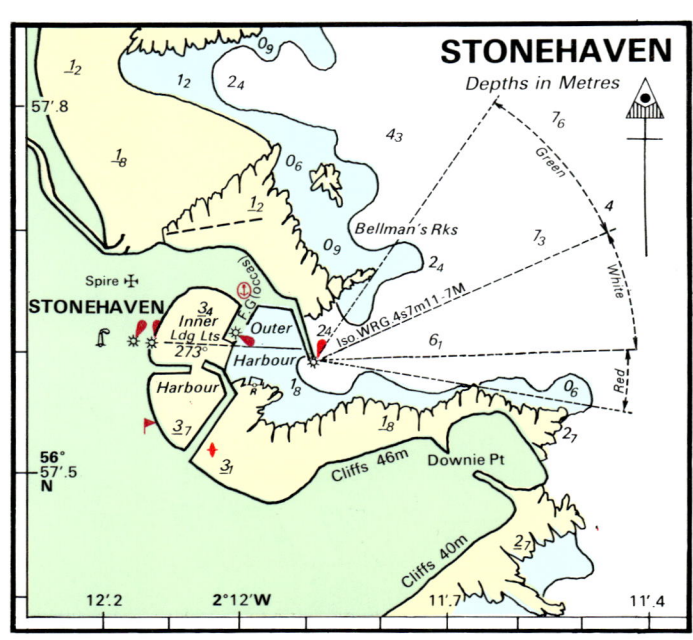

SCOTLAND, EAST COAST

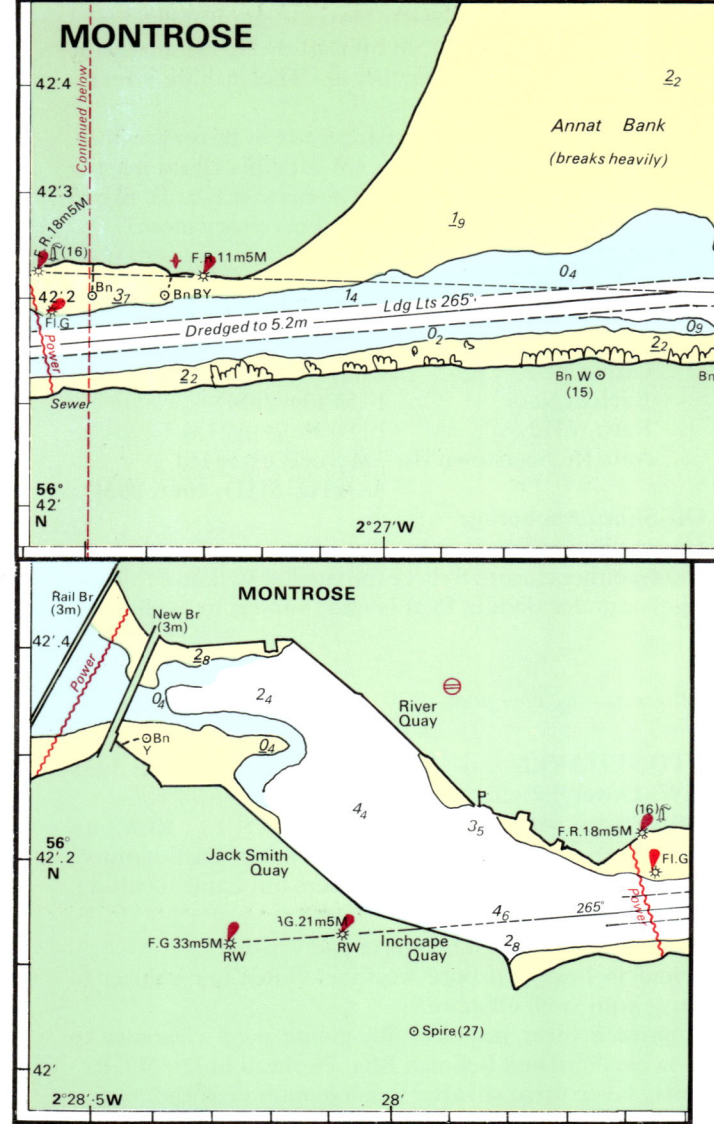

MONTROSE — Chart BA 1438

HW: Dover +3½h

MHWS 4.8m MHWN 3.9 MTL 2.8 MLWN 1.9 MLWS 0.7

A busy commercial and oil port with ship movements round the clock. Very strong tides in channel and entrance.

Approach From S or N keep minimum ½M offshore until ldg line open 271° between R and G lit buoys. 50m wide channel dredged to minimum 4m. Hold ldg line until abeam inner of two W unlit stone bns on S shore; then alter 265° onto inner ldg line.

Entry best at slack water or first hour of flood. Avoid in strong onshore weather; seas break in channel.

Berthing Normally alongside quay on N side. Previous wet dock now closed. Fender board desirable.

Facilities All. EC Wed.

Tel HM (0674) 72302 or 73153. VHF 16, 12.

Signals Traffic Signals in force. G lt by day and night from control tr prohibits entry from seaward.

Entry Contact hbr control (if no VHF loudhailer instructions from Control Tr at root of N breakwater). N Pierhead and S breakwater lit – see plan.

Berthing As directed; usually at quays in Victoria or Upper Dock.

Facilities All. Main line trains; Dyce Airpt 7M. EC Wed/Sat.

Tel/HM (0224) 592571 VHF 16, 12, 10, 11, 13 (24h).

ABERDEEN — Chart BA 1446

HW: Dover +2½h. DS: Dover −2½h SE; +3¾h NW

MHWS 4.3m MHWN 3.4 MTL 2.5 MLWN 1.6 MLWS 0.6

Busy major oil port; yachts only in emergency. Well protected from S but open to NE; do not attempt on ebb in strong NE wind.

Approach Ldg line 236° from Fairway RW lt buoy is lit FR (entrance safe) or FG (entrance dangerous). Keep S face of N pier just open.

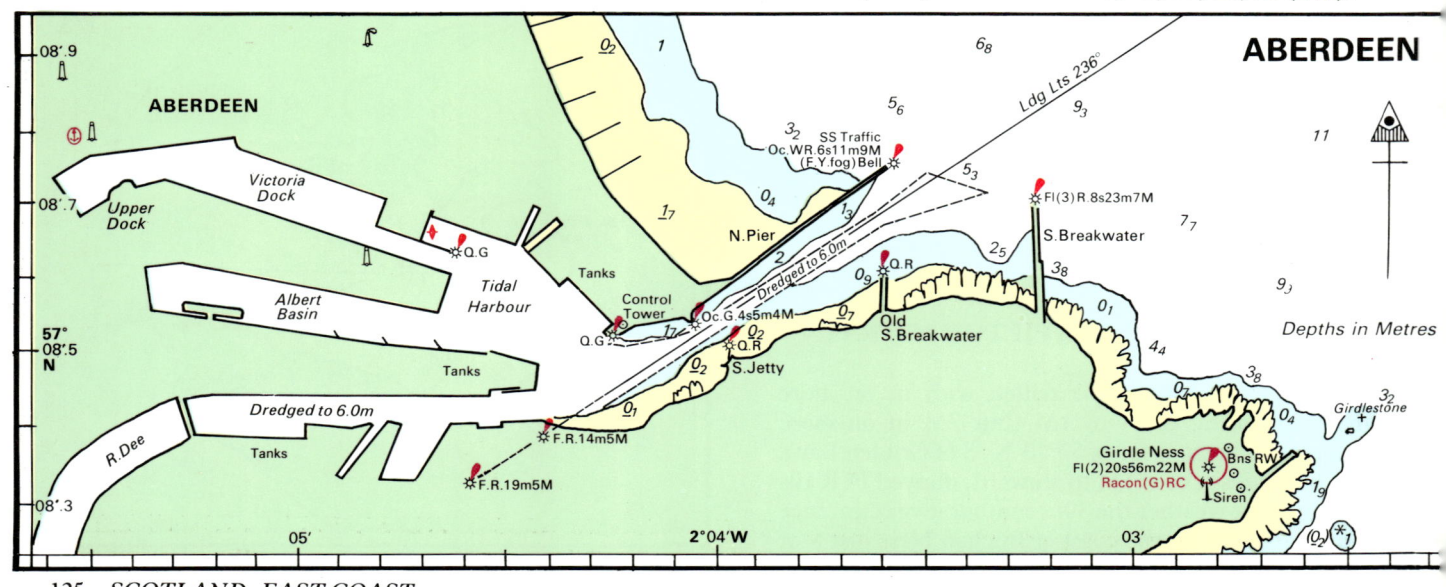

125 SCOTLAND, East Coast

PETERHEAD
Chart BA 1438

HW: Dover +2h. DS off: Dover −2h S; +3½h N
MHWS 3.8m MHWN 3.1 MTL 2.2 MLWN 1.5 MLWS 0.5

A busy fishing and oil port; little room for yachts. Power stn chy S of bay makes conspic landmark. Long breakwaters turn whole bay into hbr of refuge available in almost any weather. New Harbour extension works in progress. Care needed on approach to S Harbour. Old N entrance closed off.

Approach Headlands to N and S are foul for ¼M; then approach between SW and NW (ldg lts 314°).

Anchorage Outside in Sandford Bay in 4m, sand; considerable swell. In Harbour of Refuge in Prison Bay in SW corner, or in NW corner 150m offshore below ldg marks.

Signals Traffic signals from control tr above hbr office (See Almanac: 3 or 4 FR(Hor) prohibits entry to fishing hbrs.) Call Hbr Control before entering or leaving.

Entry and Berthing Yachts normally directed to Port Henry in NW corner through lifting and sliding bridges. Beware obscured shipping movements in S hbr. Tie up well clear of access to ice plant.

Facilities All – but geared to larger vessels. EC Wed.

Tel/HM (0779) 74020 (75281 after hours). VHF 16, 14.

Note Considerable congestion when fishing fleet in hbr, Thur-Sun. Fleet sails en masse in middle of Sun-Mon night.

PASSAGE NOTE: MORAY FIRTH TO WICK

Kinnairds Head In heavy weather keep 2M offshore; otherwise keep ¼ to ½M off R bn marking reef off Cairnbulg Pt.

Moray Firth Surprisingly heavy seas can be met in W or NW winds. Large scale charts are needed for approach to Inverness and Caledonian canal, 223, 1078. (For canal see West Coast Scotland.)

Passage Lights & DF Beacons

Kinnairds Hd	Fl 15s 25m 18M
Covesea Skerries	Fl WR 20s 49m 24/20M
Tarbat Ness	Fl(4) 30s 53m 24M
Clythness	Fl(2) 30s 45m 16M
Noss Hd	Fl WR 20s 53m 25/21M
Duncansby Hd	Fl 12s 67m 24M
RC Kinnairds Hd	301.5kHz, KD, cont, 70M
Aero RC Wick	344kHz, WIK, cont, 40M

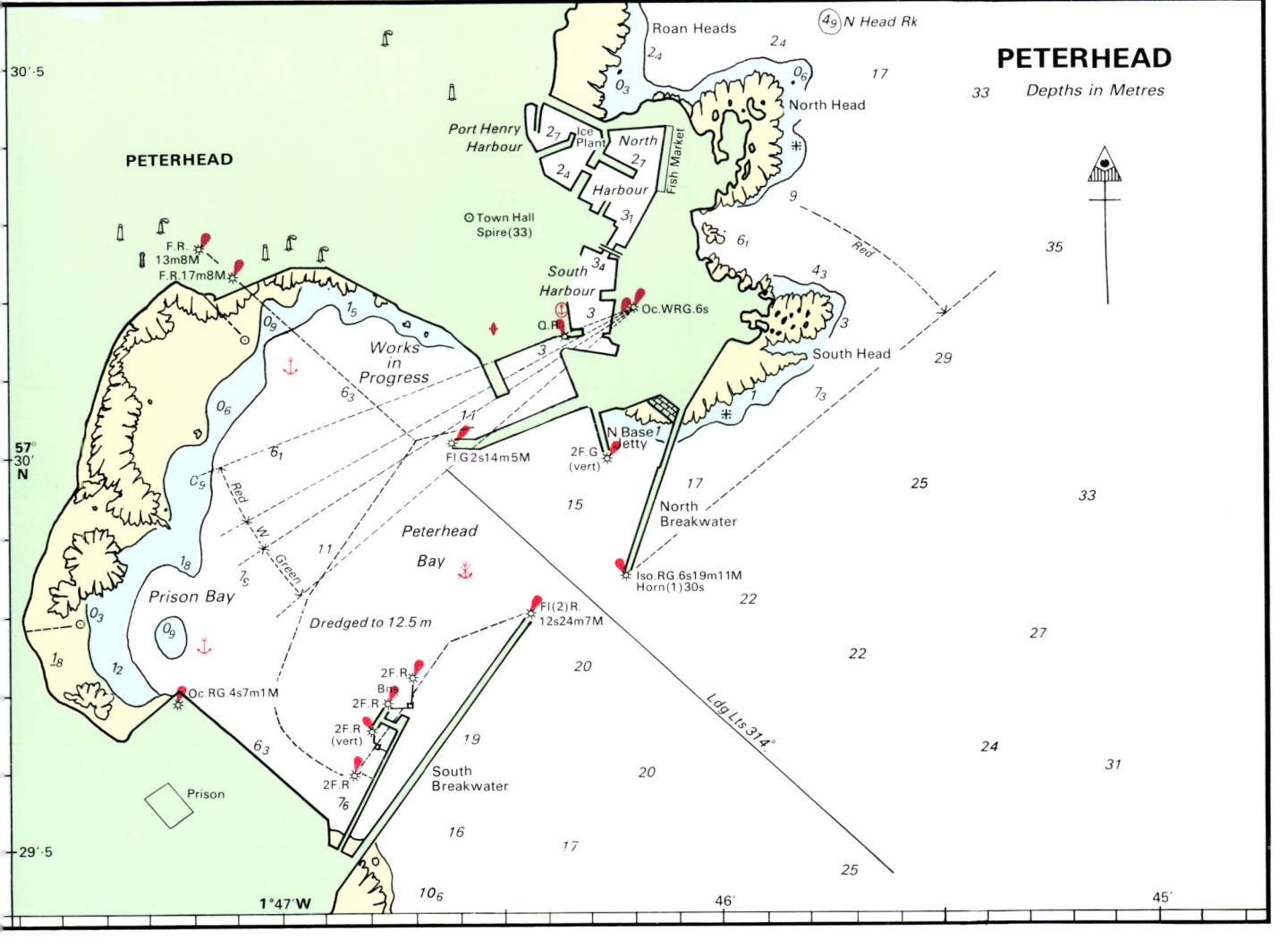

FRASERBURGH
Chart BA 1462
HW: Dover +1½h
MHWS 3.9m MHWN 3.1 MTL 2.3 MLWN 1.5 MLWS 0.6
A very busy fishing port, but a good port of call for yachts with plenty of room. Entrance dangerous in onshore gales.
Approach on 291°. Ldg lts Oc R over QR, or old Parish Ch spire (to S of dome) just open S of Balaclava Pier. Keep W silo on N Pier open S of lt on Balaclava breakwater.
Signals R flag/R lt – entrance dangerous.
2 B Balls/2 R lts vert – port closed.
Berthing usually in S Hbr on SE pier. In bad weather or if leaving boat ask to move into Winter Basin. Directions from watch-house.
Tel/HM (0346) 25858. VHF 16, 12 (24h).

PASSAGE NOTE: MORAY FIRTH
In good weather and with enough time the small hbrs on the Moray Firth are available to yachts willing to dry out: **Whitehills, Portsey, Portknockie, Findochty, Hopeman** (popular and crowded in season). **Nairn** (bars at river mouth and in channel; dredging in progress, pontoon berths). Chart 222. Similarly **Portmahomack** on S side of entrance to Dornoch Firth.
Beware stake nets and inconspic pot markers in approaches to these hbrs. Bombing range target float 4M E of Troup Hd.

MACDUFF (BANFF)
Chart BA 1462
HW: Dover +1h
MHWS 3.5m MHWN 2.8 MTL 2.0 MLWN 1.1 MLWS 0.5
Fishing hbr with 3 basins, least depth 2m; generally crowded. Good shelter but entrance very rough in winds from W to N. Not to be attempted in onshore gales or in heavy swell, when smaller Banff Hbr across bay, facing E, offers refuge. Banff Hbr dries, clean sand.
Signals Ldg lts Oct-March only. B ball/G lt – hbr closed.
Berthing In N-most basin beyond line of slipway.
Facilities All. EC Wed.
Tel/HM (0261) 32236/22014. VHF 16, 12 (24h).

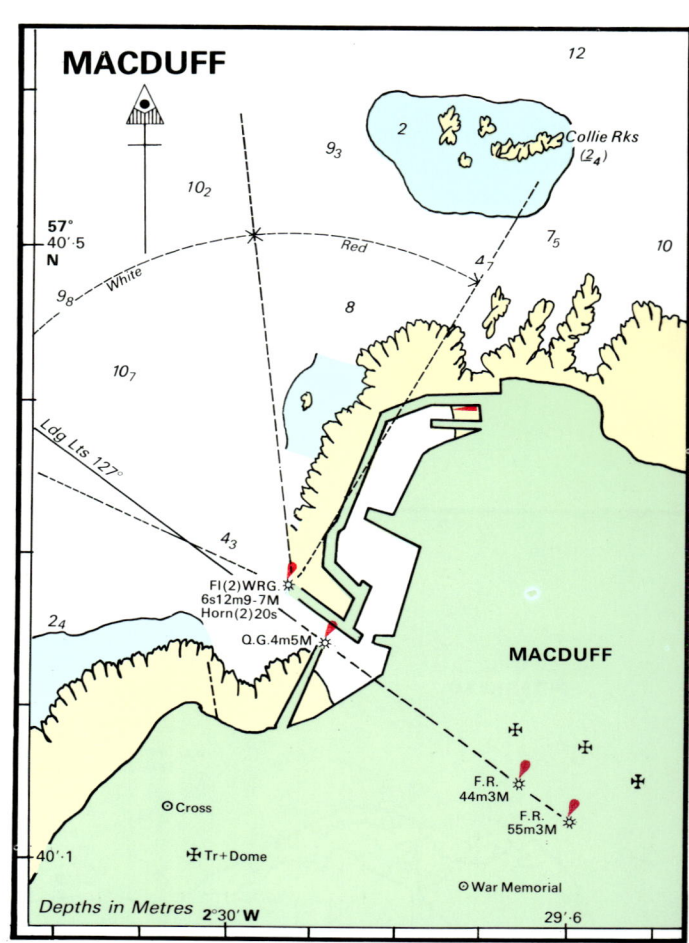

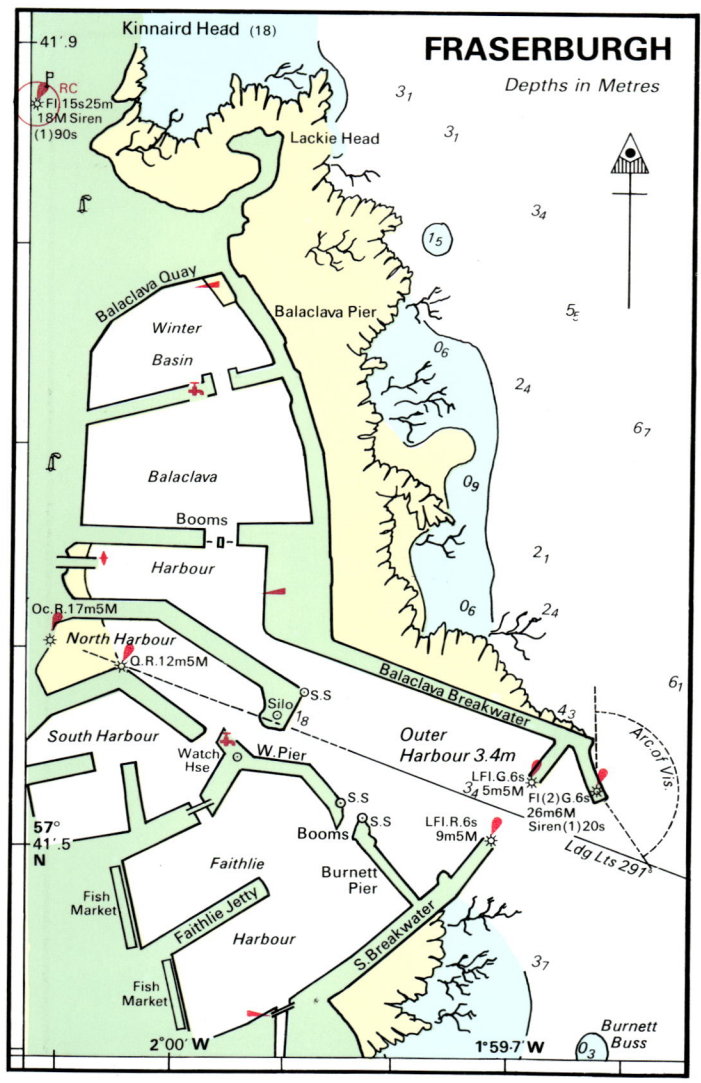

BUCKIE
Chart BA 1462
HW: Dover +1h
MHWS 3.5m MHWN 2.8 MTL 2.0 MLWN 1.1 MLWS 0.5
A busy fishing port with 4 basins, drawbridge between No. 3 and No. 4. Safe entry in all weathers. 2.2m minimum in entrance and 3m alongside.
Signals 3B balls/3 FR (vert) – hbr closed.
Berthing As directed, usually No 4 basin. Handle for bridge from HM's office.
Facilities All, diesel by can or bowser. EC Wed.
Tel/HM (0542) 31700. VHF 16, 12, 9, 11 (24h).

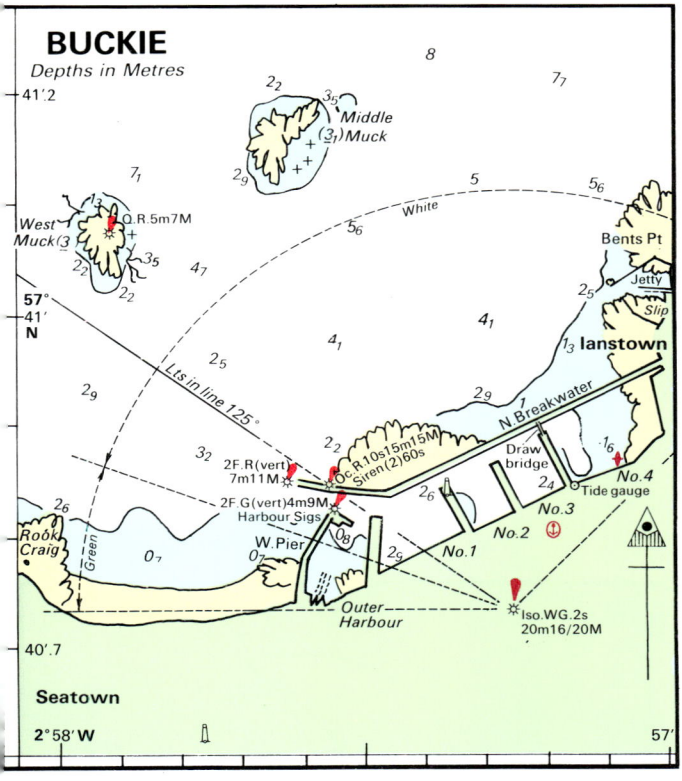

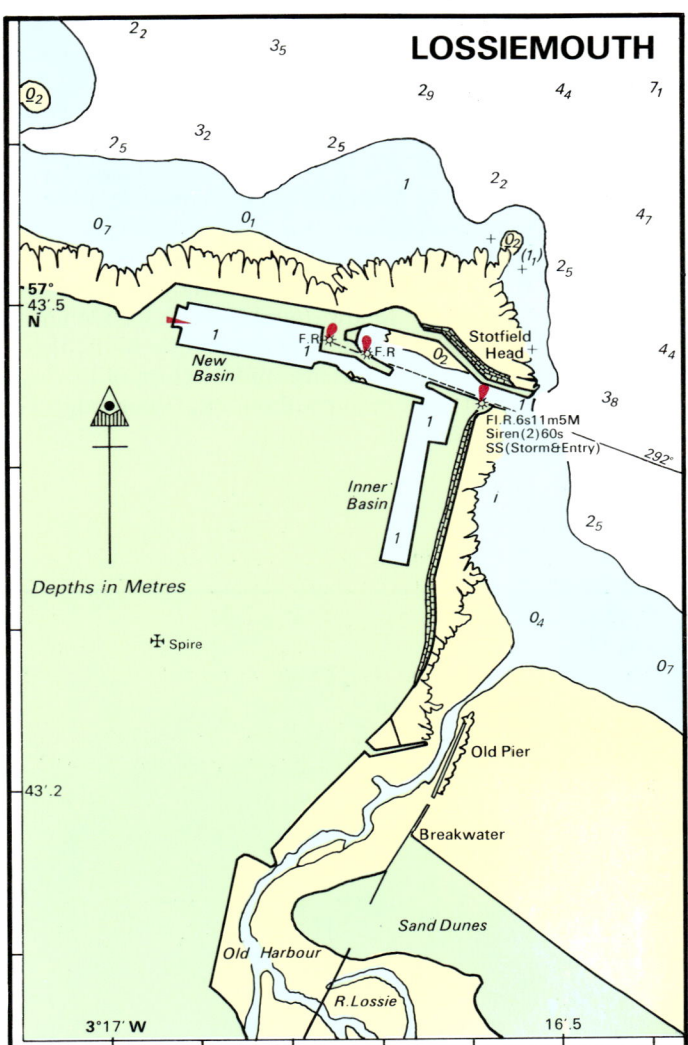

LOSSIEMOUTH Chart BA 1462
HW: Dover +¾h
MHWS 4.1m MHWN 3.2 MTL 2.4 MLWN 1.6 MLWS 0.6
Fishing hbr, identified by Covesea Lt Ho to W of town. Avoid in winds F5 or over from E or NE.
Signals Ldg lts (FR 292°) when entrance is safe. B ball/R over G lts on S pier – unsafe.
Entry and Berthing 1.8 to 2.4m, may be less in entrance after prolonged E winds. Best depth in S basin. Beware strong current setting across entrance N from river mouth.
Tel/HM (034-381) 3066. VHF 16, 12 (0800-1700).

BURGHEAD Chart BA 1462
HW: Dover +1h
MHWS 4.1m MHWN 3.2 MTL 2.2 MLWN 1.6 MLWS 0.6
Hbr offers shelter in all winds, but swell can be considerable.
Entrance 1.5m LWS. Tide gauge. Keep 15m off wooden extension of N pier hd then keep mid-channel; at night identify lts on N pier spur (QR) and S pier (QG), both vis only from SW, and keep G open S of R.
Berthing As directed or as far as possible up basin: never on N side of S pier.
Facilities Stores, chandler, water, fuel, buses.
Tel/HM (0343) 835337. VHF 16, 12, 9, 6 (occas).

FINDHORN Chart BA 223
HW: Dover +1¼h
MHWS 4.1m MHWN 3.2 MTL 2.2 MLWN 1.6 MLWS 0.6
HQ R Findhorn YC in river mouth behind shifting sand bar. Village conspic on W side of Burghead Bay; windsock E of entrance.
Bar shifts constantly, buoyage somewhat unreliable and subject to change. Telephone YC for advice, (0309) 30247; pilot recommended, (0309) 30099.
Entrance Local knowledge advisable. Enter near HW leaving YC's R buoys and poles to port.

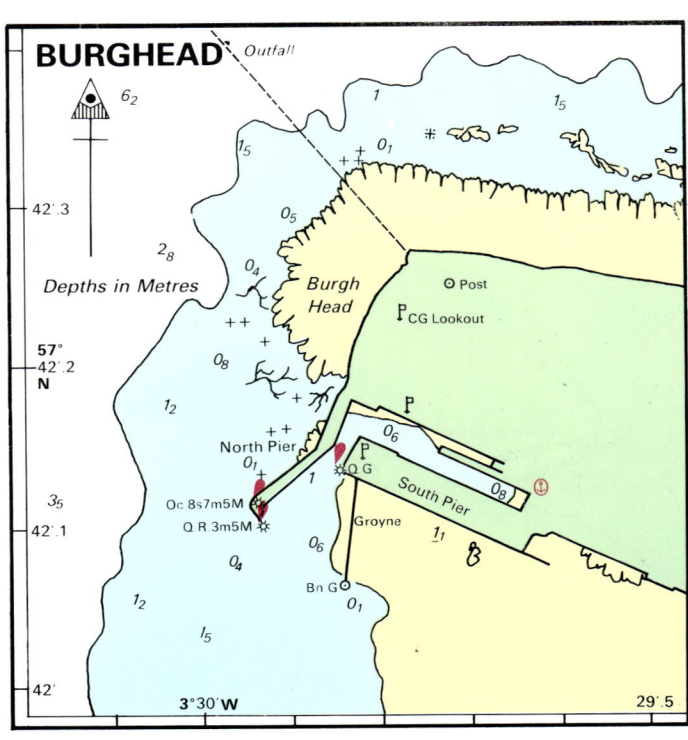

SCOTLAND, EAST COAST

INVERNESS FIRTH AND HBR   Chart BA 1078

HW: Dover +1¼h

MHWS 4.8m   MHWN 3.7   MTL 2.7   MLWN 1.8   MLWS 0.7

City docks (timber exports) in river mouth beyond rd br at head of Inverness Firth. Entrance to Caledonian Canal 1M beyond river mouth.

Approach From E or N keep to buoyed channel S or N of Riff Bank to narrows between Fort George and Chanonry Pt. With sufficient water and rising tide steer 222° for Munlochy RW buoy (Fl 10s) and G con buoy (Fl G 3s) 1M ENE of Br. Otherwise follow round N shore for 5M until Kilmuir Ch (ruins) opens up behind woody bluff; then 160° to G con buoy, and thence under centre of br (ldg lines on BA chart are difficult without local knowledge; G buoy inconspic from N).

Entrance Narrow but deep; beware strong offsets. 2 lt bns to port. From G lt on point keep 10-15m off W bank until level with jetty then cross over and follow quays.

Berthing Moor on Shore St Quay to E of training wall. Keep well over to quay as training wall slopes out below water.

Facilities None apart from city shops and garages. Fuel, gas at Muirtown Basin in Caledonian canal. (In NW winds over F6 access to Clachnaharry sea lock may not be feasible.)

Tel/HM (0463) 233291. VHF 12, 16, 14 (0900-1700 Mon-Fri). Caledonian Canal Office (0463) 233140. Clachnaharry Sea Lock 235439. VHF 16, 74.

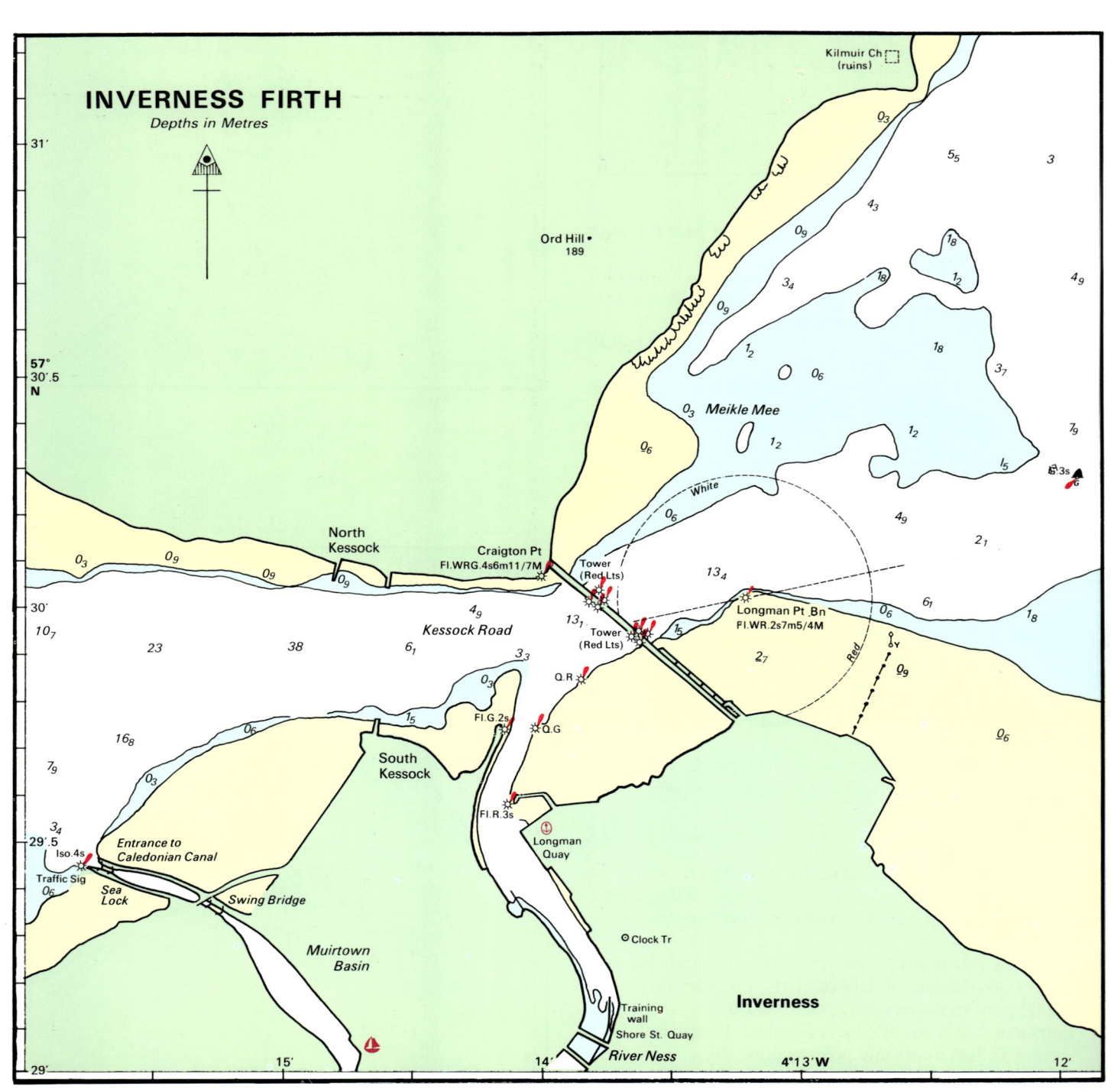

HELMSDALE
Chart BA 1462

HW: Dover +½h

MHWS 3.7m   MHWN 2.9   MTL 2.2   MLWN 1.5   MLWS 0.6

A good small hbr; avoid in strong Easterlies.

Signals Rear ldg mark FG; front FG when hbr open, but FR when hbr closed.

Bar About 2.5m on sand bar at entrance at half tide.

Entrance Ldg marks 313° two W poles near base of NW pier.

Berthing In New Hbr alongside. All facilities. EC Wed.

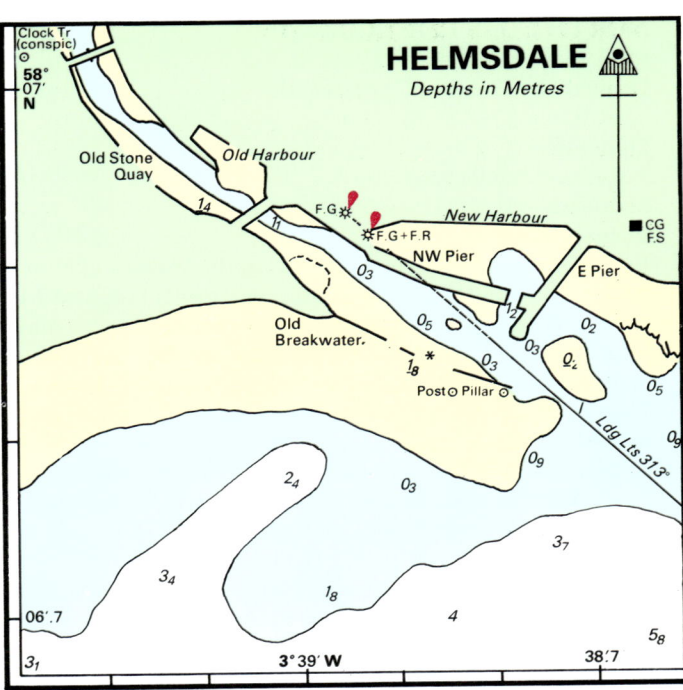

LYBSTER
Chart BA 115

HW: Dover ¼h

MHWS 3.5m   MHWN 2.8   MTL 2.1   MLWN 1.4   MLWS 0.5

Pier hbr 2½M WSW of Clyth Ness. Good refuge; entrance needs to be accurate and difficult in strong Easterlies.

Entry Steer for W pier-head (Oc R 6s occas) on 350°-005°. Keep up to W pier; beware set onto rocks and first pier to stb.

Berthing In outer hbr on innermost end of W pier or in SE corner of inner basin (W part dries).

Facilities Hotel, stores ½M. EC Thur.

WICK
Chart BA 1462

HW: Dover +½h

MHWS 3.4m   MHWN 2.7   MTL 2.0   MLWN 1.4   MLWS 0.5

Busy oil, commercial and fishing hbr at hd of Wick Bay 2½M S of Noss Hd.

Entrance dangerous in strong E winds and heavy seas run into hbr with wind between NE and S.

Approach and Entrance Hbr obscured until bay is fully opened up. Both shores of Wick Bay are foul. Enter on 290°. Fixed Dir WRG lt. Then steer for Lt Ho on S pier (W tower, Fl WRG) on 270°-285° (in W sector of this Flashing light), pass close N of pier hd and keep along N face (ldg lts FR 234°).

Berthing As directed or where space available. Inner hbr for preference, 2m. Outer hbr depths variable due to silting/dredging. Avoid River Hbr to N of entrance; privately rented; dries, bottom rough.

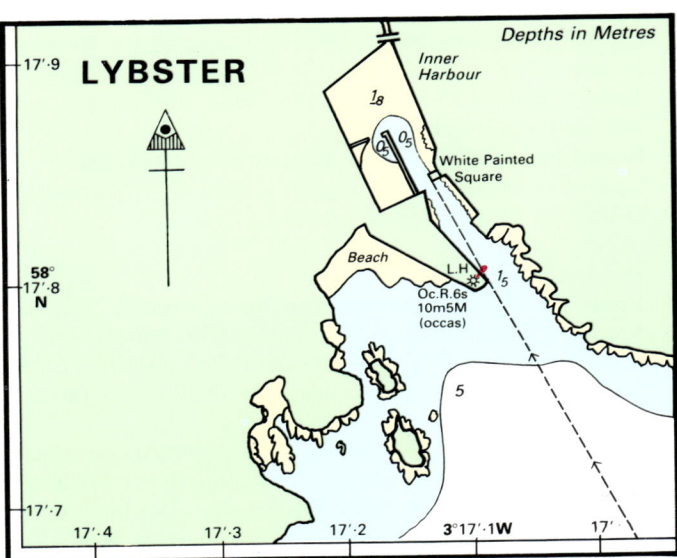

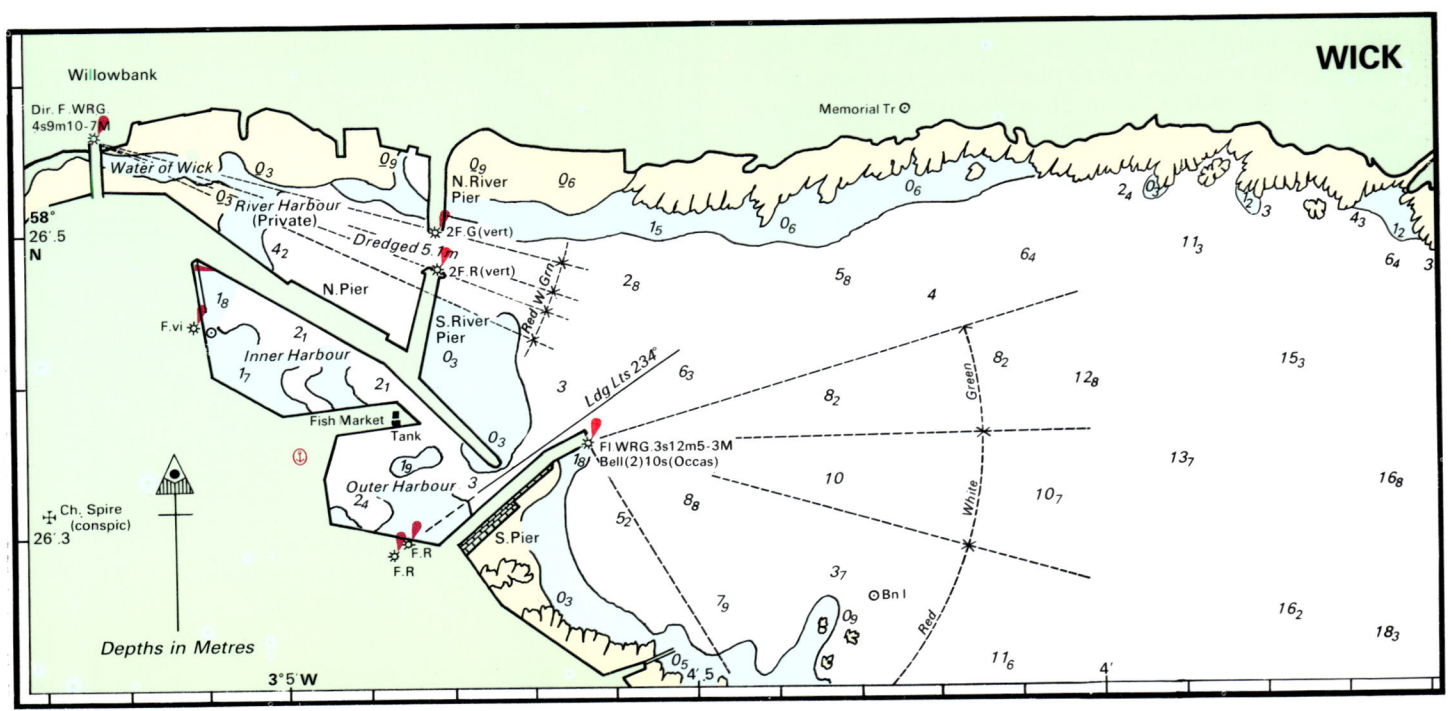

SCOTLAND, EAST COAST

NORTH COAST OF SCOTLAND

Duncansby Head to Cape Wrath

General
For more details refer to CCC SD: N and NE Coasts of Scotland.

Passage Note
From Duncansby Hd to Cape Wrath the N coast of Scotland stretches 60M E to W, rounding Dunnet Hd, Strathy Pt and Whiten Hd. Temporary anchorages in numerous sandy bays in offshore winds, but these are very dangerous if wind shifts N'ly and wind changes are often sudden. John O'Groats Hbr (2m MLWS available) could be used to wait for tide.
In winds over F7 only two anchorages can be used safely: Loch Eriboll; and Thurso Bay (Scrabster) or in winds from NE in Dunnet Bay behind Dunnet Hd.

Tidal Streams
From Freswick Bay (S of Duncansby Hd) keep inshore where there is 10h slack water.
Off Duncansby Hd: Dover +1h W; −5¾h E.
To Westward of Dunnet Hd: Dover +½h W, −6h E; but close inshore W until −4½h.
Gill's Bay: stream sets towards St John's Pt for 9h from Dover −3h.
Brough Bay: HWD NW for 4h. Eddy continues to run NW on main E-going stream.
Brimsness: HWD W for 6h at up to 8kn at Springs.
Cape Wrath: Inshore of Stag Rk always W; ½M seaward of Stag Rk Dover −1¾ W; +4¼ E.

Pentland Firth
From E to W the passage can be hazardous. Do not attempt it with tides near Springs, or with winds over F4 (if Westerly over F3), or in less than good visibility. Seek local advice; the RNLI coxswains at Wick and Scrabster are always helpful.
Round Duncansby Hd just before W-going stream starts, about HWD to +½h, keeping very close in with Dunnet Hd just open of St John's Pt. Deep water to within 30m of cliffs. Then within ½M of shore until up to St John's Pt, passing the Rocks of Mey off the point 100m off. (This keeps the boat out of the severe 'Merry Men of Mey' race which stretches right across to Tor Ness on Hoy in Orkney. On no account try to pass through the race.) Do not pass Rocks of Mey before 2h of ebb have run; anchorage available in W of Gill's Bay to await suitable conditions.
From W to E is somewhat easier, as no race forms while tide is favourable and wind with tide is more common. Leave Scrabster at Dover +4½h to arrive off Dunnet Head Dover +5½h as stream turns Easterly. Pass midway between St John's Pt and Stroma steering S to avoid being set onto rocks S of Stroma (bn, unlit). Then through middle of Inner Sd and give Duncansby Hd a wide berth.

Via Orkneys The Pentland Firth can be partly avoided by passing through Scapa Flow.

Cape Wrath
Unless in calm weather give the headland a wide berth when wind and tide are opposed; seas are then exceptionally heavy.
Stag Rk, ¼M NExE of the lt ho covers at half tide (though it may show in the hollows of swell). It can be cleared on the inside by keeping well towards the headland (steep-to); otherwise give it a wide berth.

Passage Lights
Duncansby Hd	Fl 12s 67m 17M
Stroma	Fl(2) 20s 32m 26M
Dunnet Hd	Fl(4) 30s 105m 26M
Strathy Pt	Fl 20s 45m 27M
C Wrath	Fl(4) 30s 122m 24M
Sule Skerry	Fl(2) 15s 34m 19M

SCRABSTER Chart BA 1462
HW: Dover −2½h.
MHWS 5.5m MHWN 3.7 MTL 3.0 MLWN 2.1 MLWS 0.8
Hbr can be entered at all states of tide; no bar; complete shelter. It is used by Orkney Ro-Ro ferry, coasters and fishing vessels. Two basins, outer dries in NW corner but minimum of 4.2m alongside NE wall; inner has 1.8m. Bottom sand, providing a clean comfortable berth.
Berthing Tie alongside of NE wall of inner basin and consult HM.
Facilities Repairs, slip. Water at pier. Diesel. Showers. No provisions; shops in Thurso, 2 miles, bus.
Tel/HM (0487) 62779. VHF 16, 12 (24h - contact poor from N and W.)

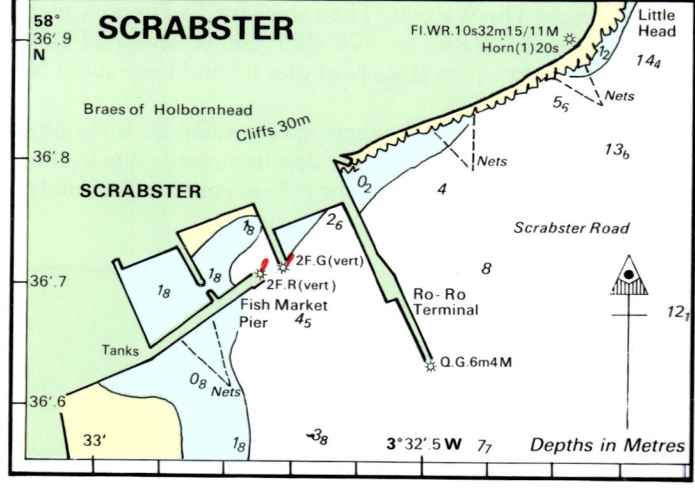

KYLE OF TONGUE
Chart BA 1954

HW: Dover −3½h

MHWS 4.7m   MHWN 3.6

The Kyle of Tongue contains a number of sheltered anchorages but entry during gales or strong Northerlies is not recommended.

Anchorage (1) Talmine, good protection except from N and E winds. Approach from N but do not turn S until W edge of the largest islet of Eiln nan Gaill (ie the westernmost) bears no less than 200°. When abeam steer in to anchor in 5m S of a small islet connected to shore by jetty. Shop 10 mins.

(2) Shelter from W and N in 5m off beach at S side of Eiln nan Gaill.

(3) Shelter from W and NW off Mol na Coinnle, a small bight on E of Eiln nan Ron. Anchorage is recognised by tin-roofed hut near foreshore. Uninhabited. Landing possible.

(4) On E side of Kyle just off small hbr of Skullomie. Entrance directly below house on hillside, best seen looking SE from Eiln nan Gaill. Keep well clear of broken wall to stb and towards E shore. Limited supplies at Coldbachie ½M.

LOCH ERIBOLL
Chart BA 2076

HW (Rispond Bay): Dover −3¾h

MHWS 4.6m   MHWN 3.5   MTL 2.6   MLWN 1.8   MLWS 0.6

Loch Eriboll lies on W side of Whiten Hd. Funnelling produces extremely strong winds in SW'ly weather, when the entrance can be very rough; but good sheltered anchorages are available.

Anchorages On E side (1) In bays N and S of Ard Neackie, good shelter.

(2) Or in 7m off white house 1M to S. Fish farm cages extend S of Ard Neackie across whole of Camus an Duin. Pass N of cages and anchor inshore. (Fish Farm VHF 14, helpful.)

On W side (3) Excellent anchor in Rispond Bay, sand, but congested by fishing boat moorings and fish-farm raft production.

(4) In S of loch. Beware mussel farming; large buoys, long ropes.

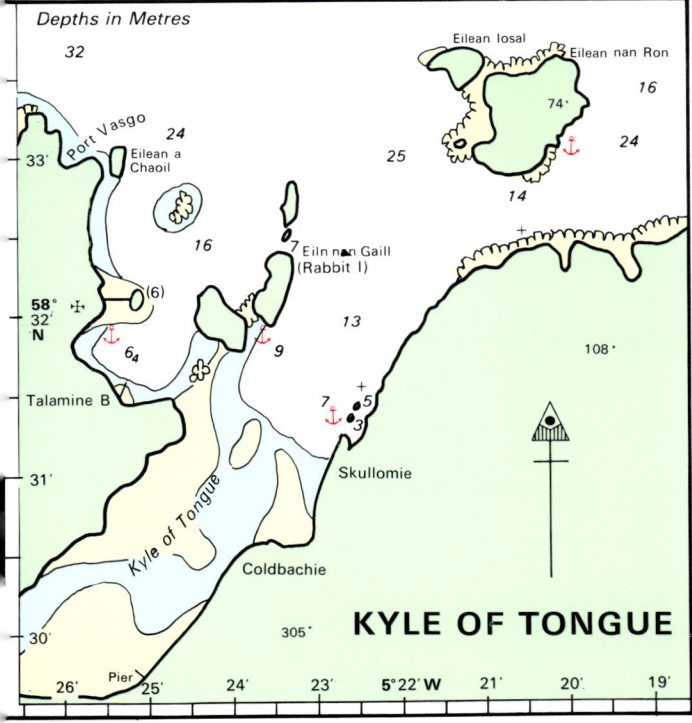

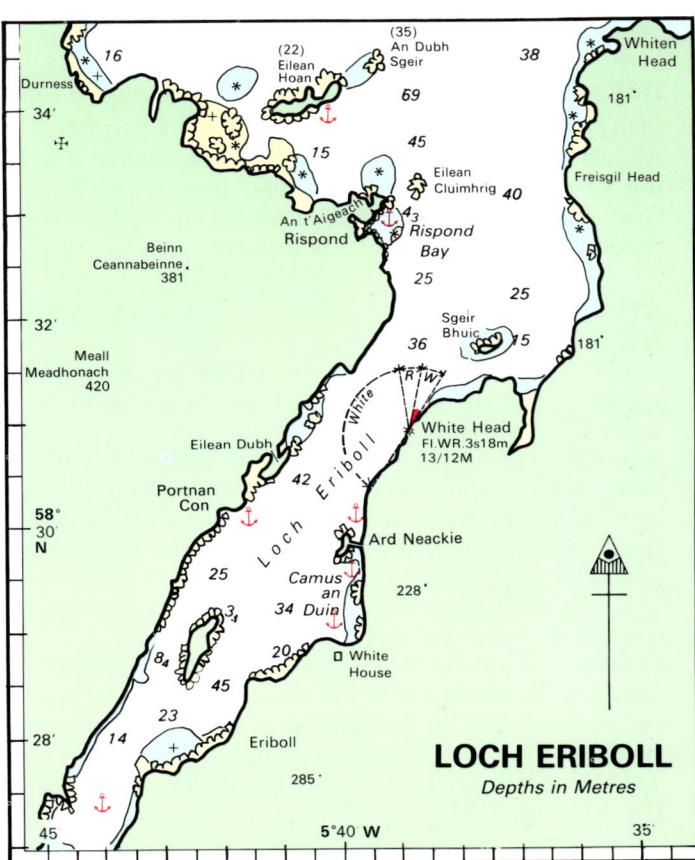

PASSAGE NOTES: MAINLAND SCOTLAND TO ORKNEY

The two straightforward routes are from Scrabster to Scapa Flow/Stromness via the Sound of Hoy and from Wick to Copinsay and the E coast. Time departure from Scrabster to reach the entrance to Sound of Hoy at slack water (Dover +5½h). From Wick keep a good 6M E of the Pentland Skerries. The tidal intricacies of the alternatives, and of the difficult passage from Scapa Flow anticlockwise to the E coast, require careful study of the CCC Sailing Directions.

SCOTLAND NORTH COAST

ORKNEY AND SHETLAND

General
For more details refer to:
CCC SD: Orkney and Shetland (separate volumes.)
Admiralty Tidal Atlas, Orkney and Shetland Is., NP209.

Anyone intending to cruise the islands should carry these sailing directions. Information given here is intended for passage-making boats.

Though the Northern Isles provide fascinating cruising grounds, sailing here calls for particular attention to barometer trends and weather information. Both tides and winds are stronger than in other UK waters: the avoidance of wind-over-tide conditions takes on special importance in entrances, between islands and off major headlands.

Lobster pot markers are numerous. In Shetland in particular mussel rafts and salmon farms abound in sheltered waters. Salmon farms are marked with Y buoys and flashing lights.

ORKNEY

SCAPA FLOW   Chart BA 35
An inland sea with many good anchorages, entered from the W through the Sound of Hoy, passing North of Graemsay, or from the South. Passages to the East are closed by the wartime Churchill Barriers.

STROMNESS   Chart BA 2568
HW: Dover −1½h
MHWS 3.4m MHWN 2.6 MTL 2.0 MLWN 1.4 MLWS 0.4
An excellently sheltered port; no tidal streams and least water 4m in harbour.
Approach Through Hoy Sound or from Scapa Flow. Very strong tides in approaches, not to be undertaken in bad weather or with wind against tide. Easiest from W with flood tide, keeping slightly towards Hoy side. Keep Hoy Sound low and high lts in transit, then the bn Fl WG 4s well open of the shore until abeam chapel ruins, then mid-channel or slightly to South.
Entrance Ldg marks lit 317° leading up buoyed channel.
Berthing Alongside one of the piers if space available or anchor just NE of Ro-Ro terminal.
Facilities Fuel, water, good shopping.
Tel/HM VHF 16, 11 'Orkney Hbr Radio'. Stromness Hbr VHF 16, 9, 11.

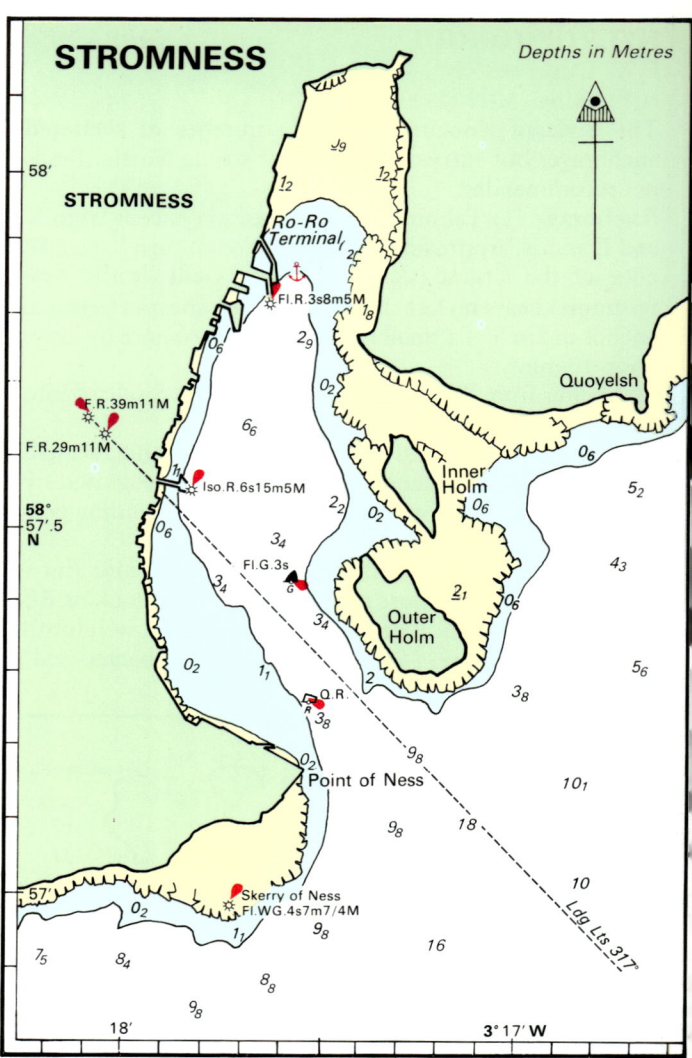

KIRKWALL   Chart BA 1553
HW Dover −¼h
MHWS 2.9m MHWN 2.2 MTL 1.7 MLWN 1.1 MLWS 0.4
Principal town of Orkney. Spire of cathedral conspic.
Approach Easiest from E through Shapinsay Sound, turning S when cathedral bears 190°. By night keep in W sectors of WRG lts on Helliar Holm and outer pier-head. Tide negligible in Kirkwall Bay.
Berthing In inner hbr, good shelter but surge at entrance in W-ly gales. Deep water along main pier outside. Anchoring possible between W pier-head and Crow Ness Pt to W but holding reported poor.
Facilities Most, fuel only in cans, no chandler. Showers at SC. EC Wed.
HM VHF 16,12.
Elwick Bay on Shapinsay, clean sand but weed round edges, offers a peaceful alternative. Approach S and W of Helliar Holm Lt Ho and anchor in 2½ to 3m off village.

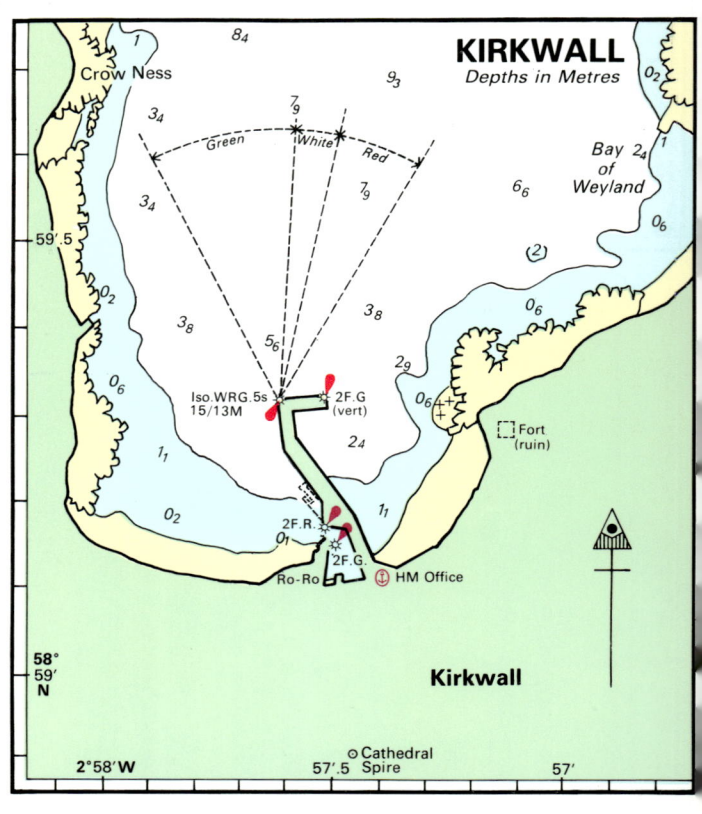

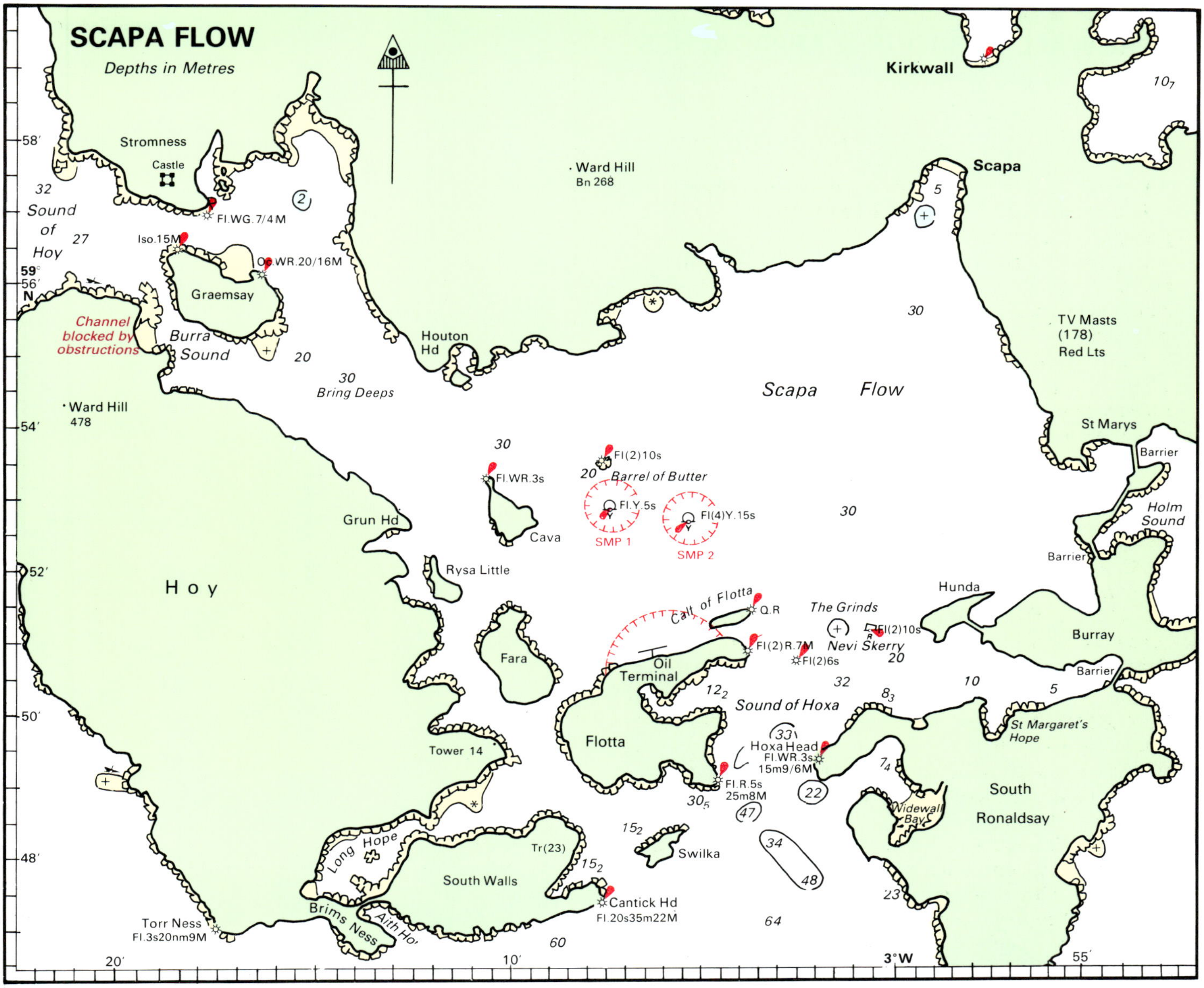

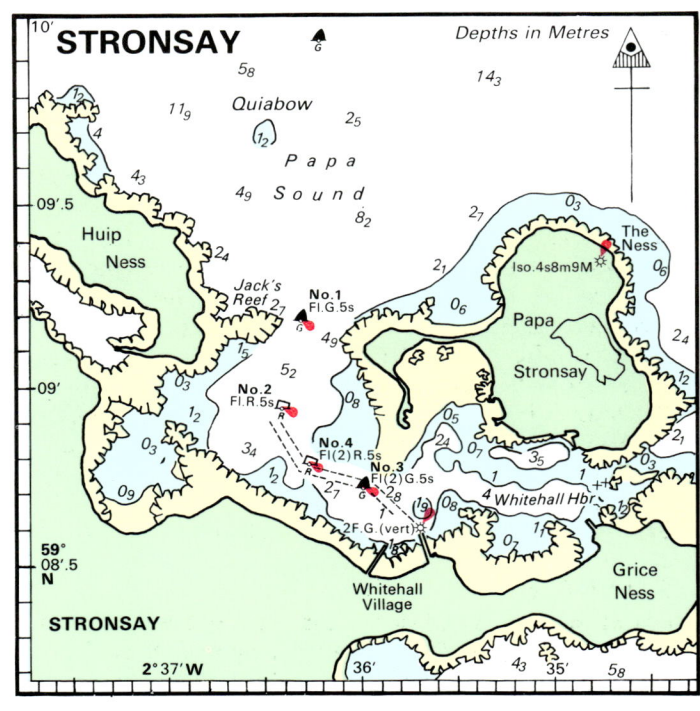

SCAPA FLOW — Depths in Metres

STRONSAY   Chart BA 2622

Whitehall Hbr off the village at the N end of Stronsay offers good shelter.

Approach Enter by N channel, dredged (3½m 1985) and buoyed 2G, 2R. Keep buoys close aboard. Do not attempt E entrance without local knowledge.

Berthing Secure along outer end of W pier and consult HM. (Ro-Ro berth on E pier.) Or anchor between pier ends or elsewhere in bay.

Facilities Provisions. Hotel. Flights and steamer to Kirkwall.

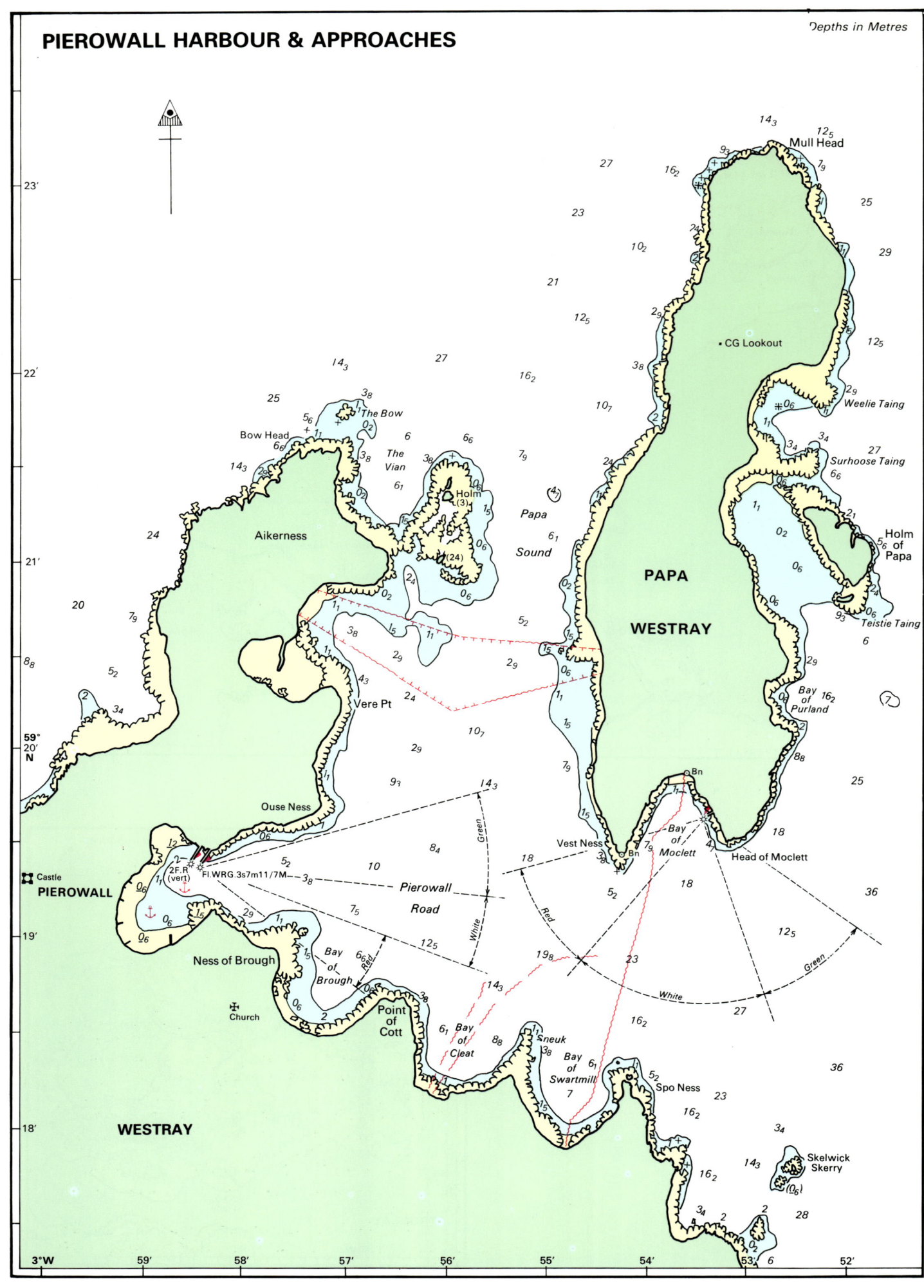

PIEROWALL, WESTRAY Chart BA 2622
HW: Dover −1¼h

MHWS 3.7m MHWN 2.8 MTL 2.1 MLWN 1.4 MLWS 0.6

Pierowall Hbr at S end of Papa Sound between Westray and Papa Westray comprises a steamer pier at Gill Point and anchorages at the head of the bay.

Approach From W and N via Papa Sound keep towards the Papa Westray shore. This entrance requires caution. CG lookout on stern bearing of 036° clears dangers. A tide race forms rapidly at N end of Papa Sound as soon as ebb sets in. From S and E note that Skerry of Skelwick extends 6 ca N from shore. White sector of lt on Gill Pt leads in, 280°, but lt is weak compared with nearby shore lights.

Anchorage 50m off Gill pier close to moorings in least depths 3.7m or on W side of bay in 1.8m. Deep water alongside Gill pier but check steamer schedule.

Facilities Village on W shore of bay, hotel. Water from fish factory. Flights and steamer to Kirkwall.
VHF 14 (daytime).

SHETLAND

Note The passage ports in Shetland covered here comprise Fair Isle; on the East, Lerwick, the main port, and Balta Sound, Unst; on the West, Vaila Sound and Gruting Voe, Scalloway and Ura Firth (Hillswick). Many Shetland anchorages have heavy loose weed.

FAIR ISLE Chart BA 2622

The secure anchorage of North Haven on the NE side offers a useful half-way stop between Orkney and the main islands of Shetland, apart from its particular charm and ornithological interest.

Both South Haven and South Hbr are full of rocks and should be avoided except with detailed local knowledge.

N Haven is uncomfortable in strong NE winds but usually tenable in summer. Enter on 199° keeping N Haven Stack on with summit of Sheep Craig behind.

Anchorage Between the stack and the pier or go alongside the lee of the pier in 2m. Check on schedule of mail boat "Good Shepherd".

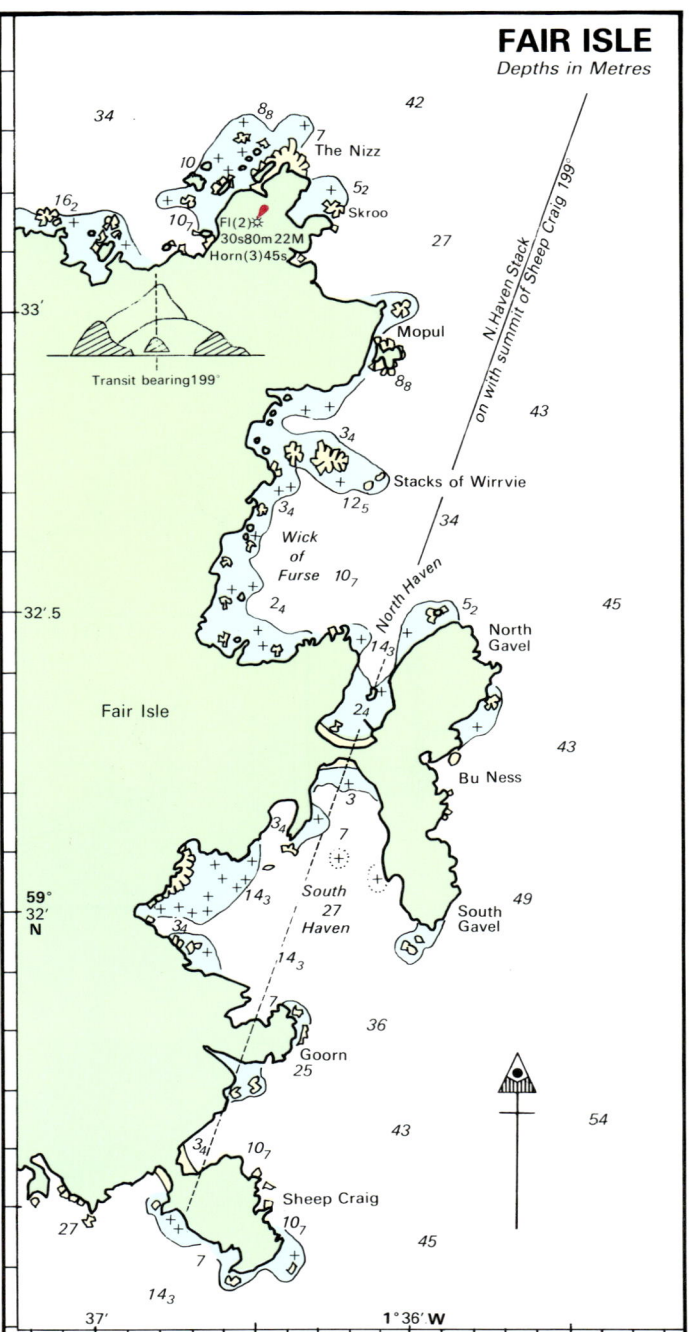

PASSAGE NOTE

The notorious race off Sumburgh Hd should be given a clearance of 3M: it is of great violence. However if proceeding round the heads from Lerwick to Scalloway it can be avoided by keeping close in under Sumburgh Hd.

Grutness Voe on the E coast just N of Sumburgh provides a convenient first anchorage arriving from S or a good point of departure Southbound.

Coming from the NW in strong winds head for the W coast harbours rather than attempt Yell Sound with its fierce tides.

Yachts entering Yell Sound and approaches to Sullom Voe should contact Sullom Voe Hbr control, VHF 10,14,20,16.

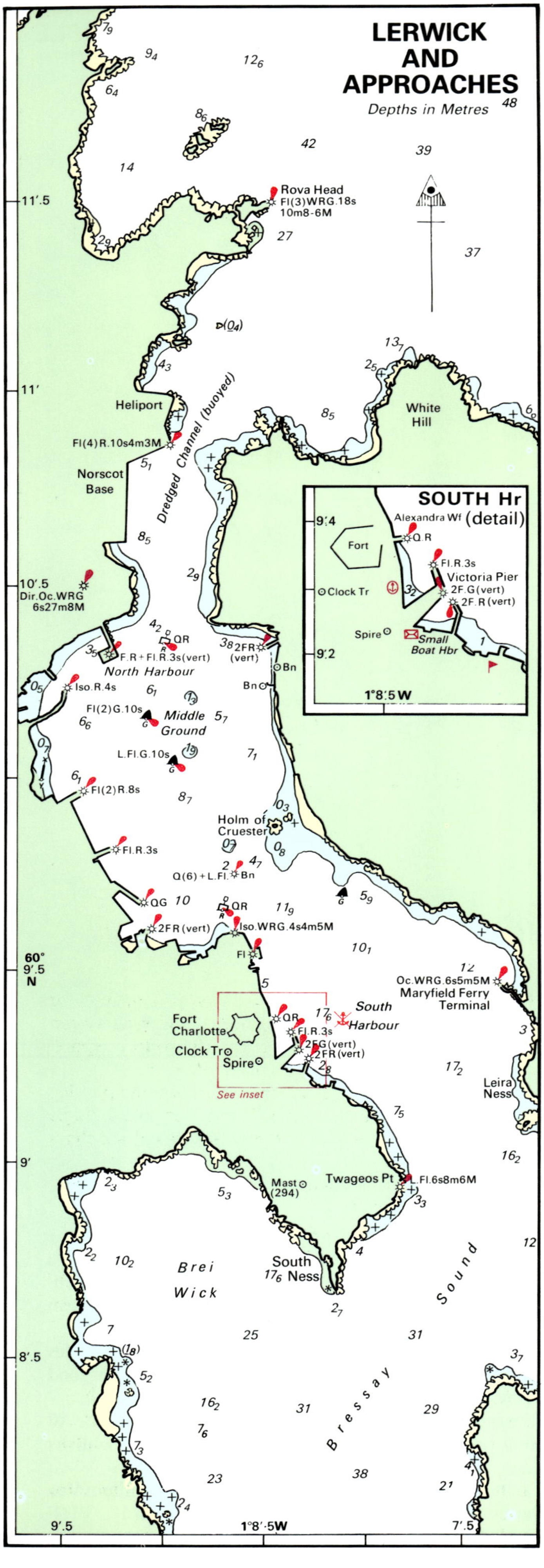

LERWICK AND APPROACHES

Depths in Metres

SOUTH Hr (detail)

LERWICK
Chart BA 3290

HW: Dover −¼h

MHWS 2.2m   MHWN 1.6   MTL 1.3   MLWN 0.9   MLWS 0.5

The capital of the Shetland Isles, a busy harbour with considerable oil, commercial and fishing traffic. Convenient and easy to enter with good berthing for yachts. Harbour of first choice bound to or from Scandinavia.

Approach High cliffs in Bressay and Noss may be visible from a long way off. Entry S of Bressay is easier, with well lit and sheltered funnel-shaped approach. N channel is narrow and much used by oil rig vessels.

Berthing In Small Boat Harbour on S side of Victoria Pier. Lie alongside Victoria Pier or outside another yacht and contact HM. Temporary anchorage possible S of Small Boat Hbr, but holding not good.

Facilities Good facilities; all repairs. EC Wed. Air and ferry daily to Aberdeen.

Tel/HM (0595) 3462. VHF 16,12.

VAILA SOUND AND GRUTING VOE

Chart BA 3295

An area of good shelter with choice of anchorages to suit wind and mud bottom, on the SW of Mainland behind Vaila Island.

Approach Do not use Wester Sound to NW of the Island. W and S sides of Vaila Island are clean and any dangers visible; give E shore a berth of ½ ca. Easter Sound divides into Vaila Sound to W, and entrance to Gruting Voe to E of Ram's Hd (WRG sectored light). Northwards of the narrows keep 1½ ca off E side of Vaila Sound, towards the island shore, to clear Galta Skerry, and the Baa of Linga. The Skerry runs NNW from the eastern shore and is marked by a concrete beacon; the Baa, a dangerous sunken rock in mid-channel, lies 2 ca NW of the Skerry, and must be passed well to the East if heading for Walls at the top of Vaila Voe.

Entering Gruting Voe keep course 055° or less and favour the West shore. Callie Taing is foul.

Anchorages Vaila Voe is better than Lera Voe. Anchor in 4-5m off Walls, N of Saltness and mid-way between it and a post in N of bay.

Browland, Seli and Scutta Voes offer a choice of anchorages. (Olas Voe is very shallow.) Keep to N entering Scutta Voe. Entrance to Browland Voe is foul on both hands, keep mid-stream but rather nearer N side.

Facilities Walls – PO, stores.

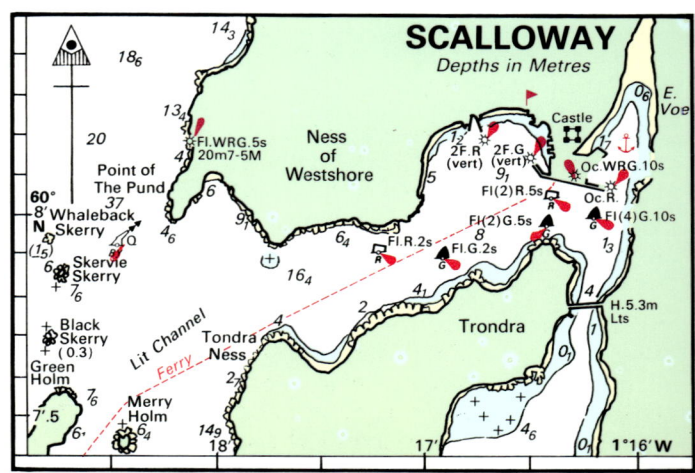

SCALLOWAY — Depths in Metres

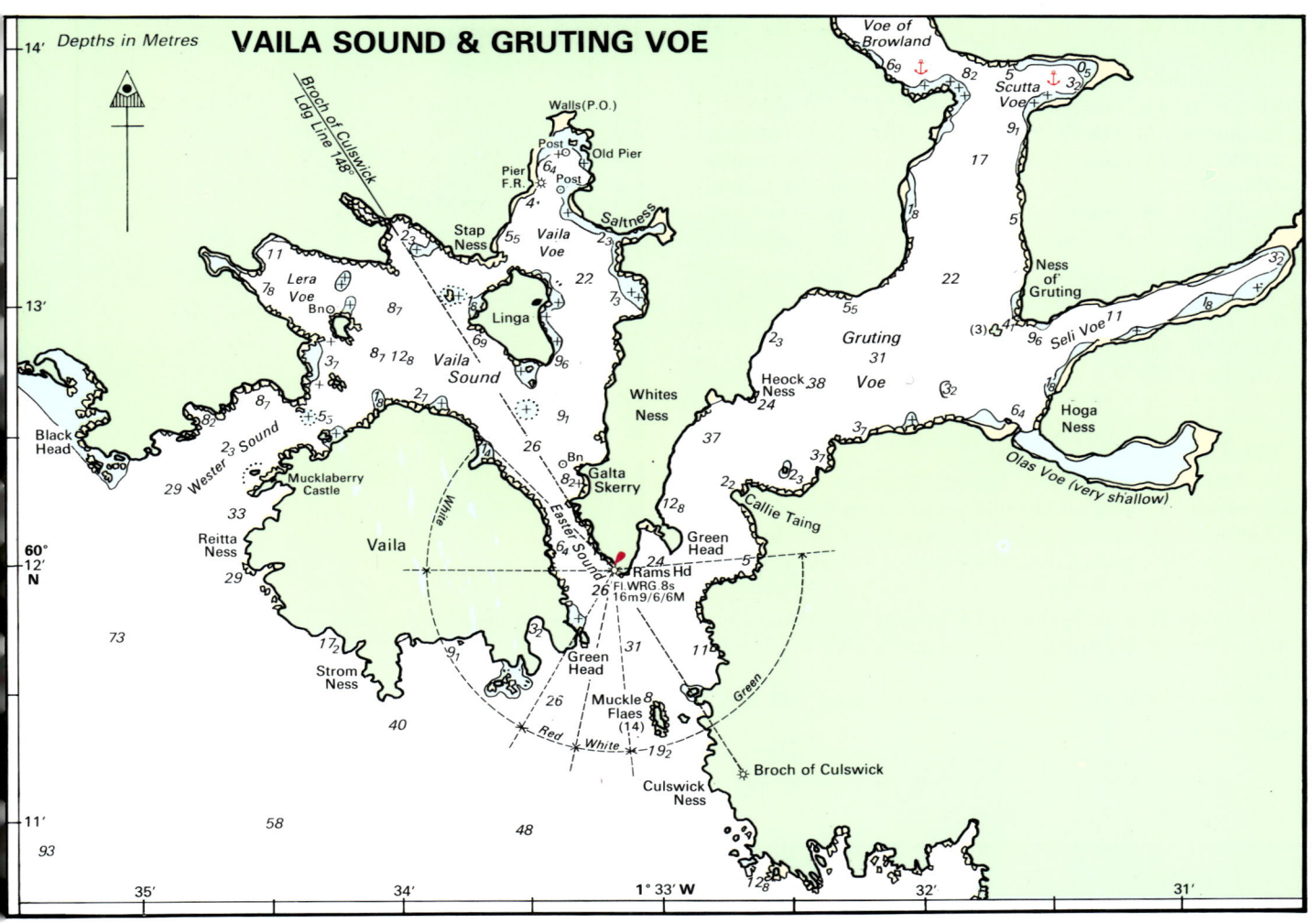

SCALLOWAY Chart BA 3294
HW: Dover −2h.
MHWS 1.6m MHWN 1.3 MTL 1.0 MLWN 0.6 MLWS 0.5
A convenient port of arrival from S and W with sheltered anchorage on W coast of mainland. Harbour protected by numerous islands. Entry should be possible in all weathers, but great care needed in strong SW winds.

Approach Of the three approaches the North Channel is the easiest and safest while the middle channel is not recommended without local knowledge and then only in good weather and daylight.

North Channel Enter between Hildasay Island and Sanda Stour keeping in mid-channel to avoid the dangerous rock close North of Hildasay. Pass between Burwick Holm and Langa keeping 2 ca off Langa to avoid the fish farm on the island's E side, and then keep 1 ca off Point of Pund to clear the drying Whaleback Skerry to starboard.

South Channel Enter between Fugla Ness and Bulia Skerry. Keep the Fugla Ness light between 032° and 082° in the W sector. Note the two dangers Bulia Skerry and Helia Baa which can cause heavy breaking seas across the entrance during SW'ly gales. At such times the South Channel is not recommended. From a position between the two dangers bring Scalloway Castle just open N of Trondra Ness on 057° and pass either between Green Holm and Merry Holm, leaving Green Holm close to port, or north about to the N of Whaleback Skerry.

At night Lighthouses on N Havra and Pt of Pund provide easy access via N Channel. For S Channel, approach Fugla Ness Lt in SW'ly white sector, thence follow lighted channel.

Entrance Keep mid-channel between Maa Ness and Trondra Ness, thence follow hbr buoyage. Note that a day/night sector light provides a white sector over the deepest part of the bar in depths of 6.6m, 057° - 059°.

Anchorages (1) Off Scalloway between Gallow Hill and Blacks Ness, 6-10m, soft mud. Better shelter E of the Castle.
(2) Scalloway BC (welcoming) located at W edge of buildings has visitors' pontoon.
(3) In Hamna Voe on W Burra just inside Fugla Ness. Almost landlocked and safe in bad summer weather; but busy fishing hbr, crowded, bottom foul with old moorings.

Facilities Scalloway – water, stores, fuel, repairs, slip, crane, diver. (EC Thur.)
Tel/HM (059 588) 547 VHF 16, 12, 9 (office hours).

URA FIRTH
Chart BA 3295

At NE of St Magnus Bay. Wide, lit, S-facing entrance approachable in any weather. Firth affords good shelter. Keep to middle entering.

Anchorages (1) Hamar Voe on E side 1M in from entrance to firth. Anchor in 4-10m anywhere just above the narrow ½M entrance channel. With detailed chart or careful sounding a pool at the head of the Voe, shallow but no hidden dangers, offers complete security. Good holding but no supplies.

(2) Hills Wick. Keep mid-firth until the bay on W shore is well open, then enter steering W for middle of bay. Anchor in 4-6m, holding poor.

Facilities Hills Wick. Hotel, PO, stores, diesel, engineer.

BALTA SOUND
Chart BA 3293

The main channel is the S Channel, 3ca wide, lit. Keep in mid-channel. Heavy seas build up in strong SE winds. N Channel is under ½ca wide but deep; keep close to Unst shore on 209° passing ½ca off the reef on Swinna Ness and ½ca E of the GW bn.

Anchorage Best off N shore in 4-8m just W of Sandison's Wharf. Elsewhere as wind dictates but head of Voe is very shoal.

Facilities Water, diesel, boatyard, hotel, shop. PO ¼M. Boat museum.

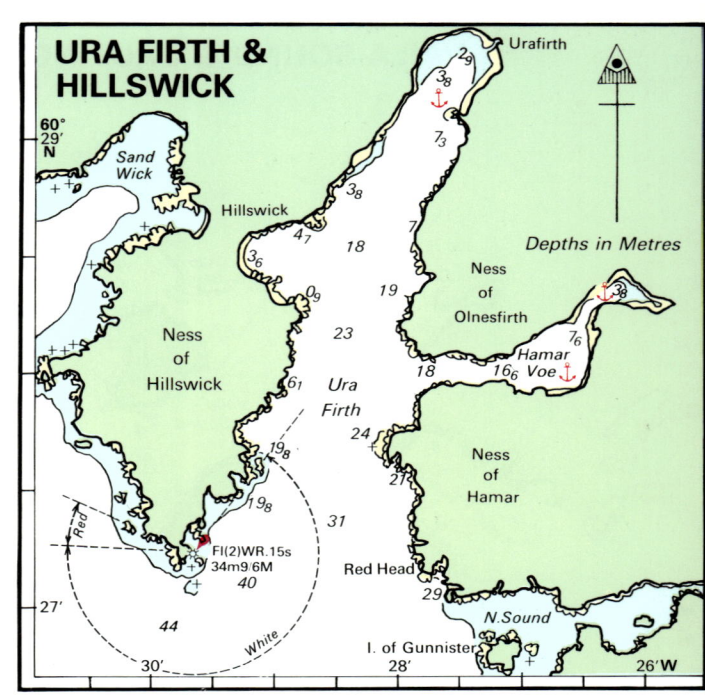

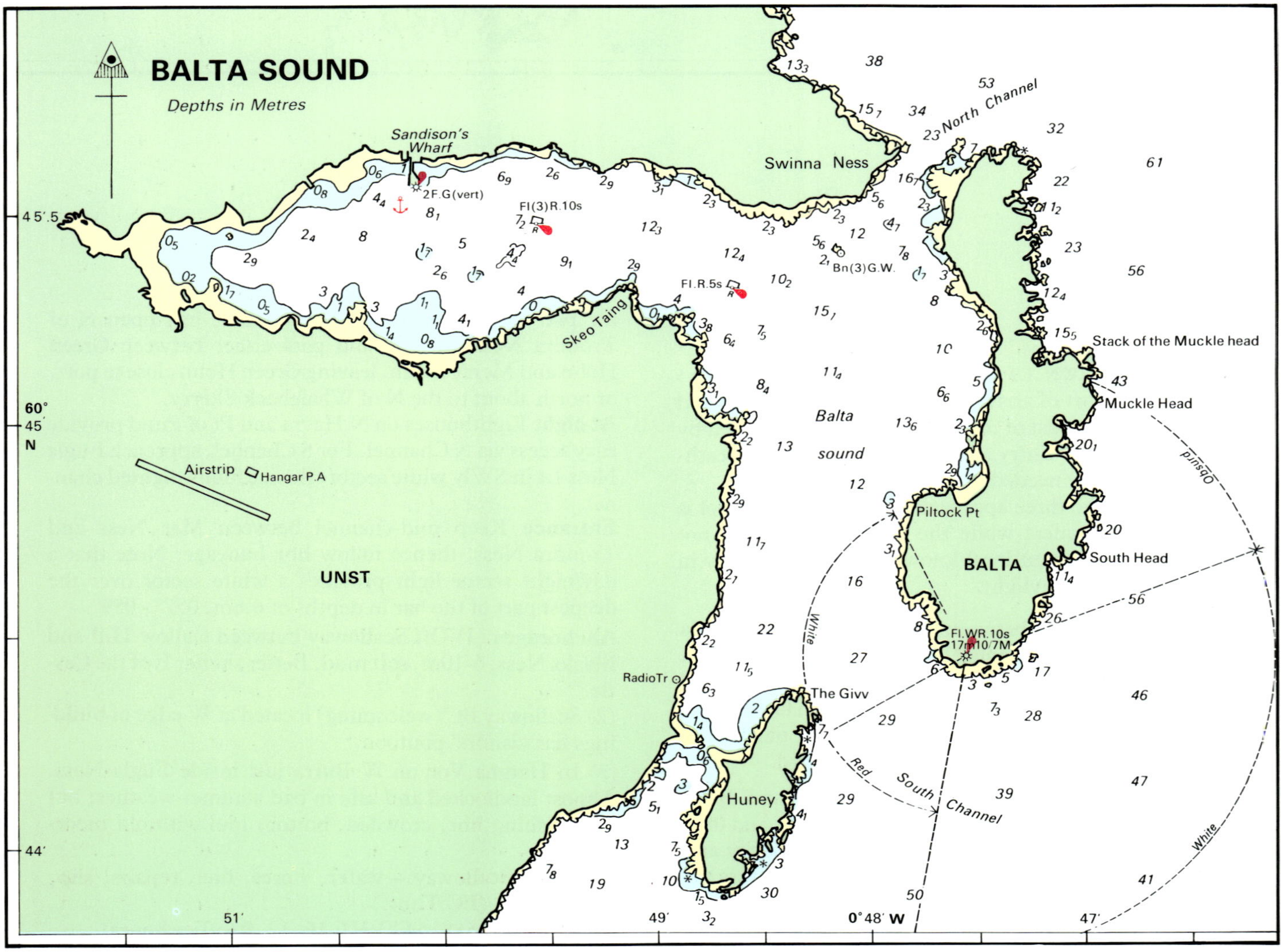

FAEROE ISLANDS (FØROYAR)

These islands lying some 200M N of Cape Wrath are delightful to visit and well worth the 48 hour passage provided one has a well found boat capable of staying out at sea if necessary. They can be approached from the hbrs of NW Scotland, the Hebrides or from the Orkneys or Shetlands. In each case the passage is of the order of 190 to 230M. If on return to the W coast of Scotland (Oban) there is a strong and sustained Sthly wind blowing then the passage back via the Orkneys and the Caledonian Canal is only 80M longer minus whatever extra distance would have had to be covered by tacking. It is therefore worthwhile having some charts of that area on board.

Apart from the use of the english 'Faeroes' for Føroyar the spelling used on the plans and in the text is that used by BA on chart 3557 and in the Admiralty Pilot, thus Streymoy (Strømø), Torshavn (Thorshavn) etc.

Tides The tides around the Faeroes are strong and very strong in the fjords between the islands. The Admiralty pilot is mostly silent about their actual strength although accurate concerning their direction. It is essential to get the book "Tidal Current around The Faeroe Islands" (Streymkort fyri FØROYAR) compiled by Fischer Heinesen and others obtainable from HN Jacobsens, Bokahandil, Torshavn, Faeroe Islands. The 1985 edition includes an English translation of the relevant parts and the diagrams are easily understood. There is a translation in the CA library of an earlier version.

Three points arise from a study of Faeroe tides. Firstly the equinoctial tides are significantly stronger (up to 11kn) than those at the solstices. Secondly with any wind against tide at the exits of the fjords a big sea will be kicked up. And thirdly in a fjord it is often possible to make way against the main stream by working along the side where contrary eddies will be found. This is possible as the sides are mostly steep-to.

The general direction of the streams run W/NW and E/SE. Off the NW coast within a mile of the shore they run at about 3kn max, 4M off at 2½kn, in Nolsoy fjord outside Torshavn at 6kn max and in Lervig fjord exceptionally up to 11kn. In both the last two instances side eddies allow navigation for most of the adverse tide. The actual rise and fall of tide is small, less than 2ft at Torshavn.

The most dangerous overfalls and races occur between Streymoy and Sandoy, off the SE end of Sandoy, Stora Dimun and Litla Dimun, and the S tip of Suderoy on the SE going stream. And between Streymoy and Sandoy, and Skuvoy and N end of Suderoy on the NW going stream.

On the outside coasts swell from the Atlantic causes problems landing on these coasts but is unlikely to in the fjords.

Weather The incidence of gales is not signicantly different in the Faeroes from other places on the W European seaboard during the summer months. However sudden strong squally winds from the high ground are common in many of the fjords. The incidence of fog is high about 6/7 days a month at Torshavn in summer which compares with 5/6 days at Ushant or 2/3 days Isles of Scilly. Occurence can be very sudden.

Navigation Around midsummer it is light all night the sun only dipping about 4° below the horizon before it rises again. All navigation lts are switched off for about three weeks either side of the summer solstice. If approaching from the S in fog the powerful RDF station at Akraberg 381kHz call sign AB serves. If passage making from the South N Rona Fl(3) 20s 114m 24M and Sule Skerry Fl(2) 15s 34m 19M are useful land marks some 50M N of C Wrath. An increase in bird life as one approaches these islands and the Faeroes themselves indicates proximity to land. The use of the echo sounder on approach is unsuitable as the land is so often steep-to. However a fog horn or whistle will produce an echo off the cliffs which will be heard from 1 to 3 ca. Obviously radar is helpful. Chart BA 117 covers all 20 islands whilst Chart BA 3557 covers 12 of the principal hbrs. Danish charts Nos 82 and 83 cover the islands as a whole and Nos 84 and 85 the hbrs.

Customs Customs clearance often given by the police soon after berthing but if not customs should be contacted at one of the clearing ports the most convenient being Vagsfjørdur or Trongisvagur on Suderoy, Torshavn or Vestmanna on Streymoy, Klaksvik on Bordoy, and Fuglafjordur on Eysturoy. The islands are dry in that alcholic drink cannot be purchased there. However small quantities for the crews' own use on board are allowed (one bottle of spirits per member) and reasonable quantities of wine. Officials are considerate but their helpfulness should not be abused by allowing alchohol to get ashore.

The Faeroese flag should be flown as a courtesy flag (Red cross lined all round with blue on a white background). The language spoken is closely related to Icelandic, Danish being the second language whilst English is quite widely understood. The currency is the Danish and Faeroese Krone. Public transport is infrequent except by air from Copenhagen, and ferry from Lerwick (Shetlands) to Torshavn (one trip each way per week). Inter island ferry service is frequent.

Supplies There is no problem at all (wine, spirits, and beer excepted) there being an excellent supermarket in Torshavn, and shops in the other main ports. Water easily available and diesel at Torshavn, Tvøroyri, and Klaksvik and probably other fishing ports. There is no sailmaker, indeed no local sailing boats. There are chandlers selling gear for small fishing boats mostly run on outboards. As there is much shipbuilding in connection with the maintenance of the fishing fleet straightforward repairs should not prove a difficulty.

Principal Lights
Akraberg	Fl(2) WRG 20s 94m 20/14M
Nolsoy	Fl 30s 71m 23M
Holn (Myggens)	Fl(3) 20s 125m 21M
Fuglo	Fl(2) 20s 445m 11M

SUDUROY-TRONGISVAGUR-TVØROYRI
Chart BA 3357   D 85
HW: Dover −4h DS in offing: Dover −3½h SSE, +2½h NW.
MHWS 1.5m   MHWN 0.8   MTL 0.6   MLWN 0.4   MLWS 0.0
This is the best fjord on Suderoy the s-most island and Tvøroyri the most suitable hbr here.

Approach There are rks off the N and S headlands forming the entrance 1M wide to Trongisvagur lying 2 ca off the N side and 1ca off the S. The Fjord narrows after 1½M to 3 ca wide with foul ground on the S side marked by port hand buoys.

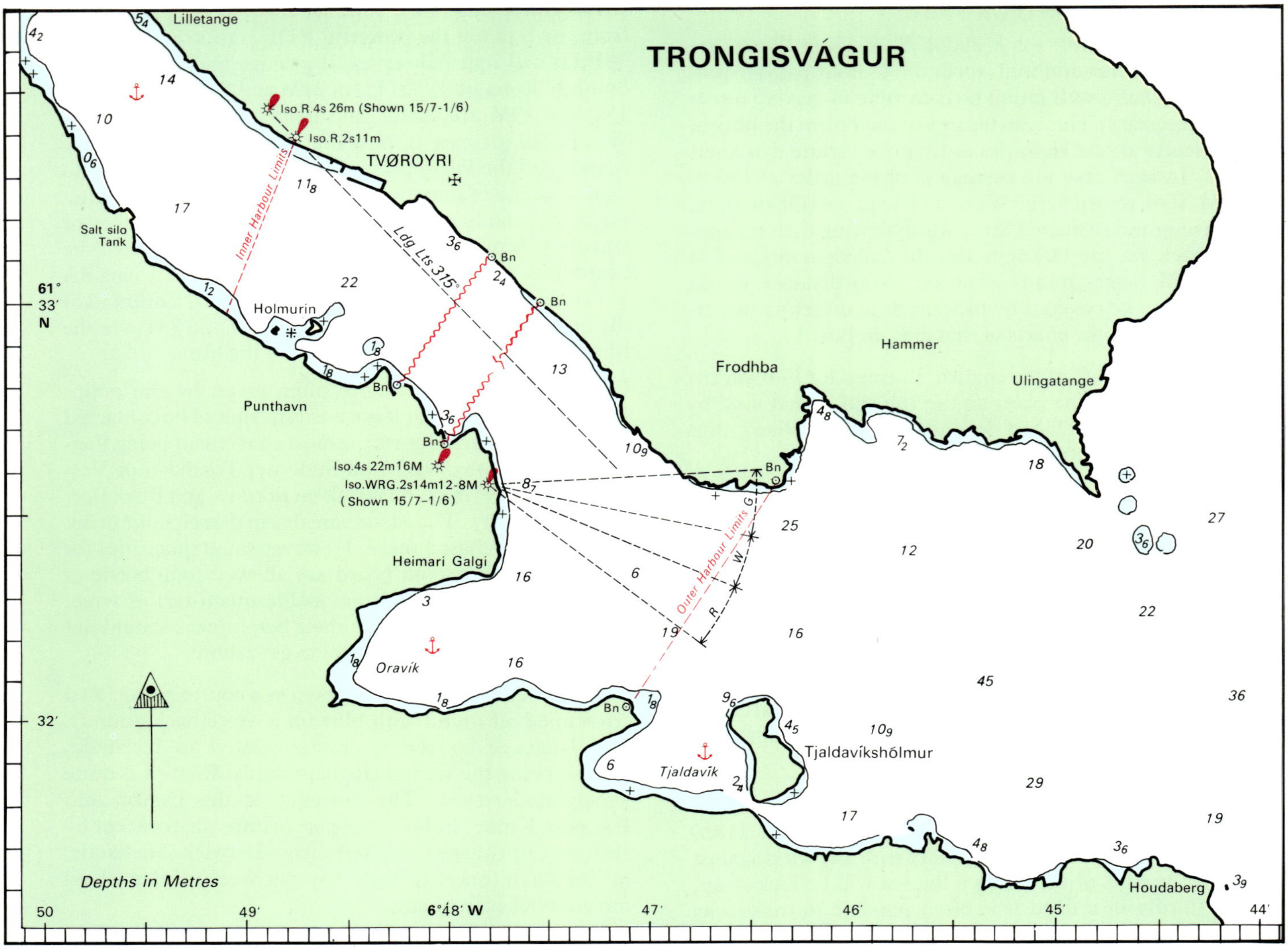

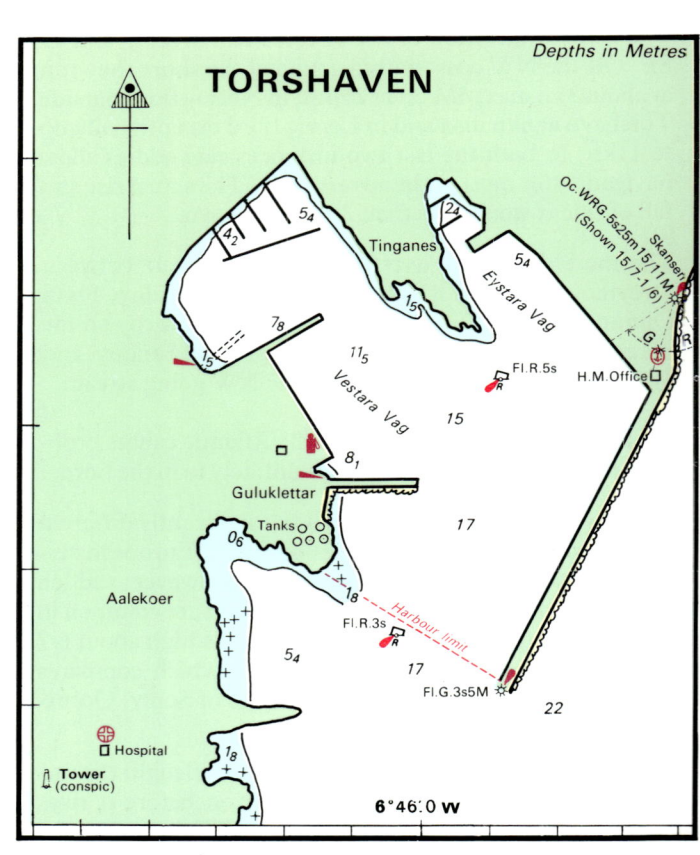

Entrance The entrance to Tvøroyri on the N side of the fjord just after the last R buoy is at the W end of the hbr wall. It is difficult to see until right opposite it. Ldg lt Iso R 4s 27m 317° brings one opposite the entrance. Ldg marks front W tr with R band 4m high and rear mark W framework tr and R band 7m high.

Berthing Alongside as HM directs. Also various anchorages in Trongisvagur at the end of the fjord or at Øravik or Tjaldavik on the W side before the fjord narrows.

Supplies Fuel and stores. Restaurant.

TORSHAVN   Chart BA 3557   D 85

HW: Dover −5¼h

MHWS 0.3m MHWN 0.2 MLWN 0.1 MLWS 0.0

DS in fjord: Dover −6¼h main stream N; −3h eddy S; −2h main stream S; −1h strong eddy N; (eddies on W side)

Approach From the S be careful not to be drawn into Hestsfjordur with a NW going tide. Enter Nolsoy fjord 2½M wide and proceed up the middle with a favourable tide or up the side if adverse in the centre. From the N approach between the N end of Nolsoy and Eystnes on the S end of Eysteroy

Entrance Entrance is well open to the S. Coming from the N give the end of the jetty a good berth as the port has a lot of ferry traffic. Enter between jetty and R can buoy marking shallow water on the W side of the entrance.

Berthing As HM directs. If not available go to W hbr and tie up to large mooring buoy or go alongside larger vessel in NW corner of hbr on N side of furthest jetty or NE

corner alongside quay. Do not use or tie up to pontoons for local boats which are too small for yachts of 20ft or over.
Supplies Fuel and water at quayside in N corner of W hbr or at quay next to fish factory. Toilets across square, showers in Seaman's hotel. All stores at supermarket ½M up hill NW of hbr. Excellent tourist information office near head of hbr where local weather forecast available.

KLAKSVIK Chart BA 3557 D 84
HW: Dover ¾h

MHWS 1.4m MHWN 0.8 MTL 0.8 MLWN 0.5 MLWS 0.0
DS related to Dover: Lervig Fjord +2h NW; −4h SE; Pollurin (outside Klaksvik) +2½h E going on N side; −3½h E going on S side and W going on N side.
Approach From the N through the Djupini and Leirvikfjordur into the S end of Kalsoy Fjord into Pollurin or direct through Kalsoy Fjord. From the S up the S end of Kalsoy fjord into Pollurin. In each case the tides must be watched carefully taking a route away from the centre of the fjords to avoid main stream tides where these are adverse. Both sides of the S end of Kalsoy are clean as is most of Djupini and Leirvikfjordur but care must be taken not to go too close inshore.
Entrance From Pollurin straight in down the centre of the hbr.
Berthing May be possible alongside in the NE corner but most quays on both sides are occupied by fishing boats. Only go alongside for short periods and do not leave unattended. Good anchorage at the S end of of the fjord in 2m or on moorings in this area. Consult HM on W side. Squally in W gales. (Fuglafjordur about 6M to the W on the NW end of Leirvikfjordur is a safer anchorage well sheltered with good holding ground and might be considered in heavy weather as it does not suffer so much from down draught).
Supplies Water, fuel and stores.

VESTMANHA Charts BA 3557 D 85
HW: Dover −2¾h

MHWS 2.0m MHWN 1.4 MTL 1.0 MLWN 0.6 MLWS 0.0
DS in Vestmanna Sound (NW section from Kvivik to sea) related to Dover: +4h NW going stream but eddies off Vagar shore; +5h Eddies of Streymoy side: −2½h SE going stream starts at SE end; −1h SE going stream starts at NW entrance but eddies start off Vagar shore and later on the Streymoy side
Approach From the SE through Hestsfjordur and Vagafjordur into Vestmanna Sound. From the NW into Vestmanna Sound between Mulin Hd and Slaettanes. Straightforward but watch for rk shelf near the shore each side of entrance.
Entrance Ldg lts 025° take one in close to the steep-to W shore. Shoal patch half way across from E shore. Beware rk off Nesidh at S end of bay on E side of hbr.
Berthing One of the most protected hbrs. Anchor in 3 or 4m in bay on E side of hbr and consult HM.
Supplies Water, fuel and stores.

FUGLAFJORDUR Charts BA 3557 D 85
MHWS 1.9m MHWN 1.0 MTL 0.9 MLWN 0.7 MLWS 0.0
DS: Dover −½h NW going stream in Leirvikfjordur starts to run into Fuglafjordur on N side and out on S side. Dover +5h SE going stream starts to run in on S side and out on N.

Approach From the N through Djupini with a SE going tide there are no problems though the stream at the entrance to Djupini must be watched. From the S through Kalsoy sound into Leirvikfjordur. Entrance to Fuglafjordur is straightforward and both sides are clean
Berthing Best at the NE end of the fjord beyond the main berth of the hbr and inside the jetty 5m. Do not tie up to pontoons in hbr N of this. Temporary berthing at the main quay but consult HM
Supplies Water, Stores. Customs

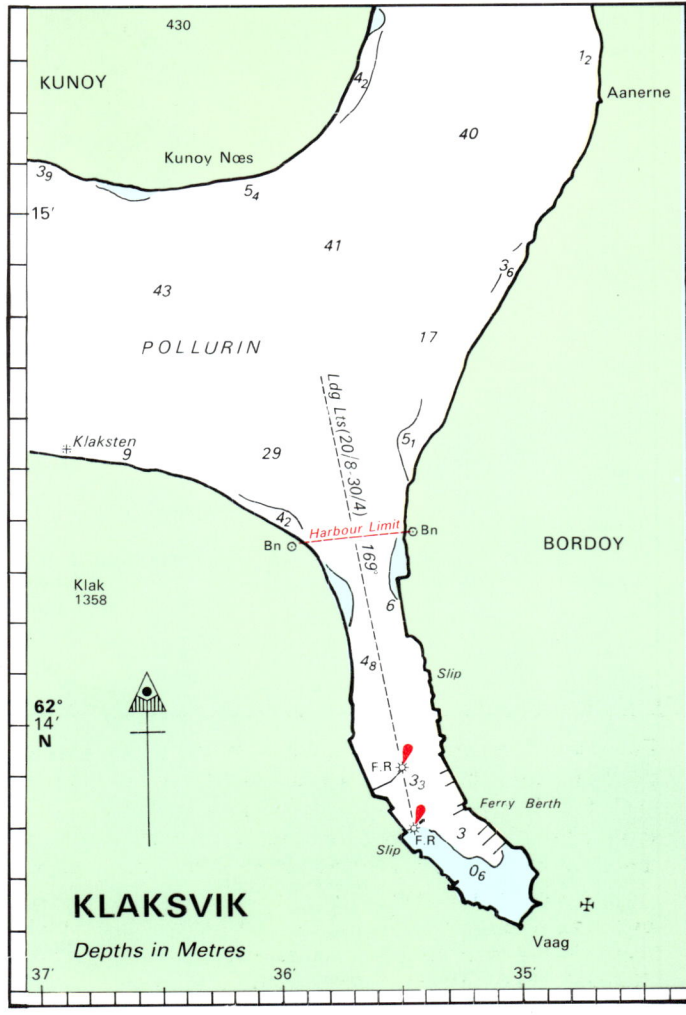

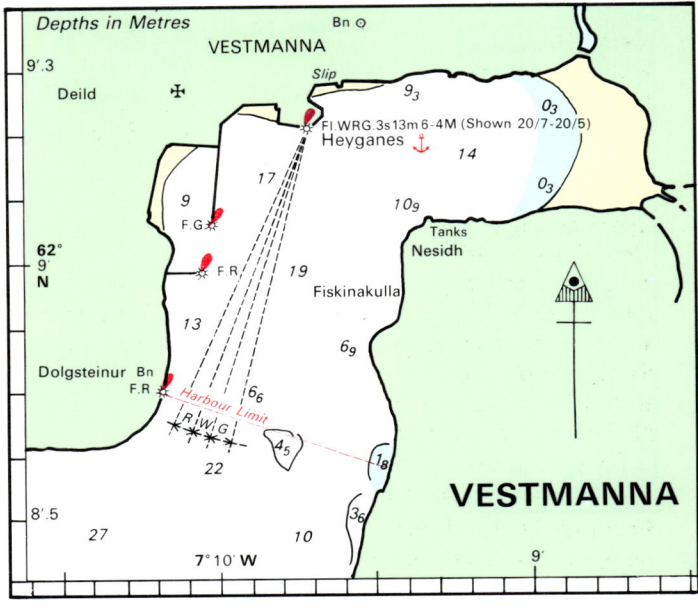

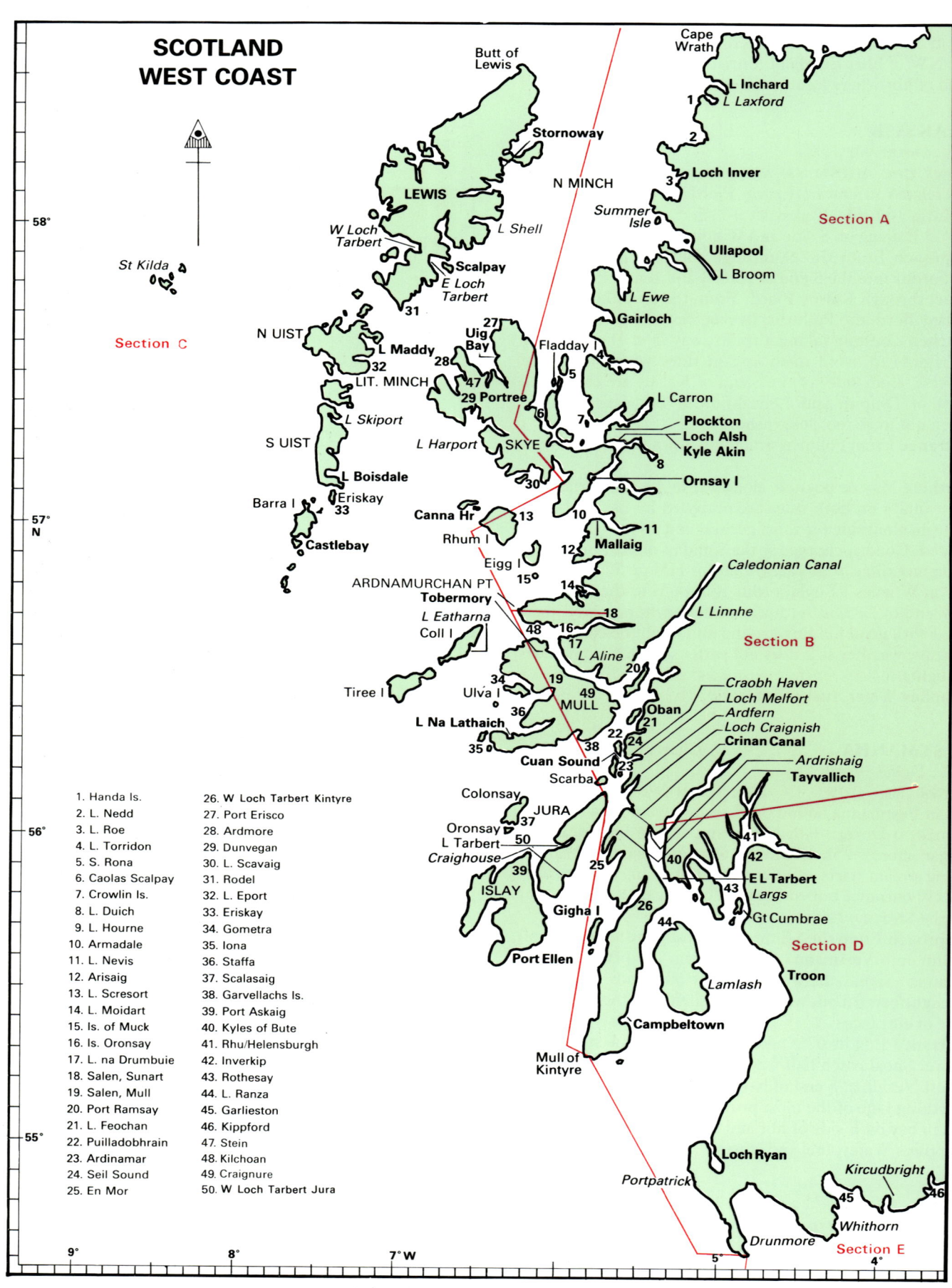

SCOTLAND WEST COAST

INTRODUCTION.

The West Coast of Scotland, with thousands of miles of highly scenic coastline, hundreds of secluded anchorages and extensive protected sailing waters, offers yachtsmen possibly the finest cruising area in Europe. Some of the coast exposed to the W and N may suffer severe conditions with strong on-shore winds and yachts sailing in these waters must be well found and well crewed. However much of the more popular cruising is either protected by off-shore islands or in sea lochs that extend many miles inland.

During the summer months the average wind strength is about the same as in the English Channel and there are marginally fewer gales. However the weather can change quickly and yachts must be prepared to clear out from some anchorages at short notice if the wind becomes onshore. In the lee of high hills and mountains squally catabatic winds may be at least two forces greater than those prevailing in open waters. Fog is rare but misty conditions with visibility down to 1-3M are not uncommon. The best weather can usually be had from mid-May to mid-July. During this period there is the added bonus of few hours of darkness so that night sailing is seldom necessary.

The flood tide flows mainly N and W. The streams may be strong with associated overfalls off prominent headlands and in some of the sounds between the islands. Details are tabulated for each section. Elsewhere the tidal streams are relatively weak. The tidal range varies from 0.3m at Islay to 4.9m at N Uist.

Navigational aids are thinly spread and many harbours are unlit. The Decca navigational system operates well in the area.

It would be quite impractical to give details in this Handbook of all the very numerous harbours and anchorages available. Therefore twenty five harbours (marked by *) which offer good access (most are lighted), secure anchorages and some facilities ashore have been selected as Passage Harbours. Chartlets and pilotage information are provided for each. In addition information and some chartlets are given for a further 24 secondary harbours. Some details of 50 other anchorages are also given in table form for cruise planning. These together with passage and tidal notes are given in five separate sections viz:

A. Mainland coast from C Wrath to Ardnamurchan Pt together with the E coast of Skye.
B. Mainland coast from Ardnamurchan Pt to Mull of Kintyre with the E coasts of the Inner Hebrides.
C. The outer passages through the Minches from the Butt of Lewis to Islay.
D. The Firth of Clyde to the Mull of Galloway.
E. The S Galloway coast.

Any yacht cruising on the W coast of Scotland should carry the Admiralty Pilot and either the appropriate volumes of Martin Lawrence's "The Yachtsman's Pilot to the West Coast of Scotland" (Imray) or the Clyde Cruising Club Sailing Directions (CCCSD). These with the appropriate medium scale Admiralty charts will provide a basic minimum but large scale charts where available are desirable in many areas.

The spelling of Gaelic names varies widely and may cause confusion. The following abreviations are used in this section of the Handbook.

Ru = Rubha or rudha   A headland
En = Eilean   An island
Bo = Bogha   A dangerous rock

Most villages have a PO/store with a freezer but fresh bread, milk and vegetables are not always available. Early closing days are often ignored in the summer months. Bank holidays are arranged locally. Calor Gas is generally easy to obtain but not Camping Gaz. Diesel can be obtained at marinas and at most fishing harbours but not always by pipe. Many anchorages are remote with no facilities. Public transport is not easy and yachts contemplating changing crews should obtain a copy of "Getting around the Highlands and Islands" published annually for the Highlands and Islands Development Board (HIDB) by F. H. G. Publications Ltd, Paisley. Yachts may be chartered from a number of centres. Details from HIDB.

Yacht marinas are virtually confined to the Firth of Clyde and to the mainland between Crinan and Oban. Repair facilities and chandlers are also concentrated in the same areas and at some fishing harbours.

Owing to the presence of heavy weed anchoring with a CQR or a Danforth may present difficulties and yachts are recommended to carry either a Fisherman or a Bruce of sufficient weight. Shallow draught yachts, and especially those that can take the ground, can often find a clean sandy bottom (visible at 7m) as well as added protection by going well up into an anchorage. The HIDB has recently laid visitors' moorings in a number of anchorages. These moorings have dark blue buoys with a ring and a weight limit of 15 tonnes. No charge is made to visitors.

In recent years there has been a huge growth in marine farming. The industry has been poorly controlled. Many popular anchorages are now partially occupied by fish farms, only a minority of which are shown on Admiralty charts. Basically there are two types of marine farm;
(1) Those for fin fish eg salmon consisting of large floating cages
(2) Those for shell fish consisting of a series of long cables suspended from buoys sometimes in a radial manner to which the shellfish attach themselves.

Both types of farm are usually marked by special yellow can buoys, occasionally lit.

Section A. CAPE WRATH TO ARDNAMURCHAN POINT.

Principal Lights.

Cape Wrath	Fl(4) 30s 122m 24M
Stoerhead	Fl 15s 59m 24M
Ru Reidh (Re)	Fl(6) 30s 37m 23M
S. Rona	Fl 12s 69m 19M
En Ban Kyle Akin	Iso WRG 4s 16m 9/6M
Isle Ornsay	Fl(2) 7s 18m 12M
Pt of Sleat	Fl 3s 20m 9M
Ardnamurchan Pt	Fl(2) 20s 55m 24M

PASSAGE NOTES

The coast from C. Wrath to Ru Reidh (Re) is exposed to the W and in heavy weather big and dangerous seas build up particularly off the headlands of Ru Stoer and Ru Re. There are many off-shore rks and islets which make running for shelter hazardous. S of Ru Re some shelter is provided by Skye and the passage through the Inner Sound E. of Rona and Raasay is free from hidden dangers. The passage down the E coast of Skye through the Sounds of Raasay, Scalpay and Pabay presents a number of hazards. Drying and submerged rks extend nearly 1M N of Rona. The Sound of Raasay is clear as far as its S end where it narrows and the channel is marked by buoys. Caolas Scalpay is obstructed by narrows which are shoal (0.1m) and only 20m wide marked by 2 small unofficial W buoys on the Scalpay side. Pass W of these to avoid a dangerous reef. There is a reef marked by a bn extending 1½M S from Pabay.

The tides are strong in Kyle Akin and Kyle Rhea but the channel is well marked and lighted. Overfalls may be encountered at Glenelg on an ebb tide with a Sly wind. From here to Ardnamurchan the passage is straightforward. Bo Faskadale 6M NE of the pt is marked by a G con buoy Fl(3) G 18s. A big sea builds up off Ardnamurchan in Wly weather and yachts rounding the pt should stand off 1M.

Tidal Streams. All related to Dover.

Cape Wrath	−5½h N	+¾h S
Stoerhead	+5¼h N	HWD S (2½kn)
Ru Reidh	+4½h NE	−1¼h SW (3kn)
Raasay Narrows	−5h N	+2h S (2kn)
Kyle Akin	−¼h W	+3¾h E (Springs 3kn)
	+1¾h W	−4¼h E (neaps)
Kyle Rhea	−1¾h N	−4¼h S (6-8kn)
Sound of Sleat	+1½h NE	−4½h SW (lkn)

LOCH INCHARD* Chart BA 2503
HW: Dover −4h

MHWS 4.9m MHWN 3.5 MTL 2.7 MLWN 1.9 MLWS 0.7

A useful passage harbour for yachts rounding C Wrath.
Approach. Entrance may be difficult to identify. Ru na Leacaig to N is bold and reddish with W concrete Lt bn Fl(2) 10s 30m 8M. There is a group of rocky islets to SW of entrance.
Entrance Keep close to N shore to avoid Bo Ceann na Saile 4m. Kinlochbervie a small inlet on N shore 1M E of Ru na Leacaig marked by lighted bns and ldg lts FG 327°.
Anchorages (1) Kinlochbervie alongside pier. Busy fishing port: yachts may not be allowed to stay.
(2) At New pier in Loch Clash.
(3) Rhiconich at head of loch. Shoals. Anchor according to depth. New fish farms proposed which may restrict anchoring.
Facilities Kinlochbervie: Diesel & water at pier. PO/shop, hotel, chandlery. Rhiconich: Hotel PO Bus to Lairg BR.

LOCH LAXFORD Chart BA 2503
HW: Dover −4¼h

MHWS 4.9m MHWN 3.5 MTL 2.7 MLWN 1.9 MLWS 0.7

A remote loch of easy access offering good shelter but no facilities.

Approach and Entrance Ru Ruadh the SW pt of entrance is reddish. Keep N of islands off S shore of loch.
Anchorages (1) Loch a Chadh-Fi. Beyond moorings of Adventure School. Pass W of En a Chadh-Fi.
(2) In bays behind islands off S shore. Beware fish farms.
Facilities None.

LOCH INVER* Chart BA 2504
HW: Dover +4½h

MHWS 5.0m MHWN 3.9 MTL 3.0 MLWN 2.1 MLWS 0.8

Approach In clear weather sugar loaf mountain, Suilven, 4M SE is a good landmark for entrance. From S give A'Chleit Is a wide berth to the W and pass close S of Soyea Is Lt Fl(2) 10s 34m 6M and steer 060°.
Entrance Leave Glas Leac Lt Fl WRG 3s to port. At night use W sector. Leave G bn Q G to stb.
Anchorages (1) W. of pier. Buoy anchor.
(2) Two visitors moorings with large yellow buoys.
Facilities Water and diesel at pier. PO, shops EC Tue, chandlery, hotel. Bus to Ullapool and Lairg BR.

ULLAPOOL LOCH BROOM* Chart BA 2500
HW: Dover −4½h

MHWS 5.0m MHWN 3.9 MTL 3.0 MLWN 2.1 MLWS 0.7

A busy ferry and fishing port. Easy access. Good protection.
Approach and Entrance Straightforward. Ru Cadail Fl WRG 6s 11m 9/6M at N pt of entrance to L Broom. Use W sector and leave R can buoy QR and Ullapool Pt Iso R 4s 8m 6M to port.
Anchorages (1) ENE of pier. May be crowded.
(2) Altnaharrie on SW shore of loch opposite Ullapool Pt. Moorings may be available. Ferry.
(3) Loggie Bay on SW shore just beyond Narrows.
Facilities Water and diesel at Fish Pier. Chandlers, charts, PO, shops EC Tue, hotel, banks, launderette. Summer Is Charters, Altnaharrie, 085483 230 some repairs and charts. Ferry to Stornoway. Bus to Inverness.

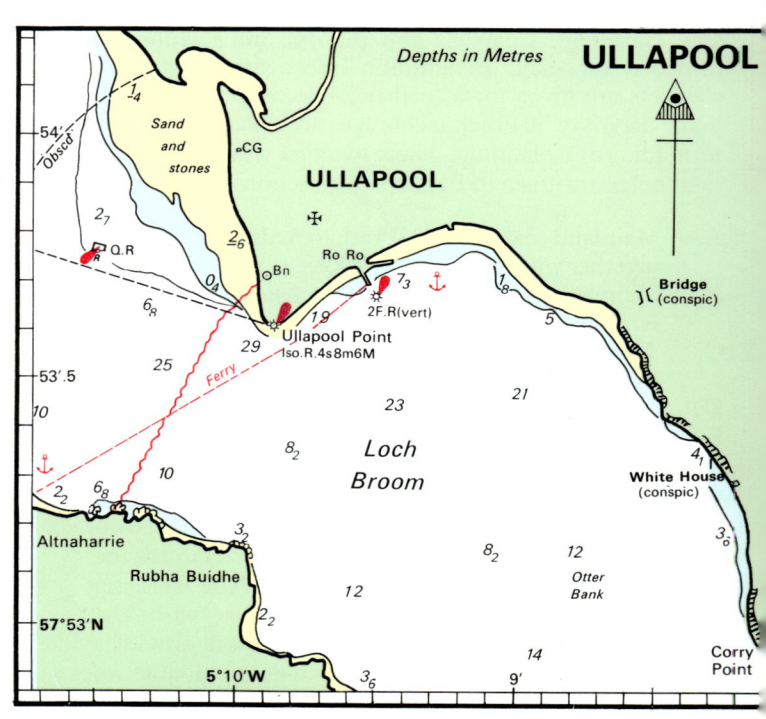

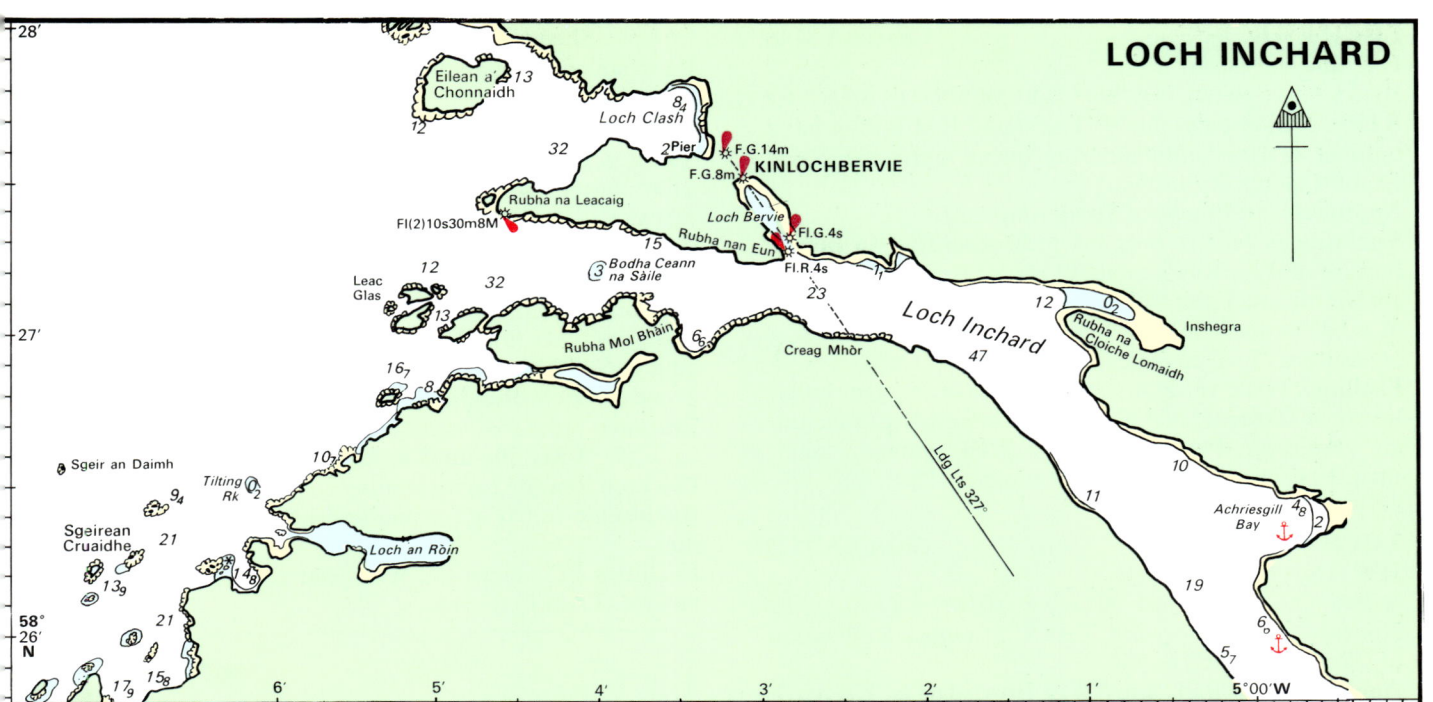

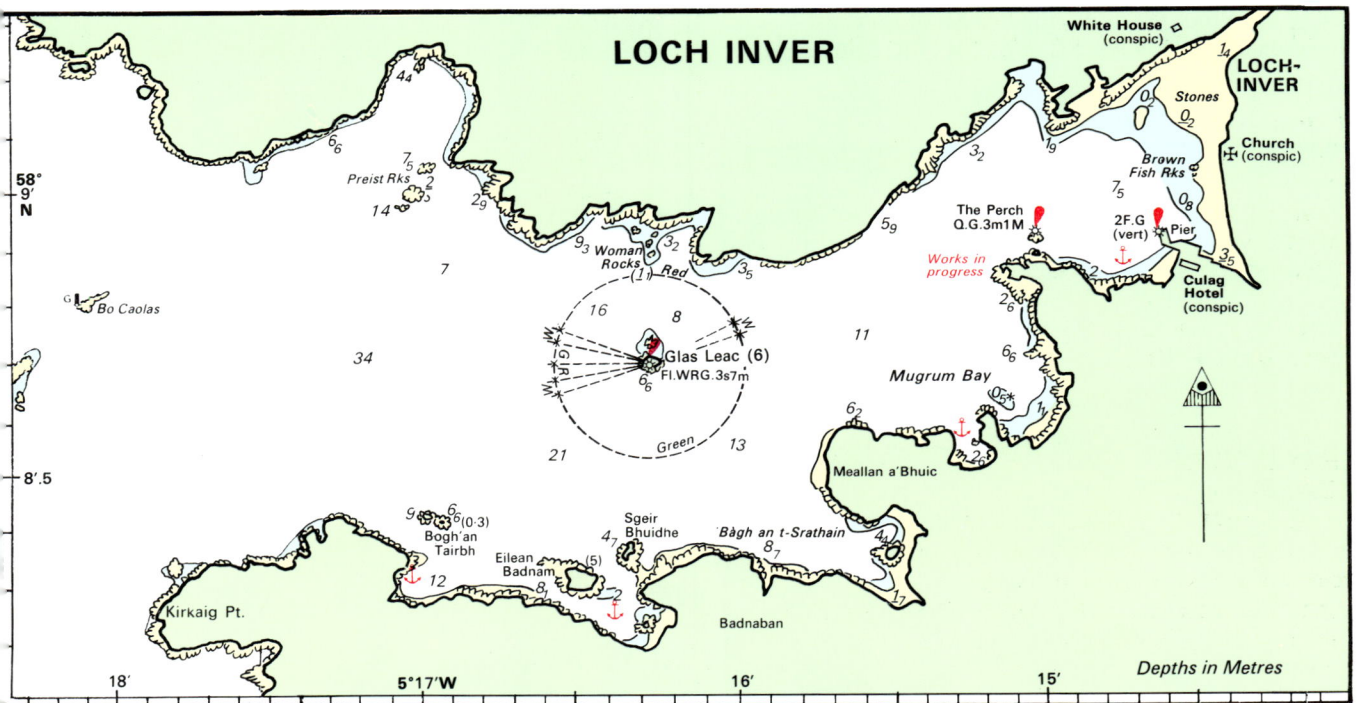

SUMMER ISLES   Chart BA 2501
HW: Dover −4¼h

MHWS 5.1m   MHWN 4.0   MLWN 2.1   MLWS 0.8

An attractive group of islands with several good anchorages. Large scale chart desirable.

Approach From NW keep towards N of Dorney Sound to avoid drying rks N of Tanera Beg but beware Iolla a Mealan (dr 0. 8m) 2 ca off mainland shore opposite N end of Tanera More. From S leave islands stretching 4½M SW of Tanera More to port.

Anchorages (1) Tanera More. In bay to E either close to stone pier or in "Cabbage Garden" S of two islands and entered between them. Uncomfortable in swell from NNE.

(2) Tanera Beg. In bight to S of En Fada Mor or NE of Tanera Beg. If approaching from N keep close to En Fada Mor.

(3) Caolas En Ristol. To E of Island. Lt Fl G 3s on mainland shore towards N end.

Facilities Water and diesel at new pier in SE corner of bay at Tanera More. Also restaurant and showers. PO/shop, Calor at Achiltibuie on mainland in Badentarbet Bay.

SCOTLAND, WEST COAST   146

LOCH EWE   Chart BA 3146
HW: Dover −4½h
MHWS 5.1m   MHWN 3.8   MTL 2.9   MLWN 2.0   MLWS 0.7
A large loch open to the N. The sound E of Is Ewe has a number of large unlit mooring buoys and some Naval establishments at Aultbea.
Approach and Entrance Straightforward.
Anchorages (1) At head of loch according to depth. Beware of Boor Rks 2 ca off W shore. If visiting gardens anchor off small pier SW of Inverewe Ho or in bay to N of pt in SE corner of loch.
(2) Aultbea. To E of pier.
Facilities Poolewe: PO, shops, EC Thur, garage, hotel. Inverewe Gardens, Nat Trust for Scotland, are outstanding. Aultbea: PO, shops, EC Wed, garage, hotel, chandlery, charts, Calor. Water at pier.

LOCH GAIRLOCH*   Chart BA 2528
HW: Dover −4¾h
MHWS 5.2m   MHWN 4.0   MTL 2.9   MLWN 1.9   MLWS 0.6
Approach Straightforward. Pass S of Longa Is in W sector of Glas En Fl WRG 6s 4M.
Anchorages (1) Badachro SW of Horrisdale Is. Keep to E side of channel. Anchor N or S of islets to SW. Note submerged rk ½ ca E of rk (dr 3.7m) 1 ca SE of islet.
(2) Flowerdale Bay. Anchor SE of pier lt Q R. Subject to swell.
(3) Loch Sheildaig E or W of En Shieldaig. Leave Fraoch En to stb and give middle island a wide berth.
Facilities PO, limited stores, small chandlery, hotel at Badachro. Water and diesel at Flowerdale Pier. Pier dues.

PLOCKTON, LOCH CARRON*   Chart BA 2528
HW: Dover −4h
MHWS 5.5m   MHWN 4.1   MLWN 1.9   MLWS 0.8
An attractive harbour with many facilities.
Approach From W straightforward. From S keep at least ¾M offshore to pass between Sgeir Bhuidhe and Nol G con buoy Fl G 3s in W sector of Lt Fl(3) WRG 10s. If passing to S of High Stone beware of Hawk Rk (0.1). High Stone on Sgeir Bhuidhe 330° clears.
Entrance Steer 164° towards castle conspic in W sector of Lt Fl(3) WRG 10s until harbour opens to SW. Beware Plockton Rks (dr 2m) extending 3 ca NNW of Castle Pt.
Anchorage In bay according to depth and clear of moorings.
Facilities PO, shops EC Wed, water, fuel, hotel, launderette. Train to Inverness.

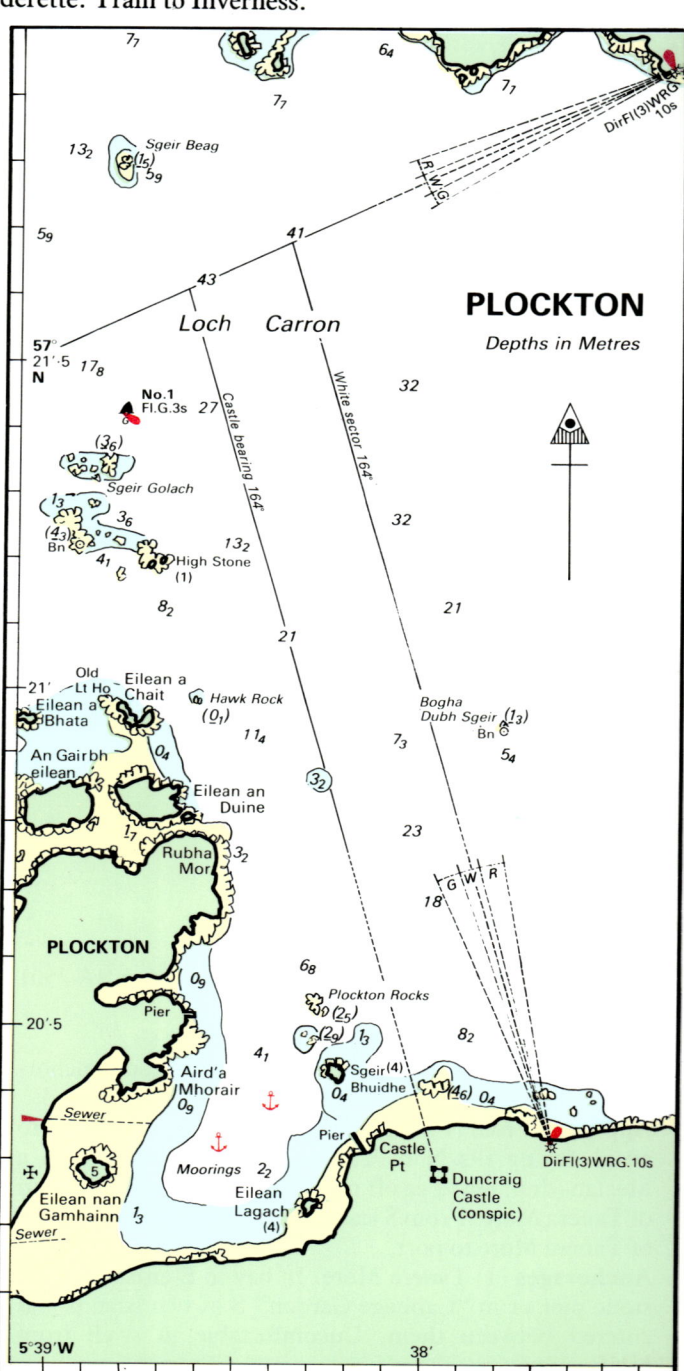

147   SCOTLAND, WEST COAST

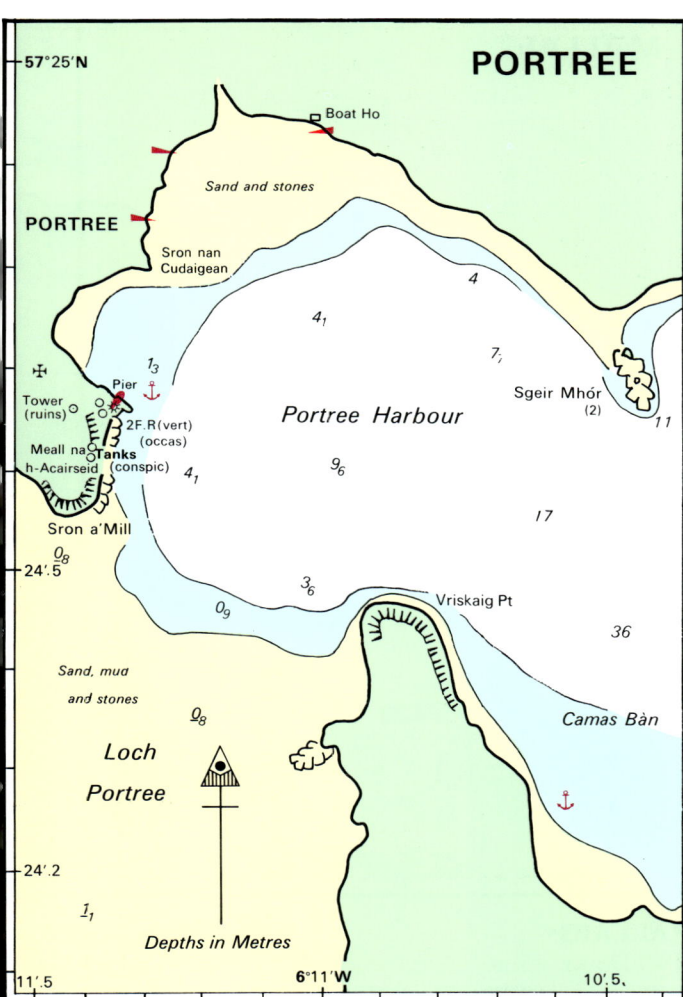

PORTREE SKYE*   Chart BA 2534
HW: Dover −4¾h
MHWS 5.3m MHWN 3.7 MTL 2.9 MLWN 1.9 MLWS 0.7
The principal town on Skye. Anchorage subject to squalls.
Approach and Entrance 2 F R (vert) occasional on pier.
Anchorages (1) 8 H.I.D.B. moorings in N of bay.
(2) To NE of pier clear of moorings. Avoid mouth of burn to N where holding poor. Exposed to SW winds.
(3) Camas Ban to SE. Protected from S.
Facilities Water at pier. Diesel by can from depot. PO, shops EC Wed. hotels, engineer, Calor. Bus to Inverness and Glasgow.

KYLE OF LOCH ALSH   Charts BA 2540 & 2498
HW: Dover −4¾h
MHWS 5.3m MHWN 3.9 MTL 3.1 MLWN 2.2 MLWS 0.8
A temporary stopping place for stores and crew changing.
Approach There are numerous hazards in Kyle Akin but these are well marked and lighted. Tides run strongly. Frequent ferries crossing to Skye.
Anchorages 1) Berth alongside of Rly pier. (temporary). Dues charged.
2) Berth alongside pier at Kyleakin.
3) Anchor or visitors mooring in Balmacarra Bay. 3M E.
Facilities Water and diesel at pier. PO, shops EC Thur, Calor, garage, hotels, banks, train to Inverness. Bus to Glasgow.

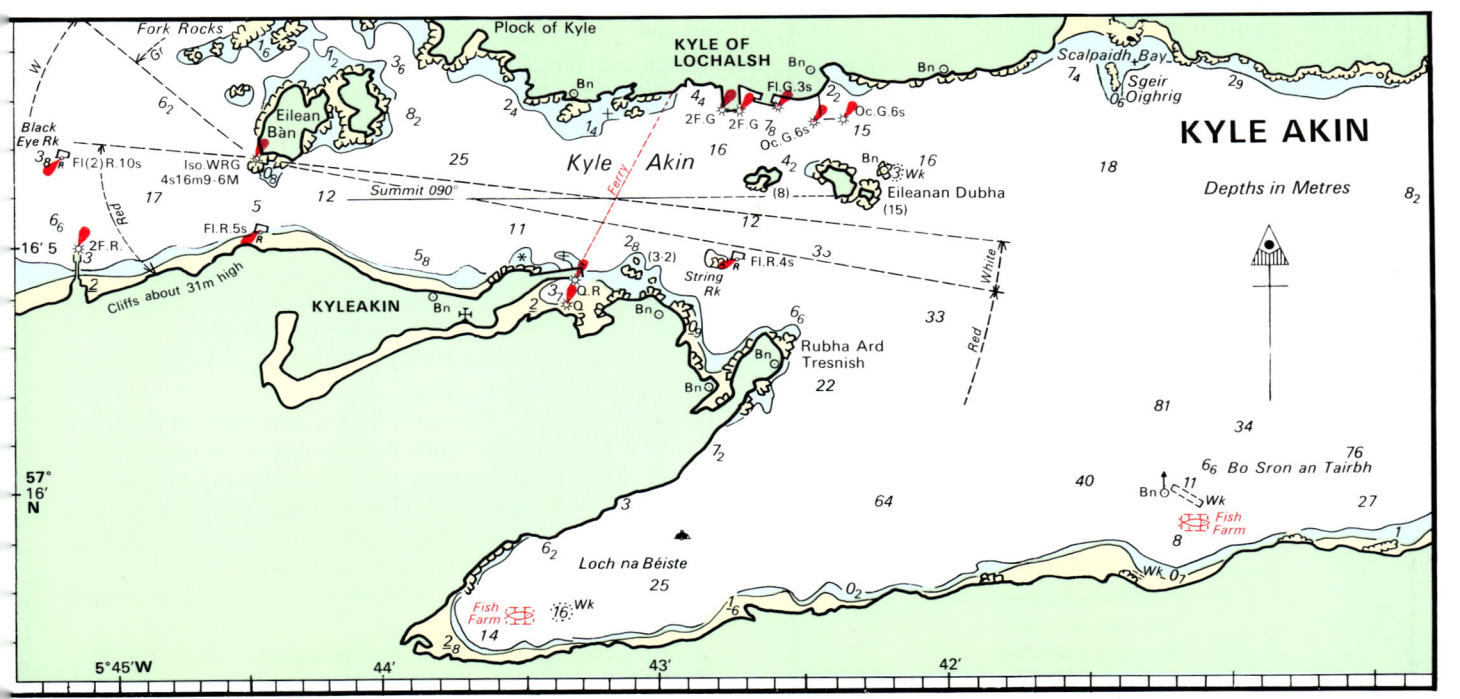

SCOTLAND, WEST COAST   148

ISLE ORNSAY SOUND OF SLEAT   Chart BA 2208
HW: Dover −5h
MHWS 5.0m   MHWN 3.8   MLWN 2.0   MLWS 0.8

An excellent alternative to Mallaig. Easy access (lighted) convenient for Kyle Rhea. Few facilities.
Approach Straightforward. Enter to N of island.
Anchorages (1) Towards head of bay according to depth.
(2) Take visitors mooring in Duisdale Bay ¾M N. Apply at hotel.
Facilities PO, store, hotel.

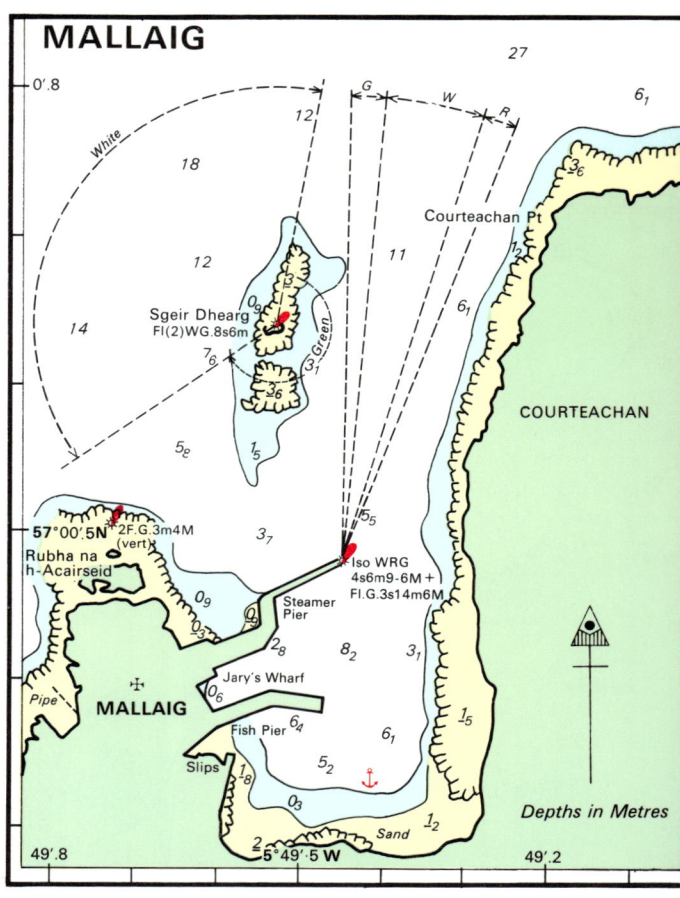

MALLAIG*   Chart BA 2541
HW: Dover −5¼h
MHWS 5.0m   MHWN 3.8   MTL 2.9   MLWN 2.1   MLWS 0.7

A busy fishing and ferry port with good facilities but little space. Open to N.
Approach Straightforward.
Entrance Pass either side of Sgeir Dhearg Fl(2)WG 8s but best to E in W sector of pierhead Lt Iso WRG 4s and Fl G 3s. Note 3 vert R lts on pierhead indicate entry or leaving prohibited.
Anchorages (1) Berth alongside Fish Pier. Limited stay. Pier dues.
(2) Anchor towards head of bay. Buoy anchor. Limited space.
Facilities Water and diesel at Fish Pier. Chandler, charts, slip, repairs. PO, shops EC Wed. hotels. Ferry to Skye. Trains to Glasgow and London.

EIGG   Chart BA 2207
HW: Dover −5h
MHWS 4.7m   MHWN 3.5   MTL 2.6   MLWN 1.6   MLWS 0.5

A pleasant and convenient anchorage about half way between Mallaig and Ardnamurchan. Exposed to swell from N to E and S. Strong tides can be uncomfortable.
Approach Identify Sgurr (391m) conspic and En Chathastail Lt bn Fl 6s 24m 8M.
Entrance From NE identify two perches-circular topmark to N and △ to S (reported missing) and pass between them. Then head for stone pier. From S keep at least 1ca W of En Chathastail. Note rks extending 1½ca SW of en.
Anchorages (1) To N of pier according to depth and clear of moorings. Sandy bottom shoals rapidly to W.
(2) S of Galmisdale Pt as close to shore as possible to avoid tide.
Facilities Water, diesel, Calor, cafe at pier. PO/store 2M. Hotel. Ferry to Arisaig and Mallaig.

CLYDE CRUISING CLUB

1. Clyde Area Sailing Directions
2. Mull of Kintyre to Ardnamurchan Sailing Directions
3. Ardnamurchan to Cape Wrath Sailing Dire tions
4. Outer Hebrides Sailing Directions
5. Shetland Sailing Directions
6. Orkney and North and North East Coasts Sailing Directions
7. Amendments to Sailing directions
8. Sketch Charts

1982 Edition. Covers West Coast of Scotland from the Solway Firth to Cape Wrath and includes the Hebrides.
Set of Chartlets - size 15" x 19"
Fully revised amendments to all seven volumes of the Sailing Directions updated annually and collected in one booklet.

**Kate Johnson, Clyde Cruising Club,
c/o RA Clement & Co
29 St Vincent Place, Glasgow G1 2DT
Tel: 041 221 0068
Fax: 041 204 3744**

OTHER HARBOURS

Harbour	Anchorages	Facilities	Comments
Handa Island 58°21′N 5°11′W	SE corner of is. Exposed to S. Poor holding.	Water tap on beach.	R.S.P.B. bird sanctuary.
Loch Nedd 58°15′N 5°09′W	Toward head of loch.	PO/shop, hotel, at Drumbeg 1½M	Easy access. Good shelter.
Loch Roe 58°10′N 5°17′W	Pool Bay to S of island at entrance.	None	Difficult entrance. Good shelter. Beautiful anchorage
Loch Torridon 57°37′N 5°47′W	1 Sheildaig. E of island. 2 Head of Upper Loch.	Water, PO/shop. Water, PO/shop.	Spectacular mountain scenery. Many anchorages. Subject to squalls.
South Rona 57°32′N 6°00′W	Acarseid Mor. Good holding.	None.	Rather difficult entrance. Attractive remote anchorage.
Caolas Scalpay 57°21′N 5°59′W	Either E or W of Narrows.	None.	Useful anchorage. Easy access from N. Dangerous narrows shoal to 0.1m
Crowlin Isles 57°21′N 5°49′W	In gut between isles. Approach from N.	None	Safe and convenient but remote anchorage in Inner Sound
Loch Duich 57°16′N 5°32′W	Totaig Bay on S. shore. SW of islet.	PO/shop, water, hotels at Dornie across loch.	Safe and attractive anchorage opposite historic En Donnan castle
Loch Hourne 57°09′N 5°40′W.	1 N or E of En Rarsaidh. 2 Off Arnisdale Village.	PO/shop, hotel. Water from tap. Bus to Kyle.	Magnificent fiord-like Inner Loch reached through four sets of narrows.
Armadale. Skye 57°04′N 5°54′W	1 HIDB visitors moorings. 2 Alongside ferry pier. Exposed from N & E. Swell from SW.	PO/shop ¾M. Ferry to Mallaig.	Convenient moorings in Sound of Sleat. Easy access from E. Lighted.
Loch Nevis 57°02′N 5°47′W.	1 Off Inverie pier. 2 In front of Glasschoille Ho.	PO/shop, water. Ferry to Mallaig.	Picturesque loch with remote Inner Loch beyond narrows.
Arisaig. L. nan Ceall 56°55′N 5°55′W.	In bay west of village.	PO, shops, hotel. Water & diesel at pier. Repairs. Trains to Glasgow and London.	Tortuous entrance marked by bns. Good shelter. Useful for stores and crew changes.
L Scresort. Rhum 57°02′N 5°55′N	In bay according to depth. Exposed to E	PO. Limited stores, water. Hotel. Ferry to Mallaig.	Owned by Nature Conservancy Access by permit only except for short Trails. For extended stay apply resident Chief Warden. No dogs.
Loch Moidart 56°48′N 5°52′W	1 Off pier at En Shona. 2 E of En Riasga	Water at Shona. PO, shops at Acharacle. 2M	Difficult entrance. Beautiful, sheltered sandy loch with historic castle ruins.
Isle of Muck. 56°50′N 6°13′W	Port Mor. Anchor clear of moorings. Somewhat exposed to S.	Hotel.	Remote and attractive island.

Section B. ARDNAMURCHAN TO MULL OF KINTYRE
Principal Lights

Ardnamurchan Point	Fl(2) 20s 55m 24M
Ru nan Gall	Fl 3s 17m 15M
Lismore	Fl 10s 31m 19M
Fladda	Fl(2)WRG 9s 13m 11-9M
Skervuille	Fl 15s 22m 9M
McArthur's Head	Fl(2)WR 10s 39m 14-11M

Passage Notes

Entering the Sound of Mull from the N keep close to the Mull shore leaving the New Rocks G con buoy to port to avoid dangerous drying reefs towards entrance of Loch Sunart. All dangers in the Sound of Mull and the Firth of Lorne are well marked. Strong tides and overfalls may be encountered off Duart Pt and in Fladda Narrows. Pass midway between Fladda Lt Ho Fl(2)WRG 9s (Sectors 169° - R - 186° - W - 337° - G - 344° - W - 356° - R - 026° - Obs - 169°) 13m 11-9M and Dubh Sgeir Fl WRG 6s (Sectors 000° - W - 010° - R - 025° - W - 199° - G - 000° 9m 6-4M into the Sound of Luing.

Alternatively the Cuan Sound provides a useful passage between the Firth of Lorne and Seil Sound and Loch Melfort but the tides run at 7kn springs and there are numerous off shore hazards. The NW entrance can be identified by overhead cables (clearance 35m) and their pylons. Beware of rks (1.1m) 1 ca W of N point of entrance. Keep in mid channel until Cleit Rk with bn is identified. Pass ¼ to ½ ca N of bn; note rk awash ¾ ca from S point of Seil. Keep in mid channel and pass either ¼ ca or 3 ca NE of Torsa.

In the Sound of Jura there are numerous islets and submerged rks W and S of Craignish Peninsular terminating in Ruadh Sgeir Lt Fl 6s. If proceeding to Crinan or Ardfern pass S of Coiresa and Craignish Pt through Dorus Mor (tide 8kn springs). If keeping W beware of being swept into very dangerous Corryvrekan between Jura and Scarba. Large scale charts are advisable if approaching Gigha or the SE of Islay owing to numerous off-lying rks. Strong tides and heavy seas may be encountered between the Mull of Kintyre, Rathlin Is and the S coast of Islay.

Tidal Streams. All related to Dover.

Ardnamurchan	+1½h N	−4½h S 1½kn
Lismore Lt Ho	+1¼h N	−5h S 2kn
Corran Narrows (L. Linnhe)	+6h NE	−5½h SW 5kn
Firth of Lorne	−1h NE	+5h SW 1½kn
Fladda Narrows	−1h N	+5h S 7kn
Cuan Sound	−1h NW	+5¼h SE 7kn
Gulf of Corryvrechan	−1¼h W	+4¾h E 8½kn
Dorus Mor	−2h W	+4¾h E 8kn

TOBERMORY*   Charts BA 2390 2392 2474
HW: Dover −5¼h

MHWS 4.4m MHWN 3.3 MTL 2.5 MLWN 1.8 MLWS 0.7

Approach From N keep close to Mull shore between Ru nan Gall Lt Ho Fl 3s and New Rks G con buoy Fl 6s.
Entrance (1) Main entrance N of Calve Is. No hazards
(2) S entrance. Narrow drying channel. Church spire on Aros Head 300°.
Anchorages (1) Off town as far S as W mark on shore according to depth: often crowded. HIDB. visitors moorings.
(2) Aros Bay according to depth.
(3) Doirlinn Narrows (S entrance)
Facilities Shops, EC Wed, hotels, chandlery, charts. Water, petrol and diesel at McBraynes Pier. Ferries to Oban, Coll and Kilchoan.

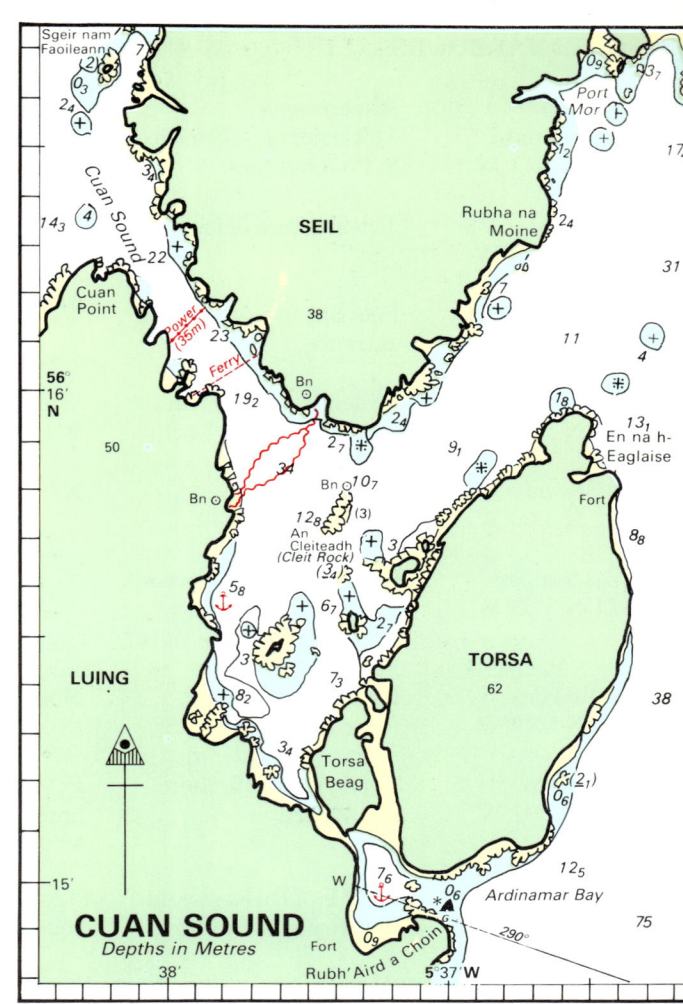

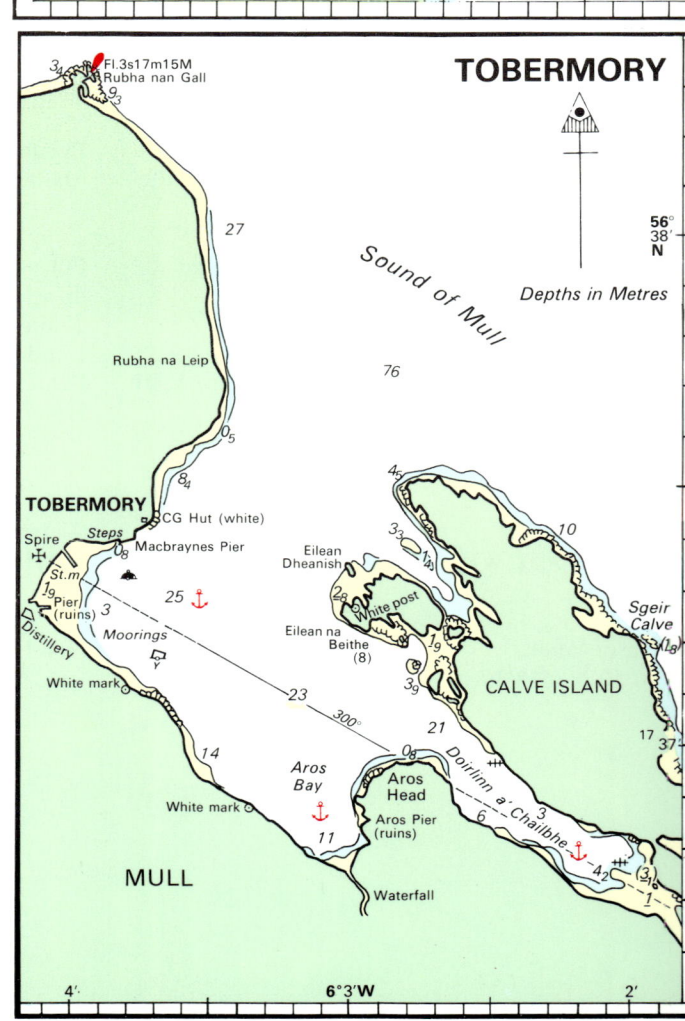

LOCH LINNHE and CALEDONIAN CANAL
Chart BA 2380 2372 1791
HW: Corpach: Dover −5h
MHWS 4.1m MHWN 3.1 MTL 2.5 MLWN 1.9 MLWS 0.9

The Northern part of Loch Linnhe has little to offer the yachtsman except as the approach to the Caledonian Canal and impressive mountain scenery. The passage through the Corran Narrows is straightforward (tidal stream 5kn). Beyond Fort William the channel to Corpach is marked by lt buoys and the canal entrance by a W lt tower Iso WRG 4s.

Anchorages (1) Corpach W of canal entrance.
(2) Camas nan Gall 1M NW of Fort William.
(3) In canal basin. Sea lock opens 4h either side of HW.

Facilities At Corpach; PO, shops, diesel. Trains to Glasgow and London. Fort William is shopping and communication centre for area.

The Caledonian Canal runs 60M NE from Corpach to Inverness via Lochs Lochy, Oich and Ness with 29 locks. Minimum passage time 2 days. All locks and bridges are manned. Vessels up to 48m LOA, 11m beam and 4m draught can use canal. Sea locks at Corpach at SW end and Beauly Firth 1M W of Inverness at NE end. Both sea locks normally operate within 4h either side of HW. Canal operates 0800-1700 daily except Sundays. Details from Manager Caledonian Canal Office, Clachnaharry, Inverness. (0463) 233140 or Corpach (039 27) 249.

OBAN*
Charts BA 1790 2387
HW: Dover −5½h
MHWS 4.0m MHWN 2.9 MTL 2.4 MLWN 1.8 MLWS 0.7

Large open bay. Rather exposed. Main harbour and centre for the area. Busy ferry and fishing port.

Approach and Entrance From N. Keep SW of Maiden Is in W sector of Dunolli Lt Ho Fl(2) WRG 6s. From S by Kerrera Sound. Avoid Sgeir Rathaid marked by N&S card buoys.

Anchorages 1. Alongside N pier. Short stay only. Heavy wash from passing vessels.
2. At Fish Quay NE of ferries.
3. Anchor N of N Pier according to depth. Beware of obstruction 1ca NNW of pier.
4. Moorings in Ardantrive Bay, Kerrera opposite.
5. Marina or anchor Dunstaffnage Bay 3M NE. Very limited space. No fuel.

Facilities Shops, EC Thur, hotels, chandlery. Water at N pier and Fish Quay. Diesel at Rly Pier and Ardantrive Pier.
Boatyards: Curries by S Quay. 0631 62102
Oban Yacht Services, Ardantrive. 0631 63666
Oban Marine, Gallanachbeg. 2M SW. 0631 63388
Trains to Glasgow and London. Ferries to Inner Hebrides, S Uist & Barra.

See next page for L. Aline

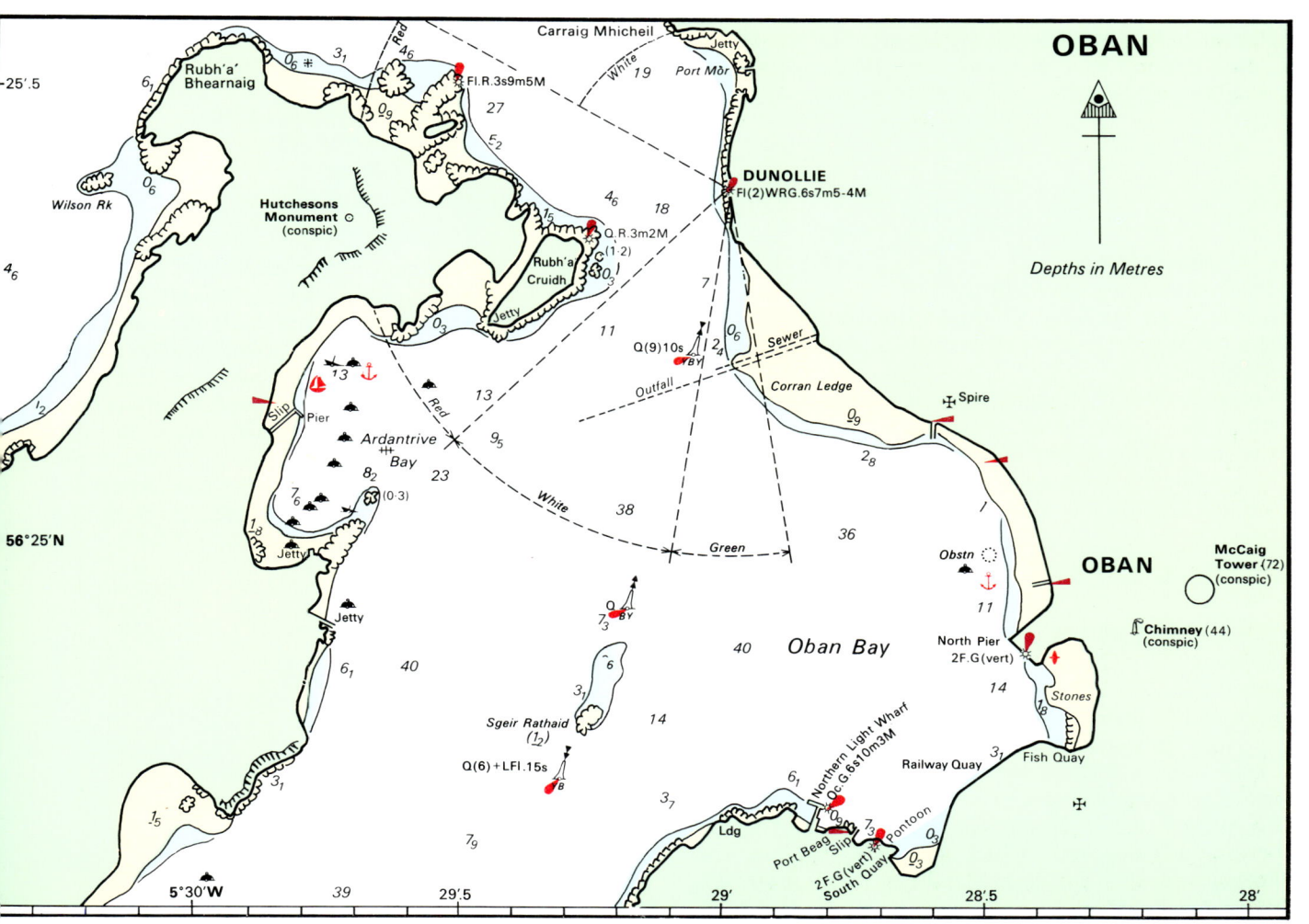

LOCH ALINE Chart BA 2390
HW: Dover −5½h
MHWS 4.5m   MHWN 3.2

A useful and protected harbour on mainland side of Sound of Mull.

Entrance Avoid reef off Bolorkle Pt to E of entrance by keeping 2 ca offshore then keep in mid-channel. 2 port and one stbd lt buoys. Ldg Bns and Lts F W 356°. Tide 2½kn in entrance.

Anchorages 1. In Miodar Bay. SE corner of loch: partially obstructed by fish farm.
2. W side of loch N of bn.
3. Head of loch: moorings or anchor according to depth.
4. Moor to stone pier on W side of entrance. (Temporary)

Facilities Store/PO, water, Calor in village. Home produce at Ardtornish garden. Small boatyard at Ardtornish.

LOCH MELFORT Chart BA 2326
HW: Dover +6h
MHWS 5.1m   MHWN 4.0   MTL 1.7   MLWN 1.3   MLWS 0.6

A very popular loch but many anchorages now filled with moorings or fish farms.

Entrance Straightforward but note Campbell Rk 1.8m ¾M NE of Ru Chnaip. Also beware of covering rk marked by bn N of pontoon in L. na Cille.

Anchorages 1. Moorings in L na Cille. Apply Yacht Haven.
2. Fearnach Bay. Moorings. Limited space for anchoring.

Facilities Water and diesel at pontoon. Boatyard, hoist 12T, repairs, engineer & chandlery. Kilmelford Yacht Haven. 08522 248/279. Shop/PO, hotel at Kilmelford 1½M. Bus to Oban. Fearnach Bay: Water, diesel and calor at pier. Shop/PO, hotel at Kilmelfort.

CRAOBH HAVEN Chart BA 2326
Tidal data as for Loch Melfort

A modern marina 7M N of Crinan formed by the construction of breakwaters between offshore islands and the mainland.

Entrance from N straightforward leaving G con buoy to stb.

Facilities Pontoon berths, water, diesel, Calor, shop, restaurant, slip & hoist.
Tel 085 25 222

LOCH CRAIGNISH and ARDFERN Chart BA 2326
Approach From N via Dorus Mor (S of Craignish Pt) Tide 8kn springs. From S keep E of Ruadh Sgeir Fl 6s 13m 8M then in L Craignish give shore and islands a berth of 1½ ca. Note Sgeir Dubh (0.6m) 2 ca E of N end of En Mhic Chrion. Enter Ardfern between Ens Mhic Chrion and Inshaig keeping well over to former.

Facilities Ardferen Yacht Centre 085 25 247. Pontoon berths and moorings. Water and diesel at pontoon. Boatyard, repairs, engineer, chandlery. Hotel, shop/P.O. Bus to Oban ½M

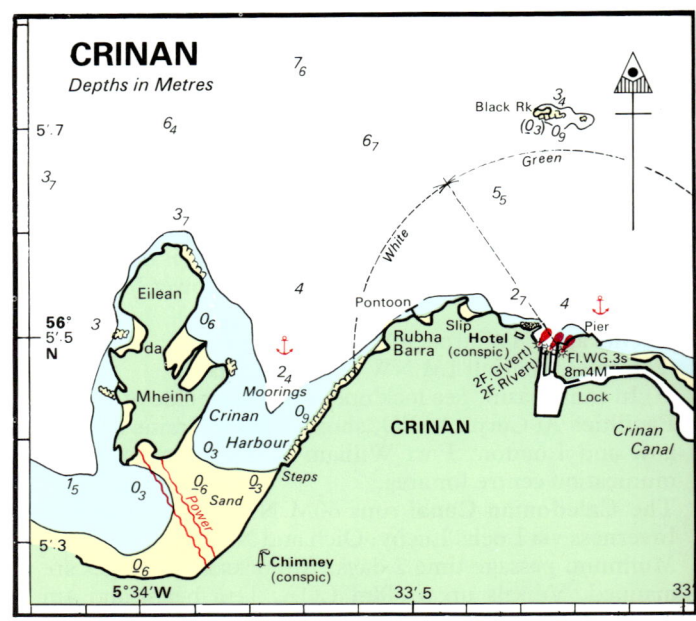

CRINAN* Charts BA 2326 2320
HW: Dover +6h
MHWS 2.4m   MHWN 1.7   MTL 1.4   MLWN 1.1   MLWS 0.3

Approach Straightforward. W hotel conspic. Lt Ho Fl WG 3s.

Entrance to canal E of hotel. Ldg Lts FW 186°. Avoid Black Rk 2 ca N.

Anchorages (1) Crinan Harbour: moorings Apply M. Murray 054 683 238 or Crinan Boats 232.
(2) Anchor outside moorings or off hotel in 4m. Exposed to NW.
(3) Moor in canal basin. Sea lock operates 0600-2130 Mon-Sat
(4) Alongside concrete pier to E of Lt Ho.

Facilities Shop (limited stores), chandlery, charts, hotel. Water and diesel at pontoon in harbour or in basin. Boatyard, slip, repairs, engineer.

CRINAN CANAL runs across the base of the Kintyre Peninsular to Ardrisaig on Loch Fyne thus saving a sometimes difficult 80M passage round the Mull to the Clyde. It is 9M long with 15 locks and 7 swing bridges and can take vessels up to 88ft LOA x 20ft beam x 9½ft draught. Through movement is restricted by bridge opening hours (0800 - 1200 & 1230 - 1630 Mon-Sat). Inland locks are operated by crew. Passage time at least 5hrs. Yachts proceeding W have right of way. Use horn when approaching bridges. Mooring pontoons established at Bellanoch. Dues payable at Ardrishaig 0546 3210.

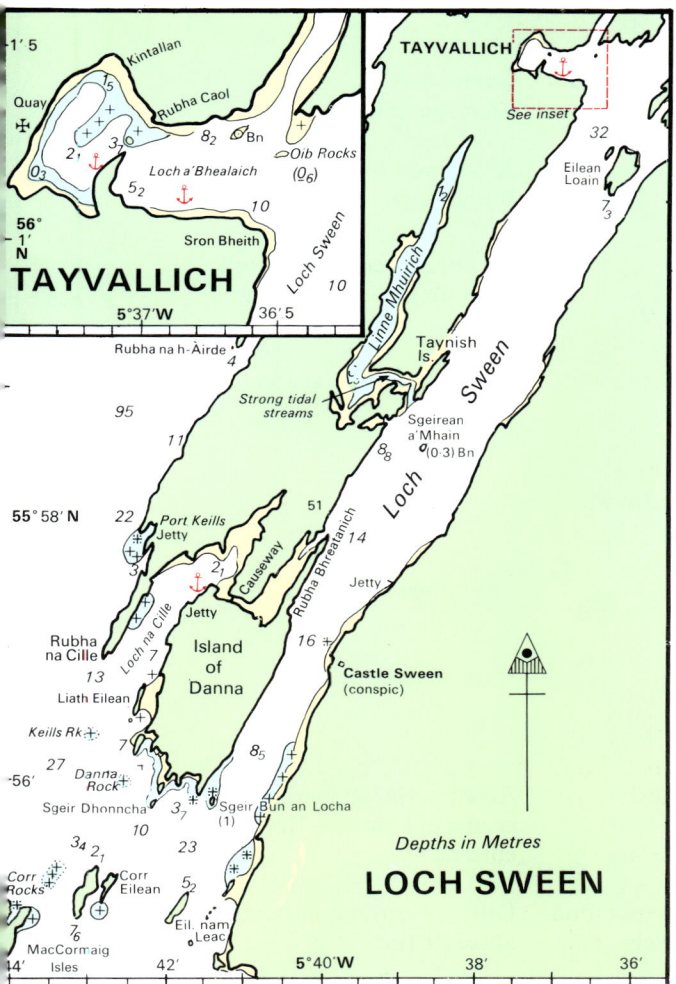
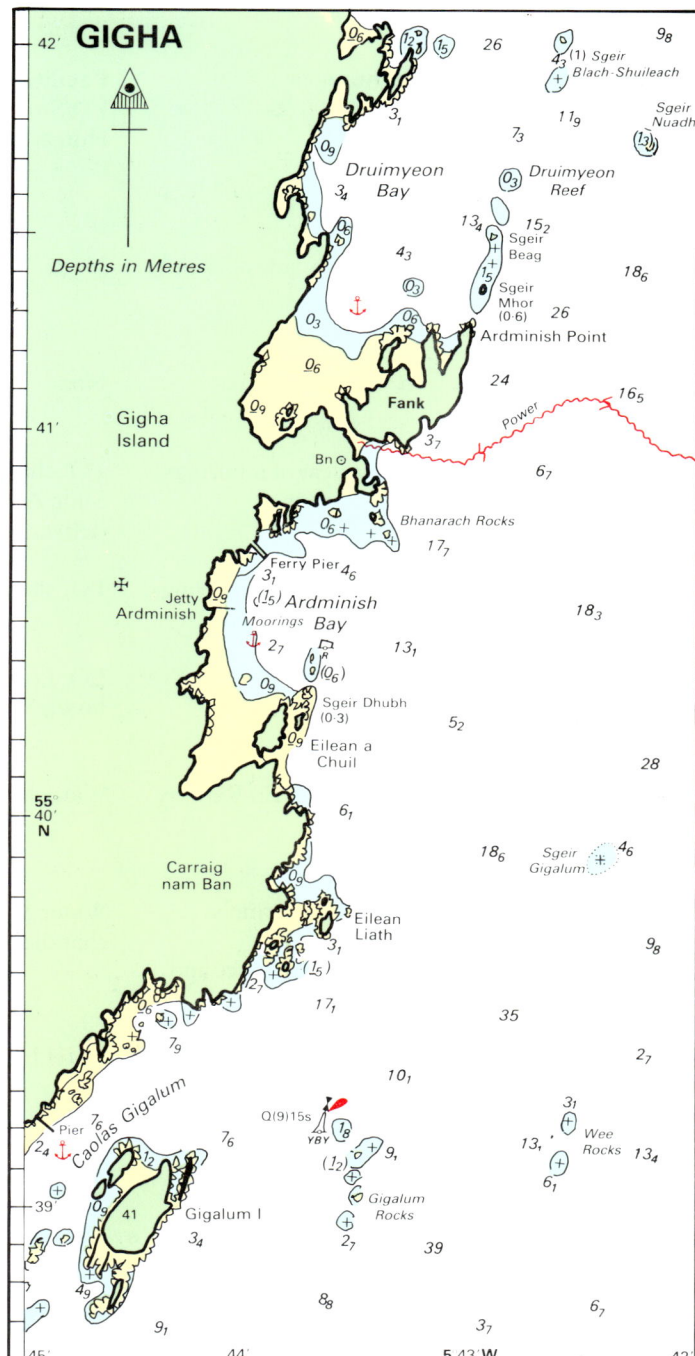

TAYVALLICH   Chart BA 2397

lst HW: Dover+3h 2nd: +6h

A popular and well protected harbour at head of L Sween. Many moorings.

Approach From N care must be taken to avoid Keills and Danna Rks to port and Corr Rks to stb. The N end of En Ghamhna on the Pt of Knapp 155° leads clear but landmarks may be difficult to identify. Avoid Sgeir Bun an Locha on W side of entrance to L Sween. In loch shores are clean but avoid mid-channel rk marked by bn awash at HW 1½M. N of Castle Sween. At head of loch keep close to Sron Bheith to port and enter harbour through narrow passage S of mid-channel islet.

Anchorages (1) Anchor close SW of central reef. Space limited. (2) In loch a'Bhealaich SE of entrance reef.

Facilities Shop/PO, restaurant, Calor. Water at tap by PO.

CRAIGHOUSE JURA (Loch na Mile)   Chart BA 2396

HW: Dover −1h

MHWS 1.2m   MHWN 0.9   MTL 0.42   MLWN 0.4   MLWS 0.3

A useful alternative to Gigha. Good shelter but subject to swell.

Approach and Entrance Na Cuiltean Fl 10s 9M lies 1½M SW of entrance. Enter between En nan Gabhar Lt bn Fl 5s to stb and perch to port.

Anchorages (1) Pick up one of HIDB visitors moorings. (2) Anchor clear of moorings off stone pier. Holding reported poor. (3) In sandy cove at SW entrance of Lowlandmans Bay N of Loch na Mile.

Facilities PO/Shop, fuel, calor, hotel.

GIGHA★   Chart BA 2475

HW: Dover 2¼h Neaps +6h Springs

MHWS 1.5m   MHWN 1.3   MTL 0.9   MLWN 0.8   MLWS 0.6

A convenient and useful passage harbour for yachts proceeding to or from the Mull of Kintyre. Exposed from NE to SE.

Approach and Entrance From S keep about 3 ca E of Cara and Gigalum and leave card W buoy Q(9) 15s to stb then keep 1 ca off En Liath. Leave R can buoy to port to enter Ardminish Bay with old pier bearing 270°. From N leave Gamhna Rks and Badh Rk card W buoy to port but keep 1M off shore to avoid Sgeir Nuadh (dr 1m) until pier bears 270°.

Anchorages (1) Ardminish Bay. HIDB visitors moorings also plenty of room to anchor according to depth. Hard sand. (2) South of Gigalum off pier.

Facilities Shop/PO, water at tap by old ferry ho. Diesel by pipe at Gigalum pier. (Contact engineer at Achamore Estate 1M), hotel, launderette. Ferry to Tayinloan connects with bus to Glasgow.

SCOTLAND, WEST COAST   154

OTHER HARBOURS

Harbour	Anchorages	Facilities	Comments
Kilchoan 56°24'.50N 6°00'.73W	8 HIDB moorings	PO/Store, Hotels	Convenient for rounding Ardnamurchan Rather exposed from S.
Isle Oronsay L. Sunart 56°40'N 5°57'W	In gut in N side of island.	None	An attractive and sheltered anchorage. Good holding.
L. Na Drumbuie 56°39'N 5°58'W	In SW corner of bay.	None	A popular anchorage S of Isle Oronsay.
Salen L. Sunart 56°43'N 5°46'W	In bay clear of moorings. Buoy anchor.	PO, chandlery, hotel. Shop Acharacle 2M will deliver.	
Salen Mull 56°31'N 5°37'W	HIDB visitors' moorings.	PO, shops, hotel.	Off-lying rks. Approach with care.
Craignure 56°28'.5N 5°42'.4W	8 HIDB moorings	PO, hotel, Shop hotel, Shop	Close to ferry pier
Port Ramsay Lismore 56°33'N 5°27'W	In bay SE of En Ramsay	Water by cottages.	An attractive anchorage at NW corner of Lismore. Rather difficult entrance.
Loch Feochan 56°21'N 5°31'W	1 Ardoran Marine's moorings. 2 Between entrance and moorings.	Water & diesel at pontoon, chandlery, showers.	Difficult entrance now marked. Shoals 0.1m
Puiladobhrain 56°20'N 5°40'W	In large pool protected by rocky islets. Good shelter and holding except in gales.	Hotel 1M	A popular and convenient anchorage. May be crowded.
Ardinamir 56°15'N 5°37'W	In pool.	Water at farm. PO/shop, restaurant 1M	Rather tricky entrance. Attractive anchorage. Irene Maclachlan at farm keeps visitors' book.
Seil Sound 56°17'N 5°36'W	1 Balvicar Bay 2 By ponton 1½M N of Balvicar.	PO/shop Water & diesel at pontoon.	Easy access. Good shelter.
En Mor, Cormach Is. 55°55'N 5'43'W	At head of gut in N coast of en. Restricted but sheltered.	None	Romantic lonely island associated with St Cormach.
West L Tarbert Kintyre 55°45'N 5°35'W	1 Head of loch. 2 N of Kennacraig ferry pier.	Hotel at head of loch. Bus to Glasgow. PO, chandlery, shops, etc. Tarbet 1½M.	Easy access. Lit. Complete shelter.

Section C. OUTER PASSAGE. BUTT OF LEWIS TO ISLAY.

Principal Lights

Flannan Is	Fl(2)30s 101m 20M
Butt of Lewis	Fl 5s 52m 25M
Tiumpan Head	Fl(2)30s 54m 24M
En Glas	Fl(3)20s 43m 23M
Uisenis	Fl WR 20s 54m 19/15M
Neist Pt	Fl(2)30s 43m 24M
Oigh Sgeir	Fl(3)30s 41m 4m 24M
Skerryvore	Fl 10s 46m 16M
Dubh Artach	Fl(2) 30s 44m 20M
Barrahead	Fl 15s 208m 21M
Ru A'Mhail	Fl(3) WR 15s 45m 24/21M

PASSAGE NOTES

The navigation of the W side of the Outer Hebrides should not be attempted without a crew capable of handling the yacht in severe conditions. Heavy seas are common along the whole 100M of the Western seaboard and the coast should only be closed in settled weather with large scale charts aboard. Shelter can be found by sailing either North or South of the chain into the lee of the islands. Off Harris, Benbecula and N and S Uist a vessel should stand off several miles. The land on the W is so low that an accurate visual fix may be difficult to obtain.

The E coast of Lewis and Harris is clear from the Butt of Lewis to the Shiant Is. There are numerous dangerous rks and islets with strong tides and overfalls extending from the Shiants to Ru Hunish (N Skye). Heavy seas may be experienced S of the Shiants. Between the Sound of Harris and the S end of N Uist the coast is clear beyond ½M offshore but Benbecula and its islets should be given a berth of at least 1M. Dangerous rks exist up to 2M S of Barra.

The W coast of Skye presents a series of prominent headlands with strong tides and overfalls. SW of Canna there are dangerous rks for over 7M and in bad weather the seas here can be very big. The Passage of Tiree is open to the SW. Great care must be taken to avoid the dangerous Torran Rks extending 4M SW of the Ross of Mull. The passage N of Colonsay to the Sound of Islay is clear.

Tidal Streams. All related to Dover

Ru Uisenish to Shiant Is	+5h NE	−1h SW 3-4kn
En Glas (Harris) to Sgeir Inoc	+5h NE	−1h SW 2½kn
Ru Hunish (Skye)	+4h NE	−2h SW 2½kn
Vaternish Pt (Skye)	+4¼h NE	−1¾h SW 2½kn
Passage of Tiree	+1h N	−5¼h S 1½kn
Ross of Mull	−1¼h N	+4¾h S 1½kn
W of Islay	−½h NE	+6h SW 2kn
Sound of Islay	−1h N	+5¼h S 5kn
Race off Onsay, SW of Islay	HW NW	−6¼h SE 8kn
Mull of Oa.	HW NW	−6¼h SE 5kn

ST KILDA   Chart BA 2524

HW: Dover −5¼h

MHWS 3.3m MHWN 2.5 MTL 1.9 MLWN 1.2 MLWS 0.4

Islands are owned by National Trust for Scotland.
Anchor in Village Bay off concrete pier. Ldg lts Oc 5s 270°. Subject to swell. Untenable in winds from ENE to SSW when Glen Bay to NW may be possible, but subject to extreme squalls.

WEST LOCH TARBERT HARRIS   Chart BA 2841

HW: Dover −5¼h

MHWS 4.2m MHWN 3.2 MTL 2.3 MLWN 1.3 MLWS 0.4

One of the few harbours on the W coast of the Outer Hebrides offering protection except from W.
Approach Either side of Taransay the N being clearer. From S keep Toe Head and summit of Coppay Is in line then in mid-channel to avoid sand spits on either side at Narrows. Keep to S shore of loch.
Anchorages (1) Head of loch at Tarbert.
(2) Taransay N of Corran Raah spit.
Facilities Shops. PO, hotel. Ferry to Skye.

STORNOWAY*   Chart BA 2529

HW: Dover −4½h

MHWS 4.8m MHWN 3.7 MTL 2.9 MLWN 2.0 MLWS 0.7

Busy ferry and fishing port.
Entrance between Arnish Pt and Holm Pt. Leave R can buoy QR off Arnish Pt to port. Leave En na Gobhail well to stb and avoid shoal to W of Inner Harbour. Leave the Parsons Rks marked by two iron perches to port. At night approach in W sector of Arnish Pt Lt Ho Fl WR 10s 17m 19M then in W sectors successively of Sandwick Oc 6s, Stoneyfield Fl 3s (astern) and Pierhead Q.
Anchorages (1) Private moorings N of Parsons Rk.
(2) In bay NW of En na Gobhail. Shoals.
(3) Berth alongside E wall of Inner Harbour. Short stay only.
(4) Glumaig Bay.
Facilities PO, shops (closed all day Wed), charts, water, diesel, slip. Ferry to Ullapool

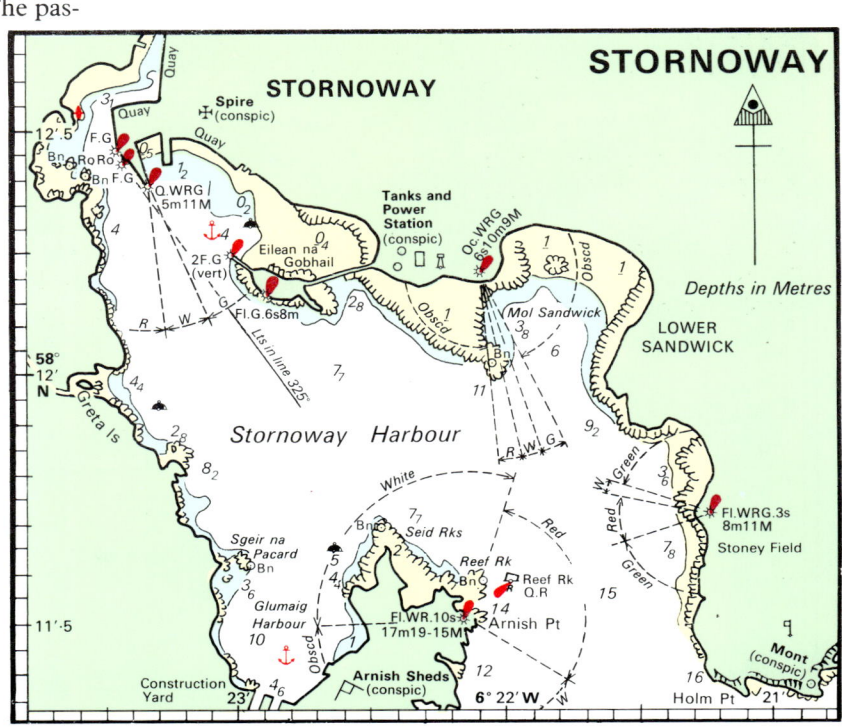

SCOTLAND, WEST COAST

LOCH SHELL Chart BA 1794
HW: Dover 4¾h
MHWS 4.8m MHWN 3.6 MTL 2.8 MLWN 1.9 MLWS 0.7
Entrance Enter S of En Lubhard. Note drying rks to NW of en.
Anchorages (1) Head of loch. Shoals. Exposed to E. Fish farms developing.
(2) Tob Eisken.
Facilities None.

SCALPAY EAST LOCH TARBERT* Charts BA 1794 2905
HW: Dover −4¼h
MHWS 5.0m MHWN 3.7 MTL 2.9 MLWN 2.1 MLWS 0.8
Approach En Glas Lt Ho Fl(3) 20s 43m 23M at E end of Scalpay. The Sound of Scalpay is clearer than the passage to the S of the island, the only danger being Elliot Rks (2.1m) 2½ca SSW of Ru Crago. To enter Scalpay N Harbour give Aird an Aiseig to NW a berth of ½ca. Ldg marks two W △ in line lead between G con buoy Fl G 2s to stb and submerged rk (1.1m) to port.
Anchorages (1) N Harbour off pier 2 vert F G Lts. Good shelter.
(2) S Harbour, difficult entrance.
(3) Tarbert. WSW of Ferry pier. Exposed to E.
Facilities Scalpay: PO/shop, water at pier. Tarbert: PO, shops EC Thur, hotel, diesel, water at pier. Ferry to Skye

LOCH MADDY* Chart BA 2825
HW: Dover −5h
MHWS 5.6m MHWN 3.6 MTL 2.9 MLWN 1.9 MLWS 0.7
Approach Straightforward. From S pass either side of Madadh Mor (26m) but note submerged rks ½ ca N of Leac nan Madadh. From N pass between Weavers Pt and Madadh Beg (6m). Thence by lighted channel between Glas En Mor Fl(2) 6s and Ru Pleach Fl R 4s and S of Ruig Liath Q G to W sector of Lt Fl(3) WRG 8s then ldg lts G 301° to pier.
Anchorages 1. 4 H.I.D.B. moorings.
2. SW of pier in soft mud.
3. SW corner of S Basin.
4. Bagh Aird nan Madadh. (Heavy visitors mooring).
5. Loch Portain 2M NNE. Keep in mid-channel NE of Flodday and 1ca off Ru nan Gall. Good holding and protection.
Facilities PO, shop EC Wed, water at pier, diesel, Calor, hotel. Ferry to Skye and Harris.

UIG BAY L Snizort, Skye* Charts BA 1795 2533
HW: Dover −5h
MHWS 5.1m MHWN 3.7 MTL 2.8 MLWN 2.0 MLWS 0.6
Bay on E side of L Snizort. Easy access. Rather exposed to W.
Approach and Entrance Straightforward but note spit extending 1 ca S from Ru Idrigill.
Anchorage NNE of pier Iso WRG 4s in 5m. Bottom foul.
Facilities PO, shops, hotel. Water and diesel at pier. Ferry to Harris and N Uist. Bus to Glasgow.

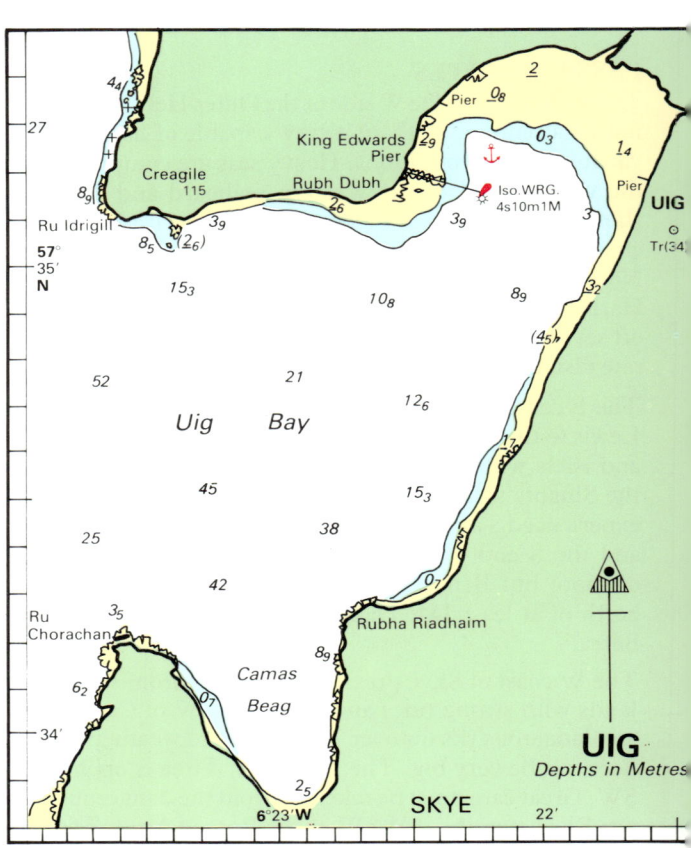

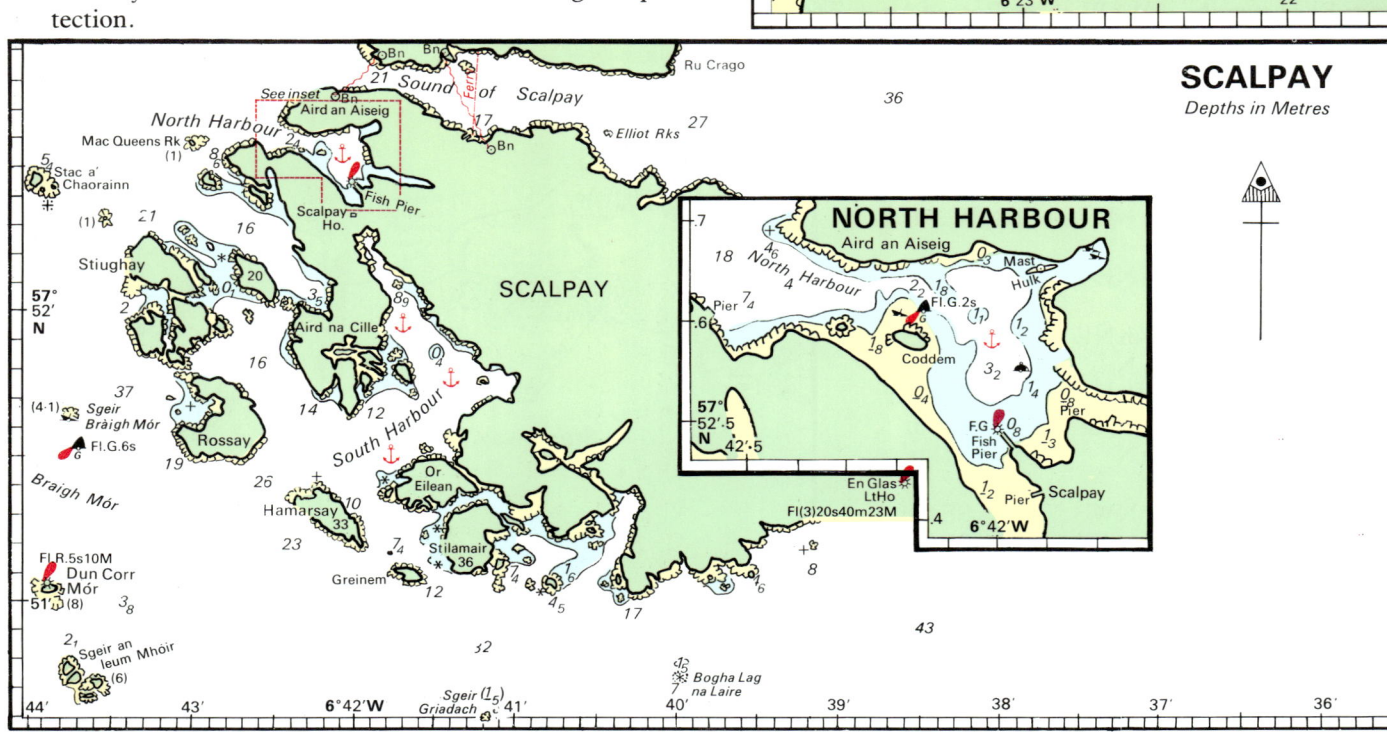

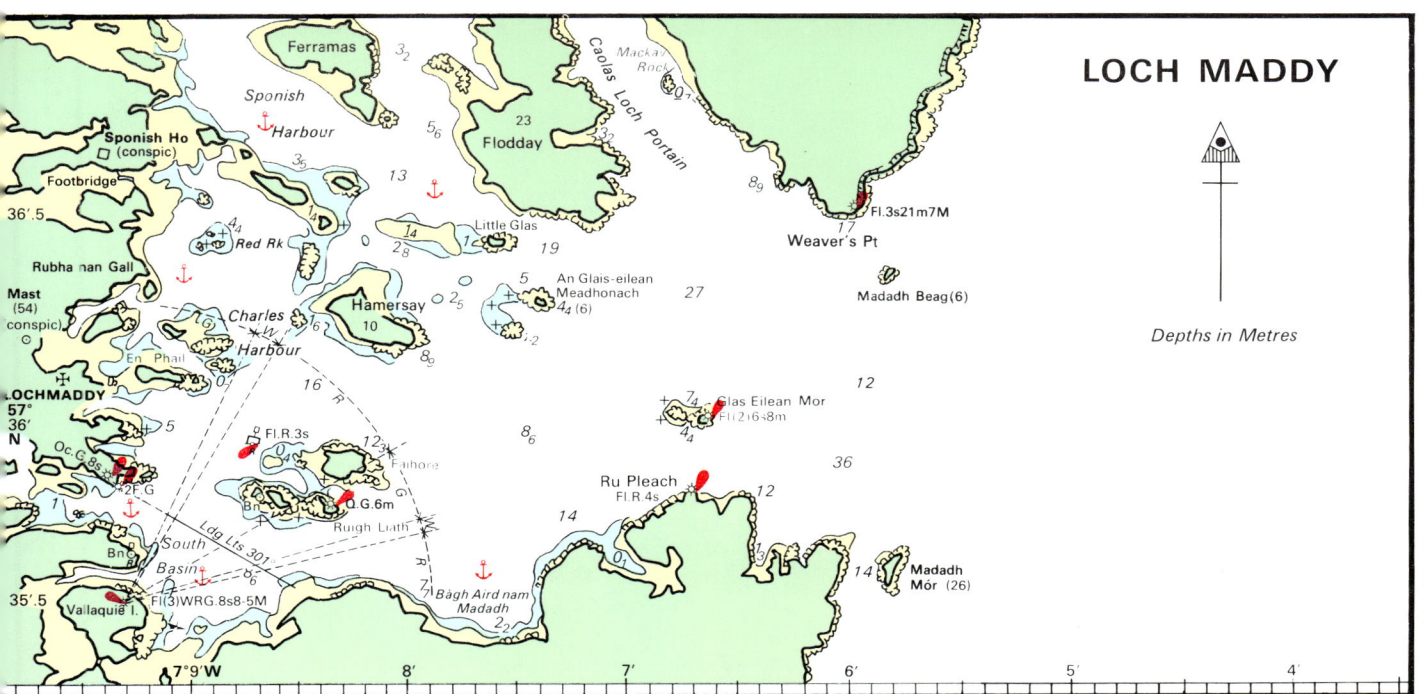

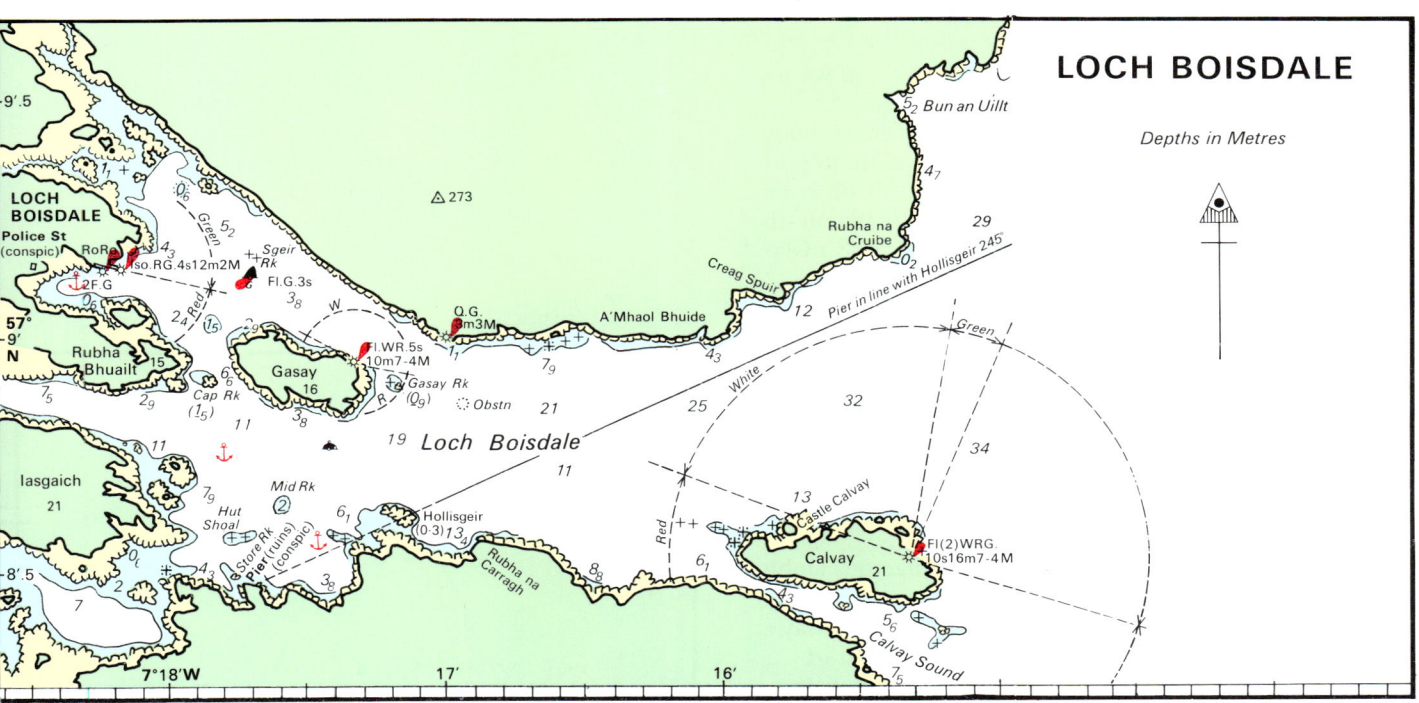

LOCH SKIPORT S UIST Chart BA 2825
HW: Dover −5¼h
MHWS 4.6m MHWN 3.3 MTL 2.5 MLWN 1.7 MLWS 0.5
Easy access N of Ornish Is. Several remote anchorages.
Anchorages (1) Wizard Pool. Keep well over towards the Shillags Mor and Beg to to avoid Float Rk dr 2. 3m thence mid channel keeping Wizard Is just open of Skillag Beg. Note drying rk 1¼ ca NW of Wizard Is.
(2) Bagh Charmaig. Note reef ½ ca off middle of W shore. Anchor at head of bay or just within E arm which shoals.
Facilities None.

LOCH BOISDALE* Chart BA 2770
HW: Dover −5¼h
MHWS 4.3m MHWN 3.0 MTL 2.4 MLWN 1.6 MLWS 0.5
Relatively easy access. Lit.
Approach and Entrance Pass between Ru na Cruibe and Calvay Is Lt Fl(2) WRG 10s then N of Gasay Lt bn at NE pt of island Fl W R 5s and to pier F RG.
Anchorages (1) 4 H.I.D.B. moorings NE of pier.
(2) SW of pier clear of moorings and pier approach. Limited space and poor holding.
(3) S of loch NE of ruined pier. Note rks 2ca NNW of pier.
Facilities PO, shop EC Tue, hotel. Water at pier, fuel at garage. Ferry to Oban.

SCOTLAND, WEST COAST 158

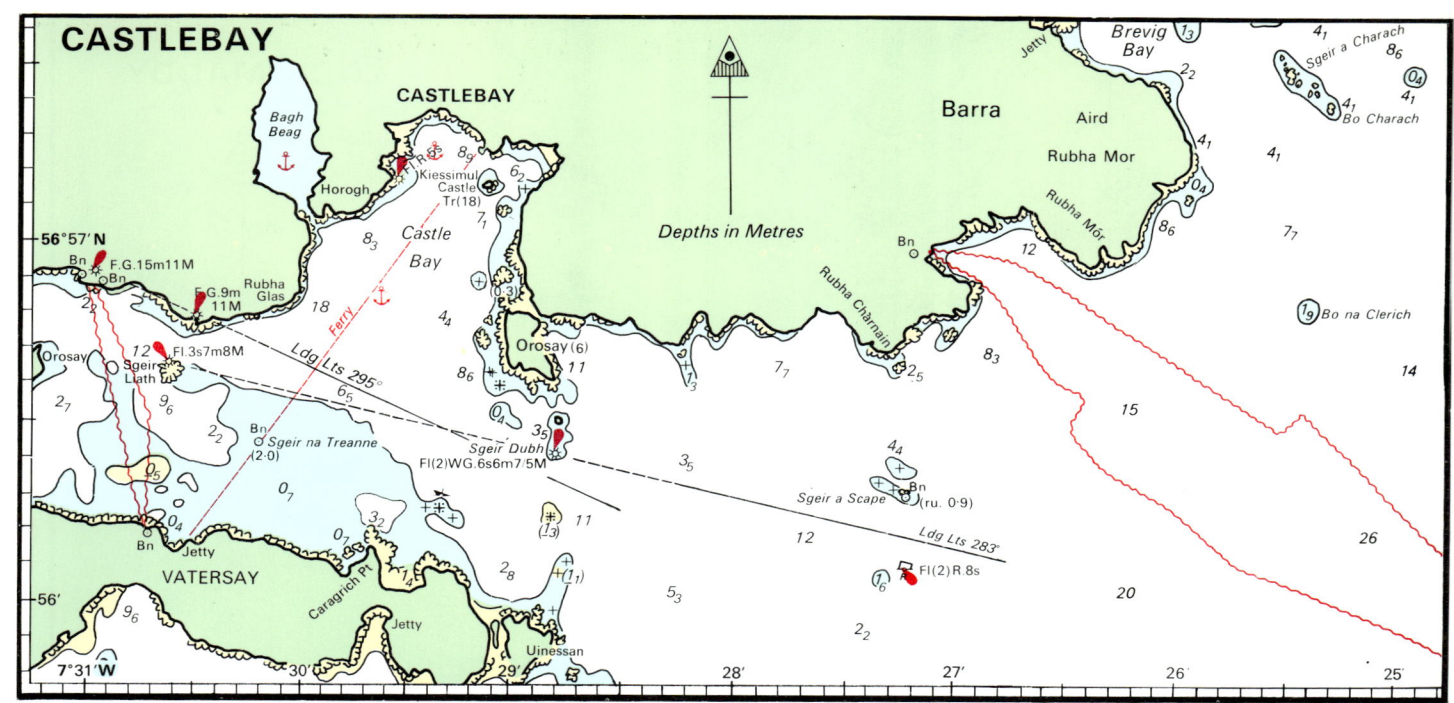

CASTLE BAY BARRA★   Charts BA 1796 2769
HW: Dover −5½h
MHWS 4.3m   MHWN 3.1   MTL 2.3   MLWN 1.7   MLWS 0.6
A valuable harbour at S end of Outer Hebrides.
Approach and Entrance From Bo Vich Chuan buoy Q(6)+LFl 15s keep R can buoy Fl(2) R 8s close to port with Sgeir Dubh Fl(2) W G 6s on Sgeir Liath Fl 3s bg 283°. Leave Sgeir a Scape with broken bn (dr 0.9m) to stb and Sgeir Dubh bn close to stb. Ldg Lts FR on Ru Glas 295°. Turn to stb when pier opens W of castle.
Anchorages (1) 8 H.I.D.B. moorings.
(2) NW of castle in 6-10m.
Facilities PO, shops, hotel. Water at pier, diesel at garage, Calor. Ferry to Oban.

LOCH HARPORT SKYE   Chart BA 1795
HW: Dover −5¼h
MHWS 5.1m   MHWN 3.8   MTL 2.9   MLWN 2.1   MLWS 0.8
The SE limb of Loch Bracadale.
Approach and Entrance From NW note dangerous Dubh Sgeir (5m) 1½M S of Ru Ruadh. Enter between Oronsay and Ru nan Clach. Give the SW and E shore of Oronsay a berth of ¼M. Leave Ardtrech Pt iso 4s 17m 9M to stb.
Anchorages (1) Portnalong. Space limited by fish farm.
(2) Carboost 1½M from head of loch.
Facilities PO, shop EC Wed.

CANNA★   Chart BA 2208
HW: Dover −5h
MHWS 4.8   MHWN 3.7
A very beautiful harbour and useful passage port when bound for the Outer Hebrides. Easy access and sheltered except from E.
Approach from N and E is straightforward. Lt at E end of Sanday Is Fl 6s 32m 9M. Steer to pass close S of Ru Carrinis. From S beware of drying reef to N of Sanday. Magnetic anomalies reported.
Entrance Beware of drying reef ¾ ca SW of pier.
Anchorage Best in line between two churches. Shoals. Hard sand suitable for bilge keelers.
Facilities PO opens as required. Ferry to Mallaig x4pw.

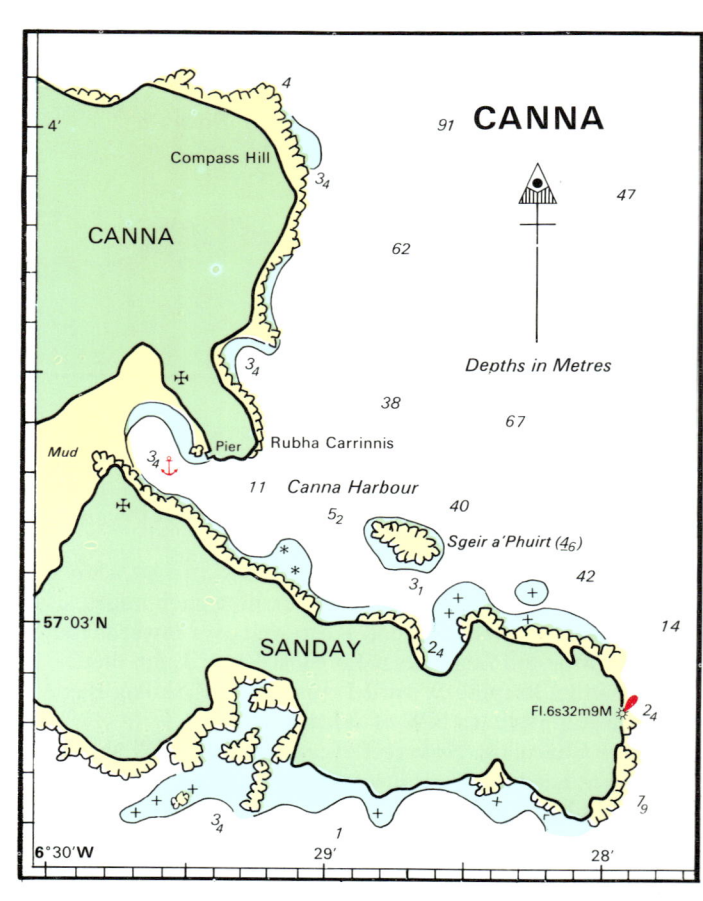

LOCH EATHARNA COLL   Charts BA 2474 2171
HW: Dover −5¼h
MHWS 4.4m MHWN 3.2
Main harbour of Coll. Exposed to winds from E to S.
Entrance Leave Bo Mor G con buoy Fl G 6s well to stbd and make for new pier 2FR then ½ ca off W shore towards old stone pier where loch shoals rapidly.
Anchorages (1) H.I.D.B. visitors moorings to N. of new pier. Untenable in winds greater than F4 from E to S.
(2) Anchor off stone pier according to depth.
(3) NE of Is Eatharna. Swinging space limited but more protected from SE.
Facilities PO, shops, hotel, launderette. Water from tap in field behind stone pier. Ferry to Oban.

LOCH NA LATHAICH*   Charts BA 2617 2171
HW: Dover −6h
MHWS 4.3m MHWN 3.0 MTL 2.4 MLWN 1.8 MLWS 0.6
An excellent harbour on N coast of Ross of Mull providing good shelter and facilities. Easy access.
Entrance Straightforward. Pass either side of En na Liathanaich Fl W R 6s 12m 8/6M. Give the En a berth of 2ca and keep to the W side of the lock.
Anchorages (1) Entrance to L Caol to W. Moorings available from boatyard.
(2) S of En Ban off pier.
Facilities Water at pontoon, diesel, chandlery, slip, showers at Bendorran Boatyard 06817-435. Shops, PO, garage, hotel at Bunessan 1½M. Bus to Craignure for Oban.

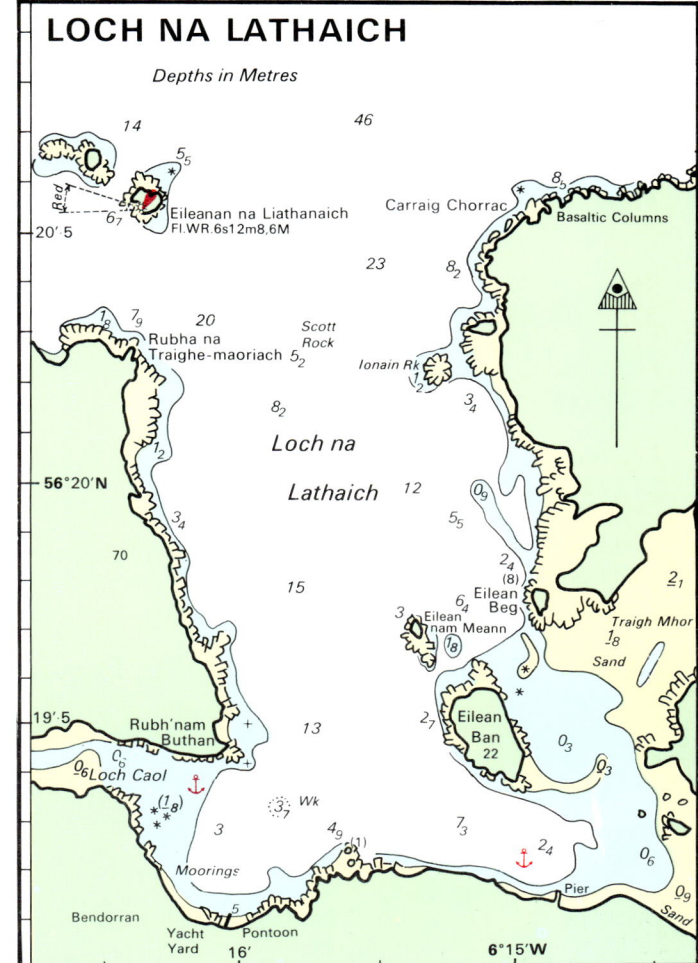

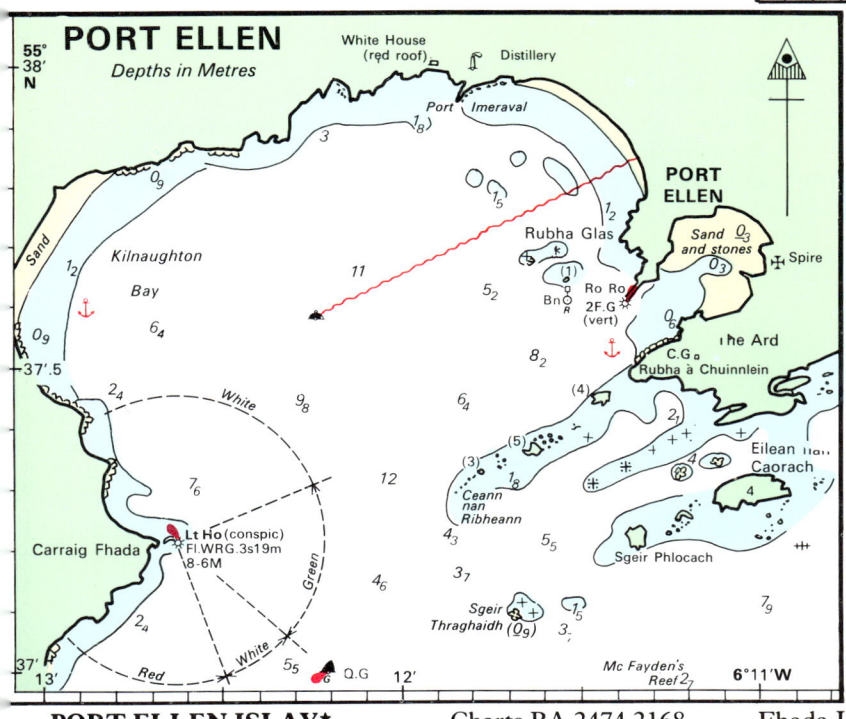

PORT ELLEN ISLAY*   Charts BA 2474 2168
HW: Dover −5¼h springs +1½h neaps
MHWS 1.9 MHWN 0.8 MTL 0.6 MLWN 0.5 MLWS 0.3
A useful passage hbr if proceeding S to Mull of Kintyre or N Ireland but exposed to swell from S. Note very small tidal range.
Approach From N keep 1½M off Islay shore and ¾M S of Texa to avoid off-lying rks. From W beware of tide races and overfalls off the Oa. From S avoid breakers over Otter Rk marked by S Card buoy Q(6)+LFl 15s. Keep Carraig Fhada Lt Ho Fl WRG 3s in line with Ro masts 330° leaving G con buoy to stb.
Anchorages
1) 10 HIDB moorings established in two trots in NE of bay. Note 3 perches with BW topmarks over underwater rks.
2) S of pier. Do not alter course until pier bears 072°. Give ferry terminal a wide berth. Harbour shoals steeply.
3) Kilnaughton Bay provides some shelter from the W.
Facilities PO, shops, hotels. Water at pierhead.

SCOTLAND, WEST COAST

OTHER HARBOURS

Harbour	Anchorages	Facilities	Comments
Port Erisco Duntulm, Skye 57°42'N 6°25'W	NE of En Tulm. Some swell.	PO/store, hotel, bus to Portree.	Convenient anchorage at NW tip of Skye.
Ardmore, L Dunvegan 57°33'N 6°39'W	At head of bay according to depth	None.	Easy access. Sheltered shoaling anchorage.
Stein 57°32'.2N 6°36'.5W	4 HIDB moorings	PO/Store. Pub	Exposed from W & S.
Dunvegan. 57°29'N 6°37'W	Head of loch beyond pier.	PO, shops, hotels, garage, diesel. Bus to Portree.	Easy access. Lit.
Loch Scavaig. Skye. 57°10'N 6°07'W	In pool NW of En Glas.	None	A most dramatic anchorage beneath the Cuillins. Subject to severe squalls.
Rodel, Harris 57°44'N 6°58'W	Poll an Tighmha. Enter by Bay channel. 4HIDB moorings Anchor in NW corner.	Water from tap, hotel Bus to Tarbert for ferry.	Landlocked anchorage accessible near HW only.
L. Eport, N Uist 57°33'N 7°09'W	Several.	None	Narrow entrance. Strong tide. Many rocks in loch.
Eriskay 57°04'N 7°17'W	In bay. 3 HIDB moorings.	Water at pier.	
Gometra 56°28'N 6°12'W	1 In S. bay between Ulva and Gometra. 2 Acarsaid Mor. N, Gometra.	None	A sheltered and secluded anchorage. Ditto. Entrance requires care.
Iona, Mull 56°19'N 6°24'W	1 Off village. (Temporary.) 2 Bull Hole. E of En Nam Ban 3 Tinker's Hole between Erraid and En Dubh.	PO, shops, hotels on island. PO/store, restaurant at Fionnphort.	A tourist centre. St Columba's cathedral (restored) and ruins interesting
Staffa 56°26'N 6°21'W	Off landing by Fingal's cave. (Temporary.)	None	Fingal's Cave. Landing only possible in calm weather.
Scalasaig, Colonsay. 56°04'N 6°11'W.	1 S. of pier. Exposed to E. 2 E. side of Oronsay. NW of En Ghaoideamal	Water, PO/shop, hotel.	A most attractive island. Priory ruins on Oronsay
Garvellach Isles 56°13'N 5°48'W.	In pool to SE of Eileach Naoimh	None	Remote anchorage. Early Christian settlement.
W L Tarbert Jura 55°57'.5N 6°50'.0W	1) Bays to N of first narrows. 2) Inner loch N of En Ard 3) Innermost loch	None	Remote attractive loch. Difficult entrance marked by series of bn transits.
Port Askaig. Islay 55°51'N 6°06'W	1 Alongside pier. Avoid ferry. 2 In small bay N of pier.	Water at pier. PO/shop, hotel. Ferry to mainland.	Strong tides and eddies. Lit.

SCOTLAND, WEST COAST

Section D. CLYDE ESTUARY TO MULL OF GALLOWAY

Principal Lights

Sanda Is.	Fl 10s 50m 15M
Davaar Ls.	Fl(2) 10s 37m 22M
Toward Pt.	Fl 10s 21m 22M
Little Cumbrae	Fl 3s 31m 23M
Holy Is	Fl(2) 20s 38m 25M
Pladda	Fl(3) 30s 40m 17M
Turnberry Pt	Fl 15s 29m 22M
Ailsa Craig	Fl 4s 18m 17M
Corsewall Pt	Al LFl WR 74s 34m 18M
Black Head	Fl(2) 30s 49m 24M
Crammag Head	Fl 10s 35m 18M
Mull of Galloway	Fl 20s 99m 28M

Unlike the rest of the West coast the waters of the Clyde Estuary are popular with many yachts and consequently offer many more facilities for yachtsmen. The passages are protected and well marked. There are restrictions to movement of vessels in Gareloch and Loch Long during submarine movements. The tidal streams are generally weak turning Nly at HW Dover and Sly at Dover +6h. There is a race with dangerous overfalls off the Mull of Kintyre and in Sanda Sound. Strong tides will also be encountered between Bennane Head (8M SSE of Ailsa Craig) and the Mull of Galloway. There is a dangerous race extending some 3M S of the Mull.

Tidal Sreams. All related to Dover.

Sanda Sound	+5h E	−1h W 5kn
Davarr Is	HWD N	+6h S 4kn
Black Hd	−1½h N	+4½h S 5kn

EAST LOCH TARBERT*   Chart BA 2381
HW: Dover +1¼h

MHWS 3.4m   MHWN 2.9   MTL 1.9   MLWN 1.1   MLWS 0.3

An excellent sheltered but crowded harbour with good facilities for yachts.

Entrance Pass N of bn Fl R 2½s marking reef off Madadh Maol then S of second G bn QG off En a Choic but give both bns a good berth then head for main quay (238°).

Berths (1) Pontoon berths on NW side of harbour near boatyard.
(2) Alongside quay.
(3) Moorings. Apply boatyard
(4) Anchor clear of moorings.

Facilities Shops EC Wed. PO, chandlers, charts, water at pontoon. Slip, repairs etc. Tarbert Boatyard 218. Bus to Glasgow.

LARGS*   Chart BA 1907
HW: Dover +1h

MHWS 3.3m   MHWN 2.8   MTL 1.9   MLWN 1.0   MLWS 0.4

A convenient modern marina with all facilities and easy access 1M S of Largs.

Approach Pass close to RW sph buoy LFl 10s and enter between breakwaters painted W.

Facilities All marina facilities. Largs Yacht Haven 0475 675333. PO, shops EC Wed, hotels 1M.

LAMLASH*   Charts BA 2126 1864
HW: Dover +1h

MHWS 3.2m   MHWN 2.7

A large natural harbour between Is of Arran and Holy Is.

Approach by either N or S channels. The flood tide sets into the S and out of the N. In strong NW winds the S channel may be difficult.

Pillar Rk Lt Fl(2) 20s 38m 25M situated SE of Holy Is.

Anchorages (1) Off Lamlash. Many moorings. Exposed to SE.
(2) NW of Holy Is.
(3) In SW of harbour.

Facilities PO, shops EC Wed, hotels. Water near pier. Diesel. Ferry to mainland.

TROON*   Charts BA 2220 1866
HW: Dover +1h

MHWS 4.4m   MHWN 3.2   MTL 1.9   MLWN 1.0   MLWS 0.4

A useful harbour and marina at Southern approach to Clyde. Easy access.

Approach and Entrance Give shore an offing of 2ca. Leave G con buoy Fl G 4s to stb and pass between pierheads. Lts Oc W R 6s 5M + Fl WG 3s 5M on West and Fl R 10s 6m 3M on E. Proceed through outer harbour to marina.

Facilities PO shops EC Wed. All marina facilities. (0292) 315553. Shipyard. Trains to Glasgow. Prestwick Airport 4M.

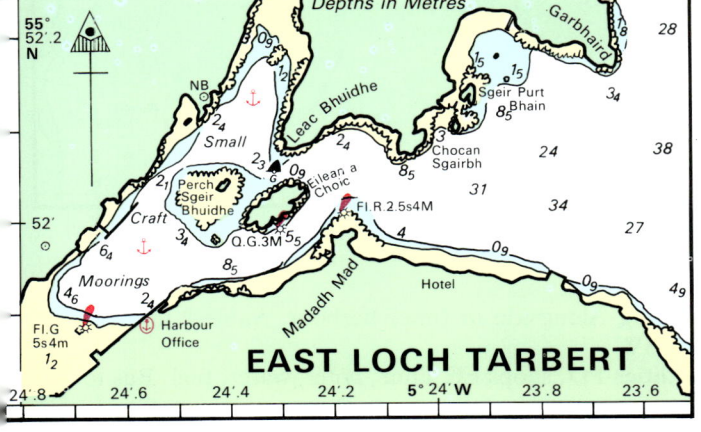

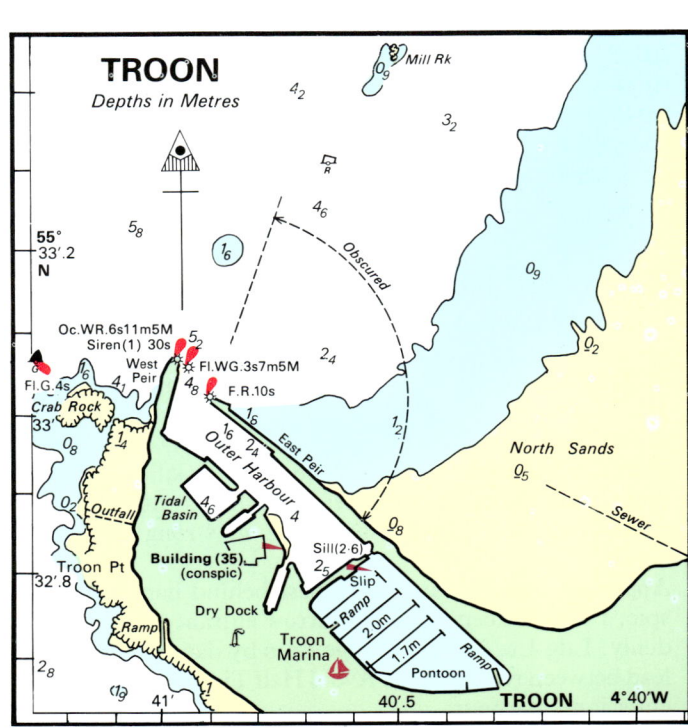

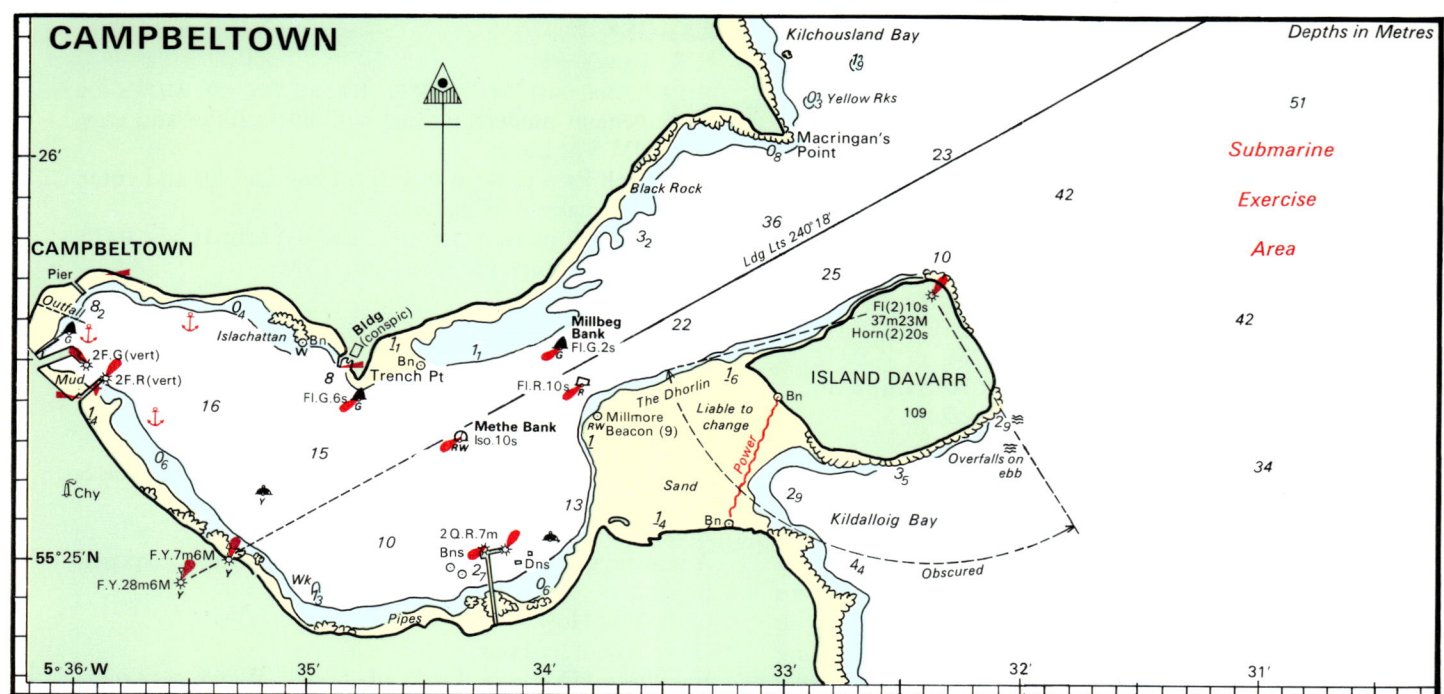

CAMPBELTOWN★ Charts BA 2126 1864
HW: Dover +¾h
MHWS 3.0m MHWN 2.5 MTL 1.7 MLWN 0.9 MLWS 0.4
A well sheltered loch. Useful if waiting to round the Mull.
Approach and Entrance From N avoid Otterard Rk marked by E card buoy Q(3) 10s 1M N of entrance. From S pass to N of Davarr Is Lt Fl(2) 10s 37m 23M then enter loch on 240° Ldg Lts F Y. Thence to harbour entrance. Lts 2FG vert & 2FR vert.
Anchorages 1 Berth at pontoon just NW of N quay.
2 Berth alongside N pier beyond elbow.
3 Anchor S of harbour.
Facilities PO, shops EC Wed. Water at pier.

LOCH RYAN★ Chart BA 1403
HW: Dover +1h
MHWS 3.0m MHWN 2.5 MTL 1.6 MLWN 0.6 MLWS 0.2
Good shelter. Easy access. Watch out for ferries.
Approach and Entrance From S give N shore of Rhins of Galloway a good berth. Leave Milleur Pt N card buoy Q to stb. Steer 145° towards Cairn Pt Lt Ho Fl(2)R 10s
Anchorages (1) The Wig. Enter bay be passing midway between Spit G con buoy Fl G 6s and No 1 bn. Holding poor.
(2) Lady Bay. W side of loch 1M S of entrance. Holding good.
(3) Stranraer. 3ca NW of W pier clear of ferries. Holding good.
Facilities PO, shops EC Wed. Water at pier. Trains to Glasgow & London.

PORTPATRICK Chart BA 2198
HW: Dover +½h
MHWS 3.8m MHWN 3.0 MTL 2.1 MLWN 0.9 MLWS 0.3
This small harbour 15M N of the Mull of Galloway is no longer maintained but provides good shelter. Strong tides across entrance. Do not approach in strong on-shore winds.
Approach and Entrance TV mast behind harbour conspic. From N keep 1ca off. Narrow entrance opens suddenly. Ldg Lts 2 F G 2 orange lines by day bearing 050° lead between ruined piers. Avoid Half Tide Rk to port and enter inner harbour.

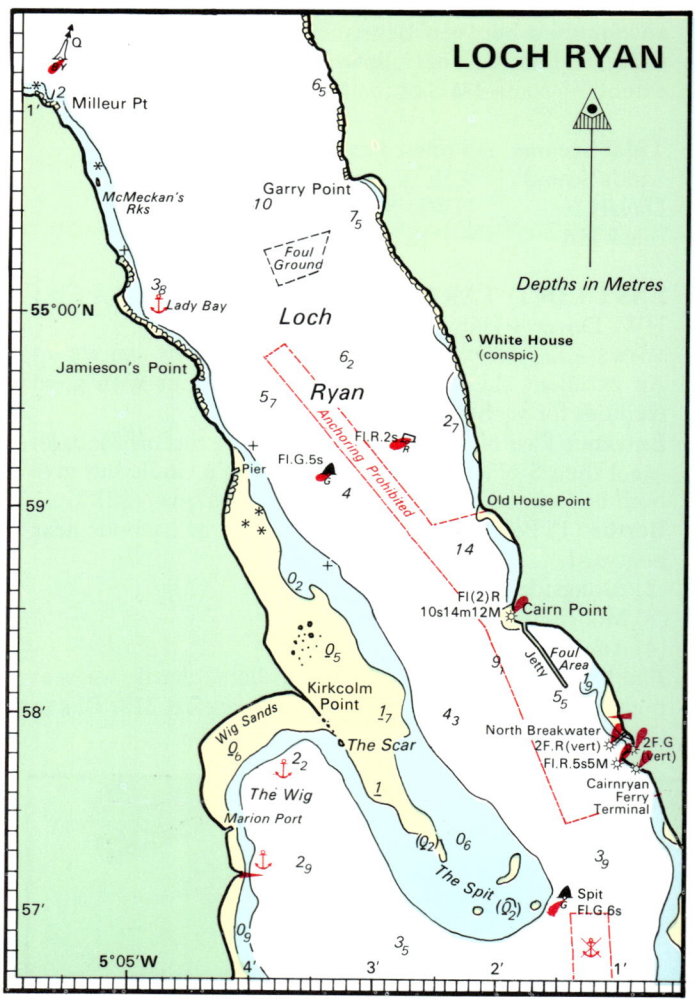

Berthing Alongside in Inner harbour. Subject to swell from SW
Facilities PO, shops EC Thur, hotel, water, fuel. Bus to Stranraer.

OTHER HARBOURS

Harbour	Anchorages	Facilities	Comments
Kyles of Bute 55°55′11 N 5°12′W	1 Tighnabruich. HIDB visitors moorings.	PO, shops, boatyard.	A popular resort. Many moorings.
	2 Blachfarland Bay Opposite.	None.	
	3 Caladh Harbour	None	Attractive secure anchorage 3M N of Tighnabruich.
Rhu/Helensburgh 55°59′N 4°45′W.	1 Rhu marina. 2 Anchor clear of moorings	All facilities	Popular yachting centre. Many moorings. Several Y.C.s
Inverkip. 55°55′N 4°53′W	Kip marina	All facilities	½M N of power station (conspic) Buoyed channel.
Rothesay. Is of Bute 55°51′N 5°03′W	1 Anchor in bay 2 Alongside in Outer Harbour	PO, shops EC Wed. Water at pier. Boatyard.	Sheltered except in strong N to NE winds.
L. Ranza. Is of Arran 56°01′N 5°37′W	Anchor off Castle.	PO, shop, hotel.	Subject to squalls in strong S1y winds.

Section E. THE GALLOWAY COAST.

Principal Lights

Mull of Galloway	Fl 20s 99m 28M
Little Ross	Fl 5s 50m 12M
Hestan Is	Fl(2)10s 38m 7M

The Galloway Coast is frequented by a small but increasing number of cruising yachts. The few harbours are small and drying and there is no port of refuge if caught out in a SW-SE blow. There are dangerous sand banks at the entrance to the Solway Firth. There is a bombing range in Luce Bay and a firing range between Kirkcudbright and Abbey Hd extending up to 14M offshore and W to Little Ross. The tidal range is over 6m and there is a dangerous race in strong winds extending 3M S of the Mull. There is also a race in strong W winds off Burrow Hd. Note Scares Rks 6M E of the Mull. There is a very useful anchorage protected from NNW through W to S in East Tarbert Bay just N. of the Mull

DRUNMORE   Chart BA 2198
HW: Dover +¾h
MHWS 5.9m   MHWN 5.4   MLWN 2.0   MLWS 0.6
Small drying harbour 4M NE of Mull of Galloway
Approach and Entrance Enter after half tide steering close to end of pier.
Berth Alongside pier. N end reserved for MOD range boat. Very limited space.
Facilities PO, shops, hotel.

ISLE OF WHITHORN   Chart BA 2094
HW: Dover +½h
MHWS 7.5m   MHWN 5.4   MTL 4.0   MLWN 2.1   MLWS 0.7
A drying harbour with 2½m at half flood.
Entrance Keep over to W watchtower to E of entrance. The stream sets SW across entrance at all times when there is 2m or more in harbour, on to Skerries marked by thin iron rod (reported missing) to W of entrance. Keep well away from both sides of entrance. Pierhead Lt QG. Ldg Lts 335°.
Anchorages (1) Alongside of quay in SE corner. Space limited.
(2) Anchor in entrance opposite slip on E. side to lie afloat. Sheltered WSW-ENE.
Facilities Water at pier. PO, shops, garage, hotel, chandlers.

KIRKCUDBRIGHT   Charts BA 1344 2094
HW: Dover +½h
MHWS 7.5m   MHWN 5.9   MTL 4.1   MLWN 2.4   MLWS 0.8
A 4M long narrow channel between sandbanks forms estuary of R Dee.
Approach and Entrance Beware of range (see above). Enquire on VHF 16 or 73. Bar (0.9m) 7 ca N of Torr Pt. Ldg marks astern on Little Ross 201°. Channel 0.0m is buoyed and lighted.
Anchorages (1) Alongside wooden jetty. Dries.
(2) Visitors moorings off jetty. 2m.
(3) Inside Little Ross. Exposed to SE.
(4) Flint Bay. N of Torrs Point in Ely winds.
(5) Off Balmangan Farm in Wly winds.
Facilities PO, shops, EC Thur. Diesel, chandlers.

OTHER HARBOURS

Harbour	Anchorages	Facilities	Comments
Garlieston Wigtown Bay 54°47′N 4°55′W	1 Alongside wall 2 Anchor in bay. Dries. Good holding.	Water at pier. PO/shops hotel	A small drying fishing harbour.
Kippford. Waters of Urr 54°51′N 3°50′W	Harbour full of moorings	Water at pier. PO/shops	A very popular yachting harbour in beautiful estuary.

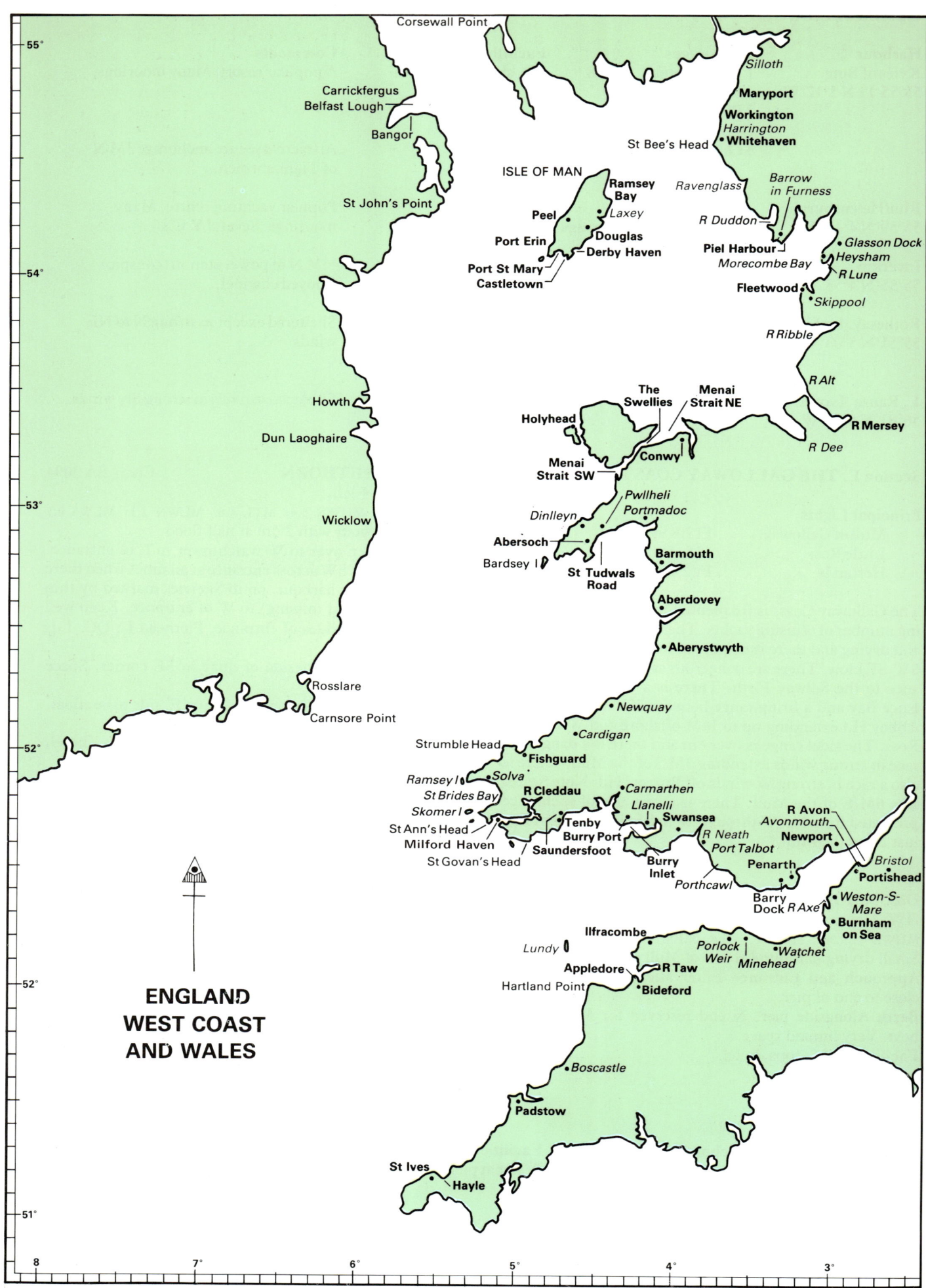

WEST COAST OF ENGLAND AND WALES

PASSAGE NOTES: NORTH CHANNEL TO MILFORD HAVEN
Chart BA 1121

Passage Lights:

Mull of Galloway	Fl 20s 99m 28M
S Rock Lt V	Fl(3) R 30s 12m 20M
Calf of Man	Fl 15s 93m 28M
South Stack	Fl 10s 60m 28M
Codling Lanby	Fl 4s 12m 22M
Bardsey Is	Fl(5) 15s 39m 26M
Wicklow Hd	Fl(3) 15s 37m 26M
Tuskar Rock	Q(2) 7s 33m 28M
Strumble Hd	Fl(4) 15s 45m 29M
S Bishop	Fl 5s 44m 24M
The Smalls	Fl(3) 15s 36m 25M

Tidal streams: all related to Dover.
The flood starts about +6h through North channel in the N and St George's channel in the S meeting between Calf of Man and Clogher Hd where there is an area of almost constant slack water.
North Channel: +6h SSE 2.2kn max, HWD NNW 2.3kn
S Stack to Strumble Hd +6h NNE 2.1kn, HWD SSW 2.1kn

Unlike the S and E coasts the W coast of England and Wales has large indentations and bays. The passage S from North Channel thus comprises a series of offshore passages, the landfalls being headlands which extend far out into the Irish Sea.

The direct route from Corsewall Pt (off L Ryan) on the E side of North Channel is almost due S, passing some 25M to the W of hbrs in the IOM (Peel, Port Erin and Port St Mary), Holyhead, and further S, Bardsey Is and Fishguard at the N and S ends of Cardigan Bay.

In heavy weather Holyhead offers complete protection and Fishguard in winds other than N or NE. The ports in the IOM offer shelter according to wind direction Douglas being the best. Those on the E side mean a considerable detour with a race round Pt of Ayre on the N tip of the Is.

On the Irish side roughly 25M to the W of the direct track there are not many hbrs of refuge; Belfast Lough (Carrickfergus or Bangor), Howth, Dun Laoghaire, and Wicklow all offer good protection.

In good visibility land can be seen on both sides simultaneously at some places as the coasts of the IOM, Wales and Ireland are high. Tidal streams in the Irish Sea are moderate except off headlands such as the Calf of Man, the Stacks off Holy Is (Holyhead), and Bardsey Is, and off the Pembrokeshire coast. On direct passage it is more important to time the tide in North Channel and off the Pembrokeshire coast than elswhere.

PASSAGE NOTE: SOLWAY FIRTH TO ST BEES HEAD
Charts BA 1346 2013

Passage Light: St Bees Hd Lt Ho Fl(2) 20s 102m 21M
Tidal streams: Dover −4h Flood into Firth, +1h Ebb out (4kn).

It is not possible to make the direct passage from Hestan Is to Maryport, nor should any attempt be made higher up the Firth where streams are strong, sands are hard and seas can be steep. When leaving Hestan Is for the English shore keep off Barnhourie Sand, Dumroof Bank and Robin Rigg by making 170° over the ground until S of the "Two Feet Bank" buoy before turning E. Workington is the only port of refuge which can be entered at all states of the tide. Wind can raise a difficult sea over Workington Bank but the passage inside the Bank is safe.

Going further S, the ebb will help to St Bees Hd: aim to get there 1h after LW and pick up the S going flood from the Hd onwards.

PASSAGE NOTE: ST BEES TO DUDDON

The tidal stream within 3M of the coast runs SE for 6h from Dover +5h. ½M off Whitehaven flood and ebb streams run until 1h after local HW and LW respectively, but 2 to 3M off until 2h after HW.

SILLOTH
Chart BA 2013

HW: Dover +¾h. DS: Dover −4h NE (4kn in Catherine Hole).
MHWS 9.2m MHWN 6.9 MTL 4.8 MLWN 2.3 MLWS 0.8
Bar 2.1m N of Ellison Scar.
Approach From the SW only. Navigation N of Silloth should only be attempted with local knowledge because of fast tidal streams and sandbanks in the estuary. Leave 'Solway' G buoy Fl(3) G 10s at least 1h after LW close to stb, then make 355° to pass close by 'Corner' G buoy Fl(2) G 5s. From here make 050° to leave 'Beckfoot' G con buoy Fl(4) G 10s to stb and then keep Lees Scar lt Q G in line with E Cote lt FG. These lts are on W piles 11m and 15m high. Leave Lees Scar lt close to stb on same bearing.
Entrance 2FG(vert) on Groyne Hd. Entrance dries. Ldg lts 115°.
Anchorage (1) Off Lees Scar lt in about 6m.
(2) Temporarily in outer hbr which dries.
(3) The wet inner hbr New Dock is commercial; see HM. Water on quays. Stores in town. EC Tues.

Maryport & Workington – see next page

HARRINGTON
Chart BA 2013

HW: Dover +½h. DS Dover −4h N for 5h; +2h S for 6h.
Approach No obstructions. From S, Workington S Card buoy Q(6) + LFl 15s the hbr bears 095° 2½M. The W clubhouse is prominent. Port only used by local fishing and sailing club.
Entrance A short training wall projects from the N side and has a BR bn at its W end. Best water is close to this. The small hbr is formed by a stone pier on the S side. Inner and outer hbrs dry.
Berthing (1) In offshore winds in settled weather anchor up to 2ca W of entrance.
(2) Contact Fishing and SC for temporary moorings in inner hbr; visitors' berths alongside marked.

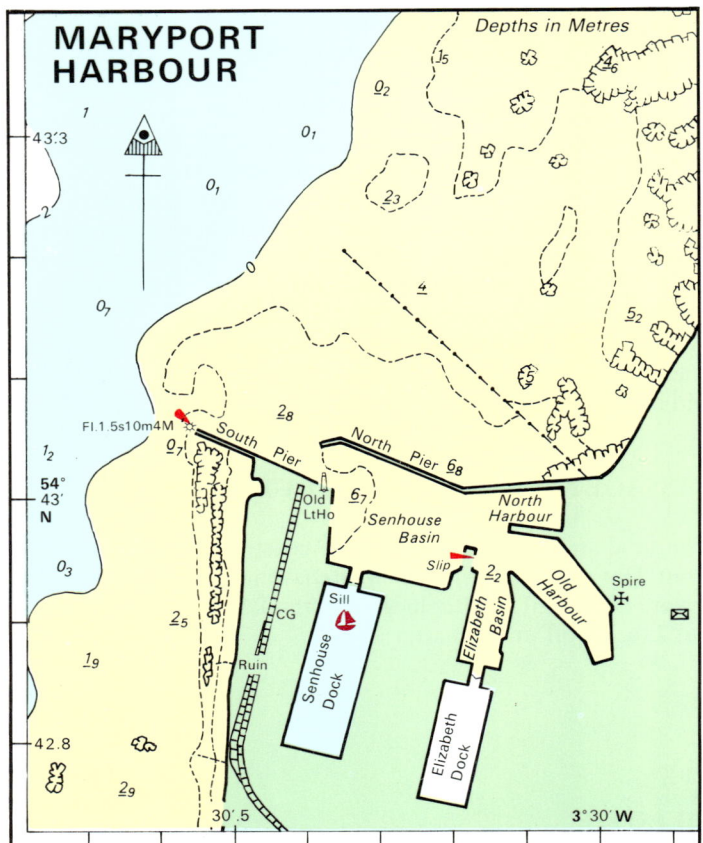

MARYPORT Chart BA 2013

HW: Dover +¾h. DS Dover −4½h NE for 5½h (2kn). Eddies off.

MHWS 8.4m MHWN 6.6 MTL 4.7 MLWN 2.5 MLWS 0.9

Bar Hbr and entrance channel dry for some distance W of S pier. There is 1.8m over the bar at S pier at half flood.

Approach Keep at least 1M off coast until in the offing because shelving bottom is clay foul with large rocks.

Entrance Lt Fl 1.5s on tr on S pier-head. Keep closer to N pier-head on entry until abreast first set of steps, then hold over to the end of the jetty with a small square building near its N end. Vessels drawing up to 2.4m can enter at HW ± 2h. Entrance dredged to combat silting on S side.

Berthing (1) In offshore winds anchor up to 1M NW of S pier-head in the Roads.

(2) The first dock (Senhouse) is now a marina with an entrance sill. Entry at HW ± 2h (approx). Visitors' berths and all facilities available.

(3) Berths alongside extensive quays, all dry outside the two docks.

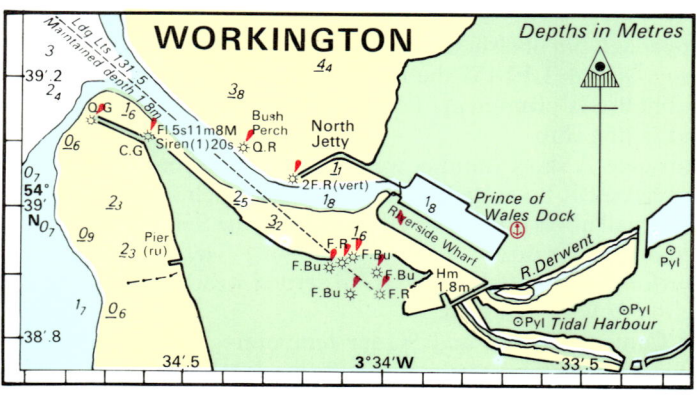

WORKINGTON Chart BA 2013

HW: Dover +½h. DS Dover −4½h NE for 5½h (2kn). Eddies off.

MHWS 8.4m MHWN 6.4 MTL 4.6 MLWN 2.5 MLWS 0.9

Bar Extends for 3ca N of R brick disused CG lt Fl 5s near end of S pier. Localised steep seas occasionally.

Approach Clear when S pier-head bears between 010° and 180°. From the S and W pick out QG lt on end of S pier and head N until the ldg lts FR are in line 131° clearly framed between two pairs of F Bu lts which mark the edge of the dredged channel to the Turning Basin.

Entrance Marked by QR lt on "Bush" perch N of dredged channel. When 2 FR (vert) on end of N jetty abeam round up to port N into Turning Basin.

Berthing (1) In offshore winds anchor 2ca NW or SW of CG.

(2) In Turning Basin sheltered from all winds but must not be left unattended as large ships pass through.

(3) Vanguard SC may have a half tide mooring free in the tidal dock S of Riverside Wharf. Trawlers, Pilot and Fishery Protection vessels take up all this dock's quay berths.

(4) With short or lowering masts, possible drying moorings on berths in tidal hbr inside rly br which no longer opens.

WHITEHAVEN Chart BA 2013

HW: Dover +¼h. DS Dover −5h E across entrance for 4½h. Eddies off.

MHWS 8.2m MHWN 6.3 MTL 4.5 MLWN 2.4 MLWS 1.2

Bar 1ca N of W pier-head.

Approach Easily identified from N by tall chimney and tall monuments on cliffs just S of hbr. No obstructions.

Entrance If tide serves even in a gale entrance is possible. Keep close to W pier-head in W gales.

Berthing (1) Outer hbr dries generally 1.5 to 2m and inner hbr 3 to 4m but both offer excellent shelter in all winds to vessels that can take the ground. Yachts mainly in S hbr or on S side of Old Quay.

(2) Queen's Dock (wet) is used by vessels up to 3000 tons. Consult HM. All stores in town. Diesel at fish quays, EC Wed.

ISLE OF MAN

Chart BA 2094

Direction of Tidal Streams (All related to Dover).
Calf of Man to Langness: −6h E; +¼h W.
Race off Chicken Rock: Eddies and a race both E and W of Langness Lt Ho.
Langness to Ayre Pt: −3½h NE for 9h; +5½h S for 3¼h.
Ayre Pt: +6h E; −¼h W race.
Contrary Hd to Calf Sound: −1¼h N; +4¾h S.
S of Narbyl Pt stream nearly continuously N.
Calf Sound +4h S; −1½h N.
With SW winds and low barometer the rise of tide is increased by up to 1m. With high pressure and E and N winds the tides are lowered to the same extent.

None of the hbrs where yachts can lie afloat is safe in all winds although with the extension of Battery pier Douglas is safe in all but NE gales. There is some commercial activity particularly at Douglas and here and at Peel and Ramsey the hbrs are crowded with fishing boats from June to Sept. If HMs are warned in advance of a yacht's probable time of arrival they take a lot of trouble to allot a suitable berth. Except at Douglas where a continuous service is maintained, it is the practice of HMs to be on duty 2h either side of HW and to meet incoming vessels and direct them to their berths. Harbour staff are extremely helpful. Hbr dues are moderate.

During Aug and Sept there may be concentrations of up to 100 fishing boats between Chicken Rock and Douglas. In good weather vessels coming from the W can find shelter in Peel hbr when there is sufficient rise. From the S make first for Port St Mary. From the N find a temporary anchorage at Ramsey at all states of the tide. These anchorages are all exposed to winds from certain directions and further details are given under the separate port headings.

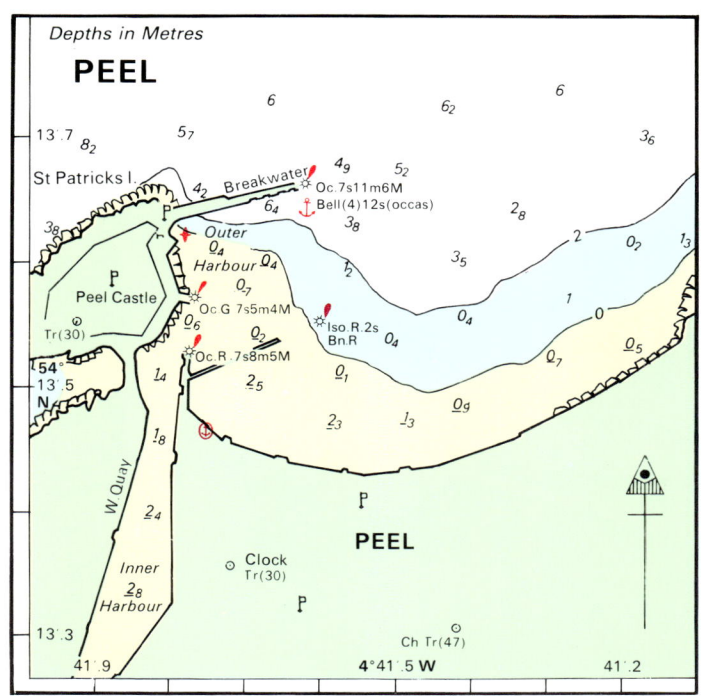

PORT ERIN
Chart BA 2696

HW: Dover +½h.
MHWS 5.2m MHWN 4.2 MTL 2.8 MLWN 1.6 MLWS 0.4
This inlet affords secure anchorage in 4 to 9m and shelter in winds from N through E to SW. Raglan Pier lt Oc G 5s on S side of bay forms a drying hbr with sandy bottom having 3.6m MHWN alongside.
Approach Rounding the Calf of Man and Chicken Rk in strong winds and weather going stream the race off the Lt Ho should be given a good berth. Close along the SW shore the stream is slight, and vessels of moderate draft may avoid the strength of the stream when weather permits by standing in. Calf Sound should not be attempted without local knowledge by any but small craft in good weather, which pass through from N with a fair tide by keeping over to the rk on port hand after passing the bn on the stb hand. Chart BA 2696 essential.
Entrance A demolished breakwater covered at HW runs out N from the SW arm of the bay and is marked by a G con buoy. In the middle of the head of the bay are ldg lts FR 099° W columns, R bands which lead into the middle of the bay.
Berthing Anchor according to draught as convenient. A good berth is close to S shore between the old breakwater and Raglan Pier. A telegraph cable runs roughly E-W across the bay so care neccessary when anchoring. Good landing at jetty shown on plan. All stores. Buses to Castletown and Douglas. EC Thur.

PEEL
Chart BA 2696

HW: Dover +¼h.
MHWS 5.3m MHWN 4.2 MTL 2.9 MLWN 1.5 MLWS 0.5
This is a convenient port on the W coast to call at for supplies when on passage from one end of the Irish sea to the other. The hbr dries and has 3.3m at MHWN. During the fishing season (June to Oct) it is rather busy. Anchorage sheltered from E through S to SW between the end of the breakwater and the R bn. The breakwater should be given good clearance and vessels should not stand in too far towards the shore as a shoal lies between the breakwater and the shore and depths on it are variable. Yachts which can take the ground safely are advised to moor alongside the W quay or at the S end of the inner hbr where it is cleaner than at most other quays and there are usually no fishing vessels. Entry should not be attempted in strong N to NW winds. All stores, fuel from garage in town in cans only. Buses to Ramsey and Douglas. EC Thur.

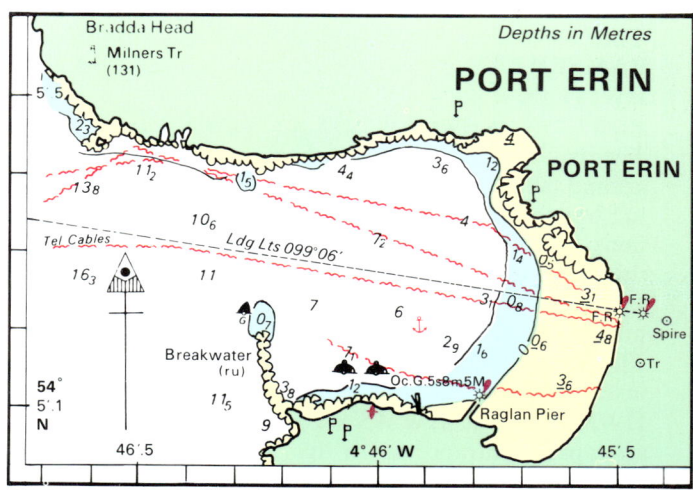

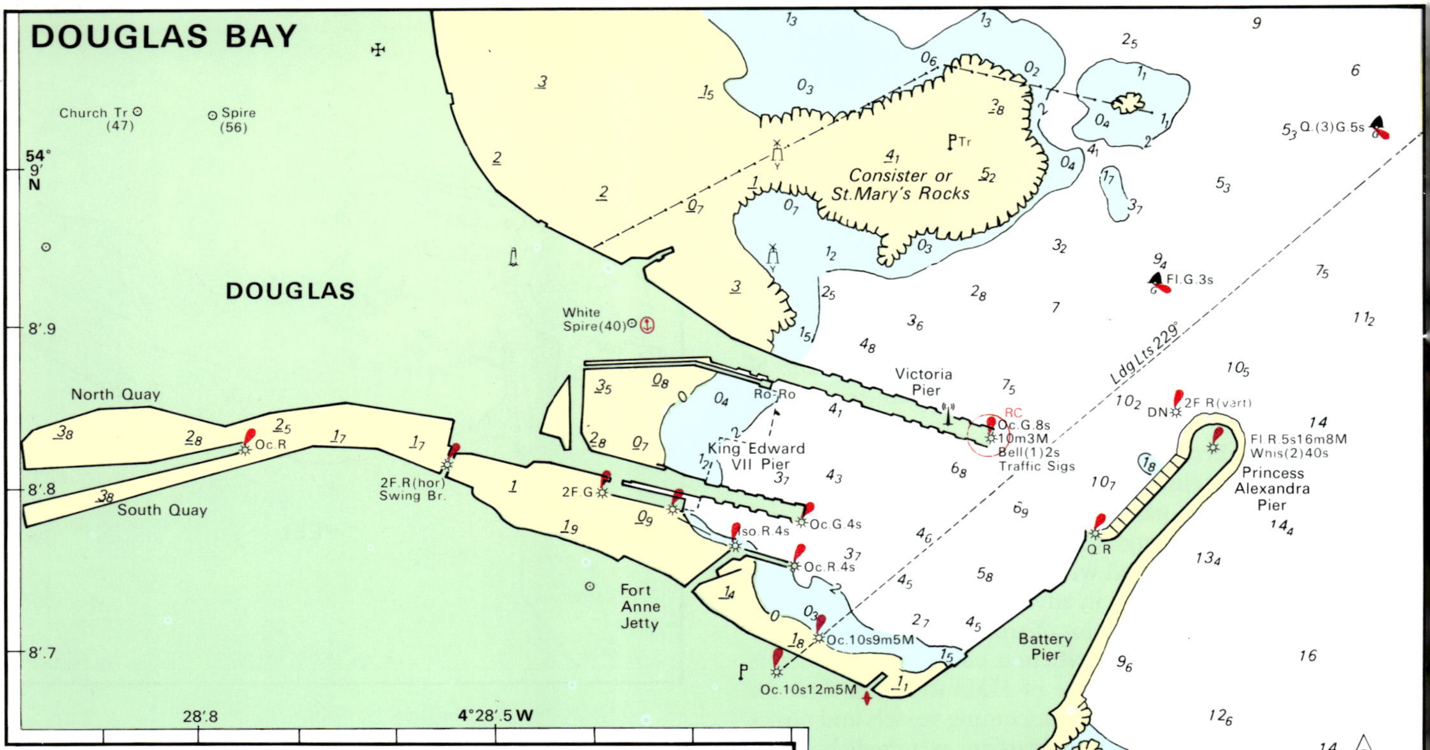

DOUGLAS BAY

DOUGLAS
Chart BA 2696

HW: Dover +¼h.

MHWS 6.9m MHWN 5.4 MTL 3.9 MLWN 2.4 MLWS 0.8

The outer hbr has 4 to 7m and a heavy sea runs in during NE gales. The inner hbr has 2 to 4m at MHWN and dries. There is a swing bridge 1¼ ca inside the inner hbr which is opened on request 3h either side of HW.

Approach Come in on 229° along approach channel with ldg marks W and R △ and lts Oc W 10s past G con lt buoys. Watch out for hbr entry signals on Victoria Pier: 3 vert R - do not proceed, GWG proceed only if informed on VHF, 3 vert G proceed.

Entrance Enter between Dolphin 2FR(vert) off Battery Pier and Victoria Pier Oc G 8s.

Berthing Outer hbr only: only a limited number of vessels are permitted to anchor, between the LBS and Fort Anne jetty, and the HM's permission must be obtained first. Exposed to the NE. One mooring buoy is laid in Summer and there is a short pontoon for visiting yachts by the steps at the inner end of the Battery pier. Inner hbr: tidal, available HW ± 2h. Extensively used by local pleasure craft, commercial vessels and coasters, and it may be difficult to find a convenient berth during the Summer. The bay affords secure anchorage especially at the N end in 10m with shelter from N through W to SW. All facilities. EC Thur.

RAMSEY BAY
Chart BA 2696

HW: Dover +¼h

MHWS 7.3m MHWN 5.8 MTL 4.1 MLWN 2.4 MLWS 0.8

The bay affords secure anchorage and good holding ground, and is sheltered with winds from NW through W to S but not necessarily in one position from all these directions. The Queen's Pier extends 685m from the shore to the S of the hbr and vessels waiting to enter hbr should anchor between this pier and the S hbr pier. Landing prohibited on Queen's pier. Sph buoy for visitors near pier. The hbr lies within two piers the ends of which are 90m inside LW mark. The hbr dries and has up to 5.5m at HWMS, 4m at HWMN. Vessels are advised not to attempt the entrance earlier than 2½ to 2h before HW, or later than 1½ to 2h after HW.

Approach From N rounding Pt of Ayre (N pt of Is) keep close inshore to avoid Whitestone Bank (7 ca E of Ayre Pt). The stream sets round the pt into Ramsey Bay at about LW Douglas, and runs for 3h. Watch for lobster pots.

Berthing Berth alongside quay as instructed by HM, usually in the channel between the piers. When entering watch the stream which sets N across the entrance for 9h from half flood to LW approx.

Most facilities. Buses to Peel and Douglas, tram to Douglas in summer. EC Wed.

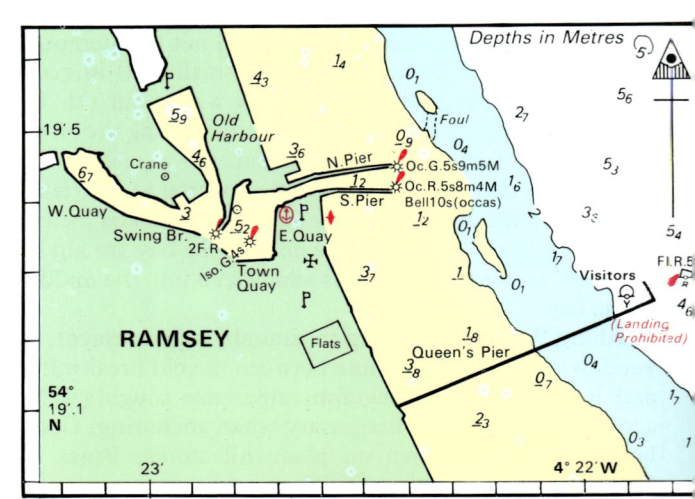

169 WEST COAST OF ENGLAND & WALES

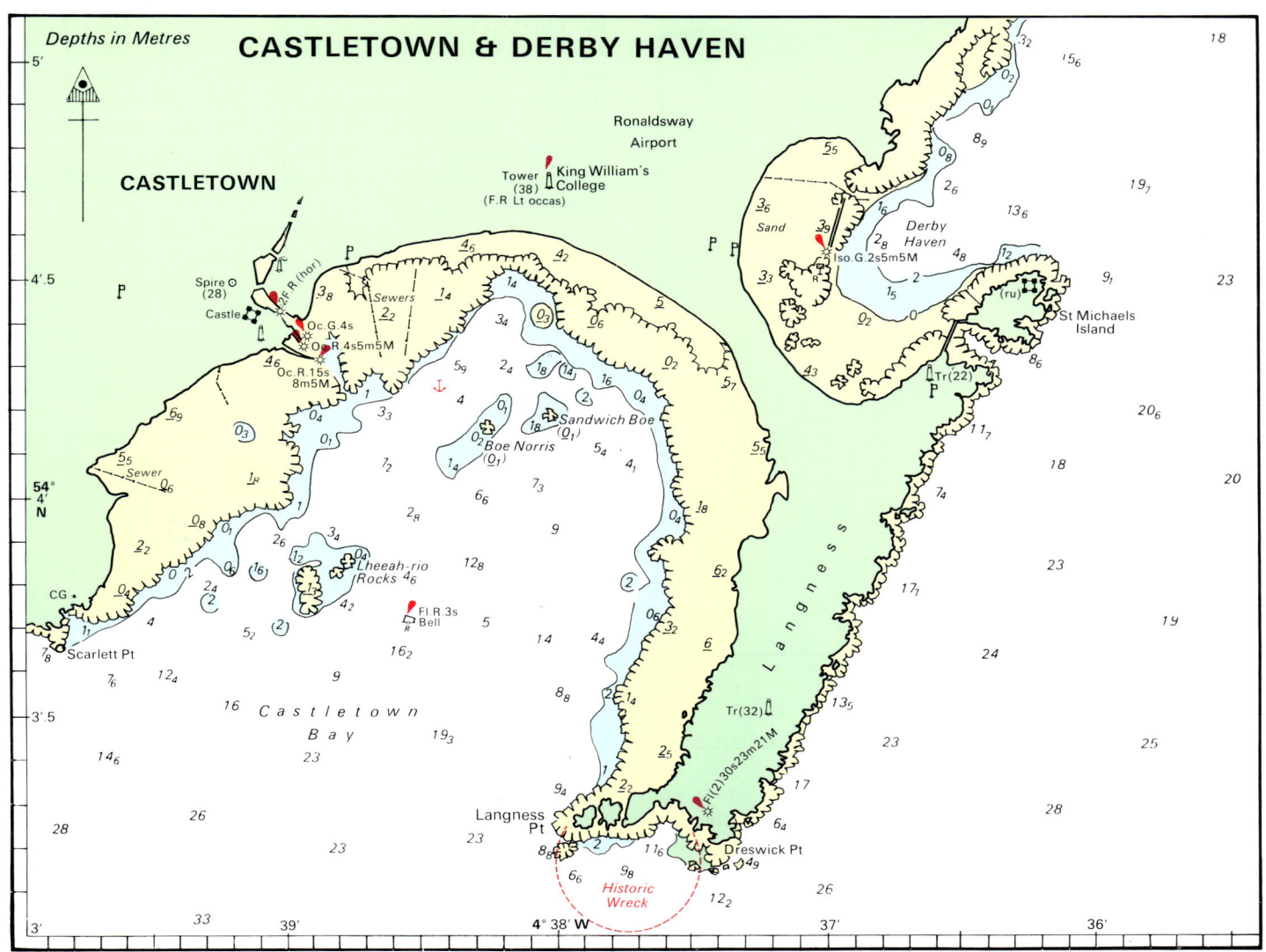

CASTLETOWN Chart BA 2696
HW: Dover +½h

The bay affords good shelter in NW through NE to E winds. The bottom is not good and the tidal streams are felt. The hbr dries.

Approach To avoid the race off Langness Pt give it a good berth in all winds. Approaching from E in heavy weather keep Clay Head well open of Douglas Head (E coast of island just S of Douglas Hbr) to clear rough ground 8ca SE of St Michael's Is.

Entrance Enter midway between Langness Pt and the R can buoy Fl R 3s which marks the Lheeah-Rio Rks which should be left to port. From abreast the buoy steer 022° till the inner jetty comes open N of the pier-head Lt Ho when steer 317° for the entrance to the hbr. At the end of the breakwater the ground consists of rocky ledges and large boulders. Beware of confusing the hbr bns with Ronaldsway Airport landing lts.

Berthing In 5.5m off the entrance to the hbr, King William College tr bearing 022°. The hbr has 2.7m MHWN; there is a basin between the outer swing and inner fixed bridges. A hard runs down from the Lt Ho towards the LW mark and stands above the level of the bottom. Yachts may also berth in basin inside the breakwater, bottom sand and shingle.

All stores. Bus to Port Erin and Douglas. EC Thur.

DERBY HAVEN Chart BA 2696
HW: Dover +½h

The bay affords shelter on a good bottom of sand and mud in 2 to 5m inside St Michaels Is and is available in N through W to S winds. Inside the breakwater the hbr which dries affords complete shelter in all winds. Bottom mud and sand, 2m MHWN.

Entrance With the S going stream which runs for 9h give N pt of St Michael's Is a good berth as the stream sets hard across a shelving rk at the entrance point. For the hbr bring the lt Iso G 2s on SW end of breakwater to bear 262° and pass between it and the R perch marking a rk to S of it.

Anchorage 2 or 3 ca from the S end of the breakwater: bottom is foul 1 ca out from it. Stores at Castletown 2M. No supplies at Derby Haven but pub serving meals if booked.

LAXEY
HW: Dover +½h

Laxey Bay offers good anchorage in N to SW winds through W. The hbr dries and has about 2m MHWN. It is available for small yachts only. Care is needed in entering the hbr which is very crowded.

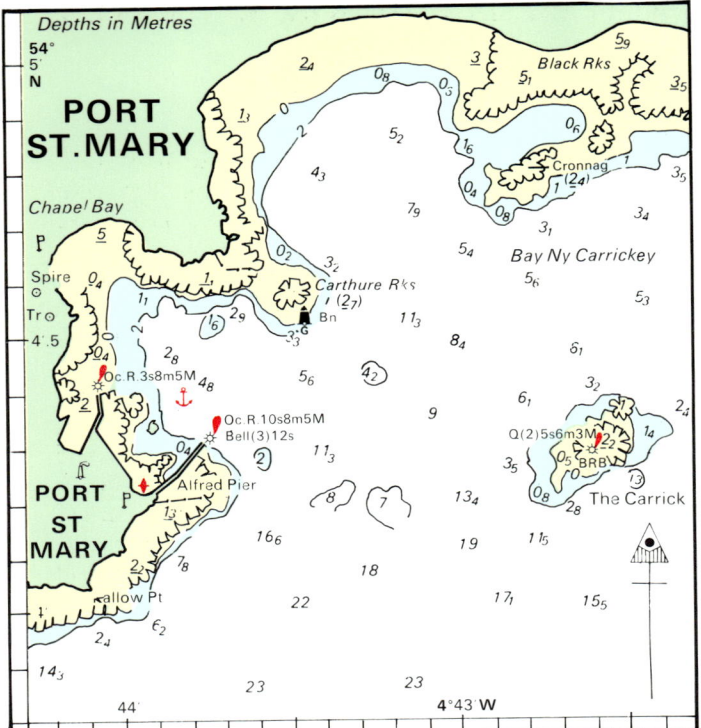

PORT ST MARY   Chart BA 2696
HW: Dover +¼h

MHWS 5.9m   MHWN 4.7   MTL 3.2   MLWN 1.7   MLWS 0.6

The hbr dries, has 3m at MHWN, 2m when the Carrick covers; bottom sand and mud. Good shelter off the entrance in 2 or 3½m in NE through NW to SW winds. The bay should not be approached in strong S winds.

Approach To clear The Carrick (lt bn Q(2) 5s) which dries 4.3m keep Langness Lt Ho well open of Scarlett Pt stack or at night when nearing the bay bring the lts of the hbr in line 303°. Approaching from the E during the first of the ebb, from Stack of Scarlett to S of The Carrick, small craft should avoid standing inshore until The Carrick shows when the sea steadies. From SW give the shore a berth of 2ca and round in to N of the Alfred Pier-head lt Oc R 10s.

Berthing Anchor 50 to 100m NW of Alfred Pier just inside the line of the two Lt Hos (one on Alfred Pier and the other on the inner pier). The outer part of Alfred Pier is often occupied by fishing vessels, but yachts may raft up afloat near its root. Keep well in to avoid reefs, marked by bns with N cones, that lie parallel. Inner hbr dries to channel, hard sand: centre is full of local moorings but yachts taking the ground can lie alongside. Six visitors' moorings off Chapel Bay. There is a landing below the clubhouse of the IOM YC which has excellent facilities and is welcoming to visitors.

All stores. Bus to Castletown and Douglas. EC Thur.

RIVER DUDDON   Chart BA 1961
HW: Dover −¼h
Duddon Bar

MHWS 8.5m   MHWN 6.6   MTL 4.6   MLWN 2.6   MLWS 0.9

The channel is unmarked and constantly changing and most of the estuary dries. Anchor at Haverigg. Pier at Askam where yachts can lie aground. Pier and small hbr at Hodbarrow on W side dries, ground foul off pier.

RAVENGLASS   Chart BA 1346
HW Tarn Pt: Dover +¼h. DS Dover −1h N, +2h S.

MHWS 8.3m   MHWN 6.4   MTL 4.5   MLWN 2.5   MLWS 0.9

The Hbr formed by estuaries of Rivers Irt, Mite and Esk dries out. It provides shelter for vessels able to take the ground although there may be difficulties on some neap tides where problems may be encountered reaching the anchorage even at HW.

There is a gun testing range at Eskmeals S of the inlet with a restricted sea area of roughly a 5M quadrant 230° to 320° from 1M S of the inlet. R flags, R lts at night, are shown on flagstaffs on shore each end of the range (about 2M apart) when firing about to begin or in progress; vessels have the right of passage through the area when firing is taking place.

Bar Dries but liable to constant change.

Approach Keep at least 2M offshore until the hbr entrance has been identified. From S avoid Selker Rks 3M from entrance. They lie 1¼M out from shore, dry at MLWS and are marked by a G con bell buoy FL(3) G 15s outside them. From N avoid Drigg Rk awash lying 1M offshore and 2M 288° from entrance and also Barnscar about 1M N, a shingle bank which now extends about ¾M seawards of the metal perch with con topmark.

Entrance Strangers should only enter at HW −1h to HW and in settled weather or offshore winds. First identify a concrete blockhouse with horizontal W band, an isolated building near the NW end of the Eskmeals Range, FG lt (occas). Then find the small G hut with W square 1½ ca E of Blockhouse on the S side of the entrance. This hut in line with a conical peak 483m 4½M E bearing 080° leads into the entrance channel. When about 2ca from the shore steer for Ravenglass village keeping close to the S shore until well inside the entrance channel.

Berthing Anchor as convenient in the estuary either in the R Irt or the Mite below rly br close to permanent moorings – holding ground poor on the village and seaward sides of moorings. PO, village shop and butcher. Water from tap outside butcher. EC Wed.

PIEL HARBOUR and BARROW-IN-FURNESS
Chart BA 3164

HW Barrow: Dover +½h

MHWS 9.1m   MHWN 7.1   MTL 5.0   MLWN 2.8   MLWS 1.0

Bar 2.1m over Piel bar, channel dredged to 3.7m. Piel hbr has 1.8 to 3.7m.

Approach Strangers should take the entrance at half flood which runs from NW. The ebb runs from S. Pick up Lightning Knoll RWVS Sph bell buoy L Fl 10s and leaving it close to stb steer 041° on first ldg lts (No 1 Q, No 2 Iso 2s). Keep on this line for just over 3M leaving Halfway R can buoy FlR 5s and Outer Bar R can buoy Fl(4)R 10s to port until Bar R can buoy Fl(2)R 5s is reached. Then bring Nos 3&4 ldg lts 006° (No 3 Q, No 4 Iso 2s) and follow line for 1¼M till abreast of Piel.

Berthing Anchor clear of fairway. Channel to Barrow 3M is well marked with lateral buoyage and further sets of ldg lts. Some moorings off town.

Landing at Piel Is and Roa Is. All facilities at Barrow. Water from HM. EC Thur. Inn at Piel Is. Ferry to mainland.

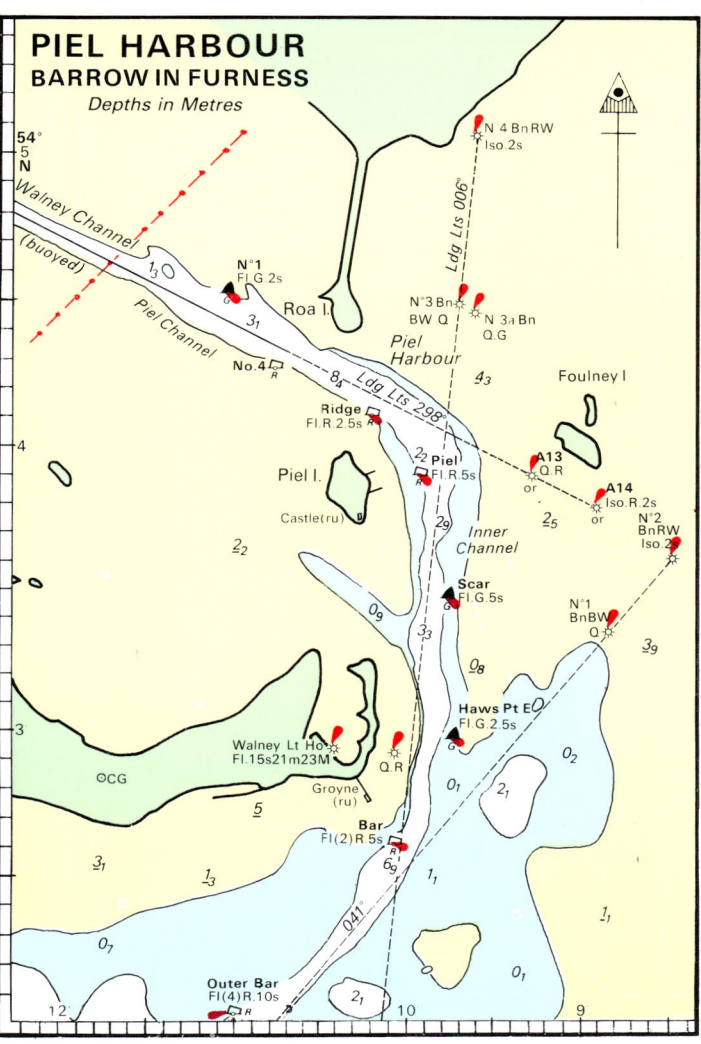

RIVER LUNE and GLASSON DOCK Chart BA 1552
HW: Dover +1h

MHWS 6.6m   MHWN 4.4m

Approach As for Fleetwood then continue to R Lune W Card Q(9) buoy.

Entrance Much of the river dries so plan to arrive at R Lune buoy 1¼h before HW and proceed up channel at 4kn to be at Glasson Dock 45 minutes before HW when gates open until HW. Channel marked by lateral buoys course 084° but channel varies until Plover Scar when it turns N past Chapel Hill and then follow river round with training wall to port until No 18 R can QR buoy whence make for lock with short length of training wall to stb.

Berthing Glasson Dock has good laying up berths and a boatyard with all facilities including electricity on quays, baths and showers, boat storage under cover and chandlery. Peter Latham (0524) 751491 Glasson Basin Yacht Hbr. Lancaster 5M above Glasson can be reached by small craft near HW. The channel is narrow and local knowledge advisable. The river has 1.5m at the town at HW.

PASSAGE NOTES: MORECAMBE BAY
Chart BA 2010

Principal Lights:

Lune Deep	S Card Q(6) + L Fl 15s
Fleetwood Fairway	No 1 N card Q
R Lune	W Card Q(9) 15s
Heysham Breakwater	2 F G (vert) 9m 5M

Streams run hard, 5kn max, and raise a short steep sea on the ebb with W winds. During Apr and May large concentrations of fishing vessels may occur up to 35M W or SW from Lune Deep buoy; smaller numbers Aug-Oct.

HEYSHAM Chart BA 1552
HW: Dover +¼h

MHWS 9.5m   MHWN 7.4   MTL 5.3   MLWN 3.1   MLWS 1.1

Although the hbr affords good shelter it is unavailable to yachts except in emergency.

Approach As for Fleetwood till past the Fairway buoy which is left to stb. Make No 1 Heysham buoy and then make good 045° to No 5 G con buoy QG and thence to hbr entrance.

Entrance Or ldg marks on S quay (not jetty) on a line 102° show the entry in middle of dredged channel. Front mark F Bu 11m, rear F Bu 14m.

Berthing Berth as directed.

RIVER RIBBLE BA Chart 1981
The port of Preston is closed to commercial traffic. Only limited navigation aids are available and entry is not advised without local knowledge. All berths dry.

RIVER ALT
This river offers a possible anchorage for those with local knowledge and is available to vessels drawing 1.8m about 1½h either side of HW. The channel shifts and it is advisable to obtain the latest information before entering which would be from the Crosby channel of the river Mersey either side of buoy C14 and crossing the training wall. Blundellsands SC maintain marks showing best water in the river.

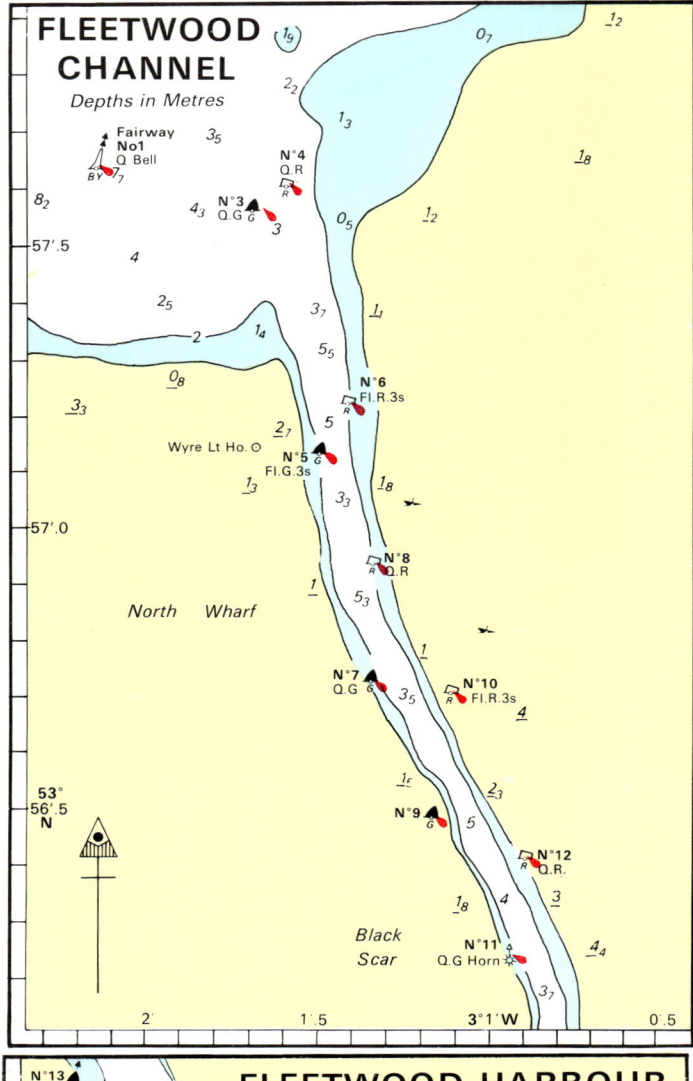

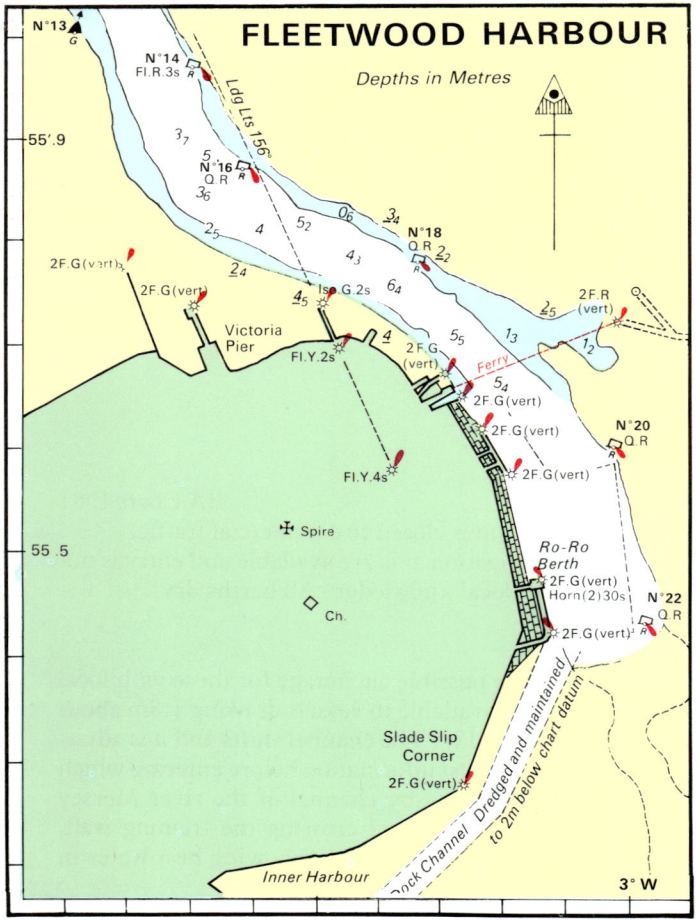

FLEETWOOD and SKIPPOOL Chart BA 2010
HW Fleetwood: Dover +¼h DS in offing: Dover +1h W
MHWS 9.5m MHWN 7.6 MTL 5.3 MLWN 3.1 MLWS 1.2
Bar 2.7 to 3.7m in main channel to Isle of Man quay.

Approach and Entrance Make the Lune Deep S Card buoy Q(6) + L Fl 15s (Whis) and set course for No 1 Fairway N Card lt buoy leaving King Scar G con buoy Q(2)G to stb and Danger Patch R can buoy Fl(3)R 10s to port and then turn SE into lighted and buoyed channel. Be careful of flood tide which sets strongly to E of these buoys.

Keep clear of Pandora RO-RO ships when they are manoeuvring. Wyre Lt Ho (disused) is on the NE elbow of the N Wharf bank at the entrance to the river. Steer on Fleetwood ldg lts 156° up the part of the channel from inside Wyre Lt Ho to abreast of No 11 buoy then alter course slightly to stb to leave No 16 R can buoy QR to port. Then alter course to port and follow the Fleetwood shore.

Berthing Watch out for car ferries which turn inside buoys 20 and 22. A Fl Y is lit on top of staging on Fleetwood side when they are manoeuvring. Do not anchor in this area. Anchor Knott End side of buoys or S of No 22. Land at jetty at Knott End or at landing stage used by local yachts ½M S of Knott End ferry slip, also on beach opposite No 2 IOM berth. Ferry Knott End to Fleetwood, EC Wed. Tram and bus to Blackpool.

SKIPPOOL is 5M above Fleetwood the headquarters of the Blackpool and Fleetwood YC. Starting 1h before HW from midstream off Fleetwood steer 180° to the NW end of the ICI pier at Burn Naze, leaving a small G stb buoy abreast of cooling trs and a large unlit G con buoy close to stb. Alter course gradually to port and steer 135° from the ICI pier to midstream at Wardleys. There is no marked channel above the ICI pier and there are sandbanks in the river which shift, mostly covered at half flood. In the narrows between Wardleys and Skippool creek the banks in mid-river are awash at 5m rise. Course to Skippool 210°.

River Ribble, River Alt – see previous page

RIVER MERSEY BA Charts 1978, 1951, 3490
HW Liverpool: Dover +¼h
MHWS 9.3m MLWN 7.4 MTL 5.1 MLWN 2.9 MLWS 0.9

Approach Tides are strong 5kn in places and wind against tide raises a steep sea in the outer reaches. There are training banks on both sides of the fairway and yachts should take care not to go or be set outside the buoys which are numerous and lit. Enter by the Queen's and Crosby channels and not by the Rock channel which is no longer buoyed.

Berthing There are few facilities for anchoring or berthing for yachts on the Liverpool side of the river. On the Birkenhead side there are:-

(1) New Brighton - Anchor only outside the fairway. Good holding but tide runs hard and this anchorage is only tenable in quiet weather. Heavy swell in W and N winds. Rly and bus to Birkenhead, rly to Liverpool.

(2) Rock Ferry - Limited anchorage S of oil tanker piers. Good holding but use trip line. Land at Rock Ferry slip. Rly and bus to Birkenhead and rly to Liverpool.

(3) New Ferry - Limited anchorage not recommended if any other berth available.

(4) On the Liverpool side – Coburg Dock new marina – Lock open HW±2h.

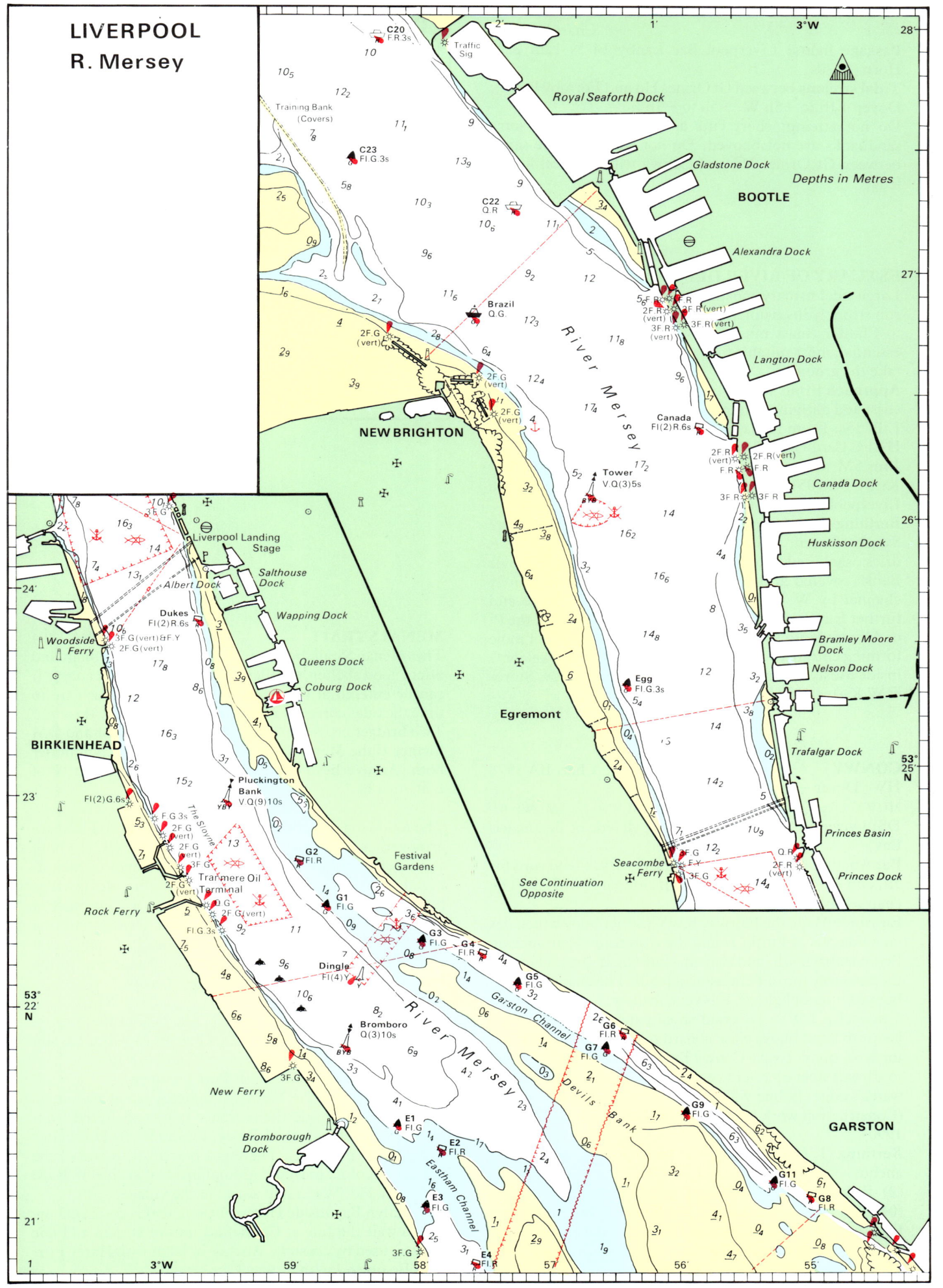

PASSAGE NOTE: LIVERPOOL TO CONWY
Chart BA 1978
Passage lights: Liverpool Bar Lanby Fl 5s 12m 22M Horn (1) 20s
Tidal streams between Gt Ormes Hd and Formby Pt run: Dover +1h to +5h W, −5h to −1h E.
Do not attempt short cuts as seaward edges of some sandbanks are not buoyed. Do not cut across the sands between Gt Ormes Hd and Conwy without local knowledge.

ESTUARY OF RIVER DEE
Large tidal estuary mostly drying at LW. Tidal streams run strongly in channels which shift. Whilst navigable up to Chester (mast must be lowered), local knowledge is essential; most suitable for shallow draft vessels which can take the ground.
Approach From W via buoyed channel between N Wales coast and outlying banks leading to Dee S Card Q Fl(6) + L Fl 15s. From N via Hilbre Swash buoyed channel past HE1 E Card Q(3) 10s turn S to leave Hilbre Is Bn Fl R 3s 14m 5M to port. Contact Captain or Boatman at West Kirby SC (051 625 5579) for latest information or call Liverpool CG on VHF.
Berthing Choice depends on direction of wind. In Hilbre Swash adjacent to Hilbre Is, Hilbre Pool close to the E dries, sheltered S to W, good holding or close to W Hoyle Bank (covered at MHWS). Drying out anchorage in N channel by W Kirby moorings S of Marine Lake and further E at Caldy. In SW channel immediately N of the Pt of Air close into the bank in Mostyn Pool, ¼M E of mole forming entrance to Mostyn Hbr. Yachts are not welcome inside Mostyn Hbr but it can be used in emergency. Stores at W Kirby and Mostyn by dinghy at HW.

CONWY
Chart BA 1978
HW: Dover −½h (Trwyn Du)
MHWS 7.6m MHWN 5.9 MTL 4.1 MLWN 2.3 MLWS 0.7
DS: Dover −5h E; −½h to +7h W (E side of Beaumaris Bay)
Bar About 0.6m at MLWS. The Scabs dry. Flood runs for 5h, ebb 7h. Vessels drawing 1.8m enter at HW−2½h. The channel shifts.
Entrance Make the Fairway RWVS spher buoy which lies on a line NE of Puffin Is and the road tunnel entrance on Penmaenbach hill, and also on a line Great Ormes Hd and the cut-away top of Penmaenbach hill. The channel is well buoyed but not lighted. It is very shallow to seaward of No 4 buoy, 1m LWS. To avoid shoal patches and the Scabs keep stb hand buoys close aboard till S of No 4 then make for No 6 buoy. Leave Conwy Bn B column Fl WR 5s well to stb and steer up river keeping Bodlondeb Pt (wooded to water's edge) in line with centre of new Conwy Road Br. (Construction work for new tunnel across hbr until about 1990).
Berthing (1) Off Bodlondeb Pt near G sewer buoy, buoy anchor.
(2) Pick up vacant mooring and inform HM Conwy (049263) 6253 or Prestatyn (07456) 6491 (house) to confirm use. N Wales Cruising Club premises with usual facilities are at Lower High St (3481) who listen on VHF M 1000-2230. All facilities. EC Wed.

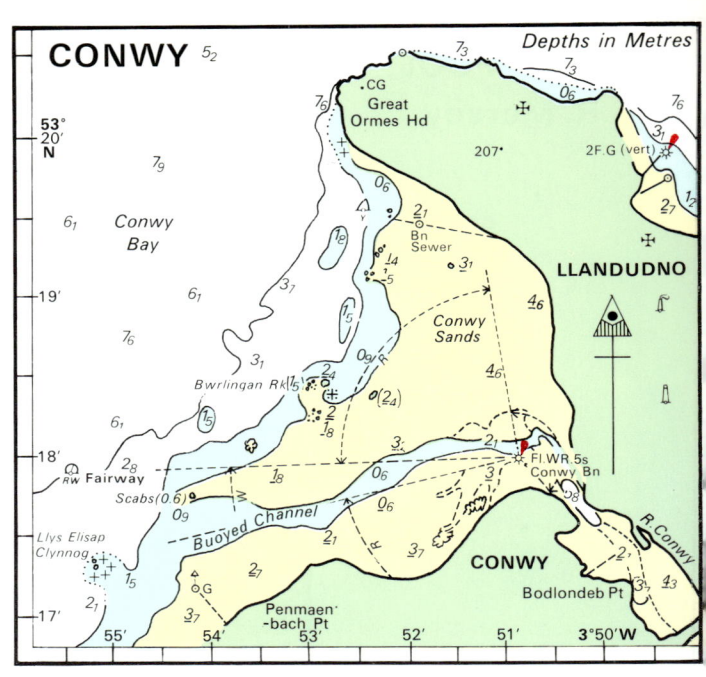

MENAI STRAIT
Chart BA 1464
The Menai Strait between Anglesey and the mainland offers good shelter, excellent facilities and fine scenery. It can be entered at either end and with particular care to time the tides correctly it is possible to pass safely through. Two bridges cross the Strait, the Britannia rly br and ¾M further E the Menai suspension br. Clearance 24m under both. An overhead cable also 24m spans the Strait W of Britannia br.

The following directions serve for craft up to 60T and are arranged as follows:- (a) inwards from the NE; (b) both ways between the bridges where the channel is encumbered with rocks and is known as the Swellies; (c) inwards from the SW. Coasters drawing 4.6m use SW entrance at MHWS; the maximum length of craft to negotiate the Swellies is 70m. Caernarvon is the head of navigation inwards from both entrances and the changeover in the buoyage is marked by a S card buoy "Change".

Good anchorages outside are: (1) 8M NW of the N entrance in NW corner of Red Wharf Bay off Moellfre LB slip sheltered from winds between SSW and NNW
(2) 13M from SW entrance at Port Dinlleyn
(3) Cemaes Bay at the N end of Anglesey, good anchorage for small craft inside the entrance points sheltered from NW in 3.7m abreast the LB slip. Round Wylfa Hd shelter may be had from NE. There is a pier at the S end of the bay, a boat of 1.8m would ground inside it at 2h ebb. Race off Wylfa Hd. Water and stores in the village.
(4) Cemlyn Bay inside Harry Furlong reef is good anchorage to wait the tide at Carmel hd, out of stream and fair shelter, used by coasters. Anchor in 1.8m with Harry Furlong Bn on end with Trwyn Cemlyn.

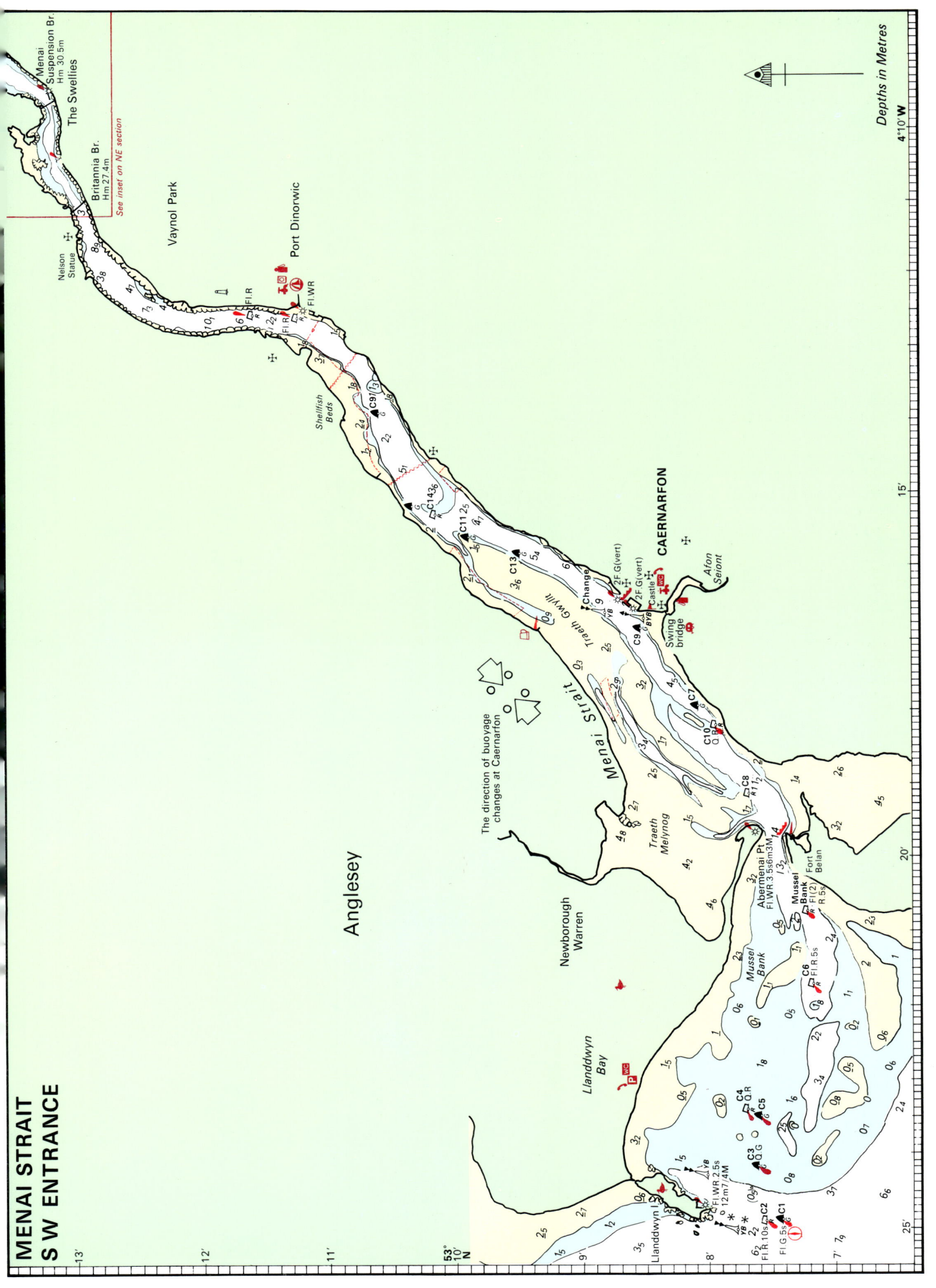

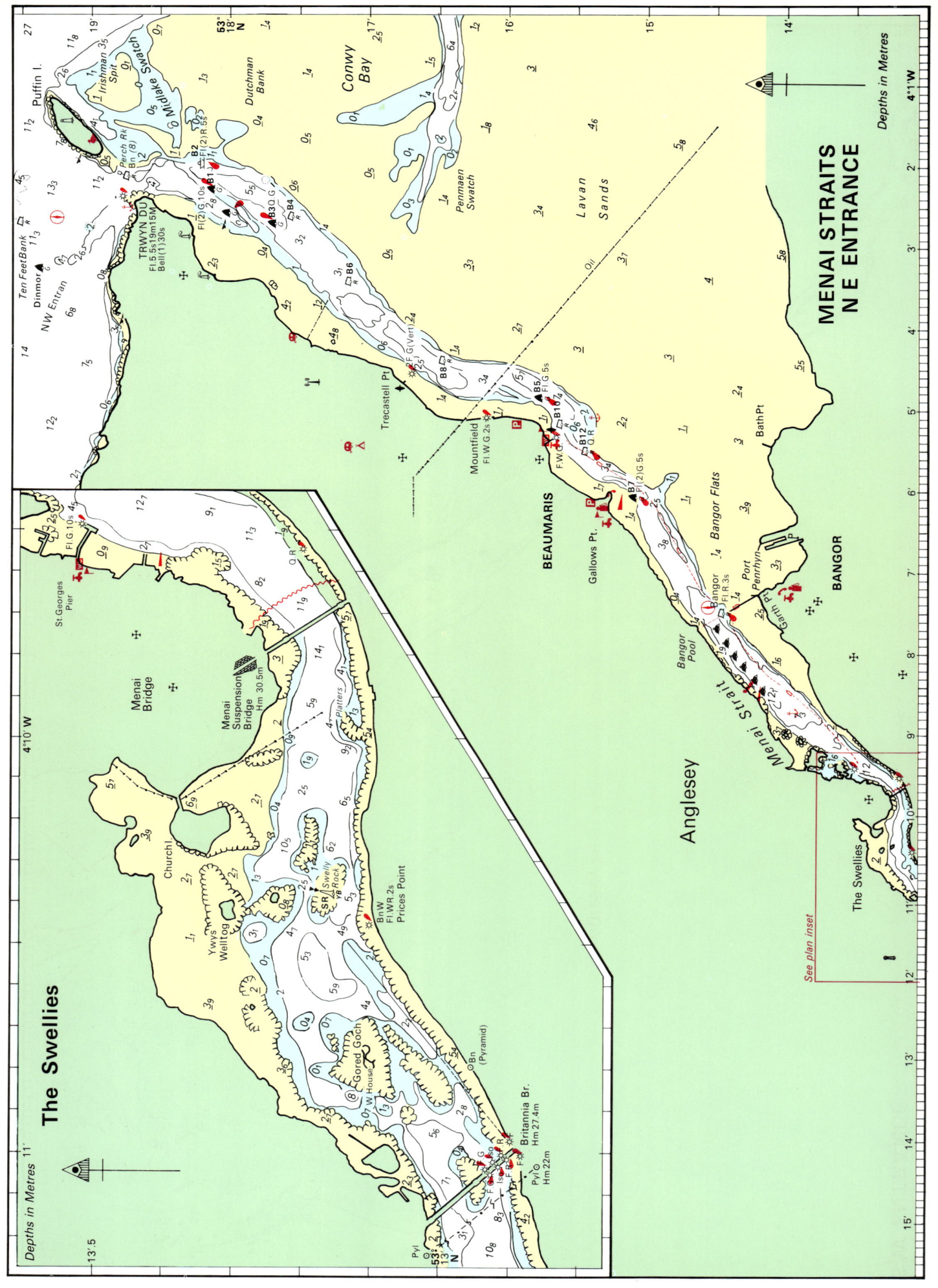

Sailing Directions
(a) NE entrance to Menai Suspension Bridge
HW Trwyn Du: Dover −½h.
MHWS 7.6m   MHWN 5.9   MTL 4.1   MLWN 2.3   MLWS 0.7
HW Menai Br: Dover −¼h
MHWS 7.3m   MHWN 5.7   MTL 4.1   MLWN 2.3   MLWS 0.8
HW Beaumaris: Dover −¼h
MHWS 7.6m   MHWN 5.8   MTL 4.1   MLWN 2.1   MLWS 0.9
DS in offing: Dover +6h E, −¼h W. In entrance at Trwyn Du: Dover −6h inward, −1¼h outward. Off Beaumaris: Dover −4½h SW, +1½h NE.
Entrance Enter W of Puffin Is between Trwyn Du, Anglesey (Menai Tr Fl 5s) to stb and Perch Rk bn SW of Puffin Is to port. The entrance on E side of Puffin Is is not recommended for strangers. Inside, the ebb sets towards the bn. The first buoy No 2 float Fl (2) R 5s is ½M S of entrance and from where the channel runs in a SW direction and is well buoyed as far as No 7 G con buoy off Gallows Pt SW of Beaumaris. At night lts at the LB slip near Trecastell Pt 2FG(vert), Mountfield bn Fl WG 2s, and Beaumaris pier FWG are useful guides. From Gallows Pt to Menai Br there are no useful navigation buoys; keep 1ca from the Anglesey shore.
Anchorages
(1) Beaumaris, between the pier-head and Gallows Pt clear of fairway and moorings in 3½m, sand. The bight dries. Land at pier-head or Gallows Pt, yard at Gallows Pt, bus, all facilities and stores, EC Wed.
(2) Bangor pier-head between fairway and mudflats in 3½m, good holding but uncomfortable with strong SW against tide. Dickie's yard, 30T travel hoist and sheds; good shops in Bangor, buses and rly 1M; EC Wed.
(3) Garth Ferry opposite Bangor pier in 5m clear of fairway and moorings; good shelter, Gazelle Hotel, bus.
(4) Off Ynys y Big (islet midway between Garth and Menai Br) in 3½m. This affords the best shelter and there are shops at Menai Br 1M.

(b) The Swellies
DS: Dover −1½h SW for 6½h, +5h NE for 5½h.
The flood runs NE here and the ebb SW. Both streams run at 4-6kn except for a short slack at HW and LW. It is essential to go through on slack water and boats have been lost through being unable to keep an accurate course over the ground when caught in the strong tides. Before making the passage it is advisable to check all the marks in the following directions and to assess the tide accurately. It is not wise to rely only on predicted times; strong SW winds postpone HW and strong NE winds have the reverse effect. If travelling SW start when boats are swinging at their moorings near Menai Br pier. If in any doubt consult local boatman at Menai marina or take a pilot.

Passage from SW: (1) From midstream pass under middle of S span of Britannia Br and steer on W bn on S shore till fixed G lts at base of S tr of br are in line.
(2) Keep lts in line astern and Swelly Rk S card buoy just open of stb bow till Price's Pt bn is close abeam to stb.
(3) Pass midway between Swelly Rk buoy and Price's Pt till Price's Pt begins to shut out centre tr of Britannia Br.
(4) Then steer on NW tr of Menai Suspension Br till on a line between Swelly Rk buoy and middle of Suspension Br
(5) Then steer to pass under middle of Suspension Br.
Passage from NE: (1) Keep in midstream past Menai Br St George's pier(jetty), Fl G 10s and rk with bn on W side.
(2) Pass under Menai Suspension Br centre.
(3) Keep Swelly Rk buoy just open of port bow till Price's Pt bn is on with centre of Britannia Br.
(4) Then steer on to Price's Pt till Swelly Rk buoy is abeam to stb; then steer to pass midway between Price's Pt and Swelly Rk buoy with bow on Gored Goch island W Ho till past Price's Pt and Swelly Rk buoy astern to stb.
(5) Steer on lts at foot of S end of Britannia Br till W bn on S shore is abeam to port.
(6) Then steer to pass under centre of S span of Britannia Br until in midstream W of Br.
(7) Keep on N side of fairway past Nelson Monument to Port Dinorwic.

(c) SW entrance of Strait to Britannia Rly Br
HW Fort Belan: Dover −1h.
MHWS 4.7m   MHWN 3.6   MTL 2.7   MLWN 1.8   MLWS 0.6
HW Caernarfon: Dover −1h.
MHWS 5.3m   MHWN 3.6   MTL 2.7   MLWN 1.8   MLWS 0.6
HW Port Dinorwic: Dover −1h.
MHWS 5.7m   MHWN 4.5   MTL 3.2   MLWN 2.0   MLWS 0.8
DS in offing: Dover +5h N, −1h S. Fort Belan: Dover +4¾h E, −1½h W.
Bar 1m. Should not be attempted in onshore winds of F5 or more. Most buoys are lit and are shifted as necessary. Up to date information from HM Caernarfon (0286) 2118.
Approach To find the outer pair of buoys marking the bar (C1 G con Fl G 5s and C2 R can Fl R 10s) make a position 5 ca S of Llanddwyn Is circular tr Fl WR 2s. A S Card marks rks off Llanddwyn.
Entrance The direction of the stream changes in different parts of the Strait at different times, but by half flood it sets fair right through to Caernarfon, Port Dinorwic and the Swellies. Proceed across the bar by the buoyed channel (C1 3 5 G con; C 2 4 6 R can). Then leave Mussel Bank buoy Fl(2) R 5s to port and the entrance is immediately ahead with Aber Menai Pt W mast Fl WR 3.5s 6m 3M to port and Belan old fort to stb. Inside the buoyed channel is on the mainland side as far as 1½M NE of Caernarfon and it is particularly narrow and near to this shore between buoys C10 and C7. Sandbanks extend from the Anglesey shore. Afon Seiont E Card buoy SE of C9 marks the channel to Caernarfon hbr (dries).

The head of navigation buoy 'Change' S card is 3ca NNE of C9 and from here onwards the buoyage is reversed; thus proceeding NE R can are stb hand buoys and G con port hand. Change buoy and C13 mark the edge of Traeth Gwyllt sands which dry and C11 its NE corner. Steer midway between these buoys and the mainland shore. Pass close on the Anglesey side of C14 then in midstream to C9 and Port Dinorwic. Between here and the bridges there are no buoys; keep on the W side of midstream.
Berthing (1) Abermenai Creek, convenient for departure to the SW. Enter close to E side of pt and anchor in 5m close to NE side opposite a hut. Sheltered except in strong NE winds. No facilities.
(2) Caernarfon. Anchor in 7m N of town and 2 ca NE of oil wharf wooden jetty with the 'Change' buoy bearing WNW; deep water mooring also available apply HM (0286) 2118. Or go into Victoria hbr S of town, mud, dries. Abfon Oceaneering slip 40T. HM allots berth. Signal for swing br to open is 1 long and 3 short blasts. All facilities, buses, EC Thur.
(3) Port Dinorwic. Anchor in 4m SW of village near moorings or go into Port Dinorwic marina (0248) 670010 through lock available HW ±2h. Berth alongside quay. All facilities bus EC Wed.

PASSAGE NOTES: SKERRIES/CARMEL HD and STACKS

Passage Lights:

    Skerries   Fl(2) 10s 36m 29M and FR 26m 16M
    S Stack   Fl 10s 26m 28M Horn 20s

DS between Skerries and Carmel Hd: Dover + 5h NE, −1h SW; 5-6kn.
1M NW of Skerries: Dover −6h NE, +½h SW; 4-5kn.
DS N and S Stacks: Dover +5½h NNE, −½h SSW. 5kn.
Race up to 1½M NW of S Stack and ½M W of N Stack on NNE stream.
Race up to ½M W of S Stack with SSW stream.

HOLYHEAD

Chart BA 2011

HW: Dover −½h

MHWS 5.7m   MHWN 4.5   MTL 3.2   MLWN 2.0   MLWS 0.7.

The hbr of Holyhead lies between Holyhead Mountain a conspic landmark 213m and Carmel Hd. It can be entered in all conditions. The depth inside the new hbr is generally 5-15m shoaling to 2m or under near the shore and over the Platters on the E side of the hbr just under 1m. The old hbr entrance is 1 ca wide 5m deep. A jetty from the N end of Salt Is is for large tankers which have right of way.

Approach From N give the Skerries a berth of at least 1M and keep S Stack well open of N Stack till breakwater Lt Ho bears SSE to avoid race over Langdon Ridge. Thence steer for breakwater. From SW give the Stacks a berth of at least 1M. Conspic chimney (Anglesey Aluminium Smelter) is a good mark. Holyhead race extending 1½M offshore is worst N of the Stacks in NW winds. At the breakwater the W going stream runs for 9h from half flood to LW by the shore.

Entrance Between the breakwater and Clipera Rks R can bell buoy Fl(4) R 15s. The breakwater and the Aluminium jetty mark the entrance to New hbr. Give breakwater ½ ca clearance as there is foul ground close in.

Berthing In New hbr only. Apply for temporary mooring from Holyhead SC. NE winds cause a chop. Area of foul ground between aluminium jetty and Salt Is. Land on beach between Trinity House buildings and Mackenzie Pier or at HYC slip. Fully equipped boatyard with 30T lift and all repair facilities. Fuel and water on quay. All stores in town within ¼M, EC Tue.

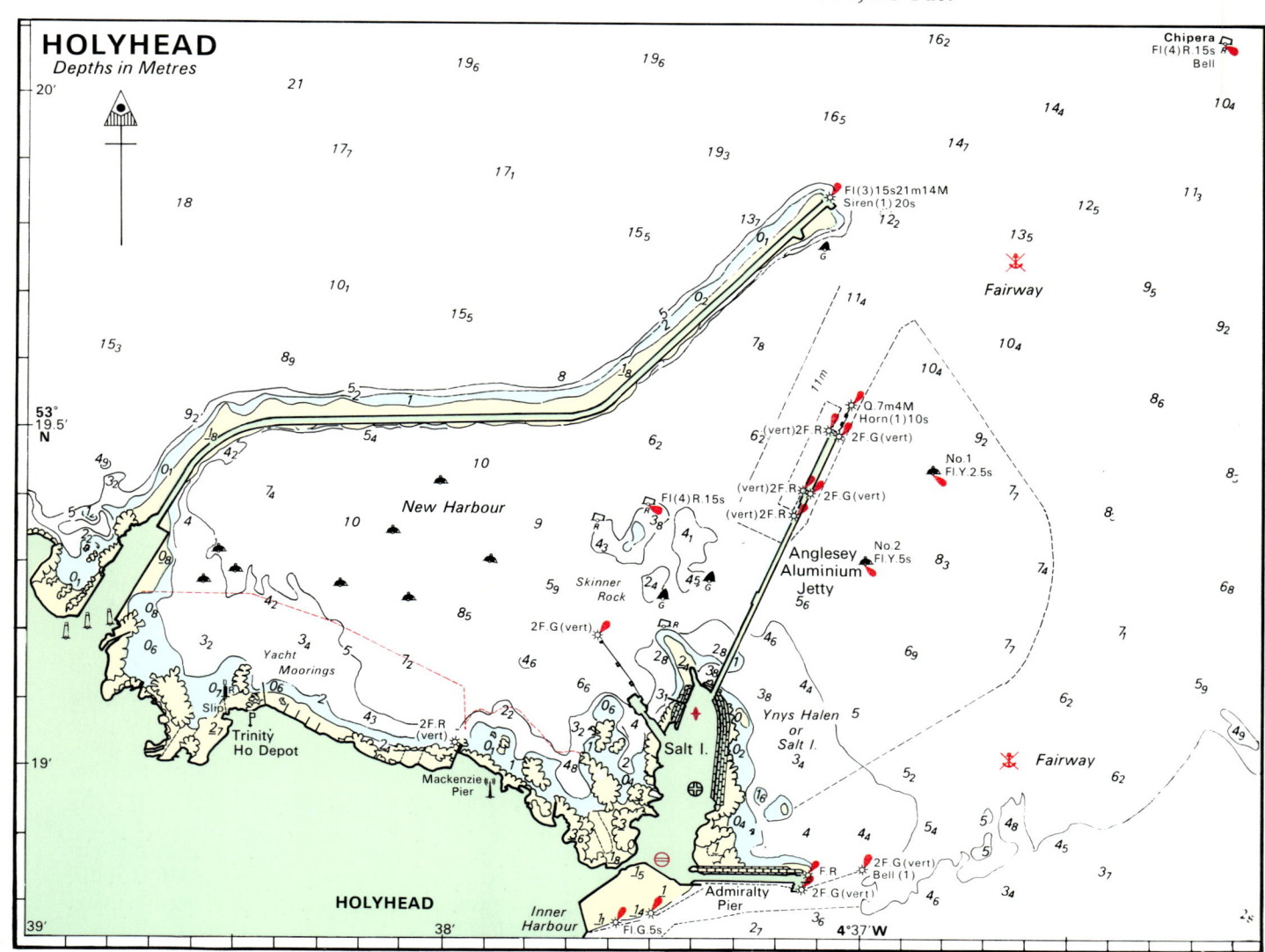

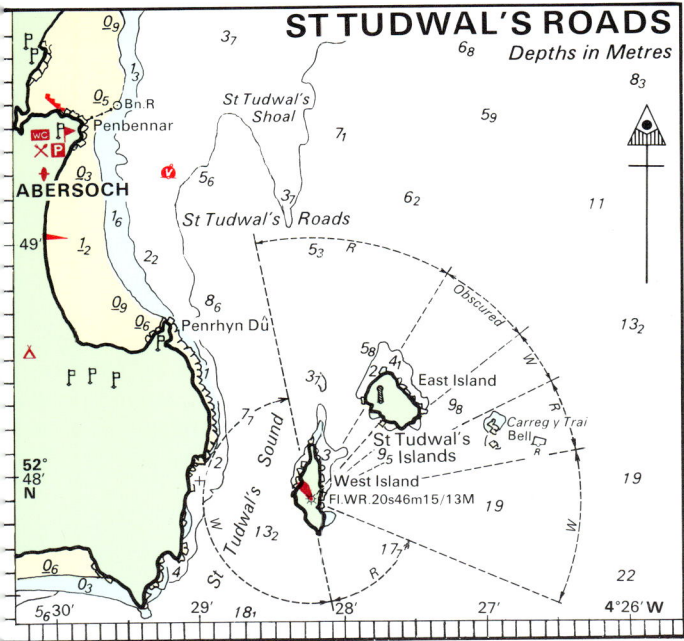

ABERSOCH and ST TUDWAL'S ROAD
Chart BA 1512

HW St Tudwal's Road: Dover −3h. DS: Dover +2h NE, −4h SW.

MHWS 4.7m MHWN 3.6 MTL 2.5 MLWN 1.3 MLWS 0.6
Hbr is small with hard bottom and dries out ½M from shore. It is a very popular yachting centre. The anchorage offshore in St Tudwal's Road is protected from SSE through SW to NE. A heavy sea comes in with winds near E.

The S Caernarvon YC on Penbennar is open from July to September landing slip and water. All stores in Abersoch, EC Wed.

PORT DINLLEYN
Chart BA 1512

HW: Dover −2h. DS in offing: Dover +6h N, HWD S. Stream runs out of bay to W for 9h at up to 2kn.

MHWS 4.6m MHWN 3.4 MTL 2.6 MLWN 1.7 MLWS 0.6
This fine bay on the N side of the Lleyn peninsular 15M SW of Caernarvon affords the only safe anchorage between there and Pwllheli in S to W winds and settled weather. With strong NW winds some shelter may be found by shallow draft boats close to the pt but strong winds from NNW to NNE send in a heavy sea.

Approach From W keep Yr Eifl (twin conspic peaks 561m) open of Porth Dinlleyn Pt to clear Careg-y-Chad dries 2m ¾M W of Pt. Give the rks off the pt a fair berth. Chwislen Rk (bn) is steep-to all round. From seaward steer for Bodfean a rounded wooded mountain 275m high 1M S of Nevin.

Anchorage About 1 ca S of LB Ho in 1½ to 3m. Better holding further out in the bay but less shelter.

Groceries at Morfa Nevin, EC Wed. For petrol and general stores Nevin 2M or in Nevin Bay 1M to E. Anchorage in Nevin Bay not recommended.

PWLLHELI
Chart BA 1512

HW: Dover −3h. DS: Dover −4¼h W by S, +2¾h E, HWD S.

MHWS 4.9m MLWN 3.7 MTL 2.7 MLWN 1.5 MLWS 0.6
A small secure crowded hbr lying in Tremadoc Bay.

Bar Varies in position and depth; has less than 0.3m.

Approach Gimlet Rk (30m, quarried) lies just E of conspic row of white houses on the promenade. The hbr entrance is E of this rk. Fresh E to SW winds cause a breaking sea offshore.

Entrance Buoyed with over 2½m at half-tide. Keep close to the buoys. The channel is narrow and follows S shore.

Berthing Anchor off YC W of Gimlet Rk and confirm with HM. All facilities and stores, boatyard, slips. Rly. EC Wed.

PORTHMADOG
Chart BA 1512

HW: Dover −2¾h.

MHWS 5.1m MHWN 4.0 MTL 2.8 MLWN 1.6 MLWS 0.7
Flood commences local LW +1h. DS in offing: HWD S.

Bar About ½m but almost entirely dependent on rainfall. Buoys 2, 3 and 4 normally span the bar. Inner hbr affords good shelter, outer exposed to southerlies.

Approach From St Tudwal's Road steer 068° to make the Fairway buoy RWVS L Fl 10s.

Entrance The channel is buoyed with unlit lateral buoys with reflectors. Enter between Nos 1 and 2 buoys in line with the Fairway buoy. Within the bar the channel has varying depths 0.6m or more, and from Fechan Pt hugs the NW shore. Safest to allow 1½h either side of HW for 1.3m draft but care required on ebb in onshore winds. A sketch of the channel available from HM 30p + postage. If in doubt contact HM or pilot before entry through coastguard or direct. Entry not hazardous in F4 (5/6 from E).

Berthing Visitors should come alongside the N wall of the inner hbr or at night pick up a vacant mooring in main stream and await instructions. HM hut on N wall; if unavailable pilot may be reached on (076 675) 684 or enquire Portmadoc SC. Rly. Extensive supplies and facilities. EC Wed.

WEST COAST OF ENGLAND AND WALES

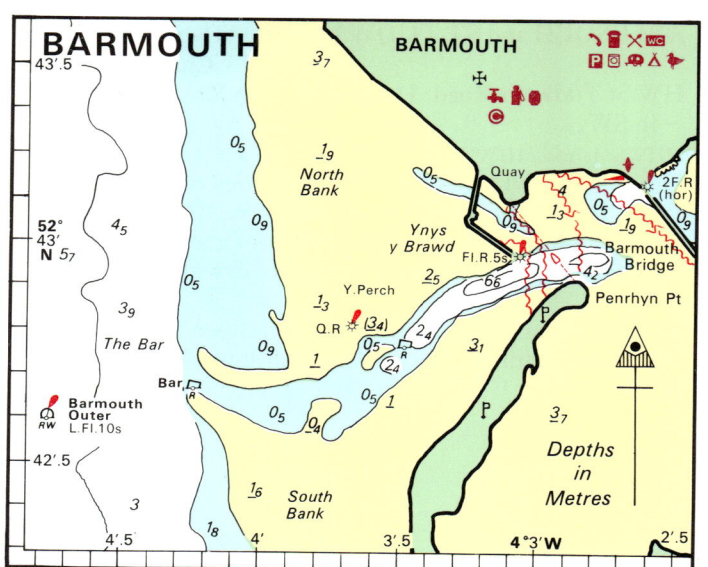

BARMOUTH
Chart BA 1484

HW: Dover −2¾h DS: HWD S, +5h N.
MHWS 4.9m MHWN 3.9 MTL 2.8 MLWN 1.7 MLWS 0.6
Bar About ½m, 1M off the town. Hbr is unapproachable in strong SW winds and should be visited in fine weather only. A very beautiful estuary.
Approach Bring Fegla Fawr hill a low turtle-back shaped hill inside S side of entrance in line with house inside Penrhyn Pt. From Barmouth Outer buoy spher RWVS LFl 10s leave R can Bar and inner buoys to port and steer for entrance which has 3½ to 5½m in channel.
Berthing Consult HM VHF 16 or 12. Electric cables prohibit anchorage near the br. Above the br suitable for power without mast. Best anchorage E of Penrhyn Pt but beware moorings. Space to lie alongside and some spare moorings Merioneth YC. Showers and bar.

ABERDOVEY
Chart BA 1484

HW: Dover −3¼h. DS: Dover −1½h S, +4½h N.
MHWS 4.8m MHWN 3.7 MTL 2.7 MLWN 1.8 MLWS 0.5
This hbr is the first major inlet S of Cader Idris. It is unlit and daylight with good visibility is essential for the approach. It can be difficult to locate the Outer buoy. If uncertain contact hbr on VHF 16 or 12.
Bar About ¼m shifts continually. There is about 3m at half-tide: it is unwise to enter with less water than this except in calm weather. In such conditions entry is possible on the ebb, but in W winds a bad sea gets up quickly on the ebb and entrance is impossible.
Approach First make the Aberdovey Outer RWVS sph buoy, moored in 9-11m at 52°32′N 4°06′W approx. About 1M to the E lies the Bar G buoy, and if no dangerous seas are breaking W of this buoy it is safe to enter. If in doubt wait until 1h before HW: if impassable shelter can be found in St Tudwal's Road.
Entrance All buoys are G con. From Aberdovey Outer steer for the Bar buoy thence for the wooden jetty. The buoys are frequently moved. At half flood the stream sets ENE across the entrance.
Berthing Alongside jetty. Local advice needed before anchoring. Note: bns with Y diamond top marks E of jetty mark a submarine cable approx 2½ca W of jetty. Water at jetty. All stores, rly, EC Wed.

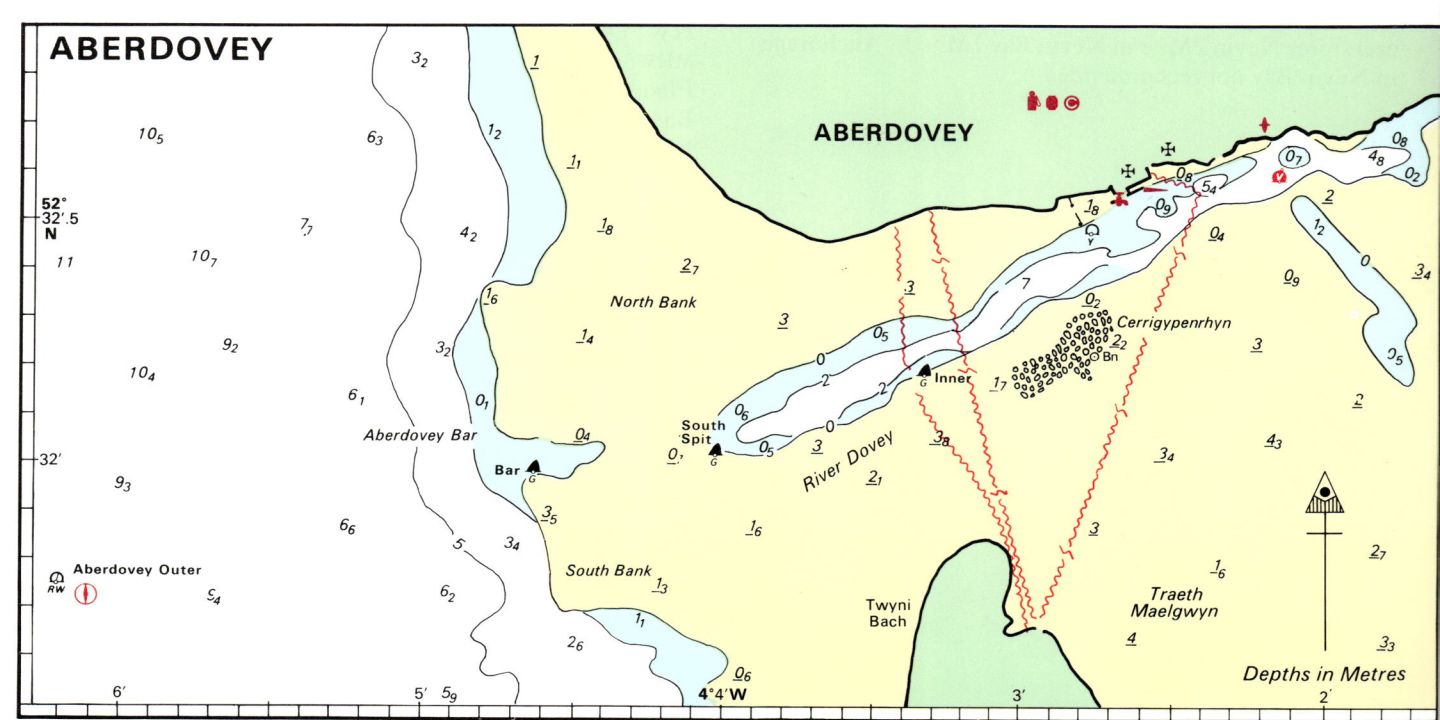

ABERYSTWYTH
Chart BA 1484

HW: Dover −3¼h DS: Dover −1h S, +5h N
MHWS 4.8m MHWN 3.7 MTL 2.7 MLWN 1.8 MLWS 0.5

The hbr may be located by Pendinas, a conspic 120m hill with Wellington monument, S of entrance.

Bar 1m off the pier. The hbr mostly dries but affords good shelter. Narrow entrance with right-angle turn inside the pier-head.

Approach Wellington monument on with lt mast will clear Castle Rks which lie N of entrance which has 3m at half-tide.

Entrance At night within W sectors of either pier-head lt (R sector of lt on N pier marking hazards to N and G sector on S pier marking hazard to S), crossing the bar 20m from N pier-head. When abreast the S pier-head steer in on FR ldg lts, then alter course to port to head up river to the town. Ldg marks are painted W for daylight entry.

Berthing Alongside quays. Visitor's berths at inner side of N pier. HM office at N end of Town quay. (0970 611433). Most supplies. EC Wed.

CARDIGAN
Chart BA 1484

HW: Dover −3¾h. DS: Dover −1h S; +5h N.

The hbr is at the mouth of the R Teifi. Entrance difficult and dangerous in strong W to NW winds, but good shelter within. No special outlying dangers.

Bar Dries and shifts. There is over 2½m at MHWS and about 1½m at MHWN.

Approach Straightforward on a course approx SE.

Entrance Prior inspection of the channel or the services of a pilot advised. Leave R can buoy to port and steel bn with crossbar to stb, passing it about 6m off.

Berthing (1) Good anchorage in soft mud with sufficient depth in several pools between St Dogmaels and Cardigan.

(2) Take ground on muddy sand alongside Spillers Quay on right bank, good shelter. Land on the beach below br. Pilot at Penrhyn. Chandlery, blacksmith. provisions, hotels, PO and launderette in town, mainly on N side of river. EC Wed.

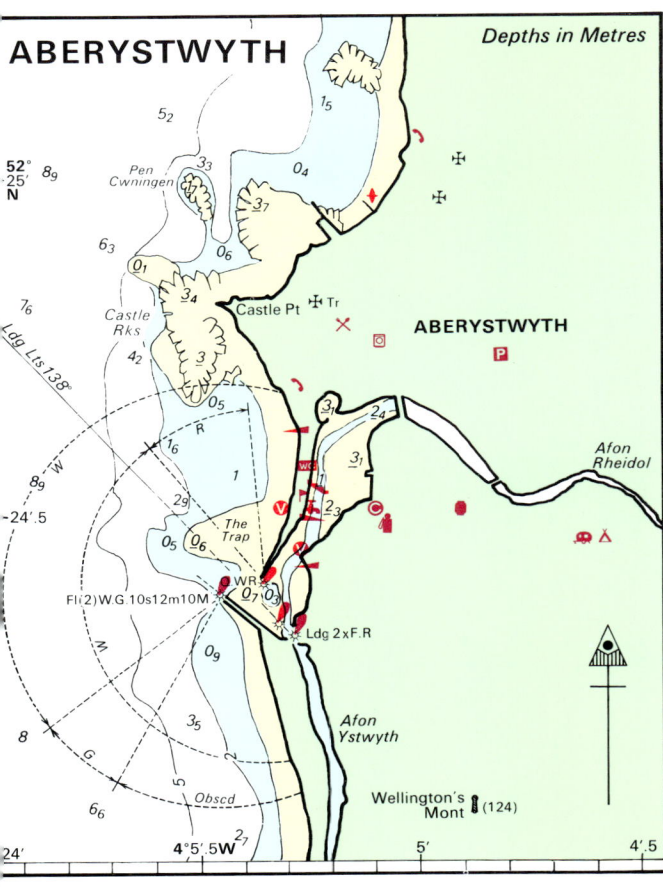

NEW QUAY CARDIGAN
Chart BA 1484

HW: Dover −3½h DS: Dover −1h S; +5h N.

Sheltered from winds W through S to NE; with N or NW wind a dangerous sea comes in. Hbr dries, bottom sand and clay. In fine weather vessels can lie head to anchor and stern to pier or outside the pier. The E side of bay off Ina Pt is foul. Pier-head has Fl WG 3s lt, W 135°-252°, G 252°-295°. A groyne runs out 45m SSE from the end of the pier and is marked by a bn with Y ball topmark.

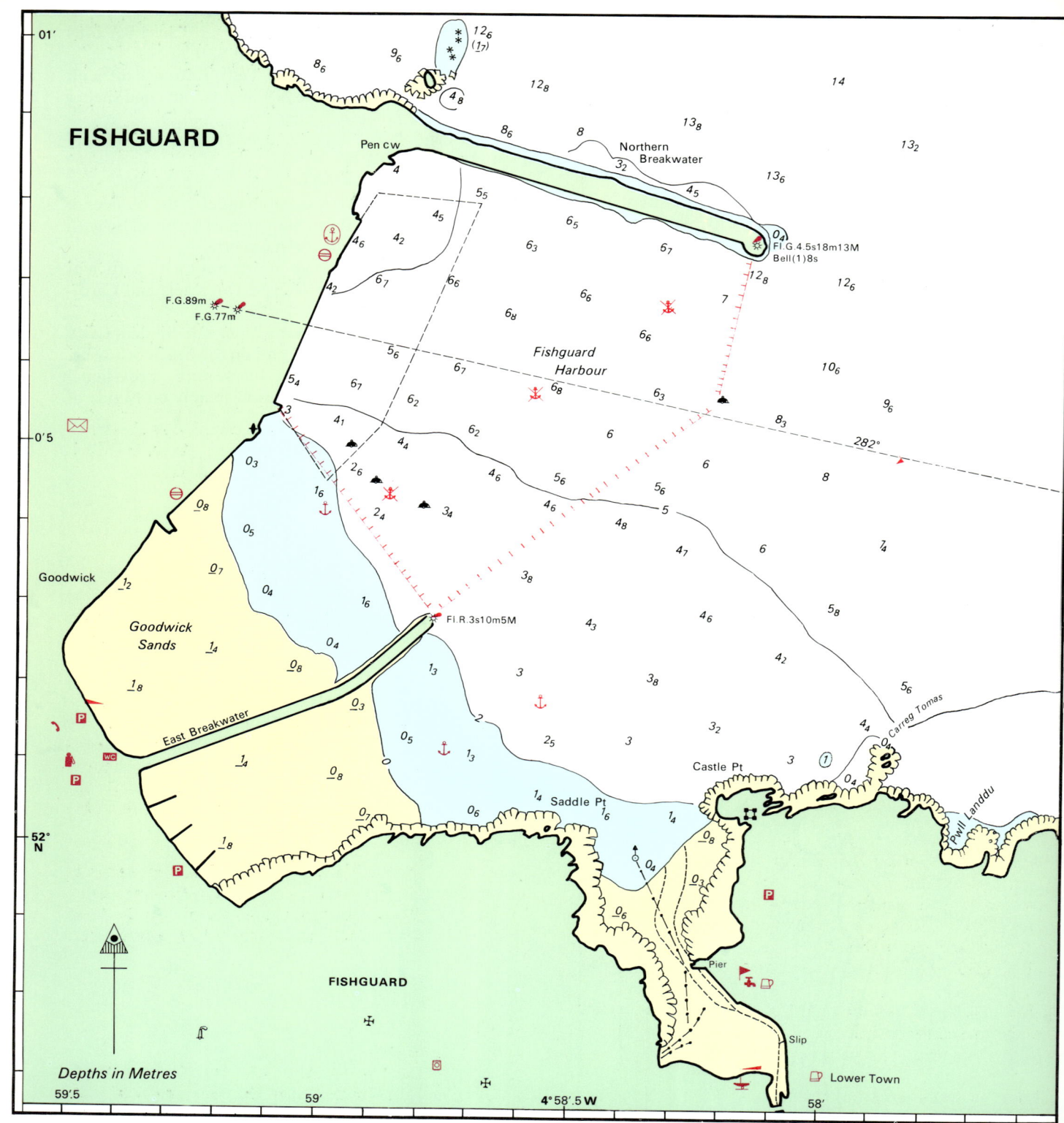

FISHGUARD
Chart BA 1484

HW: Dover −4h. DS in offing: HWD S, +6h N.
MHWS 4.8m MHWN 3.5 MTL 2.8 MLWN 2.1 MLWS 0.8
The only hbr between Holyhead and Milford Haven that can be entered in any weather at any time. Provides shelter in most winds but a considerable swell exists in winds above F5 from NNW to E.

Approach From NW after passing Pen Anglas on coast steer to leave the N breakwater lt Fl G 4.5s close to stb. This will clear the rks, dry 1.7m, off Pen Cw near the root of the breakwater. Hold course until E breakwater lt Fl R 3s is well open then proceed to anchorage watching out for fishing nets.

Anchorage Vessels should anchor S to SE of the line from end of breakwaters to large mooring buoy. Anchorage is prohibited NW of this line. Good holding no stream. If draft permits anchorage is possible inside the E breakwater SW of the three mooring buoys and also between the breakwater and Saddle Pt. All facilities, water. Rly.

OLD HARBOUR Between Saddle and Castle Pts, dries 1.2m, mud and clay. Hbr shoals to 1m 1ca inside these Pts where bottom is very stony. Heavy scend in N or NE gales when entrance is dangerous. Hbr very crowded with local moorings so advisable to enquire first at YC before entering. Pwll Gwaelod ¾M E inside Dinas Hd affords shelter to small craft in E gales.

PASSAGE NOTE: FISHGUARD TO ST. DAVID'S HD
Chart BA 1973

Bound S from Fishguard advantage can be taken of an inshore eddy by keeping fairly close to the land until Porthgain. Keep clear of rk awash off Penbwchdy Hd. After Porthgain the coast must be left ¾M to clear outlying rks. This helps to get through Ramsey Sound before the full strength of the tide develops and causes overfalls at the S end.

PASSAGE NOTES: STRUMBLE HD TO ST ANN'S HD
Chart BA 1973, 1478

Passage Lights:

Strumble Hd	Fl(4) 15s 45m 29M
South Bishop	Fl 5s 44m 24M
The Smalls	Fl(3) 15s 36m 25M
Skokholm Is	Fl R 10s 54m 17M
St Ann's Hd	Fl WR 5s 48m 23/19M

Tidal streams: all times related to Dover

Strumble Hd	−1h SW; +5h NE
Bishops and Clerks	−1½h SW; +4½h NE
Smalls	+¼h S; −5¾h N
Between Skomer and Grassholm	−1h S; −5h N
Between Skokholm and St Ann's Hd	−½h SE; +5½h NW
Inshore W of St Ann's Hd	−1½h SE; +4½h NW

This is an area of strong tides and turbulent seas. The streams run at 5kn near the Bishops, 4kn between Skomer and Grassholm, and up to 6 or 7 kn in the narrow parts of the inner sounds. 2 to 3M W of the Bishops and Smalls the streams are much weaker (2-3kn). Eddies and races form off the rks and islands, the Wild Goose Race W and SW of Skokholm being particularly dangerous.

Four routes are available. (1) Outside the Smalls but between 1-2M W of the Smalls Lt Ho to avoid the N going traffic separation lane and well S of the Wild Goose Race clears all dangers and avoids the worst of the tidal stream. It is much the longest and really suitable for passage from the middle of the Irish Sea.
(2) Outside the Bishops and between Skomer and Grassholm.
(3) Inside the Bishops along the W coast of Ramsey Is and between Skomer and Grassholm.
(4) Inshore through Ramsey and Jack Sounds.

For (2) pass N Bishop unlit 37m above HW but do not turn S for S Bishop until at least 1¼M W of N Bishop to clear heavy overfalls. Then steer to pass midway between Grassholm and Skomer and afterwards between Skomer and Skokholm to avoid the Wild Goose Race. Steer to clear St Ann's Hd.
Route (3): From N pass between St David's Hd and Carreg-trai (dries 4m) and steer to leave Gwahan to port. Pass down W coast of Ramsey Is leaving Llech Uchaf to stb and continue S across entrance of St Bride's Bay to pass W of Skomer Is. Continue as for (2). Do not attempt at night. Tides are weaker than in the Sounds.
Route (4) is a valuable short cut but should only be used by strangers in good visibility. Always go through at slack water or with a fair tide and avoid with wind over tide in F4 or over. Chart BA 1482 is absolutely essential. Directions follow for both sounds in each direction.

RAMSEY SOUND
DS: Dover −2h S; +4h N. 6kn max.

From N pass close to St David's Hd and steer to leave Carreg Gafeilog off the S end of Whitesand Bay ½ca to port. Steer towards a point midway between the Bitches and the mainland cliff at the S end of the sound being careful to leave the Horse Rk (dries 1m) to port. When Pen Dal-aderyn is abeam keep St David's Hd in sight astern so as to clear the Shoe Rk (dries 2.7m). If broken water is seen ahead in the vicinity of Sylvia Rk calmer water will be eastward.

From S leave Sylvia Rk to the W and when clear of it open St David's Hd of Pen Dal-aderyn to clear Shoe Rk. Steer midway between the E end of the Bitches and the mainland and continue due N being careful to leave the Horse Rk about a ¼ ca to stb. Steer midway between Gwahan to port and Carreg Gafeilog to stb.

There is an anchorage in the sound just N of the Bitches. The island is privately owned and permission should be obtained to land. To wait for the tide or make short expedition ashore safer to anchor in Whitesand Bay.

JACK SOUND
DS: Dover −3h S; +3h N. 7kn max.

Both ways it is advisable to have the engine running as even a fair wind can suddenly drop in the middle of the sound. Correction may be needed to avoid being swung off course from the many eddies.

From N identify Tusker Rk (1.5m) ¾ ca W of Wooltack Pt and the Blackstones 2ca S of Midland Is before entering the sound. Pass W of Tusker Rk and immediately bring the Blackstones on with the W end of Skokholm. Approach the Blackstones to pass close E of them. Rough water will be encountered on leaving the sound with a moderate S wind against tide.

From S identify the Blackstones while still S of them and Tusker Rk. Leaving the Blackstones close to port steer for Tusker Rk. When the Garland Stone off the N Pt of Skomer opens N of Midland Is you are free of all dangers W of Tusker Rk

SOLVA
HW: Dover −4¾h
MHWS 5.5m   MHWN 4.2   MTL 3.2   MLWN 2.3   MLWS 0.7

A small creek on N side of St Bride's Bay, 4m inside entrance. Hbr dries 100m inside entrance rk. Complete shelter for craft which can take the ground though swell in extreme weather. Hbr crowded.
Entrance 50m wide. Black Rk 4m showing at HW lies in centre; it is steep to on its E side. Leave close to port and proceed up the hbr keeping to outer side of bend. Beware spit of stones just inside entrance on W side at Trwyn Caws.
Anchorage Temporary anchorage in calm weather may be found in 3m just behind the rk but there is little room. In N winds better to anchor outside or behind Dinas Fach 1M E. Small craft taking the ground can go further in and lie alongside the quay or in midstream off the LB Ho or can go up further at HW. Strong winds from S render the entrance impassable. A charming village with some facilities and stores.

ST BRIDE'S BAY   Chart BA 1478

HW: Little Haven: Dover —4¾h

MHWS 5.9m   MHWN 4.4   MTL 3.3   MLWN 2.3   MLWS 0.7

It is possible to anchor in fine weather at various places in St Bride's Bay, especially with offshore winds. Avoid if any chance of strong winds from the W, as although the tides in the bay are weak, to get out one has to go either through the sounds or round Skomer Is in the S or Ramsey Is in the N, either way encountering strong tides.

Anchorage With S or E winds anchor close in between Little Haven and Borough Hd. In N or E winds anchor between Solva and Dinas Fach. In S winds North Haven on Skomer Is is suitable in about 6m. Chart 1482 advisable. Beware of the reef on the E side of the entrance.

SKOMER IS, SOUTH HAVEN   Chart BA 1482

HW: Dover —5h

MHWS 6.6m   MHWN 5.1   MTL 3.7   MLWN 2.3   MLWS 0.7

A small bay on the SE side of Skomer, giving shelter in winds from W through N to E. This is a most beautiful anchorage and although exposed to winds from the S it is normally an easy beat or fetch down to Milford Haven should winds come up from that direction

Entrance If coming from Milford Haven aim for the Mew stone a prominent rk 48m high off the S tip of Skomer. Beware of rks extending S from the Is just E of the Neck awash at MLWS.

Anchorage Right up towards the head of the bay in about 6m, sand. Do not go further in at neaps as the ground becomes rocky. Land on the Neck. Landing fee payable to the warden. Care should be taken on the Is which is a nature resrve to respect the wild life particularly where nests are marked. No facilities.

MILFORD HAVEN   Chart BA 2878, 3274, 3275

HW: Dover —5h

MHWS 7.0m   MHWN 5.2   MTL 3.8   MLWN 2.5   MLWS 0.7

One of the finest harbours in the British Isles. From Dale in the W to Lawrenny in the E is about 12M the width varying from 1½M to ½M. It is a major oil port with four terminals for very large tankers. In the entrance there are two deep-water channels and small boats must keep out of the way of deep-draft vessels which are restricted to these channels. However there is plenty of room to manoeuvre and tack between these deep-water channels and either shore.

The Port Authority is the Milford Haven Conservancy Board whose jetty and office is at Hubbertson Pt, with a Port Operations Centre with VHF and a protected boat hbr from which the Board's patrol and Pilot launches operate. These have green hulls and white upperworks and fly a blue flag with the word 'Harbourmaster' in white letters, or Pilot flag depending on duties. They are very helpful to yachts and their instructions must always be obeyed. Yachts should not approach within 300 ft of terminals or tankers.

Attention is particularly drawn to the Byelaw which makes it mandatory for small craft including sailing vessels, to keep out of the way of large vessels constrained by draft in the deep-water channels.

Approach The Turbot Bank 4M S of St Ann's Hd, marked on its W edge by a W Card Buoy VQ(9) 10s, causes a heavy sea in bad weather. There is also a confused and sometimes dangerous sea close to St Ann's Hd especially in SW gales against the ebb. In these conditions quieter water will be found in the E channel or near Sheep Is. In daytime with good visibility the first conspic mark likely to be seen from the S is the power stn chimney near Pennar Gut. At night the first lt to be seen is likely to be from one of the Angle Oil refinery stacks where oil is burnt off (51°41′N 5°01′W). This can be seen up to 30M off, beyond the range of St Ann's Lt Ho.

Entrance The entrance offers no obstructions to shallow draft vessels in most weathers but the Middle Channel Rks 5m and Chapel Rks 3m in the centre of the entrance should be avoided in very heavy weather.

Both E and W channels are well buoyed and lit, the W channel being the deeper with three separate sets of ldg lts before the two channels combine.

The most noticeable mark in the entrance is the bn 18m on Middle Channel Rks

In poor visibilty at night the ldg lts on W Blockhouse Pt may be seen before St Ann's Hd lt

Although there is never any necessity to go between Thorne Is and the mainland the channel has 3m and the overhead cables clearance of 15m at HW.

The course to be taken from the outer line of the entrance (St Ann's to Sheep Is) to the inner line (Dale Fort to Thorn Is) will vary according to the eventual destination and the need to keep out of the way of deep draft vessels. The shores on both sides are generally clean and steep to and can be safely approached within ½ca.

For vessels going to Neyland the channel is well buoyed. The S shore between Thorne Is and Popton Pt outside the line of Angle Bay is clean and it is possible to keep out of the way of commercial shipping here. After the Esso terminal the main channel must be taken although except at LWS there will be room between the channel and Milford Shelf.

The main dangers after this which may not be apparent are Wear Spit marked by a bn QR 7m and Carr Rks (strong cross tidal set) N edge marked by stb buoys. Beware of Neyland spit marked by a R Float Fl(2)R. If proceeding beyond the Cleddau Br (37m) take care to pass under main arch marked by F R and G lts. After the br the channel swings over to stb marked by a R can buoy. There is deep water to Lawrenny and nearly to Landshipping after which the river divdes into the E and W Cleddau at Picton Pt. Take care to avoid spits projecting from the outside of bends only some of which are marked. Above Lawrenny abreast Benton Castle do not approach the Castle closer than midstream to avoid rks. Navigation is possible to Haverfordwest and Slebech but only on the tide and to vessels with suitable draft. The br before Haverfordwest cannot be opened.

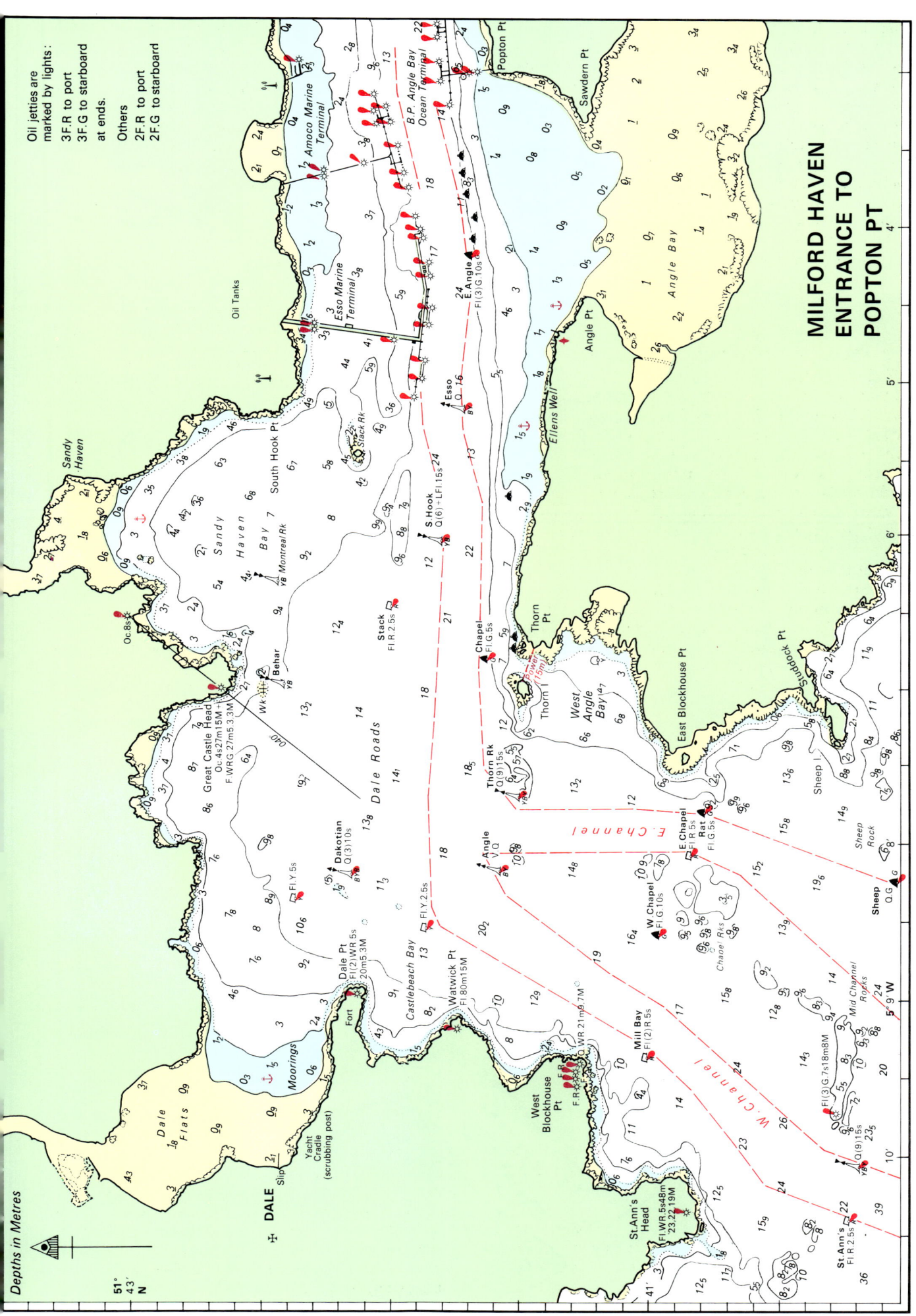

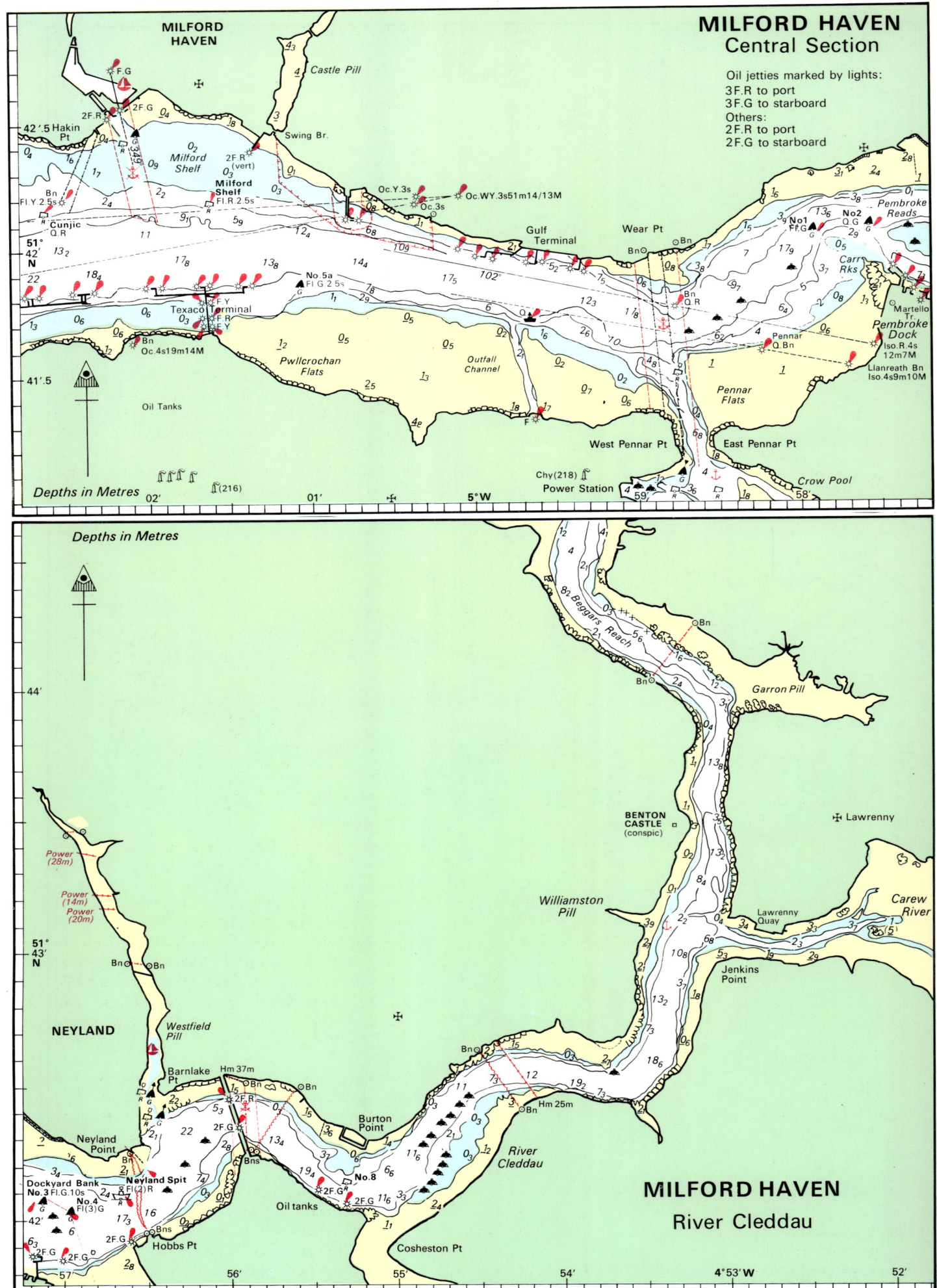

187 WEST COAST OF England & Wales

Berthing There is a marina at Neyland (450 berths) and normally there is room for visitors. If calling the marina on VHF 37 do so E of Wear Spit. The marina dredged to 2m is in Westfield Pill just before the Cleddau Br and has a buoyed channel 2m. Extensive shore facilities by Dale Sailing Co inc engine repairs and fibreglass paint workshop. Copp Sails have extensive sail loft and can undertake repairs at short notice, (0646) 601561

Milford Docks. These may be approached by a narrow cut in the mud with a depth of 2.4m MHWS, ldg lts 348°, gates open HW —2h to HW. Signal for gates to open, blue flag by day, 2G lts vert by night displayed on E entrance. Waiting pontoon on E side of entrance. On entering dock turn to stb where pontoons for yachts and usual marina facilities, boat repairs and chandlery.

Anchorages From W to E.

(1) Dale about 3ca NW of Dale Fort close to moorings. Comfortable in winds from S and W. In strong N winds anchor off N shore or in Castlebeach Bay. In strong E winds somewhat exposed and landing difficult. Scrubbing posts in corner of bay apply Dale YC. Provisions in village. Showers at YC. Water and petrol but no diesel or chandlery.

(2) Sandy Haven Bay sheltered from N and E winds

(3) Off Ellens Well and Angle Pt on S shore sheltered from S.

(4) With sufficient rise of tide Angle bay may be entered. Useful for boats that can take the ground or lie along W side of pier on S shore at W end of bay.

(5) At Milford off Hakin Pt or off MHCB jetty W of town.

(6) Pennar Gut on the S side 1M W of Pembroke Dock, entrance marked by a R can buoy. Sheltered anchorage in 4m buoy anchor. Water fuel and shop ashore.

(7) Pembroke Dock above Hobbs Pt close to moorings (the tide runs strongly). Watch out for Irish ferry which enters and leaves by channel E of Dockyard Bank. Kelpie Boat services have a few moorings for visitors and a large chandlery. Grid for drying out on inside of slipway. Diesel from E Llanion Marine in Cleddau Br approach road.

(8) Burton, off and above Trinity House pier.

(9) Off Williamston Pill opposite Lawrenny.

(10) Off the jetty at Lawrenny where moorings may be available. Secure temporarily to visitor's buoy at entrance to creek or to pontoon and go ashore to arrange a berth. Supplies available.

Yachts on passage requiring a night's shelter use (1) or (2) otherwise any anchorage according to choice, (6) and (9) being the most peaceful. The marina at Neyland is probably most convenient if fuel and water required.

Rly from Milford and Pembroke Dock. EC Milford Thur, Pembroke Dock Wed.

PASSAGE NOTES MILFORD HAVEN TO LANDS END
Chart BA 1178

Passage Lights:

St Ann's Hd	Fl WR 5s 48m W 23M, R 19/22M
Skokholm Is	Fl R 10s 54m 17M
St Gowan Lt V	Fl 20s 12m 26M
Pendeen	Fl(4) 15s 59m 27M
Seven Stones Lt V	Fl(3) 30s 12m 25
Longships	Iso WR 10s 35m W 19M, R 15/18M
Wolf Rock	Fl 15s 34m 23M

The tidal stream runs at right angles to the course to be made good although there is a slight advantage in leaving Milford Haven on the flood for the first 10M. As the coast of Cornwall is closed so the tide will be more in line with the course, especially between Cape Cornwall and Land's End where the streams run at a maximum of 2kn.

It is 110M from Milford Haven to Land's End and very little shelter offers in bad weather. Milford Haven itself is very easy to enter in any weather or state of the tide. To the E of the direct track shelter can be found under the lee of Lundy in W or SW winds; otherwise Padstow is the only harbour to offer shelter from the prevailing SW, but entry over Doom Bar would not be possible for most vessels at LW or at any time in strong NW. St Ives offers shelter in S and E winds only.

NAVIGATION IN THE BRISTOL CHANNEL E OF LINE HARTLAND PT-LUNDY-St GOWANS HD
Chart BA 1179

Passage lights:

Lundy N Pt	Fl(2) 20s 48m 15M
Lundy SE Pt	Fl 5s 53m 24M
Hartland Pt	Fl(6) 15s 37m 25M
Mumbles	Fl(4) 10s 35m 17M
Nash	Fl(2) WR 10s 56m 21/17M
Flat Holm	Fl(3) WR 10s 50m 21/17M
Lynmouth	
Foreland	Fl(4) 15s 67m 26M

Tidal streams in the channel are generally strong, a spring rate of 1.8kn midway between Lundy and St Gowans Hd increasing eastwards to 6kn at the Severn Br. The streams in the inner parts of Carmarthen and Bideford Bays are weak but there are races off many headlands in particular Hartland Pt and Bull Pt on the S side and St Gowans Hd, Oxwich Pt and Mumbles Hd on the N, together with dangerous races, the Hen and Chickens and White Horses, off the NW and NE of Lundy.

Overfalls are widespread, sometimes in mid channel, and a short steep sea sets up quickly with wind against tide, so a craft unable to stay out at sea should be considered unsafe in the Bristol Channel if far from an accessible hbr.

There is a firing range from Castlemartin between Sheep Is at the E edge of the entrance to Milford Haven and Linney Hd extending about 5M out to sea. Firing takes place on most week days 0900-1700 hours. During these times it is necessary to proceed S of Turbot Bank buoy before passage E. Range officers are in attendance and can be contacted on VHF.

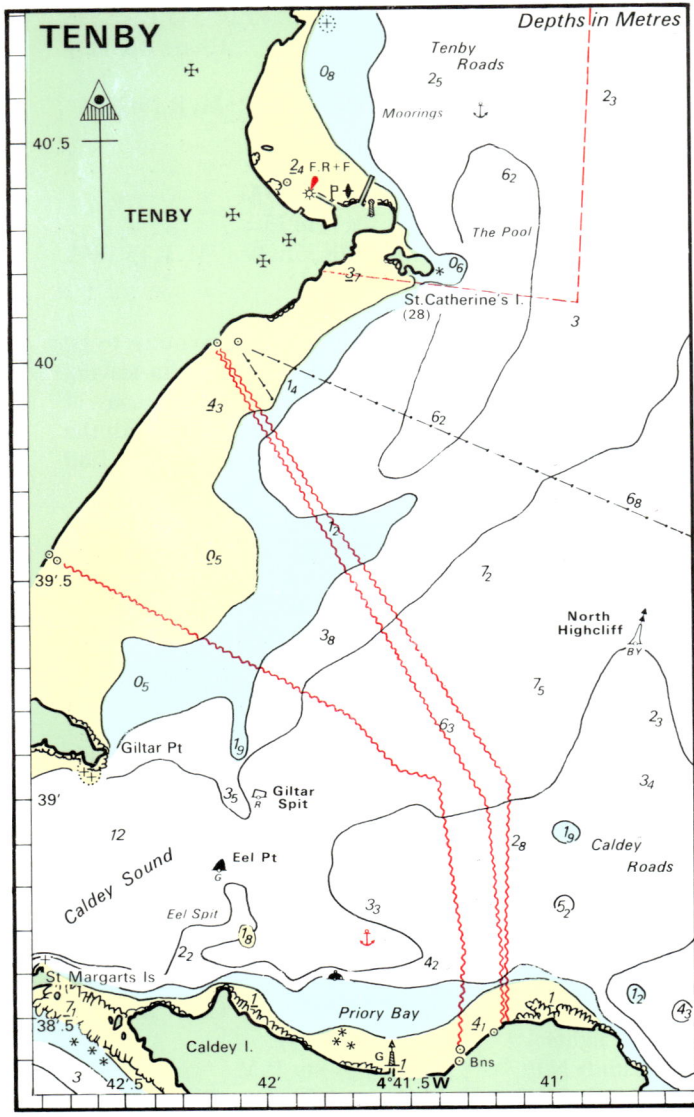

TENBY Chart BA 1482
HW: Dover −5¼h. DS in offing: Dover −5h W, +1h E.
MHWS 8.4m MHWN 6.3 MTL 4.6 MLWN 3.0 MLWS 0.9
Harbour dries 1m at the pier head; bottom hard sand
Approach From the W by day through Caldey sound. Steer ENE for Giltar Pt giving St Margaret's Is a berth of at least 2 ca. Pass between Giltar Spit R can and Eel Pt G con buoys. Then make for North Highcliff N card buoy leaving it to stb. Steer due N until abreast St Catherine Is giving Sker Rk a berth of 1 ca.

When approaching Tenby Roads it is advisable to keep outside the line of local moorings. A vessel drawing 1m should not attempt to enter the hbr until HW −2½h. By night pass S of Caldey giving it a berth of ½M. The streams run hard in Caldey sound and power may be needed if stream is foul. A weather going stream causes a tide rip at the W end of the sound.

From the S and E by day there is only Woolhouse Rk S card to avoid. From S by night vessels may pass 2 ca off E end of Caldey and thence steer NNE for DZ2 buoy Fl Y 2s keeping in W sector of Caldey lt. From DZ2 steer 290° for Tenby Roads remembering that the Woolhouse Rk is not lit.

Berthing (1) Anchor NNE of lifeboat slip on N side of Castle Hill to await tide. Safe except in strong SE winds.
(2) To enter hbr accessible about 2½h either side of HW, steer well towards an iron post on the shore S of Gosker Rk and when nearly on the line joining the rk to the pier-head round up and come alongside the pier; apply to HM for berth. There is a wooden landing jetty at the end of the pier. The pier-head can be rounded as close as desired. Hbr is always very crowded but water quiet except in strong E winds. Only one or two visitor's berths available.
(3) Caldey: small craft can bring up in Priory Bay outside the local moorings but as close inshore as draft permits to avoid the tide. An uncomfortable anchorage in any wind but offers reasonable shelter from SE through S to WSW. Land at Tenby hbr. Facilities limited, stores, water, diesel some distance. Rly EC Wed.

SAUNDERSFOOT Chart BA 1482
HW: Dover −5¼h. DS: Dover −5h W, +1h E.
MHWS 8.4m MHWN 6.3 MTL 4.6 MLWN 3.0 MLWS 0.9
Harbour dries at about 4h ebb, but there is at least 3½m inside at MHWS and 1½m at MHWN. Yachts drawing 1m can enter at half tide. Waiting to enter, good anchorage in 2½m ½M SE of the hbr lt about 3 ca offshore, keeping the glasshouses on the W shore of the bay well open. Well sheltered from winds from NNE through W to SW, good holding. Scend in strong SW and W gales.
Approach Keep about 100m NE of the entrance until the N pier-head close to stb. A variable sandbank (about 3m at MHWS) extends about 50m from the S pier-head. At night once clear of Monkstone Pt (unlit) keep S pier-head lt Fl R 5s due W then approach as above.
Berthing There may be room alongside sharp to stb inside the entrance against the NE pier or alongside the SE wall. A limited number of moorings are available in the centre of the hbr. Enquire first from HM whose office is next to the SC at the NW end of the hbr, (0834) 812094, after hrs 813313. Bottom sand and mud. A lt Fl R 5s is exhibited from a cupola on the S pier-head. Yacht yard and laying up facilities. Fuel in the town, chandlery and provisions. Water tap on the SW wall. Concrete slip for vessels up to 15m. Bus to Tenby and Haverfordwest, rly 1M EC Wed.

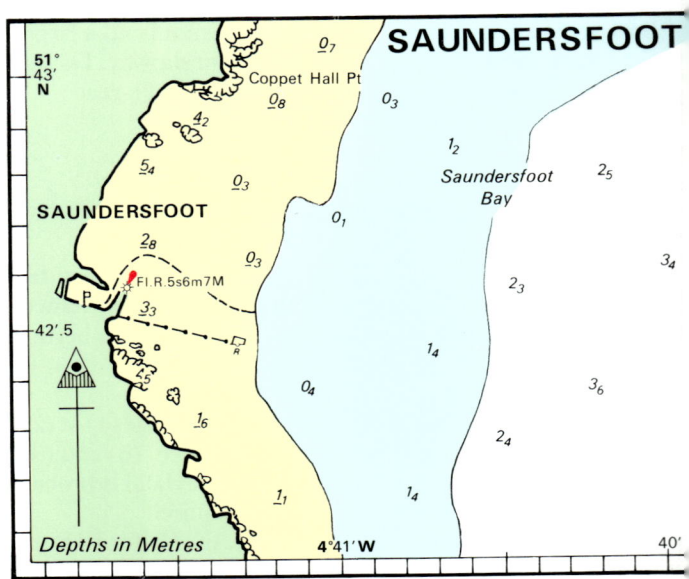

CARMARTHEN
Chart BA 1076

HW: Dover −5h. MHWS 2.6m MLWS 0.4
HW Ferryside: Dover −5h.
MHWS 6.7m MHWN 4.5 MTL 3.1 MLWN 0.8 MLWS 0.1

Bar Nearly dries; ground swell may break. Strong streams.

Approach Encumbered with shifting sandbanks: charts cannot be relied upon for the position of the fairway. In Carmarthen Bay DZ buoys mark areas used for firing practice on weekdays; tel Pendine Range Contoller (09945) 243. The channel is not buoyed and entrance is not advised without local knowledge or a pilot and certainly not at night. However if swell is not heavy the bar, 7M 047° from Spaniel Shoal E card buoy, 11M 322° from just off Worms Hd, can be crossed without difficulty for 1h either side of HW by craft drawing up to 1.5m. From a position 1½M offshore (Pendine Burrows) with Caldey Is lt bearing 232° 8M and Ragwen Pt bearing 297°, steer 072° until artillery lookout tr on Ginst Pt bears NNW. Then steer NE towards St Ishmael ch. When about 4 ca off ch steer N to distinct B post in the centre of the river below Ferryside.

Entrance Once over the bar one can proceed along this pretty river as far as the rly br about 1M below Carmarthen, but there are no berths above Blackpool below Green Castle. Various overhead cables cross, the least known ht being 15m. Except in a few pools the river is almost dry at LW. It is difficult to tell where the channel lies.

Berthing (1) At Ferryside off the Towy YC. The stream is strong. It is preferable to take the ground on the bank in the middle of the river, yacht moorings give the lie of the stream and channel.

(2) At HW one may proceed to Blackpool 2.4m at MHWN, usually water in pool at LW, good anchorage but advisable to check first at R Towy YC for up to date information.

(3) Taf River-approach close to Wharley Pt then steer WNW towards Laugharne. Anchor about ¼M due E of Laugharne. Moderate drafts can reach St Clears but beware of shallows off Laugharne.

BURRY PORT and LLANELLI
Chart BA 1167

HW (Llanelli): Dover −5h
MHWS 7.8m MHWN 5.8

Approach Free of dangers in Carmarthen Bay but the outer bar should not be attempted in W or SW winds F5 or over. Strong stream. Not advisable without local knowledge as the channel is not buoyed. There is a firing range in Carmarthen Bay marked by DZ buoys consult Pendine Range Controller (09945) 243. For shelter Caldey Is, Tenby or Saundersfoot.

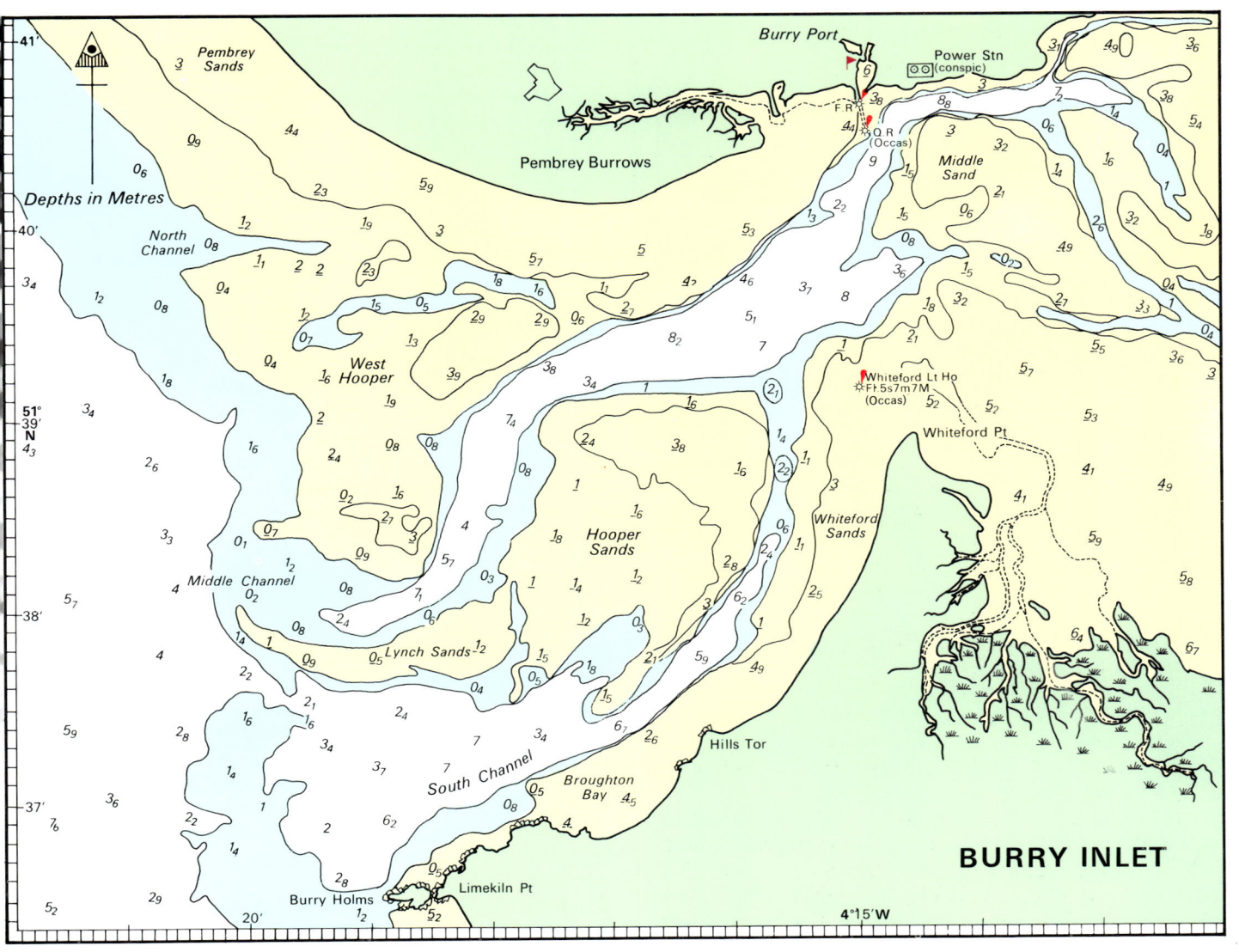

Entrance The channel through the sandbanks shifts and is not offically buoyed although there may be temporary YC marks. Enter between 4h and 5h flood 3 ca NW of Burry Holms, a conspic detached islet (32m) off Limekiln Pt. From here steer NNE allowing for the tide, Worms Hd in the centre of the Sound E of Burry Holms Islet provides a useful stern transit until Whiteford Lt Ho Fl 5s 7m 7M (occas) bears 080° about 1½M. Then alter to 040° to leave the Barrel Post, a Y perch Q R (occas) 1 ca S of hbr entrance, about 2 ca to port.
Berthing The hbr is filled with moorings but could be useful in emergncy.
There is an anchorage in 6m between the barrel post and the disused Power stn E of the entrance whose three chimneys (conspic) provide a good mark. The tide runs across the entrance at 3-4 kn at springs. EC Tue.

LLANELLI From close off Burry port the channel continues E to Llanelli following the Northernmost channel on the chart immediately S of Cefn Patrick Sand. This should not be attempted without local knowledge. The dock at Llanelli is now much silted up owing to the removal of the dock gates

SWANSEA Chart BA 1161
HW: Dover −5h.
MHWS 9.6m   MHWN 7.3   MTL 5.3   MLWN 3.2   MLWS 1.0
Available in all weathers and accomodation for yachts in marina. Port entry controlled by signals.
Approach The approach channel is dredged to 3m to King's Dock outer sill.
Make the SW Inner Green Grounds S Card buoy Q(6) + LFl 15s and steer 020° for the outer Fairway G con buoy QG and the inner Fairway G con buoy Fl G 2.5s.
Entrance With 1.8m draft entry usually possible at any state of the tide. Port entry contolled by the middle lt in the left hand vert line of 9 lts (3x3) G for entry, R entry prohibited wait in holding area W of dredged channel. Lock gate for marina is controlled by lts, 2R or none lock not operating, 1R working but closed, 1G proceed. Outgoing lts for exit S of Prince of Wales dock. Access normally after half tide.
Berthing In marina which has visitor's berths. Mooring berths in R Tawe marked SYH available for yachts waiting to enter. Call VHF M for current instructions. Good facilities, storage, repairs.

RIVER NEATH Chart BA 1161
About 3M E of Swansea. Entry HW −2h between training walls marked by posts and buoys. When inside take port branch to Monkstone Marina and Cruiser & SC. 2 holding buoys in R Neath upstream of marina entrance. YC (0639) 8722.

PORT TALBOT Chart BA 1161
HW: Dover −5h.
MHWS 9.6m   MHWN 7.3   MTL 5.3   MLWN 3.3   MLWS 1.0
Approach Difficult in strong offshore winds. Make for R can buoys marking dredged channel to new hbr but leave to stb and proceed to old hbr in R Afan keeping close to old S pier. Entry possible 1h after LW.
Berthing In channel up to the old wet dock, protected from E and N. Craft must not be left unattended due to the high range of tide and steep-sided channel nor enter the new iron ore hbr at any time.

PORTHCAWL Chart BA 1169
HW: Dover −5h.
MHWS 9.9m   MHWN 7.5   MTL 5.4   MLWN 3.3   MLWS 1.0
A small hbr full of local boats on fore and aft moorings
Approach From W find Fairy W Card buoy, from E, Tusker R can buoy Fl(2)R 5s and steer 315° to Fairy buoy making due allowance for the tide and avoiding Fairy Rks. From Fairy buoy steer 010° to end of jetty (FWRG). Tide runs at 6kn (springs) off end of breakwater.
Entrance Beware submerged old breakwater extending from E side of entrance marked by bn, also rks off lt on W entrance.
Berthing Hbr dries, soft mud. Anchorage possible in 7m 3 ca SSE of Lt Ho but poor holding.

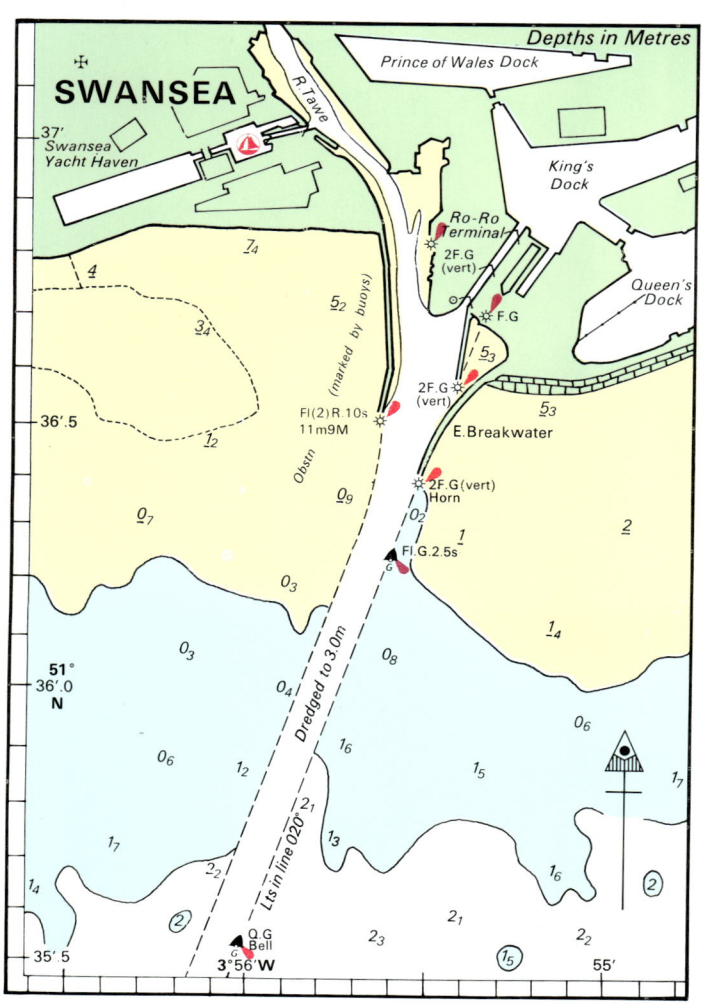

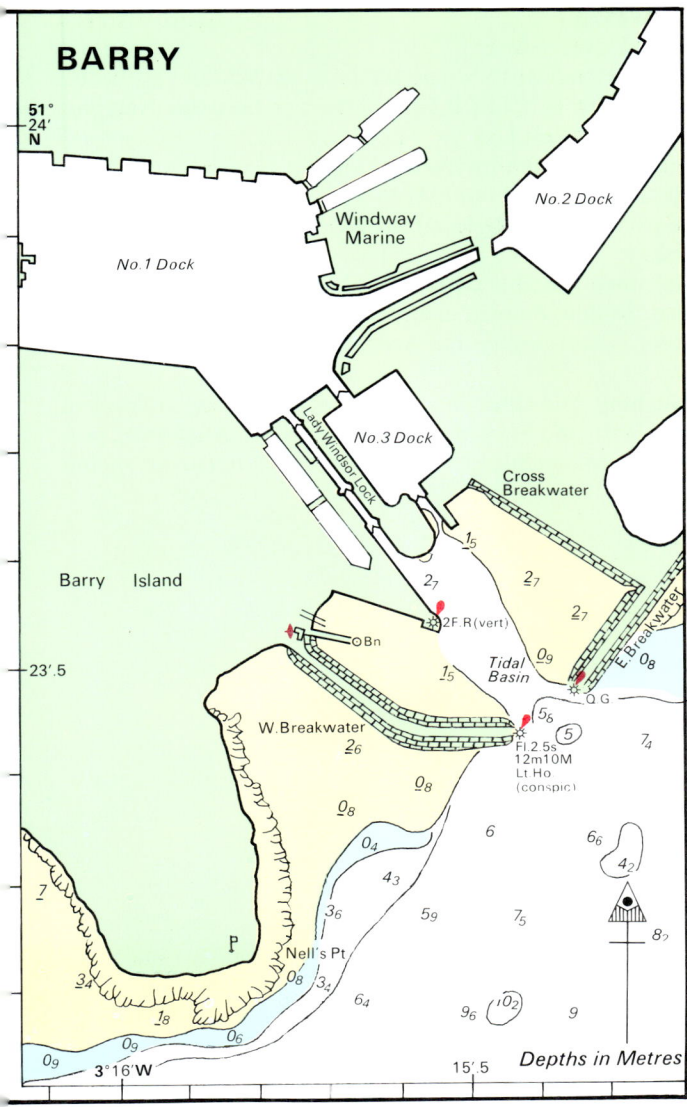

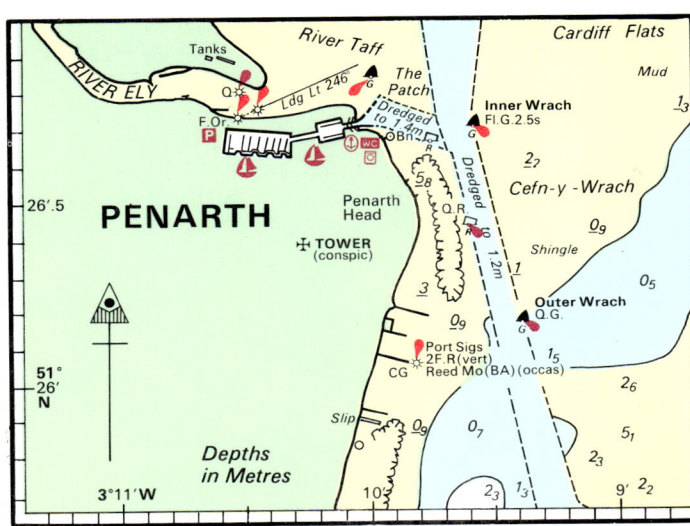

PENARTH   Chart BA 1182

HW (Cardiff): Dover −4½h.
MHWS 12.3m   MHWN 9.6   MTL 6.7   MLWN 3.8   MLWS 1.2

Approach Enter dredged channel 1.2m on 349° as for Cardiff. Turn to port about 1 ca before Inner Wrach buoy Fl G 2.5s and proceed past port hand bn.

Entrance Channel runs straight from R Ely channel 304° to lock. Watch cross tide on turning to port into marina channel. Entrance available at about 3h either side of HW but check with marina on VHF 37 (24h watch).

Berthing (1) Penarth Dock Basin is a modern marina with about 100 berths for visitors and usual facilities including chandlery.

(2) Boatyard in R Ely half tide pontoon now extended, access just below high level br. Laying up facilities available.

BARRY   Chart BA 1182

HW: Dover −4½h DS in offing: Dover −5h W
MHWS 11.4m   MHWN 8.7   MTL 6.2   MLWN 3.7   MLWS 0.9

The outer hbr is always available. There is 2m at MLWS between the piers and to the docks. Great caution is needed as traffic is heavy. Give way to all merchant vessels entering or leaving. At LW craft may anchor in the fairway but must move into the yacht area as soon as tide serves. Keep clear of Pilot launch and lifeboat on swinging moorings. Large yachts (over 11m or multihulls) cannot easily be accomodated..

Approach From the W keep S of the line of the Nash Lts to clear the Scarweather and Nash Sands. From the E give the shore a good berth.

Entrance The entrance lies between two breakwaters on the E side of Barry Is; turn hard to port inside. Due to silting the deep-dredged channel is only in line of entrance channel; steep sides. Beware cross-set of tide in entrance.

Berthing Hbr crowded: Tie up alongside local moored boats in centre of hbr and enquire at YC for berth. If anchor dropped inside, not due W of Pilot boats due to mooring chains, and in any case tripping line advisable. Yachts must not be left unattended. Area dries at LWS. Possible to go into Lady Windsor lock and through to Windway marine for laying up but heavy lock fee. The old hbr W of Barry Is dries and is no longer of any use. All facilities, water at YC. EC Wed

WEST COAST OF ENGLAND AND WALES   192

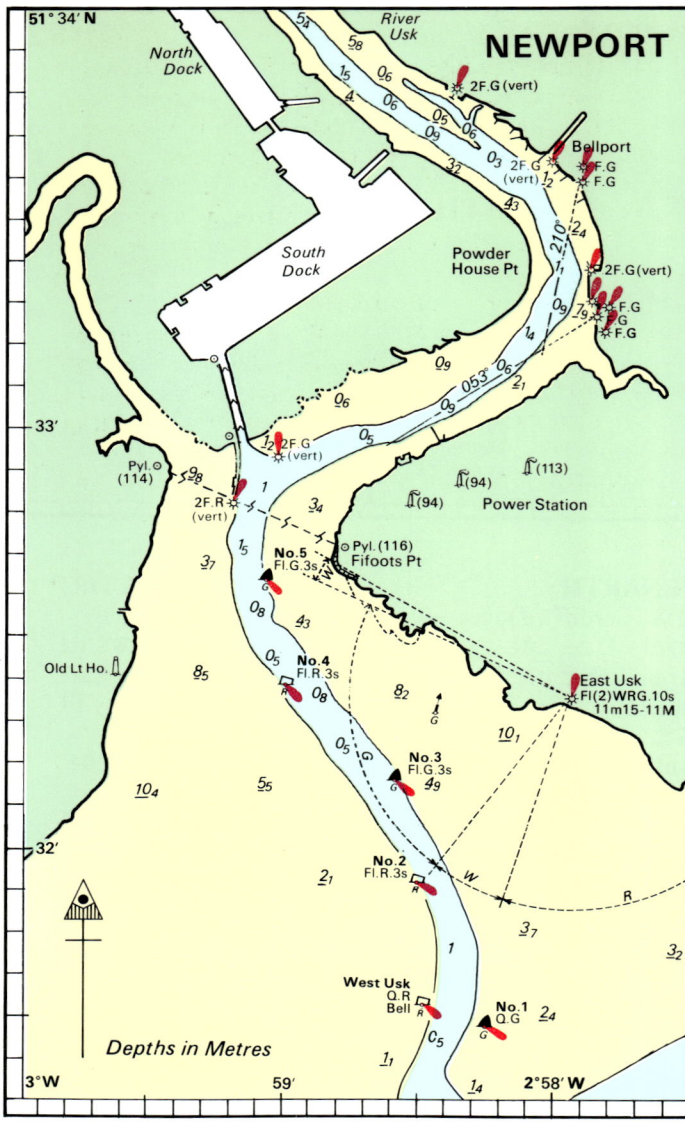

NEWPORT Chart BA 1176
HW: Dover −4½h
MHWS 12.1m MHWN 9.0 MTL 6.0 MLWN 2.9 MLWS 0.2

Bar There is about 0.5m on the bar between Newport Deep and West Usk.

Approach Make for Newport Deep G con buoy Fl(3)G 10s and leave it about ½M to stb steering 021° to pass between West Usk QR and No1 QG buoys at mouth of R Usk.

Entrance Possible within 1h of LW but tide is strong 4-5kn. Follow buoyed channel to South Lock after which there is no buoyage but keep slightly to stb of centre of river.

Berthing Moorings on S side between jetty in front of power stn and SC which dry HW + 3½h. Anchoring possible in 1m outside line of moorings essential to use anchor lt.

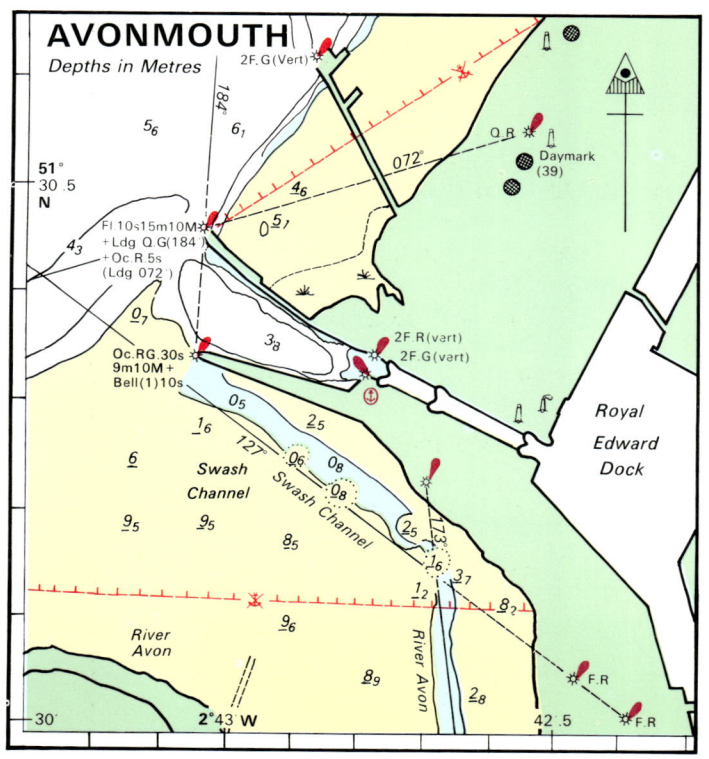

RIVER AVON, BRISTOL Chart BA 1859

The booklet entitled "Bristol City Docks-Information for Owners of Pleasure Craft" available from City Docks PBA office, Underfall Yard, Cumberland Rd, Bristol BS1 6XG (0272) 24797 will be found invaluable.

Approach Find Cockburn R can buoy and steer 098° for entry to R Avon at Swash Channel immediately S of South Pier of Avonmouth Docks which just dries at MLWS.

Entrance Proceed up R Avon taking care to keep in channel. Chart 1859 is essential. The channel is marked by ldg lts at many points along the banks and from Pill Creek Stb hand lts are OcG 5s and Port hand F Y. There are only two br, the M5 Br (30m) and Clifton Suspension Br (73m) until Plimsoll swing br at the Cumberland Basin at the entrance to the City Docks. From the Swash channel to the Basin is 6.2M

After entering R Avon inform Avonmouth Signal Stn that you are bound for the City Docks calling 'Avonmouth Radio' on VHF 16, working 12 or 14, low power. Alternatively signal or flash letter R. When in Sea Mills Reach call Bristol City Docks on VHF 16. Wait for G signal lt at Hortwells Pontoon before Dock entrance. Unless instructed to go directly into the lock tie up at the Tongue Mead just upstream of the entrance.

If too late to be locked in take the ground in soft mud in line with the entrance of the lock and not nearer than the iron ladder on port side 36m from lock gates. Locking in times are 2.35h, 1.25h and 0.15h before HW, the lock gates remaining open for ½h after these times if other craft are expected.

Berthing In the yacht basin on stb in the Floating Harbour or alongside Narrow Quay on stb side at N end of Floating Harbour.

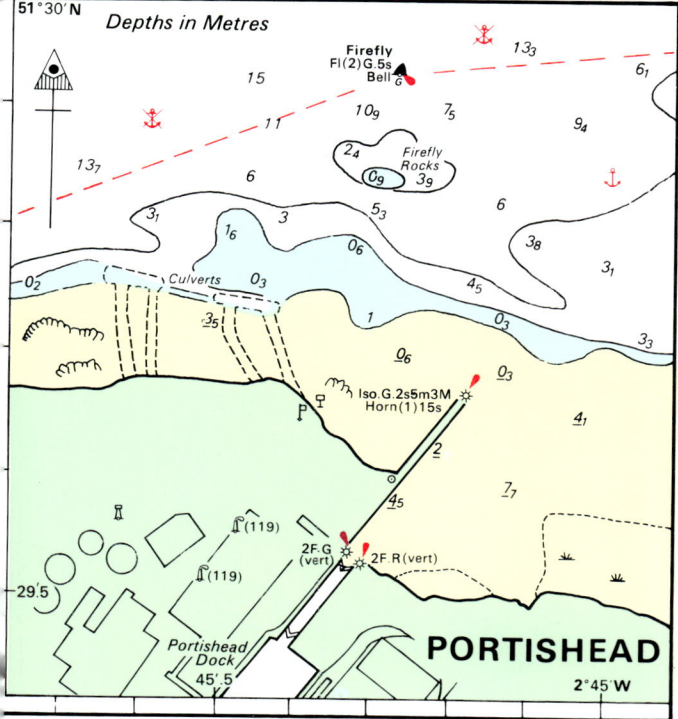

RIVER AXE   Chart BA 1152

A half tide hbr running into Weston Bay S of Weston. Fresh N-lies make the entrance difficult. To enter bring Black Rk into line with W mark on Uphill Hill. Approach the rk to within 1ca and leave it to port, then keep to mid-channel. A Weston Bay YC buoy 'Juicy' indicates the bar 4ca from Brean Down about halfway along. There are withies along N side of of the channel. The river dries.

No room to anchor: Take vacant mooring and enquire ashore. Further up at the E end of Brean Down a bend in the channel is buoyed and thereafter bns mark the channel upstream. In moderate winds anchor in shallow bay under Brean Down. There is a boatyard at the top of Uphill Pill; Chandlery, fuel and repairs. Craft up to 14m and 12T can be handled.

PORTISHEAD   Chart BA 1859

HW: Dover −4¼h. DS in offing: Dover −5h W.
MHWS 13.1m   MHWN 9.9

Approach The stream turns W close inshore 2h before HW and runs fast outside Firefly buoy, which should be rounded close to. Then head for the pier (lt at end Iso G 2s 5m 3M) which should be given a good berth. An eddy on the flood sweeps towards the pier end.
Entrance Enter close to the pier-head.

Berthing The hbr can be used as a harbour of refuge by arrangement with Avonmouth Hbr authorities: call on VHF between HW −2h to +½h. The dock may not open on every tide. Otherwise anchor in 3½ to 7m between Firefly and Flatness rks in Portishead Pool. Yachts can lie aground in the soft mud SE of the pier but the sides are steep. There is a good anchorage in line with the lock gates and opposite the pier steps. Land at landing stage.

WESTON-SUPER-MARE   Chart BA 1152

HW: Dover −4½h DS in offing: Dover −5h W
MHWS 12.0m   MHWN 9.0   MTL 6.1   MLWN 2.7   MLWS 0.7

Approach The causeway at the hbr entrance is marked by a bn and there are 2 F G lts (vert) on the Grand Pier. The hbr wall lies 2ca N of Grand Pier.

Berthing Anchorage is available from 4h flood to 2h ebb except at dead neaps, but Knightstone hbr dries out and yachts normally use legs or make fast alongside two wooden dolphins. Shelter from all winds except S. Small yachts anchor S of the old pier near the LB Ho in what is called the Cut or Sound; mainly dry at MLWS. Boatman will indicate the best berth. All stores, engine repairs. Rly. EC Thur.

THE CRUISING ASSOCIATION

Founded 1908 - Membership 5500

Library 8500 volumes - Chart Room 2500 charts

Pilots & Navigational Information

Worldwide Regional Files

250 Hon Local Representatives Worldwide

Quarterly Magazine & Navigation Notes

Bi monthly Bulletins

Crewing Service - Local Area Sections & Meets

The Cruising Association, Ivory House,
St Katharine Dock, London E1 9AT
Tel: 071 481 0881

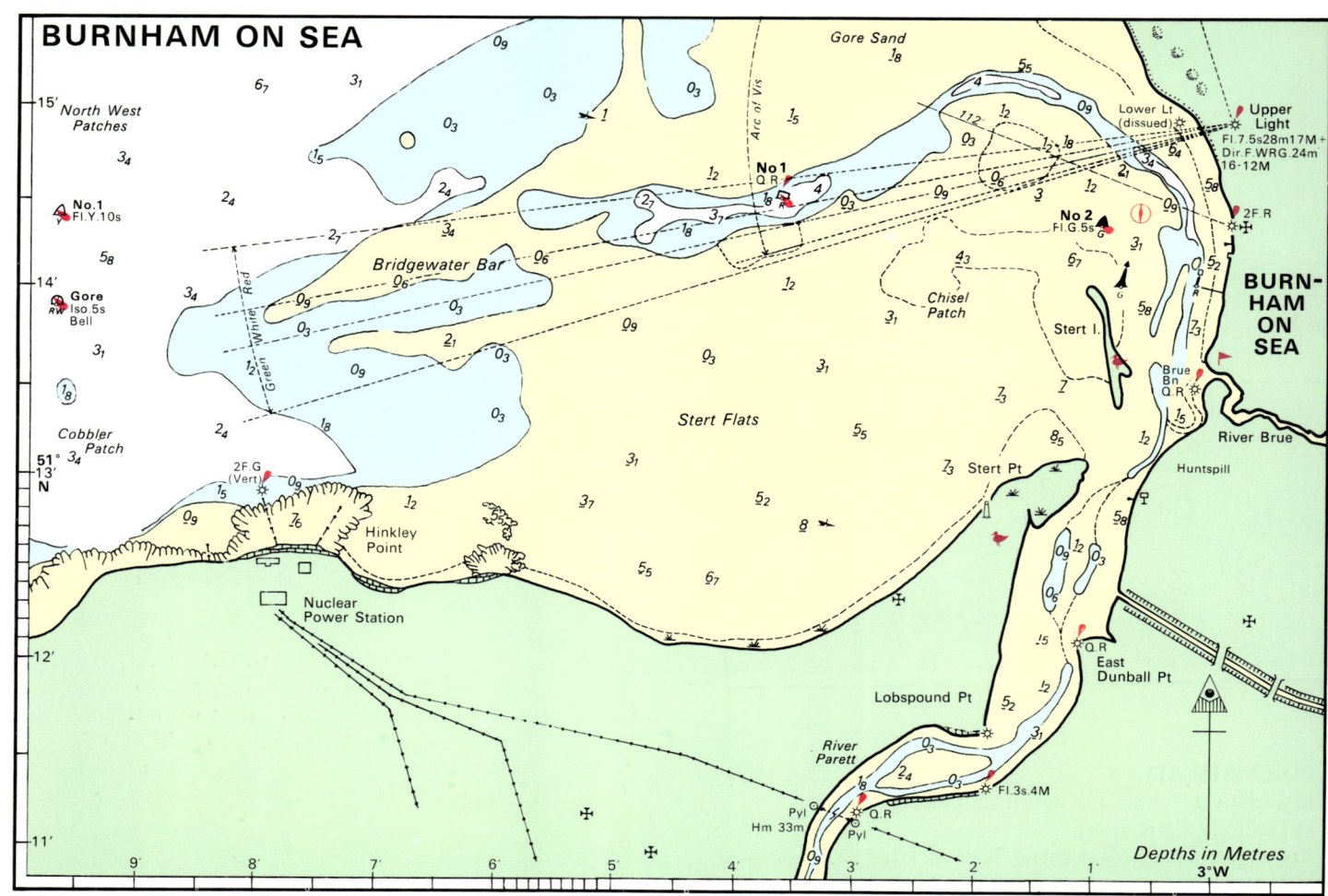

BURNHAM ON SEA   Chart BA 1152

HW: Dover −4½h. DS in offing: Dover −5h W
MHWS 10.9m   MHWN 8.1   MTL 5.2   MLWN 2.1   MLWS −0.2
Lies at the head of Bridgewater Bay. Shoals extend 5M out from the land which is flat and featureless except for Brent Knoll a conspic conical hill.

Bar Dries about 1m

Approach and Entrance From W approach Brent Knoll on an E bearing ½M S of the Gore RWVS sph buoy Iso 5s. Continue about E along buoyed channel. Buoyage is unreliable, particularly after heavy weather. No 4 R can buoy marks the swatchway through the Gore Sand to the N. The channel turns gradually to stb on nearing Burnham. From N and E within 2h of HW steering S and keeping an eye on the depth keep Flatholm Lt Ho on with the E end of Steepholm astern and cross the bank which dries about 2.4m then pass close to the buoy to join the former track.

By night steer in on the W sector of Burnham lt (077°-079°). All the buoys should be clear of the W sector. Continue until 2 R lts in line 112°. The front lt is on the esplanade (Daymark W vert stripe on sea wall) and rear lt on the SW corner of St Andrew's Ch Tr. Continue on lts until about 3ca from shore then turn S. A disused Lt Ho on piles on the foreshore painted W with R stripe is conspic by day and occasionally floodlit in summer. Anchor off Burnham or enter the R Brue, best at HW −2h when the banks will be seen. From No 9 buoy steer for Brue bn (RWHS pole). Ldg marks having B top marks will lead over the bar.

After half-flood craft drawing up to 1.8m have enough water over the sand to Burnham in moderate weather. In strong winds the whole area is a welter of broken water.

Berthing A yacht can lie afloat in 3m NW of Burnham. The bottom off Burnham is hard sand constantly shifting although there is a patch of mud between the N end of Stert Is and the shore. The R Brue dries but yachts may sit upright here in soft mud. The yard at Highbridge will assist visitors. All stores, fuel and facilities.

It is possible to go up the R Parrett to Dunball although there is no anchorage above Combwich where there is a small inlet accessible near HW. Yachts which can take the ground will find good shelter from W winds under Sterte Is or Pt.

WATCHET   Chart BA 1160

HW: Dover −5h. DS in offing: Dover −5h W.
MHWS 11.3m   MHWN 8.5   MTL 6.1   MLWN 3.6   MLWS 1.0
Available HW ±2h for av draught. The rks off the entrance dry ½M out.

Berthing Inside tie up alongside either breakwater, ground soft mud, and seek local advice. If early on the tide avoid fishing stakes. The hbr is used by small coasters. Land at either pier or slip.
A B ball on the W pier-head (FG at night) and 2 FR(vert) lts on the E pier indicate at least 2.4m on the flood, 3m on the ebb at hbr entrance. Hbr office keeps watch on VHF 12 14 and 16 from 2h before HW.
All facilities and stores. EC Wed.

MINEHEAD Chart BA 1160
HW: Dover −4¾h

Hbr is formed by a single pier curving E to SE and dries. It should not be approached earlier then HW −2½h when there is 2.1m of water at the hbr steps alongside the quay. No bar.

Approach From seaward if tide too low to enter, approach the W mark on shore abreast the hilltop 5ca E of Greenaleigh Pt and about 5ca NW of the column on the foundations of the old pier and anchor abreast the mark 2ca offshore in about 3½m. The column shows 3m above HW. If approaching from the E beware the Gables ridge extending 1M to the NW of Warren Pt.

Entrance From W round G stb hand bn with cone topmark Fl G 10s and then round the pier-head at least 10m off. Go slow as hbr crowded.

Berthing As directed or as space allows, alongside pier or other vessels. The bottom is an easy slope upwards from the entrance. HM (0643) 2566. All supplies. EC Wed.

PORLOCK WEIR Chart BA 1160
HW: Dover −5h

A delightful privately owned hbr in rural surroundings. Difficult and narrow entrance channel but safe once inside. Crowded in season. Contact HM first.

Entrance At the W end of Porlock Bay. The bar dries. The channel is about 15m wide between a pebble bank to stb and a timber piled wall to port. These are marked by G&W and R&W poles respectively. Channel available HW ±1h for 1.8m draft.

Berthing In small pool inside the entrance where 3 or 4 shallow draft boats can lie afloat otherwise inside the piers and dry out. Anchorage in Porlock Bay only in very settled conditions; holding poor except in patch of sand in line of thatched cottages to the E of the entrance channel.

Two pleasant hotels, stores on quayside. Bus to Minehead. HM Mr T Ridler in white cottage at E end of village opposite car park, (0643) 862106.

LUNDY ISLAND Chart BA 1164
HW: Dover −5½h.

MHWS 8.4m MHWN 5.9 MTL 4.3 MLWN 2.7 MLWS 0.8

DS In the vicinity clear of the land: Dover +½h ENE; −5½h WSW.

Approach Beware strong tidal races. On the E going stream a heavy race extends 1M N from the N end of the Is and 1½M E from Rat Is in the S. The White Horses race over Stanley Bank NE of the Is is severe and should be avoided. Similar races form during the W going stream extending 1M SW of Shutter Pt but that over Stanley Bank is less violent.

Anchorage The only reliable anchorage is that N of the SE point of the Is as far in as draught permits. In winds between NW and SSW the shelter is good even in gales owing to the height of the land but the anchorage is exposed to winds with any E. Good holding. It is a possible anchorage of refuge in an area with little shelter if caught out in heavy weather from the W.

In strong winds from the E or N some shelter will be found on the W or S side of the Is. Anchorage is just possible on the W side in about 10m.

From the normal anchorage in the SE part of the Is there is a landing place with a steep path and a rope to the top, or land on the beach and walk up the main track to top 145m. Landing may be difficult at HWS particularly in E or N winds even when light and in these circumstances care must be taken when returning by dinghy. Inn at top of track.

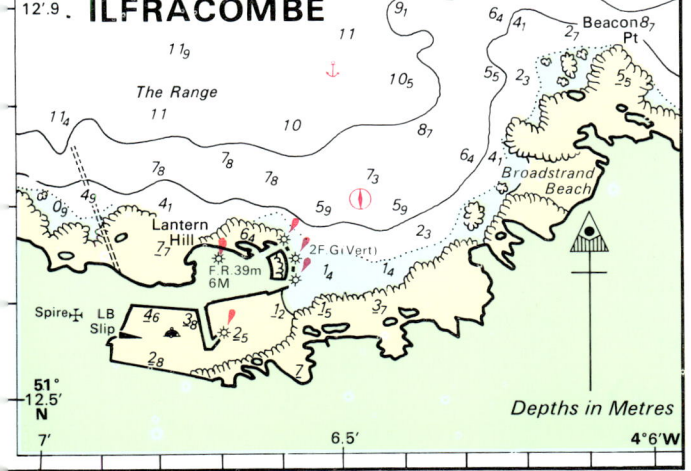

ILFRACOMBE Chart BA 1160
HW: Dover −5½h.

MHWS 9.2m MHWN 6.9 MTL 4.9 MLWN 3.0 MLWS 0.7

Half tide drying hbr, sandy bottom. There is about 1.8m along outer pier thence bottom shoals towards head of hbr. Outer hbr has 1.5 and 1.2m at 2h flood springs and neaps respectively. Ferry plies between hbr and Lundy Is and may return at HW day or night.

Berthing Go to the S side of the inner hbr for directions but do not anchor in line with the lifeboat slip. Water on pier and S side of inner hbr. Chandlery, diesel, marine engineer. Petrol 10 mins, stores 5 mins.

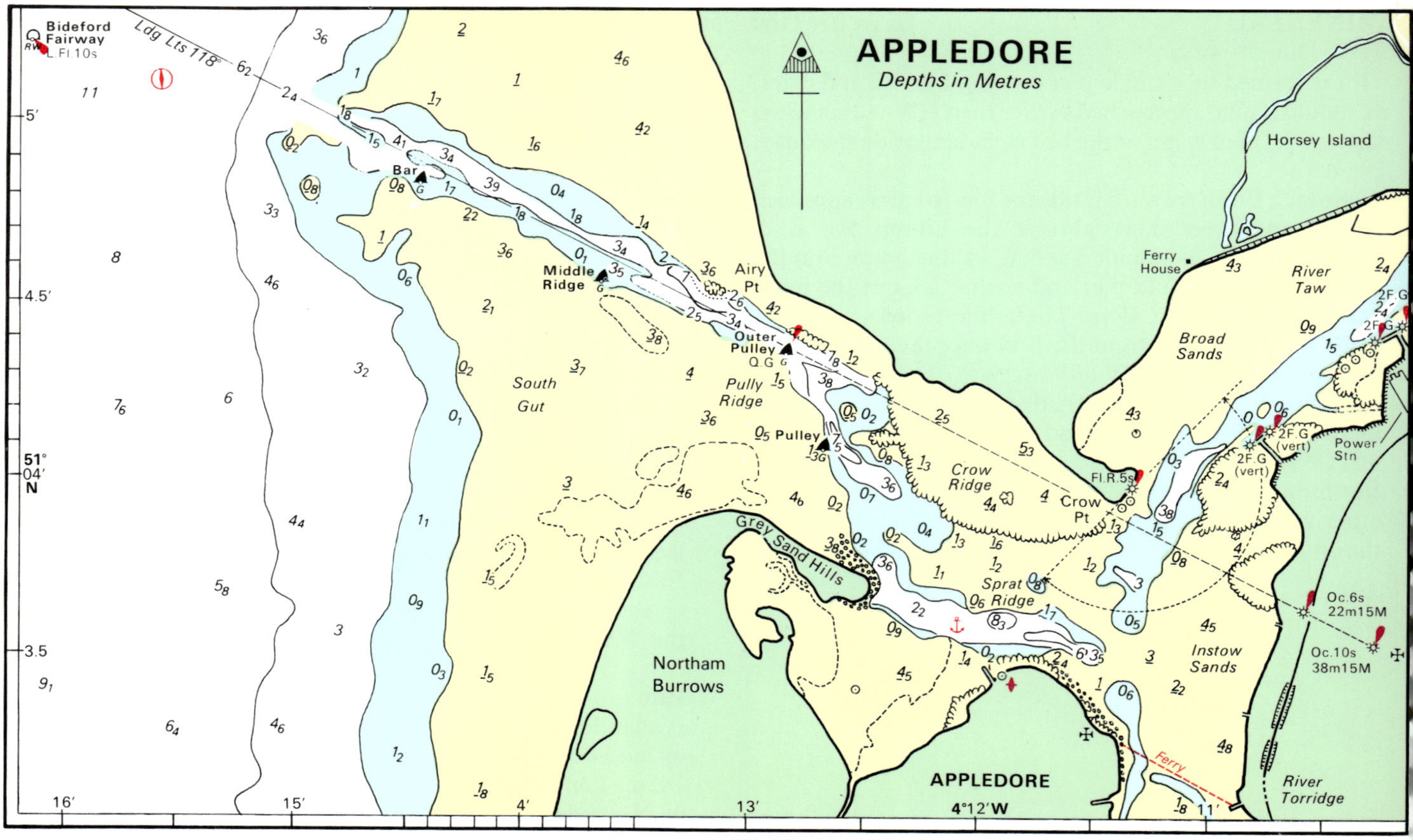

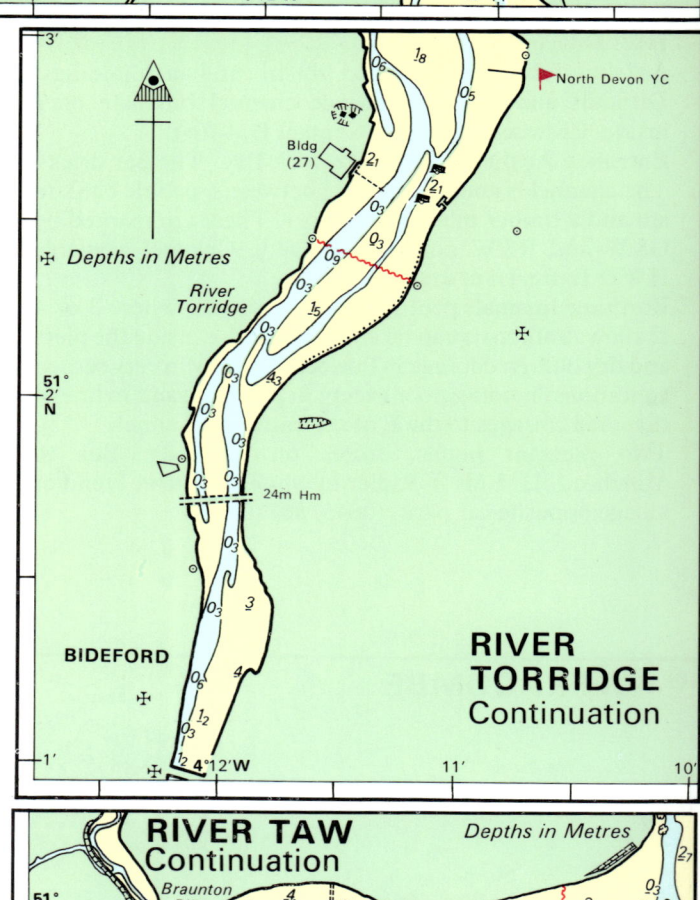

APPLEDORE Chart BA 1160

HW: Dover −5½h.

MHWS 7.5m MHWN 5.2 MTL 3.6 MLWN 1.6 MLWS 0.2

Bar Bideford bar has about 1m. It is dangerous if a heavy ground swell is running. Oc ldg lts are moved to suit the fairway. If a sea is running on the bar a good rise in tide should be awaited. Under bad conditions the entrance may be difficult and dangerous. The tide may be awaited in Clovelly Bay with wind S of W.

Approach In thick weather make Downend or Westward Ho! and thence shape a course for Bideford Fairway RWVS Sph buoy Fl 10s 3M NNW of Rock Nose, Westwood Ho! Thence make good 110° to pass Bar G con, then proceed on ldg line 118° leaving Middle Ridge and Outer Pulley G con buoys to stb. After passing Outer Pulley turn on to 160° to leave Pulley G con to stb and continue to SE end of Grey Sand Hills. Then steer 102° through Appledore Pool towards the lifeboat on a mooring buoy. After passing the slip on stb, watch out for three mooring buoys which may be partly submerged at HW.

Berthing Anchor close above or below the lifeboat and other two buoys in fine weather buoying the anchor. The stream runs strongly in this pool and is uncomfortable in N winds during early ebb. In that event better to anchor in the R Taw to NE with Crow Pt Lt Fl R 5s bearing 240° and Appledore Ch about 197° but holding only moderate. At a sufficient rise Appledore may be rounded to the S and a drying berth picked up on the mud S of the village above the shipyard or at Appledore quay.

BRAUNTON Anchor close inshore abreast the Ferry House on Broad Sands; a boat of 1.8m draft can berth in very soft sand. The vessel will make its own berth but care should be taken not to be neaped. The position is excellent if a few days' stay is desired but the berth should be located beforehand. Near midstream the sand is hard and anchor likely to drag.

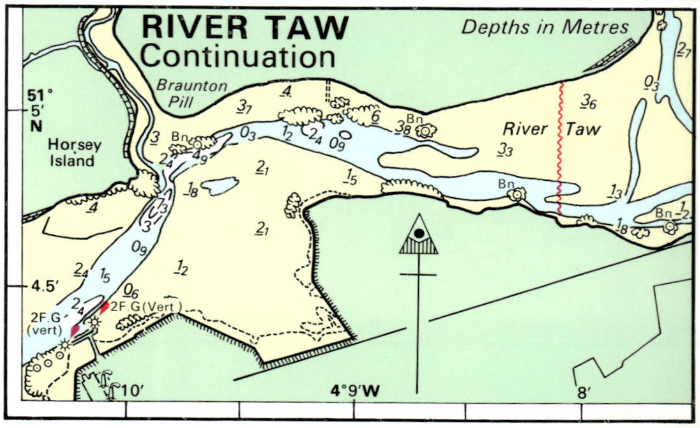

BIDEFORD The passage from Appledore to Bideford is easy for 1.8m draft from HW–2h. At Bideford anchor on sand in middle opposite the vertical section of the quay about ½ ca downstream from the br – legs needed.

BARNSTAPLE Pilots at Appledore. Approach only at HW and beware neaping. EC Wed.

BOSCASTLE
HW: Dover –5½h.
MHWS 7.3m MHWN 5.6 MTL 4.1 MLWN 2.7 MLWS 0.9
Approach only in fine settled weather. Essential to identify Meachard Rk before attempting to enter near HW. Narrow entrance with very sharp bend to stb. Berth against wall and dry out on hard sand over rk. Heavy bumping in any ground swell.

PADSTOW   Chart BA 1168
HW: Dover –6h.
MHWS 7.3m MHWN 5.6 MTL 4.1 MLWN 2.6 MLWS 0.8
Bar 1m at MLWS but liable to change. Do not attempt to cross Doom Bar at LW with any swell and entry inadvisable at any state of tide in strong NW winds.
Approach The only dangers in Padstow Bay are shoal patches of rk close E and W of the Newland Is. Stepper Pt, the W pt of the entrance has a lt L Fl 10s 12m 4M and also a daymark 12m high and 83m above sea level.
Entrance At HW sail in straight over Doom Bar leaving R can buoy Greenaway Fl(2) R 10s to port and G con Bar buoy Fl G 5s to stb. Make for R can Channel buoy FlR 5s at end of The Pool. If bound for hbr turn to stb as soon as the shore immediately beyond St Saviour's Pt opens thus leaving the Town spit to port. Turn into dock entrance lit 2 FG on N jetty and 2 FR on S. The channel up to Wadebridge has many bends and is available for 1.2m draft at MHWN.
Berthing Berth in inner hbr, lock gates open when water shows 3m at gate approx HW –1½/2h and close at HW + 1½/2h. Pick up buoy or tie up alongside moored boat in The Pool but do not anchor there. Room for visitors in dock. If anchoring do so out of the fairway taking the ground. All facilities and stores EC Wed.

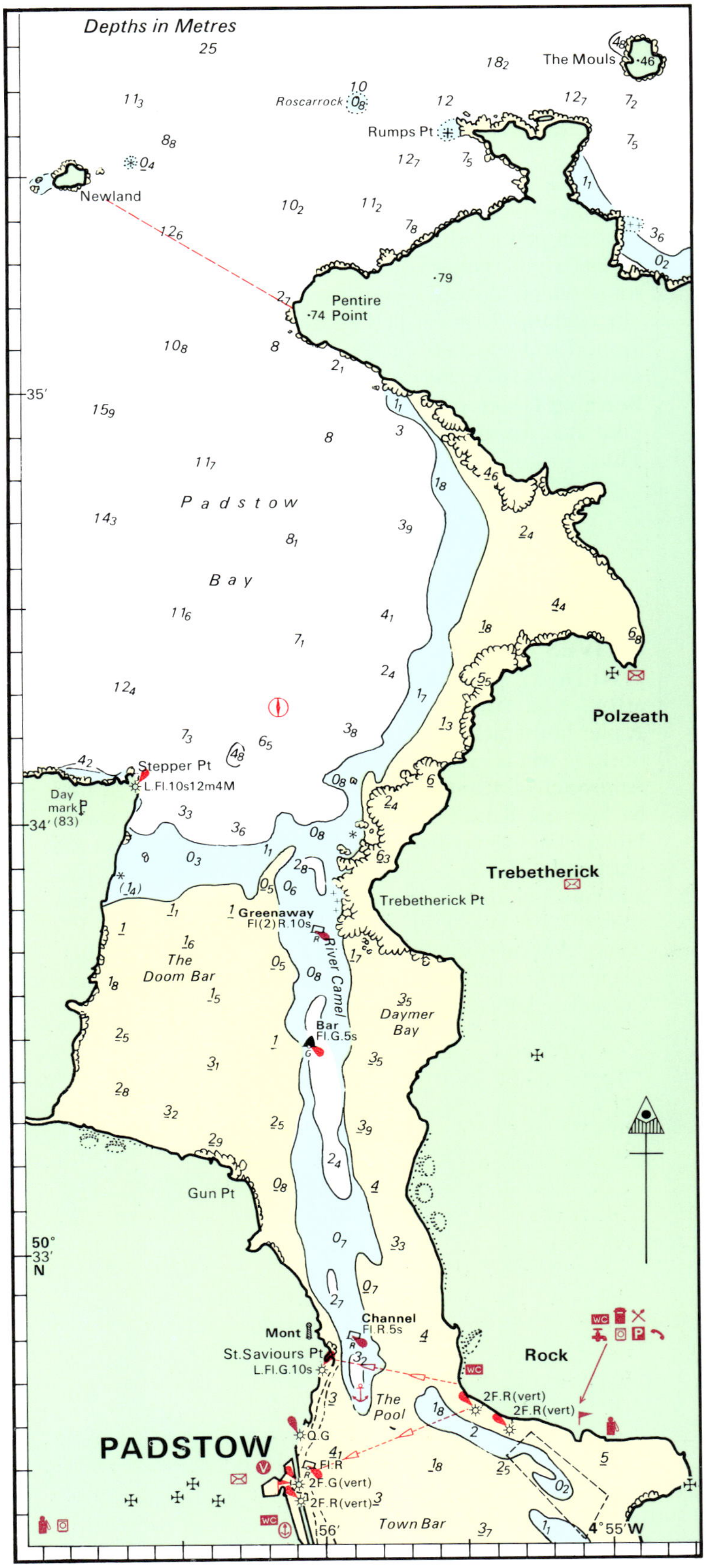

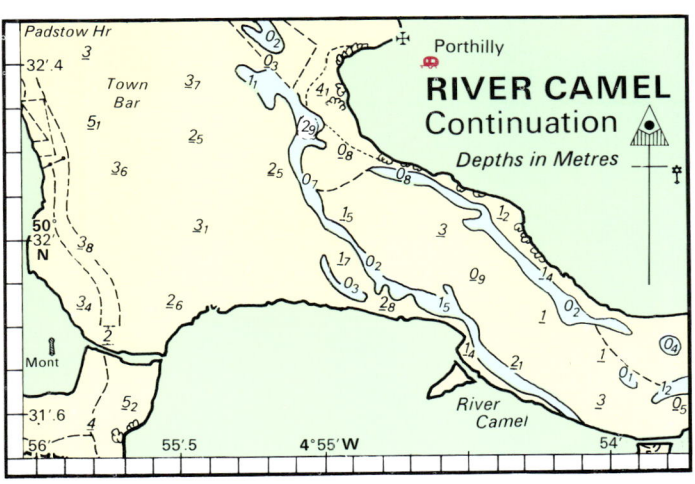

WEST COAST OF ENGLAND AND WALES 198

HAYLE
Chart BA 1168

HW: Dover −6h.
MHWS 6.6m MHWN 4.9 MTL 3.7 MLWN 2.4 MLWS 0.8

Bar Dries. Hbr dries out but affords complete shelter

Approach Accessible only in fine weather within 1h of HW.

Entrance The best water lies about 1½ca E of the line of the first 4 perches. Make to leave these to stb and pass 20m E of 5th perch. Alter course to stb and after passing 6th perch (tripod) below Chapel Anjou Pt identify the shingle shore which is steep to separating the R Hayle from the hbr channel. Leave 4 perches to port marking a middle ground and when abeam the last perch alter hard to port and then to stb to berth against quay.

Berthing Vessels dry at LW alongside quays. All facilities. Pilot may be signalled when passing St Ives. Rly. EC Thur.

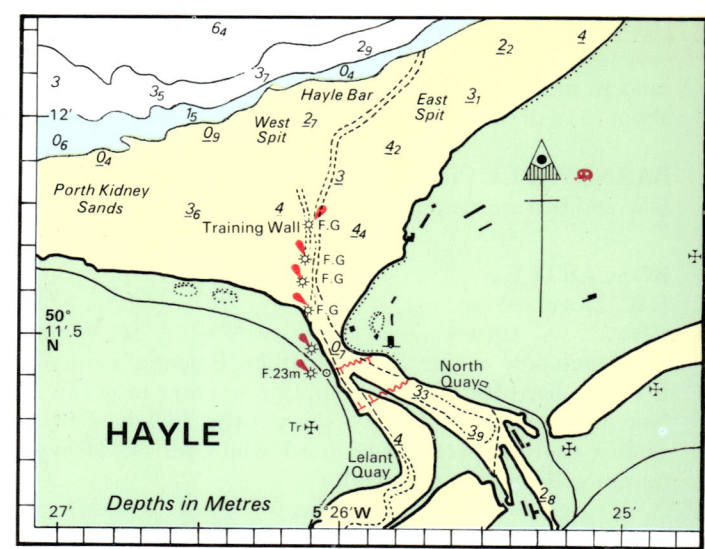

ST IVES
Chart BA 1168

HW: Dover −6h.
MHWS 6.6m MHWN 4.9 MTL 3.7 MLWN 2.4 MLWS 0.8

A pier hbr which dries 2m and is subject to heavy swell in onshore winds or continuous SW gales.

Approach and Entrance Hoe and Merran rks are cleared by keeping Knill's monument on with Tregenna Castle Hotel. The ruins of the end of the outer breakwater are marked by G con buoy. Round inner pier-head close to and moor alongside as convenient. At night the W pier shows 2 FR (vert) and the outer (Smeaton) pier 2 FG (vert). Alternatively in offshore winds anchor in 3m between the hbr and the Carracks, or in Carbis Bay S of the Carracks. All facilities. Rly. EC Thur.

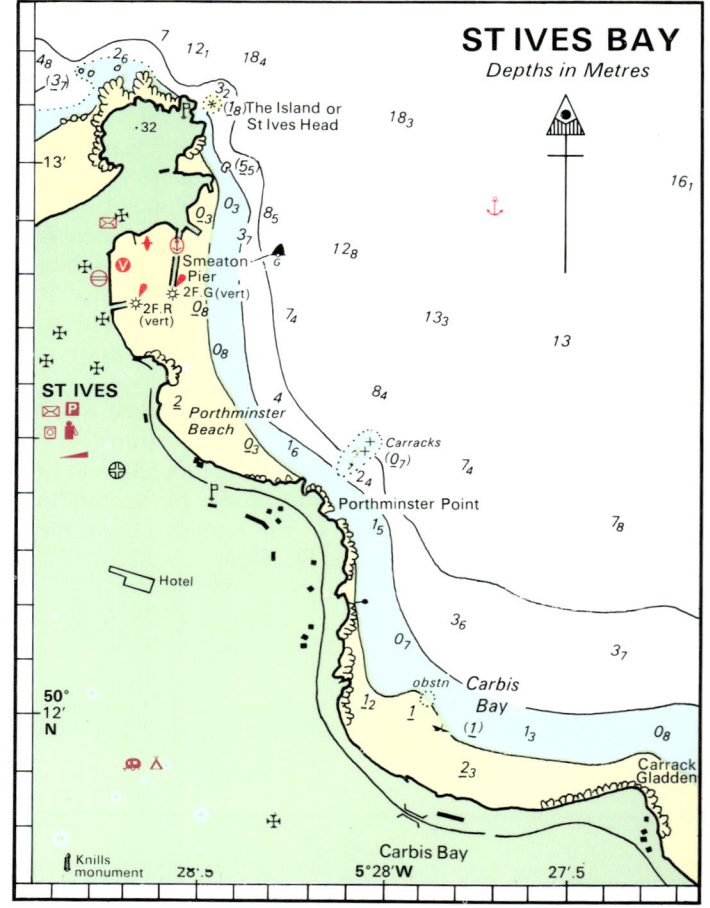

199 WEST COAST OF ENGLAND & WALES

ADMIRALTY CHARTS
and
Hydrographic Publications

The Hydrographic Department has been publishing charts and navigational publications for almost 200 years. To-day, a range of over 3000 charts provides world-wide coverage for all vessels from yachts to supertankers. Admiralty Notices to Mariners are issued weekly to allow chart users to incorporate the latest navigational information so vitally important to safety at sea.

ADMIRALTY CHARTS

Sailing directions (Pilots) · Radio Publications · Tidal Publications

Admiralty List of Lights · Admiralty Notices to Mariners Small Craft Edition

Admiralty charts and hydrographic publications are obtainable through an extensive network of appointed Admiralty Chart Agents in the British Isles and overseas.

ADMIRALTY PRODUCTS DESIGNED FOR THE SMALL CRAFT USER:
Tide Tables For Yachtsmen - 3 volumes covering various ports on the South Coast, in France and the Channel Islands.
NP159a - a version of Tidal Prediction by the Simplified Harmonic Method, for use on a home computer.
NEW FOR 1992 - Small Craft Editions of Admiralty Charts.
NOW ALSO AVAILABLE FROM GOOD CHANDLERS

HYDROGRAPHIC DEPARTMENT, TAUNTON, SOMERSET TA1 2DN
Telephone: Taunton (0823) 337900   Telex: 46274

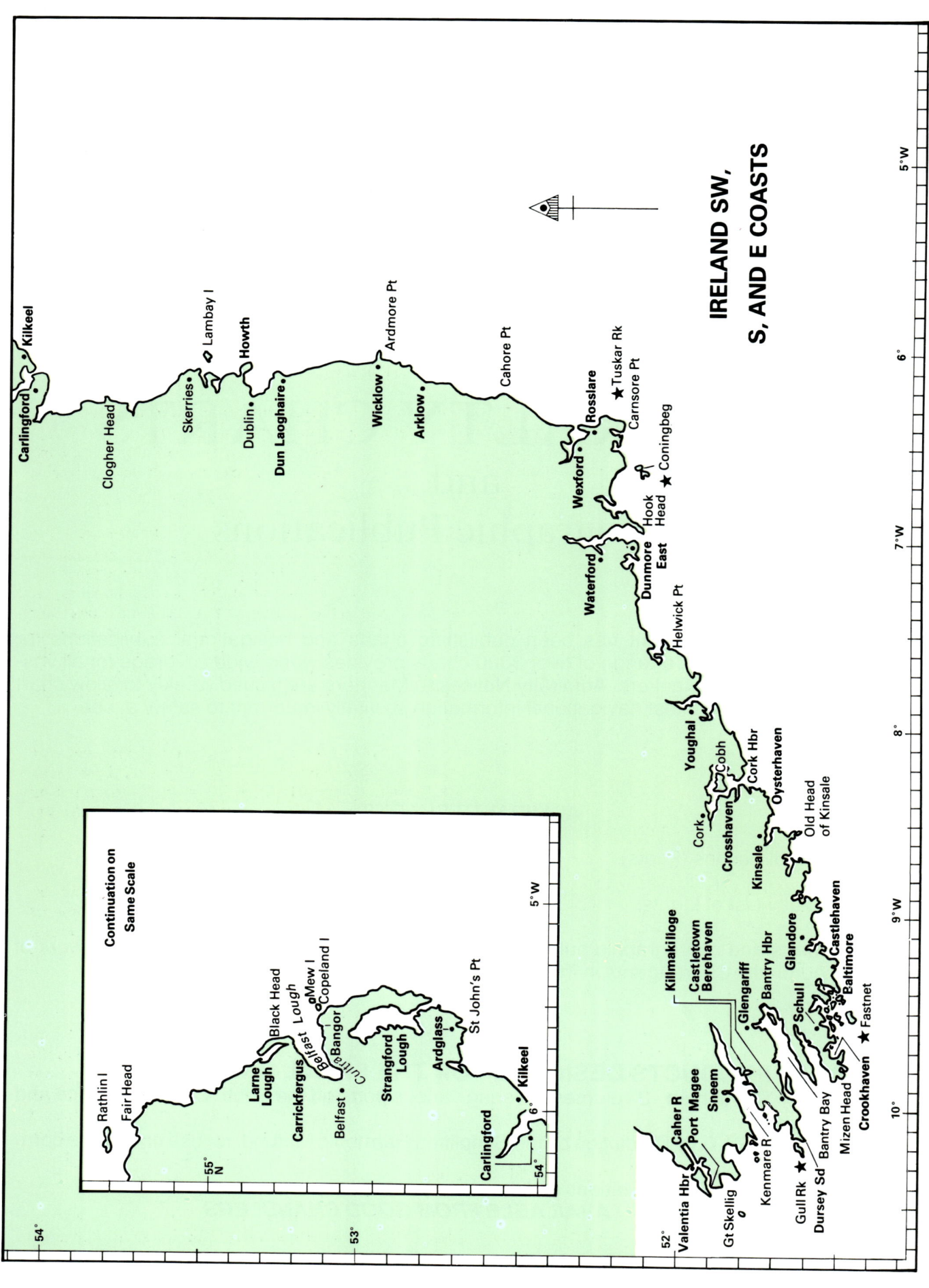

IRELAND

Yachtsmen cruising to Ireland (certainly for anything more than a fleeting visit) are recommended to obtain the Irish Cruising Club Sailing Directions (referred to below as ICC). They are published in two volumes, one for the South and West Coasts and one for the East and North, and are obtainable from Mrs. Barbara Fox-Mills, The Tansey, Baily, Co. Dublin, Eire and also from nautical booksellers. Corrections are published annually.

This section of the handbook covers the whole of the Coast of Ireland and gives directions for entering 50 anchorages together with their facilities, The ICC publications, of course, cover the area in much greater detail and mention all anchorages known to yachtsmen, many of which are remote, secluded and sometimes difficult to find but very rewarding. ICC contain further information and covers many additional harbours and anchorages, of which a few are mentioned below. The BA Irish Coast Pilot N P 40 12th Edition 1985 (supplement 1987) is also useful.

Weather forecasts for Irish coastal waters are broadcast four times daily by Radio Eireann on 567 and 729 kHz at 0630, 1155, 1755 and 2352 hours BST. There are also transmissions from Cork and Valentia on VHF giving forecasts about every four hours. These are often more accurate than the BBC forecasts covering areas extending further to seaward. The BBC forecasts are, however, essential for tracking incoming weather.

Warnings

Nets Salmon drift nets may be found all along the S, N and W coasts, often extending ½M to 2M in length. Frequently a fishing boat will mark one end, usually inshore, and a buoy the other, but sometimes there is no boat and the net is only marked by two buoys. They occur most frequently on the Connemara and Mayo coasts. Most nets are taken in at night, but some may be left out. They are a serious danger to yachts under power, which should always keep a sharp lookout for them, particularly approaching a bay or estuary. Yachts with unprotected rudders might consider carrying a stout pole with a Y end or a suitable fitting for the spinnaker boom. This danger makes it inadvisable to cruise near the coast at night. Furthermore there is no apparent "close season".

Lights Another reason for avoiding making smaller ports by night is that the lesser navigational lights, which are operated and maintained by the local authorities, have all too frequently been reported as not showing.

Gas Calor (Kosan) gas, though widely available, now comes in yellow containers different from the usual 10lb containers supplied in Britain. Though still holding 10lb the container is about 5in taller when fitted with the supply tube, wider at the base and may not fit into existing gas lockers. It has a different connection which is provided for no extra change if a British-type container is exchanged for the Irish container. Your own Calor Gas containers can be refilled while you wait at the Whitegate Gas Depot on the SE side of Cork Harbour. Standard Calor containers are available in Northern Ireland. Camping Gaz is widely available.

Safety In recent years some yachts and fishing boats have been damaged or sunk by submarines in the course of surfacing. As a submarine is visually blind until it actually raises its periscope, this is its most vunerable manoeuvre as far as small boats are concerned. However, modern submarines have a very wide range of active and passive sensors which can "see" all types of noises and electronic transmissions, it therefore follows that vessels which are stopped in the water without engines running or underway with sails only, may not be "seen" by submerged craft. A good protection for such situations is to switch on your echo sounder when passage making in deep water.

Submarines of all nationalities are about the coasts in the deep water areas, and there is a large area of the Firth of Clyde and N. Channel designated on the Admiralty Charts as a Submarine Exercise Area in which particular care should be taken.

Customs The international boundary line between the Republic of Ireland (Eire) and Northern Ireland is at the inner end of Carlingford Lough and again at the inner end of Lough Foyle. It is marked on the charts. Skippers should report to the Customs authorities at their next port of call after crossing the seaward extension of the boundary. Fly Q flag, if no customs are immediately available, report by phone to the nearest police station - Garda in the Republic and RUC in Northern Ireland. Courtesy ensigns are customary.

Naval Patrol Off the cost of Northern Ireland there are a small number of Royal Naval Patrol vessels, these are on anti-terriorist duties. If sighted you should listen out on VHF 16 and obey any instructions. Sometimes yachts are boarded but more frequently it is only an enquiry of your last and next ports of call.

Long term laying up Owners wishing to leave or lay up their vessels in the Republic for periods of over 6 months should contact the Value Added Tax authorities in Dublin Castle, Dublin 1, in order to obtain a copy of current regulations.

Hydrographic Surveys Very little surveying of the coast of the Republic of Ireland has been done since 1914. In fact many of the surveys date back to the latter part of the last century. Yachtsmen are particularly warned about depths of water in river estuaries and of sandy bays where considerably less water than shown on the charts, even if they are metric, may be encountered. Tidal information on the West Coast is incomplete and in some places unreliable.

IALA Buoyage The whole coast of Ireland is now completely converted to the standard IALA system. The Commissioners of Irish Lights are responsible for all seaward navigational marks and lights, in common with their opposite numbers in Great Britain. An increasing number of lights have a reduced range and fog signals are being discontinued.

IRELAND, SOUTHWEST COAST

PASSAGE NOTES: VALENTIA TO CROOKHAVEN

Passage Lights
- Skelligs Rk   Fl(3) 10s 53m 27M
- Bull Rk   Fl 15s 83m 31M
- Sheep Hd   Fl(2) WR 15s 83m 18/15M
- Mizen Hd   Iso 4s 52m 16M

Direction of tidal streams (all related to Dover) between Skelligs and the shores +5½h S, −¾h N; between Bull Rock and Dursey Hd +2¾h S, −3¼h N.

Dursey Sound is a useful channel between Dursey Is and the mainland, but the tides run up to 4kn. DS: Dover +1¾h S; −4¼h N. Pass very close to the island side.

In the Kenmare R above Sneem watch out for Maiden Rk in the middle, awash at LWS, marked by stb buoy (G con) 3 ca N of rk.

Between Three Castle Hd and Mizen Hd the streams run S and NW to N, becoming E and W between Mizen Hd and Crookhaven; Dover +1½h S and E and −4½h N and W. Off Mizen Hd the spring rate is 4kn, and off Three Castle Hd 3kn decreasing to 1.5kn when 4 to 5M offshore. The race off Mizen Hd can be dangerous and may extend to Three Castle Hd; on S and E-going stream it extends SE in a crescent. If caught in the race steer straight out to sea, then parallel to the edge of rough water.

VALENTIA   Chart BA 2125

HW: Dover (Knights Town) +5½h. DS Dover: −1h S; +5h N.

MHWS 3.8m   MHWN 3.0   MTL 2.1   MLWN 1.2   MLWS 0.5

The hbr affords shelter in all winds and may be entered from the NW at all states of the tide (exposed in NW gales), and, with sufficient rise, from SW through Portmagee channel. This has a bridge with opening span.

Bar By NW entrance: the Cromwell Pt entrance has 7m on the ldg line. The Doulus bar has 3m. By SW: until inside Reencaheragh Pt there is 8m; entrance channel 2m.

Approach NW entrance: make Doulus Hd, avoiding the Coastguard patch in severe conditions.

Entrance Having located Fort Pt, Fl WR 2s, bring W bns in line 141° or keep in W sector (141°-142°) of lt Oc WRG 4s leaving Harbour Rk bn Fl(3) 10s to stb, and thence to anchorage as convenient, avoiding the Caher bar between E end of Beginish Is and Reenard Pt near LW.

Anchorages In N winds, good anchorage off SE bight of Beginish Is, in 2 to 8m; or, according to wind, off Knights Town to S of jetty, or S of Reenard Pt, or as convenient in Portmagee channel. There is a pier at Reenard Pt with 3m on the SE side.

Caution Do not anchor S or W of the pecked lines S of Knights Town owing to telegraph cables.

CAHER RIVER (Valentia River)

If proceeding to Caherciveen enter over Doulus bar, 3m, leaving Doulus Rks to stb and Kay Rk to port, thence SSE passing a full ca from E end of Beginish. From the hbr, cross Caher bar, 0.3 to 1m, then close the S shore of the river till Ballycarberry castle comes abeam, then work towards N shore gradually till Caherciveen barracks open and proceed in midstream to the quay at Caherciveen. There is a series of five ldg lines up the Caher River, FG lts on rather inconspic telephone-type poles. It is essential to use these ldg marks. Streams run fast at springs. If lying afloat at Caherciveen it is not possible to berth clear of the current.

Supplies at Knights Town, limited to bread, some general stores and fuel. Water on quay at Reenard Pt. Beginish Is, farm produce and home-made bread. Caherciveen, all requirements.

PORTMAGEE   Chart BA 2125

Approach Entrance inadvisable in heavy weather owing to violence of sea under Bray Hd and baffling winds. No dangers in approach.

Entrance In strong SW winds the N entrance should be used. For 1¼M inside Reencaheragh Pt, navigation requires great care and the chart should be studied carefully.

Anchorage Below the bridge off the pier in 5m. To proceed through the bridge and through the 1m chan beyond, seek local advice. Bridge opening may or may not be possible. Consult the postmaster, tel Portmagee 1.

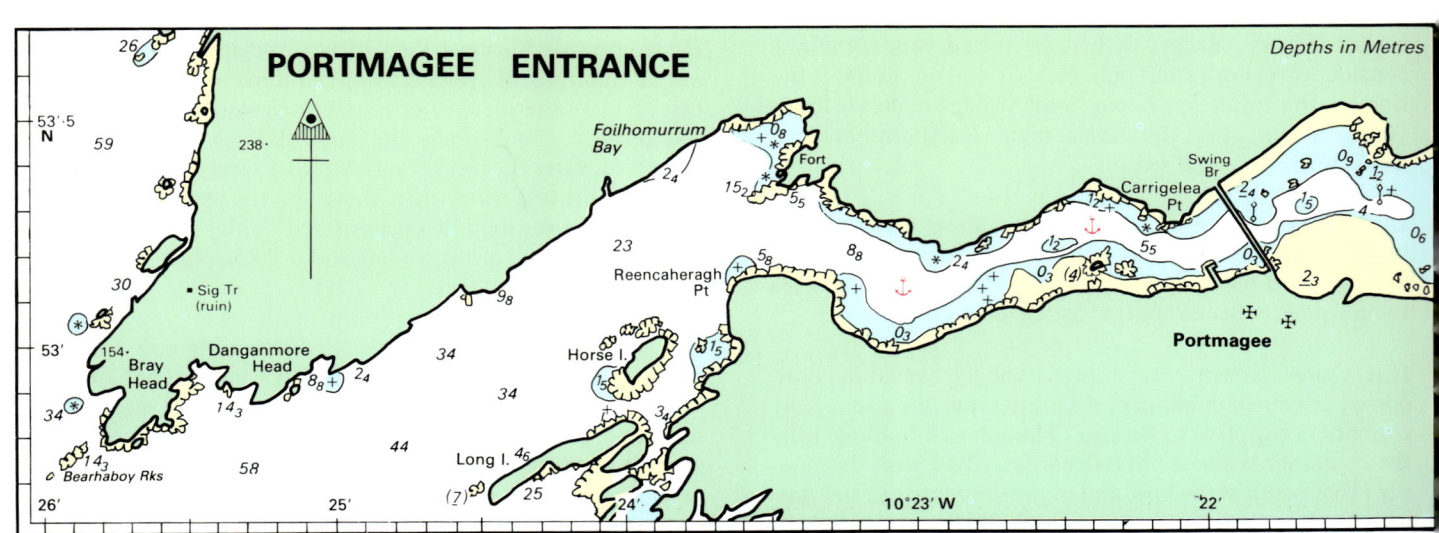

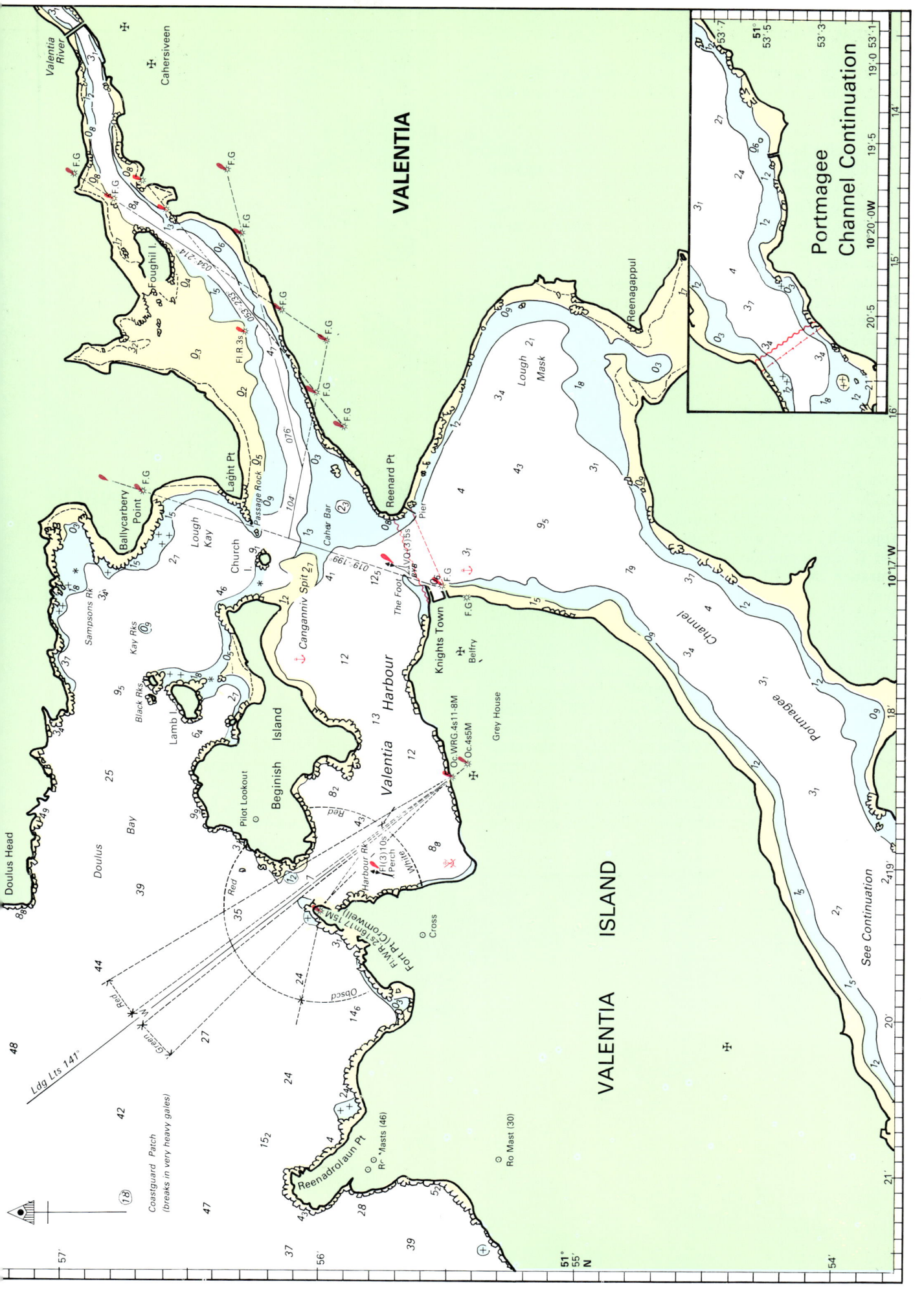

SNEEM
Chart BA 2495
HW: Dover +5¾h.
MHWS 3.5m   MHWN 2.8   MTL 2.0   MLWN 1.2   MLWS 0.5

A small hbr on N side of the Kenmare R opposite Kilmakilloge; affords anchorage for small craft in 3 to 6m and upwards; a very beautiful anchorage.

Approach Close with the SE side of Sherky Is. To pass inside Sherky Is and avoid Cottoner Rk (dries 0.3m), keep nearer to Pigeon Is to port than to Sherky Is.

Entrance Hence steer 013° on the hotel. When well past the third Is, Inishkeragh, steer 318° on the NE extreme of Garinish Is, leaving it close to port.

Anchorage In 6m between Goat Is and the pier, or in 3m inside the bay at the NE end of Garinish known as "The Bag" but beware of mooring cables on bottom.

All necessities from Sneem, 2M but only accessible at half-flood by dinghy. Water at Parknasilla Hotel.

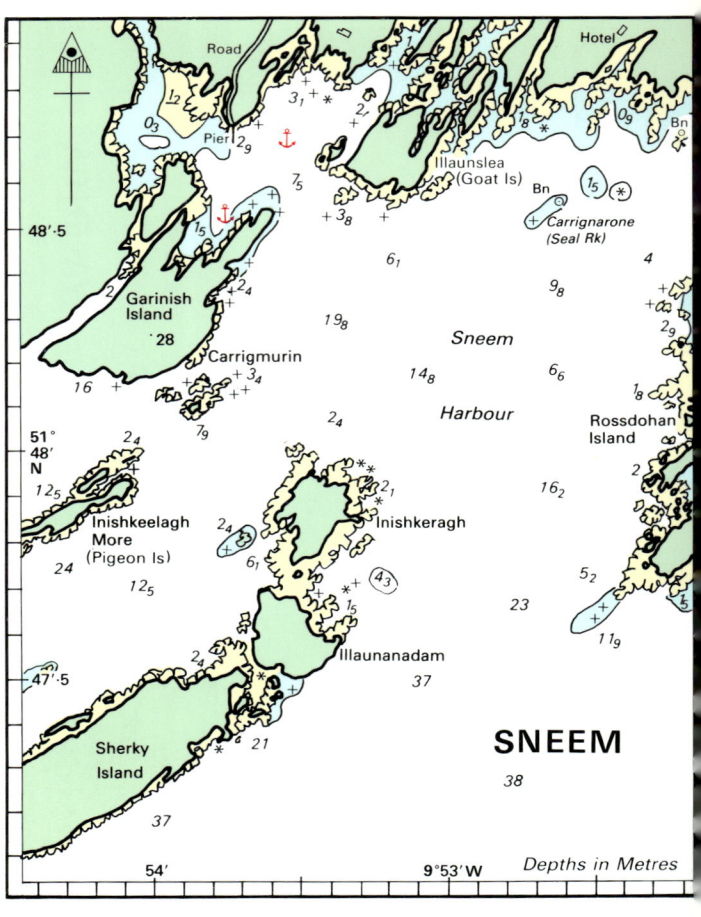

KILMAKILLOGE
Chart BA 2495
HW: Dover +5½h.
MHWS 3.5m   MHWN 2.8   MTL 2.0   MLWN 1.2   MLWS 0.5

Inside Kilmakilloge, there are three separate hbrs. Kilmakilloge, Bunaw and Collorus.

Approach From E give Laughan Pt a berth of over 2½ca; give W side of entrance a berth of 1½ca.

Entrance Book Rk, awash at LW, extends 3 ca off E shore, near a grassy precipice 53m high; off Collorus Pt on W side dangers extend 1½ ca. Enter on mid-channel course steering slightly W of Spanish Is. Thence according to anchorage.

Anchorage (1) For Kilmakilloge hbr, once past Collorus Pt alter course to 102° for the woods near Dereen Ho. Anchor in 4m SW of Yellow Rk, awash at HW. Landing at Dereen, shop 1½M E at Lauragh. Good pub lunches.

(2) For Collorus hbr, round Collorus Pt keeping a good ca off, and passing between the Pt and Spanish Is slightly nearer the former. Anchorage in middle of hbr in 5m; holding soft with kelp and unreliable. Look out for oyster fishing rafts. No shops, but some provisions might be obtained from farms.

(3) Bunaw hbr, on NE side of entrance, is entered through channel 1 ca wide between unmarked rks, with pier-head bearing 041°. There are B & Y poles with Y ldg lts on this bearing: front lt on pier-head. Anchor on ldg line in 4 to 6m. Limited stores and water available. There are numerous shrimp pots all over the hbr. Good pub.

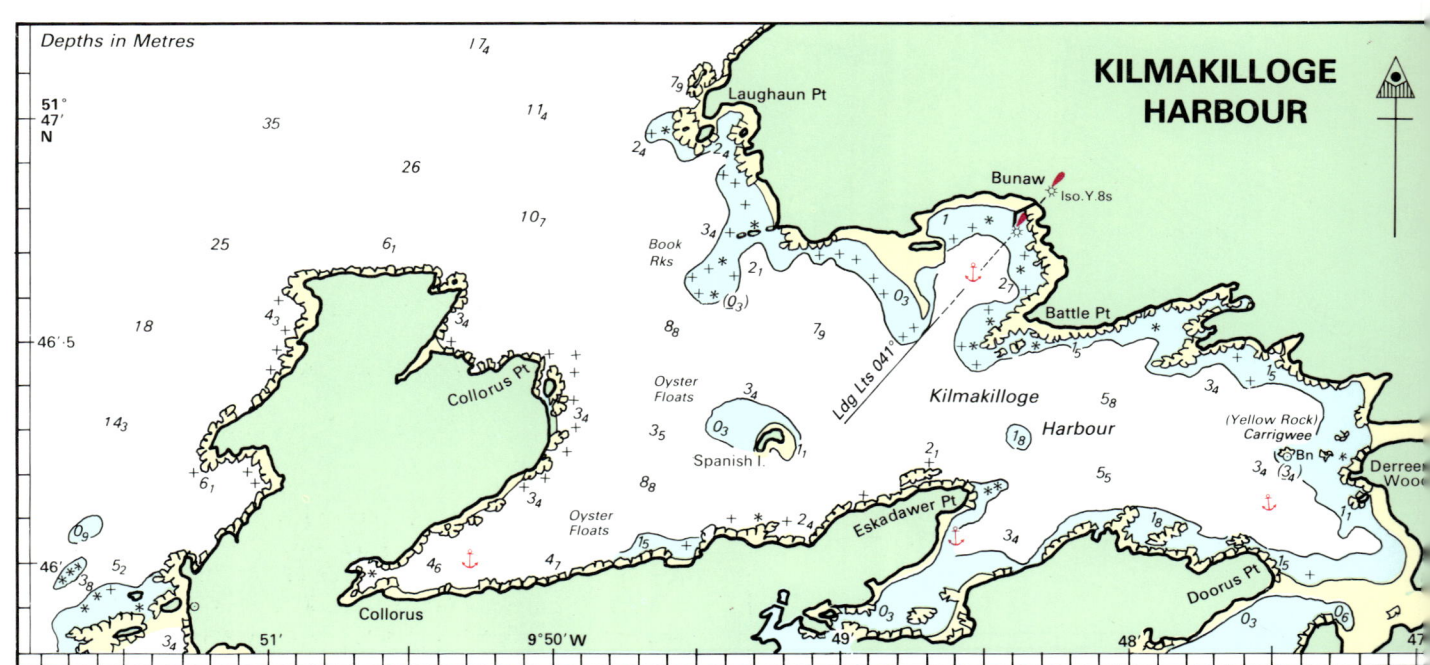

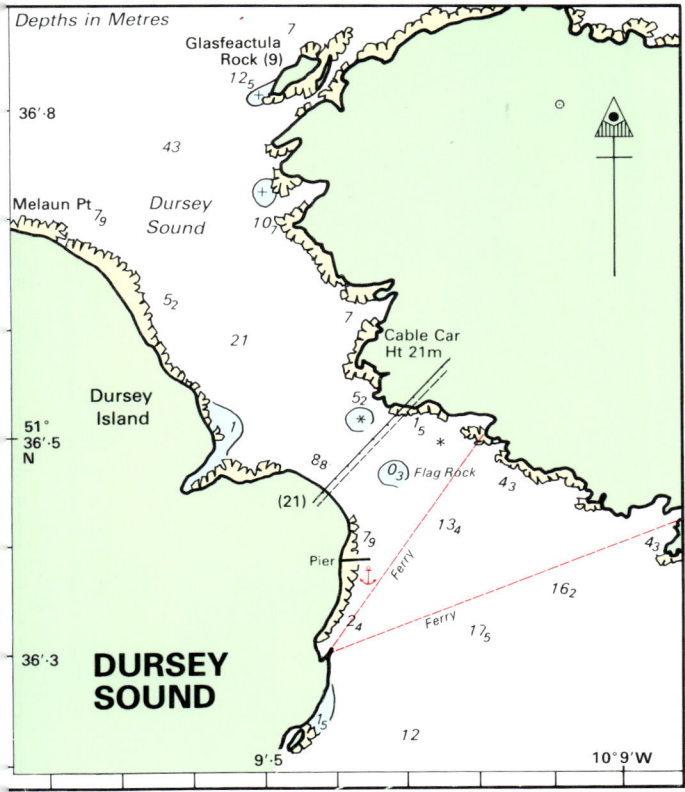

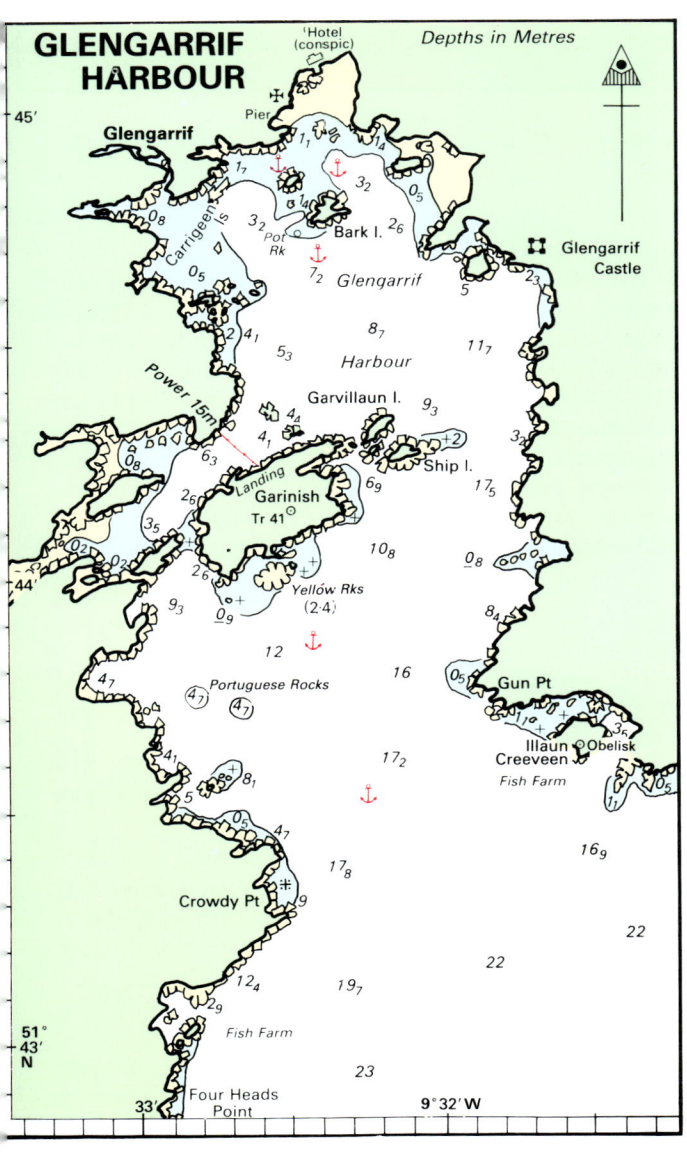

DURSEY SOUND

Tidal Stream: Dover −4¼h N going, +1¾h S going. Spring rate 4 kn with overfalls. It can be even more swift close to the shore on the spring stream. There are eddies on both sides of the S entrance during S-going stream. This is a narrow and useful channel between Dursey Island and the mainland. It is advisable to go through with a favourable tide or at least before it reaches its maximum rate. Entering the sound from the S a peculiarity about which strangers should be forewarned is that having rounded Crow Head the bay presents the appearance of a cul-de-sac as the similarity of colour of the island and the mainland shores prevents contrast where they overlap. There is a temporary anchorage off the pier on the E side of Dursay Is while waiting for the tide.

Having cleared the Bull's Forehead off Crow Head steer for Illanebeg on the island shore. Look out for lobster pots SW of the entrance. Keep very close to the island shore going through the narrows which are only 1 ca wide. Flag Rock with only 0.3m over it at LW lies almost in mid-channel in the narrowest part of the sound, thus limiting the navigable part to 90m. The N-going tide sets directly on to the rock. There is deep water close to the shore of the island so a yacht should keep very close in. The E extremity of Scariff Island in line with the E shore of the island, 339° leads W of the 0.3m rock. Note that Scariff Island, 252m, and Deenish Island, 141m, are the same shape viewed from the S. There is a cable car across the sound also a telephone wire; the least clearance at HWS is 21m under the car itself with 24m under the cables and 26m under the telephone wires. There is usually a disturbed sea at the N entrance which can become dangerous in strong to gale force N/NW winds. The sea rebounds from the cliffs of Glasfeactula Rk, 9m high, at the E side of the N entrance. Quite frequently a different wind is met on either side of the sound. Be prepared for sudden changes in wind direction going through the sound; especially near the N entrance where heavy squalls from the high ground may be met. Salmon nets may be just N of the N entrance and it would be very dangerous to foul one.

GLENGARIFF Chart BA 1838

HW: Dover (Bantry) +6h

MHWS 3.4m MHWN 2.6 MTL 1.9 MLWN 1.2 MLWS 0.5

The hbr is situated at the E end of Bantry Bay and affords complete shelter in beautiful surroundings.

Approach Leave Corrid Pt (Four Heads Pt) about 3 ca to W and steer 015°, leaving Gun Pt a short ca to E.

Entrance Give the inlet to NE within the Pt a sufficient berth to clear a patch of rks extending 1.5 ca from its hd. Continue 015° within ¾ca of the E side, leaving Ship Is and rks extending E of it well to port. There is an uncharted patch of rk, having 3m at MLWS, 30m E of Ship Rks.

Anchorages (1) S of Bark Is. This anchorage may have oyster rafts in it.
(2) NE of Bark Is.
(3) For yachts of less than 1.8m draft, close to wooden pier N of Carrigeen Is. Pier has 1m LWS. Holding in latter two unreliable. There is a wide choice of other anchorages.

Note The iron post of Pot Rock SW of Bark Is is missing. Water on pier, PO, tel, bread, petrol and good small shops in Glengariff village. Bus to Cork via Bantry.

IRELAND 206

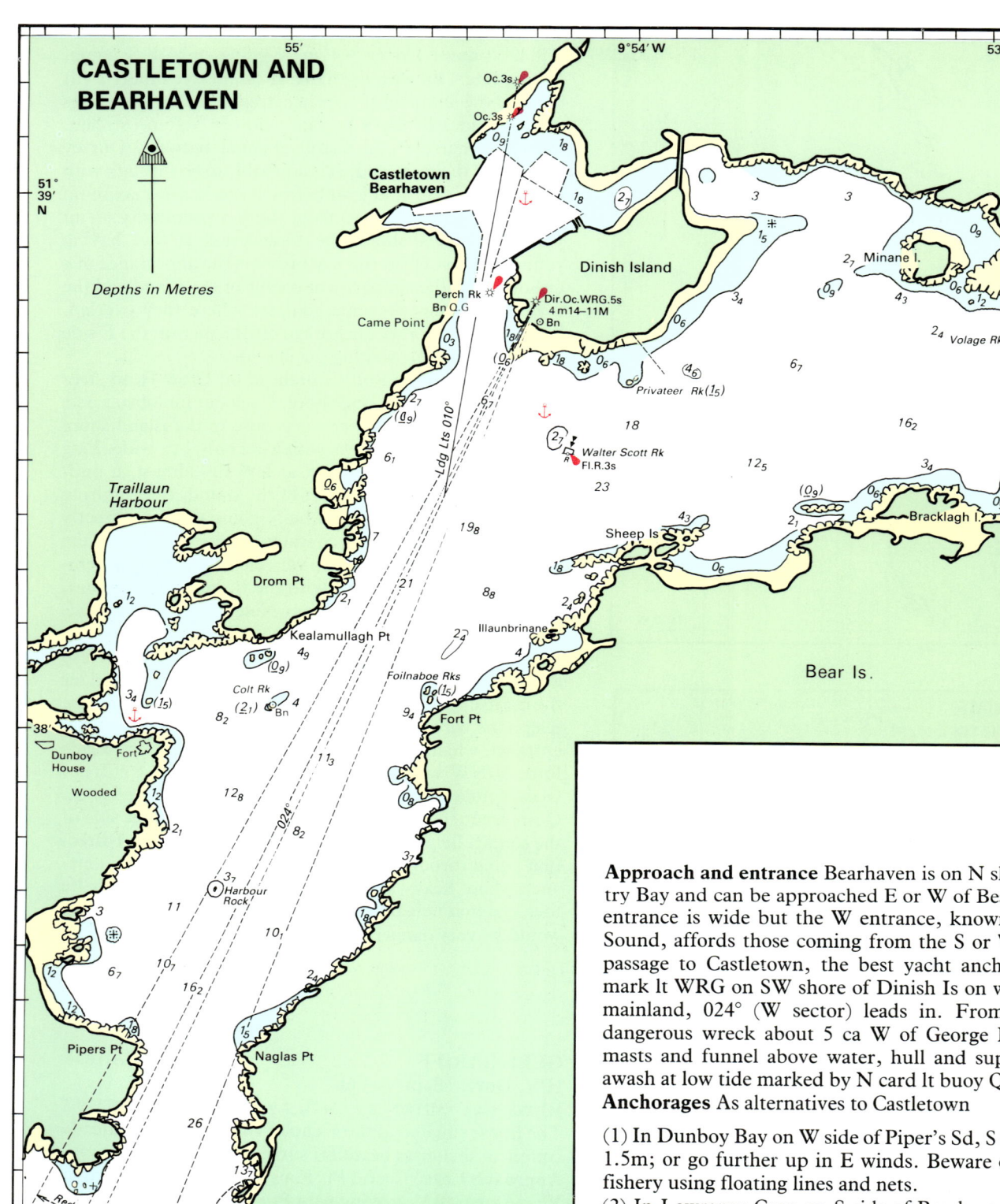

Approach and entrance Bearhaven is on N shore of Bantry Bay and can be approached E or W of Bear Is. The E entrance is wide but the W entrance, known as Piper's Sound, affords those coming from the S or W a shorter passage to Castletown, the best yacht anchorage. Ldg mark lt WRG on SW shore of Dinish Is on with a bn on mainland, 024° (W sector) leads in. From E beware dangerous wreck about 5 ca W of George Rock buoy, masts and funnel above water, hull and superstructure awash at low tide marked by N card lt buoy Q.

Anchorages As alternatives to Castletown

(1) In Dunboy Bay on W side of Piper's Sd, S of rk drying 1.5m; or go further up in E winds. Beware of an oyster fishery using floating lines and nets.
(2) In Lawrence Cove on S side of Bearhaven; sheltered except in N winds. (To E of end of plan on Bear Is.). Very pretty, soft mud bottom, no facilities.

CASTLETOWN　　　　　　　　　　　　　Chart BA 1840

Bar 3m W of Dinish Is.

Entrance The entrance channel is less than 50m wide abreast Came Pt immediately W of Perch Rk marked by G lt bn QG. Keep a little closer to this bn than to W shore. Ldg lts in line 012° on R marks with W stripe lead through the channel: rear Iso G 2s, front QG.

Berthing (1) Anchor in part dredged to 2.4m, or in a S blow closer to Dinish Is but clear of harbour works.
(2) A berth may be available at W end of Quay (alongside a fishing boat) or at NE end: avoid central part. Water on quay. Petrol and diesel, shops, hotels, banks, PO.

BEARHAVEN　　　　　　　　　　　　　Chart BA 1840

HW: Dover +6h

MHWS 3.5m　MHWN 2.7　MTL 2.0　MLWN 1.2　MLWS 0.5
Stream in offing is negligible. In entrance at HWD tide floods, from +6¼h ebbs, max rate 2kn.

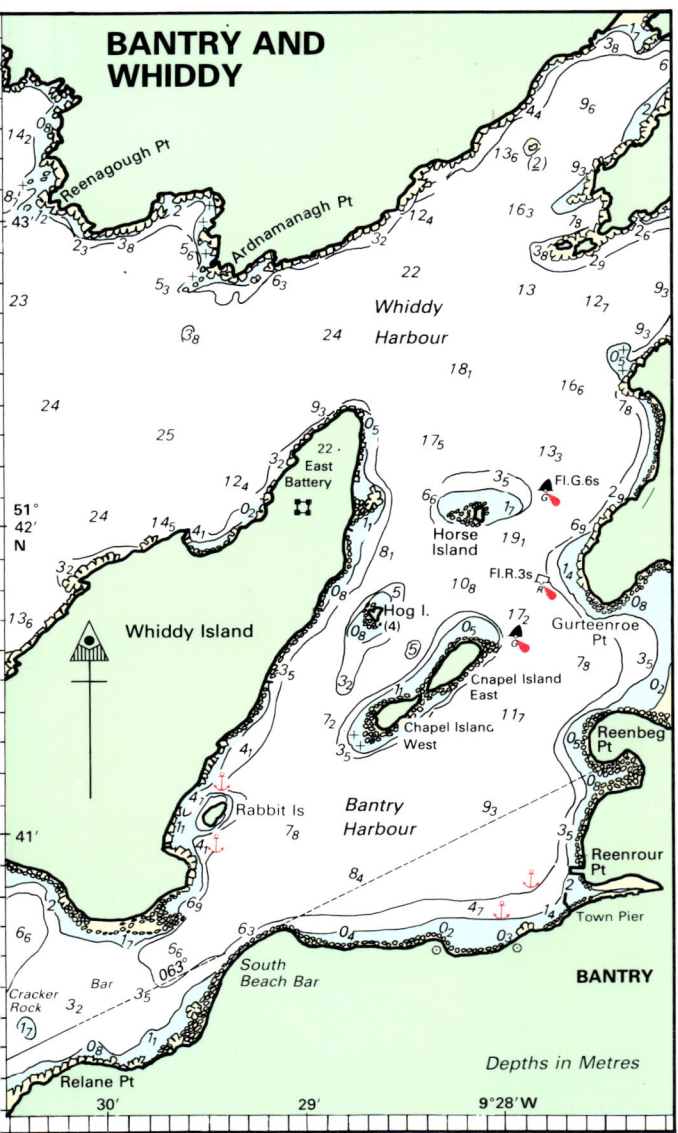

Mussel farming has started in the hbr. Rafts may be encountered in the area E of Whiddy Is, particularly outside the main buoyed channel, and sometimes quite close to it. They are low, unmarked and sometimes hard to see. Most are floating structures but some are lines of barrels. They can be moored in strings. Do not pass close as floating mooring lines may extend some distance.

IRELAND, SOUTH COAST

PASSAGE NOTES: CROOKHAVEN TO CORK
Charts BA 2424, 2129, 2092, 2184, 1765

Passage Lights
Fastnet	Fl 5s 49m 28M
Galley Hd	Fl(5) 30s 53m 28M
Old Hd Kinsale	Fl(2) 10s 72m 25M
Roche's Pt	Oc WR 20s 30m 20/16M

Tidal Streams: All related to Dover. In general the streams up to 5M offshore change at nearly the same time from Crookhaven to Old Head of Kinsale. +2¼h E-going stream; −4h W-going; spring rate 1 to 1.5kn, but 2 to 2.5kn off the Fasnet Rk and the main headlands. In Gascanane Sound: −½h SE; −5¾h NW; spring rate 3kn. Old Head of Kinsale to Cork Harbour: +¾h E; −5h W.

The channel between Fasnet Rk and Cape Clear is free of dangers apart from a rock with 3m ¼M NE of Fasnet. Galley Hd is fairly steep-to; but ½M WSW is Dhulic Rk, dries 3.4m, with Sunk Rk, less than 1.8m, 1.5 ca to SSW of it. Tides set across Dhulic Rk and it must be given a wide berth.

With wind against tide there can be a bad sea close to Galley Hd and to Seven Heads.

Off Old Head of Kinsale a potentially dangerous tide-race extends over 1M to SW on W-going stream, to SE on E-going stream. The race can be avoided by rounding the hd close up except in S winds or any strong winds; in these conditions give it a berth of over 2M.

BANTRY HARBOUR   Chart BA 1838
HW: Dover +6h
MHWS 3.4m   MHWN 2.6   MTL 1.9   MLWN 1.2   MLWS 0.5

Entrance North: Whiddy Pt East may be rounded close in, but Is in hbr are generally foul all round. Leave Horse and Chapel lt buoy to stb, Gurteenroe lt buoy to port. On approach beware of ruined, badly lit oil terminal jetty 2.5 ca N of Whiddy Is oil terminal.

West entrance: use only in good conditions. Bar has only 1.7m and sometimes breaks. Outside bar, Cracker Rk has only 1.7m. Ldg marks 090° on shore front W post (F), rear RW post (FR) lead over bar 2.5m from seaward a second set of W lts on Whiddy show when to alter course.

Anchorages (1) 1 ca NW of town pier; keep over 1 ca from pier on N side which is foul, but clear of fairway.
(2) About 3 ca W of (1), outside local yachts in 3.5m.
(3) 4 ca SW of Rabbit Is in 2 to 3.5m; oyster fisheries inside Rabbit Is. Anchorages (1) and (2) subject to wash from Whiddy Is launches. Water on pier. Petrol, diesel, engineers, some repairs. Best shopping and transport centre on this coast. Bus to Cork, Glengariff, Castletownbear and (summer only) Kenmare, Killarney, Clonakilty. Beware of unlit oyster rafts in hbr and (Sept/Oct) shrimp pots. It is unsafe to pick up moorings without permission.

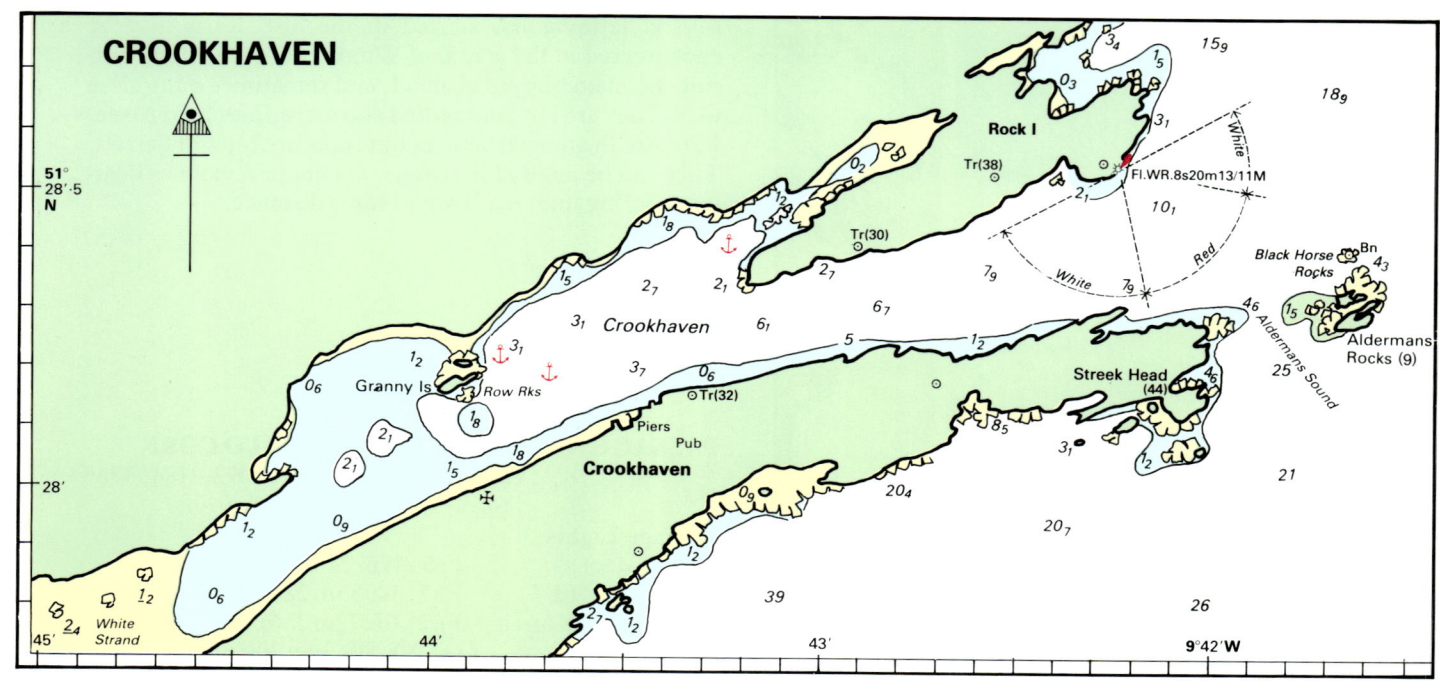

CROOKHAVEN   Chart BA 2184
HW: Dover +6h
MHWS 3.3m MHWN 2.7 MTL 1.8 MLWN 0.9 MLWS 0.4
An excellent hbr which may be entered at all states of the tide and in all weathers, is 2M long, 2 ca wide. 10m at entrance, 3m off Crookhaven village, shoaling thence gradually to its head.

Approach From the Fastnet Rock steer N to fetch the entrance. Give Alderman Rks and Black Horse Rks, which extend ½M to E of Streek Hd and are marked by a bn (N Card), a good berth, both shores being otherwise steep-to. Beware tidal set through Alderman Rks.

Entrance At night do not steer for the W lt tr (Fl WR 8s) at N point of entrance till R sector covering Alderman Rks turns to W, then enter along N shore.

Anchorage Anchor abreast village in 3m. In a SW blow shelter behind Granny Is; in E blow N of W point of Rock Is. Water from taps on both piers, PO, some stores from village shops. There is often kelp in this anchorage.

SCHULL   Chart BA 2129
HW: Dover +6¼h
MHWS 3.2m MHWN 2.7 MTL 1.9 MLWN 1.1 MLWS 0.4.
The hbr is situated between Schull Pt and Cosheen Pt and is protected by Long Is and other islands from S. It affords good shelter and may be preferred to Crookhaven in E winds and at other times. However, it is untenable in a S gale and then shelter should be sought behind Long Is; dig in the anchor with engine to ensure that it is clear of kelp. Heavy fishing boat traffic.

Approach From S, when about 3 ca S of Amelia Rk buoy (G con Fl G 3s) marking the rks W of Castle Is, steer 346° for entrance. From W, leave Cush Spit G con buoy to stb, thence for entrance

Entrance By day pass Bull Rk, dries at half-ebb, R perch, on either side: W shore is then clear apart from Baker Rk 1.5 ca N of Schull Pt but E shore must be given a berth of at least 1 ca. By night ldg lts Oc 5s lead 346° to E of Bull Rk.

Berthing Anchor according to choice but avoid area immediately SSE of end of extended pier as fishing boats pass frequently or lie alongside fishing boat on N side of pier. Water on pier, PO, all supplies.

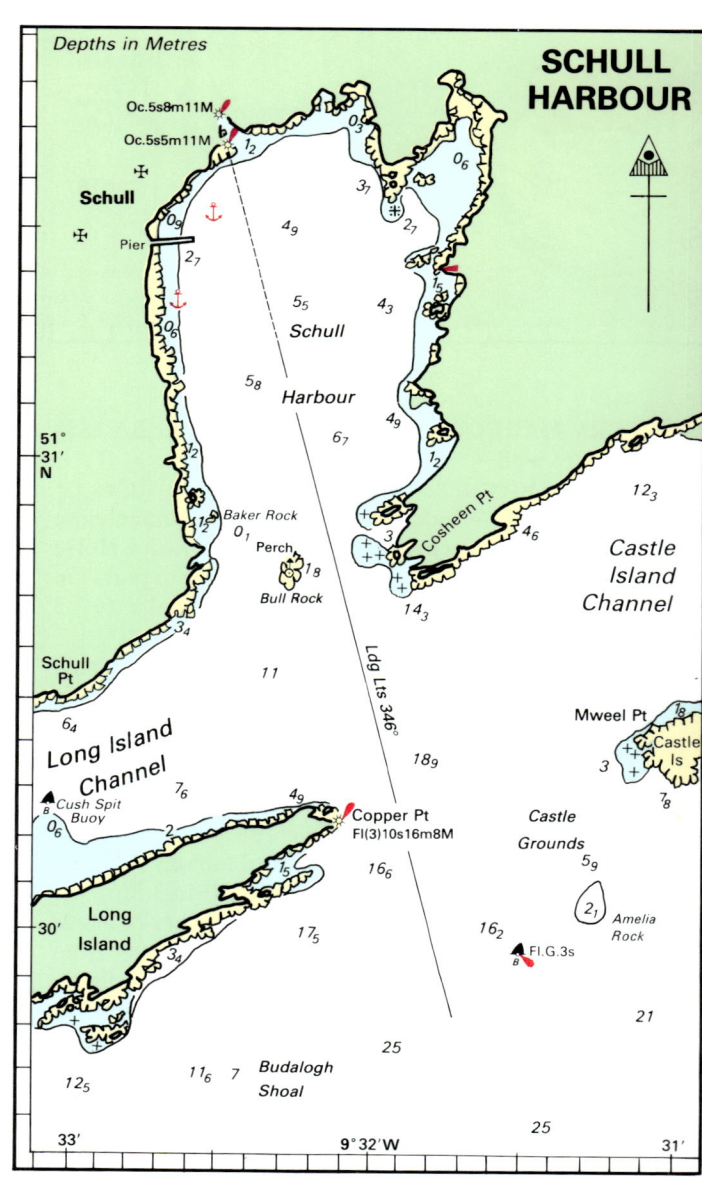

BALTIMORE Chart BA 3725
HW: Dover −6h
MHWS 3.6m MHWN 3.0 MTL 2.1 MLWN 1.4 MLWS 0.6
Approach The position of hbr may be recognised by a conspic W tr called Lot's Wife on Beacon Pt, the E pt of entrance, and by the W Lt Ho (Fl (2) WR) on Barrack Pt, the W pt of entrance. S of the Lt Ho, give the W shore a berth of fully ¾ca to clear Wilson Rk, awash at HW.
Entrance Steer in 340° between entrance pts and give the inner E entrance pt, Loo Pt, a berth of ¾ca, leaving G con buoy marking Loo Rk 0.2m to stb. Steer N, leaving Quarry Rk, 2.9m, to stb till the northerly (new) pier comes open N of Connor Pt, 060°.

Anchorages (1) N or W of New Pier.
(2) In Church Strand Bay beyond the RNLI slip (the safest place in gales). "A hurricane hole".
(3) Off Skerkin Is under Dunalong Castle ruins. Yachts can also berth alongside NW face of New Pier (1.3m) in fine weather.
Rocks Quarry Rk, 2.9m, lies 1¾ca 004° from Loo Pt. Lousy Rks, situated in the W centre of the hbr, dry, and are marked by a bn (S Card) on SE rk. Wallis Rk, 1.6m in centre of the hbr, has a R can buoy E of the rk. Other rks obstruct NW corner of the hbr along the shore.
Water on New Pier. Chandler and small yard, PO, hotels, general store, fuel, bus to Skibbereen, 8M.

IRELAND 210

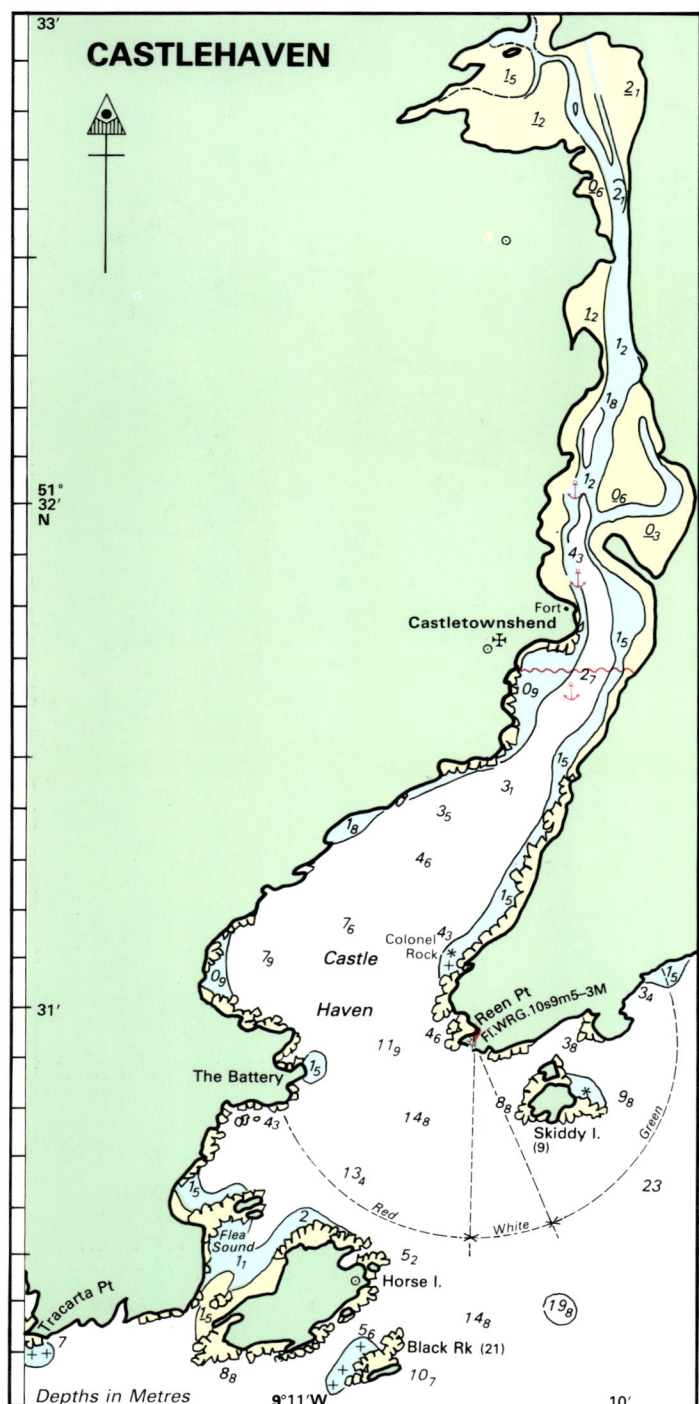

CASTLEHAVEN
Chart BA 2092

HW: Dover +6½h DS: Dover +2h E; −4h W.
MHWS 3.7m MHWN 2.9 MTL 2.0 MLWN 1.0 MLWS 0.4

Can be entered at all states of tide, and affords a protected and excellent anchorage in all weathers, with some swell in SW winds.

Approach Hbr lies 3M NE of Stag Rks.

Entrance Steer in halfway between Horse Is to port and Skiddy Is to stb. A lt is shown from W tr on Reen Pt, and at night the W sector leads in. Continue heading for NE shore until the Stags open through Flea Sd, to port, which line clears Colonel Rk, 1m, on SE shore. In hazy weather keep in mid-channel.

Anchorages Anchor abreast of Castletownshend or lower down clear of fishing boats, which enter at night along SE shore. In SW winds better shelter will be found upstream just above the Fort, where the fishermen go.

A few general shops. Skibbereen, where all stores may be obtained, is 5M.

IRISH CRUISING CLUB

Founded in 1928 to encourage cruising on the Coasts of Ireland and abroad.

Membership 540.

A Flag Officer is appointed for each of the four Provinces of Ireland. The seniority of these positions rotates at intervals of not more than three years.

Rallies and Cruising in company are organised both at home and abroad during the sailing season.

Meetings with maritime orientated speakers and visits to places of sailing interest take place during the winter months.

There are no Club premises, however, the committee meets in the main yachting centres, kindly being invited to use the facilities of existing yacht clubs in the area.

An annual dinner is organised by each of the Flag officers in turn, and takes place in the early spring.

The Annual General Meeting is held in the Dublin area in March.

Honorary Secretary:
  Cormac McHenry, 8 Heidelberg, Ardilea, Dublin 14, Republic of Ireland.
Honorary Publications Officer:
  Barbara Fox-Mills
  The Tansey, Baily, Co. Dublin,
  Republic of Ireland.

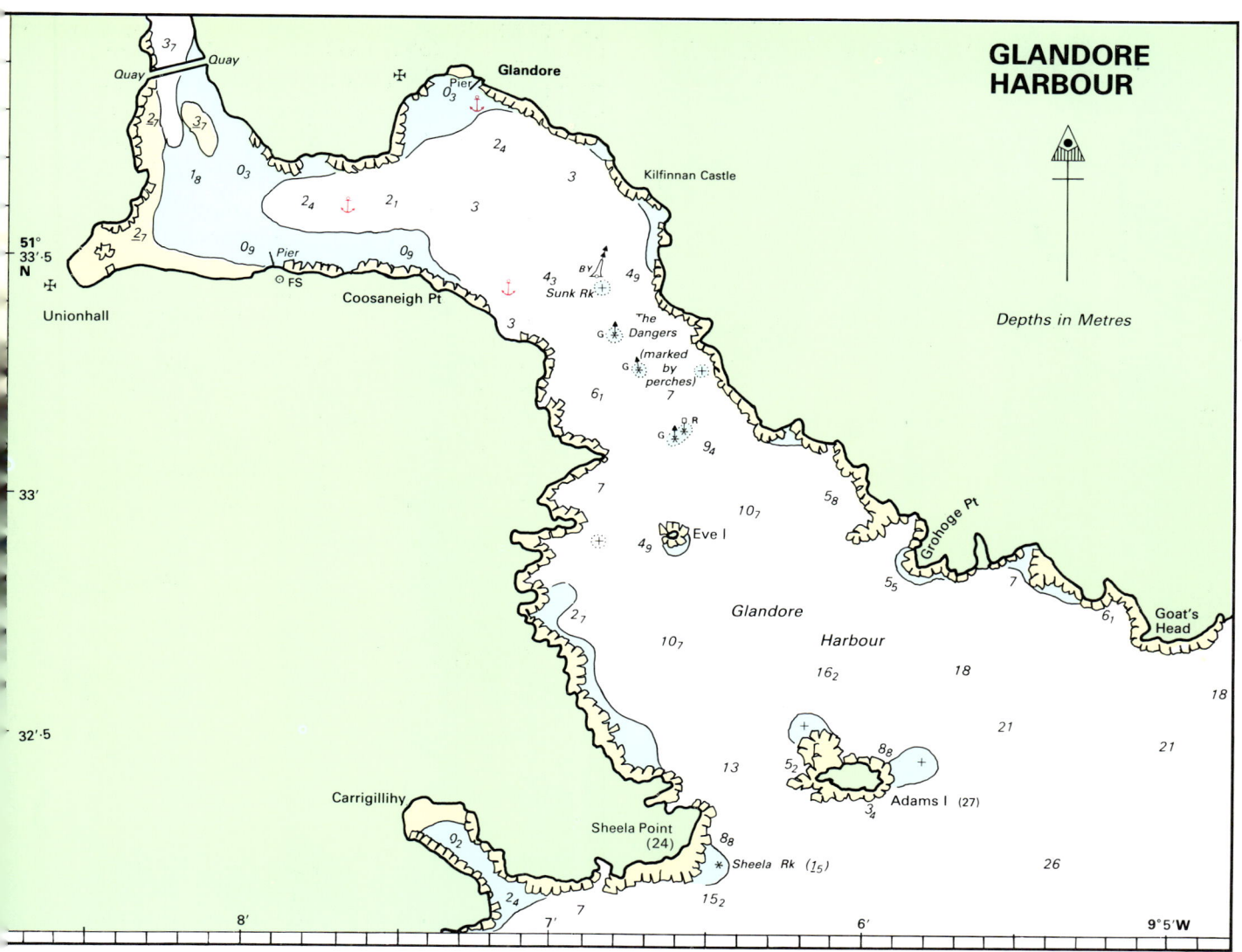

GLANDORE Chart BA 2092

HW: Dover −6¼h. DS Dover: +2h E; −4h W.
MHWS 3.7m MHWN 3.0 MTL 2.1 MLWN 1.0 MLWS 0.4

Approach The entrance lies between Foilnashark Hd on E and Sheela Pt on W and is divided into two channels by Adam Is. From SW give High Is a berth of 1 ca. From E there are no dangers on the direct course from a position S of Doolic Rk off Galley Head.

Entrance Between Adam Is and Goats Hd giving Adam Is a wide berth, or between Adam Is and Sheela Pt; then steer to pass 1 ca E of Eve Is. Pass midway between W shore and the Dangers, three separate rocks in the middle of the chan. The Outer Danger is marked by a stb perch (G, con topmark) on its W side and a port perch (R, can topmark) on its E side. The Middle Danger and the Inner Danger are each marked by one perch (G, con topmark). Sunk Rk, about 1 ca N of the Inner Danger, is marked by a buoy (N card). Strangers should not attempt to sail between the Dangers and should particularly note that the perches on the Outer Danger mark the ends of what is in effect one rock.

Anchorages (1) In W or NW winds off Glandore pier in 2.5m.
(2) In S or SW winds off Unionhall in 2.5m; give Coosaneigh Pt a good berth to avoid mudbank extending 1 ca from it. Water at both piers. Provisions and some fuel at Unionhall. Provisions also at Glandore.

IRELAND 212

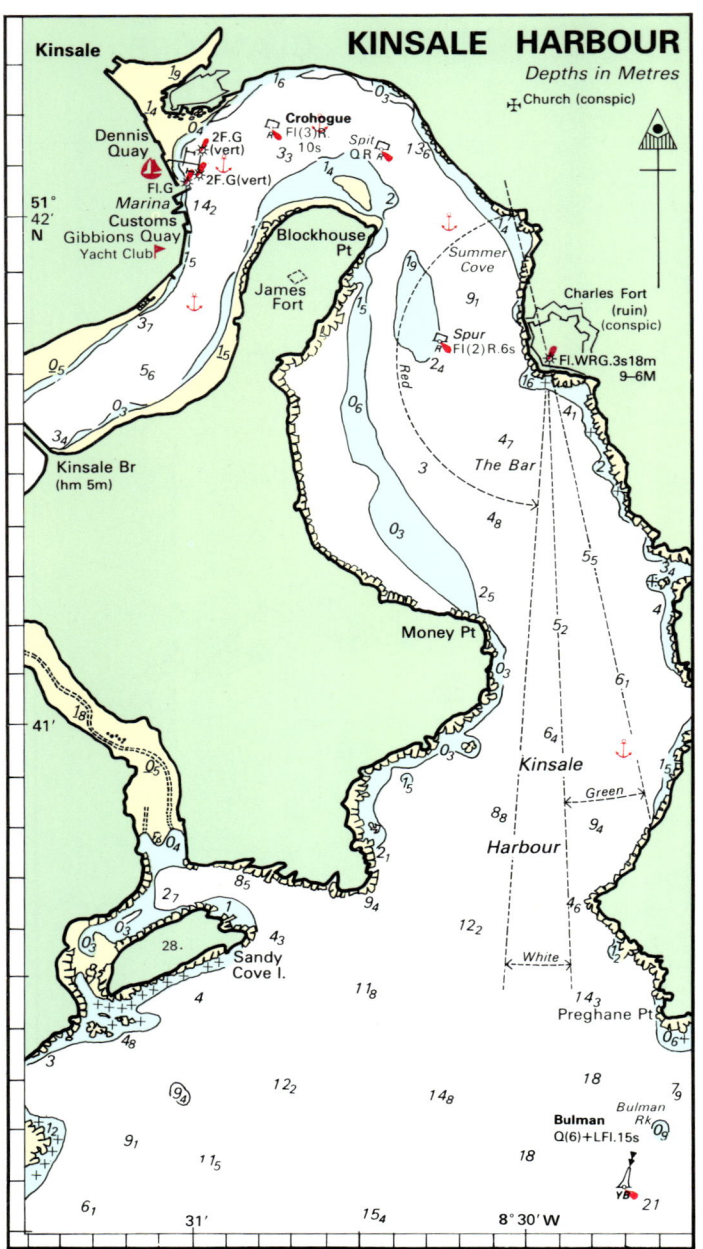
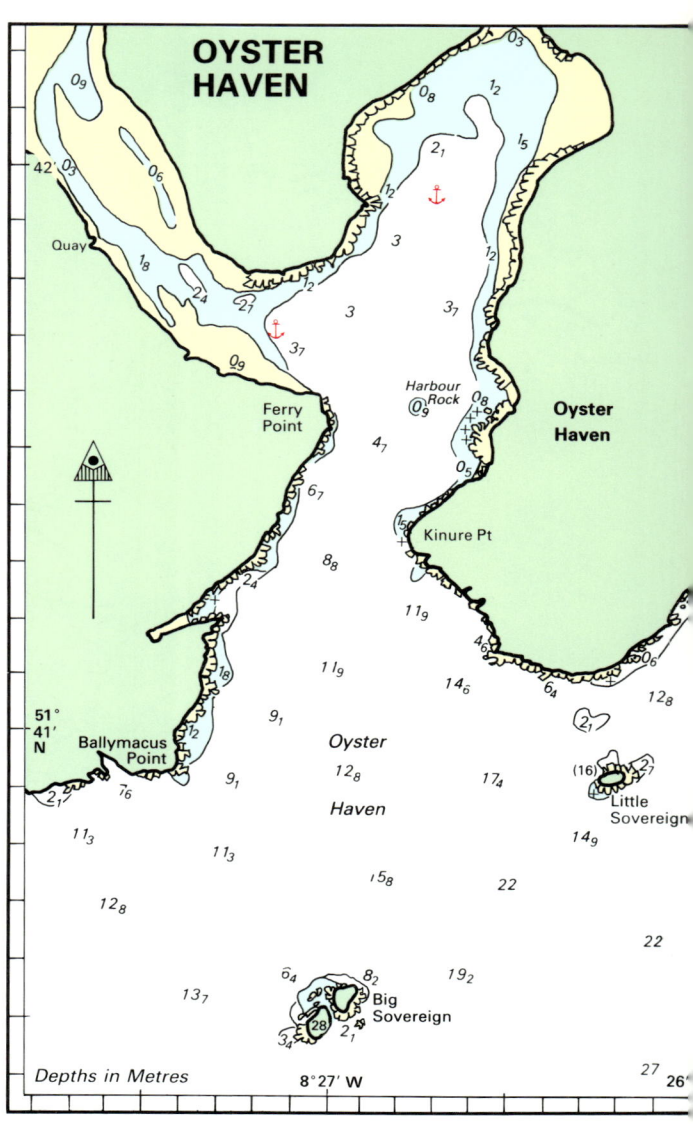

KINSALE   Chart BA 2053

HW: Dover −6h

MHWS 4.0m   MHWN 3.2   MTL 2.3   MLWN 1.4   MLWS 0.5.

Bar 3m, 2 to 3 ca S of Charles Fort.

Approach From E keep outside the Bulman Rk S Card lt buoy off Preghane Pt.

The hbr will then open up to N and when Charles Fort is visible between Money Pt and Preghane Pt, steer for it. At night the W sector of Charles Fort lt leads in.

Entrance Keep in mid-channel and cross the bar S of Charles Fort. The W side of the channel from the bar round Blockhouse Pt to the town is marked by three R can lt buoys which must be left to port.

Berthing (1) At Kinsale YC marina N of Town Quay; visitors' berths on outer pontoon, but a finger berth inside marina may be available. Berthing controlled by Marina Supervisor.

(2) Anchor on bank N of James Fort, 2 to 4m.

(3) Anchor in river between Town Quay and bridge.

Landing at Town Quay or on SE shore from (3). All stores, bus to Cork. EC Thur. Cork airport 12M. Diesel available at Gibbons Quay, water at Marina and pier hd, electricity at Marina. Many good restaurants. Interesting maritime museum.

OYSTERHAVEN   Chart BA 2053

A quiet safe harbour 2M E of Kinsale.

Entrance Approach either side of Big Sovereign and make for centre of entrance. Give Ballymacus Pt on W of entrance a berth of at least ¾ca. Harbour Rk, 1m, is 1.5 ca E of Ferry Pt and must be passed on its W side.

Anchorages (1) N of Ferry Pt midway between N and S shore in 4 to 6m, soft mud and weed. Keep Kinure Pt on E side of entrance open of Ferry Pt.

(2) In N branch of hbr in 3m, sand.

CORK HARBOUR
Charts BA 1777, 1773

HW: Dover −5¾h DS: Dover +1h E; −4½h W.

Cobh
MHWS 4.1m MHWN 3.3 MTL 2.3 MLWN 1.3 MLWS 0.5

Passage West
MHWS 4.4m MHWN 3.6 MTL 2.5 MLWN 1.5 MLWS 0.7

Cork
MHWS 4.4m MHWN 3.4 MTL 2.4 MLWN 1.3 MLWS 0.5

Hbr is accessible at all times.

Approach From Old Hd of Kinsale, Cork RWVS buoy, Fl 10s, off the entrance to the port of Cork bears 058°, 12½M. Hence Roche's Pt, the E pt of the entrance, 001°, 4¾M. The approach is clear of obstruction for small craft excepting Daunt Rk, 3.5m, marked by R buoy Fl(2)R 6s, 7 ca 140° from Roberts Hd: to leave this to W bring the high tr E of Roche's Pt Lt Ho on with tree clump in rear, 018°. By day, having left Daunt Rk about 4 ca to port, a course 009° made good will lead into the entrance between Weaver Pt and the Lt Ho. By night, a R sector from Roche's Pt Lt Ho covers Daunt Rk, and this sector should be shut in before rounding up for Roche's Pt Lt Ho. 016°.

Entrance No dangers for small craft in entrance to Cork Hbr. To make for Crosshaven, the main yachting centre, round Ram pt at a distance of fully 2ca and steer for the G con buoy C1 at entrance of Owenboy river. Enter on ldg line 252° leaving C2 perch to port. In the entrance the tidal streams follow the bends, the flood and ebb streams setting into White bay.

Berthing Crosshaven: (1) At W end of RCYC marina. (Interest: Royal Cork YC now amalgamated with Royal Munster YC is the oldest in the world.)
(2) At Crosshaven Boat Yard ((021) 831161) marina.
(3) Anchor below Town Quay clear of tel cables.
(4) Ask Crosshaven Boat Yard for a mooring. Good supplies, all facilities. Bus to Cork Airport.

Cobh: Anchor W of town. Garage, shops, hotels, PO, bank. EC Wed. East Ferry:
(1) Marina S of Belgrove Quay.
(2) Anchor on W side S or E of quay, 2 to 3m;
(3) On E side ½M further up, 3 to 4m.

Cork: A berth may be obtained by permission of Port Operations Office, Cobh. Is the second city of the Republic of Ireland. It has all facilities including rail to Dublin, Airport to UK and ferry (from Ringaskiddy) to France. In offshore winds, awaiting tide, anchorage will be found outside the entrance in Ringabella Bay.

Warning: No yacht may approach within 50m of Whitegate oil jetty.

PASSAGE NOTES: CORK TO TUSKAR ROCK
Charts BA 2049, 2740

Passage Lights
Ballycotton	Fl WR 10s 59m 22/18M
Hook Hd	Fl 3s 46m 24M
Tuskar	Q (2) 7.5s 33m 28M

Tidal Streams (All related to Dover). Cork to Waterford less than 0.5kn starting progressively later towards Waterford where they begin +5¼h ENE −1h WSW. Between the Saltees and Carnsore Pt +5¼h ENE, spring rate 2.4kn; −¾h WSW, spring rate 2.6kn.

Off Hook Hd there is a dangerous tidal race extending 1M S of the Hd, especially in strong westerlies. To avoid this race keep outside the 20m line.

E of Hook Hd, Baginbun and Bannow Bays though exposed to SE give good shelter from westerlies. The recommended offshore anchorage is at the SW end of Bannow Bay just N of Ingard Pt.

A yacht proceeding from Waterford to the E coast has the choice of the offshore or inshore passage. Using the offshore passage make for the Coningbeg LV, and thence to a position S of South Rk buoy (S Card) and E of the Tuskar Rk. Give the Tuskar a good berth as the tide sets onto it. For the inshore passage, pass between the Saltees or N of them and about ¼M S of Carnsore Pt. Chart BA 2740 and directions in ICC are essential for this passage.

Warning The sea area off the SE corner of Ireland is to be avoided in bad weather.

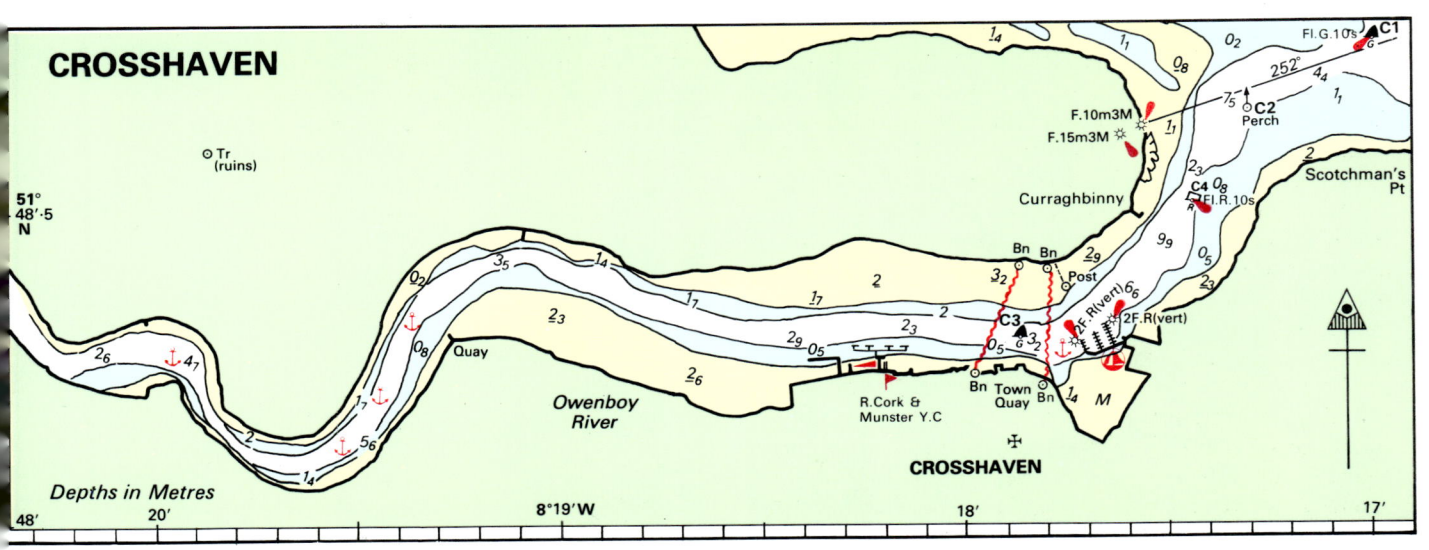

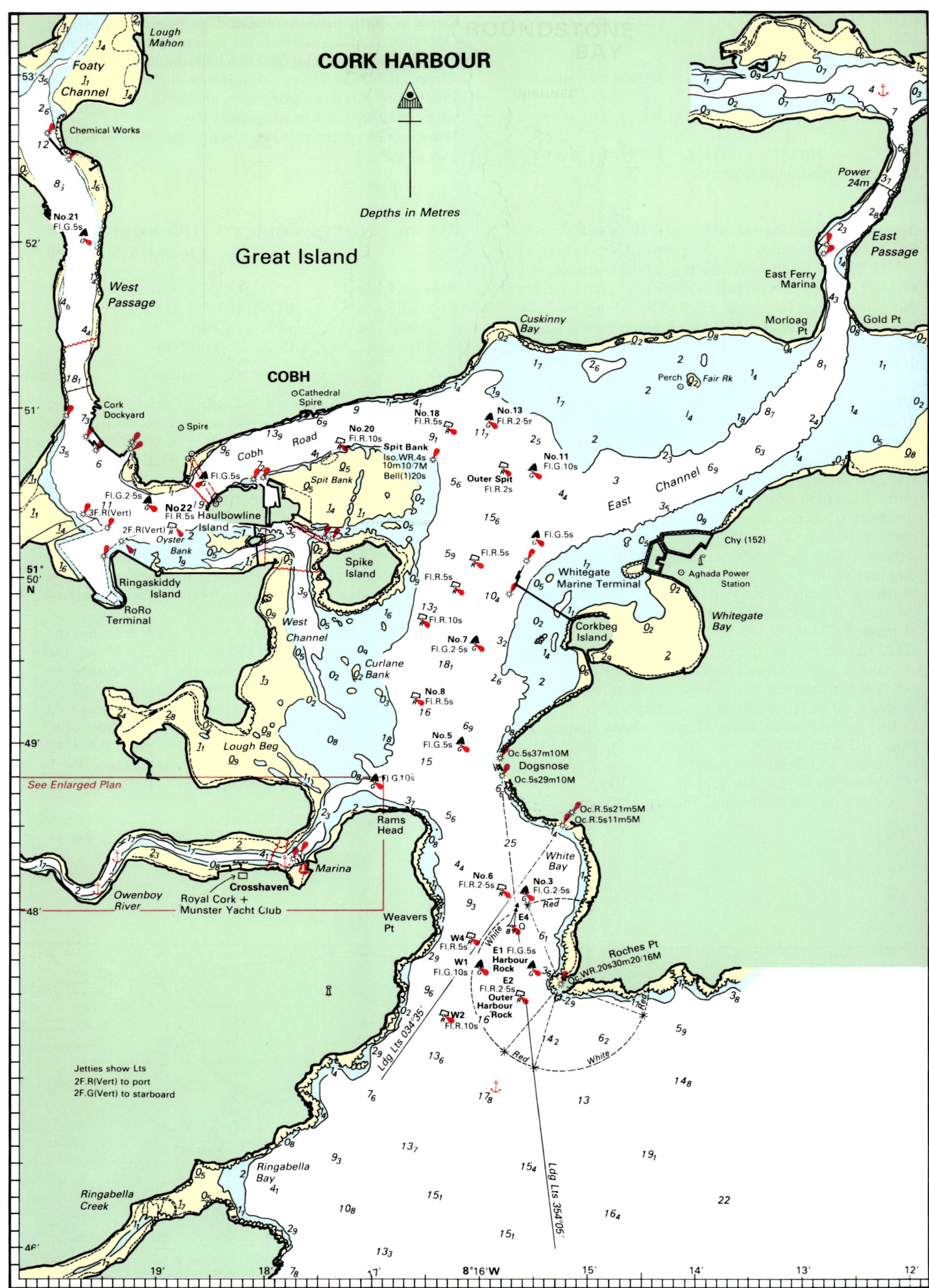

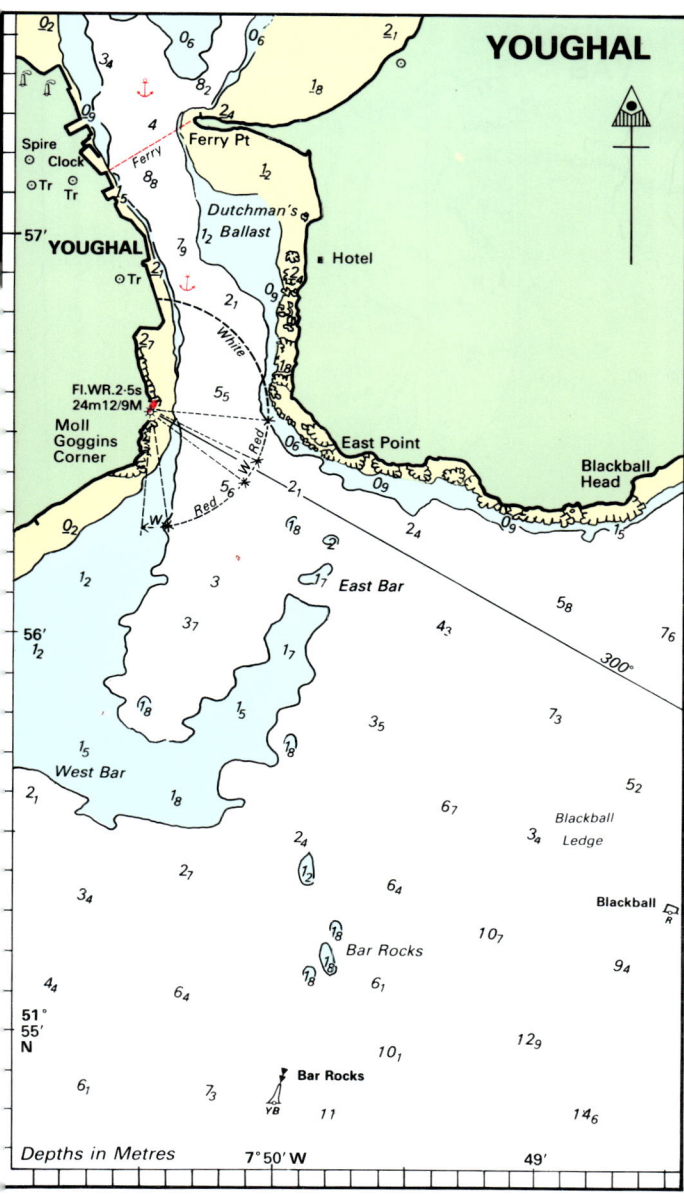

Entrance Having passed the Lt Ho, keep in towards the W shore. The E side of entrance on a transit between East Pt and Ferry Pt is shoal.

Anchorages (1) On a 3m bank off the most Nly warehouse. (2) In 2 to 4m N of Ferry Pt. (3) Off market clock. (4) N of LB slip off small landing beach.

Caution: Anchorages reported (1988) to be silting up. All stores. EC Wed.

WATERFORD   Chart BA 2046

HW Dunmore East: Dover −5½h. DS: Dover −2h to +5h W; −6h to −3h SSE.

MHWS 4.5m   MHWN 3.6   MTL 2.4   MLWN 1.2   MLWS 0.4

Dunmore East This is a small artificial hbr on the W side of the entrance which affords a convenient port of call. Lt Ho on pier LFl WR 8s; lts Fl R 2s at end of breakwater extension to E pier and Fl G 2s at N end of W quay. There are yacht moorings in the bight N of NW quay for the use of Waterford SC owners only. Berth alongside on NW side of hbr only and report to HM. Water from tap on W quay, diesel on E quay, shops and PO in village. Bus to Waterford. YC. Good showers and heads on pier.

Bar 4M inside Hook Hd, has 3m. The R Suir has 10 to 4m up to Waterford. Below Duncannon outgoing stream follows E side, the ingoing W side.

Approach The summit of Slieve Coiltia bears 000° from the entrance, which lies between Swines Hd, 60m, on the W side, and the long low-lying Hook Hd 4M to the E. It bears 296°, 11M from Coningbeg LV. In hazy weather care must be taken to distinguish Tramore Bay, which has three W trs on the W pt and two on the E pt of the bay, from the Waterford entrance.

The approach is clear of obstructions except Falskirt Rk, 2 ca S of Swines Hd, covers at 2/3 flood, and Brecaun reef, 2M NE of Hook Hd, 3 ca offshore (0.5m), to clear which keep Hook Lt Ho W of 233°. Tower Race extends 1M to the S of Hook Hd, and should be given a good berth. In fresh W winds over W-going stream conditions are severe.

Entrance Keep in buoyed channel. Abreast Duncannon the channel lies on E side, and Drumroe Bank to W must be avoided. Duncannon Dir lt Oc WRG 4s W 357° leads in. Ldg lts from Snowhill Pt show 255° over Cheek Pt bar. Ldg lts 098° indicate fairway coming out through Queen's channel.

Anchorages (1) Just above and opposite Ballyhack in 5m on E side close in out of tidal stream.

(2) W of Cheek Pt (avoid fish weirs) in 3m, ½ to 1 ca N of village quay, secure anchorage, good holding, little stream.

(3) In W side of King's Channel just N of the W bank ferry stn. No facilities. The E side is silted up and there is no passage through the wires of the ferry.

(4) Waterford town; berth at pontoon by Reginald's Tower and Tower Hotel. Strong flood stream. All stores and most repairs except sailmaker. EC. Thur. Rail to Dublin. Customs.

Beating up the river near HW, vessels must be careful to avoid old stumps of fish weirs, which extend over the mud flats toward the channel. R Suir has 2.5m at Fiddoum Is, and dries 3M below Carrick. There are two lifting bridges at Waterford. R Barrow has plenty of water in the buoyed chan to New Ross but the channel is very narrow between Red Bank and the W side. Barrow Bridge at confluence has 7m clearance MHWS, 11m MLWN, opens for 3 blasts but preferably tel Campile 37. Pilots at Dunmore East. EC Thur.

YOUGHAL   Chart BA 2071

HW: Dover −5¾h DS: HWD W.

MHWS 4.1m   MHWN 3.3   MTL 2.3   MLWN 1.2   MLWS 0.5

The tidal stream sets into hbr at Dover +1½h, out at −4¼h; 2.5 to 3kn springs.

Bar Not to be attempted in a big sea. The approach is divided by Bar Rks and Blackball Ledge, 3.4m, into two channels, E bar, having 2m, and W Bar 1.8m. Over E Bar one may expect less sea and less stream. Strong E and S winds cause a heavy and dangerous sea in the bay. N winds reduce the tidal rise, and SW gales cause a swell inside; the ebb sets on to the W bar.

Approach From W, using the W bar channel leave Bar Rks S Card buoy marking Bar Rks (0.6m) about 2ca to stb, then steer direct for the entrance about N.

Using E Bar channel, coming from S, leave Blackball Ledge R can buoy to port. From E, steer for Lt Ho when it comes well open of Blackball Hd and bears about 300°.

IRELAND 216

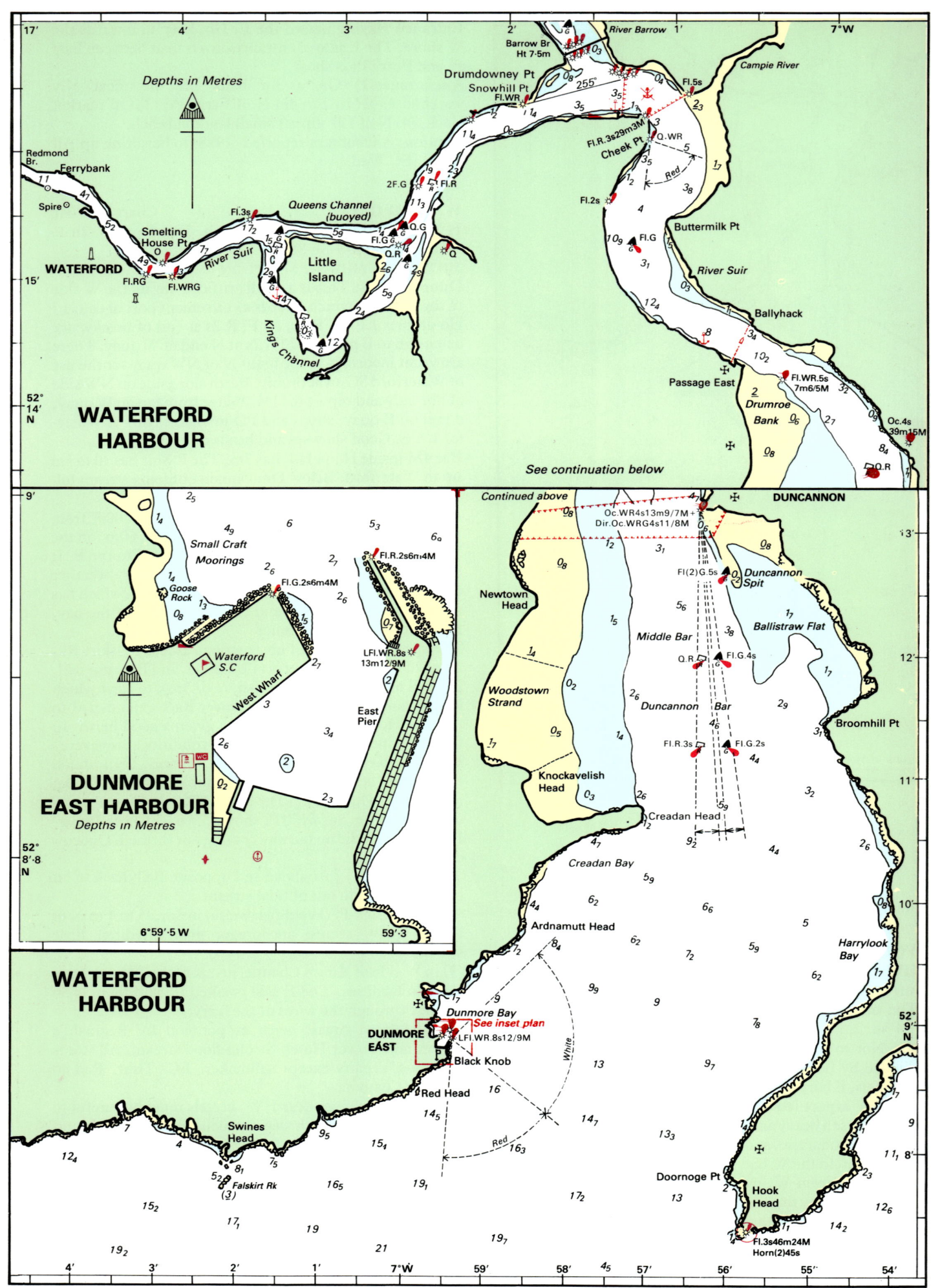

IRELAND, EAST COAST

Warning: A sharp lookout should be kept for lobster pots.

PASSAGE NOTES: CARNSORE PT TO DUBLIN BAY
Charts BA 1787, 1468, 1415

Passage Lights
Arklow Lanby	Fl(2) 12s 12m 16M
Wicklow Hd	Fl(3) 15s 37m 26M
Kish Bank	Fl(2) 30s 29m 28M
Codling Lanby	Fl 4s 12m 16M
Dun Laoghaire (E Breakwater)	Fl(2) 15s 16m 22M

Tidal Streams DS (related to Dover) in middle of St. George's Channel: +6h NE; HWD SW. Outside Tuskar Rk: −5½h NE; HWD SW, 2.5kn; there is a strong set onto the rk. Streams change about 1½h earlier between the Irish banks and the shore; they set across these banks. From Land's End it can be dangerous to come in W of the Tuskar Rk, but coming from the W yachts need not leave this rk to port.

The passage from Carnsore Pt to Rosslare should only be attempted at night with a competent navigator on board. From Tuskar to Dublin Bay the normal route is outside the Blackwater bank, inside the S Arklow Lanby, thence past Wicklow Hd and through Dalkey Sound, quite clean except close to island side, or through Muglins Sd, but this has rks with under 2m on each side. By night go outside Muglins, Lt Fl 5s 14m 8M.

Keep away from Arklow Bank, a dangerous shallow ridge. Approaching Dublin Bay from E make Kish Lt Ho Fl(2) 30s, Horn (2) 30s, thence to S Burford S Card lt buoy, Horn (1) 20s, leaving N Kish N Card lt buoy to port. In Dublin Bay, yachts are required to keep out of way of commercial shipping.

ROSSLARE
Chart BA 1772

HW: Dover −5¼h.

MHWS 2.0m MHWN 1.5 MTL 1.2 MLWN 0.9 MLWS 0.4.

The hbr, opening NW, is formed by a curved breakwater and is a very busy commercial port in which yachts are not allowed to berth alongside the main ferry pier. It is convenient for yachts bound from SW England to E coast of Ireland, however, and for yachts bound S along the Irish coast held up by headwinds. A new inner pier has been constructed.

Anchorages (1) SW of the breakwater.
(2) If (1) is fully occupied by local boats, anchor further W beyond an area of rocky bottom in 2 to 5m; safe and comfortable in winds between WSW and SE but untenable in fresh winds between W and NE.
(3) Yachts may now berth alongside SW side of new pier. Petrol and diesel, small shop, PO, hotels. Car ferry to Fishguard and France.

Wexford Harbour – See next page

ARKLOW
Chart BA 633

HW: Dover −1¾h. DS: Dover −1h SSW

MHWS 1.7m MHWN 1.0 MTL 1.3 MLWN 1.2 MLWS 0.8

Bar and river to wharves dredged to not less than 3.5m. Dock dredged to 3.7m but there is a drying part on SW side between LB and ship hoist. Note very small tidal rise.

Entrance Narrow and difficult under sail. Dangerous in gales from N through E to SW. S pier-head has 10m steel tr, Fl WR 6s; N pier-head Fl G 3s. The dock on S side provides perfect shelter against NE or SE quay with 10m wide entrance. There is approx 2m in centre to N of River as far as ASC premises where a small slip has been built. Holding poor. Liable to silting. All facilities including boat yard, except sailmaker. EC Wed.

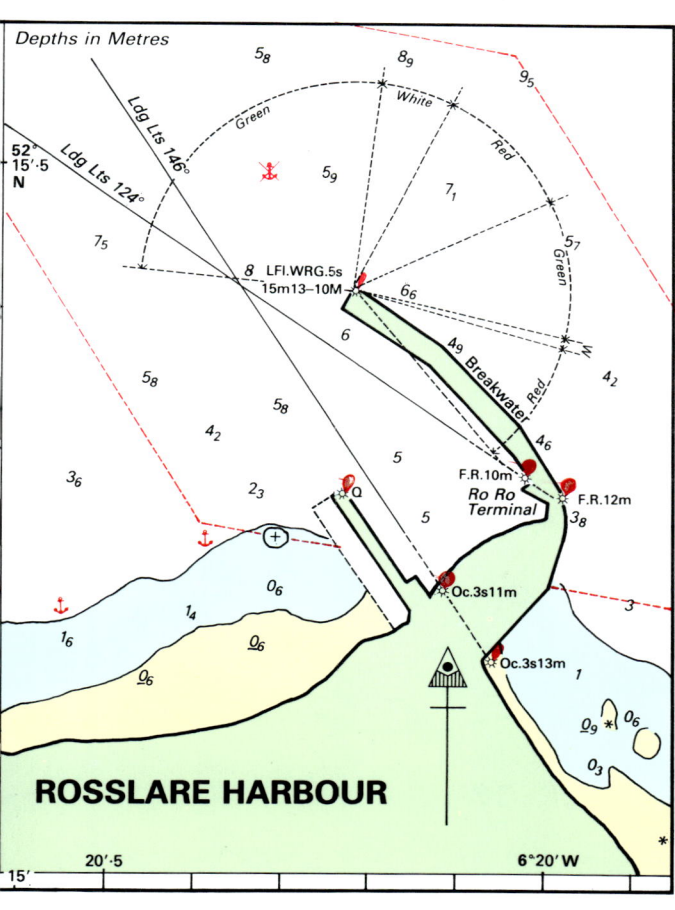

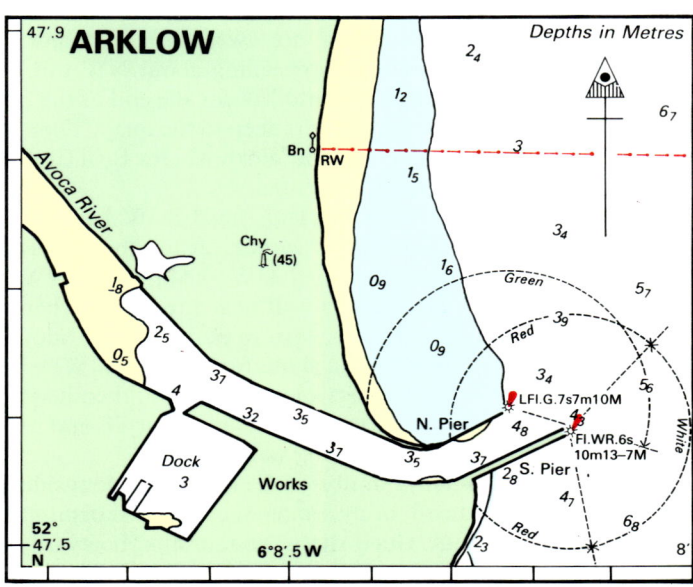

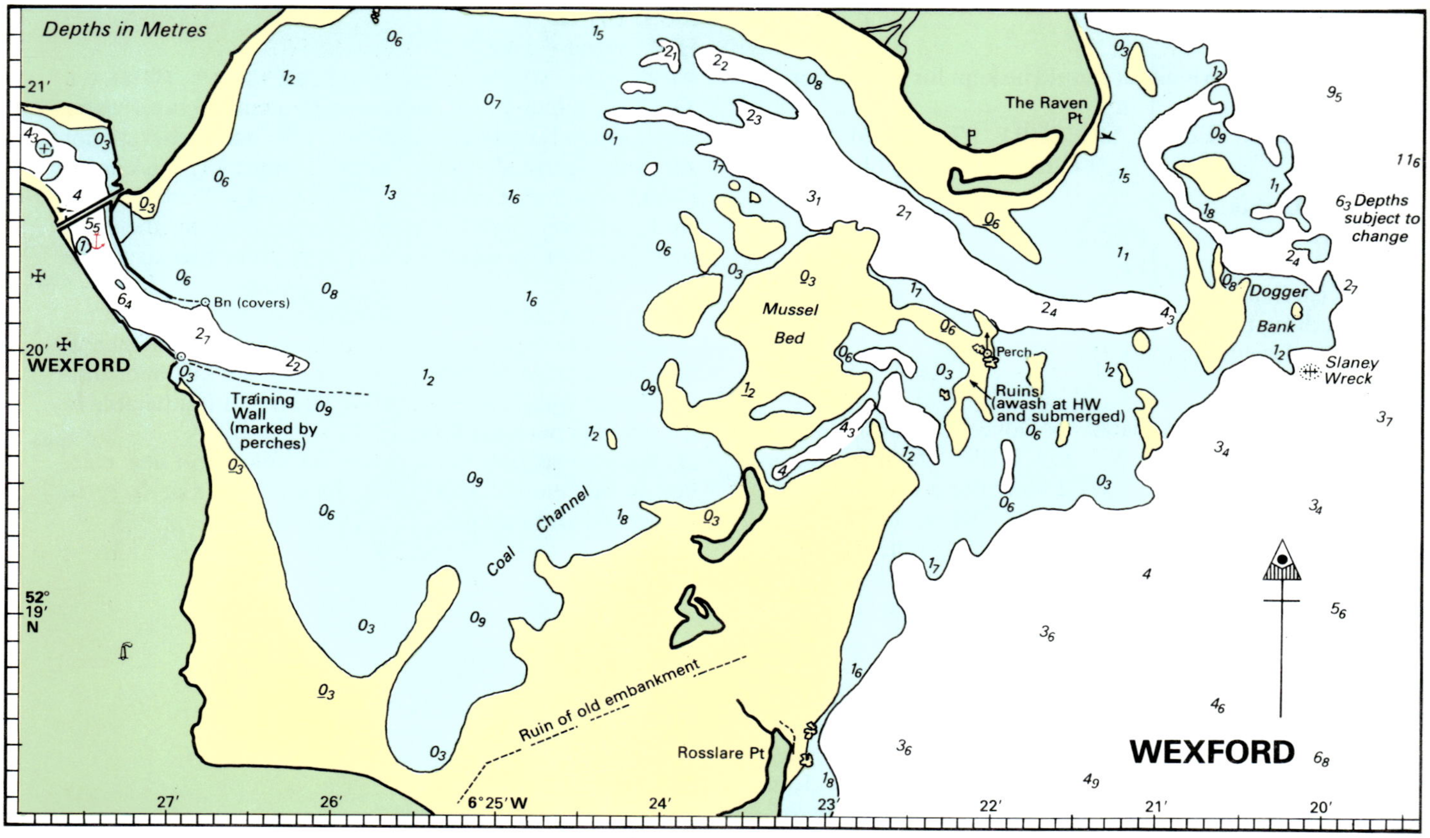

WEXFORD HARBOUR Chart BA 1772
HW Dover −3h Sp, −6¼h Np.
MHWS 1.7m MHWN 1.4 MTL 1.0 MLWN 0.5 MLWS 0.2.
Once entered, this hbr is completely safe, sheltered and charming.

Bar 1.5m (but 1m in inner chan). Subject to annual change.

Approach Dangerous in strong winds between S and E. In general visitors should not attempt to enter without local assistance (see below) but in offshore winds and settled weather a stranger with reliable power may attempt the entrance from a position about 1M E of the N end of the detached (Nly) part of Rosslare Pt. Slaney wreck, an unmarked dangerous wreck 1¼M SE of Raven Pt, lies close S of the approach to the bar.

Entrance Leave the ruins of a fort, awash at HW, to port and work in on soundings, proceeding about NW until near the shore, then turning onto SW for the end of the S training wall, whence the water is deep to the quay. There are unlit lateral buoys laid by the Wexford Hbr Boat Club (summer only) marking the channel.

When these lateral buoys are laid, head in W between them, starting outside Slaney wreck. After the 3rd R buoy, N of the ruins awash at HW, head about NW towards 2 W vert marks on a wall near the shore; when about 4 ca from these marks, turn to port past a R buoy and keep about 2.5 ca off the shore for about 1M. When off similar marks ashore pass another R buoy; then head SW towards a prominent tower on a factory at SE end of town. When 1 ca off the training wall, turn in.

Berthing Good holding in hbr on E side, or lie alongside quay in centre of town, or by arrangement against disused LV, now a museum. Good shops, restaurants, boatyard, YC.

Warning The banks in the entrance are variable in depth and position and the information on the plan must not be relied upon in detail. Strangers should telephone John Sherwood, Rosslare (053) 22875 (shop hours) or 22713 (home), or the Boat Club (22039), who will give latest information and supply Pilot if thought necessary.

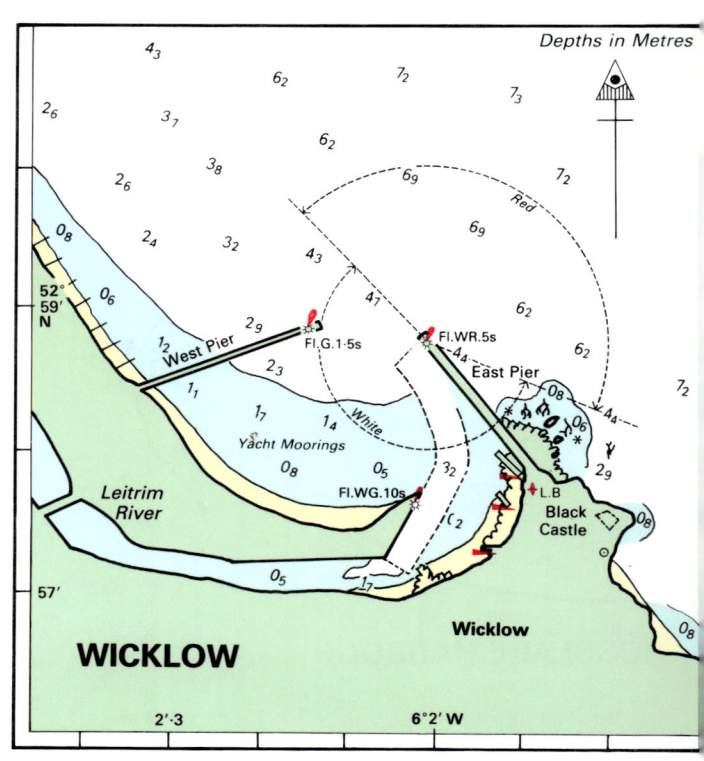

WICKLOW
Chart BA 633

HW: HWD. DS: HWD: SW.

MHWS 2.7m MHWN 2.3 MTL 1.6 MLWN 0.9 MLWS 0.5

The hbr faces N and is exposed in NE winds; inner part offers complete shelter.

Entrance For Inner hbr steer between outer piers towards W boathouse; when face of ferry quay opens turn sharp to stb. Keep front of RNLI boathouse open to avoid shallows on SE side.

Berthing (1) Anchorage in outer hbr midway between ends of W pier and quay in 2 to 3m outside YC moorings.
(2) In inner hbr the S side is being developed for use by fishing boats and yachts; if the quays there are not yet available a yacht may go alongside the steamer quay, beyond knuckle, with permission from HM office in middle of pier. Petrol on S quay. All stores and facilities except sailmaker. EC Thur.

HOWTH
Chart BA 633

HW: Dover +¼h DS: Dover −6h N, HWD S.

MHSW 4.1m MHWN 3.4 MTL 2.3 MLWN 1.2 MLWS 0.5

As the result of substantial development this hbr now affords excellent facilities.

Approach and Entrance From E leave to stb Rowan Rocks E card buoy Q(3) 10s Howth G con buoy Fl G 5s and South Rowan G con buoy (QG). Give E pier hd lt Fl(2) WR 7.5s 13m 17/13M a berth of at least 50m; do not turn into the hbr until it is well open; enter nearer W pier-head lt Fl G 3s 7m 6M.

Lts inside the hbr are:- Trawler Breakwater hd QR 7m 6M.

Berthing In marina operated by Howth YC. Yachts are recommended to call on VHF 37 (calling & working channel) before entering the hbr. A gabionade 30m long and 2ft wide is placed between the jetty and marina; essential to follow berthing instructions on VHF. Water, diesel, showers, clubhouse in hbr area. Shops, hotels, restaurants and puts within walking distance.

DUN LAOGHAIRE
Chart BA 1447

HW: Dover +¾h. DS off entrance: Dover −1½h SE; +5h NW

MHWS 4.1m MHWN 3.4 MTL 2.4 MLWN 1.5 MLWS 0.6.

A large artificial hbr on S side of Dublin Bay, always available. Major yachting centre. Exposed to NE and E gales, when anchors may drag and no good berth available, then best make for Liffey (a new marina is scheduled in the SW corner in the area of the Coal Hbr).

Entrance Allow for tide across hbr mouth. Keep well clear of ferries, which have right of way.

Berthing Anchor outside moored yachts opposite entrance off RIYC; moorings often available. Royal St. George YC has moorings inside E pier, quieter in E-ly winds. Berth alongside moored ships in coal hbr, but subject to much traffic and scend in NE wind. Inner hbr only for 4ft. draft. Water in Coal Hbr or tap at RIYC. All facilities. EC Wed. There is a floating pontoon for visitors (4 berths) at the National YC in the SE corner. Maritime Museum within a few hundred yards

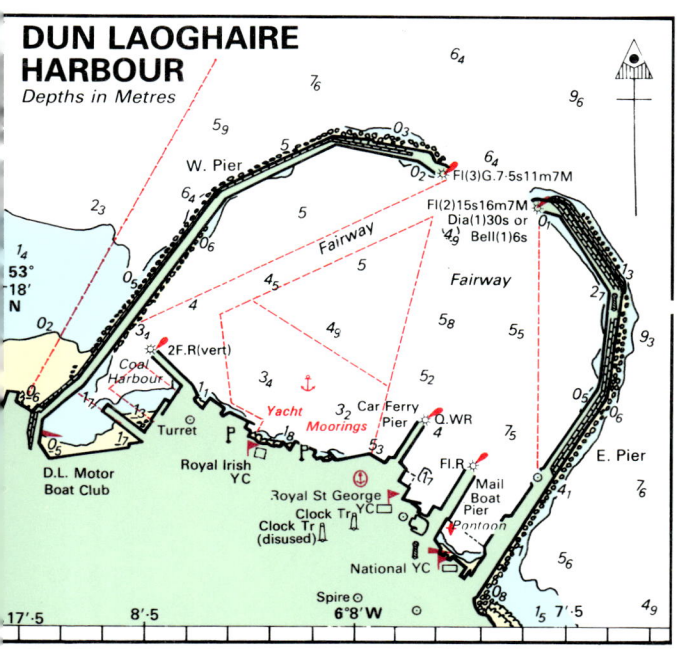

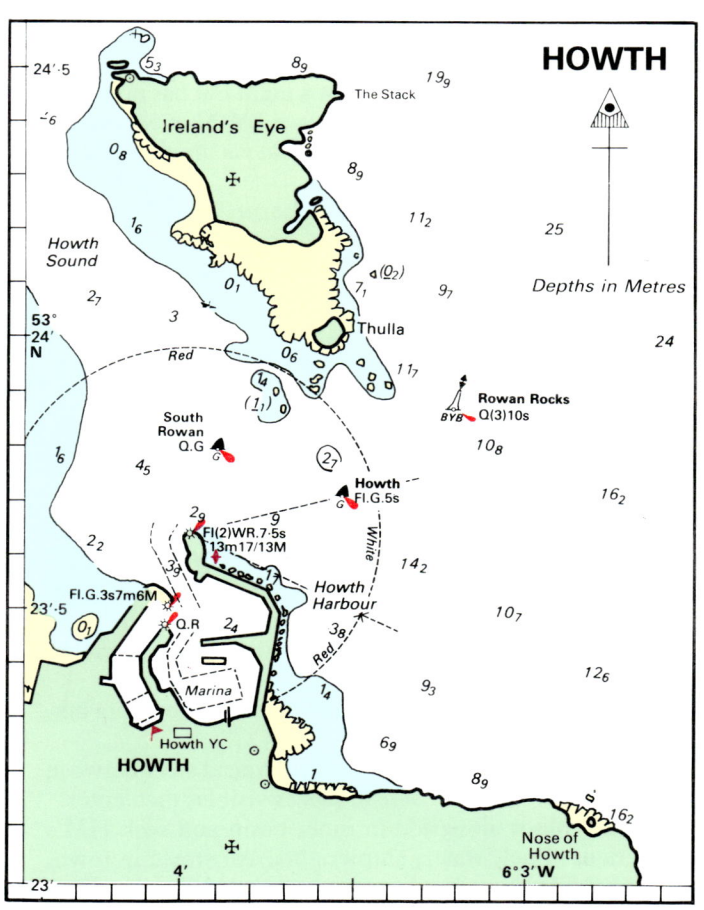

IRELAND 220

PASSAGE NOTES: DUBLIN BAY TO FAIR HEAD
Charts BA 44, 2093, 2198, 2199, 3709

Passage Lights

Ben of Howth-Baily	Fl 20s 41m 27M
Rockabill	Fl WR 12s 45m 23/19M
Carlingford - Haulbowline	Fl(3) 10s 32m 20M
St. John's Pt	Fl(2) 7.5s 37m 23
	+Fl WR 3s 15m 15/11M
South Rock Lt F	Fl(3) R30s 12m 20M
Mew Is	Fl(4) 30s 37m 30M
Black Hd	Fl 3s 45m 27M
Maidens	Fl(3) 20s 29m 23M

Tidal streams: All related to Dover.

Between Hill of Howth and St. John's Pt: DS +6h N HWD S: strong S of Rockabill Pt, weak further N and negligible S of St. John's Pt. Between St. John's Pt and Fair Hd: HWD N and NW, +6h S and SE; weak near St. John's Pt, strong N of Belfast Lough, reaching 4.5kns in entrance to North Chan. There is an inshore eddy on the SE stream between Torr Hd and Fair Hd, −4h NW for 10h.

Ballyquintin Pt, E of the entrance to Strangford Lough, should be given a berth of ½M. There are extensive rks off Kearney Pt 3¼ M NE of Ballyquintin Pt. South Rk LV is moored 2M E of South Rk, marked by a disused Lt Ho 18m high. North Rks, 1½E of Ringboy Pt, must be passed at least 1½ ca to E. Donaghadee Sound inside Copeland Is is the normal passage for yachts sailing along the coast; S entrance marked by buoys.

SE of Muck Is there is a race which should be taken with the stream. The Maidens are two dangerous groups of rks within 4M of Ballygalley Hd separated by a channel 1M wide.

Rogerstown Inlet in the bay facing Lambay Is provides sheltered anch for up to 1.7m draft. Drogheda, on R Boyne, provides good shelter for a night but has no special berths for yachts. Portavogie, some 8M N of Strangford Lough, is at present so congested that yachts should use it only in emergency.

Carnlough Hbr, some 11M N of Larne, provides shelter for yachts drawing less than 1.5m, and for these is a useful port for a passage to or from the Scottish coast.

KILKEEL
Chart BA 2800

HW:Dover +¼h, DS Dover +1h S; −5h N (weak).
MHWS 5.3m MHWN 4.4 MTL 3.1 MLWN 1.9 MLWS 0.7

A very crowded fishing port 3½M NNE of Hellyhunter buoy. Visitors are permitted to berth; useful alternative for small craft if tide into Carlingford is missed. Depth off quays is mostly 1.1m but parts of the basin and the outer end of the channel are shallower. Extensive hbr works starting 1989.

Approach From about 1M offshore with hbr bearing between 340° and 350°, or steer first for CGS.

Entrance When 100m away from pier-head steer between 010° and 015° till inner side of pier is visible, then enter.

Berthing Moor alongside in inner basin and seek HM's directions. Fuel, water, shipwrights. All stores in town, ½M. EC Thur.

CARLINGFORD LOUGH
Chart BA 2800

HW Cranfield Pt: Dover +¼h
MHWS 4.8m MHWN 4.3 MTL 2.9 MLWN 1.8 MLWS 0.7
HW Warrenpoint: Dover +½h. DS:Dover −5h N; +¼h S.

Tidal streams Weak outside, 3.5kn in buoyed approach channel, 4.5kn just E of Lt Ho, 1.5kn between entrance and Greenore, 5kn off Greenore, 2.5kn between Stalka and Watson rks, 1.5kn off Carlingford, quiet above Killowen Pt. Between Lt Ho and No.5 buoy the flood tends to N; there is a S-going eddy on flood along E side of Block House Is. Otherwise the streams follow channels. Small yachts cannot enter or leave against the tide and should have reliable power or leading wind even with fair tide. A heavy and disturbed sea occurs with a S-ly wind against the ebb immediately outside the entrance. In on shore gales the entrance is impossible.

Carlingford Lough lies 39M N of Dublin, 28M S of Strangford, and may be located by Carlingford Mt, 585m, some 5M NW of entrance and by the Mourne Mts to the N.

There are shoals E and W of the approach within 1M of the entrance pts, Ballagan on W and Cranfield on E. The whole entrance is blocked inside at LW by the Limestone Rks, except the Cut, a narrow channel 1M long on NE side.

Approach From NE or SE, leave to stb Hellyhunter buoy, S Card QG + L Fl 15s. From S, keep a mile or more of Ballagan Pt. Cranfield Pt (not conspic) with houses bearing 016° or No. 2 buoy, R, bearing N will lead to entrance.

Entrance Steer on Vidal ldg lts, RW piles Oc 3s 1M inside the Pt, 310°, along buoyed and lit chan, leaving Haulbowline Lt Ho ¼M to port, till Greenore Lt, Fl R 7.5s, bears 287°, when steer for it. Proceed between further lighted lateral buoys till abreast Killowen Pt, hence 355° to anchor off Wood House, or off Rostrevor quay, 1 to 4m.

Anchorages (1) Between quay and breakwater at Greenore just past end of old rly station in 3m.
(2) ½M N of Carlingford Hbr in 3m, or berth alongside either pier in hbr, which dries.
(3) Between Killowen Pt and Rostrevor.
(4) In SW wind, off Greer's quay.

In S wind the lough is disturbed. Squalls from the hills. Landing is impossible at Rostrevor pier at LW, but Carlingford Lough YC just N of Killowen Pt has a slip where one can always land, though caution needed at LW. Water at Greenore and Warrenpoint; stores at Greenore and Carlingford, best at Warrenpoint, there are reasonable stores at Rostrevor.

Note: The NE shore of the lough is Northern Ireland, the SW the Republic. Customs formalities are observed. EC: Carlingford Thur, Warrenpoint Wed.

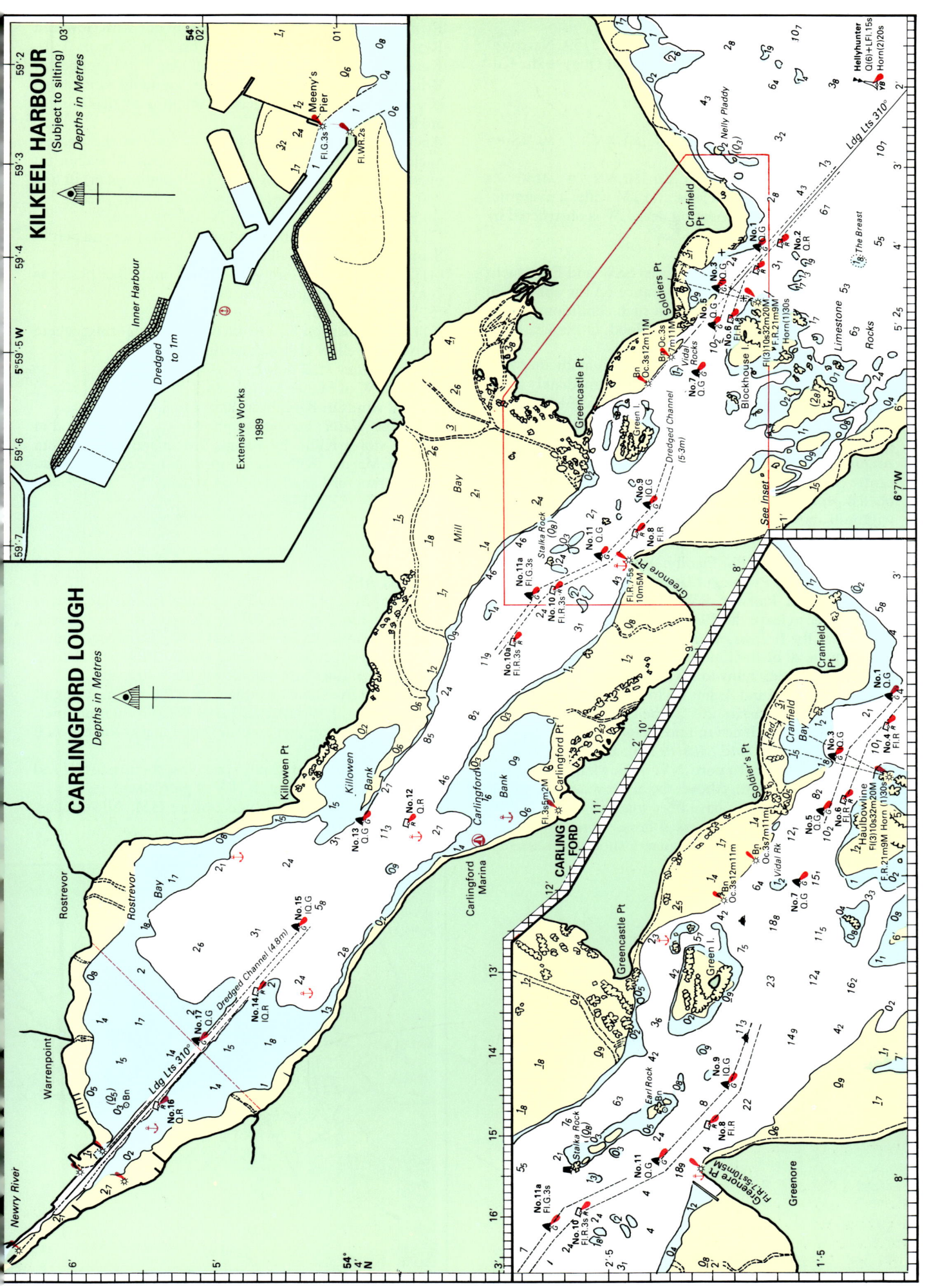

STRANGFORD LOUGH
                                Chart BA 2156 and 2159 (Narrows)
HW Killard Pt: Dover +¼h Strangford Quay +2h; Killyleagh +2¼h.
DS: Dover +2h E for 3h; +5h SW for 8h.
Killard Pt
MHWS 4.5m   MHWN 3.8   MTL 2.5   MLWN 1.2   MLWS 0.5
Strangford Quay
MHWS 3.6m   MHWN 3.1   MTL 2.0   MLWN 0.9   MLWS 0.4

Lough Strangford is 12M long and 2M wide, a magnificant small craft area. Navigation near LW is obstructed by numerous shoals called "pladdies".

Bar None in E channel.

Approach In strong winds between SSW and E no yacht should approach or leave the entrance on the ebb, when the sea breaks heavily outside. In such conditions departure should be timed for the young flood. Otherwise enter with flood and leave with ebb.
The stream runs true, out of the Narrows at 2h after HW and in at LW (Belfast) except that immediately N of Angus Rk flood and ebb run NW and SE respectively. At Bankmore Pt the spring stream runs at 7kn.
Guns Is, 30m high with W obelisk bn, is SW of entrance. Angus Tr, Fl 5s, 13m with con topmark, is visible in the centre of the entrance, with Angus Bn, a truncated obelisk, further to port. N of entrance there is a conspic windmill above Portaferry.
From S give St. Patrick's Rk bn, 3 ca off Killard Pt, a good berth. From N clear Bar Pladdy, 0.6m, S Card lt buoy, by keeping Ringfad Pt open of Guns Is. Alternatively, make for Strangford Fairway RW safe water buoy, Fl 10s; thence steer to leave Bar Pladdy buoy to stb.

Entrance: By E chan, when N end of Portaferry town comes open W of Bankmore Hill and Rue Pt steer 342°, leaving Bar Pladdy buoy to stb and Pladdy Lug W pile bn at least 1 ca to stb and Angus bn to port, into the Narrows till Kilclief castle bears 265°, when Meadows shoal has been left to port. Hence in mid-channel to pass between Gowland Rks bn Oc (2) 10s to stb, and poles and bns marking shoal water to port. NW of Gowland Rks strong eddies in midstream. Above the narrows many of the perches on the dangers have been marked with reflective tape in differing combinations of broad or narrow bands. Then anchor as required. Strangers should not attempt other channels.

By night keep Dog Tail Pt Oc(4) 10s in line with Gowland Rks Oc(2) 10s 341° until Salt Rk bn Fl R 3s bears 330°. Keep Salt Rk bn on this bearing till Dog Tail Pt is abeam. Bring this lt on a bearing of 098° and sound into anchorage (1). It is risky for strangers to attempt to make other anchorages by night.

Anchorage (1) Cross Roads on W side is the nearest anchorage to the entrance, but no landing. W anchor bn on shore, and a W bn on Tully Hill (not on plan) in line 260° lead into the anchorage; anchor in 3.5m.
(2) Ballyhenry Bay, ¼M from Portaferry town.
(3) In Audleys Roads between small stone pier and perch. S and inside of this is all shoal.
(4) Quoile R inside Gore's Is, 2 to 4m, and other places as convenient in this immediate area.
(5) S of Killyleagh, 2m or more.
(6) Inside Trasnagh Is, 2 to 4m off SLYC moorings where there are 5 yellow visitors moorings.
(7) S of Rainey Is, 2 to 6m.
(8) S and W of Mahee Is, 4 to 6m.
(9) In E winds in Kircubbin Bay, 4 to 8m.

Facilities Water: taps at Ringhaddy CC pontoon and at SLYC; stores Killinchy village, 2M inland. Diesel from Morrow Marine, Killyleagh. Stores and petrol also available at Strangford and Portaferry Village.

ARDGLASS   Chart BA 633
Pier hbr 1M N of Ringfad Pt, a conical hill with tr, always available, has 2 to 3m. SE winds send in heavy swell. There is an inner basin with 3m at HW, bottom deep mud, affording perfect shelter at all times. Rks extend from both sides of the shore outside the hbr entrance.

Approach Give shore on either side a fair berth. At night: approach in the W sector of Iso 4s WRG lt on inner pier. Opposite the outer pier an iron tripod marks the rks on E side of fairway.

Entrance Round end of outer pier close to, turn to SW and leave tripod bn marking rk NW of pier, to stb.

Berthing Berth alongside and contact HM. All supplies. Bus to Downpatrick.

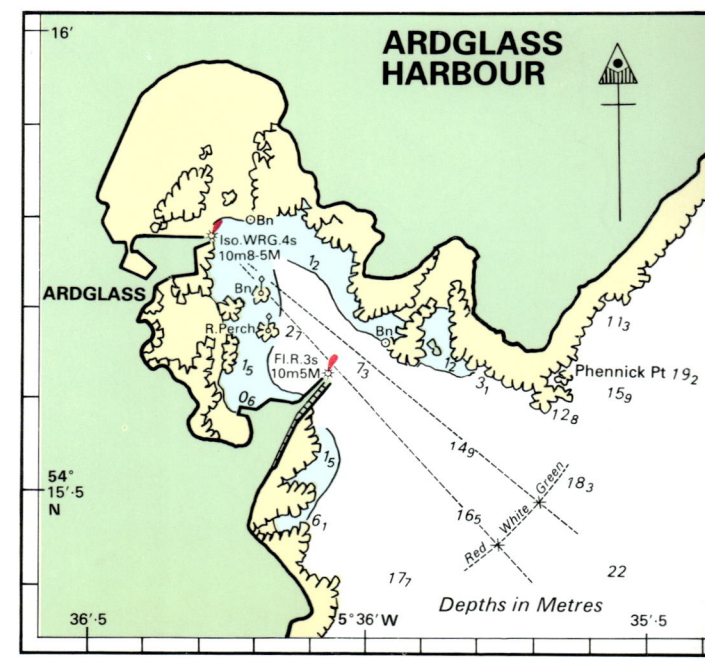

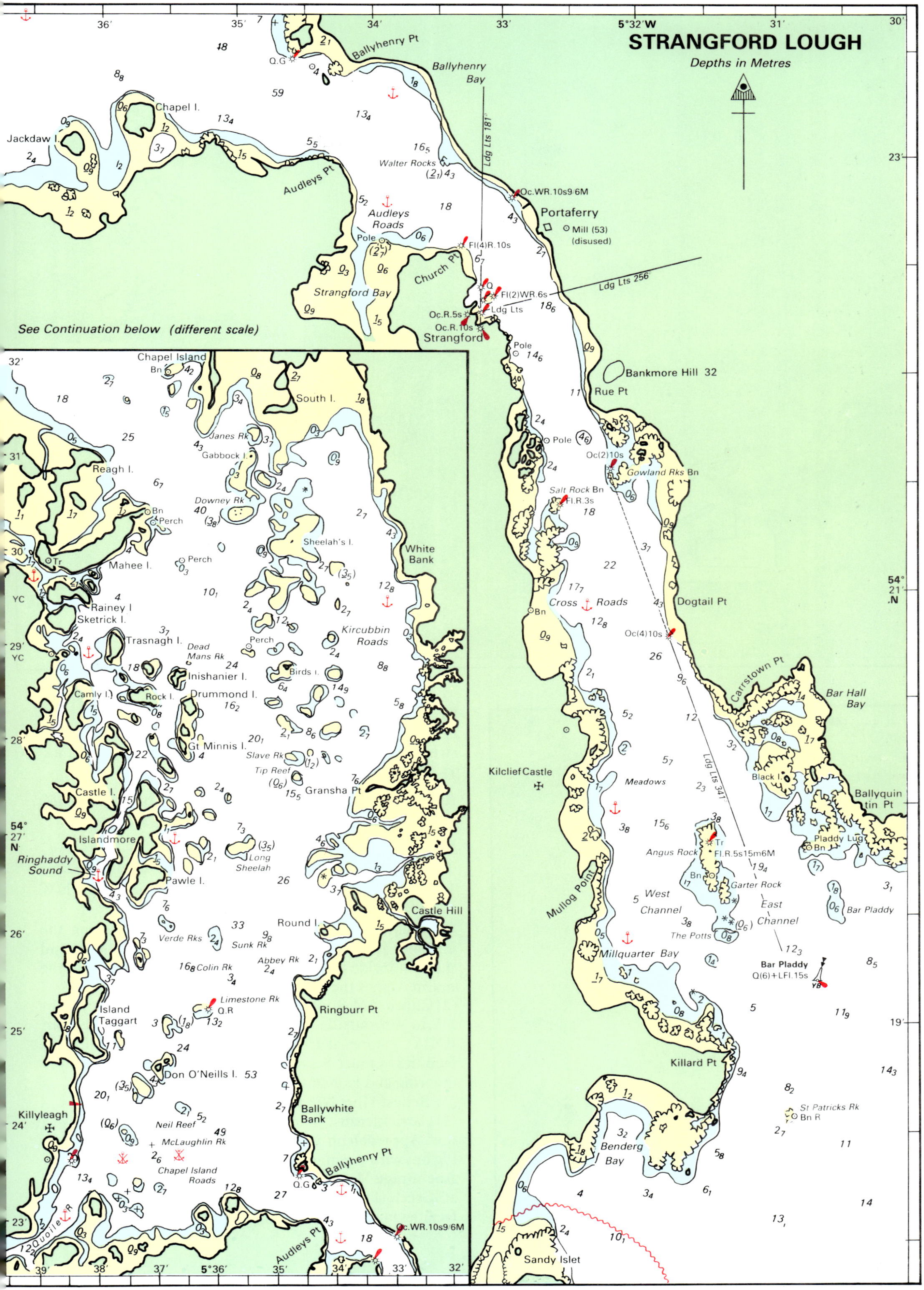
STRANGFORD LOUGH
Depths in Metres
Ballyhenry Pt
Ballyhenry Bay
Chapel I.
Jackdaw I.
Audleys Pt
Walter Rocks
Audleys Roads
Pole
Oc.WR.10s9/6M
Portaferry
Mill (53) (disused)
Fl(4)R.10s
Church Pt
Strangford Bay
Ldg Lts 181°
Ldg Lts 256°
Fl(2)WR.6s
Ldg Lts
Oc.R.5s
Oc.R.10s
Strangford
Q.G
See Continuation below (different scale)
Bankmore Hill 32
Rue Pt
Oc(2)10s
Gowland Rks Bn
Salt Rock Bn
Fl.R.3s
Cross Roads
Dogtail Pt
Oc(4)10s
Carrstown Pt
Bar Hall Bay
Kilclief Castle
Meadows
Ldg Lts 341°
Black I.
Ballyquintin Pt
Pladdy Lug
Angus Rock
Tr
Fl.R.5s15m6M
Garter Rock
Bar Pladdy
Mullog Point
West Channel
East Channel
The Potts
Millquarter Bay
Bar Pladdy Q(6)+LFl.15s
YB
Killard Pt
St Patricks Rk
Bn R
Benderg Bay
Sandy Islet
5°32'W
54° 21' N
Chapel Island Bn
South I.
Janes Rk
Gabbock I.
Reagh I.
Downey Rk
Bn
Perch
Sheelah's I.
White Bank
Mahee I.
Tr
Rainey I
Sketrick I.
Kircubbin Roads
Trasnagh I.
Dead Mans Rk
Inishanier I.
Birds I.
Camly I.
Rock I.
Drummond I.
Gt Minnis I.
Slave Rk
Tip Reef
Gransha Pt
Castle I.
Islandmore
Ringhaddy Sound
Long Sheelah
Pawle I.
Castle Hill
Round I.
Verde Rks
Sunk Rk
Abbey Rk
Colin Rk
Limestone Rk
Q.R
Ringburr Pt
Island Taggart
Don O'Neills I.
Killyleagh
Ballywhite Bank
Neil Reef
McLaughlin Rk
Ballyhenry Pt
Chapel Island Roads
Q.G
Quoile R
Audleys Pt
Oc.WR.10s9/6M
5°36'
54° 27' N

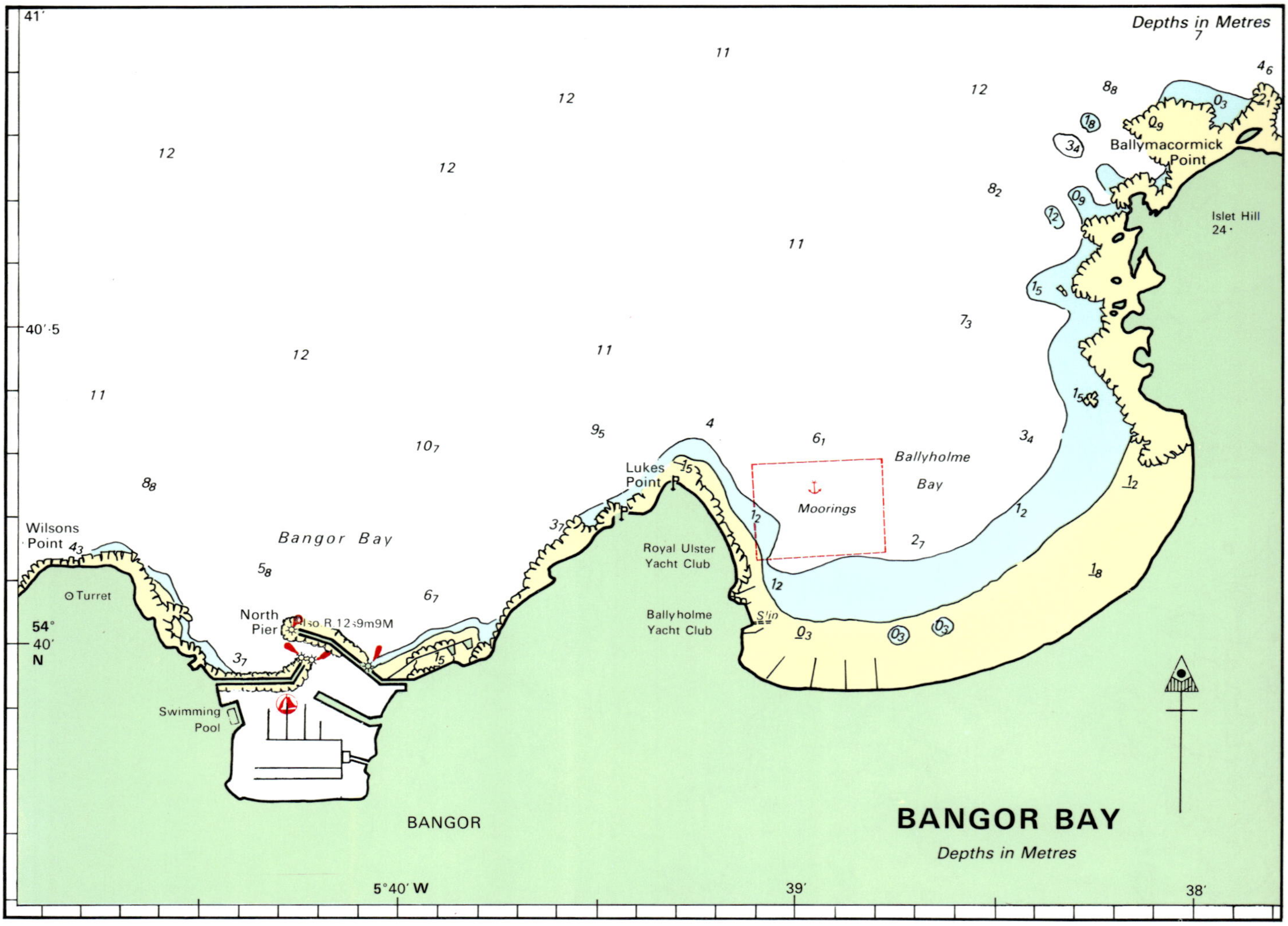

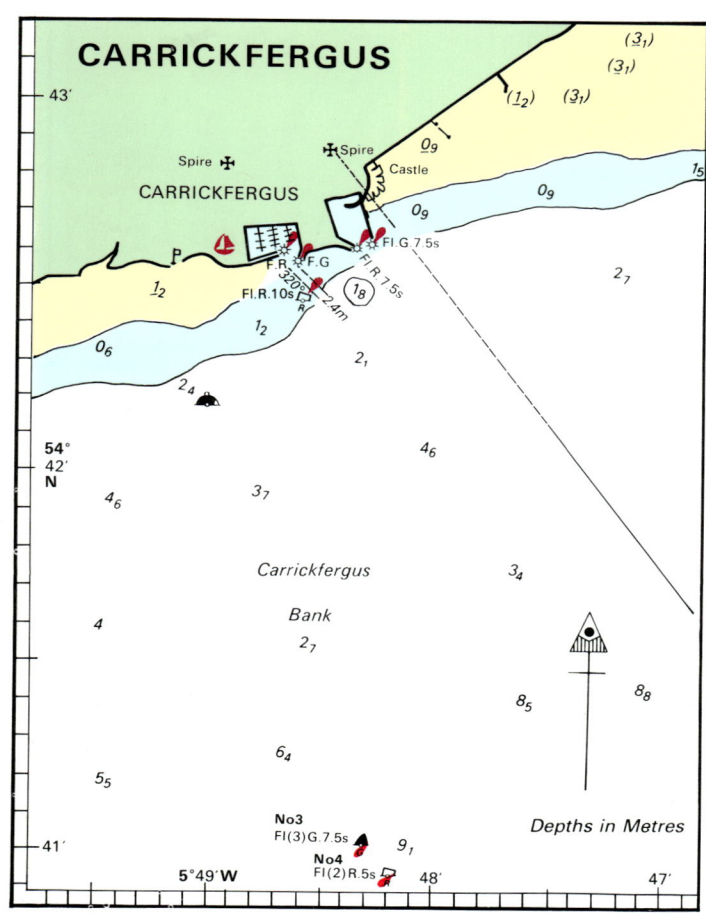

BELFAST LOUGH Chart BA 1753

HW: Dover HW DS in offing : Dover +1h N
MHWS 3.5m MHWN 3.0 MTL 2.0 MLWN 1.1 MLWS 0.4
The lough is 10½M long, depths decreasing from 12 to 3m.

Approach Rounding Orlock Pt, avoid the Briggs Rks ¾M offshore, R can buoy, Gp Fl R (2) 10s.

Berthing (1) Bangor
(a) Anchor in Ballyholme Bay in 3.5 to 5.5m, or on a Ballyholme YC visitor's mooring, exposed to winds from NW to NE;
(b) Bangor marina with all facilities. On approach the entrance is obscured; leave lt on N pier well to port and dolphin inside to stb carrying on until the entrance to the marina opens then turn sharp to stb.
(2) Cultra, 5M W of Bangor. Anchor in offshore winds in 3.5 to 4m outside yacht moorings. Water, diesel from RNIYC, stores at Holywood 1M. Boatyard and slipping facilities contact Secretary on Belfast 428041 for visitors mooring and launch service.
(3) Belfast Hbr: Not now suitable for yachts.
(4) Carrickfergus. Marina about 330m W of Carrickfergus hbr. Approach on 320° to marina retaining wall which has ldg bns with top marks Fl W. Turn sharply to stb to enter.
Anchorage W of Carrickfergus Bank in 2m 2 ca offshore at Greenisland. All stores in Carrickfergus town. All facilities including fuel, chandlery and sailmaker in marina.

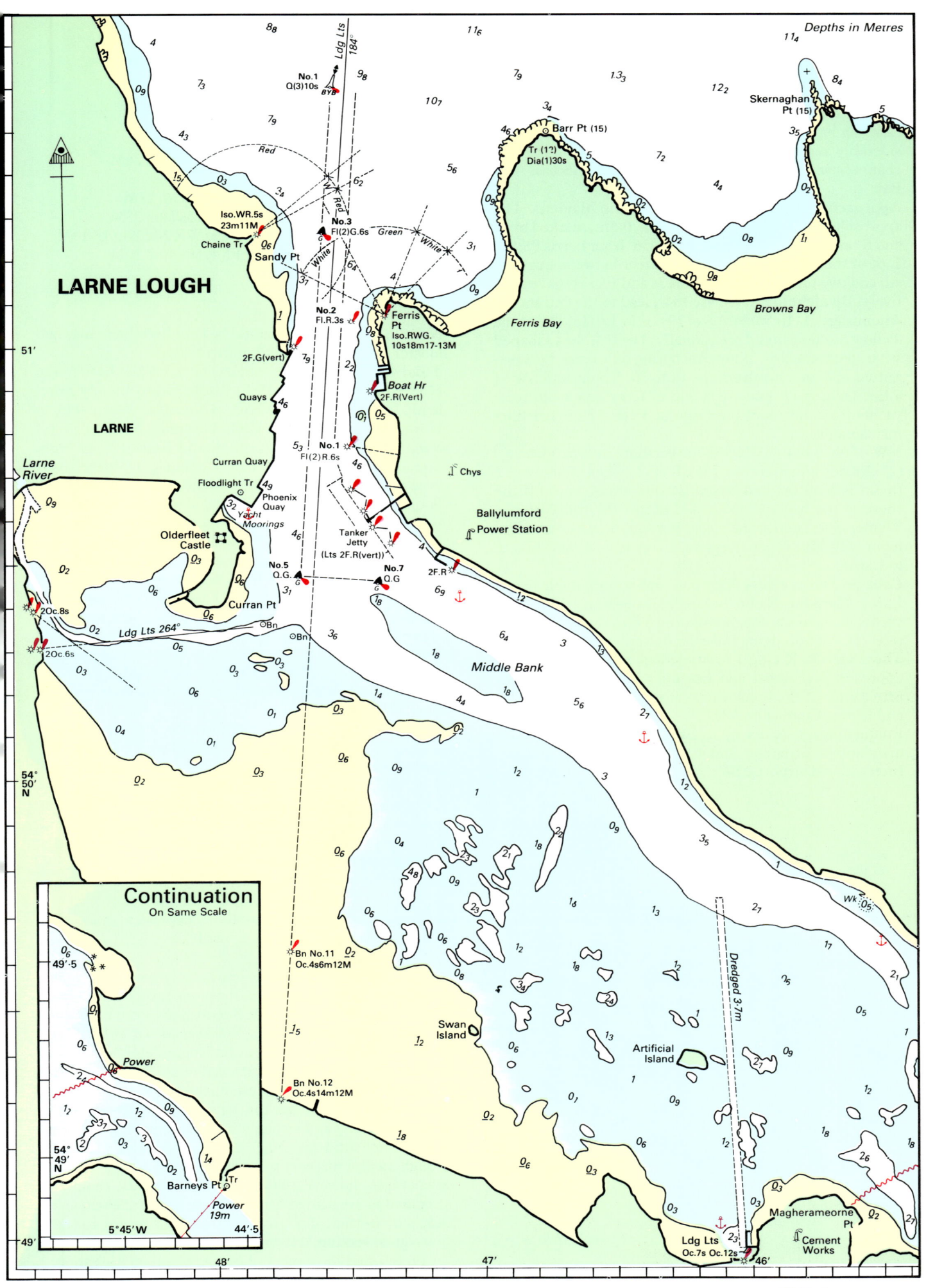

LARNE LOUGH
Chart BA 1237

HW: Dover +¼h. DS: HWD N

MHWS 2.8m MHWN 2.5 MTL 1.6 MLWN 0.8 MLWS 0.4

Larne Lough affords the best shelter between Belfast and Foyle loughs.

Tidal Streams run strongly in the offing, 4.6kn max, and raise big lop. The navigable area within the lough is considerably reduced by shoal banks on the W side. The channel carries 6m for ½M, and 4m to 2m abreast Mill Bay.

Approach The entrance lies 4M S of the Maidens. The approach is obstructed by Hunter Rk, 0.8m, marked by N and S card lt buoys, situated 2¼M 036° from Ferris Pt, the E pt of the entrance. On entering steer between quays to stb and two pile bns to port, Fl R 3s and Fl(2) R 6s respectively. By night ldg lt, Oc 4s, 184°, lead to the entrance.

Anchorage (1) In 5m ¾M S of Ferris Pt Lt Ho, SW of the Yellow Stone (painted occasionally) 1 ca E of the L-shaped wharf opposite No 7 Buoy. Anchoring off Curran Pt is permitted NW of a line from the Pt to No 5 buoy and SW of a line from No 5 buoy to S end of ferry quays but local yachts leave no room for visitors; VHF 37 for berthing instructions.

NW of No 5 buoy. VHF 37 for berthing instructions.

(2) Outside a shallow bay 1M SE of (1), ½ ca offshore in 2 to 3m NW of moored boats. Beware wreck ¾ ca off the shore of the bay and 1¼ ca SE of its NW tip. Water at Wymers Pier, petrol and stores in town, diesel by arrangement with Hbr office. Repairs. Ferry from Island Magee to Larne.

Caution This is a busy ferry port and it is advisable to call Larne Harbour Radio before approaching. There are yachts moorings at Magheramorne YC in about 2m on stb side - beware dredging holes on bottom when anchoring. There are Oc R Ldg Lts into Magheramorne YC. The approach is dredged and has unlit leading marks. The actual ends of the breakwaters at entrance have lighted R and G bns. Contact on VHF.

Frequent ferry service up to 10/12 sailings per day to UK mainland at Stranraer and Cairnryan. Train to Belfast. International airport 20M.

PASSAGE NOTES: FAIR HEAD TO BLOODY FORELAND

Passage Lights

Altacarry Hd (Rathlin East)	Fl(4) 20s 74m 26M
Rathlin West	Fl R 5s 62m 22M
Inishtrahull	Fl(3) 15s 59m 25M
Fanad Hd	Fl(5) WR 20s 39m 18/14M
Tory Island	Fl(4) 30s 40m 30M

Note: A sharp lookout should be kept for salmon nets and lobster pots when navigating this coast.

Tidal steams DS (all related to Dover): Fair Hd to Malin Hd, +1h WNW, −5h ESE. Malin Hd to Bloody Foreland, inshore, −2½h WSW, +3h ENE. Malin Hd to Horn Hd, offshore, −5½ ENE, becoming E and SE; −1½ SW, becoming W, slack −2½h and from +3h to +6h. Streams are strong near Fair Hd but get progressively weaker to W; 6kn in Rathlin Sound, 4kn in Inishtrahull Sound, 2kn in Tory Sound. Detailed tidal stream information and advice, beyond the scope of these notes, from ICC SDs. Rathlin Sound, 2 to 3M wide, is the normal approach to the N coast. A fair tide is essential; the overfall SW of Rue Pt must be avoided from +1h to +3h. Beware Carrickmannanon Rk, 3 ca NE of Kinbane Pt, across which the tidal streams set. Skerries Sd is convenient in moderate conditions but keep outside in swell or strong offshore winds.

Inishtrahull Sound should not be attempted if there is a big sea running; in bad weather it is advisable to pass 3M N of Torr Rks.

Between Lough Swilly and Mulroy Bay the coast should be given a wide berth using the clearing marks on chart BA 2699. An area of abnormal magnetic variation has been reported 1M 250° from Malin Hd.

Portstewart is a small hbr 2½ SW of Portrush which in quiet weather is convenient for a temporary visit, and advice may be obtained about entering the Bann and a berth arranged at Coleraine Marina.

Culdaff Bay provides good anchorage in winds between SE and NNW, and is useful if awaiting favourable conditions for Inishtrahull Sound. Sheephaven anchorage offers a reasonable anchorage: see ICC.

The N coast of Ireland is most beautiful, with many interesting geological formations, including the famous Giant's Causeway, and in ideal conditions it can be an idyllic cruising ground. It must, however, never be forgotten that the whole length of the coast is completely exposed to the full weight of the Atlantic swell when the wind is from between W and N, and in established strong winds from this quarter, conditions can be such as to test even the most seaworthy and strongly crewed yacht. If conditions deteriorate suddenly, the most satisfactory refuge is Lough Swilly; it is easy to enter and there are a number of anchorages, however, boats cruising the coast should be prepared to keep to sea for some time before shelter can be reached. Indeed, if a strong SW-ly wind begins to show any sign of veering, it is wise to consider putting in straight away, to avoid the danger of being caught on a lee shore.

IRELAND
NORTH AND WEST COASTS

Depths in Metres

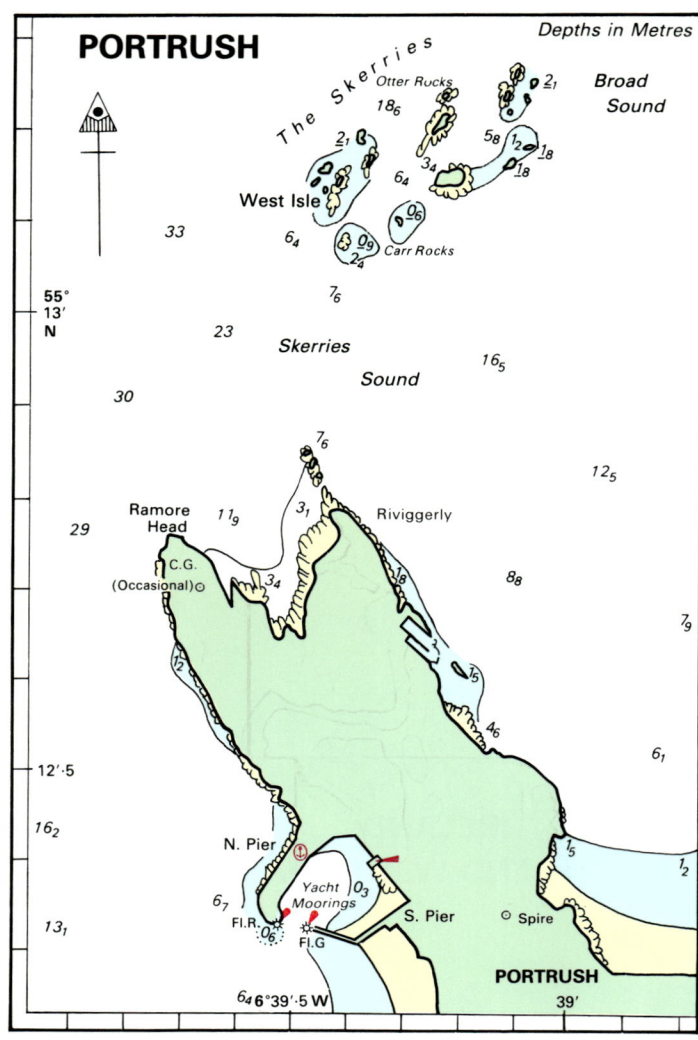

PORTRUSH   Chart BA 49

HW Dover −4¼h. DS: Dover +6h E; HWD W
MHWS 2.1m   MHWN 1.4   MTL 1.2   MLWN 1.1   MLWS 0.4
A small crowded hbr on W side of Ramore Hd, good shelter except in N gales. RNLI Station.

Approach Swell makes entrance difficult in onshore winds over F4. Beware submerged breakwater projecting 20m SW from N pier.

Entrance Hbr has 2m in entrance. 3 to 5m inside.

Berthing Berth alongside N quay and seek directions from hbr office, also temporary pontoon berthing. Rly to Belfast and Derry; all supplies. EC Wed.

RIVER BANN   Chart BA 2723, 2798

HW Coleraine: Dover −3¾h.
MHWS 2.1m   MHWN 1.6   MTL 1.2   MLWN 0.7   MLWS 0.3
Bar 3.7m.

Approach River mouth is between stone training walls projecting 2 ca N from beaches. It must not be attempted in strong onshore winds or if swell is breaking noticeably on ends of training walls.

Entrance Keep towards E wall as W wide is foul with boulders. Channel 45m wide, dredged to 3.2m, is marked with lights (which may be weak) and bns. Beware possible salmon nets across full width of river. Ebb runs at 4kn.

Berthing (1) In Coleraine Marina on NE bank 4M from entrance. Water and food on pontoons, chandlery, 15T Travellift crane. Shops ½M away.
(2) Anchor on NE side ½M upstream of old CG, clear of channel.

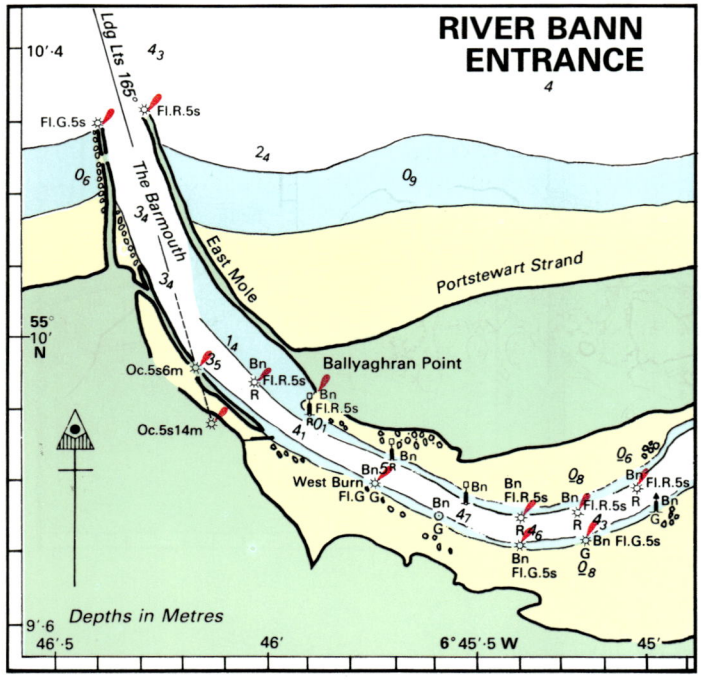

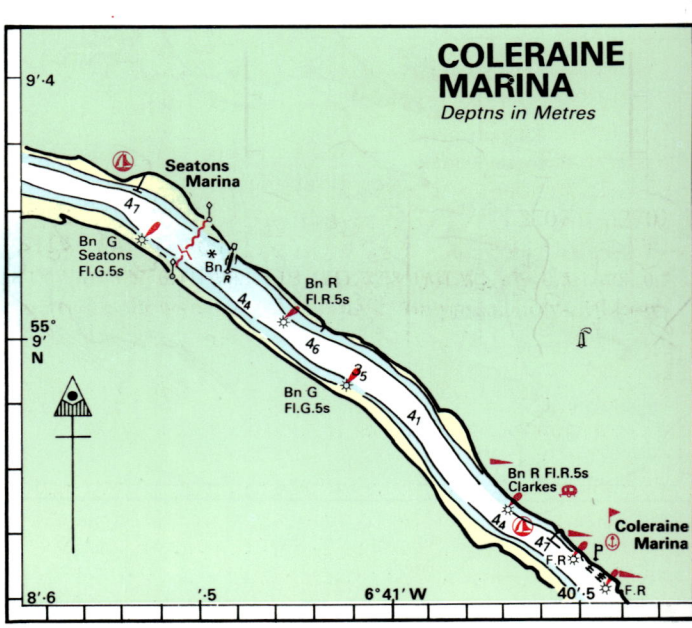

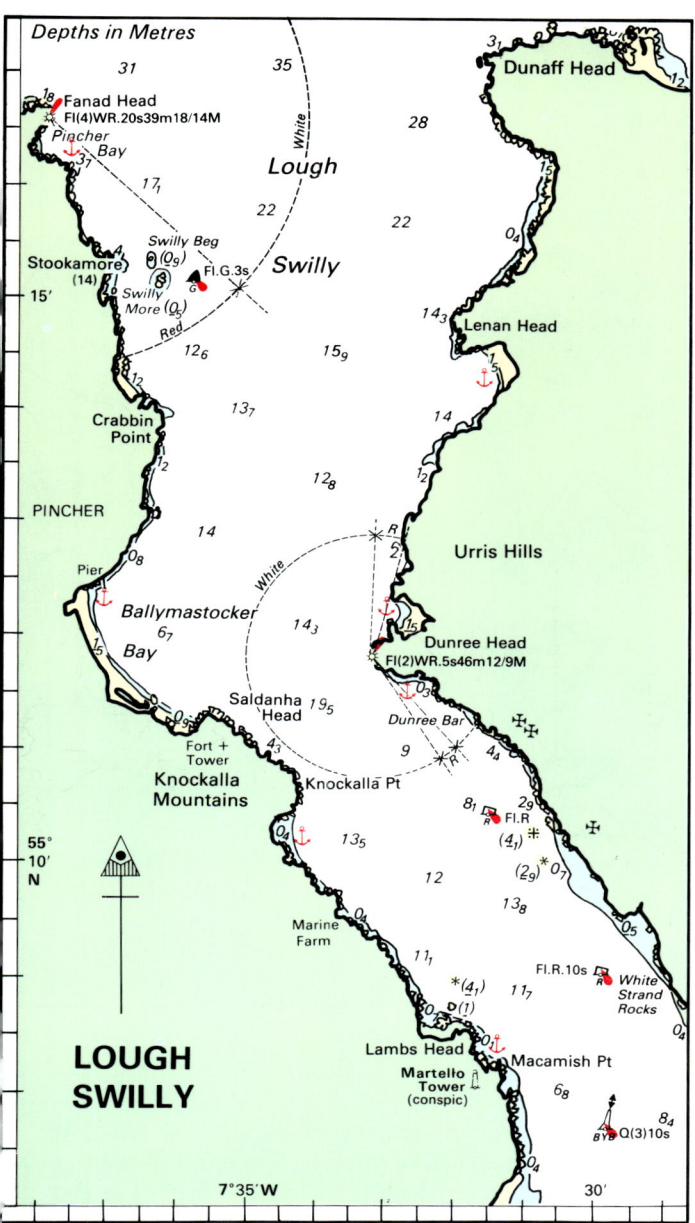

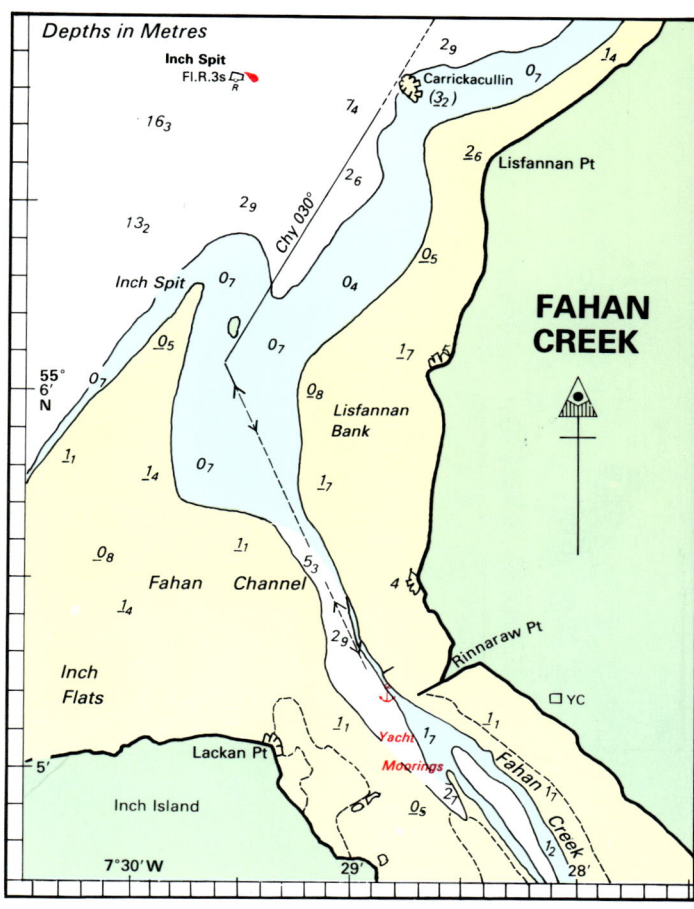

moored yachts in 2 to 5.5m. Bus to Buncrana and Londonderry. New sketch plan in ICC amendments. Sometimes the entrance is buoyed by the local YC.
(3) W of Macamish Pt sheltered from SW to N through W, 3 to 5m, sand.
(4) Rathmullan Rd, N of pier off the town. The best place for visiting yachts; water at pier-head, small grocery, petrol, good local hotels.

LOUGH SWILLY   Chart BA 2697

HW Rathmullan: Dover −4¾h.

MHWS 4.3m   MHWN 3.2   MTL 2.5   MLWN 1.9   MLWS 0.5
The lough is entered between Fanad Head Lt and the bold Head of Dunaff. It is 26M long, 3½M wide, and has 15 to 20m up to Fort Stewart; bottom sand and mud.
Approach Care should be taken to carry tide through Inishtrahull Sound, where the W-going stream runs 3h only. Give W pt of entrance a berth of ½M and leave Swilly Rks G con buoy (Fl G 3s) to stb. By night, keep out of the R sector of Fanad Lt.
Entrance Off Dunree Hd up to Buncrana Bay, keep at least ½M clear to W, or keep Dunree Hd and Fanad Lt in line.
Anchorages (1) Pincher Bay, 4½M inside Fanad Hd on W shore, anchor off the pier in 2 to 5m, small shop and pub. Exposed to E.
(2) Fahan Creek is the most sheltered anchorage although uncomfortable in NW winds; the entrance is silting and the rise of the tide irregular. Yachts drawing over 1.8m should not attempt it; others are advised to enter 1-1½h before HW and leave if they ground. Anchor SE of

MULROY BAY   Chart BA 2699

HW (bar): Dover −4.55h.

MHWS 3.9m   MHWN 2.9
Mulroy Bay affords 12M of navigable channel. A power cable across Moross channel, clearance 6m, bars North Water to yachts with higher fixed masts. Some of the finest scenery in Ireland.

IRELAND   230

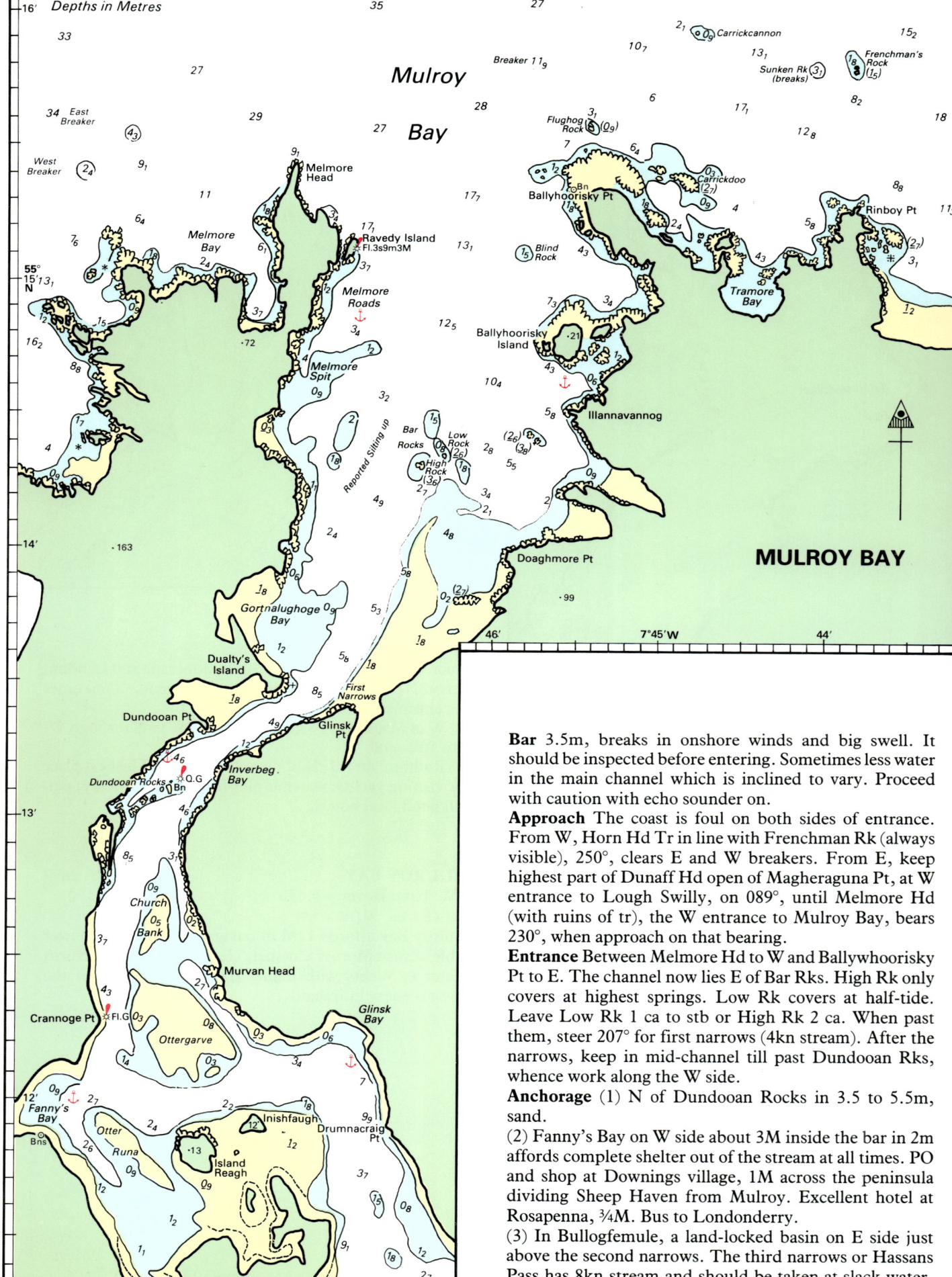

MULROY BAY

Bar 3.5m, breaks in onshore winds and big swell. It should be inspected before entering. Sometimes less water in the main channel which is inclined to vary. Proceed with caution with echo sounder on.

Approach The coast is foul on both sides of entrance. From W, Horn Hd Tr in line with Frenchman Rk (always visible), 250°, clears E and W breakers. From E, keep highest part of Dunaff Hd open of Magheraguna Pt, at W entrance to Lough Swilly, on 089°, until Melmore Hd (with ruins of tr), the W entrance to Mulroy Bay, bears 230°, when approach on that bearing.

Entrance Between Melmore Hd to W and Ballywhoorisky Pt to E. The channel now lies E of Bar Rks. High Rk only covers at highest springs. Low Rk covers at half-tide. Leave Low Rk 1 ca to stb or High Rk 2 ca. When past them, steer 207° for first narrows (4kn stream). After the narrows, keep in mid-channel till past Dundooan Rks, whence work along the W side.

Anchorage (1) N of Dundooan Rocks in 3.5 to 5.5m, sand.

(2) Fanny's Bay on W side about 3M inside the bar in 2m affords complete shelter out of the stream at all times. PO and shop at Downings village, 1M across the peninsula dividing Sheep Haven from Mulroy. Excellent hotel at Rosapenna, ¾M. Bus to Londonderry.

(3) In Bullogfemule, a land-locked basin on E side just above the second narrows. The third narrows or Hassans Pass has 8kn stream and should be taken at slack water. Flood begins at Dover +4h, ebb at −2½h.

IRELAND, WEST COAST

The coast resembles the W coast of Scotland and the Scandinavian peninsula. In an uncharacteristically 'purple' passage, H.J. Hanson, who compiled the early editions of this Handbook almost singlehanded, wrote, "The splendour of the mountains, their varying colours, whether in the rising or setting sunlight, by noonday or under the moon, the glory of the sea in fine weather at sundown, when it often resembles a lake of molten gold, the mighty cliffs, attaining in Donegal and Mayo to a height of nearly 2,000 ft, and the secure harbours scattered with few exceptions at easy intervals, will well repay the efforts required to reach these waters." That is as true today as it was when it was written over fifty years ago.

Except when crossing the mouth of Donegal Bay and between Galway Bay and the Blaskets, there is usually an easily accessible hbr close by. In unsettled weather a yacht may be held up to leeward of one or other of the headlands, but on such occasions most hbrs afford facilities for dinghy sailing or excursions.

Although a careful and experienced skipper can in general navigate this coast with ease and confidence, it is fully exposed to the Atlantic swell. If overtaken by bad weather and poor visibility, unless a familiar anchorage is close at hand it may well be necessary to get clear of the land until the weather improves. This coast should therefore be cruised only by seaworthy yachts capable of making to windward and remaining at sea in any conditions.

Local opinion is that the sailing season starts well on in May and closes early in September, on account of the heavy swell which is usually running in the Atlantic at other times of the year. So long as there is swell in the offing, only a moderate onshore breeze is needed to bring it quickly into the coast, but from the end of June the coast is usually subject only to such seas as may be caused by local breezes or a summer gale.

Many W coast anchorages have heavy growths of kelp on the bottom, and the CQR anchor (at least in weights below 30kg) tends to clog and drag, as does the Danforth. A large fisherman is the traditional solution: the Bruce is also well thought of in some quarters. Whatever is used, it is wise to ensure that the anchor is holding, particularly in calm conditions, by reversing the motor. Vessels are advised to moor on two anchors when left unattended on such ground.

Streams are not extensively charted, but are apt to be considerably stronger off headlands giving rise to confused and possibly breaking seas with any weight of wind. Headlands such as Bloody Foreland, Erris, Achill, Slyne and Loop Heads should be treated with the greatest respect and an offing of two to three miles lessens the chances of a shaking-up when rounding. Avoid, in all but calm periods, those areas in which the symbol for overfalls is indicated on the chart.

The ensuing pages of this Handbook provide, in each of three sections of the coast between Bloody Foreland and Valentia, brief general notes followed by short notes on a selection of harbours. They indicate possible harbours of refuge for cruise planning purposes only: bad weather may make it unsafe to approach any harbour. Anyone cruising the area should regard the ICC Sailing Directions as essential.

PASSAGE NOTES: BLOODY FORELAND TO ERRIS HEAD

Passage Lights
  Aranmore Rinrawros Pt Fl(2) 20s 71m 29M
  Rathlin O'Birne Is   Fl WR 20s 35m 22/18M
  Eagle Is   Fl(3) 10s 67m 26M

The Rosses, extending 15M from the Bloody Foreland to Aranmore, afford a fascinating cruising area on the direct route for a yacht sailing round Ireland, sheltered by a string of islands and with several good anchorages. The Stag Rocks and more particularly the Bullogconnell shoals must be given a good berth.

The direct course between Rinrawros Pt on Aranmore and Rathlin O'Birne some 20M to S leads clear of dangers, but there is a strong set into Boylagh Bay.
Yachts proceeding S with insufficient time to explore Donegal Bay should make for Erris Hd (47M from Rathlin O'Birne) with the option of putting into Broadhaven or carrying on. Proceeding N on the direct passage, Rathlin O'Birne is the best landfall, with the options of making for Killybegs (or Teelin in favourable weather) or for Aranmore.
For those with more time Donegal Bay contains several interesting inlets between Sligo and Killybegs. Between Killala and Broadhaven there is a 24M stretch of inhospitable coast which should be given a wide berth in all but exceptionally calm and settled conditions.
The best hbrs of refuge are Killybegs, Aran Road in W winds and Rutland hbr inside Aranmore in S or E winds although passage into the latter is intricate.

ARANMORE (Aran Roads)   Charts BA 1883, 2792
This is a very popular area of the W of Ireland having many good anchorages with good shelter. As there are many holiday homes in the area supplies and fuel are relatively easy. The approaches from the N or S are well described in the ICC sailing Directions. Most of the difficult parts of the roads are well marked by buoys, leading lights and beacons. Chart 1883 is essential and 2792 is essential for Burtonport and Rutland Hbr. The best anchorage is in the N Sound on the Aran Shore just N of the Black Rock in 4m. Other places are in Chapel Bay to S of Aran in 4m and Rossillian Bay in 2m both rather subject to swell. Both Rutland Hbr and Burtonport on the mainland are well sheltered and are approachable under power as the various channels are well marked but narrow.

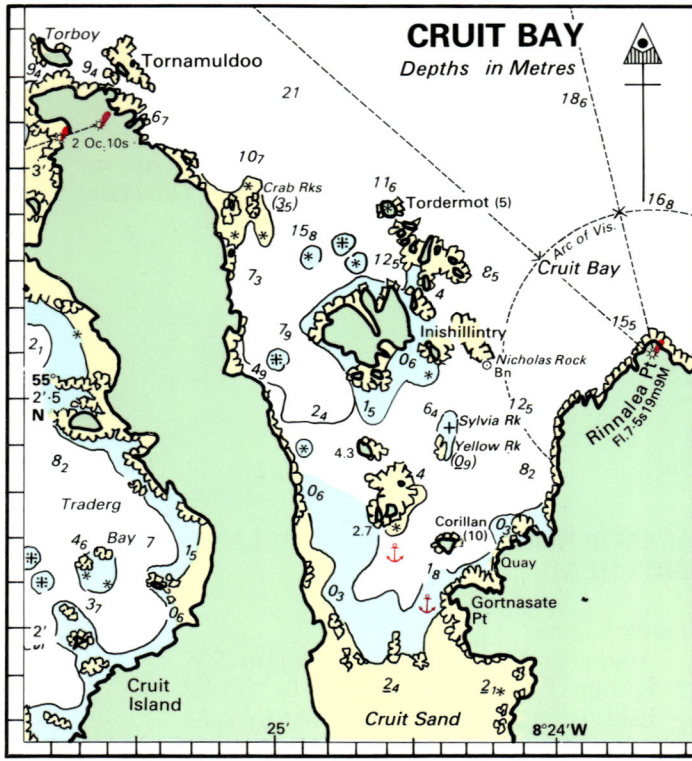
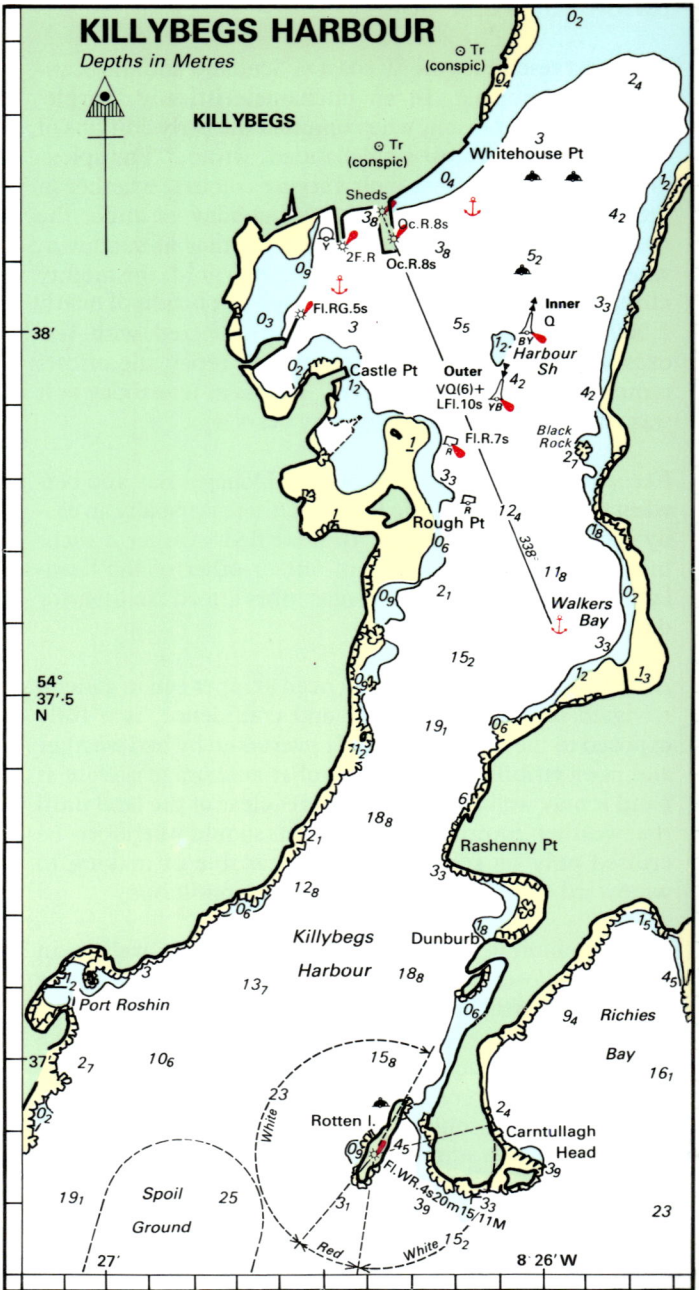

CRUIT BAY (pronounced Critch)   Chart BA 1883
HW: Dover −5¼h
MHWS 3.5m   MHWN 2.4   MTL 2.2   MLWN 1.5   MLWS 0.5
A good anchorage in all summer winds, and easy to enter, however, there is a swell particularly in N-ly winds. The ebb runs out strongly.
Approach from N. Leave Gola Island which has Knockaculleen 69m at the N end to port with a fair offing ½M and head due S to leave Inishfree also to port. This takes a yacht clear of all possible breakers. The transit for entering Cruit Bay is Gortnasate Point open E of Corillan Is 195°. The Is is well into the bay.
Entrance Keeping on the transit leave Nicholas Rock with bn to stb. This also clears the Yellow Rock. On closing Corillan turn to stb and round the islet close leaving it to port. Take care not to mistake the entrance with the bay to the W of Tordermot and Inishillintry which is very foul.
Anchorages (1) Just S of Corillan in 2m sand.
(2) To W of the above and N of existing local boats, also in sand. Take care not to get N by W of Corillan as there is a bad rock just off an unmarked Is in this area.
(3) It is possible to go alongside Gortnasate Quay while getting stores. Facilities: water at quay. PO and limited stores at Kincaslough ½M. Fuel 2M. Enquire from the locals who may be able to help with transport.

KILLYBEGS   Charts BA 2702 2792
HW: Dover −5½h.
MHWS 5.1m   MHWN 3.9   MTL 2.9   MLWN 2.0   MLWS 0.6
A very busy fishing port, yachts should not be left unattended except for very short periods. However it does provide very good shelter and can be entered day or night. New quays recently built.
Approach From the W. Pass two miles S of Muckross Head and head E until the E side of Drumanoo Head bears NE, then turn in to pass SE of it, passing midway between Ellamore Shoal or the 14.3m shoal, 1½M to the W. In heavy westerly weather it can break heavily on these shoals.
From the S Leave Inishmurray 2M to port and head for Bullockmore buoy which lies 3M W of St John's Point then alter course for Drumanoo Head to leave Ellamore shoal to stb and follow the directions above.
Entrance Keep in the mid channel leaving Rotten Island Fl WR 4s 15/11M to stb. Keeping mid channel pick up buoy off Rough Pt and head for the S card buoy VQ(6) + LFl 10s on the Harbour Shoal and when ½ ca S of this buoy turn in towards the quays. There are ldg lts Oc R 8s. bearing 338°.
Anchorages (1) To the E of the town in 2.5 to 3.5m in mud, thus avoiding heavy fishing boat traffic. Sometimes poor in SW-ly weather.
(2) To the SW of W end of the town in 4 to 7m. Subject to fishing boat traffic.
(3) In Walkers Bay if the wind is S-ly. Off the slip to NW in 5 to 8m, avoiding local moorings.
Warning: Do not anchor in Port Roshin, holding poor and an uncharted rock. Beware of lost ground tackle in all anchorages. All facilities in town except sailmaker; buses to Donegal Town and Sligo. Call HM on VHF for berth.

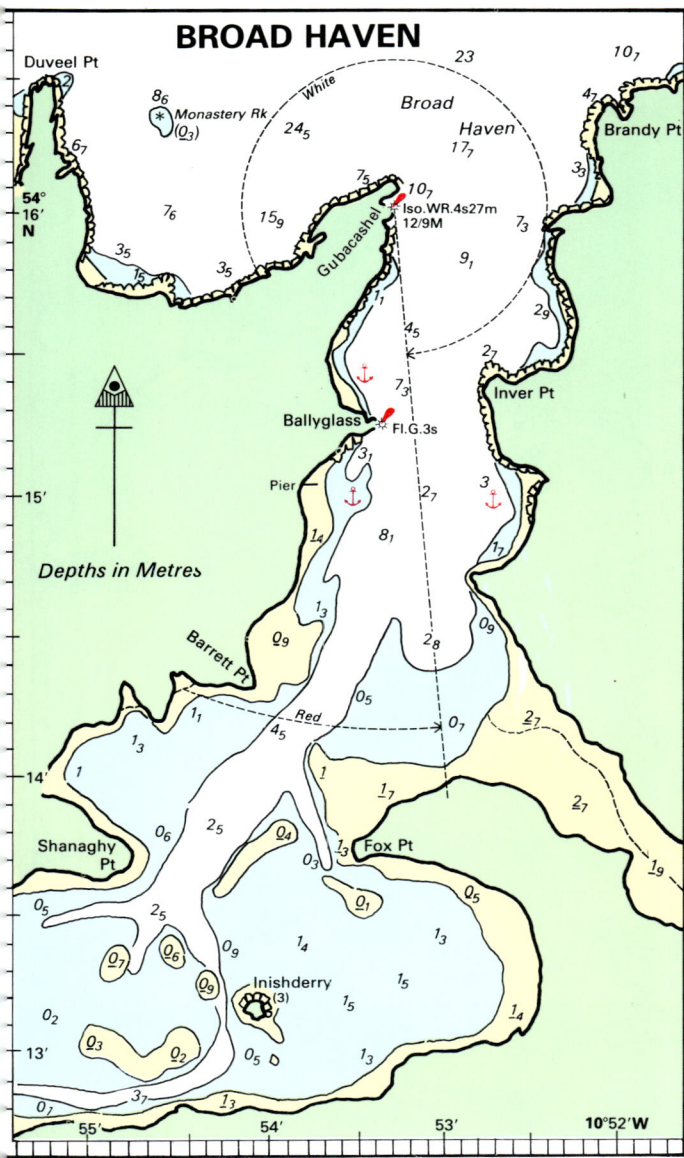

BROADHAVEN   Chart BA 2703
HW: Dover −5¼h

MHWS 3.7m MHWN 2.8 MTL 2.1 MLWN 1.6 MLWS 0.5

A good safe harbour in all summer weather. It is 5M long and 1M wide in places. In bad NW and N gales the entrance breaks and should not be attempted.

Approach From N. Pass outside the Stags and give Kidd Island a 1M berth to avoid the race. Alter course for Gubacashel Lt. This take you clear of the rk off Doonanierin Pt.

From S. Leave Eagle Is light to stb and head for a point 1M N of Erris Head – again to avoid the race. Turn into Broad Haven Bay and head for Gubacashel Lt. Do not get inside a line between this point and Duvell Point as Monastery Rock is nasty.

Entrance The entrance is clear for 1M except for a small islet just S of the Light. After that there are shallow patches on each side.

Anchorages (1) In bay N of Ballyglass in 3.5m. The line is Gubacashel Pt in line with the W side of Kidd Island. Shelter from SW to NW.

(2) Off the pier in the next bay to stb in 3m with the outer end bearing 035°. The pier has 2m alongside and it is sometimes possible to lie alongside a trawler there. Bellmulett 6M. RNLI life boat (1989). Small general store. Tel.

(3) On port side ½M S of Inver Point in 3.5m off the hamlet. Best in E winds. Small shop. Telephone 2M at Barnatra. The rest of the bay can be explored on a rising tide in a dinghy.

PASSAGE NOTES: ERRIS HEAD TO SLYNE HEAD

Passage Lights

Black Rk	Fl WR 12s 86m 22/16M
Achillbeg Is	Fl WR 5s 56m 18/15M
Slyne Head	Fl(2) 15s 35m 28M

The coast from Erris Hd to Slyne Hd is deeply indented, with long stretches fronted by islands affording some protection from the swell. It is a fine day-cruising area, although not well enough lit for sailing inshore at night. There are many sheltered bays, the pick of the anchorages being Blacksod Bay, Clew Bay, Killary and Little Killary, Ballynakill, Inishbofin and Clifden. Frenchport is handy if pressed for time.

It is theoretically possible to pass through Achill Sound, given sufficient rise of tide, and subject to mast height of less than 11m (check the clearance locally) but the channel is intricate and local knowledge is needed.

Blacksod Bay is a good refuge in bad weather, with quite a number of anchorages.

FRENCHPORT

A small inlet providing a port of call on the direct route for yachts sailing round Ireland. Not recommended if the W-ly swell is running high. No facilities, no water. Good pub and shop at Clough.

IRELAND 234

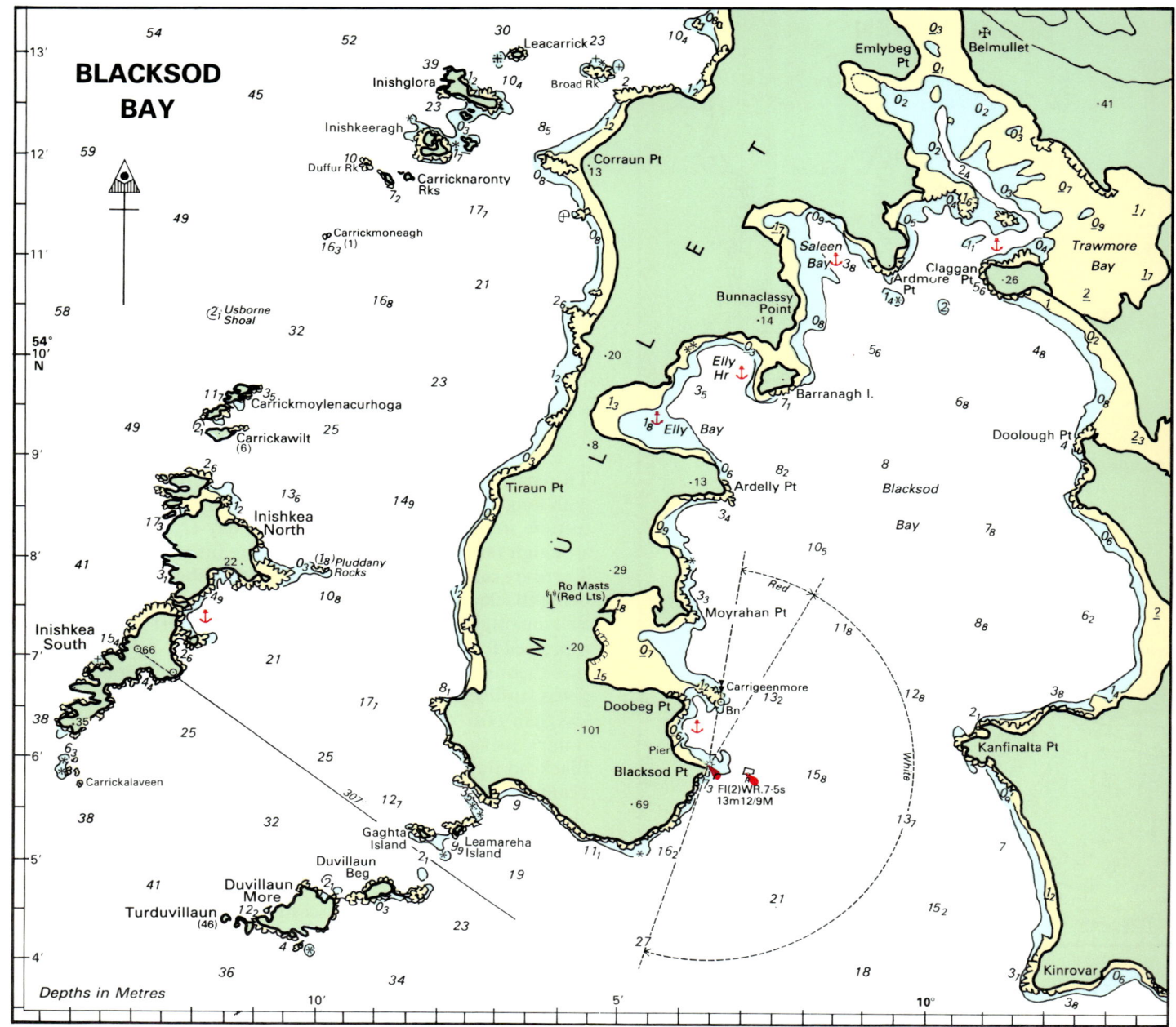

BLACKSOD BAY Chart BA 2704

HW Blacksod quay: Dover −5½h

MHWS 3.9m   MHWN 2.9   MTL 2.1   MLWN 1.4   MLWS 0.4

The tide runs strongly 2.5kn straight onto the two headlands Turduvillaun and Achill which guard the outer bay. In the bay itself the tide is weak.

This is a large open bay surrounded by low lying land and sand hills. It is about 3M wide and 9M long. Off the main bay are many smaller bays, most of which are very shoal at their heads. It is always possible to select a bay for any wind so only the main places to anchor are mentioned below. The canal at Belmullet connecting through to Broadhaven is now closed.

Approach From N through Inishkea Sound, leading mark to avoid Pluddany Rks to the E of Inishkea N is Turduvillaun in line with the Ears of Achill. It is possible in daylight to enter the bay through Duvillaun Sound. The ldg bns are on Inishkea South. At night sail S until into the white sector of Black Rock Lt then turn in to open up the white sector of Blacksod Point. 3½ ca abeam of this light is unlit R can buoy. Proceed due N until clear of the perch on Carrigeenmore and anchor until daylight.

Anchorages (1) In the bay NW of Blacksod Quay between it and Doobeg Point avoiding local boats, 3m sand. The quay itself dries and is foul, and the immediate area for 2 ca around is shallow and poor holding.

(2) Elly Bay is one of the best anchorages, give Ardelly Point a good berth and avoid the SE area of the bay as it is shoal. Anchor outside local boats.

(3) Elly Harbour just N of (2). Anchor in the middle in 3 or 4m. Subject to swell in southerlies.

(4) Saleen Bay 1 ½M N of (3) Tend towards the NE shore where there is 3m. Good landing. Subject to swell in S or SE-lies.

(5) N of Claggan Point. If possible enter at LW in order to see the drying patches to N. Avoid the dangerous rock which lies 3 ca S by E of Ardmore Point.

Facilities (1) About 1½M inland, PO, petrol, diesel and limited groceries. Possible local friendly transport.

(2) At Belmullet 3M. Shops, PO, fuel, pub, RC Church. Possible friendly local transport or taxi.

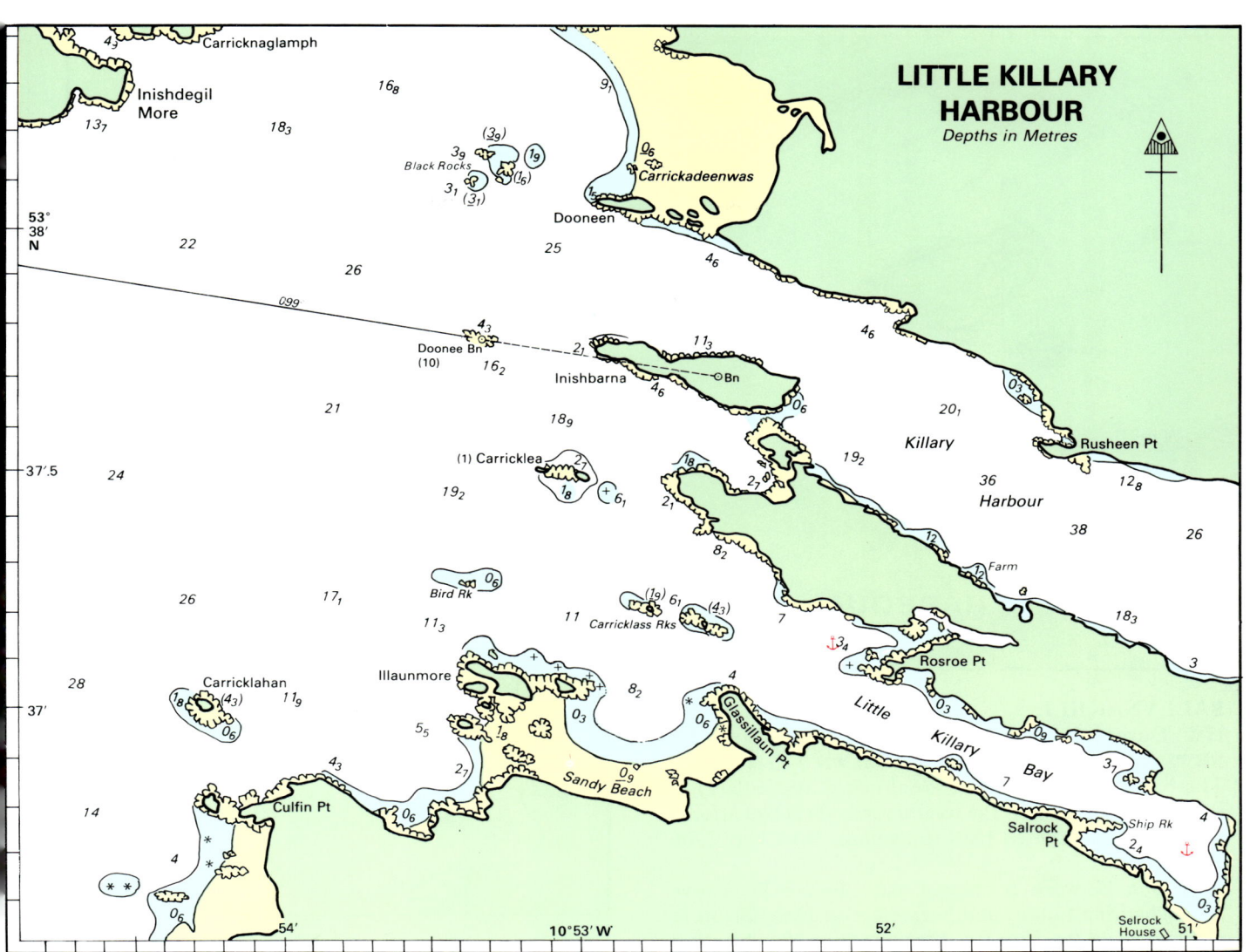

LITTLE KILLARY HARBOUR (Salruck)

BA Chart 2706

HW: Dover −5¾h

MHWS 4.1m MHWN 3.1 MTL 2.3 MLWN 1.6 MLWS 0.5

A very picturesque anchorage. Not easy in bad weather or low visibility as the various clearing lines marked on the chart are sometimes difficult to identify. There are quite a number of offlying rocks and shoals. In that event adjacent Killary Harbour which itself if well worth a visit for its magnificent fjord-like scenery offers easier access although one has to travel 3M up the lough for shallow enough water to anchor at Derrynasliggan or a further mile to anchor on the N shore at Bundorraghan. Beware of large numbers of lobster pots and fish farms in this region.

Approach From N. The line astern is Mweelaun 19m high in line with the sloping top of Clare Island 341°. However it is necessary to come to the Eastward to avoid the patch to the E of Govern Island, likewise 1M later bear to the Westward to avoid the patch to W of Inishdegil More, then turn into Little Killary Harbour.

From W, give Innishbroom Island off Rinvyle Point a fair berth of approx ½M to avoid Mweelaunatura. When Rinvyle Point shows N of Innish Broom alter course for Illaunananima (Live Island) until reaching the next transit of N side Freaghillaun with S islet of Shanvallybeg 089°. This clears the Puffin Rocks. The next transit is Cleggan Point over the E end of Inishbroon (051°) taking one clear of various dangers to stb. When the beacons on Doonee and Inishbarna come in line 099° alter course onto this bearing and proceed for 3½M when the entrance to the harbour opens up to stb.

Entrance: All dangers are above water and should be given a fair berth.

Anchorages (1) In 3.4m off Rosroe Point as shown on chart.

(2) Better still at the head beyond Ship Rk off Salruck Pt. a good berth. Anchor as convenient in perfect shelter. Mud. A good anchor is required in strong blows. Water from well with permission of the owner of Salruck House. No other facilities. An adventure school has dinghies and canoes in the bay.

Caution Only attempt this area in good visibility during daylight, there are no lights. Chart 2706 essential.

IRELAND

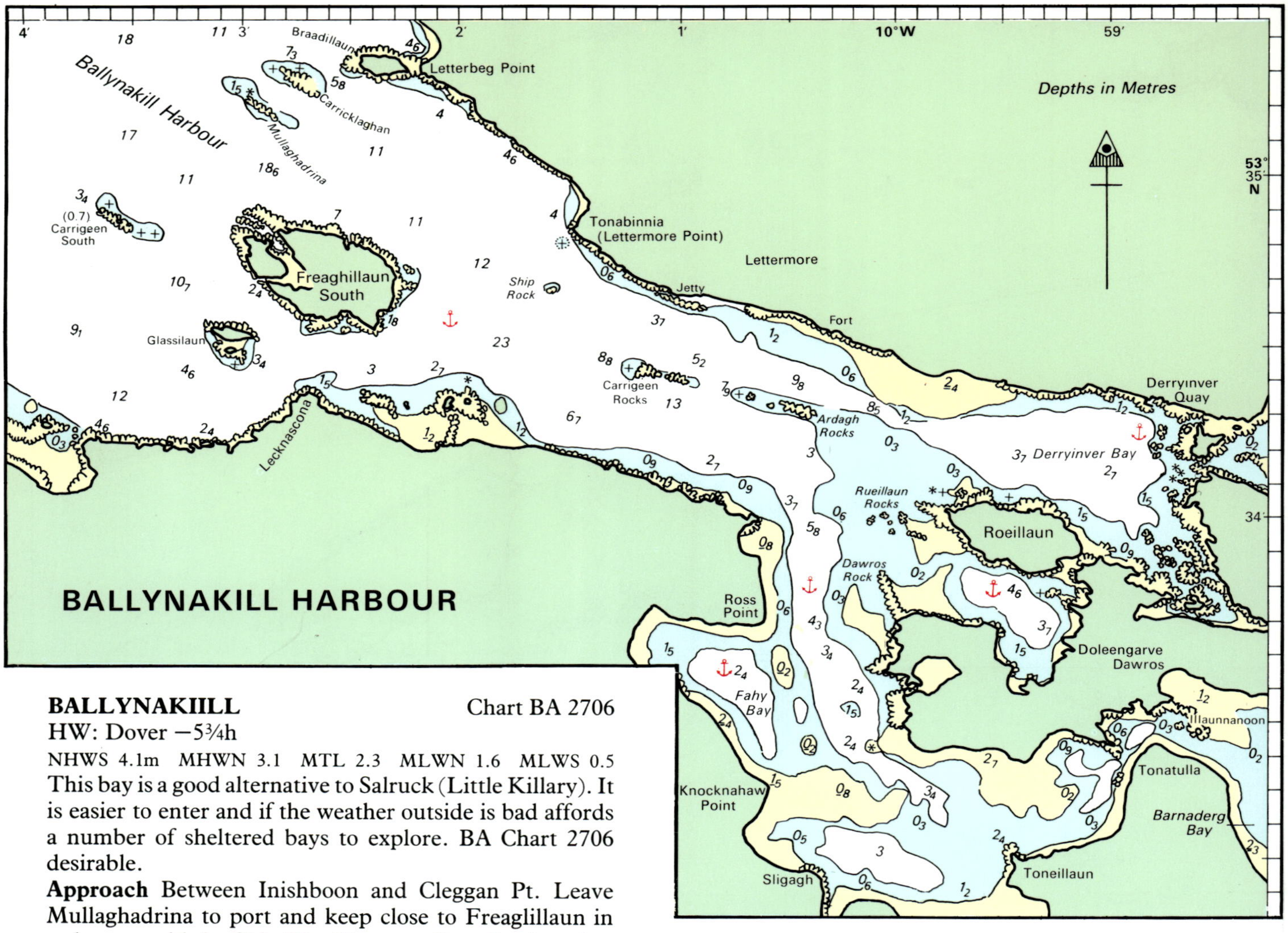

BALLYNAKIILL   Chart BA 2706

HW: Dover −5¾h

MHWS 4.1m MHWN 3.1 MTL 2.3 MLWN 1.6 MLWS 0.5

This bay is a good alternative to Salruck (Little Killary). It is easier to enter and if the weather outside is bad affords a number of sheltered bays to explore. BA Chart 2706 desirable.

Approach Between Inishboon and Cleggan Pt. Leave Mullaghadrina to port and keep close to Freaglillaun in order to avoid the Ship Rk. Clearance lines for the other dangers are shown on the chart. Fish farming in the area.

Anchorages 1. Fahy Bay in 2/3m. Good holding, beware of wind from SE.
2. Off Ross Point. Tide rode, but good shelter from W.
3. Derryinver Bay about ½ ca SW of Pier in mud.
4. In the pool W of Doleengarve, accessible at half tide.
5. Barnaderg Bay. Sound your way in on a rising tide. Very narrow entrance.

Facilities 1. Most provisions at Moyard 2M. PO. Petrol and gas.
2. Nil
3. Groceries at Tullynacross 1M. Letterfrack 2½M. Hotel 3M.
4. Nil.
5. Petrol and most supplies at Letterfrack ½M.

INISHBOFIN   Chart BA 2707

HW: Dover −6h.

MHWS 4.1 MHWN 3.1 MTL 2.3 MLWN 1.6 MLWS 0.5

A favourite port of call for yachts on passage N or S, however the area is strewn with rks so it must be approached with caution. Whilst safe inside exit would be impossible in S/SW gales.

Approach From the N leave Inishturk to port - it is clear, and steer for Davillaun Island. Pass between it and the Black Rocks which lie to the E of Inishbofin. There is a dangerous rock to W of Davillaun but it is close inshore. Lyon Head is clean, with a dir lt on it. Keep close along the shore steering to the W until the harbour opens up. Bring the w trs in line 032° and enter. Do not confuse the white gable ends of some cottages for the towers. Carrickmahoy rock lies 8ca due S of Lyon Head and should be carefully avoided.

Anchorage Having passed the fort on Port Island turn to E and anchor in the pool in 2 to 4m. Do not go further up than abreast of the building with three chimneys, as the bay shelves rapidly.

Facilities There is a shop with minimum groceries, a pub and a good hotel. The islanders are very friendly towards visitors. Ferry to Cleggan.

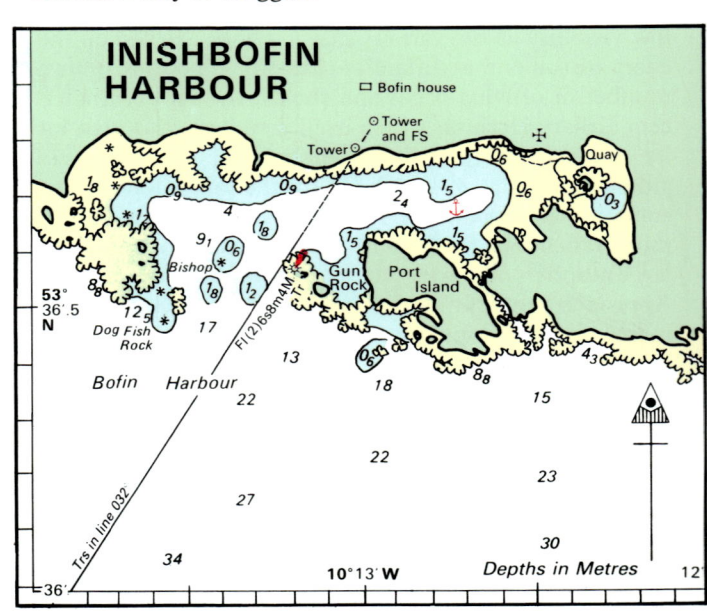

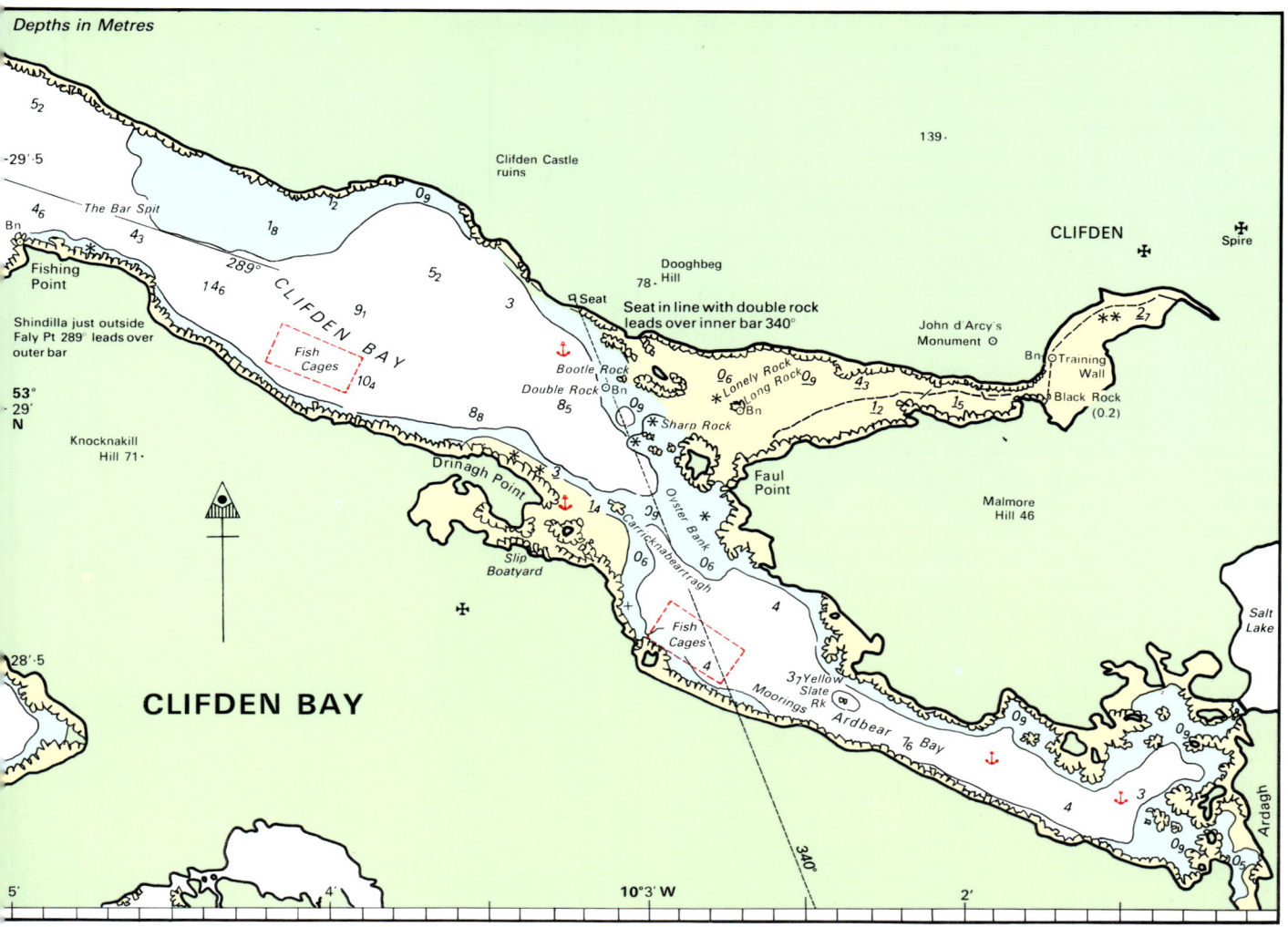

CLIFDEN BAY
Chart BA 2708

HW: Dover −6h
MHWS 4.4   MHWN 3.4

This bay is well sheltered, but now has a number of fish farms with their attendant gear. It has the added advantage of having a well known ship builder and repairer together with engineering facilities. Boats up to 80 tons can be slipped. Yachts can be laid up or looked after for prolonged periods. The town of Clifden which can be approached by dinghy on a rising tide has all facilities and is one of the best places for victualling on this coast. EC Thur.

Approach From the N. Unless in very settled weather, keep to the W of High Island and then alter course to pick up the bn (conspic) on Carrickrana Rock. This keeps one clear of the breakers to the W. About 1M past the bn alter to 180° and pick up the transit for entering Clifden Bay. Clifden Castle (ruins) appear N of Fishing Pt 080°. This avoids the outlying dangers on both Carrickrana Rocks and Doolick which stretch N'wards for a good 2 ca.

Entrance When 4ca short of Fishing Point alter course due N to pick the transit for crossing the bar. This is Shindilla on Ardmore Island just outside Fishing Point 289° astern. Approach with caution and have your echo sounder on as the bar is reported to be silting up from the N. There is a second bar guarding the entrance to Ardbear Bay. The bn on Double Rock in line with a seat on the shore 340° takes a yacht clear of Carrickbertagh Rk. Bar marked by R can buoy and rk by stb hand perch.

Anchorages (1) Off the bn which marks the entrance to Clifden Hbr, slightly to NW. Road to Clifden town approx. 1½M. Mud.

(2) Between Larmer rk and Drinagh Pt in 5m. Beware of ebb overfall from Ardbear Bay. A good place to wait for the flood tide up to Clifden hbr for shallow draft yachts. Boatyard close by on S shore which has visitor's moorings and water and diesel alongside, 3.3m HWS. A boat can be left here in the care of our HLR Adrian O'Connell.

(3) Any unoccupied place in Ardbear Bay (see above for entrance transit). Beware of Yellow Slate Rock which dries 1-2m about 8 ca up from anchorage.

(4) The head of the bay has good shelter giving the shore a fair berth. No facilities.

PASSAGE NOTES: SLYNE HEAD TO VALENTIA

Passage Lights

Rock Island (Earagh)	Fl 15s 35m 23M
Innisheer	Iso WR 20s 34m 20/16M
Loop Head	Fl(4) 20s 84m 28M
Inishtearaght	Fl(2) 20s 84m 27M

The South Connemara coast between Roundstone Bay, 15M E of Slyne Hd, and Cashla, 32M from Slyne Hd, affords a fascinating cruising ground with a wide choice of anchorages among several bays.

For 20M between Cashla and Galway the N shore of Galway Bay is exposed with no safe harbours. The S side has a number of anchorages between Galway & Black Hd. Thence the 45M of coast to Loop Hd has no safe anchorage and should be given a good offing. Passages to or from the S can be shortened by spending a night at Kilronan, Aran Is, in most weather conditions.

IRELAND

If making a direct passage between the Aran Is and Blasket Sound, note that the course from the Gregory Sound to Sybil Pt passes 7M W of Loop Hd. There is no light between Inisheer and Loop Hd (33M SW of Inisheer) and at night it is important not to get to the E of the direct course. Nor is there any major light between Loop Hd and Inishtearaght (39M). In the prevailing swell there is a pronounced set to the E for which it is wise to allow 5°.

Yachts bound between the Mayo, Sligo or Donegal coasts and the S might consider a direct Inishbofin-Valentia passage, thus eliminating considerable deviation of course to hbrs on this coast. Direct course appears to take you within 1M of Slyne Hd.

There are, however, possible anchorages between Loop Hd and Sybil Pt which, apart from Smerwick Hbr, involve varying deviations from the direct course.

If passing through or outside the Blaskets, it is especially important to note and respect those areas where overfalls are indicated on the large-scale chart. The magnetic anomaly to the N of the Blaskets is to be treated seriously: its influence is reported as very localised but extreme enough to spin the card of a compass through 360°!

The best hbrs of refuge are, in the N of the area, Roundstone and Cashla Bays, and S of Loop Hd, Smerwick in S-ly gales and Dingle in N. Yachts may also run for shelter in the R Shannon, notably at Carrigaholt.

ROUNDSTONE   Chart BA 2709

HW: Dover −6h

MHWS 4.4 MHWN 3.4 MTL 2.5 MLWN 1.7 MLWS 0.5

A well sheltered anchorage in shallow water. A good base to explore the surrounding bays. The chart is essential.

Approach From the W steer E to avoid Murvey and Caulty Rocks to be left to port and the Wild Billows Rock with Illunacroagh More and its outlying dangers to stb. Alter course for Inishnee Point light, enter the bay giving a fair berth to both sides but tend towards the W side to avoid rk which lies 3½ca SW of pier. There is a bar with 0.9m. Beware of salmon nets and fish farms.

Anchorage Anchor in 2m just off the pier where holding is dubious – take local advice. There are quite a number of alternative places to lie in the area which can best be ascertained from the chart.

Facilities: Water, groceries, hotels, PO and bus to Galway.

Zetland Hotel at the head of Cashel Bay is very well known.

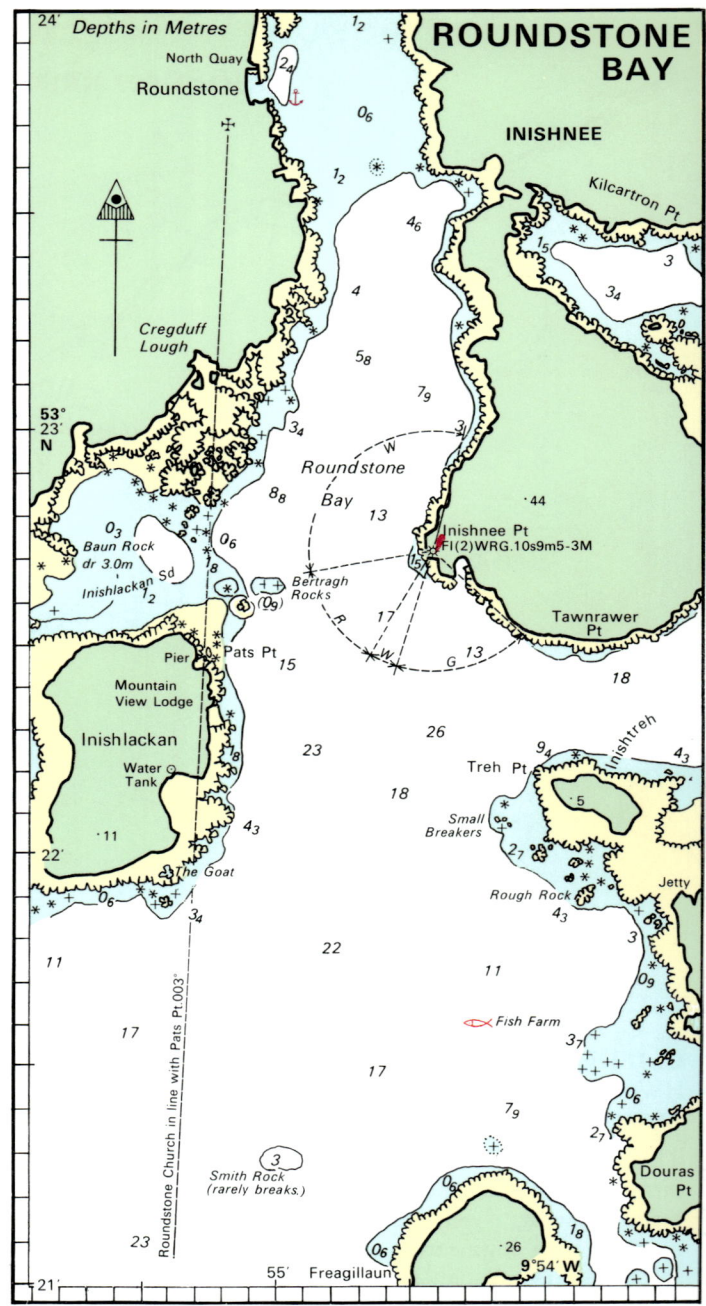

GREATMAN BAY   Chart BA 2096

This bay lies between Gorumna Island and the mainland. It is immediately to the W of Cashla and can be confused with Cashla if care is not taken. Its entrance which has no lights is relatively simple provided chart 2096 is on hand. There is an anchorage off the quay at Natawnay in approx 3m, however, it is a 2M walk to the village of Carrowe for the simplest of supplies. The best anchorage is of Maurmeen Quay approx 1½M further up the bay on the Gorumma side. It is guarded by a number of unmarked rocks. The best place to lay your anchor is 4ca NW of the quay in 3m. Supplies are limited, however there are groceries, tel, ch, bus to Galway and a pub about 1 M where petrol can be obtained. There is a further anchorage up the bay at Bealadangan which can be approached with great care on a rising tide. Again limited stores and pub. If time permits then the rest of this bay and the inlet to westward, Kilkieran, can be explored with care and a dinghy.

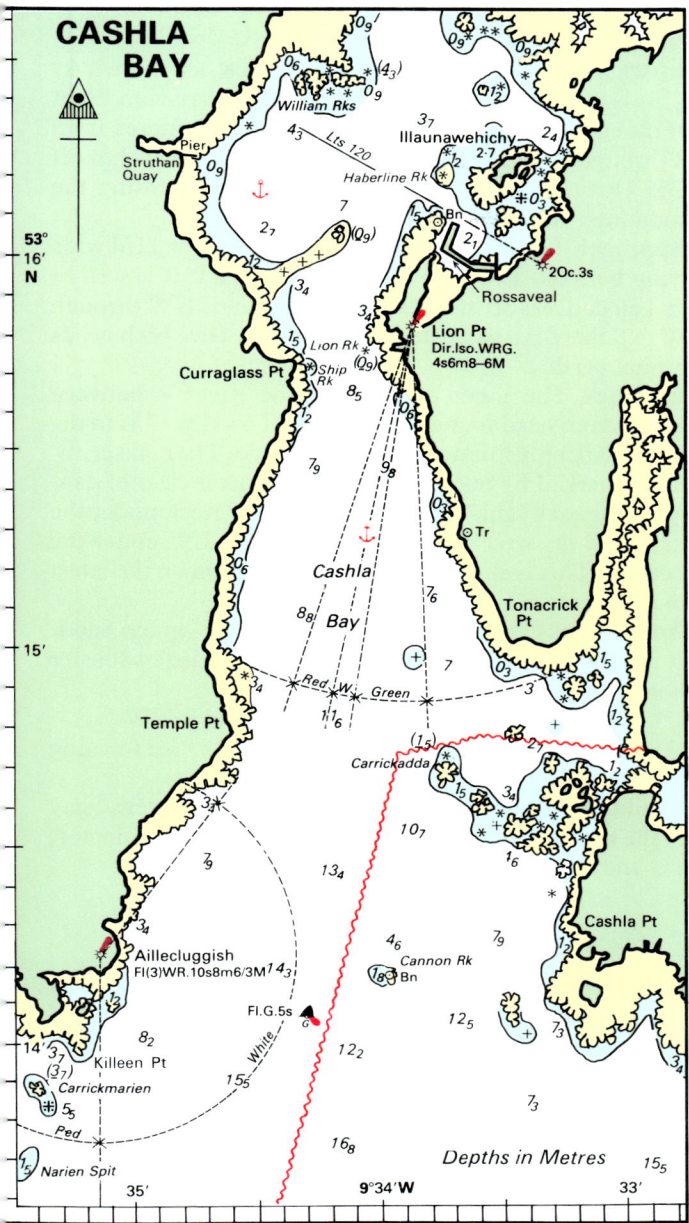

Anchorage Ldg Lt 120° takes one into Rossaveal Quay which is a busy fishing port. It is possible to lie alongside a friendly boat. This transit takes care of the bn on the rk to W of the Pier Head and Haberline Rk 1 cable due N of it. The alternative anchorage is off Struthan Quay to W of Rossaveal in 3m.

Facilities At Rossaveal: Small shop ½M, Pub 1M, Bus to Galway, Diesel and water available.

At Struthan: Shops, hotel, ch, tel, and bus to Galway at Carraroe 1M, Fuel 200 yds. water at quay.

KILRONAN HARBOUR, KILLEANY BAY, ARAN IS.
Chart BA 3339

HW: Dover +6¼h

MHWS 4.7m MHWN 3.6 MTL 2.6 MLWN 1.8 MLWS 0.5

Much the most sheltered anchorage in the Aran Islands.

Approach Pass through N Sound between Goruma Island and Inishmore. Temple Benan ruin in the SSW corner of bay in line with the sand patch 226° leads into the bay in the best water leaving the con buoy to stb. Then steer over to stb towards the pier.

Anchorage Anchor due S of pier which has a Fl WG lt in 3m. Well sheltered.

Facilities Diesel, water, limited groceries, pub, ferry and air service to Galway. There are excellent walks in the area. Bicycles and a side car can be hired to see the more remote parts of the island.

CASHLA
Chart BA 2096

HW: Dover −6h

MHWS 4.8m MHWN 3.7 MTL 2.7 MLWN 1.9 MLWS 0.6

One of the most sheltered anchorages on this part of the coast. It has the added advantage of being lit with two fixed lights and a number of lit and unlit buoys. Entry is possible in practically all weather.

Approach It is not recommended to take the inner passage to the N of Namachan and Eagle Rocks. The passage to the S requires one to have Golana Tower open S of Eagle Rock 094°. This clears Seal Rk and the Westward breaker to the N. The next transit of N end of Carricknamackan open of S end Eagle Rk on 290° takes one clear of all dangers until Cashla Bay opens up. Do not turn into the first bay – Greatmans by mistake.

Entrance Between Killeen Point with its outlying Marien Spit and Cannon Rk with Bn lt on Lion Pt. Dir, Iso WRG 4s 6m 8-6M shows way in. Off Curraghglass Pt is the dangerous Ship Rk to port and also the Lion Rk to S off Lion Pt. There is a drying patch 3 ca due N of Lion Rk usually marked by a local buoy as are the other two dangers above.

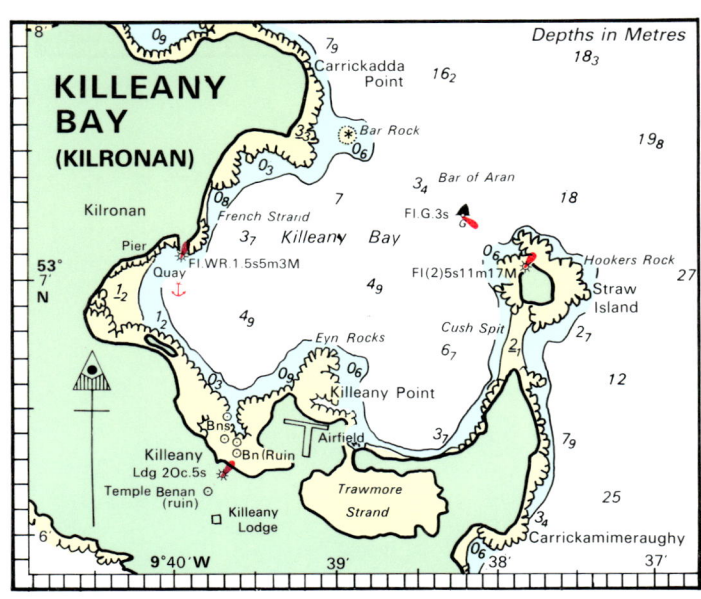

IRELAND 240

GALWAY
Chart BA 1903

This is the third largest city of the Republic of Ireland. It has very good road, rail and air connections with Dublin and other parts of the country. The approaches are well lit and buoyed to show the dredged channels.

The harbour is very much a commercial one having coasters calling frequently and there is a ferry to the Aran Islands. The dock has lock gates which open two hours before HW and close at HW. There is an area in the SW of the basin used by small craft where it would be safe to leave a yacht. Contact the HM who is very helpful (091) 62329.

All facilities including repairs to engines, hull and electronics. Although this is a long way to leeward it is a good place to change crews, with its good bus service to places further W. Galway Bay Sailing Club (091) 84527 at the head of the inlet is open at the weekends and some evenings in the summer. It sometimes has visitor's moorings.

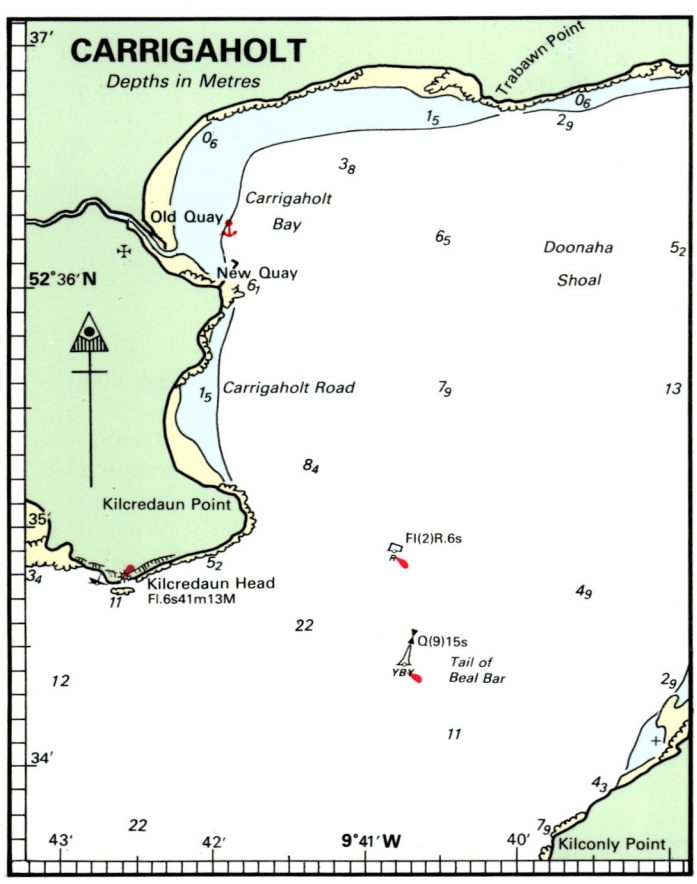

CARRIGAHOLT
Chart BA 1547

HW: Dover +6h

MHWS 4.9m   MHWN 3.7   MTL 2.7   MLWN 1.9   MLWS 0.7

This is a wide bay about 1½M north of Kilcredaun Point at the entrance to the River Shannon. Well sheltered from S through W to N. If going well into the bay to anchor off Old Quay, shallow draft only, take care regarding the soundings which date from 1842.

Approach The mouth of the Shannon is approx 11M wide lying between Loop Head and Kerry Head. It is well lit and all dangers are marked. In strong winds NW through W to S there is a bad race during the ebb. Give both heads a good berth.

Entrance The inner entrance to the River is between Kilcredaun head to the N with a Lt Fl 6s 41m 13M to the N and Kilconly Point, approx 1¾M wide. The main channel is marked by buoys. The coast to port is clear of dangers if given a cable offing to pass Ladder Rock under the light and the wreck which shows 1.2m at LW under the battery. This is shown in the wrong position on the latest metric chart.

Anchorages (1) Off the New Quay to the W in 6m Sand. It is possible to lay alongside, but it is occupied by lobster boats most of the time.

(2) About 2 ca SSW of (1) in 4m if the wind is NW.

(3) At the Old Quay for shallow draft boats. See warning above.

Facilities: It's about 10 minute walk from the New Quay to the village of Carrigaholt. Groceries, fuel, meat, doctor, PO and tel, restaurant in summer.

FENNIT
Chart BA 2739

HW: Dover +6h

MHWS 4.6m   MHWN 3.5   MTL 2.6   MLWN 1.6   MLWS 0.6

A well sheltered anchorage in all winds except S-E. Reasonable facilities in the town.

Approach Leave Kerry Head to port and steer S to enter Tralee Bay between Mullaghmore and Mullaghbeg. The former has an outlying rk which dries approx 3ca N of it. Head for Little Samphire Island which has a dir lt. Then head E to Samphire Is which forms part of the harbour being joined to the mainland by a causeway and bridge. A pier extends from Samphire Is ENE to form the rest of the harbour. It has a lt on the end.

Anchorage Having rounded the pier head N until the lt on Little Sampline Is shows through the bridge. Anchor near the local boats in 3m. Good holding and plenty of room. It is possible to go alongside pier on the N side where there is 3m with ladders and steps. However there is quite a lot of fishing traffic.

Facilities Groceries, pubs, hotels, resataurants, ch, PO. Tralee sailing club has showers and a bar open in the summer evenings. Cranes for lifting out. Bus to Tralee. Customs.

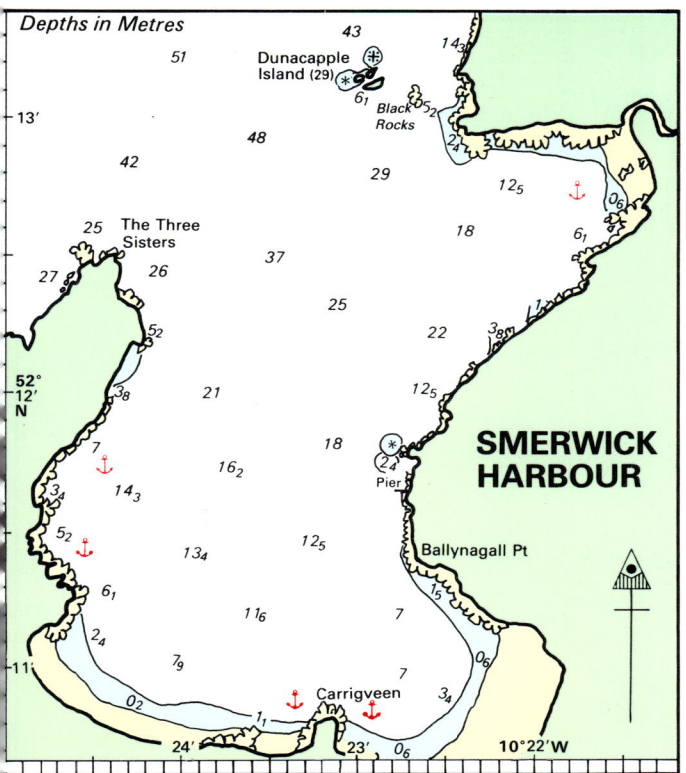

SMERWICK HARBOUR Chart BA 2789
HW: Dover +5¾h

MHWS 3.8m   MHWN 2.9

Tide sets N across the entrance at Dover −1h at 1kn. This wide bay which is open to NW and although subject to swell in N winds. some protection will be found close in on the W side in NW winds.

Approach The approach is clear from the N, however, there are no lights in the area. From the S coming from Sybil Point a rk about 3 ca due N of middle of the Three Sisters must be avoided. These cliffs are about 150m high.

Entrance Between Dunacapple Island and the northern most of the Three Sisters about 1M wide. Do not pass between Dunacapple Is and the mainland. There is a rk just to W of the island.

Anchorages (1) In Smerwick Road just N of the Boat Harbour marked on the chart in good holding.

(2) In the bay to the NE corner of the Harbour. Gives shelter in N winds. Do not go in beyond the 2m line as there are boulders. Beware of pots and nets.

(3) In the bay just S of Ballynagall Point in order to get stores at Bulltsnitty. The bottom is rk just off the pier. Further to the SW in this bay is good holding in sand, in 2m just W of Carrigveen Point.

Facilities At Ballynagall (known locally as Ballydavid) there are limited shops, pub, and tel. At Carrigveen there is petrol beyond the sandhills.

DINGLE HARBOUR
HW: Dover +5¾h.

MHWS 3.8   MHWN 2.9   MTL 2.1   MLWN 1.3   MLWS 0.5

A land-locked hbr with a safe entrance and free from swell, but most of it is shallow and the only alternative to berthing alongside a fishing boat at the pier is to anchor almost 1M from the pier and the town. Water and diesel on pier, all normal supplies in the town.

IRISH CRUISING CLUB

Founded in 1928 to encourage cruising on the Coasts of Ireland and abroad.

Membership 540.

A Flag Officer is appointed for each of the four Provinces of Ireland. The seniority of these positions rotates at intervals of not more than three years.

Rallies and Cruising in company are organised both at home and abroad during the sailing season.

Meetings with maritime orientated speakers and visits to places of sailing interest take place during the winter months.

There are no Club premises, however, the committee meets in the main yachting centres, kindly being invited to use the facilities of existing yacht clubs in the area.

An annual dinner is organised by each of the Flag officers in turn, and takes place in the early spring.

The Annual General Meeting is held in the Dublin area in March.

Honorary Secretary:
  Cormac McHenry, 8 Heidelberg, Ardilea, Dublin 14, Republic of Ireland

Honorary Publications Officer:
  Barbara Fox-Mills
  The Tansey, Baily, Co. Dublin,
  Republic of Ireland.

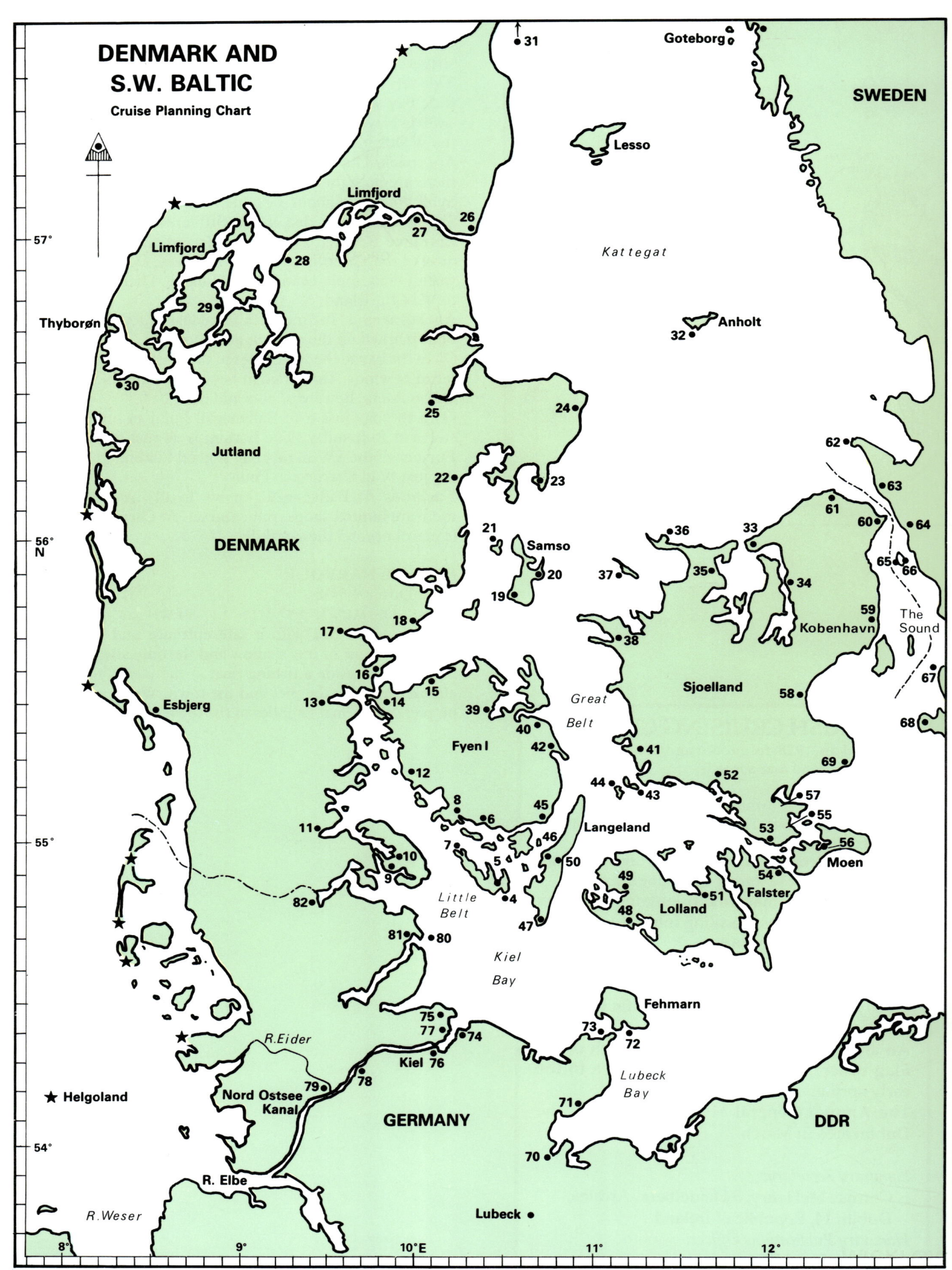

243 DENMARK, SOUTHWEST BALTIC

SOUTHWEST BALTIC

Cruise Planning Chart

It should be pointed out that the diphthong æ (Æ) and the letter ø come at the end of the Danish alphabet. This should be noted when using Danish lists. This is awkward for English speaking readers, so the alphabetical list has been printed as though æ were simply those letters as in English, and ø is treated the same as o. Broadly speaking the list leads north from Kiel up the Little Belt to the Limfjord and Skagen, south via the Great Belt, then eastward south of Sjaelland and north up The Sound on the Danish side, then south on the Swedish side, and finally across to W Germany again. The harbours are later listed alphabetically for ease of chart reference, but the numerical list aids cruise planning. Those in bold type are dealt with first and include sailing directions. The remainder are described in summary form later.

Ports on Cruise Planning Chart in Numerical Order –

Numerals 1-3 are omitted. Some Swedish harbours lie beyond the boundaries of the planning chart and so are described but not numbered.

4. Marstal
5. Ærøskobing
6. Fjaellebroen
7. Søby
8. Faaborg
9. **Sonderborg**
10. Augustenberg
11. Aabenraa
12. Assens
13. **Kolding**
14. Middelfart
15. Bogense
16. Fredericia
17. Velje
18. Juelsminde
19. Kolby Kaas
20. Langør
21. Tunø
22. Aarhus
23. Ebeltoft
24. **Grenaa**
25. Randers
26. **Hals**
27. Aalborg
28. Løgstør
29. Nykøburg (Limfjord)
30. Lemvig
31. **Skagen**
32. Anholt
33. Hundested
34. Frederickssund
35. Nykøbing (Sjaelland)
36. Odden
37. Sejerø
38. Kalundberg
39. Odense
40. Kerteminde
41. **Korsør**
42. Nyborg
43. Agersø
44. Omø
45. Svendborg
46. Rudkøbing
47. **Bagenkop**
48. Rødby
49. Nakskov
50. Spodsbjerg
51. Sakskøbing
52. Naestved
53. Vordingborg
54. Stubbekøbing
55. Kalvehave
56. Stege
57. Praesto
58. Køge
59. **København**
60. Helsingør
61. Gilleleje
62. Mölle
63. Viken
64. Raa
65. Kyrckbacken
66. Backvicken
67. Limnhamn
68. Skanør
69. **Rødvig**
70. **Travemunde**
71. **Grömitz**
72. **Burgtiefe**
73. **Heilinghafen**
74. **Laboe**
75. **Schilksee**
76. **Olympiahafen**
77. Stickenhorn BYKC
78. Rendsburg
79. Gieselau
80. **Schleimünde**
81. **Maasholm**
82. **Flensburg**
83. Rungsted

Alphabetical Key to Numbers on Chart

I DANISH HARBOURS

Æroskøbing	(5)	Kolby Kaas	(19)	Omø	(44)
Agersø	(43)	**Kolding**	(13)	Praesto	(57)
Anholt	(32)	**Korsør**	(41)	Randers	(25)
Assens	(12)	Kristiansand (see Norway)	(–)		
Bagenkop	(47)	Langelinie see		Rødby	(48)
Esbjerg (see Danish N Sea)	(–)	Kobenhavn	(59)	**Rodvig**	(69)
		Langor	(20)	Rudkøbing	(46)
Faaborg	(8)	Lemvig	(30)	Rungsted	(83)
Fjaellebroen	(6)	Løgstor	(28)	Sakskøbing	(51)
Fredericia	(16)	Mandal (see Norway)	(37)	Sejerø	
Gilleleje	(61)	Marstal	(4)	**Skagen**	(31)
Grenaa	(24)	Middelfart	(14)	Søby	(7)
Hals	(26)	Naestved	(52)	**Sonderborg**	(9)
Helsingør	(60)	Nakskov	(49)	Spodsbjerg	(50)
Hundested	(33)	Nyborg	(42)	Stege	(56)
Juelsminde	(18)	Nykøbing on Limfjord	(29)	Stubbekøbing	(54)
Kalundborg	(38)	Nykøbing in Sjaelland	(35)	**Thyborøn** (see Danish N Sea)	(–)
Kalvehave	(55)			Tunø	(21)
Kerteminde	(40)	Odden	(36)	Vejle	(17)
København	(59)	Odense	(39)	Vordingborg	(53)
Koge	(58)				

II SWEDISH HARBOURS

Bäckviken	(66)	Kyrkbacken	(65)	Utklippan	(–)
Gislovhamn (Trelleborg)	(–)	Limnhamn	(67)	Viken	(63)
		Raa	(64)	Ystad	(–)
Göteborg	(26)	Skanor	(68)		

III GERMAN HARBOURS

Burgtiefe	(72)	**Laboe**	(74)	**Schilksee**	(75)
Flensburg	(82)	**Maasholm**	(81)	**Schleimünde**	(80)
Gieselau	(79)	**Olympiahafen**	(76)	Stickenhorn	(77)
Grömitz	(71)	Rendsburg	(78)	**Travemunde**	(70)
Heilinghafen	(73)				

NORWAY, DENMARK AND THE SOUTHWEST BALTIC

PASSAGE NOTES – THAMES ESTUARY TO NORWAY OR DENMARK

TIDES

In the east of the N Sea the tides are diurnal, with the greatest range in the German Bight and decreasing progressively until scarcely perceptible in N Denmark. Persisting strong winds or unusual barometric pressure can significantly affect tidal heights.

The tidal streams in the mid- or north- N Sea have a spring rate of 1kn which diminishes as one travels north.

Currents caused by prolonged strong winds can reach 1.25kn, and perhaps twice this close into the Norwegian S coast.

The Baltic Sea is almost landlocked, with a huge inflow of fresh water. The consequent lowered salinity of its water, and the presence of the landmass, have marked effects on the behaviour of both sea and weather in Baltic waters. There is a general surface outflow to the N Sea of the lighter, less salinated, Baltic water with a deeper, saltier N Sea inflow, which can produce curious currents. The continued effects of wind, barometric pressure and freshwater may alter or even reverse current flows so that water heights may abruptly rise or fall as much as a metre in a few hours, without apparent reason, giving the appearance of a tidal effect.

A sudden rise in the water level may presage the coming of a depression. With lowered salinity and shallow waters even moderately strong winds can quickly raise short, steep, uncomfortable seas.

Entering the Kattegat, tides generally cease to be a problem. Fairly strong northerly currents may be experienced on the Danish coast south of the Skaw. Currents are mostly only of note in confined stretches of water, but are erratic in direction and can produce confused seas in a wind against current situation. Thought should always be given to the possible temporary effects of currents especially in confined waters. Winds with any east or south in them in the Kattegat will generally give a north-going current, whilst winds from west or north may possibly yield a south-going current – always providing remote conditions in the Eastern Baltic or the N Sea don't override local effects

Because of the prevailing westerlies, the eastern shore of the Kattegat, particularly between Göteborg & Helsingborg, is usually an exposed lee shore and thus not favoured for cruising. Similarly, the western side of the Kattegat is the more sheltered cruising area if time is limited.

North of Grenaa on the Danish east coast, perhaps the most interesting cruising, particularly for smaller yachts, is in the western section of the Limfjord. The Kattegat islands (Laesø and Anholt) are partially surrounded by reefs and shoals but repay the care required to visit them.

Further south, between Jutland to the west and Sweden to the east, lie the large islands of Fyn and Zealand thus forming the channels of the Little Belt, the Great Belt and Smaalands, and The Sound between Copenhagen and Sweden. If visiting The Sound the current is usually northgoing unless there are fresh north to west winds. It may reach 3kn off Elsinore. There are often inshore counter currents. The Great Belt is the main shipping channel and is crossed by the main ferry routes between Fyn and Zealand. The currents behave similarly to those in The Sound.

The Smaalands lead off from the Great Belt towards The Sound. There are numerous small islands. The current is mainly influenced by the wind prevailing and can be up to 3kn in the narrows.

The Little Belt is the least commercially used channel. Again although there is a general north-going current it is readily affected by strong winds. In the narrows at the north end of the Belt it has been known to reach a speed of 5-6kn. Of particular note is Kolding on the west side as being very useful for exchange of crews.

A particulary pleasant – but therefore in the summer particularly crowded – area leads off the Little Belt to the S of Fyn.

WEATHER

In the N Sea the predominating winds are SW-W, and on average stronger in the north than the south. Gales average 2-3% in the summer, commonly from between SW-NW, but, if they occur in summer they are mainly from the N, and most last less than 6 hrs.

Very heavy cross seas can occur if SW gales veer NW/N. Winds within 20M of the coast may decrease a little and be deflected more parallel to the coast. There should be daytime sea breezes with fine summer spells. In the Norwegian fjords these can be up to F6 and tend to veer very noticeably following the sun.

Both radiation and sea fog occur. Radiation fog shows diurnal variation and if present at 0800hrs will almost certainly clear by noon. It is more likely at night. Sea fog may occur at any time. Both are rare in Aug and Sept. However, S of 55°N poor visibility (<5M) is common, less so N of 55°N.

The incidence of fog in summer is low but increases with latitude. Fog at sea usually clears up near the land and vice versa, but onshore wind tends to blow sea fog into the Norwegian shore. If on a reasonably close approach (not less than 3M) neither shore, lighthouse nor light is clearly visible it would indeed be foolish for strangers to proceed further, particularly at night – but such conditions may be considered uncommon. However, on rare occasions one may need, unavoidably in poor visibility, to stand-off, perhaps for 24hrs or more.

In the Baltic the influence of the surrounding masses of land causes weather to undergo rapid changes and to have no regular pattern – unless in summer an area of high pressure becomes stationary over Scandinavia. Fog and bad visibility are not common or persistent, but SW winds commonly bring rain with consequent poor visibility.

DEPARTURES and APPROACHES:
England – Norway/Denmark

Taking a departure from Smith's Knoll Lt V avoids the hazards of the Norfolk and Lincolnshire coasts. Give gas/oil installations at least their obligatory 500m berth. Use RDF, Decca, Satnav, and Radar to supplement uncertain DR plots or astro fixes. Use Decca with caution when sailing into Norwegian fjords in poor visibility. High ground can give errors. If sailing close-in to the S Norwegian coast it may well be advantageous to use Danish Decca chains. When approaching the Norwegian coast do not rely on soundings as it is often very steep-to. Entrances to fjords and inner leads are generally very well marked and easy to follow. The panoramic views in the Norway Pilots (Vols.56 and 57B) are of immense help. All seamarks are in accordance with IALA System A.

Reasonable approaches from the W or SW are:-
Oksøy for Kristiansand
Ryvingen for Mandal
Lista for Listafjord and Flekkefjord
All have lights and powerful fog signals (usually diaphones with 10M+ range)
All have radiobeacons with over 50M range.

FISHING

Nets may be encountered but should not be considered as a frequent hazard. Particularly off the Danish coast watch out for trawlers working in pairs, perhaps as much as 300-400m apart, and do not pass between them.

Be aware of drift and purse net fishers. Drift nets up to 3M long, usually parallel to the coast, may be found round the SE coast from Egersund to Oslofjord, less so on the S coast. They are usually in place between 2100 and 0200hrs. Keep a sharp lookout, and listen out for radio notices.

Salmon nets up to 1M long are usually laid at right angles to the coast and up to 5M out, and left semi-permanently in place. All nets ought to be marked at each end by light buoys, flags and a radar reflector.

Collections of sea birds often indicate shoals.

DEPARTURE and APPROACHES:
England – Denmark and Baltic

If heading for Denmark or the Baltic the eastern side of the North Sea can be a relatively unwelcoming, often low-lying lee shore.

If going north, again, taking a departure from Smith's Knoll LV avoids the English offshore hazards.

If heading for the Kiel canal, Helgoland is a valuable refuge if waiting for better weather, or a favourable tide in the R Elbe.

North of Helgoland the only all weather hbr on the Danish coast is ESBJERG, invaluable for crew exchanges, with ferries from Harwich, and excellent rail links throughout Denmark. Sailing north the Horns Rev must be either traversed or by-passed. Slugen, (Chart D 94) the channel across Horns Rev, W of Blaavandshug Lt Ho, is marked inward bound from S to N by lateral marks with Lt buoys. The tidal currents usually run 2kn but can reach 5kn in strong SW or NW winds and raise a heavy sea and breakers in the channel. Between the reef and The Skaw the Danish coast is mostly low and sandy with off-lying shallows and bars subject to frequent changes of position and depth. There are some small harbours (some with inland areas of water) all with offshore bars. They may be approached in settled weather.

THYBORØN gives access to the Limfjord which traverses Jutland. The west part of the Limfjord to Aalborg has open stretches of water like meers, and is an excellent cruising ground, generally with westerlies. The eastern section is more formally canalised and industrialised and emerges at Hals on the Kattegat.

North of Thyborøn, bound for the Kattegat, the nearest all weather ports are MANDAL and KRISTIANSAND in Norway, or SKAGEN, just round the Skaw, in Denmark.

Entry to the Kattegat via The Skaw is straightforward and shelter from the prevailing winds is at hand (after negotiating the fishing stakes) in the fishing port of SKAGEN which welcomes yachtsmen, and is an artist's delight. It also has good rail links back to Esbjerg for the ferry to UK.

ARRIVAL in NORWAY

Arrive and report at a Customs-manned port such as Stavanger on the W coast; Mandal, Kristiansand or Lilliesand on the SE coast; Frederikstad, Tønsberg, or Moss at the S end of Oslofjord.

ARRIVAL in DENMARK or the SW BALTIC

On arrival in Denmark report should be made to the Customs in the usual way – probably at Skagen in the north or Sønderborg or Bagenkop in the south.

Customs and other regulations change too often to be covered in this book: up-to date notes are to be found in the "Foreign Cruising Notes" published jointly by the CA and RYA.

RETURNING HOME

A) To Shetland or Scotland: This is straightforward with a choice of Orkney or Caledonian Canal for those returning to the W Coast or Ireland.

B) To the E and S coasts: From between Egersund and Oslo one has three reasonable options (1) sailing direct (2) revisiting old or exploring new haunts in Holland en route or (3) sampling some of the attractions of Sweden's west coast north of Gothenberg (particularly to Uddevalla) then returning via Norway. To continue down the Little or Great Belts or Sound and out by the Kiel Canal is the least rewarding unless time is of no concern. Tacking out of the Elbe is not to be recommended and one may still have to tack all the way to England. Passage westward through the Limfjord usually means much motoring in the first phase, and then much beating or more motoring in the second.

CHARTS

BA 2182 A, B, C and D. NS 305, 306, 307, 308, 309 and 310.

Norwegian charts are just about essential. From Stanfords; Kelvin Hughes; Nautisk Forlag A/S, Drammensvn. 130, P.O.Box 321, Skøyen, 0212 OSLO 2. Tel.(02)558480; Fax (02)562385. Office hours 0800-1600h and from major bookshops in Norway.

The best are the 1:50,000 series but there are also small craft charts (båtsportkart), obtained in sets, with additional tourist information and covering all of the south Norwegian coast.

In Danish waters, BA charts will suffice for the Kattegat and the main belts. For smaller channels use the Danish yachtsman's charts obtainable from Ivar Weilbach or in most Danish chandlers or ships provision agents or major bookshops.

Publications

Admiralty Pilots Nos. 56, 57A, 57B, 58A and 58B
Norwegian Pilot Book: Den Norske Los Vols. 1,2,3, now available in English.
Norwegian Cruising Guide: by Mark Brackenbury/Stanford Maritime – covers S & SW Norway and SW Sweden.
Admiralty Pilot No. 55 for North Sea (East) includes the W Danish coast, and their Baltic Pilot Vol 1 covers the Kattegat to the Baltic.
Den Denske Havnelods contains many harbour plans of even the smallest ports, and Komma's Lods gives descriptions and plans for 525 Danish hbrs especially for yachtsman – but it is written in Danish.
Hafenhandbuch, Band 1, Kattegat mit Limfjord, Belte und Sund, Ostsee (Deutscher Segler-Verband) also contains many harbour plans and descriptions but in German.
Baltic Southwest Pilot by Mark Brackenbury.

The Kiel canal – BA chart 2469
The Limfjord – Danish charts 105,106,108 and 109.

DENMARK – ALS

SØNDERBORG Charts BA 3562 D152/154/155
(54°54'.6N 9°47'.2E) FLENSBERG FJORD

Busy, often crowded hbr in two parts separated by lifting bridge, on the channel between Als and Jutland. Nearest Danish Customs post on the western route from Kiel.

Approach From the N into clearly buoyed channel in Als Sund. From the S leave Oosterhage W card buoy YBY Q(9)15s to stb and Vesterhage R can Fl(2)R 5s to port. Conspic chimney with neon sign over town is good mark.

Signals Only for bridge opening: Fly Danish ensign and flag 'N' at half hoist or (white lt at bow) and blow blasts one long, one short on horn. Road/rail bridge has clearance 5m. When it opens do not delay your passage!

Responses from bridge:
Your Signal is noted – one FR, but no thoroughfare.
Passage permitted N to S – 2 FR.
Passage permitted S to N – 3 FR

N.B. the bridge marks the change of buoyage direction in the two parts of the Sund.

Berthing N, or preferably S of the bridge on the E side only of the sound, against the wooden quays as available. Beware possible 2kn current in either direction, according to wind direction, when coming alongside.

Supplies Customs. Water, WC and showers at N end of quay. Boat yard, chandler and chart agent New large yacht hbr to E of old small one S of the Sund.

PASSAGE LIGHTS

GERMANY and DENMARK

Helgoland	Fl 5s 82m 28M
Elbe 1 LV	Iso 10s 15m 17M
	Horn Mo(EL)30s Racon
Blaavandshuk (Esbjerg)	Fl(3) 20s 23M
Thyborøn	Fl(3)10s 24m 16M Horn
Hantsholm	Fl(3) 20s 66m 26M
Hirtshals	F Fl 30s 58m 25M Horn(2)
The Skaw N	Fl(3)WR 10s 31m 17M 12M Horn(3)
The Skaw S	Fl 4s 44m 23M

NORWAY

Ryvingen (Mandal)	Fl(4) 40s Dia.60s 52m 28M
Songvaar (Mandal/Kristiansand)	WRG 7s 23m 18/14M
Oksøy (Kristiansand)	Fl(2) 45s Dia. 120s 30m 30M
Lista (Lista and Flekkefjords)	Fl 4s 40m 26M Dia.

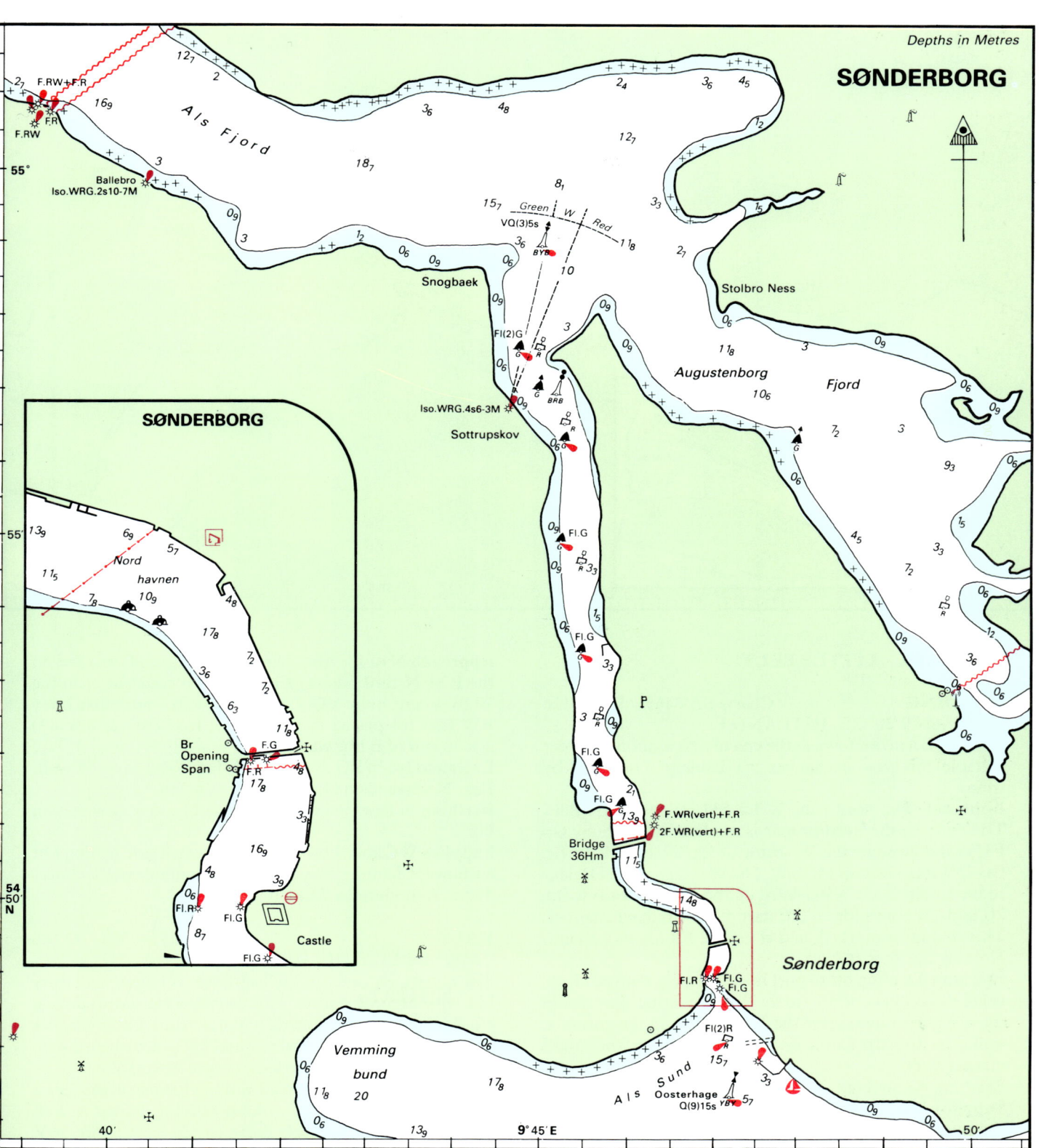

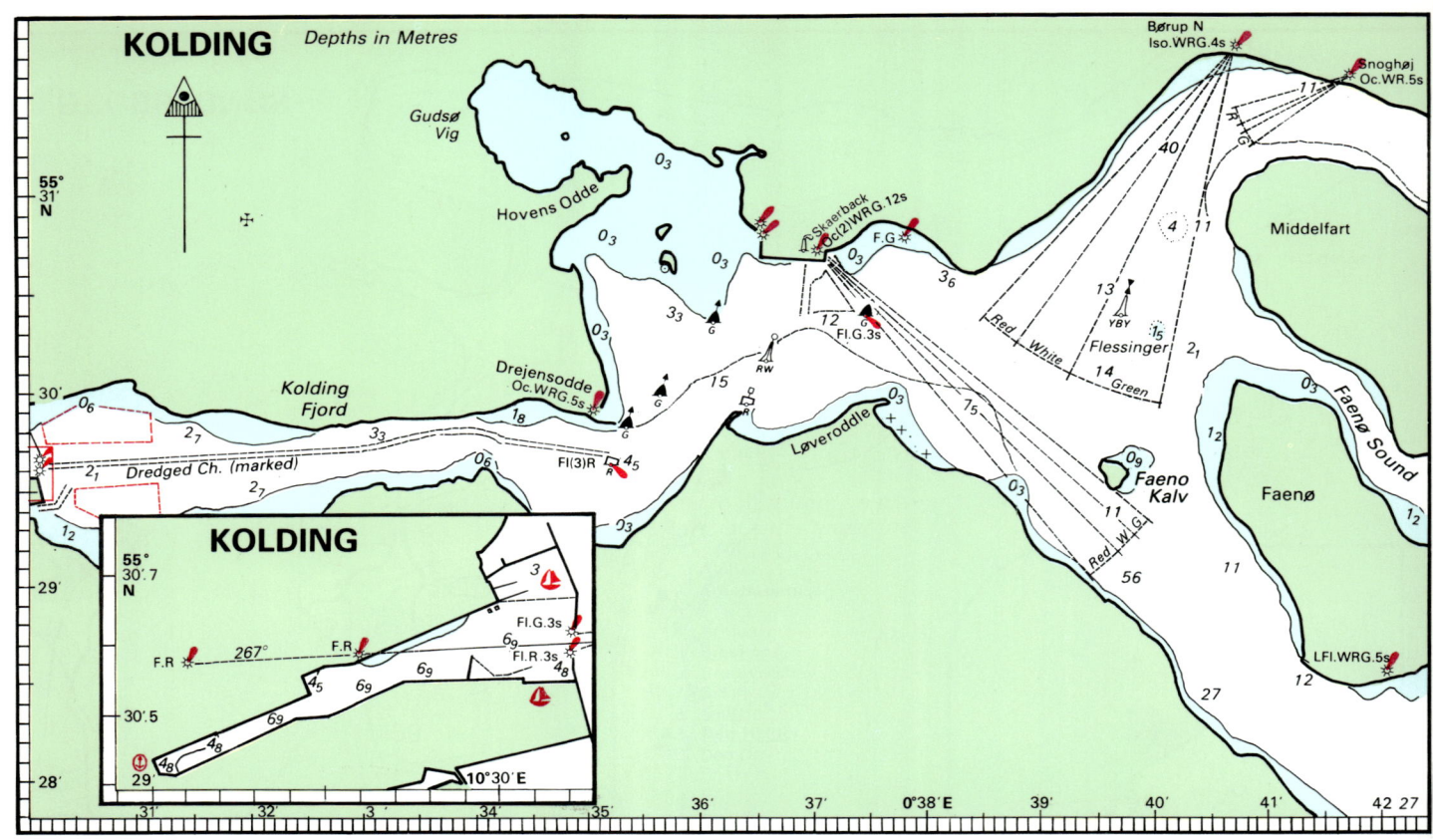

DENMARK – LITTLE BELT

KOLDING Charts BA 3465 D 151/156
(55°29′.6N 9°30′.2E) JUTLAND E.
Kolding is a major town at the end of a pleasant fjord, very suitable for crew exchanges via Esbjerg (one hour by train).
Approach The fjord runs W for 5M off the Little Belt. The entry to the fjord proper is marked by a G buoy Gp Fl(3) and at night the W sector of the Skaerbaek Lt Gp Oc(2) WRG 12s 36m 14/18M. The W sector of the Drejensodde Lt Ho Oc 5s WRG 4/2M on the N shore leads to the 2G and 1R buoys ldg to the start of the dredged channel. This channel is marked, and at night 2 FR ldg lts lead into Kolding itself on 267°
Entrance Leading off to port is a separately buoyed channel (Ldg lts 2FG on 236°) to the "new" marina. Just inside the old hbr proper, after the Fl R and G on the entrance walls, on the stb hand, on the town side, is the "old" marina & YC.
Berthing As directed.
Supplies WC, showers, fuel, water, YC and restaurant, chandlery.
For ease of baggage and crew exchange motor up the hbr and lie alongside the quay to stb at the head of the hbr opposite the pedestrian subway to the rly stn.

DENMARK – KATTEGAT

GRENAA Charts BA 2114/613 D 102
(56°24′.7N 10°55′.7E) JUTLAND E
Busy industrial fishing and ferry port and holiday resort with good beaches.

Approach N of the hbr, avoid the Kalkgrand, marked on the E by N card buoy Q Fl and unlit S card buoy; on the W by a card buoy VQ(9)10s. Follow in from pillar buoy RW LFl 10s placed in W sector of Iso WRG 2s Siren(1) 20s on end of E hbr wall.
Entrance Iso WRG 2s on E wall; Iso WRG 4s on W wall. Bear N when inside leaving Fl G 5s to stb.
Berthing In new yacht hbr placed in N end of new section hbr.
Supplies WC and showers. Diesel from S side fishing hbr entrance. Chandlery, sail repair and engine repairs. Stores 400m. Launderette. Main town 2M.

HALS Charts BA 2114, 598 D 106
(56°59′.4N 10°18′.5E) JUTLAND E.
The eastern entrance to the Limfjord. A fishing and ferry hbr with lifeboat station. Not usually a lee shore. Strong winds give a current flowing with the wind. Calm weather gives an average 0.5m tidal rise and fall synchronised with the N Sea – but subject to local surges up to 1.2m.
Approach 4.5M well marked and lit channel, across coastal drying flats, dredged to 10.4m with ldg marks/lts. Follow 317° in W sector Hals Barre Lt Ho Fl 10s 18m 26M and Oc(2) WRG 6s 15m 12-8M Horn(1) 30s, until to port Egense Lt W Iso 4s 20m 12M is seen between the Fl(3)G 10s 13m 5M and the Fl(3)R 10s 13m 5M, when turn to 294° for 3M. Then leave Fl RG 3s and Fl R 3s 5m 9M to port and close shore on Hals E Ldg Lts Iso 4s 9m on 315°. Channel is used by quite large vessels, difficult to manoeuvre at slow speeds. Do not impede their progress.
Entrance Immediately after the last two channel buoys, which have topmarks, Hals hbr lies to stb and Egense yacht hbr to port.
Berthing Easy on several quays as space allows.
Supplies Diesel and water in NE corner of outer basin. Shower and WC middle of N quay. Chandler with charts NW corner inner basin. Fish market on W quay.

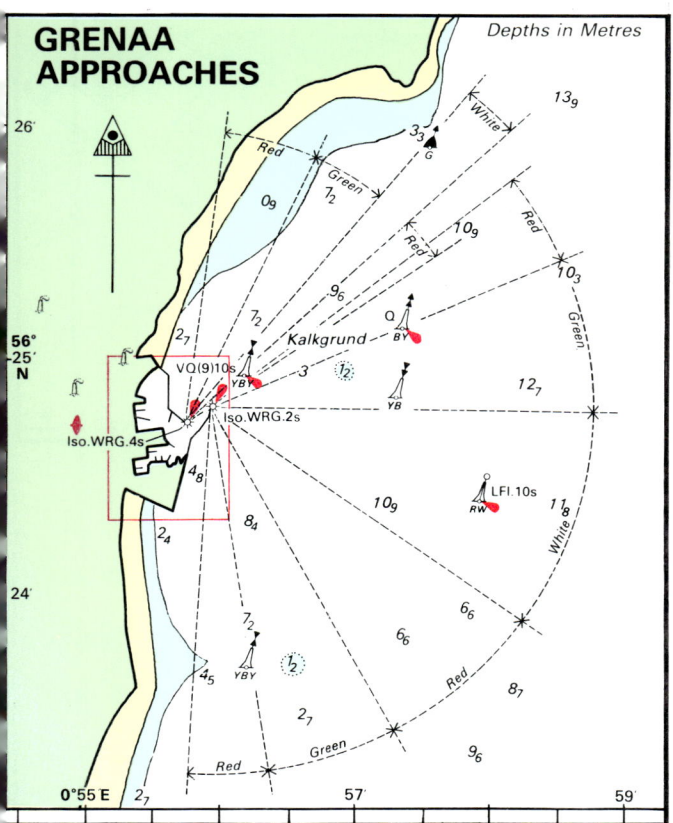
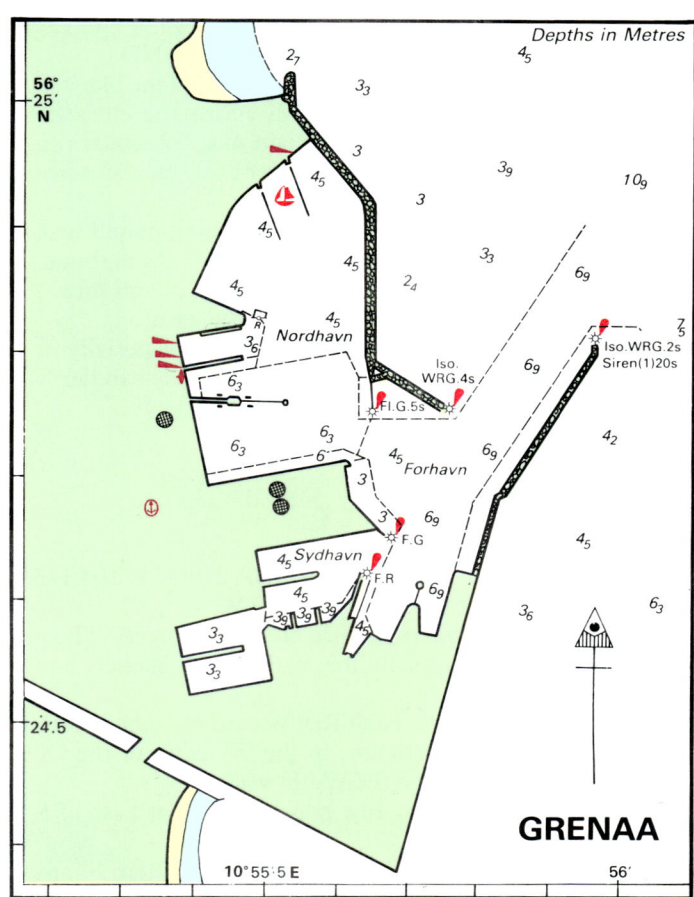

DENMARK, SOUTHWEST BALTIC 250

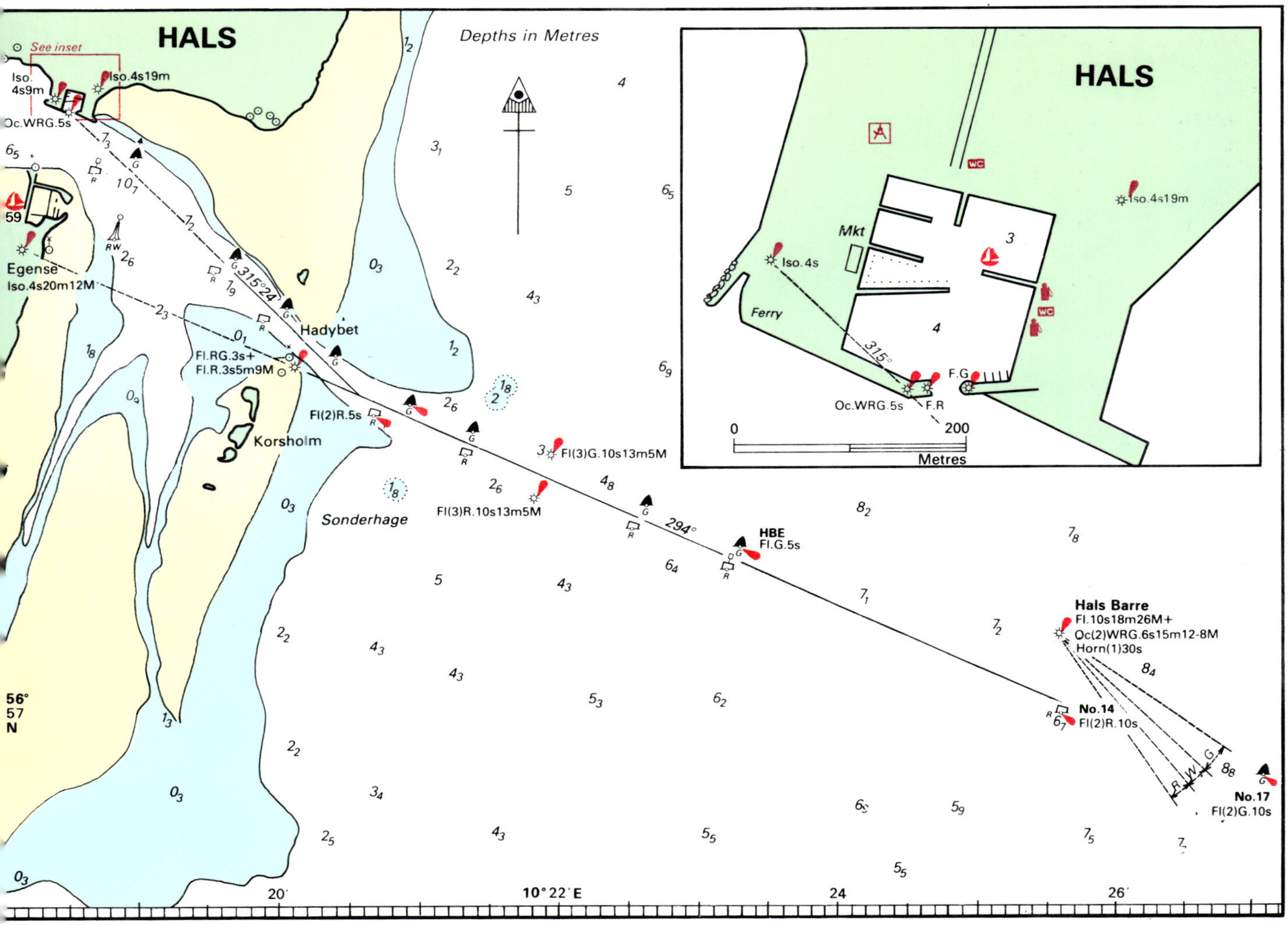

SKAGEN   Charts BA 2114   D 151
(57°43′.0N 10°35′.8E) THE SKAW, JUTLAND

A large fishing and refuge harbour just round the Skaw in the Kattegat. The current sets NE across the entrance with strong W winds and may attain 4kn. W winds can raise water by 1.4m: E winds can lower by 0.9m. Entrance has no difficulty except in SE gales.

Approach Coming from N watch for fishing pound nets and stakes which extend 2-3M offshore from the harbour. Steer 334° on R Iso ldg lts when within 2 ca of entrance.

Berthing Moor alongside Pier 1 in middle basin.

Supplies All facilities, supplies, chandlery (especially in very large galvanised sizes), charts from "skibshandler", (ship's chandler), diesel from fuel barge.

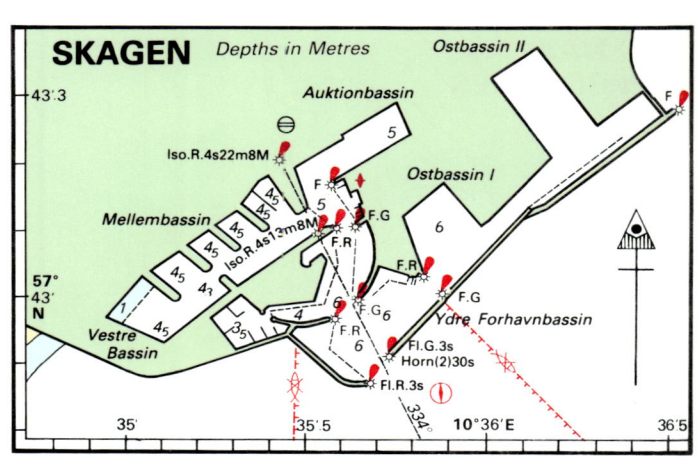

DENMARK – GREAT BELT

KORSØR   Charts BA 2596   D 104/143
(55°20′.04N 11°08′.19E) ZEALAND W.

An old ferry and naval port with interesting streets. There is a modern separate yacht hbr, with perfect shelter, S of the naval hbr.

Approach From the Badstue Rev W card buoy head NE, leaving 2G con buoys to stb, in the W sector of the Oc WRG 10s 5m 4-2M lt on the W hbr wall.

Berthing As directed by hbr master: office at base of S wall.

Supplies Water, fuel, WC and showers. Chandler. Shops 5 mins.

DENMARK – KIEL BAY

BAGENKOP   Charts BA 2597   D140/185
(54°45′.1N 10°40′.0E) LANGELAND SW

Nearest Danish hbr to Kiel en route for the Great or Little Belts.

Approach Can be rough in W winds but no hazards. At night 2 ldg lts Iso on 110°.

Entrance Fl R and G to port and stb on outer mole ends.

Berthing In the N-most Basin 3. Always room but dues rather high.

Supplies Customs. Water, fuel, WC on S side of basin. Self service store, baker and butcher. Diesel on piers between basins.

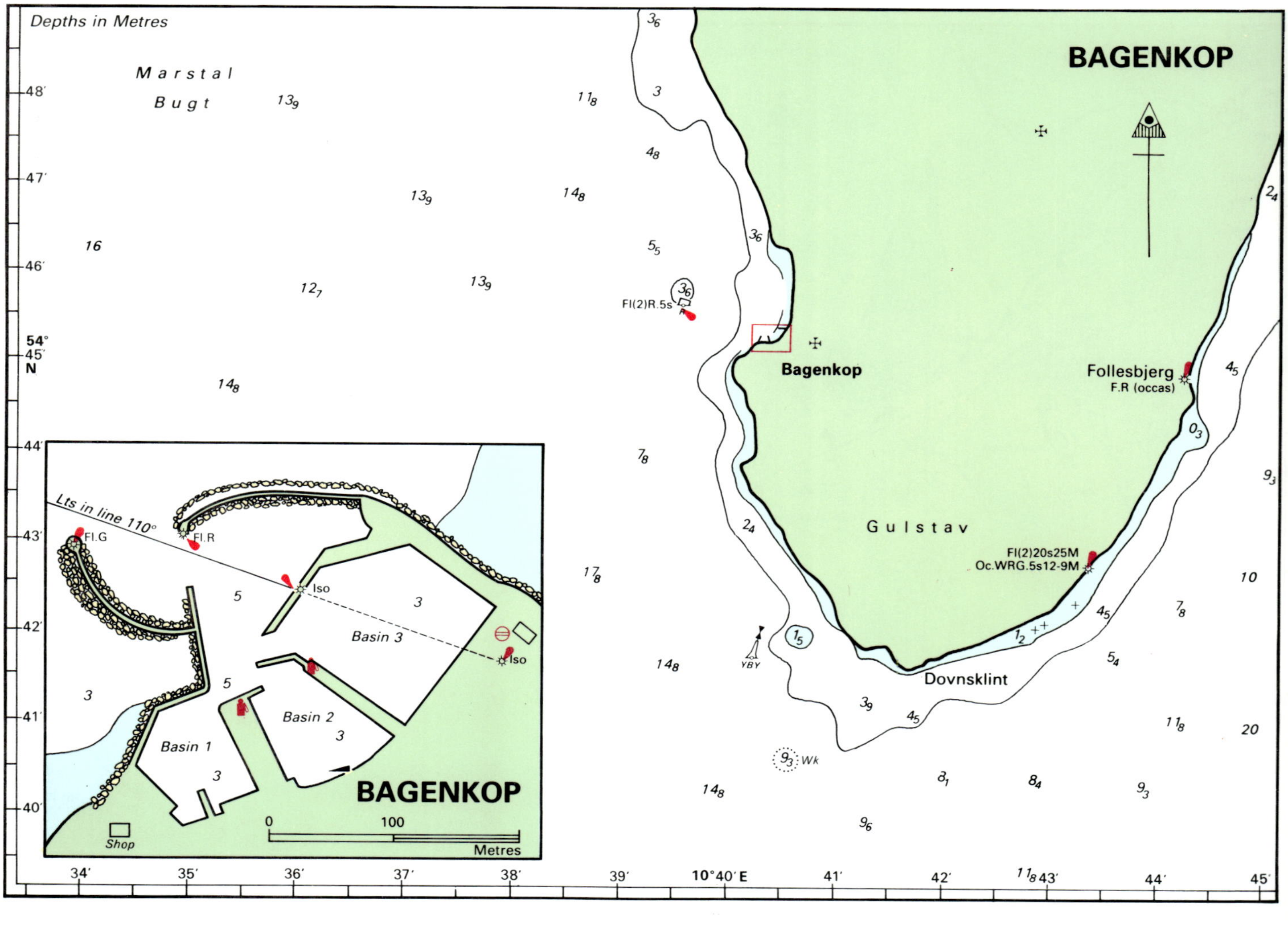

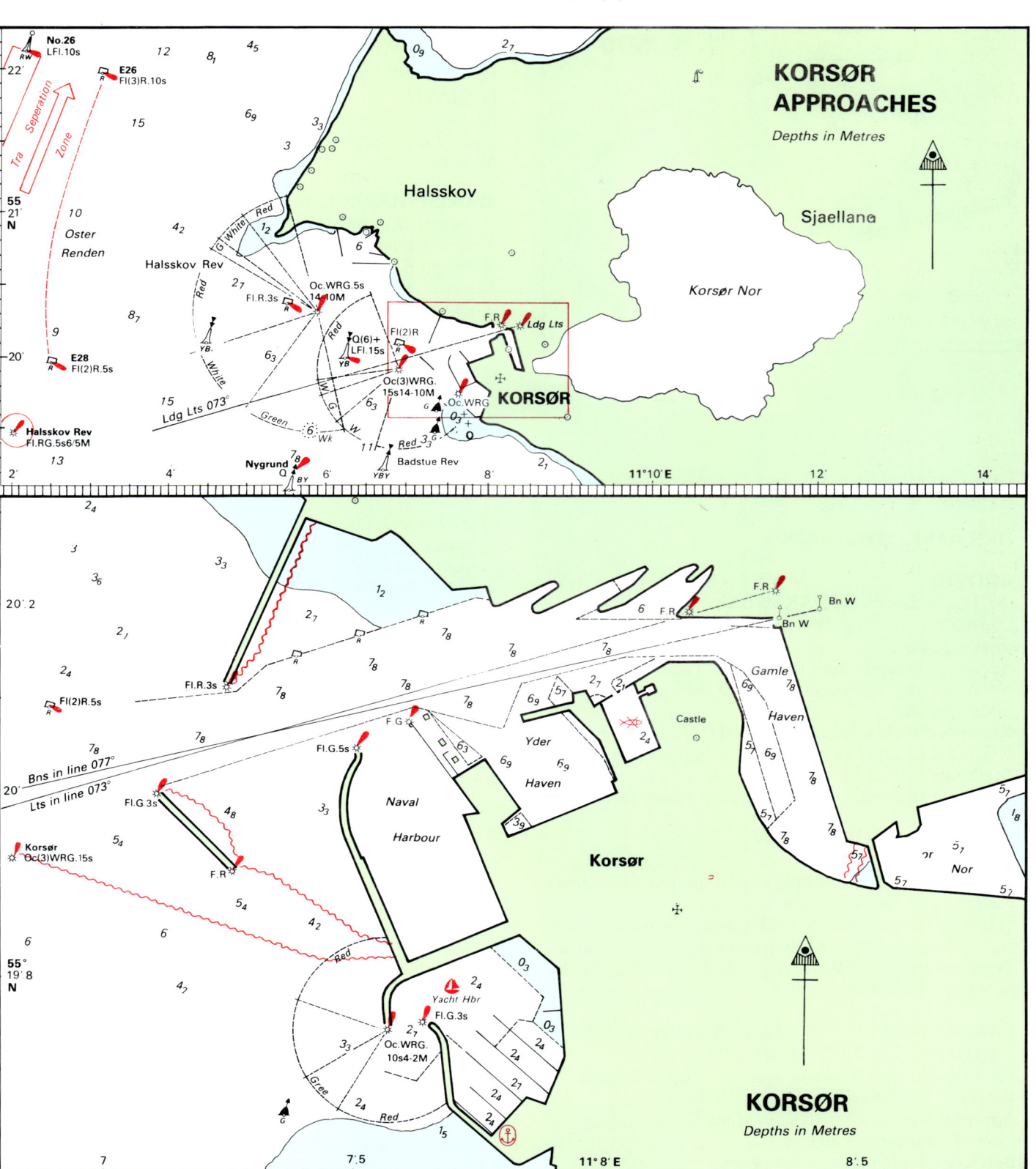

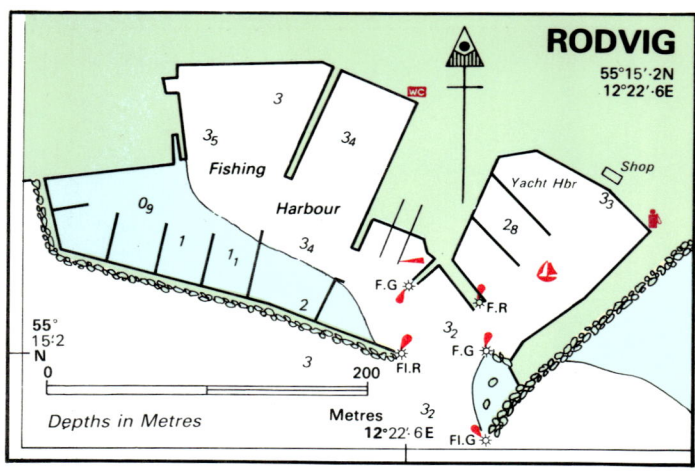

DENMARK - THE SOUND

RØDVIG   Charts BA 2115   D187/190
(55°15′.2N 12°22′.6E) FAKSE BAY
Convenient en route for Copenhagen, large, but somewhat expensive.
Approach Directly from the S out of Fakse Bay steering NNW because of the coastal belts of fishing stakes either side of the hbr.
Entrance No ldg marks/lts. Fl G and R on outer hbr walls. F G and R on inner yacht hbr walls of the E basin.
Berthing As directed
Supplies Fuel, water, WC and shower. Shop. Boatyard.

DENMARK – KØBENHAVN

There are several yacht hbrs in and around the capital. Langelinie is the most central, (even though it is a good mile from the city centre), and is therefore often crowded, and, because of passing wash, it is not always comfortable. Svanemølle is some 4M from the centre, but has good public transport and facilities and is quiet and not crowded.

LANGELINIE   Charts BA 3194   D 133/134
(55°41′.7N 12°36′.0E) THE SOUND
Set in parks and gardens near the "Little Mermaid" statue.
Approach Arrive 0900-1000hrs in the hope of taking the place of someone leaving.
Berthing Bow to quay: stern to buoy.
Supplies WC and showers: nil else. Shops ½M.

SVANEMØLLE   Charts BA 3194   D 133/134
(55°43′.0N 12°35′.5E) THE SOUND
Approach From the NE via the Kalkbraenderiløbet. After unlit E card buoy only unlit G buoys to stb. Three power station chimneys to S of hbr, illuminated at night, make a good mark. Ldg lts on 208° – Front: Iso R 2s 5m 11M; Rear: Iso R 4s 14m 11M.
Entrance Lt Fl G 5s on stb wall end.
Berthing As directed
Supplies Fuel, water, WC and showers, YC, restaurant, repairs, sailmaker. Rly stn 500m for centre city.

HELLERUP
Small hbr 1M N of Svanemllle. Lie to stern anchor. Good facilities and transport but often full.

NYHAVN
In centre of town but very noisy, not recommended overnight. Large yachts can lie alongside main quay ½M N of Nyhavn.

DANISH HARBOURS

Aabenraa (11) Busy commercial hbr at W end of fjord. Entrance marked by spars/ldg lts at night. The SC have jetties on E side of New Hbr (Nyhavn). A large yacht hbr lies S of the commercial basins, usually room. Diesel alongside, service from clubhouse. Report to club on arrival to pay dues. Except for late arrivals, 10kr extra charged for dues collected after 2000hrs. All stores.

Aalborg (27) Limfjord. Marina just W of the two bridges, 2m. All stores; food at hbr cafe/restaurant.

Aarhus (22) Second largest city in Denmark. The yacht hbr is separate, with an entrance NW of that for the main hbr. Three YCs, fuel cheaper in main hbr.

Ærøskøbing (5) On the island of Ærø: beautiful but usually crowded. The town is a famous showpiece and well worth a visit HM prefers visitors to use new yacht hbr instead of old hbr. Diesel pump below HM office in old hbr. Stores, all repairs, good facilities.

Agersø (43) The hbr lies on the E side of the Is, 2.8m. Keep to the left or right after entering to avoid slipway running down the centre of the hbr. Crowded but helpful.

Anholt (32) Hbr lies near the E side of the Is, 2.8m. The N side is all sand dunes and a mecca for visiting Danish yachtsmen. Yachts generally moor on the W mole of the inner basin, rafted alongside. Good facilities, often crowded and expensive.

Assens (12) The yacht hbr is in the SW corner of the area enclosed by the main breakwater, 2.5m. Good supplies, all facilities including Gaz.

Augustenberg (10) Well buoyed channel through Als sound to marina with all facilities.

Bagenkop (47) See notes and plan p. 251
Bogense (15) Buoyed entrance to new marina – moor pontoons to piles. Town 15min walk.

Ebeltoft (23) A charming town and has marina S of old hbr. Follow W quay of commercial hbr southwards and the marina entrance is easily found. The town is a showpiece and worth a visit. All facilities.

Esbjerg see Danish N Sea notes and plans p. 266/267
Faaborg (8) Yachts can still berth in the old hbr on NE wall less crowded since new marina opened to W. Approaches well buoyed. Interesting town. Sailmaker. All facilities.

Fjaellebroen (6) A small yacht hbr on the S coast of Fyn. Beware sharp turn into very narrow entrance (10m) Entrance buoyed, important to keep to channel. Berth on the mole at either side of the entrance, or as directed. Fuel & water, small shop.

Fredericia (16) Yachts berth in the old hbr, the most E'ly basin. Highly industrial, & Middelfart to be preferred. There is also a yacht hbr 1M to the SW. Good facilities but crowded. If no free berth, moor at fuel quay after hours and move in the morning.

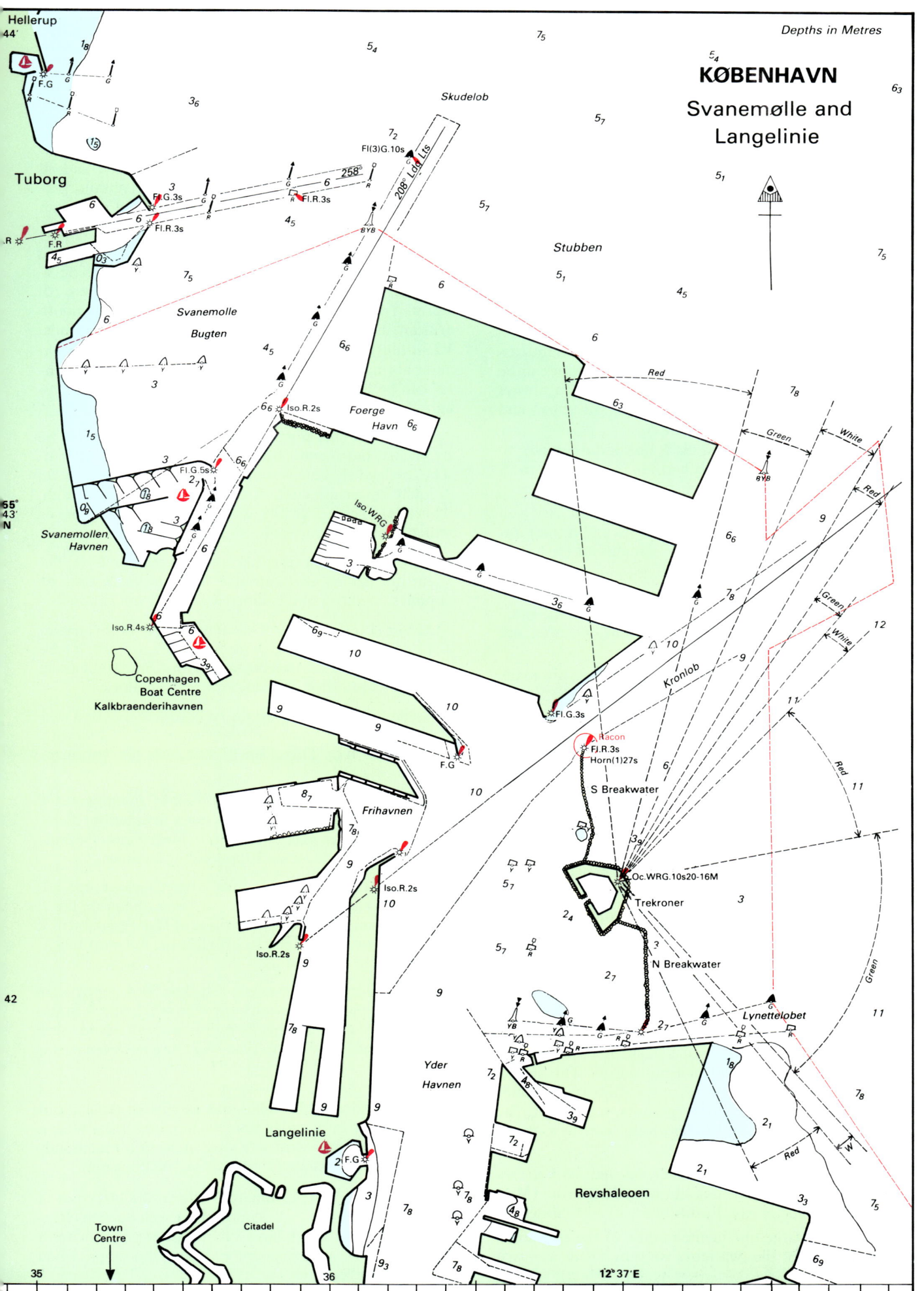

Frederickssund (34) A busy hbr in the Roskildefjord, just S of the Prince Frederick Br, which must be passed before entering the hbr. Flag 'N' (or national ensign) at half mast on the signal halyard, and N (– .) on the foghorn is the signal to open the Br. Berth in large yacht hbr on W side (Frederickssund): few facilities, diesel on inshore jetty, apply HM (closed Mon/Tue); or in Marbaek Marina on E side. All repairs, sailmaker, diesel every day.

Gilleleje (61) Crowded & busy hbr. Yachts berth in any basin S of the outer hbr, mostly bow to quay, stern to anchor. All supplies nearby. Pleasant clean town with good quality bathing.

Grenaa (24) See notes & plan p. 249/250

Hals (26) See notes & plan p. 249/250

Hellerup See København (59) p.253

Helsingør (60) This is Shakespeare's Elsinore, and the castle (Kronberg) with excellent maritime museum can be visited. Yachts use the N hbr on the N side of town, always crowded; berth as opportunity affords. All stores and facilities. YCs. Trains to Copenhagen.

Hundested (33) A busy hbr on the E side of the entrance to the Isefjord, Sjaelland. Yachts berth in the S hbr on the S or W side. Good supplies. Engine repair shop.

Juelsminde (18) A fishing/commercial hbr with easy well buoyed entrance. YC with good facilities and restaurant, diesel and water on quay. Good stores including fresh fish.

Kalundborg (38) An important ferry and commercial hbr on W Sjaelland. The YC can be approached by a buoyed channel. It lies outside the hbr beneath two large radio masts to the W. Otherwise berth in W hbr, all stores and facilities.

Kalvehave (55) A much expanded and deepened hbr in the Ulvsund with good facilities. Enter from the S. Berths mostly in E basin on N or E walls. Diesel just E of slip. Chandler. WC/showers at hbr office. Supermarket nearby.

Kerteminde (40) On the E side of Fyn. There is a yacht hbr with an entrance some 200m N of the commercial hbr, though large yachts still moor on the N side of the latter. Easy approach, good stores, chandlery, YC.

København (Copenhagen) (59) See notes & plan p.253

Køge (58) A useful hbr S of Copenhagen. Moor in the new hbr N of the old hbr. Good facilities including free loan of bicycles to town.

Kolding (13) See notes & plan p.249

Korsør (41) See notes & plan p. 252

Kristiansand see Norway and Skaggerak notes & plan p. 265

Langør 20) On the NE side of Samsø. A pretty hbr in beautiful surroundings. Buoyed but not lit. The largest scale Danish chart is essential as approaches are intricate. Berth on the quays as space permits, 2.5m but, (as elsewhere in the Kattegat) this may be lowered by as much as 1m with S winds. Modest stores.

Lemvig (30) Has a dredged channel, buoyed, with ldg lts on 171.5°. Moor in the fishing hbr or in the marina 1M N of town on W side of bay. Beautiful town, all facilities.

Løgstør (28) A large hbr in the middle of the Limfjord. Moor in either of the two more western basins as space allows. All stores.

Mandal see Norway and Skaggerak notes and plan p.264

Marstal (4) At the E end of Ærø, usually very crowded. Moor as space allows, probably at S end of hbr where there is a yacht hbr. A most beautiful town, with an interesting ship museum. All facilities.

Middelfart (14) The old hbr is uncomfortable and even dangerous owing to wash from passing ships and has few facilities other than diesel from the fishmonger and all stores. Use new marina on the S side of the isthmus, perfect shelter and not far from the town – best overnight berth in the area. Stores ¾M.

Naestved (52) An industrial hbr reached through a long dredged channel and canal. An interesting town. The W basin has 6m, the E 2m, yachts berth as space allows. All stores. Yachts mainlt berth at Karrebaeksminde at nouth of fjord. Entrance very rough in strong W to SW winds. Yacht hbr inside lifting br is perfectly sheltered: basin in outer hbr not too bad, but entering it from the main channel can be hairy. Br opens only on the hour and in daylight.

Nakskov (49) This large commercial hbr is seldom visited by yachts, but is most interesting and worth the detour. The dredged channel is well marked. Berth near E end of N quay or as directed. All stores, interesting church. There is a yacht hbr 1M W of the town at Hesthoved which provides a quieter berth for the night.

Nyborg (42) A major ferry hbr on the E coast of Fyn. The yacht hbr has its own entrance W of the main hbr. All supplies, facilities, interesting castle, well worth a visit

Nykøbing (Limfjord) (29) One of three hbrs of this name, it is a useful stop on passage through the Limfjord. There is a dredged channel, well buoyed, with 4.5m. Moor along W wall by hbr office. Pleasant town, all facilities.

Nykøbing (Sjaelland) (35) In the Isefjord, entered by a well buoyed channel. There are two large yacht hbrs with many berths free. Diesel on W side of E hbr entrance. Good stores.

Odden (36) Busy fishing town but useful staging point for yachtsmen. Deep-draught yachts moor in outer hbr along N wall, small ones may find berth in inner basin. Considerable wash. Diesel, some supplies, few facilities.

Odense (39) is Denmark's third city. D chart needed. There is a yacht basin at Stige, or moor alongside the E wall of the middle basin. Birthplace of Hans Andersen, it has impressive museums. Industrial hbr, but worth visiting.

Omø (44) Very small, but good shelter. Max depth 2.2m but with shallow patches on both sides of the hbr. It is also possible to anchor nearby. Beautiful unspoilt island. Simple stores some way away. 1986 new hbr completed beside old one.

Praestø (57) Chart D 190 advisable. Best berth alongside in enclosed basin at W end of hbr. Yacht jetties to the E have little water (1.5m). Attractive town in beautiful surroundings. Good stores, diesel from garage, 100 litres min.

Randers (25) A large commercial hbr on the NE coast of Jutland, usefully placed. Approach by well buoyed channel: use N basin which has a yacht hbr, or possibly berth at W end of basin, considerably nearer the shops. Good supplies: few facilities.

Rødby (48) Usefully placed if going to The Sound by the outside route. Heavy ferry traffic. Yachts berth in N basin, on the N or E quays, 5m. Few shops, no facilities.
Rødvig (69) See notes & plan p.253
Rudkøbing (46) Largest town on Langeland, with yacht hbr (2.2m) NE of the two commercial hbrs. Visitors berth at W end of N mole. Interesting old buildings. Good stores and facilities.
Rungsted (83) Large marina in pleasant surroundings. Kobenhavn half hour by train.
Sakskøbing (51) Approached through a dredged channel which must not be attempted at night. Posts in channel have small R or G patches to indicate to which side they should be left. Berth as space allows: good shopping close to berth.
Sejerø (37) This hbr lies on the S side of the Is, NW of Sjaelland. There is a blockship extension to the W mole which is steep-to. HM is active and allots berths. The small boat hbr should not be used without prior arrangement. Good supplies; interesting village 10 min walk. Good beaches.
Skagen (31) See notes & plan p.251
Søby (7) Useful hbr at N end of Ærø. Moor on S side of central mole, or in SE corner of inner basin. Store near hbr, otherwise supplies in village. Good bathing beach to the SW.

Sønderborg (9) See notes & plan p.247
Spodsbjerg (50) Useful hbr on the E side of Langeland. Berth in the S fishing hbr, on the S mole as opportunity offers. Often full: in W winds there is good anch 2 ca S of hbr entrance. Limited stores.
Stege (56) This hbr is approached by a dredged channel which is lit. Yacht hbr (<9m loa) first entrance on port (NE) side, 2.5m There is always room in N Havn for larger craft. HM, Customs, WCs near br. Shops very close to hbr, old houses, museum, 13C church, mediaeval ramparts and moat.
Stubbekøbing (54) Useful hbr on the way to Copenhagen from the S. Approach well lit and buoyed. Berth in E basin, at W end of S wall. Good supplies, welcoming YC.
Svendborg (45) Intricate but well buoyed approach to large town: Chart D 170 recommended. Current in sound can run at up to 5-6kn. Yacht hbr lies between Taasinge Br and the town, 2.5m, with diesel on stb side of entrance. Otherwise visitors should use wooden jetties in NW corner of commercial hbr. All supplies and facilities; popular tourist resort.

Thyborøn see Danish N Sea notes and plans p. 266

Tunø (21) A small hbr on a beautiful small Is. Crowded in season. Moor bow to quay, stern to anchor (be prepared beforehand). Arrive early, or else moor third deep like a rugby scrum. Limited supplies: a most attractive island.
Vejle (17) A rather dull town at end of a most lovely fjord; Yacht basin on N side inside entrance; supplies 10min walk. Visitors if too big for yacht hbr, or no berth available may also moor at W end of commercial hbr. Do not leave boat unattended there until berth agreed with HM. All stores.
Vordingborg (53) Use the N hbr by the buoyed channel. The first two yacht jetties have 1.5m at ML, the W-most 2.0m, or proceed to town quay, 2.4m. Winds between E-SW can cut depths by 1m. Castle and museum. Friendly clubhouse. Shopping excellent.

SWEDISH HARBOURS
The W coast is higher and more rugged than the E but does not have the "shargard" – a protective chain of islands off the mainland which makes interesting sailing possible. Navigation is intricate but rewarding.

Backviken (66) On the E side of Ven, slightly exposed to E or NE winds. Berth as space allows (only 1.5m at W end of S Mole). Surrounding area is most beautiful. There are the ruins of Tycho Brahe's observatory.
Gislovhamn (-) Yacht hbr for Trelleborg which lies close to W. Although listed as Customs port Trelleborg. has no facilities for yachts. Customs will visit Gislovhamn – a quiet unspoilt village. On entry turn sharply to stb to avoid 1.2m shoal just inside entrance.
Göteborg (62) Second city of Sweden – two yacht hbrs. One Längedrag on S side of R. Göta 5M from centre, the other, Lilla Bommen on S side of river by the square-rigged "Viking" close to shopping precinct. Göta canal, designed by Telford connects via Trollhatten canal and several large lakes to Mem about 70M S of Stockholm, traversing the country W to E in 214M and rising over 90m above SL. Dues are high but include overnight moorings for up to ten nights. Cruising from E to W is aided by flow of rivers.

Kyrkbacken (65) On the W coast of Ven, slightly open to strong W winds. Yachts berth on the W or N side of the hbr 3m. Some stores, few facilities. Beautiful area, good bathing.

Limnhamn (67) A large yacht hbr just S of large ferry hbr. Buoyed entrance; visitors berths at end of jetty K with R & G card system. Provisions from block overlooking hbr. Customs Port. Bus to Malmo which is a busy commercial hbr with no provision for yachts. Good bookshop Lundoren Bokhandel for charts.

Raa (64) A large yachting centre serving Halsingborg. Yacht hbr to stb immediately after the entrance, berths usually available. 2.5m. Larger yachts berth in old hbr. Good facilities but shops are 1000m away.

Skanor (68) A fishing hbr with considerable provision for yachts. Moor along outer end of N mole or at end of central mole. Smaller boats can berth between posts and jetty. Heavy swell in NW winds. Food at YC, good stores, good bathing.
Utklippan (-) At extreme SW of Sweden. Collection of tiny islets partially joined by concrete quays to provide completely sheltered miniscule hbr that can be entered from either E or W depending on the wind. Both entrances narrow and rock fringed. Only inhabitants the light house keepers who collect dues and sell postcards. No facilities – not even water. Idyllic - but beware aggressive sea-birds protecting their open nests within yards of the quays.

Viken (63) A pleasant hbr N of Halsingborg for small yachts. Just under 2m inside - but can be less in some conditions. Berth on W or N quays. Limited supplies, no facilities.
Ystad (-) A high walled ferry hbr gives landmark for yacht hbr with shared entrance – beware Bornholm ferries. All facilities and very convenient for town. Departure port for crossing the bight to Karlskrona and the Kalmar Sound.

FEDERAL REPUBLIC OF GERMANY

For details of entry and customs regulations see "Foreign Cruising Notes C1"

The coast of Germany is divided by the Jutland peninsula into an Eastern section in the SW Baltic and a Western section facing the North Sea. The Baltic ports are dealt with here and the N Sea section after the North Sea ports of Denmark. The Baltic coast of Germany, extending from the border with the former German Democratic Republic at Travemunde to Flensburg lies entirely within the province of Schleswig-Holstein, the whole of which is low-lying with a maximum height above sea-level of 200m. Tidal range is insignificant but persistent. Winds may produce variations in sea-level of 1m and surface currents between 1 & 2kn in light winds increase to more than 4kn in stronger blows. Due to the low salinity ice forms in most years from Jan-Mar, but the development of the central European high pressure zone during the summer produces very warm conditions with little rainfall except in the occasional thunderstorms. Winds are predominantly from the West and North West in July and Aug and although they can be strong are generally kindly for cruising yachts.

The North Sea Coast, on the other hand, extending from the sandy dune-covered islands of the North Friesian group South of the Danish frontier to the Ems estuary and the border with Holland, experiences a considerable semi-diurnal tidal range, with associated strong tidal streams making the estuaries dangerous places for small craft with wind opposing tide. In such conditions yachts have been delayed for days before being able to leave the Elbe or the Weser. Helgoland is a useful port of refuge whilst awaiting suitable conditions to enter these rivers.

PASSAGE NOTES

From Lubecker Bay, a narrow buoyed channel leads under the Fehmarn Bridge (clearance of 23m) but vessels must keep 3M North of the coast beyond Heiligenhafen to avoid the firing range which is in daily use during the summer. It is patrolled by units of the German Marine (VHF 13 call sign 'Marine boot').

The approach to the Vogelfluglinie Br is via a buoyed channel from the Fehmarn Sund buoy (RWVS with Sph topmark).

From the W, the white bldgs of Heiligenhafen will appear long before the buoys become visible. The arched span of the bridge is further confirmation of the course, but the channel underneath is only 50m wide, although dredged to 4m.

From the North and the Danish port of Sønderborg or the Flensburg fjord there are no major obstacles. The Kiel Lt Tr 30m with a red gallery surmounting white tr on an artificial island dominates the fjord and is a powerful sectored lt. On the Eastern bank of Kieler Fjord, at Laboe is the conspicuous tr of the German Naval war memorial in the form of the conning tower of a U-boat. The Friedrichsort Lt is exhibited 33m high from a W Tr with B bands. Signals are also displayed here denoting the use of the firing range. The entrance to the Kiel canal at Holtenau is marked by a collection of lights and towers just South of Stickenhorn and the British Kiel YC.

These ports are listed in the graphical index of the SW Baltic.

FLENSBURG Charts BA 3562 G 41

Approach and Entrance An old trading port which still possesses considerable commercial importance. The yacht hbr at the S end of Harniskai has a least depth of 6m. The hbr is approached through a wide and deep fairway for 4½M through Flensburg fjord. Alternative moorings may be found at Kollund pier, 1½M WSW of Kohage.

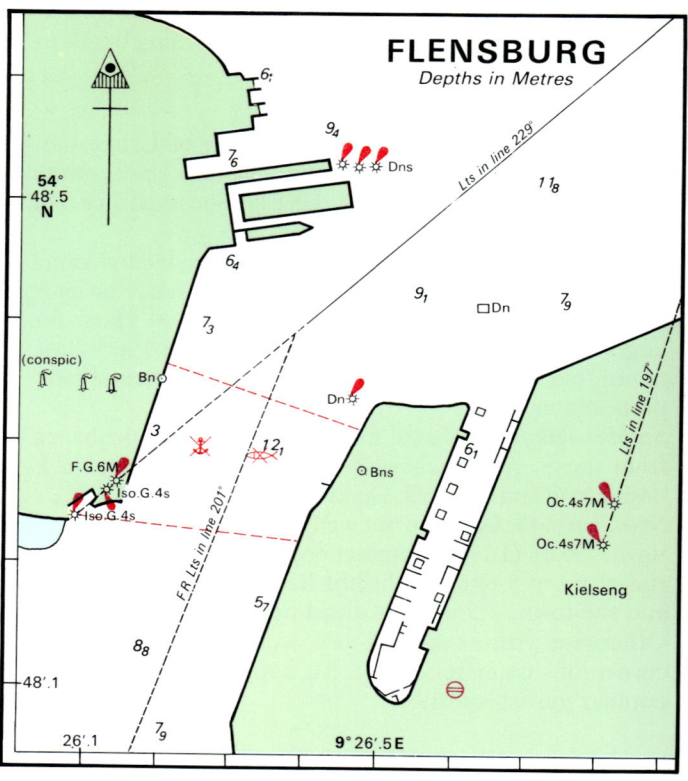

MAASHOLM Charts BA 3562 G 41

A small fishing village, 1½M inside the Schlei.

Approach and Entrance The Schleimunde Seegat is a buoyed channel dredged to 5m. Entrance to the Schlei is between two moles the heads marked by bns: the Schleimunde light is exhibited from a W Tr with a B band, and at a height of 15m. W ly gales may lower the water level by as much as 2m, whilst E ly gales may raise it up to 3m above mean level.

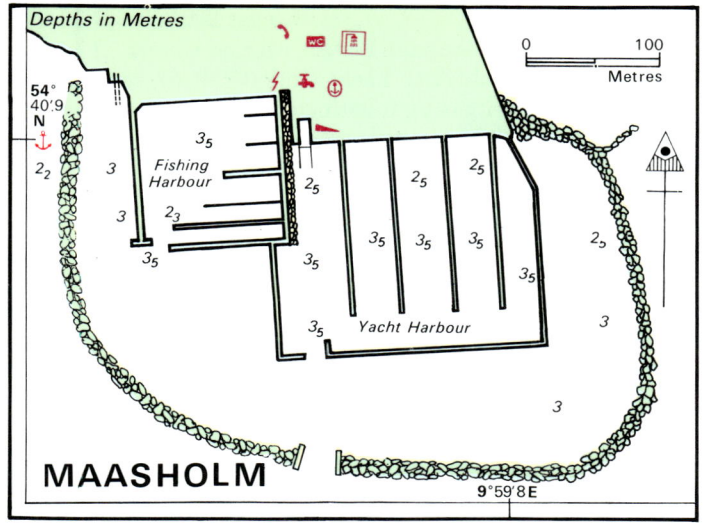
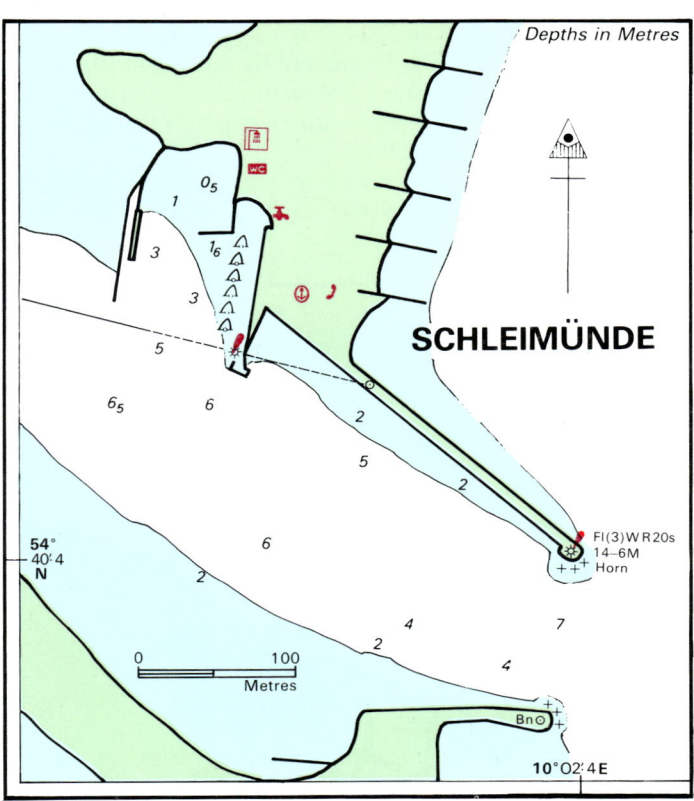

Passing Schleimunde Hafen on the North which has a small yacht hbr – least depth 2.5m, Maasholm has a yacht hbr adjoining the fishing hbr. All facilities, but fuel only obtainable in the fishing hbr. A stone breakwater with a cone-topped bn extends southwards of the hbr and must be left to stb on entering.

SCHLESWIG Charts BA 3562 G 41

The town is 22M from the entrance at Schleimunde and although an interesting and historic town has only a small yacht hbr with limited facilities and only suitable for shoal draught vessels. Water, toilets and showers available, but no fuel.

KIEL FJORD Charts BA 33

There are several yacht harbours including two Olympiahafen. It is Germany's main naval base and activity is constant.

Approach and Entrance Best made direct to the Kiel Lt Ho and thence on a course of 202° passing 1.5M off Bulk LT Ho and thus avoiding the shoals of the Kleverberg. The naval war memorial is a conspic mark fine to port.

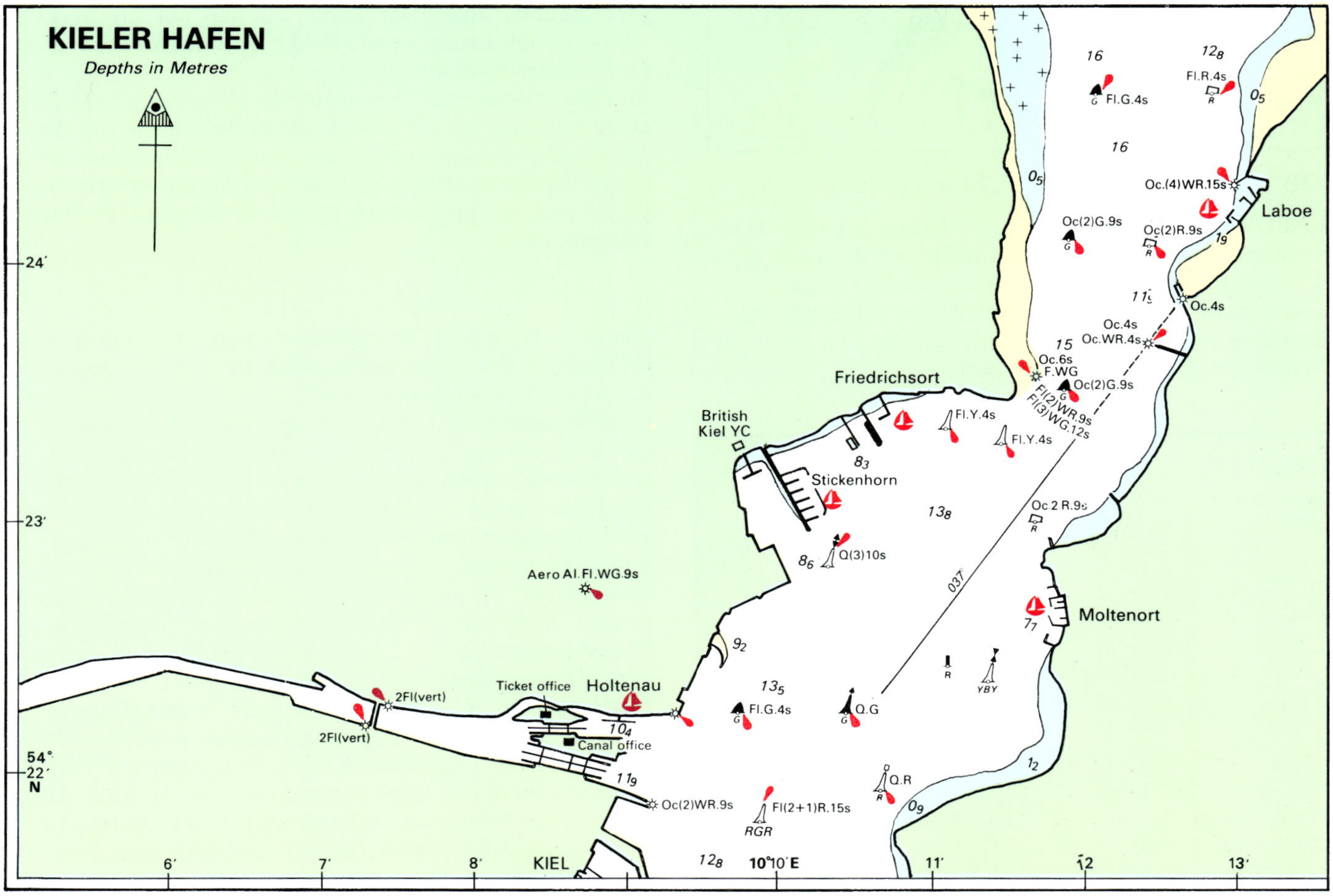

FEDERAL REPUBLIC OF GERMANY AND SOUTHWEST BALTIC 258

SCHILKSEE

Olympia Zentrum may be entered by turning to stb on to 270° after 4.5M and after 1.5M on this course the entrance is between two breakwaters with a sharp turn to stb for the visitors' berths. All facilities.

Entrance is between breakwaters with a N card bn to stb and then a sharp turn to port leaving another breakwater head to stb.

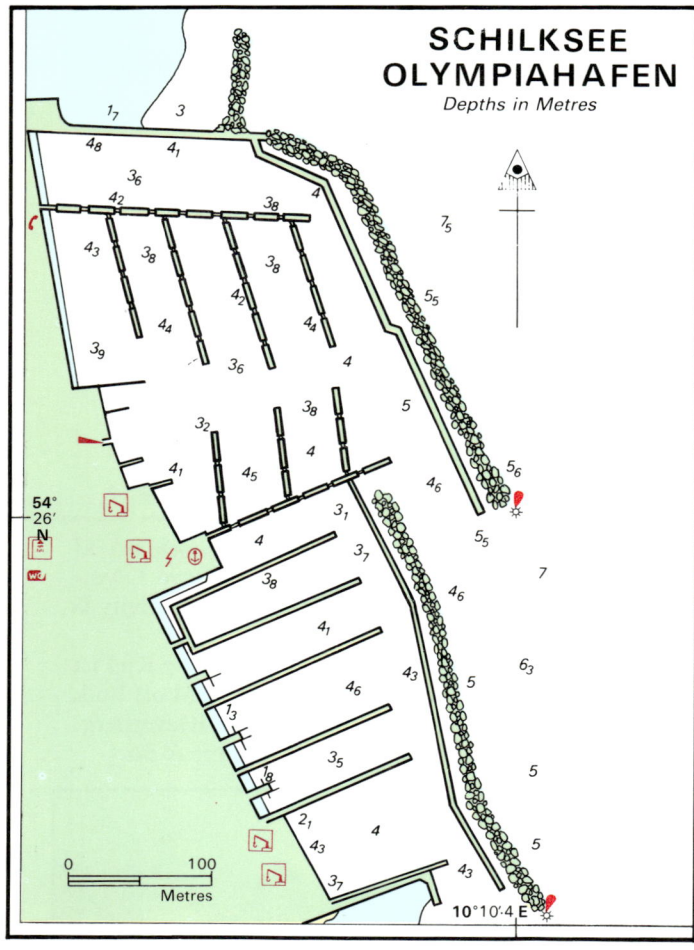

LABOE   Charts BA 696   G30

LABOE   Charts BA 969   G 30

Approach and Entrance From the direct line from Kiel Lt Ho to Friedrichsort Lt Ho. A turn to port on to a SE ly course must be made when still 1M N of Friedrichsort.

Berthing bow to quay with stern secured to a post. All facilities except fuel. Customs post.

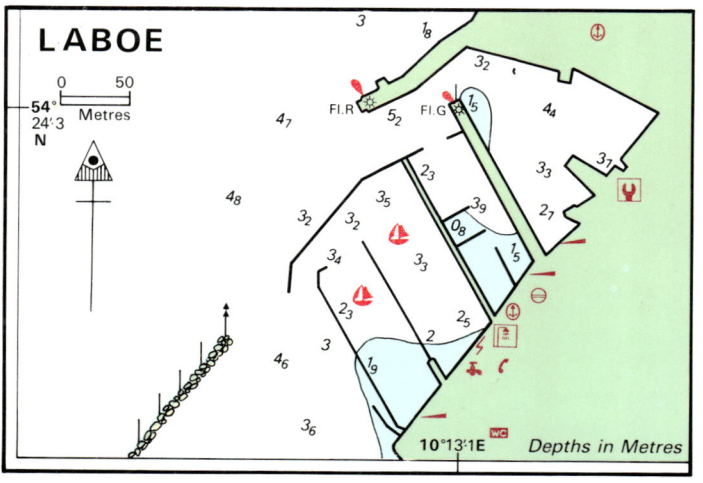

STICKENHORN   Charts BA 969   G 30

A German Naval base and British Marine Centre. The home of the British Kiel Yacht Club VHF 67 callsign "Sailtrain". Security is tight with guard dogs on the loose at night, but British visitors are made very welcome. Shops nearby. Yacht hbr is at head of enclave formed by breakwater.

Berthing Bows to the 'T' shaped pier. stern quarters secured to posts (have long ropes ready with large loops) Report to office on arrival but duty NCO usually on pier to assist. Care must be taken not to turn to N of breakwater or to attempt to secure on the southern side of the enclave as this is German naval territory.

HOLTENAU   Chart BA 969

Approach Numerous lts and trs mark the Kiel canal but there are yacht moorings on the N side of the channel. Supermarket; fuel usually available from a moored tanker. Beware large vessels manoeuvring whilst waiting to enter locks, or others emerging at a rapid rate. VHF 12 call sign Kiel canal 4.

KIEL CANAL   Chart BA 2469

The canal, opened in 1895 as the (Kaiser Wilhelm Kanaal), extends for 54M from Kiel-Holtenau to Brunsbuttel on the R Elbe. The R Eider, reached via the Gieselau locks near Oldenbuttel provides an alternative and scenically attractive, if slow and winding route to the North Sea at Tonning. It has a least depth of 2.7m.

The canal takes vessels up to 235m in length. Yachts may proceed under their own power, but may not sail except with the engine running and then only if the wind is free. Commercial tows are rarely arranged nowadays, but if they are, it is necessary to register the details with the HM at the entrance lock. Traffic is controlled by Lts and the whole canal is under radar surveillance. Police posts are established at intervals – a Y flashing Lt means that the Police post has information for the vessel passing. Stop and enquire!

The canal is marked throughout its length by Km posts to aid location. Dues are payable only at the Holtenau end, at a news kiosk N of all locks. Notify dues office, if intending to leave canal via R Eider. Tickets must be date stamped for the day of passage at the HM's office at the top of the control building situated between the locks. Passage of the canal must not be commenced unless it is possible to reach a berthing place before nightfall as small craft are not permitted to navigate the canal either during the hours of darkness or in poor visibility (unless equipped with radar). Mooring is only permitted at Rendsburg, Dukerswisch (Km 21.5), Gieselau Locks (Km 40.5), Obereidersee (Km 66), Borgstedt Narrows (Km 70) and Flemhudersee (Km 85.5). 3 R lts (vert) forbid all movement in the canal. Of the various signals exhibited, the only other one of significance to yachts is a single Fl W lt which on becoming fixed permits entry to the lock. All others relate to large commercial craft. Lt signals may be supplemented by verbal instructions through a loud-hailer, which may be difficult to hear above engine noise.

BURGTIEFE   Charts BA 2364   G31

A large yacht marina lying to the North of the Burgtiefe peninsula which protects it from all winds from southerly quarters.

Approach From the Fehmarnsund-Ost RW buoy a course of 032° leads after 1.9M to Burg 1 con buoy skirting the rocky shoals to the West. Three conspic blocks of flats appear ahead.

Entrance From Burg 1 a well-marked curving channel leads into the BurgerSee with Burgstaaken on the Northern shore. A subsidiary channel leads off from the Burgtiefe K buoy to the East to the sheltered yacht hbr. All facilities including fuel. Entrance is not recommended at night. Smaller yachts may berth inside the circular wall, larger craft lie on the outside, stern to posts.

There are also pontoons with stern posts to the east of the original yacht hbr 3m depth.

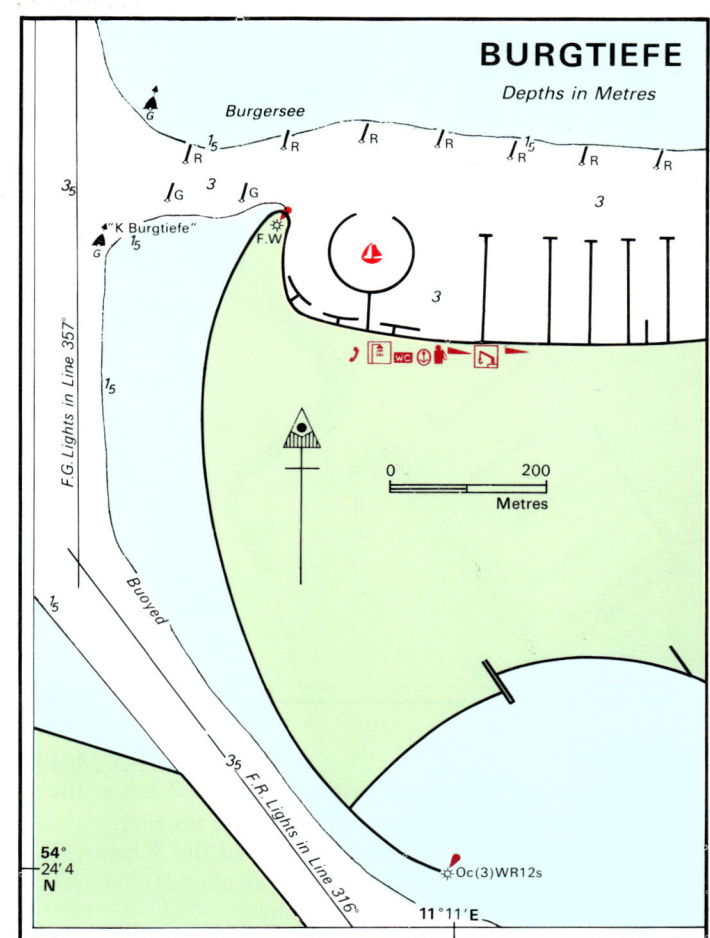

HEILIGENHAFEN   Chart BA 2364

Entrance The Heiligenhafen N card buoy marks the NE extremity of the shoals from which a SSE course should be steered until the buoys marking the entrance channel become visible. In strong NW winds the entrance is dangerous, and the island of Fehmarn provides little protection from strong winds from the NW. In such cases it is better to proceed under the bridge and either N to Burgtiefe or S to one of the ports in Lubeck Bay.

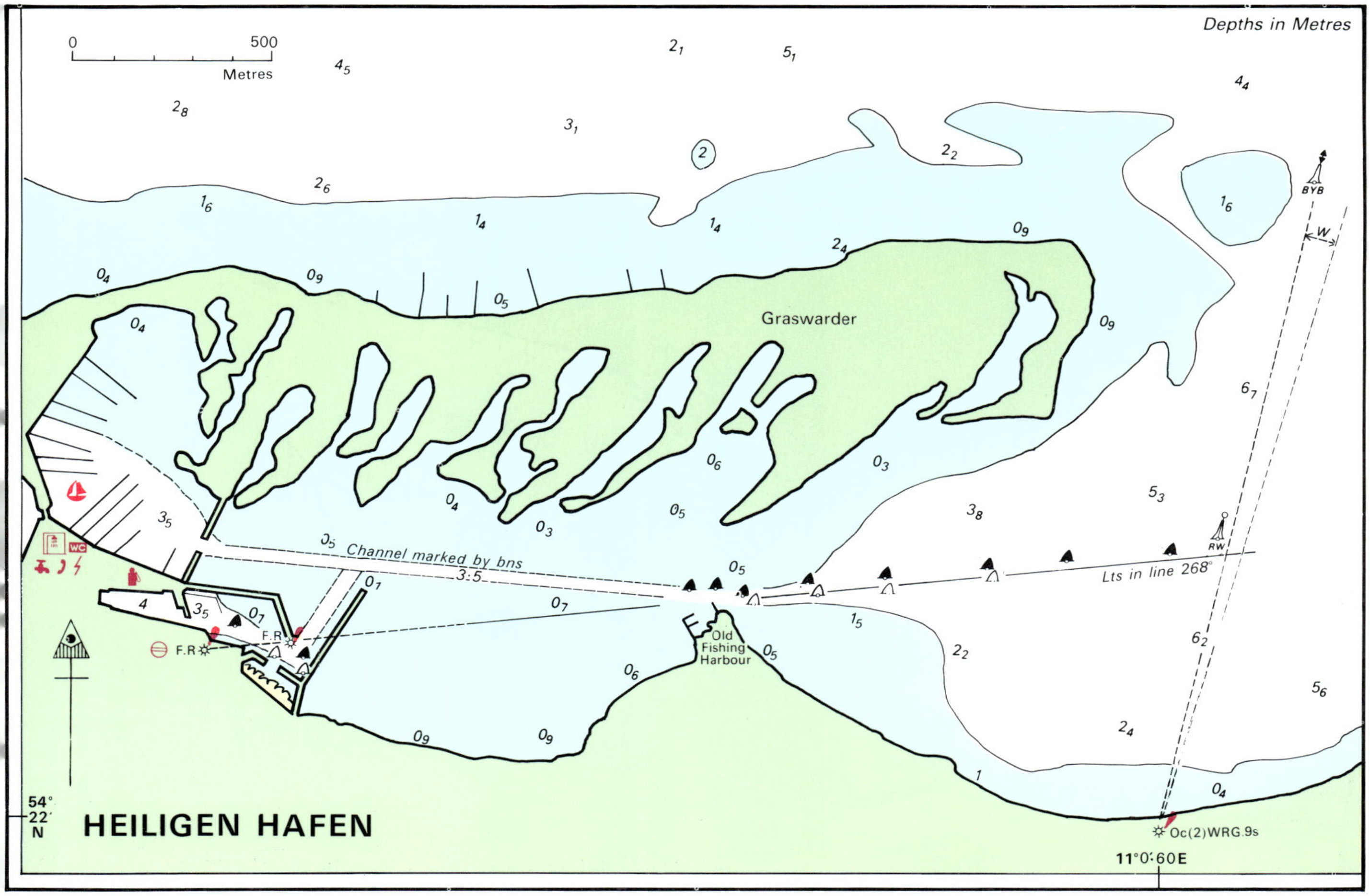

FEDERAL REPUBLIC OF GERMANY AND SOUTHWEST BALTIC

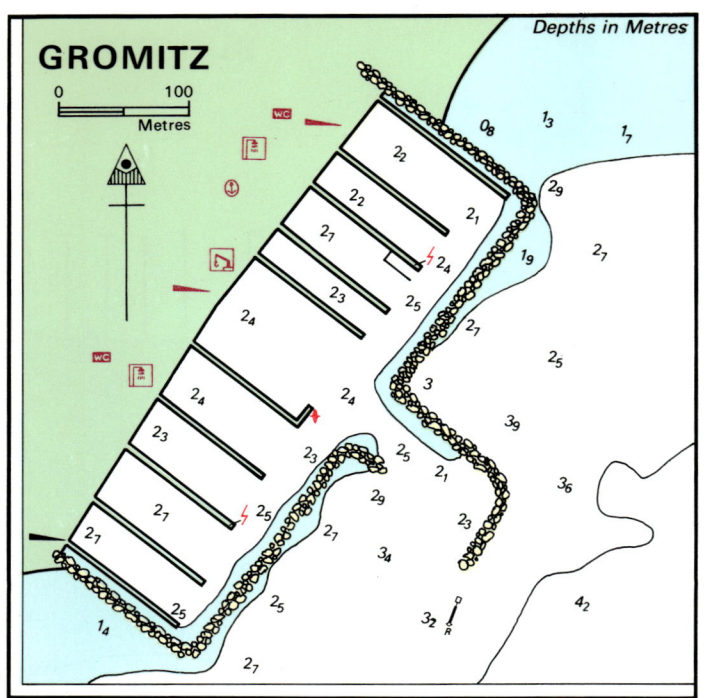

TRAVEMÜNDE
Chart BA 2364

This is the outport of the ancient Hanseatic City of Lübeck which is 11M inland and is reached by the R Trave – dredged to a depth of 8.5m and with one lifting bridge. Although of great historic and architectural interest, Lübeck has few facilities for yachts and it is better to lie at one of the yacht hbrs at Travemünde and journey overland by train or bus which takes only 30 mins. Travemünde has excellent beaches and is a good shopping centre. If proceeding to a Scandinavian country it is wise to replenish stores here as prices are generally much lower.

Approach A tall conspic tower block is visible from well out in Lubeck Bay. This bldg is situated just North of the entrance. A continuous stream of ferry traffic will be encountered. The E canal Brodten-Ost buoy 020° from the entrance at 2½M should be left to stb as the Riff Ground between here and the shore is covered with rocky boulders. The main fairway buoys may then be followed.

Entrance The Ldg lts are on a bearing of 215° and lead between the No 6 R buoy to port and the N mole-head to stb. The Passathafen with excellent facilities lies on the Southern shore with the square-rigged "Passat", permanently moored. Access to the shops, restaurants etc is by frequent ferry either from seaward of the "Passat", or the car ferry ½M upriver. Other yacht hbrs are situated on the northern shore but tend to be noisy. A fuel station is to be found just before the car ferry on the southern shore.

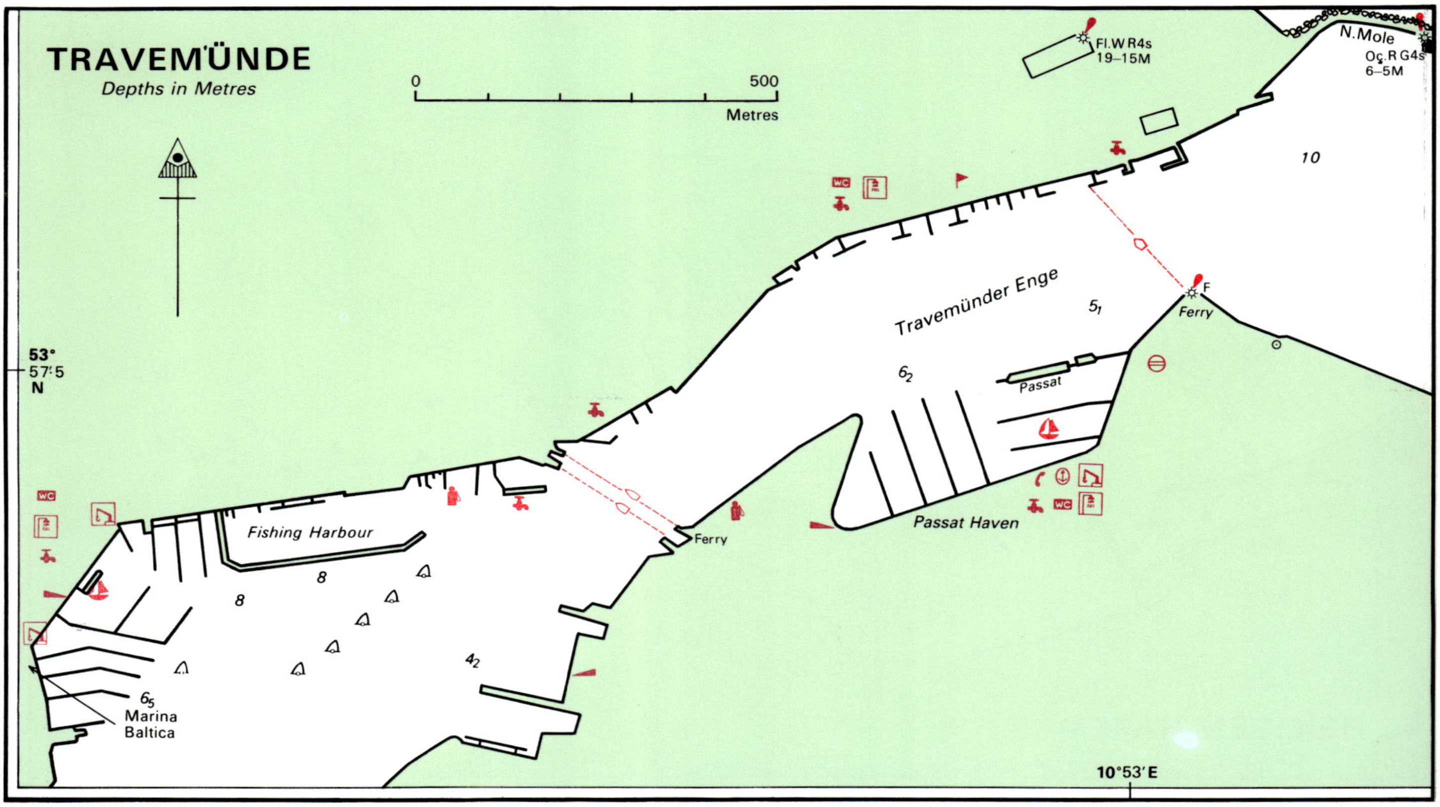

GRÖMITZ
Chart BA 2364

An artificial yacht harbour with a depth of 2.5m at the outer end has been constructed ¾M SW of the pier.

Approach From the NW, having cleared the Schwarzer Grund Ost E Card buoy, sufficient depth clear of obstacles will be found no more than ½M offshore.

Entrance An Oc G 4s Lt is exhibited at a height of 6m on the N mole head. Pontoons are equipped with water and electricity and there is a marina shop. Toilets and showers are provided.

THE KIEL CANAL Chart BA 2469
See entry after Holtenau.

RENDSBURG Charts BA 2469 G 42
This town is on the N of the canal between km 60 & 67 (Km posts along the canal).

Approach The yacht hbr is in the dammed section of the Upper Eider river and is approached via a buoyed channel from the main canal at the eastern end of the town, passing shipbuilding yards.

Entrance The yacht hbr lies 1½M along the branch and has stern-to moorings with posts. All facilities, but fuel more easily obtainable from pumps on the Northern bank of the main canal at a commercial quay in the centre of the town.

Just beyond the town is a transporter bridge, the conveyor section of which passes less than 12m above the water: the main structure like all other bridges and cables provides clearance of 40m.

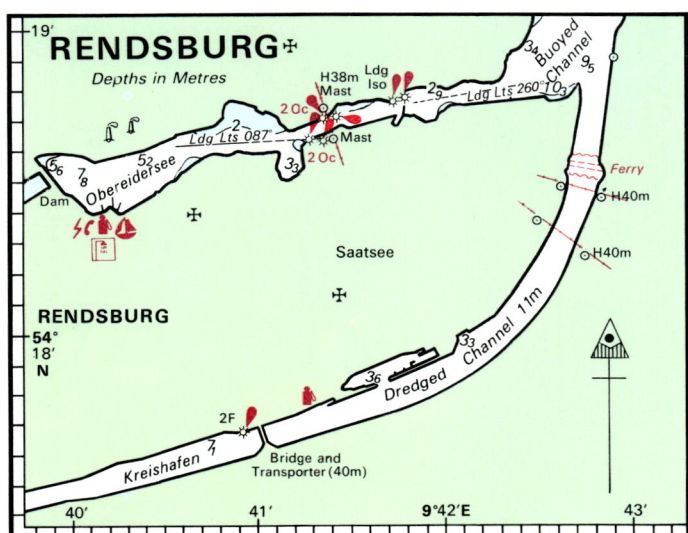

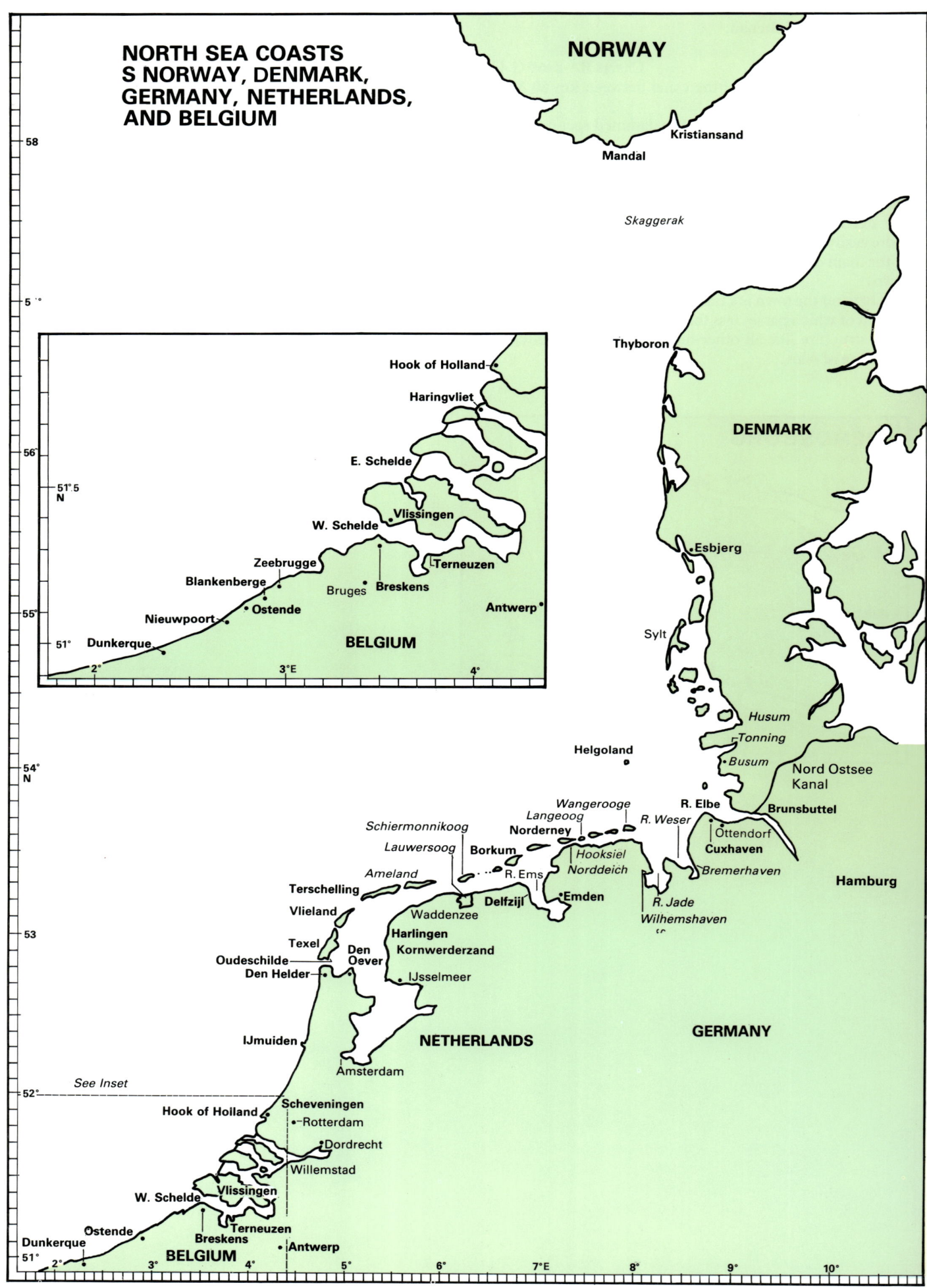

NORWAY – SKAGGERAK

For Passage Notes see p245

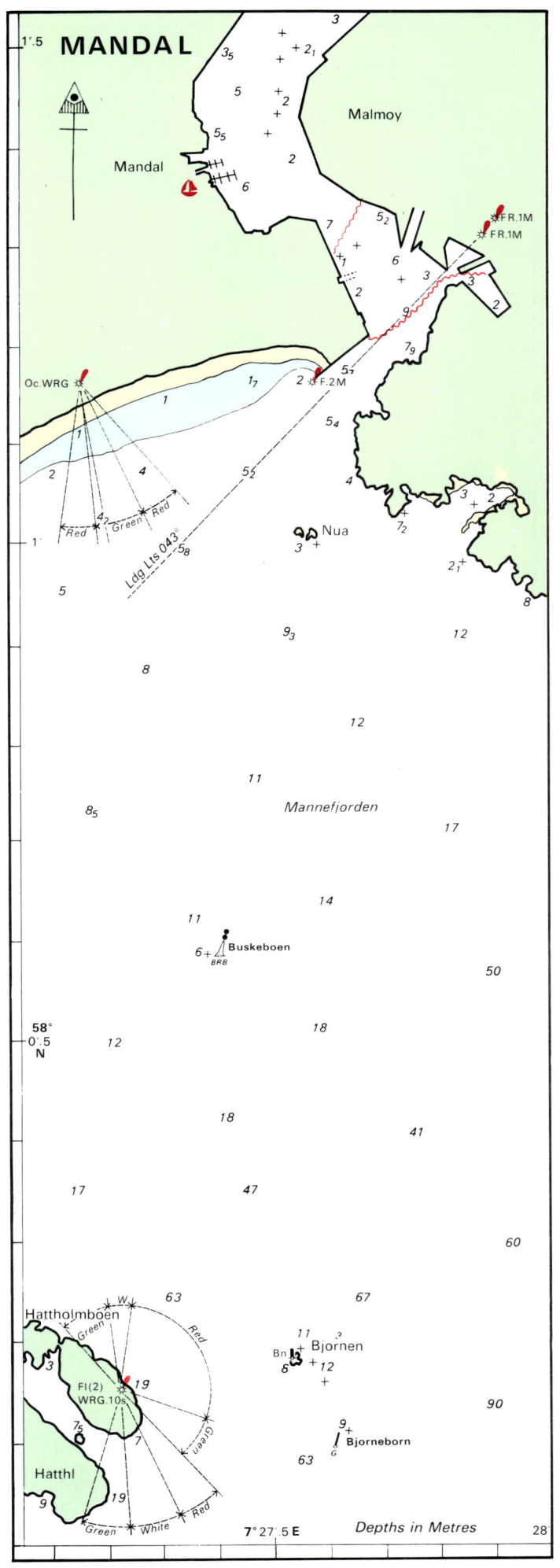

MANDAL Charts BA 2182 B   N S 457
(58°02′.0N 7°27′.0E)

No significant tidal rise or fall. No constant tidal stream, but generally a SW-going current, affected by winds. A land-locked river harbour, totally protected and available in all weathers.

Approach From seaward identify RYVINGEN Lt Ho Conspic RW 28M Fog siren. Steer 350° with major islands to stb and rocks and skerries to port altering slightly as necessary will lead in safely as all relevant hazards show above water.

Entrance There is a bar in sheltered water with 3m water. In channel keep to stb until channel turns NW, when hold to W side as E becomes shoal.

Berthing Gjestehavn on port past shipyard. 4.5m depth at quays. New pontoon berths available. Customs.

Supplies All facilities except sailmaker. Shops shut at 1600hrs.(1300 Sats.)

Customs on N side of river beyond br.

KRISTIANSAND Charts BA 2182 B   N S 459
(58°08′.5N. 8°00′.0E)

Tidal information as for Mandal.

A double harbour set in a large deep bay, associated with a Radiobeacon, and available in all weathers.

Approach The approach from SW uses OKSØY radiobeacon and lights to port and GRÖNINGEN Lt to stb. Bring GRÖNINGEN Lt Ho to bear 030° and in line with SOTISEN 85m high and the S of two easily identified wooded hills 3M NNE. This leads E of all dangers off the SE side of YTRE FLEKKERØY.

Entrance Two harbours E and W of ODDERÖ Island are separated by a fixed low bridge. Leaving ODDERÖ to port steer on a ch steeple for preferred yacht hbr.

Berthing E Hbr alongside as space allows in 1.8m. There is berthing in the W hbr should the wind be SE but it is further from town.

Supplies All services; sailmaker; excellent public baths and sauna at the "Health Studio" – a public facility. There are showers and DIY laundry facilities at the hbr. Having cleared Customs, and done any shopping (shops close not later than 4pm in summer), those seeking a quiet anchorage should try Prestöy 1.5M across the fjord. If at all possible, visit the piece of coastline between Kristiansand and Lillesand to the east, known as the Blindleie – a sheltered stretch of water behind and between offshore islands and very highly recommended for cruising.

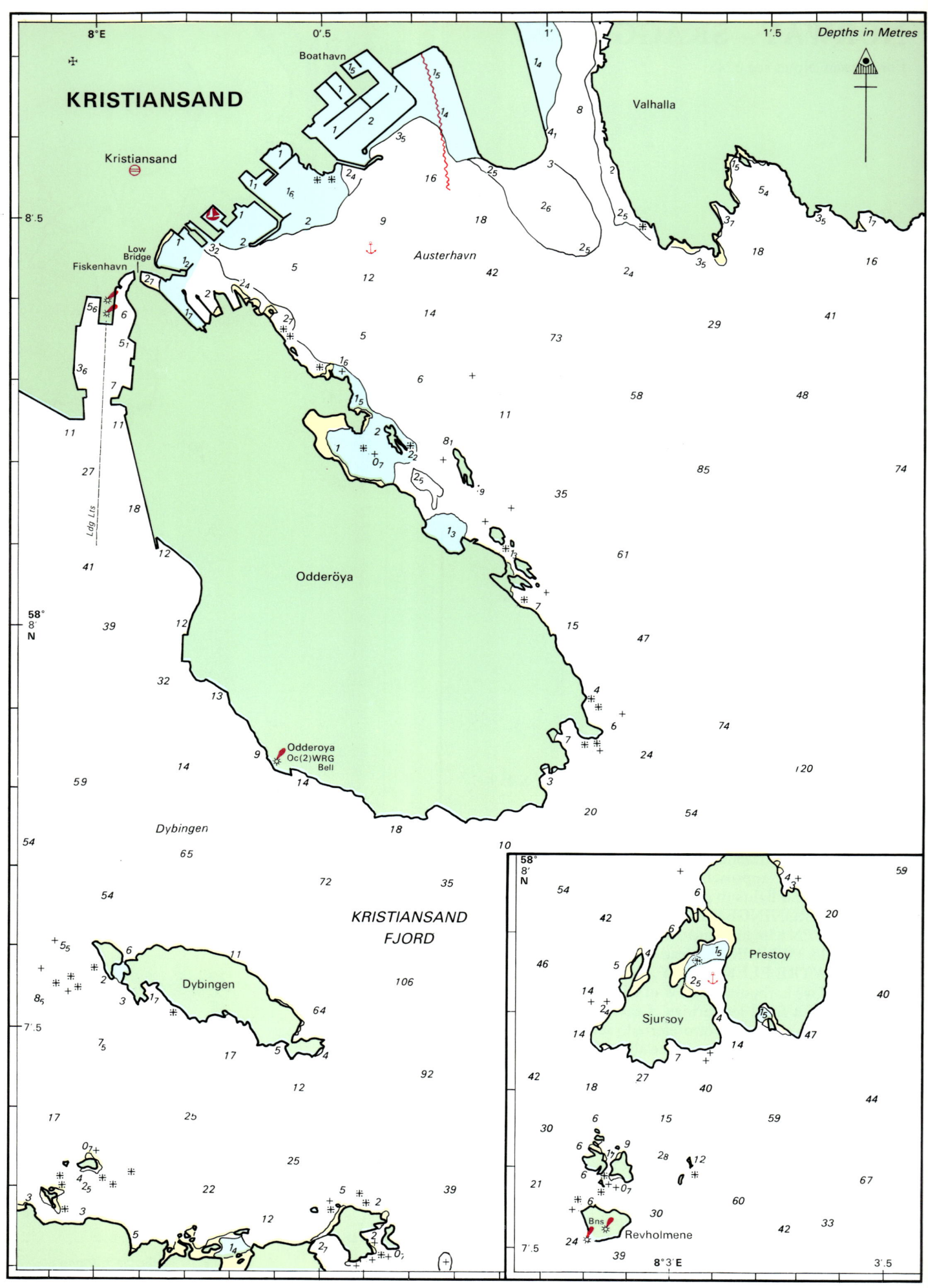

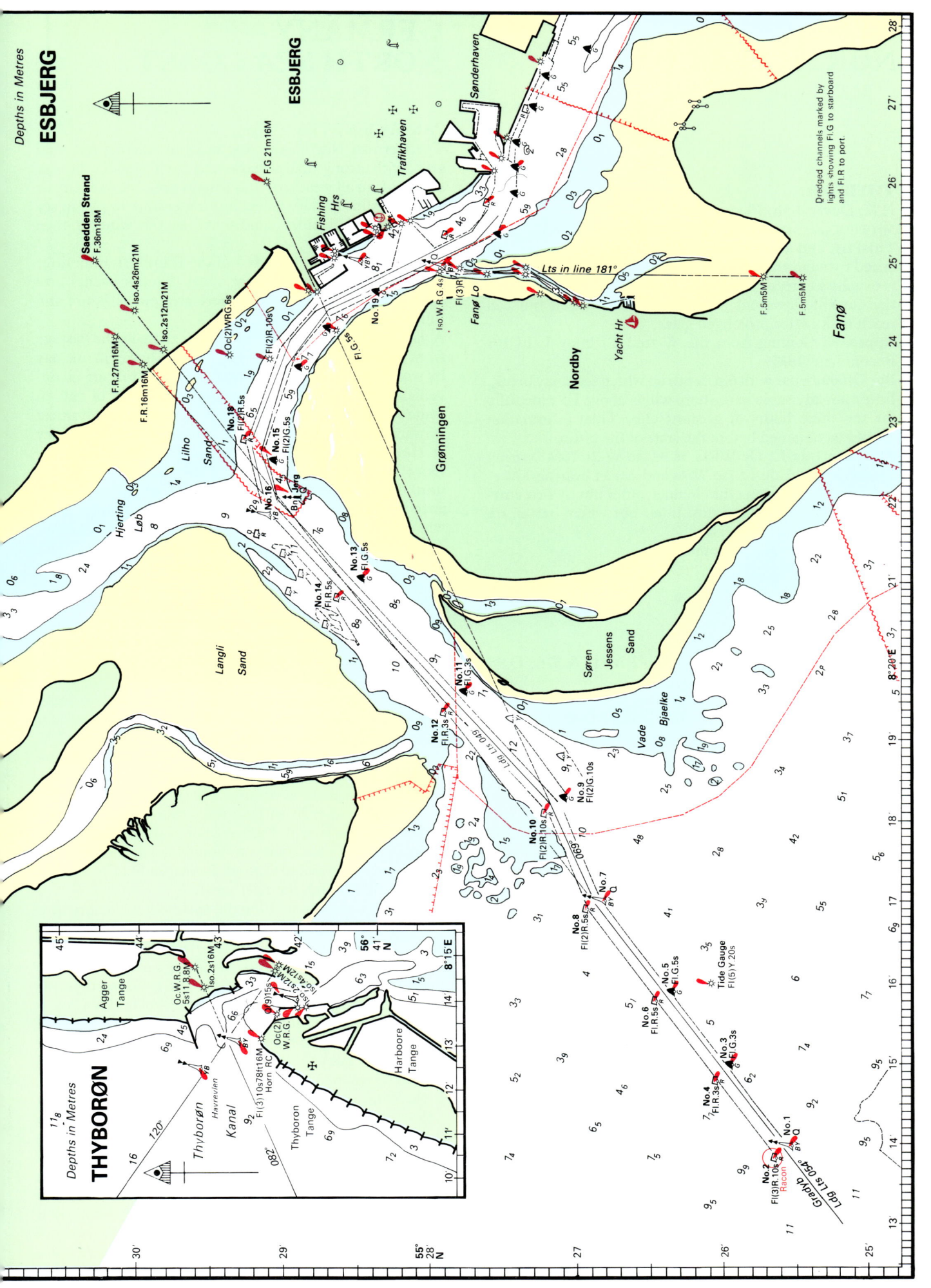

DENMARK – NORTH SEA COAST

THYBORØN Charts BA 2325 D 108
HW: Dover +5h Plan P 266
MHWS 0.4m MHWN 0.3 MTL 0.2 MLWN 0.1 MLWS 0.0
Tidal rise and fall are negligible, and stream is more influenced by wind than tide. With established W winds there is usually a current into the hbr; with established E winds the current flows out. Currents usually 1-2kn but can reach 6-8kn after prolonged gales.
Approach Coming from the W find Lt buoy L Fl 10s Racon(3cm) 10M.
Bar Offshore bar with 6m depth on which seas may break. Entry not advisable in onshore winds above F5 especially for the three hours of greatest ebb. Tidal information should be obtained before the start of the cruise.
Entrance Ldg Lt Oc WRG 5s + Iso W 2s 16M bearing 082°. Channel Ldg Lt Iso W 4s and 2s 8M bearing 120°.
Berthing Steer S along the channel, enter hbr by first entrance and go to northernmost inner hbr where berths are usually available on E wall.
Supplies All stores. Customs.

ESBJERG Charts BA 417 & 3768 D 95
HW: Dover +2h Plan P 266
MHWS 1.6m MHWN 1.4 MTL 0.8 MLWN 0.2 MLWS −0.1
The only all weather port on the Danish N Sea coast.
Approach Via Fanø Bay with Horns Reef to the north. Sandbanks off the low-lying shore make radio navigational aids useful. Identify the Gradyb Bar Lt buoy Fl(3) R 10s Racon(3cm) 10M. The Gradyb channel has a bar with a dredged crossing 200m wide. Strong W-SW winds raise a heavy sea and breakers on the bar and in the 5M long channel especially against a 2kn ebb.
Entrance The channel is dredged to 9.5m and 200m wide: well marked and lit. The first Ldg Lt is one F and two Iso 21M bearing 054°. A 24hr watch is kept on VHF.
Berthing Call HM VHF 12 no charges.
Supplies All stores. Customs.

GERMANY – NORTH SEA COAST

PASSAGE NOTES
The German North Sea coast is an interesting but wild area, with strong tidal streams and few harbours that are accessible in all weathers. It is usually possible to enter the main ones in onshore gales, but impossible to put to sea from them in similar conditions, as the wind is then against the stream.
The North Friesian Islands S of the Danish frontier offer interesting cruising for those shoal draught yachts prepared to take the ground as there are few harbours and tidal ranges are considerable.
A yacht capable of maintaining 6 kn can make the passage from either Borkum or Nordeney to Cuxhaven in one day by working the tides, but when the times of tide are inconvenient, Helgoland is a very convenient port of call en route at which to await a favourable tidal stream. The most favourable conditions will be found by leaving Nordeney at Helgoland HW −1½h and taking a course from the Dove Tief buoy parallel to the islands and approx 3M out until the Otzumer Balje buoy N or the Wangerooge entrance is reached. At which point a decision must be made whether to proceed to the Elbe or to make for Helgoland. The latter requires a course to be made good of 025° with weak tidal streams requiring little adjustment and with the benefit of several sea-marks on the way. This route will cut across the SE tip of the Precautionary Area of the Jade approach but clear the restricted channels of the Neue and Alte Weser. The passage should be completed not more than 8 hours after departing Nordeney or 14 hours from Borkum.

If continuing to the Elbe, course needs to be set to make good 061° to clear the Scharhorn Riff and enter the stb side of the Elbe approach channel 1½ to 2M S of the Elbe 1 LV, thereby avoiding most of the traffic. There are numerous sea-marks along the route but BA chart 1875 is essential. The ETA at a position with the Elbe LV abeam should be HW Helgoland −5h to take full advantage of the tidal stream into the Elbe to Cuxhaven or even to Brunsbuttel. From Nordeney to Cuxhaven should take no more than 12 hours and it is possible to reach Brunsbuttel in 14 hours if proceeding through the Kiel canal.

From Helgoland to the Elbe the optimum departure time is Helgoland HW −5h. Going W, the problem is, as already stated, getting out of the River Elbe, as the seas become dangerous in strong winds against the tide. To make the best use of the tidal streams in good weather, the optimum departure time from Brunsbuttel is HW Cuxhaven +1h when the Elbe 1 LV can be reached in 4 hours. It is essential to keep to the starboard side of the channel, but close to the buoys to keep clear of shipping. Helgoland should be reached in a further 2h or Nordeney in 6h.

If the wind is from a W or NW quarter and is anything above F4 a more comfortable passage may be achieved by departing Cuxhaven at HW Cuxhaven −2h and keeping to the port side of the Elbe but out of the shipping channel thereby averting the wrath of the Port Control who monitor all vessels on radar. When the Lt Tr "C" is abeam course must be set directly across the river to the starboard side before continuing Westward, but by then the seas are less steep and the tidal stream will only just have commenced to oppose the wind.

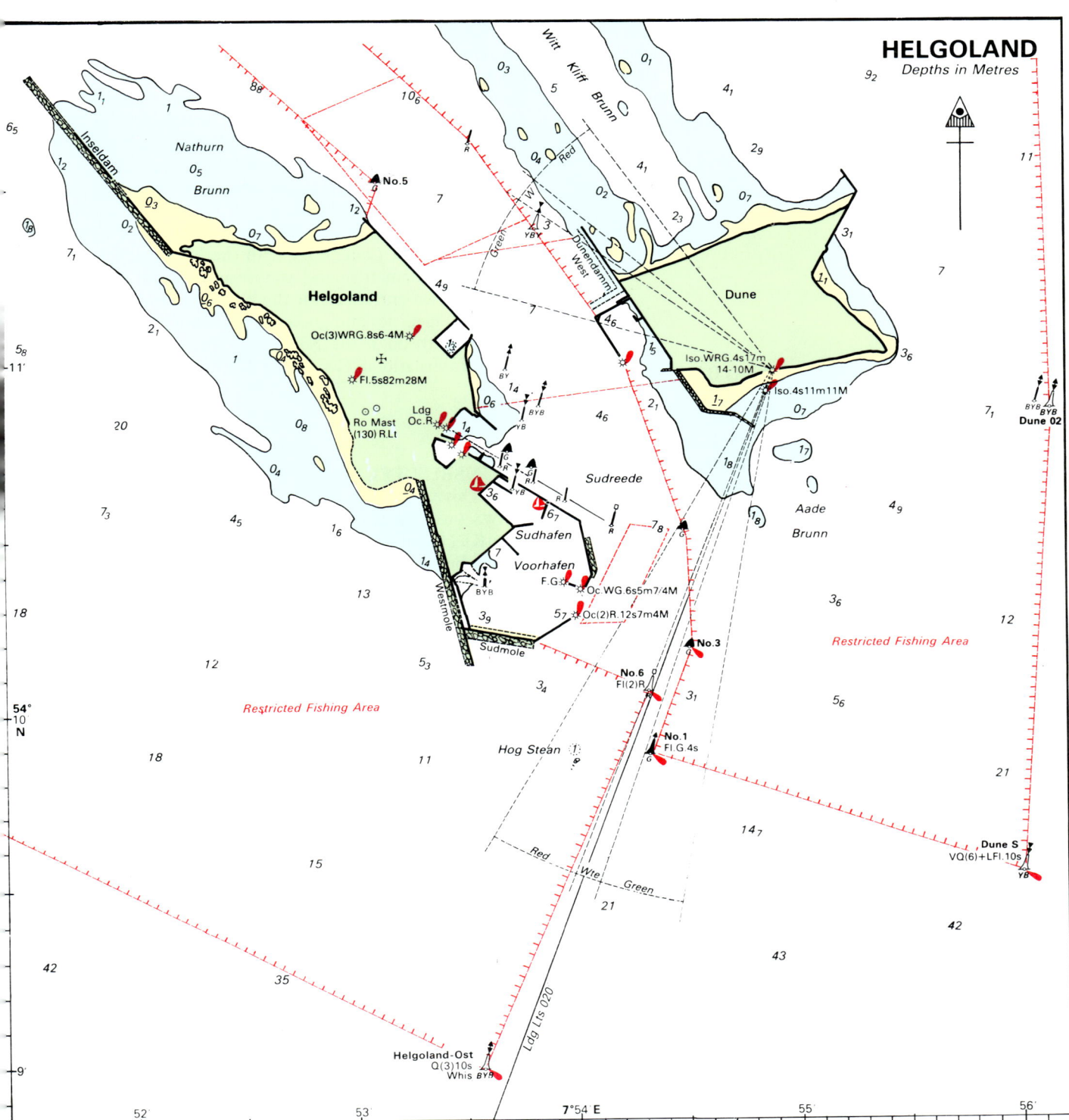

HELGOLAND Charts BA 126 & 1875
HW: Dover −¼h

MHWS 2.6m MHWN 2.3 MTL 1.4 MLWN 0.4 MLWS 0.0
A conspic red rock rising to 55m above sea level with a Fl 5s lt exhibited at a height of 81m and radio masts extending to 130m makes a good landmark.

Once an English possession, this is an all-weather hbr in the SE part of the North Sea. It can be approached from either the N or S, and one of these approaches is always sufficiently sheltered to permit entry.

Approach The channels from both directions are well buoyed.

Entrance Yachts use the southernmost basin on the main Is, entered between two pier-heads; no hazards.

Berthing Yachts proceed into Sudhaven immediately to the N, where there are pontoons. This gives shelter and is safe but has severe swell in E gales, then the E side is more protected. A short walk to the shops. All facilities, fuel and supplies, are inexpensive as this is a low-tax island but crowded in summer and essentials like bread and milk more difficult to find than duty free drink etc. Berthing is expensive.

NORTH SEA GERMANY 268

HUSUM
Chart BA 3767
HW: Dover +1½h
MHWS 3.8m MHWN 3.4 MTL 2.1 MLWN 0.5 MLWS 0.0
Husum is approachable near HW but has only 0.3m at MLWS and vessels must be prepared to take the ground in soft mud in the hbr at LW. VHF 11.

TONNING
Charts BA 3767 G 105
HW: Dover +2½h

Approach From the W a course of 084° leads in 5½M from the Aussen Eider buoy (071° from Helgoland 15M) to the Eider buoy and at first in an ESE direction and then following a winding course along a well marked channel for 15M to the Eiderdamm. Good visibility and settled weather are required, and the flood tide must be taken. The tidal stream then sets across the sands and care is needed not to pass outside the buoys as they are placed at the edges of the channel and silting produces incursions into the channel.

Entrance is by means of a lock (VHF 16 & 14) which operates throughout the day and night. Two long blasts is the appropriate sound signal requesting opening. There is a further lock at Nordfeld, but Tonning 5M from the Eiderdamm has a depth of 3.0m.

Berthing is alongside the quay but there are no facilities for yachts or their crews, other than water. The Eider connects with the Kiel canal at Gieselau. There are several locks with fixed charges for each opening shared by all the craft using it at the time. It is thus more expensive to go through alone, but dues are not high.

Custom clearance must be obtained here if travelling via R Eider to Kiel Canal.

BUSUM
Charts BA 1875, 3767 G 105
HW: Dover +1¼h
MHWS 3.7m MHWN 3.2 MTL 1.81 MLWN 0.5 MLWS 0.0

Approach This hbr has a deep water approach at all states of the tide and a least depth at MLWS of 2.3m in the hbr entrance. A buoyed channel leads in from the Sudfahrwasser and the Suderpiep buoy which is 095° from Helgoland 15M.

Entrance Strong eddies set across the entrance which is between two breakwaters leading through a lock which usually stands open to the hbr basins. The yacht hbr is the southernmost and is entered by turning sharply to stb through a channel marked by withies on the northern side and bns on the south. Yachts lie afloat moored to a pontoon. All facilities. YC.

Westwards from the Elbe, the coast is inhospitable, fringed with low-lying islands and shifting sandbanks. Fog is a frequent hazard. Traffic into and out of the Elbe and Weser is heavy.

RIVER ELBE
The river is bounded by shoals and sandbanks that run far out to sea. Very severe seas occur in wind over tide conditions and with W or NW winds the river must not be entered until the flood has begun. Until then keep W of the Elbe 1 LV. The channel is well buoyed, but traffic is very heavy and yachts must keep right over to the stb side of the channel. The Elbe is navigable for ocean going ships as far as Hamburg 80M from Elbe 1 LV, and for a further 27M for small craft of less than 1.8m draught and 4.2m air ht to connect at Lauenburg with the Elbe-Lubeck canal and other German inland waterways. Wedel on the N bank has two entrances for the yacht hbr and a depth of 2.5m. All facilities and good rail conections to Hamburg. If passing through the Kiel canal without visiting Germany, International Code Flag 3rd Substitute should be flown.

BRUNSBUTTEL
Charts 2469, 3362 G 45
HW: Dover +1¾ DS: Dover −2¾h E, +2h W
MHWS 3.0m MHWN 2.7 MTL 1.4 MLWN 0.2 MLWS -0.1

The Kiel canal joins the Elbe here. There is a small very noisy hbr with limited facilities on the N bank just inside the locks. The Elbe has very strong tidal streams up to 3 kn in each direction at Brunsbuttel and exceeding that rate lower down the river. Flood stream commences HW Cuxhaven -3h; ebb stream commences +2⅝h. For locks VHF 13 (callsign Kiel canal 1) Duty free diesel can be obtained on the N bank ¼M inside the locks.

CUXHAVEN
Charts BA 3261 G 44
HW: Dover +¾h DS: Dover −3¼h SSE, −1¼h NE, +2¼h NW.
MHWS 3.4m MHWN 3.0 MTL 1.7 MLWN 0.4 MLWS 0.0

This hbr now has one of the largest of all the German North Sea yacht fleets, and an excellent yacht hbr safe to enter in all weathers.

Approach The channel is well buoyed from both directions, and the yacht hbr entrance lies immediately NW of the conspic radar tr in front of the lt ho. At night the conspic Ro-Ro terminal is easier to see than the radar tr. Upriver traffic should have no problem, but going downstream from Brunsbuttel the need to cut across the busy traffic requires reliable power.

Entrance 2 ca SE of Ro-Ro terminal is straightforward but beware of the strong stream across the entrance which can reach 5kn+. There is room inside to round up and lower sails.

Berthing Pontoon berths as space allows. Diesel in the Altenhafer, the next basin to the SE. Stores from town, YC, showers, toilets.

Port Control and Elbe channels – VHF 12.

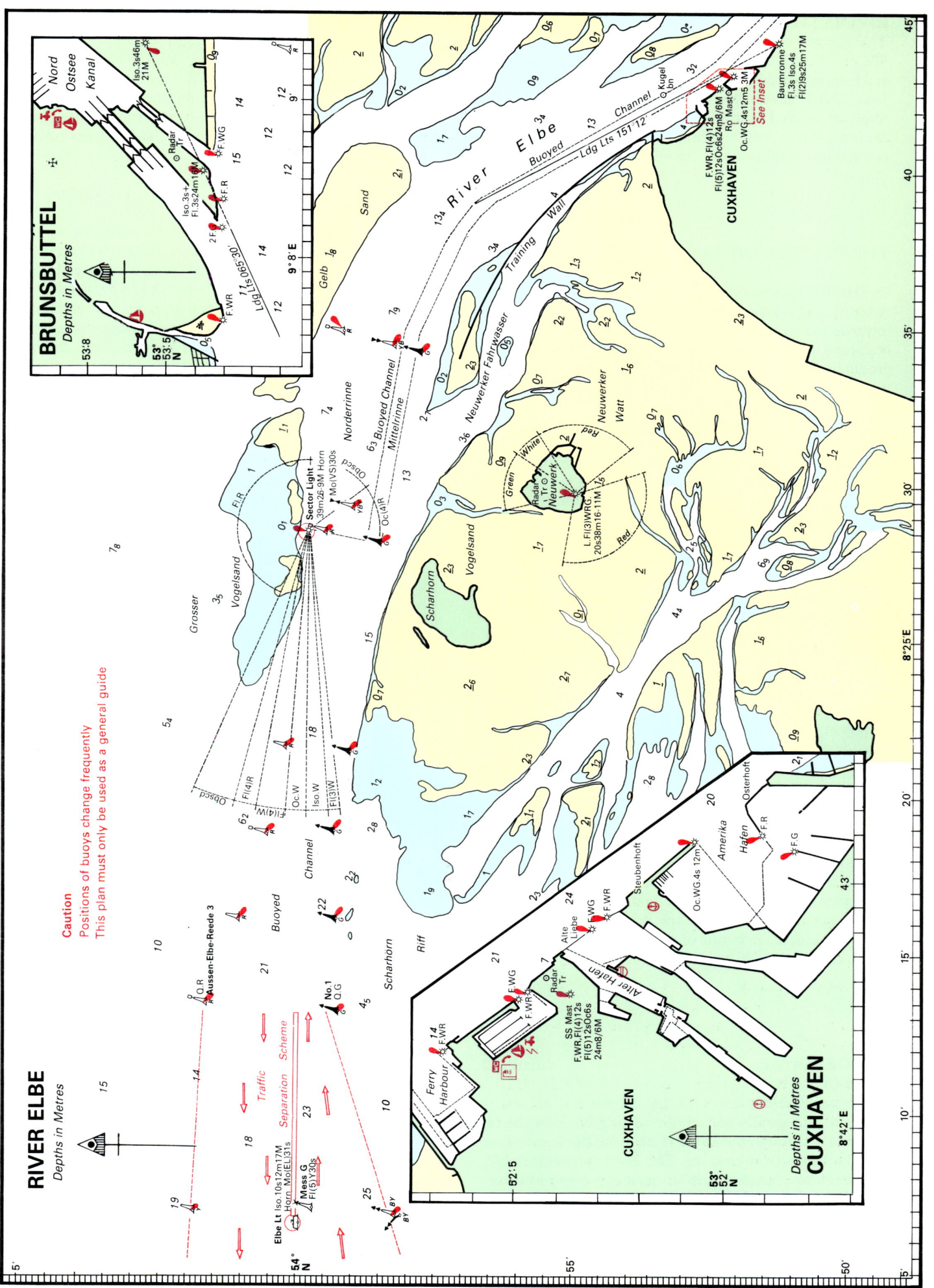

RIVERS JADE AND WESER   Charts BA 3368   G 2

The buoyed channels into both these rivers begin at the Weser LV, N of Wangerooge. There are good yacht hbrs at Horumersiel, Hooksiel and Wilhelmshaven on the R Jade, and Bremerhaven on the R Weser. Both rivers can safely be entered in strong onshore winds once the flood is running, but as with the Elbe it is almost impossible to get out in these conditions on the ebb.

THE GERMAN FRISIAN ISLANDS –

INSHORE PASSAGES

After passing between the islands the flood stream fans out towards the mainland and into channels parallel to the mainland between the Is and the shore. The channels gradually become shallower and the tide becomes slacker until a place behind each Is is reached where the tides round its two ends meet and there is never any tidal stream to speak of. These regions tend to silt and banks form which dry about a metre. These are called "Hohe watts" (high flats) in German waters and "wantij" banks (weak tide banks) in Dutch waters. Owing to the timing of the tides, the watershed behind each Is occurs at a point roughly two-thirds of its length from the W end.

The main watersheds behind the German Frisians between the Weser and the Ems have 1½ to 1m at MHW. The Memmert Waltfahrwasser channel between Norderney and the Ems has 2m. Passage is only possible in daylight with good visibility. Channels are marked at intervals with withies on the N side. Double withies mark channel entrances and junctions. With the possible exception of the Baltrum-Norderney and Langeoog-Spiekeroog watersheds, only one watershed can be passed on a tide. The tide floods up to the watersheds from both sides. In an emergency the mainland hbrs (Harlesiel, Bensersiel, Norddeich) offer shelter.

Note: the sands change constantly and up-to-date German charts are essential. Where possible obtain local advice before each passage. "Frisian Pilot" by Mark Brackenbury gives detailed descriptions of all the inshore passages behind both the German and Dutch Is. However, boats of draught up to 1.5m can negotiate the main channels at HW. Although it would be most unwise to attempt any of these passages at night without detailed local knowledge, it is worth mentioning that the withies marking all the main channels have bands of reflective tape round them, which enable them to be seen by torchlight.

WANGEROOGE   Chart G 2
HW: Dover –½h

MHWS 3.4m   MHWN 2.9   MTL 1.6   MLWN 0.5   MLWS 0.0

This is a strategically placed hbr at the SW tip of the Is. Entrance is through the Dove Harle from the seaward, or over the banks from inshore. The hbr is uncomfortable, and sometimes dangerous, in strong winds from any direction except between NW and NE, in which circumstances it is safer to make for Harlesiel, the mainland hbr to the S; however, there is only 0.4m at LWS in the approach to this hbr. No facilities at Wangerooge, stores and water at Harlesiel.

271 NORTH SEA GERMANY

LANGEOOG   Chart G 89
HW: Dover –½h

MHWS 3.1m   MHWN 2.7   MTL 1.5   MLWN 0.5   MLWS 0.0

This well sheltered hbr at the SW corner of the Is has a small marina dredged to 1.2m. Enter between pier-heads and leave all withies to stb before steering for the pontoons. YC and restaurant at the hbr, stores from town, 1½M.

NORDERNEY   Chart G 89
HW: Dover –¾h

MHWS 2.9m   MHWN 2.5   MTL 1.4   MLWN 0.5   MLWS 0.0

Approach may be made either through the Schlucter or Dove Tief channels, but although both are buoyed, the Schlucter has the deeper water 1.8m at LWS. In onshore winds above F4 the approach is dangerous and with any onshore wind the seas break heavily on either side of the winding channel so that at times it appears one is sailing directly towards broken water. If the channel is followed, however, the seas do not usually break.

One of the best hbrs in the German Frisians. Beware of strong cross-tides in the entrance; proceed northwards up the hbr keeping towards the W side, when the extensive yacht moorings become visible. YC and some supplies at the hbr; full supplies, hotel etc in town, 1M. Diesel, water. Supermarket adjacent to nearby Ferry terminal.

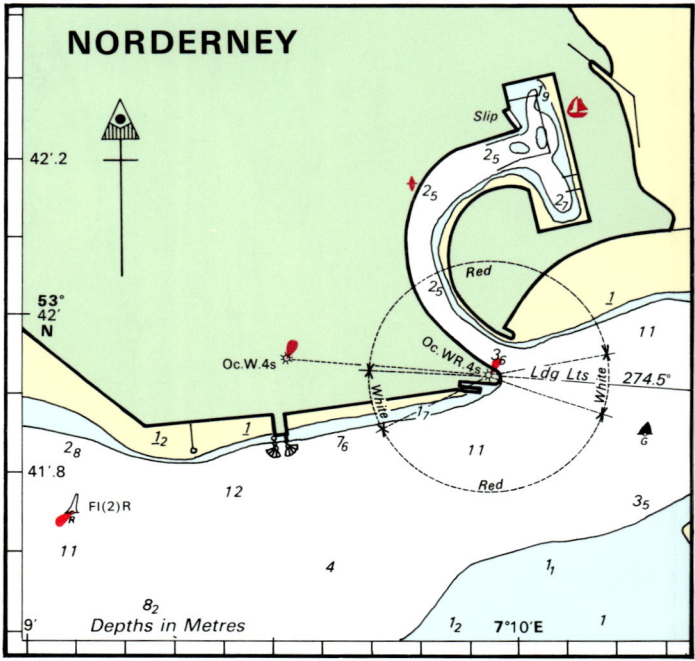

NORDDEICH   Chart G 89
HW: Dover –¾h

MHWS 2.9m   MHWN 2.5   MTL 1.4   MLWN 0.5   MLWS 0.0

The mainland port S of Norderney, reached between two breakwaters more than a mile long. Proceed S between them and take the E arm where the channel divides. Yacht moorings at the E end of the hbr. A yacht hbr with several hundred berths is W of the breakwaters. All stores and facilities.

BORKUM
Chart G 90
HW: Dover −1h

MHWS 2.7m MHWN 2.3 MTL 1.3 MLWN 0.4 MLWS 0.0

One of the few Frisian hbrs that can safely be approached in onshore gales, although even here wind over tide conditions must be avoided. The hbr is at the extreme S tip of the Is, approached by a buoyed channel running along the S side of a training wall which covers at HW. Yachts berth at the pontoon on the W side of the hbr. Fuel and all facilities, some stores; the main town is over 3M to the NW. A new yacht hbr is situated 3 ca to the W of the Schutzhafen, entered from the approach channel to the main hbr.

EMDEN
Charts N 1812
HW: Dover +¼h

MHWS 3.5m MHWN 3.1 MTL 1.86 MLWN 0.4 MLWS 0.0

Approach Emden lies 25M inland from Borkum on the R Ems which is navigable for a further 22M as far as Papenburg by sea-going vessels. Emden is the main port for the industrial products of the Ruhr to which it is connected by the Dortmund-Ems canal. There is also canal connection to the Jade by the Ems-Jade canal and to the Weser by the Kustencanal. Part of Emden hbr is a duty-free area. It is accessible at all states of the tide, but tidal streams are strong and passages should be planned to reach Emden 1h before local HW.

Entrance There are several training walls on the northern side of the Ems within 5M of the town, but the buoyed channel leads clear of them. They are awash at half-tide and should on no account be crossed.

Berthing The Outer hbr leads by a lock into a series of inner hbrs but the yacht hbr is on the Eastern side just before the lock. For longer stays another yacht hbr is to be found after passing the lock and after 4 ca turning 180° to stb and following the basin round to port into the Jarssumerhafen. Entry may sometimes be made from the Vorhafen locks by turning to stb on entering the outer hbr.

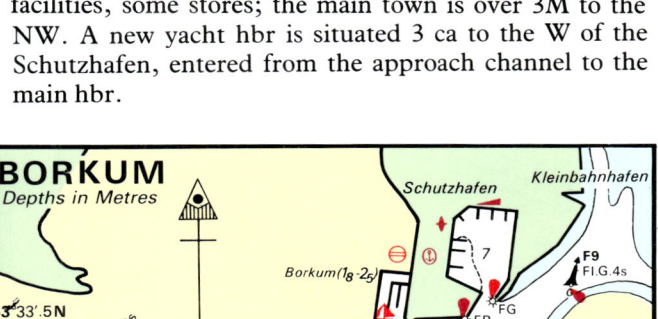

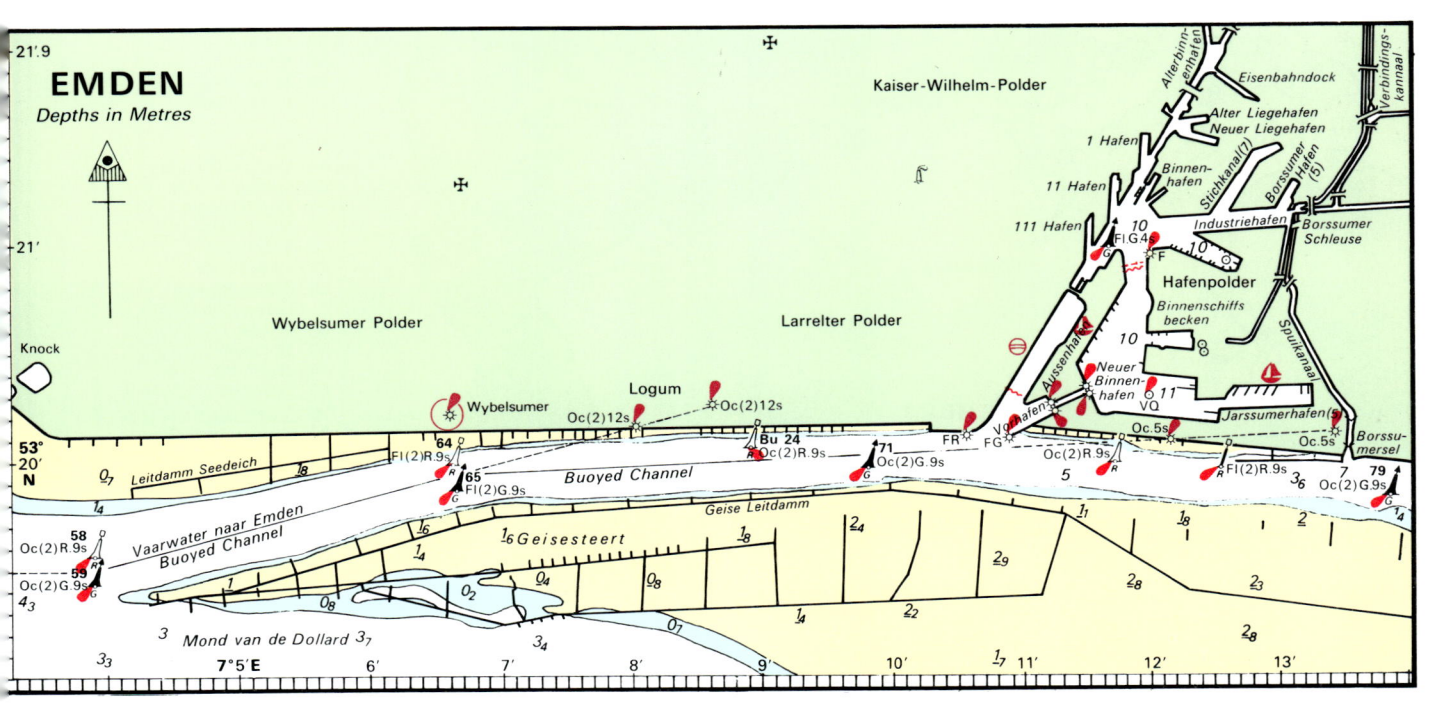

HOLLAND

Unlike most of the countries dealt with in this book, Holland - or more strictly The Netherlands - for Holland is only two provinces of that country - also has an "inside". The coastline of the Netherlands has few attractions apart from some magnificent beaches, but the inland waterways of rivers, canals and lakes provide some of the most sheltered cruising ground in Europe. Weather patterns in the Netherlands are similar to those in Britain but the sheltered water can often permit safe, dry sailing in conditions which would confine most yachts to their moorings in British coastal waters.

Although the shores are bounded by numerous sandbanks, which may change their shape and position continuously, these are well-marked. Up-to-date Dutch charts are a requirement for safe navigation, particularly in the Frisian Islands and the Waddenzee. The Algemeen Nederlandse Wegbruickers Bond (ANWB), which is the equivalent of the AA in the UK, publishes the Almanak voor Watertoerisme Vol 2 which contains invaluable information about the opening times of bridges and locks, bridge clearances, VHF channels, fuel and water supplies etc. It can be bought from chart agents in England but is more cheaply obtained from most bookshops or chandlers in the Netherlands. It is written in Dutch but the essential information can usually be understood with the help of a dictionary and this is the only way to avoid frustrating delays. A supplement to the Almanak Vol 2 entitled Spoorbruggen-Openingstijden is published annually in June and gives the latest information about opening times of railway bridges.

Entry Requirements
Yachts are required to enter The Netherlands at an official "Port of Entry" shown on the plan opposite and the skipper must go ashore and report to the local Customs and Immigration offices, taking the ship's registration document and the passports of all on board. A "Verklaring" certificate which is valid for twelve months will then be issued in respect of the boat. Failure to observe this procedure may lead to heavy fines and the imposition of VAT on the boat. If you are carrying duty-free supplies, make sure that you do not have more than the EEC allowance. A "Q" flag need not be flown unless you are carrying dutiable goods.

Dutch laws require all vessels to carry a copy of the police regulations for the navigation of rivers and canals and these are contained in the Almanak voor Watertourisme Vol 1. They are, however, written entirely in Dutch!

Regulations and Requirements for Yachts
1. Do not obstruct the passage of commercial vessels either under sail or power even when the yacht would otherwise have right of way.
2. When crossing shipping lanes proceed with the engine running, even if under sail, and cross these lanes as quickly as possible by the shortest route available.
3. Keep to the starboard side of all channels at all times unless directed otherwise by sign boards.
4. Do not attempt to tack along the rivers or canals.
5. Observe the speed limits indicated by sign boards.
6. When towing, even a dinghy, display a red flag with a white rectangular centre, and keep a sharp look-out for larger vessels displaying such flags.
7. Verey Pistols are forbidden without a licence from the country of origin. (For UK citizens, a British firearms certificate.) This must be presented to Dutch Customs when entering for the first time to obtain a "Transit Permit".

Precautions to be Observed
1. Watch out for vessels displaying a W Fl lt and a blue flag (or board) usually on the stb side of the wheelhouse. This indicates that they wish to pass you starboard to starboard.
2. Where dredgers are operating, apart from the International Signals, they may exhibit a R and W board to indicate their "clear" side on which it is safe to pass them, their dangerous side being marked by two B balls.
3. Yachts must be prepared to moor frequently to await the opening of bridges or locks and to move off smartly when signalled through. If you tie up in the vicinity of a lock or bridge without intending to pass straight through it is accepted practice to moor with the bows pointing away from the bridge or lock to make your intentions clear.
4. Light signals on locks and bridges are standardised throughout Holland. A single R lt means "wait". A R lt over a G lt means "stand by". One or two G lts give permission to proceed. Two vertical R lts mean "no passage possible". This signal is shown outside the normal opening hours. The navigable span of fixed bridges is marked with a yellow diamond or lt. The air-height is usually shown on posts or piers some distance ahead of the bridge.
5. When entering locks allow the commercial vessels to enter first, even if they arrive last, but in any event obey the instructions of the lock-keeper. Lines should be secured immediately one is inside a lock and held secure until commercial shipping has left. Otherwise, the wash from propellers can swing craft round with consequent damage.
6. Yachts need to be equipped with adequate fenders, and the larger the better. Towed dinghies in a lock can be a nuisance to the owner and other yachts.
7. Railway bridges and the busiest road bridges open only at fixed times. Others usually open on approach. Sound morse letter "K" (-.-) on your horn if you do need to request opening during normal opening hours.
8. Some very large vessels use the main commercial water routes. Powerful "pusher" tugs propelling up to four barges each of up to 4,000 tons are the equivalent of a ship of some 18,000 tons and need to be treated with extreme caution. Always keep well clear and never attempt to race them into a lock or through a bridge.

CHARTS
BA charts give excellent coverage of the passages to the Netherlands and along the coast. The Dutch Hydrographic Department publishes a series of conveniently sized charts in booklet form especially for small craft. They are highly recommended; chart symbols are explained in English and harbour plans are included. The booklets are:

1801	North Sea Coast from Oostende to Den Helder
1803	Westerschelde from Vlissingen to Antwerp, the Walcheren Canal and Terneuzen - Gent canal.
1805	Oosterschelde, Veerse Meer and Grevelingenmeer.
1807	Zoommeer, Volkerak, River Spui, Haringvliet and Hollandsch Diep.
1809	Europoort, Rotterdam, Dordrecht and surrounding rivers.
1810	IJsselmeer and Randmeren.
1811	Waddenzee & Frisian Islands (West)
1812	Waddenzee & Frisian Islands (East)

The ANWB publish a series of charts for inland waterways in the remaining areas of the Netherlands and these are generally available from chandlers. Both series of Dutch charts show details of the location of locks and bridges, their dimensions, and whether the bridges are opening (beweegbare) or not.

The Dutch Hydrographic Office publish a number of tidal atlases (stroomatlases). The ones for the Waddenzee, the Oosterschelde and the tidal rivers around Rotterdam (Stroomatlas Benedenrivieren) are particularly useful.

Language Dutch people are generally very appreciative of foreign visitors' attempts to speak their language and a little effort goes a long way towards making new friendships. It doesn't take long to discover that the town of Goes is pronounced "hoose" or that IJmuiden is pronounced "Ay-mowd-en". The following translations may be found useful when trying to interpret notes in the almanaks or on Dutch charts:

Dutch		English
aanlegplaatsen	=	temporary berthing places
afval	=	rubbish
ankerplaats	=	anchorage
bakboord	=	port
bediening	=	opening times of bridges & locks
ma. t/m zat	=	monday through saturday
zo. en fd	=	sundays and public holidays
di,wo,do,vr	=	tuesday,wednesday,thursday,friday
betonning	=	buoyage
beweegbare	=	opening(bridge)
brug	=	bridge
douane	=	customs
gat	=	channel
geen	=	no, none
gesloten	=	shut
havengeld	=	harbour dues
havenmeester	=	harbourmaster
jachthaven	=	yachtharbour, marina
ligplaatsen	=	overnight berths
oost (abbr O)	=	east
sluis	=	lock
spoorbrug	=	railway bridge
vast	=	fixed(bridge)
veer	=	ferry
verboden	=	forbidden
wassalon	=	launderette
zuid (abbr Z)	=	south

Weather Forecasts The BBC shipping forecast for Thames area is a good guide to weather in The Netherlands and it can be received on Radio 4 (198 kHz) anywhere in the country. Scheveningen Radio broadcasts forecasts in English on 1862 kHz and 1890 kHz (Single Side Band) at 0340, 0940, 1540, 2140 (all G.M.T.) There are many daily radio forecasts in Dutch on VHF and on domestic radio channels. These are referred to inside the front cover of Dutch chart booklets. Local sailors are a particularly helpful source of information about the weather and it is a useful topic of conversation while you are rafted up waiting for a lock or br to open.

Fuel Petrol (benzine), diesel (diesel or gas-olie) and paraffin (petroleum) are readily available at waterside pumps throughout the Netherlands. Calor Gas is not used on the Continent but bottles can be replaced at chandlers in some of the harbours more popular with tourists such as Middelburg. It makes sense either to take sufficient gas for the trip or to take a Camping Gaz adaptor. This allows the use of Camping Gaz which is available throughout Europe.

Publications NP 28 Dover Strait Pilot (Hydrographer to the Navy)
NP 55 North Sea (East) Pilot (Hydrographer to the Navy)
North Sea Harbours (Calais to Den Helder) by Jack H Coote. (Barnacle Marine) ISBN 0 948788 21 6
North Sea Passage Pilot by Brian Navin. (Imray) ISBN 0 85288 102 9
Cruising Guide to the Netherlands by Brian Navin. (Imray) ISBN 0 85288 131 2
Dutch Inland Sailing Pilot by Henry Levison. (Stanford) ISBN 0 540 07432 2
Frisian Pilot by Mark Brackenbury. (Stanford) ISBN 0 540 07185 4
"Vargids" Voor de Nederlandse en Belgische Kust (Dutch Hydrographic Office) ISBN 906611.4215. This publication is written in Dutch but the essential information can be deduced without too much effort and it does contain some excellent plans and aerial photographs.

PASSAGE NOTES

Yachts from the UK crossing the North Sea may arrive at any of the ports which have Customs posts such as Breskens, Vlissingen, Hoek van Holland, Scheveningen, IJmuiden or Den Helder (see plan on p.273). Each has its advantages, depending on the starting point, but it should be noted that making a landfall anywhere on the low lying Netherlands coast is not easy. It is probably best to plan to be off the coast one hour before sunrise so that the lighthouses may still be identified.

From the Crouch, Blackwater or Orwell the first stage of a passage to the Westerschelde is to make the Long Sand Head lt buoy by local LW and from there to head for the W Hinder Lt V passing S of the S Galloper buoy and crossing the main TSS at right angles. The West Hinder TSS can then be crossed and the buoyed S edge of the TSS followed to the Kwintebank N card buoy. There is then likely to be a full 6 hrs of unfavourable tide followed by 1 or 2 hours of fair tide into the Westerschelde.

IJmuiden is 125 M from Harwich on a course of 076° from the Shipwash LV. There are no hazards other than oil and gas platforms and occasional incinerator ships. Oil rigs must be given a berth of at least 500m and it is not advisable to pass downwind of incinerator ships as they are employed in disposing of toxic wastes.

Alternatively, some boats prefer to make a shorter sea crossing to, for example, Calais, Dunkerque, Nieuwpoort, Oostende or Zeebrugge before port-hopping to Breskens, Vlissingen, Terneuzen or Hansweert. Yachts leaving Oostende, Blankenberge or Zeebrugge for the Schelde have a maximum of 4 hours of favourable tide. Those departing from Vlissingen or Breskens down the Belgian coast have up to 9 hours of favourable tide. It is possible to reach Vlissingen from Oostende on one tide but crucial to reach the Schelde before the tide turns because the ebb is very strong. There is a traffic separation scheme in force on the northern side of Westerschelde must be crossed at right angles in compliance with Rule 10 of the Collision Regulations. The Schelde Information Service on VHF 14 broadcasts in English at 10 minutes before each hour.

THE DELTA PROJECT

Dyke building began in the Netherlands over 1000 years ago and land reclamation was carried on throughout the Middle Ages. However, with the land around the North

Sea progressively sinking and the average sea level rising there were repeated flooding disasters. The storm on the night of Jan 31st, 1953, breached the dykes in 89 places and 1,853 people lost their lives. In order to prevent similar disasters the Delta Project, a revolutionary programme of hydraulic engineering, was begun in 1958. This aimed to seal off the seaward entrances of many tidal waterways, especially in Zeeland and South Holland, and allow the levels of water in the inland lakes and rivers to be controlled. The project was finished in 1987 when the Oosterschelde storm surge barrier was completed, taming the flooding power of the sea and creating vast improvements in road communications and recreational amenities.

Harbours Around the Coast

DELFZIJL Charts BA 3510 N 1812
HW: Dover +¼h DS: Dover -4¾h ESE, +1¼h NW
MHWS 3.5m MHWN 3.1 MTL 2.0 MLWN 0.7 MLWS 0.3
This is the most important commercial and fishing port in the N of Holland with aluminium and chemical processing plants. Direct access via the Eems Kanaal and Groningen leads to inland water routes for yachts with fixed masts to the IJsselmeer and hence to the N sea at IJmuiden. Alternatively, the canal system gives access to the ports in the S of Holland. A further route leads to the R Schelde, Antwerp and the canals of Belgium and France. It is an official "port of entry". Customs 15060.
Approach The outer part of the Eems estuary is divided by the island of Borkum and large drying areas into the Westereems and Oostereems. From the Oostereems buoy there is a difficult passage across the shoals S of Memmert to join the Westereems 7M N of Delfzijl. A safer approach from the E is to continue to either the Riffgat, Huibertgat or Westereems, all of which are marked at their seaward ends by safe-water buoys bearing the names of the respective channels. From the W the main approach channel is the Huibertgat which is well buoyed. At night the fixed W sector of Borkum lt ho leads in until the first of the lit buoys on a bearing of 090° with any deviation to the N taking one into a Fl(4s) sector, or to the S into a Fl sector. The channel turns slightly to the N at H11 G buoy and joins the Ranselgat at the 15/H15/A1 G pillar buoy IQ 13s. Follow the Ranselgat buoyed channel SE guided by the leading sector lt of Campen lt ho, keeping just outside the shipping channel. Change course slightly to stb after the No 27 G pillar buoy (Fl 4s) to follow the buoyed and lit Doekegat channel into the Oostfriesche Gaatje. After the second R sector of the multi-sector Knock lt ho, the W sector guides you towards the R ldg lts on a heading of 203°. In any event, keep N of the PS3/BW26 GRG buoy Fl(2+1)12s on approach.
Entrance is between F R & F G pierhead lts followed by a turn to stb between bns exhibiting G lts to stb and R to port for 3M. The Balkenhaven Yacht hbr is on the stb side and is entered between bns 21 (G Fl 5s) and 23 (Q G). HM office is on stilts at the end of the first pontoon above the fuel berth. HM 05960-15004. Water and electricity are available on the pontoons. Sailmakers, engineers, and chandlers/chart agents are in the town.
The Eemskanaalsluizen (VHF 11) give access to the Eems canal leading to Groningen. Port Control VHF on 14 listens 24h and gives traffic reports in fog. Alternative berths may be found at the seaward end of the Oude Eemskanaal but there are few facilities. The Farmsumerhaven is not recommended as it is usually full with commercial shipping.

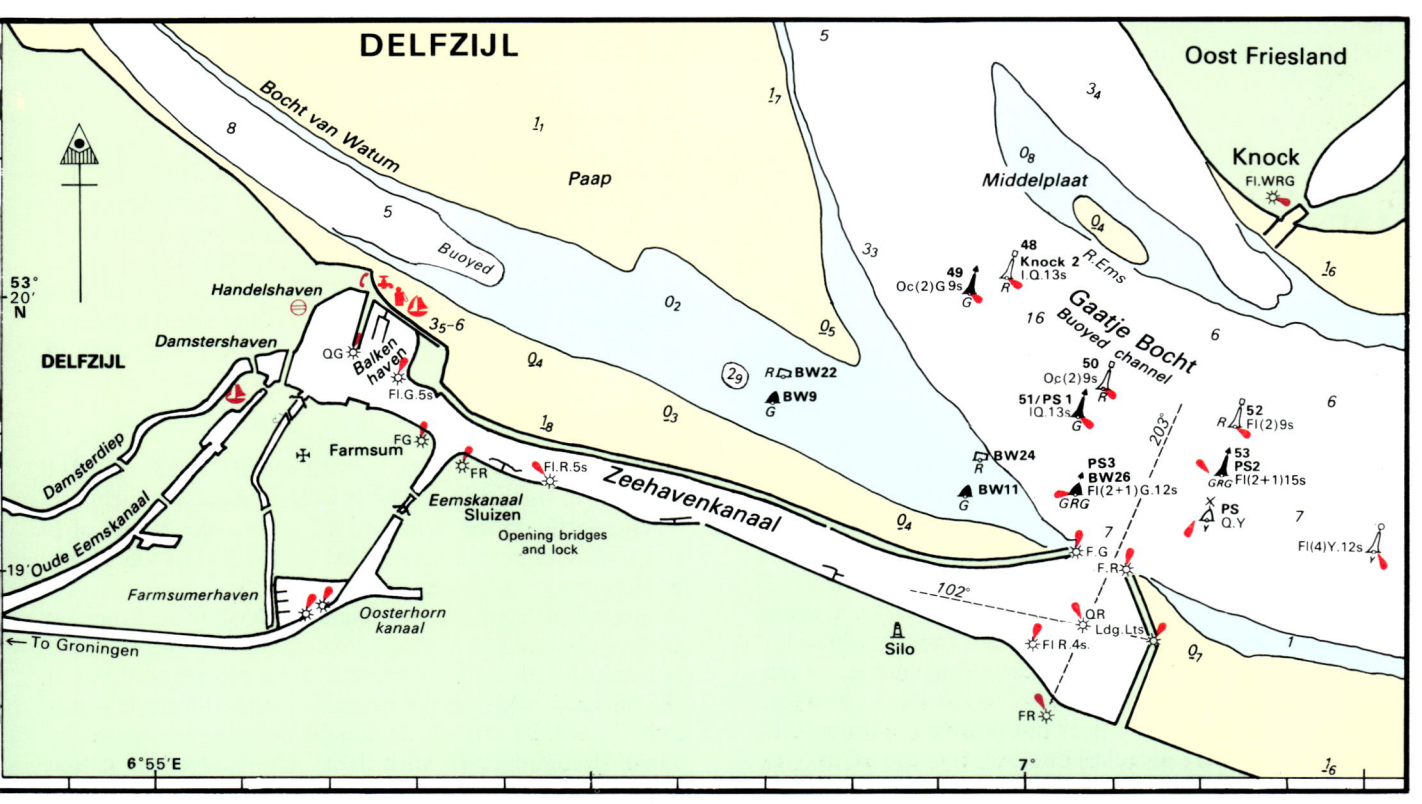

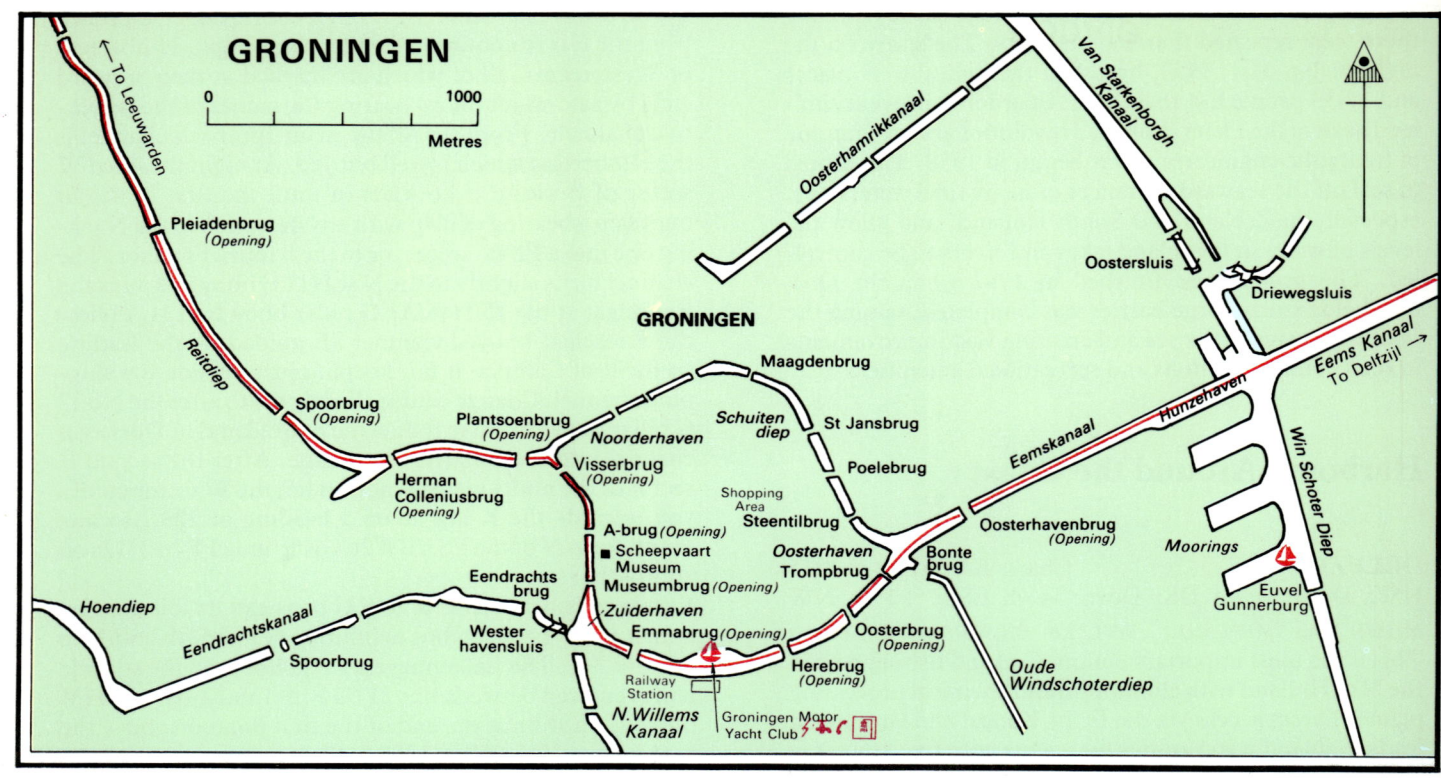

WESTEREEMS TO FRIESCHE ZEEGAT
Chart BA 3761   N 1812

Any passage into or out of the Zeegats (channels to the sea) must be undertaken with due regard to weather as fresh winds opposing the tidal stream create short steep seas that rapidly become not merely uncomfortable, but dangerous. The effect is most noticeable with W winds over the ebb tide. As tidal streams run strongly, "working the tides" is important in this area. From Delfzijl (or Borkum) to Lauwersoog, it is wise to plan to be at the WG buoy Iso marking the entrance between Schiermonnikoog and Ameland, at local LW (Helgoland -5h) to carry the full flood stream into Westgat. The WG buoy lies some 6M WSW of the Hubertgat buoy and a further ¾M to the SW lies the WG1 buoy at the seaward end of Westgat. The return passage should be commenced at local LW -2h.

LAUWERSOOG   Charts BA 3761   N 1812
HW: Dover -1¾h
MHWS 3.2m   MHWN 2.8   MTL 1.7   MLWN 1.0   MLWS 0.6

Approach The Westgat runs through a buoyed channel for 6M until the low-lying Engelsmanplaat is abeam. Then from Z1-PR8 GRG buoy follow the buoyed and partly lit Zoutkamperlaag. Approach the harbour from N of the unlit G Z15 buoy.

Entrance The entrance is between piers with F G & F R lts into a small outer hbr. The entrance to the fishing hbr which lies to the E is marked by a F R lt on the N pierhead. The lock keeper of the Robbengatsluis is on VHF 22. If arriving too late for the lock (hours in the Almanak Vol 2) it is sometimes possible to lie alongside the ferry on the W pier just before the lock. Permission is usually given, but it is wise and courteous to ask. Water is available at a tap. Immediately to the W of the lock is a Customs office (enquire of lock-keeper if officer not present). Through the lock, the Noordergat yacht hbr lies 3 ca to the SE and has water, diesel, electricity, telephone, showers, toilets and launderette (Tel: 05193 9040). Over the sea wall, to the E of the lock, is a restaurant, fish cafés, chandlers and a small supermarket. An alternative is to proceed S through the Lauwersmeer to Oostmahorn. Keep the Is to stb and follow the channel marked by beacons and withies. Water, fuel, toilets and showers are available at Jachthaven Oostmahorn (05193 1445/1880). Stores are not available at this hbr but if proceeding through the canal to Leeuwarden, and entering through the lock at Dokkumer Nieuwezijlen there is a shop by the second br. Dokkum is reached after 7M and is a pretty town with easy mooring facilities on a quay to the S after the br. Good shopping. From the E side of the Lauwersmeer, the Reitdiep connects with Groningen and is a fixed mast route of 18M, but slow because of the bridges.

SCHIERMONNIKOOG   Charts BA 3761   N 1812
Hbr lies in the SW of the Is. From the Zoutkamperlaag follow the buoyed Gat van Schiermonnikoog to the RGR GvS18/R1 buoy. Head W of N to leave R3 G buoy to stb and follow withies across the "Siege wal" drying area. It is advisable to approach and leave on a rising tide within 2hrs of HW. No entrance lts. The harbour has min depth of 1.3m. Necessary to reserve a berth in busy summer months. HM 05195-1544.

AMELAND   Charts BA 2593   N 1811
Hbr lies in the mid-S of the Is at Nes. Access is difficult. Yachts settle on the firm bottom against the N end of E hbr wall with permission of HM (05191 2304/4305/2729). Shelter except in strong S winds.

Approach is from seaward from the Zeegat van Ameland through the narrow Westgat leading into the Borndiep. It is marked with unlit buoys and has a pronounced bar at the entrance which is dangerously rough during E winds and flood tidal stream. It should only be attempted by shoal draught craft with local knowledge in settled weather.

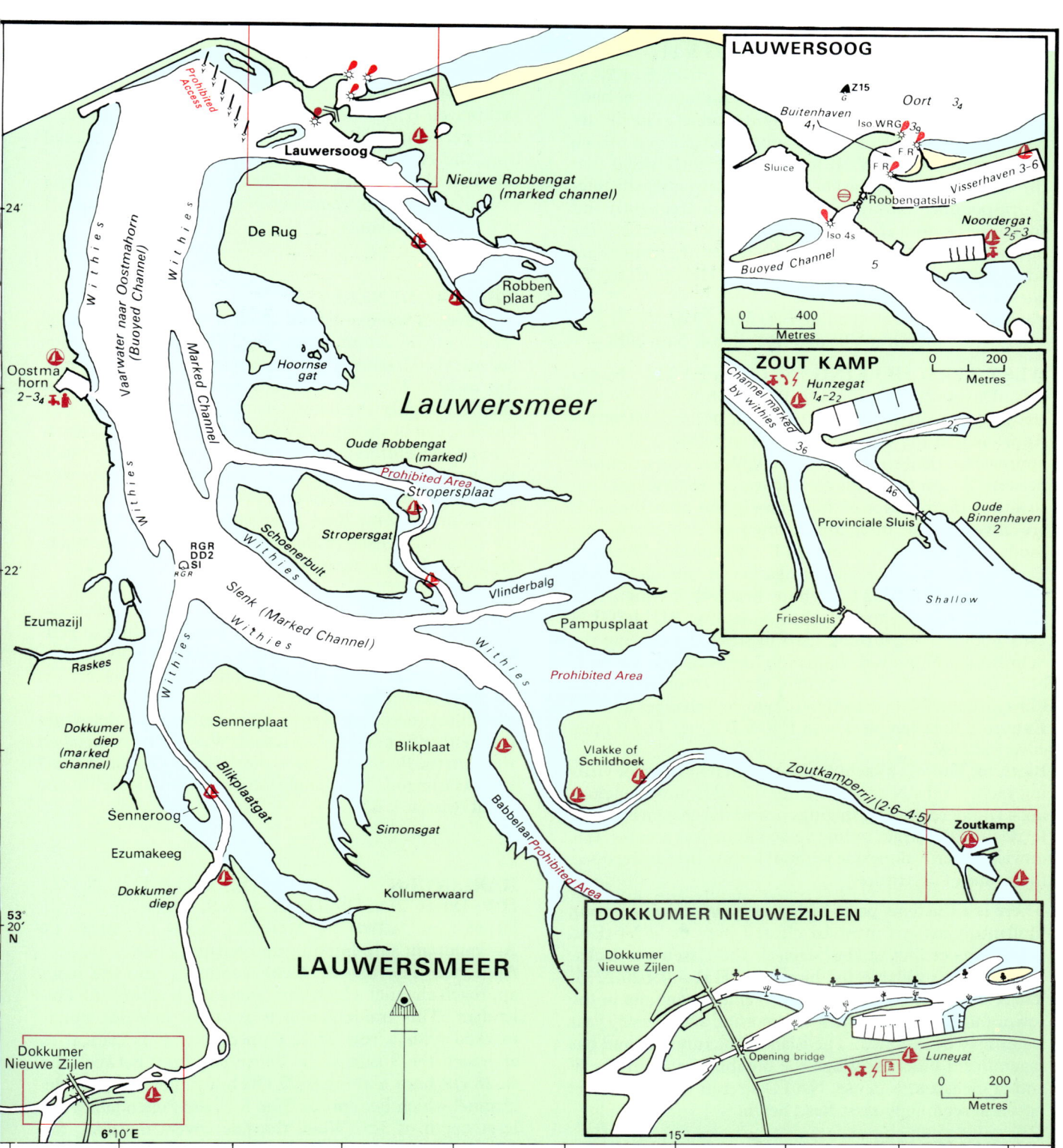

ZEEGAT VAN TERSCHELLING
Charts BA 2593 & 112   N 1811
The only safe approach, whether coming from E or W, is via the Stortemelk and from the SM Iso 4s safe-water buoy a course of 090° leads into the buoyed channel. The Zuider Stortemelk can be extremely uncomfortable in strong winds from W to NW. It must also be emphasised that throughout this area the channels are constantly shifting. Corresponding buoyage changes are made frequently and sometimes before chart amendments can be notified: the buoyage pattern should always be followed. Visitors are advised to contact the traffic centre on VHF 2 or 67 for the latest navigational information.

Passage Lights: Terschelling Fl5s 55m 29M
               Oost Vlieland (RTr)Iso 4s 54m 20M

WEST TERSCHELLING   Charts BA 112   N1811
HW: Dover -2¼h DS: Dover -1h E, +5h W

MHWS 2.9m MHWN 2.6 MTL 1.3 MLWN 1.2 MLWS 0.8

Approach In the channels S of Terschelling and in the approaches, tidal streams run strongly and with a complex pattern. Whilst the sands are uncovered, the streams tend to flow in the direction of the channels, but when the sands are covered, the direction is often directly across the sands. The Dutch Stroomatlas K (Waddenzee Westelijk Deel) is essential for safe navigation of this fascinating area. From ZS13/VS2 GRG buoy head NE leaving ZS20/BD17 S Card buoy to port, then N, leaving BD14/SG1 N card buoy to stb, turning hard to stb and following the Schuitengat N buoyed channel to just N of SG13 lt bn L Fl5s. Ldg lts F W & Iso 5s 053° lead in from here to the hbr entrance. Note direction of buoyage changes at SG1.

Entrance Between piers with F R & F G lts. The E mole covers at HW.

Berthing There is a yacht harbour with pontoons for visiting yachts at the N end of the hbr. Good facilities, including a launderette. The stagings nearer the entrance are for ferries and the larger sailing vessels known as schalks. It is unwise to berth alongside without having first ascertained their time of departure.

There is a Customs post (1 May - 1 Nov) and, if entering Holland, Customs must be cleared here or at Vlieland before proceeding to Harlingen or the IJsselmeer locks. Bicycles are available for hire from HM - 05620-2235. There is a good selection of shops and restaurants in the town, but fuel is not available alongside and in a dry year water may be rationed. The island is picturesque and has magnificent beaches. When the bombing range at the W end of the island is in use, NATO aircraft make low-level passes at seemingly mast-head height.

OOST VLIELAND   Charts BA 112   N 1811
Tidal data as for West Terschelling.

The well-sheltered yacht hbr is at the SE corner of this picturesque Is. Small shops and restaurants are available in the town at 15 mins walk away. Bicycles and/or trailers may be hired from the HM. A travelling shop visits daily. Ferries ply to Harlingen. Customs office (1 May - 1 Nov) is at the NW end of the yacht hbr. The hbr tends to be crowded in the holiday period and may then be closed. Yachts may anchor in the channel, marked by floating beacons, to the W of the hbr entrance. It is as well not to leave the yacht unattended until satisfied that it will remain afloat at LW! The sand is hard.

Approach From the Zuid Stortemelk, the ZS13-VS2 GRG con (isigny) lt buoy marks the entrance to the Vliesloot buoyed channel. Keep to W side of channel near unlit G buoys at first and then make for VS10 LFl 8s until ldg lts (276.5°) are in line.

Entrance The entrance, marked by F R & F G lts is between massive wooden moles. Port HM 05621-1563. Jachthaven HM 05621-1729. HM office only open for a short period morning and evening. Fuel may be ordered from the HM for delivery by tanker. Superb beaches, excellent walks, wonderful views from the lt ho, and the scent of the pines on a summer evening make this the pearl of the Frisian Islands.

THE WADDENZEE
This area of sandbanks and shallow channels is the tidal remnant of the former Zuider Zee. The non-tidal S section became the IJsselmeer with the completion of the Afsluitdijk in 1932. It is an inhospitable expanse of wild seascape and frequently-changing channels which, although buoyed, can be difficult to follow. It requires particularly careful concentration in the reduced visibility to which this area is liable during the summer. For yachts with fixed keels the only area for reasonable sailing until one has acquired some local knowledge is the area between Terschelling, Texel (pronounced "Tessel") and the mainland from Harlingen to Den Helder.

From Terschelling or Vlieland the Vliestroom leads S and after 4M divides into the Blauwe Slenk, leading to Harlingen, and the Inschot which leads via the Zuidoostrak to Kornwerderzand and the locks into the IJsselmeer. On the flood tide either route may be taken, but in the reverse direction proceeding N from Kornwerderzand, departure must either be made before local HW, or a diversion taken through the Boontjes close to the dykes to join the channel from Harlingen. This avoids the Zuidoostrak which at one point dries at LW.

HARLINGEN   Charts BA 2593 & 112   N 1811
HW: Dover -2¼h DS: Dover -1¼h S, -6h N

MHWS 3.0m MHWN 2.7 MTL 1.3 MLWN 1.2 MLWS 1.0

An important ship-building and repairing port.

Approach The Blauwe Slenk continues into the main approach channel which runs along the S side of the Pollendam. This training wall is awash at half-tide but is marked with a row of R topped bns. It is critical to approach the S side of the Pollendam from between the BS28 QR buoy and the BS27 QG buoy. The centre of the channel which lies approx 50m S of the Pollendam has a least depth of 3m. When the tide covers the wall, the stream sets strongly across it. The Hanerak is an alternative yacht channel marked with spar buoys and with a depth of 1.5m. The final approach is marked by ldg lts on 112°, the rear lt being the main Harlingen lt ho - Oc W 6s 19m 14M visible 097°- 127°. Port VHF 11.

Entrance Between the mole-heads on 170° turning immediately to port to make for the Oude Buitenhaven and into the Noorderhaven (2 brs - depth 1.1m) or turning further to port through the Nieuwe Voorhaven (min depth 2.7m) to the lock leading into the Van Harinxmakanaal. There is a small yacht hbr to stb at the inner end of the lock.

Supplies Both hbrs have good facilities, but fuel is available only in the commercial Zuiderhaven. Chandlers, sail-makers, engineers and electricians.

Tel HM 05178-5666. Customs 05178-5241.

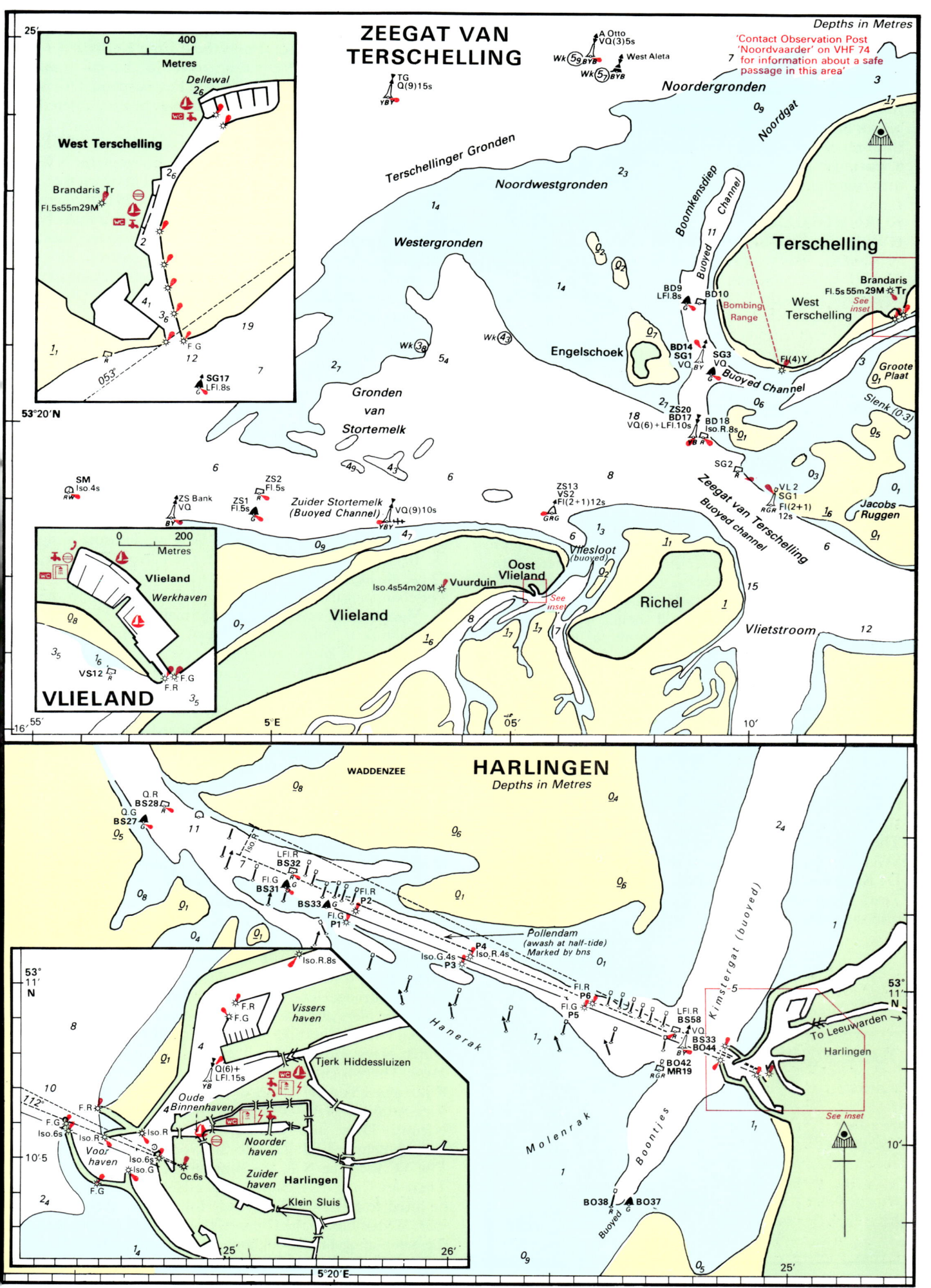

It is 17M from Harlingen to Leeuwarden along the Van Harinxmakanaal. At or near LW the lock stands open and there is an outward current up to 2kn. Care is needed when passing through, especially if outward bound. All the brs on the canal open. From Leeuwarden there are fixed mast routes to Grouw or Sneek and beyond to Lemmer or Stavoren on the IJsselmeer. It is quicker to use the short sea-route from Kornwerdenzand and enter the canal at Harlingen, but more picturesque to sail from the IJsselmeer through Stavoren or Lemmer. Least depth 1.5 m.

KORNWERDERZAND   Chart N 1810.6 & N 1811
HW: Dover -2h DS: -5¾h SW, +2h NE

MHWS 2.9m   MHWN 2.8   MTL 2.0   MLWN 1.3   MLWS 1.0

The NE entry point for the IJsselmeer.

Approach From the E by the Boontjes channel from Harlingen with a minimum depth of 1.3m. The channel is well marked at regular intervals, but very narrow. From the N by the Inschot and Zuidoostrak (but see earlier note under "The Waddenzee") with a turn to an E course at the KWZ W Card buoy VQ (9) 10s, some 12 ca to the W of the entrance. There is also an approach channel - The Doove Balg - from the W and Texel. This is a deep and well- marked route leading to the KWZ buoy. The sea-dyke is featureless with the occasional ch spire showing above.

Entrance There are two opening and only the E leads to the locks. The W or Spuihaven is not used for navigation. The Buitenhaven piers have F R & F G lts. Enter on a course of 225° taking care to avoid the shoal to port. A swing br opens to enable yachts to enter the Voorhaven where there are mooring posts if it is necessary to wait for a lock opening. The Lorentzsluizen operates 24h - VHF 18. On the S side are mooring posts with good shelter which may be used for a few hrs or overnight. No other facilities.

EIERLANDSCHE GAT

This Zeegat between Vlieland and Texel is unmarked and should not be attempted. The latest edition of the Dutch chart 1811.6 is marked "vessels should not attempt to negotiate this entrance".

OUDESCHILD   Charts BA 191   N 1811
HW: Dover -4h DS: Dover +4h NE, -1¾h SW, up to 3kn

MHWS 2.7m   MHWN 2.5   MTL 1.9   MLWN 1.4   MLWS 1.1

The main hbr of Texel - there is a small ferry hbr 3M to the SW. Good bus services to Den Burg at the centre of Is and De Koog and its beaches on the N Sea coast. The sturdy Texel sheep roam the dykes; much of the Is is devoted to bird sanctuaries.

Approach From seaward through the wide and deep Marsdiep. From SE and the Den Oever locks at the NW corner of the IJsselmeer. From the E from Kornwerderzand or from the ENE via an intricate channel from Terschelling. All routes lead into the Texelstroom. This is a Naval exercise area and submarines may be encountered on the surface.

Entrance is from between a R lt buoy (T14) and a RGR buoy (T16/OS1) followed by R & G spar buoys on the NW side of the Texelstroom. Keep the Oc 6s lt between the 2 F R and 2 F G pierhead lts for approach of 291° through the stone moles. Strong currents across the entrance. N end of hbr is Jachthaven Oudeschild. Very good facilities, but tends to be crowded at the height of the season. Bicycles available for hire. Fuel from pumps, water, electricity and telephone. HM VHF 9 (02220-2710). There are no Customs facilities on Texel.

DEN HELDER   Chart BA 191   N 1811
HW: Dover -4½h DS: Dover +3¼h E, -3h W

MHWS 2.6m   MHWN 2.5   MTL 1.2   MLWN 1.4   MLWS 1.1

This is the principal Naval hbr of Holland: there is also a large fishing fleet.

Approach From the N the Molengat buoyed channel lies between 1M and ½M W off the coast of Texel and has at least 6m. From the S the Schulpengat buoyage commences at the SG buoy situated 3M W of the Grote Kaap Oc 10s RWG lt ho and is within the narrow W sector. There are ldg lts of daylight intensity on Texel (026.5°). The channel runs NW through the Breewijd for 7M to join the Marsdiep between Texel and the mainland. The Noorderhaaks is an uninhabited area of sand with off-lying banks to the W of Marsdiep and presents a major hazard in the approach. There is a S card lt buoy off the E end of Noorderhaaks from which an E course for 2M leads to the entrance. The North Sea coast, both of Texel and the mainland, is low-lying and dune-fringed and landmarks are difficult to identify. If making a landfall here, and tidal considerations permit, an arrival one hour before dawn enables the lts to be distinguished, and then an entry to be made in full daylight.

Entrance There are 2 sets of ldg lts, one on 207° for the ferry hbr to the W of the main harbour and the other on 191° (Oc 5s) for the Marinehaven. Signals apply only to commercial shipping, but permission to enter should be requested on VHF 14. Tidal streams run fast across the Marinehaven entrance and reference to Dutch Stroomatlas J is recommended. Keep a sharp look-out for ferries entering and leaving the Veerhaven as you approach. There are two successive sets of port and stb lts marking the hbr entrance. The yacht hbr is to stb after entering the main hbr piers and has water and electricity to the pontoons. The Koninklijke Marine Jachtclub is part of the Dutch Navy and toilets and showers are in the Officers' Mess. There is another yacht hbr reached by entering the Rijkzeehaven on the W side of the hbr passing through the Vice-Admiral H.V. Moorman Br (VHF 18) into the Nieuwe Diep and locking through the Koopvardersschutsluis (VHF 22) into the Noord-Hollands canal. The YC is to the N in the Binnenhaven (02230-17076). There are Customs facilities at Den Helder. Bicycles may be hired from HM. The Noord-Hollands canal connects with Medemblik to the E and Alkmaar and Amsterdam to the S (opening brs throughout, but a fixed br N of Purmurend limits heights to 7m in Edam branch).

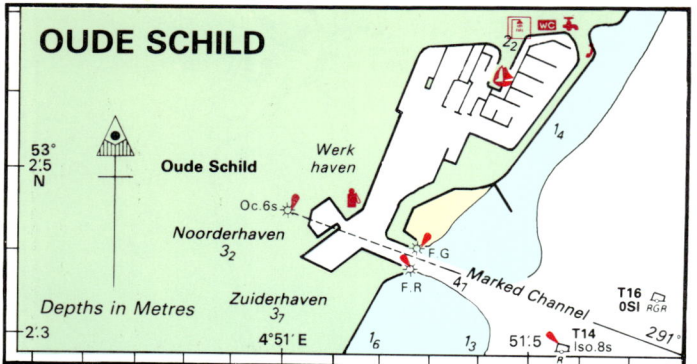

DEN OEVER   Charts BA 2593   N 1810 & 1811

HW: Dover -2¾h to -3¾h.
Average tidal range approx 1.5m.

One of four old villages on the former island of Wieringen which was joined to the mainland by a dyke in 1924. The Stevinsluis links the Waddenzee and the IJsselmeer at the W end of the Afsluitdijk.

Approach There is no deep water approach from the E on the seaward side of the Afsluitdijk. This area is well-buoyed but the streams run fast and the edges of the channels dry out. The mean spring rates off Den Helder reach 3½ knots. Strong winds create difficult and sometimes dangerous conditions in these shallow waters. From the Texelstroom, follow the buoyed Malzwin channel to the bar (less than 2m) at the N end of the Wierbalg channel. It is advisable to make the approach near the top of the tide. The channel is narrow, has drying banks either side, and is constantly changing. It winds through the sands until the final approach (ldg lts on the Afsluitdijk) on 131° leads S of the Liedam.

Entrance Turn to stb just before the O12 buoy (R Iso 4s) and keep in the W sector of the GWR Iso 2s lt on the end of the inner hbr wall, entering the outer hbr between F R & F G lts. The outer hbr is well sheltered by moles on each side. Turn to port, keeping between the port and stb buoys, towards the Afsluitdijk where it may be necessary to tie up to the piles while waiting for the two bridges to open. Enter the Voorhaven and the lock (VHF 20). The channels are lit, but a first time passage at night is inadvisable. The fishing hbr N of the locks is unsuitable for yachts. After passing through the locks a temporary berth may be found on the W side of Binnenhaven. For overnight stays the Jachthaven Den Oever, with all facilities, is at the S end of the Zuiderhaven.

PASSAGE NOTES

IJmuiden is 40M from Den Helder, Scheveningen is 66M and the Hoek of Holland is 75M. Apart from the shoals off Den Helder there are no obstructions along the coast. This whole stretch of coast has few landmarks apart from the nuclear reactor off Petten, the steelworks at IJmuiden and a few isolated lt trs.

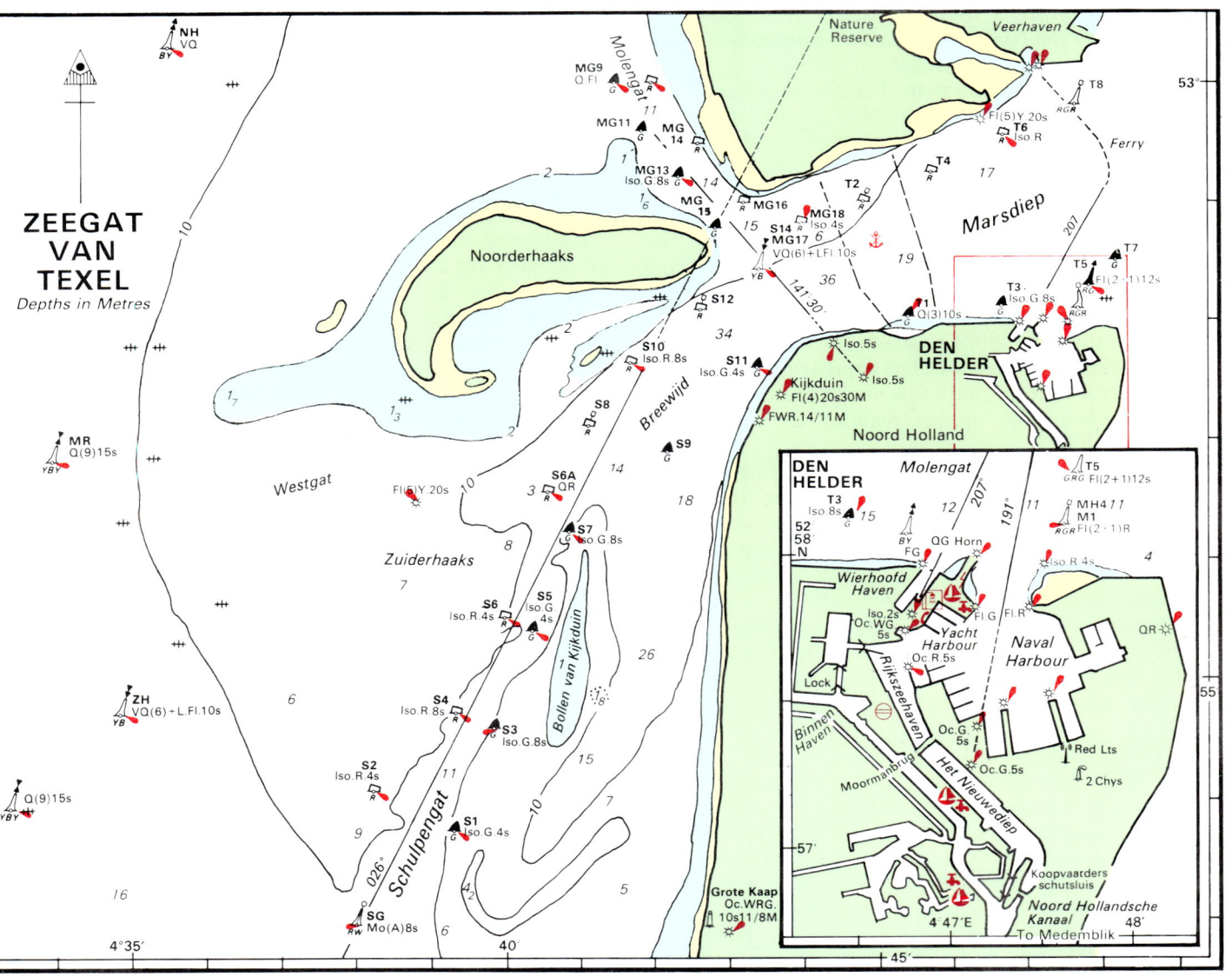

HOLLAND 282

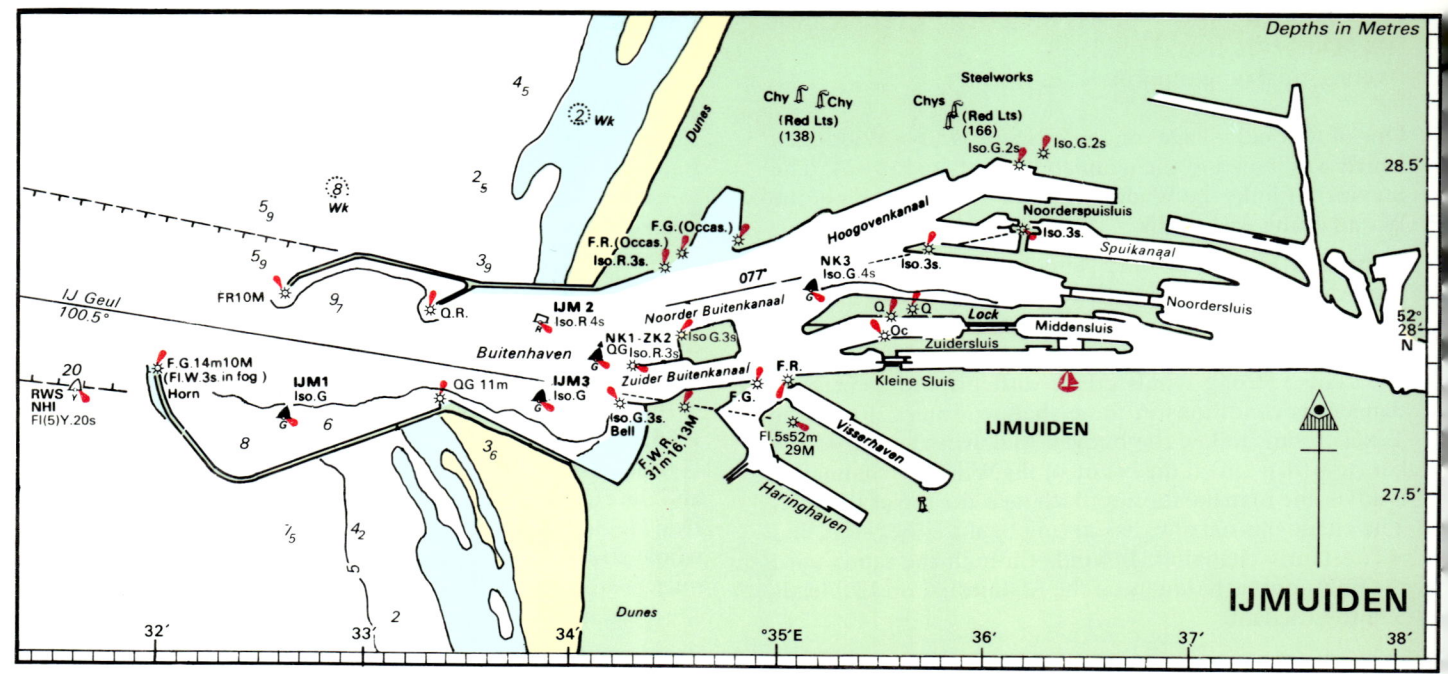

IJMUIDEN
Chart BA 2322 & 124   N 1801
HW: Dover -4¼h   DS: Dover -4h S, +2h N Max 2kn
MHWS 2.0m   MHWN 1.7   MTL 1.1   MLWN 0.3   MLWS 0.2
Considerable fishing traffic. Apart from providing an entry port to the Noordzee Kanaal to Amsterdam, it has little significance for yachting.

Approach There are steel works N of the town and the coloured smoke often provides the first positive identification by day. The S arm of the hbr extends 1M offshore. Strong tidal streams run across the entrance.

Entrance From the IJmuiden IJM racon buoy Morse(A)8s a course of 100° on the ldg lts for 5M takes one through the outermost pierheads and through the Buitenhaven towards the Zuider Buitenkanaal. Yachts generally use the Zuidersluis where a Customs post is established at the seaward side on the N bank. IJmuiden Port Control should be contacted on VHF 9 when approaching from seaward. The approach and outer hbr and even the Buitenhaven can be rough in onshore winds. Take care before leaving that conditions are suitable outside.

Berthing If arriving from abroad, after clearing Customs as required, a comfortable berth may be found at the W.V. IJmond marina on the W side of the Zijkanaal C which opens to the S of the Noordzee Kanaal, 4½M on. The Buitenrust br at the entrance to this canal opens on request. The marina has water, electricity, toilets and showers and also a launderette. There is also a useful club restaurant, but there are no shops. 1M further along the Noordzee Kanaal, the Zijkanaal D on the N side has a smaller yacht hbr with facilities, at Nauerna.

NOORDZEE KANAAL

This 13M canal is the main shipping thoroughfare to Amsterdam and was opened in 1876 in response to the silting of the Zuiderzee. Traffic regulations are enforced by the water police. Yachts must keep close to the stb side of the canal and although sailing is permitted, tacking is not. However, the canal is over 175m wide and shipping does not present a problem. There is more than 3m depth, 10m from the bank. The Zeekanaal C leads to Spaarndam and Haarlem to the S, and the principal yacht route from Amsterdam to Rotterdam. The Zijkanaal D joins with the Noord-Hollands Kanaal and Den Helder as also does the Zijkanaal G at Zaandam.

AMSTERDAM
Charts BA 124   ANWB G & I
This principal city of the Netherlands, constructed on the dam between the Amstel and IJ rivers, is a natural mecca for all visitors to Holland. The Noordzee Kanaal continues through the city as the R IJ. Just E of the central rly stn, which is built on piers over the water and resembles a vast domed glasshouse, lies a small hbr on the S bank. It is very uncomfortable due to the wash of passing vessels. To the N the lofty Shell tr is a good landmark beyond which, after the locks leading to the Noord-Hollands Kanaal, lies the sheltered Sixhaven marina which is ideally situated for the free ferry to the city centre which operates 24h every few mins. Amsterdam Port Control VHF 14. Although there is a Customs office at Amsterdam (010255383), yachts cannot obtain clearance either inward or outward, but can embark dutiable stores after notifying them.

To the E the IJ continues past cargo and passenger quays to the Oranjesluizen (VHF 18) operating 24h and enabling craft to enter the IJsselmeer. Beyond the Oranjesluizen and after the lifting Schellingwouderbrug (VHF 18) the small hbr of Durgerdam is reached through a narrow buoyed channel to the N. It is only a short bus ride from the city centre. Anchoring is possible in the bay if the hbr is full.

A further alternative to the Amsterdam hbrs, and yet within a short bus ride, are the hbrs to the S of the city on the Nieuwe Meer. For those coming from the S and not intending to proceed N from Amsterdam these save a tedious route through 14 opening brs, two of which are rly brs which open only between 0100 and 0430. Vessels over 5m air draft take this route in convoy during the night. It is an interesting experience. Vessels travelling N towards Amsterdam must gather at the Nieuwemeersluis at 2300hrs. If you are going S from Amsterdam, go into the SE corner of the Oude Houthaven, pay dues at the br

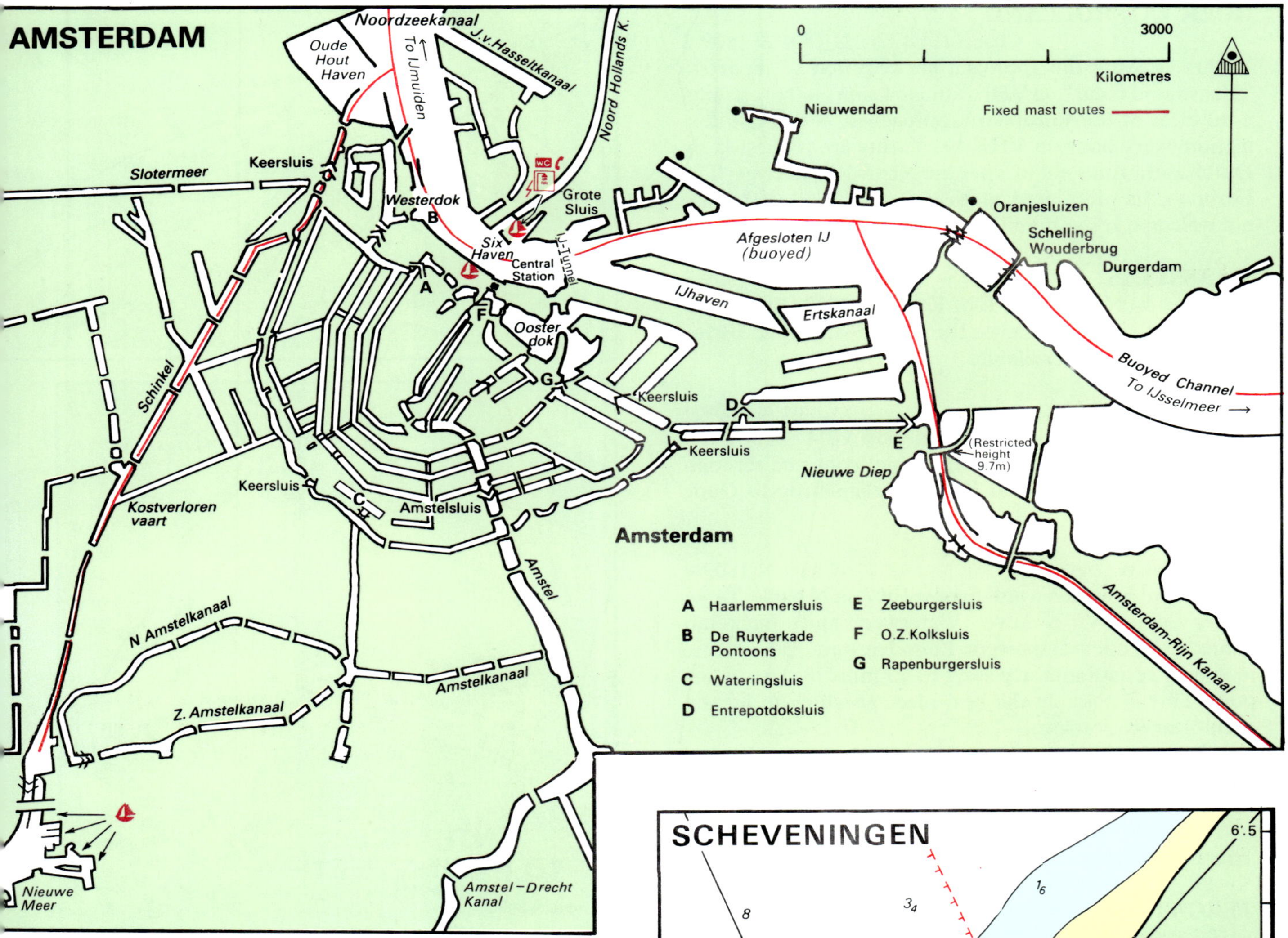

AMSTERDAM

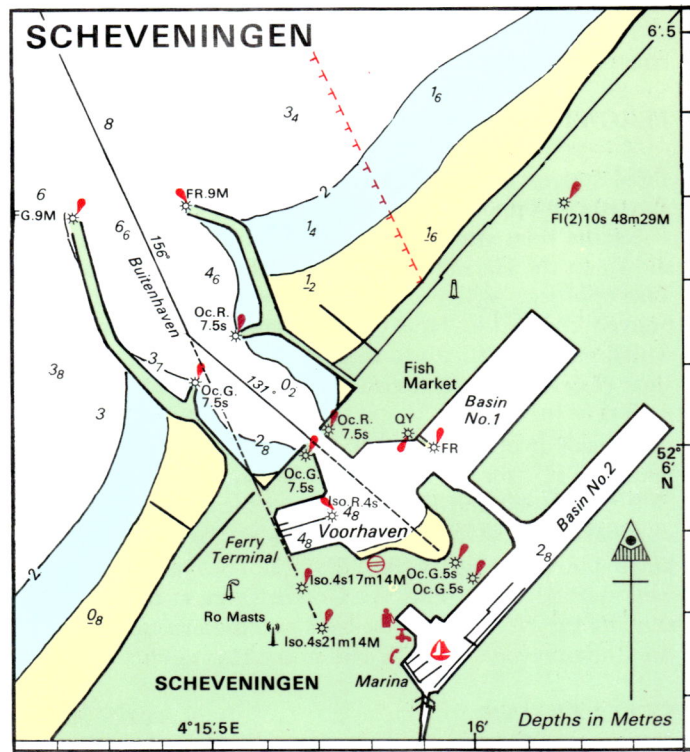

A Haarlemmersluis
B De Ruyterkade Pontoons
C Wateringsluis
D Entrepotdoksluis
E Zeeburgersluis
F O.Z.Kolksluis
G Rapenburgersluis

office and pass into the Singel to await the opening of the rly br. The Authorities prefer yachts to enter the Singel not later than approx 2200h so that they can determine the size of the convoy and make arrangements for all the brs to be opened by the mobile team of br keepers. Contact the Nieuwemeersluis or Westerkeersluis on VHF 22 for instructions. Vessels cannot stop or the convoy will pass ahead but, after crossing the Nieuwe Meer at dawn and passing under the Schiphol motorway br at its morning opening, you may anchor in the Westeinder Plas to recover! Keep a watch for plastic debris on the water if propeller problems are to be avoided. Craft with less than 7m air-draught may use the Amsterdam-Rijn canal as an alternative route to the S. Entrance is through a buoyed channel opening to the S from the IJ just before the Oranjesluizen.

SCHEVENINGEN Chart BA 122 & 2322 N 1801.5
HW: Dover +3¼h DS: Dover -5h SW, + 1h NE
MHWS 2.1m MHWN 1.8 MTL 1.1 MLWN 0.3 MLWS 0.2
A busy fishing port. There is no access to the inland waterways but it is a lively seaside resort and convenient for visiting the Hague. Customs post 070-514481. The outer hbr entrance faces N, is uncomfortable in strong N winds and dangerous in NW winds of F6 or more. Tidal streams, especially the N-going stream near the time of HW, run strongly across the entrance (Stroomatlas J). Approach Scheveningen lt ho Fl(2) 10s 29M lies ½M E of the entrance. From the safe water buoy (Iso 4s) 2M NW of the hbr a course of 156° on ldg lts (Iso 4s) leads in to the outer hbr.

Entrance All yachts are required to call Scheveningen hbr on VHF 14 before entering or leaving. The outer hbr moles are marked by FR & FG lts. Course should be altered to 131° to enter the Buitenhaven and Voorgaven before turning NE into the No 1 Basin and then hard to stb along a narrow cut into the No 2 Basin. Turn to stb again for the WV Marina Scheveningen (070 520017) at the S end of the No 2 Basin. There is a good clubhouse (070-520308), bar, restaurant and showers, toilets and washing machines.

HOEK VAN HOLLAND
Charts BA 122   N 1801 & 1809.2

Yachts crossing the approach are required to report to "Maasmond radar" on VHF 3 and to listen on that channel until clear of the Europoort approaches. Weather information every hour on VHF 14. Yachts are requested by Dutch authorities not to enter the Nieuwe Waterweg. The Europoort is prohibited to pleasure craft and yachts are not welcome at the Berghaven just inside.

MAASSLUIS
Chart N 1809.2

Entrance on N bank just E of Km post 1019. Enter Binnenhaven from Buitenhaven through a road br and rly br. Water and fuel are available.

VLAARDINGEN
Chart N 1809.4

Entrance on N bank just after Km post 1011 - E of Delta Hotel. Buitenhaven is uncomfortable; continue through Keersluis, railway br and Prinses Julianabrug to Oude Haven.

SCHIEDAM
Chart N 1809.4

Entrance to Spuihaven at Km post 1007 on N bank. Yacht Haven of WV Nieuwe Waterweg and Jachtclub Schiedam. Toilets & showers. Launderette at 750m. Close to shops, restaurants, rly station. 10 mins by taxi to airport. This is possibly the best place at which to leave a yacht near Rotterdam.

ROTTERDAM

Little remained of the old town after the German bombing of 1940 but the new town and port are well-planned. There are no recommended yacht hbrs.

ZEEGAT VAN GOEREE - HARINGVLIET
Charts BA 2322   N 1801 & 1807

Tidal streams in the approach are complex and currents may run in opposing directions. Sluicing operations can affect the tidal streams and R lts in triangular form are shown on the Haringvlietdam when they are in progress. The approach will be helped by being at the Slijkgat buoyed channel at Hoek van Holland HW -4h to -2h, which may be difficult to achieve after a North Sea crossing. (Leave the Goereesesluis at Hoek van Holland HW +1h to +3h).

Approach From the Goeree lt tr Fl(4) 20s 32m 28M a course of 117° for 8M brings one to the safe-water SG buoy (RWVS Iso 4s) and the entrance to the Slijkgat buoyed channel on 108° within the narrow W sector of the Kwade Hoek lt ho Iso 4s WRG 10m 12/9/8M. The channel is very well marked and follows the Goeree shore at first before skirting the Noord Pampus shoal and then turning SE to the Buitenhaven at the SW end of the Haringvliet dam.

STELLENDAM
Chart N 1801

A course of 232° gives entrance between the moles with an alteration to port after passing the S pierhead leading to the Goereesesluis (VHF 20). From half an hour before, until the end of sluicing. R lts in a △ pattern are exhibited on the dam. Yachts must keep within the buoyed channels and well clear of the sluices. From 1 April - 1 Nov a Customs post is staffed by Customs Officers from Vlissingen between 1400hrs and 1900hrs. There are two opening brs across the lock. The seaward one has clearance of NAP + 14.3m and is left closed whenever possible. Call the bridge (VHF 20) for information about exact clearance. The 150

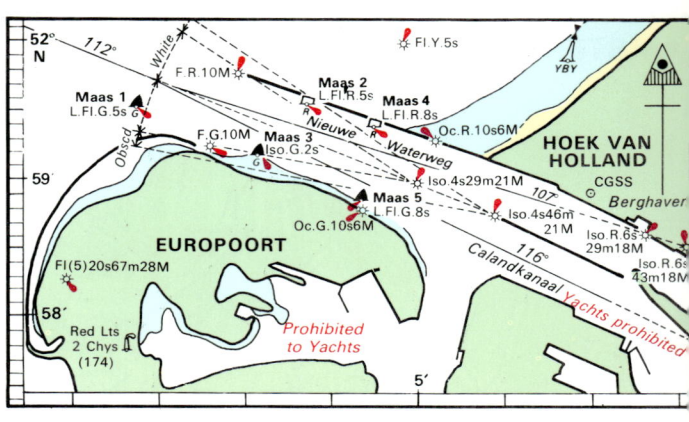

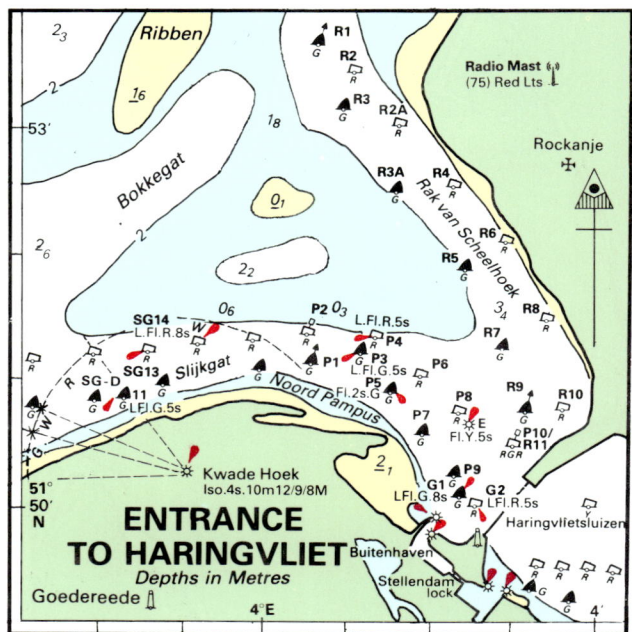

berth Aqua Pesch marina in the Buitenhaven has water, fuel, toilets, showers, launderette and is a convenient place from which to visit the Delta Exhibition. Stellendam town is 3km away. To reach Hellevoetsluis - only 4M away - follow the R can buoys through the Deltageul on the edges of the R (to port) and W (to stb) sectors of Hellevoetsluis lt ho - Iso WRG 10s 16m 11/8/7M on a general course of 096°.

HELLEVOETSLUIS
Chart N 1807.6

A busy yachting centre with a choice of hbrs. The Heliushaven is entered directly from the Haringvliet and contains three yacht club hbrs. It is a fifteen minute walk from the centre of town. The W side of the entrance to the inappropriately named Industriehaven in the Groote Dok is marked by a W lt ho with a black base. Pass through the Haaven and a swing br to reach the Hellevoetsluis YC (01883-14640) and the Arie de Boom Marina (01883-12166), both of which have full facilities, including a launderette and chandlery. Fuel is available opposite the HM's office. Shops are 10 mins walk. To the E, the Koopvaardijhaven forms the entrance to the Voornsche Kanaal and there is a mooring stage to the W of the harbour with summer toilets and showers.

MIDDELHARNIS

On the S side of the Haringvliet opposite the entrance to the R Spui. Entrance is between harbour moles through a lock and br (HM VHF 12). Opening times are Mon-Sat 0700-2100h; Sun, hols 0800, 1000, 1700, 2100h. The pleasant old town harbour is reached along a 1M canal.

INLAND FROM THE HARINGVLIET

The Haringvliet ends 15M inland at the Haringvliet br with a lifting section (VHF 13). Max ht under fixed span 12m at LW. E of the Haringvliet br lies the Hollandsch Diep and to the S, after passing the N end of the Volkeraksluizen, the old fortified town of Willemstad. The Hollandsch Diep leads on to the Dordtsche Kil and to Dordrecht and the Oude Maas. For yachts with fixed masts navigation of the Hollandsch Diep further to the E is blocked by the Moerdijkbrug with maximum clearance of 9m. For craft able to continue, the Biesbos is a fascinating area of reeds, islands and navigable channels, leading into the R Maas, Venlo, Maastricht and the canal system of Belgium and France.

THE OOSTERSCHELDE   Chart N 1801 & 1805

Approach With tidal streams running at up to 2½kn it is worth planning to arrive at the Middelbank buoy between HW Zierikzee +3h and +6h (Dover -6h and -3h to carry the tidal stream towards the lock and into the Oosterschelde. The Roompot should be approached with great care and only in fair weather as there are numerous off-lying sandbanks and shoals. Between these the streams run swiftly and with rapidly changing directions. Entrance is only possible via the Roompotsluis (VHF 18) (01115 9265) over which there is a fixed br with a minimum clearance of 18m. The lock opens 24 hrs and there are mooring pontoons with plenty of sheltered sea room at each end. In unsettled weather it is safer to stand off.

Entrance The areas either side of the Roompotsluis are dangerous owing to the rapid streams and underwater obstructions. The buoyed channels converge about 1M from the entrance to the Buitenhaven which is entered between F R & F G lts on a course of 73.5° (leading lts Oc 5s) with a turn to stb after passing the S molehead. There is a summer Customs post at the Roompotsluis open 0900hrs - 1630hrs from 1 April to 1 Nov. When this is closed, boats with a valid Verklaring certificate have been known to enter here and clear Customs at Vlissingen by telephone.

PASSAGE NOTES   Charts BA 110 & 3371

From the UK, course should be set for the Middelbank safe water buoy Fl Iso 8s situated in a line of lt buoys. Westkapelle lt ho Fl 3s and the Noorderhoofd lt ho Oc 10s are leading lts on a bearing of 149.5°. By steering on this course the Steenbank can be crossed near the MSB W card buoy Q(9)15s in 6m of water. E of this, the partly lit Westgat and Oude Roompot channel leads to the Roompot lock entrance. In daylight the unlit Roompot channel to the S of the Hompels bank is an alternative with a final buoyed dogleg leading N to the lock between E and W card buoys.

ZIERIKZEE   Chart N 1805.8

MHWS 3.0m   MHWN 2.7   MTL 1.6   MLWN 0.4   MLWS 0.3

On the N bank of the Oosterschelde, 8M from the Roompotsluis. A picturesque old fishing port. Tidal set across the entrance to the Havenkanaal (min depth 2.4m). After the open flood barrier there are box moorings to port and the WV Zierikzee with toilets and showers (tel: 01110 14700). Then, a floating pontoon with a ramp leads to the HM office, toilets and showers. Beyond this is a further floating pontoon and toilet/shower block. Two chandlers on the quayside, sailmakers and most repair facilities. Calor gas cylinders can be re-filled at the fuel pontoon.

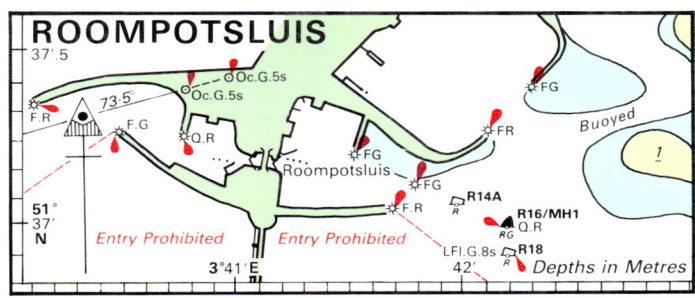

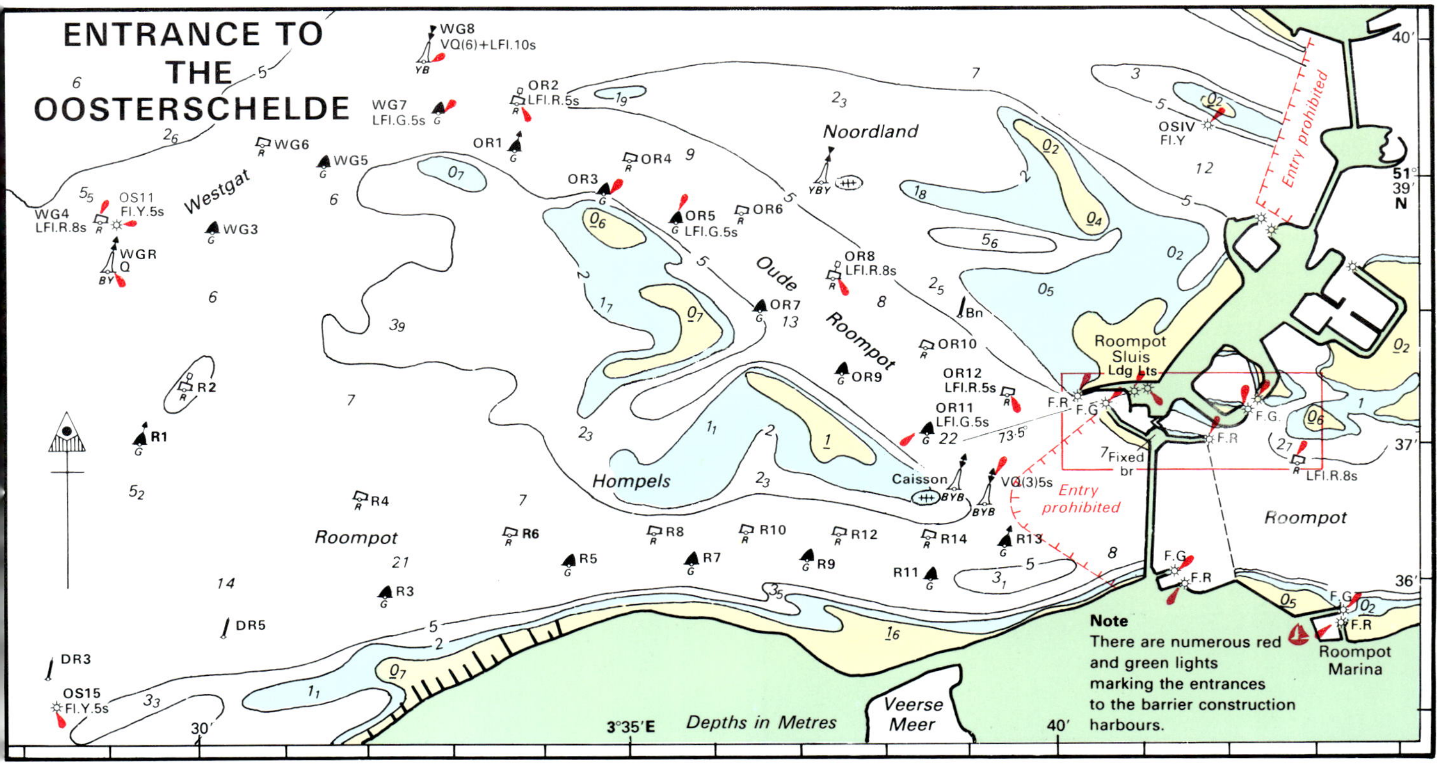

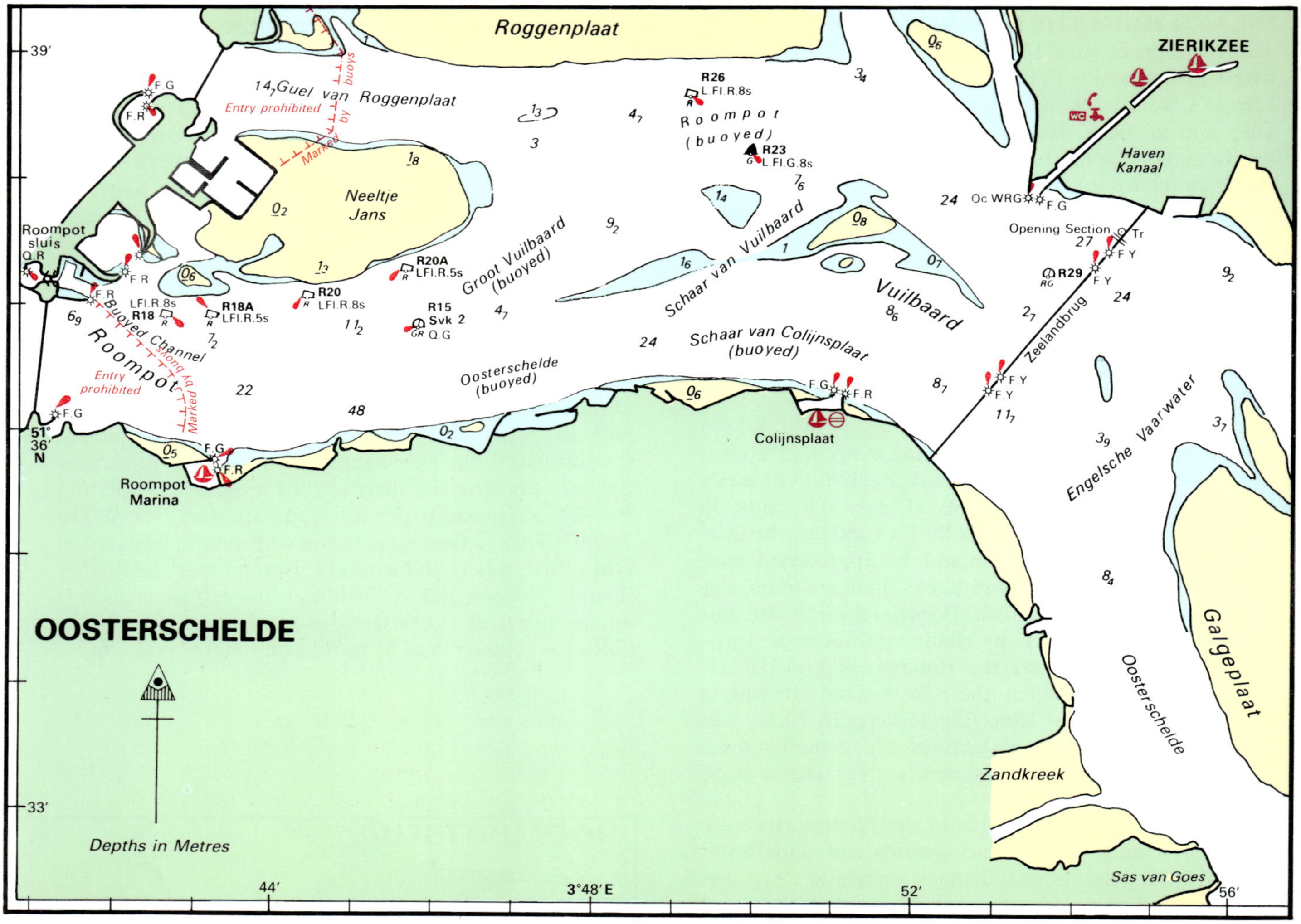

COLIJNSPLAAT

A modern Marina opposite Zierikzee on the S shore of the Oosterschelde and 6M from the Roompot. Tide runs across the very narrow entrance which is from the NE. WV Noord Beveland is at W end of hbr (01199-762). Good shelter. All facilities including water and electricity on pontoons. Launderette and restaurants. Village shops nearby.

1M beyond Colijnsplaat/Zierikzee is the 3M long Zeelandbrug with an average clearance range of 13.3m - 16.9m. Opening span at the N end of the br (VHF 18). After the br, the N arm of the Oosterschelde leads to the locks into the Grevelingenmeer at Bruinisee, or through the Krammer locks to the Volkerak and Willemstad. The SE arm leads towards the Zandkreek and the locks into the Veerse Meer. It continues further SE to Goessche Sas and a lock into a tree-lined canal which ends at Goes.

GOES   Chart N 1805.5

The Havenkanaal passes through a br at Wilhelminadorp. Then, on the edge of the town, the Ringbrug opens on the hr, Mon-Fri 07-21h (except 12h), Sat, Sun, hols 08-11, 17-20h. After this, the entrance to the yachthaven of WV de Werf, with depth of 1.4m, is immediately to port. The attractive Town Harbour, with quayside and box moorings lies beyond a quaint lifting wooden bridge which operates in partnership with the Ringbrug.

WEMELDINGE   Chart N 1805

This small town lies 7M SE from the Zeelandbrug, and is at the N end of the S Beveland canal which leads to the Westerschelde at Hansweert, and hence the N Sea. It provides an alternative to the route via the Veerse Meer and the Kanaal door Walcheren to Vlissingen. At the N end, a new branch of the canal is under construction to the E of the existing locks. This is planned to open in 1992 and the canal will then become tidal, although the locks at the S end will remain in use. There should be fewer delays at the N end of the canal to allow better timing for the rly br (opens 10mins before the hour) ¾M N of the Hansweert locks. A new marina is planned to occupy the existing approaches to the locks.

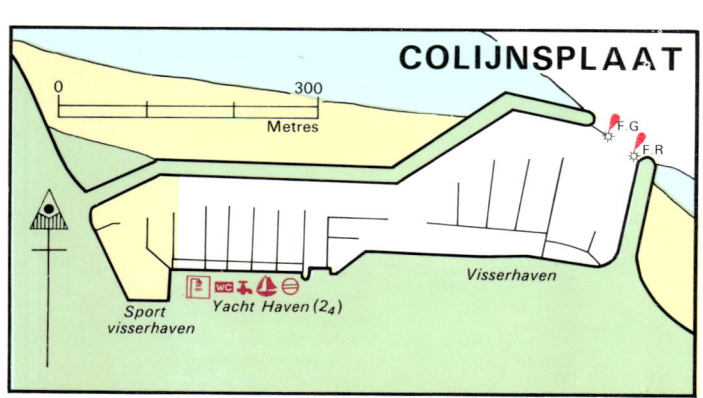

VLISSINGEN Charts BA 1872 & 235   N 1801, 1803
HW: Dover +2h DS: Dover -3¼h E, -1h W, up to 4kn
MHWS 4.9m   MHWN 4.0   MTL 2.6   MLWN 1.0   MLWS 0.5

The principal entry port in S Holland with ferry connections to Sheerness and good rail links with Amsterdam. On the Westerschelde special traffic regulations apply - notably that yachts must have their engine running when under sail; shall cross the shipping lanes at right angles; shall not obstruct commercial craft and shall maintain a minimum speed of 3½ knots. As Vlissingen is a pilot station, ships may slow down, stop or even swing through 180° in the offing and yachts must be prepared for these manoeuvres. The Breskens - Vlissingen ferries also have right of way but these symmetrical vessels do, however, serve to indicate the point of entrance to the locks at Vlissingen.

Approach From the N the Oostgat may be entered by running in on 149° - the ldg line of the Noorderhoofd Oc 10s 20m lt ho in transit with Westkapelle Fl 3s 50m 28M lt ho until within ½M of the shore. The off-shore (SW side) of this channel is marked by G con buoys as far as the OG-DL E Card buoy which marks the confluence with the Deurloo channel. From this point inwards care is needed to avoid the Spleet shoal to the SW which dries. Approaching from the S the Wielingen channel is wide, well-buoyed, and much used by shipping bound to and from Antwerp. It is entered through the Scheur channel N of Zeebrugge and runs in an E direction through lt buoys. There is deep water which is free of obstructions apart from one well-marked wreck, the "Seablue", and yachts are recommended to remain outside the shipping lane until past the B & W banded Nieuwe Sluis lt ho Oc WRG 10s 28m 14/11/10M at the N tip of the mainland at the entrance to the river. With the engine running and minimum speed of 3½kn as required by law, course should be set across the river for the large R W10 buoy - Q. Maintain radio watch on VHF 14. There is a TSS just S of Vlissingen which requires considerable care and attention to the rules. The W-going lane lies 3ca offshore and the E-going lane 2ca further S.

Entrance The Michiel de Ruyter Marina in the former Visserhaven shares an entrance with the pilot launch hbr, just W of the conspic windmill. There is a footbridge over the entrance which limits access. Entrance is possible from 1 April to 1 Oct between 0800 - 2200 local time. The marina is tidal and there is a gauge at the port side of the entrance showing the depth of water over the sill which is at 0.85m above chart datum. The marina accommodates 100 boats and has good facilities, including diesel. It is close to the centre of town but a long walk from the Customs post and is not connected to the inland waterways. If planning to enter the inland waterways it is more convenient to arrive via the ferry harbour and the locks leading to the Walcheren canal.

Entrance The Buitenhaven is 1M E of the marina and is easily identified by the frequent ferries entering and leaving. The sea locks (VHF 22) operate 24h. It is not necessary to report to port control VHF 9 but the information broadcasts on VHF 14 every h+50 (Dutch and English) are worth monitoring. The Customs office is on the S side of the locks and it is obligatory to report there on first entry. It is never easy to get ashore just inside the locks, but a U-turn to port leads into a quiet backwater where you may tie to the wall very close to the building labelled "Douane".

Vlissingen yacht hbr is on stb, just before the first br over the Walcheren canal (01184-65912). All facilities including launderette and clubhouse serving food. The town centre is a good half hour's walk. The restaurant in the rly stn is worth trying. There are five bridges between Vlissingen and Middelburg, the first of which is remote controlled. The bridge keeper can be called on VHF 22, call sign "Sloebrug". Middelburg has restaurants, chandlers, fuel barge and an excellent shopping centre. Veere, 3M further, on the enclosed Veerse Meer is easily reached with only 1 more lock.

The **VEERSE MEER** leades eventually to the Zandkreeksluis and the Oosterschelde. It winds round a series of natural and man-made Is, some with free mooring facilities, some restricted to wild-life, and there are several large marinas on the N and S shores.

HANSWEERT   Chart N 1803.3
This is the S end of the South Beveland canal offering an alternative route to the Oosterschelde at Wemeldinge. No yacht facilities at Hansweert apart from the locks (VHF 22) and Customs post (1 May - 1 Nov).

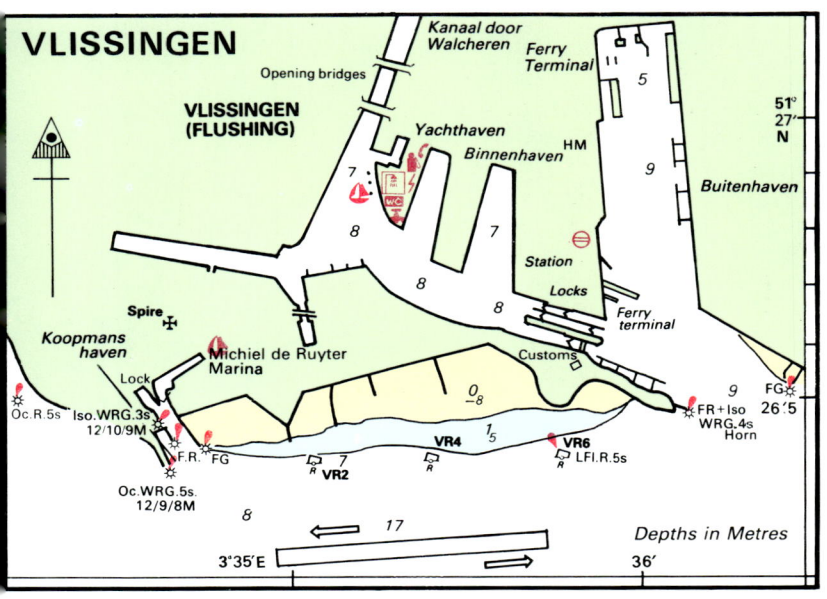

HOLLAND 288

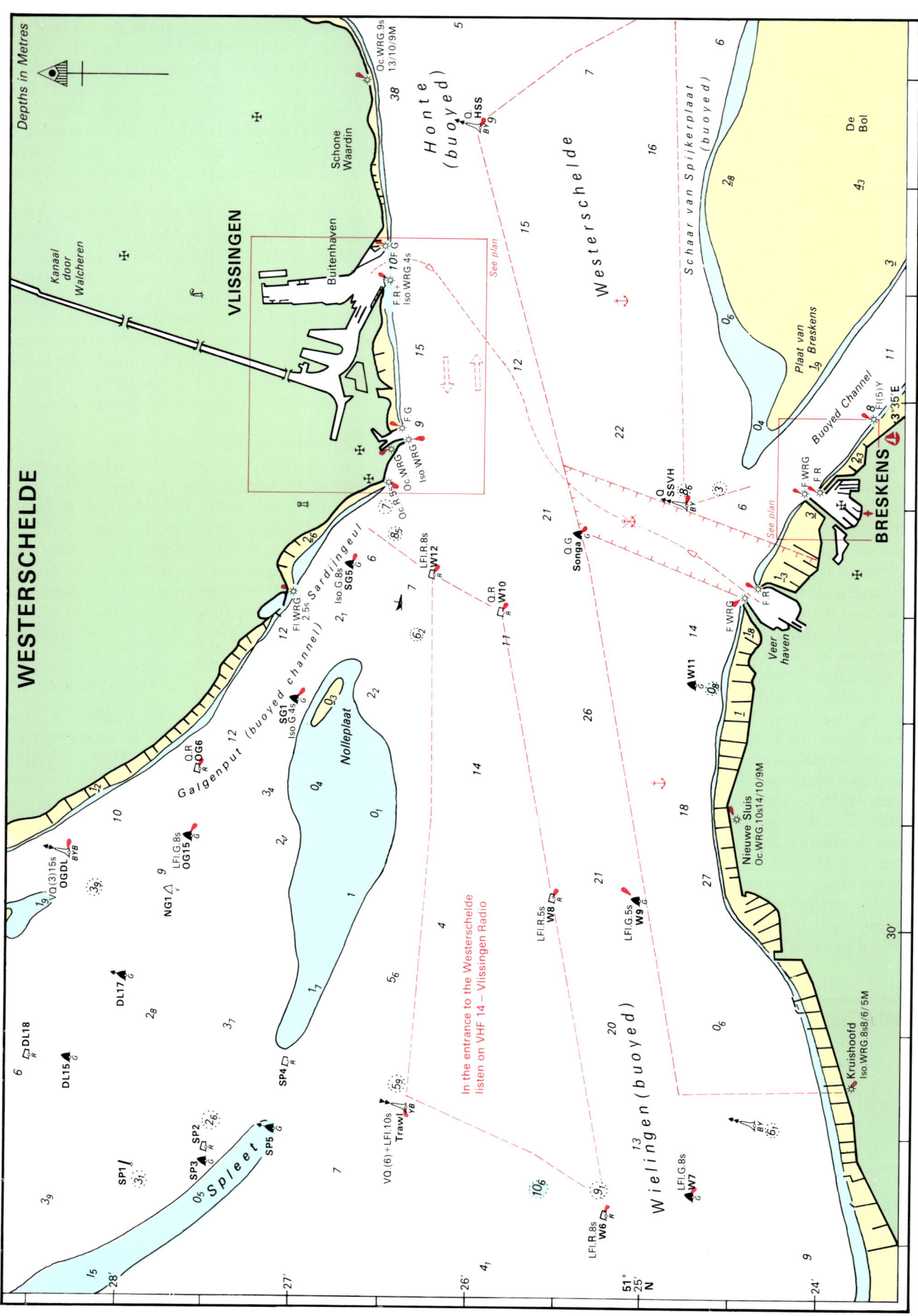

TERNEUZEN   Charts BA 120   N 1803
HW: Dover +2½h DS: Dover -1½h ENE, -½h W
MHWS 5.1m MHWN 4.2 MTL 2.6 MLWN 0.9 MLWS 0.4

A picturesque town on the S shore of the Westerschelde. It is possible to reach Ghent (18M and 3 lifting brs) from Terneuzen with a fixed mast.

Approach The buoyed channel must be followed carefully, taking the S channel through the Pas van Terneuzen on 125° using the ldg lts N of the large chemical plant. Alter course parallel to the shore at a range of 3 ca and continue for 2M past the entrance to the W Buitenhaven (prohibited to yachts). The Belgian canal system joins the Schelde here and there is heavy barge traffic. The tidal stream runs strongly across the hbr entrances.

Entrance If bound for Ghent, enter the E Buitenhaven and through the locks (VHF 11) and lifting brs. Moorings can be found S of the locks by turning 180° to port after 5 ca. The YC is at the N end of Zijkanaal A. (01150-96331). Customs (01150-12377) at the lock. If bound for the yacht hbr, enter the Veerhaven between two sea walls topped with port and stb lt beacons. There are two marinas at the S end of the Veerhaven each with similar facilities.

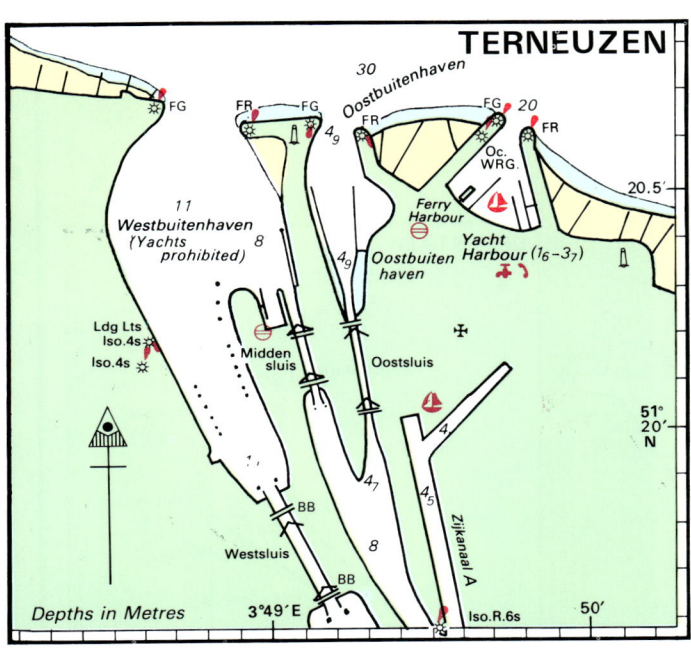

BRESKENS   Charts BA 325   N 1803
Tidal information as for Vlissingen.

A large marina, accessible at all states of the tide. It is a useful alternative to Vlissingen as there are no locks to cause delays.

Approach as for Vlissingen, but maintaining course 1 ca off the S shore, passing the ferry hbr and rounding the high steel-shuttered wall.

Entrance Streams set strongly across the entrance, but once within the outer pierheads the effect is lost. The sands extend seaward off the NW mole head which must be given a good berth. The way to the pontoons is partially blocked by a moored barge which acts as a wave-break and must be left to port on entering. The modern clubhouse is at the SE corner (01172-3278), (for berths 01172-1902). Customs (01172-1837) in a building labelled "Transport Vooruit" across the sea-wall from the HM office. Hbr is well sheltered except in strong NW winds and HW. High spring tides lap the outer seawalls. Facilities here are above average but so are the prices.

THE IJSSELMEER   Chart N 1810
An inland fresh water sea formed in 1932 by the completion of the 21M long Afsluitdijk and divided in 1975 by the Houtribdijk which stretches from Enkhuizen to Lelystad. It is a superb sailing area but with its shoal depths, which are generally less than 3m, and its low-lying shores, it is subject to the rapid development of dangerous short steep seas in fresh to strong winds. It is an area to be treated with respect and not thought of as merely a lake. It is over 40M from N-S and as wide as the Dover Straits. Look out for the fishing nets which are usually well marked and charted. Hbrs are listed in clockwise order, commencing in the NE.

MAKKUM   Chart N 1810.6
Only 2M SE from Kornwerderzand locks.

Entrance Enter on 092° following a buoyed channel between shoals. One of the few places in the IJsselmeer with sandy beaches used for swimming. If visiting the town, the most convenient place to stay is the Visserhaven beyond the industriehaven and its conspic ship-building shed. There is a yacht mooring stage beyond the fishing boats. For craft drawing less than 2m it is possible to enter the Friesland canal system here and join the fixed mast route to Leeuwarden and beyond. There is a chandlers, a small supermarket and fried fish take-away in the town.

WORKUM
5M further S is entered from the Workum-Hindeloopen middle ground buoy RGR Iso 2s through a narrow buoyed channel and 1M long entrance canal. This is another entrance to the Frisian canals and lakes. A large marina on the N bank (It Soal) has all facilities. Between It Soal and the lock are a number of additional moorings and another marina; Jachthaven Anne Wever B.V. The entrance canal, Het Zool, has a min depth of 1.7m and ends in a quaint circular basin before the lock where it is possible to moor overnight. The basin has a toilet block with showers and a water hose and is just a short walk into the town. It is hardly worth entering the lock unless proceeding to the lakes.

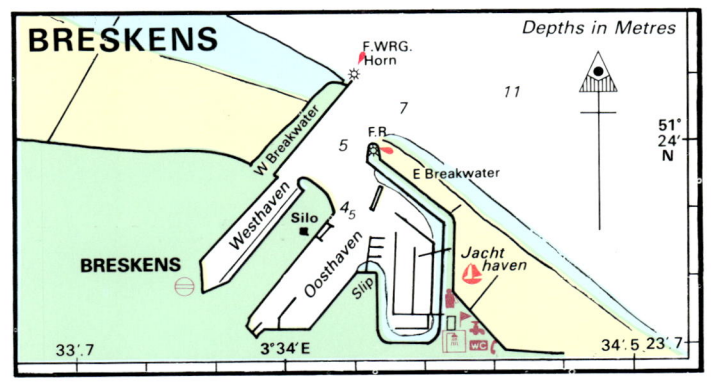

HOLLAND

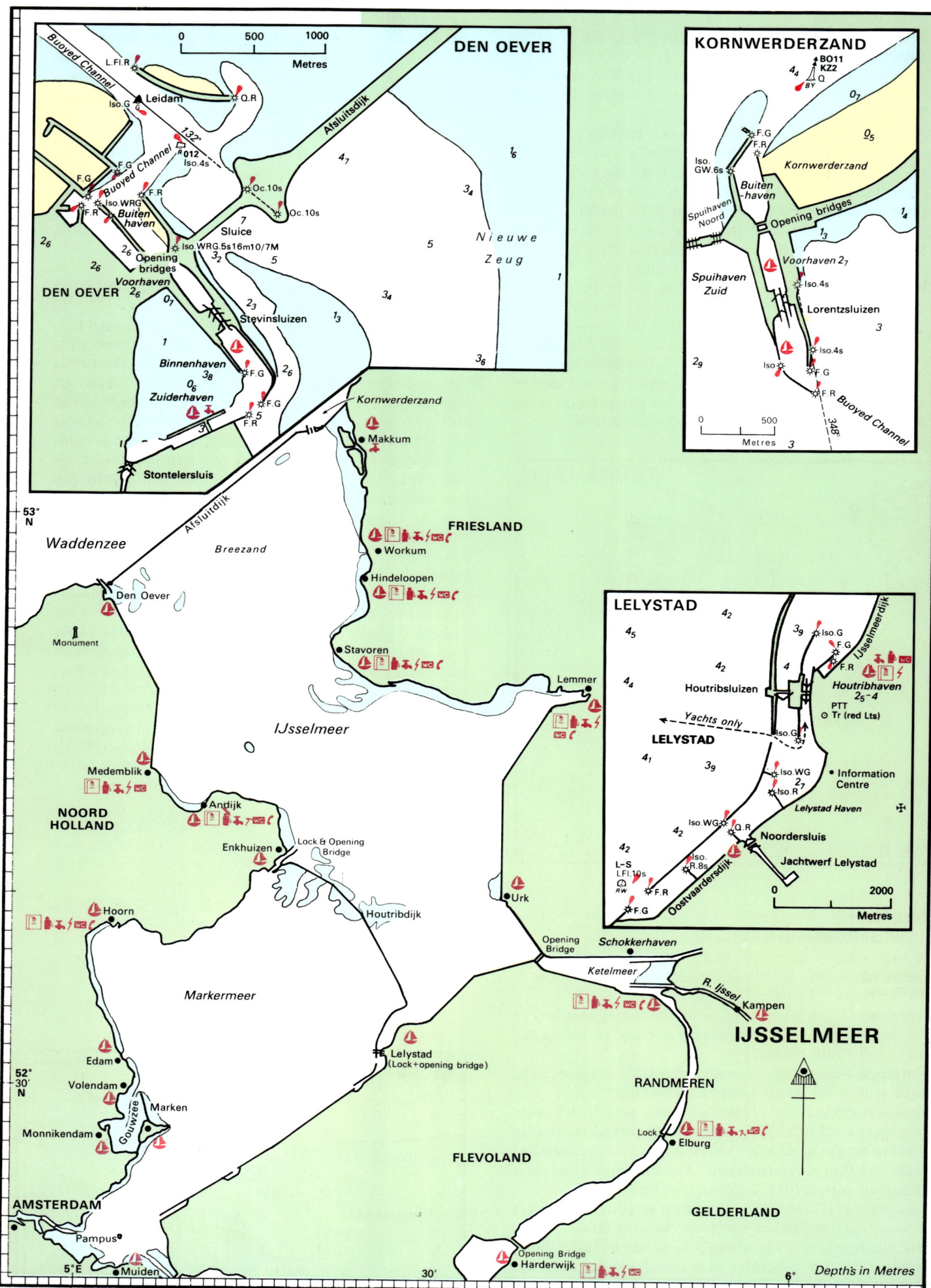

HINDELOOPEN

Formerly an island this beautiful town is famous for its enamelled woodware. No access to the inland waterways, but the small canals and tiny bridges are very attractive.
Entrance Enter from the H2/W1 buoy RGR Iso 2s on a general SE course, keeping to the channel. Enter between high wooden piers and turn to port immediately for the large Jachthaven Hindeloopen which has all facilities including fuel, launderette, 20 ton travel-lift, swimming pool, engineers and hairdressers. Moorings can also be found in the old hbr to the S of the entrance. Stores from the town close by. The Church with its leaning tr and graves of servicemen of both sides from the 1939-45 War should not be missed. Although there is full shelter from the seas in the marina, strong winds from the N blow right across. HM 05142-2009.

STAVOREN

A busy ferry port, 4M S of Hindeloopen. There are 2 hbrs; the one to the N is the Spoorhaven and used by the ferries and larger craft. The S hbr is the Nieuwe Voorhaven and ends at the Johan Frisosluis forming one of the main entrances to Friesland for craft not over 2m draught. From off-shore, the distinctive concave roof of the pumping station provides a useful steering mark. Although there are mooring rails outside the locks these are principally for waiting craft and more pleasant moorings will be found inside by grassy but protected banks. Stores from shops in the town. Fuel alongside.

LEMMER

The Prinses Margriet canal, 1M W of the town harbours, provides access to the Friesland canals for craft not exceeding 3m draught. However, there is also a route via the town which is well worth visiting. The Prinses Margrietsluis (VHF 20) does not operate on Sundays and public holidays.
Approach is E between Friesland and the Nordoost Polder with a buoyed channel close to the S shore. The small Friese Hoek lt ho on the NW corner of the Noordoost Polder provides a steering mark until the channel buoys, less than 2 ca from the steep-to shore, can be identified. Lemmer is a large yachting centre and there are many yacht hbrs and mooring places both outside and inside the locks through the town. Full facilities. Fuel is available at the Friesehoek hbr on the N shore outside the locks and at the marinas on either side of the canal after the Flevobrug. Opening times for the locks are: Mon-Fri 0700-2100, Sat 0700-2000, Sun, hols, 0830-1200, 1400-1730, 1800-2000h. All the town brs open on approach. A fee for the lock and town brs is collected by the HM in the lock.

URK Another former island, now linked by dykes to the polders, Urk retains its individuality and, surprisingly for Holland, has steep streets. A large fishing fleet now operates mainly from coastal ports, but some boats still work from here. The entrance, which is only possible from the S, requires care. There are more mooring places than the single marina symbol on the chart indicates. Visiting yachts can moor on the N, S and W sides of the Nieuwe Haven, all three walls of the Westhaven and the S wall of the Oosthaven. Fuel is available in the Westhaven. Small shopping centre.

THE RANDMEREN

3M SE from Urk the Ketelbrug - clearance 10m, but with a lifting span, separates the IJsselmeer from the Ketelmeer and Randmeren. The Randmeren is all that is left of the SE part of the Zuiderzee after reclamation of the Noordoost and Flevoland polders. It provides a continuous navigable waterway, with a buoyed channel 3m deep, between the Flevoland polder and the original Zuiderzee coast. However, yachts with more than 12.5m air-draught will not be able to pass under the fixed Hollandse br at Muiderberg and so would have to retrace their track to the Ketelmeer.

KAMPEN

This interesting medieval town, about 6M up the R IJssel from the Ketelmeer, has four yacht marinas and a good shopping centre. The channel has a minimum depth of 3.2m and is well marked.

ELBURG, HARDERWIJK, SPAKENBURG & HUIZEN

Elburg is a 13th century town with impressive ramparts and a moat. Moorings alongside the S bank of the canal and in the town hbr. Harderwijk is an old Zuiderzee trading port with several 13th and 14th century buildings and a choice of three hbrs. Spakenburg has a very picturesque old hbr with many traditional Dutch sailing barges. The townsfolk are noted for their wearing of traditional dress. Huizen has two buoyed entrance channels, the W one leading to three marinas while the E leads through an opening br to the old fishing hbr. The town has suffered much development.

LELYSTAD

This port was constructed subsequent to the draining of Flevoland in the 1970s. It has a lock - the Houtribsluis (VHF 20) through the dyke separating the N IJsselmeer from the proposed Makerward polder. A good yacht marina is to the N of the lock. IJsselmeer museum close by.
Approach This is clearly defined by the dyke and the sea-wall whilst the two very conspic chimneys of the electricity generating station are passed close to port. These chimneys provide an excellent navigating mark for the whole of the S part of the IJsselmeer. The S exit from the locks is between the sea-wall and offshore training dykes, but yachts are expected to use only the first of the gaps to the IJsselmeer by turning sharply to stb after rounding the stb mole from the lock. There is a small yacht hbr 1½M further S by the Noordersluis.

MUIDEN

At the S end of the IJsselmeer, Muiden is approached from the main shipping channel leading to Amsterdam by leaving the channel at the IJM WR buoy, 11 ca N of the old fort of Pampus Is. The narrow buoyed channel is then followed on 142° until the Pampus is abeam to stb. A course of 202° for a further 12 ca leads to the spar buoys marking the channel into Muiden. The E mole (port hand on entry) is submerged for the first 2 ca and considerable caution should be exercised in keeping on 181° in the entrance and close to the W training wall. Even greater care is needed on leaving if other vessels are entering. The Muiden YC has good facilities in the shadow of the castle. N of the Pampus the buoyed channel leads SW to the Buiten IJ and the approach to Amsterdam (see p 283).

MARKEN
Between 1164 and 1957 Marken was an Is which is now joined to the mainland by a causeway. From the N end of the Is there is a wall stretching 1M NNW to the 2m contour, and on the E tip there is a prominent white lt ho. Enter the Gouwzee from N of Marken and follow the buoyed channel (2.2m) into any of the three hbrs.

MONNICKENDAM
A picturesque town with four marinas. However, the closest berths to the town are beyond the marinas in the Town Harbour which has toilets, showers and fuel.

VOLENDAM
Very commercialised. No marina berths for visitors who moor to the quayside in the NE half of the hbr.

EDAM
Edam is one of the loveliest and best preserved of all the Zuiderzee ports and the town deserves to be explored. Narrow entrance through a lock and br to a canal with mooring space on both banks. Water hose on N bank.

HOORN
The home of the discoverers of the S Cape of S America has many signs of its former glory as a Hanseatic town. The former warehouses now serve as private dwellings or restaurants and the bronze statues of the "Boys from the Bontehoe" still look out for a suitable ship on which to stow away.
Entrance From the S on 352° from a R can buoy 1 ca to the S of the rough stone walls forming the outer hbr walls. You may anchor in the outer hbr (2m) or moor in the Town hbrs or the quieter modern marina to the W. All facilities at the marina.

ENKHUIZEN
This is the largest port of the Zuiderzee and lies at the N end of the Houtribdijk. It is also a busy ferry port. The Zuiderzee Museum consisting of an outdoor village and an indoor marine museum is an essential visit.
Approach from the S, the channel to the Krabbersgatsluis is well buoyed and the course to the entrance is marked by ldg lts (Iso 4s) on 037°. There are good mooring places on each side of the lock approaches (VHF 22), but there are often long delays here. The N approach is from the EZ1/KG2 RGR(Iso 2s) buoy into the Krabbersgat on a course of 230° (ldg lts - Iso 8s).
Entrance Going N from the locks there are three yacht hbrs. The first to port is the Buyshaven which has a marina at the S side. Fl Y lt on N pier of hbr forbids all movement while the ferry enters or leaves. There is a well-appointed toilet/shower block but the box moorings are the furthest from the town. The second is the Buitenhaven which is adjacent to the rly stn and is therefore convenient for crew changes. This hbr is often very crowded and you may have to raft alongside several boats. Toilets and showers are next to the HM office on the N side. The third hbr, the Compagnieshaven, houses the largest marina. It is beyond the town to the NE and has showers, toilets, water, fuel, chandlery and a launderette. It is a short walk to the town and very conveniently situated for the Marine Museum near the Stavoren Gate (Staverse Poortje).
Enkhuizen has a good shopping centre, boatyards, sail-maker and engine repairs. Calor gas cylinders can be refilled at De Wit's in Vyrelstraat.

ANDIJK (Kerkbuurt)
A large, well equipped marina but fairly isolated (visiting shop). Apart from the small village of Andijk there are no other attractions nearby. Entrance is obtained by following the sea wall round from the N tip at Andijk and continuing along the W of the breakwater before turning its S end and heading N through the hbr entrance between breakwaters. A sharp turn to stb brings one to the end of the first pontoon where a reporting telephone is provided. The helpful HM usually sees yachts entering and hails them over the loud-hailer with berthing directions. Chandlery and restaurant.

MEDEMBLIK
3M to the NW is identified at a distance by its collection of spires. Approach the narrow entrance on 232° (Oc 5s lt between FR & FG on wooden piers). There are submerged rocks either side. The first part of the hbr (Oosterhaven) is not available to visiting yachts. The Middenhaven has no facilities but yachts can lie alongside on either side of the hbr. Access to the marina in the Westerhaven is through an opening road br. The HM office, showers, toilets and launderette are all in one building. The Noordhollands canal can be entered here via the Westerhavensluis at the SW of the hbr. This port hosts international dinghy regattas and is the home of the Royal YC of Holland.

BELGIUM

ENTRY REQUIREMENTS
A "Q" flag should be flown at the first port of entry until Customs Officers board. If they do not board, enquire at the marina or YC.

PASSAGE NOTES
Charts BA 1872, F 1348, B 11, N 1801

Passage Lights:
Nieuwe Sluis	Oc WRG 10s 28m 14/11/10M from a W tr with black bands
Kruishoofd	Iso WRG 8s 15m 8/6/5M from a metal tr
Zeebrugge	Oc WR 15s 24m 20/18M from a tr on end of inner hbr mole
Blankenberge	Oc(2) 8s 32m 20M from a W tr with black band at top
Oostende	Fl(3) 10s 65m 27M from a W tr (partially obscured to SW)
Nieuwpoort	Fl(2) R 14s 26m 21 M from a W tr

The coast of Belgium is fringed by a number of sandbanks, running roughly parallel to the coast. The sea breaks heavily over them in strong winds, especially when those winds oppose the tidal streams. Tidal streams run parallel to the coast with the East-going stream commencing at Dover $-1\frac{1}{4}$h and the W-going stream at Dover $+4\frac{3}{4}$h. The average rate in both directions is 2kn.

Yachts from the Dover Strait may enter the buoyed Dunkerque approach channel and continue via the Passe de Zuydcoote, with a least depth of 3m, in a NE direction and into the Westdiep. From Nieuwpoort there is unhindered navigation no more than one mile off-shore as far as Blankenberge, but the breakwaters of Zeebrugge harbour produce reflected waves and disturbed seas for up to two miles out. To avoid these, and the commercial shipping into and out of Zeebrugge, it is advisable to pass at least 1M off the outer moles of the hbr. If bound N for the Schelde, follow a course just inshore of the buoyed Wielingen shipping channel when well clear.

Passages through the banks from the North are well buoyed for Oostende and Zeebrugge, from the W or N Hinder LVs. The whole coast is low-lying and fringed with dunes. The various seaside resorts present very similar appearances from seaward making identification difficult. The traditional technique of planning to make a landfall before dawn and before the lights are extinguished has much to commend it.

Caution is needed in using MTL to calculate LW as Mean Sea Levels may vary by as much as 0.5m for up to a month. For precise information Admiralty Tide Tables should be consulted.

The following guides will be found useful in navigating this coast:
"North Sea Harbours - Calais to Den Helder" by Jack Coote, (Barnacle Marine - ISBN 0 948788 21 6)
"North Sea Passage Pilot" by Brian Navin, (Imray - ISBN 0 85288 102 9).

ANTWERP   Charts BA 139   N 1803
HW: Dover $+3\frac{3}{4}$h

MHWS 5.8m MHWN 4.2 MTL 2.7 MLWN 1.0 MLWS 0.0

Approach via the Westerschelde some 45M from Vlissingen and 33M from Terneuzen. At the mouth of the Westerschelde spring tidal streams can exceed 4 knots and rates are almost as high between sandbanks further into the estuary. Tidal timing is therefore critical and it may be desirable to break the passage at Terneuzen. At Nieuwe Sluis the ingoing stream starts at HW Vlissengen -5h and there is then 8hrs of favourable tide for the passage up river. There is between $4\frac{1}{2}$ and 5hrs of favourable tide for the return passage. The river is well-buoyed and lit, but there is heavy commercial traffic. Maintain listening watch successively on VHF 14 (Schelde entrance) VHF 21 (Post Vlissingen), VHF 3 (Post Terneuzen), VHF 71 (Post Hansweert) and VHF 12 (Zandvliet Radio). Keep to stb side of channel. Give way to commercial craft. Have engine ready for immediate use and hoist a cone if motorsailing.

Entrance Keep N of the Stroomleidam, the N end of which is marked by an 82m pylon, and follow the winding channel until a sharp bend to stb at the 109 G buoy (Iso 8s) brings the waterfront and churches of Antwerp into view. Keep the next buoy (Y unlit) to stb. The entrance to the Nic Haven is marked by a Y con buoy to stb and a Y can buoy to port. The gate operates approx HW ± 1h between 0600hrs and 2000hrs depending on tides. Yachts may anchor between the two con Y buoys while waiting for the gate, or moor to the Y waiting buoy opposite the entrance. Call Nic Haven on VHF 9(71). Tel:(03) 219-08-95. All facilities including fuel. On the return journey, yachts should leave the marina at the first opening of the hbr gate. From the marina the city of Antwerp on the opposite bank is reached either by a pedestrian and cycle tunnel or by another tunnel for motor vehicles.

ZEEBRUGGE   Charts BA 325 & 97, B 11. N 1801.2
HW: Dover +1½h DS: HWD E, +5h W
MHWS 4.8m   MHWN 3.8   MTL 2.4   MLWN 1.1   MLWS 0.4

The major fishing port of Belgium and an important ferry port with heavy large commercial traffic.

Approach and Entrance If you have VHF radio it is mandatory to call Zeebrugge Port Control - VHF 71 - before entering or leaving and to maintain a listening watch on that channel while inside the harbour. Because of reflected waves, confused seas may be encountered if approaching too close inshore from the W and to a lesser extent from the E. The entrance can be very rough in strong onshore winds. Tidal stream across the entrance up to 4kn.

Berthing Within the outer moles keep to the E side of the buoyed channel passing close to the series of three R Fl lt buoys until opposite the end of the old hbr mole marking the second inner entrance. Then turn to stb following a series of R channel lt buoys, keeping NW of them until a conspic memorial cross on the E bank. Then, hard to port and port again to the pontoons of the Royal Belgian Sailing Club at the W end of the Visserhaven. At night there are four sets of ldg lts to assist. All facilities and several restaurants near the hbr, but some shops are 15 mins walk away.

The entrance to the Boudewijnkanaal is now through the Pierre Vandamme sea lock approached from the Toegangsgeul. Call the lock on VHF 13. Boats with fixed masts can reach the centre of Brugge from Zeebrugge along this route.

BLANKENBERGE   Charts BA 325, B 11, N 1801.2
HW: Dover +1½h DS: HWD E, 5h W
MHWS 4.9m   MHWN 4.0   MTL 2.5   MLWN 1.0   MLWS 0.5

Approach and Entrance An important yachting centre, Blankenberge provides an easier entrance and quieter berthing than Zeebrugge except in strong NE to NW winds. The entrance is narrow, between two piers (F R & F G), neither of which should be confused with the Casino pier at the E end of the town. The lt ho Oc(2)8s32m20M is near the root of the E pier. The channel is dredged to more than 1.5m but is subject to silting, especially after onshore gales. It is safer not to enter within 1½ hours either side of low water. Ldg lts (F R) on 134° assist at night and are marked with red crosses for visibility during daylight. VHF 16 & 8.

Berthing The old yacht hbr lies at the end of the port arm, but the marina is reached through a narrow passage to stb, just after the main channel turns to port, marked by dolphins. Limited facilities, but water, electricity and fuel available on pontoons. Shops and restaurants are close at hand. Three YCs. Good bathing from the beaches. Fl Bu lt prohibits departure of craft of less than 6m LOA.

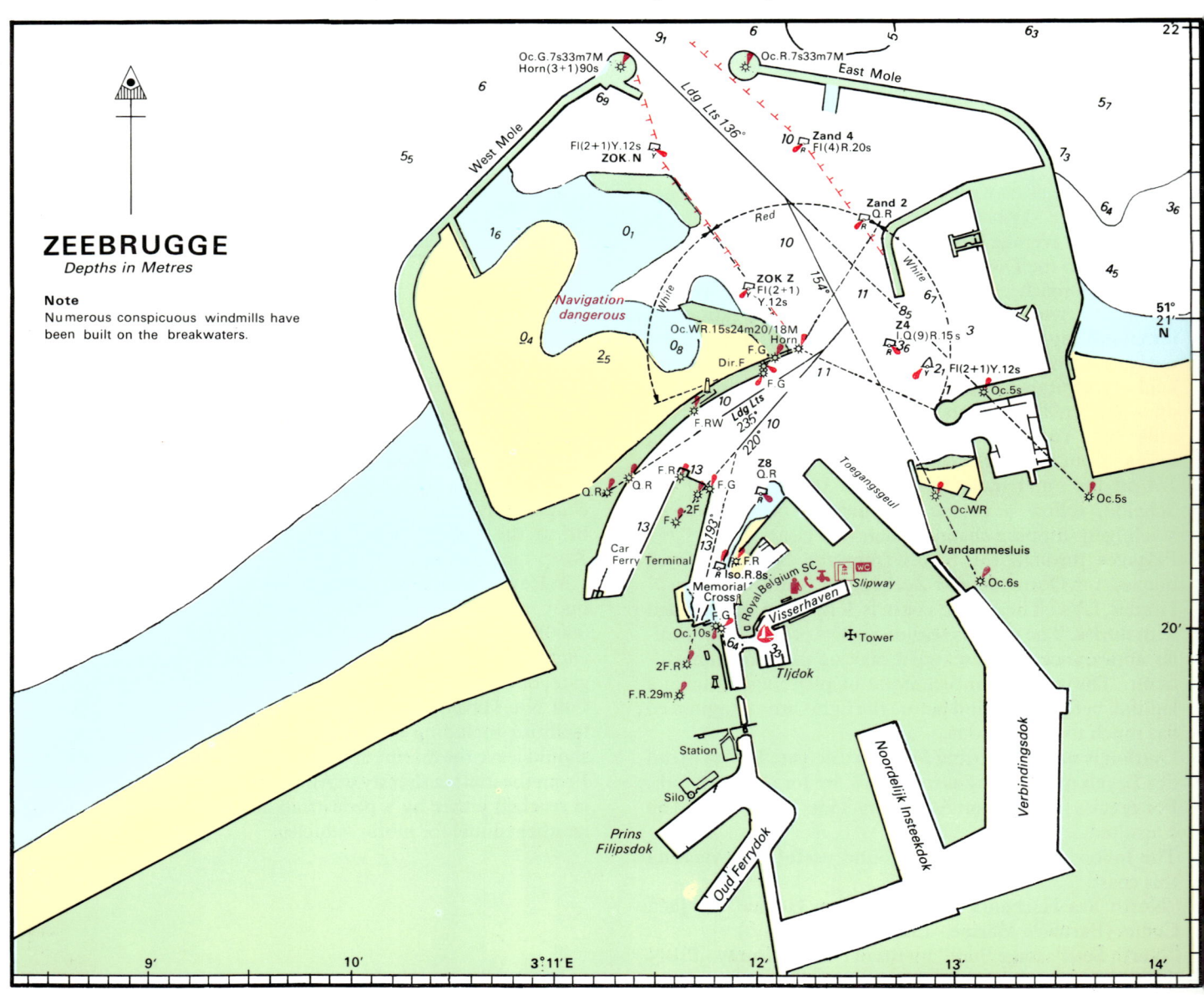

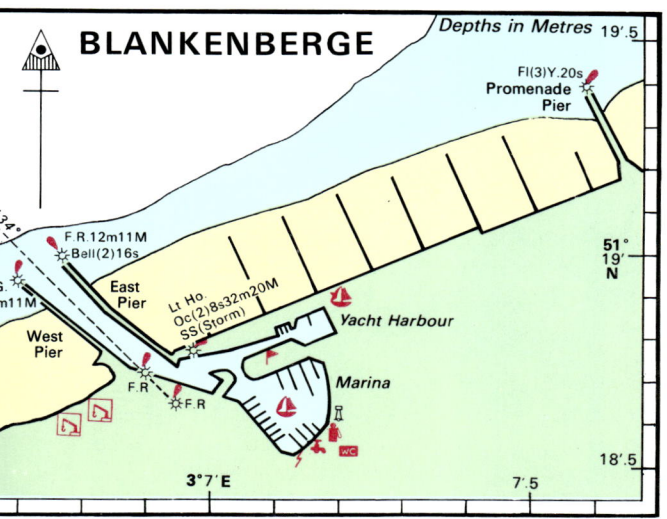

OOSTENDE   Charts BA 125, B11, N 1801.2
HW: Dover +3¼h   DS: Dover +¾h E, +4¾h W
MHWS 5.1m   MHWN 4.2   MTL 2.4   MLWN 1.1   MLWS 0.3

Approach and Entrance Oostende is a very busy commercial and ferry port with jetfoil services to Dover. A Fl Y Lt on the E pierhead, the YC and the entrance to Montgomerydok indicates that a large vessel is about to leave or enter, and small craft are not permitted to move. Apart from traffic, there are no navigational hazards in the approach, which may be made from the W close inshore via the Kleine Rede, or further out through the Grote Rede taking care to avoid the shoals on the Stroombank. From the E, the coastal passage is clear from Zeebrugge, whilst from the N the passage is buoyed through the banks until the N card (Q) Buitenstroombank and E card Q(3)10s Binnenstroombank buoys are reached. Port Control VHF 9.

Berthing There are tidal berths at the North Sea YC at the seaward end of the Montgomerydok which are liable to be affected by a disturbing scend from the harbour channel and the entry and departure of fishing vessels. A lock gives access to two basins of the Mercator yacht hbr in the centre of the town by the Central Station. It has limited facilities, but is cheaper and quieter if staying for more than one night. The Royal YC of Oostende has pontoon moorings at the SE end of the Voorhaven and good facilities with nearby shops. Mercator Yacht hbr VHF 14.

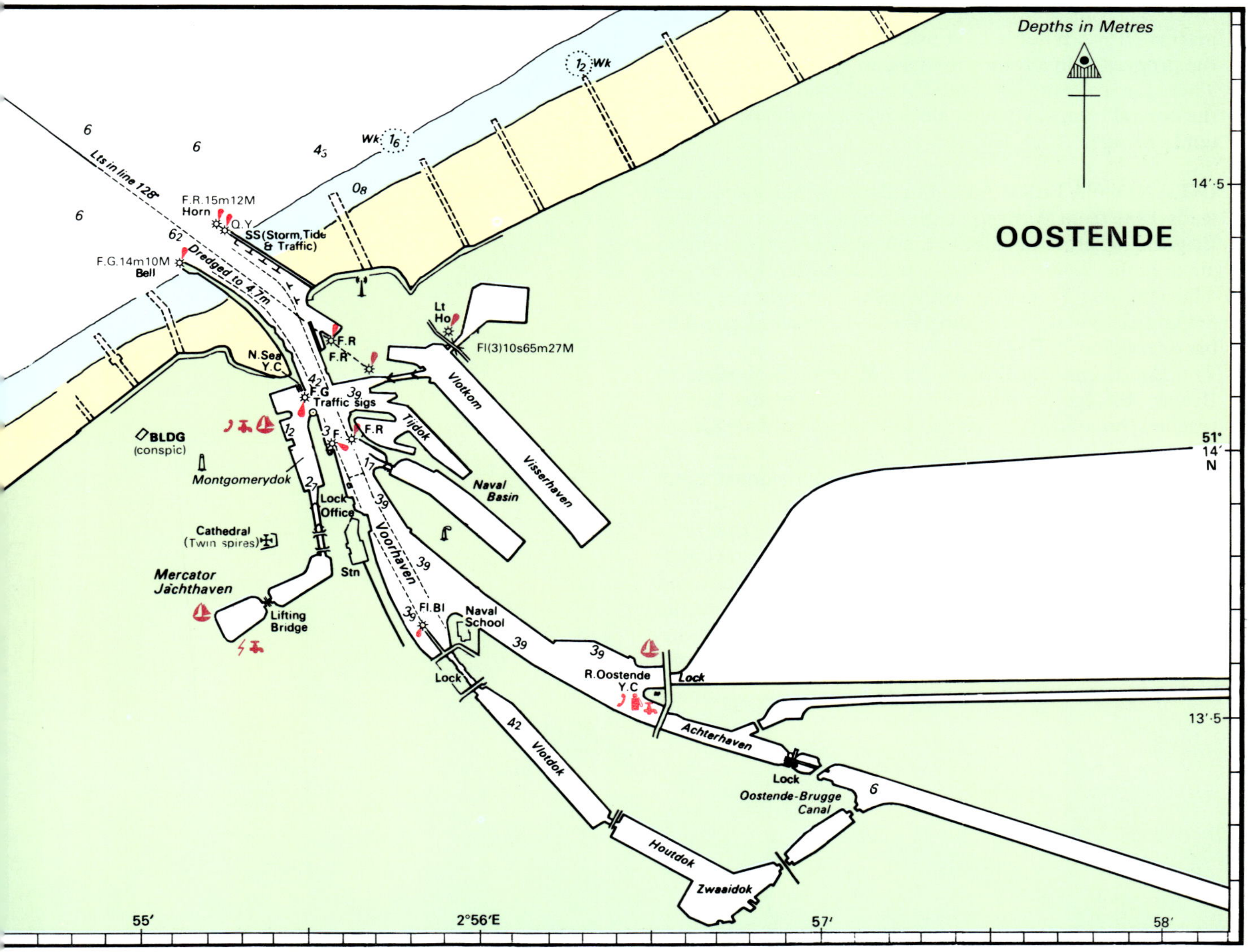

BELGIUM 296

NIEUWPOORT

Charts BA 1872 & 125, B11

HW: Dover +1h DS: Dover -1½h E, +5¾h W

MHWS 5.2m MHWN 4.3 MTL 2.4 MLWN 1.1 MLWS 0.2

Approach and Entrance The hbr entrance between two lattice piers is dredged to more than 1.5m but is subject to silting. The main lt ho Fl(2)R14s26m21M is a red tr with W horizontal bands and is situated at the root of the E pier. Take care to avoid the wreck, marked with a N card buoy, ½M N of the entrance. Enter parallel to the piers between the two white entrance trs (F R & F G lts). Beware cross-set off entrance. VHF 9.

Berthing The entrance channel divides after 1M with YCs and marinas in each branch. The channel to the E also leads to the fuel barge near the fishing hbr. The Nieuwpoort YC on the W branch has large premises with a restaurant. Showers, toilets, water and electricity are available, but shops are more than 20 mins walk away. Visiting yachts should moor alongside the HM office at the outer end of the first pontoon to obtain berthing instructions.

The second, much larger, yacht basin on the E branch houses the 2400 berth VVW marina. The town is reached by road and a br ½M away. However, bicycles are made available free of charge for shopping trips and can be hired for extended journeys. The YC has an excellent and reasonably priced restaurant. In the NE corner of the basin, and directly ahead on entering, is the Royal Belgian Air Force YC which has its own facilities including two restaurants.

Fuel is obtained from a grey-painted barge on stb as you enter the fishing hbr which is 200m up-river from the marina. It is advisable to consult the HM and telephone the proprietor in advance to make an appointment.

There is a frequent service to Oostende and Zeebrugge on the coastal tramway which also gives access close to Oostende airport.

INLAND WATERWAYS The Brussels Maritime canal leads 18M from Antwerp with opening bridges as far as Brussels, where the bridge to the Avant port has only 6.7m air-draught. There are 3 locks and a least depth of 5m.

The 34M long Terneuzen-Ghent canal has a least depth of 8m and allows large sea-going vessels to reach Ghent. The brs operate on VHF 11.

The Boudewijnkanaal leads for 5M from Zeebrugge to Bruges (Brugge) with a depth of 7m. Brugge may also be reached from Oostende via the 40M long Oostende-Ghent canal which has a least depth of 3.4m to Brugge and 2.3m between Brugge and Ghent. This is a mast-down route with several fixed bridges and a max air height of 4m.

The most important inland waterway system is that linking the Schelde to the waterways of The Netherlands, Belgium and France through the Antwerp-Rotterdam and Albert canals respectively. The latter connects with the Meuse and so to the extensive canal system of France. (See "Notes on French Inland Waterways" - published by the C.A.)

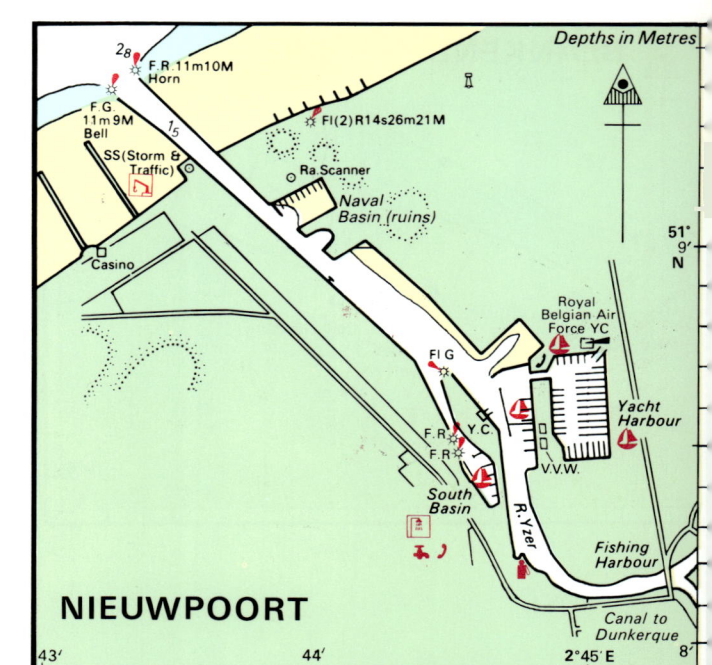

Other publications by the Cruising Association include:

Notes on the French Inland Waterways (1988)
Edited by Vernon Marchant

Yachtsman's Guide to the London River (1987)
Compiled by Donald Willis

and jointly with the Royal Yachting Association:

Planning a Foreign Cruise CI/91
Covers England, Sweden, Norway, Denmark, Germany, Netherlands, Belgium, France & Ireland.

Planning a Foreign Cruise C2/92
Covers Spain, Portugal, Gibraltar, Mediterranean France, Italy, Yugoslavia, Malta, Greece, Cyprus & Turkey

Available direct from the Cruising Association, Ivory House, St. Katharine Dock, London E1 9AT

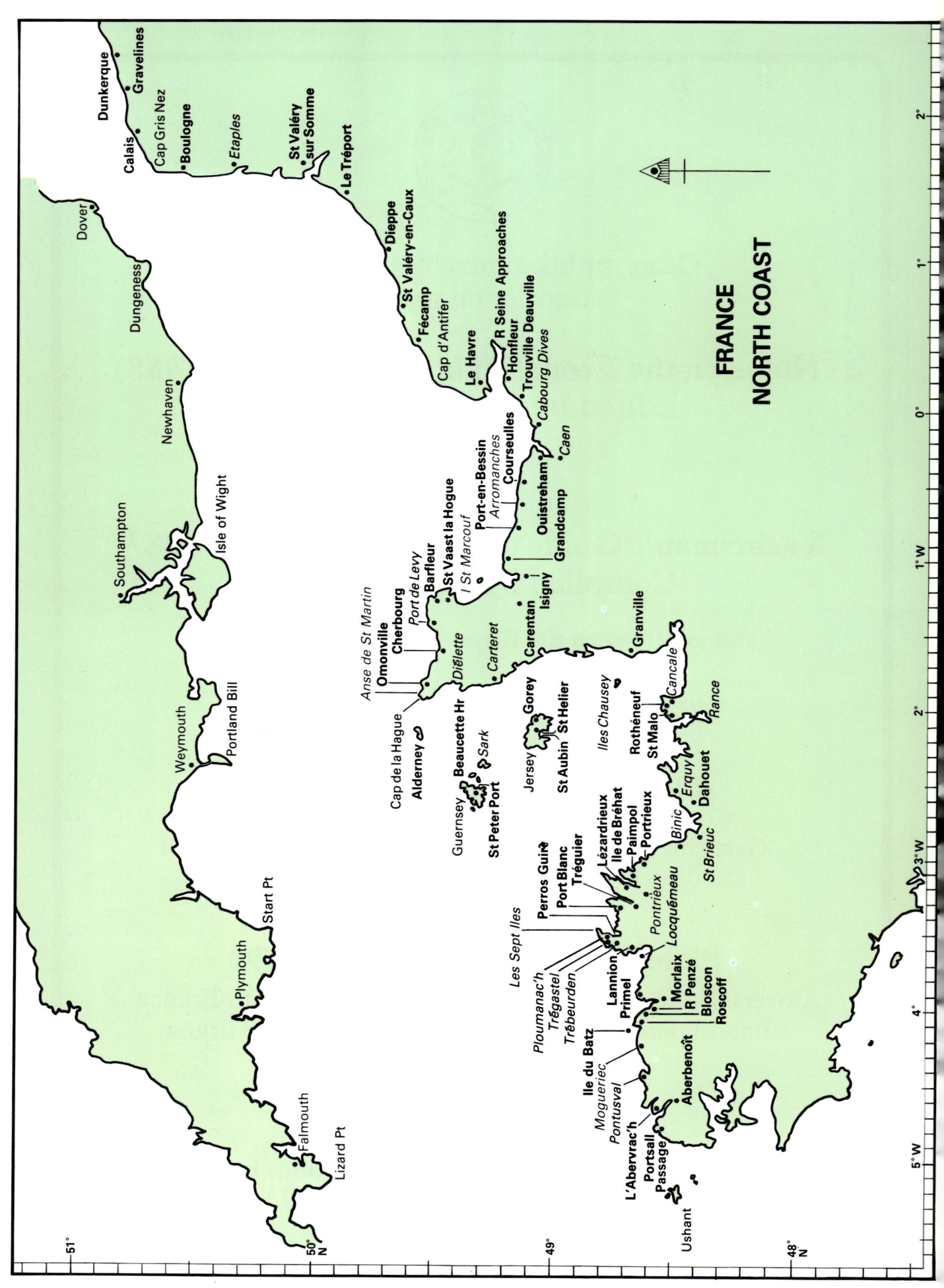

FRANCE

For many British yachtsmen France is the nearest foreign country to which to cruise. It also has simple entry formalities, good buoyage, excellent shore lights and a wide range of harbours, marinas and anchorages. The navigation required varies from fairly straightforward in Normandy to very challenging in some passages off Brittany.

Basically any pleasure craft under the command of its owner, not being used for commercial purposes and not carrying dutiable stores in excess of the normal allowances, is free to come and go without formality: for such a craft it is not necessary to fly a Q flag. But it is essential to carry a copy of the current edition of CA/RYA 'Planning a Foreign Cruise' to know the complications that may arise if the owner wishes to leave the boat, change crews, stay more than six months or carry excess dutiable stores; and to know what documents are required and what background literature is available.

Pink-dyed fuel at the lower tax rate as supplied to fishing boats cannot be bought for yachts; nor can domestic fuel oil. Fuel carried in a boat's fixed tanks is not charged duty but fuel carried in spare cans may be.

If crossing to France E of the Greenwich meridian the Dover Straits Traffic Separation Lanes must be crossed. Rule 10 of the Collision Regulations must be observed – traffic in this area is closely supervised. Remember that the lanes must be crossed at right-angles: that is the course to steer, not the course made good. Listen on VHF 16 and also, if possible, on VHF 11 for broadcasts from the Information Service.

The following books may be found to be of particular value as supplementing the information in this Handbook. 'Normandy and Channel Islands Pilot' by Mark Brackenbury (Adlard Coles); 'French Pilot' Vols 1 to 4 and 'Channel Islands Pilot' both by Malcolm Robson (Nautical Publishing Co), very good on transit lines and inshore passages; Votre Livre de Bord (Mer du Nord - Manche - Atlantique) (Bloc Marine). Also recommended are the Admiralty 'Channel Pilot' and 'Pilote Côtier Fenwick' by Alain Rondeau (Praxys Diffusion), in French; Vols 4 to 7 cover the W coast of France from the Spanish frontier to Dieppe. Excellent illustrations.

Charts for coastal passages will be required. There are those of the British Admiralty and the French Service Hydrographique et Océanographique de la Marine; and proprietary charts published by Imray (Imray, Laurie, Norie & Wilson), or Stanford Maritime; and the French 'Cartes Guides Navigation Côtière' (by Editions Maritimes et d'Outre Mer). The latter have an ingenious system for showing the characteristics of lights.

FRENCH INLAND WATERWAYS

GENERAL INFORMATION AND CRUISE PLANNING

Only a brief summary can be included here. For more detailed information see the separate Cruising Association publication "Notes on French Inland Waterways" edited by Vernon Marchant.

The inland waterway system of France is an extensive network which covers a great part of the country and connects with the waterways of Belgium, Holland and Germany. From a yachtsman's point of view it has a twofold attraction: as a route between sea cruising areas and as an interesting cruising area in its own right.

When planning an inland voyage, remember that locks and sections of canals are sometimes closed for repairs and maintenance. It is essential to obtain the current programme of closures (chômages) which is available about the end of March each year from the French Government Tourist Office, 178 Piccadilly, London, WIV OAL.

Dimensions: The maximum dimensions for a yacht going from the UK to the Mediterranean via the main French canals are: length 38.50m, beam 5.05m, draught 1.80m, height 3.50m. On the Burgundy route the maximum height is only 3.10m.

For the Canal du Midi between the Atlantic and the Mediterranean maximum dimensions are: length 30.00m, beam 5.50m, draught 1.60m, height 3.00m at the centre of bridge arches reducing to 2.00m at the sides.

On the Brittany route between the English Channel and the Atlantic maximum dimensions are: length 25.80m, breadth 4.50m, draught 1.20m, height 2.50m.

The Seine as far as Paris is navigable by boats drawing up to 3.00m with height up to 6.00m.

N.B. Do not place too much reliance on published figures for depths. On some canals silting has taken place, and water levels are sometimes reduced in very dry weather. Even in normal conditions there are not many mooring places with full depth alongside.

Through Routes (see map)

The popular route southwards through France is from Le Havre up the River Seine via Rouen to Paris, 368km, 6 locks. Thence to the R Saône by one of the following routes.

The Bourbonnais (Western) Route Paris to Lyon, 643 km, 157 locks. Some locks are automatic. Moderate commercial and pleasure traffic. The easiest and quickest route.

The Burgundy Route Paris to Lyon, 629km, 219 locks. Beautiful but slow. Locks have restricted opening arrangements on certain days of the week. Almost no commercial traffic but many hire boats during the summer season.

The Marne (Eastern) Route Paris to Lyon, 713km, 155 locks. Carries a fair amount of commercial traffic at times. Some locks are closed on Sundays. A pleasant route, quicker than the Burgundy but slower than the Bourbonnais.

All these routes involve the passage of the rivers Saône and Rhône. From Lyon to the mouth of the Rhône is 321km, 12 locks.

Inland Waterways of France
Cruise Planning Map

FRENCH INLAND WATERWAYS

1. CANAL DE CALAIS
2. LA LIAISON AU GRAND GABARIT
3. CANAL DE BOURBOURG
20. CANAL DE L'OISE A L'AISNE
21. CANAL DES ARDENNES
22. CANAL DE L'EST NORTH BRANCH
23. CANAL DE LA MARNE AU RHIN
24. CANAL DES HOUILLÈRES DE LA SARRE
25. GRAND CANAL D'ALSACE
26. CANAL DE L'EST (SOUTH BRANCH)
27. CANAL DU RHÔNE AU RHIN
28. CANAL DU NORD
29. CANAL DE ST QUENTIN
30. CANAL DE LA SAMBRE A L'OISE
31. CANAL DE LA SOMME
32. TANCARVILLE CANAL
33. CANAL DE L'OURCQ
34. CANAL LATÉRAL À LA MARNE
35. CANAL DE LA MARNE À LA SAÔNE
37. CANAL DE BOURGOGNE
38. CANAL DU NIVERNAIS
39. CANAL DU LOING
40. CANAL DE BRIARE
41. CANAL LATÉRAL À LA LOIRE
43. CANAL DU CENTRE
45. CANAL DU RHÔNE A SETE
46. CANAL D'ILLE ET RANCE
47. CANAL DU BLAVET
48. CANAL DE NANTES À BREST
49. CANAL LATÉRAL A LA GARONNE
50. CANAL DU MIDI

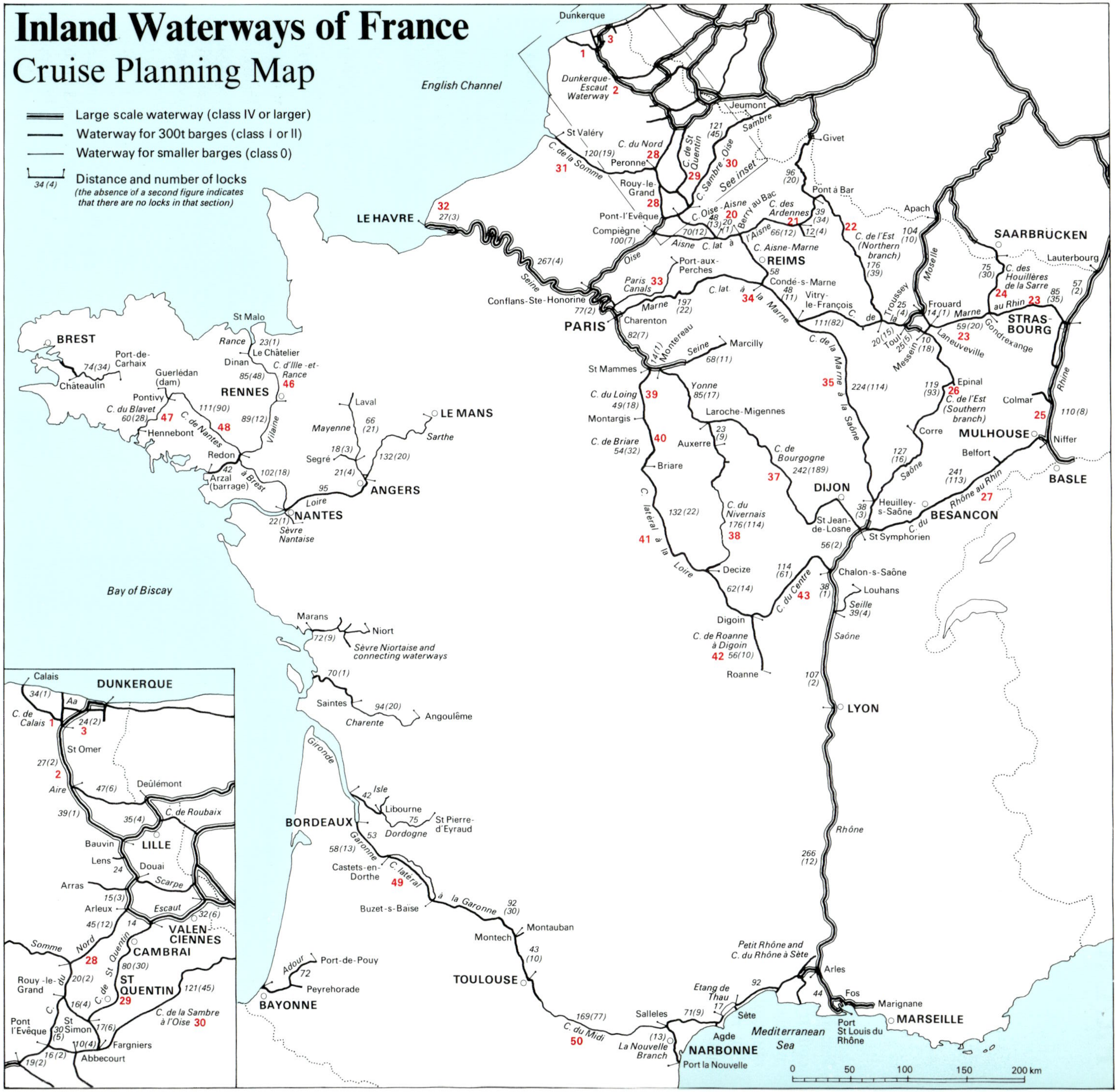

301 *FRANCE, NORTH COAST*

The Rhône is now completely canalised but there is still a considerable current in places. In normal times this nowhere exceeds 4kn but when flood water is coming down it may reach 6kn. Strong winds can create difficult conditions on some stretches. At such times the river is dangerous.

Do not attempt to go out to sea through the Rhône delta; there are constantly shifting dangerous sandbanks. If eastbound, lock out of the river at Port St Louis from where a short canal leads into the Golfe de Fos.

If westbound in the Mediterranean, vessels drawing not more than about 1.50m can turn out of the Rhône 2km upstream of Arles into the Petit Rhône. This leads into the Canal du Rhône à Sète and so into the sea either at Aigues Mortes or Sète.

Other Routes

The Midi Route From Bordeaux to the Mediterranean at Sète, 503km, 139 locks, This provides a direct route from the Atlantic to the Mediterranean. From Bordeaux to Castets, where the canal begins, the R Garonne is still tidal and there are shallows. From Castets the Canal Latéral à la Garonne leads to Toulouse and from there the Canal du Midi runs to Sète.

Brittany Canals From the English Channel to the Bay of Biscay via St Malo, Dinan, Rennes, Redon, and the R Vilaine, 254km, 63 locks.

Routes from Northern France It is also possible to enter the waterways at Dunkerque, Gravelines, Calais or St Valéry-sur-Somme.

Charts should be taken, at least for the major rivers, e.g. the Seine and Rhône, or the Garonne. They are less important for other waterways, but they add to the interest of the voyage.

Two series of strip charts are available, the 'E.C.M. Cartes-Guides' and the 'Vagnon Cartes-Guides'. Both series have English translations and contain much useful information. They are available from specialist book-sellers in England.

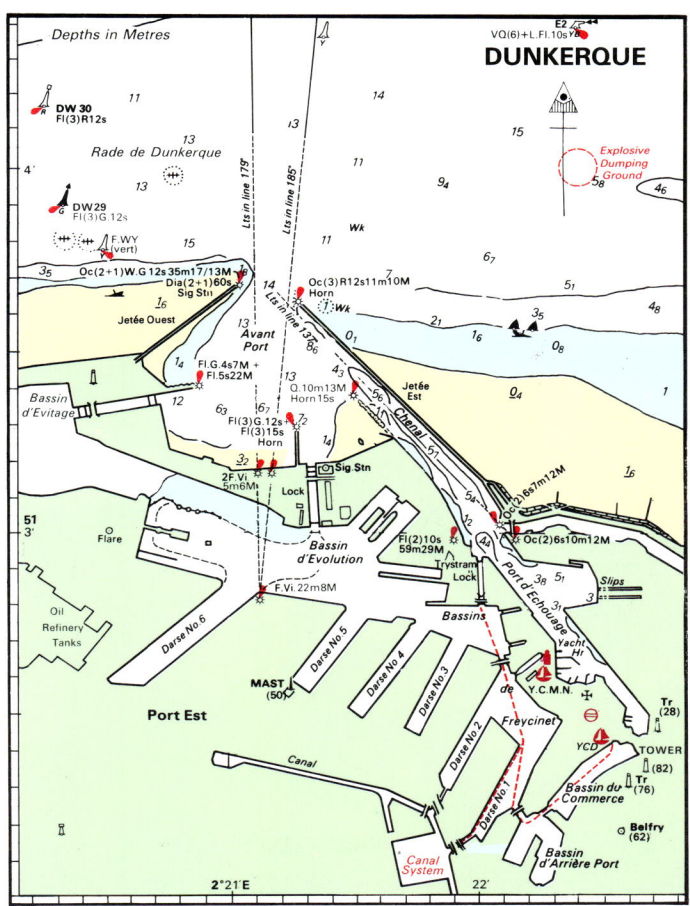

FRENCH CHANNEL PORTS

DUNKERQUE   Charts BA 1350, F 7057
HW: Dover +1h. DS: Dover −2h E; +4h W.
MHWS 5.8m   MHWN 4.7   MTL 3.2   MLWN 1.5   MLWS 0.6
A busy commercial hbr, good shelter for yachts and good facilities. A possible entry to the canal system.

Approach from E or W along one of the inshore buoyed channels. The offshore banks dry at LAT and should not be crossed even at HW except in light winds.

Signals Traffic signals (full Fr code) from main lt ho.

Entrance Straightforward except for strong cross-set across entrance. At night enter on one of two ldg lines 179° and 185° (both F Vi 6M) and then keep along E breakwater on ldg lts both Oc(2) 6s 12M, 137°, through Avant Port (the two locks out of this basin lead into W hbr – yachts not allowed). Trystram lock, to stb just past lt ho leads into inner basins, canal system and non-tidal marina. Otherwise continue to tidal marina. Trystram lock opens at fixed times between 0800 and 1930. Consult Capitainerie, VHF 73.

Canal Entry Clearing the lock, make for the first lifting br (opening co-ordinated with locking); avoid the basin immediately to stb but continue past it round to stb into Darse No 1 at the end of which is the canal lock.

Berthing (1) Yacht Club de la Mer du Nord tidal marina. About 60 visitors' berths, 3.85m. (Two private marinas further up have no visitors' berths.)

(2) Yacht Club de Dunkerque marina, non-tidal, 5m. Follow instructions for canal entry but about 1½ ca before the far lock turn to port under a second lifting br (opens a few minutes after the first) and then turn to port again into Bassin du Commerce. Moor at first pontoon. Advisable to book in first week of June when racers congregate.

Supplies Fuel at YCMN, water at both marinas.

Tel/VHF YCD (28) 66-11-06; YCMN (28) 66-79-90; Port Control (28) 65-99-22/ ch 12, 73, 16; Customs (28) 65-14-73.

DUNKERQUE OUEST, 7M W of Dunkerque is a tanker and ferry terminal; yachts are forbidden except in emergency. (N.B. Crew arriving on the ferry from Ramsgate will land here and not at Dunkerque.)

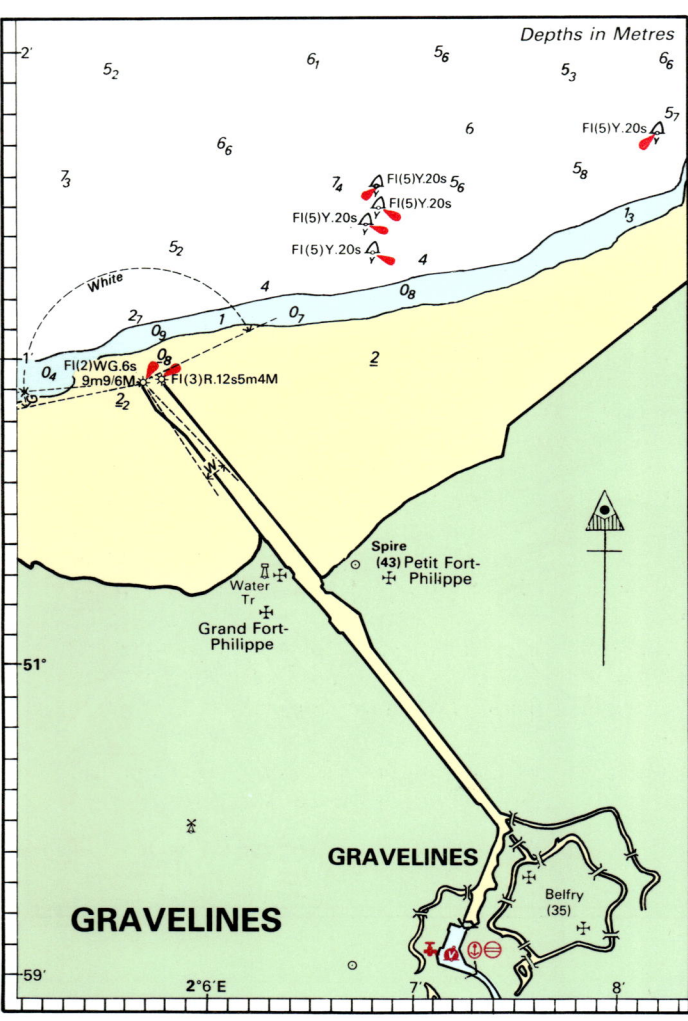

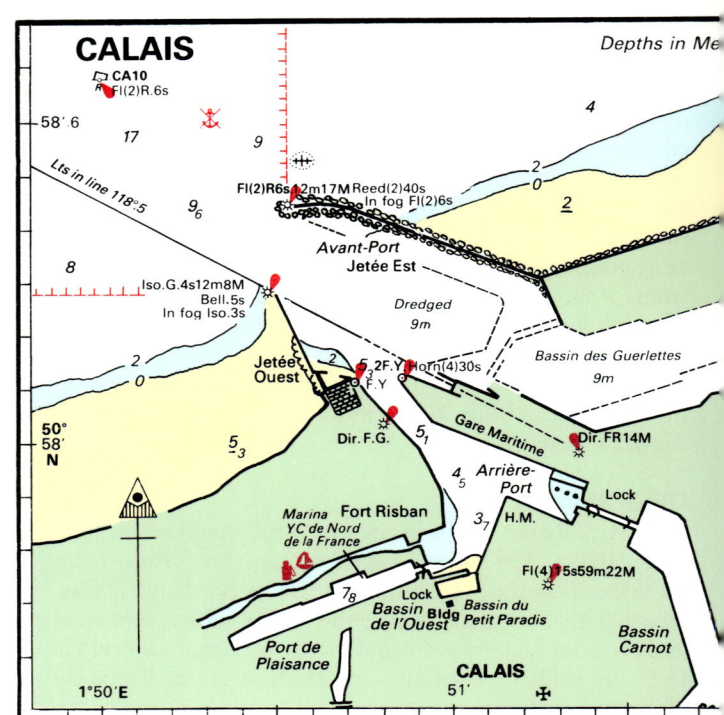

GRAVELINES   Chart BA 1350, F 7057
HW: Dover +¾h. DS: Dover −4h W; −1h E. Slack +5h to −5h

MHWS 5.9m MHWN 4.8 MTL 3.2 MLWN 1.4 MLWS 0.5
A small fishing port on the mouth of River Aa with long drying entrance, a non-tidal basin and access to canal system.

Approach Entrance, 2½M W of Dunkerque Ouest, can be identified by water tower to W of entrance and spire to E, with villages of Grand- and Petit-Fort-Phillipe on either side.

Entrance dries; access is only possible from HW−3h to HW, is difficult in fresh onshore winds and should not be attempted in such winds over F5. Beware strong E-going set across entrance. Lock opens from ¾h to 1h either side of HW between neaps and springs. Canal lock at far end of basin open HW±1½h.

Berthing there are drying pontoons (soft mud) off Petit-Fort-Phillipe on E bank and also outside the lock while waiting. In the non-tidal basin there are seven visitors' berths; sometimes part of the basin dries when level is lowered to take flood water from Aa but 2m is available at some of them.

Supplies Fuel from garage, water at marina.
Tel/VHF HM (28) 23-13-42/ch 24, 61; Customs (28) 23-08-52.

CALAIS   Charts BA 1352, F 6474
HW: Dover +½h. DS: Dover −2h E; +3½h W
MHWS 7.2m MHWN 6.0 MTL 4.1 MLWN 2.2 MLWS 1.0
A busy ferry and commercial port with a non-tidal basin for yachts and access to the canal system.

Approach To the N of the entrance is the bank Ridens de la Rade which at MLWS has only ½m in places. In winds of F6 or more from NW to NE it is wiser to make for Boulogne; otherwise the bank may be crossed safely at H±3h. With less water keep S of the R buoys S of the shoal when coming from W; from E keep at least 2M offshore and do not make for the entrance until the W jetty head bears about 100° – in bad weather keep on round SW end of the bank.

Signals The full French code of three lts (R and/or W, G) at signal station applies to ferries and large craft only; but if more than three lights are on display yachts should not enter or leave. The additional lts are for ferries (R leaving, G entering) or tankers (2R leaving, R/G entering), when movement by all other craft is forbidden. A single R lt denotes dredging – movement allowed with care. It is possible to follow an entering ferry, keeping to stb. If in doubt call Port Control on VHF 12.

Entrance Beware strong cross current; keep W jetty close to stb and bear to stb round Fort Risban (beware shallows) for entrance to yacht basin. For the canals lock into Bassin Carnot, then a second lock into Bassin de la Batellerie and thence under br to port.

Berthing Yachts berth in Bassin de l'Ouest (Calais YC); br opens at HW−2h, HW and HW+1h. Amber lt gives 10 min warning of opening. There are waiting buoys in Avant Port; if full, wait alongside quays on E and S sides of Avant Port (dry); concrete blocks are reported at foot of wall opposite Fort Risban, dangerous at less than half tide. Scend can be severe in Avant Port.

Supplies Diesel and water at marina; petrol from garage. Crane for demasting at YC.
Tel/VHF (21) 96-31-20/ch 12; Port de Plaisance (21) 34-55-23; YC (21) 34-60-00.

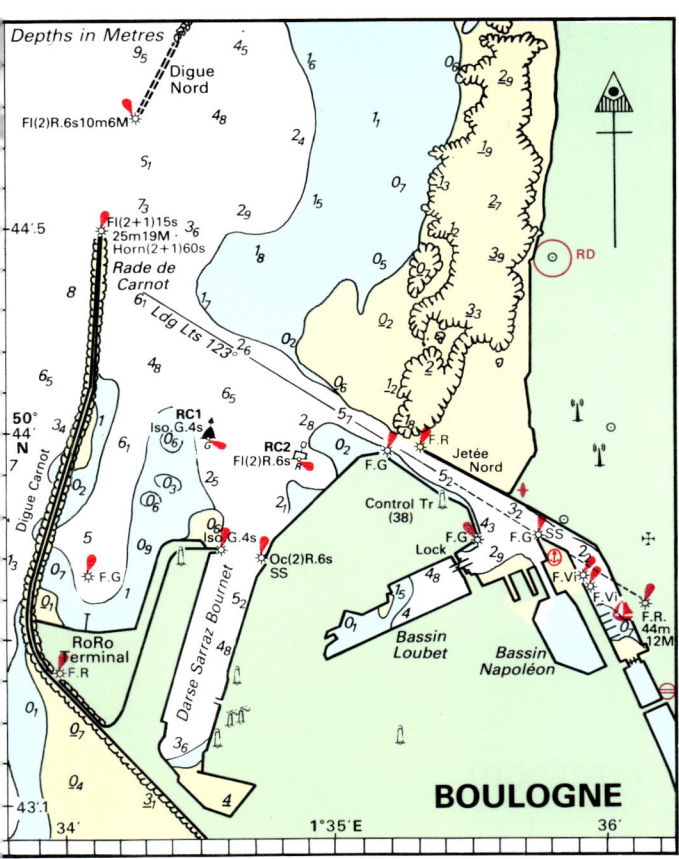

ETAPLES (and Le Touquet)   Chart F 6795
HW: Dover. DS: Dover −2¾h N; +3¼h S
MHWS 8.8m   MHWN 7.1   MTL 4.8   MLWN 2.6   MLWS 0.9
The drying estuary of the River Canche. Le Touquet is a popular holiday resort: beware sailboards, dinghies and swimmers.

Approach The approach is impracticable with strong winds from SW through W to NE because of breakers. It should be attempted only in daylight in settled weather between HW −1h and HW, preferably before springs to avoid the risk of being neaped. (There is 3m at springs but only 1m at neaps.) Identify La Canche lt tr (Or octagonal with brown band) at Le Touquet, S of entrance, and the heights of Terres de Tourmont, 175m, to N.

Entrance Channel is marked by buoys and beacons, altered to meet changes. The first pair is usually about ½M W of Pte de Lornel, whence the course is on the N side of the estuary. After the buoys, usually four pairs, the channel to Étaples is marked by port bns. If bound for Le Touquet, make for the YC, on E side of Pte du Touquet, after the first bn.

Berthing There is a small drying basin at Le Touquet. At Étaples, there is a marina for small yachts; mooring difficult save at slack HW. Accessible HW±2h, open to NW.

Supplies Water at Le Touquet YC or on quay at Étaples. Fuel from garages. Good shops at Le Touquet.

BOULOGNE   Chart BA 438, F 6436
HW: Dover. DS: Dover +4¼h S; −2½h N
MHWS 8.9m   MHWN 7.1   MTL 5.0   MLWN 2.8   MLWS 1.1
A busy ferry, fishing and commercial port with marina. Accessible at all times.

Approach The sea breaks heavily on the Bassure de Baas shoals, N and S of the entrance in gales from SW to NW, when it is best to keep 3M offshore until entrance bears E; otherwise from S keep about 1½M offshore inside the shoal. From W make for ZC1 Y buoy, Oc(3) Y 6s, and head E. The cathedral tr is prominent behind the town as is the tall Colonne de la Grande Armée (145m).

Signals Full code (three lts, R and/or W, G) is shown from signal mast at Darse Sarraz Bournet for entry to outer hbr and from SW pierhead of inner hbr for entry to the latter, G over W over R prohibits all movements in inner hbr.

Entrance Yachts over 10m must get permission to enter and berthing instructions on VHF 12. The N breakwater is submerged for its outer ½M with the outer end marked by a wooden tr, Fl(2) R 6s, (Ldg lts front F G, rear F R, 197°, lead on to Ro Ro berth). 1 ca inside S pier steer S until inner piers open (ldg lts 123°), then steer for inner hbr.) Follow round the N side for the marina but be alert for movements of ferries and fishing boats to stb.

Berthing Yachts up to 10m moor at pontoons of YC Boulonnais on stb side past ferry terminal; 2.4m at outer ends but only 1m near quay. Grid at far end. Moorings are rarely available in Arrière Port.

Supplies Fuel from garage; water at marina.

Tel/VHF HM (21) 30-10-00; Control Tr (21) 31-52-43/ch 12; Port de Plaisance (21) 31-70-01. Fuel delivery (21) 31-63-29. Customs (21) 30-14-24.

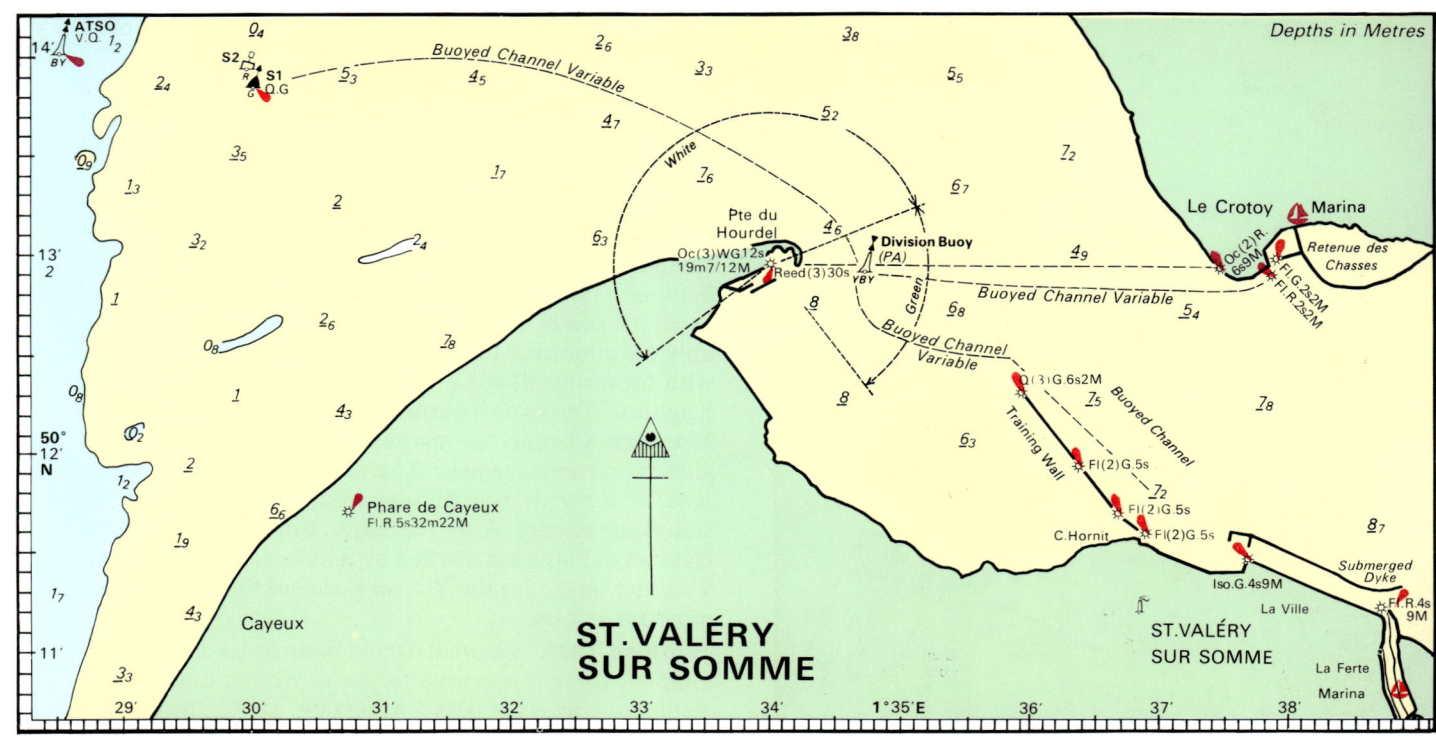

SOMME ESTUARY
Chart F 7084.

HW: Le Hourdel, Dover +¼h; St Valéry +½h. DS: Dover −2¼h NNE, +3¼h SW

MHWS (Le Hourdel and St Valéry) 9.8m   MHWN 7.9

The approaches and the estuary up to St Valéry dry; Le Crotoy is a small fishing village. St Valéry is somewhat larger with a marina and a lock giving access via the R Somme to the canal system. Only a few cottages at Le Hourdel.

Approach should not be attempted in strong onshore winds or in poor visibility. Coast is low-lying, prominent features being the lt ho of Ault (W tr, R top, 95m) 8M S of entrance and Cayeux (W tr, R top, 32m) about 3M SE of landfall buoy. Accurate navigation and timing are essential, to allow 2h (at 4kn) to reach St Valéry from the entrance.

Entrance Make for the Baie de Somme buoy, N card BY VQ, about 2¾M 325° from Cayeux lt ho. The positions of the channel buoys vary and the first pair (S1 and S2) may be anywhere from SE to NE of the card buoy. The channel winds — it is easy to mistake which pair to make for. It leads round Pte du Hourdel, ½M E of which a W card buoy separates the E-going Crotoy branch (1m MHWN), buoys marked C, from the SE major branch to St Valéry. Keep in the fairway of latter to clear submerged groynes off the land. Opposite St Valéry lt tr (W, G top) Iso G 4s, is a submerged groyne marked by R bns which should be given a clear berth. It leads to the embankment lt tr (W, R top) Fl R 4s opposite Pte La Ferté where the channel runs E of S to St Valéry and the lock and sluice of R Somme.

Berthing Anchor at Le Hourdel (dries, soft mud) or Le Crotoy (shallow draft boats may remain afloat). St Valery marina is after the quay. Visitors' moorings at end of each pontoon, 1.5m, accessible HW±2h; mooring difficult when stream running. If waiting for lock it is generally possible to tie alongside the work boat opposite the marina. Gate opens on request at HW − 1h to HW.

Supplies Water and petrol at marina. Diesel at garage. Shops at St Valéry and Crotoy; nothing at Le Hourdel.

Tel/VHF Marina (22) 26-91-64/ch 9.

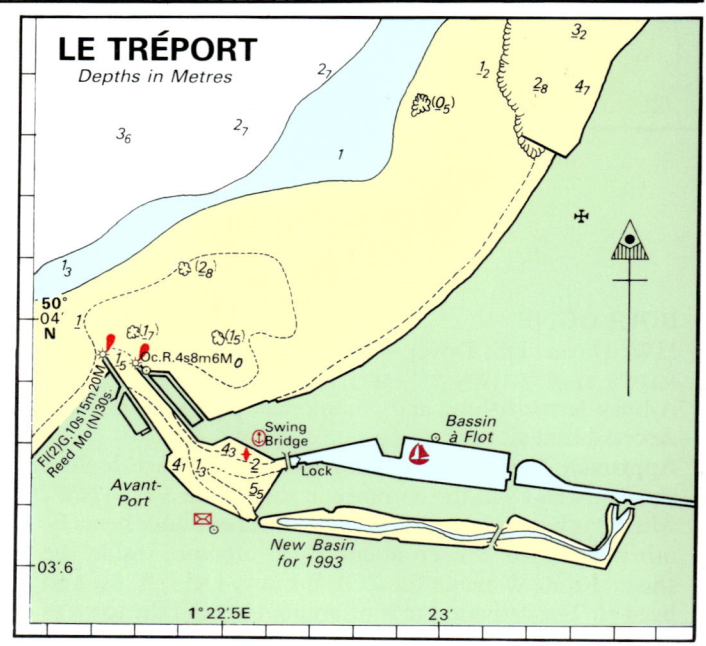

LE TRÉPORT
Chart BA 1352; F 934, 5928

HW: Dover. DS: Dover +2h SW; −4½h NE

MHWS 9.2m   MHWN 7.3   MTL 4.9   MLWN 2.3   MLWS 0.6

A small drying fishing port and holiday resort with wet basin.

Approach Difficult to identify by day. Distinguishable from adjacent towns by two clock trs or at night by W jetty lt Fl(2) G 10s 15m 20M. Difficult in strong onshore winds; severe scend in outer hbr in such conditions.

Entrance dries 1.5m, Avant Port dries 4.3m. From W keep E pierhead, lt Oc R, open of W pierhead, Fl(2) G, to clear off-lying rks. Allow for NE set, and squalls in entrance.

Berthing Yachtsmen must report to Capitainerie for instructions before entering inner hbr. Lie alongside NE wall (Quai Béllot), soft mud to await lock opening (HW −1½h to HW). Visitors' pontoon inside, limit 48h.

Supplies Water on quay; stores.

Tel/VHF Capitainerie (35) 86-17-91/ch 16, 12. Customs (35) 86-15-34.

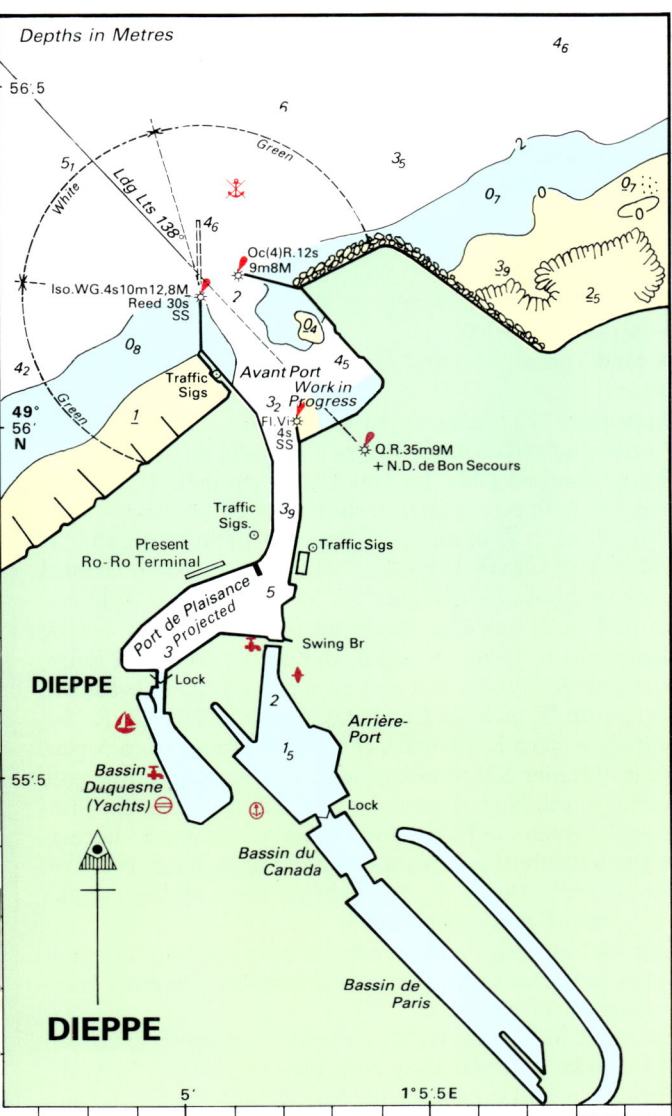

DIEPPE
Charts BA 2147   F7084

HW: Dover −¼h. DS: Dover −4¾h ENE; +1¼h WSW
MHWS 9.1m   MHWN 7.1   MTL 4.8   MLWN 2.4   MLWS 0.6

A busy ferry, fishing and commercial port with yacht berths. Accessible at all states of tide.

Approach is straightforward. Easily identified by ships in approaches and urban sprawl on land.

Signals must be obeyed by yachts (no room to pass a ferry at LW). Full code of entry displayed on W jetty ½ ca from seaward; for leaving, display is on W bank at N end of Avant Port, opposite signal mast; additional lts may be shown above normal signals; R or G for ferry entering or leaving, W for dock gates open, 2R dredger in channel. Simplified code at entry to inner basins.

Entrance Steer for W jetty hd and follow W wall to br and lock at end of Avant Port. Heavy swell in outer hbr in strong onshore winds. Some ferries turn in Avant port - listen on VHF 12.

Berthing in Bassin Duquesne; from Avant Port wait at pontoon W of br across entrance to the basin (swell from ferries and wind). Gates open HW −2h to +1h: bridge opens on hour and half hour, depending on road traffic. Pontoons and YC.

Work is in hand to provide new quays in the entrance for commercial traffic and for a Port de Plaisance in Avant Port. Ready possibly by 1995.

Supplies Fuel, water and all facilities.

Tel/VHF Port de Commerce (35) 84-10-55/ch 12, 6, 16; Port de Plaisance (35) 84-32-99; Customs (35) 82-24-47. Duquesne br VHF 9.

ST VALÉRY-EN-CAUX
Chart F 6794

HW: Dover −½h; DS: Dover −5h ENE; +1h WSW
MHWS 8.7m   MHWN 7.0   MTL 4.7   MLWN 2.3   MLWS 0.8

A holiday resort with non-tidal marina.

Approach Dangerous in strong winds from N to NE. From NE keep 1½M off to avoid shoals (0.6m) ENE of entrance. Hbr not easily identified: the Paluel nuclear power stn is 2½M W of entrance and there is a disused signal tr 1M W of lt ho (W, B top) Oc(1+2) G 12s.

Entrance dries 2.5m. Leave R posts marking wave-break ramp close to port to avoid shingle bank off W pier, then keep to mid-channel. On the flood there is an eddy across the entrance from E to W until HW +½h.

Berthing Possible to moor to quay at end of Avant Port (reputedly possible to remain afloat off the sluices on port side) or on buoys to wait for gates to inner harbour to open, HW±3h. Inside tie to pontoon on stb and report to hbr office.

Departing After the lock opening there can be a strong tidal surge in the outer hbr, especially at springs. It may be prudent to await the second br opening (½h intervals).

Supplies Fuel, water, shops.

Tel/VHF HM: (35) 97-01-30/ch 9.

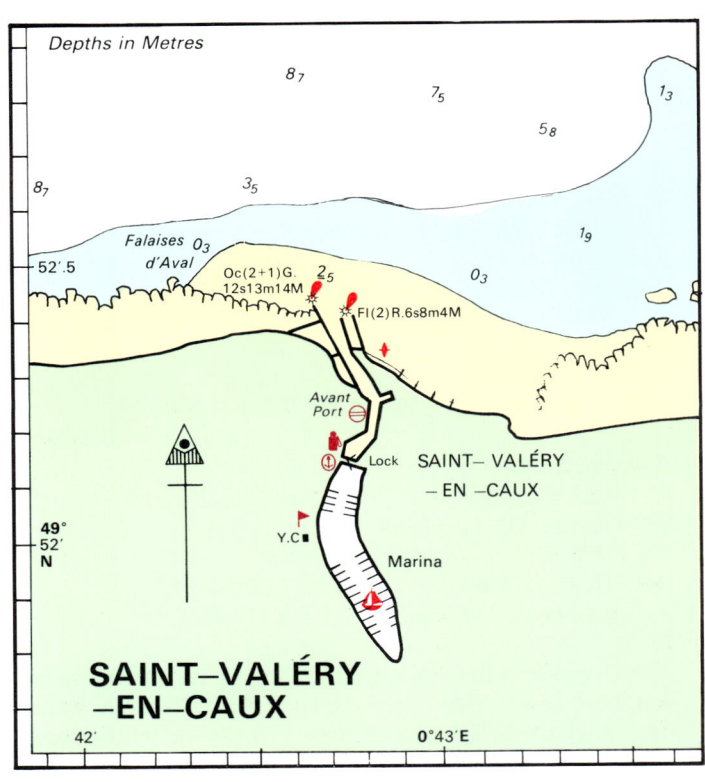

FRANCE, NORTH COAST   306

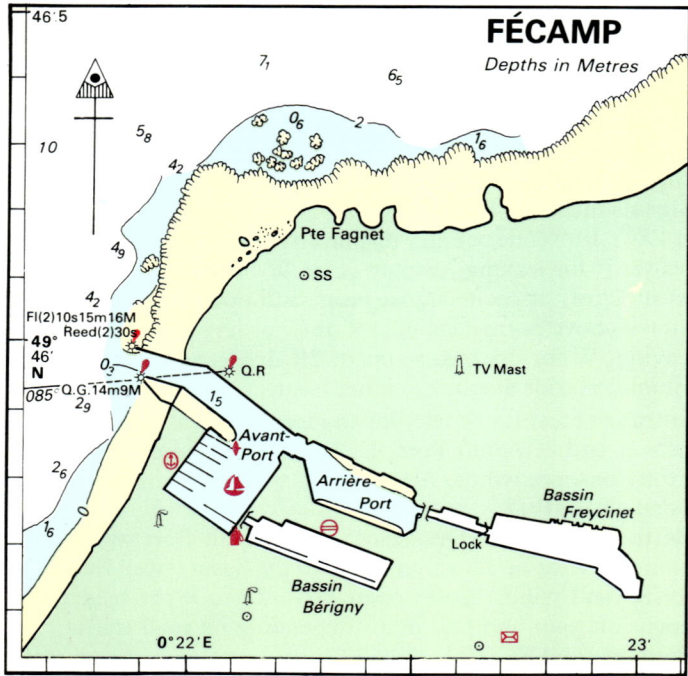

LE HAVRE   Chart BA 2990, 2146; F 6683

HW: Dover −1¼h

MHWS 7.8m   MHWN 6.5   MTL 4.5   MLWN 2.8   MLWS 1.1

DS off Le Havre is complicated by the flow from the Seine and an eddy close N of the entrance.

DS 3M W of Cap de la Hève: Dover −4¼h NE; +¾h SE; +2¾h SW

Close inshore of Cap de a Hève: Dover −3¼h NE; +¾h NW; +3¾h S

2M S of entrance: Dover −6¼h S; −4¼h E; −2¼ NE; −¼h slack; +¾h W

A busy commercial and ferry port and a major yachting centre.

Approach If coming down channel do not mistake the Antifer buoyed channel (buoys with letter A) for Le Havre (buoys marked LH). Le Havre has Cap de la Hève to N and two high power station chimneys, 250m on its S side. From N keep W of the spoil ground Y pillar buoy, Fl Y 4s 3M NW of Cap de la Hève, to enter the approach channel between buoys 10, Q R, and 12, VQ R. The area E of buoy 12 and N of the channel is uncomfortable and can be dangerous in fresh SW winds due to the Banc de l'Eclat, 0.1m, which produces a violent scend off the N breakwater. From W pick up Le Havre Lanby (RW Fl(2) R 10s) and then steer E for main channel. Coming from S pass close to Ratier NW G pillar buoy, VQ G; coming down the Seine, round No 6 R buoy, VQ R, to clear the shoals. Shoaling between Le Havre and Chenal de Rouen is increasing as a result of completion of the Digue Basse Nord on the N side of the latter. By night the same applies; ldg lts 107°, both F and intensified.

Signals Simplified code at head of N breakwater does not apply to yachts but it is essential to keep well away from ships near the entrance.

Entrance Ships have right of way in the channel; keep well to the side. After entering turn hard to port for the yacht hbr, and round the short spur beakwater running SE from Digue N, Fl(2) R 6s. For the Tancarville Canal pass the Thoresen Ferry quay to enter the small lock at the end of Bassin de la Manche (Arrière Port), cross the Bassin de la Citadelle into Bassin de l'Eure; turn hard to stb and take the first opening to port through the br into Bassin Fluvial, thence to Bassin Vétillart and into the canal. Get advice about opening times. If making for Le Havre from the Seine when conditions in the outer estuary are bad, it is better to enter the Canal at Tancarville; locks open HW (Le Havre) −4h to +3¼h.

Berthing Visitors on outer side of outer pontoon in outer basin of yacht hbr, stern to buoys. For longer stays the Bassin du Commerce is reserved for yachts and is more comfortable. In Avant Port bear to port for Bassin de la Manche; past the ferry terminals turn to port where two opening brs and a lock (sill 1.1m) open HW −2½h to −½h, and lead to the Bassin de Commerce, 3.5m.

Supplies Water at pontoons, fuel at SE corner of outer basin of yacht hbr, grid, and crane for unstepping masts.

Tel/VHF HM (35) 21-74-00/ch 12, 20; Port Ops ch 67, 69; Port de Plaisance (35) 21-23-95/ch 9; Customs (35) 41-24-34.

FÉCAMP   Chart BA 1352, F 932

HW: Dover −½h; DS: Dover +¼h SW; −5h NE

MHWS 7.7m   MHWN 6.4   MTL 4.3   MLWN 2.5   MLWS 0.7

A major fishing port with good tidal yacht moorings.

Approach Dangerous in strong onshore winds. SW of hbr are two square church trs (one with sloping top) and a water tr (conspic). Give wide berth to rks N of entrance; Pte Fagnet semaphore in view guarantees 3.7m.

Signals Simplified code from mast on SW jetty (not always used). Additional flag P when dock gates open.

Entrance is dredged 1.5m. Heavy swell frequent; in strong onshore winds attempt only from HW −2h to +1h. Outside anchorage in good conditions for deep draught yachts waiting for water; holding poor. Best approach 085°; ldg lts 085° QR (rear) and QG on SW jetty hd; beware spit running W from latter and cross-set onto rks during flood. At end of entrance channel turn to stb for yacht berths.

Berthing at pontoons in Avant Port (outer end of Pontoon C, 1.2m, severe scend at times) or in Bassin Bérigny (gates open HW −2h to HW). If Avant Port berths full report to Capitainerie.

Supplies Diesel, water, shops.

Tel/VHF HM (35) 28-13-58/ch 9. Yacht hbr (35) 28-16-35.

PASSAGE NOTES: FÉCAMP TO LE HAVRE
        Chart BA 2613.

Passage Lights

Cap d'Antifer	Fl 20s 128m 29M
Antifer Oil Terminal	
SW jetty	QR 9M
Cap de la Hève	Fl 5s 123m 24M
Le Havre RW Lanby	Fl(2) R 10s 20M

Give a good berth to oil terminal S of Cap d'Antifer; there can be a vicious tide race for up to 2M off. Tankers leave the entrance at speed and have priority in the buoyed channel. The coast is then clean to Cap de la Hève.

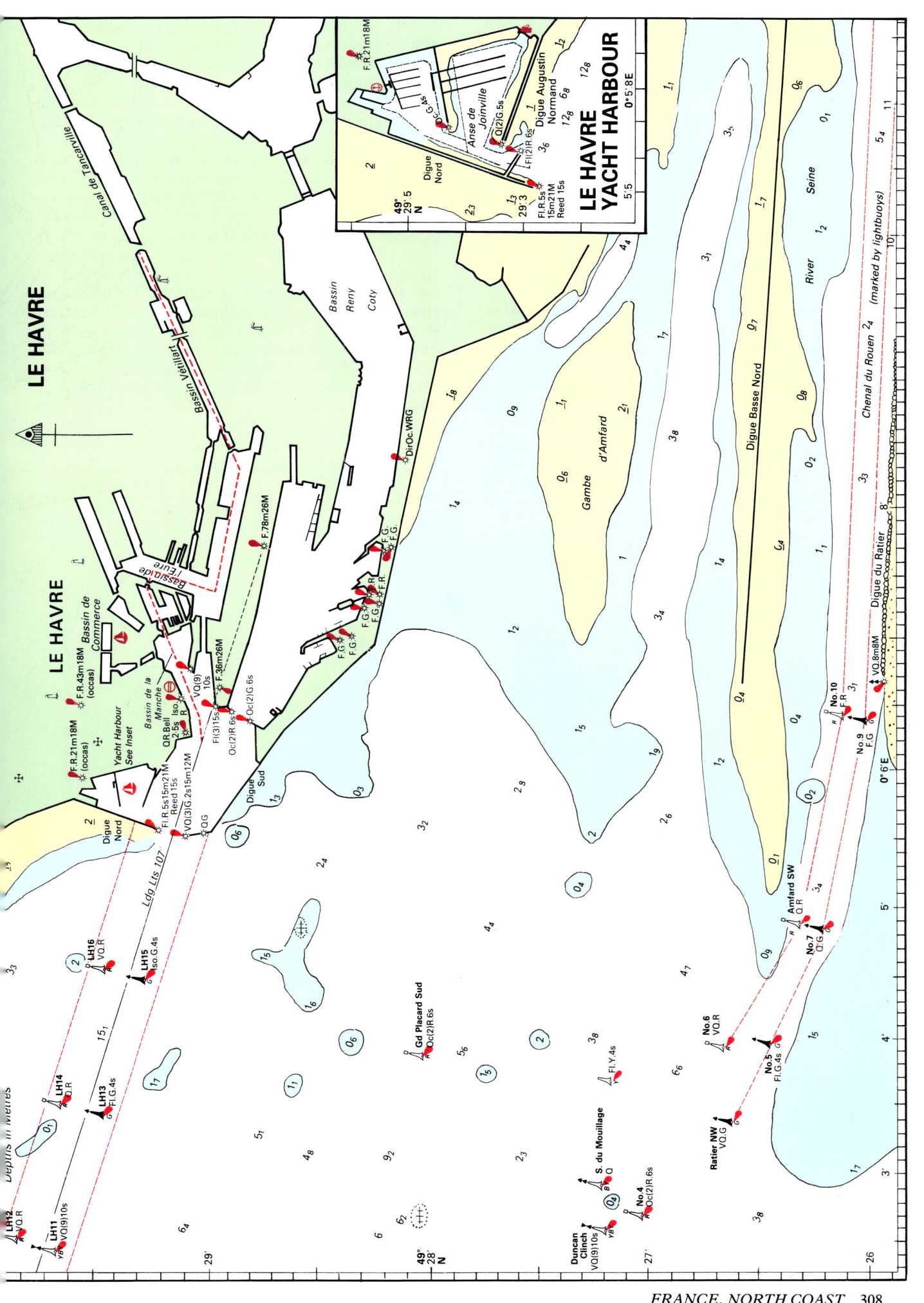

SEINE ESTUARY
Charts BA 2994, F 6796

Navigation of the Seine to Rouen and Paris is described in outline in Cruising Association booklet 'Notes on French Inland Waterways' and in detail in the Carte-Guide Navigation Fluviale, 'La Seine aval du Havre à Paris' (Editions Cartographiques Maritimes). It is navigable with masts stepped to Rouen maritime docks where basic facilities in Bassin St Gervais exist only for short stay to lower masts. With masts only 5.7m above WL yachts can pass the Rouen brs at Highest Navigable Water Level and berth in the marina on the N side of the island above the fourth bridge; a height of 12m is said to be passable at MLW, but it would be prudent to check this with the sea or river port authorities at Rouen. It is important to clear Le Havre by LW; at 5½kn Rouen can be reached in 12¾h.

Leaving Honfleur at the first br opening the journey takes about 8½h at 7kn. The return journey takes about the same time at that speed if departure is calculated for arrival off Honfleur when the flood has passed its fiercest – about 6h after LW Le Havre. At slower speed it would be necessary to stop somewhere, if a safe mooring can be found, or continue against the flood. (It is dangerous to moor against quays because of wash from passing ships.) Navigation by pleasure craft is forbidden at night between Rouen and R Risle to E of Honfleur. Listen on ch 11 (Rouen Port Radio).

Tel/VHF Port de Rouen (sea port; excludes brs) (35) 88-81-55/ch 11 – do not call on ch 16; Port Fluvial de Rouen (river port; includes brs) (35) 89-44-72; Tancarville locks ch 18.

PASSAGE NOTES: SEINE TO CHERBOUG
Charts BA 2613, F 6857

Passage Lights

Trouville	Fl(4)WR 12s 10/7M and Fl WG 4s 12/9M
Ouistreham	Oc WR 4s 16/12M
Pointe de Ver	Fl(3) 15s 26M
Port-en-Bessin ldg lts	Oc(3) 12s (synchronised) 9/10M; siren 20s
Grandcamp	Oc 4s 13M; siren 30s
Iles St Marcouf	VQ(3) 5s 9M
Morsalines ldg lts	Oc 4s 11M and Oc (3+1) WRG 12/8M
Pointe de Saire	Oc(1+2) 12s 13M
Cap Barfleur	Fl(2) 10s 27M; reed(2) 60s
Cap Levi	Fl R 5s 20M

Streams related to HW Dover

9M WSW of Cap de la Hève −5¼ E; +¾h W; 1½kn.
9M NE of Grandcamp −5¼h SE; +¾h NW; 2kn.
Inshore W of Iles St Marcouf −5¼h S going to SE; −¼h NE going to NW; 1kn
Between Pte de Saire and Pte de Barfleur +4¼h SSE; −3¼h NNW; 2¾kn.
3M N of Pte de Barfleur −5¼h SE; +¾h WNW; 5¼kn.
Pte de Barfleur slack water. +4½h and −2h.

In strong onshore winds there is no easily accessible port of refuge between the Seine and St Vaast. The streams in Baie de la Seine are weak until rounding Pte de Barfleur. Approaching Iles St Marcouf keep clear of Banc du Cardonnet, extending 6M to SE, marked by E card buoy, VQ Fl(3) 5s at SE end, with another E card (wreck) buoy QFl(3) 10s halfway along N edge; and of Banc de St Marcouf extending 2½M NW, marked at NW end by W card buoy VQ Fl(9) 10s.

In the Barfleur race the sea breaks heavily especially at Springs with wind against tide. It extends 3-4M E and NE from the point and should be given a wide berth. In settled conditions and in the absence of winds from E to NE it is possible to pass close round the point at slack water. Leaving to port La Grotte G buoy (½M NE of Barfleur entrance), aim to leave La Jamette E card bn (3 ca NE of the lt ho) about 100m to port and make good about 335° to round Les Equets N card buoy, Q, and then Basse du Rénier N card buoy, VQ, whistle. (The Hédouin Channel leads W close inshore from La Jamette bn, but it has to be taken at slack water, in calm conditions and with at least 5M good visibility and a large scale chart.) From Basse du Rénier buoy to Cherbourg, keep well N of Pierre Noire W card buoy, QFl(9), 15s to clear the shoals off Cap Levi. (Leaving Cherbourg with the E-going tide, the stream sets hard onto the shoals.)

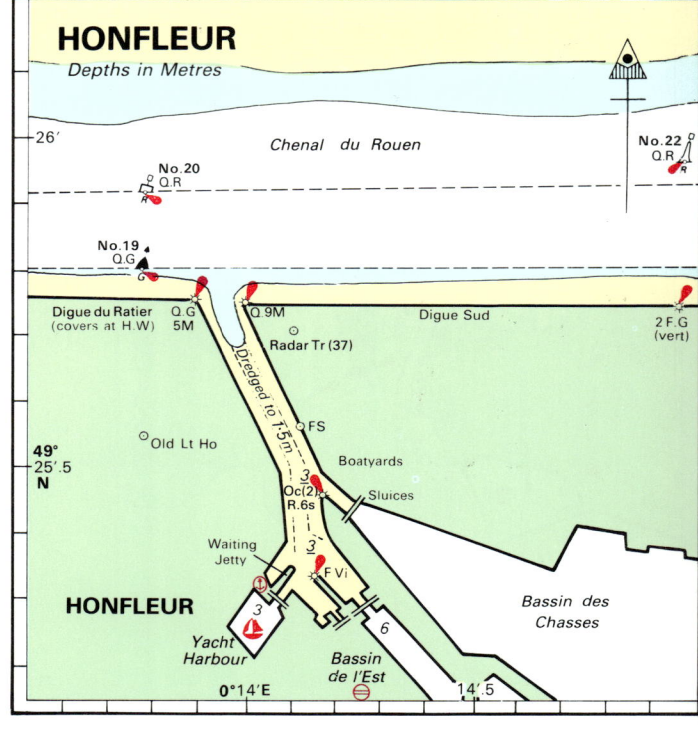

HONFLEUR
Charts BA 2146, 2994; F 6796

HW: Dover −1½h. DS: (In Seine) LW Le Havre +1½h E; +7h W (approx HWD −5h at springs; +5½h neaps.)
MHWS 7.8m MHWN 6.4

A drying fishing port with two non-tidal basins, one for yachts. A picturesque town and popular tourist attraction.
Approach Via Chenal de Rouen, buoyed and lighted with submerged training banks either side marked by bns. Yachts are required to keep outside the buoyed channel, close N of R buoys (2m). Coming from W, round Ratier NW G buoy, VQ G to clear Banc du Ratier. It is possible to take a short cut through the Digue at 'Passe des Pêcheurs' 600m from E end, N of Falaises des Fonds lt ho(14m). This gap can be used **only** at HW Le Havre ± 1h; at other times the stream runs strongly SW or NE reaching 7 or 8kn. The gap is 100m wide and is marked by a perch on each side.

Entrance Entrance dries CD (subject to silting) and Avant Port 1.5 to 3m, soft mud. There is a conspic radar tr on E side. Cross Chenal de Rouen just to E of buoys 19, 20. Beware craft emerging at speed and strong cross-set at entrance – sides rocky. After 3¼ ca take stb branch (leave quay head, Oc(2) R 6s, to port); follow wall on stb side and, avoiding cul-de-sac to stb, leave next mole to stb for entrance to yacht hbr in Vieux Bassin (Bassin de l'Ouest).
Berthing in Vieux Bassin, controlled by Honfleur YC. The moorings to port and at far end are for local boats only; immediately to stb is an area reserved for fishing boats. Visitors raft up alongside pontoon about a third of the way down the SW (stb) quay. The lock opens either side of HW but the lifting br opens only once an hour when the lock is open. Times are posted on the end of Lieutenancy at NE end of basin. Times of first opening vary from, springs to neaps, HW Havre −2h to −1¼h; br opens three times, four at weekends. Waiting outside, tie to stb quay – soft mud; beware rush of boats leaving as br opens. Enter or leave smartly – br will not wait for ditherers.
Larger boats may lie in Bassin de l'Est – consult HM.
Supplies Water on pontoons; fuel only at garages. Good shops; boatyard.
Tel/VHF Capitainerie (31) 89-20-02/ch 11, 16 (HW −2h to +4h).

THE CRUISING ASSOCIATION

Founded 1908 - Membership 5500

Library 8500 volumes - Chart Room 2500 charts

Pilots & Navigational Information

Worldwide Regional Files

250 Hon Local Representatives Worldwide

Quarterly Magazine & Navigation Notes

Bi monthly Bulletins

Crewing Service - Local Area Sections & Meets

The Cruising Association, Ivory House,
St Katharine Dock, London E1 9AT
Tel: 071 481 0881

CABOURG DIVES   Charts BA 2146, F 6928.

The estuary of R Dives dries 3m but is accessible to small craft HW±2½h. Two buoys mark entrance channel; dir lt Oc(2+1) WRG 12s 6m 9M. Inside, the quays are occupied by fishing boats; the drying area is almost fully taken up by moorings. Up-river at Cabourg it is possible to anchor in soft mud but landing is impossible below half-tide. Limited resources; water on quay at Cabourg.

DEAUVILLE – TROUVILLE   Charts BA 1349; F 6928
HW: Dover −1¾h. DS: Dover −4½h NE; +¼h SW
MHWS 7.7m   MHWN 6.3   MTL 4.3   MLWN 2.5   MLWS 0.8
Deauville is a sophisticated and expensive holiday resort with a modern marina. Trouville is an old port with a yacht basin.
Approach dries for 6 ca. In good weather, approach can be made after half-tide; in strong onshore winds, from HW −2h to HW or avoid altogether. From N keep W of the town to avoid Banc du Ratier (S side of Seine estuary) and inshore shoals. From W keep 1½M offing to Trouville SW buoy, W card VQ (9) 10s, then steer about 150° for the entrance. At night keep in W sectors of two outer lts until on ldg line, Oc R 4s. The front ldg lt is obscured NE of the line of the E outer breakwater; coming from N it will not be seen until close in.
Entrance At night keep on the ldg line; by day clear the posts on E and W training walls. Turn to stb round end of Digue du Large, Iso G, for lock to Port Deauville, or straight on for gate to Trouville basin, avoiding shoals at the sides. (Do not continue up-river past the entrance.)
Berthing (1) Port Deauville marina. Lock opens HW −3h to +4h.
(2) Trouville yacht basin. Gate opens HW±2½h.
Supplies Fuel, water; shops at Trouville.
Tel/VHF Capitainerie, public port (31) 88-28-71/ch 9; marina (31) 88-56-16; closed Monday/ch 9.

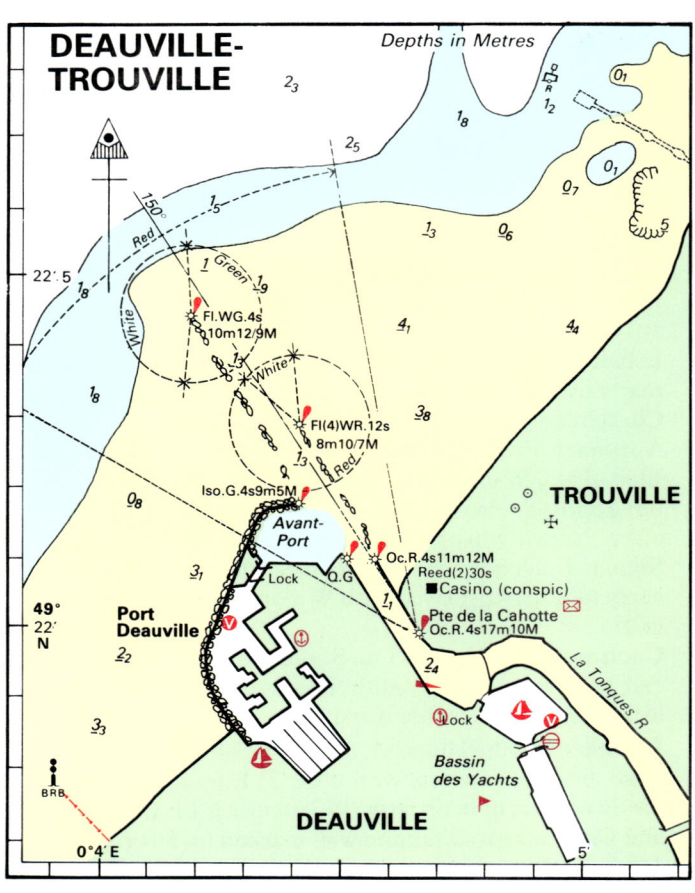

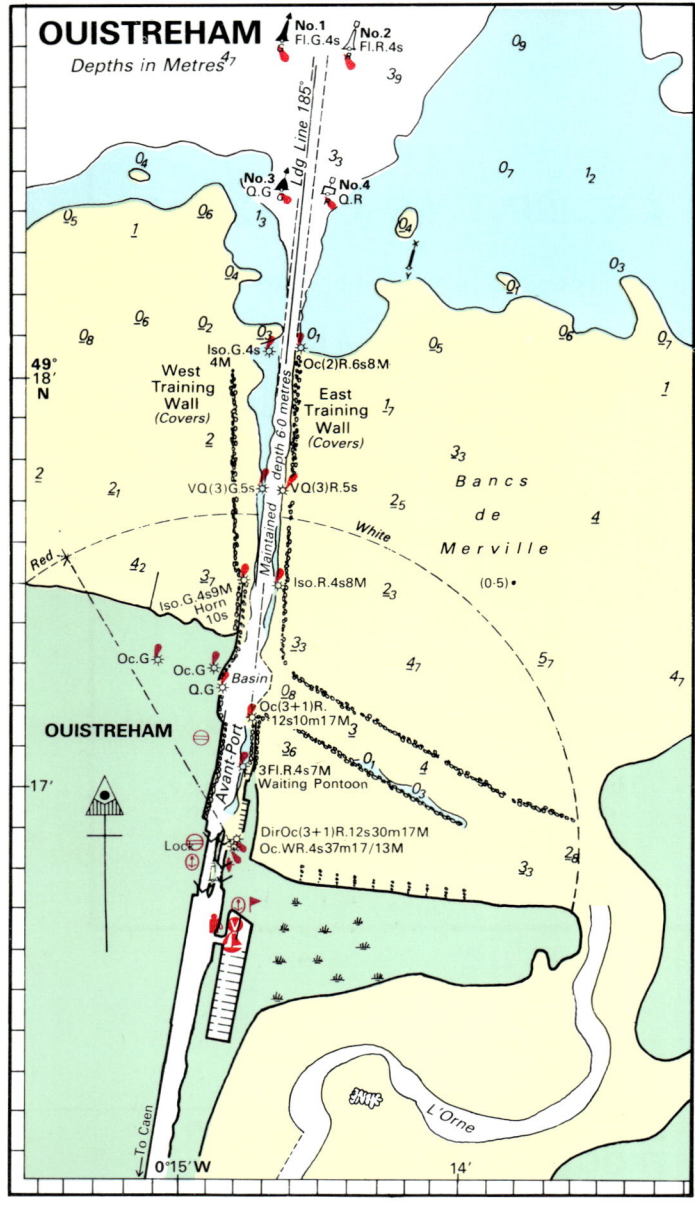

Locks Open HW −2h to +3h; small craft generally use smaller E lock, entrance dredged to CD. From mid-June to mid-Sept, and at weekends from 1 April to 31 Oct this lock opens for exit to the sea at HW −3h, −2h, +1¾h, and +2¾h; and to lock into the canal at HW −2½h, −1½h, +2¼h, and +3¼h. Congested on summer Sun evenings. Wait at pontoon outside lock on E side, up to 6 abreast, max stay 7h, wash.

Caen The canal is 7½M long, is dredged to 9.9m and has four movable brs. Yachts go free in convoy, 5½kn, once a day in each direction (enquire at Control Tr or marina for times); otherwise pay. Pontoons for yachts awaiting convoy.

Berthing (1) Marina to E of canal just through the locks. (2) Moor to bank on W side, above boatyard, opposite marina entrance; wash. (3) Caen: yacht basin in Bassin St Pierre (4.5m draught); well situated. (4) Drying anchorage at Franceville, 1M up R Orne.

Supplies Ouistreham: Water on pontoons; fuel N of marina entrance. Shops limited. Caen: water; shops.

Tel/VHF HM (31) 97-14-43; Customs (31) 97-18-62; VHF: Ouistreham Port 12, 16, 68 in lock opening times; Caen Canal 12; Caen port 8, 68.

OUISTREHAM & CAEN Charts BA 1349; F 7055
HW: Dover −1½h. DS: Dover −6h ESE; HWD WNW
MHWS 7.5m MHWN 6.1 MTL 4.2 MLWN 2.5 MLWS 0.7
Estuary of R Orne (non-navigable) and canal to Caen with marina either end. The only hbr between Le Havre and Cherbourg with deep water access at all times.

Approach Prominent lt ho: W tr, R top, Oc WR 4s, (R 115° - 151°, W elsewhere) 37m 17/13M. Sands dry for 2M but approach channel is dredged 3m; make for 'OC' RW buoy, Iso 4s, whistle and steer 187° for entrance, 2½M.

Signals Full code; small craft enter when G/W/R (forbids entry to ships) displayed with W alongside (exempts small craft).

Caution: G/W/R with G or R alongside forbids entry or exit to all but specially authorised ships. W alone means lock will open 1h before usual time.

Entrance Channel buoyed, ldg lts Oc(3+1) R 12s, 185°. E dyke extension covers, with lt Oc(2) R 6s at head, nearly 1M N of head of main jetty. W jetty has lt Iso G 4s at head and Oc G at root. Training wall marked by bns runs 360° 1M from the root.

COURSEULLES Charts BA 1349; F 5598
HW: Dover −2½h. DS: Dover +5½h E; −1¼h W
MHWS 7.0m MHWN 5.5 MTL 3.8 MLWN 2.2 MLWS 0.7
A drying hbr with congested yacht basins; entrance dangerous in strong onshore winds.

Approach Courseulles lies 2½M E of Pte de Ver lt ho, W square tr, Fl(3) 15s 42m 26M, and 1½M W of Bernières ch spire. Calvados Plateau shoals extend 2M off shore and dry to ½M off pier-heads. From W steer with Bernières spire on with twin trs of Délivrande, 134° to Fosse de Courseulles pillar buoy, Iso 4s. If necessary anchor there (6m) to await rise in tide for entry.

Entrance Dries 3.5m; approach only from Fosse de Courseulles buoy, thus avoiding nets and buoys, to enter between HW -2h and +1h. There are training walls either side of entrance marked by bns, leading to a jetty on E and a spur on W. W side has a wooden tr, W with G top, Iso WG 4s (W 135° to 235°) on dolphin at head of W training wall; E side has brown pylon, R top, Oc(2) R 6s at head of E jetty. During fog a horn sounds 30s from west tr at HW ±2h. Keep to E side until the end of the wooden part of the E pier, then continue in mid channel.

Berthing (1) Yacht basin in R La Seulles for shallow draught boats. Access under br to stb in Avant Port (opens from HW±2 to 3h). First three berths on NW belong to YC and should be avoided. River dries 3.5m but sill retains 1.2m in basin.
(2) In Bassin Joinville marina at end of Avant Port, 2m. Gates open HW±2h. Limited space for visitors.

Supplies Water on pontoons; fuel W side of Bassin Joinville.

Tel Capitainerie (31) 37-51-69.

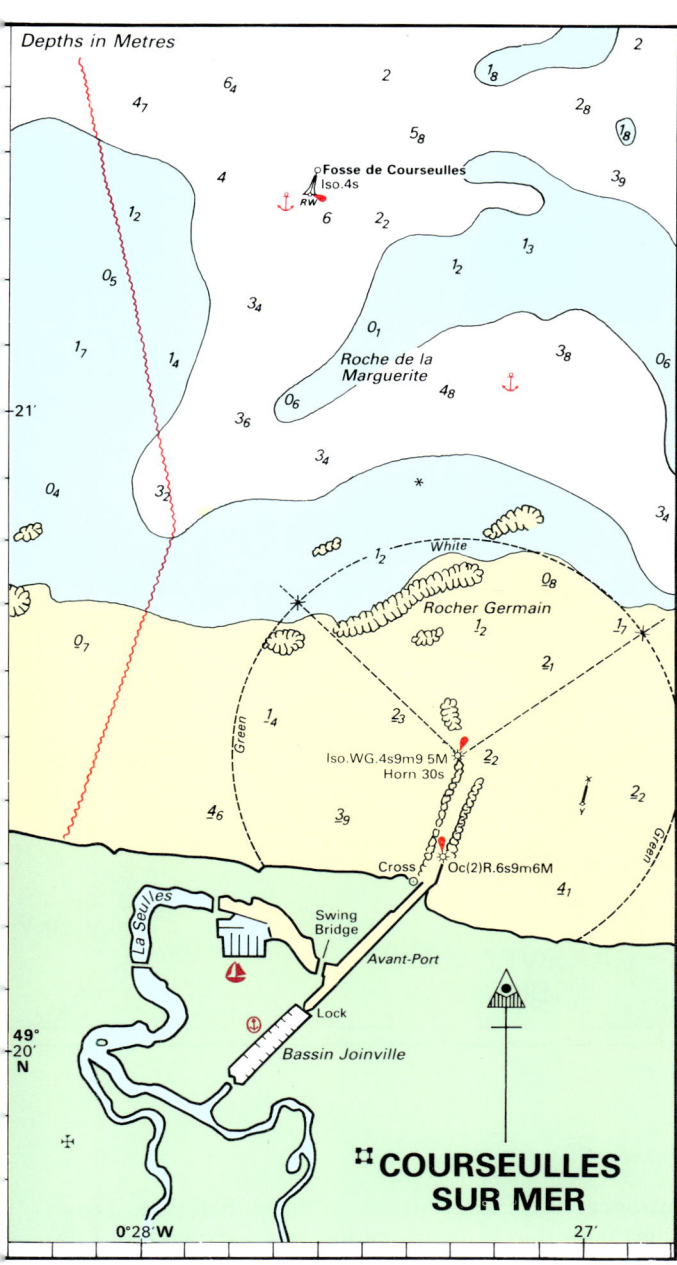

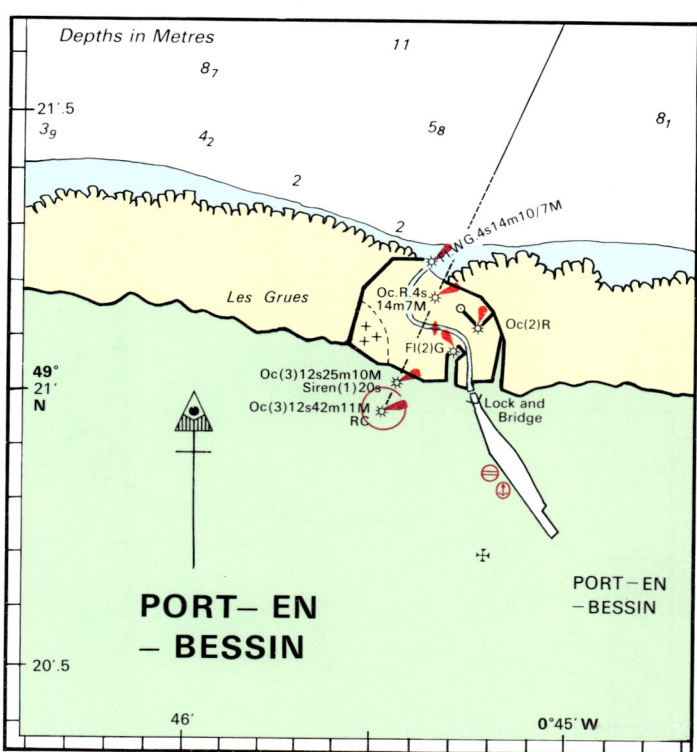

PORT-EN-BESSIN Charts BA 2613, F 7056.
HW: Dover −2h. DS: Dover −¾h W; +6¼h E
MHWS 7.1m MHWN 5.9 MTL 4.1 MLWN 2.5 MLWS 1.0
An important but drying fishing port with very limited accommodation for visiting yachts in wet basin.
Approach should not be attempted in winds from NW to NE over F5; otherwise approach at half-tide or over. Anchor off in 3m, good holding, subject to swell, while waiting. Ro Bn 'BS' 313.5khz continuous, 5M.
Entrance Pier heads are painted white, visible a long way off. Ldg lts Oc(3) 12s 204°. Channel through Avant Port dries 2m; at end is a long passage, 10m wide, leading through a lock into wet basins.
Signals Blue flag at lock gates (see below). Signal station ½M W of entrance shows traffic signals on simplified code.
Berthing Wet basin is crowded with fishing boats but there are berths for 12 visiting yachts above fishing vessels on E quay. Locks open HW±2h but swing br only opens for yachts on hour and half hour in this period. After gates close, level may fall by 1m if sluices are opened to scour outer hbr (24h warning is given by blue flag at lock gates). Yachts may be limited to 24h stay.
Supplies Water on quay; fuel at garage. Shops.
Tel/VHF Capitainerie (31) 21-70-49/ch 18.

ARROMANCHES Charts BA 2613, F 6927.
Remains of wartime Mulberry Hbr provide an interesting daytime anchorage, uncomfortable in strong onshore winds, particularly when the caissons cover. Approach from E has Roche du Calvados, dries 5m, ½M to NNE. Keep 2M offshore until near approach because of fishing pot chains. Make for E card BY wk buoy 'Harpagas' then steer 160° for entrance marked by port and stb buoys near W end of N side of hbr. Avoid wks on E side and anchor near the W end, sand, gradually shoaling, clear of obstruction marked by W buoys. Foul patches, buoy anchor. E part is foul with wks.

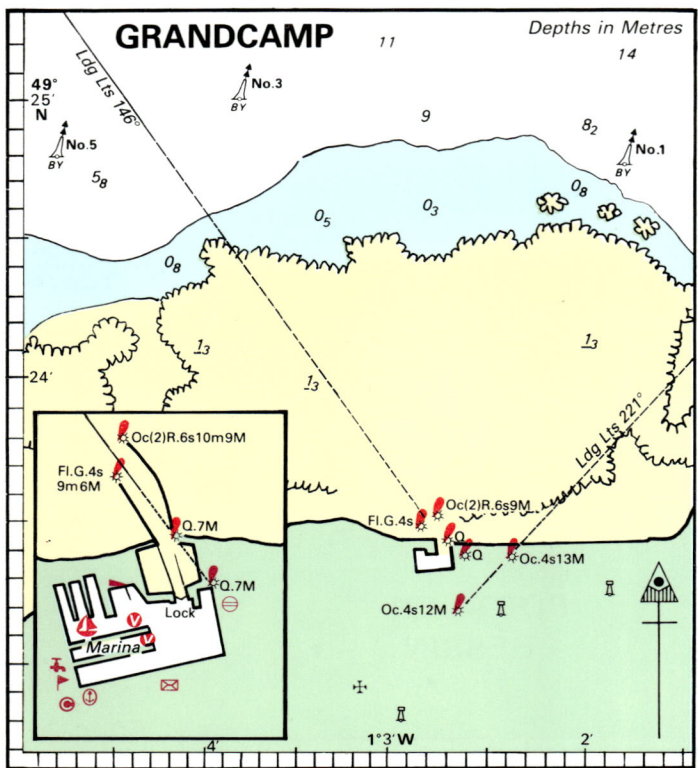
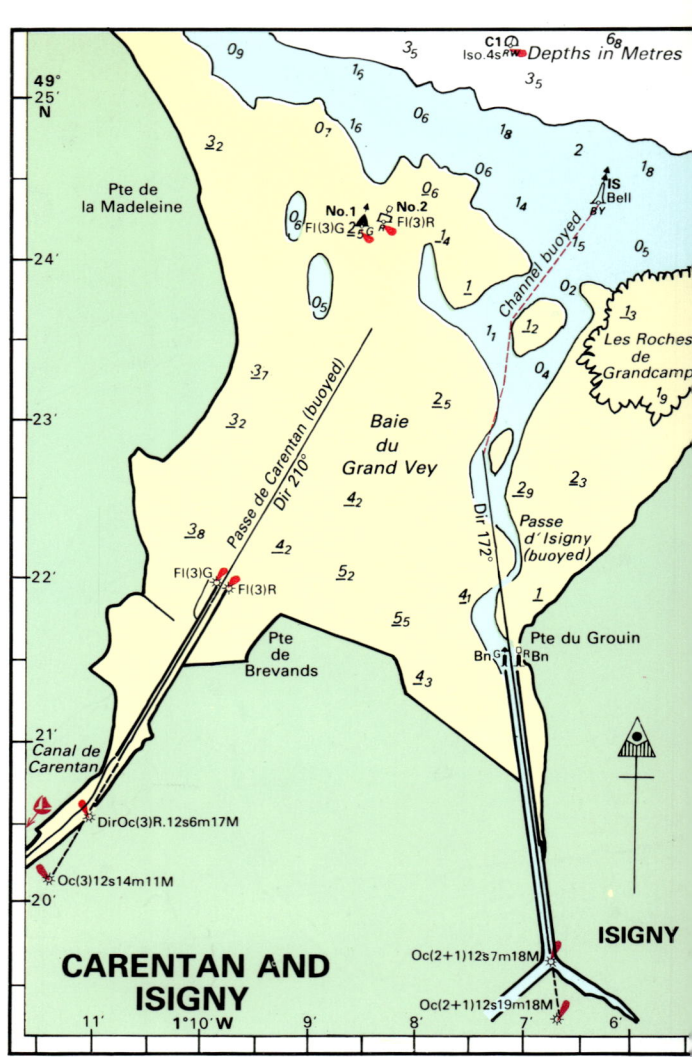

GRANDCAMP Charts BA 2613, F 7056.
HW: Dover −2¼h. DS: Dover +2h NW; −5h SE
MHWS 6.8m   MHWN 5.5
A fishing port with a wet basin.
Approach Roches de Grandcamp dry 1.6m for 1M. N limit marked by three BY N card unlighted buoys marked Nos 1, 3, 5 from E to W. Approach from any of these at HW±2h.
Entrance is exposed to winds from NW to NE, has lts Fl G 4s 6M and Oc(2) R 6s 9M on jetty hds. Ldg lts Q 7M 146°. Much Japanese seaweed reported.
Berthing Do not wait in front of the gates; considerable surge. Berths for 25 visitors at N pontoon (stern to buoys) in wet basin. Gates open HW±2½h. Sill dries 2m; basin has 2.5m. Mass exodus when gates open.
Supplies Water at pontoons; fuel at garage.
Tel/VHF Port de Plaisance (31) 22-63-16/ch 9.

ISIGNY Charts BA 2613, F 7056.
HW: Dover −2¼h (springs; maybe later at neaps). DS: in Rade de la Capelle, off the entrance: Dover +5h SSW; −1½h NNE. In Chenal d'Isigny: Dover +5h S; −1½h NNE.
E-going stream begins S and quickly changes to E; W-going stream begins SW and quickly changes to W.
MHWS 7.3m   MHWN 6.0
LW is at HW−2¾h; tide comes with a rush.
Small town with drying quays on R Aure.
Approach should not be attempted in winds of F5 or more; otherwise approach HW ±3h. From E make for the three BY N card buoys N of Grandcamp (marked 1, 3, 5); from No 5 (W-most) bear SW for N card buoy IS 1M N of W end of Roches de Grandcamp. From NW make for Carentan RW pillar buoy, Iso 4s and then steer SE for the Isigny buoy.

Entrance dries; passable for 2.7m at half-tide. From Isigny buoy the channel is marked by buoys and bns. Ldg lts Oc(1+2) 12s 18M (front W post on W hut 7m, rear W pylon on W hut 19m) 173°. At junction with R Vire (at front ldg lt) turn to port for Isigny but beware mud bank off left bank just short of the division.
Berthing Visitors berth (soft mud; dries 3m) at pontoon on W bank near Spar warehouse. E bank quay slopes, hard bottom, and spaces mostly taken by work boats.
Supplies Water on quay; fuel from garage. Shops.
Tel/VHF None.

CARENTAN Charts BA 2613, F 7056.
A small town with pleasant marina at end of long drying approach; good rail connections.
HW: Dover −2½h (springs); −1¼h (neaps). DS in Rade de la Capelle: Dover +5h SSW; −1½h NNE.
MHWS 4.1m   MHWN 2.1
Flood last for 2h springs, 3h neaps.
Approach Make for Carentan C1 RW safewater buoy Iso 4s, 4M SSE of Iles St Marcouf with ch conspic on a hill (28m) on W side of estuary. The Baie du Grand Vey dries 2m in the Carentan channel (more on the banks) and should not be attempted in fresh or strong onshore winds or with a falling tide.

Entrance N.B. The ldg lts for the canalised section are NOT appropriate for the approach channel. From Carentan safewater buoy steer SW for the entrance channel, marked with buoys and bns. There is 1.2m at half-tide. As the channel changes so does the buoyage system; certain buoys are lit, generally the first pair and at a turn; Fl G or R 2s. Currently at buoys 9 and 10 turn to stb and at 12 to port for the entrance to canalised section, entrance bns lit Fl(3) R or G 4s, then 210° on ldg lts front Dir Oc(3) R 12s 17M, rear Oc(3) 12s 11M. Canal is shallowest at buoys 2b and 6b which have 1.6m at Cherbourg height of tide 4.8m. Immediately in front of the lock gates (8M from the safewater buoy) R Douve enters from stb and R Taute from port: there can be a strong cross current and boats have been swept up the Taute onto a br.
Berthing At pontoons in ¾M long locked section of canal. Gates open HW−2 to +3; sill 1.8m above CD.
Supplies Water on pontoons; fuel; shops.
Tel/VHF Capitainerie (33) 42-24-44/ch 9.

ILES ST MARCOUF   Charts BA 2613, F 7056.
Two uninhabited fortified islands. Avoid in bad weather, especially from SW.
Approach Keep clear of Banc de Saint-Marcouf, extending 2½M to NW, on which there are breakers with fresh winds from N to NE; and of Banc du Cardonnet running 6M SE.
Anchorage 3-4m, to SE of S card bn, 10.1m, on rks 1 ca WSW of larger Is, Ile du Large, and SW of lt ho. Buoy anchor, stream strong. Land between HW±2h at boat hbr on W side of Is; when rks to bn are awash there is 1.3m in entrance.
Ile de Terre, smaller Is, is a bird sancturary; landing forbidden without permission.
Supplies Nil.

Saint Vaast – see next page

BARFLEUR   Charts BA 1349, F 7090.
A small picturesque drying hbr.
HW: Dover −2¾h. DS: Dover −4¾h N; +4½h S.
MHWS 6.4m   MHWN 5.1   MTL 3.7   MLWN 2.3   MLWS 0.9
Approach See Passage Notes re Barfleur Race. From a position about 1¼M ESE of Pte de Barfleur, steer 219° on the 7m W square lt tr (ldg lts Oc(3) 12s). Do not confuse this tr with the squat W tr at end of S breakwater: ldg line passes about 50m S of the latter.
Entrance Ldg line is 219°, front W square tr Oc(3) W 12s 7m; rear Grey and W square tr, G top, Oc(3) W 12s 13m, synchronised. Channel is marked by buoys and bns and has a strong cross-current. Near HW adjacent rks are awash and it is most important to keep on the ldg line and not steer direct for the entrance. When 2 or 3 ca off the entrance the ldg lts will be hidden by the hbr wall; at this point, about abreast of the last port bn, head for the entrance. There is a tide gauge on concrete base close SW of lifeboat slip: when the base is covered there is 1.6m along the quay.
When leaving at night have compass course prepared as ldg lts are not visible for first 250yds.
Anchoring Waiting to enter, near the ldg line, 5-6m, sand and mud, poor holding. Also in bay N of town, except with winds E to NE. Approach 256° from Roches des Anglais G con buoy.

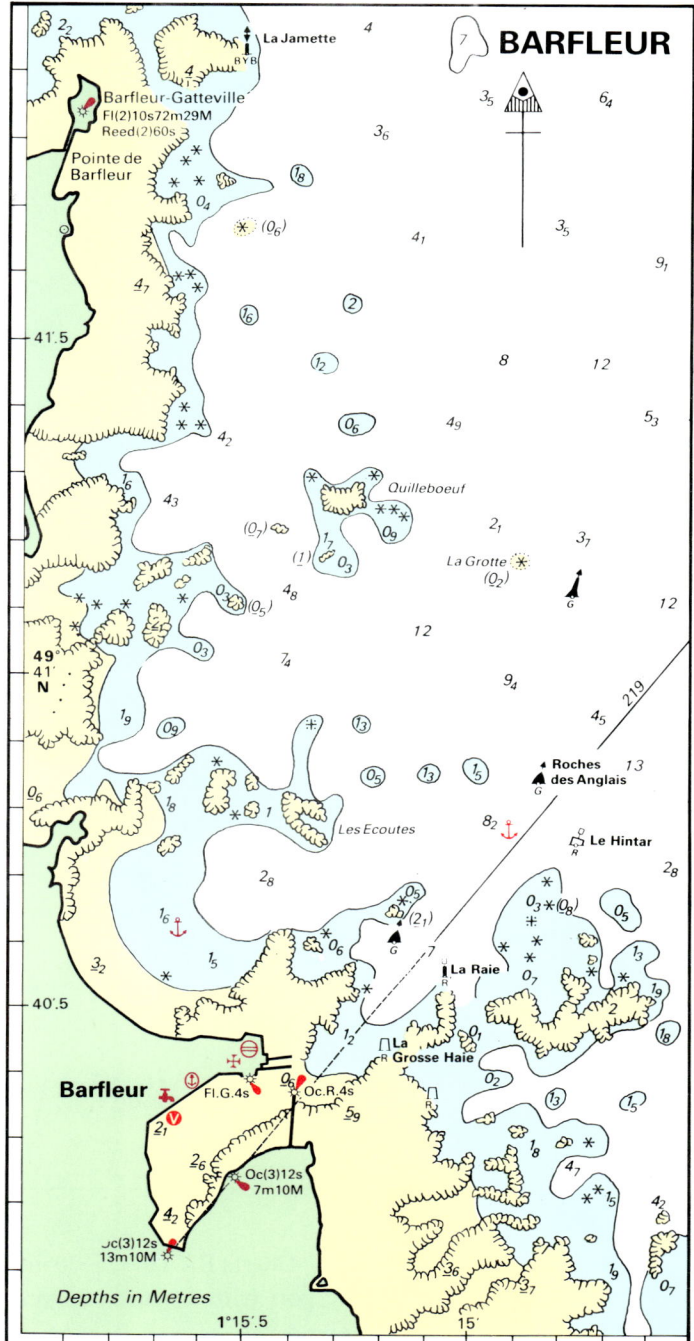

Berthing along SW part of NW quay, dries 2-3m, level mud, sand and gravel. 'Yachts' on wall separates yachts from fishing boats. E side is rocky. There is a strong surge with fresh winds E to NE.
Supplies Fuel and water, shops.
Tel Capitainerie (33) 54-08-29.

PORT DE LÉVI & LE BECQUET   Chart BA 1106.
Small drying hbrs (1.5m plus) generally full of local boats and floating lines. No facilities; not recommended.

FRANCE, NORTH COAST   314

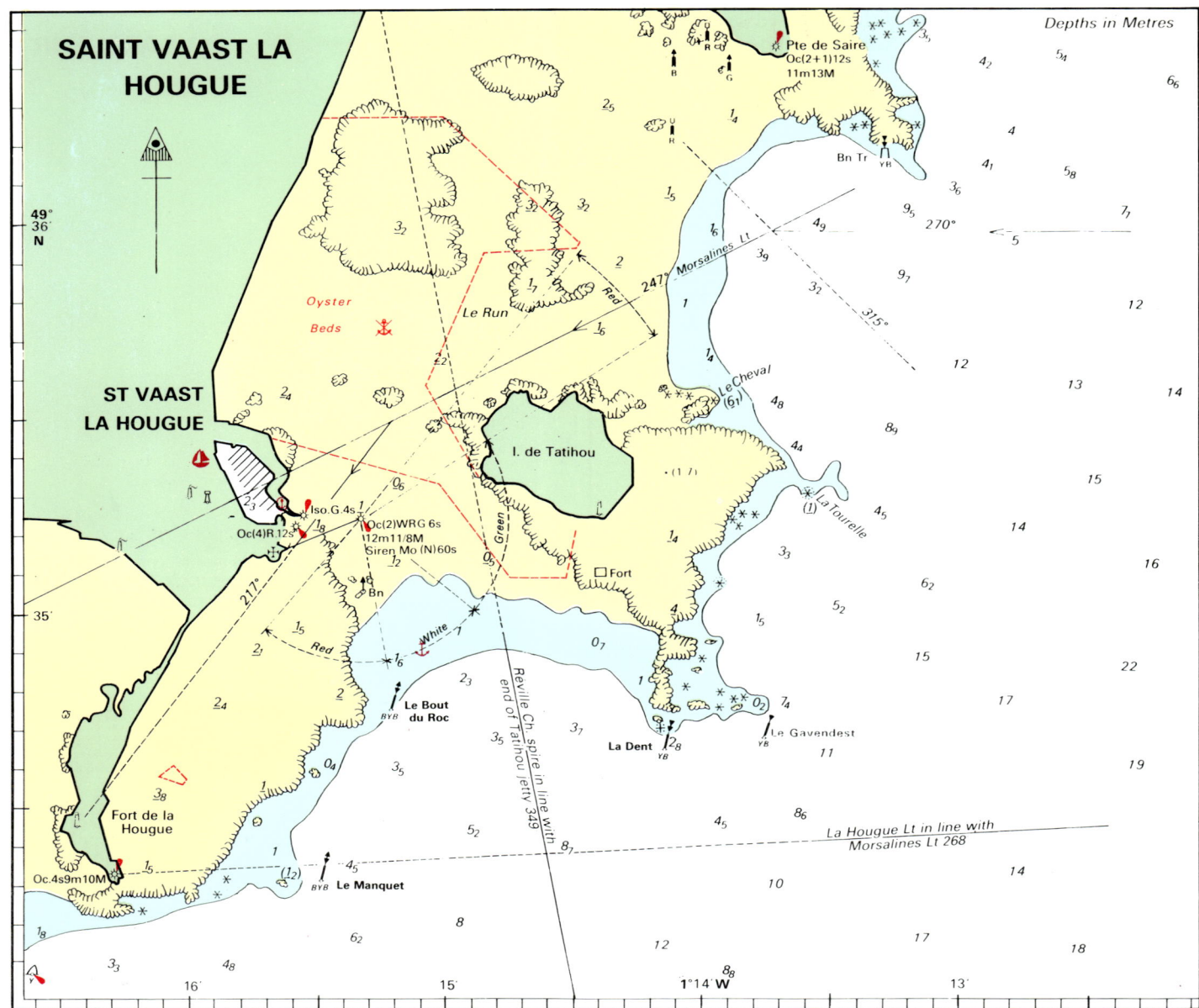

ST VAAST
Charts BA 1349, F 7056.

A busy but attractive fishing port with a marina in wet basin; good oyster beds.

HW: Dover −2¾h. DS: in Grande Rade: Dover −5½h SW; +½h NE; 2½kn

An eddy runs N during the English Channel E-going stream.

MHWS 6.0m   MHWN 5.1   MTL 3.4   MLWN 2.1   MLWS 0.6

Approach From N leave Pte de Saire 1M to stb and continue for 1¾M W of S past Ile Tatihou (broad tr on S end with low detached fort to S); steer W round two unlit YB S card pillar buoys, then bear NW for entrance. From S go between Iles St-Marcouf and mainland to leave to port two W card buoys and Y buoy Fl 2s E of Fort de la Réville bell tr on with jetty at SW corner of Tatihou.

By night: from N keep Barfleur-Gatteville lt, Fl(2) 10s, open until on the line La Hougue lt Oc 4s with Morsalines Oc(3+1) WRG, 267°. Keep on the latter until in W sector of St Vaast lt Oc(2) WR 6s 7M bearing NW. From S leave Quinéville lt buoy, VQ(9) 10s, well to stb; do not cross La Houge-Morsalines line until in W sector of St Vaast lt. Leave this lt to port and enter between R and G lts at lock.

There is another, more hazardous approach from the N, via 'Le Run' and suitable only for HW±2h. Clear the S card bn to SE of Pte de Saire, steer 270°, ½M, until R bn bears 315°, about 3 ca off, when Morsalines lt ho (W octagonal with G top) comes on line with large house at root of N breakwater. Follow this line (247°) to get La Hougue tr just open to E of 2 W trs conspic at entrance to basin (208°); follow this line and turn off when appropriate.

Entrance Port side of approach to the jetty head from S is marked by buoys and bns; exposed to strong winds from NE and SE. Dries 1½m but sandbank outside the gates covers at half flood – draught over 1.6m will touch; stay within 15m of wall until just past first (stone) bollard.

Berthing (1) anchor SSW of Ile Tatihou clear of the eastern half of the white sector of Oc WR lt.

(2) Waiting for lock, tie up on N side of jetty. As this is used by fishing boats to unload when lock is shut it is more comfortable to anchor off but waiting area is limited to western half of the white sector of Oc WR lt. (N.B. anchoring N of the jetty is forbidden - oyster beds.)

(3) Pontoons in marina. Gates open HW -2¼h to +3h (may close 1¼ earlier according to wind and tide). Entry traffic lts.

Supplies Fuel and water at marina. Good shops.
Tel/VHF Capitainerie (33) 54-48-81/ch 9.

Imray Charts and Books
... The first choice for yachtsmen

We are Admiralty chart agents.

Imray Yachting Charts

- The most extensive series published especially for yachtsmen from Scotland to France – North Biscay – East Coast and North Sea – English Channel – West Coast and Ireland.
- Two series are available – Small and medium-scale C Charts and large-scale Y Charts – providing the safest coverage for cruising and passage making.
- All charts are published folded, flat or waterproofed.
- Imray charts are corrected to the date of despatch.
- Hand correction service or correction slips available. Nories Bulletin of Corrections published quarterly.
- Notes on the reverse of each chart.
- Overprinted lattice for Decca users, large-scale plan insets, tidal stream information and radio information on most charts in each series.
- Most charts are revised and reprinted annually.

Imray Books

The finest series of pilot books available. Coverage includes the North Sea, English Channel, Scotland, the West Coast, Netherlands and France. Imray pilots also offer unbroken coverage for Southern Europe from Northwest Spain via Gibraltar to the Eastern Mediterranean as well as the Atlantic Islands.

We also publish inland waterway maps and guides, Imray Iolaire charts of the Caribbean Sea and supply Street's Guides to the Caribbean.

Imray, Laurie, Norie & Wilson Ltd
Wych House The Broadway St. Ives Huntingdon
Cambridgeshire PE17 4BT England

☎ St. Ives (0480) 62114 (2 lines) (24 hours)
Telex 329195 IMRAYS G
Fax (0480) 496109

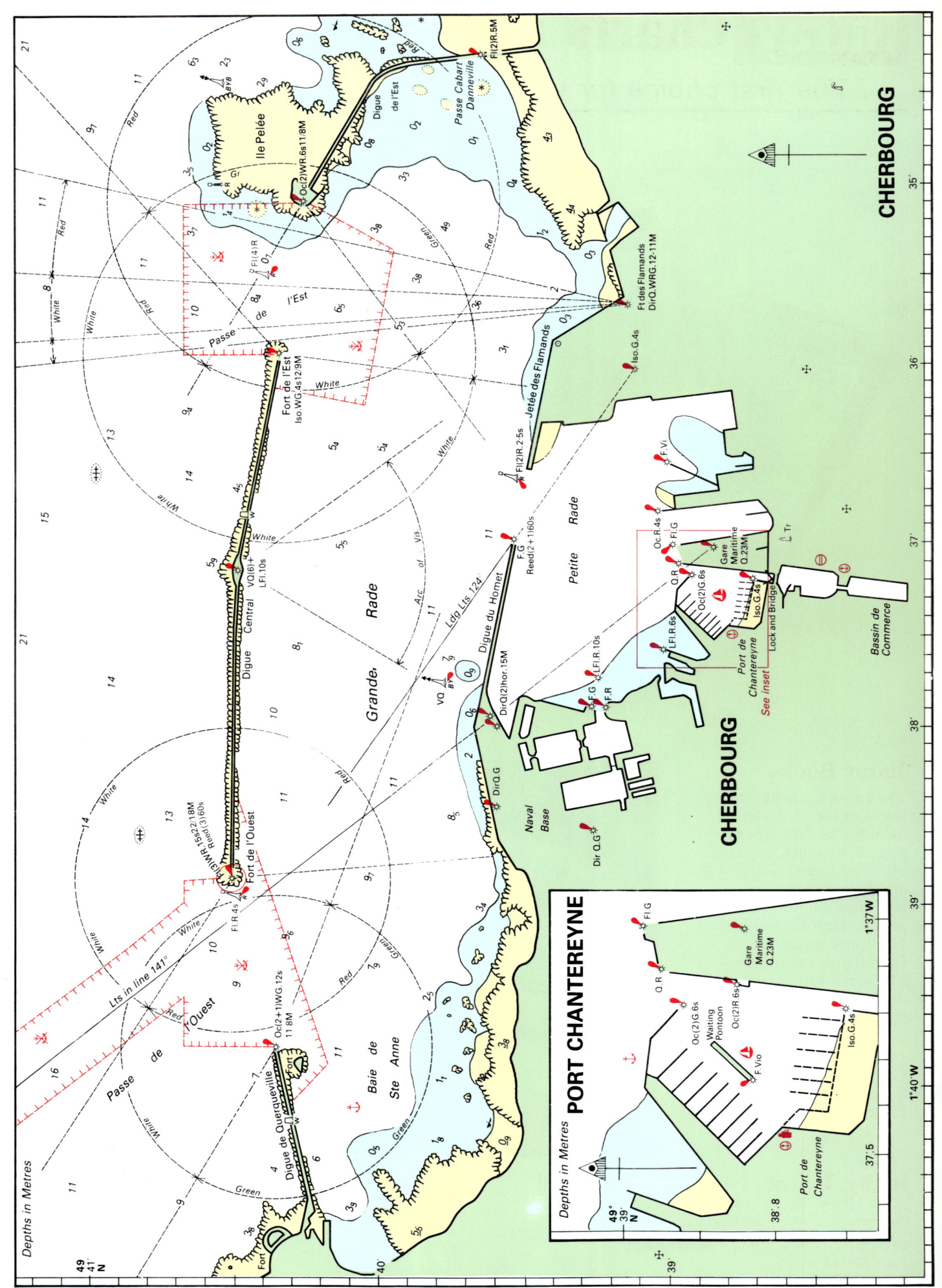

CHERBOURG
Charts BA 2602, F 6737D.
HW: Dover −3¾h. DS: Dover +4¾h ENE; −2h WSW. Tidal streams change 2–3h later in mid-channel than along the shore.

MHWS 6.2m MHWN 4.8 MTL 3.5 MLWN 2.3 MLWS 0.8

A major commercial, naval and yachting port which can be entered at all times.

Approach To E and W keep at least 2½M off the land; and keep well clear of Raz de Lévy in E, end of which is marked by W card YB buoy Q(9). Cherbourg can be located by atomic power station on high ground to W, a cliff behind the town, a long low breakwater with prominent circular forts, and Cap Levi lt ho (27m) to the E. There is a Ro Bn on Fort de l'Ouest, 312.6khz, RB, 20M. CH1 RW pillar buoy, LFl 10s, whistle lies 3M NW of W entrance.

Entrance The main, W, entrance (ldg lts Dir Q, 141°) is marked on its E side by the Fort de l'Ouest, Fl(3) WR 15s, showing W from 122° over the centre breakwater to 355°, R elsewhere. The W side is marked by the Querqueville lt Oc(3) WG (120° to 290°, G elsewhere); there is a R port buoy Fl R 4s close inside the entrance. Keep well to stb on entry to avoid emerging craft. From here the ldg line for Petite Rade is 124°, front F G, rear Iso G, leaving front lt on Digue du Homet to stb.
Passe de l'Est should be approached from W of N to clear the shoals near Ile Pelée. At night W sector of Fort des Flamands, Dir Q WRG, leads in 180°. From the entrance, ldg line is twin spires of Notre Dame (rear) to right of small tower of Ste Trinité (front) 211°.
Passe Cabart Danneville at E end of Grande Rade is narrow with strong streams; not recommended.

Petite Rade: The NE breakwater, Jetée des Flamands, covers. Its W end is marked by R pillar buoy, Fl R 2.5s. Once clear of breakwater, steer 196° for marina and entrance to inner hbr (at night ldg lts Q R front, Iso G 4s 4m 2M rear, leaving former to port).

Departing If heading for Passe de l'Est it is imperative to leave to stb the R pillar buoy Fl(2)R 6s in the entrance to clear Jetée des Flamands.

Berthing At marina. If arriving at night and outer berths are full, raft up or anchor off, clear of fairway to inner hbr. Anchoring is also possible in Petite Rade close N of marina breakwater (wash and uncomfortable in N winds) or at W end of Grande Rade (isolated and considerable swell). The inner hbr is for local boats only unless prior arrangements are made.

Supplies All.

Tel/VHF Port de Plaisance (33) 53-75-16/ch 9; Customs (33) 53-79-65; Naval Port Control ch 11.

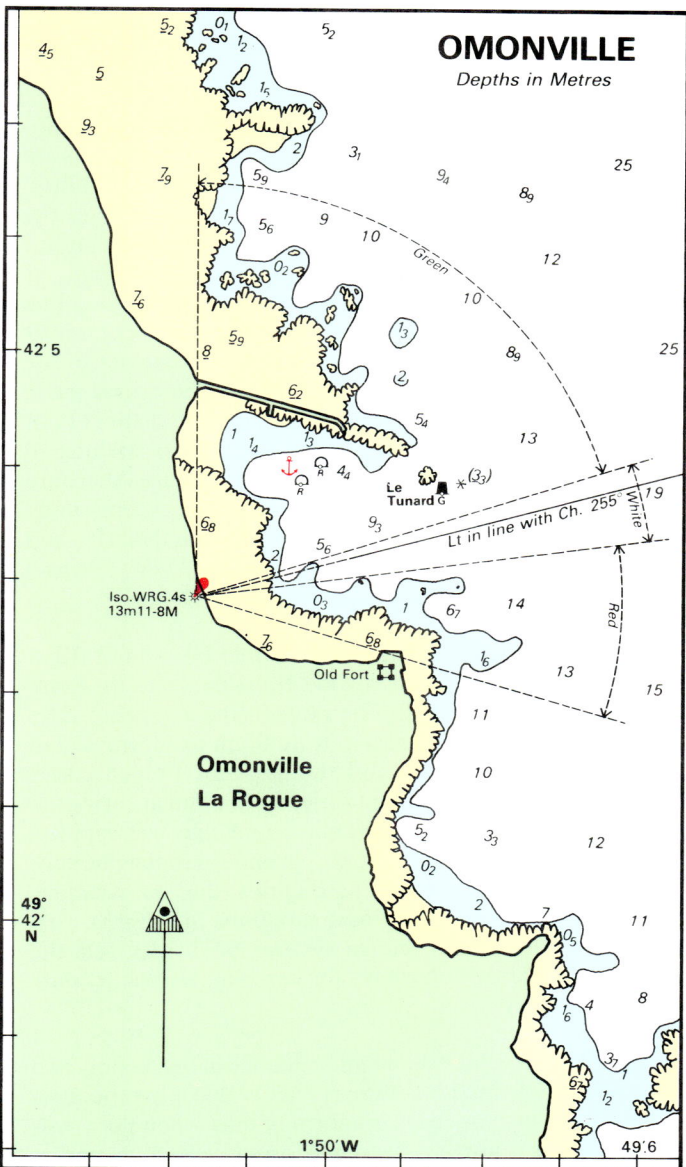

OMONVILLE-LA-ROGUE
Charts BA 1106; F 5631
HW: Dover −3¾h. DS: (1M N): Dover −6h E; −1½h W

MHWS 6.1m MHWN 4.7 MTL 3.5 MLWN 2.4 MLWS 0.8

A small hbr, 4M ESE of Cap de la Hague, useful if missing the tide E-bound to Cherbourg or wanting an early passage through Alderney race. Sheltered from SSE through W to NNW.

Approach From W keep at least 1M off until Omonville has been identified. The entrance is marked by Le Tunard G bn tr and to the S are the ruins of an old fort. Keep well to the E of the transit of these (194°) to clear the rks of Les Tataquets and allow for strong stream, usually WNW. From E keep at least 1M offshore.

Entrance ½ ca wide between a submerged rk off the old fort and Le Tunard bn. On the shore between them is W tr Iso WRG 4s. Bring this on with Omonville ch, 255°. At night enter in W sector.

Berthing Two large visitors' buoys, each taking several yachts. Moor bow to buoy with stern anchor, or anchor SE of short breakwater, 5m, sand, foul. Beware of rks E of breakwater.

Supplies a few shops.

ANSE DE ST MARTIN
Chart BA 1106
This is a passage anchorage, 2M E of Cap de la Hague, convenient in settled weather. It is unlit and departure at night is difficult. Dangerous in onshore winds and to be avoided in strong SW with implicit threat of swing to NW.

Approach from E: best at HW when offlying rks are covered; clear Marti-au-Roc, dries 9.4m, 1 ca to port and steer SW, with ch tr on with jetty, 242°. From W keep a good ½M offshore. NE of the W point of the bay is a group of rks awash at LW. If approaching before half-tide, keep going E until Jobourg ch tr is on with a group of houses nearer the shore, 204° and steer on that line. Otherwise identify the point at W end of sandy beach at head of the bay and steer on that 187°; not easy with strong cross stream. Do not approach until position certain.

Anchor off Port Racine in SW corner, good holding, sand and mud.

Supplies None.

CHANNEL ISLANDS Charts BA 2669

These islands afford fascinating sailing for the well equipped yacht with an experienced navigator. The hazards are concealed rocks, strong tidal streams and poor visibility. Good up-to-date charts are essential. BA 2669 gives the outlines of CI and is adequate if passing round them; but for inter-island navigation larger scales are needed, as shown at the head of each island entry. A good pilot guide is also highly desirable because of the importance of transit lines when navigating in these waters; in some places the difference between a course steered and the course made good can be as much as 60°. The Admiralty Channel Pilot is a mine of detailed information. For those wishing to make the most of inshore routes and anchorages there are Malcolm Robson's *Channel Islands Pilot*, exceptionally well provided with sketches of transit lines and marks, and the French *Pilote Côtier Fenwick, vol 7 (St Malo – Dieppe)* with simple charts and good photos.

The Admiralty Tidal Atlas for Channel Island and Adjacent Coasts of France, or a good equivalent such as Stanford's, is also essential. The range of mean spring tides shows a remarkable variation from 5½m to 11½m within the area of the Islands and the adjacent French coast; within the islands the range varies from 9.8m at springs to only 2.1m at neaps. Tides make and take off rapidly; streams run rapidly even at neaps; and there may be considerable variation from predictions due to weather. There may also be many local variations in streams, particularly eddies, not shown on the tidal atlas. Of the twenty five hbrs with quays for berthing alongside, only five do not dry.

The Admiralty Pilot shows an incidence of fog on only two days a month in the summer; this is deceptive because there are also many days of morning mist when poor visibility makes it impossible to pick up some leading marks. Radar and a Decca navigator are most helpful if caught by mist or fog when at sea; but neither is sufficiently reliable to keep on transit lines and their possession does not justify leaving hbr in poor visibility.

There is complete shelter at all times at St Peter Port in Guernsey and at St Helier in Jersey. Elsewhere there are very many anchorages which provide shelter in settled weather or offshore winds – but all are subject to swell.

Finally it must be remembered that although the Channel Islands are Crown Dependencies they are not part of UK. Customs requirements for yachts are more rigorous than in France: Q flags must be flown and it is necessary to report to Customs (usually by depositing a form) not only when arriving from France but also from UK and when moving from one Island administration to another (eg from Guernsey to Jersey). Clearance can be given at Braye in Alderney; St Peter Port, St Sampson or Beaucette marina in Guernsey; and St Helier or Gorey in Jersey. Normal EC duty free limits apply.

PASSAGE NOTES: CHERBOURG AND THE CHANNEL ISLANDS Charts BA 2669

Passage Lights

Cap de la Hague	Fl 5s 24M horn 30s
Quénard Pt	Fl(4) 15s 28M Siren(4) 60s
Casquets	Fl(5) 30s 25M horn(2) 60s;
Cap de Carteret	Fl(2+1) 15s 26M horn(3) 60s
Sark	Fl 15s 18M horn (2) 60s
Platte Fougère	LFl WR horn 45s; R sector over rks to NW
Les Hanois	Q(2) 5s 23M horn(2) 60s
St Martin's Pt	Fl(3) WR 10s 14M horn(3) 30s; R sector over rks to SW
Grosnez Pt	Fl(2) WR 15s R sector over rks to NE;
Corbière	Iso WR 10s 16M horn 60s; R sectors over rks to N and SE
Roches Douvres	Fl 5s 28M siren 60s

Streams related to Dover:
Alderney Race HWD SW; +6h NE.
Between Guernsey and Jersey the stream is rotatory anti-clockwise, HWD W; +3h S; +6h E; −3h N.
The Alderney Race is 7M wide and presents no difficulty in reasonable weather although there are overfalls, marked on the chart, which should be avoided, especially with wind against tide. Tidal streams can reach 10kn and it is essential to time one's passage accordingly, taking advantage where necessary of the inshore eddies round Alderney.

From Cherbourg to CI, leave Cherbourg at about HWD−4h to catch the start of the inshore W-bound eddy. Between Cherbourg and CI, Omonville is a convenient passage port; the eddy running W inshore from there begins at HWD−5½h. If bound for Alderney or the Casquets, a generous allowance must be made for tidal set. If bound through the Race for Jersey or Guernsey, the most comfortable passage will be made at HWD before the overfalls have built up.

Southbound from Alderney, the shortest route to Guernsey is through the Swinge. Depart Braye Hbr at local HW+2 to 2½h (Dover −2 to −1½h) to avoid the overfalls S of Burhou. Leave Corbet Rk about 100m to port and then change course to keep Great Nannel just open E of Burhou, 003°, until Les Etacs are on the port beam.

Northbound from St Peter Port Leave as soon as the stream in the Little Russel turns N at about HWD+4¾h. This should give a favourable tide through the Swinge or the Alderney Race. If bound for Alderney note that the tide runs NE in the Race longer than in the Swinge and change course if you run out of tide before entering the Swinge. Approaching the Swinge keep Great Nannel just open E of Burhou, 003°, to clear Pierre au Vraic (dries 1.2m) and to clear Les Etacs at SW end of Alderney. Keep to E side of Swinge to avoid the overfalls, about 100m W of Corbet Rk.

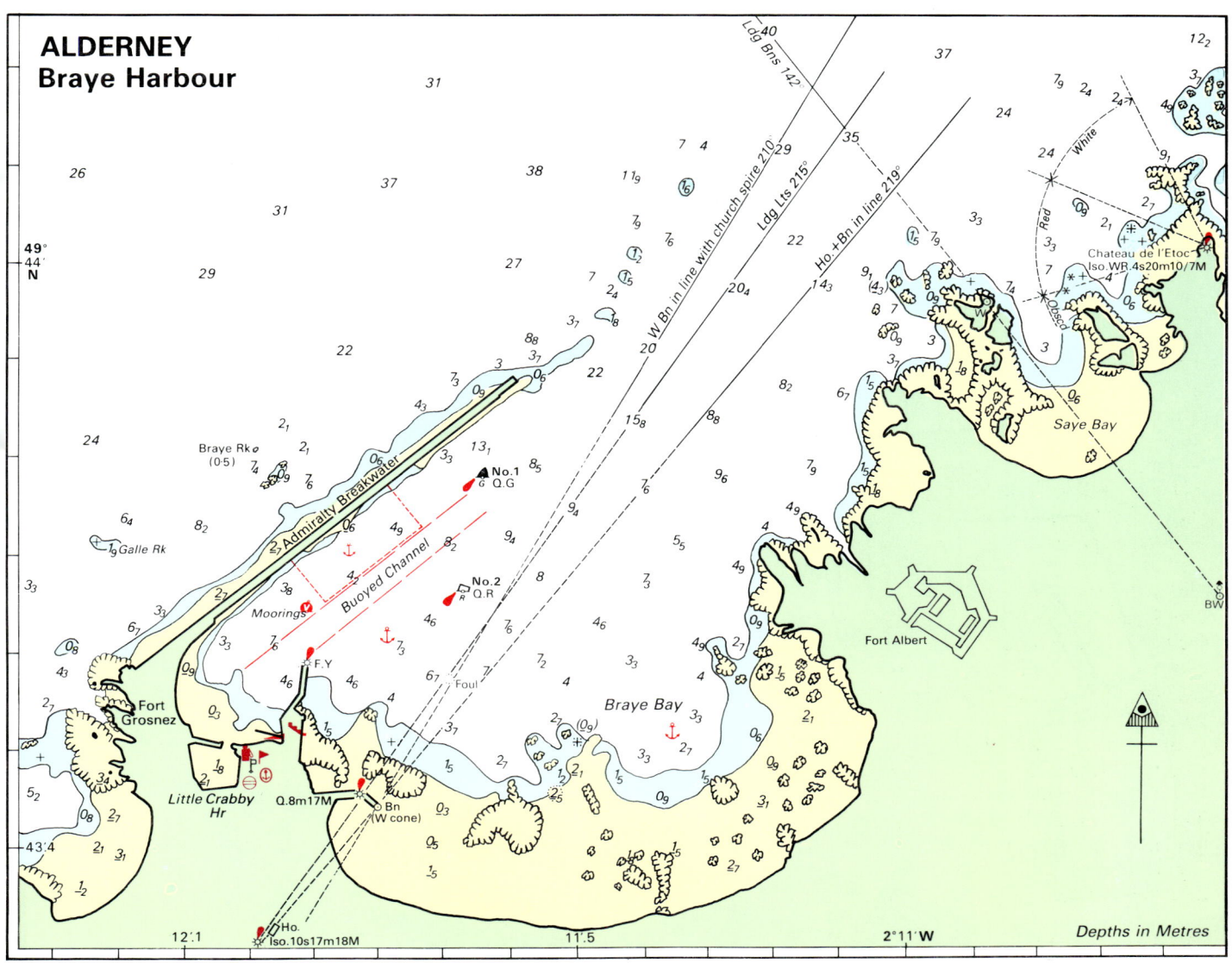

ALDERNEY
Braye Harbour

To Cherbourg from Alderney leave at about HWD+5h to catch the start of the NE-going stream. If coming from Guernsey note that the early W-going stream along N coast of Cherbourg Peninsula is stronger than suggested in Tidal Atlas. Avoid it by keeping well offshore.

BRAYE, ALDERNEY Charts BA 2845, 60.
HW: Dover −4h. DS (Race): Dover −3½h SW; +5¼h NE

MHWS 6.3m MHWN 4.7 MTL 3.6 MLWN 2.6 MLWS 0.8

Alderney is an unspoilt island with reasonable facilities. The artificial hbr is exposed to NE. No animals may be landed. Air connections to UK, Cherbourg and other islands.

Approach is best from NE at HWD+5h when the stream off the entrance is least. From NW either pass N of the Casquets and Burhou Is or, if the SW stream is running, leave them to N, pass S of Alderney and go NE through the Race with flood tide.

From S see Passage Notes; but at night it is prudent to use the Race approach rather than the Swinge because in the latter it is difficult to establish the clearance off rks to the side.

Entrance Beware sunken continuation of the breakwater running NE for 3 ca. The W-going stream sets strongly onto it for 9½h. When rounding it, if coming from SW, keep E of ldg line of two bns: front W with W globe on islet on W side of Saye Bay, rear BW △ top, 142°; then bring W con bn near hd of Old Hbr pier on with St Anne's spire, 210° (this transit leads 1 ca E of the submerged breakwater).

At night to clear the breakwater extension keep in W sector of Château à l'Etoc lt Iso WR (111° to 151°); R sector covers the shoals 071° to 111°. Ldg lts into hbr are front Q intense 210° to 220°, rear Iso 10s, intense over same sector.

Berthing Moor to any Y buoy or anchor clear of moorings with a riding lt, 8m. Little Crabby Hbr is used for local boats except for visitors when re-fuelling, HW±2h. Land at steps or slipway below HM office (keep it clear).

Supplies Fuel, water, gas, 12T crane, adequate shops.

Tel/VHF HM (041 82) 2620/ch 16, 74 (office hours). Water taxi 'Mainbrayce' ch 37.

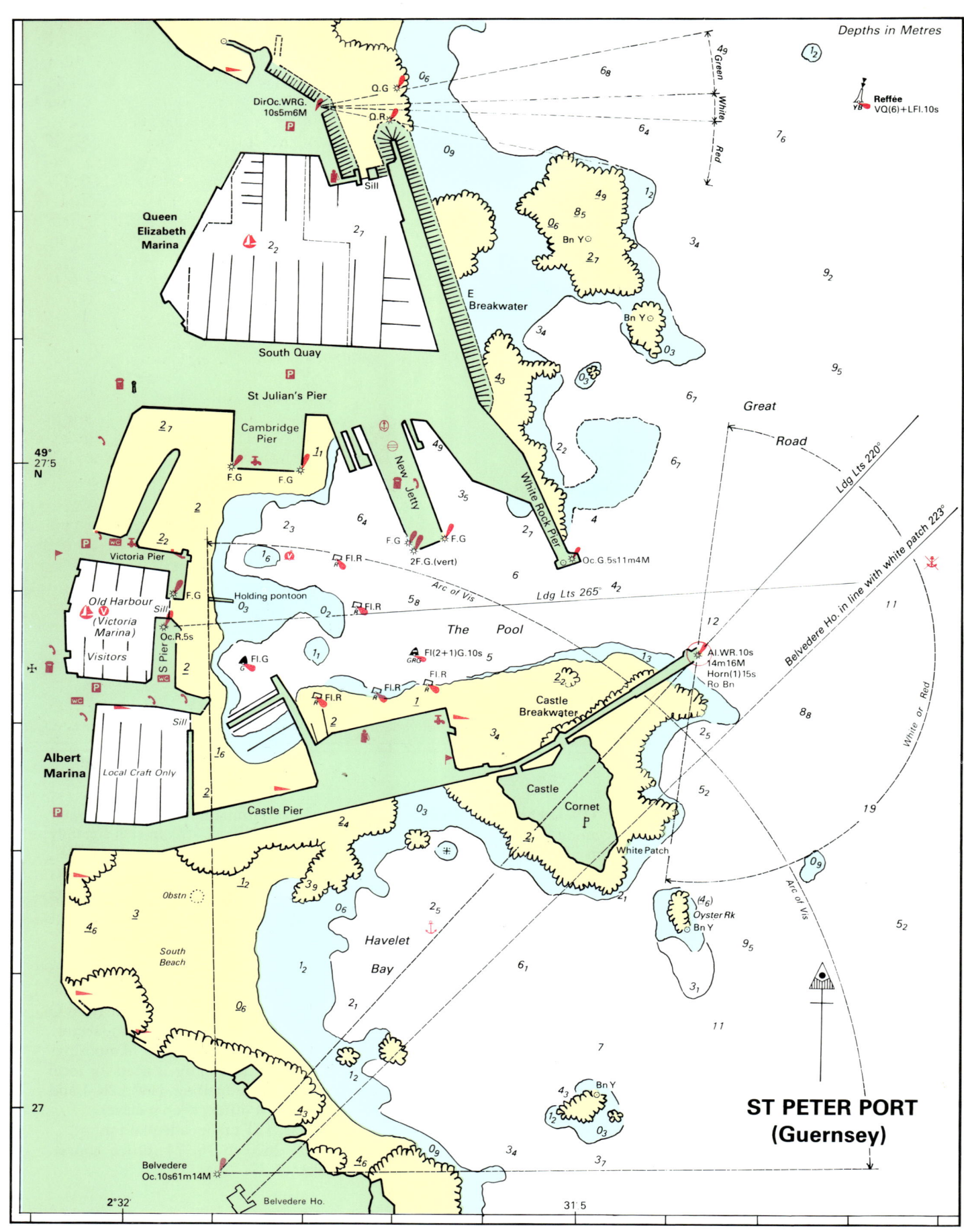

GUERNSEY   Charts BA 3654

DS off E side: Dover −1h SW; +5½h NE
off W side: HWD SW; +6h NE
The W coast is rocky and inhospitable; the E coast offers better shelter and facilities.

Approach There are three main lines of approach to the E coast and St Peter Port: (1) by Little Russel Channel; (2) by Great Russel Channel; (3) from W and S.

Approaching from N, as from the Solent, the simplest pilotage is to make for the Casquets, then make good 224° down W coast to Les Hanois lt ho and follow S coast 1M off to pick up approach (3). In bad visibility this route is strongly to be preferred.

Warning: with the SW-going tide there is a considerable inset SE across the N end of Guernsey.

(1) **Little Russel Channel** entrance is marked on W by Platte Fougère grey octagonal lt tr, Fl WR 10s (R over area W to NW) and on E by Tautenay lt tr, BW vert stripes, 7m Q(3) WR 6s (R over area to E, 215° to 050°). It provides the most direct route from N, and can be used at LW with good visibility, but the streams run at up to 6kn and it can be very rough, with overfalls, with wind against tide. At NE end of channel, between the Braye Rks and Amfroque, the stream sets directly towards the N end of Herm from Dover +1¾h to +3¾h. Do not approach Platte Fougère grey octagonal lt tr from W on a bearing less than 165° or from E on a bearing greater than 255°. Make for a position about 2M NE of Platte Fougère and then bring Brehon tr (low, squat) just to the E of St Martin's Pt, 208°. Keep on this line until Roustel tr, BW, is 1¼ ca to stb, then get on transit of Belvedere House, W, on with W patch on Castle Cornet, 223°. If these letter marks are difficult to pick out against the sun or in poor visibility, steer 220° from Tautenay, adjusting as necessary to clear Roustel tr, BW chequered stone, to port; Platte tr, G con stone, to stb; and Brehon tr, squat circular fort, ½M to port.

At night from a position NE of Platte Fougère Fl WR 10s, pick up ldg lts front Castle Breakwater Alt WR 10s 16M, rear Belvedere Ho Oc 10s 14M, 220°. When St Sampson front ldg lt FR is obscured, bear to E of line to open Castle Breakwater and Belvedere lts by about 2° to clear Agenor shoal, 1.8m.

(2) **Great Russel Channel** is 2M wide, easy of access, and has weaker streams than Little Russel. In rough weather or poor visibility it is safer. Enter it with W edge of Little Sark open E of the E side of Brecqhou. When St Martin's Pt comes well open S of Goubinière Rk (243°), make good 230°, allowing for tide, round Lower Heads S card buoy to make for St Peter Port. At night keep in the W sector of Noire Pute lt, Fl(2) WR 15s (W 220°-040°) as far as Lower Heads S card buoy, Q(6)+LFl 15s. Leave this close to stb and make directly for the Castle Breakwater lt, Al WR 10s, 16M.

(3) **From W and S** give the NW shore of Guernsey a berth of 3½M, Les Hanois lt 1½M and the S shore about 1M. At night do not let Les Hanois lt bear more than 164° until Casquet lt bears 051°. Round St Martin's Pt about a mile off and bring E side of Castle Cornet in line with White Rock lt ho (round, 11m) 350° and make good this line to clear the drying rks to port. If beating, keep Brehon tr E of N to avoid the Great Russel indraught. Remember that the E-going tide does not set N round St Martin's Pt till about Dover +3h. At night, from a position off St Martin's lt, Fl(3) WR 10s, keep the Old Hbr Oc R lt, 5s, just open of Terres Pt, 342°. When St Martin's lt bears 215°, steer 015° until White Rk Pier lt, Oc G 5s, comes on with Castle Breakwater lt, Alt WR 10s, 308°, when steer 330° until the Old Hbr lt bears 265°, thence enter.

Anchorages There are several anchorages suitable for use in offshore winds:
(1) **Icart Bay** and **Petit Port** on SE (each has drying rks in it and is subject to swell);
(2) **Havelet Bay** adjacent and S of St Peter Port is useful when the latter is crowded but swell can be a problem;
(3) **Grande Havre** and **L'Ancress Bay** on N side, the latter being more protected from SW winds. Clearance at St Peter Port or Beaucette is required before anchoring in any of these places.

ST PETER PORT   Chart BA 3140

HW: Dover −4¾h. DS: Dover −2h S; +4h N.
MHWS 9.0m MHWN 6.7 MTL 5.0 MLWN 3.5 MLWS 1.0
A good centre with all facilities.

Signals R lt from White Rock Pierhead: entry and exit from main hbr prohibited.
R lt from New Jetty: exit prohibited.
R lt from S pier of Old Hbr: entry/exit from marina prohibited.

Entrance Contact Port Control on VHF 12 ½h before arrival. Yachts are generally met by Hbr Patrol on or soon after entering. If waiting for marina opening, go straight ahead to holding pontoon at entrance to it. Ro Bn on Castle Breakwater lt ho transmits continuously on 285khz, 'GY', 10M.

Berthing Victoria Marina in Old Hbr is for visitors; it has a sill, drying 4.2m. Open HW−2½ to +2h. Albert Marina immediately to the S of it and North Beach Marina immediately N of main hbr are for local craft only.
There are also visitors' moorings in NW of main hbr, preferred by some to the marina especially if capable of taking the ground. Consult Port Officers.

Supplies Fuel point on S side of hbr, dries 2.5m; water in marina, at fuel pt and at root of Victoria Pier. All supplies and services.

Tel/VHF Hbr Office (0481) 20229/ch 16, 62, 78; Marina 25987/'Port Control' ch 12. Customs 26911. Link calls ch 62; DF bearings ch 16, 67.

ST SAMPSONS dries and is mainly a commercial hbr. Shipyard.

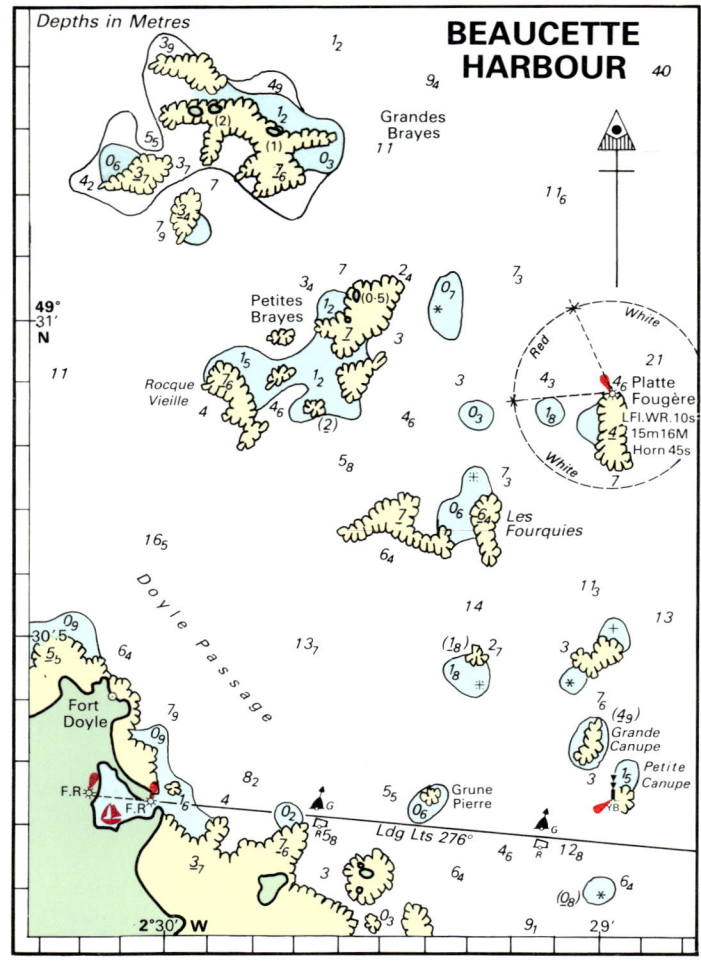

BEAUCETTE MARINA Charts BA 807, 808.
At NE corner of Guernsey in an old quarry.
Approach from NW in day by Doyle Passage: from 1M W of Platte Fougère Tr get Corbette d'Amont Y con bn midway between Herm and Jethou, 146°, 15m depth. Otherwise enter from Little Russel.
Entrance Channel buoyed, first pair lit, 1M N of Platte lt tr. Ldg lts front FR (W column R stripe), rear FR (R column W stripe) 276°. Can be dangerous in strong NE to E winds. Sill dries 2.4m, has about 2.7m at half-tide. 2 Y buoys for waiting entry.
Supplies Fuel, water, repairs, small shop.
Tel/VHF Marina (0481) 45000/ch 37.

SARK Chart BA 808
HW: Dover −4¾h. DS: NE coast is slack at half-tide and HW; SW coast is slack at half-tide and LW.
Off W coast, Dover +5h NE; −1h SW. Off E coast +6h NE; −1h SW
MHWS 9.7m MHWN 7.1 MTL 5.4 MLWN 3.6 MLWS 1.1
An unspoilt island with basic facilities and good anchorages, sometimes subject to swell.
Approach Should not be attempted by night. The safest, but longest, route from St Peter Port is to go S, round Lower Heads S card buoy; bound for La Grande Grève, Musé Passage (29m), Victoria Tr in line with N face of Castle Cornet 291°, is more direct; and if going N of Sark, use the mailboat route, Tobars passage. The transits are: (1) Grande Fauconnière bn (or, better, Bec du Nez of Sark) seen just over the S slope of Jethou, 090° (or 093°), (2) 2 ca short of Jethou, get Vale Mill in line with W edge of Brehon tr, 321°; hold this course for 2 ca. (3) Noire Pute just SE of Grande Fauconnière, 061°, leaving Quarter rks of Jethou ½ ca to port, and bearing off to leave Grande Fauconnière (steep-to) also ½ ca to port. Beware cross tides; these shorter routes are best taken near slack water.
Anchorages All may be subject to swell. None should be considered in onshore winds except the lightest.
(1) **La Grande Grève** on W coast has good sandy bottom but with a rock drying 0.3m in the middle and a group of drying rks in the S. Approaching from W keep S end of La Coupée on with N end of Pt de la Joue, 090°. From the S, first round Les Hautes Boues by keeping W end of Givaude bearing at least 355° or, if visible, on with middle of Grand Amfroque, 355°. Anchor 1 ca NE of Pt de la Joue. Long steep flights of steps to the top.
(2) **Havre Gosselin.** Approach from N with W-ly rk of Little Sark seen through Gouliot Passage 188° (half-tide is slack). Through Gouliot, head E leaving Moie de Gouliot (50m) ½ ca to port. Hbr is clear of dangers, no stream. Anchor in 5m, shingle and sand, as near to landing (300 steps) as convenient.
(3) **Dixcart and Derrible Bays** From SE with Sark Mill (no vanes) open W of Pt Chateau in Dixcart Bay 337°. Both are clear of danger in middle, sand 3 to 5m. Path at Dixcart to hotels and village.
(4) **Creux Hbr** dries and is full of local boats. It is sometimes possible for yachts to lie, with HM's permission, against one of the walls. Anchoring outside is difficult owing to local moorings and need to leave a passage for launches from Guernsey.
(5) **Maseline Hbr** is the main arrival place for supply ships and tourist boats. There is no room for yachts at the quay but it is possible to anchor in the bay, 10m. Approach from NE with E side of L'Etac de Sark in line with W side of Les Burons, 211°. When Pt Robert lt ho opens to S of Grande Moie, alter course to leave Grande Moie 1 ca max to N.
(6) **Grève de la Ville** is a good anchorage with cliff path to village. Approach from N with Noire Pierre (3.7m) midway between Grande Moie (30m) and NE face of Les Burons (22m) 153°. Noire Pierre is clean all round beyond 10m so pass either side and anchor in the bay, 11m sand.
Supplies Diesel is available in cans from the electricity company above Creux; water is difficult – there is a pipe in Creux. General stores, butcher, bank, pub and hotels.

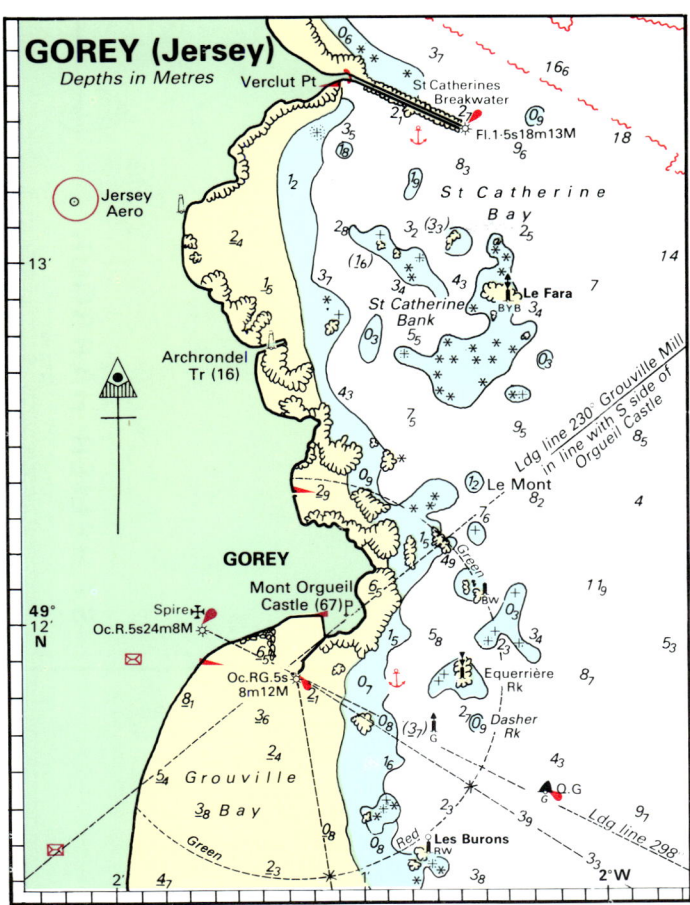

JERSEY
Chart BA 3655

A very popular holiday island, Jersey has a large marina, a number of drying hbrs and several good anchorages for offshore winds.

The SE corner has reefs extending for over 3M but the Is may be readily approached from SW to NW, and from N between the Paternosters and Dirouilles groups.

At N and S of Jersey it is slack water at local HW and HW+5h by the shore. At E and W ends of the Is it is slack water at about half-tide by the shore.

Yachts arriving from outside the Bailiwick, unless from the Minquiers or Ecrehous, must clear at either St Helier or Gorey.

GOREY
Charts BA 1138, 3655

An attractive drying (3 to 5m) hbr but generally very crowded.

Approach From NE, the ldg line is Grouville white mill (rear) over SE slope of Mont Orgeuil Castle (front), 230°. At night use the ldg lts (see 'Entrance'). From SE, at a position 1M E of Grande Anquette Refuge BW bn, steer on line pierhead with Gorey ch spire, 305°. When abeam of Le Giffard R can buoy, alter course to N for leading line.

Entrance Ldg line 298°, front W frame tr Oc RG 5s 8m, rear WR patch on stone wall with Oc R 5s 24m. When leaving, if bound N go at half flood with N-going inshore eddy.

Anchorage There are some drying visitors' moorings. Otherwise anchor E of pier, stream runs fast; or take the ground inside, hard sand, mooring bow and stern; or lie alongside pier inside staging at pierhead. Also at St Catherine's Bay inside breakwater off Verclut Pt, sand and weed, 3 to 9m, moderate holding.

Supplies Fuel and water at end of pier. Shops.

Tel/VHF HM (0534) 53616/ch 74 at HW±3h.

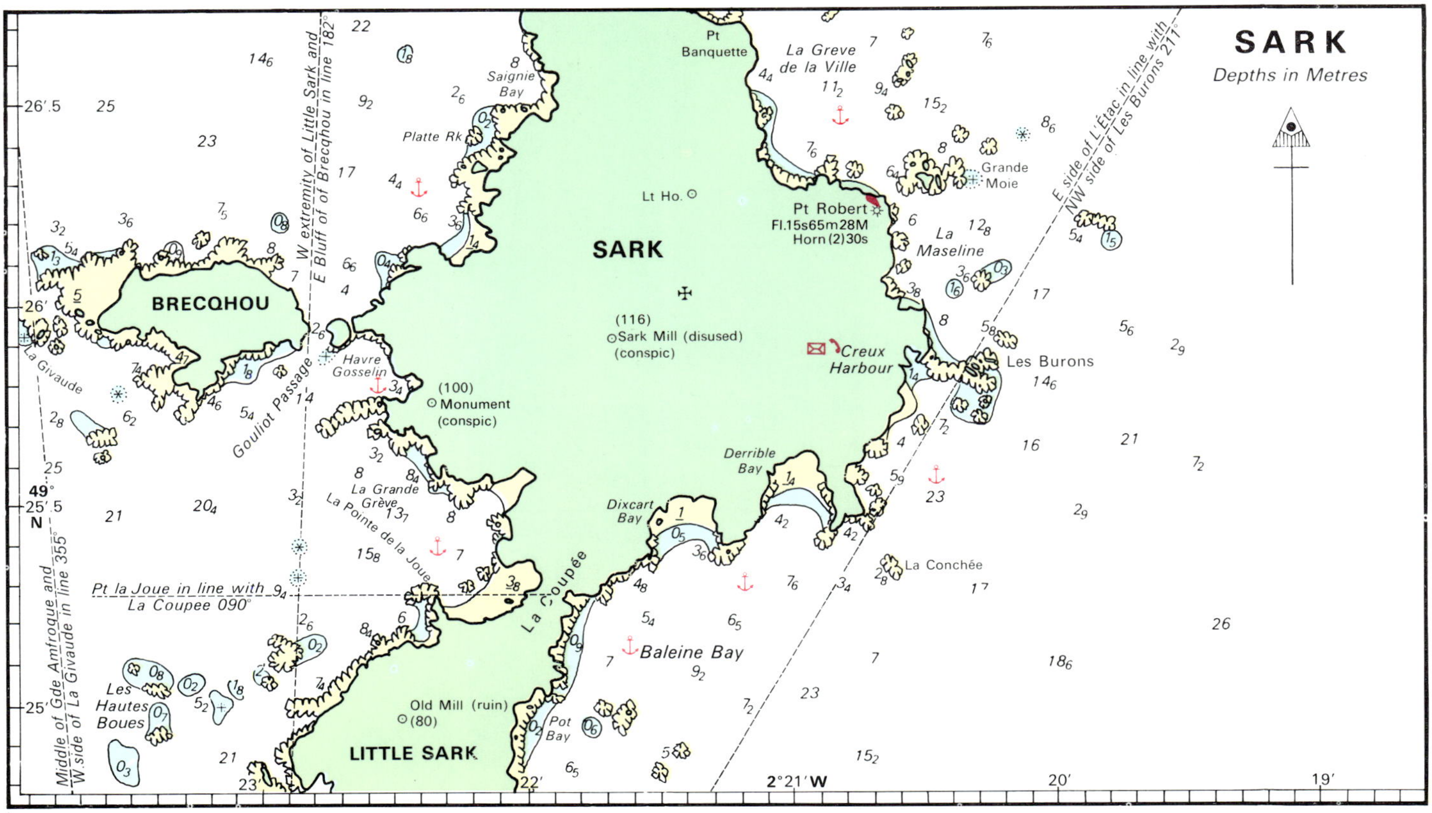

FRANCE, NORTH COAST 324

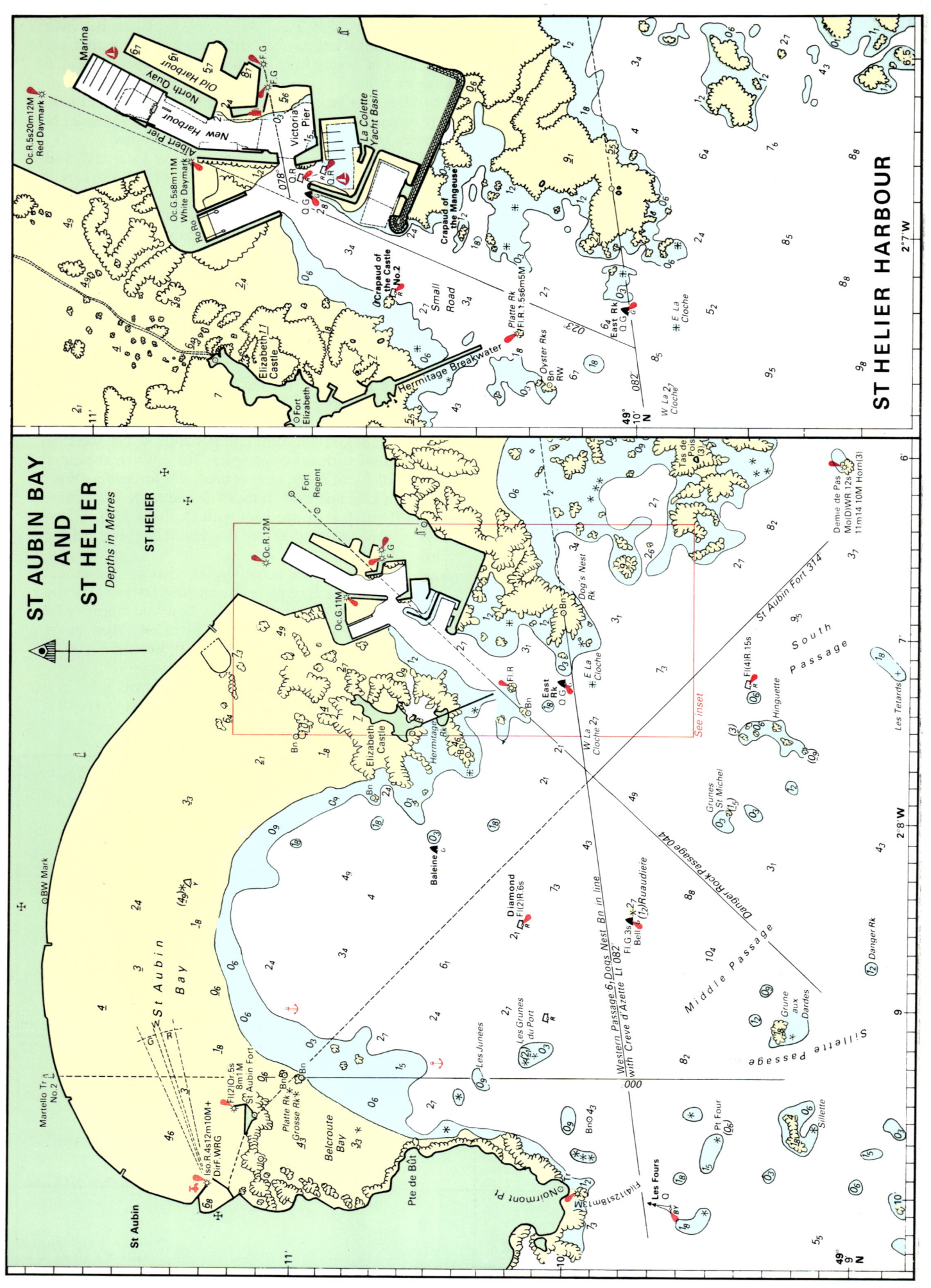

ST HELIER
Charts BA 1137; hbr 3278
HW: Dover −4¾h. DS (2M S): Dover −4½h W; +2¼ E
MHWS 11.1m MHWN 8.1 MTL 6.2 MLWN 4.1 MLWS 1.3

Approach from NW, rounding La Corbière, keep the summit of Jersey high land in line with or above the lantern of the lt ho, but in bad NW weather keep 1½M off; at night keep the FR lt to the NE at the level of Corbière lantern. Once round keep ½M off S coast until just E of Noirmont Pt it is possible to get on the Western Passage ldg line, front Dog's Nest W bn, globe top; rear la Grève d'Azette RW lt tr, 082°.

At night (1) keep Noirmont Pt lt ho bearing 095° until La Corbière lt ho is touching La Moye Pt, 290°.

(2) Then steer 110° on that back bearing to pass about 2 ca S of Noirmont Pt.

(3) When Noirmont Pt is abeam, steer 082° on Western Passage ldg lts: front La Grève d'Azette lt ho, Oc 5s; rear Mont Ubé lt tr Oc R 5s. This passage passes N of Les Fours N card buoy Q; N of Ruaudière G bell buoy, Fl G 3s; and S of RW Oyster Rk bn.

(4) Soon after passing Oyster Rk bn, and before reaching East Rk G con buoy Q G, alter course to port round Platte bn, Fl R, to bring ldg lts in transit: front Oc G 5s, rear Oc R 5s synchronised (W patches by day), 023°.

From Gorey come down E coast on line La Coupé Turret open E of Verclut Pt 332° until about ½M N of Violet pillar buoy, RWVS Fl 10s. Steer about 240° to leave this buoy close to port and continue to pick up the line Icho BW Tr, 14m, open S of Conchière bn, 2m, disc top. After about ½M on this line steer W to pass mid-way between Conchière bn and Canger W card buoy, Q(9) 15s and continue so as to pick up line Noirmont lt ho B tr W band, Fl(4) 12s open S of Demie de Pas YB tr 11m Mo(D) WR (R 130° to 303°), 290°. Follow this line until ½M from Demie de Pas, then pass 2 ca to the S to get St Aubin Fort bearing 314°. Keep on this bearing, leaving Hinguette R can buoy, Fl(4) R 15s to port and East Rk G con buoy, Q G, to stb until on hbr ldg line, (see above), 023°.

Signals at Victoria Pier Hd: FG/Fl G: vessels may enter but not leave; FR/Fl R: vessels may leave but not enter. Q amber in addition: power craft under 25m may proceed contrary to signals.

Entrance Yachts exceeding 14m loa or 1.8m draught should call Port Control on VHF 14 to confirm there is berthing space. All should watch on this ch. Keep on ldg marks until entrance opens: two G lts in line 078°. Beware strong cross-set.

Berthing Visitors are directed by Port Control to marina in N part of hbr. There is a fixed sill 3.6m above CD; on this a hinged gate rises 1.4m to maintain 5m inside. The flap is lowered when there is 5.7m and raised at 5.8m. FG shows when flap is down, FR when raised. Fl R denotes gate is being raised or lowered, when it is highly dangerous to attempt to pass. Depth gauges and an electric indicator board show when entry and exit are possible, approx HW±3h. Visitors normally berth at piers E, F or G at N end. Marina sometimes full in Aug. Two weeks maximum stay.

When marina is closed yachts should go to La Collette basin, entrance 1m, immediately S of hbr entrance after G con buoy Q G. Wait at first, 'D', pontoon, dredged 1.8m. Anchoring outside in Small Roads is not recommended owing to shipping movements.

Supplies Water at pontoons; fuel at E side of main hbr, opposite entrance. All facilities.

Tel/VHF Port Office (0534) 34451/ch 16, 14. Marina 79549/ch 14 (Port Control). Customs 73561.

ST AUBIN
Chart BA 1137

A pleasant but drying hbr, much quieter than St Helier.

Approach as for St Helier but from Ruaudière G con buoy, Fl G 3s, turn N to leave Diamond R can buoy, Fl(2) R 6s, close to port and steer 332° for 1.3M leaving two bns SSE of fort well to port.

Entrance A causeway between the fort and the shore dries 5.1m. The channel has small port and stb buoys, 252°. At night steer 252° in W sector of lt Dir F WRG on N pier head with lt Iso R 4s. Tide gauge on N pierhead; enter HW±1½h.

Berthing There are berths for about 10 visiting yachts alongside N quay: dry, mud. Anchorage E of Platte Rk bn SE of fort, 2m. RCIYC has three moorings for visitors in Belcroute Bay, 3½ ca S of fort, 0.9m.

Supplies Water on quay, fuel, shops, boatyard.

Tel RCIYC (0534) 41023.

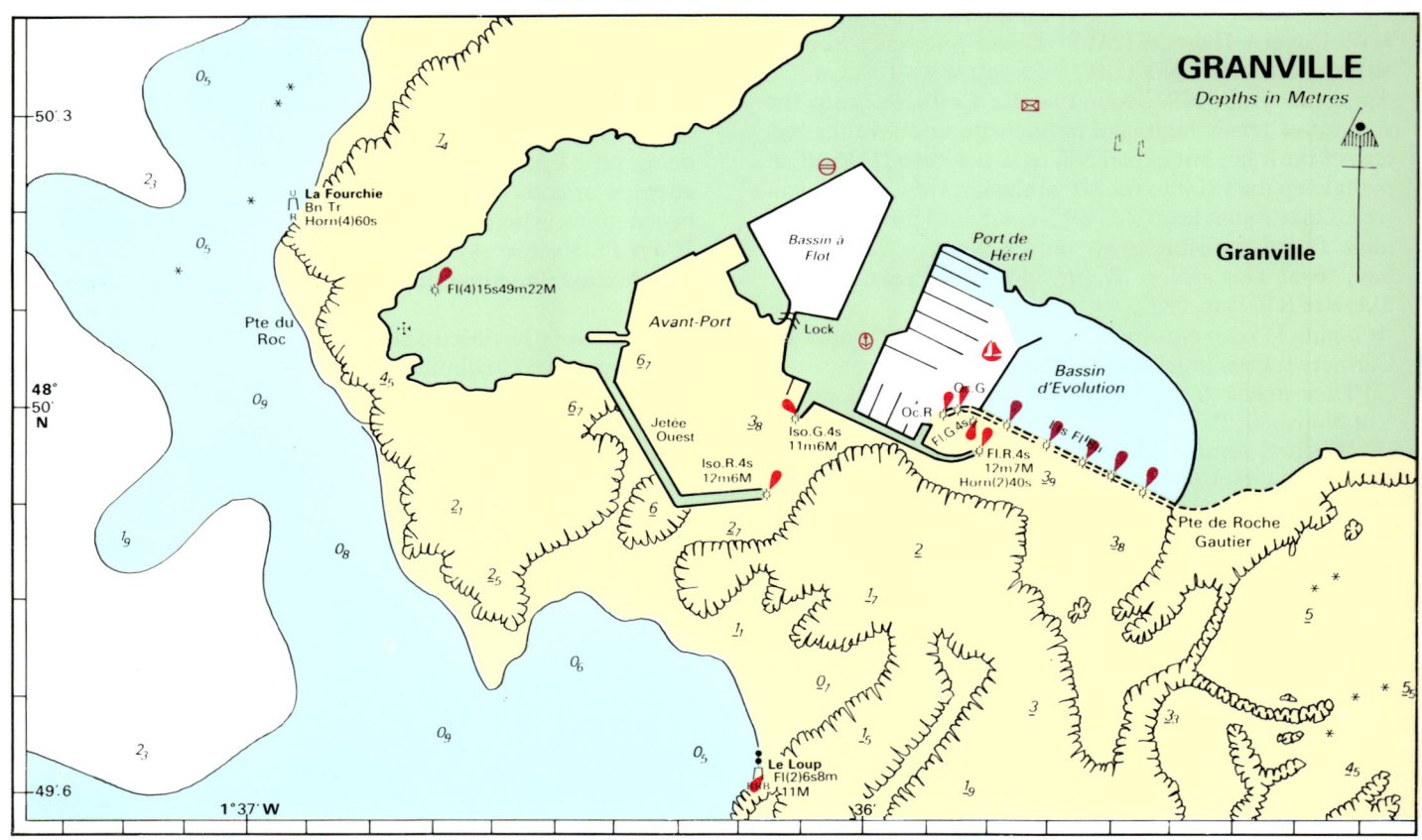

FRANCE, NORTH COAST

PASSAGE NOTES: W COAST OF THE CHERBOURG PENINSULA

Charts BA 2669; F 6966 or 824 to 828
The W side of the Cherbourg Peninsula is an inhospitable and rocky coast, with shoals and mussel and oyster parks extending far offshore, exposed to winds with any W in them. There is no sheltered anchorage and Granville, the only port with a wet basin, can be approached only after half tide. Landmarks are few and difficult to identify and fog may occur at any season. Tides run strongly and the westerly swell breaks heavily on the shoals. There is an area of abnormal magnetic variation around Cap Flamanville. Nevertheless although it is simpler to go W of Jersey and Les Minquiers, this inshore passage provides the most direct route between Cherbourg, St Malo and Granville, for which there are two channels: Passage de la Déroute and Déroute de Terre.

Passage de la Déroute leads from Cap de la Hague between Les Ecrehou and Basses de Taillepied; between Basse Occidentale des Boeufs and S Anquette (beware dangerous wreck position (doubtful) 49°05′.00N, 1°50′.00W); W of Basse Le Marié; E of Les Ardentes; over Banc de la Corbière and through Entrée de la Déroute between Les Minquiers and Iles Chausey. In the narrows the flood runs at 4 to 5kn, the ebb at 3½ to 4kn.

Déroute de Terre should be attempted only near HW there being only 0.9m at the S end. It passes inshore between Trois Grunes and Cap Carteret; between Bancs Félés and Basses de Portbail; between Basse Jourdan lt buoy and the buoy NW of Le Sénéquet; close E of special buoy, marking outer edge of oyster beds, 4M SW of Sénéquet lt; E of La Catheue buoy; E of a wreck buoy to 1M W of Pte du Roc and so to Granville.
The night passage involves eight transits on shore lights; details in Admiralty Pilot.

DIELETTE
Chart F 6059.
Dielette is a small drying hbr about 11M S of Cap de la Hague, sheltered between ENE and S. Entrance dries 2.1m.

CARTERET
Chart F 825.
Carteret is a small fishing port 10M S of Cap de Flamanville Approach dries 4m for ½M. Berth at N part of quay, N of slip; or mooring area dries 8m.

GRANVILLE
Charts BA 3672; F 5897
HW: Dover —5h. DS (1½M offshore): Dover —5h NE; HWD SW

MHWS 12.8m MHWN 9.6 MTL 7.1 MLWN 4.6 MLWS 1.4
A commercial and fishing port; also a popular holiday resort and yachting centre. Accessible only after half-flood.

Approach is rough in strong winds between W and NW. Pte du Roc has a steep cliff under grey, circular lt tr with R top, Fl(4) 15s. 3½M to W is a W card buoy, VQ(9) 10s, marking Videcoq Rk (dries 1m).

Entrance Best to arrive at HW −½h. From Videcoq buoy steer 090° to leave Le Loup BR lt tr, Fl(2) 6s to stb and W jetty head, Iso R 4s, to port. Continue easterly past Avant Port and double back round the southern breakwater, Fl R 4s, leading to the Port de Herel marina basin. Keep clear of line of R posts, Fl Bu, marking the submersible breakwater of the dinghy basin.

Berthing Access to the marina is over a hinged gate, 16m wide, between R and G bns, Oc R or G 4s. The gate opens and closes at HW ±3 to ±3½h when there is 1.40m on the sill. An illuminated panel on the breakwater shows the depth of water on the sill. If the panel shows «0», entry is forbidden as the gate is closed. Moor to ends of first two pontoons, in front of office, 2.5m (but only 1.3m in N end of basin).
Supplies Fuel on quay; water on pontoons. All facilities.
Tel/VHF Capitainerie du Port (33) 50-17-75/ch 12, 16. Port Herel (Marina) (33) 50-20-06/ch 9. Customs (33) 50-19-90.

ILES CHAUSEY Charts BA 3656, F 829, 830
HW: Dover −5h. DS 1M N and S: Dover +1½h E; −5h W
1M E and W: Dover +4¼h N; −2½h S. Up to 3¾kn.
MHWS 12.9m MHWN 9.8 MTL 7.4 MLWN 4.9 MLWS 1.9

A beautiful archipelago of islets and rocks. Grande Ile, the largest island, with anchorage and moorings in the Sound on its NE side. Much frequented in summer.
Approach is straightforward from the S. The N is more difficult; marks are harder to distinguish and the approach dries.
Entrance from a position SE of the grey square lt ho, Fl 5s, 38m (horn 30s), on SE tip of Grande Ile, steer 332° with La Crabière Est S card bn, Oc RWG 4s (W 329° to 335°) in line with L'Enseigne W tr, to leave Epiettes G con bell buoy, Fl G 2s, to stb. Keep La Crabière close to stb, and bear 30° to port to leave next RW bn to stb.
Berthing Moorings are normally available in the Sound, sheltered at LW, apart from swell from SE winds; but exposed at HW and uncomfortable with wind against tide. Anchorage is restricted by moorings but craft that dry out can find large stretches of flat sand, but beware rocky outcrops and poor holding with strong streams. The N part dries at springs but there is 2m in S. Anchorage is also possible in the bay to the W of the lt ho, sheltered from NW to E.

CANCALE Chart BA 3659.
Cancale dries and is considerably obstructed by oyster parks and stakes. It is suitable for smaller yachts only. There is an anchorage, in suitable weather, between Pte de la Chaine and Ile des Rimains, 5m; strong stream.

ROTHÉNEUF Charts BA 2700, F 5645
HW: Dover −5¼h. DS (Chenal de la Bigne): Dover +1¾h NE; −5h SW
MHWS 12.1m MHWN 9.1

A drying hbr about 3M E of St Malo, offering good shelter.
Approach and Entrance The approach is dangerous near HW when the rks are covered; and the flood, crossing the approach, is at its strongest just after half-tide. It is best to approach before then and if necessary anchor outside to await more water.
Leave St Malo by Chenal de la Bigne; after passing La Petite Bigne G bn 50m to port, continue on that line (042°) to leave Le Durand (dries 10m) and le Roger (dries 4.7m) to stb, until the entrance bn, G cone up, is about 7 ca off bearing 175°. Steer on that course to leave the bn close to stb. If too early to enter, anchor to await the tide about 50m N of this bn, 3-4m.
Anchorage The whole hbr dries about 8m, good flat sand.
Supplies Shops in village.

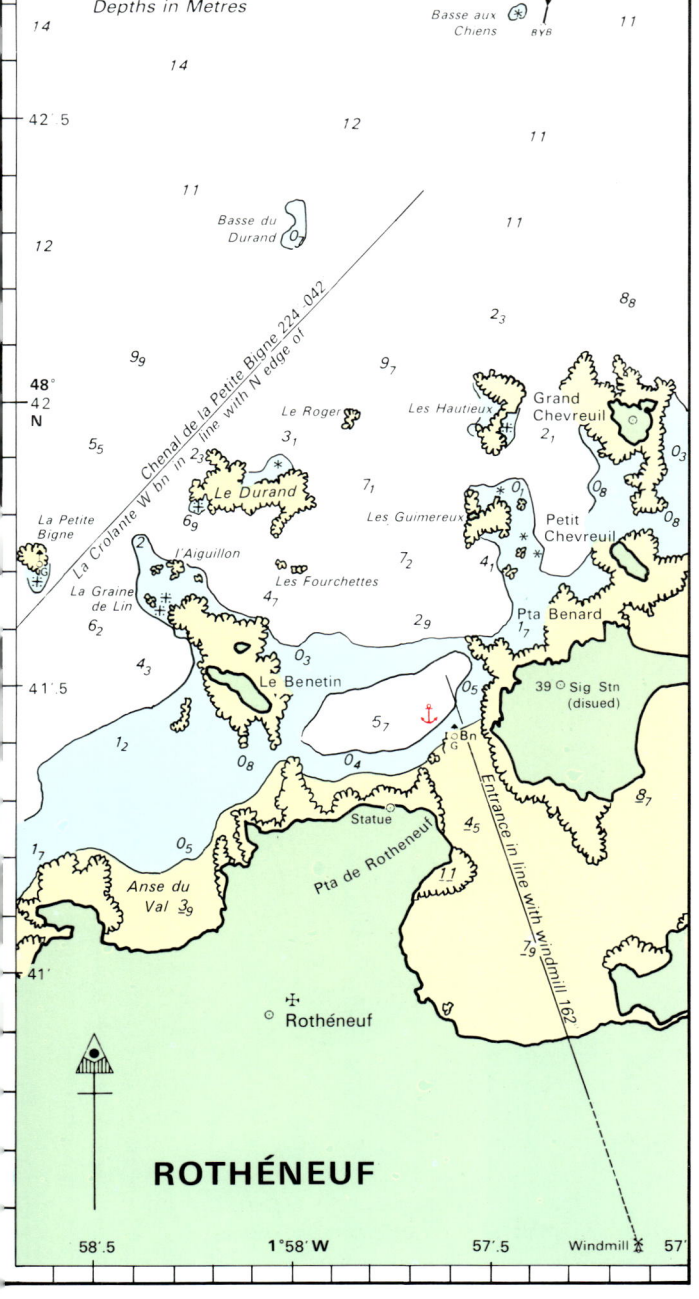

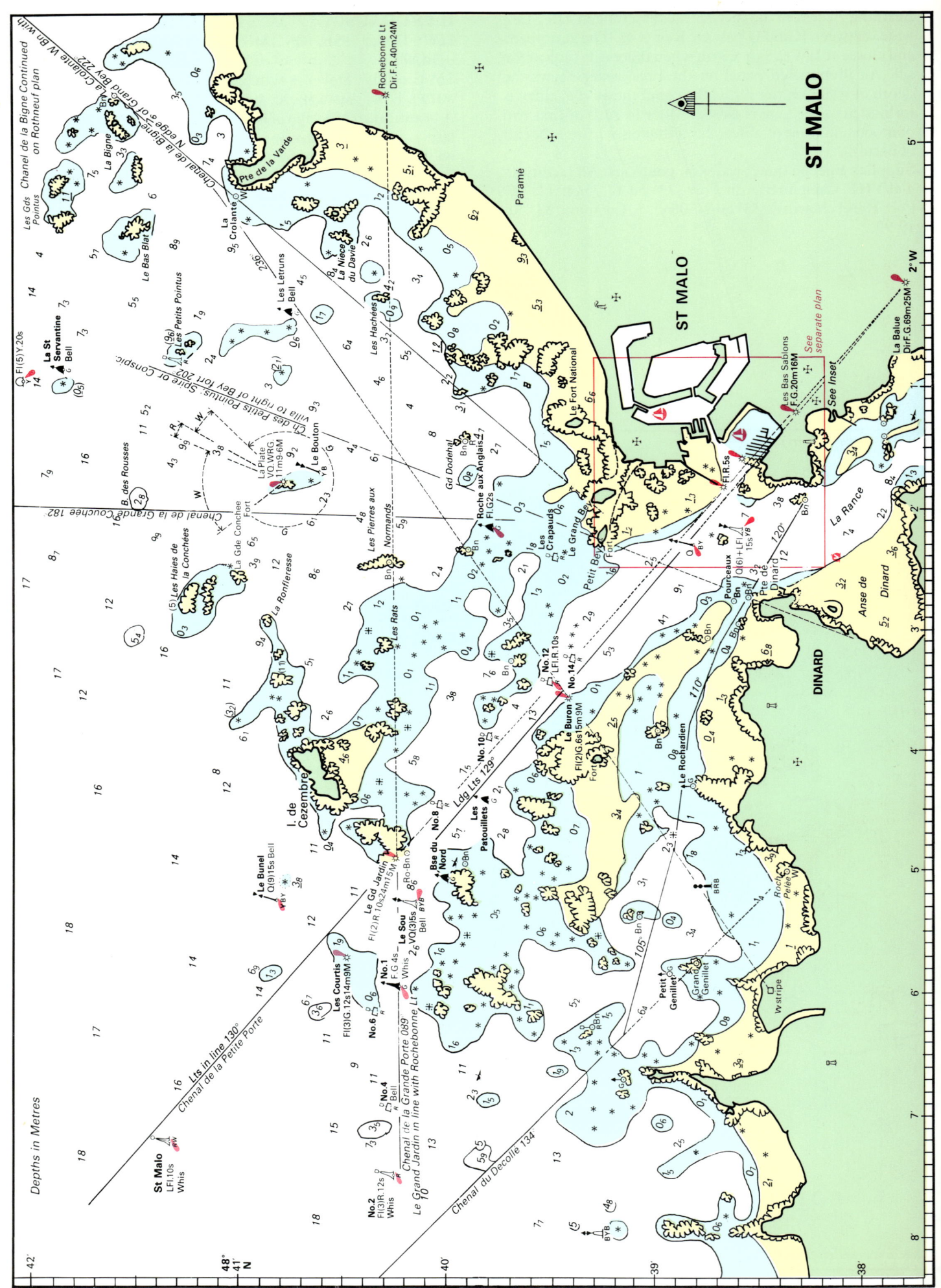

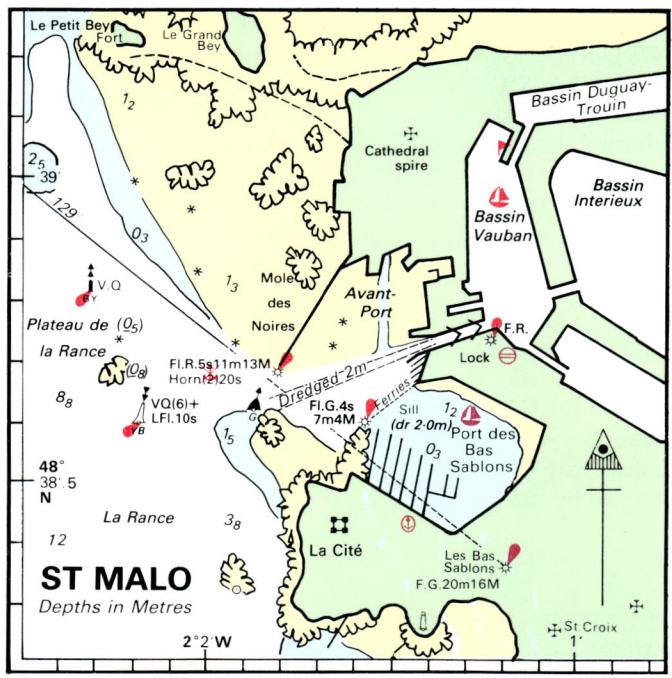

ST MALO Charts BA 2700, F 4233, 5645
HW: Dover −5¼h. DS In Grande and Petite Port channels: Dover +2¼h E; −4½h W
In Chenal des Petits-Pointus: Dover +1¾h E; −5h WSW
MHWS 12.1m MHWN 9.1 MTL 6.7 MLWN 4.4 MLWS 1.4
St Malo is an attractive old town with good shops and yacht moorings in the locked docks and an outside marina.
Approach There are six approach channels, of which only the second and third are lighted. Beware strong cross-streams. From W to E they are as follows:

Chenal du Décollé is the shortest approach from the W but is unlit. Starting about 3½ ca SW of No 2 R buoy, get W pyramid on Roche Pelée in line with W bn tr Grand Genillet, 134°. From this line steer with Pte de Dinard bn on with Rochardien bn 105°, altering course to N to round the latter to get on line of Ste-Croix ch round belfry with Pourceaux bn, 110° to round Pte de Dinard, marked by two stb bns.

Chenal de la Grande Porte (7.2m) is the main approach from W. Le Grand Jardin grey tr, Fl(2) R 10s, 24m, in line with Rochebonne W square tr, R top, Dir F R (intense 088°-090°) 40m, 089°. The latter is difficult to distinguish by day; the buoyed channel can be followed. In mist use Grand Jardin Ro bn, 294.2khz, GJ, 2 and 6 min, until at Buharats No 2 whistle port buoy, VQ R, then No 4 R can bell buoy and to stb No 1 whistle buoy, Fl G 4s. Finally No 3 Le Sou bell buoy Q(3) 5s marks the turn into Chenal de la Petite Porte.

Chenal de la Petite Porte (7.2m) is the approach from NW. From the RW safewater whistle buoy, L Fl, get Le Jardin lt tr in line with La Balue grey square lt tr (on high ground behind town), FG, 130°. Beware strong cross-streams. When about 4 ca off Le Jardin, bear S to get Bas-Sablons W square lt tr, B top, F G (intense 128°-131°) 20m, in line with La Balue, 129°.

Chenal de la Grande Conchée can be taken by day at all times save LWS; least depth 0.5m. Identify La Grande Conchée, a rk with round ruined fort on top, 5m, 1M E of Ile de Cézembre.
From a position 3ca E, steer 182° to leave La Plate BY N card lt tr, VQ WRG, to port. At night keep in W sector; R sector covers La Servantine Rk. Beware strong cross-stream and alter course if necessary to leave Roche aux Anglais G stb buoy, Fl G, clear to stb and bear SW to leave Les Crapauds R can buoy to port to join Chenal de la Petite Porte. Shallows are E and SE of Roche aux Anglais and W of Les Crapauds - about 0.5m, but easily passable after half-tide.

Chenal des Petits Pointus is another day channel for good visibility, with 0.3m but is the most direct from Iles Chausey. From a position 1¼M W of Rochefort bn tr steer 202° on line of W edge of small fort on Petit Bey with either high W house with four chimneys or with bell tower of Dinard ch to join Chenal de la Bigne NE of Roche aux Anglais.

Chenal de la Bigne (0.5m) is a useful short cut bound from Granville or Cancale. Start about ¾M E of Rochefort bn tr and steer 222° with La Crolante W bn tr in line with N edge of Grand Bey. Be careful to be on this line when passing the narrow gap E of La Bigne stb bn. ¼M after La Bigne bn, steer 236° with Le Buron G lt tr in line with W stripe under a villa on Pte Bellefard (if the latter not visible, keep Buron just left of Ile Harbour fort behind Buron). In rounding La Crolante keep at least 200m to NW to clear unmarked drying rk (3.2m) to SW of it. When La Plate tr comes on with Conchée fort, bear to port, 222°, to S of Roche aux Anglais buoy to join Chenal des Petits Pointus.

Entrance In the main channel get leading lts, front Bas-Sablons W square tr, B top; rear La Balue grey square tr, both FG, in line 129°; channel is well marked. This leads N of N card Rance buoy, Q, to head of Môle des Noirs, Fl R 5s. Port des Bas Sablons (St Servan marina) is to stb of approach to the locks (dredged 2m).

Berthing (1) **Port des Bas Sablons** (marina) has a sill, drying 2m, from the ferry terminal (forming S approach to the lock) linked to a jetty off the Fort de la Cité. Entry is possible at 1h to 1½h after LW with tidal coefficient over 70. Passage is possible at all times at neaps (coefficient 40). There are three waiting buoys; entry is suspended when a ferry is clearing the lock. A tide gauge at the head of the ferry pier, with large illuminated repeater on NW wall, shows depth on the sill, which is unmarked when covered. The head of the jetty is lit, Fl G 4s, but there is no corresponding R lt at the far end of the sill. Inside tie to end of first pontoon and report. Sheltered at LW but surge when sill is covered, especially with strong NW-lies.

(2) **Bassin Vauban** in the docks, reached via L'écluse du Naye, gates work between HW±2½h, varied according to tide. Simplified code of signals. Possible to wait for opening in Port des Bas Sablons. Yachts enter after ships and fishing boats; high lock sides require keepers' help with mooring lines. Yachts are moored to quay and pontoons at N end of Bassin Vauban; when full it is necessary to pass the lifting br into bassin Duguay-Trouin and moor to quay immediately to left after the br. Well protected and near old town.

Supplies Fuel from garages. Water on pontoons at both marinas.
Tel/VHF Port Captain (at lock) (99) 81-62-86/ch 12; Bas Sablons Y Hbr (99) 81-71-34/ch 9 (0800-1200, 1400-1700); Vauban Port de Plaisance (99) 56-51-91/ch 12; Customs (99) 81-65-90.

RIVER RANCE   Chart F 4233

The Rance is dammed by a hydro-electric barrage 1M above St Servan. A lock at the W end gives access to the river which with a reasonable engine and less than 1.6m draught and 16m head height is navigable to Dinan, above Le Châtelier lock, and thence to Brittany canal system. Above Dinan the canal has max 1.2m draught and 2.5m headroom.
Approach, dredged 2m, is along W shore by La Jument G lt tr, Fl(5) G 20s 4M, leaving to port an exclusion safety zone below the barrage, marked by R conical buoys, cylinder topmarks, lettered ZI with a number. ZI 12 is lit, Fl R 4s.
Signals at the lock:
Ball or R lt: No entry from N. Cone pt down or G lt: No entry from S.
Ball and cone or R and G lts: No entry either way.
Signals near the centre of the barrage:
W cone over B cone, pts up or G over W lts: Flood stream through sluices.
B cone over W cone, pts up or W over G lts: Ebb stream through sluices.
Entrance The lock is 65m by 13m with 2m depth on the sill, and has floating bollards. It works from 0430h to 2030h and opens on the hour when height of tide on each side of it exceeds 4m. Yachts should arrive 20 min before opening (30 min if leaving). There are dolphins for waiting but bases dry 1.2m. Boats with no masts enter last (first when descending) as they may be berthed under the lowered br.
Water levels do not follow the tide times. They are given 24h in advance at St Malo office and at the locks at the barrage and at Châtelier. The channel dries at LW between St Suliac and Le Châtelier. Le Châtelier lock, 3M below Dinan, opens when the depth exceeds 7.3m, giving about 5h working per tide. When the lock is working there is 2m in the approach. Boats with 1.8m draught can lock through and berth to stb, but cannot get to Dinan. To Châtelier from seaward, leave HW−3h to have the best conditions above Mordreuc. From Châtelier to the sea, leave at HW.
Headroom: Pont St Hubert 23m; De Lessard viaduct 18.9m.
Anchorage anywhere up to St Suliac clear of main channel; holding variable. Deep water moorings off St Juliac and Mordreux.

BAIE DE ST BRIEUC   Charts BA 3674, F 833.

The hbrs dry except Le Légué and Binic which have wet basins. The best anchorage in westerly winds is in the Anse de Bréhec, 48°43'N, 2°56'W.

ERQUY   Charts BA 3672, F 5724, 833

HW: Dover −5¼h. DS (Chenal D'Erquy): Dover +1½h ENE; −5h WSW
MHWS 11.2m   MHWN 8.5   MTL 6.3   MLWN 4.1   MLWS 1.3
A drying hbr whose roadstead provides a useful passage anchorage.
Approach From E, steer 229° through Chenal d'Erquy (dangerous with strong wind against tide) with Cap d'Erquy in line with Le Verdelet Rk, leaving two S card buoys to stb. When Rohein YB lt tr, VQ RWG 10s, is behind La Basse de Courant S card buoy, bear to stb to round the headland about 2 ca off. From W, from a ca S of Rohein lt tr make good 100° until the jetty W lt tr, R top, Oc(2+1) WRG bears 090°: Enter in W sector.
Anchorage Good holding ½M W of jetty. Not recommended with fresh SW winds. Berths at or in lee of jetty are taken by fishing boats.

ST BRIEUC (LE LÉGUÉ)   Charts BA 3674, F 833

HW: Dover −5¼h
MHWS 11.2m   MHWN 8.5   MTL 6.3   MLWN 4.1   MLWS 1.3
Approach W of Grand Léjon RW lt tr, Fl(5)RW 20s, 17m, and 1½M W of Le Rohein YB lt tr, VQ RWG 10s. At night keep in W sector of Grand Léjon (350°-015°) leading between Roches de St Quay and Le Rohein, to the landfall RW buoy, Mo(A) 10s; thence make good 220°.
Entrance Channel dries 5.6m, buoyed and lit. Entrance lock opening times between HW−2h and +1½h according to tide.
Berthing at end of basin beyond the swinging bay.
Supplies Fuel from tanker or garage; water; shops.
Tel/VHF Capitainerie (99) 33-35-41/ch 12 (during locking times).

BINIC   Chart F 5725

HW: Dover −5¼h
MHWS 11.2m   MHWN 8.5   MTL 6.3   MHLWN 4.1   MLWS 1.3
A small port with drying avant port and wet basin.
Approach from the NW is easier offshore of St Quay Portrieux rocky plateau rather than by the inshore passage.
Entrance to avant port dries 5m; W tr, Oc(3) 12s on N mole. Wet basin has a single pair of gates; entry is possible between HW±1h at springs but not at all at neaps with a HW less than 9.5m (coefficient 65).
Berthing in wet basin on pontoons or to dolphins. Outer harbour has hard flat sand; space limited. N jetty mostly occupied by fishing boats; S has rocky base.
Supplies Petrol; water; shops.
Tel/VHF Capitainerie (96) 73-61-86/ch 9.

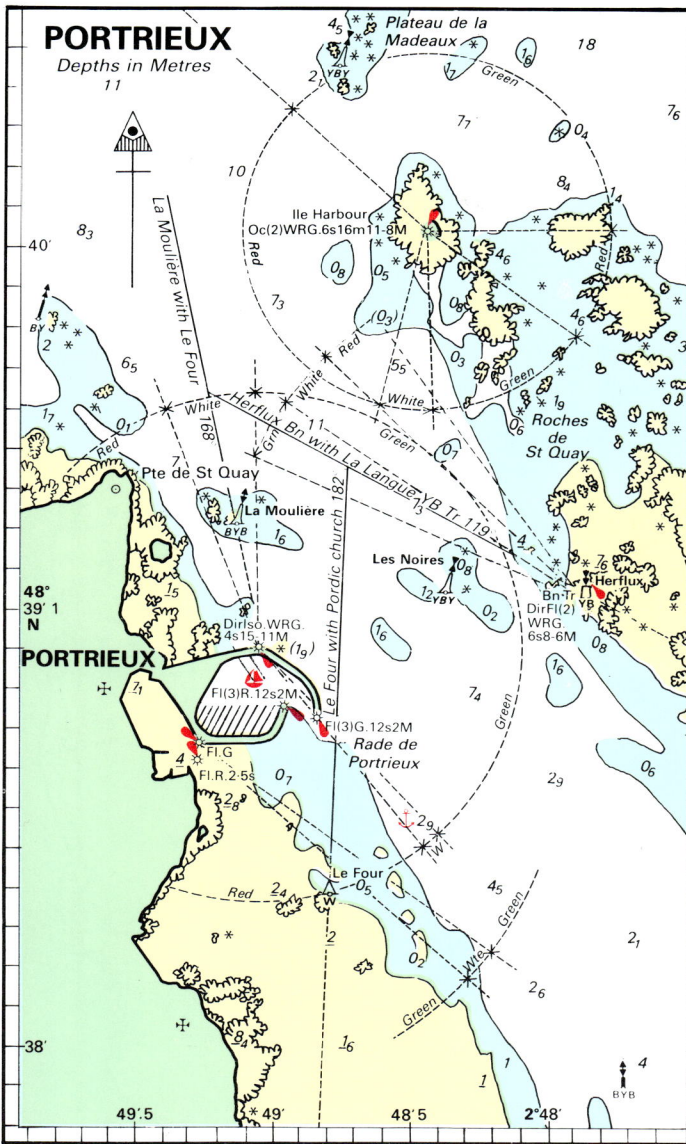

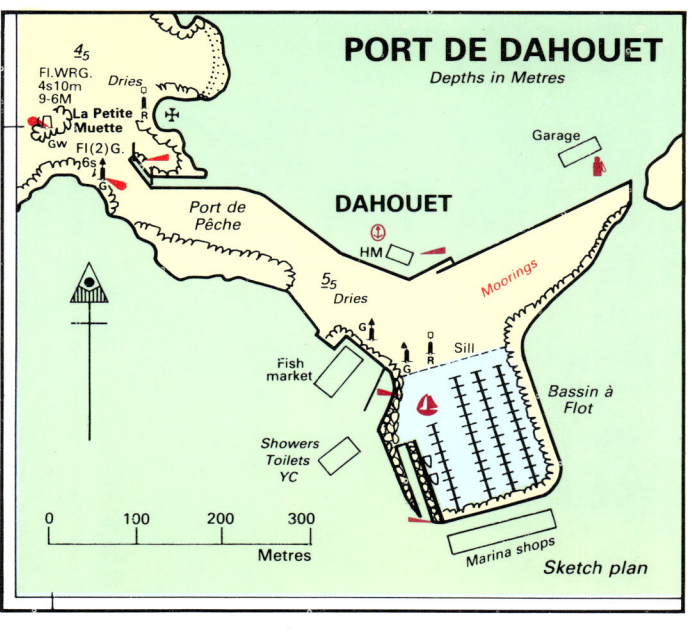

SAINT QUAY, PORTRIEUX Charts BA 3672, F 5725
HW: Dover −5¼h. DS (W of Roches St Quay): Dover +1h SSE; −5¼h NW, 2kn
MHWS 11.2m MHWN 8.5 MTL 6.3 MLWN 4.1 MLWS 1.3
A 950-berth marina, 10% reserved for visitors opens mid-summer 1990; dredged to 3.5m. There is also a drying hbr where it is not easy in summer to find a place to moor.
Approach Transit lines are, from N: at 1½M N of Ile Harbour W lt ho, Oc(2) RWG, La Moulière YB E card tr with slender lt tr on N mole of marina, 168°; Herflux S card tr with La Longue YB S card tr, 119°; Le Four tr with Pordic ch 182° to entrance. From S, La Hergue W tr with the Pte St Quay (W ho and FS), 317°. The marina is built on to the NE side of the old hbr.
Entrance to the marina is accessible at all states of the tide; entrance lts are Fl(3) G (stb) and Fl(3) R (port) each 12s. Entrance to the old hbr dries 3m; entrance lts are Fl G (stb) and Fl R (port) each 2.5s.
Berthing to pontoons in marina, max 18m loa. Anchorage in Rade. Good holding but exposed at HW to N through E to S.
Supplies Petrol and water on quay. Fuel and water in marina.
Tel Marina office (96) 70-96-67.

DAHOUET Charts BA 3674, F 833.
HW: Dover -5¼h. DS Plateau des Jaunes Dover +1½h ESE; -5h. W.
MHWS 11.3m MHWN 8.7 MTL 6.3 MLWN 3.9 MLWS 1.3.
A small fishing port with drying anchorage and wet basin.
Approach from NW leaving Rohein W card bn tr, VQ(9) WRG 10s 8M and Plateau des Jaunes W card bn tr both to port and Dahouet N card buoy to stb. At night keep in W sector, 114°-146° of Petite Muette lt Fl WRG 4s 9/6M.
Entrance Lies in a gap in the cliffs 1M SW of Pte Pléneuf. Bar is dangerous with strong NW winds and on the ebb with any sea. Await HW for entry, otherwise accessible at half-tide with 1m draught. La Petite Muette lt tr may be passed on either side but ldg line 133°, pagoda just open N of tr, leaves it to stb, then steer S between tr and port bn at edge of shore, then to SE as entrance opens. The S approach with tr to port is on line of two ldg bns, 100°.
Berthing Avant port reserved for fishing boats. NE branch of inner hbr has 180 drying moorings on buoys. On the S side the wet basin has pontoons with 15 visitors' berths up to 12m o.a. and 2.4m draught at neaps. Sill passable HW ± 2h. Fair weather anchorage W of Petite Muette 2m.
Supplies Water, fuel, gas, provisions.
Tel HM 96.72.82.85.

FRANCE, NORTH COAST 332

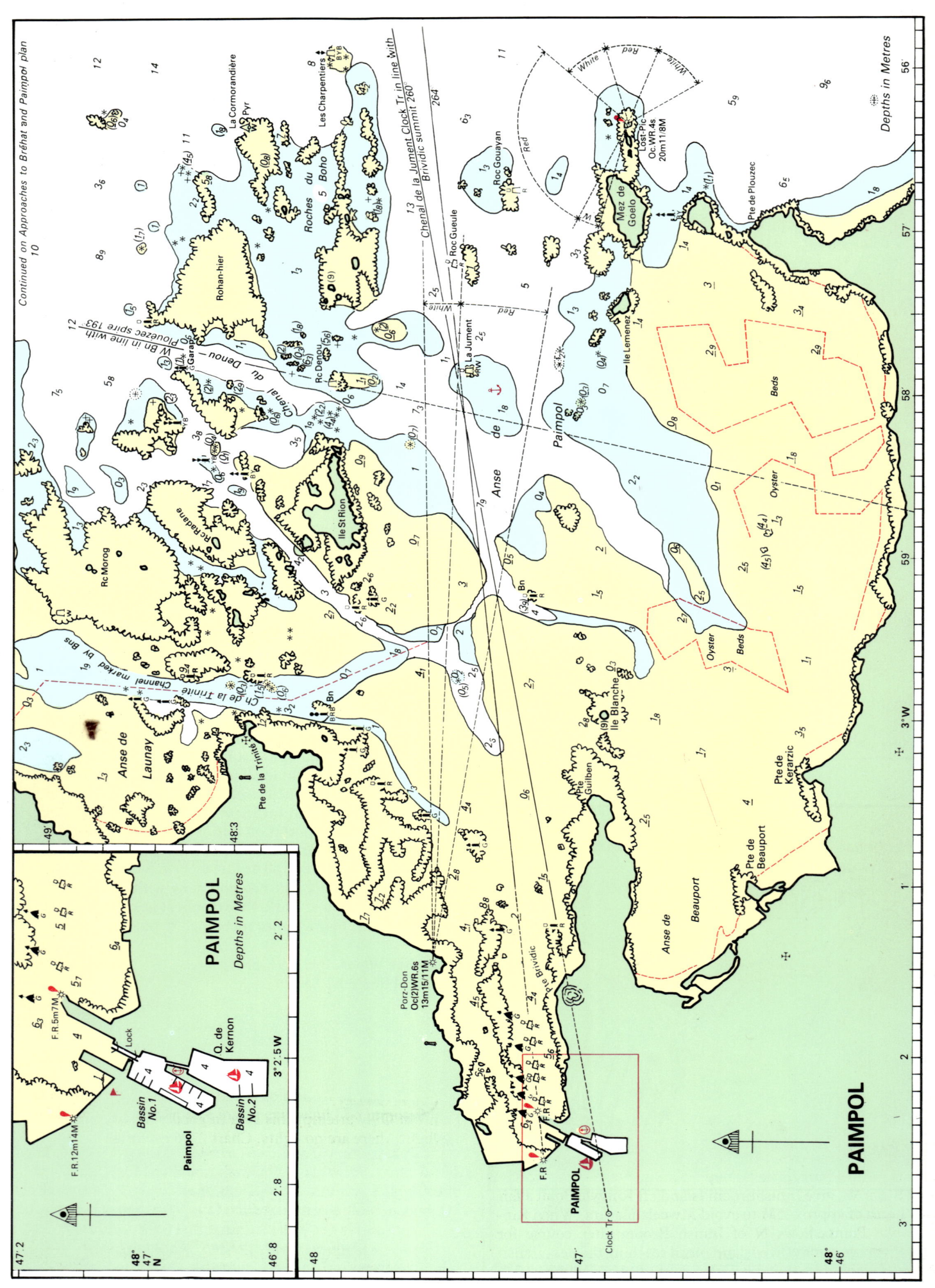

PAIMPOL
Charts BA 3673, F 3670

HW: Dover −5¼. DS (W of La Jument): Dover +1h SE; −6¼h NW.

In Chenal du Denou, Dover +¾h SE; −5¾h NW

MHWS 10.3m MHWN 7.8 MTL 5.4 MLWN 3.2 MLWS 0.5

A pleasant small town with marina in wet basin.

Approach From the E by Chenal de la Jument. At 1¾M NE of Lost-Pic lt, 2 W trs R tops, Oc WR (W 221°-253°, 291°-329° and 105°-116°), follow line of Paimpol spire over wooded Pte de Brividic, 260°, but N of La Jument RW tr steer 264° on ldg line, front W hut R top, FR 5m; rear W pylon R top, Dir FR (262°-267°) 12m.

By night keep in W sector of Porz Don, Oc(2) 6s, past R sector of Lost-Pic until the latter changes to W when the ldg lts can be followed.

From N by Chenal du Denou (2.8m). At ¾M E of Men-Gam BYB E card tr, make good 193°, allowing for cross-set, with W Denou tr in line with Plouézec ch spire. ¾M N of Denou tr it is essential near LW to keep on this line which passes E of Garap stb bn and only 50m E of a rk drying 1m close E of Garap, and W of Rohan-Hier port bn. Pass about ½ ca W of Denou bn.

Alternatively, Chenal de la Trinité is well marked by bns but start from position at least 1¼ ca E of Les Piliers BY bn (plan on this page) to avoid drying rks E of bn. Anchor to await the tide 1 ca SW of La Jument.

Entrance Continue on ldg line to the buoys marking last 800m. Lock gates open between HW±1½h (less at neaps) with sometimes free flow around HW, with a current up to 2kn. Boats under 10m moor in No 1 basin, immediately after the lock; larger ones go through the narrow passage to port into No 2 basin and moor at two pontoons at the far end. If in doubt enquire at office on central mole between the two basins.

Supplies Water at entrance jetty and in No 2 basin. Good shops.

Tel/VHF HM (96) 20-80-77.

TRIEUX RIVER LÉZARDRIEUX & ILE DE BRÉHAT
Charts BA 3673, F 832; 882, 2845

HW Les Héaux: Dover −5¼h, Lézardrieux: Dover −4¼h

DS (near La Horaine): Dover +1½h SE; −4¾h NW

MHWS 10.0m MHWN 7.5 MTL 5.4 MLWN 3.4 MLWS 0.9

A beautiful river with many anchorages and good shelter.

Approaches The coastline is low-lying and the marks are not easily distinguished against the sun or in a haze. Landfall from the N is best made towards the end of the night, when an excellent system of lights gives good fixes, followed by mooring in the light of dawn. The main approach channels are the Grand Chenal (6m) from NE; the Chenal du Ferlas (2.4m) from the E and Chenal de la Moisie (less than 2m), unlit, from NW.

From the N if W of Roches Douvres, get in the W sector of Paon square lt tr, F WRG (W 181°-196°) 22m 11M and head S until on ldg lts of Grand Chenal, 225°.

Coming from N, E of Roches Douvres, or coming offshore from E, get in W sector of Les Héaux grey lt tr, Oc(3)WRG 12s (W 247°-270°) 48m 15M until on Grand Chenal ldg line. Both of these approaches leave to port La Horaine W octagonal lt tr, B diag stripes, Fl(3) 12s. By day make for a position 9 ca NW of Basse du Nord N card buoy, 1M N of La Horaine, thence make good SW to Grand Chenal.

From NW, there is a more direct daytime approach via the **Moisie Passage,** dangerous in strong onshore winds. At 1¾M E of Les Héaux lt tr, steer 159° with Rosédo W pyramid in line with the chapel, both on Ile de Bréhat. Keep exactly on this line when passing close NE of La Moisie bn tr and Noguejou bn, both E card, to clear drying rks to port, until in the Grand Chenal.

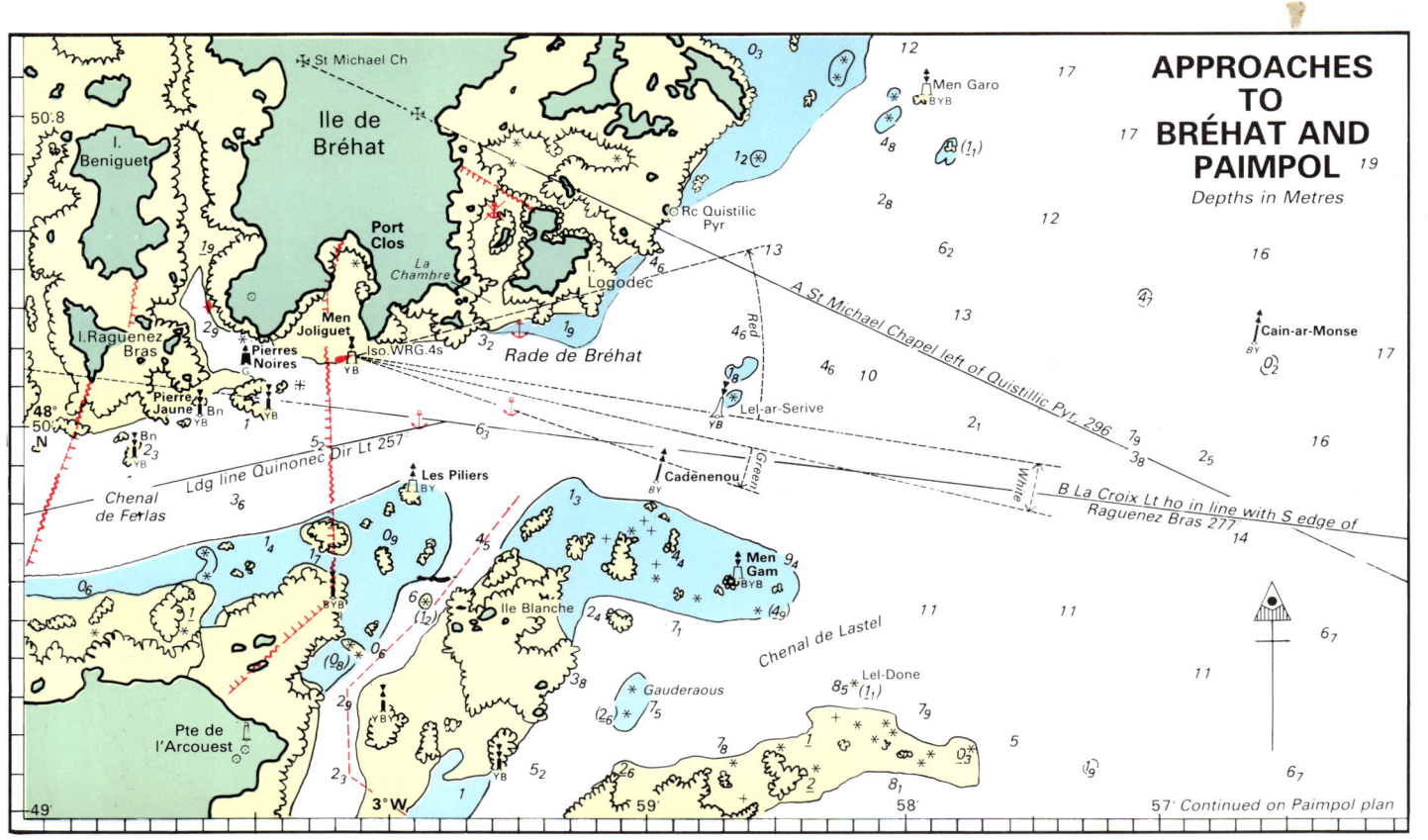

APPROACHES TO BRÉHAT AND PAIMPOL
Depths in Metres

FRANCE, NORTH COAST 334

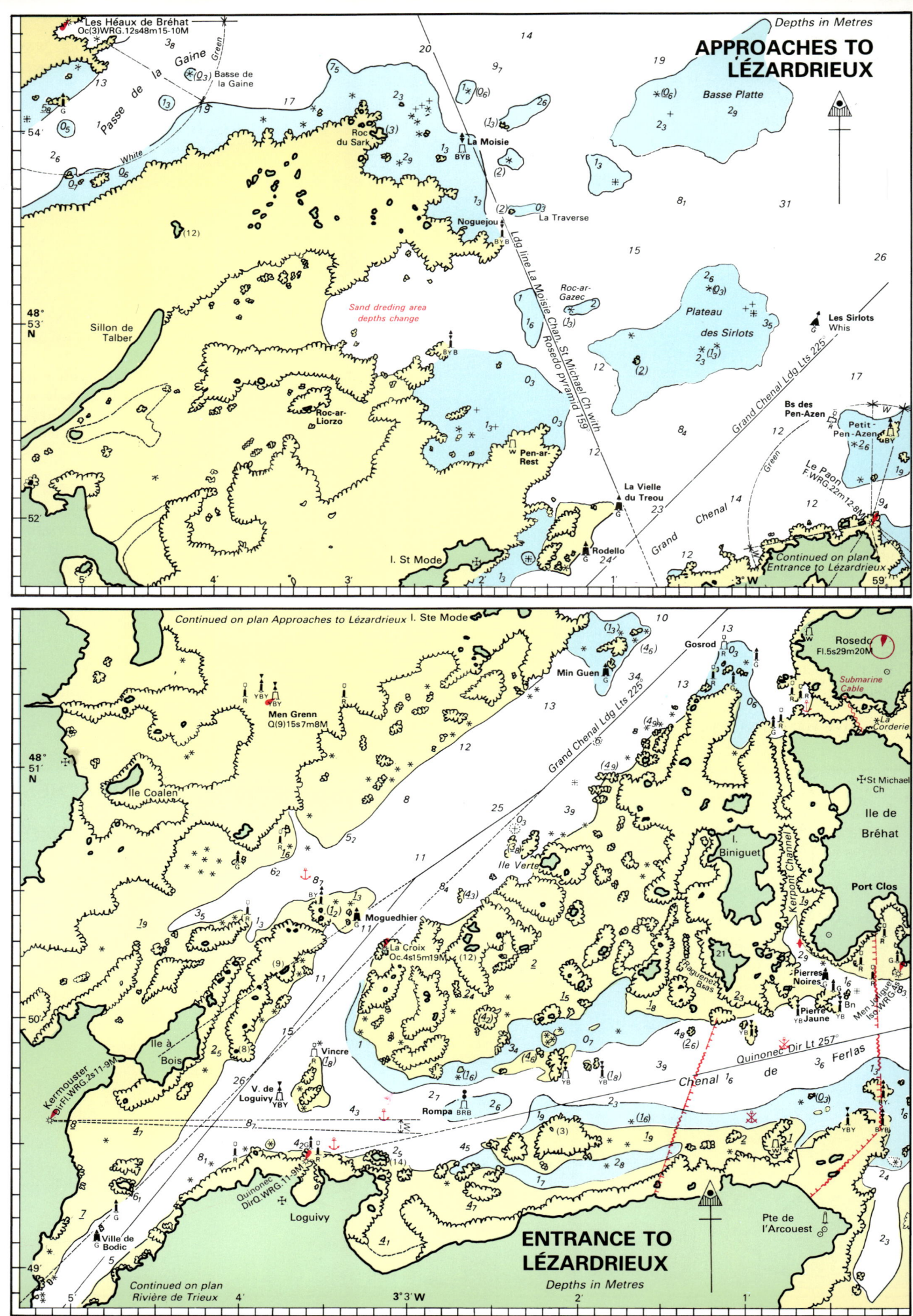

Coming inshore from E take the **Ferlas Channel** (See Plans for Approaches to Bréhat and Approaches to Lézardrieux.) Transit lines are Bréhat chapel to the left of Quistillic W pyramid 296°; La Croix lt ho (two trs joined) in line with S side of Raguenez-Bras (small islet off SW tip of Bréhat) 277° and into well-marked Ferlas Channel. At night, steer for Paon lt, F WRG (W 307°-316°) in its W sector until in W sector of Men-Joliguet lt, Iso WRG 4s (W 279°-283°). Steer in this sector past unlit Piliers tr and pick up the narrow W sector of Quinonec lt, Dir Q WRG, (W 257°-257.7°). Near Rompa tr pick up the W sector of a third dir lt on W bank of Trieux River – Kermouster Fl WRG 2s (W 270°-272°) which comes onto Coatmer ldg line.

Le Grand Chenal. From Les Sirlots G con whistle buoy the Channel is clearly marked by day. At night the ldg lts are front La Croix (two trs joined) Oc 4s (intense 215°-235°) 15m 19M; rear Bodic W ho with gable, Dir Q (intense 221°-229°) 55m 22M. When Bodic dips behind La Croix, bear slightly W to keep it at the W edge of the tr. When Men-Grenn lt Q(9) 15s is abeam to stb, steer 235° until on Coatmer ldg line, front F RG (R 220°-250° to seaward; G 250°-053° up-river); rear F R 219° 9M. When Olenoyère unlit R tr is abeam to port head for W sector of Perdrix lt Fl(2) WG (W 197°-203°). Leave Perdrix about 60m to stb; 3 F Bu lts ahead mark marina pontoons.

Berthing There are W visitors buoys on west edge of channel N of Perdrix and fore and aft buoys off Lézardrieux marina. With care it is possible to anchor in the estuary between Ferlas Channel and Perdrix (although the best places are taken by buoys); above the suspension br (17.7m, 20m above CD) at Lézardrieux; and in the Ferlas Channel off Loguivy.

Rivière de Pontrieux is navigable at HW to Pontrieux lock and quays above it. The channel is clearly marked, with an anchorage at Roche Jagu chateau, 4M above Lézardrieux. Take the stb cuts at the next two branches to Pontrieux lock (sill 3.5m above CD): gates open by day nominally HW ±1h (St Malo) but often soon after HW only. Waiting buoy. Lock is open by day and night with a free flow when tide exceeds 8.8m. Moor to bank at small port de plaisance about ¾M above the lock.

Ile de Bréhat has three main anchorages.
(1) **La Chambre**, off Ferlas Channel, E of Men Joliguet tr. Very popular but uncomfortable at HW with a strong N wind. Anchor as far in as tide height allows.

(2) **La Corderie**, off the Kerpont Channel which dries 1.5m and leads off Ferlas Channel past SW tip of the island; it is passable only after 2h of flood. The tide runs at up to 5kn. Enter leaving Pierres Noires bn to port (N.B. There is no passage between Pierres Noires bn and Pierre Jaune bn to SW). Steer 352° for 2 ca and then slightly W of N between visible rks and bns (leave cones to W, cans to E). La Corderie is well marked with bns. At springs it is impossible to stay afloat out of the strong tide in the Kerpont, but at neaps a quiet berth can be found. Yachts can take the ground on hard flat sand.

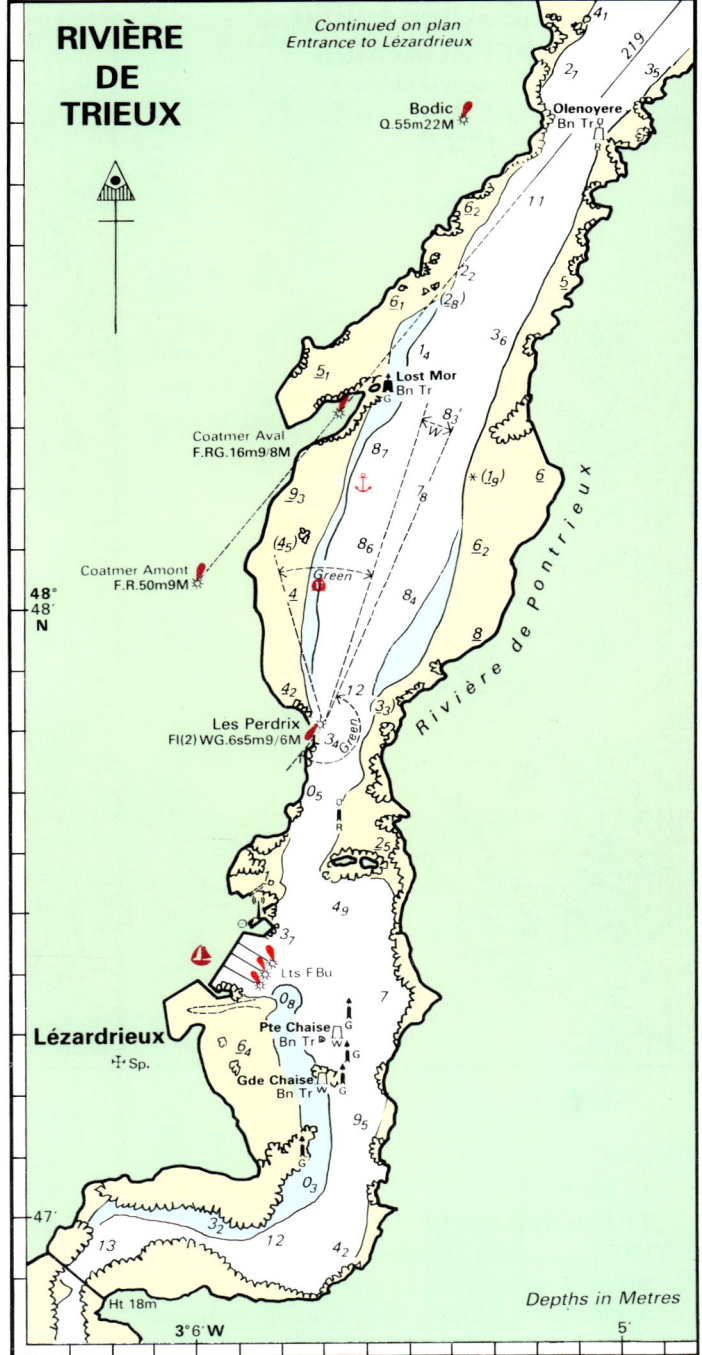

(3) **Port Clos** at the SW tip of Bréhat is the main landing place for tripper launches and room to anchor is limited. Not recommended.

Supplies Fuel and water at marina. Water at Pontrieux. Shops at Lézardrieux, Pontrieux and Loguivy and some small ones on Ile de Bréhat.

Telephone/VHF Lézardrieux HM (96) 20-14-22/ch 9; Pontrieux Capitainerie (96) 95-66-66; Ecluse de Pontrieux VHF 12/16.

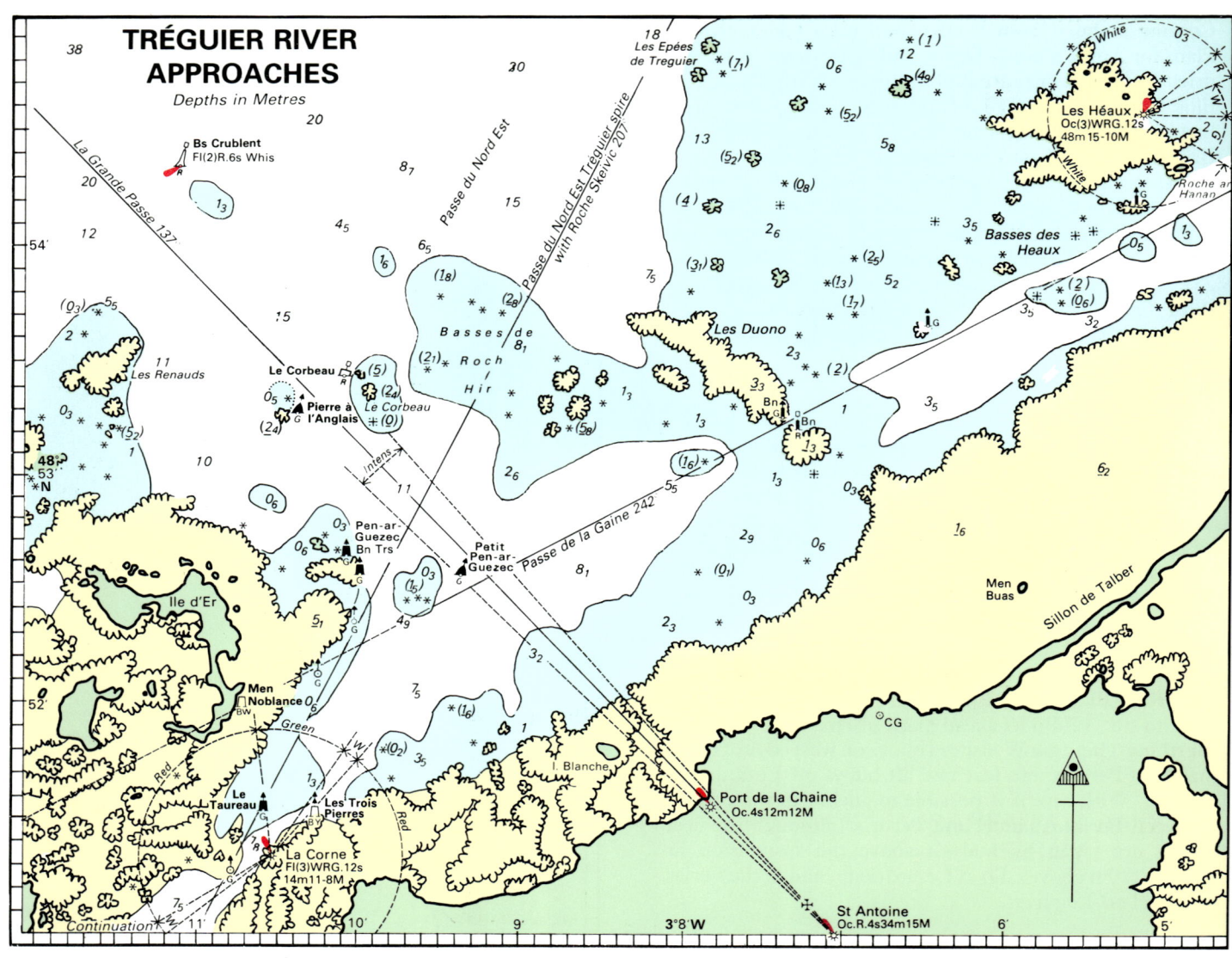

TRÉGUIER RIVER   Charts BA 3672, F 972, 973

HW (Tréguier): Dover −5¾h

MHWS 9.7m   MHWN 7.4   MTL 5.3   MLWN 3.3   MLWS 0.9

A pleasant sheltered river leading to the old cathedral town of Tréguier and marina.

Tidal Streams 5M N of Les Héaux: Dover +1¾h E; −4½h W, 4kn.

La Jument buoy: +1¼h E; −5h W, 4kn.

Grande Passe N of Les Renauds: +½h E; −5¾h W, 4kn.

Passe de la Gaine +¼h ENE; +4¾h WSW, 3kn.

N of La Corne lt tr: +½h SW; −5¾h NE, 3kn.

Approach From the N and E the dominant feature is Les Héaux grey lt ho, Oc(3) WRG 12s 48m. From W get 7M WNW and enter by Grande Passe. From E, either pass N of the lt ho and La Jument des Héaux N card bell buoy VQ to enter by Grande Passe or by day and in good visibility, get 2M ENE of Les Héaux and enter by Passe de la Gaine. The latter is shorter and may seem more attractive if conditions round Les Héaux are uncomfortable, but the marks are difficult to see and the line must be strictly kept to. From Trieux River, in good weather leave by the Moisie Passage (details under Trieux) for Passe de la Gaine.

Entrance There are two main entrances, only one lighted, and a third more difficult.

La Grande Passe (4.4m) can be taken at any time with reasonable visibility. From Basse Crublent R buoy, Fl(2) R 6s, the ldg line is 137°: front, Port de la Chaine W ho Oc 4s 12m, and rear, Ste Antoine W ho, R roof, Dir Oc R 4s 34m. It can be hard to identify by day, in which case pick up the entrance buoys (Pierre à l'Anglais G con and Corbeau R can) and steer 137° to Petit Pen ar Guezec G con buoy and alter course to stb when La Corne bears 217°. Strong cross-set.

Passe de la Gaine (0.3m) is not easy and is unlit; the ldg marks require 8M good visibility, but if there is enough, about 1M, to see the first bn before starting the passage, after half flood there are few difficulties. At 1¾ ca S of Roche ar Hanap (7m), which is 3 ca SE of the lt ho, get Men Noblance BW pyramid in line with Plougrescant mark (W wall with B vert band, 1¾M behind it), 242°. Pass two stb bns into the Duono narrows between port and stb bns Petit Pen ar Guezec G con buoy.

Chenal du Nord-Est (0.8m) is to the E of Corbeau rks. W and NW seas break across it; the ldg marks are often not visible and with a strong cross-tide this entrance can be dangerous. At a position SW of La Jument N card buoy, VQ, ldg line is Skeiviec W tr in line with Tréguier cathedral spire, 207°. When the latter disappears, follow buoys and bns. Not recommended.

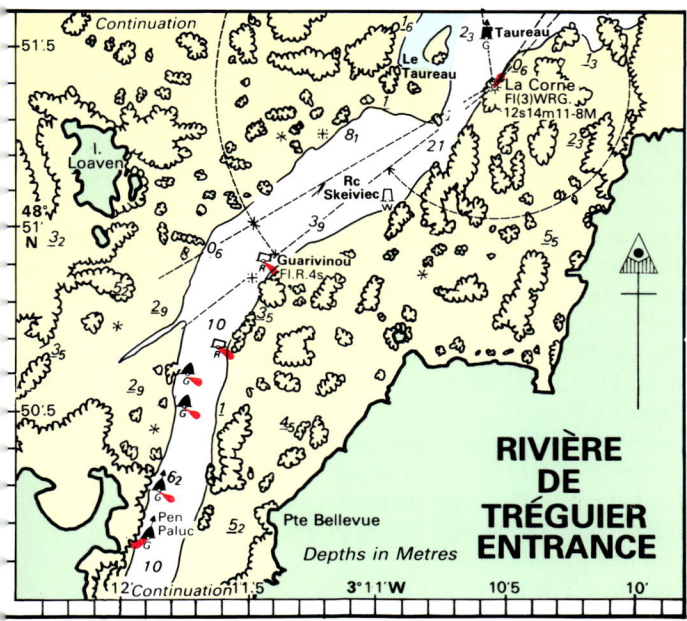

River From La Corne the channel is clearly buoyed. At night on the Grande Passe line, when G sector of La Corne light, Fl(3) WRG 12s, changes to W, steer in that sector 217°. Leave La Corne close to port and follow its W sector on the SW side, 052°-059°, being careful to avoid Banc du Taureau G con buoy, unlighted, to Guarivinou lt buoy, Fl R 4s, whence come S into the lighted channel. Approaching the marina, the channel follows the E bank on outside of the bend: do not aim straight for the marina lts. The br has 3m headroom at HW, when river is navigable for 3M above it.

Berthing. There is a marina at Tréguier on stb side before the br over the main channel. The stream is strong around half-tide: it is essential not to attempt to enter between the lines of pontoons across the stream. On arrival moor to end of a pontoon against the stream until slack water. It is equally important not to leave other than at slack water. There are also two rows of W buoys, 2.5m depth. The town quays dry. Anchoring is not permitted in sight of the town but is otherwise possible in the river, out of the fairway, especially off Roche Jaune village (off small shingle beach 1½ca S of ramp); at Pen Paluc on W bank 1½M to the N; or anchor close inshore under the château near No 10 buoy, 5m (crowded in season; charge).

Supplies Water at marina and Roche Jaune; diesel at marina. Shops at Tréguier and Roche Jaune.

Tel/VHF HM (96) 92-42-37/ch 9.

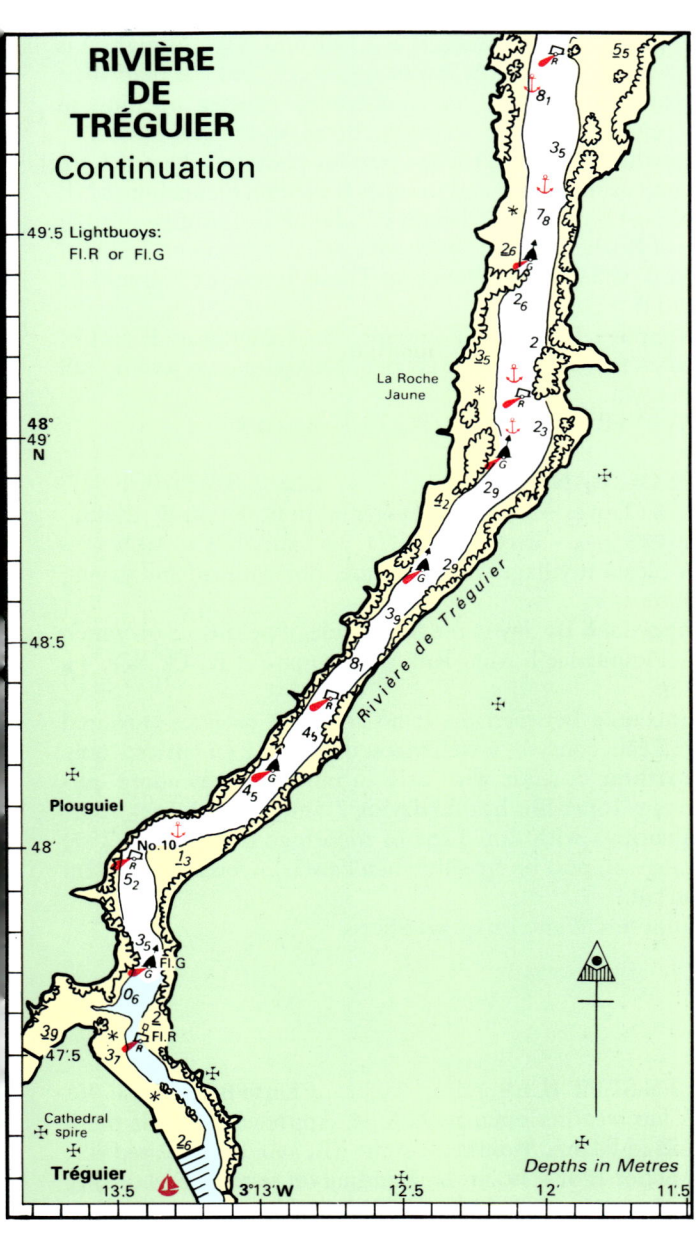

FRANCE, NORTH COAST

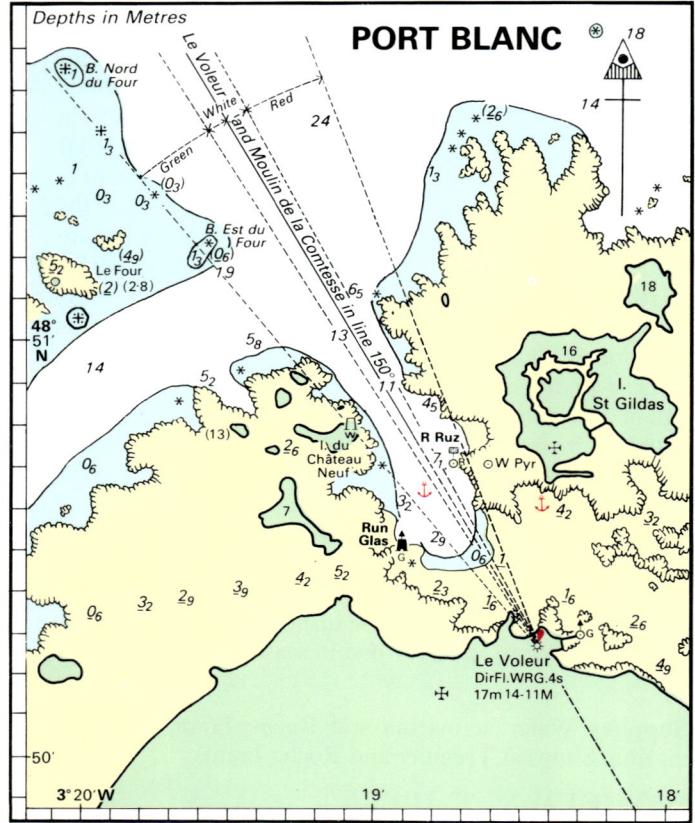

PORT BLANC Charts BA 3672, F 974
HW (est): Dover −5¾h. DS: Dover +¼h E; −6h W, 2½kn

MHWS 9.5m MHWN 7.3 MTL 5.3 MLWN 3.3 MLWS 0.9

A pleasant small holiday and fishing village, open NW to NE.

Approach To the E are rks extending 1½M offshore as far as Pte du Château, and Ile Ziliec with a large house. To NW the Plateau du Four has a R can whistle buoy on its NW side.

Entrance (7m) lies between Ile du Château Neuf to W and Ile St Gildas to E, both with conspic W pyramids. Ldg line is, front, Le Voleur W tr, Fl WRG 4s 17m, with rear, Moulin de la Comtesse on the hill, 150°. Marks in gap in trees are difficult to see until on the line, the rear mark being covered by trees. Best line is with Ile St Gildas twice as far to port as Ile du Château Neuf is to stb.

Berthing Anchor SW of ldg line, SW of Roc'h Ruz R bn, 7m, or closer in, sand and shell. There are W visitors' buoys in the W part of the hbr, offshore of small craft moorings, and also in the E, drying, part of the hbr with room to anchor clear of them. If taking the ground in shallower area, beware of some deep holes.

Supplies Water at tap on drying ramp E of the lt tr. Small shops in surrounding villages.

Tel Capitainerie (96) 92-64-96.

TRÉGASTEL Charts BA 3669, F 967
About a mile W of Ploumanac'h, this hbr provides moorings afloat. Rk La Pierre Pendue conspic E of entrance which is marked by bns. Inner buoys dry but outer ones have 2m; 10 are for visitors. Uncomfortable in winds between W and N, especially near HW when outer rks cover. Some shops.

PERROS-GUIREC Charts BA 3672, F 974
HW (est): Dover −5¾h. DS NW of Ile Tomé and in channels: Dover +½h E, 4¾kn in E channel, 2¾kn in W; −4½h W, 4¼kn and 2¾kn respectively.

MHWS (est) 9.3m MHWN 7.2 MTL 5.2 MLWN 3.4 MLWS 0.9

A popular holiday resort with a marina and drying approach.

Approach Ile Tomé with its surrounding plateau separate the E and W channels.

Passe de l'Est From Guazer R whistle buoy, 2½M NE of Ile Tomé, pick up ldg line 225°: front Le Colombier W ho Dir Oc(4) 12s, intense (217°-233°), 28m; rear Kerprigent W tr, Dir Q (221°-228°), 79m 22M.

Passe de l'Ouest (0.9m) is entered between Bilzic R tr and La Fronde G con buoy with Kerjean W tr, grey top, Dir Oc(2+1) WRG (W 143°-144°) 12s 78m, bearing 144°. By day have it in line with Nantouar W disused lt ho on the shore, 143°. When ¼M SW of Pierre du Chenal BR bn tr, turn SW into Passe de l'Est.

Entrance The Passe de l'Est leads to the hbr to stb. Entry between the pierheads (lts Fl(2) 6s, R or G) is possible after half-flood with 1.5m draught. R buoy Fl 2s close W of jetty marks drying sand. There are some waiting buoys. The basin has a sill on the SE side, drying 7m marked by R and G perches and a gate, 6m usable width at E end. The gate is open by day at springs between HW−2h and +1h; at neaps between HW−1½h and HW. At night it is open only at HW. At low neaps, coefficient less than 40, it may not open at all. Sometimes shorter opening at weekends. Beware of strong current as the gate opens.

Berthing On entry turn to port for pontoons. Depth 2.4m decreasing to NW and towards the shore. Or anchor to NE of port according to height of tide; on E side of peninsula, S of Roche Bernard (swell with NE winds); or on E side of Ile Tomé (beware Platier du Tomé, 0.6m, 1 ca off middle of Is).

Supplies Water on pontoons. Fuel station at E end of basin serves when gate is open. Shops on quay and up hill to town.

Tel/VHF Capitainerie (96) 23-37-82/ch 9.

PLOUMANAC'H Charts BA 3670, F 967.
HW: Dover −5½h. DS: Dover +½h E; +4¼h W, 2¾kn

MHWS 8.9m MHWN 7.0 MTL 5.0 MLWN 3.4 MLWS 0.9

A pleasant village with wet inner hbr with sill and drying outer hbr.

Approach By day make for W side of peninsula on which is Ploumanac'h Men Ruz pink square lt tr, Oc WR 4s, 26m.

Entrance between the lt ho and Ile Costaeres (towered château, conspic) is well marked by bns. S end dries 1.6m.

Berthing Anchor with care in outer hbr, avoiding outcrops. Inner hbr has sill drying 2.5m, giving 1.5m – some moorings with 2m. Line of moorings for visitors. Tide gauge on port bn by sill; when base is covered there is 2m on sill.

Supplies Water on quay. Shops.

LES SEPT ILES Charts BA 3670, F 967
A fair weather open anchorage. Approach towards the E end of Ile aux Moines from the SE, avoiding isolated rks. Anchor E of lt ho on Is. Landing on steps at end of slip. Path to lt ho and old fort at W end of Is.

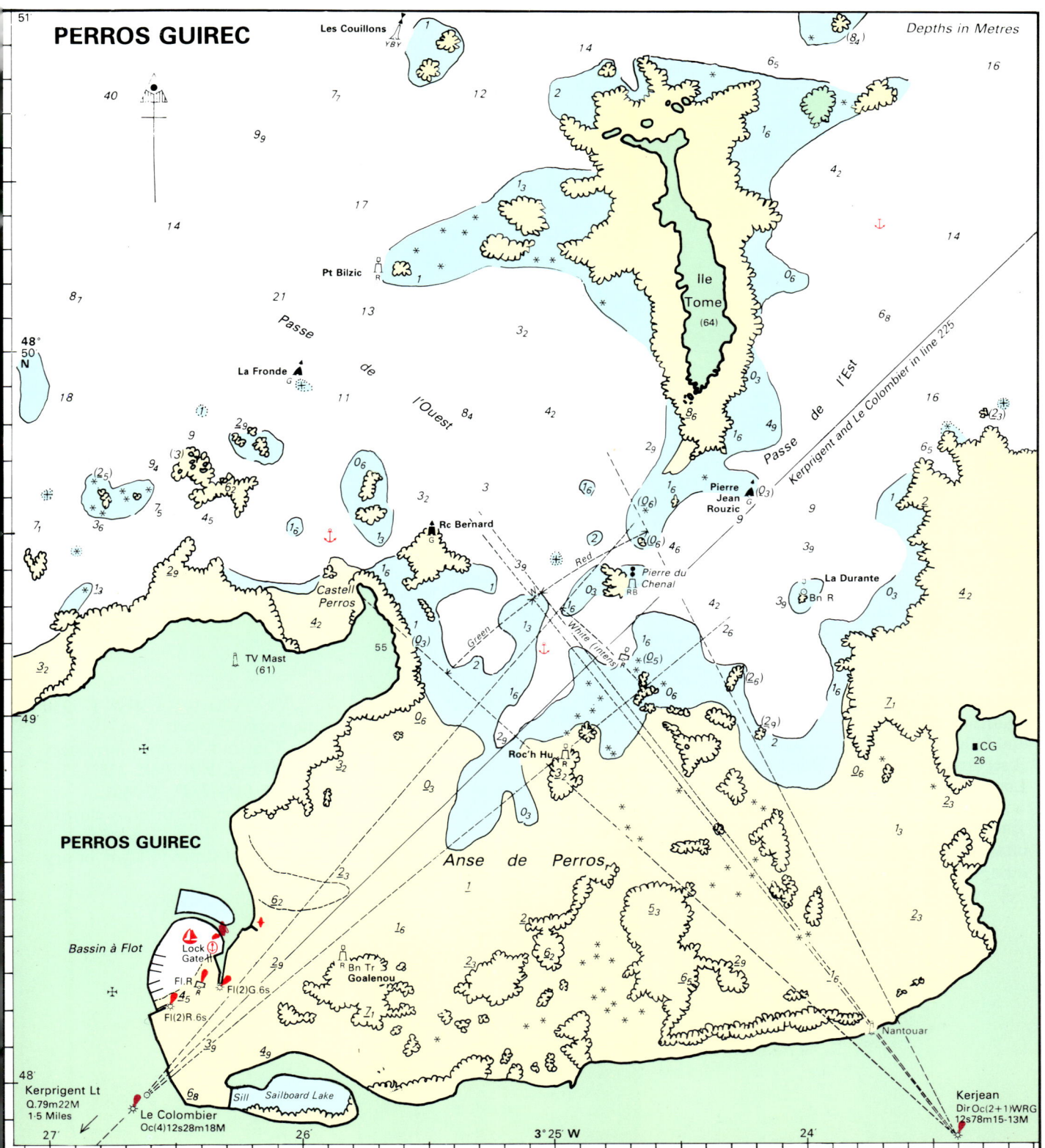

TREBEURDEN Charts BA 3669, F 7151.
HW: Dover −6h. DS at Basse Blanche buoy: Dover +1h SE-E; +5h SW-W, 2kn.
MHWS 9.0m MHWN 7.0 MTL 5.2 MLWN 3.5 MLWS 1.2
A popular holiday resort with good anchorages, except in W and NW winds.

Approach on the W side of Le Crapaud shoal. The marks for the passage to the E are difficult to identify and it cannot be recommended.

Entrance From a position 1¼M S of Le Crapaud W card buoy, steer 070° between Ar Goureudec S card lt buoy, VQ(6)+Fl 10s, and NW tip of Ile Milliau (50m), leaving latter about 1½ca to stb; continue past the bns to required anchorage.

Berthing There are anchorages (1) N of Ile de Milliau, W of a line joining the Is slipway to the white high-rise apartment block at Trébeurden, 2m; also visitors' buoys.
(2) NW of that, as close in as tide allows to the edge of the beach SE of Il Molène. Exposed at HW.

Supplies Water on quay. Shops.
Tel HM (96) 23-66-93.

FRANCE, North Coast 340

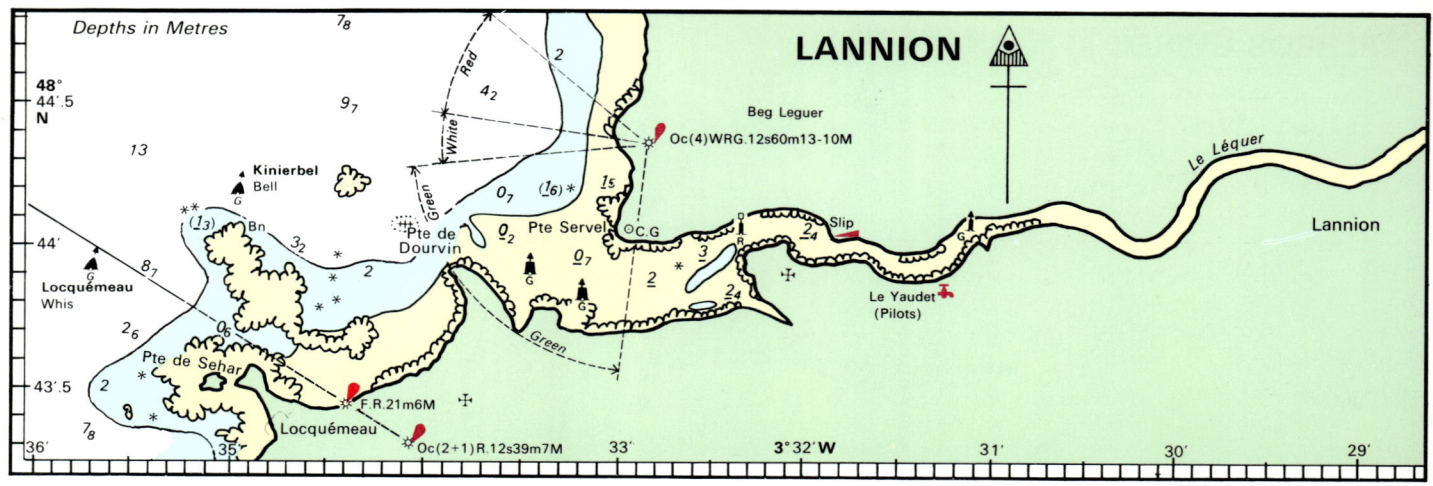

LANNION RIVER   Charts BA 3669, F 5950
HW: Dover −6h. DS at Le Crapeau: Dover +1h ESE; −5h WSW, 2kn
MHWS 9.0m MHWN 7.0 MTL 5.2 MLWN 3.5 MLWS 1.2

A mainly drying river in a wooded valley leading to Lannion about 4½M from the entrance. Le Taureau rk, 2m, 2M offshore is a good guide.

Approach should not be attempted with winds from WNW to NW, when shelter can be sought under Pte de Locquirec, 3M to SW. From W keep Ben Leguer W lt ho, R top, Oc(4)WRG 12s 60m 13/10M, bearing 090° (at night keep in the W sector, 084°-098°), leaving Kinierbel G bell buoy to stb. From NW the two G trs in the entrance in line, 123°, lead N of Le Taureau rks (11m), but the line leaves close to stb the Ar Boulier rk, 4.9m, 4 ca N of Le Taureau. When Beg Leguer lt ho bears 095° make for it and follow instructions for entrance. By night keep W of R sector (339°-010°) of Triagoz lt, Oc(2)WR 6s to pick up Locquémeau ldg lts, front F R, rear Oc(2+1)R 12s 6M, and then follow W sector of Beg Leguer.

Entrance dries 0.4m. Do not come S of Beg Leguer, or into its G sector, until Locquémeau F R lt is just W of S to miss rk drying 0.1m ¾M to its N; then bear SE to leave two G trs close to stb. If waiting for the tide to rise, anchor in the bay N of Locquémeau front lt, keeping E of N of it. River is clearly marked to Lannion but is unlit. There is a br at Lannion, headroom 2.5m. If going above the br by dinghy, beware large masonry blocks in the channel.

Berthing Anchor E of low quay at Le Yaudet, dries 1.2m; the pools just upstream of it, 1-3m, have many moorings leaving little swinging room, two anchors necessary. At Lannion moor to short quay on S bank by the first houses, dries 5m.

Supplies Water on quay, fuel from garage and shops at Lannion.

LOCQUÉMEAU   Charts BA 3669, F 5950
A drying hbr with anchorage open to winds W to NW.

Approach At ¾M S of Le Crapaud W card buoy, steer 122° on ldg line: W frame, R top, F R (068°-228°) 21m front; W gabled ho Oc(2+1)R (016°-232°) 12s 6M.

Entrance Leave Locquémeau G con whistle buoy close to stb and enter N of G Séhar bn.

Berthing Anchor E of bn off end of slipway, 1.5m; or dry further in E of second, short, slipway.

PRIMEL
Charts BA 2745, F 7124
HW: Dover −6¼h. DS: See Morlaix
MHWS 9.0m MHWN 7.0 MTL 5.2 MLWN 3.5 MLWS 1.3
A small fishing village in a rocky bay exposed to NW.
Approach At ½M NW of Pte de Primel pick up ldg marks, three W rectangles with vert R stripes, two lit FR, 35 and 56m, (visible 134°-168°), 151°.
Entrance Leave Zamégues rk (painted bright G on seaward side) to stb and enter between two conspic rks marked by bns. Gap is 27m wide, 7m depth.
Berthing Some visitors' buoys. Anchor in channel, 2-9m, but not more than 2 ca inside the entrance, or dry out clear of the outcrops. The dredged area behind the jetty is used by fishing boats; the rest of the jetty is rocky.
Supplies Water and stores at Le Diben and Primel.
Tel/VHF HM (98) 72-38-76/ch 9.

PENZÉ RIVER
Charts BA 2745, F 7095, 7151.
HW (Roscoff): Dover −6¼h. DS: Dover −¼h ingoing; +5¼h outgoing, 1kn
MHWS 8.8m MHWN 6.8 MTL 5.0 MLWN 3.3 MLWS 1.2
A wide estuary, approached through a maze of rks. The narrow channel has good depths but is open to N and the banks dry. Small drying hbr of Penpoul is convenient for St Pol-de-Léon.
Approach With the aid of a large-scale chart various lines of approach can be followed.
Entrance From Bloscon N card buoy, VQ, the transits are Guerheon G tr with Trébunnec G tr, 169°; Benven W tr with Mazarin W tr, 137°; La Tortue R port perch with Caspari isolated danger bn 171°, to pass midway between Trousken R tr and La Petite Fourche G tr. Leave Trébunnec tr 2 ca to stb and when about 3 ca S of it with enough water make for the trumpet-shaped bn off the end of the breakwater at Penpoul.
The River dries below La Corde br (15m) with 1m at the first of the St Yves slipways. At HW it is navigable above the br as far as Penzé; small quay dries 5m.
Berthing Anchor
(1) In channel (11m, poor holding) off Penpoul; drying hbr is full of moorings.
(2) Mouillage de Carantec, S of Figuier isolated danger bn, 4m sand; difficult to land at low water.
(3) Off St Yves, 1-2m.
Supplies Fuel from garage at Carantec. Shops at St Pol-de-Léon.

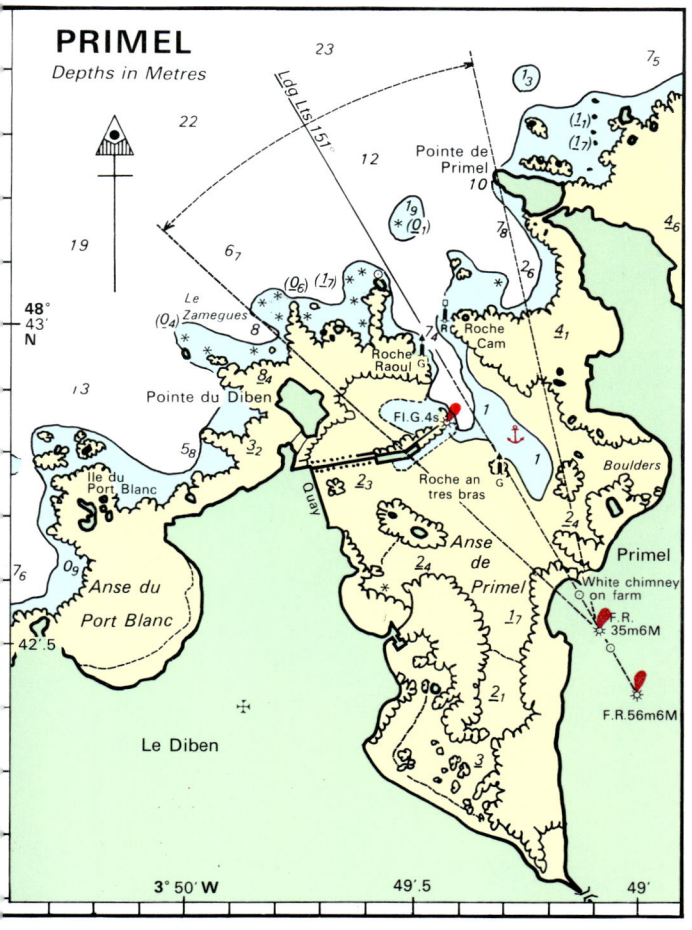

Morlaix — *see next page*

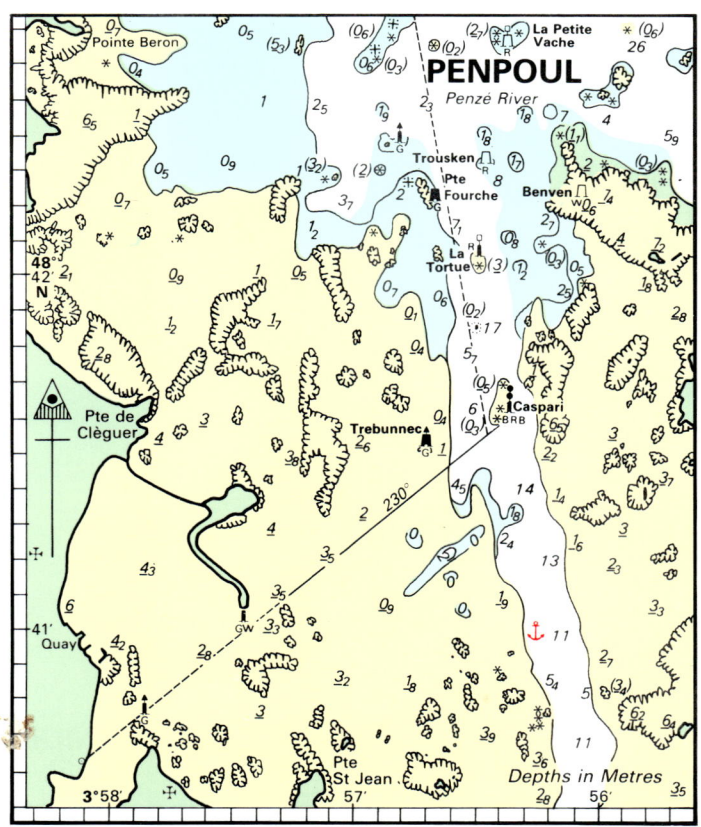

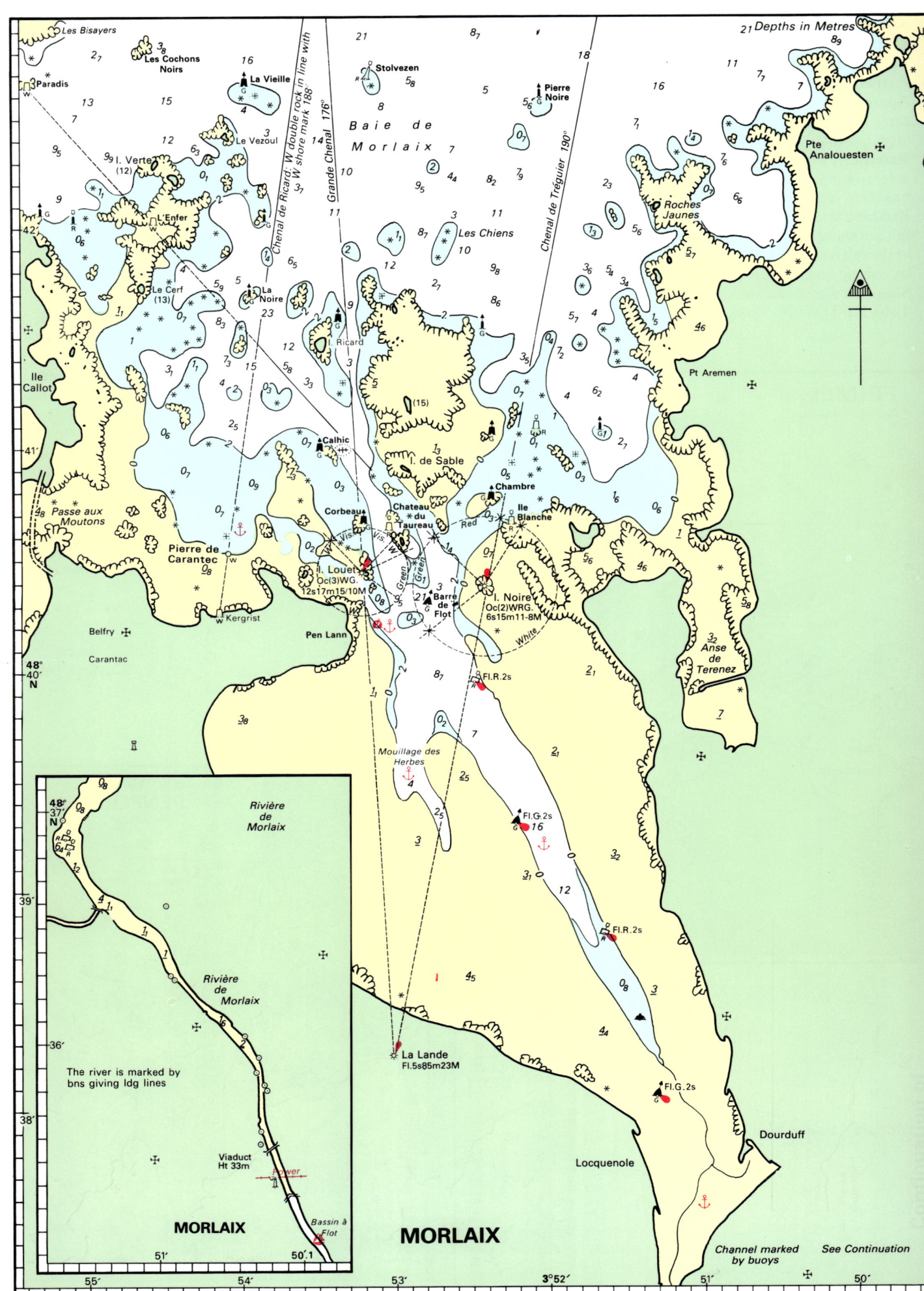

MORLAIX ROADSTEAD AND RIVER

Charts BA 2745, F 7095, 7151.
HW (Morlaix): Dover −6h. DS: Dover +6h W; −½h E.
MHWS 8.9m MHWN 6.9 MTL 5.1 MLWN 3.5 MLWS 1.2

A wide estuary, available at all times except by night in strong onshore winds, leading by a drying channel to Morlaix, where there is a wet basin with marina.

Approach Prominent marks are: Ile de Callot with chapel, 18m, and small W tr off Carantec peninsula; Château de Taureau, a large square fort; Ile Noire W lt tr, R top, Oc(2)WRG 6s 15m, 4 ca ESE of Le Taureau; and Ile Louet W lt tr, Oc(3) WG 12s 17m.

From Roscoff keep Piguet W bn tr in line with steeple of Notre Dâme among trees on Ile de Batz 293° (at night in W sector of Charden lt Q(6) and Fl WR 15s, W 288°-294°) until on ldg line of Grand Chenal, just W of Stolvezen R buoy. From the N pass between Plateau des Duons, grey bn tr 10m, and Plateau de la Méloine, W card whistle buoy, for any of the three entrance channels.

From NE pass between la Méloine and Pte de Primel. At night from E keep in W sector of Triagoz lt Oc(2) WR 6s, bearing at least 063° astern to pass N of Méloine bank.

Entrance There are three main entrance channels, of which only the first is available at all times, and even that is difficult at night, especially with strong onshore winds.

(1) **Grand Chenal** (2m) E of Ile Ricard. Get Ile Louet lt tr in line with La Lande rear W lt tr, B top, Fl 5s 85m, 2M behind it, 176°. On this line, abreast Calhic G bn tr, steer 160°, leaving Corbeau G tr to stb and pass between Château de Taureau and Ile Louet. Hence keep edge of the Château on with W edge of Ile Ricard astern steering 153° past La Barre de Flot stb buoy into the estuary. At night get the two ldg lts, front Ile Louet Oc(3) WG 12s 13M, rear La Lande Fl 5s 23M, in line 176°, leaving Ile Ricard G tr close to stb. When Ile Noire lt, Oc(2) 6s, changes from R to G, steer 160°, leaving Taureau fort and bn to port and entering G sector of Louet. It is then prudent to round the lt at just over 1 ca off, leaving unlit Barre de Flot buoy well clear to port and anchor or pick up W buoy off Pen Lann until daylight.

(2) **Chenal de Ricard** l(5.8m) is a wider variant of Grand Chenal going W of Ile Ricard. It is a safer choice when an onshore swell is breaking on the rks bordering Grand Chenal but it is unlit. From a position on the Grand Chenal ldg line, N of Stolvezen R buoy, bring La Pierre de Carantec, an isolated double rk, in line with a W mark, Kergrist, 4 ca E of Carantec ch tr, 188°. The channel is well marked by G stb bns. After La Noire stb bn bear round to SSE with a back bearing of L'Enfer W bn tr in line with Paradis W bn tr, 319° to join Grand Chenal NE of Calhic bn.

(3) **Chenal de Tréguier** dries 0.8m and should not be attempted before half-tide. Steer with Ile Noire W lt tr, R top, in line with La Lande W lt tr, B top, 190°. Having passed between La Chambre G tr and Ile Blanche R tr, steer SW until E edge of Château de Taureau comes on with W edge of Ile Ricard and with this line astern continue past Barre de Flot buoy into the estuary. By night keep Ile Noire lt Oc(2) WRG and La Lande lt Fl 5s in line 190° until Ile Louet lt Oc(3) WG changes from W to G, 244°, then steer for it until Ile Noire lt, Oc(2) WRG 6s, turns from R to G, 135°, then round to 180°. Leaving Barre de Flot to stb, Ile Noire will change from G to W, 051°; continue for 1 ca. The channel continues 153°: find a berth as convenient either side.

Morlaix River from Barre de Flot the river is marked by buoys and stakes, including 2 G and 2 R lt buoys, Fl(2) 2s. The channel dries about 1M NNW of Dourduff. It is 5½M from Pen Lann anchorage to Morlaix lock. Leaving at half-tide or HW−2h will give sufficient time. The narrow part is entered at Dourduff and is clearly buoyed; unlit but many of the buoys have reflectors. As the river narrows there are ldg marks, with St Andrew crosses, showing the deeper water.

Anchorages (1) Between Barre de Flot and Pen Lann; 5 W visitors' buoys; land near NE corner or at fish quay on S side of Pen Lann.

(2) Mouillage des Herbiers, a creek between mud banks, ½M S of Barre de Flot, on W side of channel, 4m.

(3) Between Barre de Flot and Dourduff, just outside the channel clear of oyster beds; exposed to NW.

(4) At neaps, in the entrance to Dourduff river; br has 3m headroom.

(5) Off Locquénolé on W side, if space allows among the moorings. Sand barges pass close and good anchor lt is essential. Anchoring is forbidden above this point. Below Morlaix are an overhead cable (32m) and a viaduct (33m).

Morlaix The wet basin is formed by a weir with lock at W side; the inner sill is 3.1m above CD, the lock 63m by 16m. The gates operate only by day at HW −1½h HW and HW+1h. Moor to quay on E side (dries 3m) while waiting. N part of the basin is for commercial use; yachts moor to pontoons in S part, run by Morlaix YC; or moor on W quay. If leaving after HW, clear the river before ebb sets hard.

Supplies Water on pontoons; fuel from café on E side of basin or garage; shops.

Supplies Water on pontoons; fuel from garage; shops.
Tel Locks (98) 88-54-92. YC (98) 88-01-01. Customs (98) 88-06-31.

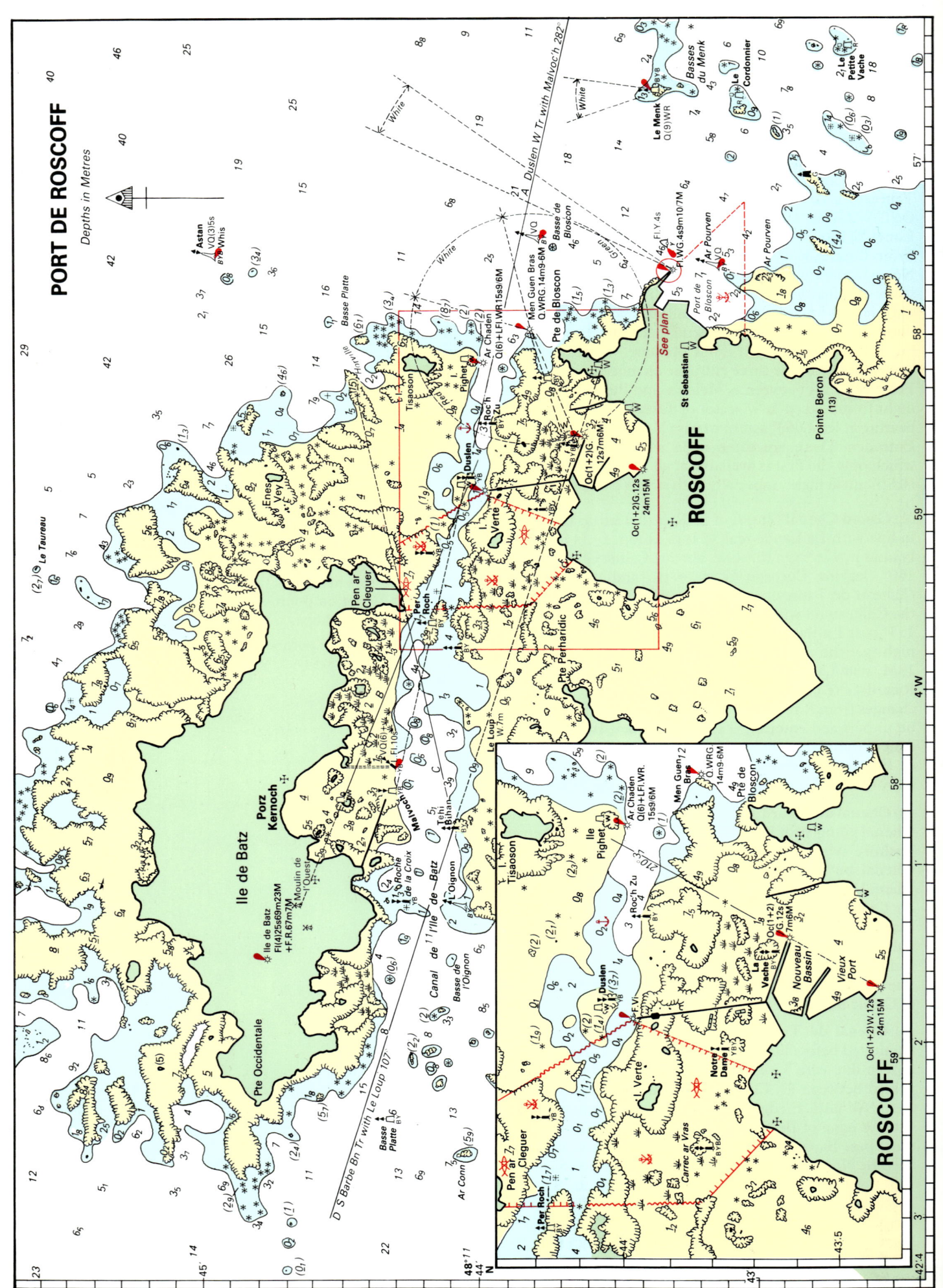

PORT DE BLOSCON
Charts BA 2745, 3669, F 7095, 7151.
HW (Roscoff): Dover −6¼h. DS: Dover −¼h S; +5¼h N, 1kn
MHWS 8.9m MHWN 7.0 MTL 5.2 MLWN 3.5 MLWS 1.3
A new hbr, on NE side of Roscoff peninsula, built primarily for car ferries and commercial shipping but which provides a satisfactory but unattractive anchorage for yachts. It can be entered at any state of the tide and provides good shelter in winds from N through W to SE.
Approach The W side of the channel is bordered by Ile de Batz with a prominent grey lt ho, Fl(4) 25s 69m 23M, and two lt trs: Ar-Chaden S card YB, Q(6) and Fl WR 15s 12m 9/6M; and Men-Guen Bras N card BY, Q WRG 14m 9/6M.
Entrance From N leave Basse de Bloscon N card buoy, VQ, to stb. The entrance, ½M to the S of it, has a jetty on the N, W col at head Fl WG 4s, with a N card buoy VQ 2ca to the S. At night enter in W sector, 206°-216°.
Anchorage On S side of hbr as close inshore as possible. Anchoring is prohibited to N of a line drawn W from the N card entrance buoy. Uncomfortable with E to NE winds. Land at slip.
Tel/VHF Capitainerie (98) 61-27-84/ch 12.

ROSCOFF
Charts BA 2745, 3669, F 7095, 7151.
HW: Dover −6¼h. DS: Dover +½h E; −6h W, 3¾kn.
MHWS 8.9m MHWN 7.0 MTL 5.2 MLWN 3.5 MLWS 1.3
An interesting old town and popular holiday resort, with drying hbr.
Approach From W by Chenal de Batz. From N leave Astan E card buoy, VQ(3) 5s 8M, clear to stb and then approach in W sector (197°-257°) of Men-Guen Bras BY N card lt tr, Q WRG. Align it with Roscoff rear ldg lt OC(2+1) 12s (grey tr, W on NE side) and when Ar Chaden R lt appears, Q(6)+L Fl WR 15s, steer to leave that close to stb. Continue for a short distance to W for the ldg lts. From Baie de Morlaix follow directions for Chenal de l'Ile de Batz; by night approach in W sector of Ar Chaden Q(6)+LFl WR, 291°.
Entrance dries 3.2m and should not be attempted until after half-tide. Steer on the ldg lts 210°, front W rectangle with B stripe on W column with G top at head of NW mole, Oc(2+1) G 12s 7m; rear grey tr, W on NE side, Oc(2+1) (synchronised with front) 12s, 2 ca to SW. This line leaves rks drying 7m close to port. Nearing the front lt, bear away to leave it to stb and round second pierhead to Vieux Port.
Berthing in outer hbr (Port Neuf) is discouraged as quays are for fishing vessels. Inner hbr, drying 3-5m, is available for yachts. Moor alongside rough jetty or anchor in centre. Jetty to E has rks at base. Surge in strong NE winds. Anchoring outside possible while awaiting tide on line between Roch Zhu N perch and Ar Chaden lt tr, 2-3m, but uncomfortable with weather-going tide. Buoys sometimes available.
Supplies Water on quay. Fuel from tanker. Shops.
Tel/VHF Capitainerie (98) 69-76-37/ch 9.

CHENAL DE L'ILE DE BATZ
Charts BA 2745, 3669, F 7095, 7151.
HW: Dover −6¼h. DS (W entrance): Dover −4¼h SSW; +¼h NE, 1-2½kn, reaching 3kn on ebb.
(E entrance): Dover +½h E; −6h W, 3¾kn
MHWS 8.9m MHWN 7.0 MTL 5.2 MLWN 3.5 MLWS 1.4
The channel is unlit W of Roscoff. The transits pass close to shoals and one almost dries in the area of Per Roch, ½M NW of Roscoff landing stage. It should not be attempted 2h either side of LWS.
Directions From E to W the transits are as follows, with E-most mark of each pair quoted first:
A. Duslen W tr with Malvoch S card tr 282°. Passes close S of Ar Chaden S card YB lt tr, Q(6)+L Fl WR 15s, and N of Men Guen Bras N card BY lt tr, Q WRG. Before coming abreast of Roc'h Zu N card bn steer 270° to clear rks from Duslen W tr to mid-stream N of long Roscoff landing stage, conspic. Keep close to the former to:
B. W pyramid in Kernoch hbr in line with E-most of the two mills (named Moulin de l'Ouest!) SE of Batz lt ho, 291°. This leaves Per Roch N card BW bn to port.
C. About 1 ca past Per Roch, steer on rear on bearing 078° with Pte Pen Ar Cléguer in line with Horville rk (dries 15m) to just N of Tehi Bihan N card bn.
D. At Tehi Bihan bn steer W to get on rear bearing 106° with Le Loup W rk in line with W pyramid at Ste Barbe to clear the entrance.
From W to E the transits are reversed.
Anchorages (1) While awaiting the tide to enter at the W end, off Ar Skeul W card YBY bn tr SW of Ile de Siec; beware drying rk to its SW.
(2) Porz Kernoch on Ile de Batz. Level ground N and NW of W Kernoch pyramid, dries 5m. Area S of pyramid has rks. Slipway to E used by passenger boats.
(3) W of Roscoff entrance on line joining Roc'h Zu bn and Ar-Chaden tr.
Supplies Small shops in Kernoch village.

PASSAGE NOTES: CHENAL DE BATZ TO L'ABER VRAC'H
Charts BA 2644 or 3668 and 3669, F 964 and 966

Passage Lights
Ile de Batz	grey tr Fl(4) 25s 69m 23M, with F R (024°-059°) 66m 7M
Pontusval	W tr Oc(3)WR 12s 16m 10/7M (R over rks to SW)
Amann Ar Rouz	N card buoy, Q, whistle
Lizen van Ouest	W card buoy, VQ(9) 10s, whistle
Ile Vierge	grey tr Fl 5s 77m 27M siren
Le Four	grey tr Fl(5) 15s 28m 20M

Streams related to HW Dover:
2M N of Ile de Batz +3¾ E; −5¼h W, 3¾kn. Off Le Libenter +¼h E; −6h W, 2½kn
On arriving from or leaving to UK allowance must be made for the tidal streams which are stronger nearer the coast.
There are no sheltered hbrs or anchorages in this 26M stretch; such hbrs as there are dry, the best being:
Mogueriec SW of Ile de Siec. Rks to NE are in Ile de Batz R sector. Ldg lts 162° front W tr G top Iso WG 4s, rear W column G top F G; 6M. Shelter by quay taken by fishing boats. Entrance impossible LW±2h or with fresh N winds.

Pontusval (Brignogan) HW Dover +6h. MHW 8.4-6.4m; MTL 4.8. Dries 2-5m; open to N and accessible only by day after half-tide. Lies 1M to E of Pontusval lt tr with conspic W lookout tr to W of entrance. From Toullcoz BR buoy approach on 178° with Coatanguy W tr in line with Plounéour-Trez spire passing G con buoy and R An Neudden tr. Anchor SW of the latter, 4m, or dry further in. Stores at Brignogan.

L'ABERVRACH Charts BA 1432, F7150, 7094.
HW: Dover +5¾h. DS at entrance to Grand Chenal: Dover HW SE; +6h NW, 1½kn.
MHWS 8.0m MHWN 6.1 MTL 4.5 MLWN 2.9 MLWS 1.1
An estuary accessible at all times, open to NW but with shelter in the upper reaches.
Approach From W or N make for a position ½M W of Libenter W card buoy, Q(9) 15s, whistle, 3M WSW of Ile Vierge lt. From NE, with good visibility and reasonable sea, make a position 1½M W of the light for the Malouine Channel.
Entrance There are three entrance channels of which only the first is usable at all times.
(1) **Grand Chenal** (3m) From 2 ca S from W of Libenter buoy pick up the ldg line, 100°, of front, Ile Vrac'h W lt ho, R top, Q R 20m 8M; rear Lanvaon W lt tr, Dir Q (091°-111°) 55m 10M; and also on this line, Plouguerneau belfry. Beware of cross tide in entrance – the flood sets hard on Libenter. After Petit Pot de Beurre E card bn tr, steer 128° following the line of buoys and trs; at night change course from 100° at La Croix lt buoy, Fl(3) G 12s, and follow W sector of La Palue molehead lt, Dir Oc(2) WRG 6s, (W 127°-129°). This leads past Breac'h Ver G tr, Fl 2.5s, Fort Cézon and Roche aux Moines G tr (ignore the W tr to SW of it) all to stb; and there bear E for moorings.
(2) **Chenal de la Malouine** (3m, ½ ca wide at entrance). Coming from E this saves the distance round Libenter. 4M visibility is needed. It passes between La Pendante rk (6m) to W and La Malouine (17m) to the E. At 1½M W of Ile Vierge lt pick up the ldg marks 176°: front BY E card tr, 5m, and rear Petite Ile de la Croix W tr, 6m and 4 ca to its S. Beware strong cross tide, up to 3kn, in entrance and pass ¼ ca W of Carrec Bazil R tr. At Bar-ar-Bleis R buoy bear SSE between Plate de L'Aber Vrac'h and Petit Pot de Beurre, at which steer 128° as in Grand Chenal.
(3) **Chenal de la Pendante** (0.3m) can be used only by day with good visibility. At 2½M W of Ile Vierge, leave La Pendante 1½ ca to port, making good 136° (cross-set 2½kn) on line of front W mark on Fort Cézon, rear Pendante B tr (Tourelle des Anges) 1¼M SE. When 1½ ca off Grand Pot de Beurre R bn, 2m, come to port and make for Bar-ar-Bleis R buoy; when close, steer SSE past Plate de L'Aber Vrac'h R buoy into the main channel.
The River is navigable (2.7m) to Paluden which is more sheltered with winds from W to NW. When past Touris R tr, steer for the quay upriver on N shore. Nearing it turn to stb up centre of river, with stakes on the edges. Give Beg-an-Toul a wide berth and keep to W side of channel until near the quays.
Berthing Boats under 10m may find a place on the pontoons; otherwise there are 30 visitors' buoys. Anchoring is prohibited within hbr limits, incl Beg an Toul. In bad weather, especially from W to N, it is more comfortable to moor to fore-and-aft buoys at Beg an Toul or anchor above the bend at Paluden, below the br, in 6m (anchor lt is essential). The quay dries 2.5m.

Supplies Water and fuel at the quay. Small shop in the village; more at Landéda, 1M.
Tel/VHF Capitainerie (98) 04-91-62/ch 9/16. Customs (98) 04-90-27.

L'ABER BENOIT Charts BA 1432, F7150, 7094.
HW: Dover +5¾h. DS: Dover +½h ingoing; +6¼h outgoing, 3kn
MHWS 8.1m MHWN 6.4 MTL 4.7 MLWN 3.1 MLWS 1.2
A wide estuary, less developed than L'Aber Vrac'h. Unlit but providing good shelter.
Approach by the W of Le Libenter W card bn, Q(9) 15s, whistle, which is 3M WSW of Ile Vierge lt.
Entrance should not be attempted in strong NW winds. From close W of Petite Fourche W card buoy, ½M SSW of Libenter buoy, make good 170°, to Rusven Est G buoy. Here steer 190° on line of front Ven Bihan rk (19m) in line with Lampaul-Ploudalmezeau spire (W-most of two). When R Orvil buoy is in line with Jument de Garo alter course to leave the buoy close to port, 130°. Bear to port to clear Ar Gazel G buoy SE of La Jument de Garo and leave Le Chien BR isolated danger tr to port. Thereafter follow the channel.
Berthing Anchor by the ferry or off the bay on N bank where river turns southward. This is as far as one can remain afloat.
Supplies Small shops up the hill on S side of the ferry. Water on S quay.

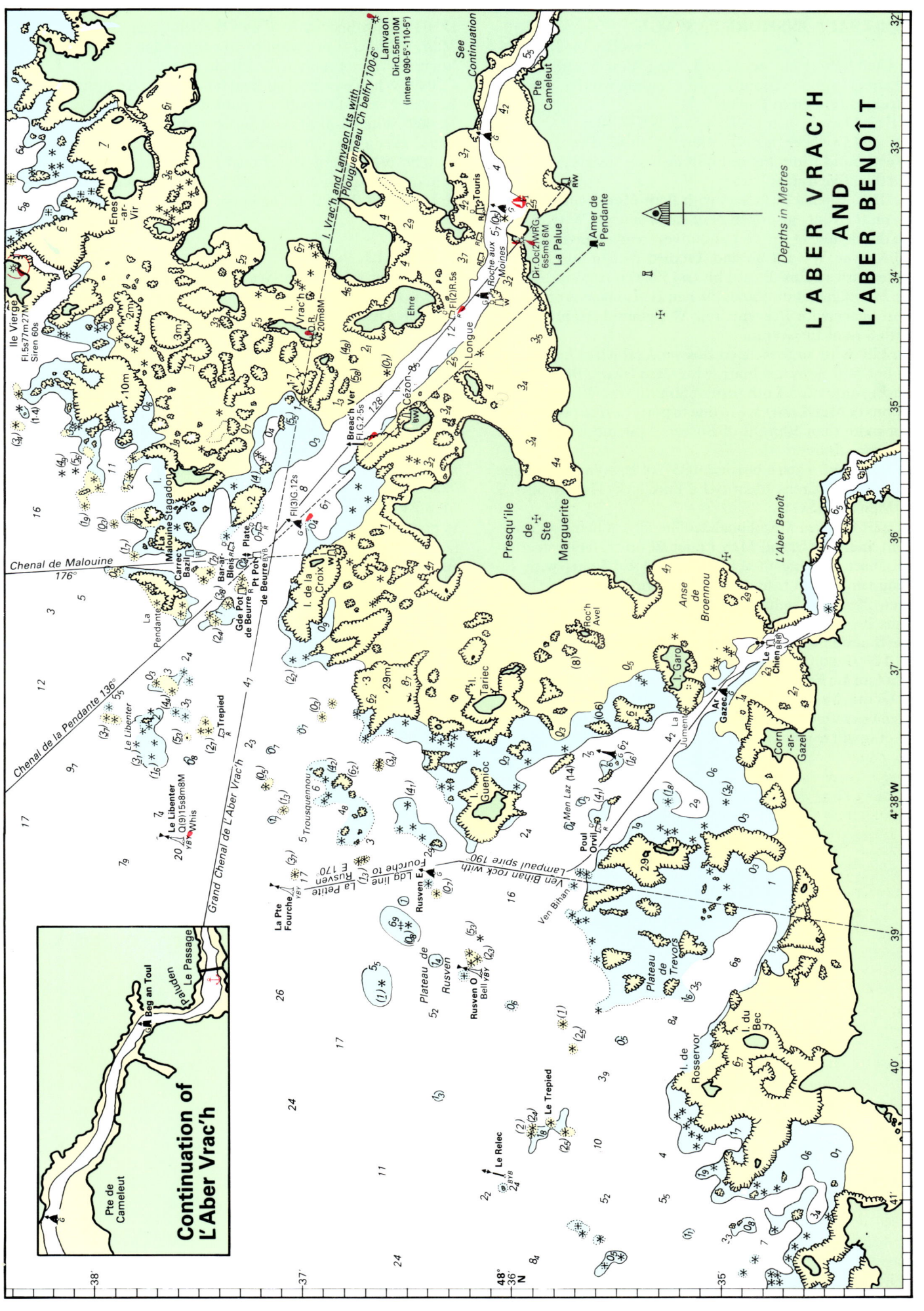

PORTSALL INSHORE PASSAGE
Charts BA 1432, F7094.

A useful short cut between L'Aber Vrac'h and le Four Channel in good visibility with a leading wind or power.

Streams related to Dover:
NE end Dover −1h ENE; +5¼h WSW, 4kn
SW end Dover −1h ENE, 4kn; +5¼h W, 5kn

Westbound From Petite Fourche buoy steer 255°. There are then five transit lines:

A. 219° (Chenal du Rélec) with Petit Men Louet conspic W bn tr (front) just open N of small conspic W tr, R top, on the skyline of Pte de Landunvès (rear). Leaves Plateau de Rusven W card bn and Trépied reef to port and Le Relec (dries 5.2m) E card bn and Bosven Amont to stb.

B. 249° (Chenal du Raous) When Ile Longue is abeam to port, steer with Bosven Creiz W pyramid (front) in line with S rk of Le Gremm.

C. 229° with large isolated Bosven Aval Rk (13m) (front) in line with grey Le Four lt ho, 28m (rear). Beware tide setting onto Men Luth (dries 5.2m) to stb. When the two W bns of Men Louet are in line to port, bear to port to pass not more than 50m SE of Bosven Aval and when past it come to stb to:

D. 215° with a stern bearing (035°) of Bosven Aval in line with Bosven Creiz. Identify Le Yurc'h rk (17m) to port, S of Men Ar Pic G tr.

E. 229° (Chenal Méridional de Portsall). When Le Yurc'h is in line with Grand Men Louet W bn tr, 049°, steer on this back bearing to come out S of Le Four, with Le Taureau W card tr to port. It is important to keep Grand Men Louet in sight through the cleft in the top of Le Yurc'h.

Eastbound needs 4M visibility for the front marks.

E. 049° Get on this line about 1 ca S of Grand Château rks, 4 ca E of Le Four, and leave Le Taureau W card bn to stb. If Grand Men Louet cannot be seen above Le Yurc'h, Men Gouzaine rk (12m), ¾M SW of Le Yurc'h, open just W of it will lead on the right line.

D. 035° with Bosven Aval and Bosven Creiz in line until Men Ar Pic G tr is abeam to stb; then edge to E to leave Bosven Aval not more than 50m to port.

C. 049° When past Bosven Aval follow the stern bearing of Bosven Aval in line with Le Four lt ho, 229°.

B. 069° When S-most rk of Le Gremm is in line with Bosven Creiz on the port quarter, follow this stern bearing.

A. 039° When Petit Men Louet bn is in line with W tr, R top, on Pte de Landunvès, 219°, follow that stern bearing to ½M W of Petite Fourche buoy.

PORTSALL
Charts BA 1432, F7094.

HW: Dover +5½h. DS: See Portsall Inshore Passage.
MHWS 8.1m MHWN 6.5 MTL 4.9 MLWN 3.4 MLWS 1.5

A drying fishing hbr open to NE, accessible after half-tide.

Approach from Chenal de Men Glas, S of Portsall rks or from Chenal Méridional.

Entrance (1) From W, at 1M SSW of Basse Paotr Bihan W card buoy, steer 108° with Le Yurc'h rk S of Men Ar Pic tr in line with Ploudalmezeau spire. When Bosven Aval rk (4.9m) bears 068°, steer on ldg marks ½M N of Portsall: front W column, R top, Oc(3+1) WRG 12s 9m (W 084°-088°) 16/13M; rear RW rectangle on wall, 085°; leaving Men Ar Pic to stb and Ile Verte and both Men Louet bns to port.

(2) Calerec Passage (dries 1m) From NE when Bosven Amont bears N steer 191° with, front, Losquet WY pyramid in line with Calerec bottle shaped W pyramid, R top. When Enes Scoune is abeam borrow a few yards to NW to avoid a rk awash at MLWS.

Anchorage (1) At springs, in the roads clear of ldg line with Petit Men Louet W tr bearing N, 10m. Suitable only in settled weather.
(2) NW of La Pendante N card BY tr, 2m.
(3) Dry out inside the hbr. Surge in NW gales.

Supplies Water on quay. Supplies very limited.

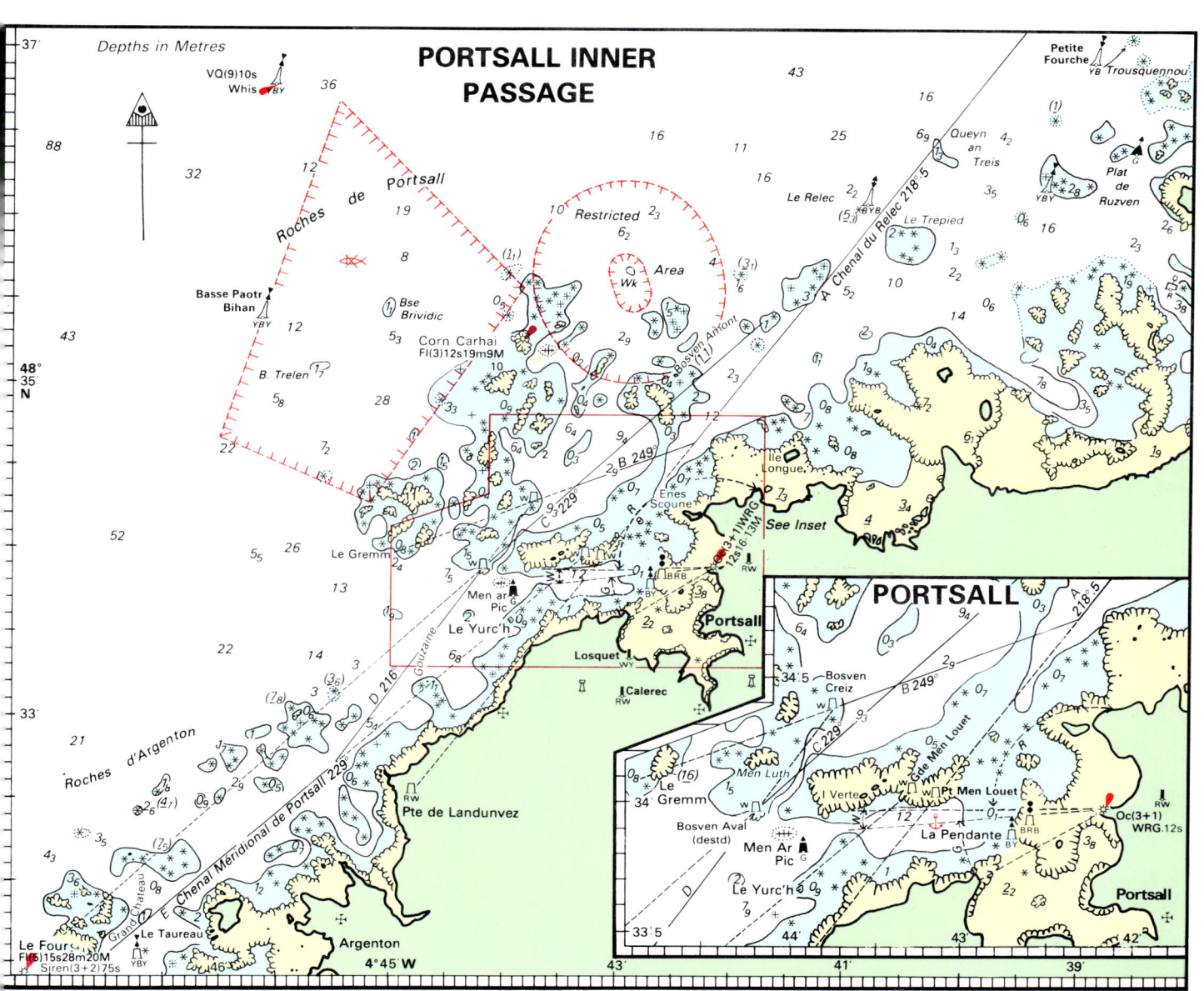

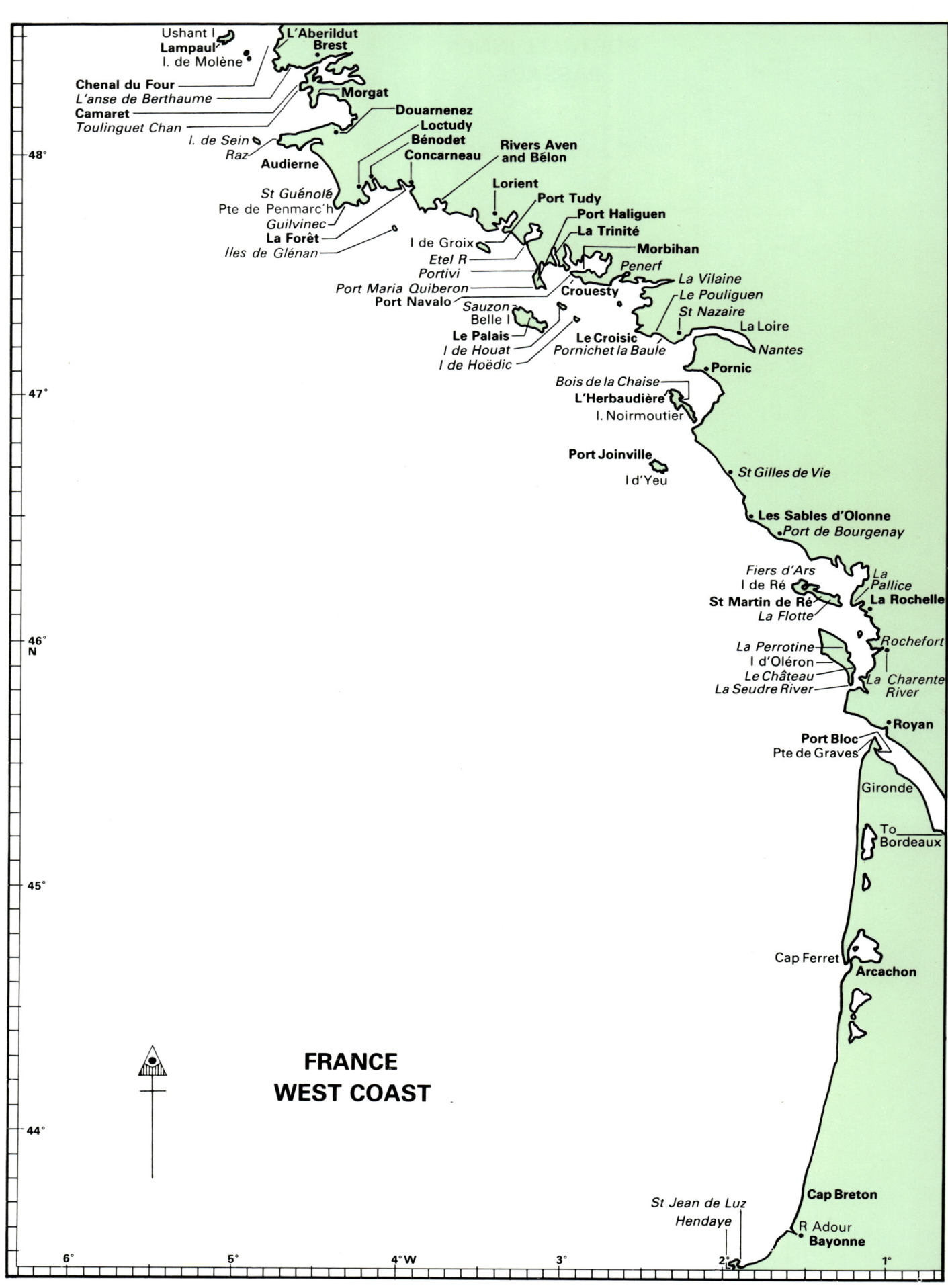

FRANCE
WEST COAST

FRANCE – WEST COAST

The West Coast of France may be considered as three separate cruising areas:-

1. The area from Ushant to St. Nazaire which includes the cruising areas of the Rade de Brest, the Baie de Douarnenez, the rivers Odet and Vilaine, the Baie de Quiberon and the Morbihan inland sea. This is probably the finest, most interesting area for cruising yachtsmen in the whole of France.

2. The area from St. Nazaire to the Gironde with the offshore islands of Noirmoutier, Ré and Oléron enclosing sheltered but shallow inshore waters, the rivers Loire and Gironde leading to inland waterways and most importantly La Rochelle the principal yachting centre on the W coast of France.

3. The area from the Gironde to the Spanish Frontier just beyond Hendaye, a low-lying featureless coast of lesser interest to yachtsmen except those on passage to the N coast of Spain. One particular hazard on this section is the French rocket range which may restrict passage between the Gironde and the Franco-Spanish Frontier (see note under Arcachon).

The flood stream up the coasts of Spain and Portugal flows SE into the Bay of Biscay, producing HW first in the SE corner and then travelling to W and N. The inshore tidal streams extend about 12M off the coast. The normal current, emanating from the Gulf Stream, also runs into the SE corner of the Bay turning W along the N coast of Spain. This however is reversed after prolonged W or NW gales which cause a strong current to run E along the N coast of Spain and then N up the coast of France extending as far as the entrance to the Gironde. Such currents may reach 4-5kn if current and tidal stream coincide.

North Biscay Pilot by K. Adlard Coles and A.M. Black and the South Biscay Pilot by Robin Brandon are useful volumes to have on board when cruising this coast, and essential for visiting the smaller ports. The annual French publication Votre Livre de Bord (Mer du Nord-Manche-Atlantique) by Bloc Marine covers the whole of the N and W coasts of France and contains much useful annually updated information including harbour chartlets. It is readily available from main French chandleries or direct from Interval Editions, 3 rue Fortia, 13001 Marseille (91) 54 38 97. Imray Laurie Norie and Wilson are U.K. distributors of this publication.

CHANNELS BETWEEN USHANT AND THE MAINLAND
Charts BA 3345;   F 7149, 7122, 7123

There are three channels between the Is and the mainland: the Fromveur, where the streams run at 9kn at springs, the Helle, the channel of approach from NW, and the Four, which is the most frequented and best buoyed and lit, 13M long. At the N end of this channel the stream runs at 3-6kn at springs, while in the narrows at the S end it attains 6-7kn.

Vessels bound for W France from the English Channel and vice versa usually avoid passing W of Ushant by using one of these channels. This shortens the passage and avoids the heavy swell often found W of Ushant. However, it is important to note that with strong winds against tide, severe steep seas build up in the Four Channel which may be beyond the capabilities of the average small yacht. This channel carries 6½m of water, and may be navigated without difficulty in hazy weather so long as visibility is not less than 2M.

Traffic separation lanes operate W of Ushant and are regularly patrolled and strictly enforced by French naval vessels (see charts).

FOUR CHANNEL (CHENAL DU FOUR)
Charts BA 3345;   F 7122
MHWS 7.4m MHWN 5.7 MTL 4.4 MLWN 3.0 MLWS 1.4

Direction of Streams The offing stream between the N end of the Four Channel and the Ile de Batz, 43M to the E, at Dover +2h turns ENE; at −4h WSW. Close inshore the stream turns 1½h earlier. The flood stream sets round the Four Rk from the SW and across the Portsall plateau, and the ebb stream in the reverse direction.

DS (all times relate to Dover). At S end of Channel: −½h N 5½kn; +5¼h S 4¾kn. Off Pt de Corsen: −1¼h N; +4½h S, 3kn. Abreast Les Plâtresses: −¼h NNE, +5½h SSW, 2kn; N of Les Plâtresses: −¼h NNE, +5½h SSW, 3kn.

Approach Nearing the N end of the Four Channel from the N or NE the principal landmarks visible in clear weather are as follows. To the SW, the cliffs of Ushant with Le Stiff Lt Ho Fl(2) R 20s 84m 24M and Créac'h Lt Ho Fl(2) 10s 70m 34M. To the E, Ile Vierge Lt Ho Fl 5s 77m 27M; the ch and spire of Plouguerneau; and at the E side of the entrance to the channel itself Le Four Lt, Fl(5) 15s 28m 20M.

Entrance From N by day, having given the Portsall plateau (Basse de Porsal W card buoy) a sufficient berth, leave the Four Lt Tr well to port and keep it open to S of Portsall Lt Tr, till Kermorvan and St Mathieu Lt Trs come in line, bearing 158°. The Kermorvan W square Lt Tr rises from the rks at the foot of Kermorvan Pt and will be seen against the heights behind Le Conquet. The St Mathieu W circular Lt Tr stands high on the cliff against the skyline, and near it the old lt tr now used as a signal stn, and the ruins of the ancient abbey.

Enter the well marked channel from N with these trs in line, 158° and carry on passing close to La Valbelle R buoy and St. Paul buoy to port until the Grand Vinotière Lt Tr, 15m, bears 180°. Then steer 180° to pass W of Grand Vinotière and E of the G buoy le Rouget abreast of the tr. When past the tr bring it in line astern 011° with Corsen Lt and keep it so until the lantern of St Mathieu secondary lt comes on with the main rear lt of St Mathieu, 128°, then steer with it so till Kermorvan and Trézien Lt Trs are nearly in line, 007°, then round out clear of the Pt of St Mathieu with them in line astern leaving Les Vieux Moines Lt to port.

From S by day, after rounding Les Vieux Moines Lt Tr from SE the above procedure is reversed using reciprocal compass bearings.

From N by night, having made the Four Lt bring it to bear E astern till St Mathieu Lt (intensified sector 157.5°-159.5°) and Kermorvan Lt are in line, 158°, then steer on them till the W sector of Corsen Lt to port is entered. Then steer 190° and be careful to remain in the W sector

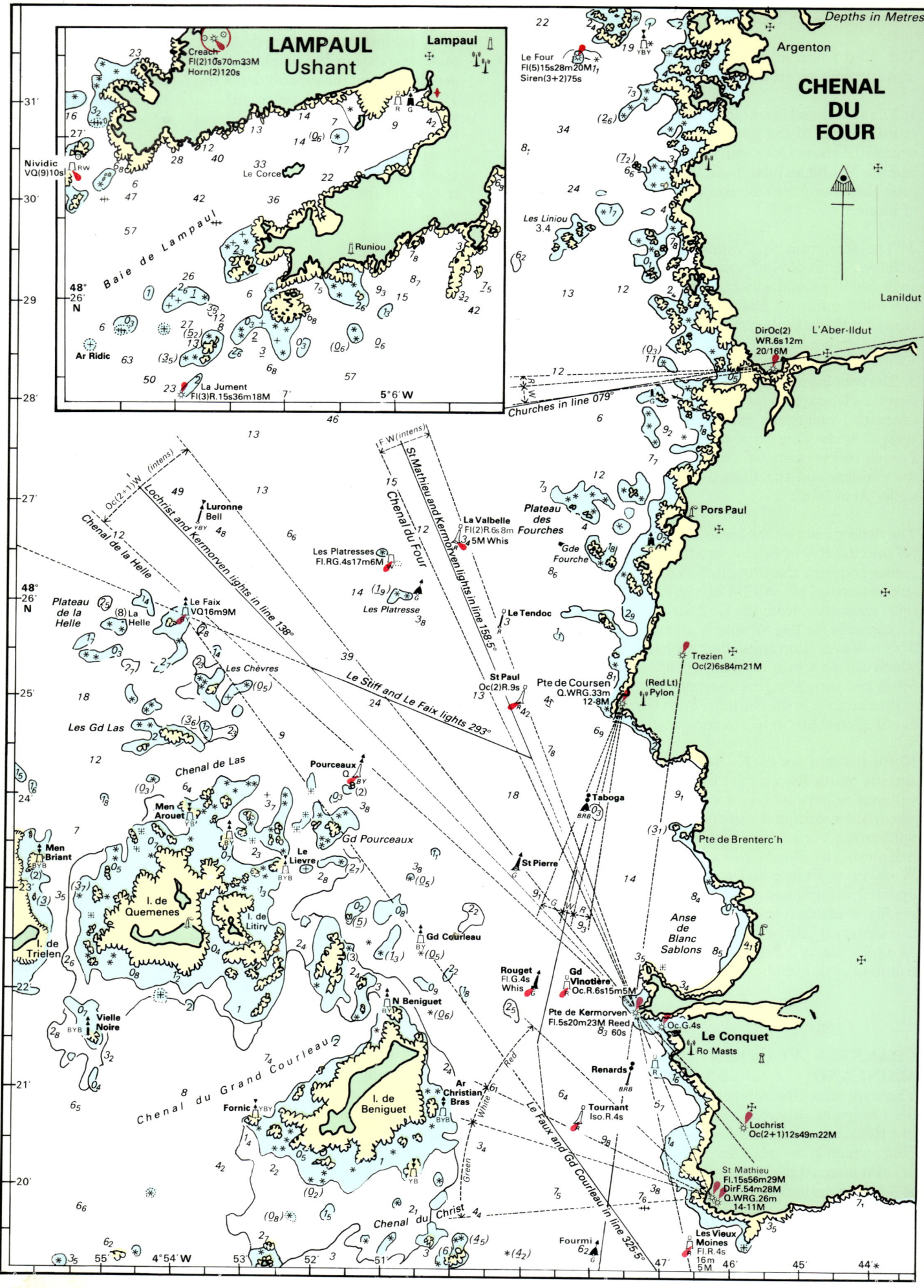

of Corsen Lt astern which will lead between the Grande Vinotière Lt to port and the lt buoy to stb abreast of it Continue 190° in the W sector of Corsen till the R sector of St Mathieu secondary lt is entered, when alter course according to stream and wind till the R sector of Corsen Lt comes on with Grande Vinotière Lt bearing 010°. Then steer with Corsen and Grande Vinotière Lts in line 010° astern, till the W sector of St. Mathieu secondary lt is entered, when alter course and bring this lt in line with St Mathieu main rear lt, 118° or nearly so, leaving the Tournant lt buoy to port. Carry on with St Mathieu lts in line till Trézien Lt comes nearly on with Kermovan Lt, 007° when turn to bring them in line astern and keep them so till the lt of Les Vieux Moines comes abeam, when alter course for the SE, keeping within visible sector of Les Vieux Moines until Portzic and Le Minou lts come in line, 068°, for Brest.

From S at night, enter the channel with Kermorvan and Trézien Lts in line, 007°, and steer so until the G sector of St Mathieu secondary lt is entered. Then steer a point or two to stb, and continuing so enter the W sector of St Mathieu secondary lt and bring the main and secondary St Mathieu lts in line, 118° astern. Steer on this line, leaving the Tournant lt buoy to stb. Continue thus till the R sector of Corsen Lt is entered. Bring this lt on with Vinotière Lt, 010° ahead. As soon as the Vieux Moines Lt or the R lt of St Mathieu are shut out, alter course to enter the W sector of Corsen Lt steering about 343° till this W sector is entered. Then steer on the lt, 013° leaving lt buoy to port and Grande Vinotière Lt to stb till Kermorvan and St Mathieu lts come in line. Keep them in line astern, 158°, till Le Four Lt bears E, when take your departure.

Anchorages (1) L'Aberildut. See separate entry, below.
(2) Anse de Porzmoguer, a good fine weather anchorage in 4½m or more, 1M S of Corsen Pt. Bring the two houses inside the bay in line and anch on this transit, with the belfry of Le Conquet open to right of Pte de Brenterc'h in 4½m, sand.
(3) Blancs Sablons Bay, a good fine-weather anchorage 7½m, sand, in N part of the bay, clear of stream but exposed to W and N. There is an eddy stream in S part of the bay.
(4) Le Conquet, a picturesque inlet between Kermorvan and Pt St Barbe for visiting in settled conditions. Strong cross tides in entrance. Hbr dredged to 2m but little room for visitors. Exposed to W. Outside anchorage between La Louve rk and the jetty head is protected NE to SE through E. Fuel available at jetty by arrangement. All stores.
(5) Ile de Molène, a rather desolate but attractive island, has an anchorage sheltered in winds from E through S to WSW. Numerous outlying rks and fierce currents. From ½M N of Le Faix Lt Bn N Card steer due W until N mill tr (RW) on Molène is in line with Les Trois Pierres Lt Ho. Leave Lt Ho 1 ca to port and steer between card buoys on ldg line of S mill with white mark on quay 190° leaving Baz Ourial to stb. Watch shingle bar when S of quays and anchor as far in as possible, or lie alongside quays. No fuel, water available daily. PO, small shops. Ferry and hydrofoil to mainland.

L'ABERILDUT Charts BA 3345; F 7122
HW: Dover +5½h
MHWS 7.6m   MHWN 6.0
DS as Chenal du Four. Bar carries 2m approx at low water.
Approach Keep Brélès ch tr, 2M inland, on with Lanildut ch tr, 079°. Brélès ch tr is 3M from Le Lieu Tr; the latter is easily identified, being shaped like a bottle. Leave Le Lieu tr 1 ca to port. Continue with rectangular Lt Ho Oc(2) WR on the N side of the entrance bearing 083°. Await tide 3 ca ESE of Le Lieu. Enter with sufficient water, and from a position 50m from the N shore steer to cross gradually towards the S shore and when over the bar round up for the quay. Halfway up the hbr an obstruction runs out from the E shore to the middle of the channel. Anchor 1 ca off the quay if room available (buoy anchor), 8m, in line with telegraph poles running down the the root of pier on NW side of hbr, keeping Lanildut ch well open of the prominent house on the N foreshore. Very crowded, but locals cooperative in use of buoys including dredgers. Shops, small restaurant, shipyard.

LAMPAUL, USHANT Charts BA 2694; F 7149, 7123
HW: Dover +5¼h
MHWS 7.4m   MHWN 5.7   MTL 4.4   MLWN 3.0   MLWS 1.4
An interesting place to visit in good weather, but to be avoided in strong W-lies. Lampaul is Ushant's main ferry harbour.

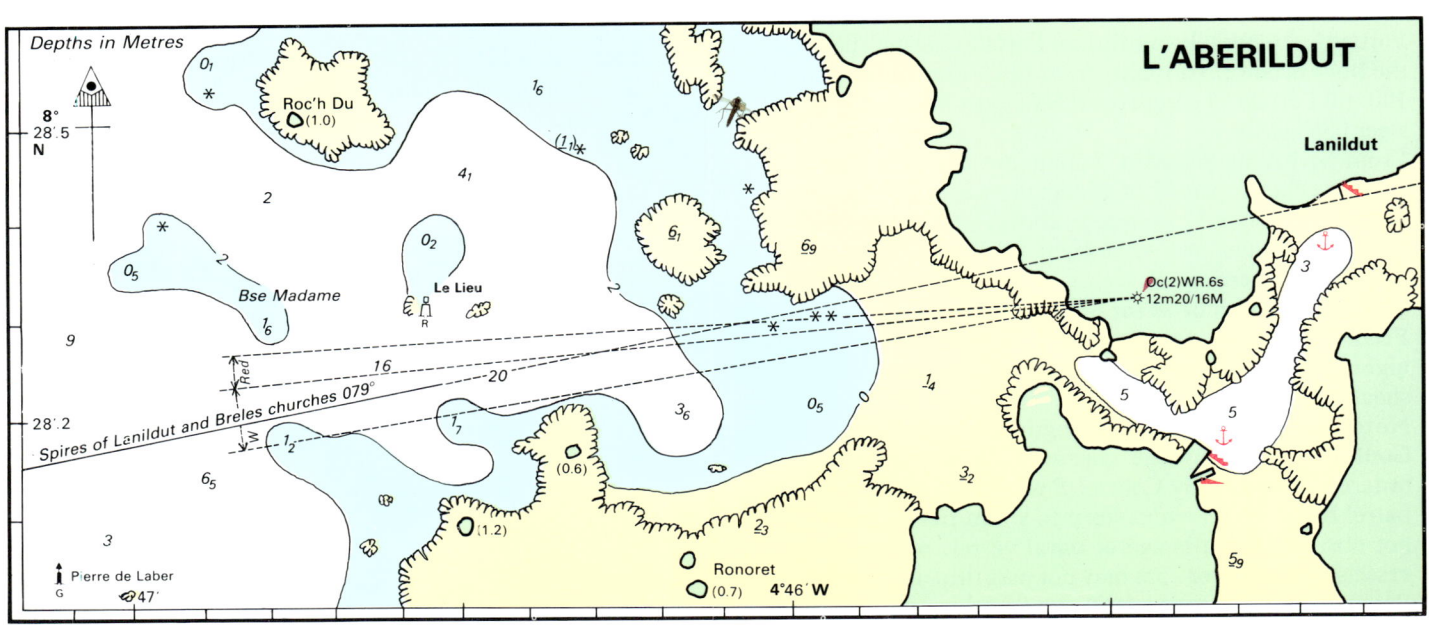

Approach With the Le Corce Is in line with Stiff Lt Ho, 055° then passing ½ ca S and E of Le Corce.
Anchorage. (1) At E end of Lampaul Bay, near the mooring buoys. Completely exposed to the W.
(2) In 2m just inside the outer hbr, clear of the ferry. The inner hbr dries.
Supplies Water, fuel from garage, PO, hotel, restaurants. Ferry to Brest.

L'ANSE DE BERTHEAUME Chart BA 3427; F 6678
Lying only 3½M ENE of Pte St Mathieu and being sheltered from winds between N and SW, under suitable conditions the W side of this bay offers a useful passage anchorage. However, as it is unlit and there are offliers, it should only be entered in daylight. Should the wind shift, Camaret and the Rade de Brest are within a short distance. On approaching from the W, keep clear of the offliers which run from E of Les Vieux Moines as far as the bay itself. Avoid also the drying rk close NE of Le Coq buoy. The Château de Bertheaume on the W headland of the bay is conspic. Give the château a berth of 2 ca to avoid offliers, including the drying rk Le Chat to the NE. This rk will have been cleared before the sandy cove just N of the château bears W. Anchor in about 5m close in, outside local moorings. Beware the rocks stretching out 4 ca to the SE from the Trez Hir Hotel (on the seashore and marked on the chart); these lie among the Nly moorings. Beware also rks and patches in other parts of the bay.

BREST Charts BA 3427, 3428; F 6542, 6427, 6426
HW: Dover+5¼h
MHWS 7.4m MHWN 5.8 MTL 4.4 MLWN 3.0 MLWS 1.3
Tidal streams in the Goulet de Brest. In Passe Sud the flood stream begins ½h after local LW and flows E; the ebb soon after HW to W. The ebb sets obliquely between Pt des Espagnols and Pt de Dellec. During the ebb an E-running eddy flows inshore along the S side of the Goulet, attaining its greatest strength during the latter half. In the Passe Nord the streams begin about ½h later. Contrary wind and tide produce a steep sea.
Approach From W leave Les Vieux Moines to port, steer 100° for 3½M, passing S of Le Coq (3.6m) and Beuzec (1.8m), and carry on till Portzic Lt comes in line with Petit Minou Lt, 068°, when steer 070° up the pass, to leave Portzic Lt to port. From abreast Portzic continue 064° for the hbr entrance. At night, from Les Vieux Moines steer 100° till Portzic Lt comes open N of Petit Minou Lt, when steer 070° as above.
From S, having rounded Toulinguet Pt, steer 010° till Portzic comes open N of Mengam, when steer to leave Portzic to port and continue as above; by night steer 010° from Toulinguet to Petit Minou till Portzic comes well open N of Mengam R sector, when head to pass S of Portzic and continue so for hbr entrance.
From Toulinguet, to pass S of Mengam, steer 037°. At night keep in W sector of Mengam Lt; R sector leads over shoals.
Note: Vessels less than 25m length may pass through the Goulet de Brest by the course of their choice unless ordered otherwise by Control Post (VHF 24,28) or by a patrol boat. Vessels must keep to stb in passes and must not obstruct free passage of naval vessels or other large vessels. Vessels over 25m may not pass thro' the Goulet de Brest without prior permission.

Entrance The breakwater heads are marked by R and G lts. Beware numerous large mooring buoys.
Berthing The Port du Commerce is available for yachts but visitors may prefer to use the marina about 2M E of the Port du Commerce in Anse du Moulin Blanc. Leave Moulin Blanc buoy Fl(3) R 12s to port and steer NNE into buoyed and lighted channel. Leave floating wavebreaker FlG to stb. (Bassin N 2m, deepest water Bassin S 5m). HM, diesel, no petrol. Restaurant, chandlery, water, toilets. Basic provisions only in village; bus service to Brest every 20 mins Mon-Sat Hm (98) 02 20 02, VHF 9. Customs at Brest (98) 44 35 20.
Anchorages within the Goulet de Brest.
Landerneau River. May be ascended at sufficient rise of tide as far as Landerneau, 12M. There is 24m clearance under the bridge; use the N arch. 4m least water as far as St Jean. 3m draught can reach Landerneau at HW. It is advisable to leave early on the ebb or before HW. There is much mud exposed at LW and a permanent barrier which covers at half tide between the sand quays and the main town quay.
Entrance Leave the buoy off Moulin Blanc to port, buoy with con topmark close to stb. A buoy marks the rk off Pt Ste Barbe. To enter by S side of the Deraliou bank at sufficient rise, keep the fort of I Longue in line with Pt Marloux astern, 220°. This line nearly dries at LW.
Anchorage A good berth at Le Passage. Vessels anchor also at St Jean and can lie alongside the quay at Landerneau.
Auberlach Bay Affords good anchorage, mud, in 3½m ¼M offshore S of jetty. Vessels of 1.8m draught can enter within 2h of HW and dry alongside the jetty. Bay exposed to W. At the head of the bay there is a lagoon, dries, soft mud. A shingle spit runs down from the N shore, leaving a narrow entrance close to the S shore through which the tide runs hard. Enter at slack water, round the end of the spit and hug the spit on its inner side till close to the N shore. Keep close inshore till abreast the village; anchor there in complete shelter.
Daoulas River Vessels of 2.7m draught can reach Daoulas at HWS. There is an anchorage in 2½m, mud, ¾M from entrance, close to S bank off a little cove where fishing boats lie. Stores 1M.
Bay of Poulmic Good anchorage to S of the shoal area, close inshore, with Plougastel on with the middle mill of Traoulior and Pt des Espagnols, to N of Penar Vir, in 3m.
Bay of Le Fret Anchor in 3½m, mud and clay, off quay.
Bay of Roscanvel On W side about half way down prominent headland in 2m (mud) exposed from N through E. Much of remaining area in bay prohibited anchorage due to French naval activity.

355 FRANCE, WEST COAST

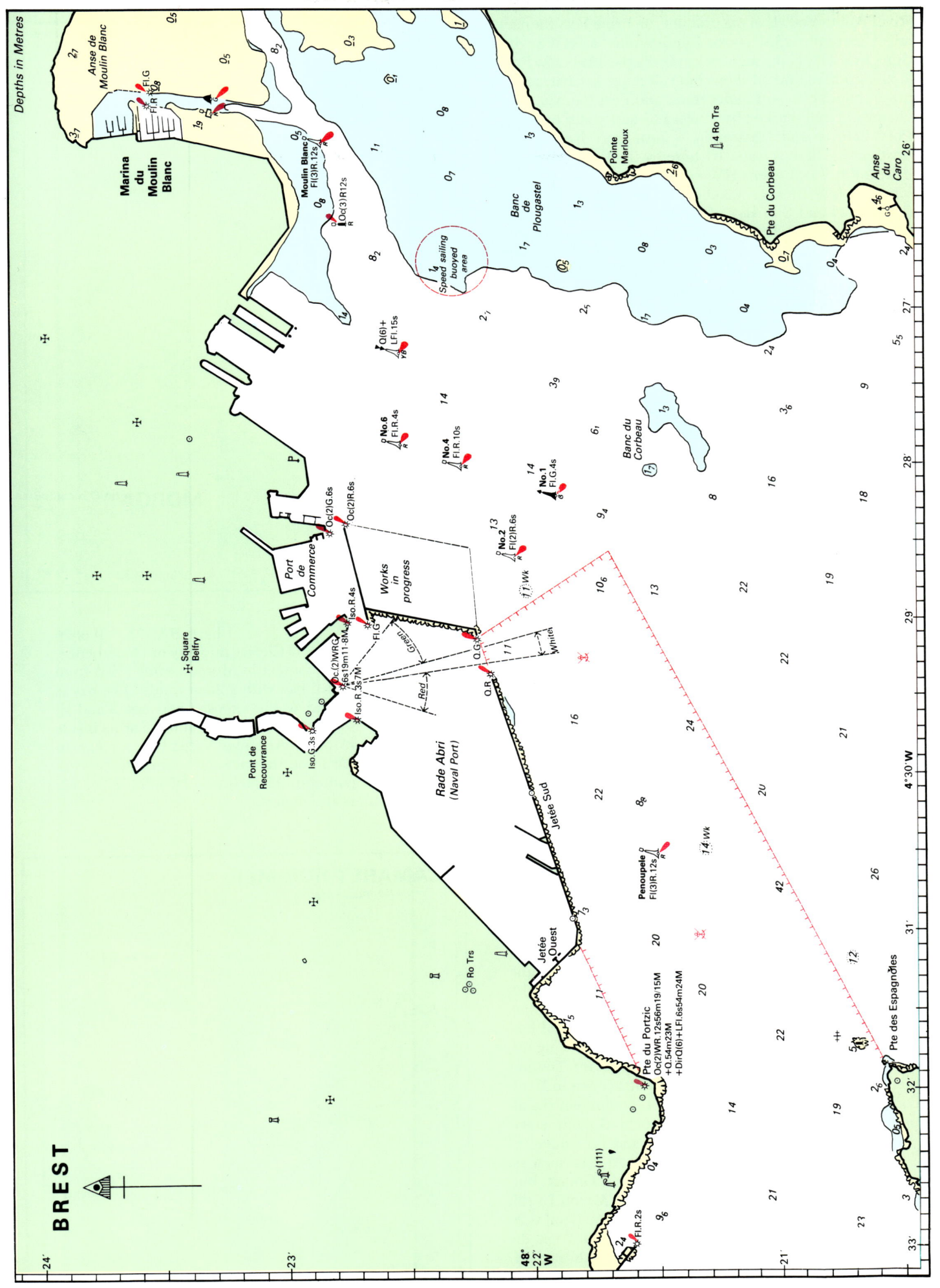

River Aulne Vessels of 4m draught can reach Port Launay and Chateaulin 13M above Landevennec at HWS, 3m draught at HWN, through lock at Guilyglas 1M below Port Launay where limited shops but full range at Chateaulin, no supplies between Landevennec and Port Launay. The channel is well marked by buoys and best water between Port Launay and Chateaulin is near port bank going upstream. There is water by hose by the lock, upper sill dries 2.7m. Lock opens HW −2h. HW at Port Launay is ½h after HW Brest. A good anchorage may be found in the bays N and S of Bay of Folgoat round first bend in river, in line with horns of bay, out of stream. Clay bottom, soft mud further in. There is a bridge at I de Terenez 27m above HW. Recognised anchorage at Tregervan and at Dineault, clear of stream. Restaurants at Folgoat, Port Launay and Chateaulin.

PASSAGE NOTES: BISCAY COAST

HW throughout the length of the coast occurs approx at Dover +4½h to 5½h.

In spring and summer prevailing winds between Ushant and the Gironde are from between W and NE through N, but in the neighbourhood of Brest SW winds are frequently experienced. Gales are not frequent during June through August, but at no time can freedom from W gales be relied on, and in unsettled weather small craft are well advised not to stray too far from shelter. In the autumn, E winds are slightly more frequent. Fog rarely lasts long on most of this coast, but is quite frequent around Ushant and Brest.

CAMARET   Charts BA 3427,   F 6678

HW: Dover +5¼h

MHWS 6.9m   MHWN 5.3   MTL 4.0   MLWN 2.8   MLWS 1.2

Hbr is sheltered from all directions except E, but there is sometimes a swell. Yachts berth at pontoons which are situated under N breakwater in up to 5.4m or anchor in bay. Water from tap, at top of pontoon gangway as well as at head of slip alongside S mole, where fuel is also obtainable. This slip must be left clear. Some buoys for visitors and room for anchoring S of entrance to inner hbr. All facilities, toilets and showers available below Vauban Tower, also pay phones. Shops ½M, HM (98) 27 95 99. Customs (98) 27 93 02.

THE TOULINGUET CHANNEL

At Dover +5½h the stream sets S, and at −½N. The passage is narrow, but may be made with care by day or night with a fair tide, in clear weather, as the tide sets straight through the fairway at 2 to 3kn. From N, pass midway between La Louve rk tr and Le Pohen rk. Channel has 4½m. From the S make W of Les Tas de Pois allowing for the inset into Douarnenez Bay. Hence steer for Toulinguet Lt with the Petit Minou Lt Ho a little open to W of Toulinguet Pt, 011°. When abreast of Toulinguet rks at night when St Mathieu Lt is hidden behind them, steer about 335° to pass between Le Pohen and La Louve tr. When clear to the N of them, round up to E as soon as Portzic Lt Ho comes open of the S side of the Goulet, but if bound for the N channel hold on for the Minou Lt till well clear to N of the Fillettes, on to which the flood tide sets. There are fair weather anchorages in the Anse de Penhir and Anse de Dinan sheltered NW to E through N after rounding Les Tas de Pois heading S.

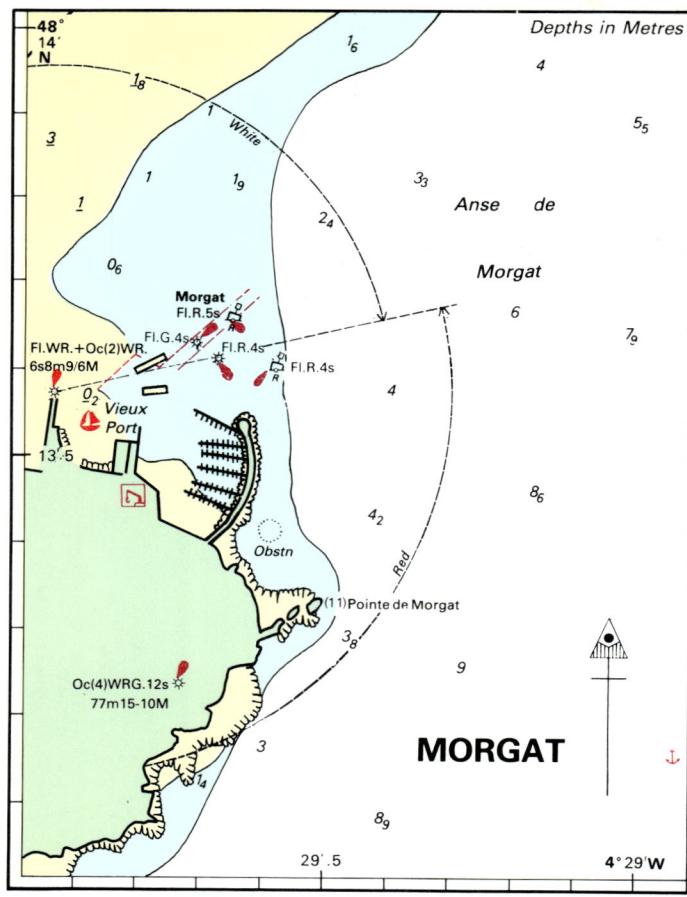

MORGAT   Charts BA 798,   F 6676

After rounding Cap de la Chevre into Bay of Douarnenez, there is a pleasant anchorage at Morgat, some 3½M from the cape in a wooded bay with golden sands. The bay is sheltered from N and W but exposed between S and E; however there is complete protection at the marina inside mole N of Pt de Morgat. Although Vieux Port dries, with sandy bottom, marina berths have at least 2m. Visitors use outside of first pontoon. All facilities. HM (98) 27 01 97, VHF 9. Customs at Camaret.

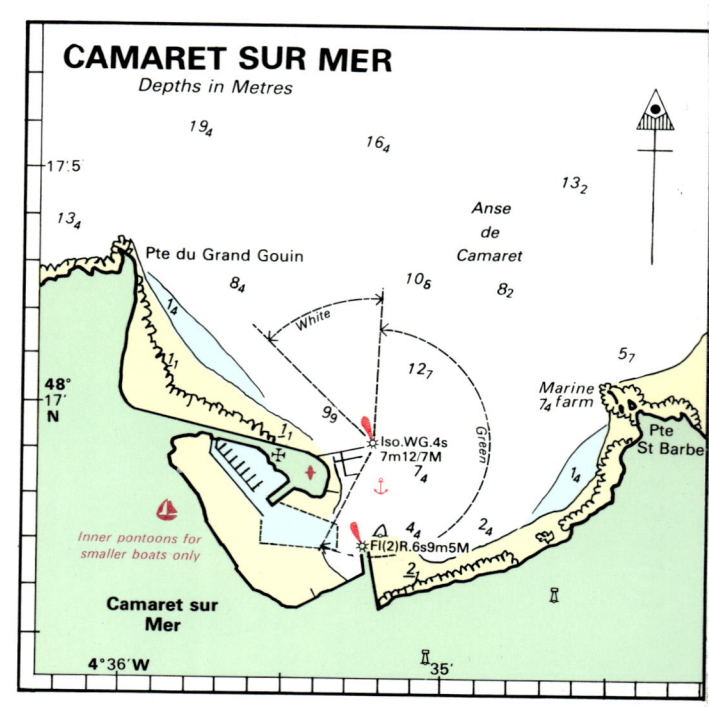

DOUARNENEZ-TRÉBOUL Charts BA 798, F 6677
HW: Dover +5¼h

MHWS 6.9m MHWN 5.4 MTL 4.1 MLWN 2.8 MLWS 1.3

A fascinating spot, 16M inside Pt du Van. Marina at Tréboul.

Approach To clear the Basse Veur, 4m, keep the Millier Lt open of La Jument Pt until Ploare ch comes open to the E of Douarnenez ch. At night keep in the W sector of Millier Lt, Oc(2) WRG 6s, until the R sector of Ile Tristan Lt, Oc(3) WR 12s has been crossed.

Anchorage Yachts are not allowed in the fishing hbr but anchor off Rosmeur S of the hbr dredged to 5m. There are lts Iso G 4s and Oc(2)R 6s on N and S sides of the hbr entrance and an Oc G lt on the end of Rosmeur mole. There are extensive fish farming tanks in this area outside local moorings. Anchoring space is very limited.

There is an anchorage exposed from NNW to NE in the Rade de Guet with many mooring buoys for visitors. The entrance to Pouldavid R is through the Grande Passage, dredged to be available at all tides, overhead cable 30m clearance. Past the Tréboul jetty head, QG, turn to stb into enlarged marina in the Tréboul inlet, dredged to 1½m, with ample visitors' berths, sheltered from all winds. Water and electricity on pontoons, fuel on quay, WC and showers in building below HM office. (98) 74 02 56, VHF 9. Marina crowded during August but visitors' buoys outside marina, also drying quays further up river at Port Rhu. Good shops at Tréboul and all facilities at Douarnenez. Customs (98) 92 01 45.

ILE DE SEIN Charts BA 798,2351, F 5252

An interesting port of call if the weather is settled, but chart F 5252 essential. Approach is best made by the N channel guarded by a whistle buoy, Iso G. Anchor off entrance in clear water or take the ground in SW of harbour or alongside quay on S side. Better visited at neaps and with winds other than from the N.

RAZ DE SEIN Charts BA 798 F 5252

Tidal Streams. HW: Dover +5h. The stream runs 6-7kn at springs, 3-4kn at neaps. In the middle of the Raz at Dover −1½h, the NE-going flood begins, and at +4¾h the SW ebb, attaining 7 and 6kn respectively. There is a period of slack water for about ½h at the end of the flood stream.

The passage is better taken at slack water, except at neap tides and in fine weather. With wind against tide, the passage is rough in moderate winds, but when the wind and stream are together the sea is smooth in the Raz, though it can then be rough outside. Between the Ile de Sein and Tévennec at Dover −1¾h the stream runs NW, and at +4½h SE, 3kn; at La Vieille −1½h NNW, +4½h SSE; there are eddies inshore.

Directions By day from S. When within 2M of La Vieille bring Tévennec rk five times its own width to W of La Vieille and keep it so, till Ile de Sein bears about 280°, then round La Vieille at ½M or more. Keep La Vieille 180° astern till Tévennec and Ile de Sein come in line. By day from

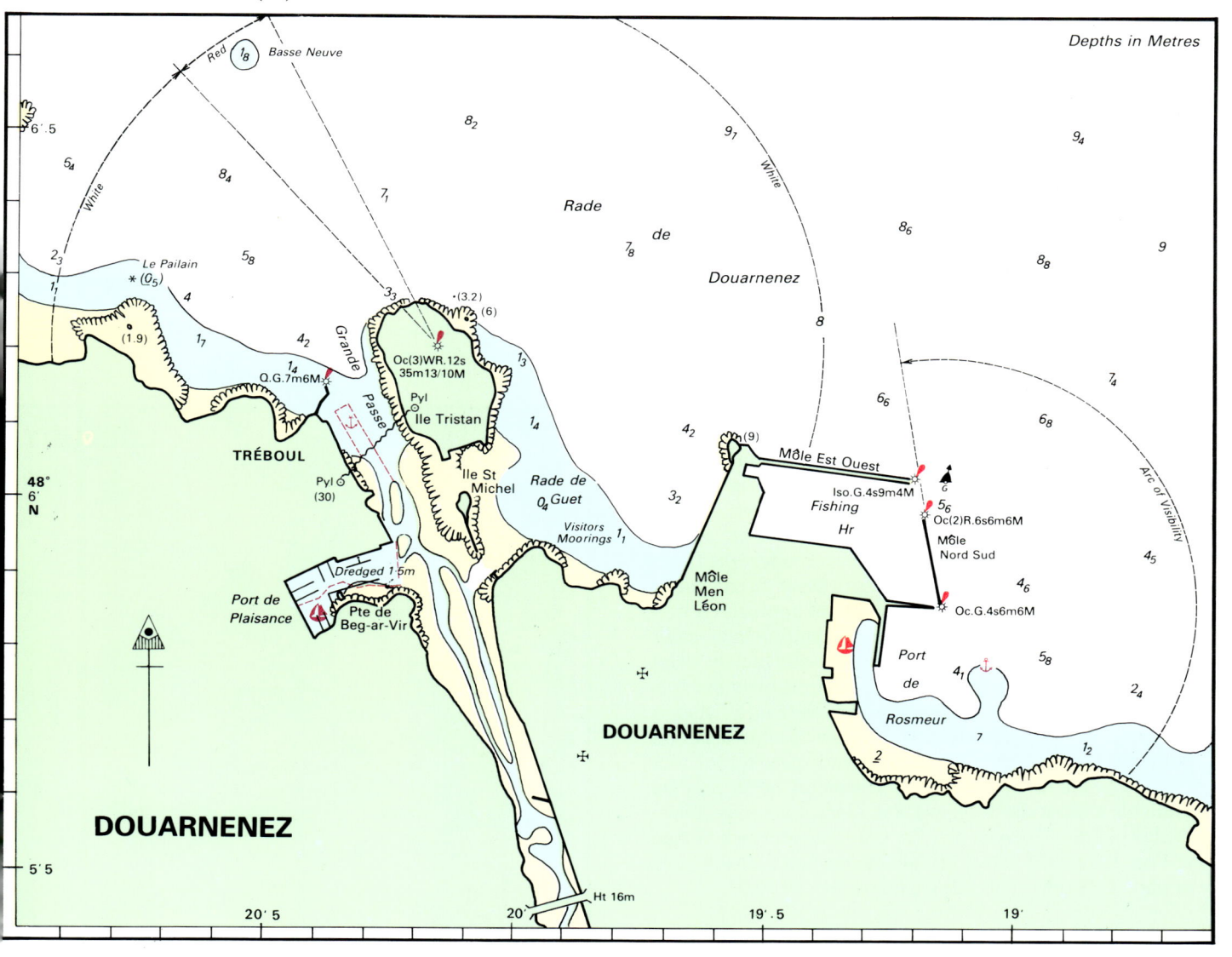

the N, steer for La Vieille 180°, round it and bring Tévennec rk five times its width open W of La Vieille astern for 2½M.

At night from S, approach La Vieille Lt in its W sector 325°-355° and, with the aid of Tévennec Lt, round it. When the NW sector of La Vieille is reached steer 013°. Allowance should be made for the tidal stream to avoid La Vieille on the ebb and Les Barillets on the flood. At night from the N, steer for La Vieille, 180°, pass close W of La Platte Lt, bring Tévennec to bear 328°, and steer 148°.

AUDIERNE AND ST EVETTE ANCHORAGE
Charts BA 3640, F 7147
HW: Dover +5h
MHWS 5.2m MHWN 3.9 MTL 3.0 MLWN 2.0 MLWS 0.8

Hbr is 9M SE of La Vieille, and may be approached in all but established bad weather from S; an attractive spot in fine weather. The river is only accessible after half-flood and strong S winds produce a dangerous sea in the entrance. However, the breakwater 3 ca NE of Le Sillon rk protects a useful anchorage, known as the Anse de St Evette, to the W of the river entrance. It is safe in all but strong SE winds though subject to some swell when there is any S in the wind. It is accessible at any state of the tide and thus recommended for starting a passage through the Raz towards the N.

Approach From the E keep Kergadec Lt Tr FR upper, Q WRG lower in line with lt Oc (1+2) WG on pierhead at W of river mouth, 331°; from W after rounding Pt de Lervily, Fl WR 12s ½M off, enter by the Grand Chenal between Pt de Lervily and La Gamelle rks (W card) and keep Kergadec Lt Tr and the old Lt Ho W of entrance in line, 006°. When making for St Evette anchorage keep on this until the end of the breakwater bears NW, then alter course to round it ½-1 ca off to avoid the rks off its foot and the shallow patch to the E. For the hbr, whose entrance almost dries, keep on the transit till the pier-head lt, Oc WG 12s, bears 034°, when steer 042° till the river comes open to E of the pier head, or at night till the pier-head lt turns W. Then steer 039° to leave the pier-head lt fairly close to port and Le Corbeau rk, YBY tr well to stb. Inside, the channel runs along the W side, not far from the pier; then to midstream. From the Poulgoazec corner it lies along the W side to the bridge; in the apex of the angle 2 ca below the bridge there is less water.

Anchorage In the St Evette anchorage, a number of the buoys are used by fishermen but may be picked up when not in use. There are also several visitors' buoys (W) marked 'Payant Visiteurs' suitable for boats up to 10m length, restricted swinging room. The least swell will be found between these buoys and the breakwater, and as close to the LB slip as possible. At certain tides, the Ile de Sein ferry arrives at another slip with a bn at its end parallel to and N of the LB slip, and its line of approach is between the breakwater and the buoys. Landing at steamer slip at all states of the tide. Audierne hbr mostly dries below the bridge. In the inner hbr the best quay berth is where quay runs NW-SE but this is nearly always occupied by fishing boats. Local smaller yachts berth on pontoons opposite the town centre, and space for visitors may be available in 2m, out of season. A berth may be available abreast the hotel in 1.8m. Good anchorage above bridge in 3.6m. Vessels of 1.8m draught can reach village of Pont Croix 3M above bridge. Water and fuel available in port. HM (98) 70 07 91, Customs (98) 70 70 97.

ST. GUÉNOLÉ
Charts BA 2351, F 6645
HW: Dover +5h
MHWS 5.2m MHWN 3.9 MTL 3.0 MLWN 2.0 MLWS 0.8

A fishing hbr just N of Pt de Penmarc'h protected by a breakwater on W side. Entrance dries but about 1.8m can be found inside. Entrance difficult and large scale chart essential. Not recommended unless in an emergency situation.

PASSAGE NOTE: PENMARC'H POINT TO LA GIRONDE RIVER

Penmarc'h lies low and may be identified by the octagonal Lt Ho 60m high standing 120m from the old tr, which is shorter and smaller.

About 4M S of Penmarc'h Pt the stream is rotatory: Dover −1h WSW; +1¾h N; +4¾h E; −4½h S. About 2M SW on Penmarc'h Pt the stream is rotatory clockwise. The flood stream runs N changing to E through NE; the ebb is SE changing to W through S.

The general direction of the tidal streams offshore along the coast between Penmarc'h and the R Gironde is as follows:

Time on Dover	Direction	Time on Dover	Direction
HWD	N	−6h	SW
+1h	NE by N	−5h	SW by W
+2h	E	−4h	W
+3h	E	−3h	W
+4h	SE by E	−2h	NW by W
+5h	SE by S	−1h	NW by N

At certain times the stream flows straight on and offshore.

GUILVINEC
Charts BA 3640, F 6646
HW: Dover +5h
MHWS 5.2m MHWN 3.9 MTL 3.0 MLWN 2.0 MLWS 0.8

A crowded fishing harbour not recommended unless in an emergency situation. Entrance difficult and large scale chart essential. A safe anchorage in settled weather may be found in bay NW of White Rock. Marine farm established in this area, centered on position 47°47'.55 N 4°18'.19 W so caution required. HM (98) 58 05 67, VHF 16-12.

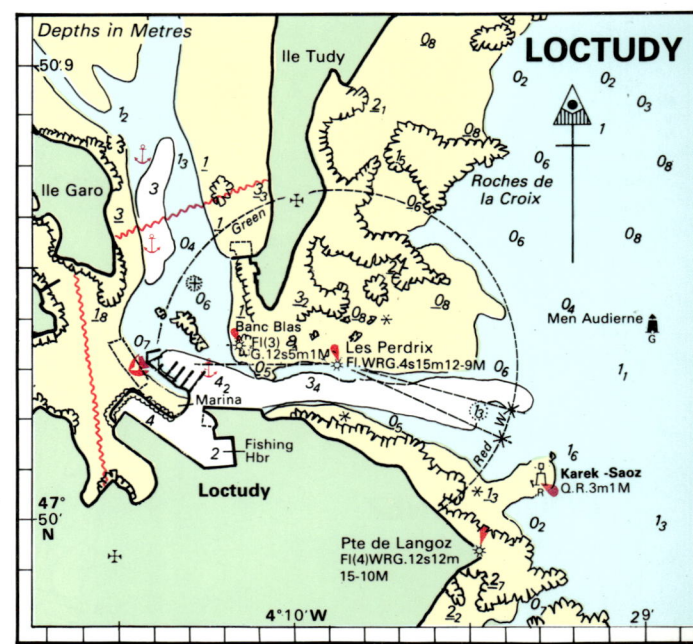

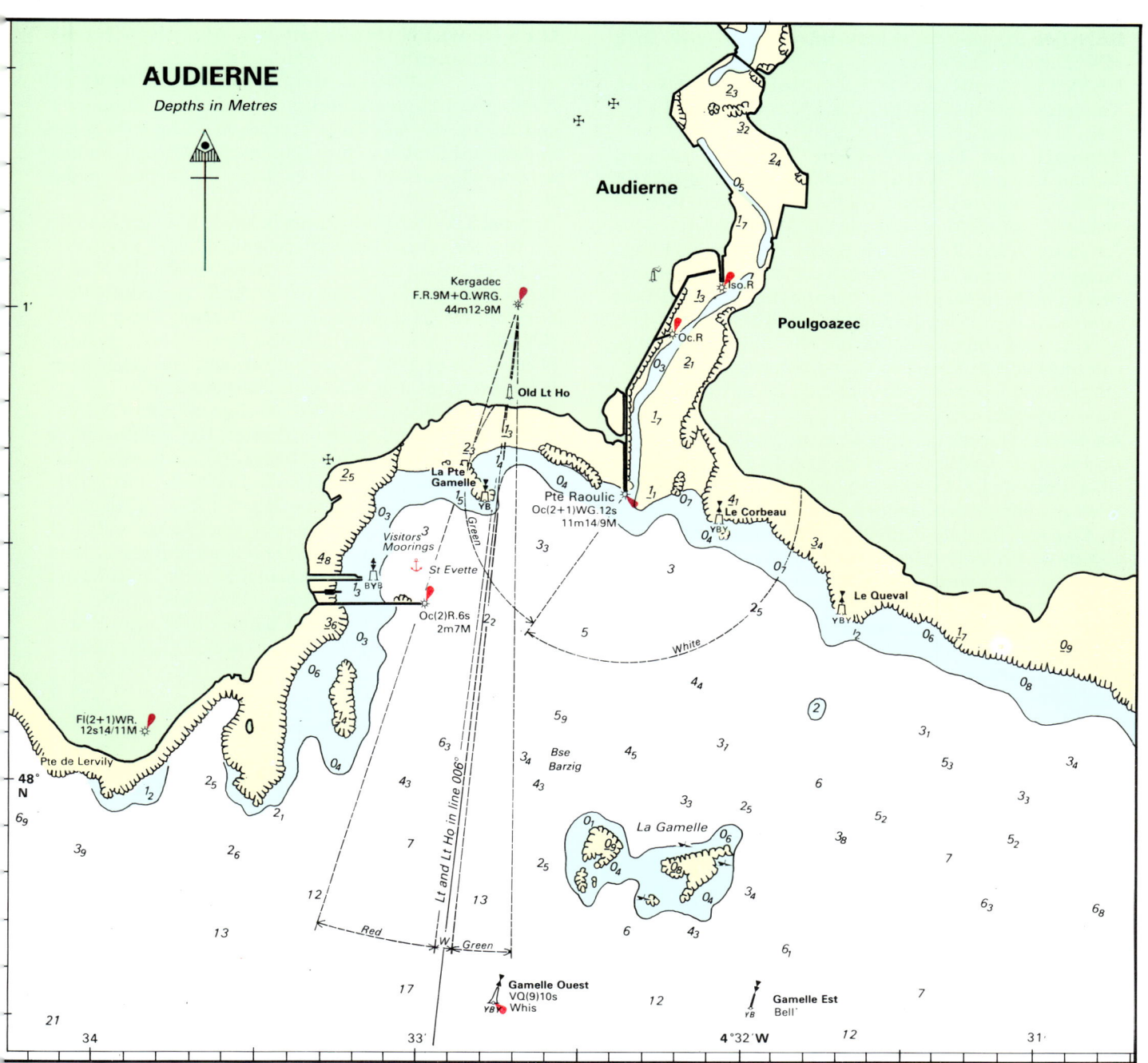

LOCTUDY   Charts BA 3641,   F 6649
HW: Dover +5h

MHWS 5.0m MHWN 3.6 MTL 2.7 MLWN 1.7 MLWS 0.5

Bar Outside the entrance the S part of the bar has about 1½m; the N part almost dries. Moorings in 3½m inside; a charming spot. Shops, hotels, restaurant.

Approach As for Bénodet. After Basse du Chenal buoy is abeam to port, steer 312° for the entrance about 2M distant, leaving Basse Bilien buoy to port.

Entrance Leave Karek Saoz, R tr, well to port, Men Audierne G bn well to stb, and stand in with the Perdrix Tr bearing 286°, open to S of Ile Tudy promontory. This transit clears Karek Croisic rk close on its N side. When the entrance comes fully open on nearing the Perdrix Tr, steer 272° on Château Laubrière, further westward among the dark trees, leaving the quay fairly close to port. If proceeding to Ile Tudy anchorage turn to stb after passing Banc Blas G bn taking care to leave middle ground to port.

Anchorage Beyond the fishing hbr on port side is a new 600 berth marina facing towards Ile Garo. On arrival moor outside first pontoon to port. There are mooring buoys beyond the LB; or anchor outside the moored boats NW of Loctudy quay or above the jetty at Ile Tudy leaving space for ferry to manoeuvre. Ebb runs 3kn, kedge essential and care required to avoid drying shingle bank 1ca N of jetty. Water on quay at Loctudy or from root of jetty at Ile Tudy. Pont l'Abbe is 3M up river; visit on the tide (vessels up to 3m draught sometimes get up). Rly to Quimper and buses from Pont l'Abbé. Outside anchorage sand, good in W winds. HM (98) 87 40 11, VHF 12.

BÉNODET   Charts BA 3641,   F 6649, 6679
HW: Dover +5h

MHWS 4.8m   MHWN 3.6   MTL 2.6   MLWN 1.7   MLWS 0.5

The entrance to the Odet R is E and N from Menhir Lt Tr; 5.4m in channel.

Approach and Entrance From W having rounded Menhir Lt Tr Fl(2) WG 6s 19m 8/5M a course of 135° for 4½M will lead to a position S of Basse Spinec S card, when steer 081° for 8¼M towards Ile aux Moutons Lt, leaving Ar Guisty S card, Karek Greis E card and Rostolou E card buoys to port until La Pyramide lt comes in line with Combrit Lt, 000°; round in on this bearing about 5M until near approach, then bring Le Coq and La Pyramide Lt Hos on E side of entrance in line on 346° and keep them so entering buoyed channel between La Rousse and Les Verres port and stb buoys. At night ldg lts and sectored lts make the approach simple.

Anchorage Outside the narrows in the Anse de Trez, open La Pyramide Lt Ho E of Pt du Coq Lt Ho and anchor when Loctudy Lt Ho is hidden by Pt de Combrit in about 5½m Anchorage is prohibited in the fairway between Pt du Coq and Anse de Penfoul, and permanent moorings occupy all available space outside the channel. There are some visitors' moorings opposite town and on marina pontoons in Anse de Penfoul, and at Port de St Marine marina opposite town. Water at marinas, fuel and toilets on quay at marina in Anse de Penfoul. High level bridge clearance 30m 2½ca NW of Anse de Penfoul. Anchorages in river out of stream above bridge at Anse de Kerandraon (stb), Anse de Combrit (port) and Anse de Keratren (port). The Odet R above Keratren is marked by bns in the upper reaches and dries above Lanros. Lower down the ebb runs strongly.

At Pors Meillou, halfway to Quimper, berth alongside the quay near its W end, bottom sand and mud. The quay covers at MHWS and there is about 1.3m at half-tide. There are other anchorages at Rosaves, Keramblais, Lanros, 1¾m and a sheltered quiet inlet to stb ½M below Lanros in Anse de St Cadou 2-3m (sounding necessary). A fixed low level bridge ½M below Quimper makes access by river with fixed mast impossible, but yachts can anchor below bridge, if visiting Quimper on the tide. At Quimper the best berth is at first quay to port 3½m MHWS. Water from hose. HM St Marine (98) 56 38 72, VHF 9. HM Penfoul (98) 57 05 78, VHF 9.

PORT LA FORÊT   Charts BA 3641,   F 6650
HW (Concarneau): Dover +5h

MHWS 4.9m   MHWN 3.8   MTL 2.8   MLWN 1.9   MLWS 0.7

A picturesque village with a marina of 800 berths

Approach Stand in with the end of Cap Coz breakwater, Fl(2) R6s, bearing about 334° and enter the approach channel which is marked by buoys outside and bns inside. Leave Cap Coz breakwater head to port and Kerleven breakwater, Fl G 4s, to stb. At head of the channel turn to stb leaving the dock head, Iso G 4s, to stb and enter marina. Depth in approach channel 1.2m; no anchorage in channel, speed limit 3kn. Marine farm (buoyed) established in centre of Baie de la Forêt to stb of entrance line to marina, caution required at night or in poor visibility.

Berthing Yachts are normally met by HM's launch and allotted a berth. Depth in marina 2m. Fuel, electricity and showers. Bus service to Concarneau and Quimper; shops and hotel. HM (98) 56 98 45 VHF 9. Customs at Concarneau.

ILES DE GLÉNAN   Charts BA 3640,   F 6647, 6648
HW (Concarneau): Dover +5h

MHWS 4.9m   MHWN 3.8   MTL 2.8   MLWN 1.9   MLWS 0.7

A most picturesque archipelago, well sheltered in summer and having the only coral beaches in Europe. It is the home of the famous Centre Nautique des Glénans Sailing School, whose boats are in evidence everywhere among the Is.

Approach A safe approach can be made from the N to Ile Penfret, the eastern Is (easily recognised by the Lt Ho FlR 5s) which has no dangers until within ½ ca at the N end. If proceeding to St Nicolas follow the W coast of Ile Penfret until off the coral beach about halfway down the W side, whence, above half tide, steer for the houses on Ile St Nicolas, about 276°. There are various approaches from other directions, but large scale chart essential.

Anchorage Outside the CNG moorings off SW of Ile Penfret, 1¾m; off coral beach on Penfret; La Chambre off St Nicolas, some white visitors' buoys, 3½m, at neaps; midway between chimney on Ile du Loc'h and fort on Ile Cigogne (2.5m MLWN); moorings S or E of St Nicolas. If leaving La Chambre for Bénodet, steer for the middle of Ile Penfret 096° and go round the E mark of Bananec then steer 325° close to isolated mark of the La Pie bn (BRB) on Ile de Brunec leaving Les Pierres Noires well to stb. Chenal des Bluiniers from La Chambre to W dries ½m. Two small cafes on St Nicolas serving meals in summer, no other facilities.

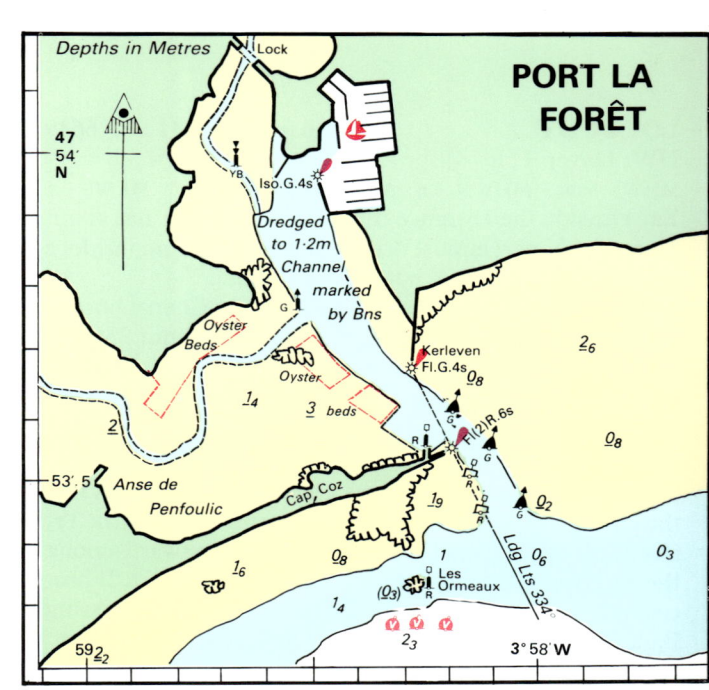

361   FRANCE, WEST COAST

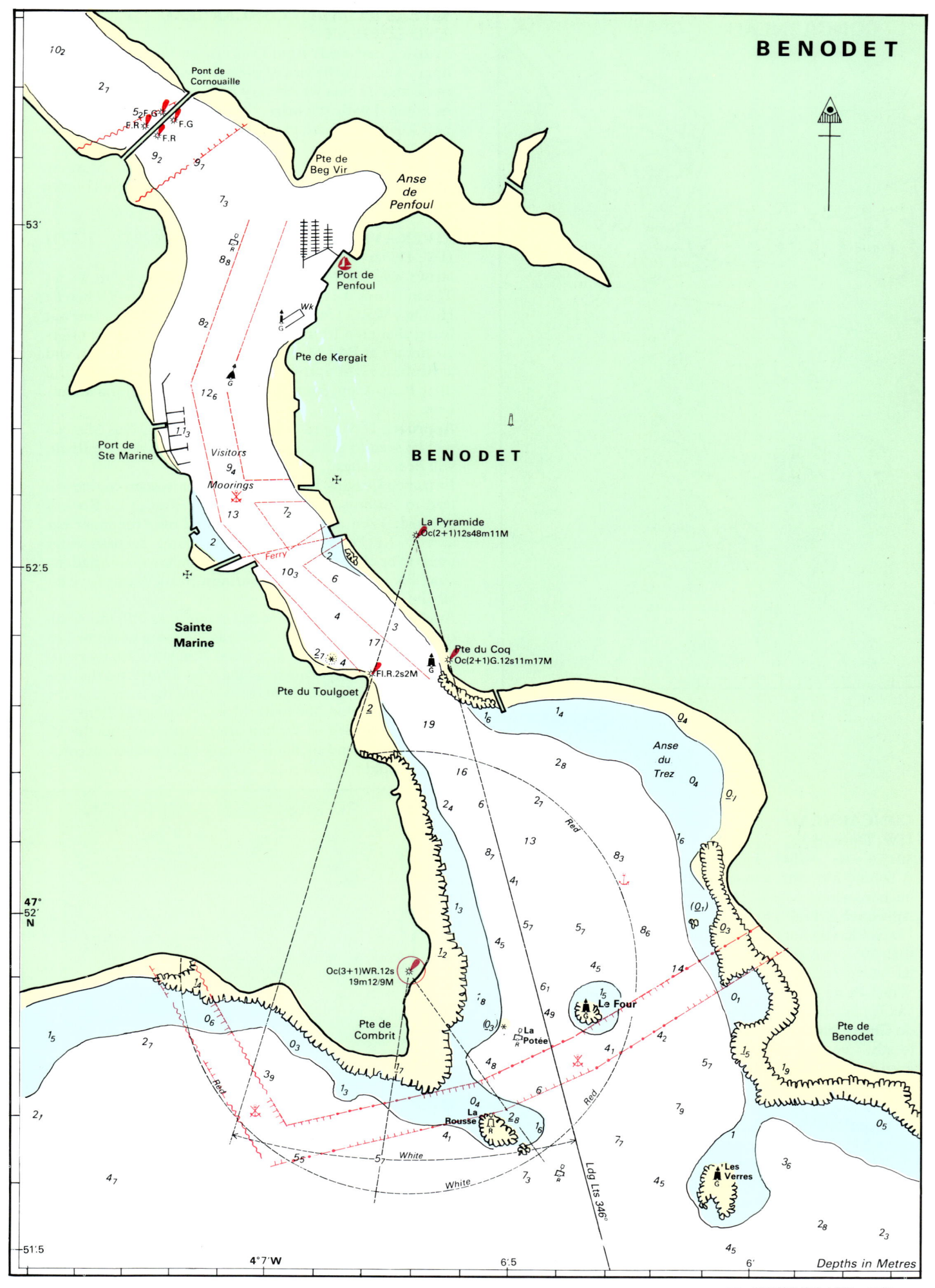

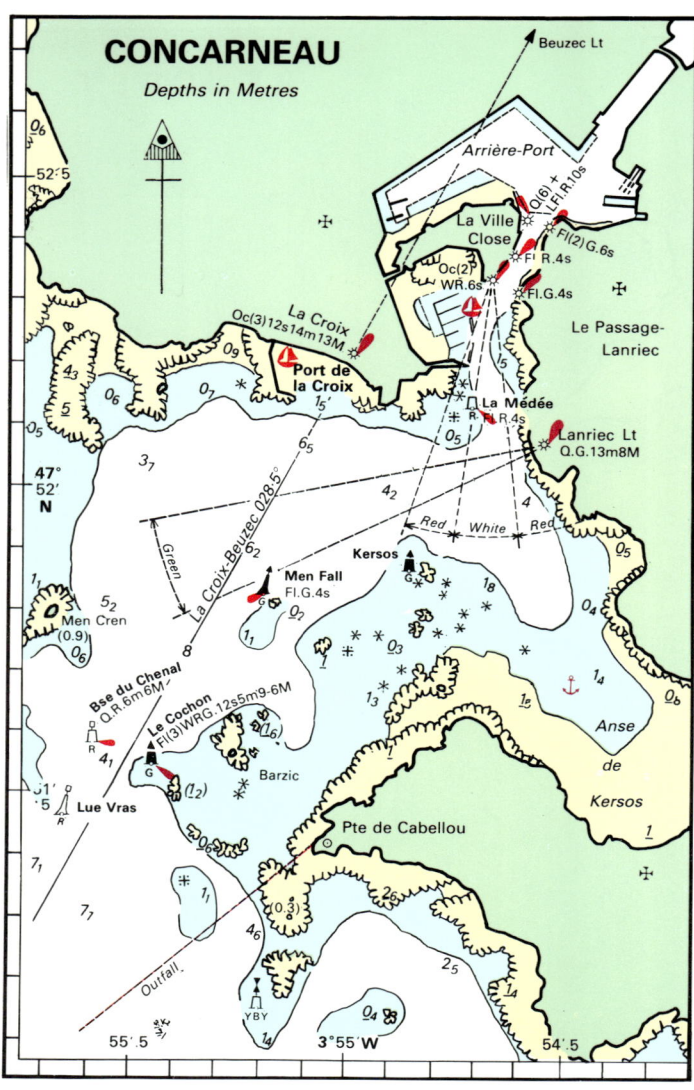

RIVERS BETWEEN CONCARNEAU AND LORIENT

Cruising eastwards from Concarneau there are six small hbrs which may be visited in settled weather. They are all protected by bars which vary in position and should only be entered with the help of the North Biscay Pilot. The best known of these harbours to cruising yachtsmen are the Aven and Bélon rivers details of which are given below. The other four harbours, Brigneau, Merrien, Doëlan and Le Pouldu (R. Quimperlé) are less well known and infrequently visited.

RIVER AVEN Charts BA 2352, F 7031
HW: Dover +4½h
MHWS 4.9m MHWN 3.9 MTL 2.7 MLWN 1.5 MLWS 0.5
The mouth of the river is situated inside Beg-ar-Vechen Lt Ho Oc 4 WRG 12s. The bar in the entrance dries 1m, but being sheltered from SW rarely breaks. The Aven offers anchorage at Port Manech, outside the bar, in 2.5m, and at Rosbras 1¼M upriver in 2m. The river is very beautiful up to Pont-Aven, 3¾M, but is not well marked above Rosbras.
Approach Having rounded Beg-ar-Vechen, Port Manech will be seen to port, and the bn of the bar rks, Le Roch, will be seen ahead.
Entrance Leaving Le Roch to port, midstream course will lead to Rosbras. When the base of the bn of Le Roch is covered, 1¾m of water will be found over the inner bar abreast Le Poulguen. Going upstream, deepest water tends to be close to the port hand perches: sounding advisable. Pools crowded with moorings, so anchoring is virtually impossible.
Anchorage At Port Manech, about 1 ca off the small breakwater; sound in. At Rosbras, between or up to 1 ca below the quays, which dry; flood 2kn, ebb 3kn. At Pont-Aven, a picturesque town, a long quay affords berths drying 2-3m. The best quay to use is round the corner, on the last straight before the footbridge. Moorings in 2½m.
Approaching Beg-ar-Vechen after dark, keep in the W sector of the lt and anchor in 3½m to SE, or inside, according to draught.

CONCARNEAU Charts BA 3641, F 6650
HW: Dover +5h
MHWS 4.9m MHWN 3.8 MTL 2.8 MLWN 1.9 MLWS 0.7
A fishing hbr with a major yacht marina. Some swell in onshore winds.
Approach From S, to clear the Corven de Trévignon and Les Soldats do not let Pt de la Jument W pyramid bear less than 005°; at night keep in the intensified sector of the ldg lts.
When Pt de la Jument is abeam bring the ldg lts (front Oc(3) 12s, rear Q) in line, 029°. This leads between Basse du Chenal bn to port and Le Cochon Tr, Fl(3) WRG 12s, to stb. Continue until past Men Fall buoy, Fl G 10s or until Lanriec Lt Q G becomes visible, then enter between Lanriec Lt and La Médée R Tr, Fl R 4s.
Entrance A 0.9m rk lies abreast the N Lanriec pyramid.
Berthing The Avant Port is a yacht marina; visitors moor at the E end of the second last pontoon to the N or as space allows. Fuel, water, showers. Double ended mooring buoys on N side of La Ville Close in inner hbr 2.4m; quays reserved for fishing and commercial boats. Anchor in Anse de Kersos if space available, or outside off La Croix mole in 5½m; ebb runs hard, mud is strong. The old walled town is worth a visit. All facilities. HM (98) 97 57 96.

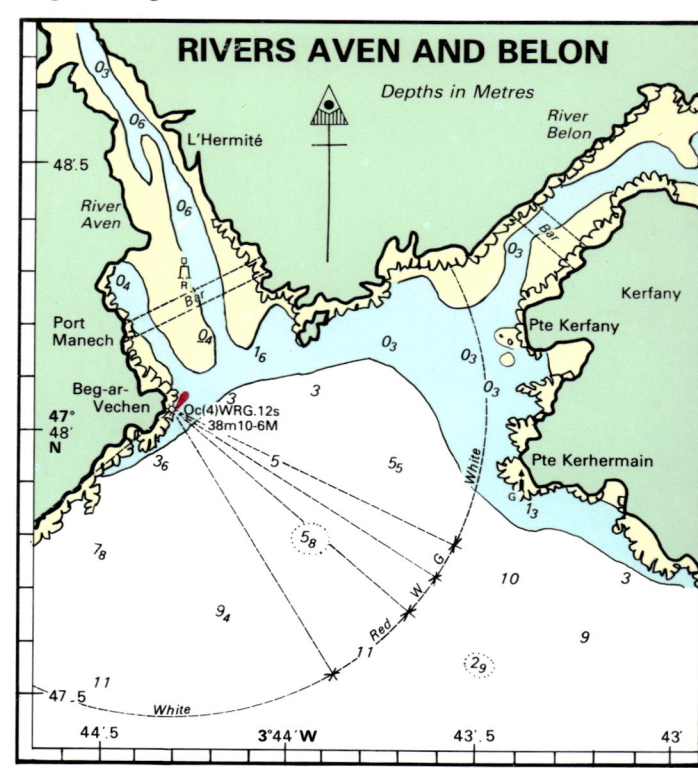

363 FRANCE, WEST COAST

RIVER BÉLON   Charts BA 2352,   F 7031
HW: Dover +4½h
MHWS 4.9m   MHWN 3.9   MTL 2.7   MLWN 1.5   MLWS 0.5

The entrance is open to SW, and the bar which dries 1½m is much more exposed than that of the R Aven, and impassable in bad weather. There is an inner bar, same depth, abreast the first bend in the river, ½M inside the entrance. Attractive scenery as far as Bélon.

Approach Leave the bn on Bec-Lerzou rk off Pt Kerhermain to stb, and steer to pass ½ ca off the next point, Pt Kerfany, on the stb side. (Caution off-lying rks)

Entrance. The channel then crosses to the N shore, whence bring Beg-ar-Vechen Lt to bear 240° astern till abreast next pt to stb, where the channel turns somewhat S of E and then 030°; when the next bend comes open to stb, round the pt and proceed thereafter in midstream.

Anchorage Obligatory fore and aft mooring buoys below the quays at Bélon and Lanriot, in 2 to 3½m. Some room to anchor at neaps below moorings. Quay dries 1¾m. Oyster beds above Bélon. Stream runs 2kn on the flood and 3kn on the ebb. Restaurant at Lanriot.

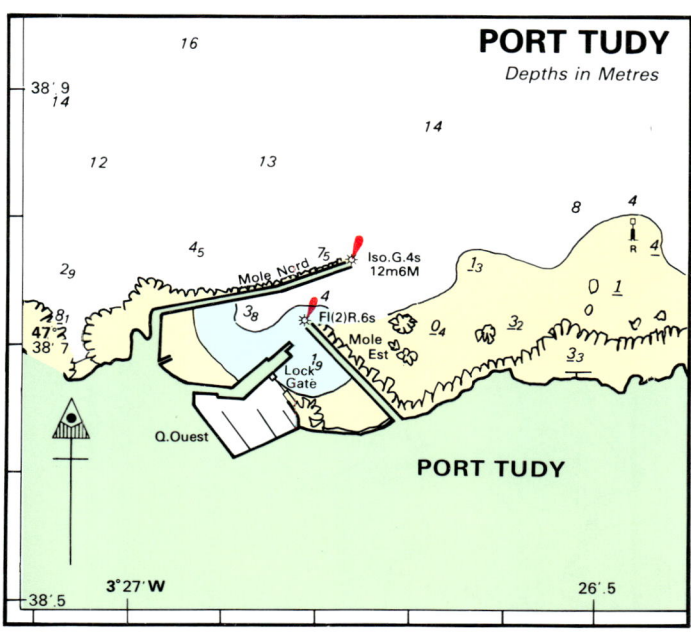

PORT TUDY, ILE DE GROIX
                 Charts BA 2352,   F 5912, 7031
HW: Dover +4½h
MHWS 5.0m   MHWN 3.9   MTL 2.8   MLWN 1.7   MLWS 0.6

A small hbr affording shelter in 3m, but some swell in NE winds.

Approach Approaching the NW corner, Pen Men Pt, with Pen Men W square Lt Ho, Fl(4) 25s, should be given a berth of about 1M. From NE keep the semaphore of Beg Melen, Pen Men Pt, open N of the Grognon battery (conspic).

Entrance Nearing the port, bring the spire of St Tudy ch in line with the W end of the N jetty, 220°. This leads between the rks which lie on either side of the approach.

Berthing Steer in between the pier heads, Lt Ho on each, and proceed to wet basin (marina) in inner hbr to port available 2h either side of HW, or moor bow to large communal mooring buoys in outer harbour, crowded in season. Water and electricity on pontoons, showers on quay in season. Cafes, stores, PO in village.

HM (97) 86 52 64 VHF9.

ETEL RIVER   Charts BA 2352,   F 7032
HW: Dover +5h
MHWS 5.0m   MHWN 3.9   MTL 2.8   MLWN 1.7   MLWS 0.6

The entrance is a few miles SE of Lorient.

Bar Variable in depth and position, dries, and may be crossed in quiet weather after half flood with 1¾m draft. Entrance requires great caution, and is best taken 1½ to 2h before HW. It should not be attempted at night nor on the ebb. The flood stream sets across the bar to NE. The streams inside turn 1½h after HW and LW, and attain 4-5kn at springs. Anchoring prohibited outside river within ½M radius centred on Lt Ho Oc(2) WRG 6s 6M. ½M.

Approach Keep two water trs in line, 042°, after leaving Roheu Tr to port. Call VHF 16 for directions for crossing the bar from the Fenoux signal stn (mast over shed and W gable end 1ca W of Lt Ho). Crossed bar signal indicates no entry or leaving, B ball no entry, R flag wait for more water.

Entrance Leave Chaudronnier Tr ½ ca to port and keep close to the W bank to avoid the midriver shoal Le Banc du Stang. When nearing Etel town, the channel is in midriver.

Berthing Anchor just S of LB Ho on SW end of quays. Alongside inside of quay 1½ to 2½m, but the dredged part is narrow and the end of the quay must be left for ferries. Small marina inside town quay. Visitors welcome, HM office at W end of long building at W end of quay. Anchorage also above town on either side of river or off Magouer on port side. Do not go much above Vieux Passage 1M above town. Shops in Etel or Magouer. Caution tides are strong and river deep (15-20m HWS). All facilities. HM (97) 55 46 62.

PORTIVI   Charts BA 2352, F 7032
HW: Dover +5h
MHWS 5.3m   MHWN 4.1   MTL 3.0   MLWN 1.9   MLWS 0.7

A pretty corner in fine weather and moderate winds from W and offshore. On the N end of the W side of Quiberon.

Approach Bring Carnac spire in line with Pen Goc'h rk 052°, and keep it so leaving Men Melein to N and Roch-Vidic-Bihan to S, till Portivi mill comes on with end of jetty, 127°, when keep it so, passing S of Guedic bn and Keroustaing bn. Having passed the two bns, turn to port a little to pass N of jetty.

Anchorage Between Keroustaing bn and Roch-Vidic-Bihan in 1½ to 3m, or at mooring buoy abreast bn. Inside at the end of the slip, bottom dries 1.2m.

PORT MARIA, QUIBERON
                 Charts BA 2352, 2353, F 5352
HW: Dover +5h
MHWS 5.1m   MHWN 3.9   MTL 2.9   MLWN 1.8   MLWS 0.7

Artificial hbr, sheltered from all winds, at S end of Quiberon Peninsula. Used by many fishing vessels and the ferries to Belle Ile and Houat. Half the hbr dries so there is not much room. Not recommended, better to proceed to Port Haliguen, La Trinité or Belle Ile.

Lorient – see next page

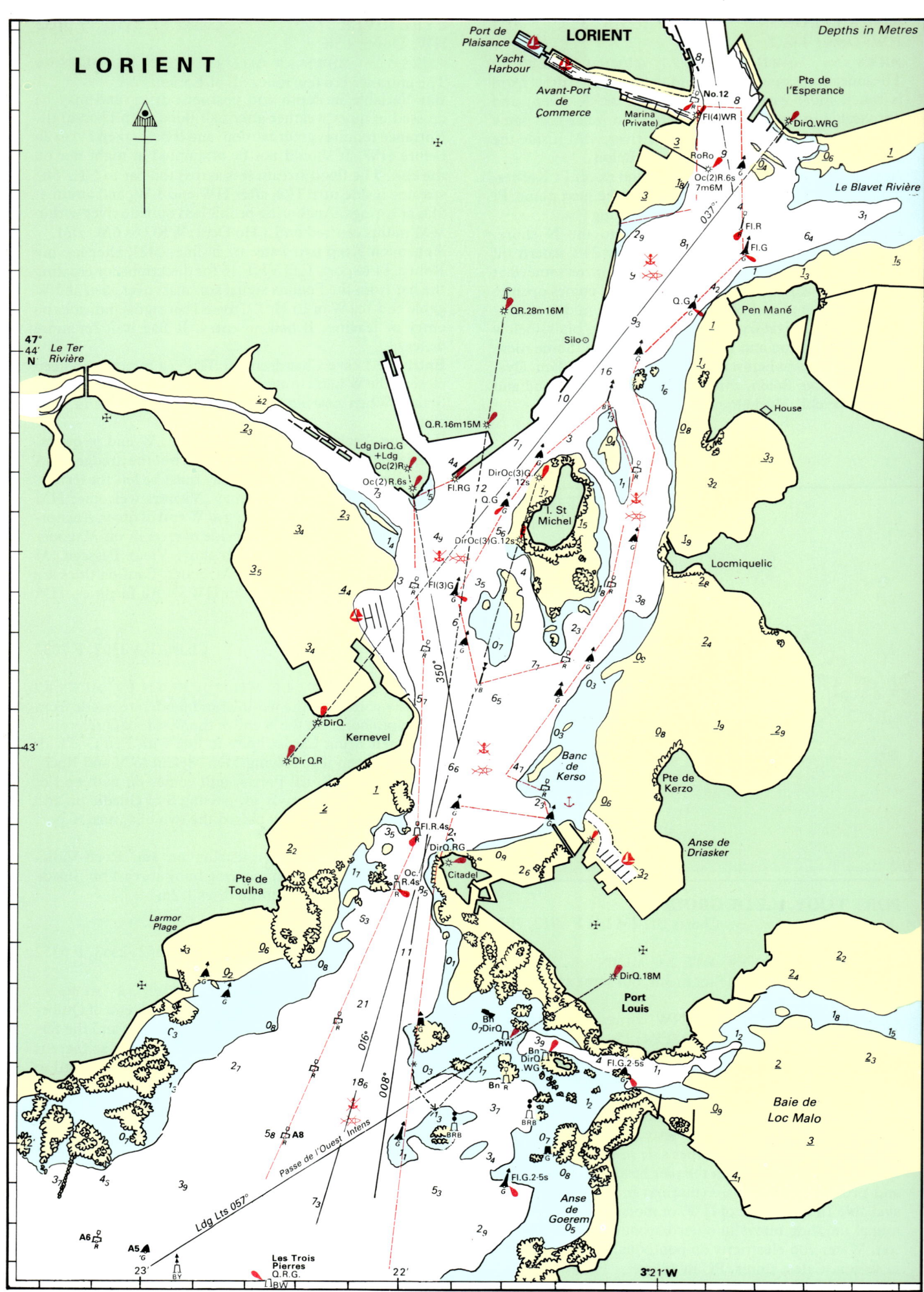

LORIENT   Charts BA 304,   F 5912, 6470
HW: Dover +5h
MHWS 5.0m   MHWN 3.9   MTL 2.9   MLWN 2.0   MLWS 0.8

A major commercial and naval hbr with considerable yachting development. The approach is sheltered from the SW by the Ile de Groix.

Approach By the W passage, give the N shore a berth of about 1M, bring Les Soeurs RW Bn Tr Dir Q 13M and Port Louis Dir Q 18M ldg lts Q in line 057°, and steer so until N of Les Trois Pierres bn tr. For the S passage, leave the two buoys off Les Bastresses 100m to stb, then steer to pass close E of Les Trois Pierres bn tr. From here, steer to pass close W of the Citadel NW of Port Louis and take the buoyed channel into the harbour.

At night use ldg lts. By the W passage turn on to 016° when lt intensifies and from S 008°.

Berthing Anchor NE of the citadel and towards the mole of Port Louis in about 3½m; at marina Port Louis, crowded; at marina to port N of Kernevel 2-3m, protected by breakwater, water and electricity on pontoons; opposite Pen Mané on W side of channel in 3½m; or off N end of Pen Mané S of the large mooring buoys. Can also lock into wet basin (HW-2h to +1h) in middle of town (marina). Entrance to port just above R Blavet and opposite Pt de l'Esperance. There are also pontoon berths outside the lock. All facilities. HM (97) 21 10 14, VHF 9. Customs (97) 37 29 57. HM Kerneval (97) 65 48 25, VHF 9.

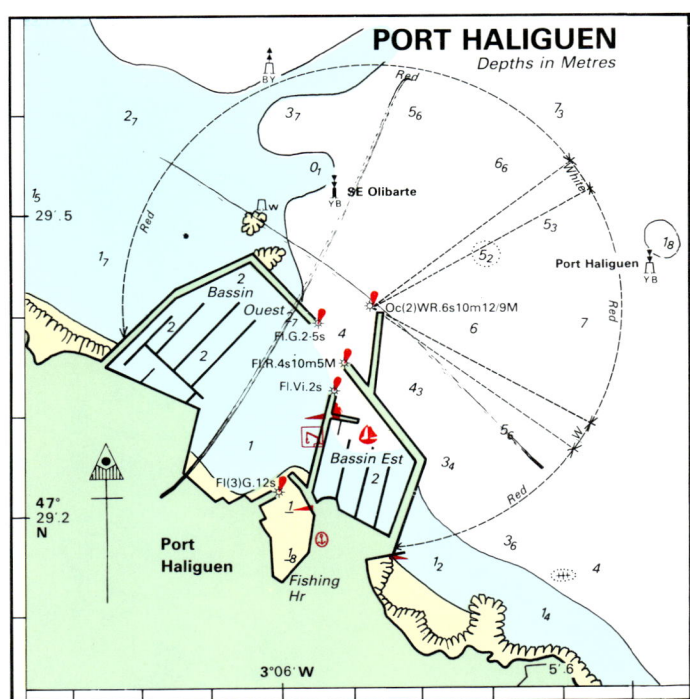

PORT HALIGUEN, QUIBERON BAY
    Charts BA 2352, 2353,   F 5352
HW: Dover +5¼h
MHWS 5.2m   MHWN 3.9   MTL 2.9   MLWN 1.9   MLWS 0.6

Pleasant yacht hbr with moorings and marina, 3.5m in entrance, to E of old drying hbr and village on E side of Quiberon Peninsula. Complete shelter. Adjacent beach.

Approach No difficulties except in heavy SE-ly weather. From about 1M ESE, steer approximately 300° on Lt Ho, Oc(2) WR 6s, keeping in W sector. Avoid unlit naval buoys and floats in line NW to SE 6 ca from entrance. Leave S Card buoy SW of these to stb; RB buoy marks a wreck about ½ ca S from entrance.

Entrance Leave R buoy to port and enter between breakwater heads into E basin.

Berthing Report to pontoon A (pontoon d'Accueil) at end of W pontoon, or HM launch in outer hbr. Met reports daily. Shops, hotels, restaurants, buses, rly and flights from Quiberon (1M, no transport but pleasant walk). HM (97) 50 20 5, VHF 9 and 16. Customs at La Trinité.

HARBOURS ON BELLE ILE
    Charts BA 2353,   F 5911
HW: Dover +5½h
MHWS 5.1m   MHWN 3.9   MTL 2.9   MLWN 1.9   MLWS 0.7

SAUZON Port de Sauzon is entered 3 ca S of Pt du Cardinal, which is 1½M SE of Pt des Poulains. Steer in, 224°, on the 9m W circular Lt Tr Oc (3+1) 12s. At night, enter in W sector.

Anchor inside N part of outer hbr sheltered from NW through S to SE by breakwaters. Inner hbr entrance has 1¾m at half tide. Best berth, dries, is inside outer quay to port on entering, bottom flat sand, clean. Some fore and aft mooring buoys laid in outer harbour during summer.

LE PALAIS Entrance has 2m. The inner hbr dries. Wet basin. Swell in E winds in outer harbour.

Entrance Midway between pier-heads, W Lt Hos on pier-heads; S:Oc(2) R 6s; N: Fl(2+1) G 12s

Anchorage Outside anchor to E clear of fairway; heavy sea in strong NW and SE winds, sheltered from W and SW. Anchoring between the N jetty at Le Palais and the approaches to Sauzon is prohibited. Ferry to Quiberon (rly). In outer harbour yachts lie to 22 white mooring buoys laid in two rows parallel to Mole Bourdelle. Boats lie quay to first line of buoys, between the two lines and outer line to anchor. Considerable confusion when hbr crowded. There is a wet basin approached through inner harbour, gate and footbridge open intermittently between HW-1½h to +1h between 0600 hrs and 2200hrs. HM at Quai Bonnelle (97) 31 42 90. Water near lock gate, all shops. Customs (97) 31 85 95

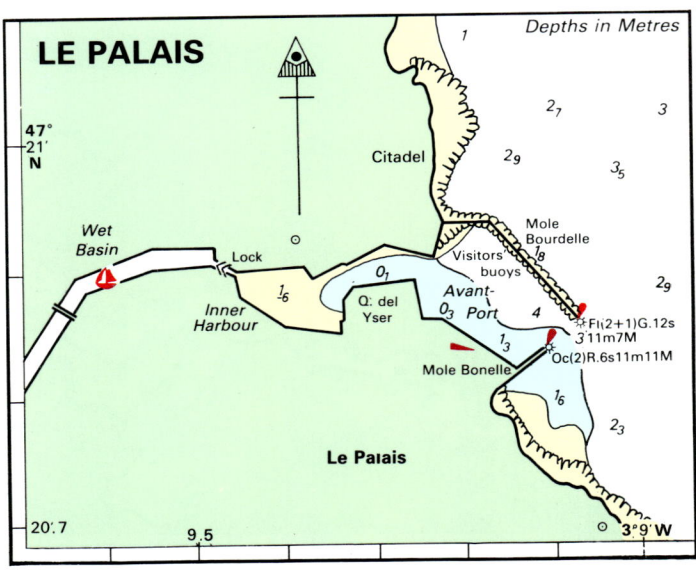

FRANCE, WEST COAST

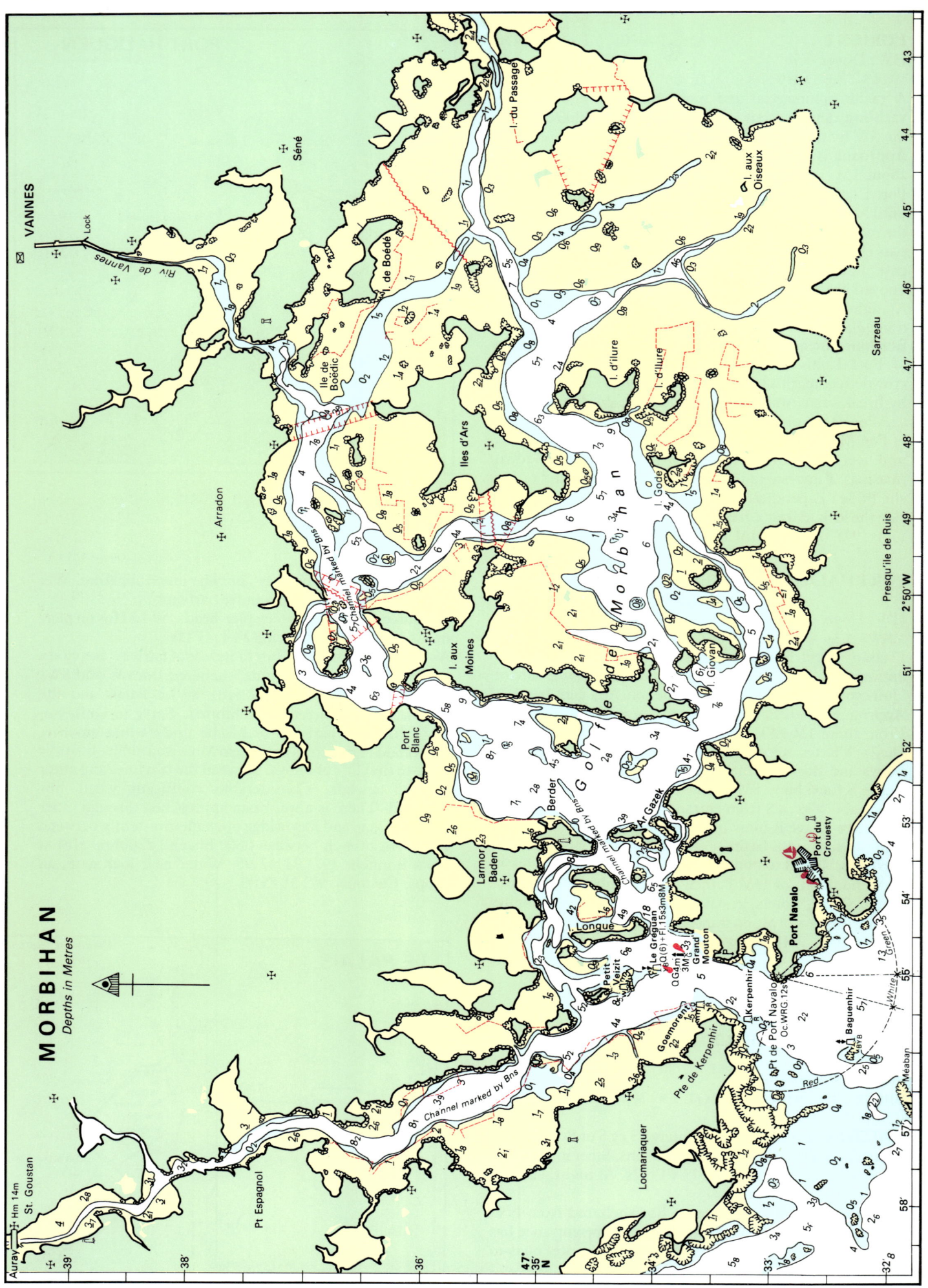

La Trinité – see next page

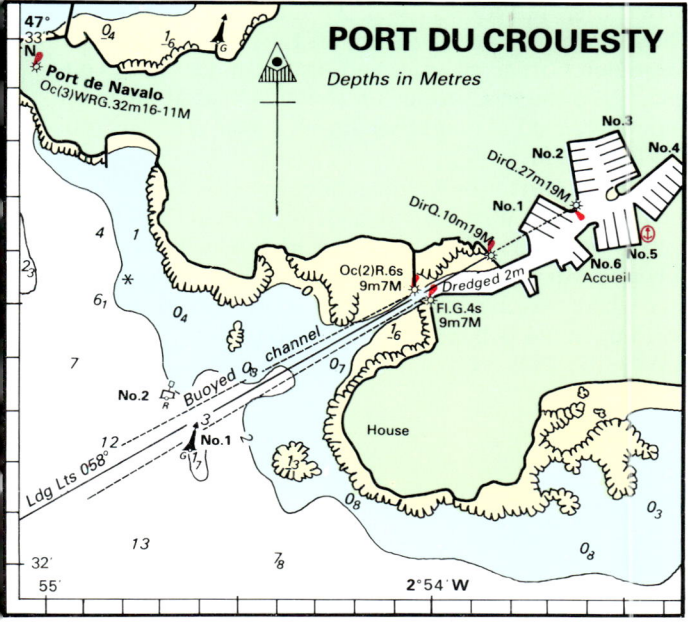

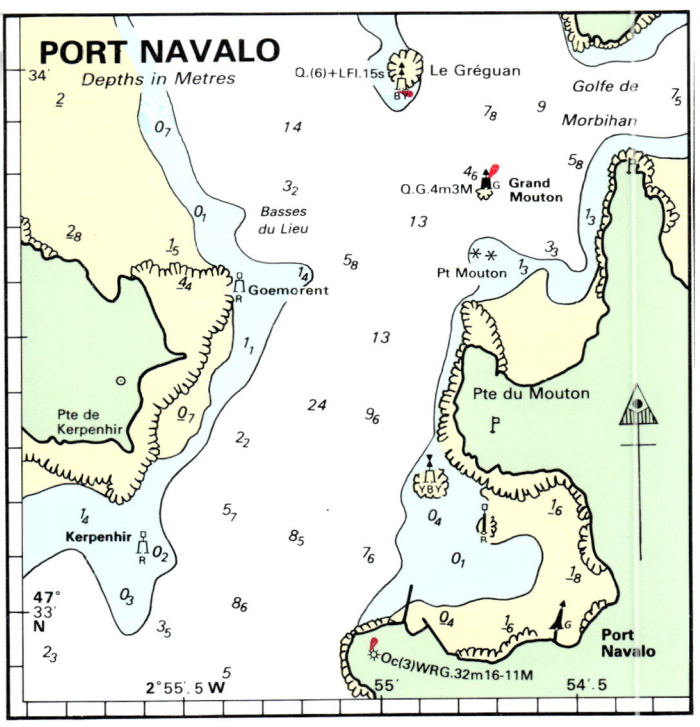

THE MORBIHAN (INLAND SEA)
Charts BA 2358, F 7034, 6992
HW (Pt Navalo): Dover +5¼h
MHWS 4.9m MHWN 3.7 MTL 2.7 MLWN 1.7 MLWS 0.5
Off Pt de Navalo, the flood stream at Dover +½h runs N and the ebb at +6h S spring rate for both 7½kn. In Auray R, the flood stream begins at HWD, the ebb at +5½h; both attain about 3kn at springs.

HW (Ile aux Moines): Dover +6h The flood stream starts 1¾h after LW, and the ebb 1½h after HW

Approach The E pt of the entrance to the Morbihan may be identified by the tall W tr of the Navalo Lt Ho, Oc(3) WRG 12s. From S keep Crac'h steeple in line with the E end of Méaban Is, 355°, to clear the Plateau du Grand Mont. From W steer 055° for the Butte de Thumiac, a mound-shaped hill 30m high, about one-third of the way between Navalo and Pt du Grand Mont. Bring Baden spire (conspic on a hilltop N of entrance) just open W of Pt Navalo and in line with Petit Veisit, 001°, White pyramid which shows near the waterline W of Navalo. Continue so, 6.5m least water, rounding Navalo Pt a reasonable distance off. Between Méaban and Petit Mont, more water will be found to E of this transit.

Entrance Slack water may be awaited in the bay SE of Petit Mont. Entering on the flood, the stream sets strongly on to the Grand Mouton, G bn QG 4m 3M. Past Pt de Port Navalo at slack water, bring the tr of Le Gréguan Q(6)+LFl 15s on with middle of Ile Radenec, 011°.

Port du Crouesty Large marina SE of Port Navalo. Useful if waiting for flood to set into the Morbihan. From the W, after rounding Méaban, the entry is just to the N of Petit Mont. From the S the Marina Lt Ho (W tr) is clearly visible over the beach S of Petit Mont. Channel into the hbr (minimum depth 1.8m) is marked by G and R buoys. Pass between the breakwaters and watch for G and R bns marking ends of obstacles. Continue past fuel pontoon to stb to pontoon marked 'Visiteurs'. Inner basins Nos. 2-5 have minimum depths 2-3m. At night enter on intensified sector of Marina lt ho 058°. All facilities, stores at Arzon. HM (97) 53 73 33, VHF 9.

Port Navalo Some moorings and space to anchor in the bay out of the tide. All facilities, but the port is exposed to W and NW winds which can raise a very steep sea quickly.

Anchorages Note: other than Port de Crouesty or Port Navalo, the BA or F large scale charts must be carried if visiting the Morbihan anchorages.

Western arm
River Auray. HW (Auray): Dover +5¾h
MHWS 5.2m MHWN 4.0 MTL 2.9 MLWN 1.9 MLWS 0.7
The R Auray runs into the W end of the Morbihan, Leaving Le Gréguan bn tr to stb, bring Pt Espagnol open of Pt du Bler, 335°, and pass E of Le Grand Harnic and a R bn. Past Pt du Bler keep the spire of Arzon on with the Château of Ile Renaud astern, 141°. After passing R buoy to port and the Catis buoy to stb, steer in a gradual curve round the mud on stb hand until heading midway towards the narrows off Pt Espagnol. From Pt Espagnol keep to E side till Anse de Kerdreau opens, when keep to W bank. LW navigation ceases 2M below Auray, above which the channel is well marked. Br at Auray 14m above HWS.
Anchorage Secure but crowded anchorage at Le Rocher, 6M up the river, 2M below Auray 2½m. Cafe and shops at Le Bono, ½M by dinghy. At Auray, fore and aft moorings, crowded in season, 3½m in centre of river opposite low quay at St Goustan, which dries alongside, 2m at HW. There is very little room to anchor. All facilities.

Eastern arm.

Larmor Baden SE of Pt be Balis close to village of Larmor Baden. Anchor in 2-4½m; perfect shelter from wind and tide, but bottom foul in places.

Kerdelan Roads NE of Ile Berder, 3½ to 5½m.

Ile aux Moines (off N end) Perhaps the best anchorage in the Morbihan, in 3 to 6m, halfway between Les Réchauds and Pt de Drech, with Le Petit Logoden just hidden behind Pt de Drech; or to N of W buoy near Les Réchauds. Landing at Pt de Drech or Pt des Réchauds, handy for Le Bourg. Good holding, sand and mud, close to but out of tideway. At Port Blanc, opposite, to NW, good anchorage but no facilities. Restaurant on Ile aux Moines. Restricted anchorage off NW corner between Pt de Toulindac and Port Blanc.

Ile Piren To S of Is in 3 to 6m, but tidal stream cannot be avoided. Landing Ile aux Moines at Pt de Brouhel within easy reach of Le Bourg.

Arradon Opposite the mainland village ½M NE of Pt d'Arradon.

Ile de Boëdic Opposite Roguédas, also nearer Penbock.

N of Ile d'Ars NE of Pt de Beluré in 2m with E side of Ile Lerne on with W side of Ile Tascon, and Roche d'Arradon on with N pt of Dronec. Landing at Pt de Beluré.

Conleau In the bight on W side of channel just S of Conleau.

Vannes HW: Dover −5h

MHWS 4.6m MHWN 3.9 MTL 2.9 MLWN 2.1 MLWS 1.2

Proceeding to Vannes, care is required rounding the Réchauds where the stream is fierce: keep in the W centre of the running stream and avoid the eddies; see chart F 7034 or BA 2358. LW navigation ceases above Conleau. Vannes, 10M above Navalo, can be reached by vessels of 3m draught at springs, 2½m at neaps. Swing bridge and lock gate open HW ±2h into town basin marina. (Opening hrs 0800-2200). Pontoons available above and below bridge while waiting for it or lock gate to open, indicated by R & G lts. All facilities inc toilets, showers and launderette available through marina office. HM (97) 54 16 08 VHF 9.

Noyalo River Good anchorage off Ile du Passage.

La Grange In 1¾m with mill of Larmor twice its width open of Pt de Nicolas, 1 ca, or more N of Pt de Beché.

Ile Longue Good anchorage out of tide on E side off SE pte. Good holding ground and quiet.

Kernés E of Pt de Kernés off the Anse in 3 to 6m with S end of Ile Berder on with Pt de Kérnes and its NE end on with mill of Larmor.

Ar Gazek (Ile de la Jument) ½ ca E of the Is in 3 to 6m. Good shelter but exposed to northerly winds.

LA TRINITÉ, CRAC'H RIVER

Charts BA 2353, 2358, F 5352

HW: Dover +5¼h

MHWS 5.3m MHWN 4.1 MTL 3.0 MLWN 2.0 MLWS 0.6

The river provides good shelter off La Trinité in 2-2½m.

Approach Carnac ch spire and nearby water tr are conspic. Keep the road bridge on about 344° until the outer buoy is reached. At night ldg lts 347°, rear Q 15M, front QWRG 10/7M.

Entrance From the outer buoy the entrance is well buoyed and lit by Dir Q WRG and then Oc WRG lts at La Trinité: keep in W sectors. Oyster beds are marked with perches.

Berthing Moor on pontoons in front of or behind slatted jetty where possible and report to marina office. Marina depth up to 3m. All facilities, launderette ½M.

HM (97) 55 7149 VHF 9. Customs (97) 55 73 46.

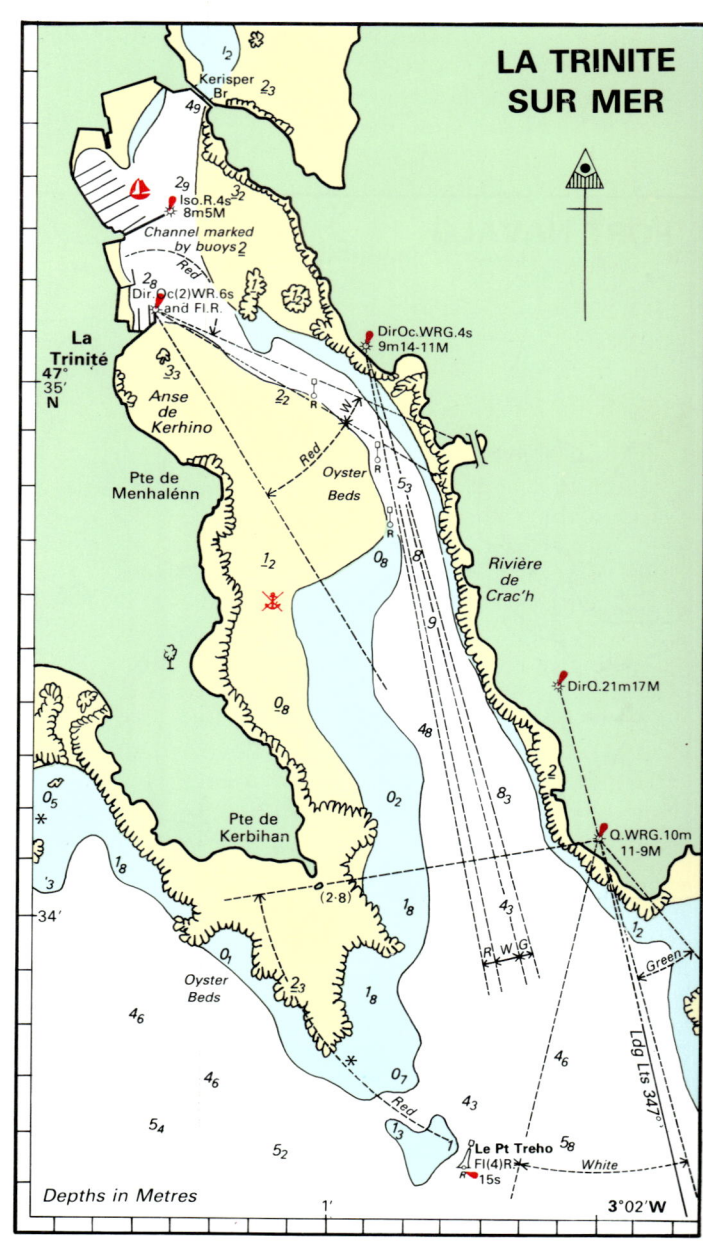

ILE DE HOËDIC
Charts BA 2353, F 7033
HW: Dover +5h
MHWS 5.1m MHWN 3.9 MTL 2.8 MLWN 1.9 MLWS 0.5

The W of the N coast of Hoëdic is a prohibited anchorage. Enter Argol hbr between the two moles which enclose a delightful sandy bay available at all states of the tide. Turn to stb and moor to communal buoys or stern to quay. Crowded July and Aug. Water from tap beside toilets. Only a small village ashore.

Port de la Croix on S side of island, drying harbour crowded in season. Anchor outside in settled weather.

ILE DE HOUAT
Charts BA 2353, F 7033
HW: Dover +5h
MHWS 5.2m MHWN 4.0 MTL 2.9 MLWN 1.8 MLWS 0.6

Towards the E end of the N coast of the Is, La Vieille rk is very conspic and the hbr is ¾M from it bearing 200°.

Approach From either side of La Vieille. From W, transit is breakwater lt ho in line with ch. Turn sharply around end of breakwater, leaving it 20m to stb and anchor in fairway, taking stern lines to breakwater. Keep the stern about 6m off breakwater, which protrudes under water, and avoid a rocky patch between third and fourth vertical ladder from end of breakwater. Once clear of the shallow 0.9m patch near outer end, there is 1¾-2½m most of the way along. Some fore-and-aft mooring buoys for visitors. Good shelter. Pier-head lt Fl(2) WG 6s. Two small shops, hotel. Fine weather anchorage in Treach er Gouret to E of island exposed to E and S. Also in SE corner of island sheltered from N and NE.

PENERF
Charts BA 2353, F 5418
HW: Dover +5¼h
MHWS 5.4m MHWN 4.1 MTL 3.0 MLWN 1.9 MLWS 0.6

The river enters Quiberon Bay 3M W of Vilaine R.

Approach Between R buoy off Pt de Penvins to W and Borenis G con buoy to E. The conspic W Tour de Penerf will be seen to NE.

Entrance There are three passes. (1) E pass, marked but narrow and winding, has 1¾ to 3½m.
(2) Central pass, La Traverse, has 0.3m and is not safe with any swell.
(3) W pass has 4½m, narrow and poorly marked with a bar inside (dries).
E pass: from 2 ca W of Borenis buoy steer 354° for the R La Traverse bn (opposite Viodec rk), keeping La Tour du Parc steeple in transit until within ½ ca, the G La Traverse bn is 1 ca further W. Leave the R La Traverse bn 20m to port. Continue on 354° for a further 50m then turn NW and N leaving Pignon Tr (R) and Men Dréan bn (R) to port, and two G buoys and the G Bayonelle bn to stb, whence round in, 066°, past a G bn and the R bn on the rk du Chenal for the Penerf quay G bn.
Central pass: at sufficient rise of tide approach with the Pignon Lt Tr (R) in transit with Tour du Parc steeple, 001°, leaving La Traverse bn (G) to stb and join E pass at Pignon Lt Tr.
W pass: not before half tide, pass close E of l'Artimon, leave two G bns to stb, and curve eastward onto 066°, to Penerf Quay.

Anchorage Outside in 7m between the buoys. Inside near the quay, 3½m, mud, clear of oyster beds or just above slip on Cadenic Pt clear of moorings. Minimal facilities, small hotel.

LA VILAINE
Charts BA 2353, F 2381
HW: Dover +5¼h
MHWS 5.5m MHWN 4.4 MTL 3.2 MLWN 2.0 MLWS 0.8

The river is 135M long, and is dammed at Arzal where one can lock into a tideless lake as far as Redon. Entry to the Brittany canal system can be made at Bellions Lock, shortly below Redon. The bar has 1m.

Approach Good visibility essential. In strong onshore winds it is best to approach by the Varlingue passage, 2m, with the mill of Avalec, the Prières Tr and the W wall of Port des Barques (E of Penlan Pt) in line 023° (the latter two marks are difficult to pick out from seaward). When Basse Kervoyal Tr Dir Q WR comes on with the mill of Billiers (4½M E of Penerf) 270°, steer with it so astern, until picking up the W Petit Sécé Tr which is left to stb and then follow the buoyed channel, R & G dayglo buoys. From W, Penlan lt Oc(2) WRG open S of the Prières Tr, 052°, leads towards entrance in 1.5m, whence proceed as above. At night, keep in the W sector of Penlan lt until the Basse Kervoyal lt can be used as a back bearing W 269°-271°, leading to the lighted buoyed channel.

Anchorage Off Tréhiguer in soft mud, exposed to W and NW. At Vieille Roche, just below the dam, outside the moorings on S bank, complete shelter.

Arzal lock opens several times daily in summer. For timetable contact HM (99) 90 05 86. Out of season lock opens irregularly on request. Marina to stb immediately after passing through lock. Fuel, chandlers and engineers to port. Also marina berths and buoys in river at St Antoine Quay, La Roche-Bernard HM (99) 90 62 17. Launderette and showers at camp site. Deep water to Pont Tournant de Cran and marina at Redon. Canal connections with Nantes and St Malo.

LE CROISIC   Charts BA 2353, F 6826

HW: Dover +5h

MHWS 5.6m MHWN 4.2 MTL 3.2 MLWN 2.0 MLWS 0.9

A popular holiday resort and fishing hbr which dries but has good though crowded anchorages off it in the pool. Yacht hbr in Chambre Herv'Rielle (see below). The entrance channel is dredged to 1¼m but the tides are strong, exceeding 4kn at springs, when entry should be made 1h before HW. At neaps entry possible at any time. There is a gauge (difficult to read) at the head of the Tréhic jetty indicating depth of water at quayside.

Approach The port may be located by its position S of La Turballe and by the 15th century walled town of Guérande, with its spire, on the heights 3M behind, and by the ch trs of Le Croisic and Batz, 46m and 55m respectively. Keep Le Croisic ch bearing 157° until it is possible to identify the first ldg marks: orange dayglo chevrons, lit DirOc(2+1) 12s. Keep these in transit 156° until the elbow in Tréhic jetty.

Entrance Turn a little to stb on the second ldg marks, G dayglo, QG. Keep these in transit 174° until the final ldg marks come into line, R pylons, both DirQR. Steer on this transit, 134°, until well past the first front ldg mark and leave quays about 50m to stb. At sufficient rise of tide to clear rks which dry, the second transit may with caution be disregarded provided the R tr, FlR 2.5s 6m 5M on Grand Mahon rk is left to port.

Anchorage The pool has 1½m and a 2m hole, and good shelter, with end of Penbron jetty on with E middle of the Hospital and the signal mast on with the quay, but streams are strong and holding only fair, sand. Best berth is under Penbron jetty in about 2-3m in E edge of the Penbron channel, where the stream is not so strong, 3kn; sound carefully and do not go too far up. Beyond the Croisic quays are drying-out berths, about 1¼m above datum, called chambres; these are formed and protected by islets called jonchères. Visitors berth in the last one, Chambre des Vasés, converted to a marina, dries, not suitable for vessels over 8m length. Great care is required in approaching the quay if the stream is running. The fishing boats sometimes ground at the entrance to the chambres on the flood and haul in as the tide rises. All facilities at marina HM (40) 23 10 95 Customs (40) 23 05 38. Rly connections. Outside anchorage: N of transit of W seamark on shore and Trévaly mill, 058°, and on line of ldg lts.

Entrance From Basse Martineau leave R bns to port and G to stb. Then enter with the ch spire open between the pier heads (lt on S pier head QR), keeping a little to the W of the middle to avoid a high bank of sand on E side. It is not advisable to enter at night.

Anchorage Apply to HM office near YC on stb quay above bridge for berth HM (40) 60 37 40 VHF 9 Customs (40) 42 33 74. The Le Pouliguen (W) port side sometimes dries, bottom hard sand. Yacht yards, engineers shops. Transport to St Malo airport. (Note: In view of the difficult entrance most cruising yachtsmen prefer the easy entrance and full marina facilities at Pornichet-La Baule.)

LE POULIGUEN - LA BAULE   Charts BA 3216, F 6825

HW: Dover +5h

MHWS 5.3m MHWN 4.0 MTL 2.9 MLWN 1.8 MLWS 0.5

The hbr is exposed to the SE and a S-ly swell breaks in the shallow water. The 1M channel leading to the port dries 1½m. While 1¼m draught can enter at half tide, yachts drawing 1¾m should enter just before HW and only when swell is absent.

Approach Make the R Penchâteau buoy, Oc R, ½M SE of Pt de Penchâteau (the w-ly pt of the bay), and 6M E of Le Croisic. Thence steer N to leave the R Basse Martineau buoy to port. A cable NW of this buoy there is anchorage in 2½-3m.

PORNICHET-LA BAULE   Charts BA 3216, F 6797

HW: Dover +5h

MHWS 5.3m MHWN 4.0 MTL 2.9 MLWN 1.8 MLWS 0.5

This large artificial harbour 4M E of Le Pouliguen is available for draughts up to 4½m at all states of the tide in any conditions. The entrance is absolutely straightforward, having been built out beyond all inshore hazards. Mole heads have R & G fl lts. 1100 berths, but crowded in season. Visitors berth at ends of walkways rafting if necessary. Fuel and all marina facilities. HM (40) 61 03 20 VHF 9. Customs in port office (40) 61 32 04. Shops and restaurants within marina complex or in Pornichet village nearby. Easy access to beaches adjacent to marina.

ENTRANCE TO RIVER LOIRE, ST NAZAIRE

Charts BA 3216, 2989, 2985,
F 6797, 6493, 6260, 6261, 5992

HW: Dover +5½h

MHWS 5.4m MHWN 4.0 MTL 2.9 MLWN 1.6 MLWS 0.5

Bar 4.8m: in strong winds should only be approached during second half of the flood. The approach is divided into two channels by La Banche bank.

Approach From NW bring Du Four lt, 293° astern, and pass about a mile S of Gd Charpentier lt, Q WRG. Then with the ldg lts QW in line, steer 025° for the bar. From SW, having given the Pilier Lt Ho a good berth to SE bring the ldg lts in line 025°.

At night do not enter the R sector of La Banche lt until past the G sector of Gd Charpentier. The top ldg lt is the high Portcé lt, a rectangular building with gable at the edge of the cliff, and the low lt is close to it at the foot of the cliff, its lt being visible only on a narrow sector close to the ldg line.

Entrance The entrance hugs the NW shore. Having passed between three pairs of lt buoys, keeping on the ldg line, Aiguillon lt tr is left to port. The channel into the river is dredged and well lighted. Good temporary anchorage at Bonne Anse between La Rougeole and the Lt Ho in about 3m. No stream, but 2M from St Nazaire.

Berthing The docks are not available to yachts, but a short stop is generally allowed alongside the E Péreire quay (NE corner of St Nazaire basin), entering by the (old) lock, which opens as demanded by traffic. The outer hbr, Penhoet basin and the main S lock and the drydock are reserved exclusively for large commercial vessels.

The passage from St Nazaire to Nantes, 30M, can easily be completed on the flood tide. A canal runs from Nantes N and W, affording connection with the Vilaine and St Malo through Redon, and with Lorient by the Blavet at Pontivy.

At Nantes there is a quiet and sheltered anchorage in 5½m in the Bras de Pirmil just below rly br at Houte Ile. From Trentemoult along the S bank of Bras de Pirmil there is a small marina, yacht moorings and a yacht yard. A more convenient mooring for the city of Nantes is on the N bank of the N arm of the river where possible. Caution bridge under construction (clearance 56m) nr Trentemoult joining positions 47°11'.693N, 1°36'.748W (Quai de Roche Maurice) and 47°11'.588N, 1°36'.750W (S bank of river). Depths amended see latest charts F5992, BA2985, Plan de Port de Nantes. All facilities at St Nazaire and Nantes. HM at Trentemoult marina (40) 84 09 14 Customs (40) 73 39 55.

PORNIC

Charts BA 3216, F 5039

HW: Dover +5h

MHWS 5.3m MHWN 4.1 MTL 2.9 MLWN 1.6 MLWS 0.7

The old port dries 1¾m, sand and mud. The N side is rocky and there is a breakwater off Goumalon Pt, which covers at HW. The end is marked by a bn.

Anchor offshore in fine weather in 3½m W or SE of Noëvéillard jetty. The extended breakwater off Noëvéillard encloses a large modern marina. Least depth 2m: up to 3m - but little water in entrance 2 hrs either side of MLWS. Access from SE: safe under most conditions. Entrance channel marked by port hand buoy and perch. R and G Fl lts on piles either side of entrance. Visitors pontoon is nearest the entrance but side facing entrance uncomfortable in a swell. HM (40) 82 05 40 Customs (40) 82 01 69 and (40) 82 03 17.

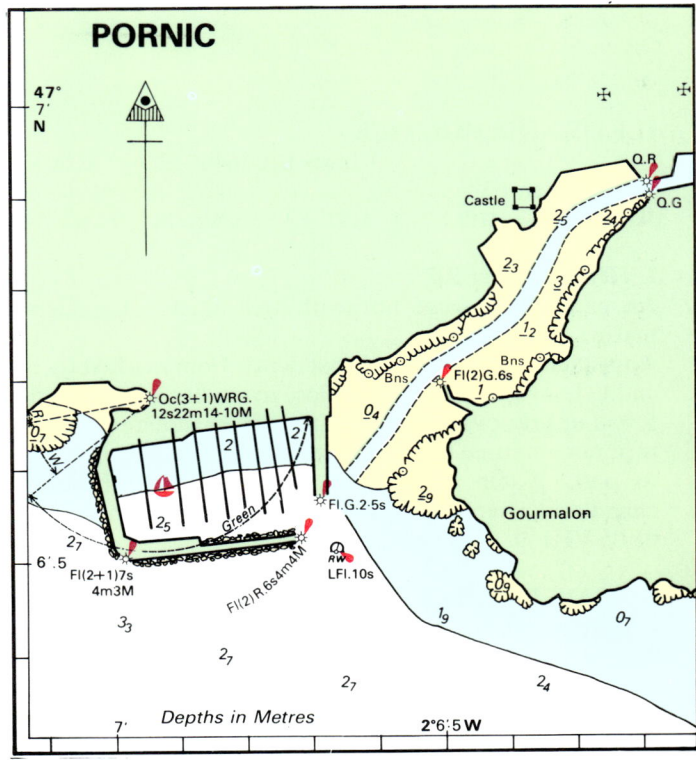

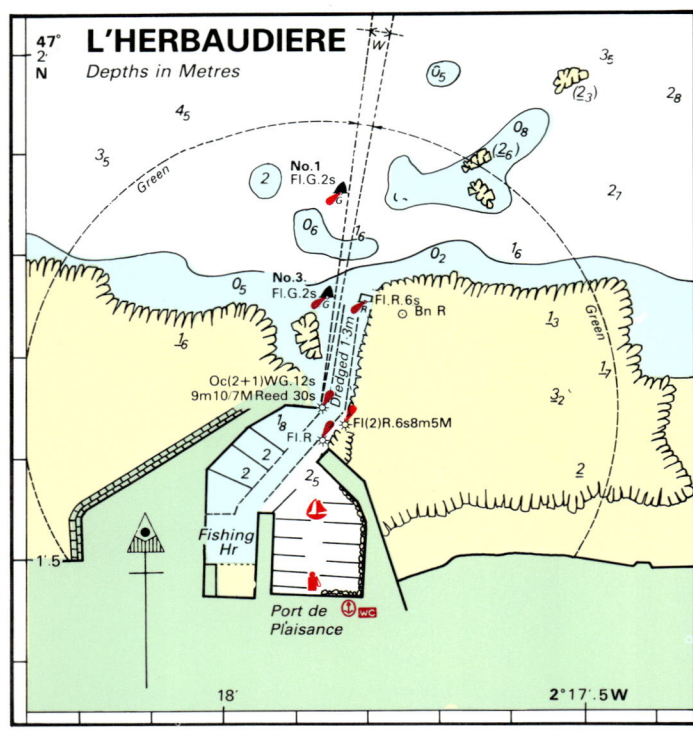

ILE D'YEU, PORT JOINVILLE

Charts BA 3640, F 6613, 6890

HW: Dover +5h

MHWS 5.2m MHWN 4.0 MTL 2.9 MLWN 1.9 MLWS 0.7

The outer hbr, which partly dries, is exposed to NW, N and NE, and winds from these directions bring in a swell. The high water tr just W of the town is more conspic than the Lt Ho. The marina has 2.5m.

Approach Ch bearing 202° lined up with W Lt Tr (G top) on NW jetty head, Oc(3) WG 12s, or at night there are ldg lts QR 219°, W trs with R tops.

Entrance Keep on these ldg marks, 1m, until it is necessary to turn sharply at the end of the jetty to port to enter the marina.

Berthing In marina in E hbr, 2½m, immediately to port after hugging inner mole heads, well sheltered but very crowded with extensive rafting in season. All facilities.

W inner hbr is reserved for ferries and fishing boats. Anchoring in outer hbr forbidden except to wait for tide. When marina full can use E basin to port (Darse de la glacière) mooring or rafting to quay. This basin has a sill which covers at half tide, caution required. There are anchorages outside the hbr in Anse de Ker Chalon, 3½m, 6ca SE of entrance, in settled weather and also in the Anse des Vieilles on the S side of the island, exposed to E, much used by French yachts. Ferries from Ile d'Yeu to mainland (Fromentine). HM (51) 58 38 11, VHF 9. Customs (51) 58 37 28.

ILE DE NOIRMOUTIER

Charts BA 2646, 3216, F 5039

HW: Dover +5h

MHWS 5.3m MHWN 3.9 MTL 2.8 MLWN 1.6 MLWS 0.4

L'HERBAUDIÈRE

An excellent passage hbr with well sheltered modern marina, depth 2-3m.

Approach and Entrance Least depth 1¼m marked by R and G buoys and bns. Keep close to stb hand buoys with E end of breakwater in line with L'Herbaudière ch clock tr (if not obscured by trees). Reporting point at Pontoon F to port. Water and power at berths: fuel, showers, chandlery, caretaking. Shops, PO in village. HM (51) 39 05 05 VHF 9. Customs (51) 39 06 80.

BOIS DE LA CHAISE

Small craft anchor in 3m, mud, with Pt Charniers open to S of Le Cobe rk and with Fort St Pierre bearing 187°; sheltered from a NW blow but a good deal of swell comes round the pt. The hbr of Noirmoutier dries 1¾m to 2½m. The channel is marked by bns; there is a lt Gp Oc at the jetty head.

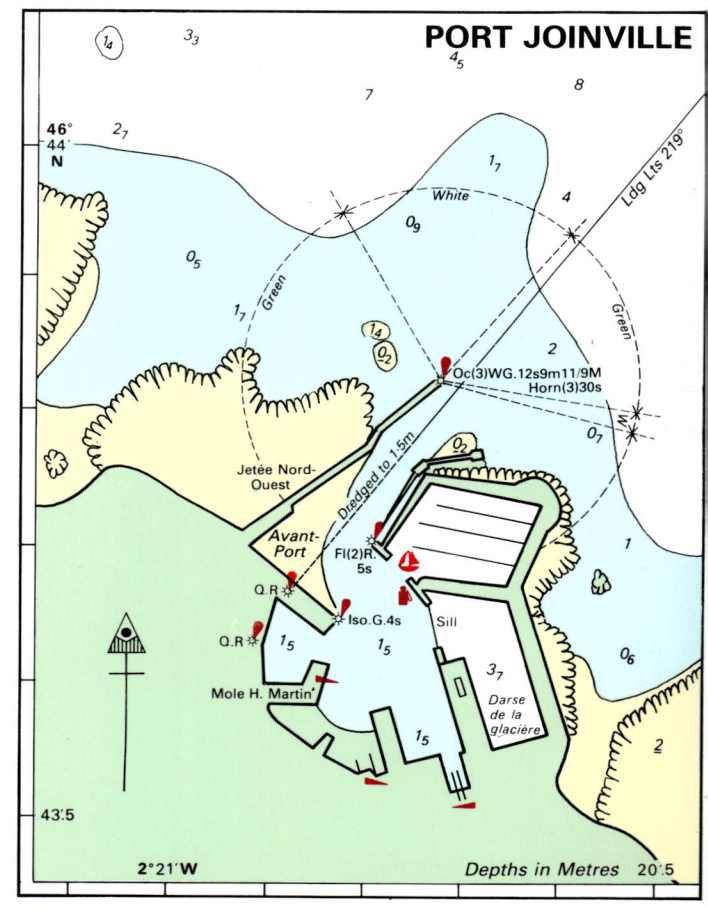

ST GILLES CROIX-DE-VIE

Charts BA 3640, F 6613

HW: Dover +5h

MHWS 5.2m MHWN 4.1 MTL 3.0 MLWN 2.0 MLWS 0.7

A small tidal hbr which may be located by the two spires of La Croix and St Gilles, the high Lt Ho at Croix de Vie, and the low rock headland of Gross Terre off which lie the Pilours, a conspic rk marked by a S Card lt buoy. Swell breaks heavily in the entrance. Ebb runs 6kn springs, 4kn neaps. Channel dredged to 1½m. Enter after half flood except in fine weather. Swell can be dangerous. Sheltered outside between NW and NE.

Approach Give the Pilours, off Pt de Grosse Terre, a good berth. At night there are ldg lts at 043°, the high Lt Ho at Croix de Vie Dir Oc(3+1)R, and a lower Lt close W of Mole de l'Adan Dir Oc(3+1)R.

Entrance At sufficient rise pass between the pier-heads, with QWG 20s to stb and Fl(2) WR to port, and continue between buoys until beyond the Gd Mole. At N end of the Garenne jetty steer to pass between the buoys off Croix-de-Vie; then the channel bears 132° for 3½ca to the R buoy marking the Bank de l'Adon. Bear to port for St Gilles. Flood sets hard on to Mole de l'Adon and ebb on to La Rotonde.

Berthing At marina on port bank beyond fishing hbrs (1½m) but beware of a strong tide running through outer berths when turning in to it. Access near HW, alongside quays (0 to ½m) outside the fishing hbrs or at quay (dries ½m) to stb at St Gilles sur Vie just below the bridge, where the streams are not so strong. Anchoring in the channel is prohibited and the Adon hbrs are reserved for fishing vessels. All facilities at Croix-de-Vie. Rly. HM at marina (51) 55 30 83, VHF 9. Customs (51) 55 10 18.

LES SABLES D'OLONNE   Charts BA 3640, F 6551

HW: Dover +5¼h

MHWS 5.2m MHWN 4.1 MTL 3.0 MLWN 2.0 MLWS 0.7

An important fishing port and popular holiday resort. The hbr has 1.5m throughout.

Approach In strong SE, S or SW winds, especially when there is a swell, the shoals make the approach rough. In bad weather the SE approach is safer. Keep the GW tr on the hd of Jetée des Sables (QG) in line with grey square Tour de la Chaume with W turret top Oc(2+1)12s, 320°, until W jetty hd is abeam to port, when bear to port for jetty and the entrance. At night, ldg lts 033° IsoR 4s.

Entrance Bring the two inner bns, FR, near La Chaume Lt Ho in line and steer on them, 327°, until well inside the jetties and then keep to stb; there are rocks and shallows on port side.

Berthing The Bassin à Flot is limited to commercial traffic. Marina (beyond main hbr) in Bassin des Chasses available at all states of tide. Safe but less convenient for town. Water and electricity. All facilities. Rly. HM (51) 32 51 16, VHF 9 and 16. Customs (51) 32 02 33. In fine weather there is an anchorage outside the line of buoys in sand off the casino. Breakwater gives protection from W and coast protects from NW through N to SE.

PORT DE BOURGENAY

Charts BA 2641, F 6522

6 miles SE of Les Sables D'Olonne

Approach Make for safe water pillar buoy in position 46°25'.33N 1°41'.83W approx 1M SW of marina entrance. Entrance dredged to 1m and hazardous due to sand banks at LWS and in strong swell. Inside depth 2m. Ldg lts QG 040°, R & G lts on jetty heads and Fl(2)R 6s on breakwater spur.

Berthing In modern well-sheltered marina. All facilities and access to swimming pool, lake and beaches. Buses to Talmont St Hilaire, all shops. HM (51) 22 20 36, VHF9. Customs at Les Sables d'Olonne.

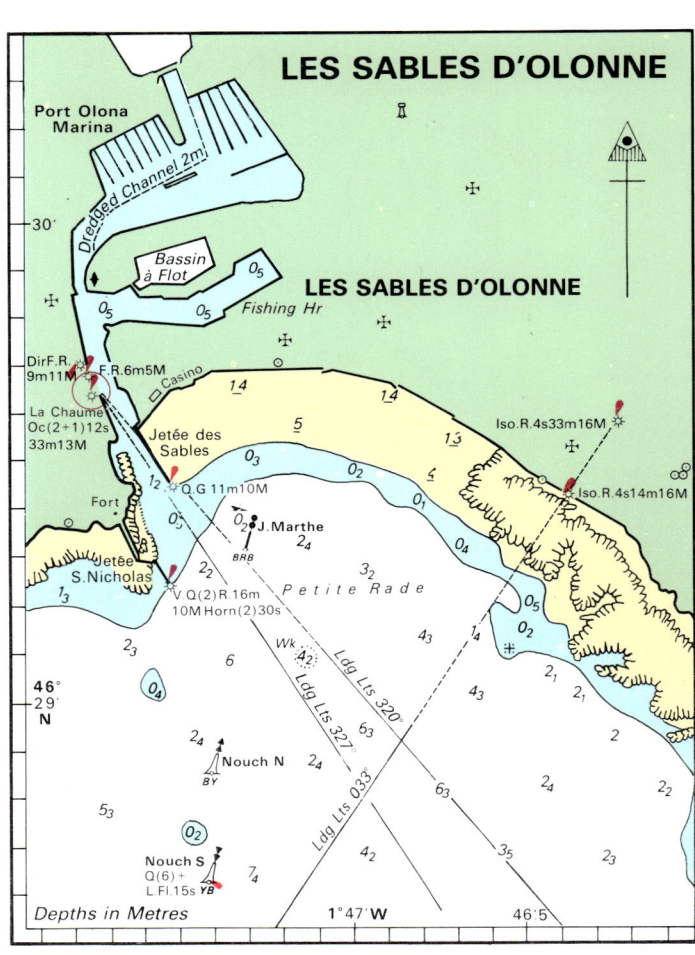

ILE DE RÉ Charts BA 2641, 2746, F 6521, 6668
HW: Dover +4½h
MHWS 6.2m   MHWN 4.6   MTL 3.4   MLWN 2.2   MLWS 0.6
In Pertuis Breton the flood or ESE stream begins about 6h before HW Pt de Graves (Dover +5¼h); the ebb stream begins at or shortly after HW. A marine farm has been established 4½M N of Ile de Ré between the island and the mainland: caution requied if approaching from this direction.

ST MARTIN A battlemented fortress port, most picturesque, with wet dock 3m. Approach and entrance dry 1½m about 1 ca from mole head.
Approach From NW to clear Rocha bank and leave it to W, leave N Card lt buoy to S and W, and bring ch and Lt Ho of St Martin in line 210°. From SE give St Martin shore a berth of 1M, pass well N of Le Couronneau N card bn. Leave breakwater Fl R 2.5s to port, rounding mole head IsoG at distance of 5 or 6m.
Entrance Proceed in mid-channel between bastions. When the hbr opens out the cut to the lock will be seen to stb. Tie up in the cut to await locking. Inside the dock, 3m, proceed to port, and tie up alongside the low wall in the W corner of the basin. The lock opens approx HW +1h (longer in season) list available in Bureau shows times of opening of bridge on each tide. Lock cut dries. Pontoons inside, usually very crowded.
Anchorage The outside anchorage in the Rade de St Martin is well sheltered from S and SW, 2 to 4m, with Le Frier upper lt on the Pt du Frier 274°, and St Marie and La Flotte chs in line 163°. The outer hbr dries. Ferry to La Rochelle. HM (46) 09 26 69.

LA FLOTTE The basin dries, mud. Good anchorage offshore sheltered from S to SW wind, 1¾ to 3m. Bring La Flotte and Chassiron lts in line, 204°, and Baleines lt open of St Martin lt, 282°.
Approach Keep La Flotte Lt Ho 215°. If approaching from E leave bn off Pt des Barres at least 1 ca to port until Lt Ho bears 215°.
Entrance Leave R can buoy to port and steer straight for centre of narrow entrance between jetties.
Berthing Moor alongside jetty (dries 2m) immediately to stb on entering inner hbr. Provisions, hotels, fuel in town. Water from tap on E quay near YC. HM (46) 09 67 66 Customs at St Martin.

FIER D'ARS
A very agreeable summer anchorage, strong tides.
Approach. After half-tide, on transit of two Lt Hos on Pt du Fier in line 265°. The Lt Hos are not conspic, but appear in a nick in the trees: rear, G turret on a pink house; front, a square board on a pylon, which can be moved as and when the channel shifts. Be careful not to confuse with Les Baleines Lt Ho 5M further W. Approaching on the transit, a stb buoy and a stb bn mark the end of the drying Banc du Bucheron, extreme caution required owing to tendency for this bank to shift.
½M further in the channel shoals and dries ½m, then deepens again to a hole about ¼M long with up to 3m. This is the outer anchorage, exposed to N and E but sheltered from S and W. In another ½M on the transit, just before the Roche Eveillon bn (port), Ars en Ré ch spire will be seen bearing 231° and open of Roche L'Abbesse bn. A conspic chimney bears 232° of the bn. Following this alignment, leave the Roche Eveillon bn 1 ca to port over a rock bottom, dries 1½m, running parallel to the Pt du Fier shore, at the inshore end of which there is a landing slip. The second deep pool of the main anchorage begins here, with 1¾m. After leaving L'Abbesse bn close to port, the channel is buoyed until the hbr entrance, dries 3m.

Berthing Outer anchorages in pools as above, exposed to NE at HW. Inner hbr is a wet basin with a single gate open each side of HW, has quays on both sides but is usually crowded in season. Gate sometimes left open when boats settle into soft mud. Water, restaurant and boatyard in hbr; shop ½M.

LA PALLICE   Charts BA 2743,   F 6468
HW: Dover +5¼h
MHWS 6.2m   MHWN 4.8   MTL 3.6   MLWN 2.5   MLWS 0.9
La Pallice is now entirely commercial and is not recommended for cruising yachtsmen unless in an emergency when access to the wet dock may be available ½h before HW. There is restricted passage between La Pallice and Ile de Ré due to road bridge recently completed, clearance 30m, lights and buoyage established. (Lt on Pt de Sablanceaux now discontinued).

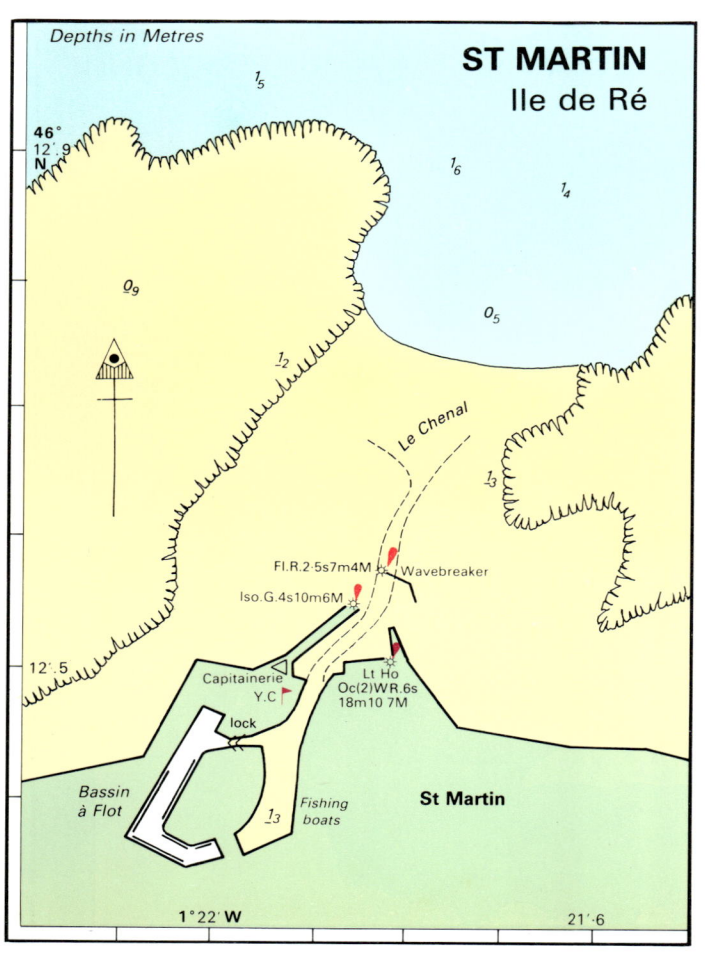

LA ROCHELLE Charts BA 2746, 2743, F 6468
HW: Dover +5¼h
MHWS 6.2m MHWN 4.8 MTL 3.6 MLWN 2.5 MLWS 0.9

There is 0.3m in channel to the main hbr; the outer hbr has 0.3m and the basin has 3m. Channel to Port des Minimes marina has 1m; 2m inside.

Approach From a position 1M S of Le Lavardin T steer 059°; from off Pt de Chef de Baie continue on ldg lts, RW tr front, W rear Dir Q 059°. E of Tr Richelieu (Fl(4) R 12s) the channel is narrow. Rocky flats dry to N, mud banks to S. Anchor to await tide just S of Pt de Chef de Baie. See (3) below for approach to Port des Minimes marina.

Entrance To old hbr between the old trs, Tour St Nicolas (stb) and Tour de la Chaine (port).

Berthing (1) Visitors' pontoons (1¼m) in outer (tidal) hbr, dredged 1¾m

(2) Lock in HW ±1½h to inner wet basin (3½m) on E side. Footbridge opened as required and berths allocated by bridge keeper. While waiting for lock, moor temporarily between dock entrance and Tour St Nicolas, alongside fishing boats if necessary.

(3) In marina, at Port des Minimes on stb hand immediately after passing Tr Richelieu, with 1m least depth in channel and 2m inside. Entrance channel on 133° is 160m E of Tr Richelieu and before first R main channel buoy (LR2) channel marked by three buoys: 'M' W Card, 'M2' and 'M4' both R, all to be left to port. Entrance is marked by bns with R and W posts: square R topmarks with W borders to port, B △ topmarks with W borders to stb. By night lts Fl(2) R to port, Fl G to stb. Full marina facilities, bonded stores. Transport to town by hourly bus or launch service in summer. Rail connections. HM (46) 44 41 20 VHF 9 Customs (46) 41 11 73.

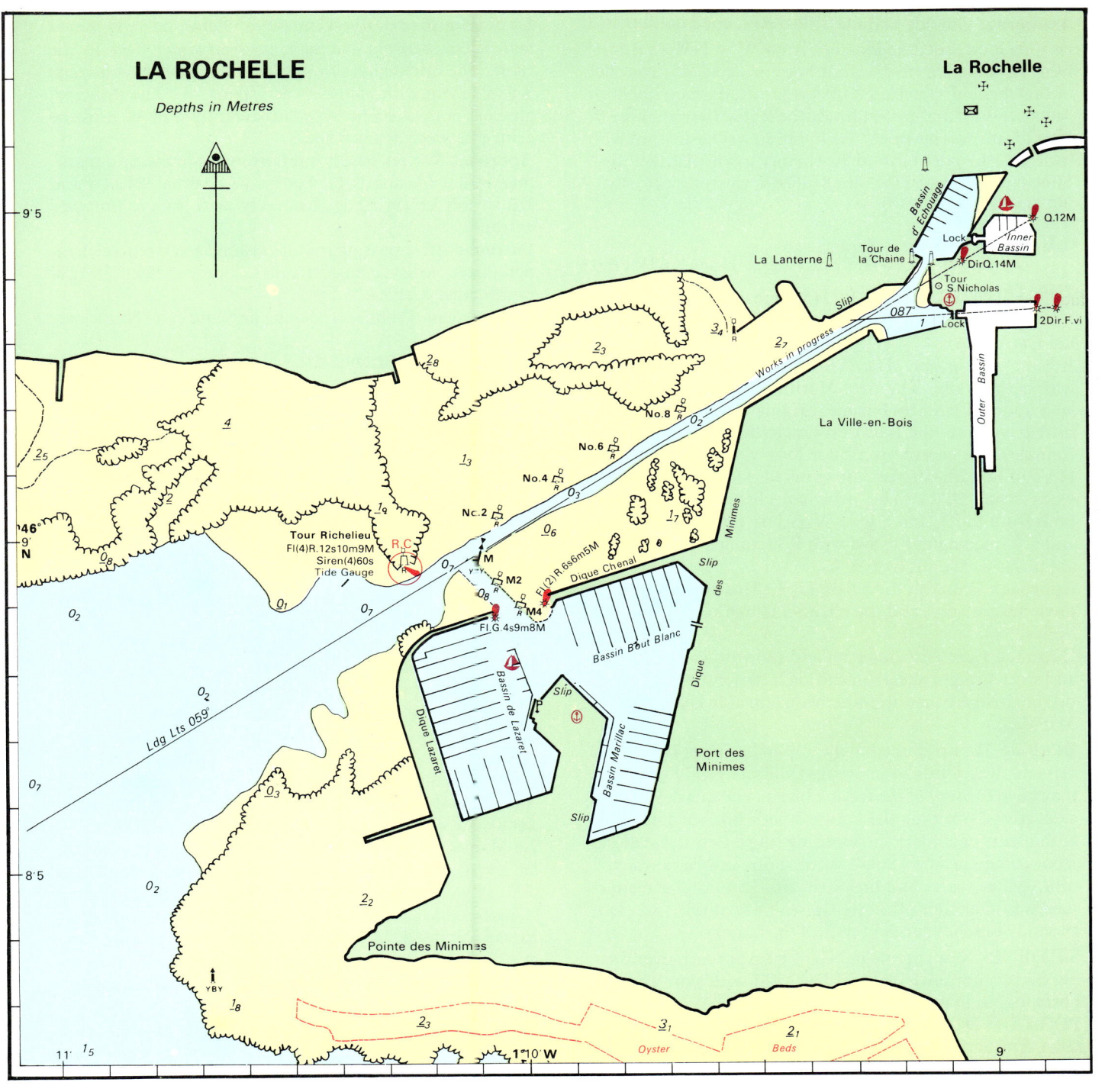

LA CHARENTE RIVER, ROCHEFORT
Charts BA 2748, F 4333 6334
HW: Dover +5½h
MHWS 5.5m   MHWN 5.1   MTL 3.5   MLWN 2.2   MLWS 1.3

Bar Fouras bar, outside entrance, has about 0.9m. In the river there are bars at Lupin and Charras which do not affect the 50m wide dredged channel, 1¾m. In the river, tidal streams attain 4kn at springs, where it is confined between embankments, and 2kn elsewhere. There is a bore at high spring tides.

Entrance The river is entered between Fouras Tr (conspic) and Sig Stn on the N bank and Ile Madame. Steer 115° with the RW square trs (QR) of Fouras leading lts in line until nearly abreast Fouras when ldg lt trs on the S bank E of Port des Barques come in line, 135°. Front is W square tr, rear has black gable and band, both Iso G 4s. Thence pairs of bns mark the dredged channel, when it does not run in midstream. Navigation in river prohibited during night.

Anchorage Outside in Rade d'Ile d'Aix, good holding in 5 to 10m mud, sheltered except from W to NW. Visitors' buoys available in the river at Soubise or at Martrou, out of the channel. There is a lift bridge at Martrou open for yachts HW±1h (times on La Rochelle) for 10 min: three W lts indicate passage open. Yacht hbr in wet basin (3m) with lock gate to port beyond Rochefort town. All facilities. Shops in Martrou. HM (46) 84 30 30. Customs (46) 99 03 90.

ILE D'OLÉRON
Charts BA 2663, 2743, 2746, F 4333, 6335, 6913
HW: Dover +5¼h
MHWS 6.0m   MHWN 4.9   MTL 3.5   MLWN 2.3   MLWS 0.9

LE CHÂTEAU
A busy fishing hbr. The 17th century town lies entirely within the walls. The first Maritime Laws, the basis of laws adopted later by Europe, originated on the Is. A 2M bridge connects the Is at Pt d'Ors to the mainland SW of Bourcefranc, centre span 80m long gives a clearance at HAT of 12.15m between the spans 14-34 with 15.10m between spans 20-24. The principal channels are marked both from the N and S by a W △ board with G △ to stb, and a W rectangular board with R rectangle to port. Both are marked at night by FW lts.

Approach From N, the Juliar Tr, Lt Hos and walls of the town are conspic, and the channel is marked by bns and buoys.

Entrance Leave the outer bn and the withies close to stb and steer straight ahead for the ldg lt structures to proceed up the dredged channel, 40m wide; 2m at MLWN, ¾m at MLWS

Berthing Tie up immediately to port in inner hbr, 1¼m soft and deep mud (2¼m draught will sit upright), but this may be in the way of the fishing boats. The quay on the stb side dries 2¾m near the seaward end, bottom soft mud, with plenty of ladders and mooring rings. Petrol and diesel from garage nearby. Small yard; shops and restaurants 5 min. Water scarce and brackish. Bus and ferry. An alternative is to anchor off Pt de Gatseau out of tide and close to sandy beach, sounding to find the hole.

ST DENIS New marina in NE of Is. Approach over drying banks; entrance channel has a sill with port and stb posts; depth in marina 1½ to 3½m.

PORT DU DOUHET New marina in NE of Is. Dredged 2.7m. Entrance sill has 2m at HW±2h. Unlit. Caution: shallow water near G bn post N of entrance.

LA PERROTINE (BOYARDVILLE)
A small tidal port, with drying bar.

Approach The entrance is about 2M, 200° from Fort Boyard. Leave the buoy well to port and approach the end of the jetty keeping the NW side open, until about ¼ ca from its end, when keep close to it until the river is entered.

Entrance Keep to stb of mid-channel, once in the river.

Berthing Marina to stb with 2m, lock opens HW±1½h, crowded in season. There are also four short quays to stb beyond marina entrance where yachts able to take ground may find a mooring. All facilities in marina. HM (46) 47 23 71 VHF 9

LA SEUDRE RIVER, MARENNES AND LA TREMBLADE
Charts BA 2663, F 6912
HW: Dover +5¼h
MHWS 5.8m   MHWN 4.7   MTL 3.5   MLWN 2.4   MHWS 1.2

La Seudre R runs into Coureau d'Oleron near the S end and offers secure anchorages in deep water once in the river. The bridge gives a clearance at HAT between spans 3-9 of 12½m with 15m between spans 5-7. The principal channel is marked by W boards and by a Fl W lt in the centre between spans 6 and 7.

Approach Well marked, but narrow channels with markings rather far apart. La Soumaille channel, N of Barat Bank, and La Garrigue channel to its S, join at the river entrance.

Entrance After passing middle ground buoy where channels meet, keep to mid-channel. There is 18m at HW under power cables.

Anchorages (1) Off La Cayenne de Seudre, on N side near ferry.
(2) Canal at La Cayenne dries 2½m, lock in (HW ±1h) to the basin at Marennes, used only by yachts.
(3) Off La Grève, ½M upstream from La Cayenne, on S side near the ferry.
(4) Canal on stb side opp La Cayenne, dries 2½m, to crowded drying-out stone piers, soft mud, at La Tremblade.

All facilities, including yards at Marennes and La Tremblade, but limited at ferry wharves.

PASSAGE NOTE: ILE D'OLÉRON TO GIRONDE RIVER
With wind against tide the Pertuis de Maumusson can be very dangerous, breaking right across. Even in calm weather, on approach from seaward the outer buoys are not identifiable in the confused seas, and the broken water is not apparent until one is committed. The flood stream sets into and the ebb stream out of Coureau d'Oleron at both ends; the streams meet and separate in the strait and differ greatly according to their position. The complete details are given in the BA Bay of Biscay Pilot NP22.

La Mauvaise bank, N of the Gironde R entrance, should be given a wide berth. Enter by Grand Passe de l'Ouest (7¾m), well marked, or Passe Sud, adequately marked. It is inadvisable to enter with a strong NW wind. In Rade de Royan the flood, SE, begins approx +½h; the ebb, NW, at +6h, 4kn springs. There are eddies. Frequent buoyage changes in the river make the use of up to date charts essential.

Offshore anchorage to port under Pt de la Coubre inside Barre a l'Anglais or better further into river on stb side inside Pt de la Chambrette.

ROYAN
Charts BA 2910, F 7028
HW: Dover +5½h
MHWS 5.2m MHWN 4.0 MTL 3.0 MLWN 1.9 MLWS 0.8
Entrance dredged to 1½m, marina dredged 2½m. Although generally packed, full marina facilities in basin beyond fishing hbr. Berth temporarily at visitors' pontoon outside hbr entrance and report to HM office nearby. Crane for masts if entering canal system. Recommended staging post. Clear police and customs here if necessary rather than Bordeaux. HM (46) 38 72 22 VHF 9. Customs (46) 38 51 27.

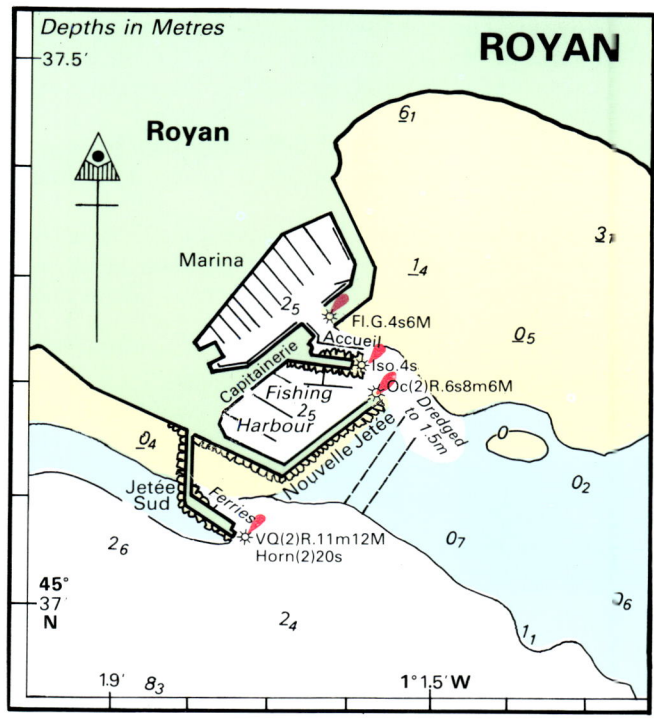

PORT BLOC
Charts BA 2910, F 7028
HW: Dover +5¼h
MHWS 5.3m MHWN 4.2 MTL 3.1 MLWN 2.0 MLWS 1.0
A well sheltered hbr with 2¾m.
Entrance About 4 ca S of Pt de Grave. Very strong streams and currents may be encountered between the Pt and the hbr.
Berthing Moor between buoys on W side of hbr (shallow). Small marina-type pontoon with water hose. Space at premium during high season. HM (56) 09 63 91 VHF 12, 6, 16 Customs (56) 09 65 14. Minimal facilities. Bus to Verdon-sur-Mer, 2M; ferry to Royan, ½h; train to Bordeaux. Basic provisions, restaurant. Good base for exploring vineyards.

GIRONDE RIVER
Charts BA 2910, 2916, F 7028, 7029, 7030
HW: Dover +5½h DS (main ent): Dover +½h SE; −5½h NW. Flood 2.5kn ; Ebb 4kn
MHWS 5.2m MHWN 4.1 MTL 3.0 MLWN 1.9 MLWS 0.9
From the mouth of the Gironde River to Bordeaux is 50M. The Gironde R becomes the Garonne above the junction with the Dordogne. The river is well buoyed but has extensive mud banks outside the buoyed channels – detailed charts required.
Anchorages Possible in many places in soft mud but the current is strong. (1) Mortagne-sur-Gironde to port. Entrance to channel across marshes is marked by conspic dolphins and beacons, dries 0.6m to quay. Lock in whenever water permits. Water, yacht yard, fuel in village, diesel by lorry. Locks open 1h before HW in daylight. Pontoons. Wintering possible.
(2) Trompeloup to stb. Anchor in up to 7m in mud about ½M W of Ile Pauillac. Berth alongside pontoons off jetty, or inner side of moored barges. Provisions in town.
(3) Pauillac, marina to stb 4m at pontoons. All facilities, restaurants. HM (56) 59 12 16 VHF 9
(4) Blaye on port bank off upriver end of Ile Nouvelle, very commercial. Mooring buoys off town near ferry jetty or berth alongside, much disturbed by ferry wash and uncomfortable in strong wind. Anchoring possible. Provisions in town, water, fuel.

BORDEAUX
Charts BA 2916, F7029, 7030
HW: Dover −4½h
MHWS 5.2m MHWN 4.0 MTL 2.4 MLWN 0.4 MLWS 0.0
Anchor or berth at marina, Point du Jour (suspension bridge) 4M outside city on W bank opposite Lormont; berth on outer pontoon preferably inside to avoid strong current, quite secure and landing easy; Rly (10 min). Shower, toilets and restaurant in YC. Water by hose. Crane on jetty head operated very efficiently by HM for masts. Good place to acquire or discard tyres for use as fenders for use in canals (essential). HM (56) 50 84 14. Canal pilot book available from HM office. The dock basin, No. 2, at Bordeaux is dirty and charges are high. Lock opens HW −2h to +½h.

PASSAGE NOTE: BORDEAUX TO CASTETS
At Castets is the first lock into the Canal Lateral à la Garonne which joins the Canal du Midi at Toulouse.
The R Garonne to Castets, 35M, is unbuoyed with extensive mudbanks, and rocky ledges. Garonne pilots do not operate above Bordeaux. Without a detailed chart or a pilot, a barge should be followed; barges moor just above the Bordeaux bridge. Castets can generally be reached on

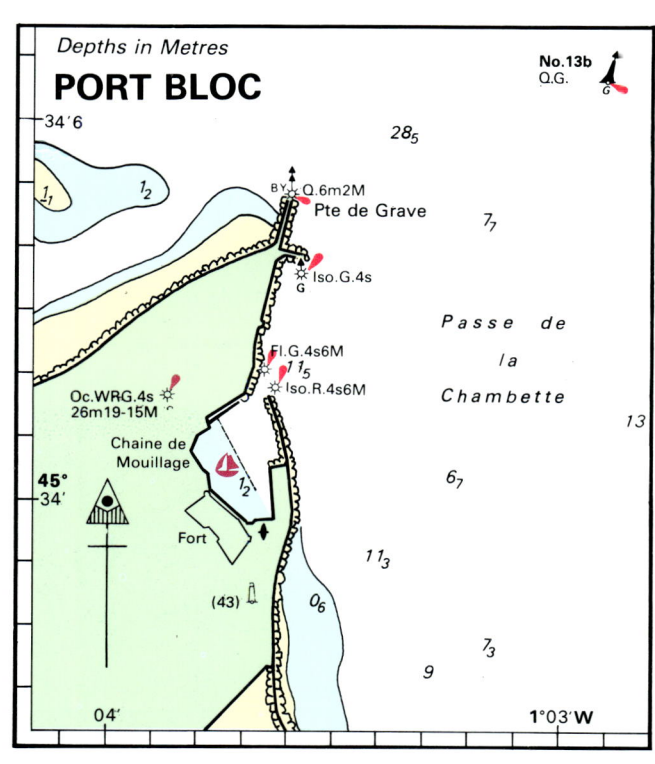

FRANCE, WEST COAST 378

one tide. The flood comes up at over 5kn, the water suddenly rising 0.3m with a 1½m wave; the last of the ebb goes down at 2kn. The lock at Castets is to stb. If, with the Garonne in spate and the upstream current therefore weakened, it should prove impossible to make Castets on one tide, ask permission to tie to a barge (they do not move overnight) or alongside the pontoon at Cadillac.

ARCACHON Charts BA 2664, F 6766
HW: Dover +6¼h
MHWS 4.3m MHWN 3.1 MTL 2.2 MLWN 1.1 MLWS 0.2
Fairway entrance is about 7M S of Cap Ferret, thence 12 M to the marina. Hbr is not accessible in heavy onshore weather or at night. It is essential to enter at half flood. The landfall buoy ATT-ARC is moved frequently and is sometimes withdrawn.
Entrance Channel varies in depth and position, usually running E then turning N with about 3m. It is marked by lateral unlit buoys, moved as the banks change. Application should be made to the Service Maritime at Royan, 35 Rue Pierre Jonain (46) 38 32 75 for latest information on buoyage. Do not attempt to go outside the buoyed channel.
Berthing Anchor in channel N of Cap Ferret (strong currents) or on pontoons in marina to stb at the E end of the town. HM (56) 83 22 44, VHF 9. Customs (56) 83 05 89. All Facilities. Buoys are also sometimes available off town in 5-6m, caution strong currents. There are a number of smaller ports within the basin accessible using large scale charts on the tide to craft of shallow draught. Channels marked by white numbered posts. Rly and boatyards.
Warning Care must be taken of the FIRING DANGER AREA (rockets) that lies off the coast between Cap Breton and La Négade bns. Yachts must keep beyond 45M or inside 3M from the coast. The areas that are dangerous and forbidden are broadcast each day after each weather bulletin by Bordeaux-Arcachon Radio.

CAP BRETON Charts BA 1102, F 6586
A hbr with three marinas. Entrance and exit is possible at half flood, but impracticable in strong onshore winds.
Entrance Enter between wooden pile to S and stone jetty to N, avoiding shallow patch in middle of entrance - tides run strongly. Opposite the entrance to the canal d'Hossegor, turn to stb through narrow gap to enter river.
Berthing. Marina immediately to stb (2m), and two more further on. All facilities Deep water moorings also available. HM (58) 72 21 23 VHF 9. Customs at Bayonne.

BAYONNE Charts BA 1343, F 6536
HW (Boucau): Dover +5h
MHWS 4.3m MHWN 3.3 MTL 2.5 MLWN 1.8 MLWS 0.7
A large town and surprisingly clean for a commercial port, about 3M up R Adour.
Entrance Close to breakwater, then midstream between jetties. Traffic signals from conspic tr to stb. After first bend, keep to stb.
Berthing (1) YC Adour Atlantic ½M above traffic signal tr welcomes visitors, and may allocate pontoon berth or mooring. Water, fuel on pontoons. Showers, shops and chandlers nearby. Bus to Bayonne.
(2) At Port d'Anglet marina to stb (2½m) all facilities, bus to Bayonne. HM (59) 63 05 45 and (59) 63 09 72. Customs at Bayonne (59) 25 58 32. There are ldg lts and bns if proceeding up river beyond marina.
(3) Alongside small wooden piers to stb just short of bridge near town hall (conspic) – strong currents on ebb. HM (59) 63 11 57

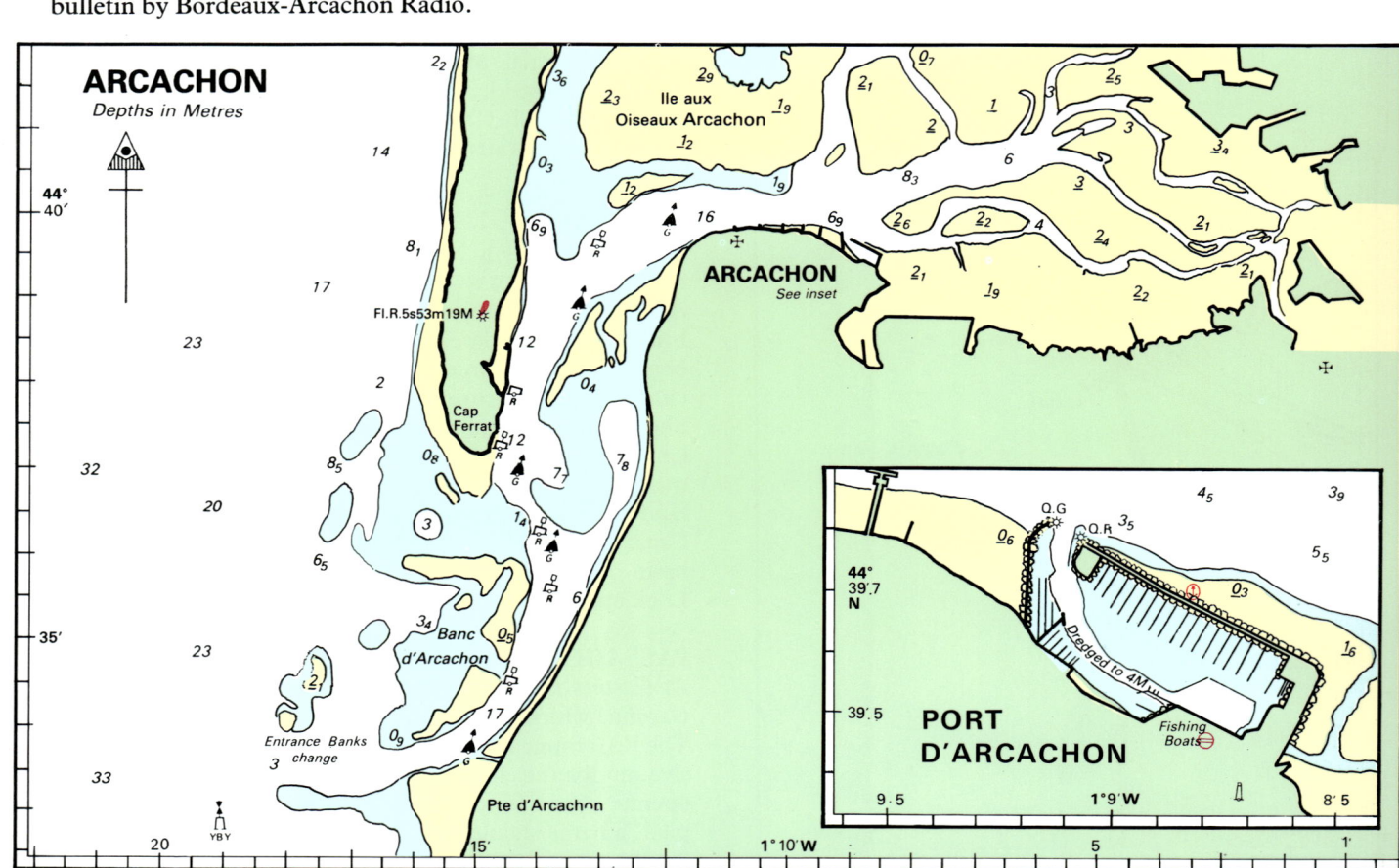

379 FRANCE, WEST COAST

ST JEAN DE LUZ Charts BA 1343, F 6526
HW: Dover +5h
MHWS 4.4m MHWN 3.2 MTL 2.4 MLWN 1.6 MLWS 0.5
Yachts may not stay in fishing port. Anchor off Socoa, hbr dries. Larraldénia Marina in inner hbr at Ciboure; all facilities but small and crowded. HM (59) 47 26 81. Customs at Ciboure (59) 47 18 44.

HENDAYE Charts BA 1343, F 6556
HW: Dover +5h
MHWS 4.3m MHWN 3.1 MTL 2.3 MLWN 1.5 MLWS 0.4
Approach is impracticable in heavy weather.
Entrance Keep close to stb (W) training wall until its root at Pt de Roca, where turn to port, following line of deep-water moorings and passing 75m S of large con bn to yacht moorings S of landing stage. YC on landing stage, with limited facilities. HM (59) 20 16 97. Reporting to customs (next to YC, (59) 20 01 98) essential as this is frontier between France and Spain. Water and diesel on quay, petrol nearby. Good restaurants and shops, 1M.

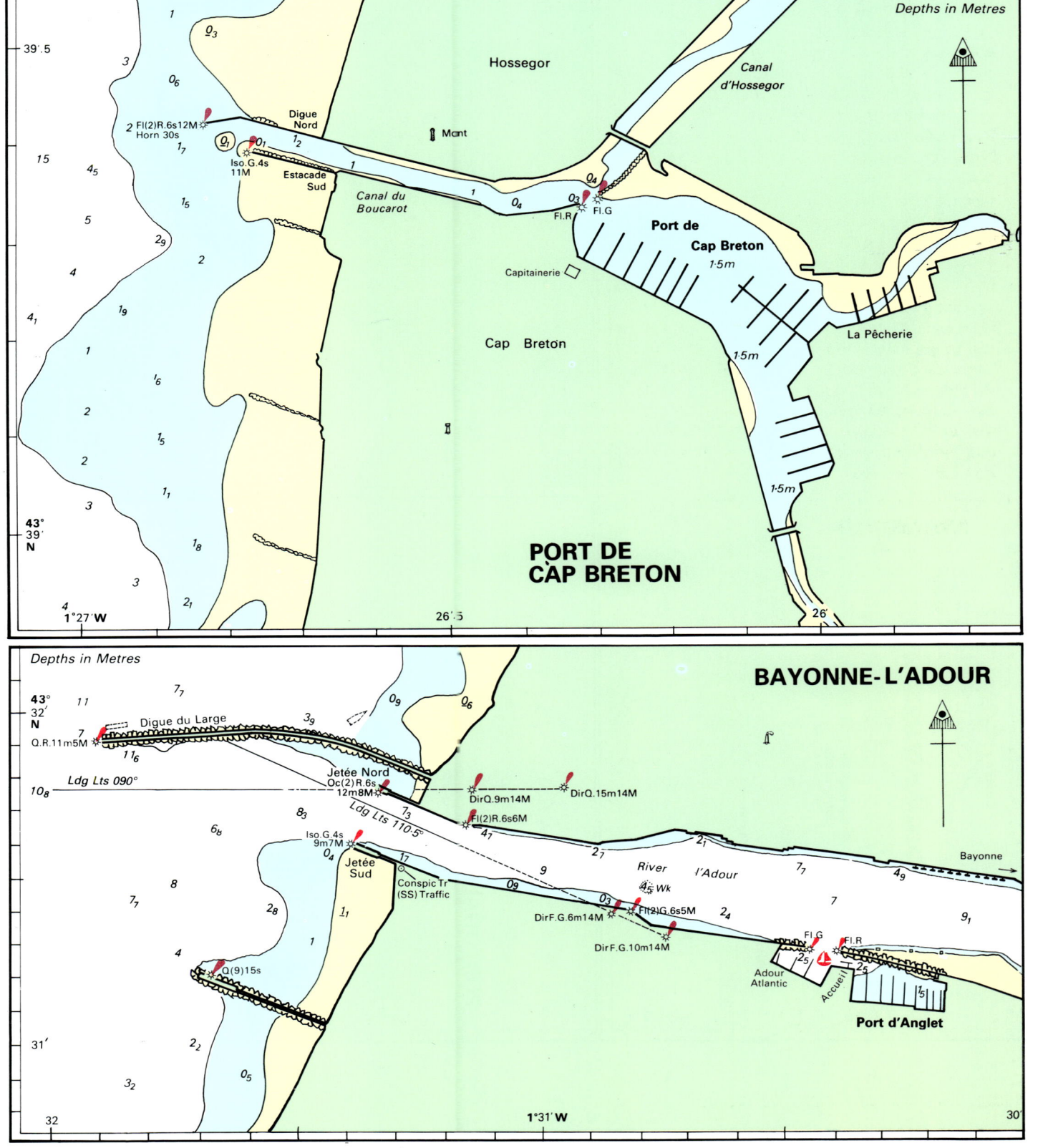

FRANCE, WEST COAST 380

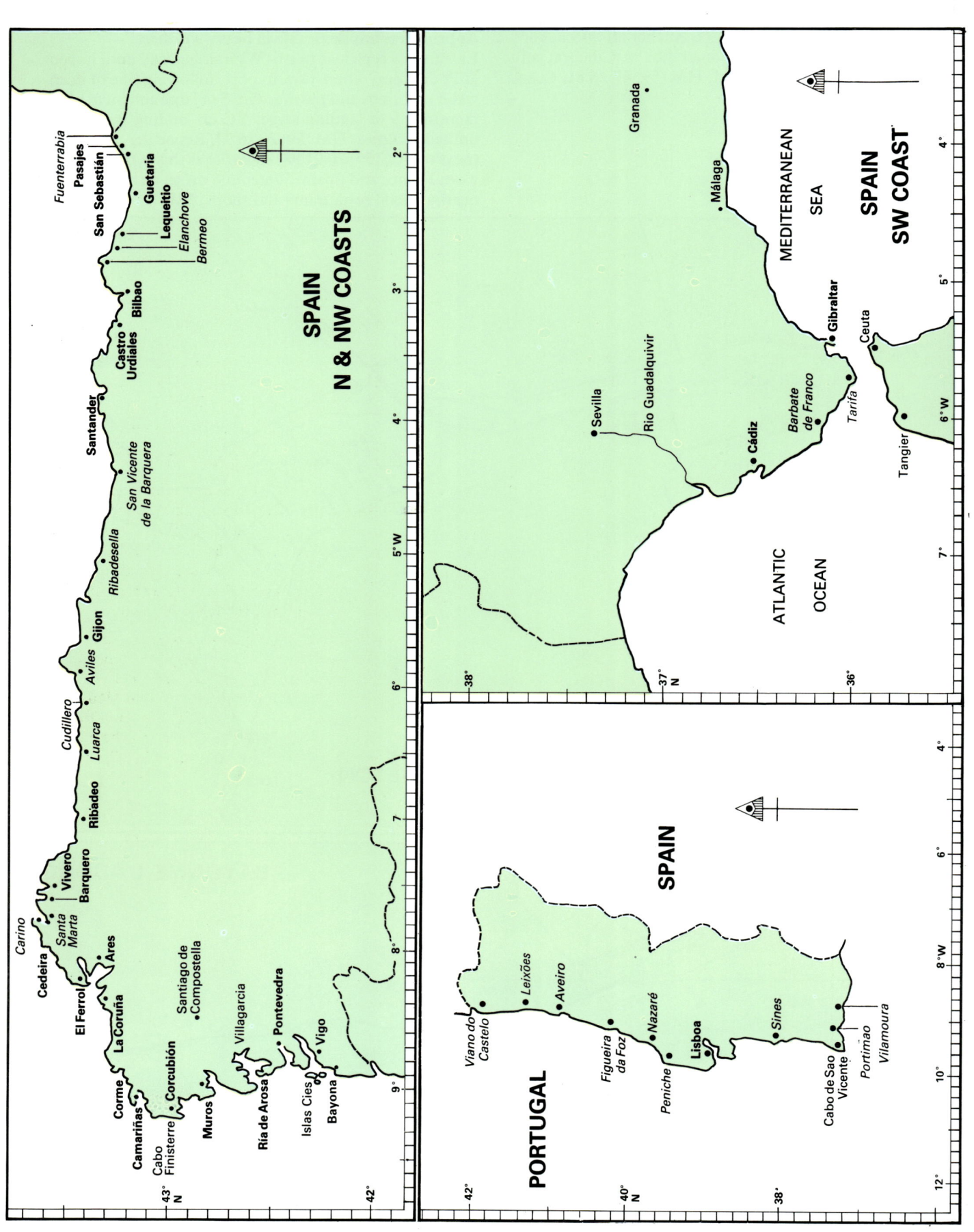

SPAIN AND PORTUGAL

PASSAGE NOTES

Routes to Spain
In summer the Bay of Biscay rarely deserves its awesome reputation. With a well-found yacht and a good crew the crossing can provide an enjoyable and memorable experience. Periods of calm are not unknown: plenty of fuel may be useful.

Routes:
Direct from SW England, Scilly Isles or Ireland. A landfall at Vigo with powerful Ro Bn at Cabo Silleiro and a return northwards exploring the rías makes a good short summer cruise. Falmouth to Vigo approx 550M.

NW France (e.g. L'Abervrac'h or Camaret) is a good point of departure, with landfall at one of the major harbours of La Coruña, Gijon or Santander. Approx. 300-350M. Another useful option is the Ría de Vivero, just E of Estaca de Bares which has a powerful Ro Bn.

Coasting down Brittany as far as Belle Ile or Ile d'Yeu reduces the open-sea distance and offers pleasant cruising. Belle Ile to Santander approx 240M; Ile d'Yeu to Santander approx 215M.

The last option, via La Rochelle, Arcachon and Fuentarrabía round the SE corner of the Bay of Biscay, has two disadvantages:
- The French rocket-firing range extends up to 45M offshore and restricts a yacht's freedom between the Gironde and Cap Breton.
- The area is a lee shore without harbours of refuge until Pasajes and therefore requires settled conditions.

Pilot Books:
Two excellent volumes to have on board are:-
"South Biscay Pilot" by Robin Brandon (A Coles Ltd.)
    The Gironde Estuary to La Coruña
"Atlantic Spain and Portugal" by RCC Pilotage Foundation (Imray Laurie Norie & Wilson)
    El Ferrol to Gibraltar

Good helpful brochures are available for every region from:

Spanish National Tourist Office	Portuguese National Tourist Office
57/58 St. James Street	1 New Bond Street
London SW1	London W1

PLANS
Deep water is coloured white. In some parts of Spain it is not possible to include a 2m contour line. Where this is so, the blue colour will be inside the 5m contour or, in certain cases, the 3m contour.

NORTH AND NORTH-WEST SPAIN

The whole coast is dominated by the mountains which lie a few miles inland from the French border at Fuentarrabía to Vigo near the Portuguese border. It is a cruising area of great natural beauty still relatively undeveloped and uncrowded. There are very few marinas or harbour charges. At night small unlit fishing boats may be found up to 15M offshore

From Fuentarrabía to Puerto de Luarca there are numerous (man-made) harbours, and small fishing ports in the Cornish style. There are also some shallow rivers (Ríos) with bars, which are available to yachtsmen with large-scale charts and shallow-draught boats; these are not covered in this text. The N coast of Spain has few off-lying dangers.

From Ribadeo to Vigo, deep bays and estuaries (the Rías of Galicia) offer a variety of sheltered anchorages and harbours. On the W coast of Spain a few unmarked reefs, often revealed by breaking waves, extend up to 4M offshore. Unlit mussel rafts are moored in shallow parts of some Rías.

In general the weather is similar to that experienced in the English Channel but about 5°C (10°F) warmer. The prevailing winds in summer are between NW and NE. Reduced visibility is not uncommon, and mist or low cloud can obscure hills and the lighthouses on them. Spanish TV shows a good meteorological chart, and local newspapers have a page for 'El Tiempo' which includes forecasts of sea conditions.

There are few buoys or beacon towers. On this coast of Spain, Decca is not as reliable as in the English Channel, and in places may be in error by as much as 2M. However, there are powerful and reliable radio beacons, with a range of 100 miles or more, at Cabo Machichaco, Estaca de Bares, Cabo Villano, Cabo Finisterre and Cabo Silleiro.

Swell is a feature of the coast. It presents few problems offshore, but in heavy swell only ports with deep-water entrances should be used. There is a west-going current along the north coast of Spain which may be modified greatly by wind-induced surface currents. Tidal streams are weak except around headlands and in the narrow entrances to some Rías. Their strength and direction are indicated by the numerous fishing-floats. The range of tides is approximately 3.0m at Springs, 1.5m at Neaps.

Formalities have been greatly eased in Spain, but yachts should be prepared to provide at any port the normal Ship's Papers and Passports for Skipper and Crew. Piped diesel fuel is only available to yachts at Gijon (Musel), El Ferrol, La Coruña, Muros, Villagarcia, Vigo and Bayona. (Diesel by the can from garages). There may be a charge for water. Calor gas is not available; Camping Gaz is universal and cheap.

Passage Charts: BA 1104 Bay of Biscay 1:1,000,000
    BA 1102, 1105, 1108, 1111, 3633 1:200,000
    S 927 to 944 inclusive all 1:40,000

Principal Lights:

Igueldo San Sebastián 43°19'.3N 2°00'.7W	Fl(2+1) 15s 132m 26M
Cabo Machichaco 43°27'.2N 2°45'.2W	Fl 7s 120m 24M
Pta Estaca de Bares 43°47'.2N 7°41'.1W	Fl(2) 7.5s 99m 25M
Cabo Prior 43°34'.1N 8°18'.9W	Fl(1+2) 15s 105m 24M
Torre de Hercules, La Coruña 43°23'.2N 8°24'.3W	Fl(4) 20s 104m 23M
Cabo Villano 43°09'.6N 9°12'.7W	Fl(2) 15s 102m 28M Racon M
Cabo Toriñano 43°03'.2N 9°17'.9W	Fl(2+1) 15s 63m 24M
Cabo Finisterre 42°52'.9N 9°16'.3W	Fl 5s 141m 23M
Cabo Silleiro 42°06'.2N 8°53'.8W	Fl(2+1) 15s 83m 24M

FUENTERRABÍA   Charts BA 1343   S 3912
HW: Dover +5h

MHWS 4.3m   MHWN 3.1   MTL 2.3   MLWN 1.5   MLWS 0.4

An old fortified Spanish town on E side of Río de Bidasoa opposite the sophisticated resort of Hendaye on the French side. Customs officials may be very active. Strong ebb tide at Springs at mouth of Río de Bidasoa.

Approach Conspic Lt Ho Fl(2) 10s on Cabo Higuer at W end of bay. Give wide berth to Les Briquets in E of bay.

Entrance Enter river on top half of tide, in normal weather only, between breakwater heads FG and LFl R 10s. Keep close to stb training wall until its root at Roca Punta where turn to port and follow dredged channel with mooring buoys.

Anchorage (1) 1 ca SW of landing place at Hendaye Plage near YC in 3.5m clear of buoys.
(2) In the river N or S of Roca Punta in 3m.
(3) 1-2 ca S of Puerto Gurutzeaundi (½M S of Cabo Higuer) W of extended breakwater FlG 3s in 2.5m clear of buoys (or inside hbr if room, FG & FR at entrance).

A first time night entry to the Río de Bidasoa is not recommended. Use (3).

PUERTO DE PASAJES   Charts BA 1181   S 9440
HW: Dover +5h

MHWS 4.1m   MHWN 3.0   MTL 2.3   MLWN 1.5   MLWS 0.5

A busy commercial hbr which can be entered in all conditions. In heavy swell enter in last quarter of flood. Well-sheltered but subject to wash from large vessels.

Approach There is a Lt Ho (conspic from E) on Cabo La Plata Oc 4s above Pta del Arando Chico, and on opposite E headland a conspic rock El Fraile.

Entrance From a position 1 mile N of the narrow steep-sided entrance steer 155° between headlands, with the Lt Ho and two concrete bns on Pta de las Cruces in line. By night ldg lts 155°; Front Oc(2) WRG 15s; Centre Q; Rear Oc 3s. When Pta del Arando Grande Fl(2) R 6s is abeam change to 144°, leaving Pta de las Cruces FG to stb, Pta Teodoro Arroca Q(4) 6s to port, Pta de Mirador QR to port, and Pta Calparra Fl(3) G 10s and Pta de la Torre FG to stb.

Anchorage (1) Off village of Pasajes de San Juan outside moorings in 4m mud.
(2) Off village of Pasajes de San Pedro outside moorings in 4m mud.
(3) In cove opposite Pta de las Cruces (Ensenada de Cala Bursa) in quiet weather only.

Facilities Major repairs possible.

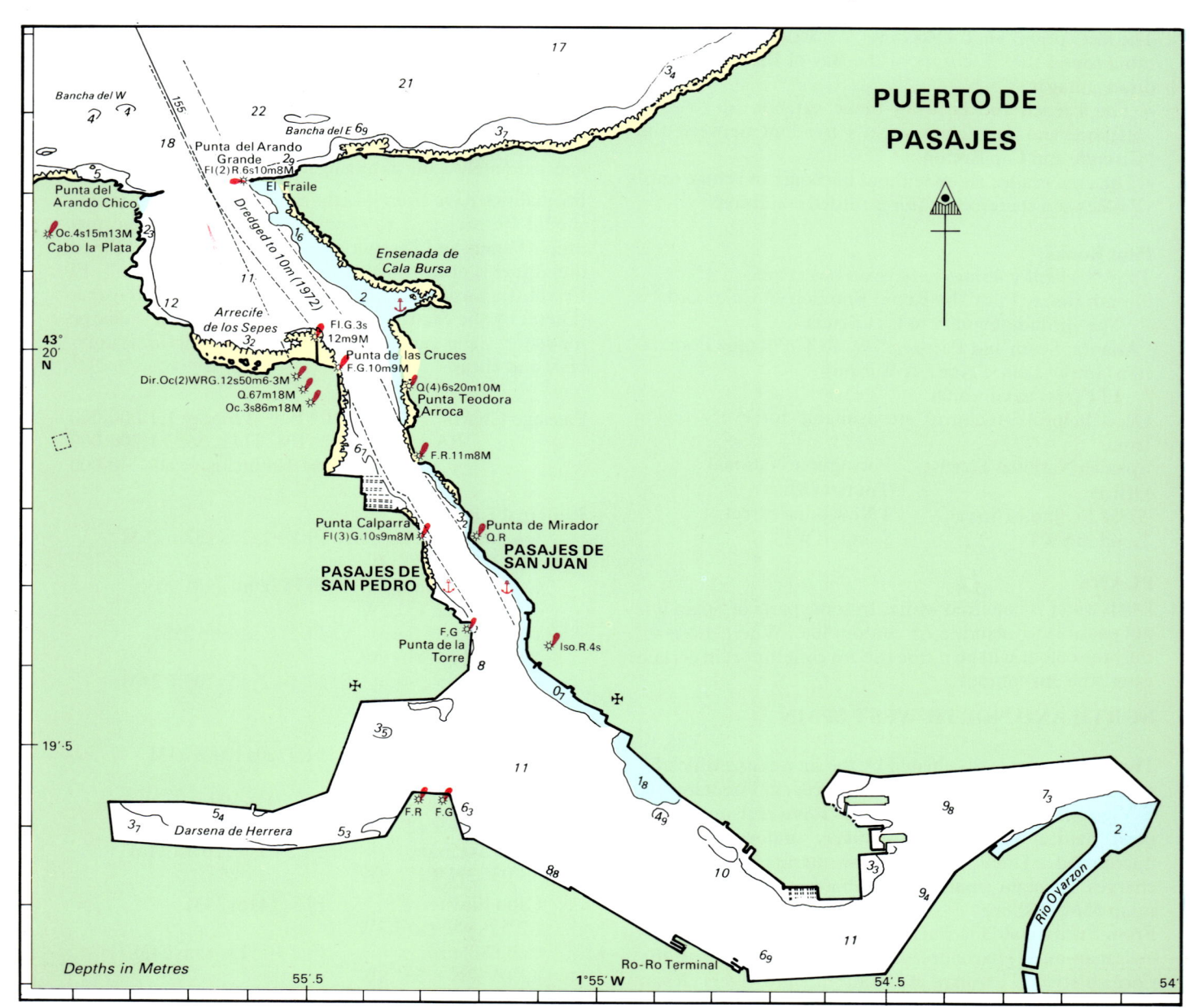

383   SPAIN AND PORTUGAL

SAN SEBASTIÁN   Charts BA 1181   S 19B

HW: Dover +4¾h

MHWS 4.2m   MHWN 3.0   MTL 2.3   MLWN 1.5   MLWS 0.5

An elegant city around a beautiful bay. Crowded.

Approach Identify Mte Urgull with large statue, Mte Igueldo Fl(2+1) 15s and Is de Santa Clara Fl 4s. In poor visibility take care not to confuse Mte Urgull and Is de Santa Clara. Avoid La Bancha shoal in heavy swell.

Entrance From a position ½M off, follow centre of passage between Mte Urgull and Is de Santa Clara on 158°. By night, intensified ldg lts FlR 1.5s and Iso R 6s on 158°.

Anchorage S of Is de Santa Clara in sand 4m, clear of local moorings, close in to avoid swell. Buoy anchor.

Berthing Very restricted space in yacht hbr Darsena de la Concha, E mole FG, W mole FR, with regular ferry.

PUERTO DE GUETARÍA   Charts BA 1171   S 303A

HW: Dover +4¾h

MHWS 4.1m   MHWN 3.1   MTL 2.3   MLWN 1.5   MLWS 0.5

A small fishing port with easy entrance.

Approach San Sebastián Fl(2+1) 15s is 9M to E. Conspic Lt Ho Zumaya Oc(1+3) 12s is 2½M to W.

Entrance Identify conspic Is de San Anton Fl(4) 15s and leave to stb. Outer hbr affected by strong gusts from NW over Is de San Anton.

Berthing Marina in outer hbr. Visitors also tie between mooring buoys.

Facilities YC.

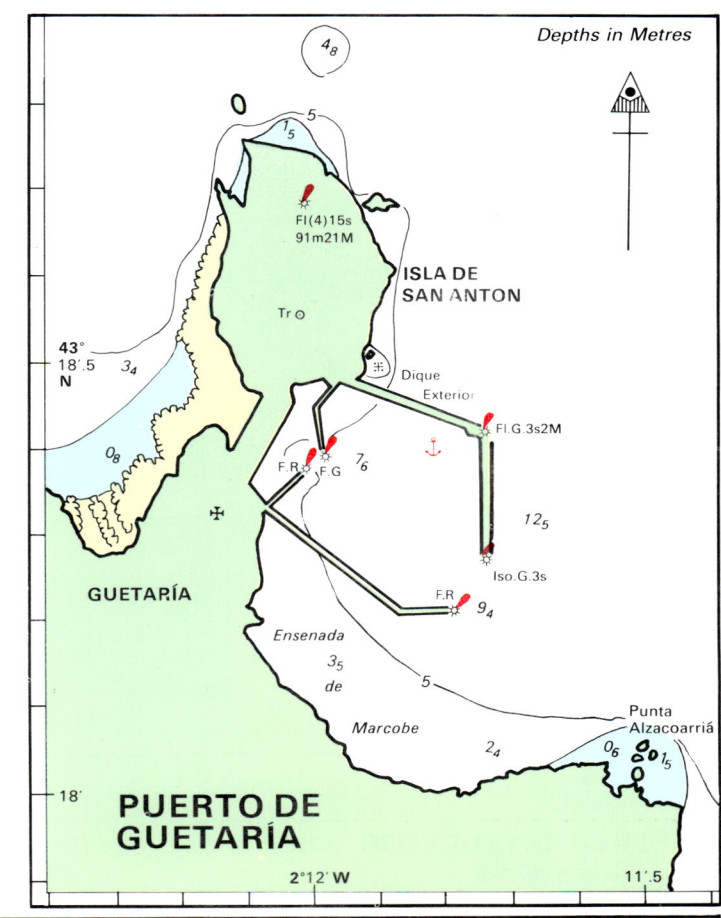

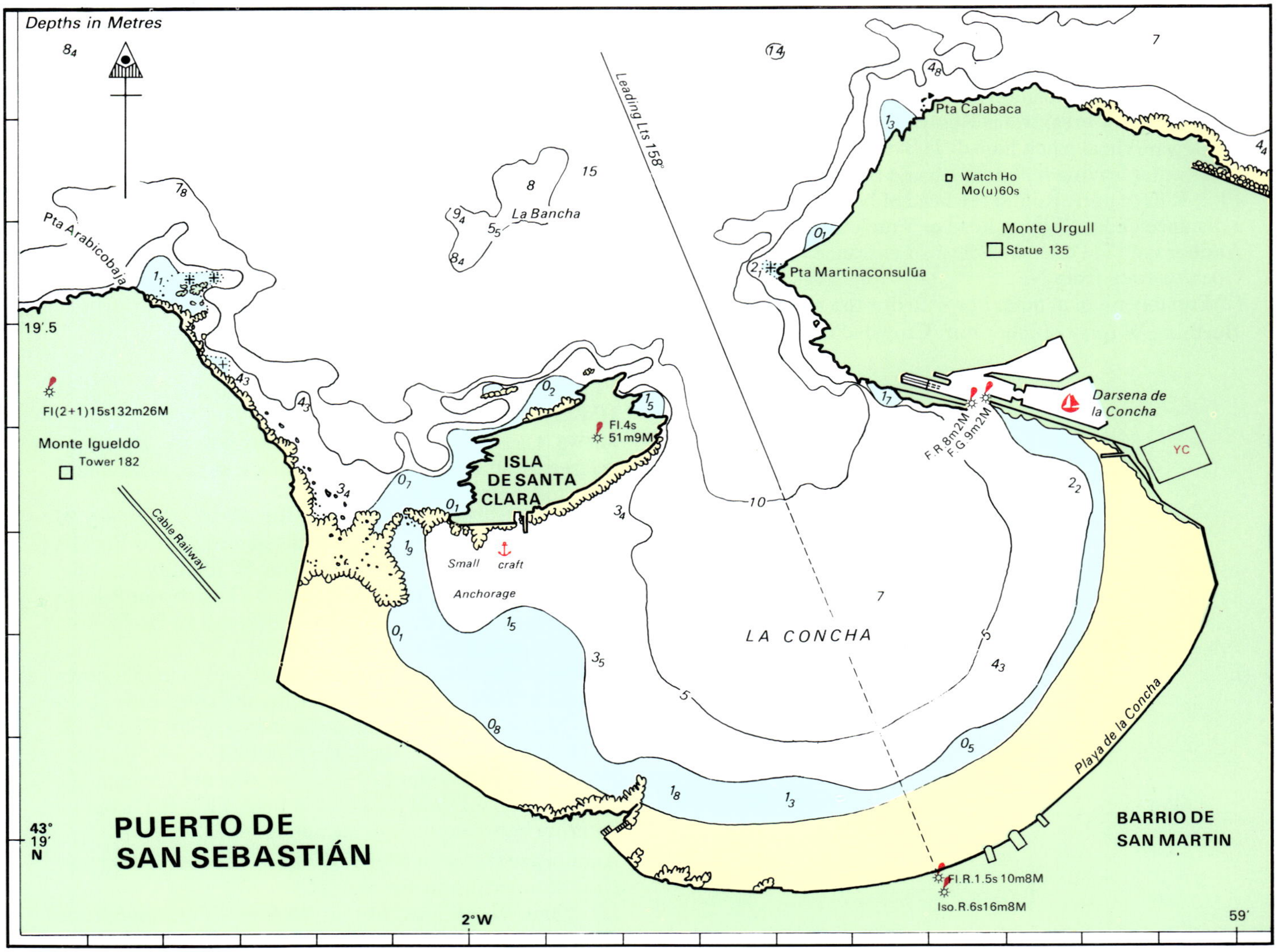

PUERTO DE LEQUEITIO Charts BA 1171 S 642A
HW: Dover +4¾h

MHWS 4.1m MHWN 3.1 MTL 2.3 MLWN 1.5 MLWS 0.5
A small picturesque fishing port and holiday resort.
Approach From W, identify Pta de Santa Catalina Fl(1+3) 20s.
Entrance From a position 2 ca N of Is de San Nicolas steer 212° on end of breakwater Rompeolas de Amandarri FlG 4s. Beware shoal patch Bajo de la Barra to port. Follow the breakwater leaving it 30m to stb and bn tr Dirque Aislado Fl(2) R 8s to port. Round the head of N mole of hbr FG at a distance of 3m, leaving head of S mole FR to port.
Anchorage (1) Outer hbr clear of entrance to inner hbr. Open to swell from N.
(2) Possibly room in inner hbr with line to a mooring buoy.
Berthing W quay of inner hbr. Crowded in season.

PUERTO DE ELANCHOVE Charts BA 1171 S 321A
HW: Dover +5h

MHWS 4.5m MHWN 3.3 MTL 2.4 MLWN 1.5 MLWS 0.4
A tiny hbr under a village perched on a cliff. Exposed to NE.
Approach The high vertical-sided Cabo Ogoño lies 3M to W.
Entrance Approach hbr on a course between 200° and 270°. The hbr wall and houses are readily visible by day but the entrance will not be seen until close in. Enter between breakwater heads slowly and take sharp turn to port into inner hbr.
Anchorage Anchor with line to a mooring buoy. Beware ledge, which dries at Springs, inside S breakwater.

PUERTO DE BERMEO Charts BA 1171 S 917
HW: Dover +5h

MHWS 4.5m MHWN 3.5 MTL 2.5 MLWN 1.5 MLWS 0.5
A busy fishing port with a well-protected hbr and easy entrance.
Approach Cabo Machichaco Fl 7s (Ro Bn MA 296.5 kHz 100M) is 2½M to NW.
Entrance Approach hbr between 150° and 270° and round the end of the new breakwater FlG 4.5s, leaving it 50m to std, into the Antepuerto. By night use white sector of Rosape Pta Lamiaren Oc(2) WR 6s for approach to breakwater lt. Enter Puerto Mayor between moleheads FG & FR. The Puerto Menor is to stb but shallow and crowded with fishing boats.
Anchorage N or S side of Antepuerto in 4 to 6m.
Berthing Alongside wall just inside entrance to Puerto Mayor to port or stb.

PUERTO DE BILBAO Charts BA 74 S 3941
HW: Dover +5h

MHWS 4.0m MHWN 3.1 MTL 2.3 MLWN 1.4 MLWS 0.5
A large commercial port which can be entered in all conditions for shelter.
Approach Bilbao continuous Air Bn. 43°19.5′N 2°58.5′W BLO 370kHz 70M. Cabo Machichaco Fl 7s (Ro Bn MA 296.5kHz 100M) is 15M to E. From W identify Pta Lucero and Dique de Pta Lucero head FlG 4s. From E identify Pta Galea with light-coloured cliffs and Lt Ho Fl(3)8s, and Dique de Pta Galea head Fl R 6s.
Entrance Between breakwater heads and steer SE down middle of outer hbr. Give inner breakwater heads clearance of 25m leaving Dique de Santurce to stb Fl(2)G 12s and Contramuelle de Algorta to port Fl(4) R 14s. By night follow the white sector 119° - 135° on root of Contramuelle de Algorta QWR and pass near R buoy Fl(3) R 11s before entering between inner breakwaters.
Anchorage (1) 100m N or NW of Las Arenas landing pier clear of moorings in 4m near YCs.
(2) 200m W of boat hbr at root of Contramuelle de Algorta.

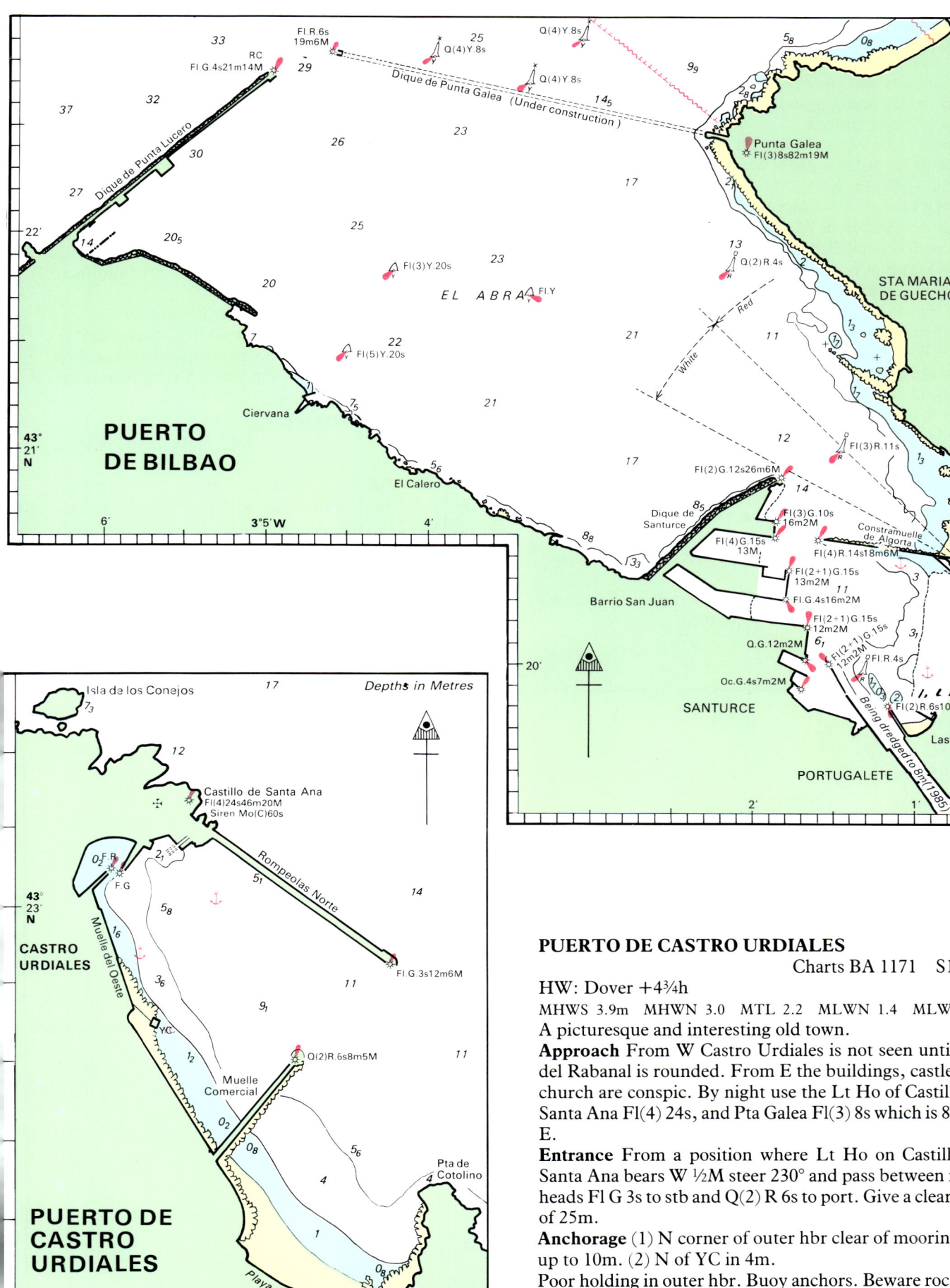

PUERTO DE CASTRO URDIALES

Charts BA 1171   S165A

HW: Dover +4¾h

MHWS 3.9m   MHWN 3.0   MTL 2.2   MLWN 1.4   MLWS 0.4

A picturesque and interesting old town.

Approach From W Castro Urdiales is not seen until Pta del Rabanal is rounded. From E the buildings, castle and church are conspic. By night use the Lt Ho of Castillo de Santa Ana Fl(4) 24s, and Pta Galea Fl(3) 8s which is 8M to E.

Entrance From a position where Lt Ho on Castillo de Santa Ana bears W ½M steer 230° and pass between mole heads Fl G 3s to stb and Q(2) R 6s to port. Give a clearance of 25m.

Anchorage (1) N corner of outer hbr clear of moorings in up to 10m. (2) N of YC in 4m.

Poor holding in outer hbr. Buoy anchors. Beware rocks in NW corner.

Berthing (1) Alongside moles of inner hbr much of which dries.

(2) Inside N breakwater Rompeolas Norte of outer hbr in calm weather.

SPAIN AND PORTUGAL

SANTANDER   Charts BA 1155   S 663A   660
HW: Dover +5h

MHWS 4.4m   MHWN 3.5   MTL 2.7   MLWN 1.9   MLWS 0.9

A pleasant city and large port on an estuary which can be entered by day or night under all conditions. Ebb stream can reach 3kn at Springs.

Approach Cabo Mayor conspic Lt Ho Fl(2) 10s (Ro Bn MY 296.5kHz 50M) is 2M NW of entrance to Santander. Cabo Ajo Oc(3) 16s is 7M NE.

Entrance Identify Is de Mouro Fl(1+2)21s.
(1) Pass between Is de Mouro and Peninsula de la Magdalena with conspic Palacio Real (now a University).
(2) Pass ¼M E of Is de Mouro.
From both entrances pass 1-2 ca S of La Cerda Lt Ho on Pta del Puerto Fl(1+4) 20s, then S of Is Horadada Fl G 6s into lighted buoyed channel. Ldg lts 260°, Front Iso 3s Rear Oc R 4s.

Anchorage 50-100m to SW or SE of YC nr Darsena de Molnedo in 3m clear of moorings and race start line. Convenient to town but subject to wash from ferries.

Berthing (1) At marina del Cantabrico 2M upriver. Follow buoyed channel leaving conspic oil terminal to port and No 15 G buoy FlG 4s to stb. Turn to stb round next E card buoy and approach hbr entrance on 241°. (Subject to change. Channel dredged to 3m but silting.) Sheltered. Long way from town.
(2) A YC berth in Darsena de Molnedo is sometimes available.

Facilities Good English-speaking chandler 'Yates & Cosas' near E end of Darsena de Molnedo.

PUERTO DE SAN VICENTE DE LA BARQUERA
43°24'N 4°23'W   Charts BA 1150   S 4021
HW: Dover +5h

MHWS 4.0m   MHWN 3.1   MTL 2.3   MLWN 1.5   MLWS 0.5

A pleasant town and ría in beautiful surroundings. Enter at or near HW by day in the absence of swell. No inner lights for night entry the first time.

Approach Pta Silla Oc 3.5s is ½M to W and Pta San Emeterio Fl 5s is 6M to W. Both are conspic. Steer to a position where hbr entrance bears SW ½M.

Entrance Enter on 225° halfway between breakwater to stb and training wall to port. Follow round the small cliffs of Pta de la Espina to stb at a distance of 25m and then steer for new fish quay on 237°.

Berthing (1) Alongside new fish quay if room.
(2) It may be possible to moor alongside a fishing boat on a buoy below the bridge. It is not recommended to anchor and take bow warps to the bridge piers. Strong current on Spring ebb.

PUERTO DE RIBADESELLA
43°28'N 5°04'W   Charts BA 1150   S 4031
HW: Dover +5h

MHWS 4.0m   MHWN 3.1   MTL 2.3   MLWN 1.5   MLWS 0.5

Small fishing port with a bar and good shelter inside. Enter HW−2 to HW. A beautiful mountainous setting.

Approach Conspic Lt Ho Pta de Somos Fl(1+2) 12s is ¾M to W. Conspic flat sloping cliffs of Pta del Caballo with white hermitage on top immediately to E of entrance. Steer to a position where Pta de Somos Lt Ho is due W and the concrete Lt Ho Fl(2) R 6s on the breakwater head at Pta del Caballo bears 140° ½M off.

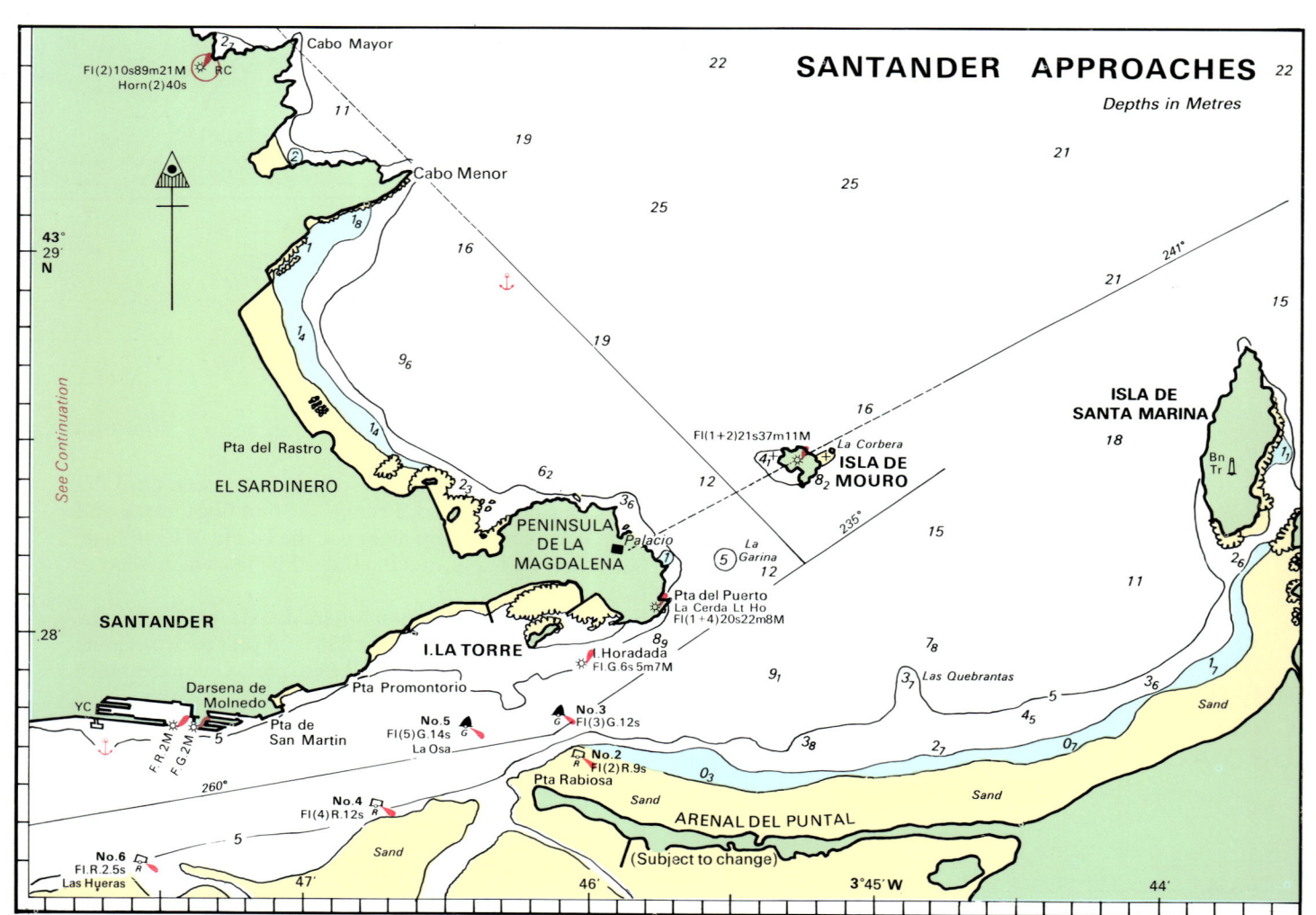

Entrance Approach the breakwater head on 140°, leave it 25m to port and follow the quay round at a distance of 25m for 4 ca into the hbr.

Berthing Alongside quay wall to port. Avoid pilings if solid wall is available. Berths near W end of bridge dry 1m.

PUERTO DE GIJON   Charts BA 1151   S 4042
HW: Dover +4¾h

MHWS 4.0m   MHWN 3.1   MTL 2.3   MLWN 1.5   MLWS 0.5

The huge new commercial hbr at Puerto de Musel affords shelter in all conditions. The old hbr with pontoon berths at Muelles Locales near the town has a bar which makes entry difficult in strong N winds.

Approach Gijon continuous Air Bn 43°33.3′N 6°01.37′W AVS 325kHz 60M. Cabo Peñas Fl(3) 15s (Ro Bn PS 301.1 kHz 50M) 9M to NW. Cabo de Torres Fl(2) 10s and the high exterior breakwater Dique Principe de Asturias of Puerto de Musel Fl G 3s are conspic.

Muelles Locales - Entrance From a position near end of Dique Principe de Asturias sail S for 1¼M and then leave rocky shoal Serrapio de Tierra with bn Fl G 1.3s to stb. Enter hbr between Dique de Liquerica Q(2) R 6s to port and Malecon de Fomento Fl G 3s to stb.

Berthing Municipal pontoon berths inside Dique de Liquerica dredged to 2m. Water, Electricity, YC, all facilities of a town, Diesel in Musel.

Puerto de Musel - Berthing Yachts are not encouraged but a berth may be found in or near the Darsena Pesquera. Few facilities. Diesel by hose to yachtsmen in SW corner of hbr.

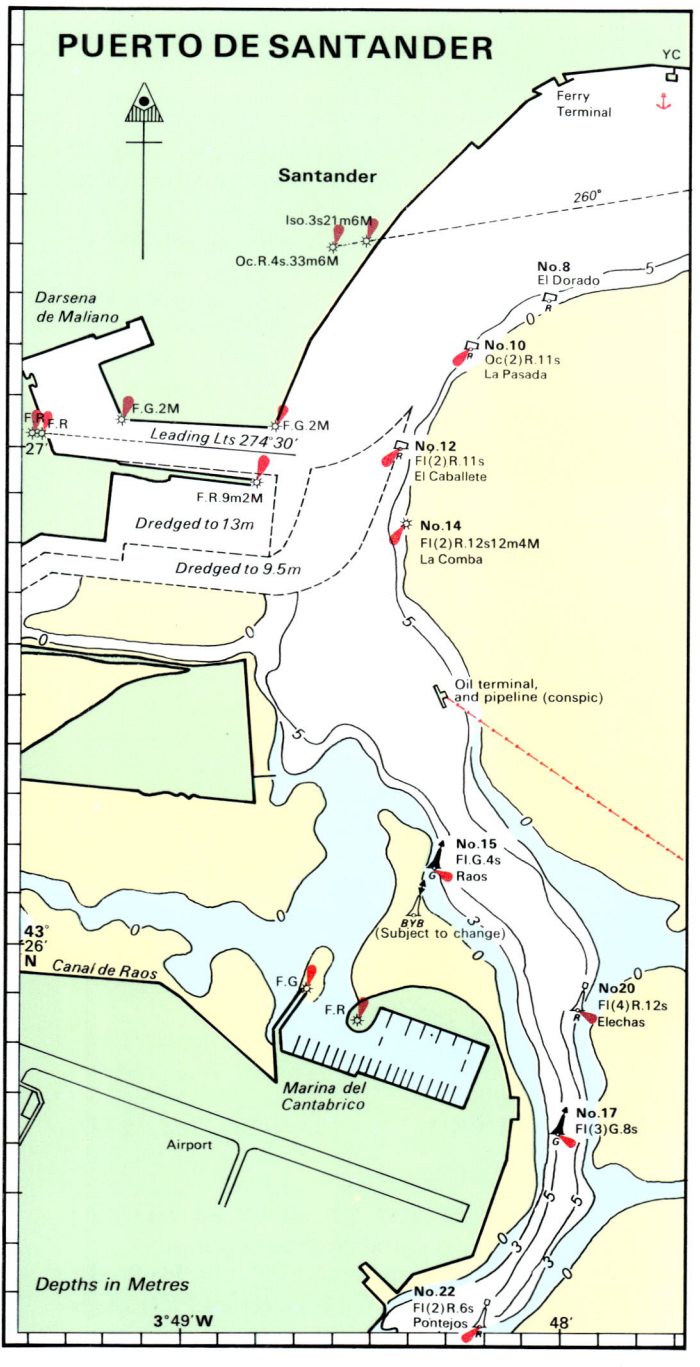

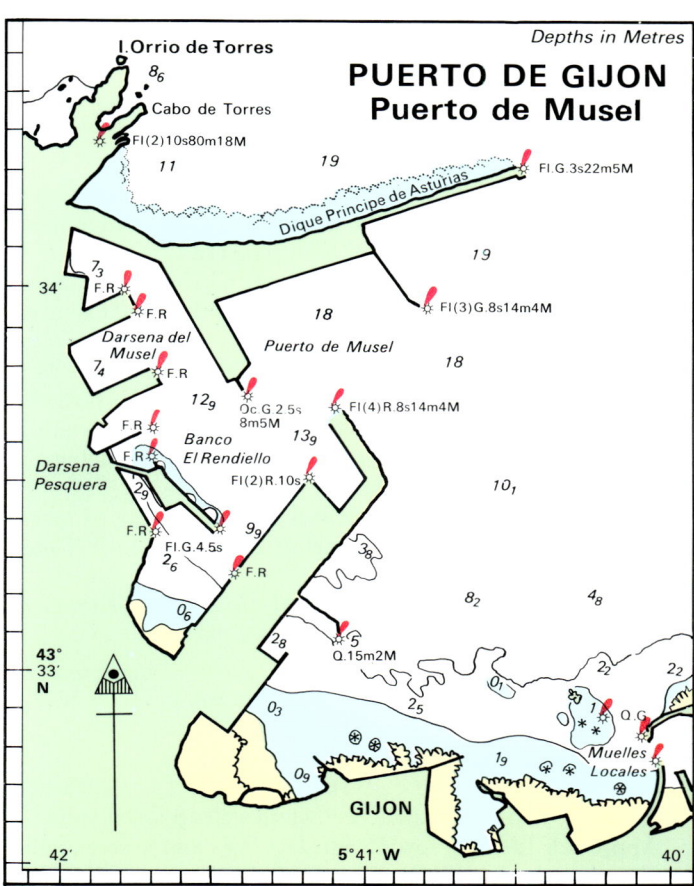

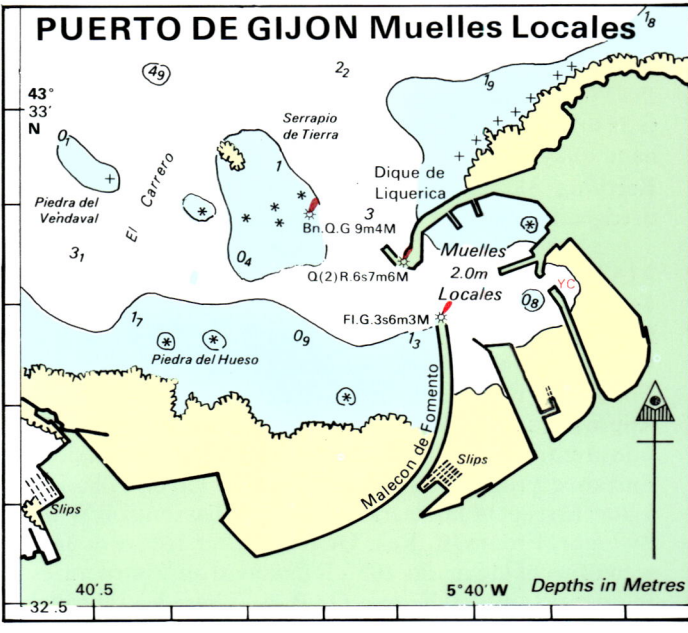

SPAIN AND PORTUGAL

RÍA DE AVILES   Charts BA 1133   S 9350
HW: Dover +4¾h

MHWS 4.0m   MHWN 3.1   MTL 2.3   MLWN 1.5   MLWS 0.6

A commercial hbr surrounded by heavy industry but with an easy approach and entrance, and a sheltered anchorage.

Approach Cabo Peñas Fl(3) 15s (Ro Bn PS 301.1kHz 50M) 5M to NE. Pta de Castillo Oc WR 4s at entrance to Aviles.

Entrance From a position 2 ca W of Lt Ho on Pta de Castillo enter lighted channel on 095°, in White sector, midway between cliffs to port and training wall and breakwater to stb.

Anchorage At Fondeadero del Monumento 1½M from entrance on port side in 4m, 100m SW of small café. Take dinghy to S end of quay (Muelle de Raices) on stb side of channel. Buses to Aviles.

PUERTO DE CUDILLERO   Chart S 934
43°34′N 6°09′W
HW: Dover +5h

MHWS 4.1m   MHWN 3.1   MTL 2.3   MLWN 1.5   MLWS 0.4

A tiny picturesque old hbr in a gap in cliffs. Huge new fishing hbr 2 ca to W. Enter on top half of tide.

Approach Identify Pta Rebollera Oc(4) 15s at E of entrance. The new high breakwater Nuevo Dique del Oeste is conspic by day.

Entrance From a position where Pta Rebollera Lt Ho bears 200° at ½M steer 200° and leave Lt Ho to port, E breakwater FG to stb. For old hbr turn hard to port round breakwater FR. For new hbr turn hard to stb through narrow entrance behind Is Osa.

Anchorage SE corner of new fishing hbr clear of local yacht moorings. Buoy anchor. Excellent shelter. Take dinghy or walk to old hbr.

Berthing Alongside E wall of old hbr in 2m, uneven rocky bottom.

PUERTO DE LUARCA   Charts BA 1133   S 731A
43°33′N 6°32′W
HW: Dover +5¼h

MHWS 3.9m   MHWN 3.0   MTL 2.2   MLWN 1.5   MLWS 0.5

A fishing port and attractive town in a steep-sided valley.

Approach Identify low Lt Ho Oc(3) 8s and conspic tall church tr on Pta Blanca 2 ca E of hbr entrance, and Pta Mujeres 4 ca NNW of hbr. By night car headlights around Lt Ho may confuse.

Entrance From a position 3ca N of Pta Mujeres steer on end of port-hand breakwater 170°. By night ldg lts both FG 170°. Enter between breakwaters Fl(2) R 6s to port, Fl G 3s to stb. Turn to port and follow breakwater and port-hand quay 25m off leaving head of jetty Fl G to stb.

Berthing Alongside quay in inner hbr which has been dredged to 2m. New busy fishing quay to stb.

RÍA DE RIBADEO   Charts BA 1122   S 550A
43°34′N 7°02′W
HW: Dover +5h

MHWS 4.0m   MHWN 3.1   MTL 2.3   MLWN 1.5   MLWS 0.5

The first of the Rías of Galicia, in a lovely setting.

Approach Is Pancha Lt Ho Fl(3+1) 20s is conspic on W side of entrance to Ría. Pta de la Cruz Fl(2) 7s is on E side.

Entrance From a position ½M N of Lt Ho on Is Pancha follow first set of ldg marks on 140°, R diamond on W trs. By night, Front QR, Rear Oc R 4s. After 1M, turn on to second set of ldg marks 205°, R diamond on W structures. By night, front VQR, rear Oc R 2s. These lead through

the new road bridge (air ht 30m), leaving two R buoys to port. Leave Pta de la Cueva Fl(3) G 9s close to stb and steer for the quay of Muelle de Mirasol FG.

Berthing (1) Alongside the outer side of Muelle de Mirasol. Beware strong Spring ebb.
(2) Inner side of NE extension of this quay, probably outside a fishing boat. First position inside is reserved for pilot boat.

Anchorage (1) Figueras in 4m, 250m W of shipyard.
(2) 300m W of Pta Castropol in 4m.

RÍA DE VIVERO   Charts BA 1122   S 4082
HW: Dover +5h

MHWS 3.9m   MHWN 3.0   MTL 2.2   MLWN 1.4   MLWS 0.4

A beautiful ría with an easy entrance.

Approach Pta de la Estaca de Bares Fl(2) 7.5s (Ro Bn BA 301.1kHz 100M) is 6M to NW. Is Coelleira Fl(4) 24s is 3M to NW. Conspic high headland Mte Faro Juances on E side of Ría.

Entrance Leave Pta de Faro Fl(2) R 14s to port, Pta Socastro Fl G 7s to stb and steer towards Cillero breakwater head FR, 2M to S.

Anchorage (1) S of Cillero quay clear of fishing boats.
(2) Between Insua d'Area and Congreiras Rock.
(3) Off Playa de Abrela in up to 10m. Open to NE.
(4) Ensenada de San Juan in up to 8m.

Berthing (1) Alongside at Cillero temporarily.
(2) At Vivero alongside quay with bow 10m below bridge. Go up the Rio at HW between two training walls. Strong ebb.

RÍA DEL BARQUERO   Charts BA 1122   S 18A
43°46′N 7°39′W
HW: Dover +5h

MHWS 4.1m   MHWN 2.9   MTL 2.2   MLWN 1.4   MLWS 0.3

A beautiful ría with easy entrance and steep-to sides.

Approach Pta de la Estaca de Bares Fl(2) 7.5s (Ro Bn BA 301.1kHz 100M) is 2M to NW. Is Coelleira Fl(4) 24s is ½M to E.

Entrance By night identify position of Pta del Castro Q(2) R 6s on port hand and Pta de la Barra FlG 3s on stb.
Anchorage (1) Puerto de Bares in 6m. Open to NE.
(2) Is Vilela in 5m. Open to NE.
(3) Playa Campelo in 6m. Open to NE.
(4) Pta del Castro in 5m NNE of Lt Ho. Open to W and NW.
(5) Playa Arenal de Valle in 5m. Open to W-NW-N.
(6) Río Sor in 3m. Enter Río near HW from Pta de Barra and follow stb bank to small cove beyond Puerto de El Barquero. Limited swinging room.
(7) Dry out alongside quay at Puerto de El Barquero.

RÍA AND ENSENADA DE SANTA MARTA with PUERTO DE CARIÑO

43°44′N 7°51′W   Charts BA 1122   S 4084
HW: Dover +5½h
MHWS 3.7m MHWN 2.9 MTL 2.1 MLWN 1.3 MLWS 0.4
A large bay and ría with wide entrance.
Approach Pta de la Estaca de Bares Fl(2) 7.5s (Ro Bn BA 301.1kHz 100M) on E side, Cabo Ortegal Oc 8s on W side. Conspic line of sharp-pointed rocks Los Aguillones off Cabo Ortegal.

Anchorage (1) Puerto de Cariño on W side of bay behind extended breakwater Fl G 2s 3M in 6m.
(2) Ensenada de Espasante in 6m in SE of bay. Open to NW and W.
(3) In Ría de Santa Marta at Santa Marta de Ortiguera. The river has a bar and strong currents. Engage a pilot at Cariño.

RÍA DE CEDEIRA   Charts BA 1122   S 930
HW: Dover +4½h
MHWS 3.8m MHWN 2.8 MTL 2.1 MLWN 1.4 MLWS 0.4
Attractive ría with easy access and a small fishing port.
Approach Conspic Lt Ho Pta Candelaria Fl(3+1) 24s is 3M to NNE. From N leave Pta Candelaria to port and keep ¼M offshore until ria opens up. From SW steer 055° towards Pta Candelaria and when 2 miles from this headland identify to stb Pta Chirlateira and its offlying rocky shoals. Steer towards Pta Lameda on 070° until the lt on Pta Promontorio Oc(1+3) 16s is just clear of Pta del Sarridal (Pta del Castillo) on 150°.
Entrance Pass close to Pta del Castillo to avoid the rocky shoal Piedras de Media Mar to stb in centre of ria, and round the breakwater Fl(4) R 13s to port.
Anchorage (1) E of jetty in 4m, clear of fishing boats. Supplies at Cadeira ½M.
(2) S of Pta Xian. Fair weather daytime only.

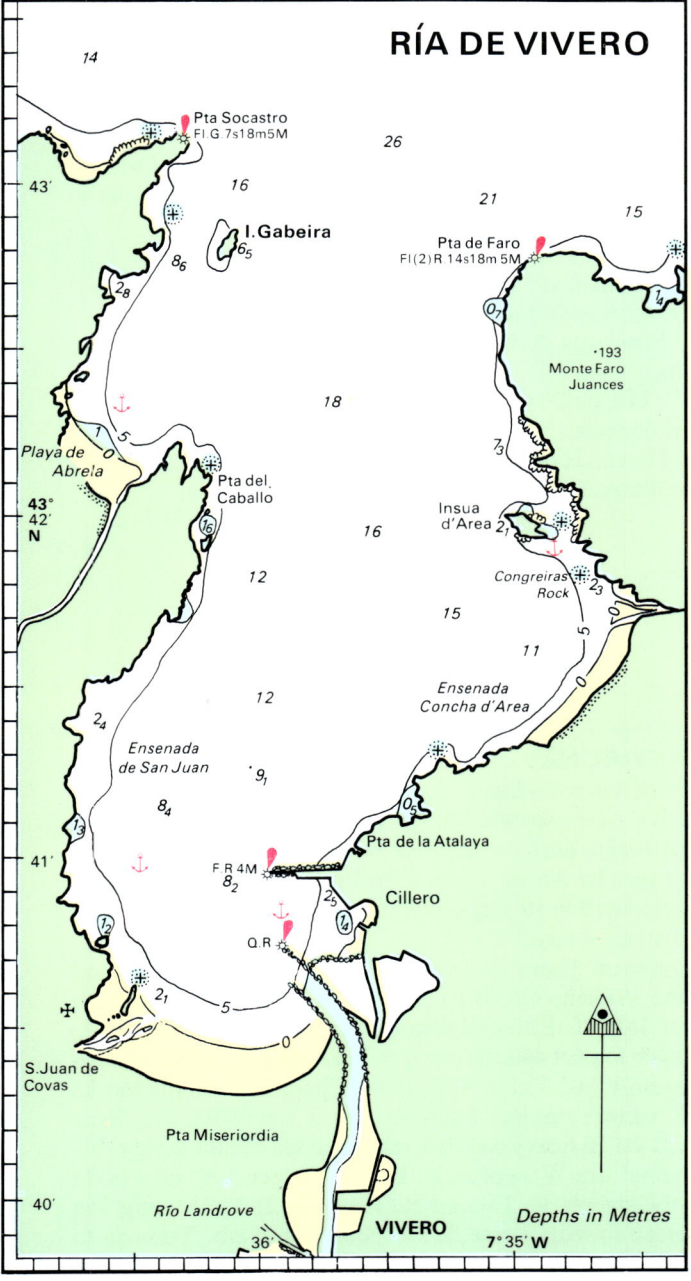

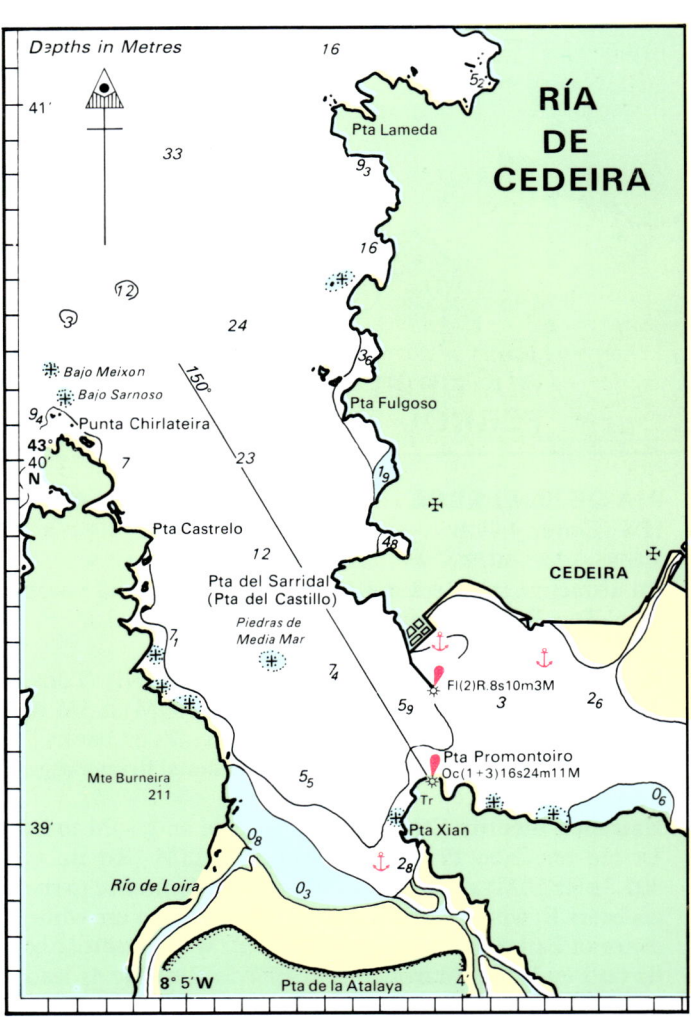

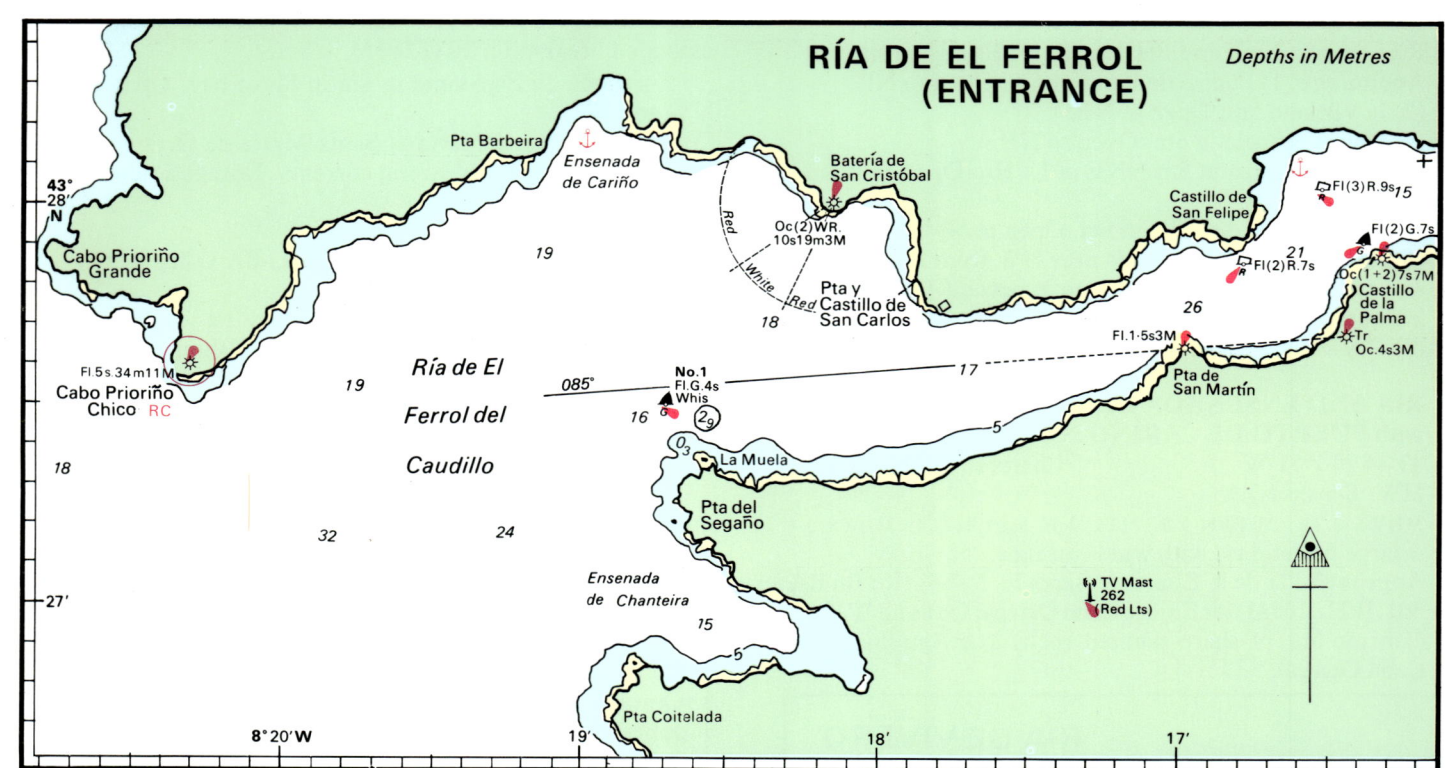

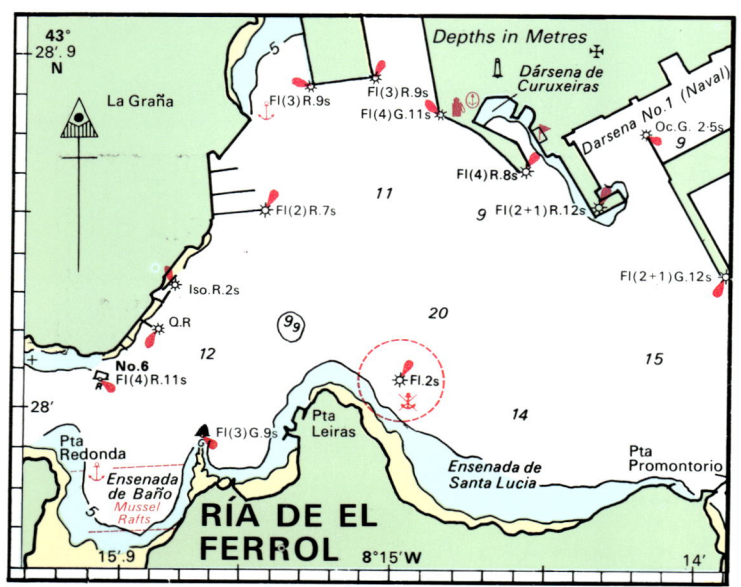

Berthing Alongside NE wall of commercial dock Darsena de Curuxeiras in 2m. Leave head of jetty Fl(4) R 8s to port. Wash from ferry boats.

Anchorages Subject to naval toleration.
(1) Ensenada de Malata NE of La Graña in 4m. Keep clear of new jetty and hbr on E side of Ensenada.
(2) Ensenada de Baño, E of Pta Redonda clear of mussel rafts.
(3) E of Castillo de San Felipe inside R can buoy No 4 clear of moorings.
(4) Ensenada de Cariño, 1M NE of C Prioriño Chico.
Facilities Repairs and piped diesel at El Ferrol.

RÍA DE EL FERROL Charts BA 1115   S 412A
HW: Dover +4½h
MHWS 3.7m   MHWN 2.9   MTL 2.1   MLWN 1.3   MLWS 0.6
An attractive steep-sided ría with a large port and naval base. Two Ro Bns useful in fog.

Approach Cabo Prior Fl(1+2) 15s is 6M to NNE. Torre de Hercules Fl(4) 20s (Ro Bn C 305.7kHz 30M) is 5M to SW. From N in rough weather the sea breaks on banks S of Cabo Prior up to 4M off. Beware occasional firing range near Cabo Prior.
Entrance Identify Cabo Prioriño Grande and, ½M to S, Lt Ho on Cabo Prioriño Chico Fl 5s 11M (Ro Bn C 305.7kHz 50M) and leave 2ca to port. The entrance to the ría bears E, with Pta del Segaño to stb. By night use white sector of Batería de San Cristobal Oc(2) WR 10s until ldg lts on Pta de San Martin, Front Fl 1.5s Rear Oc 4s lead into ría and lighted buoyed channel.

LA CORUÑA Charts BA 1114   S 412A   4126
HW: Dover +4½h
MHWS 3.6m   MHWN 2.8   MTL 2.1   MLWN 1.3   MLWS 0.5
The major port on the NW coast of Spain with an easy entrance by day or night. Two Ro Bns useful in fog. Subject to swell in strong winds from N and NW. Picturesque old areas of city.
Approach From N leave Cabo Prior Fl(1+2) 15s and Cabo Prioriño Chico Fl 5s (Ro Bn C 305.7kHz 50M) to port 1M off. Enter in mid-ría on S leaving Pta del Seijo Blanco to port and the conspic Torre de Hercules Fl(4) 20s (Ro Bn L 305.7kHz 30M) to stb. Steer 182° on ldg marks (W sector) on Pta Fiaiteira Front Iso WRG 2s, Rear Oc R 4s. In heavy weather when the sea breaks across this channel use W approach. From W steer 108° on Pta de Mera ldg marks Front FR, Rear Oc(2) 10s leaving Pta Herminio with Torre de Hercules 2ca to stb. Turn on to ldg marks on Pta Fiaiteira 182°.

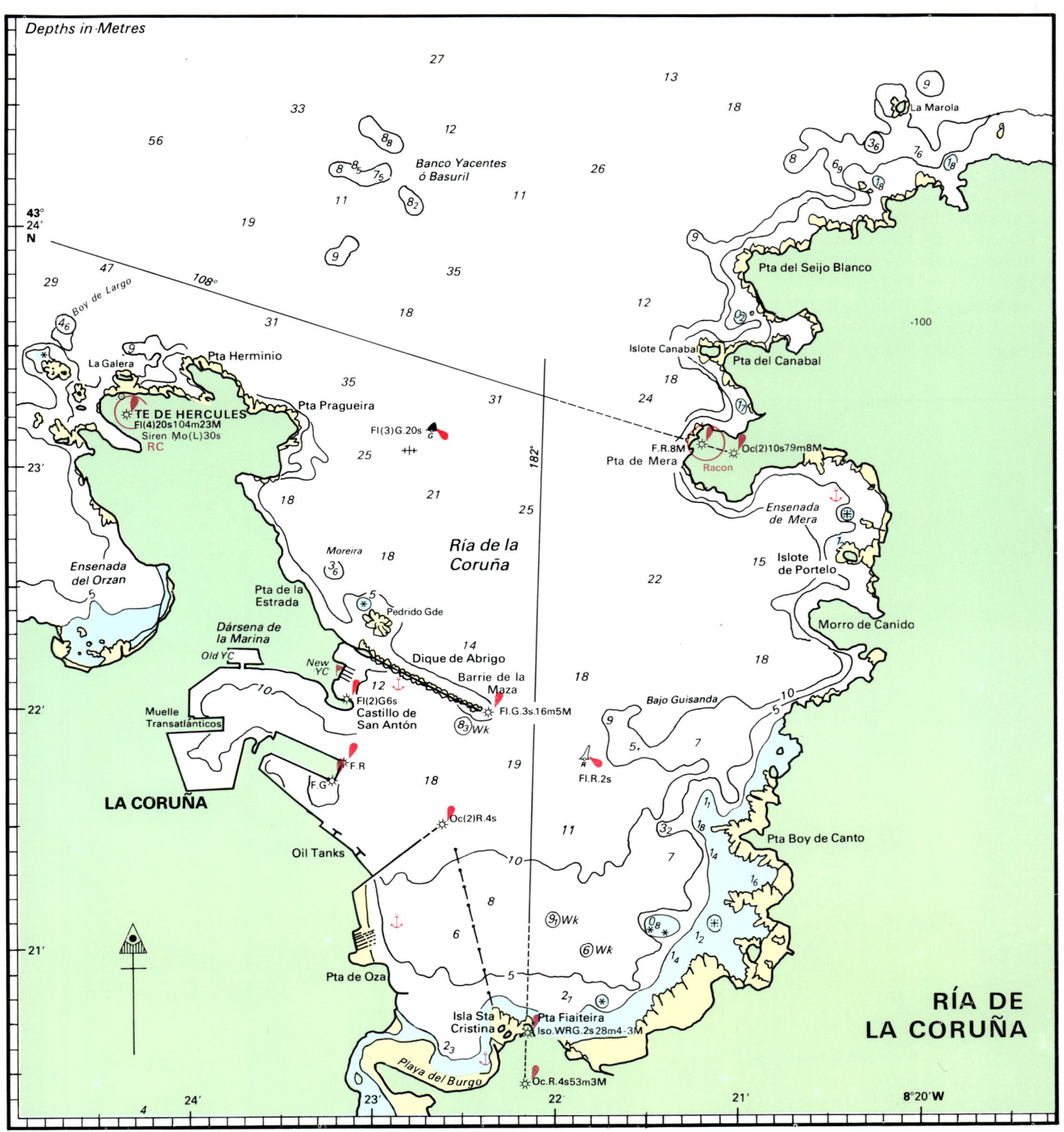

Entrance Round end of breakwater Dique de Abrigo Fl G 3s to stb and follow SW side of mole towards new YC 1 ca N of Castillo de San Anton Fl(2) G 6s.

Anchorage (1) E of Castillo de San Anton in 10m mud clear of YC moorings and unlighted wave breaker.
(2) In small bay NW of Pta de Oza in 6m sand.
(3) W of Is de Santa Cristina clear of slip and rocks.
(4) Ensenada de Mera, clear of rock off head of jetty. Sheltered N to SE.

Berthing (1) A pontoon berth may be available. Apply to new YC.
(2) Alongside W wall of Darsena de la Marina near old YC. Wall projects at LW. Wash from fishing boats.

Facilities Market, shops, restaurants. Piped diesel at new YC jetty – beware 1m at LWS. All repairs – apply to helpful HLR or YC. International airport at Santiago de Compostela, 1hr by 'bus.

Ría de Betanzos & Ría de Ares next page

RIA DE BETANZOS & RIA DE ARES   Charts BA 1114   S412A

HW Dover +4½h
MHWS 3.6m   MHWN 2.8   MTL 2.0   MLWN 1.3   MLWS 0.4

Two quiet attractive rías with easy entrance within short distance of El Ferrol and La Coruña.

Approach Cabo Prioriño Chico Fl 5s (Ro Bn C 305.7kHz 50M). Torre de Hercules Fl(4) 20s (Ro Bn L 305.7kHz 30M).

Entrance Identify Pta Coitelada to port and Pta del Seijo Blanco to stb. Pass between them, clearing coast by 2ca. Leave Is de la Miranda to port and Pta de San Amede to stb.

Anchorage (1) Fontán, Ría de Betanzos. Inside extended breakwater Fl(3) G 9s, clear of fishing boats. Holiday resort of Sada ¾M to S.

(2) Ensenada de Ares in 2-3m off landing stage on W shore.

(3) Ensenada de Redes, S of village near small headland in 2m clear of mussel rafts.

(4) Ensenada de Cirno, clear of mussel rafts.

RIA DE CORME & LAGE   Charts BA 1113   S 9280

HW: Dover +5¼h
MHWS 3.2m   MHWN 2.4   MTL 1.8   MLWN 1.1   MLWS 0.3

Two small fishing villages. Choose anchorage according to wind.

Approach From N identify Pta del Roncudo Fl 6s and pass 1M offshore before turning S to Pta de Lage Fl(1+4) 14s. From SW keep 1M off coast NE of Cabo Villano Fl(2) 15s and round Pta Lage between ½M and 1M off.

393 SPAIN AND PORTUGAL

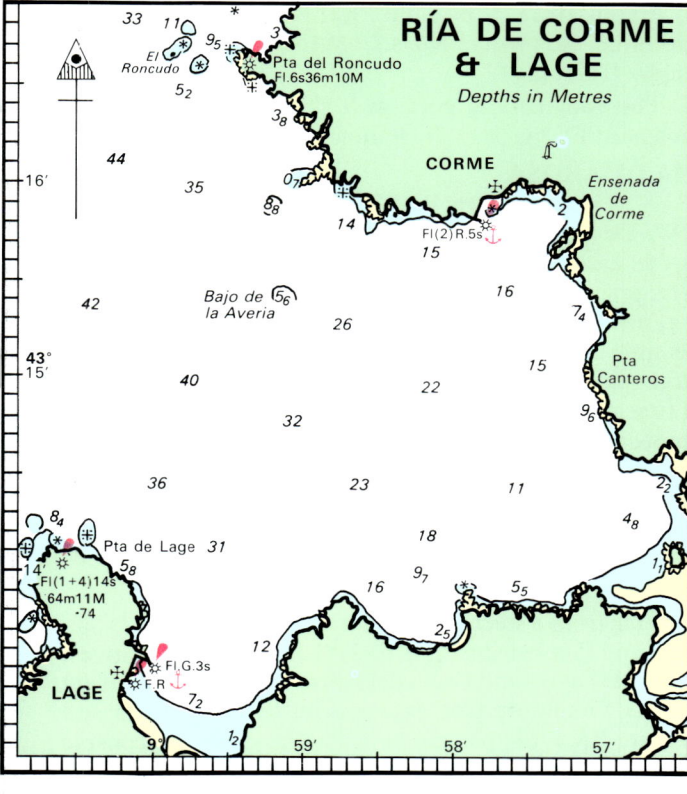

Entrance Avoid Bajo de la Averia shoal in heavy weather. From a position 1M N of Pta de Lage steer E until Corme mole Fl(2) R 5s bears less than 045°.

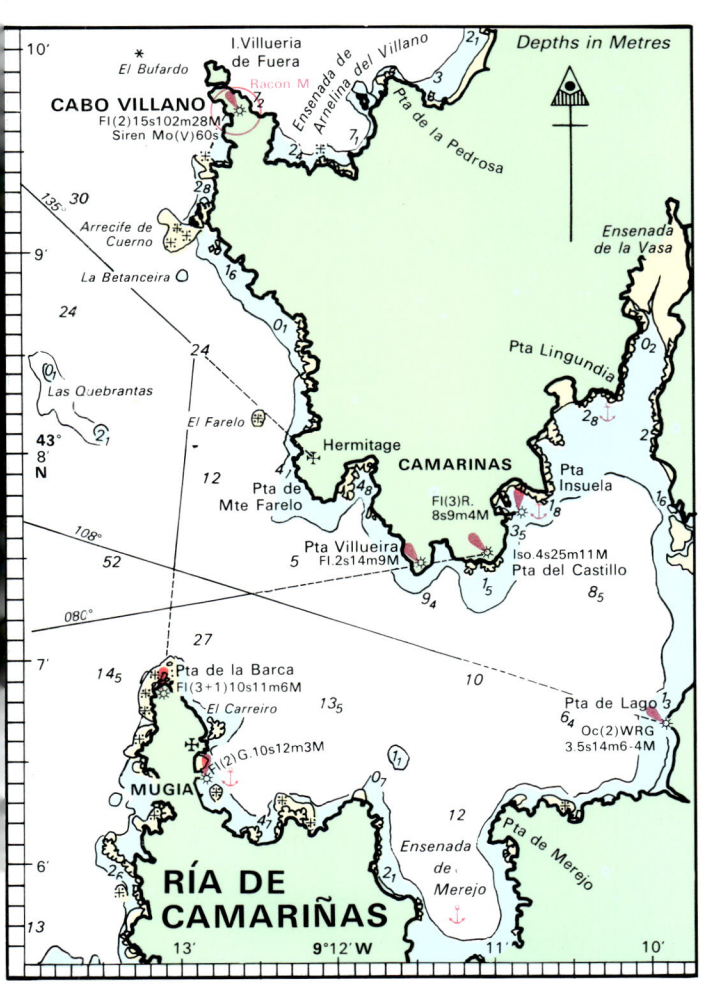

Anchorages (1) CORME. 100-200m NE-E-SE of molehead 12-14m sand clear of moorings and reefs inshore marked by bn. Exposed SW-W and to NW swell.
(2) LAGE. S end of new mole FlG 3s clear of hbr entrance in 6-8m sand.

RIA DE CAMARIÑAS   Charts BA 1113   S 9272
HW: Dover +4½h
MHWS 3.3m   MHWN 2.5   MTL 1.9   MLWN 1.2   MLWS 0.4
An attractive ria with two villages. Entry by day or night in reasonable visibility. Note Traffic Separation Scheme Cabo Villano to Cabo Finisterre.

Approach Cabo Villano conspic Lt Ho Fl(2) 15s (Ro Bn VI 310.3kHz 100M Racon M) is 2M N of ría. Pass outside or inside El Bufardo, rock awash 3ca off Cabo Villano.

Entrance By day (1) From NE round Cabo Villano and steer SW to avoid Las Quebrantas shoal until white hermitage on Mte Farelo bears E and the middle of the ría entrance is open on 108°, the line of Pta de Lago ldg marks, two concrete trs in line but difficult to see.
(2) From NE pass inshore of Las Quebrantos by heading 135° towards hermitage on Mte Farelo until ¾M from shore. Then steer for Pta de la Barca until Pta de Lago ldg marks come in line.
(3) From SW pass ½M NW of Pta de la Barca to join Pta de Lago ldg line.
By night (1) From NE pass 1½M NW of Cabo Villano to clear isolated rock El Bufardo, then steer not less than 200° until the white sector of Pta de Lago light is visible on 108°. If Pta de Lago cannot be seen continue on 200° until the more powerful ldg lts of Pta Villueira Fl 2s and Pta del Castillo Iso 4s come into line on 080°. Follow this line until Pta de Lago ldg lts are seen.
(2) From SW steer to pass ½M NW of Pta de la Barca Fl(3+1) 10s. Follow ldg lts on Pta Villueira and Pta Castillo, and Pta de Lago.

Anchorage (1) CAMARIÑAS. From Pta de Lago ldg line steer for Camariñas molehead Fl(3) R 8s when it bears 340°. Anchor off mole in 3-4m clear of hbr entrance and avoid reef from Pta Insuela 1ca to E.
(2) Further up ría near Pta Lingundia.
(3) Ensenada de Merejo. Exposed to N & NW.
(4) MUGIA. From Pta de Lago ldg line steer for Mugia molehead Fl(2) G 10s when it bears 220°. Anchor in 3-4m S of end of new breakwater. Beware two rocks off beach to S.

RIA DE CORCUBÍON   Charts BA 3764   S 9271
HW: Dover +4½h
MHWS 3.4m   MHWN 2.6   MTL 1.9   MLWN 1.2   MLWS 0.3
A small ría 5M to NE of Cabo Finisterre. Exposed to S.

Approach From N keep 2M off shore to avoid shallow patch La Carraca NW of conspic rocky islet Centola de Finisterre and leave Cabo Finisterre Fl 5s ½M to port. Steer 060° for mouth of ría leaving Carrumeiro Chico Q(2) 6s to stb and Cabo Cée Fl(4) 8s to port. From S give Pta Insua FWR and Oc(1+2) WR 20s an offing of 5M to clear extensive rocky shoal Bajo de los Meixidos. Leave Islote Lobeira Grande Fl(3) 15s to stb and steer between Carrumeiro Chico and Cabo Cée.

Anchorage (1) Off quay at Corcubíon, to N or SE.
(2) In NE corner of ría, off new quay. Both (1) & (2) give variable holding in rock and sand.
(3) Ensenada del Sardiñeiro. Good shelter from W-N-E.
(4) Puerto de Finisterre (2M to NE of Cabo Finisterre) 100m NE of molehead FlR 2s 13m 4M. (QR 8m 1M on inner elbow of mole.) Little room behind mole.

SPAIN AND PORTUGAL

RIA DE MUROS
Charts BA 1756 S 9264

HW: Dover +4½h

MHWS 3.5m MHWN 2.7 MTL 2.0 MLWN 1.3 MLWS 0.4

A pleasant ría with picturesque old fishing port of Muros.

Approach From N keep 5M off Pta Insua FWR and Oc(1+2) WR 20s to avoid extensive rocky shoal Bajo de los Meixodos and visible group of rocks Los Bruyos 3M to W of Pta Queixal Fl(2+1) 12s. The inshore passage through the Canal de los Meixodos may be taken in good weather with chart BA 1756. Leave Pta Carreiro and Pta Queixal ¾M to N to clear rocky islet Leixoes. From S give Cabo Corrubedo Fl(3+2) R 20s and Fl(3) R 20s (sectored lt) an offing of 3M until it bears E, and then steer 020° on Pta Queixal and Mte Louro behind it, to clear two groups of rocks, Banco las Basoñas and La Baya. Leave Leixoes 1M to N and turn into ría.

Entrance For town of Muros, steer NE into ría until Cabo Reburdiño Lt Ho Fl(2) R 6s comes into view and leave it 1 ca to port.

Anchorage (1) Muros, outside hbr, NW of molehead Fl(4) R 13s, clear of mussel rafts. Pontoon for small boats outside N mole. Exposed to NE.

(2) Ensenada de Bornalle, clear of rocks. Sheltered from NE.

(3) Ensenada de Esteiro for daytime stop in good weather.

(4) Freijo, 100m N of mole Fl(2) R 5s. From here the interesting old town of Noya 2½M to E can be reached by dinghy HW±1h.

(5) Portosin, fishing port on S shore of ría. Extended molehead Fl(2)G 5s. New E mole FR.

RIA DE AROSA
Charts BA 1768 1757 S 9261 9262 9263

HW: Dover +4¼h

MHWS 3.6m MHWN 2.8 MTL 2.1 MLWN 1.4 MLWS 0.5

A large ría with buoyed channels, sheltered waters for sailing, and a variety of attractive anchorages. Night entry possible into Villagarcia and Puebla del Caraminal. With large-scale chart 1768 pilotage is much easier than would at first appear.

Approach The Canal Principal between Is Salvora and Pombieriño is the easiest and safest approach. From N pass 5M offshore from Cabo Corrubedo Fl(3+2) R 20s and Fl(3) R 20s (sectored lt) to clear rocky shoal patch Bajos de Corrubedo. Leave Is Salvora Lt Ho Fl(3+1) 20s and Fl(3) 20s (sectored) to N at a distance of 1M.

Coming from S steer to a position mid-way between Is Salvora and Pombeiriño bn tr Fl(2) G 12s. Two alternatives, Canal de Sagres and Canal del Norte to the N of Is Salvora and Is Vionta are best explored on leaving the ría and require BA 1768, passing N of Piedras del Sargo conspic bn tr QG.

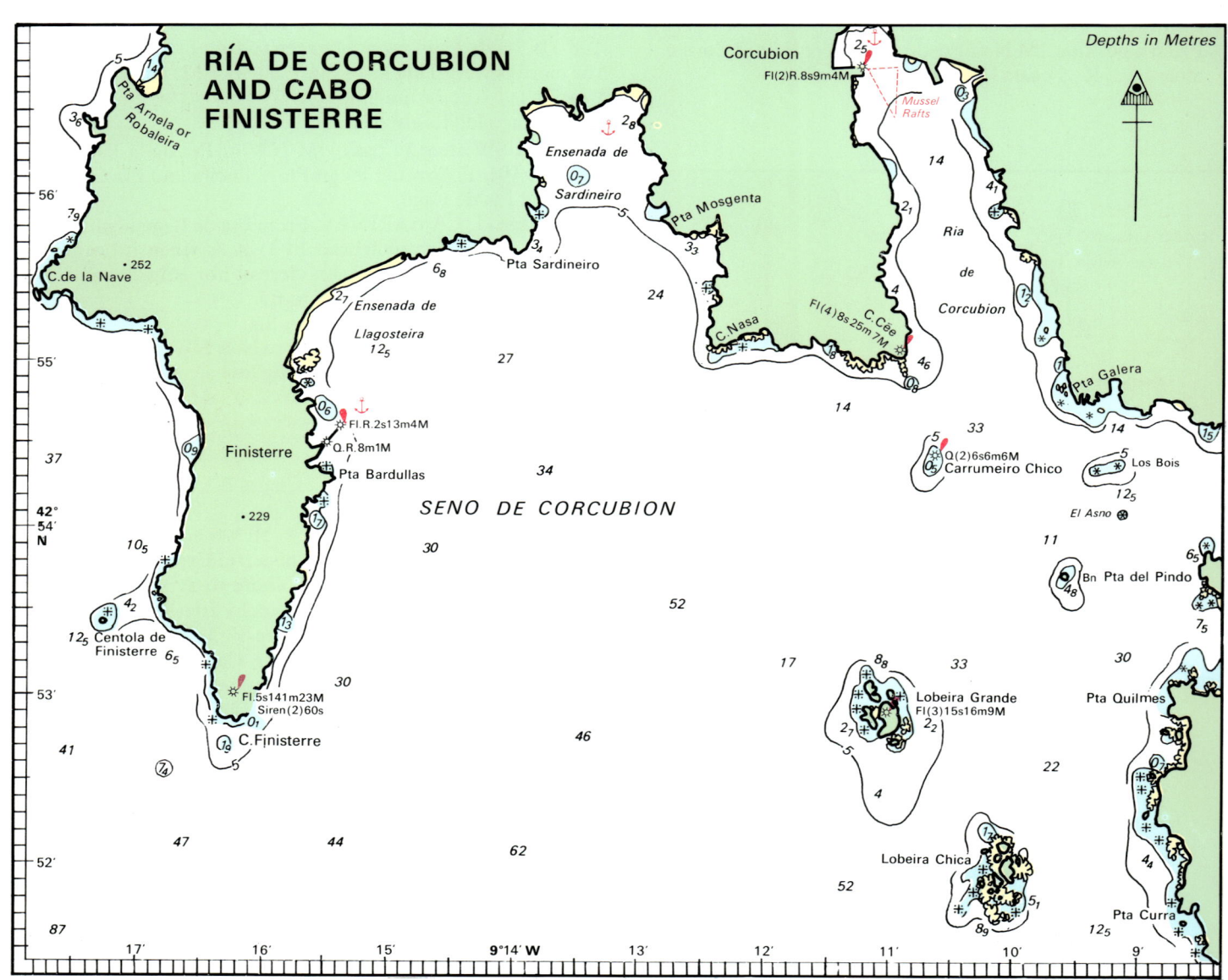

395 SPAIN AND PORTUGAL

Entrance Steer for Is Rua Lt Ho Fl(2+1) WR 10s on conspic rocky islet and leave to port, passing between Is Rua and Bajo Piedra Seca W tr Fl(3) G 15s. Continue on 030° for 2M to clear bank Sinal del Maño with R unlit buoy.

Anchorage (1) Puerto de Puebla del Caramiñal. Leave bn tr Sinal de Ostreira Fl(3) R 15s 1ca to port and approach new mole at Caramiñal Fl(2) WR 6s in white sector. Anchor inside mole clear of fishing boats in 4-5m, or 100m S of old jetty. Good shelter.
(2) Cabo Cruz, to E of rocky peninsula in centre of bay, or N of new hr on W side of peninsula, exposed to N.
(3) Is de Arosa, in bay N of village of San Julian.
(4) Is de Arosa, SW of Pta Caballo Fl(4) 8s inshore of mussel rafts and inside Pta Barbafeita. Exposed to W.
(5) Is Toja Grande, on E side, in 4-6m. Attractive but requires BA 1768 and careful pilotage on top half of tide.
(6) San Martin del Grove. Approach as for (5). Anchor S of end of breakwater in fair weather.
(7) Santa Eugenia de Riveira, a large crowded fishing port on W side of ria. Anchor outside hbr mole Fl(2) R 8s. Beware unlit bn marking Camouco 1M to E.

Berthing Villagarcia de Arosa. New marina with pontoons and friendly YC. No room for anchoring. Piped diesel and water. International airport at Santiago de Compostela. Buses, trains.

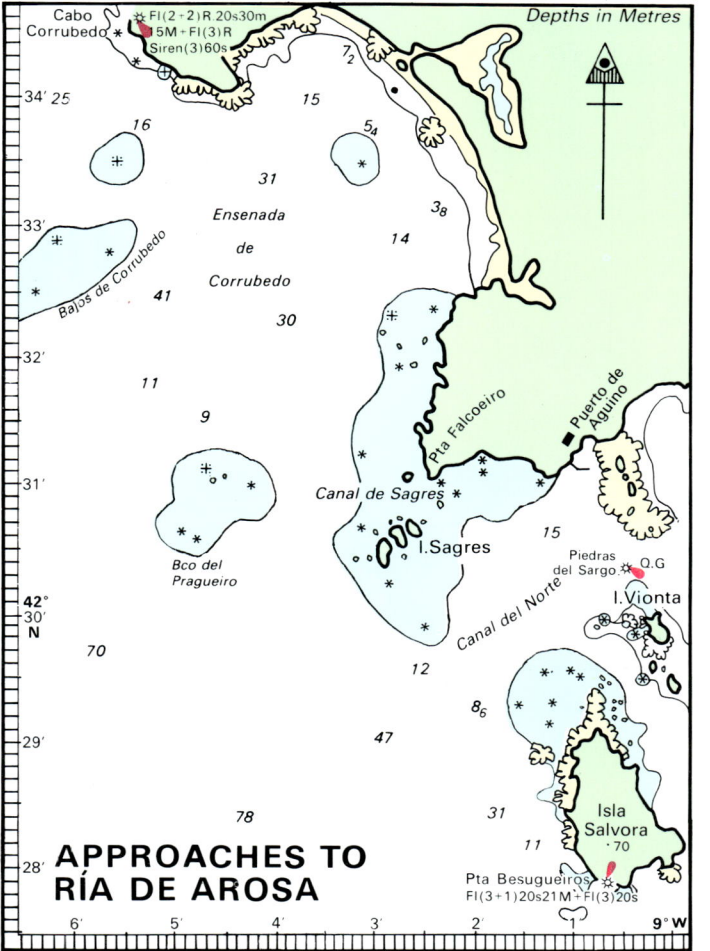

APPROACHES TO RIA DE AROSA

RIA DE PONTEVEDRA   Charts BA 1758   S 9251
HW: Dover +4½h
MHWS 3.4m   MHWN 2.6   MTL 2.0   MLWN 1.3   MLWS 0.5
A ría with several anchorages, and a naval college at Marin. No landing on Is Tambo (military zone).

Approach Identify Is Ons Fl(4) 24s
(1) N of Is Ons through Paso de la Fagilda, passing either side of Picamillo bn tr Oc(2) G 6s, and leaving R buoy Q R to port. Leave Los Camoucos rocky shoal Fl(3) R 18.4s to stb.
(2) S of Is Ons. Steer 040° half way between Is Ons and Pta Couso Fl(3) WG 9s.

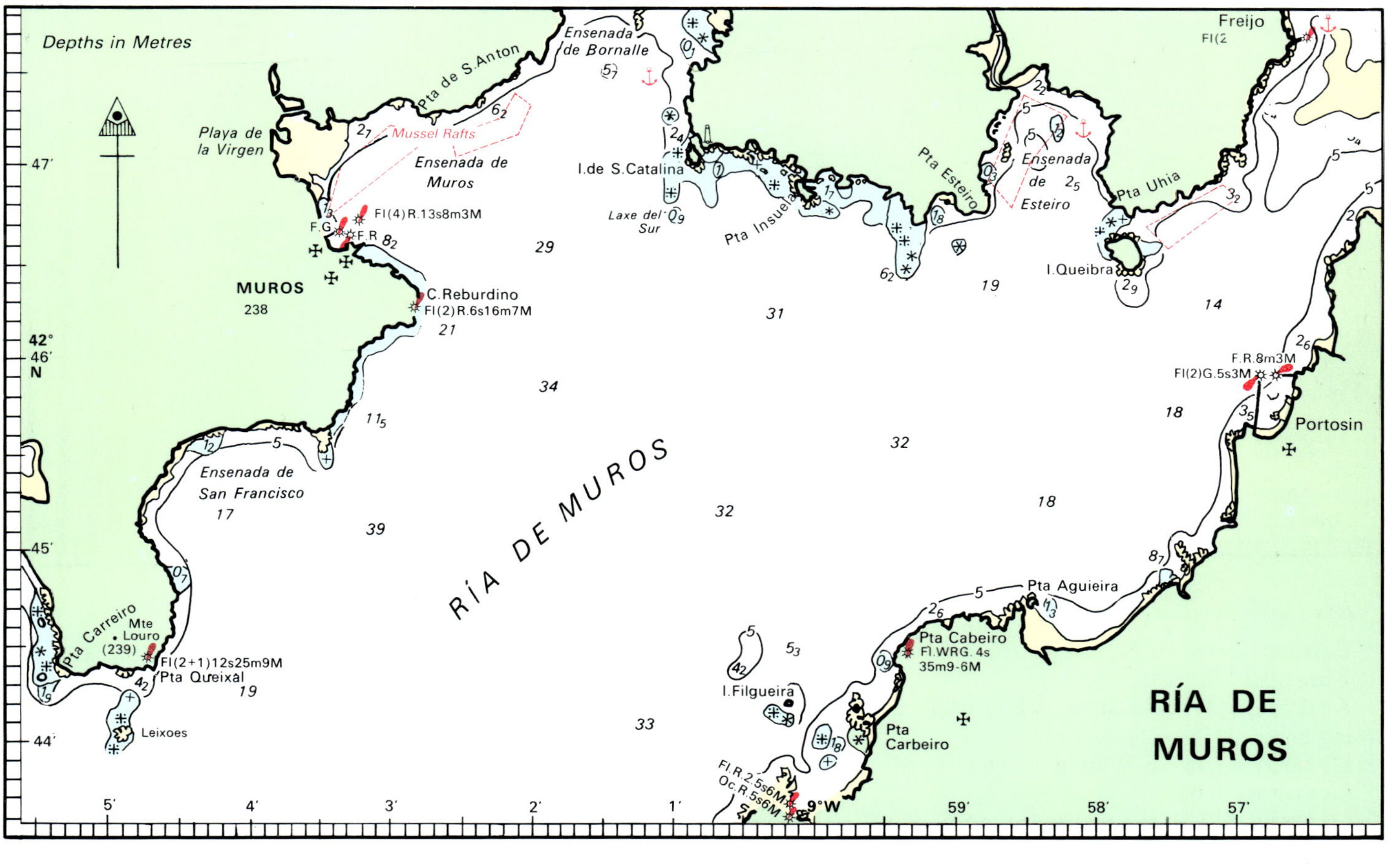

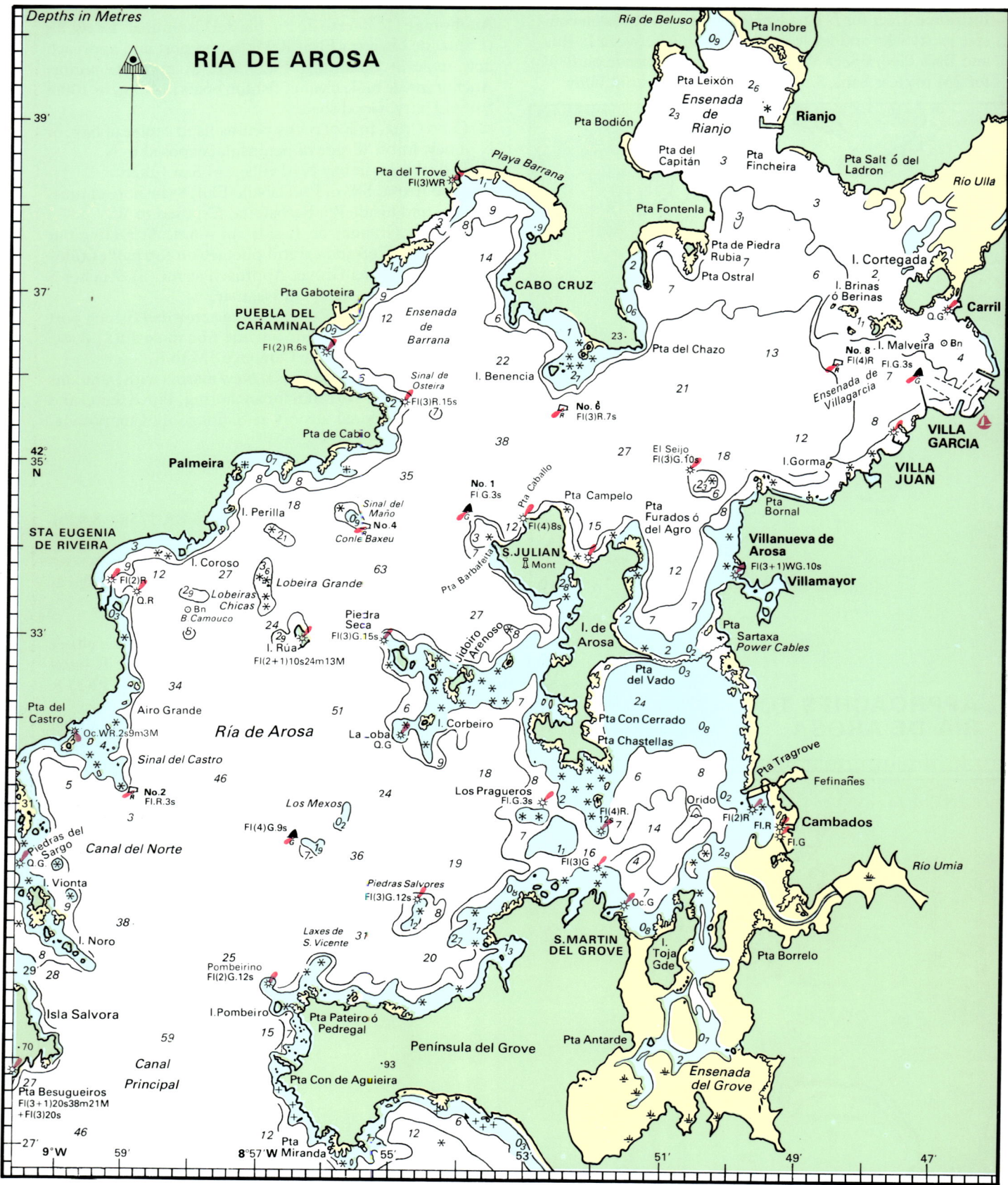

Ría De Pontevedra (Continued)

Entrance Between Pta Cabicastro on N side and Cabo de Udra on S.
Anchorage (1) Porto Novo. In E of small bay, clear of fishing boats.
(2) Sangenjo, in bay W of mole. Open to SW. Little room for visitors in hbr.
(3) Marin. Off W mole, exposed to SW and W.

(4) Combarro. A delightful old fishing village. Anchor S of jetty in 3m, clear of mussel rafts. Useful base for a visit to Pontevedra town.
(5) Bueu. Small pleasant fishing port. E of E jetty Fl(2) R 6s clear of fishing boats on buoys, close to beach in 3-4m. Good shelter from SW-W.
(6) Is Ons. Pleasant day anchorages on E side.

397 SPAIN AND PORTUGAL

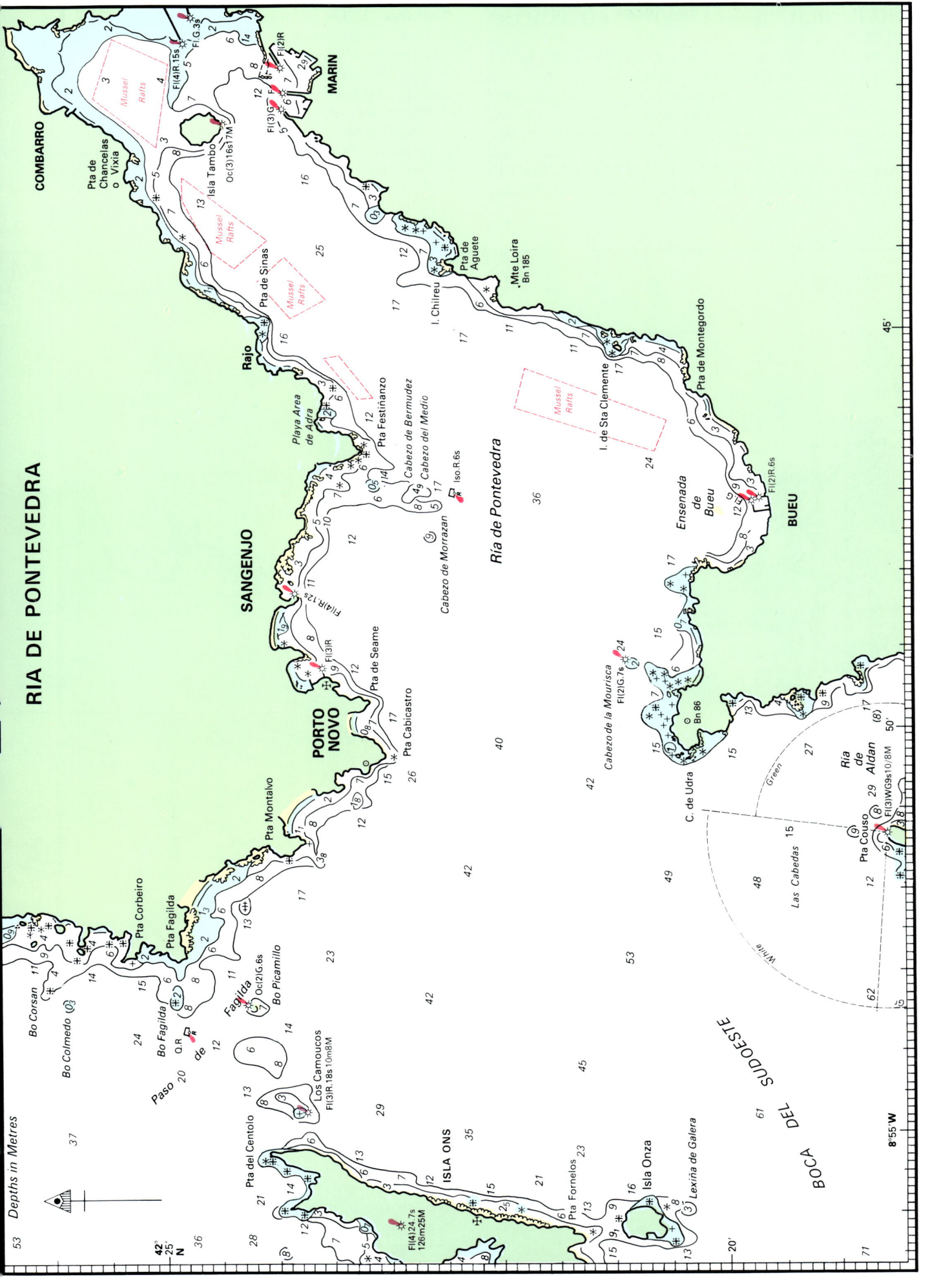

RÍA DE VIGO Charts BA 2548 1757 S 9240 9241 9242
HW: Dover +4¼h

MHWS 3.5m MHWN 2.7 MTL 2.0 MLWN 1.3 MLWS 0.4

There is a wide deep-water entrance S of Is Cies with directional Ro Bn. The ría is dominated by the large commercial port of Vigo but has attractive anchorages. Bayona is delightful as well as convenient, with easy access by day or night.

Approach Use Cabo Silleiro Fl(2+1) 15s (Ro Bn RO 310.3kHz 200M) and Mte Faro Fl(2) 8s on conspic Is Cies.

Entrance (1) The main entrance, Canal del Sur, lies between Islote Boeiro or Agoeiro Fl(2) R 8s, off the most S island of Is Cies, and Pta Lameda Fl(2) G 8s. From N leave Is Cies 1M to E and give 1M berth to Is Boeiro. From S, round Cabo Silleiro ¾M off and pass Las Serralleiras Fl G 4s at a distance of ½M. Steer on ldg lts of Cabo Estay Front Iso 2s, Rear Oc 4s on 069° (Ro Bn VS 296.5kHz 20M). In reduced visiblity, that is at night and in daytime fog, continuous tone on 069° ±3°: N of this tone changes to Mo(N) and S of it to Mo(A).

(2) The N entrance between Is Cies and Cabo del Home in clear weather.

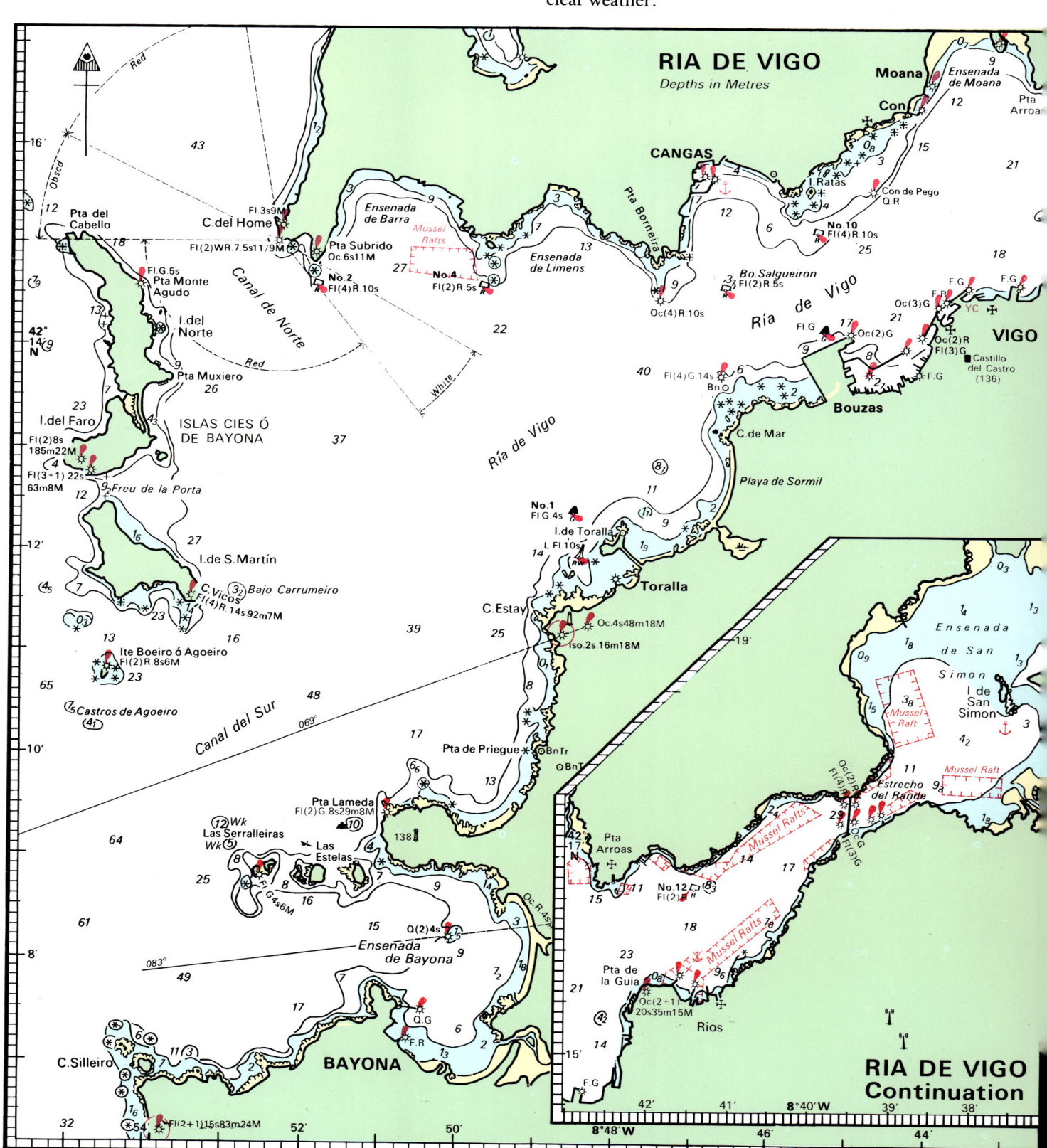

BAYONA Enter between Cabo Silleiro and Las Serralleiras on 083°, ldg lts Front Q(2) 4s, Rear OcR 4s. Rear lt difficult to see in daylight. Beware rocky shoals which extend up to ½M S of Las Serralleiras Lt Ho. Steer for molehead QG on not less than 160°. Anchor S of mole. Also YC moorings and pontoon berths. Piped diesel and water. Repairs. Good YC.

VIGO New marina with pontoons near YC in basin immediately beyond conspic former transatlantic terminal buildings. Beware frequent ferries to Cangas from adjacent basin. Good YC. Piped diesel and water. Major repairs at Astilleros Lago Carsi.

Other Anchorages (1) Cangas, outer hbr, little room. Pleasant town.
(2) Ensenada de Cangas, off beach.
(3) Ensenada de San Simon, beyond the suspension bridge.
(4) E of Is Cies, N or S of Pta Muxiero or NE of Is de San Martin, off beach. Delightful. Beware rock 1m at LWS off ferry jetty S of Pta Muxeiro.
(5) Ensenada de Barra, clear of mussel rafts, sheltered NE.

PORTUGAL

From the Rio Minho southwards to São Vicente the coast flattens progressively and becomes one of sand beaches backed by dunes or low cliffs. The rivers have sand bars and in any swell should only be entered shortly before High Water. Some of the fishing harbours have been improved and extended; ports free of a bar include Leixões, Sines, Nazaré and Peniche.

There are traffic separation schemes off Cabo da Roca and Cabo de São Vicente.

After Cabo São Vicente is rounded, the influence of the Mediterranean is increasingly felt. The Algarve is crowded and busy in summer, the weather hot and dry. With large scale charts of the ports, the Algarve coast can make a pleasant cruising area. In summer, the influence of the Azores high tends to produce northerlies, often reinforced in the afternoon by a sea breeze, and allowance should be made for strong winds if planning to return northwards at the end of a cruise to this area.

Formalities are more rigidly observed in Portugal than in Spain. At the first port of call it is necessary to enter with Policia Maritima and obtain a Transit Log (Declaraçao Geral de Entrada de Barcos de Recreio) which is used at each port visited. Piped diesel is available at most ports. Camping Gaz is widely available. There may be a charge for water.

PASSAGE CHARTS: BA 3634 3635 3636 1:200,000
89 1:175,000
P 1 to 8 inclusive 1:150,000

Principal Lights:
Leça Fl(3) 15s 57m 28M
41°12′.0N 8°42′.6W
I Berlenga FL(3) 20s 113m 27M
39°24′.8N 9°30′.6SW
C da Roca Fl(4) 20s 126m 26M
38°46′.8N 9°29′.8W
C Espichel Fl 4s 167m 26M
38°24′.8N 9°12′.9W
C de Sines Fl(2) 15s 40m 28M
37°57′.5N 8°52′.7W
C de São Vicente Fl 5s 84m 32M
37°01′.3N 8°59′.7W

VIANA DO CASTELO Charts BA 88 P 53
HW: Dover +4¼h
MHWS 3.5m MHWN 2.7 MTL 2.0 MLWN 1.4 MLWS 0.5
A fishing port with good shelter. Entrance dredged but in heavy swell the sea may break on bar.
Approach Montedor Lt Ho Fl(2) 7.5s Siren(3) 25s is 5M to N.
Entrance The ldg lts on 013° Front Iso R 4s, Rear Oc R 6s now lead very close (10m) to the extended Molhe Exterior Fl 3s, and then into the Antepuerto leaving Molhe de Bugio to port Fl R 5s. Turn to stb through small inner basin to lock and opening bridge leading to yacht basin, Doca de Flutuação
Berthing Alongside Doca de Flutuação. No ladders. Use dinghy and dock steps.

LEIXÕES Charts BA 3254 P 58
HW: Dover +4¼h
MHWS 3.5m MHWN 2.7 MTL 2.0 MLWN 1.3 MLWS 0.5
A good port of refuge with helpful YC.
Approach Oil refinery 2M to N conspic by day and night. Leça Lt Ho Fl(3) 15s is 1½M to N. From N round end of extended breakwater Fl WR 5s (sectored), at distance of 200m.
Entrance Steer 350° between inner moleheads, leaving Fl G 4s to stb, FlR 4s to port.
Anchorage W of old fishing hbr in N corner of main hbr. A mooring may be available in old fishing hbr. Apply YC. Water and diesel. Buses to Porto. International airport at Porto.
Berthing With a large-scale chart in good weather yachts can go up the Rio Douro and berth near Luis I bridge in Porto. Buoyed channel. Strong ebb.

RIA DE AVEIRO Charts BA 88 P 59 60
HW: Dover +4¾h
MHWS 3.2m MHWN 2.6 MTL 2.0 MLWN 1.4 MLWS 0.7
Enter only in daylight in good weather just before HW. Strong tidal streams. Strong winds SW-NW produce a dangerous sea.
Approach There are few marks along the low sandy coast. Aveiro Lt Ho Fl(4) 15s.
Entrance Between extended N mole FlR 3s and S Mole FlG 3s on ldg lts 065° Front concrete tr Oc R 3s, Rear silo Oc R 6s. When ¾M inside entrance turn to port into Canal de San Jacinto and follow buoyed channel to Aveiro 7M.
Anchorage Canal de S Jacinto, inside training walls.
Berthing Alongside YC quay (1m) or fish quay at Aveiro. Lock under construction.

FIGUEIRA DA FOZ   Charts BA 88   P 64
HW: Dover +4½h
MHWS 3.4m   MHWN 2.6   MTL 2.0   MLWN 1.4   MLWS 0.6
Extended breakwaters and recent dredging of bar to 5m have improved the entrance but beware swell from the W. Strong ebb at Springs.
Approach Cabo Mondego Lt Ho Fl 5s is 2½M to N. Conspic suspension bridge 1½M upriver from entrance.
Entrance Between N mole Fl R 6s and S mole Fl G 6s on ldg lts both FR 074°. Ldg marks difficult to see by day. Keep to N shore. When ¾M inside moleheads turn to port into Doca de Figueira.
Mooring Fore-and-aft between buoys in Doca de Figueira which shoals at W end. For diesel apply to Capitania.

PORTO DE NAZARÉ   Chart P 65
HW: Dover +4h
MHWS 3.2m   MHWN 2.5   MTL 1.8   MLWN 1.3   MLWS 0.5
A new, well-sheltered major fishing port 1M to S of old town and beach. Useful as a port of refuge.
Approach Pontal da Nazaré Oc 3s is 1M to N.
Entrance Between N mole LFl R 5s and S mole LFl G 5s.
Anchorage Near two jetties in S of hbr, clear of fishing boats or alongside jetty if room. Water and diesel on fish quay near control tr. 1½M walk to town. Little provision for yachts.

PENICHE   Charts P 69   68
HW: Dover +4h
MHWS 3.5m   MHWN 2.7   MTL 2.0   MLWN 1.3   MLWS 0.5
A large, well-sheltered fishing port with easy entrance on S side of peninsula of Peniche.
Approach From N identify two islands, Os Farilhão Fl 5s and Ilha Berlenga Fl(3) 20s, also Cabo Carvoeiro Fl(4) R 15s. By day, the peninsula of Peniche can be mistaken for an island. Traffic separation zone to W of islands.
Entrance The W mole FlR 3s extends 1 ca S of E mole Fl G 3s. Narrow entrance 100m.
Anchorage (1) Inside hbr, in bay N of E mole, or alongside new jetty on E side of bay.
(2) On N side of peninsula in 3-5m at Peniche de Cima. Open to N, and to swell from NW. By night, ldg lts both LFl R 7s on 215°.
(3) SE of Ilha Berlenga near Lt Ho Fl(3) 20s in 15m.

LISBOA & RIO TEJO
     Charts BA 3263 3264   P 71 72 73
HW: Dover +4½h
MHWS 3.8m   MHWN 3.0   MTL 2.2   MLWN 1.4   MLWS 0.5
A pleasant and interesting capital city. Tidal streams in river 2-3 knots at Springs, more after heavy rain. In strong SW winds, enter only on flood.
Approach From N identify Cabo de Roca conspic Lt Ho Fl(4) 20s (Ro Bn RC 308kHz 100M) 20M from Lisbon, Cabo Raso Fl(3) 15s and Guia Iso WR 2s. From S, Cabo Espechel Fl 4s. Traffic Separation Zone 9M to W of Cabo de Roca.
Entrance Steer between conspic Fort Bugio Fl G 5s on a sandbank to stb and Fort São Julião OcR 5s to port. By night Gibalta Oc R 3s and Esteiro Oc R 6s give ldg lts 047° between Bugio and São Julião. Keep well on to Gibalta before turning upriver.

Berthing There are 4 hbrs on N bank of river used by yachts. All have cross currents at entrance. Only (1) & (4) welcome visitors.
(1) Doca de Bom Sucesso, just past ornate Torre de Belem floodlit at night. Pontoons under construction with electricity and water. Crowded.
(2) Doca de Belem, 4ca E of Bom Sucesso, just past conspic floodlit monument. Reserved for local yachts. Water and diesel on fuelling pontoon. YC, showers, telephone. Travel-lift. Scrubbing grid.
(3) Doca de Santo Amaro 1ca E of bridge. Close to hbr authorities. No facilities. Noise from bridge traffic. Fore-and-aft buoys.
(4) Doca de Terreiro do Trigo. Continue upriver past busy ferry terminals. Enter second of pair of Navy docks. E end reserved for visiting yachts. Showers. Diesel. Shallow at LWS in places but soft mud.
International and national air, rail and bus connections.
Anchorage (1) CASCAIS. 38°41′.5N 9°25′.0W. Anchor in bay. Open to S. Helpful YC. Water. Diesel. Frequent trains to Lisboa.
(2) CANAL DO MONTIJO. Round Ponta de Cacilhas 1½M E of suspension bridge and steer 108° for buoyed Canal da Cuf. After 1M the buoyed Canal do Montijo leads off at 073°. No landing at military airfield.

SINES   Charts BA 3276   P 84
HW: Dover +3¾h
MHWS 3.4m   MHWN 2.6   MTL 2.0   MLWN 1.4   MLWS 0.6
A new port and oil terminal, well protected except from SW, surrounds the old fishing hbr.
Approach 1½M to N is Cabo de Sines Lt Ho Fl(2) 15s (Ro Bn SN 308kHz 50M).
Entrance From N keep 1M offshore and leave to port R pillar buoy FlR 10s off unlit end of breakwater. From S the entrance is wide. At night a variety of sectored lights lead into hbr and may confuse:-
(1) Ldg lts front Iso R 6s, rear Oc R 5.6s.
(2) Dir Oc(2) WRG 6s bearing 020°.
(3) Dir Oc WRG 3s bearing 348°.
Anchorage (1) In bay on N side of hbr 1¼M from end of breakwater, near fish hbr.
(2) For shelter from S & SW, behind mole, which is not lit, of fish hbr.
(3) Near YC on E side of hbr. Sheltered from S & SW. Dinghy landing.

PORTIMÃO   Charts BA 83   P 88 89
HW: Dover +3¾h
MHWS 3.5m   MHWN 2.7   MTL 2.1   MLWN 1.4   MLWS 0.6
A busy fishing port and resort town on the Algarve coast. New hbr with good shelter.
Approach Ponta da Piedade Lt Ho Fl 7s is 7½M to W. Alfanzina Lt Ho Fl(2) 15s is 4½M to E.
Entrance Ponta do Altar Lt Ho L Fl R 5s is ½M to E of hbr entrance. Pass between W mole FlR 5s and E mole FlG 5s on bearing 020°. Ldg lts on 020° Front OcR 5s, Rear Oc R 7s lead to port-hand R buoy and buoyed channel. If entering at night anchor at (1) until daylight.
Anchorage (1) Inside the E mole, clear of rocks along mole. Best shelter.
(2) Off Ferragudo on E shore in 3m mud. Supplies at Ferragudo. 1M from town quay for landing at Portimão.

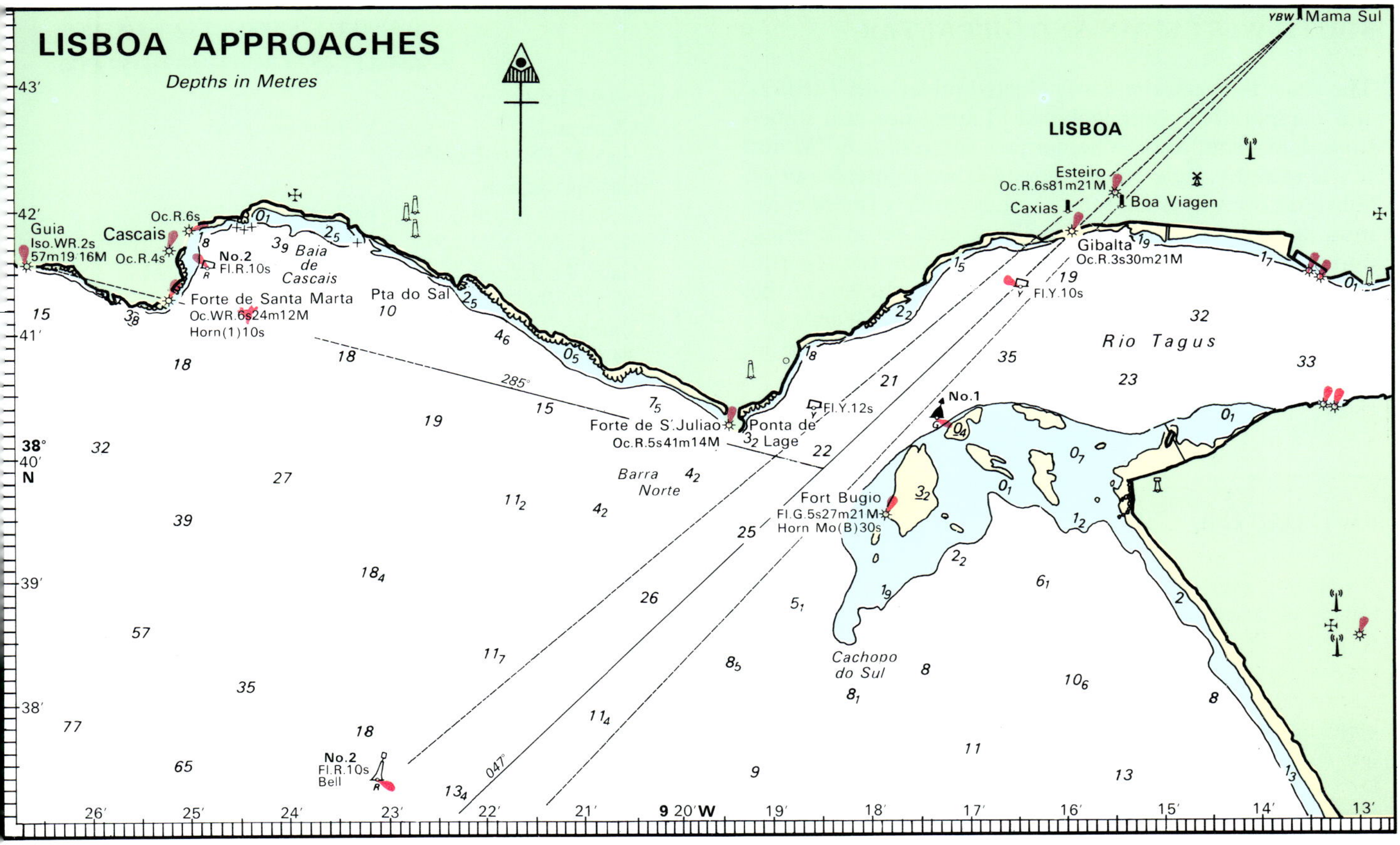

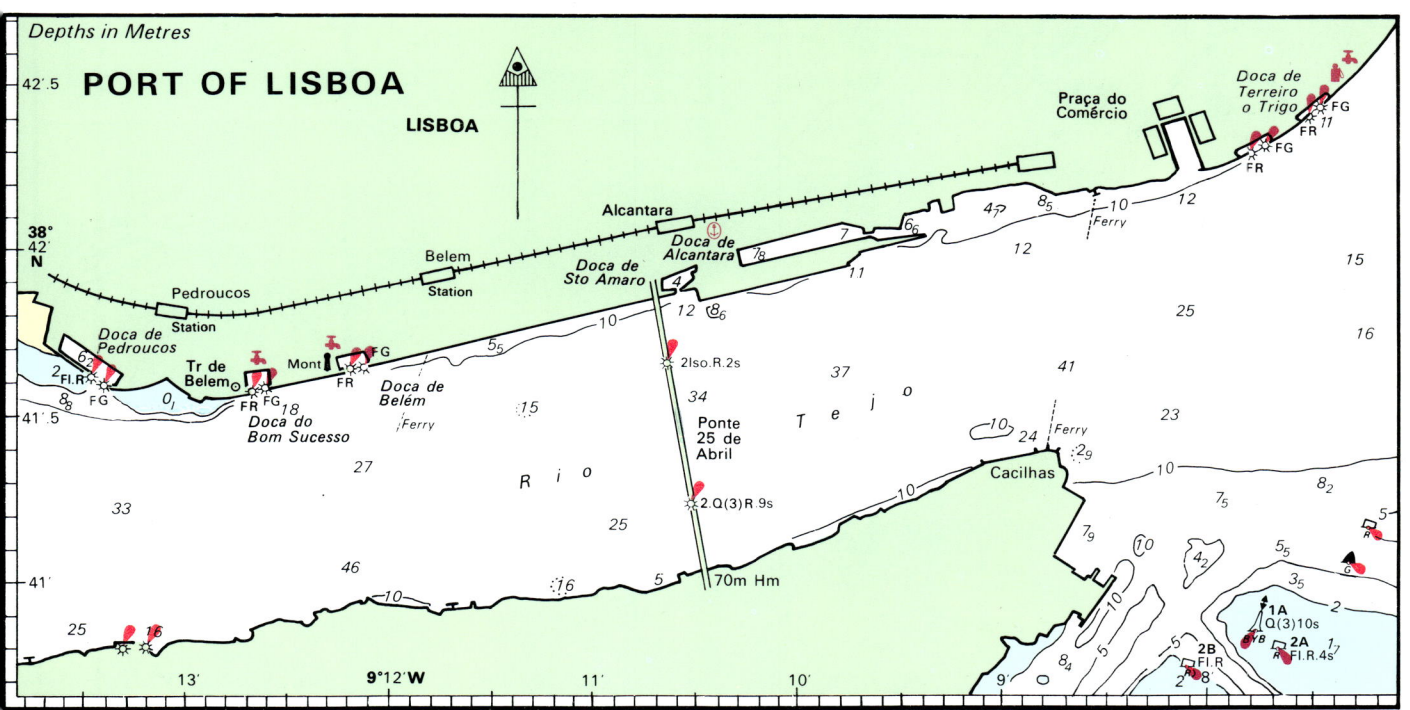

VILAMOURA Chart P 1052
HW: Dover +4h
MHWS 3.6m MHWN 2.8 MTL 2.2 MLWN 1.5 MLWS 0.7
A well-developed marina with good facilities, including laying-up. English spoken. Formalities may be observed strictly.
Approach Vilamoura Lt Fl 10s on control tr of marina.

Entrance Between W molehead Fl R 4s and E molehead Fl G 8s. In strong winds and swell seas may break at LW near W molehead. Width between moles 100m. Steer for entrance to inner basin 60m wide and moor to first pontoon to port alongside control tr to obtain clearance.
Facilities Diesel, repairs, scrubbing grid, hoist, crane, International airport at Faro, ½–1h by taxi/bus.

SPAIN AND PORTUGAL 402

SOUTH-WEST SPAIN AND GIBRALTAR

BA 90 1:175,000 142 1:100,000
S 443 445 452 630 631 633 1:52,000

The coast between the River Guadalquiver and Tarifa is still comparatively undeveloped. Tunny nets are sometimes laid, from May to September, stretching 6-7M out to sea at right angles to the coast. Towards the Strait of Gibraltar the winds tend to be either easterly (more common in summer) or westerly. There may be an E-going current at the Strait of 2 or 3kn. Tidal streams can also run up to 3kn at Springs. Traffic Separation in the Strait: the S limit of the inshore passage is only 1½M off Tarifa Lt. The range of tides at Cadiz is approximately 2.9m at Springs and 1.3m at Neaps.

Principal Lights
- Chipiona 36°44′.3N 6°26′.4W Fl 10s 68m 25M
- Castillo de San Sebastian (Cadiz) 36°31′.8N 6°18′.9W Fl(2) 10s 38m 25M
- Cabo Trafalgar 36°10′.7N 6°02′.1W Fl(2+1) 15s 50m 22M
- Tarifa 36°00′.1N 5°36′.5W Fl(3) 10s 40m 25M
- Europa Point, Gibraltar 36°06′.7N 5°20′.6W Iso 10s 49m 21M ⎫
   Oc R 10s 49m 17M ⎬ Sectors
   FR 44m 17M ⎭

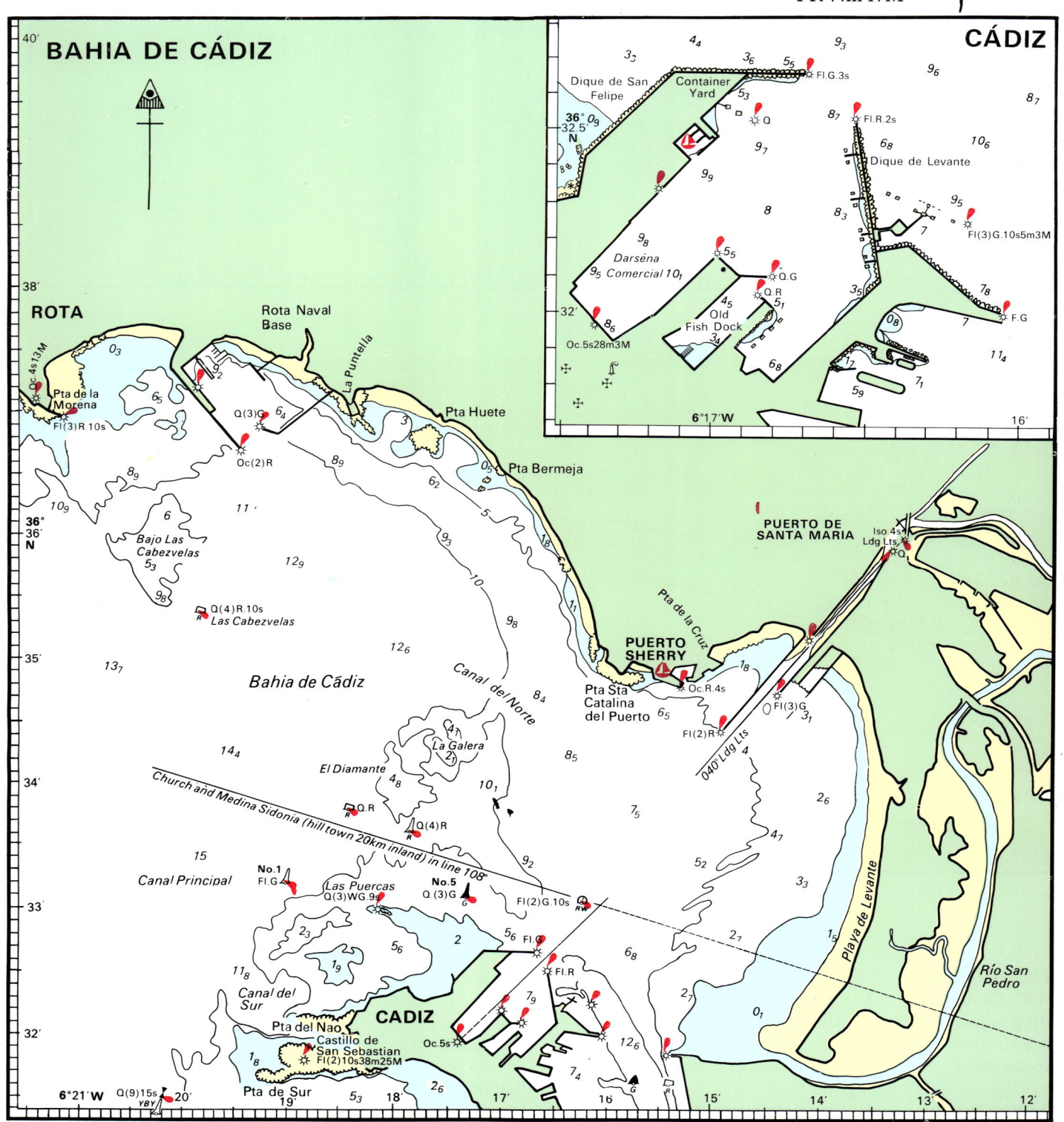

403 SPAIN AND PORTUGAL

CÁDIZ & CÁDIZ BAY   Charts BA 86   S 443A   4432
HW: Dover +3¾h
MHWS 3.3m   MHWN 2.5   MTL 1.8   MLWN 1.2   MLWS 0.4
Approach From N pass 2M off Pta del Chipiona Fl 10s. A buoy Fl(2) R 6s marks Bajo El Quemado at 36°36′N 6°24′W. From S keep more than ¾M off conspic Castillo de San Sebastian Fl(2) 10s and leave W card pillar lt buoy Q(9) 15s off Pta de Sur to stb.
Entrance The main lit channel into Cádiz lies close N of bn tr Las Puercas Q(3) WG 9s. G sector marks rocky shoal to SW of Las Puercas. From S make well up to No.1 buoy Fl G 3s before turning into white sector and channel.
Berthing: CÁDIZ. Moleheads are lit Fl G 3s and Fl R 2s. (1) Keep to W side after entry past container park to small crowded yacht hbr. Boats up to 11m might find room. 2km from town. (2) Old fish hr at E quay alongside fishing boat.
PUERTO SHERRY. A large new marina ½M to NW of training walls of Puerto de Santa Maria Fl(2) R 9s and Fl(3) G 11s. Conspic W tr at marina entrance Oc R 4s.
Anchorage At Puerto de Santa Maria. At night ldg lts Q and Iso 4s on 040° lead between training walls. Anchor off YC on W side.
Facilities All yacht repairs and diesel at Puerto Sherry. Spanish charts from Instituto Hydrografico, Tolosa Latour 1. Cádiz (Take passport for entry). International airport at Seville.

BARBATE DE FRANCO   Chart S 621A
HW: Dover +3¾h
MHWS 1.9m   MHWN 1.5   MTL 1.2   MLWN 1.0   MLWS 0.6
A new fishing port 1½M to W of shallow Río de Barbate.
Approach From W keep 3M off Cabo Trafalgar Fl(2+1) 15s. From E clear the shoal Los Cabezos with conspic wreck 3M to S of Pta Paloma Fl(2) 5s. Unlit tunny nets May to Sept.
Entrance Steer on ldg lts 298°, both Q, and enter between W molehead Fl(2) R 6s and E molehead FlG 3s. Turn to stb round E molehead into hbr.
Berthing Alongside a pontoon in SE corner of hbr.

TARIFA   Charts BA 1542   S 628A 10
HW: Dover +3¼h
MHWS 1.4m   MHWN 1.0   MTL 0.8   MLWN 0.5   MLWS 0.2
A small fishing port 16M from Gibraltar.
Approach From W beware the shoal Los Cabezos with conspic wreck 5M to W of Tarifa, covered by R sector of conspic Lt Ho on Is de Tarifa Fl(3) 10s and FR sector. There is also a 2m shoal patch NW of Tarifa at 36°02′.52N 5°40′.62W (approx). From E clear Pta Carnero Oc(1+3) WR 20s by 1M. The S limit of the inshore passage of the traffic separation scheme in the Strait of Gibraltar is 1½M to S of Tarifa Lt Ho. Unlit tunny nets May to Sept.
Entrance Steer for head of outer (E) mole Fl G 3s of hbr on NE side of Is de Tarifa.
Berthing E mole to stb, or in Naval pens (charge made).
Anchorage Temporary shelter from E on NW side of Is de Tarifa and its causeway.

GIBRALTAR   Charts BA 1448 144   S 3500 3501
HW: Dover +3½h
MHWS 1.0m   MHWN 0.7   MTL 0.5   MLWN 0.3   MLWS 0.1
A convenient port of call on passage to and from the Mediterranean, and a good place to fit out, repair and to lay up ashore unattended.
Approach Gibraltar Europa Point Lt Ho Iso 10s, Oc R 10s and FR
Entrance All yachts must report to customs station at the N end of the Rock, just to the S of airfield runway. Pass round the N end of the N mole or so-called 'E' Head. Customs station flies 'Q' flag. Reclamation operations in progress N of N Mole ('E' Head) in approaches to marinas.
Berthing Two marinas, Sheppards and Marina Bay, inshore of customs station.
Anchorage Immediately N of runway.
Supplies Diesel and water by customs station. BA chart agent. Air services to UK.

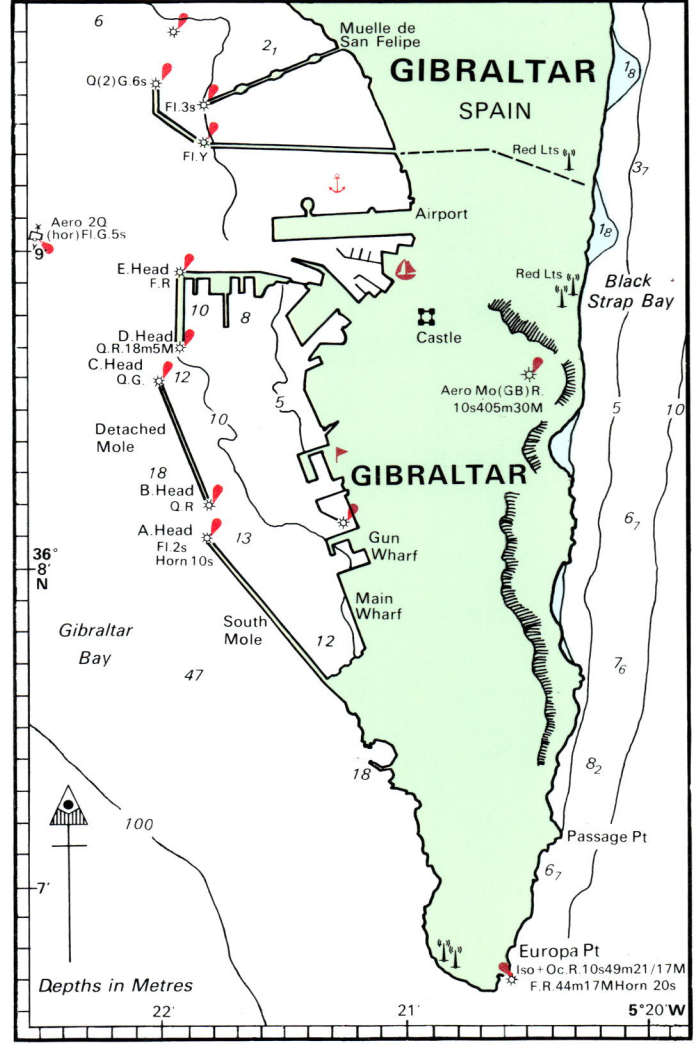

SPAIN AND PORTUGAL   404

Notes on the use of the index: All entries are indexed under their individual names; geographical descriptions are put after the name, as are words such as The, La etc. Page numbers of plans normally are not indexed as these will be found in close proximity to the text references. Entries are arranged in word-by-word order. Abbreviations used are: B - Bay; Hbr - Harbour; Is – Island(s); R - River.

Aabenraa, 253
Aalborg, 253
Aarhus, 253
Aber Benoît, L', 347
Aber Vrac'h, L', 347
Aberdeen, 125
Aberdovey, 181
Aberildut, L', 354
Abermenai Creek, 178
Abersoch, 180
Aberystwyth, 182
Aerøskøbing, 253
Agersø, 253
Aldeburgh, 93
Alderney, 320
Aline, Loch, 153
Alt R, 172
Ameland, 277
Amsterdam, 283-284
Ancress B, L', Guernsey, 222
Andijk, 293
Anholt, 253
Anstruther, 121
Antwerp, 294, 297
Appledore, 197
Aran Is, 240
Aranmore, 232
Arbroath, 122
Arcachon, 379
Ardfern, 153
Ardglass, 223
Ardinamir, 155
Ardmore, 161
Ares, Ría de, 393
Arisaig, 150
Arklow, 218
Armadale, 150
Arosa, Ría de, 395-6
Arran, Is of, 162
Arromanches, 312
Assens, 253
Audierne, 359
Augustenberg, 253
Aulne R, 357
Auray R, 368
Aveiro, Ría de, 400
Aven R, 363
Aviles, Ría de, 389
Avon R, 193
Axe R, 194

Bäckviken, 256
Bagenkop, 246, 251
Ballynakill, 237
Balta Sound, 139
Baltimore, 210
Banff, 127
Bangor, Co. Down, 225
Bangor, Menai Strait, 178
Bann R, 229
Bantry Hbr, 208
Barbate de Franco, 404
Barfleur, 314
Barmouth, 181

Barnstaple, 198
Barquero, Ría de, 390
Barra, 159
Barrow-in-Furness, 171
Barry, 192
Batz, Ile de 346
Bayona, 400
Bayonne, 379
Bearhaven, 207
Beaucette, 323
Beaulieu R, 44
Beaumaris, 178
Becquet, Le, 314
Belfast Lough, 225
Belle Ile, 366
Bélon R, 364
Bembridge IoW, 50
Bénodet, 361
Bermeo, Puerto de, 385
Bertheaume, L'Anse de, 355
Berwick-upon-Tweed, 116
Betanzos, Ría de, 393
Bideford, 198
Bilbao, Puerto de, 385
Binic, 331
Birdham Pool, 57
Birkenhead, 173
Blacksod B, 235
Blackwater R, 83
Blakeney, 98
Blankenberge, 295
Blyth, 113
Bogense, 253
Bois de la Chaise, 373
Boisdale, Loch 158
Bordeaux, 378
Borkum, 267, 272
Boscastle, 198
Bosham Channel, 59
Boston, 102
Boulogne, 304
Boyardville, 377
Bradwell, 83
Brancaster Staithe, 100
Braunton, 197
Braye, 320
Bréhat, Ile de, 334-336
Breskens, 290
Brest, 355
Bridlington, 106, 107
Bridport, 30
Brightlingsea, 85
Brighton, 61
Brignogan, 347
Bristol, 193
Bristol Channel, 188
Brixham, 25
Broadhaven, 234
Broom, Loch, 145
Brue R, 195
Brunsbüttel, 267, 269
Buckie, 127
Buckler's Hard, 44
Bunaw, 205
Burghead, 128

Burgtiefe, 260
Burnham Overy Staithe, 100
Burnham-on-Crouch, 79
Burnham-on-Sea, 195
Burntisland, 121
Burry Port, 190-91
Burtonport, 232
Busum, 269
Butley R, 93

Cabourg, 310
Cadgwith Cove, 8
Cádiz, 404
Caen, 311
Caernarfon, 175, 178
Caher R, 203
Calais, 303
Caldey Is, 189
Caledonian Canal, 152
Camaret, 357
Camariñas, 394
Camel R, 198
Campbelltown, 163
Cancale, 328
Canna, 159
Caolas Scalpay, 150
Cap Breton, 379
Caramiñal, Puerto de Puebla del, 396
Cardigan, 182
Carentan, 313
Cariño, Puerto de, 390
Carlingford Lough, 221
Carrigaholt, 241
Carron, Loch, 147
Carrickfergus, 225
Carmarthen, 190
Carteret, 327
Cascais, 401
Cashla, 240
Castlebay, 159
Castlehaven, 211
Castletown, Ireland, 207
Castletown IoM, 170
Castro Urdiales, Puerto de, 386
Cattawater, 16
Ceall, Loch nan, 150
Cedeira, Ría de, 390
Channel Is, 318-326
Chapman's Pool, 33
Charente R, 377
Château, Le, 377
Chateaulin, 357
Chausey Is, 328
Chenal du Four, 352
Cherbourg, 318, 320, 327
Christchurch, 36,37
Chichester, 57
Clamerkin Lake, 44
Clifden B, 238
Cobh, 214
Coleraine, 227, 229
Colijnsplaat, 287
Collorus, 205
Colne R, 85
Colonsay, 161
Concarneau, 363
Conwy, 175
Copenhagen, 253
Corcubion, Ría de, 394
Cork, 214
Cormach Is, 155
Corme, Ría de, 394
Corpach, 152
Coruña, La, 391-2

Courseulles, 311
Cowes, 46
Crac'h R, 369
Craighouse, 154
Craignish, Loch, 153
Craobh Haven, 153
Crinan, 153
Croisic, Le, 371
Cromer, 100
Crookhaven, 208, 209
Crosshaven, 214
Crouch R, 79
Crowlin Is, 150
Cruit B, 233
Cuan Sound, 151
Cudillero, Puerto de, 389
Cuxhaven, 267, 269

Dahouet, 332
Dale, 188
Dartmouth, 24
Deauville, 310
Deben R, 92
Dee R, 175
Delfzijl, 276, 277
Den Helder, 281
Den Oever, 282, 291
Derby Haven, 170
Dielette, 327
Dieppe, 306
Dingle Hbr, 242
Dittisham, 24
Dives R, 310
Douarnenez, 358
Douglas, 169
Dover, 65
Drambuie, Loch na, 155
Drunmore, 164
Duddon R, 171
Dun Laoghaire, 220
Dunbar, 119
Duncansby Head, 131
Dungeness, 63
Dunkerque, 302
Dunmore East, 216
Duntulm, 161
Dunvegan, 161
Dursey Sound, 206

Eatharna, Loch, 160
Ebeltoft, 253
Edam, 293
Eigg, 149
Eirlandische Gat, 281
Elanchove, Puerto de, 385
Elbe R, 267, 269
Elburg, 292
Elly Hbr, 235
Emden, 272
Emsworth Channel, 57
En Mor Cormach Is, 155
Enkhuizen, 293
Eport, Loch, 161
Eriboll, Loch, 132
Erquy, 331
Esbjerg, 246, 267
Etaples, 304
Etel R, 364
Ewe, Loch, 147
Exe, River, 29, 30
Eyemouth, 119

Faaborg, 253
Faeroe Is, 140-42
Fahan Creek, 230
Fair Isle, 136
Falmouth, 8, 9

406

Fambridge, 79
Fareham Lake, 54
Fécamp, 307
Fennit, 241
Feochan, Loch, 155
Ferrol, Ría de El, 391
Fiers D'Ars, 375
Figuera da Foz, 401
Filey, 106
Findhorn, 128
Fishguard, 183, 184
Fjaellebroen, 253
Fleetwood, 173
Flensburg, 257
Flotte, La, 375
Folkestone, 65
Føroyar, 140-42
Fosdyke, 102
Four Channel, 352
Fowey, 14
Fraserburgh, 127
Fredericia, 253
Frederickssund, 255
French Inland Waterways, 300-302
Frenchport, 234
Fuenterrabía, 383
Fuglafjordur, 142

Gairloch, Loch, 147
Galway, 238, 241
Garlieston, 164
Garth Ferry, 178
Garvellach Is, 161
Gibraltar, 404
Gigha, 154
Gijon, Puerto de, 388
Gillan Creek, 8
Gilleleje, 255
Gironde R, 378
Gislovhamn, 256
Glandore, 212
Glasson Dock, 172
Glénan, Iles de, 361
Glengariff, 206
Goes, 287
Goldhanger Creek, 83
Gometra, 161
Gorey, 324
Göteborg, 256
Grandcamp, 313
Grande Grève, Sark, 323
Grande Havre, Guernsey, 322
Granton, 119
Granville, 327
Gravelines, 303
Gravesend, 75
Great Yarmouth, 97
Greatman B, 239
Greenhithe, 75
Grenaa, 249
Grève de la Ville, Sark, 323
Grimsby, 103
Groix, Ile de, 364
Grömitz, 261
Groningen, 276
Gruting Voe, 137
Guernsey, 322-323
Guetaría, Puerto de, 384
Guilvinec, 359

Hals, 249
Hamble R, 51
Hamford Water, 87
Hamoaze, 16
Handa Is, 150

Hansweert, 288
Harderwijk, 292
Haringvliet, 285, 286
Harlingen, 279
Harport, Loch, 159
Harrington, 166
Hartlepool, 110
Harty Ferry, 74-5
Harwich, 89, 91
Havelet B, Guernsey, 322
Havengore Creek, 78-9
Havre, Le, 307
Havre Gosselin, Sark, 323
Hayle, 199
Hayling Is, 57
Heiligenhafen, 260
Helensburgh, 164
Helford R, 8
Helgoland, 246, 267, 268
Hellerup, 253
Hellevoetsluis, 285
Helmsdale, 130
Helsingør, 255
Hendaye, 380
Herbaudière, L', 373
Heybridge Basin, 83
Heysham, 172
Hillhead Haven, 51
Hindeloopen, 292
Hoëdic, Ile de, 370
Hoek van Holland, 285
Holehaven, 78
Holtenau, 259
Holy Is, 116
Holyhead, 179
Honfleur, 309-10
Hoorn, 293
Houat, Ile de, 370
Hourn, Loch, 150
Housel B, 8
Howth, 220
Huizen, 292
Hull Marina, 103
Humber R, 100, 103-6
Hundested, 255
Husum, 269

Icart B, Guernsey, 322
Ijmuiden, 275, 283
Ijsselmeer, 290
Ilfracombe, 196
Inchard, Loch, 145
Inishbofin, 237
Inishtrahull Sound, 227
Inver, Loch, 145
Inverkip, 164
Inverness, 129
Isigny, 313
Itchenor, 57

Jack Sound, 184
Jade R, 271
Jersey, 324-6
Juelsminde, 255

Kalundborg, 255
Kalvehave, 255
Kampen, 292
Kerteminde, 255
Keyhaven, 39
Kiel Canal, 246, 259
Kiel Fjord, 258
Kilkeel, 221
Killary, 236
Killeany B, 240
Killybegs, 233
Kilmakilloge, 205
Kilronan, 238, 240

Kingsbridge, 21
King's Lynn, 102
Kinsale, 213
Kippford, 164
Kirkcudbright, 164
Kirkcaldy, 121
Kirkwall, 133
Klaksvik, 142
Knights Town, 203
København, 253
Køge, 255
Kolding, 245, 249
Kornwerderzand, 281, 291
Kørsor, 251
Kristiansand, 246, 264
Kyle of Lochalsh, 148
Kyle of Tongue, 132
Kyles of Bute, 164
Kyrkbacken, 256

Laboe, 259
Lage, Ría de, 394
Lamlash, 162
Lampaul, 354
Landerneau R, 355
Langelinie, 253
Langeoog, 271
Langør, 255
Langstone Hbr, 54-7
Lannion R, 341
Largs, 162
Larne Lough, 227
Latchingdon Hole, 83
Lathaich, Loch na, 160
Lauwersoog, 277
Lawling Creek, 83
Lawrenny, 188
Laxey, 170
Laxford, Loch, 145
Légué, Le, 331
Leixões, 400
Lelystad, 292
Lemmer, 292
Lemvig, 255
Lequeitio, Puerto de, 385
Lerwick, 137
Lézardrieux, 334-6
Limfjord, 246, 249
Limnhamn, 256
Linnhe, Loch, 152
Lisboa, 401
Lismore, 155
Littlehampton, 60
Liverpool, 173
Llanelli, 191
Locquémeau, 341
Loctudy, 360
Loe Pool, 8
Løgstør, 255
Loire R, 372
London R, 77-8
Looe, 14
Lorient, 366
Lossiemouth, 128
Lowestoft, 95, 96
Luarca, Puerto de, 389
Lulworth Cove, 33
Lundy Is, 196
Lune R, 172
Lybster, 130
Lyme B, 27
Lyme Regis, 30
Lymington, 42

Maasholm, 257-8
Macduff, 127
Maddy, Loch, 157
Makkum, 290
Maldon, 83, 85
Mallaig, 149
Man, Isle of, 168-171
Mandal, 246, 264
Marennes, 377
Margate, 72
Marken, 293
Marstal, 255
Maryport, 167
Mayflower Marina, Plymouth, 16
Medemblik, 293
Medina R, IoW, 46
Medway R, 72-4
Melfort, Loch, 153
Menai Strait, 175-8
Mersea Quarters, 84
Mersey R, 173
Methil, 121
Mevagissey, 12
Middelfart, 255
Middelharnis, 285
Mile, Loch na, 154
Milford Haven, 185-8
Millbay Docks, Plymouth, 167
Minehead, 196
Moidart, Loch, 150
Moines, Ile aux, 369
Monnickendam, 293
Montrose, 125
Morbihan, 368
Morgat, 357
Morlaix, 344
Mousehole, 6
Muck, 150
Muelles Locales, 388
Mugia, 394
Muiden, 292
Mullion, 8
Mulroy B, 230
Muros, Ría de, 395
Mylor Creek, 9

Naestved, 255
Nakskov, 255
Nantes, 372
Nazaré, Porto de, 401
Neath R, 191
Nedd, Loch, 150
Needles Channel, 37
Nevis, Loch, 150
New Grimsby Hbr, 6
New Quay Cardigan, 182
Newhaven, 61-3
Newlyn, 6
Newport, 193
Newtown IoW, 44
Neyland, 188
Nieuwpoort, 297
Noirmoutier, Ile de, 373
Noordzee Kanaal, 283
Norddeich, 271
Norderney, 267, 271
Norfolk Coast, 98
Nyborg, 255
Nykøbing, Limfjord, 255
Nykøbing, Sjaelland, 255

Oban, 152
Odden, 255
Odense, 255
Oléron, Ile d', 377
Omø, 255

Omonville-La-Rogue, 318
Oost Vlieland, 279
Oostende, 294, 296
Oosterschelde, 286
Orford Haven, 93
Orkney, 132, 133-6
Ornsay, Isle, Sound of Sleat, 149
Oronsay, Isle, L. Sunart, 155
Orwell R, 91
Ouedeschild, 281
Ouistreham, 311
Ouse R, 106
Oysterhaven, 213

Padstow, 198
Paignton, 26
Paimpol, 334
Palais, Le, Belle Ile, 366
Pallice, La, 375
Parrett, R, 195
Parn Voose, 8
Pasajes, Puerto de, 383
Pauillac, 378
Peel, 168
Pembroke Dock, 188
Penarth, 192
Penerf, 370
Peniche, 401
Pennar Gut, 188
Penpoul, 342
Penryn R, 9
Pentland Firth, 131
Penzance, 7
Penzé R, 342
Perros-Guirec, 339
Perrotine, La, 377
Peterhead, 126
Petit Port, Guernsey, 322
Piel Hbr, 171
Pierowall, 136
Pin Mill, 91
Plockton, 147
Ploumanac'h, 339
Plymouth, 16, 19
Polperro, 14
Pontevedra, Ría de, 396-7
Pontrieux R, 336
Pontusval, 347
Poole Hbr, 34
Porlock Weir, 196
Pornic, 372
Pornichet, 371
Port Askaig, 161
Port Blanc, 339
Port Bloc, 378
Port de Bloscon, 346
Port de Bourgenay, 374
Port Du Crouesty, 368
Port Dinlleyn, 180
Port Dinorwic, 178
Port Edgar. 119
Port Ellen, 160
Port Erin, 168
Port Erisco, 161
Port Haliguen, 366
Port Joinville, 373
Port La Forêt, 361
Port Launay, 357
Port de Lévi, 314
Port Maria, 364
Port Navalo, 368
Port Ramsay, Lismore, 155
Port St. Mary, 171
Port Talbot, 191
Port Tudy, 364
Port-en-Bessin, 312

Portchester Lake, 54
Porthcawl, 191
Porthleven, 8
Porthmadog, 180
Porthoustock Cove, 8
Portimão, 401
Portisead, 194
Portivi, 364
Portland Bill, 27
Portland Hbr, 32
Portmagee, 203
Portpatrick, 163
Portree, 148
Portrieux, 332
Portrush, 229
Portsall, 349
Portsmouth, 54
Portstewart, 227
Pouliguen, Le, 371
Praestø, 255
Primel, 342
Puerto Sherry Marina, 404
Puiladobhrain, 155
Pwllheli, 180

Queen Anne's Battery Marina, Plymouth, 16
Queenborough, 74, 75
Quiberon, 364, 366
Quimper, 361

Raa, 256
Ramsey B, 169
Ramsey Sound, 184
Ramsgate, 68
Ramsholt, 92
Rance R, 331
Randers, 255
Ranza, Loch, 164
Rathlin Sound, 227
Ravenglass, 171
Raz de Sein, 358-9
Ré, Ile de, 375
Redon, 370
Rendsburg, 262
Restronguet Creek, 9
Rhu, 164
Rhum, 150
Ribadeo, Ría de, 389
Ribadesella, Puerto de, 387
Ribble R, 172
Roach R, 79
Roche Bernard, La, 370
Rochefort, 377
Rochelle, La, 376
Rødby, 256
Rodel, 161
Rødvig, 253
Roe, Loch, 150
Roscoff, 346
Rosslare, 218
Rothéneuf, 328
Rothesay, 164
Rotterdam, 285
Roundstone, 239
Royan, 378
Rudkøbing, 256
Rungsted, 256
Rutland Hbr, 232
Ryan, Loch, 163
Ryde, 50
Rye, 64

Sables d'Olonne, Les, 374
St Abbs Hbr, 119
St Alban's Head, 32-3

St Aubin, 326
St Bees Head, 166
St Bride's B, 185
St Brieuc, 331
St Evette, 359
St German's R, 19
St Gilles Croix-de-Vie, 374
St Guénolé, 359
St Helen's Pool, Scilly, 6
St Helier, 326
St Ives, 199
St Jean de Luz, 380
St Just Creek, 9
St Kilda, 156
St Malo, 330
St-Marcouf Is, 314
St Martin, Ile de Ré, 375
St Martin, Anse de, 318
St Mary's Is, Scilly, 6
St Mawes Creek, 9
St Michael's Mount, 8
St Monance, 121
St Nazaire, 372
St Peter Port, 322
St Sampsons, 322
St Tudwal's Road, 180
St Vaast La Hougue, 315
St Valéry-en-Caux, 305
Sakskøbing, 256
Salcombe, 21
Saleen B, 235
Salen, L. Sunart, 155
Salen, Mull, 155
San Sebastián, 384
San Vicente de La Barquera, Puerto de, 387
Sandwick, 67-8
Santa Maria, Ría de, 390
Santander, 387
Sark, 323
Saundersfoot, 189
Sauzon, Belle Ile, 366
Scalasaig, 161
Scalloway, 138
Scalpay, E. Loch Tarbert, 157
Scalpay, Caolas, 150
Scapa Flow, 133
Scarborough, 106, 107
Scavaig, Loch, 161
Scheveningen. 284
Schiedam, 285
Schiermonnikoog, 277
Schilksee, 259
Schleimünde, 258
Schleswig, 258
Schull, 209
Scilly Is, 3-6
Scrabster, 131, 132
Scresort, Loch, 150
Seaham, 111
Seil Sound, 155
Sein, Ile de, 358
Seine Estuary, 309
Sejerø, 256
Sept Iles, Les, 339
Seudre R, 377
Sharfleet Creek, 74
Shell, Loch, 157
Shetland, 133, 136-9
Shoreham, 61
Shotley Point, 89
Silloth, 166
Sines, 401
Skagen, 246, 251
Skanör, 256
Skiport, Loch, 158
Skippool, 173

Skomer Is, 185
Sleat, Sound of, 149
Smerwick Hbr, 242
Sneem, 205
Søby, 256
Solva, 184
Somme Estuary, 305
Sønderborg, 246, 247
South Ferriby, 106
South Rona, 150
Southampton Water, 48
Southwold, 95-6
Spakenburg, 292
Spodsbjerg, 256
Staffa, 161
Stangate Creek, 74
Stavoren, 292
Stege, 256
Stellendam, 285
Stickenhorn, 259
Stonehaven, 124
Stornoway, 156
Stour R, Essex, 89
Stour R, Kent, 67-8
Strangford Lough, 223
Stromness, 133
Stronsay, 134
Stubbekøbing, 256
Studland B, 33
Suduroy, 140-41
Suffolk Yacht Hbr, 91
Sumburgh Head, 136
Summer Isles, 146
Sunart, Loch, 155
Sunderland, 112
Sutton Hbr, Plymouth, 16
Svanemølle, 253
Svendborg, 256
Swale R, 74-5
Swanage, 33
Swansea, 191
Swanwick, 51
Swellies, The, 178
Swilly, Lough, 230

Tamar R, 19
Tarbert, E Loch (Harris), 157
Tarbert, E Loch (Kintyre), 162
Tarbert, W Loch (Harris), 156
Tarbert, W Loch (Kintyre), 155
Tarifa, 404
Taw R, 197
Tay R, 124
Tayport, 124
Tayvallich, 154
Teddington, 77-8
Tees R, 110
Teignmouth, 28
Tenby, 189
Terneuzen, 290
Terschelling, 279
Thames Estuary, 70-72
Thames R, 77-8
Thirslet Creek, 83
Thorney Channel, 57
Thyborøn, 246, 267
Titchfield Haven, 51
Tobermory, 151
Tollesbury, 84
Tonning, 269
Torquay, 26
Torridge R, 197
Torridon, Loch, 150
Torshavn, 141-2
Totnes, 25
Toulinget Channel, 357
Travemünde, 261

408

Trébeurden, 340
Tréboul, 358
Trégastel, 339
Tréguier R, 337-8
Tréhiguier, 370
Tremblade, La, 377
Trent R, 106
Tréport, Le, 305
Trieux R, 324
Trinité, La, 369
Trongisvagur, 140-41
Troon, 162
Trouville, 310
Truro R, 9
Tunø, 256
Tvøroyri, 140-41
Tynemouth, 112

Uig B, 157
Ullapool, 145
Unionhall, 212
Ura Firth, 139
Urk, 292
Urr, Waters of, 164
Ushant, 354-5
Utklippan, 256

Vaila Sound, 137
Valentia, 203
Vannes, 369
Vejle, 256
Veerse Meer, 288
Vestmanha, 142
Viana do Castelo, 400
Vigo, 399, 400
Viken, 256
Vilaine, La, 370
Vilamoura, 402
Villagarcia, 396
Vivero, Ría de, 389
Vlaardingen, 285
Vlissingen, 288
Volendam, 293
Vordingborg, 256

Waddenzee, 279
Waldringfield, 92
Walton Backwaters, 87
Wangerooge, 271
Wareham Channel, 34
Warkworth Hbr, 113
Warsash, 51
Wash, The, 100

Watchet, 195
Waterford, 216
Wellington Dock, Dover, 65
Wells-next-the-Sea, 99
Wemeldinge, 287
Weser R, 271
West B (Bridport), 30
Weston-super-Mare, 194
Westray, 136
Wexford, 219
Weymouth, 32
Whitby, 106, 108
Whitehaven, 167
Whithorn, Isle of, 164
Whitstable, 72
Wick, 130, 132
Wicklow, 220
Wigtown B, 164
Wisbech, 103
Wivenhoe, 85
Woodbridge, 92
Woolverstone, 91
Wootton IoW, 50
Worbarrow B, 33
Workington, 167
Workum, 290
Wrabness, 89

Yarmouth IoW, 39
Yealm R, 19-21
Yeu, Ile d', 373
Yns y Big, 175
Yorkshire Coast, 106
Youghal, 216
Ystad, 256

Zeebrugge, 275, 294, 295
Zeegat van Goeree, 285
Zierikzee, 286